CENGAGE ADVAN

THE ENDURING VISION

A History of the American People

SEVENTH EDITION

Paul S. Boyer
University of Wisconsin

Clifford E. Clark, Jr.
Carleton College

Karen Halttunen
University of Southern California

Joseph F. Kett
University of Virginia

Neal Salisbury
Smith College

Harvard Sitkoff
University of New Hampshire

Nancy Woloch
Barnard College

WADSWORTH
CENGAGE Learning·

Australia • Brazil • Japan • Korea • Mexico • Singapore • Spain • United Kingdom • United States

The Enduring Vision: A History of the American People, Seventh Edition
Paul S. Boyer, Clifford E. Clark, Jr., Karen Halttunen, Joseph F. Kett, Neal Salisbury, Harvard Sitkoff, Nancy Woloch

Senior Publisher: Suzanne Jeans

Senior Sponsoring Editor: Ann West

Assistant Editor: Megan Chrisman

Editorial Assistant: Patrick Roach

Senior Media Editor: Lisa Ciccolo

Senior Marketing Manager: Katherine Bates

Marketing Coordinator: Lorreen Pelletier

Marketing Communications Manager: Caitlin Green

Project Management: PreMediaGlobal

Senior Art Director: Cate Rickard Barr

Print Buyer: Sandee Milewski

Rights Acquisition Specialist/ Text: Katie Huha

Rights Acquisition Specialist/ Image: Jennifer Meyer Dare

Cover Designer: Gary Ragaglia

Cover Image: Carl Rakeman, *Railroad Crossings Bridged*, 1934. Oil on canvas. Munson-Williams-Proctor Arts Institute/ Art Resource, NY

Compositor: PreMediaGlobal

For product information and technology assistance, contact us at **Cengage Learning Customer & Sales Support, 1-800-354-9706**

For permission to use material from this text or product, submit all requests online at **www.cengage.com/permissions**. Further permissions questions can be emailed to **permissionrequest@cengage.com**

Library of Congress Control Number: 2010936834

ISBN-13: 978-1-111-34155-8

ISBN-10: 1-111-34155-9

Wadsworth
20 Channel Center Street
Boston, MA, 02210
USA

Cengage Learning is a leading provider of customized learning solutions with office locations around the globe, including Singapore, the United Kingdom, Australia, Mexico, Brazil, and Japan. Locate your local office at **international.cengage.com/ region**.

Cengage Learning products are represented in Canada by Nelson Education, Ltd.

For your course and learning solutions, visit **www.cengage.com**.

Purchase any of our products at your local college store or at our preferred online store **www.cengagebrain.com**.

Printed in the United States of America
1 2 3 4 5 6 7 13 12 11 10

Brief Contents

Contents

14

FROM COMPROMISE TO SECESSION, 1850–1861   412

15

CRUCIBLE OF FREEDOM: CIVIL WAR, 1861–1865   443

22

GLOBAL INVOLVEMENTS AND WORLD WAR I, 1902–1920   675

23

COPING WITH CHANGE, 1920–1929   709

30

A CONSERVATIVE REVIVAL AND THE END OF THE COLD WAR, 1980–2000   938

List of Maps

Preface

America and the world have changed dramatically since we began planning *The Enduring Vision* more than twenty-five years ago. Some developments have been welcome and positive; others deeply unsettling. This new Seventh Edition fully documents all these changes, as well as the continuities that offer reassurance for the future.

Although the United States of today differs markedly from the nation of even a few decades ago, the values that give meaning to America—among them individual freedom, social justice, the rule of law, openness to diversity, respect for minority rights, and equality of opportunity—remain constants in our life as a people. The desire to convey the strength of this enduring vision in a world of change continues to guide our efforts in writing this book.

The Enduring Vision, Seventh Edition, builds on the underlying strategy that has guided us from the beginning. We want our history to be not only comprehensive and illuminating, but also lively, readable, and true to the lived experience of earlier generations of Americans. Within a clear political and chronological framework, we integrate the best recent scholarship in all areas of American history. Our interest in social and cultural history, which shapes our own teaching and scholarship, has suffused *The Enduring Vision* from the outset, and it remains central. We integrate the historical experience of women, African-Americans, Hispanic Americans, Asian-Americans, and American Indians—in short, of men and women of all regions, ethnic groups, and social classes who make up the American mosaic.

As we pursue these purposes in this Seventh Edition, we welcome Karen Halttunen to the team of authors. A distinguished historian of nineteenth-century American social and cultural history who teaches at the University of Southern California, Professor Halttunen brings impressive strengths to our mission.

IMPROVEMENTS AND CONTINUITIES

This edition of *The Enduring Vision* brings the work fully up to date, incorporating major developments and scholarship since the Sixth Edition went to press. We have included the best of the new political history, stressing the social, cultural, and economic issues at stake in political decisions and debates. Religious history remains an important focus, from the spiritual values of pre-Columbian communities to the political activism of contemporary conservative Christian groups.

A fresh new design gives the Seventh Edition a strikingly contemporary look. New paintings, photographs, and other illustrations reinforce the narrative throughout the text.

REORGANIZATION OF THE POST-1945 CHAPTERS

In our continuing quest to make the text clear and reader-friendly, we have rearranged some sections and reorganized some chapters. The post-World War II chapters, in particular, have been heavily reorganized to consolidate topical coverage and tighten the narrative. We have edited rigorously but without sacrificing any substantive material. As a result, we have reduced the chapter total from 32 to 31 and shortened the text by about 10 percent.

RENEWED EMPHASIS ON ENVIRONMENTAL HISTORY

Understanding history requires a firm grasp of geography, and *The Enduring Vision* has always emphasized the significance of the land in the interplay of historical events. The book's unique *Prologue* on the American Land solidly establishes that theme early on, and our extensive coverage of environmental history, the land, and the West is fully integrated into the narrative and treated analytically—not simply "tacked on" to a traditional account. We have retained these elements while re-dedicating ourselves to making environmental history even more evident in the Seventh Edition. An upgraded map program offers maps that are rich in information, easy to read, and visually appealing. And our new primary source feature (described in more detail below) features a number of primary sources involving the land, including excerpts from Meriwether Lewis's Journal, the *Book of Mormon*'s Land of Promise, and a Dust Bowl diary.

"BEYOND AMERICA" AND "TECHNOLOGY AND CULTURE"

In the Seventh Edition we again underscore the global context of American history throughout the narrative and in the special feature "Beyond America—Global Interactions" introduced in the Sixth Edition. From the origins of agriculture ten millennia ago to the global impact of environmental changes today, we have emphasized how all facets of our historical experience emerge with fresh new clarity when viewed within a broader world framework.

In the popular "Technology and Culture" feature, and throughout the text, we continue to highlight the historical importance of new inventions and technological innovations. In addition to discussing the applications of science and technology, we note the often unanticipated cultural, social, and political consequences—as, for instance, with the development of the hunting implements of the Paleo-Indians and today's breakthroughs in information processing. Medicine and disease receive extensive coverage, and we look at the epidemics brought by European explorers and settlers as well as today's AIDS crisis, bioethics debates, and controversies over health-care financing.

NEW PRIMARY SOURCE FEATURE: "GOING TO THE SOURCE"

To bring American history vividly alive and offer an opportunity for analysis of historical evidence, we have added a new chapter feature called "Going to the Source." This feature includes a rich selection of primary source material drawing on speeches, diaries, letters, and other primary source materials created by

Americans who lived through and helped shape the great events and historical changes of successive periods. In selecting documents, we focused especially, but not exclusively, on environmental themes. A brief introduction places each selection in context, and focus questions suggest assignment and discussion possibilities. The people who "speak" through "Going to the Source" represent a cross-section of Americans, including presidents (from Abraham Lincoln to Barack Obama), national leaders in various fields, and "ordinary" men and women reflecting on their often extraordinary historical experience, such as Anna Marie Low, a North Dakota farm girl who endured the terrible dust storms of the 1930s, and Beatrice Morales Clifton, who worked at Lockheed during World War II.

VISUAL RESOURCES AND AIDS TO THE STUDENT

To help students grasp the structure and purpose of each chapter, outlines are included at the beginning of each chapter. The chapter Conclusion summarizes the key issues. As a further pedagogical aid, each chapter includes Key Terms that appear in boldface in the text where first introduced. Key Terms are defined in an alphabetical glossary on *The Enduring Vision* website.

Chronologies appear at the end of each chapter to facilitate review.

REVISIONS AND INNOVATIONS IN EACH CHAPTER

We have carefully assessed the coverage, interpretations, and analytic framework of each chapter to incorporate the latest scholarship and emerging themes. This is reflected both in our textual revisions and in the new titles listed in the end-of chapter bibliographies. A chapter-by-chapter glimpse of some of the changes highlights new content and up-to-the-minute scholarship.

The text of **Chapter 1** has been tightened to make it more concise and readable.

Chapter 2 deepens the analysis of the role of environmental factors in the early struggles of the English colonists at Jamestown. The discussion of the Chesapeake colonies and of Quakerism in **Chapter 3** has been made more concise. The "Going to the Source" feature in **Chapter 3** documents a tense exchange between dissenter Anne Hutchinson and Massachusetts governor John Winthrop.

In **Chapter 4**, the section on "The Rise of Colonial Elites" has been reorganized to highlight and sharpen the central point. Several sections in **Chapter 5** have been reworked to give the discussion a smoother narrative flow. In Chapter 5's "Going to the Source" feature, the Ottawa leader Pontiac describes a message from the Great Spirit promising a restoration of vanished animal species if the Indians cease their dependence on whites.

Chapter 6 offers new information on the impact of the American Revolution on African-Americans and on Native Americans, and reframes the discussion of post-Revolutionary state constitutions and the Articles of Confederation.

The conclusion of **Chapter 7** offers a more explicit consideration of the implications of developments in the 1790s for white women and for non-whites. The "Going to the Source" feature reinforces the latter theme as Benjamin Banneker, a free African-American, reminds Thomas Jefferson of the glaring inconsistency between the lofty language of the Declaration of Independence and Jefferson's ownership of slaves.

Chapter 8 extends the discussion of President Jefferson's foreign policy with a fuller treatment of the First Tripolitan War and its sequel—an early U.S. encounter with a Muslim society. The "Going to the Source" document, from Meriwether Lewis's journal, recalls a stressful moment in charting a course through an unfamiliar landscape during the Lewis and Clark Expedition.

Chapters 10 and 11 have been freshly recast in particularly exciting ways. **Chapter 10** is now organized around the theme of *improvement,* both individual and social, that underlay the ferment of antebellum politics, religion, reform, and utopian communitarianism. The complex connections between antislavery and women's rights have been clarified, and the "Going to the Source" selection from *The Book of Mormon* discusses America as the promised land.

Chapter 11 now highlights the theme of Americans' conflicting responses, often expressed in their own voices, to technological innovations. The treatment of mass entertainment elaborates the importance of sensationalism in a range of media, from newspapers and the theater to the writings of Poe, Hawthorne, and Melville. The "Going to the Source" selection, from Thoreau's *Walden,* expresses his views of Nature, wildness, and the American West.

The new "Going to the Source" features in **Chapter 12** offers an extract from a book by Daniel R. Hundley, a southern defender of the slave system.

Chapter 15's "Going to the Source" feature describes life in an African-American regiment during the Civil War.

Chapters 17–20, on the Gilded Age, all stress the environmental and human toll of industrialization. **Chapter 17** incorporates new material on worker accidents in the mining industry. **Chapter 18** offers new material on the cigarette industry and its advertising practices—still a timely topic today. In **Chapter 19** coverage of reform and the working class has been reorganized to enhance the flow and clarity of the narrative. **Chapter 20** consolidates our coverage of politics in this period by incorporating discussion of urban political bosses, and expands our coverage of the Populist movement.

Turning to the twentieth century, **Chapter 21**'s "Going to the Source" feature is from *Our National Parks,* by Progressive-era environmentalist John Muir. **Chapter 22** offers a more in-depth treatment of the long-term causes of World War I; expanded coverage of homefront vigilantism during the war; and a "Going to the Source" feature drawn from the vivid memoirs of a World War I flying ace. **Chapter 23** draws on recent scholarship for an expanded discussion of the ideology of mass consumption and advertising in the 1920s and of the economic theory underlying Treasury secretary Andrew Mellon's tax-cut proposals.

Chapter 24, on the Great Depression and the New Deal, again reflecting new scholarship, deepens the analysis of the New Deal's role in promoting infrastructure development, encouraging long-term economic expansion, and providing a template for post-World War II public-housing and interstate-highway programs.

The coverage of World War II in **Chapter 25** is enhanced by a "Going to the Source" feature recording the memories of women war workers.

Chapters 26–29, treating the 1945-1980 era, have been extensively reorganized to draw together the coverage of the Cold War, the civil rights movement, and the

Vietnam War in a cohesive, topical way, rather than dispersing the treatment of these subjects over four separate chapters.

Chapter 26 now addresses the domestic politics and foreign policy of the Truman and Eisenhower presidencies.

Chapter 27 now covers American society from 1945 to 1960, with expanded treatment of racial changes and the early civil-rights movement.

Chapter 28, beginning with John F. Kennedy's tragically short presidency, focuses in a clear and comprehensive way on the black freedom struggle, Lyndon Johnson's domestic program, and the full span of the Vietnam War.

Chapter 29 examines the political and social ferment of the 1960s and 1970s, including the rise of the New Left and the counterculture, and the crisis-ridden years 1968–1970. The coverage of the 1970s, formerly split between two chapters, is now consolidated into one, offering a clear view of this crucial transitional decade, including the feminist, gay-rights, and environmental movements; the Watergate crisis; and the political, diplomatic, and economic developments of the Ford and Carter presidencies.

Chapter 30, dealing with the years 1980–2000, continues the environmental theme with a "Going to the Source" excerpt from Al Gore's *Earth in the Balance.* This chapter expands coverage of the cultural trends of these years and of the Reagan administration's covert military involvement in Afghanistan—another topic of contemporary interest.

Chapter 31, extensively revised and expanded, focuses on the brief but fateful period from 2000 to the present, including the disputed 2000 presidential election, the Bush administration's response to the attacks of September 11, 2001, the controversial invasion of Iraq and its aftermath, the historic election of Barack Obama in 2008, the ensuing national debates over health-care reform and the deployment of U.S. troops in Afghanistan, and the severe economic recession that tested the American people and the nation's political leadership. This final chapter also explores the long-term economic developments and social and demographic trends that will influence the nation's history well into the future. The "Beyond America" feature newly examines the timely issue of global warming from a transnational perspective.

SUPPLEMENTARY RESOURCES

A wide array of supplements is available to help students master the material and guide instructors in setting up and managing their courses with *The Enduring Vision,* Seventh Edition. For more information on viewing or ordering these materials, please consult your sales representative.

FOR STUDENTS:

- **Companion Website for *The Enduring Vision*** features a rich assortment of resources to help students master the subject matter. The website includes a glossary, flashcards, crossword puzzles, tutorial quizzes, essay questions, critical thinking exercises, web links, and additional suggested readings. To access these course materials, please visit www.cengagebrain.com. At the CengageBrain.com home page, search for the ISBN of your title (from the back cover of your book) using the search box at the top of the page. This will take you to the product page where these resources can be found.

- **Wadsworth American History Resource Center** gives your students access to a "virtual reader" with hundreds of primary sources including speeches, letters, legal documents and transcripts, poems, maps, simulations, time-lines, and additional images that bring history to life, along with interactive assignable exercises. A map feature including Google Earth™ coordinates and exercises will aid in student comprehension of geography and use of maps. Students can compare the traditional textbook map with an aerial view of the location today. The American History Resource Center is an ideal resource for study, review, and research.

FOR INSTRUCTORS:

- **Companion Website for *The Enduring Vision*, 7e** offers instructors access to all of the features of the Student Companion Website, plus access to History-Finder, **the American History Resource Center**, and the Instructor's Resource Manual. The manual includes instructional objectives, chapter outlines and summaries, lecture suggestions, suggested debate and research topics, cooperative learning activities, and suggested readings and resources. To access these materials, please visit http://login.cengage.com.

- HistoryFinder is a searchable online database from which instructors can quickly and easily download thousands of assets, including art, photographs, maps, primary sources, and audio/video clips. Each asset downloads directly into a Microsoft® PowerPoint® slide, allowing instructors to create exciting PowerPoint presentations for their classrooms.

- PowerLecture with ExamView and Join In for *The Enduring Vision*, 7e. This dual platform, all-in-one multimedia resource includes the Instructor's Resource Manual; Test Bank (with key term identification, multiple-choice, short answer, essay, and map questions); Microsoft® PowerPoint® slides of lecture outlines and images and maps from the text that can be used as offered, or customized by importing personal lecture slides or other material; and JoinIn® PowerPoint® slides with clicker content. Also included is ExamView, an easy-to-use assessment and tutorial system that allows instructors to create, deliver, and customize tests in minutes. Instructors can build tests with as many as 250 questions using up to 12 question types, and using ExamView's complete word-processing capabilities, they can enter an unlimited number of new questions or edit existing ones.

- WebTutor™ on Blackboard® and WebCT® for The Enduring Vision provides text-specific, pre-formatted content and total flexibility, allowing instructors to create and manage their own custom course website. WebTutor's course management tool gives instructors the ability to provide virtual office hours, post syllabi, set up threaded discussions, track student progress with the quizzing material, and much more.

ADDITIONAL SUPPLEMENTS

- *Rand McNally Atlas of American History,* 2/e is available for packaging with this text. This comprehensive atlas features more than 80 maps, with new content covering global perspectives, including events in the Middle East from 1945 to 2005, as well as population trends in the U.S. and around the world. Additional maps document voyages of discovery; the settling of the colonies; major U.S. military engagements, including the American Revolution and World Wars I and II; and sources of immigrations, ethnic populations and patterns of economic change.

- **Enduring Voices Document Set.** A two-volume document collection *Enduring Voices* can be packaged with the text.

- **Other United States History Readers.** Wadsworth, Cengage Learning publishes a wide variety of primary and secondary source readers that would complement this text. These include collections focusing on cultural history, political documents, social history essays, biography, and readers with specific methods of primary source analysis. Contact your Wadsworth, Cengage Learning sales representative for more details about the readers that would work best for you and your students.

ACKNOWLEDGMENTS

In undertaking this major revision of our textbook, we have drawn on our own scholarly work and teaching experience. We have also kept abreast of new work of historical interpretation, as reported by our U.S. history colleagues in their books, scholarly articles, and papers at historical meetings. We list much of this new work in the books cited at the close of each chapter, and in the Additional Bibliographies on *The Enduring Vision* website. We are much indebted to all these colleagues.

We have also benefited from the comments and suggestions of instructors who have adopted *The Enduring Vision;* from colleagues and students who have written us about specific details; and from the following scholars and teachers who offered systematic evaluations of specific chapters. Their perceptive comments have been most helpful in the revision process.

Cara Anzilotti, *Loyola Marymount University*
Robert Berta, *Northern Kentucky University*
Troy Bickham, *Texas A&M University*
Michael Brattain, *Georgia State University*
Kim Brinck-Johnsen, *University of New Hampshire*

Roger Bromert, *Southwestern Oklahoma State University*
Michael Colomaio, *Alfred State College*
Scott Cook, *Motlow State Community College*
Frederick B. Gates, *Southwestern Oklahoma State University*
Stephanie Holyfield, *University of Delaware*
George Jarrett, *Cerritos College*
Steven Kite, *Fort Hays State University*
Michael Krenn, *Appalachian State University*
Lisa Lane, *MiraCosta College*
John Leiby, *Paradise Valley Community College*
Edith MacDonald, *University of Central Florida*
Steven Miller, *Goshen College*
Uraina Pack, *Clarion University*
Christopher Phelps, *Ohio State University*
Steven Reiss, *Northeastern Illinois University*
Donald Rogers, *Central Connecticut State University*
Steve Stein, *University of Memphis*
Patricia Thompson, *University of Texas at San Antonio*
Paul Vandermeer, *Arizona State University*
Keith Volanto, *Collin County Community College*
William Whisenhunt, *College of DuPage*
Paul C. Young, *Utica College*

In addition, Clifford Clark would like to acknowledge the research assistance of David B. Hirsch.

Finally, we salute the skilled professionals at Wadsworth/Cengage Learning Company whose expertise and enthusiastic commitment to this new Seventh Edition guided us through every stage and helped sustain our own determination to make this the best book we could possibly write. Ann West, Senior Sponsoring Editor, presided over our initial planning meeting with good nature and wise suggestions, and has been a reassuring presence throughout. Development Editor Jan Fitter, with an unfailing upbeat outlook and a wealth of experience, masterfully managed the day-to-day challenges of keeping us all on track. Pembroke Herbert and Sandi Rygiel of Picture Research Consultants & Archives again brought their creative skills to bear in seeking out fresh and powerful visual images for the work. Senior Content Project Manager Jane Lee ably shepherded the work through the crucial stages of production, while Assistant Editor Megan Curry oversaw the increasingly important Web-based resources. Megan Chrisman, the Senior Editorial Assistant, worked with reviewers and provided support through all phases of development. Charlotte Miller of Mabou Studio brought a wealth of cartographic experience to upgrading the *Enduring Vision*'s map program. Katherine Bates, Senior Marketing Manager, offered insights that helped us prepare a work that would not only represent the best in historical scholarship, but would also appeal to instructors and to the students who give meaning to the entire undertaking.

We also recall with warm appreciation a host of gift ed and dedicated editors, staff members, marketers, and sales representatives at D. C. Heath & Co. and Houghton Mifflin Company who have worked with us over the years to make *The Enduring Vision* the enduring success it has been.

Paul S. Boyer
Clifford E. Clark, Jr.
Karen Halttunen
Joseph F. Kett
Neal Salisbury
Harvard Sitkoff
Nancy Woloch

About the Authors

PAUL S. BOYER, Merle Curti Professor of History emeritus at the University of Wisconsin, Madison, earned his Ph.D. from Harvard University. An editor of *Notable American Women, 1607–1950* (1971), he also coauthored *Salem Possessed: The Social Origins of Witchcraft* (1974), for which, with Stephen Nissenbaum, he received the John H. Dunning Prize of the American Historical Association. His other works include *Urban Masses and Moral Order in America, 1820–1920* (1978), *By the Bomb's Early Light: American Thought and Culture at the Dawn of the Atomic Age* (1985), *When Time Shall Be No More: Prophecy Belief in Modern American Culture* (1992), and *Promises to Keep: The United States since World War II,* 3rd ed. (2003). He is also editor-in-chief of the *Oxford Companion to United States History* (2001). His articles and essays have appeared in the *American Quarterly, New Republic,* and other journals. He has been a visiting professor at the University of California, Los Angeles; Northwestern University; and the College of William and Mary.

CLIFFORD E. CLARK, JR., M.A. AND A.D. HULINGS Professor of American Studies and professor of history at Carleton College, earned his Ph.D. from Harvard University. He has served as both the chair of the History Department and director of the American Studies program at Carleton. Clark is the author of *Henry Ward Beecher: Spokesman for a Middle-Class America* (1978), *The American Family Home, 1800–1960* (1986), *The Intellectual and Cultural History of Anglo-America since 1789* in the *General History of the Americas,* and, with Carol Zellie, *Northfield: The History and Architecture of a Community* (1997). He also has edited and contributed to *Minnesota in a Century of Change: The State and Its People since 1900* (1989). A past member of the Council of the American Studies Association, Clark is active in the fields of material culture studies and historic preservation, and he serves on the Northfield, Minnesota, Historical Preservation Commission.

KAREN HALTTUNEN, professor of history at the University of Southern California, earned her Ph.D. from Yale University. Her works include *Confidence Men and Painted Women: A Study of Middle-Class Culture in America, 1830–1870* (1982) and *Murder Most Foul: The Killer and the American Gothic Imagination* (1998). She edited *The Blackwell Companion to American Cultural History* (2008) and co-edited, with Lewis Perry, *Moral Problems in American Life: New Essays on Cultural History* (1998). As president of the American Studies Association and as vice-president of the Teaching Division of the American Historical Association, she has actively promoted K16 collaboration in teaching history. She has held fellowships from the Guggenheim and Mellon Foundations, the National Endowment for the Humanities, the Huntington Library, and the National Humanities Center, and has been principal investigator on several Teaching American History grants from the Department of Education.

JOSEPH F. KETT, James Madison Professor of History at the University of Virginia, received his Ph.D. from Harvard University. His works include The Formation of the American Medical Profession: The Role of Institutions, 1780–1860 (1968), Rites of Passage: Adolescence in America, 1790-Present (1977), The Pursuit of Knowledge under Difficulties: From Self-Improvement to Adult Education in America, 1750–1990 (1994), and The New Dictionary of Cultural Literacy (2002), of which he is coauthor. A former History Department chair at Virginia, he also has participated on the Panel on Youth of the President's Science Advisory Committee, has served on the Board of Editors of the History of Education Quarterly, and is a past member of the Council of the American Studies Association.

NEAL SALISBURY, Barbara Richmond 1940 Professor Emeritus in the Humanities (History), at Smith College, received his Ph.D. from the University of California, Los Angeles. He is the author of *Manitou and Providence: Indians, Europeans, and The Making of New England, 1500–1643* (1982), editor of *The Sovereignty and Goodness of God,* by Mary Rowlandson (1997), and co-editor, with Philip J. Deloria, of *The Companion to American Indian History* (2002). With R. David Edmunds and Frederick E. Hoxie, he has written *The People: A History of Native America* (2007) (also published by Cengage). He has contributed numerous articles to journals and edited collections, and co-edits a book series, Cambridge Studies in North American Indian History. He is active in the fields of colonial and Native American history, and has served as president of the American Society for Ethnohistory and on the Council of the Omohundro Institute of Early American History and Culture.

HARVARD SITKOFF, professor of history at the University of New Hampshire, earned his Ph.D. from Columbia University. He is the author of *A New Deal for Blacks* (1978), *The Struggle for Black Equality, 1954–1992* (1992), and *Postwar America: A Student Companion* (2000); coauthor of the National Park Service's *Racial Desegregation in Public Education in the United States* (2000) and *The World War II Homefront* (2003); and editor of Fifty Years Later: The New Deal Reevaluated (1984), A History of Our Time, 6th ed. (2002), and Perspectives on Modern America: Making Sense of the Twentieth Century (2001). His articles have appeared in the American Quarterly, Journal of American History, and Journal of Southern History, among others. A frequent lecturer at universities abroad, he has been awarded the Fulbright Commission's John Adams Professorship of American Civilization in the Netherlands and the Mary Ball Washington Professorship of American History in Ireland.

NANCY WOLOCH received her Ph.D. from Indiana University. She is the author of *Women and the American Experience* (4th ed., 2006), editor of *Early American Women: A Documentary History, 1600–1900* (2nd ed., 2002), and coauthor, with Walter LaFeber and Richard Polenberg, of *The American Century: A History of the United States since the 1890s* (6th ed., 2008). She is also the author of *Muller v. Oregon: A Brief History with Documents* (1996). She teaches American history and American Studies at Barnard College, Columbia University.

1

NATIVE PEOPLES OF AMERICA, TO 1500

CHAPTER OUTLINE

• The First Americans, ca. 13,000–2500 B.C.E. • Cultural Diversity, ca. 2500 B.C.E.–C.E. 1500 • North American Peoples on the Eve of European Contact

---

THE FIRST AMERICANS, CA. 13,000–2500 B.C.E.

Exactly how and when the Western Hemisphere was first settled remains uncertain. Many Indians believe their ancestors originated in the Americas, but most scientific findings point to the arrival of the first humans from northeastern Asia sometime during the last Ice Age (ca. 33,000–10,700 B.C.E.). These earliest Americans traveled by two different routes when land linked Siberia and Alaska (see Map 1.1). Thereafter, as the Ice Age waned and global temperatures rose, Native Americans dispersed throughout the hemisphere, adapting to environments ranging from tropical to frigid. Though divided into small, widely scattered groups, they interacted through trade and travel. Over several thousand years, Indians learned from one another and developed ways of life that had much in common despite their diverse backgrounds.

Peopling New Worlds   Most archaeologists agree that humans had arrived in the Americas by 13,000 B.C.E. Traveling in small foraging bands in search of food, they apparently traveled by watercraft, following the then-continuous coastline from Siberia to Alaska and progressing southward along the Pacific coast. Along the way, groups stopped and either settled nearby or traveled inland to establish new homes. Coastal sites as far south as Monte Verde, Chile, reveal evidence from about 12,000 B.C.E. of peoples who fed on marine life, birds, small mammals, and wild plants, as well as an occasional mastodon. (Archaeologists estimate dates by measuring the radioactive carbon 14 [radiocarbon] in organic materials such as food remains.) Some later migrants

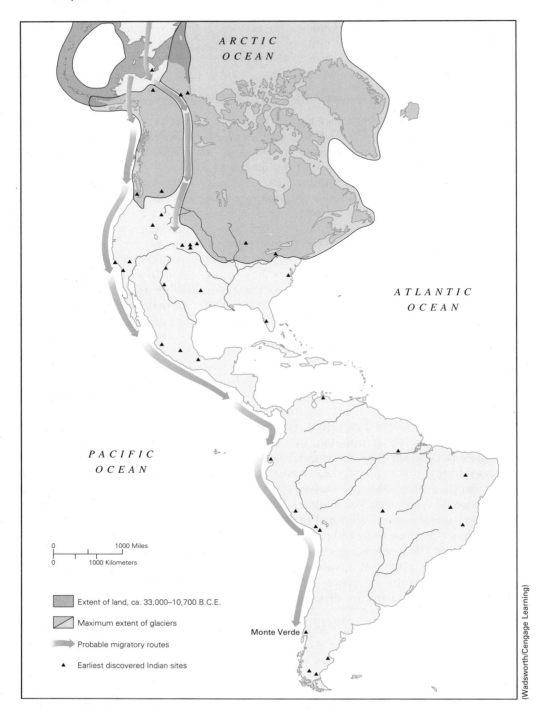

ARCTIC
OCEAN

ATLANTIC
OCEAN

PACIFIC
OCEAN

0 ——————— 1000 Miles
0 ——————— 1000 Kilometers

Extent of land, ca. 33,000–10,700 B.C.E.

Maximum extent of glaciers

Probable migratory routes

▲   Earliest discovered Indian sites

Monte Verde

(Wadsworth/Cengage Learning)

MAP 1.1 The Peopling of the Americas

Scientists postulate two probable routes by which the earliest peoples reached America. By 9500 B.C.E., they had settled throughout the Western Hemisphere.

reached North America by land. As the glaciers gradually melted, a corridor developed east of the Rocky Mountains through which these travelers passed before dispersing themselves over much of the Western Hemisphere.

Scientists have determined that most Native Americans are descended from these early migrants. However, the ancestors of some native peoples came later, also from northeastern Asia, after the land connecting Siberia with Alaska had submerged. Speakers of a language known as Athapaskan settled in Alaska and northwestern Canada in about 7000 B.C.E. Some of their descendants later migrated to the Southwest to form the Apaches and Navajos. After 3000 B.C.E., Inuits (Eskimos) and Aleuts crossed the Bering Sea from Siberia to Alaska.

Native American oral traditions offer conflicting support for scientists' theories, depending on how the traditions are interpreted. Pueblos and Navajos in the Southwest tell how their forebears experienced perilous journeys through other worlds before emerging from underground in their present homelands, while the Iroquois trace their ancestry to a pregnant woman who fell from the "sky world." Among the Iroquois and other peoples, the original humans could not settle the water-covered planet until a diving bird or animal brought soil from the ocean bottom, creating an island on which they could walk. Still other traditions recall large mammals, monsters, or "hairy people" with whom the first people shared Earth. Many Native Americans today insist that such accounts confirm that their ancestors originated in the Western Hemisphere. However, others note that the stories do not specify a place of origin and may well reflect the experiences of their ancestors as they journeyed from Asia, across water, ice, and unknown lands, and encountered large mammals before settling in their new homes. If not taken literally, they maintain, the traditions support rather than contradict scientists' theories.

Paleo-Indians, as archaeologists call the earliest Americans, established the foundations of Native American life. Paleo-Indians appear to have traveled within well-defined hunting territories in **bands** consisting of several families and totaling about fifteen to fifty people. Men hunted while women prepared food and cared for the children. Bands left their territories when traveling to quarries to obtain stone for making tools and other objects. There they encountered other bands, with whose members they exchanged ideas and goods, intermarried, and participated in religious ceremonies. As in nonmarket economies and nonstate societies throughout history, these exchanges followed the principle of **reciprocity**—the mutual bestowing of gifts and favors—rather than the notion that one party should accumulate profits or power at the expense of the other. These encounters enabled Paleo-Indians to develop a broad cultural life that transcended their small bands.

The earliest Paleo-Indians found a hunter's paradise in which large mammals—mammoths, mastodons, and giant species of horses, camels, bison, caribou, and moose—roamed America, innocent of the ways of human predators. Around 9000 B.C.E., the megafauna quickly became extinct. Although some scholars believe that Paleo-Indian hunters killed off the large mammals, most maintain that the mammals were doomed not just by humans but by the warming climate, which disrupted the food chain on which they depended. Human beings, however, were major beneficiaries of environmental changes associated with the end of the Ice Age.

**Archaic
Societies**

After about 8000 B.C.E., Native Americans began modifying their Paleo-Indian ways. The warming of Earth's atmosphere continued until about 4000 B.C.E., with far-reaching global effects. Sea levels rose, flooding coastal areas, while glacial run-off filled interior waterways. The glaciers receded northward, along with the arctic and subarctic environments that had formerly extended into what are now the lower forty-eight states of the United States. Treeless plains and evergreen forests gave way to deciduous forests in the East, grassland prairies on the Plains, and desert in much of the West. The regional environments we know today emerged during this period.

Archaic peoples, as archaeologists term Native Americans who flourished in these new environments, lived off the wider varieties of flora and fauna that were now available. With more sources of food, communities required less land and supported larger populations. Some Indians in temperate regions now resided in year-round villages. From about 3900 to 2800 B.C.E., for example, the 100 to 150 residents of a community near Kampsville, Illinois, obtained ample supplies of fish, mussels, mammals, birds, nuts, and seeds—without moving their homes.

Over time, Archaic Americans expanded women's and men's roles. Men took responsibility for fishing as well as hunting, while women procured wild plant products. Gender roles are apparent in burials at Indian Knoll, Kentucky, where tools relating to hunting, fishing, woodworking, and leather-working were usually buried with men and those relating to cracking nuts and grinding seeds with women. Yet gender-specific distinctions did not apply to all activities, for objects used by religious healers were distributed equally between male and female graves.

Archaic Indians—usually women in North America—honed their skills at harvesting wild plants. Through generations of close observation, they determined how to weed, prune, irrigate, transplant, and otherwise manipulate their environments to favor plants that provided food and medicine. They also developed specialized tools for digging and grinding as well as more effective methods of drying and storing seeds. The most sophisticated early plant cultivators lived in **Mesoamerica** (central and southern Mexico and Central America), where maize agriculture was highly developed by 2500 B.C.E. (see Beyond America).

CULTURAL DIVERSITY, CA. 2500 B.C.E.–C.E. 1500

After about 2500 B.C.E., many Native Americans moved beyond the ways of their Archaic forebears. The greatest change occurred among peoples whose environments enabled them to produce food surpluses by cultivating crops or other means. Some of these societies transformed trade networks into extensive religious and political systems linking several—sometimes dozens of—local communities. A few of these groupings evolved into formal confederacies and even states. In environments where food sources were few and widely scattered, mobile hunting-fishing-gathering bands persisted.

**Mesoamerica
and South
America**

As Mesoamerican farmers refined their practices, their crops improved. When they planted beans alongside maize, the beans released an amino acid, lysine, into the maize that heightened its nutritional value. Higher yields and improved nutrition led societies to center their lives around farming. Over the next eight centuries, maize-based farming societies spread throughout Mesoamerica.

After 2000 B.C.E., some Mesoamerican societies produced crop surpluses that they traded to less populous, nonfarming neighbors. Expanding their trade contacts, a number of these societies established formal exchange networks that enabled them to enjoy more wealth and power than their partners. After 1200 B.C.E., a few communities, such as those of the Olmecs in Mesoamerica and Chavín de Huántar in the Andes developed into large urban centers, subordinating smaller neighbors. Unlike in earlier societies, the cities were highly unequal. A few wealthy elites dominated thousands of residents, and hereditary rulers claimed kinship with religious deities. Laborers built elaborate temples and palaces—including the first American pyramids—and artisans created statues of rulers and gods.

Although the earliest hereditary rulers exercised absolute power, their realms consisted of a few closely clustered communities. Anthropologists term such political societies **chiefdoms**, as opposed to **states** in which a ruler or government exercises direct authority over many communities. Besides Mesoamerica and the Andes, chiefdoms eventually emerged in the Mississippi and Amazon valleys. A few states arose in Mesoamerica after C.E. 1 and in South America after C.E. 500. Although men ruled most chiefdoms and states, women served as chiefs in some Andean societies until the Spanish arrived.

The capital of the largest early state, Teotihuacán, was situated about fifty miles northeast of modern-day Mexico City and numbered about a hundred thousand people between the second and seventh centuries C.E. At its center was a complex of pyramids, the largest of which, the Sun Pyramid, was about 1 million cubic meters in volume. Teotihuacán dominated the peoples of the valley of Mexico, and its trade networks extended over much of present-day Mexico. Although Teotihuacán declined in the eighth century, it exercised enormous influence on the religion, government, and culture of its neighbors.

Teotihuacán's greatest influence was on the Maya, whose kingdom-states flourished from southern Mexico to Honduras between the seventh and fifteenth centuries. The Maya developed a calendar, a numerical system (which included the concept of zero), and a system of phonetic, hieroglyphic writing. Maya scribes produced thousands of books on bark paper glued into long, folded strips. The books recorded religious ceremonies, historical traditions, and astronomical observations.

Other powerful states flourished in Mesoamerica and South America until the fifteenth century, when two mighty empires arose to challenge them. The first was the empire of the **Aztecs** (known at the time as the Mexica), who had migrated from the north during the thirteenth century and settled on the shore of Lake Texcoco as subjects of the local inhabitants. Overthrowing their rulers in 1428, the Aztecs went on to conquer other cities around the lake and extended their domain to the Gulf Coast. Aztec expansion took a bloody turn in the 1450s during a four-year drought, which the Aztecs interpreted as a sign that the gods, like themselves, were hungry. Aztec priests maintained that the only way to satisfy the gods was to serve them human blood and hearts. From then on, conquering Aztec warriors sought captives for sacrifice in order, as they believed, to nourish the gods.

A massive temple complex at the capital of Tenochtitlán formed the sacred center of the Aztec empire. The Great Temple consisted of two joined pyramids and

BEYOND AMERICA — GLOBAL INTERACTIONS

The Origins and Spread of Agriculture

For most of their two and a half million years on Earth, human beings lived as hunter-gatherers or foragers, subsisting on wild plants and animals. It was only between ten thousand and four thousand years ago that scattered groups of people transformed a few dozen wild plant species into domesticated crops. The grain, pulse (peas and beans), root, and melon/squash crops they produced remain the principal sources of plant food for humans and their domestic animals today.

The transformation of wild plants into crops was a gradual process. Through careful observation, gatherers selected varieties of plants that produced the highest yields. After planting the largest seeds of these varieties, they eliminated nearby, competing plants and harvested the favored plants when the food was ripe. As crop production intensified, farmer-gatherers developed specialized tools, such as digging sticks and hoes, to facilitate the planting of seeds and elimination of weeds. Over time, the new foods replaced many wild sources of food in farming peoples' diets.

Gatherers domesticated plants in just a few, widely separate parts of the world. In about 8000 B.C.E., people began cultivating wheat, barley, and peas in the Middle East; sugar cane in New Guinea; and squash in Peru. Within 500 years, similar processes had begun with rice in southern China; bananas and taro, a root crop, in New Guinea; and sorghum, a grain, in the eastern Sahara region of Africa. (Climatic warming would later turn the Sahara into a desert, ending farming there.) Maize cultivation began in Mesoamerica in about 5000 B.C.E. By around 3500 B.C.E., Native Americans had domesticated potatoes in the Andes Mountains and manioc— a starchy root crop—in the Amazon Basin. Within another one thousand years, women in parts of eastern North America had begun cultivating favored varieties of squash, sunflowers, and grasses.

In domesticating wild plants, early farmers shaped the evolution of plant species. The most complex example of domestication occurred in the highland Mexican valley of Tehuacan, where Native Americans experimented with a lowland plant called *teosinte*. Through an intricate process of trial and error, they selected mutated seeds that flourished at higher elevations and yielded favorable characteristics such as larger cobs and kernels and better taste. By continuing to plant preferred seeds, the Indians eventually produced a new, much larger species— maize—with dozens of varieties. In so doing, geneticist Nina V. Federoff has written, they achieved "arguably man's first, and perhaps his greatest, feat of genetic engineering."

From its few points of origin, agriculture spread to other parts of the world. In some cases, nonfarming societies acquired seeds and agricultural know-how through trade or from immigrating farmers. Wheat and barley moved beyond the Middle East to Europe, reaching Greece by 6000 B.C.E., Central Europe by 5000 B.C.E., and parts of western Europe by 4000 B.C.E. Similarly, maize cultivation expanded in all directions from the Tehuacan Valley. By 2500 B.C.E., Indians were growing it elsewhere in Central America, in the Amazon River basin, and as far northward as what is now

was surrounded by several smaller pyramids and other buildings. Most of the more than two hundred deities the Aztecs honored originated with earlier and contemporary societies, including those they had subjugated.

To support the nearly two hundred thousand people residing in and around Tenochtitlán, the Aztecs maximized their production of food. They drained swampy the American Southwest. In other cases, whole societies of farmers invaded new lands, subordinating or expelling hunter-gatherers. For example, southern Chinese rice farmers took over favorable lands in northern China and Southeast Asia.

As agriculture spread, farmers adapted plants to new environments. Maize arrived in eastern North America in about 300 B.C.E., but remained a minor crop for another thousand years until women there developed a strain that produced high yields in climates with as few as one hundred frost-free days per year. Thereafter, it was a dietary mainstay for eastern North American Indians. Once they adopted crops originating elsewhere, some farmers then domesticated local plants, further diversifying their diets. For example, only after adopting wheat and barley from the Middle East did western Europeans discover how to cultivate indigenous oats and poppies.

Climate, topography, soil composition, and availability of water limited agricultural production to certain, mostly temperate areas. Within these areas, farming required that people have access to and knowledge of the few plants that could be effectively cultivated on a large scale. In the absence of these conditions, many people remained foragers and did not attempt to farm. Even where farming was a realistic option, its adoption was not inevitable. When members of a hunting-gathering band began to rely on crops, they had to remain in one place for longer periods of each year in order to tend the fields, thereby foregoing other food-gathering practices that had proven reliable. A decision to cultivate often was dictated by the shortage of a wild food source on which a group had

depended, but in other cases people took a risk that unfamiliar crops would flourish and not succumb to fluctuations in climate or to blight. While evidence is hard to come by, a group's cultural values and beliefs about their place in nature undoubtedly influenced their decisions.

In many parts of the world, as people began cultivating plants, they also domesticated animals. Although hunters had long used dogs to track prey, it was only after 8000 B.C.E. that people in the Middle East began to tame wild sheep, goats, and cattle. Soon people in the Eastern Hemisphere domesticated other species, including water buffalo, donkeys, pigs, chickens, and—much later—horses and camels. Animals supplied people not only with meat but also with milk, eggs, wool, labor (including in agricultural fields), and transportation. Animal domestication was severely limited in the Western Hemisphere. Ancestral species of horses and camels flourished in the Americas when humans first arrived but soon became extinct. By the time Native Americans began farming, the only species suitable for taming were dogs, llamas, turkeys, and guinea pigs.

Until C.E. 1492, domesticated plants (and animals) spread strictly within either the Eastern Hemisphere or the Western Hemisphere. Thereafter a "Columbian exchange" would transform many species into global crops (see Chapter 2).

Questions for Analysis

- *By what processes were plants first domesticated?*
- *Why were domesticated crops a primary source of food in some parts of the world and not in others?*

areas and created artificial islands with rich soil from the lake bottom. Aztec farmers grew food on the islands to supply the urban population. Aztec engineers devised an elaborate irrigation system to provide fresh water for both people and crops.

Sun Pyramid, Teotihuacán *Built over several centuries, this pyramid remained the largest structure in the Americas until after the Spanish arrived.*

(Richard Alexander Cooke III)

The Aztecs collected taxes from subjects living within about a hundred miles of the capital. Conquered peoples farther away paid tribute, which replaced the free exchanges of goods formerly carried on with neighbors. Trade beyond the Aztec domain was conducted by *pochteca*, traders who traveled in armed caravans. The *pochteca* sought salt, cacao, jewelry, feathers, jaguar pelts, cotton, and precious stones and metals, including gold and turquoise, the latter obtained from the American Southwest.

The Aztecs were still expanding in the early sixteenth century, but rebellions constantly flared within their realm. They had surrounded and weakened, but not subjugated, one neighboring rival, while another blocked their westward expansion. Would the Aztecs have expanded still farther? We will never know because they were violently crushed in the sixteenth century by another, even more far-flung empire, the Spanish (see Chapter 2).

Meanwhile, a second empire, that of the **Incas**, arose in the Western Hemisphere. From their sumptuous capital at Cuzco, the Incas conquered and subordinated societies over much of the Andes and adjacent regions after 1438. One key to the Incas' expansion was their ability to produce and distribute a wide range of surplus crops, including maize, beans, potatoes, and meats. They constructed terraced irrigation systems for watering crops on mountainous terrain, perfected freeze-drying and other preservation techniques, built large storehouses, and constructed a vast network of roads and bridges. The Incas were still expanding when they too were overcome by Spanish invaders in the sixteenth century.

The Southwest

The Southwest is a uniformly arid region with a variety of landscapes. Waters from rugged mountains and forested plateaus follow ancient channels through vast expanses of desert on their way to the gulfs of Mexico and California. The amount of water has fluctuated over time, but securing water has always been a challenge for southwestern peoples. In spite of this challenge, some of them became farmers.

Maize reached the Southwest via Mesoamerican trade links in about 2500 B.C.E. Yet full-time farming began only after 400 B.C.E., with the introduction of a more drought-resistant strain. Thereafter, southwestern populations rose and Indian cultures were transformed. The two most influential Southwestern cultures were Hohokam and Ancestral Pueblo.

Hohokam culture emerged in about 300 C.E., several centuries after ancestors of the Akimel O'odham and Tohono O'odham Indians began farming in the Gila and Salt River valleys of southern Arizona. Hohokam peoples built irrigation canals that enabled them to harvest two crops a year. To construct and maintain their canals, the Hohokam organized large, coordinated work forces. They built permanent towns, usually consisting of several hundred people. Although many towns remained independent, others joined confederations in which several towns were linked by canals. The central village in each confederation coordinated labor, trade, religion, and political life for member communities.

Although a local creation, Hohokam culture drew on Mesoamerican materials and ideas. From about the sixth century C.E., the large villages had ball courts and platform mounds similar to those in Mesoamerica at the time. Mesoamerican influence was also apparent in the creations of Hohokam artists, who worked in clay, stone, turquoise, and shell. Archaeologists have uncovered rubber balls, macaw feathers, cottonseeds, and copper bells from Mesoamerica at Hohokam sites.

Ancestral Pueblo culture originated in about C.E. 1 in the Four Corners area where Arizona, New Mexico, Colorado, and Utah meet. By around C.E. 700, Ancestral Pueblos were harvesting crops, living in permanent villages, and making pottery. Thereafter, they expanded over a wide area and became the most powerful people in the Southwest.

A distinguishing characteristic of Ancestral Pueblo culture was its architecture. Ancestral Pueblo villages consisted of extensive complexes of attached apartments and storage rooms, along with *kivas*—partly underground structures in which male religious leaders conducted ceremonies. To this day, similar apartments and kivas remain central features of Pueblo Indian architecture in the Southwest. Ancestral Pueblo culture reached its height between about 900 and 1150, during an unusually wet period in the Southwest. In Chaco Canyon, a cluster of twelve large towns forged a powerful confederation numbering about fifteen thousand people. A system of roads radiated from the canyon to satellite towns as far as sixty-five miles away. The roads were perfectly straight; their builders even carved out stairs or footholds on steep cliffs rather than go around them. By controlling rainwater runoff through small dams and terraces, the towns fed themselves as well as the satellites. The largest town, Pueblo Bonito, had about twelve hundred inhabitants and was the home of two Great Kivas, each about fifty feet in diameter. People traveled over the roads from the satellites to Chaco Canyon's large kivas for religious ceremonies. The canyon was also a major trade center, with links to Mesoamerica, the Great Plains, the Mississippi valley, and California.

Ancestral Pueblo culture, as manifested at Chaco Canyon, Mesa Verde in southwestern Colorado, and other sites, declined in the twelfth and thirteenth

(© Bettmann/Corbis)

Cliff Palace, Mesa Verde *Modern tourists help demonstrate the scale of this remarkable Ancestral Pueblo community site.*

centuries. Although other factors contributed, the overriding cause was drought. As often has happened in human history, an era of abundant rainfall ended abruptly. Without enough water, the highly concentrated inhabitants abandoned the great centers, dispersing to form new, smaller communities, many of them on the Rio Grande. Their modern Pueblo descendants would encounter Spanish colonizers three centuries later (see Chapter 2). Hohokam communities also dispersed when drought came. With farming peoples now living in the few areas with enough water, the drier lands of the Southwest attracted the nonfarming Apaches and Navajos, whose arrival at the end of the fourteenth century ended their long migration from the far north (mentioned earlier in this chapter).

The Eastern Woodlands

In contrast to the Southwest, the Eastern Woodlands—stretching from the Mississippi valley to the Atlantic Ocean—had abundant water. Water and deciduous forests provided Woodlands Indians with a rich variety of food sources, while the region's extensive river systems facilitated long-distance travel. As a result, many eastern Indians established populous villages and complex confederations.

By 1200 B.C.E., about five thousand people lived at **Poverty Point** on the lower Mississippi River. The town featured earthworks consisting of two large mounds and six concentric embankments, the outermost of which spanned more than half a mile in diameter. During the spring and autumn equinoxes, a person standing on the larger mound could watch the sun rise directly over the village center. As elsewhere in the Americas, solar observations were the basis for religious beliefs and a calendar.

Poverty Point was the center of a larger political and economic unit. The settlement imported large quantities of quartz, copper, obsidian, crystal, and other materials from long distances for redistribution to nearby communities. These communities almost certainly supplied some of the labor for the earthworks. Poverty Point's general design and organization indicate Olmec influence from Mesoamerica. Poverty Point flourished for about three centuries and then declined, for reasons unknown. Nevertheless, it foreshadowed later developments in the Eastern Woodlands.

A different kind of mound-building culture, called **Adena**, emerged in the Ohio valley around 400 B.C.E. Adena villages were smaller than Poverty Point, rarely exceeding four hundred inhabitants. But Adena people spread over a wide area and built hundreds of mounds, most of them containing graves. The treatment of Adena dead varied according to social or political status. Some corpses were cremated; others were placed in round clay basins; and still others were given elaborate tombs.

After 100 B.C.E., Adena culture evolved into a more complex and widespread culture known as **Hopewell**, which spread from the Ohio valley to the Illinois River valley. Some Hopewell centers contained two or three dozen mounds within enclosures of several square miles. Hopewell elites were buried with thousands of freshwater pearls or copper ornaments or with sheets of mica, quartz, or other sacred substances. These and other materials originated in locales throughout America east of the Rockies. Through far-flung trade networks, Hopewell religious and technological influence spread to communities as far away as Wisconsin, Missouri, Florida, and New York. Although the great Hopewell centers were abandoned by about 600 B.C.E. (for reasons that are unclear), they had an enormous influence on subsequent developments in eastern North America.

The peoples of Poverty Point and the Adena and Hopewell cultures did little farming. Indian women in Kentucky and Missouri had cultivated small amounts of squash as early as 2500 B.C.E., and maize first appeared east of the Mississippi by 300 B.C.E. But agriculture did not become the primary food source for Woodlands people until between the seventh and twelfth centuries C.E.

The first full-time farmers in the East lived on the floodplains of the Mississippi River and its major tributaries. Beginning around C.E. 700, they developed a new culture, called **Mississippian**. The volume of Mississippian craft production and long-distance trade dwarfed that of Adena and Hopewell peoples. As in Mesoamerica, Mississippian centers, numbering hundreds or even thousands of people, arose around open plazas. Large platform mounds adjoined the plazas, topped by sumptuous religious temples and the residences of chiefs and other elites. Religious ceremonies focused on the worship of the sun as the source of agricultural fertility. The people considered chiefs to be related to the sun. When a chief died, his wives and servants were killed so that they could accompany him in the afterlife. Largely in connection with their religious and funeral rituals, Mississippian artists produced highly sophisticated work in clay, stone, shell, copper, wood, and other materials.

After C.E. 900, Mississippian centers formed extensive networks based on riverborne trade and shared religious beliefs, each dominated by a single metropolis. The largest, most powerful such system centered on **Cahokia,** located near modern St. Louis, Missouri, where about twenty thousand people inhabited a 125-square-mile metropolitan area.

For about two and a half centuries, Cahokia reigned supreme in the Mississippi valley. After C.E. 1200, however, Cahokia and other valley centers experienced shortages of food and other resources. As in the Southwest, densely concentrated societies had taxed a fragile environment with a fluctuating climate. Competition for suddenly scarce resources led to debilitating warfare and undermined Cahokia and its allies. The survivors fled to the surrounding prairies and westward to the lower valleys of the Plains, where they regrouped in decentralized villages. Mississippian chiefdoms and temple mound centers persisted in the Southeast, where Spanish explorers would later encounter them as the forerunners of Cherokees, Creeks, and other southeastern Indian peoples (see Chapter 2).

Despite Cahokia's decline, Mississippian culture profoundly affected Native Americans in the Eastern Woodlands. Mississippians spread new strains of maize and beans, along with techniques and tools for cultivating these crops. Life for Indians as far north as the Great Lakes and southern New England revolved around village-based farming. Only in more northerly Eastern Woodlands areas was the growing season usually too short for maize (which required one hundred or more frost-free days) to be a reliable crop.

Woodland peoples' method of land management was environmentally sound and economically productive. Indian men systematically burned hardwood forests, eliminating the underbrush and forming open, parklike expanses. Although they occasionally lost control of a fire, so that it burned beyond their hunting territory, the damage was not lasting. Burned-over tracts favored the growth of grass and berry bushes that attracted a profusion of deer and other game. The men then cleared fields so that Indian women could plant corn, beans, and squash in soil enriched by ash. After several years of abundant harvests, yields declined, and the Indians moved to another site to repeat the process. Ground cover eventually reclaimed the abandoned clearing, restoring fertility naturally, and the Indians could return.

Nonfarming Societies

Outside the Southwest and the Eastern Woodlands, farming north of Mesoamerica was either impossible because of inhospitable environments or impractical because native peoples could obtain ample food from wild sources. On the Northwest coast, from the Alaskan panhandle to northern California, and in the Columbia Plateau, Native Americans devoted brief periods of each year to catching salmon and other spawning fish, which they dried and stored in quantities sufficient to last the year. As a result, their seasonal movements gave way to a settled lifestyle in permanent villages. From there they had ready access not only to fish in both rivers and the ocean but also to whales and other sea mammals, shell-fish, land mammals, and wild plants.

By C.E. 1, most Northwest coast villages numbered several hundred people who lived in multifamily houses built of cedar planks. Trade and warfare with interior groups strengthened the wealth and power of chiefs and other elites. Leading families displayed their wealth in the potlatch—a feast at which they gave their goods to guests or destroyed them. From the time of the earliest contacts, Europeans were amazed by the artistic and architectural achievements of the Northwest coast Indians. "What must astonish most," wrote a French explorer in 1791, "is to see painting everywhere, everywhere sculpture, among a nation of hunters."

At about the same time, Native Americans on the coast and in the valleys of what is now California were clustering in villages of about a hundred people to coordinate the processing of acorns. After gathering millions of acorns from California's extensive oak groves each fall, tribal peoples such as the Chumash and Ohlones ground the acorns into meal, leached them of their bitter tannic acid, and then roasted, boiled, or baked them prior to storage. Facing intense competition for acorns, California Indians combined their villages into chiefdoms and defended their territories. Chiefs conducted trade, diplomacy, war, and religious ceremonies. Along with other wild species, acorns enabled the Indians of California to prosper. As a Spanish friar arriving from Mexico in 1770 wrote, "This land exceeds all the preceding territory in fertility and abundance of things necessary for sustenance."

Between the Eastern Woodlands and the Pacific coast, the Plains and deserts were too dry to support large human settlements. Dividing the region are the Rocky Mountains, to the east of which lie the grasslands of the Great Plains, while to the west are several deserts of varying elevations that ecologists call the Great Basin. Except in the Southwest, Native Americans in this region remained in mobile hunting-gathering bands.

Plains Indian hunters pursued a variety of game animals, including antelope, deer, elk, and bear, but their favorite prey was buffalo, or bison, a smaller relative of the giant bison that had flourished when humans first arrived. Buffalo provided Plains Indians with meat and with hides, from which they made clothing, bedding, portable houses (tipis), kettles, shields, and other items. They made tools from buffalo bones and containers and arrowheads from buffalo horns, and they used most other buffalo parts as well. Limited to travel by foot, Plains hunters stampeded herds of bison into small box canyons or over cliffs, killing dozens, or occasionally hundreds. Since a single buffalo could provide two hundred to four hundred pounds of meat and a band had no means of preserving and storing most of it, the latter practice was especially wasteful. Yet humans were so few in number that they had no significant impact on the bison population before the arrival of Europeans. There are no reliable estimates of the number of buffalo then roaming the Plains, but the earliest European observers were amazed. One Spanish colonist, for example, reported a "multitude so great that it might be considered a falsehood by one who had not seen them."

During and after the Mississippian era, groups of Eastern Woodlands Indians moved to the lower river valleys of the Plains, where over time the rainfall had increased enough to support cultivated plants. In contrast to Native Americans already living on the Plains, such as the Blackfeet and the Crow, farming newcomers like the Mandans and Pawnees built year-round villages and permanent earth lodges. But they also hunted buffalo and other animals. (Many of the Plains Indians familiar today, such as the Sioux and Comanches, moved to the region only after Europeans began colonizing North America [see Chapter 4].)

As Indians elsewhere increased their food production, the Great Basin grew warmer and drier, further limiting already scarce sources of foods. Ducks and other waterfowl on which Native Americans formerly feasted disappeared as marshlands dried up after 1200 B.C.E., and the number of buffalo and other game animals also dwindled. Great Basin Indians such as the Shoshones and the Utes countered these trends by relying more heavily on *piñon* nuts, which they harvested, stored, and ate in winter camps. Hunting improved after about C.E. 500, when Indians in the region adopted the bow and arrow.

In western Alaska, where the first Americans had appeared thousands of years earlier, Inuits and Aleuts, carrying sophisticated tools and weapons from their Siberian homeland, arrived after 3000 B.C.E. Combining ivory, bone, and other materials, they fashioned harpoons and spears for the pursuit of sea mammals and—in the case of the Inuits—caribou. Through continued contacts with Siberia, Inuits introduced the bow and arrow in North America. As they perfected their ways of living in the cold tundra environment, many Inuit groups spread westward across upper Canada and to Greenland.

The very earliest contacts between Native Americans and Europeans occurred in about C.E. 980, five centuries before the arrival of Columbus, when Norse expansionists from Scandinavia colonized parts of Greenland. The Greenland Norse hunted furs, obtained timber, and traded with Inuit groups. They also made several attempts, beginning in about 1000, to colonize Vinland, as they called Newfoundland. The Vinland Norse initially exchanged metal goods for ivory with the local Beothuk Indians, but peaceful trade gave way to hostile encounters. Beothuk resistance soon led the Norse to withdraw from Vinland. As a Norse leader, dying after losing a battle with some natives, put it, "There is fat around my belly! We have won a fine and fruitful country, but will hardly be allowed to enjoy it." Although some Norse remained in Greenland as late as the 1480s, it was later Europeans who would enjoy, at the expense of native peoples, the fruits of a "New World."

NORTH AMERICAN PEOPLES ON THE EVE OF EUROPEAN CONTACT

By C.E. 1500, native peoples had transformed the Americas into a dazzling array of cultures and societies (see Map 1.2). The Western Hemisphere numbered about 75 million people, most of them in Mesoamerica and South America. Between 7 million and 10 million Indians were unevenly distributed across North America. As they had for thousands of years, small, mobile hunting bands peopled the Arctic, Subarctic, Great Basin, and much of the Plains. More sedentary societies based on fishing or gathering predominated along the Pacific coast, while village-based agriculture was typical in the Eastern Woodlands and the river valleys of the Southwest and Plains. Mississippian urban centers still prevailed in much of the Southeast. North American Indians grouped themselves in several hundred nations and tribes, and spoke hundreds of languages and dialects.

Despite the vast differences among Native American societies, all were based on kinship, reciprocity, and communal ownership of resources. Trade facilitated the exchange not only of goods but also of technologies and ideas. Thus, the bow and arrow, ceramic pottery, and certain religious values and practices characterized Indians everywhere.

MAP 1.2 Locations of Selected Native American Peoples, A.D. 1500

Today's Indian nations were well established in homelands across the continent when Europeans first arrived. Many would combine with others or move in later centuries, either voluntarily or because they were forced.

Kinship and Gender

Like their Archaic forebears, Native North Americans were bound together primarily by kinship. Ties among biological relatives created complex patterns of social obligation and interdependence. **Nuclear families** (a husband, a wife, and their biological children) never stood alone. Instead, they lived with one of the parents' relatives in multi-generational **extended families**. Customs regulating marriage varied considerably. Some male leaders had more than one wife, and either husbands, wives, or both could terminate a marriage. In most cultures, young people married in their teens, usually after engaging in numerous sexual relationships.

In some Native American societies, such as the Iroquois, the extended families of women took precedence over those of men. Upon marriage, a new husband moved in with his wife's extended family. The primary male adult in a child's life was the mother's oldest brother, not the father. Other Indian societies recognized men's extended families as primary, and still others did not distinguish sharply between the status of female and male family lines.

Kinship was also the basis for armed conflict. Indian societies typically considered homicide a matter to be resolved by the extended families of the victim and the perpetrator. If the perpetrator's family offered a gift that the victim's family considered appropriate, the question was settled; if not, political leaders attempted to resolve the dispute. Otherwise, the victim's family members and their supporters might seek to avenge the killing by armed retaliation. Such feuds could escalate into wars between communities. The potential for war rose when densely populated societies competed for scarce resources, as on the Northwest and California coasts. Yet Native American warfare generally remained minimal, with rivals seeking to humiliate one another and seize captives rather than inflict massive casualties or conquer land. A New England officer, writing in the seventeenth century, described a battle between two Indian groups as "more for pastime than to conquer and subdue enemies." He concluded that "they might fight seven years and not kill seven men."

Women did most of the cultivating in farming societies except in the Southwest (where women and men shared the responsibility). With women producing the greater share of the food supply, they gained power in their communities. Among the Iroquois, for example, women collectively owned the fields, distributed food, and played a decisive role in selecting chiefs. In New England, women often served as sachems, or political leaders.

Spiritual and Social Values

Native American religions revolved around the conviction that all nature was alive, pulsating with spiritual power. A mysterious, awe-inspiring force, such power united all nature, including human beings, in an unbroken web. Native Americans endeavored to conciliate the spiritual forces in their world—living things, rocks and water, sun and moon, even ghosts and witches. For example, Indian hunters prayed to the animals they killed, begging their pardon and thanking them for the gift of food.

Native Americans had several ways of gaining access to spiritual power. One was through dreams and visions, which most Native Americans interpreted as spiritual instructions. Sometimes, a dreamer received a message for his or her people. Native people also sought power through physical ordeals. Young men in many societies gained recognition as adults through a vision quest—a solitary venture that entailed fasting and envisioning a spirit who would endow them with special powers. Some tribes initiated girls at the onset of menstruation into the spiritual world from which female reproductive power flowed. Entire communities often practiced collective power-seeking rituals such as the Sun Dance, performed by Indians of the Plains and Great Basin.

Native American societies demanded a strong degree of cooperation. Using physical punishment sparingly, if at all, Indians punished children psychologically, by public shaming. Communities sought unity through consensus rather than

Big Horn Medicine Wheel, Wyoming *The medicine wheel was constructed between three and eight centuries ago as a center for religious ceremonies, including those relating to the summer solstice.*

(Wyoming State Archives)

tolerating lasting divisions. Political leaders articulated slowly emerging agreements in dramatic oratory. The English colonizer John Smith noted that the most effective Native American leaders spoke "with vehemency and so great passions that they sweat till they drop and are so out of breath they scarce can speak."

Native Americans reinforced cooperation with a strong sense of order. Custom, the demands of social conformity, and the rigors of nature strictly regulated life and people's everyday affairs. Exacting familial or community revenge was a ritualized way of restoring order that had broken down. On the other hand, the failure of measures to restore order could bring the fearful consequences experienced by the Iroquois—blind hatred, unending violence, and the most dreaded of evils, witchcraft. In fearing witchcraft, Native Americans resembled the Europeans and Africans they would encounter after 1492.

The principle of reciprocity was central to Native Americans. Reciprocity involved mutual give-and-take. Its aim was to maintain equilibrium and interdependence even between individuals of unequal power and prestige. Most Indian leaders' authority depended on the obligations they bestowed rather than on coercion. By distributing gifts, they obligated members of the community to support them and to accept their authority, however limited. The same principle applied to relations between societies. Powerful communities distributed gifts to weaker neighbors who reciprocated with tribute in the form of material goods and submission. A French observer in seventeenth-century Canada clearly understood: "For the savages have that noble quality, that they give liberally, casting at the feet of him whom they will honor the present that they give him. But it is with hope to receive some reciprocal kindness, which is a kind of contract, which we call ... 'I give thee, to the end thou shouldst give me.'"

CHRONOLOGY
13,000 B.C.E.–C.E. 1500

ca.13,000 B.C.E.	People present in Americas.
ca.9000 B.C.E.	Paleo-Indians established throughout Western Hemisphere. Extinction of big-game mammals.
ca.8000 B.C.E.	Earliest Archaic societies. Domesticated squash grown in Peru.
ca.7000 B.C.E.	Athapaskan-speaking peoples enter North America.
ca.5000 B.C.E.	First maize grown in Mesoamerica.
ca.3000–2000 B.C.E.	Inuit and Aleut peoples enter North America from Siberia.
ca.2500 B.C.E.	Archaic societies begin giving way to a more diverse range of cultures. First maize grown in North America.
ca.1200–900 B.C.E.	Poverty Point flourishes in Louisiana.
ca.400–100 B.C.E.	Adena culture flourishes in Ohio valley.
ca.100 B.C.E.–C.E. 600	Hopewell culture thrives in Midwest.
ca. C.E. 1	Rise of chiefdoms on northwest coast and in California. Ancestral Pueblo culture begins in Southwest.
ca.300	Hohokam culture begins in Southwest.
ca.700	Mississippian culture begins.
ca.900	Urban center arises at Cahokia.
ca.1000	Norse attempt to colonize Vinland (Newfoundland).
ca.1200	Ancestral Pueblo and Hohokam peoples disperse in Southwest.
ca.1200–1400	Cahokia declines and inhabitants disperse.
ca.1400	Iroquois Confederacy formed.
1428	Aztec empire expands.
1438	Inca empire expands.
1492	Christopher Columbus reaches Western Hemisphere.

CONCLUSION

When Europeans "discovered" the Americas in 1492, they did not, as they thought, enter an unchanging "wilderness" inhabited by "savages." American history had begun with the arrival of people thousands of years earlier during an Ice Age, when Asia and North America were directly connected. As Earth's climate warmed, the earliest Paleo-Indians exploited wider ranges of food sources that could support larger populations. They also learned from one another through inter-band exchanges. These developments resulted in the emergence of new, regional cultures, termed Archaic. After 2500 B.C.E., Native Americans in several regions moved beyond Archaic cultures, clustering in seasonal or permanent villages where they produced food surpluses by growing crops, fishing for salmon, or processing acorns. Some built larger towns or cities. While people in the smallest bands were equal, political leaders in most societies came from prominent families. In a few, very large societies, hereditary chiefs, kings, and even emperors ruled far-flung peoples.

Underlying their diversity, North American Indians had much in common. First, they usually identified themselves as members of extended families rather than as individuals or political subjects. Second, most emphasized reciprocity rather than hierarchical authority as the underlying principle for relations within and between communities. Third, they perceived the entire universe, including nature, as sacred, and regarded humans as part of nature. These core values arrived with the earliest Americans and persisted beyond the invasions of Europeans and their sharply contrasting ideas. Throughout their long history, Native Americans reinforced shared beliefs and customs through exchanges of material goods, new technologies, and religious ideas.

Although they had much in common with one another, Native Americans had never thought of themselves as a single people. Only after Europeans arrived and emphasized the differences between themselves and indigenous peoples did the term "Indian" come into usage. (The term originated with Columbus, who thought in 1492 that he had landed in the Indies [see Chapter 2].) The new America in which people were categorized according to continental ancestry was radically different from the one that had flourished for thousands of years before 1492.

2

THE RISE OF THE ATLANTIC WORLD, 1400–1625

CHAPTER OUTLINE

• African and European Backgrounds • Europe and the Atlantic World,
1400–1600 • Footholds in North America, 1512–1625

AFRICAN AND EUROPEAN BACKGROUNDS

When the Atlantic world emerged in the fifteenth and sixteenth centuries, all
the continents facing the Atlantic Ocean were undergoing internal change. In the
Americas, some societies rose, others fell, and still others adapted to new circumstances (see Chapter 1). West Africa and western Europe were also being transformed;
a market society emerged on each continent alongside older systems of barter and
local exchange. Wealthy merchants financed dynastic rulers seeking to extend their
domains.

Western Europe's transformation was thoroughgoing. Its population nearly
doubled in size, the distribution of wealth and power shifted radically, and new
modes of thought and spirituality undermined established beliefs and knowledge.
The result was social, political, and religious upheaval alongside remarkable expressions of creativity and innovation.

**West Africa:
Tradition and
Change**

Before the advent of Atlantic travel, the broad belt of grassland, or savanna, separating the Sahara Desert from the
forests to the south played a major role in long-distance
trade between the Mediterranean Sea and West Africa. The
trans-Saharan caravan trade stimulated the rise of grassland kingdoms and empires, whose size and wealth rivaled any in Europe at the time. The richest grassland
states were in West Africa, with its ample stores of gold. During the fourteenth and
early fifteenth centuries, the empire of **Mali** was the leading power in the West

African savanna. Through ties with wealthy Muslim rulers and merchants in North Africa and the Middle East, Mali's Muslim rulers imported brass, copper, cloth, spices, manufactured goods, and Arabian horses. Their major exports were gold and slaves.

With gold having recently been made the standard for nearly all European currencies, demand for the precious metal rose. During the fifteenth century, this demand brought thousands of newcomers from the savanna and Central Africa to the region later known as Africa's Gold Coast. New states emerged to take advantage of the opportunities afforded by exporting gold, though none was as extensive or powerful as Mali at its height.

Immediately south of the grassland empires lay a region of small states and chiefdoms. In Senegambia, at Africa's westernmost bulge, several Islamic states took root. Infestation by the tsetse fly, the carrier of sleeping sickness, kept livestock-herding peoples out of Guinea's coastal forests, but many small states

Sankore Mosque, Timbuktu, Mali

Sankore was one of three great mosques built during the fourteenth century when Timbuktu became the center of Islamic worship and learning in West Africa.

arose here, too. Among these was Benin, where artisans had been fashioning magnificent metalwork for centuries.

Still farther south, a welter of chiefdoms consolidated into four major kingdoms by the fifteenth century. Their kings were chiefs who, after defeating neighboring chiefdoms, installed their own kin as local rulers of the newly conquered territories. Of these kingdoms, **Kongo** was the most powerful and highly centralized.

West African political leaders differed sharply in the amounts and kinds of political power they wielded. Some kings and emperors enjoyed semigod-like status. Rulers of smaller kingdoms depended largely on their ability to persuade, to conform to prevailing customs, and to satisfy their people when redistributing wealth.

As did Native Americans, West Africans lived within a network of mutual obligations to kinfolk (see Chapter 1). Not just parents but also aunts, uncles, distant cousins, and persons sharing clan ties formed an African's extended family and claimed his or her first loyalty. In centuries to come, the tradition of strong extended families would help enslaved Africans in the Americas endure the forced breakup of nuclear families by sale.

West Africans viewed marriage as a way for extended families to forge alliances for mutual benefit. A prospective husband made a payment to his bride's kin before marriage. He was not "buying" a wife; in effect, he was posting bond for good behavior and acknowledging the relative prestige of his own and his bride's extended families. West African wives generally maintained lifelong links with their own families. As among Native Americans, children in many societies traced descent through their mother's forebears, rather than their father's. These practices reinforced the status and power of women.

A driving force behind marriage in West Africa was the region's high mortality rate from frequent famines and tropical disease epidemics. The shortage of people placed a high premium on the production of children. Children contributed to a family's wealth by increasing its food production and the amount of land it could cultivate. Men of means frequently married more than one wife in order to produce more children, and women generally married soon after reaching puberty.

West Africans depended on farming by both men and women for most of their food. The abundance of land relative to population enabled African farmers—like many Native Americans and unlike Europeans—to shift their fields periodically and thereby maintain high soil quality. Before planting new fields, men felled the trees and burned off the wild vegetation. After several years of intensive cultivation, largely by women, farmers shifted to a new location. After a few years, while the soil of the recently used fields was replenished, they returned to repeat the cycle. In the coastal rain forests, West Africans grew such crops as yams, sugar cane, bananas, okra, and eggplant, among other foods, as well as cotton for weaving cloth. On the grasslands, the staff of life was grain—millet, sorghum, and rice—supplemented by cattle raising and fishing.

By the fifteenth century, the market economy, stimulated by long-distance trade, extended to many small families. Farmers traded surplus crops at local marketplaces for other food or cloth. Artisans wove cotton or raffia palm leaves, made clothing and jewelry, and crafted tools and religious objects of iron and wood. While gold was the preferred currency among wealthy rulers and merchants, cowry shells served as the medium of exchange for most people.

Religion permeated African life. Like Native Americans and Europeans, Africans believed that another world lay beyond the one people perceived through their five senses. This other world was only rarely glimpsed by living persons besides priests, but the souls of most people passed there at death. Deities spoke to mortals through priests, dreams, religious "speaking shrines," and magical charms. Unlike Islam and Christianity, indigenous West African religions emphasized the importance of believers' continuous revelations as sources of spiritual truth. Like both Native Americans and Europeans, Africans explained misfortunes in terms of witchcraft. But African religion differed from other traditions by emphasizing ancestor worship, in which departed forebears were venerated as spiritual guardians.

Africa's magnificent artistic traditions were also steeped in religion. The ivory, cast iron, and wood sculptures of West Africa (whose bold designs would influence twentieth-century western art) were used in ceremonies reenacting creation myths and honoring spirits. A strong moralistic streak ran through African folk tales. Storytellers transmitted these tales in dramatic public presentations with ritual masks, dance, and music of a highly complex rhythmic structure—now appreciated as one of the foundations of jazz.

Among Africans, Islam appealed primarily to merchants trading with North Africa and the Middle East and to kings and emperors eager to consolidate their power. Some Muslim rulers modified Islam, retaining elements of traditional religion as a concession to popular opinion. By 1400, Islam was just beginning to affect the lives of some ordinary people in the savanna.

European Culture and Society

When Columbus reached Guanahaní in 1492, western Europe was undergoing a cultural **Renaissance** (literally, rebirth). Intellectuals and poets rediscovered Europe's descent from a classical tradition originating in ancient Greece and Rome but obscured for a thousand years. Western European scholars found scores of forgotten ancient texts in philosophy, science, medicine, geography, and other subjects, and a rich tradition of commentary on them by Muslim, Eastern Orthodox, and Jewish scholars. Armed with the new learning, Renaissance authors strove to reconcile ancient philosophy with Christian faith, to explore the mysteries of nature, to map the world, and to explain the motions of the heavens.

The Renaissance was also an era of intense artistic creativity. Wealthy Italian merchants and rulers—especially in the city-states of Florence and Venice, and in Rome (controlled by the papacy)— commissioned magnificent architecture, painting, and sculpture. Artists such as Leonardo da Vinci and Michelangelo created works rooted in classical tradition and based on close observations of nature (including the human body) and attention to perspective. Europeans celebrated these artistic achievements, along with those of writers, philosophers, scientists, and explorers, as the height of "civilization" to which other cultures should aspire.

But European society was also quivering with tension. Renaissance creativity was partly inspired by intense social and spiritual stress. Europeans groped for stability by glorifying order and hierarchy in the universe and in society. Writing near the end of the Renaissance, William Shakespeare (1564–1616) expressed these values with eloquence:

The heavens themselves, the planets and this center [earth]
Observe degree, priority, and place...
Take but degree away, untune that string,
And hark, what discord follows!

Gender, wealth, inherited position, and political power defined every European's status, and few lived outside the reach of some political authority's taxes and laws. But this order was shaky. Conflicts between states, between religions, and between social classes constantly threatened the balance.

Beneath these conflicts lay deep-seated forces of change. By the end of the fifteenth century, strong national monarchs in Spain, France, and England had consolidated royal authority at the expense of the Catholic Church and the nobility. The "new monarchs" cultivated powerful merchants by promoting their enterprises in exchange for financial support. King Ferdinand of Aragon had married Queen Isabella of Castile in 1479 to create the Spanish monarchy. France's boundaries expanded as a series of kings absorbed neighboring lands through interdynastic marriage and military conquest. England's Tudor dynasty gradually suppressed the aristocracy's ability to plunge the nation into deadly civil war.

Most Europeans—about 75 percent—were peasants, frequently driven to starvation by taxes, rents, and other dues owed to landlords and Catholic Church officials. Not surprisingly, peasant revolts were frequent, but the authorities mercilessly suppressed such uprisings.

Conditions among European peasants were made worse by a sharp rise in population, from about 55 million in 1450 to almost 100 million by 1600. Neighboring families often cooperated in plowing, sowing, and harvesting as well as in grazing their livestock on jointly owned "commons." But with new land at a premium, landlords, especially in England, wanted to "enclose" the commons—that is, convert the land to private property. Peasants who had no written title to their land were especially vulnerable to these pressures.

Environmental factors further exacerbated peasants' circumstances. Beginning in the fourteenth century, lower-than-average temperatures marked a "Little Ice Age" that lasted for more than four centuries. During this time, many European crops were less abundant or failed to grow. Hunger and malnutrition were widespread, and full-scale famine struck in some areas. One consequence of population growth was deforestation resulting from increased human demand for wood to use as fuel and building materials. Deforestation also deprived peasants of wild foods and game, whose food sources disappeared with deforestation.

Pressures on peasants accelerated their exodus to towns and cities. European towns were numerous but small, typically with several thousand inhabitants each. A great metropolis like London, whose population ballooned from fifty-five thousand in 1550 to two hundred thousand in 1600, was exceptional. But all towns were dirty and disease-ridden, and townspeople lived close-packed with their neighbors.

Unappealing as sixteenth-century towns might seem today, many men and women preferred them to the rural poverty they left behind. Immigration from the countryside—rather than an excess of births over deaths—accounted for towns' expansion. Most people who flocked into towns remained at the bottom of the social order as servants or laborers and could not accumulate enough money to marry and live independently.

The consequences of rapid population growth were particularly acute in England, where the number of people doubled from about 2.5 million in 1500 to 5 million in 1620. As throughout western Europe, prices rose while wages fell during the sixteenth and early seventeenth centuries, widening the gap between rich and poor. Although English entrepreneurs expanded textile production by assembling spinners and weavers in household workshops, the workers were competing for fewer jobs. Enclosures of common lands severely aggravated unemployment, forcing large numbers of people to wander the country in search of work. To the upper and middle classes, these poor vagabonds seemed to threaten law and order. To control them, Parliament passed laws that ordered vagrants whipped and sent home, but most offenders only moved on to other towns. Some English writers viewed overseas colonies as places where the unemployed, landless poor could find opportunity, thereby enriching their countries rather than draining resources.

As in America and Africa, traditional society in Europe rested on maintaining long-term, reciprocal relationships. European reciprocity required the upper classes to act with self-restraint and dignity, and the lower classes to defer to their "betters." It also demanded strict economic regulation to ensure that no purchaser paid more than a "just price"—one that permitted a seller a "reasonable" profit but that barred him from taking advantage of buyers' misfortunes to make "excessive" profits.

Yet for several centuries Europeans had been compromising the ideals of traditional economic behavior. "In the Name of God and of Profit," thirteenth-century Italian merchants had written on their ledgers. By the sixteenth century, nothing could stop lenders' profiting from interest on borrowed money or sellers' raising prices in response to demand. New forms of business organization emerged—especially the **joint-stock company,** a business corporation that amassed capital through sales of stock to investors. Demand rose for capital investment, and so did the supply of accumulated wealth. Gradually, a new economic outlook justified the unimpeded acquisition of wealth and insisted that individuals owed one another nothing but the money necessary to settle their transactions. This new outlook, the central value system of capitalism or the "market economy," rejected traditional demands that economic activity be regulated to ensure social reciprocity and maintain "just prices."

Sixteenth- and seventeenth-century Europeans therefore held conflicting attitudes toward economic enterprise and social change, and their ambivalence remained unresolved. A restless desire for fresh opportunity kept European life simmering with competitive tension. But those who prospered still sought the security and prestige provided by high social status, whereas the poor longed for the age-old values that would restrain irresponsible greed.

Perhaps the most sensitive barometer of social change was the family. Throughout Europe, the typical household consisted of a small nuclear family—two parents and several children—in which the husband and father functioned as a head whose authority was not to be questioned. The role of the wife and mother was to bear and rear children as well as assist her husband in providing for the family's subsistence. Children were regarded as potential laborers who would assist in these tasks until they left home to start their own families. The household, then, was not only a family but also the principal economic unit in European society. Peasants on their tiny farms, artisans and merchants in their shops, and even nobles in their castles all lived and worked in households. People who did not live with their own families resided as dependents in the households of others as servants, apprentices, or relatives. Europeans regarded those who lived outside family-based households with extreme suspicion, often accusing them of crime or even witchcraft.

Europeans frequently characterized the nuclear family as a "little commonwealth." A father's authority over his family supposedly mirrored God's rule over Creation and the king's over his subjects. Even grown children knelt for their father's blessing. "Wives," according to a German writer, "should obey their husbands and not seek to dominate them; they must manage the home efficiently. Husbands... should treat their wives with consideration and occasionally close an eye to their faults." Repeated male complaints, such as that of an English author in 1622 about wives "who think themselves every way as good as their husbands, and no way inferior to them," suggest that male domination had its limits.

Religious Upheavals   Although Europe was predominantly Christian in 1400, it was also home to significant numbers of Muslims and Jews. Adherents to these three religious traditions worshiped a single supreme being, based on the God of the Hebrew Bible. While they often coexisted peacefully in lands bordering the Mediterranean, hatred and violence also marked their shared history. For more than three centuries, European Christians conducted numerous Crusades against Muslims in Europe and the Middle East, and Muslims retaliated with "holy war." Each side labeled the other "infidels." Eventually, ambitious rulers transformed the religious conflicts into wars of conquest. While the Islamic Ottoman Empire seized Christian strongholds in southeastern Europe, the Catholic monarchies of Portugal and Spain undertook a "reconquest" of the Iberian Peninsula, and in 1492 Spain drove the last Muslim rulers from Iberia and expelled all Jews who refused to convert to Catholicism.

The Spanish reconquest completed the Roman Catholic Church's domination of western and central Europe. The Catholic Church taught that Christ's sacrifice was repeated every time a priest said Mass, and that divine grace flowed to sinners through the sacraments that priests alone could administer—above all, baptism, confession, and communion. The Church was a vast network of clergymen and religious orders, male and female, set apart from laypeople by the fact that its members did not marry. At the top was the pope, the "vicar [representative] of Christ" on earth.

Besides conducting services, priests heard the confessions of sinners and assigned them penance, usually devotional exercises and good works that would demonstrate repentance. Recently the Church had assumed the authority to grant extra blessings, or "indulgences," to repentant sinners. Indulgences promised cancellation both of penance and of time in purgatory, where the dead atoned for sins they had already confessed and been forgiven. (Hell, from which there was no escape, awaited those who died unforgiven.) Given Catholics' anxieties about sinful behavior, indulgences became popular. By the early sixteenth century, many religious authorities granted them in return for such "good works" as donating money to the Church.

The jingle of one enterprising German friar promised that

As soon as the coin in the cash box rings,
The soul from purgatory's fire springs.

The Muslim Conquest of Eger, Hungary *Turkey's Ottoman Empire seized Eger in 1596 during the course of expanding across southeastern Europe. Nearly a century later, European Christian forces took back the city.*

The sale of indulgences provoked charges that the materialism and corruption infecting economic life had spread to the Church. In 1517, German monk Martin Luther (1483–1546) openly attacked the practice. When the pope censured him, Luther broadened his criticism to encompass the Mass, purgatory, priests, and the papacy. After Luther refused to recant, the Roman Church excommunicated him. Luther's revolt initiated what became known as the **Protestant Reformation,** which changed Christianity forever. (The word *Protestant* comes from the *protest* of Luther's princely supporters against the anti-Lutheran policies of Holy Roman Emperor Charles V.)

To Luther, indulgence selling and similar examples of clerical corruption were evil not just because they bilked people. The Church, he charged, gave people false confidence that they could earn salvation simply by doing good works. His own agonizing search for salvation had convinced Luther that God bestowed salvation not on the basis of worldly deeds, but solely to reward a believer's faith. Luther's spiritual struggle and experience of being "reborn" constituted a classic conversion experience—the heart of Protestant Christianity.

Other Protestant reformers followed Luther in breaking from Catholicism, most notably John Calvin (1509–1564), who fled his native France for Geneva, Switzerland. Whereas Luther stressed faith in Christ as the key to salvation, Calvin insisted on the stark doctrine of **predestination.** Calvin asserted that an omnipotent God predestined most sinful humans to hell, saving only a few in order to demonstrate his power and grace. It was only these few, called the "elect," "godly," or "saints," who would have a true conversion experience. At this moment, said Calvin, a person confronted the horrifying truth of his or her unworthiness and felt God's transcending power.

Despite their differences, Protestants shared much common ground. For one thing, they denied that God had endowed priests with special powers. A proper church, Luther claimed, was a "priesthood of all believers." Protestant reformers insisted that laypeople take responsibility for their own spiritual and moral conditions. Accordingly, they placed a high value on reading. Protestants demanded that the Bible be translated from Latin into spoken languages so that believers could read it for themselves. The new faith was spread by the recently invented printing press. Wherever Protestantism became established, basic education and religious study followed. Finally, Protestantism (initially) condemned the replacement of traditional reciprocity by marketplace values. Protestantism's greatest appeal was to all those—ordinary individuals, merchants, and aristocrats alike—who brooded over their chances for salvation and valued the steady performance of duty.

In the face of the Protestant challenge, Rome was far from idle. Reformers like Teresa of Ávila (1515–1582), a Spanish nun from a *converso* (converted Jewish) family, urged members of Catholic holy orders to repudiate corruption and to lead the Church's renewal by living piously and austerely. Another reformer, Ignatius Loyola (1491–1556), founded a militant religious order, the Society of Jesus, whose members (Jesuits) would distinguish themselves in coming centuries as royal advisers and missionaries. The high point of Catholic reform came during the Council of Trent (1545–1563), convened by the pope. While denouncing Protestants, the council reformed Church administration to combat corruption and broaden public participation in religious observances. This revival, the **Catholic or Counter-Reformation,** brought the modern Roman Catholic Church into existence.

The Protestant Reformation changed the religious map of Europe. Lutheranism became the state religion in the Scandinavian countries, while Calvinism made significant inroads in France, the Netherlands (which a royal marriage had brought under Spanish rule), England, and Scotland. The tiny states comprising the modern nations of Germany and Switzerland were divided among Catholics, Lutherans, and Calvinists.

The Reformation in England, 1533–1625   England's Reformation was started not by a theologian or cries of the people, but by a king and Parliament. King Henry VIII (ruled 1509–1547) wanted a male heir, but his queen, Catherine of Aragon, failed to bear a son. Henry asked the pope to annul his marriage, but the pope refused. Frustrated and determined, Henry persuaded Parliament to pass a series of acts in 1533–1534 dissolving his marriage and proclaiming him supreme head of the **Church of England** (or Anglican Church). The move justified Henry's seizure of income-producing Catholic Church properties, further consolidating royal power and financial independence.

Religious differences divided England for more than a century after Henry's break with Rome. Under Edward VI (ruled 1547–1553), Henry's son by the third of his six wives, the church veered sharply toward Calvinism. Edward's half-sister and successor, Mary I (ruled 1553–1558), tried to restore Catholicism, in part by burning several hundred Protestants at the stake.

The reign of Elizabeth I (ruled 1558–1603), a half-sister of both Edward and Mary, marked a crucial turning point. After the reign of "Bloody Mary," most English people were ready to become Protestant; *how* Protestant was the divisive question. Elizabeth took a middle road by affirming the monarch's role as head of the Anglican hierarchy of archbishops, bishops, and parish priests while allowing individuals and parish churches wide latitude in deciding which customs and practices to follow.

Militant Calvinists, whose opponents derisively called them **"Puritans,"** wanted a more thorough purification of the Church of England from "popish [Catholic] abuses." Puritans insisted that membership in a congregation be limited to those who had had a conversion experience and that each congregation be independent of other congregations and of the Anglican hierarchy. Thus, they repudiated the Anglican (and Catholic) practices of extending membership to anyone who had been baptized. Some "nonseparating" Puritans remained nominally within the Church of England, hoping to reform it. Others, called Separatists, withdrew, insisting that a "pure" church had to be entirely free of Anglican "pollution."

The severe self-discipline and moral uprightness of Puritans appealed to few among the nobility and the poor. Puritanism appealed primarily to the small but growing number of people in the "middling" ranks of English society—landowning gentry, yeomen (small independent farmers), merchants, shopkeepers, artisans, and university-educated clergy and intellectuals. Self-discipline had become central to both the secular and spiritual dimensions of these people's lives. From their ranks, and particularly from among farmers, artisans, and clergy, would later come the settlers of New England (discussed in Chapter 3).

Elizabeth distrusted Puritan militancy; but, after 1570 when the pope declared her a heretic and urged Catholics to overthrow her, she regarded English Catholics as even more dangerous. Thereafter, she courted influential Puritans and embraced militant anti-Catholicism.

Although opposed by Elizabeth, most Puritans still hoped to transform the Church of England into independent congregations of "saints." But her successor, James I (ruled 1603–1625), a distant cousin of Elizabeth who was king of Scotland, bitterly opposed Puritan calls to eliminate Anglican bishops. Yet while insisting on outward conformity to Anglican practice, James tolerated Calvinists who did not publicly proclaim their dissent.

EUROPE AND THE ATLANTIC WORLD, 1400–1600

The forces transforming Europe quickly reverberated beyond that continent. During the fifteenth and sixteenth centuries, dynastic monarchs and allied merchants organized imperial ventures to Africa, Asia, and the Americas. Besides seeking wealth and power, expanding Europeans proclaimed it their mission to introduce Christianity and "civilization" to the "savages" and "pagans" of alien lands. Two prominent outcomes of the new imperialism were a transatlantic slave trade and the colonization of the Americas. The multiple exchanges that resulted gave rise to a new Atlantic world.

Portugal and the Atlantic, 1400–1500

During the fifteenth century, some European merchants sought to enhance their profits by circumventing costly Mediterranean-overland trade routes to and from Asia and Africa. Instead, they hoped to establish direct contacts with sources of prized imports via the seas. Tiny Portugal led the way in overcoming impediments to long-distance oceanic travel.

Important changes in maritime technology occurred in the early fifteenth century. Shipbuilders and mariners along Europe's stormy Atlantic coast added the triangular Arab sail to their heavy cargo ships. They created a more maneuverable vessel, the caravel, which sailed more easily against the wind. Sailors also mastered the compass and astrolabe, by which they got their bearings on the open sea. Without this maritime revolution, European exploration would have been impossible.

Renaissance scholars' readings of ancient texts enabled fifteenth-century Europeans to look at their world with new eyes. The great ancient Greek authority on geography was Ptolemy, but Renaissance cartographers corrected his data when they tried to draw accurate maps based on recent European and Arabic observations. Thus, Renaissance "new learning" helped sharpen Europeans' geographic sense.

Led by Prince Henry "the Navigator" (1394–1460), Portugal was the first nation to capitalize on these developments. Henry gained the support of merchants seeking to circumvent Moroccan control of the African-European gold trade. He encouraged Portuguese seamen to pilot the new caravels southward along the African coast, mastering the Atlantic's currents while searching for opportunities to trade or raid profitably.

By the time of Henry's death, Portugal was exporting substantial quantities of gold and slaves from south of the Sahara. The Portuguese were also expanding their vision of a trading empire beyond Africa. In 1488, Bartolomeu Días reached the Cape of Good Hope at Africa's southern tip. A decade later, Vasco da Gama led a Portuguese fleet around the Cape of Good Hope and on to India (see Map 2.1).

Although the Portuguese did not destroy older Euro-Asian commercial links, they showed western Europeans a way around Africa to Asia. In the process, they brought Europeans face-to-face with West Africans and an already flourishing slave trade.

The "New Slavery" and Racism

Slavery was well established in fifteenth-century Africa. The institution took two basic forms. Many Africans were enslaved because of indebtedness. Their debts were purchased by kings and emperors who made them servants or by families seeking additional laborers. They or their children were either absorbed into their new families over time or released from bondage when they worked off their debts. But a long-distance commercial trade in slaves also flourished. For several centuries, Middle Eastern and North African traders had furnished local rulers with a range of fine, imported products in exchange for black laborers. Some of these slaves had been debtors, while others were captured in raids and wars.

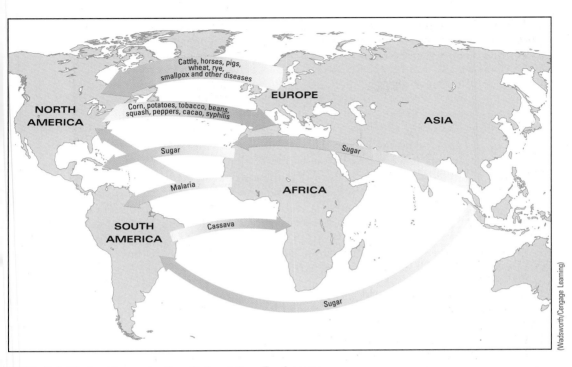

MAP 2.1 Major Items in the Columbian Exchange

As European adventures traversed the world in the fifteenth and sixteenth centuries, they initiated the "Columbian Exchange" of plants, animals, and diseases. These events changed the lives of the people of the world forever, bringing new foods and new pestilence to both sides of the Atlantic.

One fifteenth-century Italian who witnessed Muslim and Portuguese slave trading noted that the Arabs "have many Berber horses, which they trade, and take to the Land of the Blacks, exchanging them with the rulers for slaves." Portuguese traders quickly realized how lucrative the trade in slaves could be for them, too. The same observer continued, "Slaves are brought to the market town of Hoden; there they are divided ... [Some] are taken ... and sold to the Portuguese leaseholders. As a result every year the Portuguese carry away ... a thousand slaves."

In 1482, the Portuguese built one outpost, Elmina, on West Africa's Gold Coast; however, they primarily traded through African-controlled commercial networks. The local African kingdoms were too strong for the Portuguese to attack, and African rulers traded—or chose not to trade—according to their own selfinterest.

Despite preventing the Portuguese from directly colonizing them, West African societies were profoundly affected by the new Atlantic slave trade. Portuguese traders enriched favored African rulers not only with luxury products but also with guns. As a result, heavily-armed slave raiders would capture yet more people for sale to the Portuguese as slaves. In Guinea and Senegambia, where most sixteenth-century slaves came from, small kingdoms expanded to "service" the trade. Some of their rulers became comparatively rich. Farther south, the kings of Kongo (from where many American slaves came) used the slave trade to expand their regional power and voluntarily adopted Christianity, just as rulers farther north had converted to Islam.

Although slavery had long been practiced in many parts of the Eastern Hemisphere, including in Europe, there were ominous differences between these older practices and the **"new slavery"** initiated by Portugal and later adopted by other western Europeans. First, the unprecedented magnitude of the trade resulted in a demographic catastrophe for West Africa and its peoples. Before the Atlantic slave trade finally ended in the nineteenth century, nearly 12 million Africans would be shipped in terrible conditions across the sea. Slavery on this scale had been unknown to Europeans since the collapse of the Roman Empire. Second, African slaves were subjected to new extremes of dehumanization. In medieval Europe, the Middle East, and in West Africa itself, most slaves had lived in their masters' households and primarily performed domestic service. But by 1450, the Portuguese and Spanish created large slave-labor plantations on their Atlantic and Mediterranean islands (see Technology and Culture on page 38). These plantations produced sugar for European markets, using capital supplied by Italian investors to buy African slaves who toiled until death. In short, Africans enslaved by Europeans were regarded as property rather than as persons of low status; as such, they were consigned to labor that was unending, exhausting, and mindless. By 1600, the "new slavery" had become a central, brutal component of the Atlantic world.

(AKG Photos)

Elmina, Portuguese Slave Trading Fortress *Thousands of enslaved Africans passed through Elmina while it was controlled by Portugal and, after 1637, by the Netherlands.*

Finally, race became the ideological basis of the new slavery. Africans' blackness, along with their alien religions and customs, dehumanized them in European eyes. As their racial prejudice hardened, Europeans justified enslaving blacks as their Christian duty. From the fifteenth century onward, European Christianity made few attempts to soften slavery's rigors, and race defined a slave. Slavery became a lifelong, hereditary, and despised status.

To the Americas and Beyond, 1492–1522   Europeans' varying motivations for expanding their horizons converged in the contradictory figure of Christopher Columbus (1451–1506), the son of a weaver from the Italian port of Genoa. Columbus's maritime experience and keen imagination led him to conclude that Europeans could reach Asia more directly by sailing westward across the Atlantic rather than around Africa and across the Indian Ocean. Underestimating Earth's size, he became obsessed with this idea. Religious fervor led Columbus to dream of carrying Christianity around the globe and liberating Jerusalem from Muslim rule, but he also burned with ambition to win wealth and glory.

Columbus was unique in the persistence with which he hawked his "enterprise of the Indies" around the royal courts of western Europe. John II of Portugal showed interest until Días's discovery of the Cape of Good Hope confirmed a sure way to the Indies. Finally, in 1492, hoping to break Portugal's threatened monopoly on direct trade with Asia, Queen Isabella and King Ferdinand of Spain accepted Columbus's offer. Picking up the westward-blowing trade winds at the Canary Islands, Columbus's three small ships reached Guanahaní within a month. After his meeting with the Tainos there, he sailed on in search of gold, making additional contacts with Tainos in Cuba (which he thought was Japan) and Hispaniola, the Caribbean island today occupied by Haiti and the Dominican Republic. Finding gold on Hispaniola, he returned to Spain to tell Isabella and Ferdinand about his discovery.

Returning to Hispaniola to found a colony, Columbus proved to be a poor administrator. Although he made two more voyages (1498–1502), he was shunted aside and died an embittered man, still convinced he had reached Asia only to be cheated of his rightful rewards.

Meanwhile, word of Columbus's discovery caught Europeans' imaginations. To forestall competition between them and to deter potential rivals, Isabella and Portugal's King John II in 1494 signed the Treaty of Tordesillas. The treaty drew a line in the mid-Atlantic, dividing all future discoveries between Spain and Portugal.

Ignoring the Treaty of Tordesillas, England attempted to join the race for Asia in 1497 when Henry VII (ruled 1485–1509), sent an Italian navigator, John Cabot, to explore the North Atlantic. Sailing past Nova Scotia and Newfoundland, Cabot claimed everything he saw and the lands beyond them for England. But England failed to follow up on Cabot's voyage for another sixty years.

The more Europeans explored, the more apparent it became that a vast landmass blocked the route to Asia. In 1500, a Portuguese voyage headed for India unexpectedly stumbled on Brazil (much of which lay east of the Tordesillas line). Other voyages soon revealed a continuous coastline from the Caribbean to Brazil. In 1507, this landmass got its name when a publisher brought out a collection of voyagers' tales. One of the chroniclers was an Italian named Amerigo Vespucci. With a shrewd marketing touch, the publisher devised a catchy name for the new land: America.

TECHNOLOGY & CULTURE

Sugar Production in the Americas

Beginning with Christopher Columbus's first expedition, organisms ranging from bacteria to human beings crossed the Atlantic in both directions. This Columbian exchange had wide-ranging ecological, economic, political, and cultural consequences for the lands and peoples of the Americas, Africa, and Europe. One significant set of consequences arose from the transfer of Mediterranean sugar production to the Americas. Out of this transfer came the single-crop plantation system, based on enslaved African labor, and a new consumer product that revolutionized diets and, quite literally, taste in Europe and its colonies.

Domesticated in New Guinea before 8000 B.C., sugar cane was one of the earliest wild plants harvested by human beings (see Beyond America, Chapter 1). By 350 B.C., sugar was an ingredient in several dishes favored by elites in India, from where it spread to the Mediterranean world. It became a significant commodity in the Mediterranean in the eighth century A.D. when expanding Arabs carried it as far west as Spain and Morocco. The Mediterranean would remain the center of sugar production for Europe over the next seven centuries.

The basic process of making sugar from the sugar cane plant changed little over time. (Sugar made from sugar beets did not become widespread until the nineteenth century.) The earliest producers discovered that one of the six species of cane, *Saccharin officinarum,* produced the most sugar in the shortest span of time. The optimal time for harvesting was when the cane had grown twelve to fifteen feet in height, with stalks about two inches thick. At this point, it was necessary to extract the juice from the plant and then the sucrose (a carbohydrate) from the juice as quickly as possible or risk spoilage. Sugar makers crushed the cane fibers in order to extract the liquid, which they then heated so that it evaporated, leaving the sucrose—or sugar—in the form of crystals or molasses, depending on its temperature.

Sugar production was central to the emerging Atlantic world during the fifteenth century, after Spanish and Portuguese planters established large sugar plantations in the Madeira, Canary, and Cape Verde islands off Africa's Atlantic coast. Initially, the islands' labor force included some free Europeans, but enslaved Africans soon predominated. The islands were the birthplace of the European colonial plantation system. Planters focused on the production of a single export crop and sought to maximize profits by minimizing labor costs. Although some planters used servants, the largest, most profitable plantations imported slaves and worked them as hard as possible until they died. Utilizing such methods, the island planters soon outstripped the production of older sugar makers in the Mediterranean. By 1500, the Spanish and Portuguese had successfully tapped new markets across Europe, especially among the wealthy classes.

On his second voyage in 1493, Columbus took a cargo of sugar from the Canaries to Hispaniola. Early efforts by Spanish colonists to produce sugar failed because they lacked efficient milling technology, because the Taino Indians died so quickly from epidemic diseases, and because most colonists mined gold. But as miners exhausted Hispaniola's limited gold, the enslaved Africans brought to work in the mines became available for sugar production. In 1515, a planter named Gonzalo de Vellosa hired some experienced sugar masters from the Canaries who urged him to import a more efficient type of mill. The mill featured two vertical rollers that could be powered by either animals or water, through which laborers passed the cane in order to crush it. With generous subsidies from the Spanish crown, the combination of vertical-roller mills and slave labor led to a rapid proliferation of sugar plantations in Spain's island colonies, with some using as many as five hundred slaves. But when Spain discovered gold and silver in Mexico and the Andes, its interest in sugar declined almost as rapidly as it had arisen.

Portugal's colony of Brazil emerged as the major source of sugar in the sixteenth century. Here, too, planters established the system of large plantations and enslaved Africans. By 1526, Brazil was exporting shiploads of sugar annually, and before the end of the century it supplied most of the sugar consumed in Europe. Shortly after 1600, Brazilian planters either invented or imported a three-roller mill that increased production still further and became the Caribbean standard for several more centuries. Portugal's sugar monopoly proved short-lived. Between 1588 and 1591, English privateers captured and diverted thirty-four sugar-laden vessels during their nation's war with Spain and Portugal. In 1630, the Netherlands seized Brazil's prime sugar-producing region and increased annual production to a century-high 30,000 tons. Ten years later, some Dutch sugar and slave traders, seeking to expand their activity, shared the technology of sugar

production with English planters in Barbados, who were looking for a new crop following disappointing profits from tobacco. The combination of sugar and slaves took hold so quickly that, within three years, Barbados's annual output rose to 150 tons.

Sugar went on to become the economic heart of the Atlantic economy (as further discussed in Chapter 3). Its price dropped so low that even many poor Europeans could afford it. As a result, sugar became central to European diets as they were revolutionized by the Columbian exchange. Like tobacco, coffee, and several other products of the exchange, sugar and such sugar products as rum, produced from molasses, proved habit-forming, making sugar even more attractive to profit-seeking planters and merchants.

More than any other single commodity, sugar sustained the early slave trade in the Americas, facilitating slavery's spread to tobacco, rice, indigo, and other plantation crops as well as to domestic service and other forms of labor. Competition between British and French sugar producers in the West Indies later fueled their nations' imperial rivalry and eventually led New England's merchants to resist British imperial controls—a resistance that helped prepare the way for the American Revolution (these topics are covered in Chapters 4 and 5).

Questions for Analysis

- *What role did Spain's and Portugal's island colonies play in revolutionizing sugar production?*
- *How did developments in mill technology interact with other factors to make sugar the most profitable crop in the Americas?*

Getting past America and reaching Asia remained the early explorers' primary aim. In 1513, the Spaniard Vasco Núñez de Balboa came upon the Pacific Ocean when he crossed the narrow isthmus of Panama. Then in 1519, Ferdinand Magellan, sailing for Spain, went around the stormy straits (later named for him) at South America's southern tip. In an incredible feat of endurance, he crossed the Pacific to the Philippines, only to die fighting with local natives. One of his five ships and fifteen emaciated sailors finally returned to Spain in 1522, the first people to have sailed around the world.

Spain's Conquistadors, 1492–1536   Columbus was America's first slave trader and the first Spanish conqueror, or conquistador. He made his assumptions and his plans clear when recording his very first encounter with the Tainos. "They should be good servants," he wrote, "... and I believe that they would easily be made Christians." When the Tainos gave the Spanish gifts in return for "trifles," Columbus thought they were simplistic, failing to realize they were engaging in the kind of reciprocal exchange Native Americans had conducted among themselves for thousands of years (see Chapter 1).

Placed in charge of Spain's first colony on Hispaniola, Columbus and the settlers there started the first American gold rush. While fighting among themselves, they forced Native people to mine gold and supply the Spanish with food and other needs. After the crown took direct control of Hispaniola, Spain extended the search for gold to nearby islands, establishing colonies at Puerto Rico (1508), Jamaica (1510), and Cuba (1511).

Tainos and other Native Americans in the Caribbean colonies died off in shockingly large numbers from smallpox, measles, and other imported diseases. To replace the perishing Indians, the colonists began importing enslaved Africans to perform labor. Spanish missionaries who came to Hispaniola to convert Native Americans had sent back grim reports of Spanish exploitation of Indians. But while the missionaries deemed Native Americans potential Christians, they joined most other colonizers in condemning Africans as less than fully human and thereby beyond hope of redemption. Blacks could therefore be exploited without limit. In Cuba, Puerto Rico, and other colonies, they were forced to perform backbreaking work on Spanish sugar plantations (see Technology and Culture).

Meanwhile, Spanish colonists fanned out even farther in search of Indian slaves and gold. In 1519, a restless nobleman, Hernán Cortés (1485–1547), led six hundred troops to the Mexican coast. Destroying his boats, he enlisted the support of enemies and discontented subjects of the Aztecs (see Chapter 1) in a quest to conquer that empire. Besides military support, Cortés gained the services of Malintzin (or Malinche), later known as Doña Marina, an Aztec woman brought up among the Maya. Malintzin served as Cortés's interpreter, diplomatic broker, and mistress.

Upon reaching the Aztec capital of Tenochtitlán, the Spanish were stunned by its size and wealth. "We were amazed and said that it was like the enchantments they tell of [in stories], and some of our soldiers even asked whether the things that we saw were not a dream," recalled one soldier. Certainly, the golden gifts that

Aztec emperor Moctezuma II (ruled 1502–1520) initially offered the invaders were no dream. "They picked up the gold and fingered it like monkeys," one Aztec recalled. "Their bodies swelled with greed, and their hunger was ravenous. They hungered like pigs for that gold."

The Spanish ignored Moctezuma's offer, raiding his palace and treasury, and melting down all the gold they could find. Despite their emperor's imprisonment, the Aztecs regrouped and drove the invaders from the city, killing three hundred Spanish and four thousand of their Indian allies. Yet just as the Aztecs took back Tenochtitlán, a smallpox epidemic struck. Lacking any previous contact with the disease, the Aztecs' immune systems were ill-equipped to resist it. When the Spanish finally recaptured the city, wrote one Spanish chronicler, "the streets were so filled with dead and sick people that our men walked over nothing but bodies." In striking down other Indians, friends as well as foes, the epidemic enabled the Spanish to consolidate their control over much of central Mexico. By 1521, Cortés had overthrown the Aztecs and began to build a Spanish capital, Mexico City, on the ruins of Tenochtitlán.

Over the remainder of the sixteenth century, other conquistadors and officials established a great Spanish empire stretching from New Spain (Mexico) southward to Chile. The most important of these later conquests was that of the Inca empire (see Chapter 1) between 1532 and 1536 by a second reckless conquistador, Francisco Pizarro (c. 1478–1541). As with the Aztecs, smallpox and native unfamiliarity with

(Oronoz)

Spanish Conquistadors vs. Aztec Defenders *After the Spanish conquest, a Mexica (Aztec) artist recalled this moment before the disastrous smallpox epidemic destroyed the Indians' ability to resist. (Oronoz)*

European ways and weapons enabled a small army to overpower a mighty emperor and his realm. The human cost of the Spanish conquest was enormous.

> *Broken spears lie in the roads;*
> *We have torn our hair in our grief*
> *The houses are roofless now ...*
> *And the walls are splattered with gore ...*
> *We have pounded our hands in despair*
> *Against the adobe walls.*

When Cortés landed in 1519, central Mexico's population was between 13 and 25 million. By 1600, it had shrunk to about seven hundred thousand. Peru and other regions experienced similar devastation. The Americas had witnessed the greatest demographic disaster in world history.

THE COLUMBIAN EXCHANGE

The emerging Atlantic world linked not only peoples but also animals, plants, and germs from Europe, Africa, and the Americas in a **Columbian exchange.** After 1492, vast numbers of Native Americans died because they lacked antibodies that could resist infectious diseases brought by Europeans and Africans—especially deadly, highly communicable smallpox. From the first years of contact, epidemics scourged defenseless Indian communities. A Spanish observer estimated that the indigenous population of the West Indies declined from about 1 million in 1492 to just five hundred a half century later. Whole villages perished at once, with no one left to bury the dead. Such devastation directly facilitated European colonization everywhere in the Americas, whether accompanied by a military effort or not.

The biological encounter of the Eastern and Western Hemispheres affected the everyday lives of peoples throughout the Atlantic world. Besides diseases, sixteenth-century Europeans introduced horses, cattle, sheep, swine, chickens, wheat and other grains, coffee, sugar, numerous fruits and garden vegetables, and many species of weeds, insects, and rodents to America. In the next century, enslaved Africans carried rice and yams with them across the Atlantic. The list of American gifts to Europe and Africa was equally impressive: corn, many varieties of beans, white and sweet potatoes, tomatoes, squash, pumpkins, peanuts, vanilla, cacao (for making chocolate and cocoa), avocados, pineapples, chilis, tobacco, and turkeys. Often, several centuries passed before new plants became widely accepted. For example, many Europeans initially suspected that potatoes were aphrodisiacs and that tomatoes were poisonous.

European weeds and domestic animals drastically altered many American environments, impinging directly on Native American ways of life. Especially in temperate zones, livestock devoured indigenous plants, enabling hardier European weeds to take over. As a result, wild animals that had fed on the plants stayed away, depriving Indians of a critical source of food. Free-roaming livestock, especially hogs, also invaded Native Americans' cornfields. Settlers' crops, intensively cultivated on lands never replenished by lying fallow, often exhausted American soil. But the worldwide exchange of food products also enriched human diets and later made enormous population growth possible.

Another dimension of the Atlantic world was the mixing of peoples. During the sixteenth century, about three hundred thousand Spaniards immigrated, 90 percent of them male. Particularly in towns, a racially blended people emerged as these men married Indian women, giving rise to the large mestizo (mixed Spanish-Indian) population of Mexico and other Latin American countries. Lesser numbers of *métis,* as the French termed people of both Indian and European descent, would appear in the French and English colonies of North America. Throughout the Americas, particularly in plantation colonies, European men fathered mulatto children with enslaved African women, and African-Indian unions occurred in most regions. Colonial societies differed significantly in their official attitudes toward the different kinds of interracial unions and in their classifications of the children who resulted.

The Americas supplied seemingly limitless wealth for Spain. More important sources of wealth than gold and sugar were the immense quantities of silver that crossed the Atlantic after rich mines in Mexico and Peru began producing in the 1540s. But Spanish kings squandered this wealth. Bent on dominating Europe, they needed ever more American silver to finance their wars there. Several times they went bankrupt, and in the 1560s their efforts to squeeze more taxes from their subjects helped provoke the revolt of Spain's rich Netherlands provinces (discussed later in this chapter). In the end, American wealth proved to be a mixed blessing for Spain.

FOOTHOLDS IN NORTH AMERICA, 1512–1625

Most European immigrants in the sixteenth century flocked to Mexico, the Caribbean, and points farther south. But a minority extended the Atlantic world to North America. Except for a tiny Spanish base at St. Augustine, Florida, the earliest attempts to plant colonies failed, generally because they were predicated on unrealistic expectations of fabulous wealth and natives who would be easily conquered.

After 1600, the ravaging of Indian populations by disease and the rise of English, French, and Dutch power made colonization possible. By 1614, Spain, England, France, and the Netherlands had established North American footholds (see Map 2.2). Within another decade, each colony developed a distinct economic orientation and its own approach to Native Americans.

Spain's Northern Frontier   The Spanish had built their American empire by subduing the spectacularly wealthy Aztecs and Incas. The dream of more such finds drew would-be conquistadors northward to what would later be called Florida and New Mexico. "As it was his object to find another treasure like that ... of Peru," a witness wrote of one such man, Hernando de Soto, he "would not be content with good lands nor pearls."

The earliest of these invaders was Juan Ponce de León, who had founded Puerto Rico. In 1513, he explored the coast of a peninsula he named "La Florida." Returning to Florida in 1521 to found a colony, Ponce de León was killed in a skirmish with Calusa Indians.

The most astonishing early expedition began in Florida in 1527. After provoking attacks by Apalachee Indians, the three hundred explorers separated into several parties. All were thought to have perished until eight years later, when four survivors, led by Alvar Nuñez Cabeza de Vaca and including an African slave, Esteban, arrived in northern Mexico. They had been shipwrecked on the Texas coast and

MAP 2.2 European Imperial Claims and Settlements in Eastern North America, 1565–1625

By 1625 four European nations contended for territory on North America's Atlantic coast. Except for St. Augustine, Florida, all settlements established before 1607 had been abandoned by 1625.

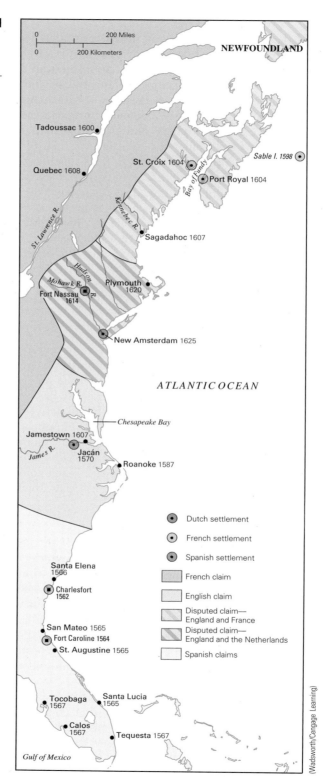

made the rest of the journey on foot, living in dozens of Native American communities along the way.

Cabeza de Vaca provided direct inspiration for two more formidable attempts at Spanish conquest. Hernando de Soto and his party in 1539–1543 blundered from Tampa Bay to the Appalachians to the southern Plains, scouring the land for gold and alienating Native people wherever they went. "Think, then," one Indian chief appealed to de Soto in vain,

> *what must be the effect on me and mine, of the sight of you and your people, whom we have at no time seen, astride the fierce brutes, your horses, entering with such speed and fury into my country, that we had no tidings of your coming—things so absolutely new, as to strike awe and terror into our hearts.*

In 1540, a coalition of Native Americans gathered at the Mississippian city of Mábila to confront de Soto. Although the Spanish were victorious militarily, their own losses doomed them. Most of their horses died from arrow wounds while their livestock (their principal source of food aside from the corn they seized) scattered. Thereafter, the expedition floundered.

Although de Soto died without finding gold or extending Spanish rule, his and other expeditions spread epidemics that destroyed most of the remaining Mississippian societies (see Chapter 1). By the time Europeans returned to the southeastern interior late in the seventeenth century, only the Natchez on the lower Mississippi River still inhabited their sumptuous temple-mound center and remained under the rule of a Great Sun monarch. Depopulated groups like the Cherokees and Creeks had adopted the less centralized village life of other eastern Indians.

Meanwhile Cabeza de Vaca had reported hearing of golden cities in the Southwest. In 1540–1542, Francisco Vásquez de Coronado led a massive expedition northward from Mexico to find and conquer these cities. Coronado plundered several pueblos on the Rio Grande and wandered from the Grand Canyon to present-day Kansas before returning to Mexico, finding no gold but embittering many Native Americans toward the Spanish. Other expeditions along the California coast and up the Colorado River likewise proved fruitless.

For several decades after these failed ventures, Spain's principal interest in North America lay in establishing strategic bases to keep French and English intruders away from Mexico and the Caribbean. In 1565, Spain established the first lasting European post in North America, a fortress at **St. Augustine, Florida.** While remaining a lone military stronghold, St. Augustine also served as a base for a chain of Catholic missions on the Florida peninsula and Atlantic coast as far northward as Chesapeake Bay. Rejecting missionary efforts to reorder their lives, the Guale, Powhatan, and other Indians rebelled and forced the closing of all the missions before 1600. Franciscan missionaries renewed their efforts in Florida in the early seventeenth century and secured the nominal allegiance of about sixteen thousand Guale and Timucua Indians. But epidemics in the 1610s killed about half the converts.

Meanwhile, in the 1580s, Spanish missionaries had returned to the Southwest, preaching Christianity and scouting the area's potential wealth. Encouraged by their reports, New Spain's viceroy in 1598 commissioned Juan de Oñate to lead five hundred Spaniards, mestizos, Mexican Indians, and enslaved Africans into the upper Rio Grande Valley. Oñate seized a pueblo of the Tewa Indians, renamed it San Juan, and proclaimed the royal colony of **New Mexico.**

The Spanish encountered swift resistance at the mesa-top pueblo of Ácoma in December 1598. When the Ácoma Indians refused Spanish demands for corn and other provisions, fifteen Spanish soldiers ascended the mesa to obtain the goods by force. After Ácoma defenders killed most of the soldiers, Oñate ordered massive retaliation. In January, Spanish troops captured the pueblo, killing eight hundred inhabitants. Oñate sentenced surviving Ácoma men to have one foot cut off and forced them, along with the women and children, to be servants of the soldiers and missionaries. Two prominent leaders also had their right hands amputated.

Despite having crushed Ácoma and imposed **encomiendas**—grants awarding Indian labor to wealthy colonists—on other Pueblo Indians, New Mexico barely survived. The Spanish government replaced Oñate in 1606 because of mismanagement and excessive brutality toward Native Americans, and seriously considered withdrawing from New Mexico altogether. Franciscan missionaries, aiming to save Pueblo Indian souls, persuaded the authorities to keep New Mexico alive. By 1630, Franciscans were present in more than fifty pueblos. Prompted by deadly epidemics and believing that Catholic rituals could be reconciled with traditional practices, a few thousand Indians accepted baptism. But resistance was common because, as the leading Franciscan summarized it, "the main and general answer given [by the Pueblos] for not becoming Christians is that when they do … they are at once compelled to pay tribute and render personal service." New Mexico began, then, amid uneasy tensions between colonists and natives.

France: Colonizing Canada   France entered the imperial competition in 1524 when King Francis I (ruled 1515–1547) dispatched Giovanni da Verrazano to find a more direct "northwest passage" to the Pacific. Verrazano explored the North American coast from the Carolinas to Newfoundland. His several encounters with Native Americans ranged from violent to friendly. In 1534 and 1535–1536, French explorer Jacques Cartier probed the coasts of Newfoundland, Quebec, and Nova Scotia and sailed up the St. Lawrence River as far as present-day Montreal. Cartier encountered large numbers of Native Americans (some of whom called the land "kanata," or Canada) but found neither gold nor a northwest passage.

France made its first colonizing attempt in 1541 when Cartier returned to the St. Lawrence Valley with ten ships carrying four hundred soldiers, three hundred sailors, and a few women. Cartier had earned Native Americans' distrust during his previous expeditions, and his construction of a fortified settlement on Stadacona Indian land (near modern Quebec City) removed all possibility of friendly relations. Over the next two years, the French suffered heavy losses from Stadacona attacks and harsh winters before abandoning the colony.

The failed French expedition seemed to verify one Spaniard's opinion that "this whole coast as far [south] as Florida is utterly unproductive." The next French effort at colonization began in 1562 when French Huguenots (Calvinists) seeking religious freedom attempted to settle in Florida. In 1564, the Huguenots founded a settlement near present-day Jacksonville. Sensing a Protestant threat to their control of the Caribbean, Spanish forces destroyed the settlement a year later, executing all 132 male defenders. These failures, along with a civil war in France between Catholics and Huguenots, temporarily hindered France's colonizing efforts.

Meanwhile, French and other European fishermen were working the plenteous Grand Banks fisheries off the coast of Newfoundland. Going ashore to dry their fish, some sailors abused local Beothuk Indians, but others bartered with them for skins of beaver. By the late sixteenth century, European demand for beaver hats was skyrocketing, and a French-dominated fur trade blossomed. Before the end of the century, French traders were returning annually to sites from Newfoundland to New England and along the lower St. Lawrence.

Unlike explorers such as de Soto and colonizers such as those at Roanoke (discussed in the next section), most fur traders recognized the importance of reciprocity in dealing with Native Americans. Consequently, they were generally more successful. In exchange for pelts, they traded axes, knives, copper kettles, cloth, and glass beads. Usually dismissed by Europeans as "trinkets," glass beads were valued by northeastern Indians for possessing spiritual power comparable to that of quartz, mica, and other sacred substances they had long obtained via trade networks (see Chapter 1). By the next century, specialized factories in Europe would be producing both cloth and glass for the "Indian trade."

Seeing the lucrative Canadian trade as a source of revenue, the French government dispatched Samuel de Champlain to establish the colony of **New France** at Quebec in 1608. The French concluded that a colony was the surest means of deterring English, Dutch, and independent French traders. Familiar with Indian politics and diplomacy from earlier voyages in the region, Champlain shrewdly allied with the Montagnais and Algonquins of the St. Lawrence and the Hurons of the lower Great Lakes. He agreed to help these allies defeat their enemies, the Mohawks of the Iroquois Confederacy, who sought direct access to European traders on the St. Lawrence. The Indians were equally shrewd in recognizing the advantage of having armed French allies when facing the dreaded Mohawks.

In July 1609, Champlain and two other Frenchmen accompanied sixty Montagnais and Huron warriors to Lake Champlain (which the explorer named for himself). Soon they encountered two hundred Mohawks at Point Ticonderoga near the lake's southern tip. As the main French-Indian column neared its opponents, Champlain stepped ahead and felled the Mohawks' three war leaders with a single shot. The two other Frenchmen began firing, causing the Mohawks to beat a hasty retreat. The French and their allies pursued the fleeing Mohawks, killing about fifty and capturing a dozen prisoners. A few pro-French Indians suffered minor arrow wounds.

The battle at Lake Champlain marked the end of an era in Indian-European relations in the Northeast. Except in a few isolated places, casual encounters between small parties gave way to trade, diplomacy, and warfare coordinated by Indian and European governments. Through their alliance with the powerful Hurons, the French gained access to the thick beaver pelts of the Canadian interior while providing their Indian allies with European goods and armed protection from Iroquois attacks. These economic and diplomatic arrangements, and Iroquois reactions (discussed later in this chapter), defined the course of New France's history for the rest of the seventeenth century.

England and the Atlantic World, 1558–1603   When Elizabeth I became queen in 1558, Spain and France were grappling for supremacy in Europe, and England was a minor power. But largely Protestant England resented Spain's suppression of Calvinists in the Netherlands and the pope's call for Elizabeth's overthrow. Elizabeth adopted a militantly anti-Spanish foreign policy, with Anglicans and Puritans alike hailing England as an "elect nation" whose mission was to elevate "true" Christianity and to overthrow Catholicism, represented by Spain. Secretly, she stepped up her aid to Dutch Calvinists and encouraged English privateers (armed private ships), commanded by "sea dogs" like John Hawkins and Francis Drake, to attack Spanish ships.

The Anglo-Spanish rivalry extended to Ireland after 1565, when Spain and the pope began directly aiding Irish Catholics' longtime resistance to English rule. In a war that ground on to the seventeenth century, the English drove the Irish clans off their lands, especially in northern Ireland, or Ulster, and established their own settlements ("plantations") of English and Scottish Protestants. The English practiced "scorched earth" warfare to break the rebellious population's spirit, inflicting starvation and mass slaughter by destroying villages in the winter.

Elizabeth's generals justified these atrocities by claiming that the Irish were "savages" and that Irish customs, religion, and methods of fighting absolved the English from guilt in waging exceptionally cruel warfare. Ireland thus furnished precedents for later English tactics and rationales for crushing Native Americans.

England had two objectives in the Western Hemisphere in the 1570s. The first was to find the northwest passage to Asia and discover gold on the way; the second, in Drake's words, was to "singe the king of Spain's beard" by raiding Spanish fleets and ports. The search for the northwest passage led only to such embarrassments as explorer Martin Frobisher's voyages to the Canadian Arctic. Frobisher returned with several thousand tons of an ore that looked like gold but proved worthless. However, privateering raids proved spectacularly successful and profitable for their financial backers, including merchants, gentry, government leaders, and Elizabeth herself. The most breathtaking enterprise was Drake's voyage around the world (1577–1580) in quest of sites for colonies, including on the northern California coast, where he traded with Miwok Indians.

Now deadly rivals, Spain and England sought to outmaneuver one another in North America. In 1572, the Spanish tried to fortify a Jesuit mission on the Chesapeake Bay. They failed, largely because Powhatan Indians resisted. Sir Walter Raleigh obtained a royal patent (charter) to start an English colony farther south, closer to the Spanish—a region the English soon named Virginia in honor of their virgin queen. After an exploratory expedition returned singing the praises of Roanoke Island, its peaceable natives, and its ideal location as a base for anti-Spanish privateers, Raleigh persuaded Elizabeth to dispatch an expedition in 1585 to found Roanoke colony.

At first all went well, but by winter, the English had alienated the Roanoke Indians with their incessant demands for food. Fearing that the natives were about to attack, English soldiers killed Wingina, the Roanoke leader, in June 1586. When Drake visited soon after on his way back to England, the starving colonists joined him.

The determined Raleigh dispatched a second group of colonists, including seventeen women and nine children in 1587. The civilian leader, John White, soon returned to England for supplies. Thereafter, the Anglo-Spanish conflict repeatedly prevented him from returning to Roanoke. When White finally arrived in 1590, he found only rusty armor, moldy books, and the word CROATOAN cut into a post. Although the stranded colonists were presumably living among the Croatoan Indians of Cape Hatteras, the exact fate of the "lost colony" remains a mystery to this day.

In 1588, while Roanoke struggled, England won a spectacular naval victory over the Armada, a huge invasion fleet sent into the English Channel by Spain's Philip II. This famous victory preserved England's independence and confirmed its status as a major power in the Atlantic.

Failure and Success in Virginia, 1603–1625
Anglo-Spanish relations took a new turn after 1603, when Elizabeth died and James I succeeded her. The cautious, peace-loving James signed a truce with Spain in 1604. Alarmed by Dutch naval victories, the Spanish now considered England the lesser danger. Consequently, Spain's new king, Philip III (ruled 1598–1621), renounced Spanish claims to Virginia, allowing England to colonize unmolested.

In 1606, James I granted a charter authorizing overlapping grants of land to two separate joint-stock companies. The Virginia Company of Plymouth received a grant extending south from modern Maine to the Potomac River, while the Virginia Company of London's lands ran north from Cape Fear, North Carolina, to the Hudson River. Both companies dispatched colonists in 1607.

The Virginia Company of Plymouth sent 120 men to Sagadahoc, on the Maine coast. After bickering among themselves, alienating nearby Abenaki Indians, and enduring a hard New England winter, the colonists returned to England and the company disbanded.

The Virginia Company of London barely avoided a similar failure. Its first expedition included many gentlemen who, considering themselves above manual work, expected Native Americans to feed them and riches to fall into their laps. Choosing a site on the James River, they called it Jamestown and formally named their colony **Virginia.** Discipline quickly fell apart, and, as at Roanoke, the colonists neglected to plant crops. The local Powhatan Indians sold them some corn but, with their own supplies running low, declined to offer more. By December, the English were running out of food. As with Roanoke and numerous Spanish ventures, Virginia's military leader, Captain John Smith, led some soldiers in an attempt to seize corn from the Powhatans. After capturing and releasing Smith, the Powhatan *weroance* (chief), also named Powhatan, did share some of his people's remaining supplies with the English. (Many years later, Smith would claim that Powhatan's ten-year-old daughter, Pocahontas, saved him at the last minute from execution. Because Smith claimed to have been similarly rescued by females on two other occasions during his military adventures, the story's accuracy is doubtful.)

Powhatan's gesture was intended to remind the English that his people were the stronger force and that reciprocity was preferable to force in their dealings with one another. In releasing Smith and giving him more corn, he expected the English to support him in return, particularly by allying with the Powhatans against local Indian enemies.

Powhatan recognized the early Virginians' weaknesses. When relief ships arrived in January 1608 with reinforcements, only thirty-eight survivors remained out of 105 immigrants. By September 1608, three councilors had died, and three others had returned to England, leaving Smith in complete charge of the colony. Smith shrewdly noted that the healthy Powhatans moved away from the James River each spring after planting their crops, not returning until the fall at harvest time. Without understanding why moving left the Powhatans healthier, Smith ordered the colonists to do the same. (Scientists have determined that tidal patterns at Jamestown at the time were such that the colonists were drinking salty, contaminated water, and that even more died from dysentery, typhoid fever, and salt poisoning than from starvation.) During the next winter (1608–1609), Virginia lost just a dozen men out of two hundred. Smith prevented Virginia from disintegrating as Sagadahoc had. But when he returned to England in 1609 after being wounded in a gunpowder explosion, discipline again crumbled and the deadly diseases returned. Of the 500 residents at Jamestown in September 1609, about 400 died by May 1610.

An influx of new recruits, coupled with renewed military rule, enabled Virginia to recover enough to assert its supremacy to the Powhatans. When Powhatan refused to submit to the new governor's authority, the colony waged the First Anglo-Powhatan War (1610–1614). After the English captured Powhatan's daughter, Pocahontas, and she converted to Christianity, the war ended when the aging weroance agreed that she could marry a colonist named John Rolfe. Nevertheless, the English population remained small—just 380 in 1616—and had yet to produce anything of value for Virginia Company stockholders.

Tobacco emerged as Virginia's salvation. Rolfe spent several years adapting a salable variety of Caribbean tobacco to conditions in Virginia. By 1619, tobacco commanded high prices, and Virginia exported large amounts to a newly emergent European market.

To attract labor and capital to its suddenly profitable venture, the Virginia Company awarded a fifty-acre "headright" for each person ("head") entering the colony, to whoever paid that person's passage. By paying the passage of prospective laborers, some enterprising planters accumulated sizable tracts of land. Thousands of young men and a few hundred women calculated that uncertainty in Virginia was preferable to continued unemployment and poverty in England. In return for their passage and such basic needs as food, shelter, and clothing, they agreed to work as **indentured servants** for fixed terms, usually four to seven years. The Virginia Company abandoned military rule in 1619 and provided for an assembly to be elected by the "inhabitants" (apparently meaning only the planters and not the laborers). Although the assembly's actions were subject to the company's veto, it was the first representative legislature in North America.

By 1622, Virginia faced three serious problems. First, local officials systematically defrauded the shareholders by embezzling treasury funds, overcharging for supplies, and using company laborers to work their own tobacco fields. They profited, but the company sank deep into debt. Second, despite massive immigration, the colony's population continued to experience an appallingly high death rate. Most of the 3,500 immigrants entering Virginia from 1618 to 1622 died within three years, primarily from malnutrition or from the diseases that had plagued earlier colonists. Finally, relations with Native Americans steadily worsened after Powhatan died. Leadership passed to Powhatan's younger brother, Opechancanough, who at first sought to accommodate the English. But relentless English expansion provoked Indian discontent and the rise of a powerful religious leader, Nemattenew, who urged the Powhatans to resist the English. After some settlers killed Nemattenew, the Indians launched a surprise attack in 1622 that killed 347 of the

Pocahontas *A Dutch artist engraved this portrait of the Powhatan woman when she traveled to England in 1616.*

(The Library of Congress)

1,240 colonists. With much of their livestock destroyed, spring planting prevented, and disease spreading through cramped fortresses, hundreds more colonists died in the ensuing months.

After the Virginia Company sent more men, Governor Francis Wyatt reorganized the settlers and took the offensive during the Second Anglo-Powhatan War (1622–1632). Using tactics developed during the Irish war, Wyatt inflicted widespread starvation by destroying food supplies and driving Indians from their homes during winter. By 1625, the English had effectively won the war, and the Powhatans had lost their best chance of driving out the intruders.

The clash left the Virginia Company bankrupt. After receiving a report critical of the company's management, James I revoked its charter in 1624 and made Virginia a royal colony. Only about five hundred colonists now lived there, including a handful of Africans who had been brought in since 1619. With its combination of fabulous profits, unfree labor, and massive mortality, Virginia was truly a land of contradictions.

New England Begins, 1614–1625

The next English colony, after Virginia, that proved permanent arose in New England. John Smith, exploring its coast in 1614, gave New England its name. "Who," he asked, "can but approve this most excellent place, both for health and fertility?" Smith hoped to establish a colony there, but in 1616–1618 a terrible epidemic spread by fishermen or traders devastated New England's coastal Native American communities by about 90 percent. Later visitors found the ground littered with the "bones and skulls" of the unburied dead and acres of overgrown cornfields.

Against this tragic backdrop, the Virginia Company of London gave a patent to some merchants headed by Thomas Weston for a settlement. In 1620, Weston sent over twenty-four families (a total of 102 people) in a small, leaky ship called the *Mayflower*. The colonists promised to send lumber, furs, and fish back to Weston in England for seven years, after which they would own the tract.

The expedition's leaders, but only half its members, were Separatist Puritans who had withdrawn from the Church of England and fled to the Netherlands to practice their religion freely. Fearing that their children were assimilating into Dutch culture, they decided to emigrate to America.

In November 1620, the *Mayflower* landed at Plymouth Bay in present-day Massachusetts, north of the Virginia Company's grant. Knowing they had no legal right to be there, the expedition's leaders insisted that all adult males in the group (including non-Puritans) sign the Mayflower Compact before they landed. By this document, they constituted themselves a "civil body politic," or government, and claimed the land for King James, establishing **Plymouth** colony.

Weakened by their journey and unprepared for winter, half the Pilgrims, as the colonists later came to be known, died within four months of landing. Those still alive in the spring of 1621 owed much to the aid of two English-speaking Native Americans. One was Squanto, a Wampanoag Indian who had been taken to Spain as a slave in 1614 but was freed and then traveled to England. Returning home with a colonizing expedition, he learned that most of the two thousand people of his village had perished in the recent epidemic. The other Indian, an Abenaki from Maine named Samoset, had experience trading with the English. To prevent the colonists from stealing the natives' food, Squanto showed them how to grow corn, using fish as fertilizer. Plymouth's first harvest was marked by a festival of thanksgiving, "at which time…we exercised our arms, many of the Indians coming amongst us, … some 90 men, whom for three days we entertained and feasted." Plymouth's relations with the Native Americans soon worsened. The alliance that Squanto and Samoset had arranged between Plymouth and the Wampanoags, headed by Massasoit, had united two weak parties. But news of the Powhatan attack in 1622 hastened the colony's militarization. Miles Standish, its military commander, threatened Plymouth's "allies" with the colony's monopoly of firepower. For although Massasoit remained loyal, other Indians were offended by the colonists' conduct.

Plymouth soon became economically selfsufficient. After the colony turned from communal farming to individually owned plots, its more prosperous farmers produced corn surpluses, which they traded to nonfarming Abenaki Indians in Maine for furs. Within a decade, Plymouth's elite had bought out the colony's London backers and several hundred colonists had arrived.

Although a tiny colony, Plymouth was significant as an outpost for Puritans dissenting from the Church of England and for proving that a self-governing society consisting mostly of farm families could flourish in New England. In these respects, it proved to be the vanguard of a massive migration of Puritans to New England in the 1630s (covered in Chapter 3).

A "New Netherland" on the Hudson, 1609–1625

Among the most fervently Calvinist regions of Europe were the Dutch-speaking provinces of the Netherlands. The provinces had come under Spanish rule during the sixteenth century, but Spain's religious intolerance and high taxes drove the Dutch to revolt, beginning in 1566. Exhausting its resources trying to quell the revolt, Spain finally recognized Dutch independence in 1609. By then, the Netherlands was a wealthy commercial power. The Dutch built an empire stretching from Brazil to South Africa to Indonesia, and played a key role in colonizing North America.

Just as the French were routing the Mohawk Iroquois at Lake Champlain in 1609, Henry Hudson sailed up the river later named for him, traded with Native Americans, and claimed the land for the Netherlands. When Dutch traders returned the following year, some of their most eager customers were—not surprisingly—Mohawks. Having established lucrative ties with Indians on the lower Hudson River, Dutch traders in 1614 built Fort Nassau near what would become Albany, and established the colony of **New Netherland.** In 1626, local Munsee Indians allowed the Dutch to settle on an island at the mouth of the Hudson. The Dutch named the island Manhattan and the settlement, New Amsterdam.

The earliest New Netherlanders lived by the fur trade. Through the Mohawks, they relied on the Five Nations Iroquois, much as the French depended on the Hurons, as commercial clients and military allies. To stimulate a flow of furs to New Netherland, Dutch traders obtained from coastal Indians large quantities of wampum—sacred shells like those used by Deganawidah and Hiawatha to convey solemn "words" of condolence in rituals (see Chapter 1)—for trade with the Iroquois. The Dutch-Iroquois and French-Huron alliances became embroiled in an ever-deepening contest to control the movement of goods between Europeans and Indians (discussed in Chapter 3).

CHRONOLOGY
1400–1625

C. 1400–1600	European Renaissance.
C. 1400–1500	Coastal West African kingdoms rise and expand.
C. 1440	Portuguese slave trade in West Africa begins.
C. 1450	Songhai succeeds Mali as major power in West African grassland.
1492	Christian "reconquest" of Spain. Columbus lands at Guanahaní.
1498	Vasco da Gama rounds the Cape of Good Hope and reaches India.
1517	Protestant Reformation begins in Germany.
1519–1521	Cortés leads Spanish conquest of Aztec empire.
1519–1522	Magellan's expedition circumnavigates the globe.
1532–1536	Pizarro leads Spanish conquest of Inca empire.
1534	Church of England breaks from Roman Catholic Church.
1541–1542	Cartier attempts to colonize eastern Canada.
1539–1543	De Soto attempts conquests in southeastern United States.
1540–1542	Coronado attempts conquests in southwestern United States.
1558	Elizabeth I becomes queen of England.
1565	St. Augustine founded by Spanish.

1585–1590	English colony of Roanoke established, then disappears.
1588	England defeats the Spanish Armada.
1591	Moroccan forces defeat Songhai in West Africa.
1598	Oñate founds New Mexico.
1603	James I becomes king of England.
1607	English found colonies at Jamestown and Sagadahoc.
1608	Champlain founds New France.
1609	Henry Hudson explores the Hudson River.
1610–1614	First Anglo-Powhatan War.
1614	New Netherland founded.
1619	Virginia begins exporting tobacco. First Africans arrive in Virginia.
1620	Plymouth colony founded.
1622–1632	Second Anglo-Powhatan War.
1624	James I revokes Virginia Company's charter.

Conclusion

The sixteenth century marked the emergence of an Atlantic world linking Europe, Africa, and the Americas. Kings and emperors in West Africa competed ferociously for the wealth brought by long distance trade, including trade in slaves. Western Europe entered a new era in which nation-states drew on Renaissance knowledge, merchants' capital, and religious zeal to advance national power and overseas expansion.

The Atlantic world brought few benefits to West Africans and Native Americans. Proclaiming that civilization and Christianity rendered them superior, Europeans denigrated Native Americans and Africans as savages whose land and labor Europeans could seize and exploit. Initial Portuguese incursions promised to expand West Africa's trade ties with Europe. But Europe's overwhelming demand for slave labor depleted the region's population and accelerated the reshaping of trade, politics, warfare, and societies. Africa's notorious underdevelopment, which persists in our own time, had begun.

After 1492, the Atlantic world spread to the Americas. Indigenous peoples in the Caribbean and in Central and South America were the first to be ravaged by European epidemic diseases, leaving them vulnerable to violent conquest and exploitation. The forced and unforced movements of people, as well as of animals, plants, and disease-causing germs constituted a Columbian exchange that transformed environments throughout the Atlantic world.

Native peoples north of Mexico and the Caribbean held would-be colonizers at bay until after 1600. Thereafter, they too suffered the effects of European-borne diseases. Native North Americans cooperated with Europeans who practiced reciprocity while resisting those who tried to dominate them. By 1625, Spain had advanced only as far north as seemed necessary to protect its prized Mexican and Caribbean conquests. Meanwhile, French, English, and Dutch colonists focused on less spectacular resources. New France and New Netherland existed primarily to obtain furs from Indians, while the English in Virginia and Plymouth cultivated fields recently belonging to Native Americans. All these colonies depended for their success on maintaining stable relations with at least some Native Americans. The transplantation of Europeans into North America was hardly a story of inevitable triumph.

3

THE EMERGENCE OF COLONIAL SOCIETIES, 1625–1700

CHESAPEAKE SOCIETY

Building on the tobacco boom of the 1620s, the English colonies on the Chesapeake Bay—Virginia and neighboring Maryland—were the first to prosper in North America. Despite differences between their political and religious institutions, Virginia and Maryland had similar economies, populations, and patterns of growth that gave them a distinct regional identity.

Chesapeake society was highly unequal and unstable before 1700. Life for most colonists was short, good health was rare, and the familiar comforts of family and community were missing. After a civil conflict, Bacon's Rebellion, the English seized yet more Native American land for growing tobacco and shifted from white indentured servitude to black slavery as the principal source of labor. On this racial foundation, Chesapeake colonists finally achieved stability, harmony, and at least minimal prosperity within their own ranks.

State and Church in Virginia

King James I had reorganized Virginia as a **royal colony**, in which a crown-appointed governor would name leading planters to an advisory council. James did not reconvene Virginia's elected assembly. With civil war threatening in England, James's successor Charles I (ruled 1625–1649) in 1639 restored the assembly as a means of securing tobacco revenues and the support of Virginia's planters. The elected representatives initially met as a single body with the council

("Jamestown, 1614" by Sidney King, Colonial National Historical Park)

View of Jamestown, 1625 *As Virginia's tobacco production boomed, the capital expanded beyond the fort that had originally confined it.*

to pass laws. During the 1650s, the legislature split into two chambers—the House of Burgesses and the Governor's Council, whose members held lifetime appointments.

Virginia adopted England's county-court system for local government. Justices of the peace served as judges and, along with sheriffs, as executives who administered local affairs. These officials were chosen by the governor. Everywhere south of New England, unelected county courts became the basic unit of local government.

As in England, Virginia's established church was the Church of England to which taxpayers were legally obliged to pay fixed rates. In each parish, six vestrymen managed church finances, distributed poor relief, and prosecuted moral offenses such as fornication or drunkenness. Vestries were elected until 1662, when the assembly made them self-perpetuating and independent of the voters.

Because Anglican priests could only be trained in England and usually found pulpits there, few were attracted to Virginia. Consequently, Virginia experienced a chronic shortage of clergymen, and most priests rotated among two or three parishes. But when a minister was conducting services in a parish, church attendance was required (as in Puritan New England); violators were subject to fines payable in cash or labor on public works projects.

State and Church in Maryland After 1632, the crown created new colonies by awarding portions of the Virginia Company's forfeited territory to wealthy, trusted English elites. One or more proprietors, as they were called, were responsible for peopling, governing, and defending each **proprietary colony**.

In 1632, Charles I awarded the first such grant to a Catholic nobleman, **Lord Baltimore**, for a large tract of land north of the Potomac River and east of

Chesapeake Bay. The grant guaranteed Lord Baltimore freedom from royal taxation, the power to appoint sheriffs and judges, and the privilege of creating a local nobility. The only checks on the proprietor's power were the crown's control of war and trade and the requirement that an elected assembly approve all laws.

Naming his colony Maryland, Lord Baltimore intended it as a refuge for English Catholics, who constituted about 2 percent of England's population. Although many English Catholics were wealthy and a few held political office, they could not worship in public and (like other dissenters) paid taxes to support the Anglican Church.

To avoid antagonizing English Protestants, Baltimore introduced the English institution of the manor—an estate on which a lord could maintain private law courts and employ a Catholic priest as his chaplain. Local Catholics could go to the manor to hear Mass and receive the sacraments privately. Baltimore adapted Virginia's headright system (see Chapter 2) by offering a two thousand-acre manor to anyone transporting five adults (a requirement raised to twenty by 1640).

Maryland's colonization did not proceed as Baltimore envisioned. In 1634, the first two hundred immigrants landed. Maryland was the first colony spared a starving time, thanks to Baltimore's careful study of Virginia's early history. The new colony's success showed that English overseas expansion had come of age. Baltimore, however, stayed in England, governing as an absentee proprietor, and few Catholics went to Maryland. From the outset, Protestants formed the majority of the population. With land prices low, they purchased their own property, thereby avoiding becoming tenants on the manors. These conditions doomed Baltimore's dream of creating a manorial system of mostly Catholic lords collecting rents. By 1675, all of Maryland's sixty nonproprietary manors had evolved into plantations.

Religious tensions soon emerged. In 1642, Catholics and Protestants in the capital at St. Mary's argued over use of the city's chapel, which the two groups had shared until then. As antagonisms intensified, Baltimore drafted the **Act for Religious Toleration**, or Toleration Act, which the Protestant-dominated assembly passed in 1649. The act affirmed toleration of Catholics and Protestants but did not protect non-Christians.

The Toleration Act also failed to secure religious peace. In 1654, the Protestant majority barred Catholics from voting, ousted Governor William Stone (a pro-tolerance Protestant), and repealed the Toleration Act. In 1655, Stone raised an army of both faiths to regain the government but was defeated. The victors imprisoned Stone and hanged three Catholic leaders.

Lord Baltimore resumed control of Maryland in 1658, but he and his descendants would encounter continued Protestant resistance to Catholic rule (as discussed in Chapter 4).

Death, Gender, and Kinship   Tobacco sustained a sharp demand for labor that lured about 110,000 English to the Chesapeake from 1630 to 1700. Ninety percent of these immigrants were indentured servants, and because men were more valued as field hands than women, 80 percent of arriving servants were males. So few women initially immigrated to the Chesapeake that only a third of male colonists found brides before 1650. Male servants married late because their indentures forbade them to wed before completing their term of labor. Women's scarcity gave them a great advantage in negotiating favorable marriages. Some female servants found prosperous planters who would buy their remaining time of service and marry them.

The high death rates that characterized the early Chesapeake persisted after tobacco production became routine. The greatest killers were typhoid fever and, after 1650, malaria. Malaria became endemic as sailors and slaves arriving from Africa brought a particularly virulent form and carried it into marshy lowlands, where mosquitoes spread it rapidly. Life expectancy in the 1600s was about forty-eight for men and forty-four for women—slightly lower than in England and nearly twenty years lower than in New England. Servants died at horrifying rates, with perhaps 40 percent going to their graves within six years of arrival, and 70 percent by age forty-nine. Such high death rates severely crippled family life. Half of all people married in Charles County, Maryland, during the late 1600s became widows or widowers within seven years. The typical Maryland family saw half of its four children die in childhood.

Chesapeake widows tended to enjoy greater economic power than widowed women elsewhere. Instead of leaving widows the one-third of an estate required by English law, Chesapeake husbands usually were more generous and often gave their wives complete control of their estates. A widow in such circumstances gained economic independence yet still needed to marry a man who could produce income by farming her fields. But because there were so many more men than women, she had a wider choice of husbands than widows in most societies.

The combination of predominantly male immigration and devastating death rates sharply limited population growth. Although the Chesapeake had received about 110,000 English immigrants by 1700, its white population stood at about seventy thousand that year. By contrast, a benign disease environment and a more balanced gender ratio among the 28,000 immigrants to New England during the 1600s allowed that region's white population to grow to ninety-one thousand by 1700.

The Chesapeake's dismal demographic history began improving in the late seventeenth century. By then, resistance acquired from childhood immunities allowed native-born residents to survive into their fifties, ten years longer than immigrants. As a result, more laborers lived beyond their terms of indenture instead of dying before tasting freedom.

Tobacco Shapes a Region, 1630–1675

Compared to colonists in New England's compact towns, Chesapeake residents had few neighbors. A typical community contained about two dozen families in an area of twenty-five square miles, or about six persons per square mile. Friendship networks typically extended for a two- to three-mile walk from one's farm and included about fifteen other families.

The isolated folk in Virginia and Maryland shared a way of life based on the production of tobacco. The plant grew best on level ground with good internal drainage, so called light soil, which was usually found beside rivers. Locating a farm along Chesapeake Bay or one of its tributary rivers also minimized transportation costs by permitting tobacco to be loaded on ships near home. Approximately 80 percent of early Chesapeake homes lay within a half-mile of a riverbank, and most were within just six hundred feet of the shoreline.

From such waterfront bases, the wealthiest planters built wharves that served both as depots for tobacco exports and as distribution centers for imported goods. Planters' control of commerce stunted the growth of towns and the emergence of a merchant class. Urbanization proceeded slowly in the Chesapeake; even Maryland's capital, St. Mary's, had just thirty scattered houses as late as 1678.

Tobacco had dominated Chesapeake agriculture since 1618, when demand for the crop exploded and prices spiraled to dizzying levels. The boom ended in 1629 when prices sank a stunning 97 percent. After stabilizing, tobacco remained profitable for most growers as long as it sold for more than two pence per pound. But after 1660, it fell to a penny a pound. Large planters offset their tobacco losses through income from rents, trade, interest on loans to small planters, and fees earned as government officials. Small planters had no such options.

Taking advantage of the headright system, a few planters built up large landholdings and grew wealthy from their servants' labor. The servants' lot was harsh. Most were poorly fed, clothed, and housed, and masters often extended servants' terms as penalties for even minor infractions. The exploitation of labor in the Chesapeake was unequaled anywhere in the English-speaking world outside the West Indies, and the gap between rich and poor whites far exceeded that of New England.

Although by 1660 servants increasingly lived to complete their terms, their futures remained bleak. Having received no pay, they entered into freedom impoverished. Virginia obliged masters to provide a new suit of clothes and a year's supply of corn to a freed servant. Maryland required these items plus a hoe, an ax, and the right to claim fifty acres—if the freed-man paid to have the land surveyed and deeded. Thus, Maryland's policy enabled many freedmen to become landowners. Two-thirds of all Chesapeake servants lived in Virginia, however, where no such entitlement existed. Moreover, large planters and absentee English speculators monopolized the best planting land in Virginia. Lacking capital, and with tobacco selling for less than ever, many freedmen toiled as tenants or wage laborers on large plantations.

Freedmen who managed to obtain land nevertheless remained poor. A typical family inhabited a shack barely twenty feet by sixteen feet and owned no more property than Adam Head of Maryland possessed when he died in 1698: three mattresses without bedsteads, a chest and barrel that served as table and chair, two pots, a kettle, "a parcell of old pewter," a gun, and some books. Most tobacco farmers lacked furniture, lived on mush or stew because they had just one pot, and slept on the ground—often on a pile of rags. Having fled poverty in England for the promise of a better life, they found utter destitution in the Chesapeake.

Bacon's Rebellion, 1676   By the 1670s, whites in Virginia seeking land focused on nearby Native Americans. Virginia had been free of serious conflict with Indians since the **Third Anglo-Powhatan War** (1644–1646). Resentful of tobacco planters' continued encroachments on their land, a coalition of Native Americans led by Opechancanough, then nearly a century old but able to direct battles from a litter, killed five hundred of the colony's eight thousand whites before being defeated. By 1653, tribes encircled by English settlement began agreeing to remain within boundaries set by the government—in effect, on reservations. Thereafter, white settlement expanded north to the Potomac River, and by 1675 Virginia's four thousand Indians were greatly outnumbered by forty thousand whites.

Tensions flared between Native Americans struggling to retain land and independence and expanding settlers, especially white freedmen who often squatted illegally on tribal lands. The conflict also divided white society because both Governor Berkeley and Lord Baltimore, along with a few wealthy cronies, held fur-trade monopolies that profited from friendly relations with some Indians. The monopolies alienated not only freedmen but also wealthier planters who wished to expand their own landholdings. As a result, colonists' resentments against the governor and proprietor became fused with those against Native Americans. In June 1675, a dispute between some Doeg Indians and a Virginia farmer escalated until some Virginia and Maryland militiamen pursuing the Doegs instead murdered fourteen friendly Susquehannocks and then assassinated the Susquehannocks' leaders during a peace conference. The Susquehannocks retaliated by killing an equal number of settlers and then offered to make peace. But with most colonists refusing to trust any Indians, the violence was now unstoppable.

Tensions were especially acute in Virginia, reflecting the greater disparities among whites there. Governor Berkeley proposed defending the panic-stricken frontier with a chain of forts linked by patrols. Stung by low tobacco prices and taxes that took almost a quarter of their yearly incomes, small farmers preferred the less costly solution of waging a war of extermination. Nathaniel Bacon, a newly arrived, wealthy planter and Berkeley's distant relative, inspired them. Defying the governor's orders, three hundred colonists elected Bacon to lead them against nearby Indians in April 1676, thereby initiating **Bacon's Rebellion**. Bacon's expedition found only peaceful Indians but massacred them anyway.

Returning in June 1676, Bacon demanded authority to wage war "against all Indians in general," which an intimidated Berkeley granted. The assembly defined as enemies any Indians who left their villages without English permission (even if they did so out of fear of attack by Bacon), and declared their lands forfeited. Bacon's troops were free to seize enemy Indians' food and possessions and to keep Indian prisoners as slaves.

Berkeley soon had second thoughts and called Bacon's men back. The thirteen hundred rebels returned with their guns pointed toward Jamestown. Forcing Berkeley to flee, the rebels burned the capital, offered freedom to any Berkeley supporters' servants or slaves who joined the uprising, and looted their enemies' plantations. But at the very moment of triumph in late 1676, Bacon died of dysentery and his followers dispersed.

A royal commission dispatched from England in 1677 found that Berkeley had mismanaged the crisis but also that some lands seized by Bacon's followers were the reservations guaranteed to now-peaceful tribes in the 1650s. In a series of treaties, the tribes and the colony renewed their peace, English-held captives were freed, and tribal lands were guaranteed in perpetuity. The leading tribe, the Pamunkeys, agreed to present the governor of Virginia with three arrowheads and twenty beaver pelts annually, a provision they honor to this day.

Most Indian-held land seized during Bacon's Rebellion was not protected by formal treaties. The colony retained most of this land and opened it to settlers. Captives from nontreaty tribes fed a growing trade in Indian slaves.

Bacon's Rebellion revealed a society under stress. It was an outburst of long pent-up frustrations by marginal taxpayers and former servants seeking land, but also by wealthier planters. Although land-hunger was one motive for the uprising, the willingness of whites to murder, enslave, or expel all Native Americans, no matter how loyal, made clear that racial hostility was also a motive.

From Servitude to Slavery   Race was also fundamental in the reshaping of Chesapeake society that followed Bacon's Rebellion. Even before the uprising, planters had begun substituting black slaves for white servants. Racial slavery had developed in three stages in the Chesapeake since the first Africans arrived in 1619. Until about 1640, colonists distinguished between blacks and whites in official documents, but did not assume that every African sold was a slave for life. The same was true for Native Americans captured in the colony's early wars. Some Africans gained their freedom during this period, and a few owned their own tobacco farms.

During the second phase, from 1640 to 1660, growing numbers of blacks and some Indians were treated as slaves for life, in contrast to white indentured servants who had fixed terms of service. Slaves' children inherited their parents' status. At the same time, white and black laborers on their own often cooperated as equals. They frequently ran away or rebelled against a master together, and occasionally married one another.

Apparently in reaction to such incidents, the colonies began legally distinguishing whites from blacks and consigning the latter to slavery. Maryland first defined slavery as a lifelong, inheritable racial status in 1661. Virginia followed suit in 1670. By 1705, strict legal codes defined the place of slaves in society and set standards of racial etiquette. By then, free blacks had all but disappeared from the Chesapeake. Although this period saw racial slavery become fully legalized, many of the specific practices enacted into law had evolved into custom earlier.

In formally codifying slavery, planter elites were attempting to stabilize Chesapeake society and defuse the resentment of whites. In deeming nonwhites unfit for freedom, the elites created a common, exclusive identity for whites as free or potentially free persons. This process began before slavery became economically significant. As late as 1660, fewer than a thousand slaves lived in Virginia and Maryland. The number in bondage first became truly significant in the 1680s when the Chesapeake's slave population almost tripled, rising from forty-five hundred to about twelve thousand. By 1700, slaves made up 22 percent of the inhabitants and over 80 percent of all unfree laborers.

As slavery developed, it replaced indentured servitude as the principal labor system in the Chesapeake. First, it became more difficult for planters to import white laborers as the seventeenth century advanced. Between 1650 and 1700, wages rose in England by 50 percent, removing poor people's incentive to move to the Chesapeake. Second, before 1690 the Royal African Company, which held a monopoly on selling slaves to the English colonies, shipped most of its cargoes to the West Indies. Some of these slaves were then transported to the Chesapeake and other mainland regions of English America. During the 1690s, this monopoly was broken, and rival companies began shipping large numbers of Africans directly to the Chesapeake.

The rise of a direct trade in slaves between the Chesapeake and West Africa exacerbated the growing gap between whites and blacks in another way. Until 1690, most blacks in the Chesapeake had either been born, or spent many years, in West African ports or in other American colonies. As a consequence, they were familiar with Europeans and European ways and, in many cases, spoke English. Such familiarity had enabled some blacks to carve out space for themselves as free landowners, and had facilitated marriages and acts of resistance across racial lines among laborers. But after 1690, far larger numbers of slaves poured into Virginia and Maryland, arriving directly from the West African interior. Language and culture now became barriers rather than bridges to mutual understanding among blacks as well as between blacks and whites, reinforcing the overt racism arising among whites.

The changing composition of the white population also contributed to the emergence of race as the foundation of Chesapeake society. As increasing numbers of immigrants lived long enough to marry and form their own families, the number of such families slowly rose, and the ratio of men to women became more equal, since half of all children were girls. By 1690, an almost even division existed between males and females. Thereafter, the white population grew primarily through an excess of births over deaths rather than through immigration, so that by 1720 most Chesapeake colonists were native-born. Whites' shared attachments to the colony heightened their sense of a common racial identity vis-à-vis an increasingly fragmented and seemingly alien black population.

From its beginnings as a region where profits were high but life expectancy was low, the Chesapeake had transformed by 1700. As nonwhites' conditions deteriorated, Virginia and Maryland expanded their territories, and their white colonists flourished.

PURITANISM IN NEW ENGLAND

After the Chesapeake, New England was the next colonial region to prosper in North America. Separatist Puritans had established Plymouth in 1620 (see Chapter 2), but Plymouth was dwarfed after 1630 when a massive Puritan-led "Great Migration" to New England began. By the time England's civil war halted the migration in 1642, about twenty-one thousand settlers had arrived. The newcomers established the colonies of Massachusetts Bay, Connecticut, New Haven (absorbed by Connecticut in 1662), and Rhode Island. New England's leaders endeavored to build colonies based on religious and social ideals. Although internal divisions and social-economic change undermined these ideals, Puritanism gave New England a distinctive regional identity.

New England offered a sharp contrast to the Chesapeake colonies. The religious foundations, economies, social structures, local communities, families, and living standards in the two regions differed completely. Chesapeake and New England colonists did, however, share English nationality and a determination to expand at Native Americans' expense.

A City upon a Hill   After becoming king in 1625, Charles I reversed James's policy of tolerating Puritans (see Chapter 2). Beginning a systematic campaign to eliminate Puritan influence within the Church of England, Anglican authorities insisted that services be conducted according to the Book of Common Prayer, which prescribed rituals similar to Catholic practices. Bishops dismissed Puritan ministers who refused to perform these rites, and church courts fined or excommunicated Puritans who protested.

In the face of such harassment, a group of wealthy Puritans successfully petitioned the crown for a charter to colonize at Massachusetts Bay, north of Plymouth, in March 1629. Organizing as the Massachusetts Bay Company, they sent four hundred colonists to Salem, Massachusetts. Like Plymouth, Massachusetts Bay would be a Puritan-dominated, self-governing colony rather than one controlled from England by stockholders, proprietors, or the crown. In 1630, eleven ships and seven hundred passengers under Governor **John Winthrop** arrived at the new capital of Boston, where Winthrop distributed an essay (perhaps already delivered as a shipboard address) titled "**A Model of Christian Charity**." In it, he boldly declared that Massachusetts "shall be as a city upon a hill, the eyes of all people are upon us." The settlers would build a harmonious, godly community in which individuals would subordinate their personal interests to a higher purpose. The result would be an example for all the world and would particularly inspire England to live up to its role as God's "elect nation."

In outlining this ideal society, Winthrop denounced the economic jealousy that bred class resentments. God intended that "in all times some must be rich and some poor," he asserted. The rich had an obligation to show charity and mercy toward the poor, who should humbly accept rule by their social superiors as God's will. God expected the state to keep the rich from exploiting the needy and to prevent the poor from burdening their fellow citizens. In outlining a divine plan in which all people, rich and poor, served one another, Winthrop expressed a conservative European's understanding of social hierarchy (see Chapter 2) and voiced Puritans' dismay at the forces of individualism and class warfare that were battering—and changing—English society.

By fall 1630, six towns had sprung up around Boston. During the unusually severe first winter, 30 percent of Winthrop's party died, and another 10 percent went home in the spring. By mid-1631, however, thirteen hundred new settlers had landed, and more were on the way. The worst was over. The colony would never suffer another starving time. Like Plymouth, Massachusetts Bay primarily attracted landowning farm families of modest means, most of them receptive if not actively committed to Calvinism. There were few indentured servants and almost no slaves. New Englanders quickly established a healthier, more stable colonial region than their Chesapeake contemporaries. By 1642, more than fifteen thousand colonists had settled in New England.

Political participation was broader in New England than elsewhere in Europe and its colonies. Instead of requiring voters or officeholders to own property, Massachusetts permitted voting by every adult male church member. By 1641, about 55 percent of the colony's twenty-three hundred men could vote. Because the other Puritan colonies based voting on property ownership, an even higher proportion of men voted. By contrast, English property requirements allowed fewer than 30 percent of adult males to vote.

In 1634, after protests that the governor (Winthrop) and council held too much power, the General Court (legislature) allowed each town to send two delegates. Initially resisting this effort, Winthrop was defeated for reelection and did not return to the governorship for three years. In 1644, the General Court became a bicameral (two-chamber) lawmaking body when the towns' elected deputies separated from the appointed Governor's Council.

New England
Ways

Although most New Englanders nominally belonged to the Church of England, their self-governing congregations, like those in Separatist Plymouth, ignored Anglican bishops' authority. Control of each congregation lay squarely in the hands of its male "saints," as Puritans termed church members. By majority vote, these men chose a minister, elected a board of elders to handle finances, and admitted new members.

Although congregations were supposedly independent and controlled by their male members, the clergy quickly asserted its power in New England's religious life. Upon arriving in New England, many ministers feared that complete congregational independence would undermine Puritan unity and lead to religious disorder. Religious disharmony would as effectively undermine "the city upon a hill" as would the social disharmony feared by Winthrop. Accordingly, the ministers established a set of official practices—the "**New England Way**"—that strengthened their authority at the expense of that of laypersons (nonclergy) within their congregations.

In its church membership requirements, the New England Way diverged from other Puritans' practices. English Puritans accepted as saints any adult who correctly professed the Calvinist faith, repented his or her sins, and lived free of scandal. New England Puritans, however, insisted that candidates for membership stand before their congregation and provide a convincing, soul-baring "relation," or account, of their conversion experience (see Chapter 2). Many colonists shared the reluctance of Jonathan Fairbanks, who refused for several years to give an account before the church in Dedham, Massachusetts, until the faithful persuaded him with many "loving conferences." The conversion relation would prove to be the New England Way's most vulnerable feature.

One means of ensuring orthodoxy was through education. Like most European Protestants, Puritans insisted that conversion required familiarity with the Bible and, therefore, literacy. In 1647, Massachusetts Bay ordered every town of fifty or more households to appoint a teacher to instruct its children, and every town of at least one hundred households to maintain a grammar school. This and similar laws in other Puritan colonies represented New England's first steps toward public education. But none of these laws required school attendance, and boys were more likely to be taught reading and especially writing than were girls.

To ensure a supply of ministers trained in the New England Way, Massachusetts founded Harvard College in 1636. From 1642 to 1671, its 201 graduates included 111 ministers, making New England the only part of English America to produce its own clergy and college-educated elite before 1700.

Puritans agreed that the church must be free of state control, and they opposed theocracy (government by clergy). But Winthrop and other New England leaders insisted that a holy commonwealth required cooperation between church and state. Except for Rhode Island, the colonies obliged all adults to attend services and levied taxes to support local churches. Thus these colonies, like England and Virginia, had an established church. The established clergy did not welcome Puritans whose views threatened to divide churchgoers. Roger Williams and Anne Hutchinson led movements considered especially dangerous by authorities because they attracted popular followings.

Roger Williams, a Separatist minister who arrived in 1631, aroused elite anxieties by advocating religious toleration and the complete separation of church and state. He opposed any civil government connection to religious matters, even swearing oaths on the Bible in court, as well as any kind of compulsory church service or government interference with religious practice. His objection was not that all religions deserved equal respect, but that the state (a creation of sinful human beings) would corrupt the church.

As Williams's popularity grew, Winthrop and other authorities declared his opinions subversive and banished him in 1635. Williams moved south to a place he called Providence, which he purchased from the Narragansett Indians. At Williams's invitation, a steady stream of dissenters drifted to the group of settlements near Providence, which in 1647 joined to form Rhode Island colony. (Other Puritans scorned the place as "Rogues Island.") True to Williams's ideals, Rhode Island was the only New England colony to practice religious toleration. Growing slowly, the colony's four towns had eight hundred settlers by 1650.

A second major challenge to the New England Way began when **Anne Hutchinson**, a deeply religious member of the Boston congregation, publicly criticized the clergy for judging prospective church members on the basis of "good works"—the Catholic standard for salvation that Protestants had repudiated during the Reformation (see Chapter 2). Supposedly, Puritans followed John Calvin in maintaining that God had "predestined" all persons for either salvation or damnation. But Hutchinson argued that ministers who scrutinized a person's outward behavior for "signs" of salvation, especially when that person was relating his or her conversion experience, were substituting their own judgment for God's. Hutchinson charged that only two of the colony's ministers followed appropriate procedures; the rest held their posts illegitimately.

By repudiating the clergy's practices, Hutchinson undermined its authority over laypersons. Critics charged that her beliefs would lead people to think they were accountable to no one but themselves. Winthrop branded her followers Antinomians, meaning those opposed to the rule of law.

Hutchinson also defied gender norms. As a woman steeped in Scripture, Hutchinson had led other women in discussions of ministers' sermons. But she went beyond that prescribed role by asserting her own opinions, including her criticisms of the clergy. As one of her accusers put it, "You have stepped out of your place; you [would] have rather been a husband than a wife, a preacher than a hearer; and a magistrate than a subject."

By 1637, Massachusetts Bay had split into two camps. Hutchinson's supporters, primarily Bostonians, included merchants (like her husband) who disliked the government's economic restrictions on their businesses, young men chafing against the rigid control of church elders, and women impatient with their second-class status in church affairs. Even the colony's governor, Henry Vane, was an Antinomian. But most colonists outside Boston were alarmed by what they regarded as religious extremism. In the election of 1637, they rejected Vane and returned Winthrop to the governorship.

The victorious Winthrop brought Hutchinson to trial for heresy before a panel of magistrates and ministers, whose members peppered her with questions (see Going to the Source). Hutchinson's knowledge of Scripture so exceeded that of her interrogators, however, that she would have been acquitted had she not claimed to be converted through a direct revelation from God. Like most Christians, Puritans believed that God had ceased to make himself known by personal revelation after New Testament times. Thus, Hutchinson's own words condemned her.

The General Court banished the leading Antinomians from the colony, and others followed them into exile. The largest group, led by Hutchinson, settled in Rhode Island. Some Rhode Island Antinomians later converted to Quakerism (discussed later in this chapter), returning to Massachusetts and again defying political and religious authorities.

Antinomianism's defeat was followed by new restrictions on women's religious independence that increasingly prohibited the kind of public religious roles claimed by Hutchinson. To minimize their influence, women were required to relate their conversion experiences privately to ministers rather than publicly before their congregations.

Towns, Families, and Farm Life   To ensure that colonists would settle in communities with congregations, all New England colonies provided for the establishment of towns, which would distribute land. Legislatures authorized a town by awarding a grant of land to several dozen landowners. These men then laid out the settlement, organized its church, distributed land among themselves, and established a town meeting—a distinctly New England institution. At the center of each town lay the meetinghouse, which served as both church and town hall.

Whereas appointed justices of the peace in England and Virginia administered local government through county courts, New England's county courts served strictly as courts of law; the town meeting conducted local administration. Town meetings decentralized authority over political and economic decisions far more than in England and its other colonies. Each town determined its own qualifications for voting and holding office in the town meeting, although most allowed all male taxpayers (including nonsaints) to participate. The meeting could exclude anyone from settling in town and granted newcomers the right to share in future land distributions.

Few aspects of early New England life are more revealing than the first generation's attempt in many towns to promote unity by keeping residents tightly clustered. They did so by granting house lots near the town center and by granting families no more land than they needed to support themselves. Dedham's forty-six founders, for example, received 128,000 acres from Massachusetts Bay in 1636 yet gave themselves just 3,000 acres by 1656, or about 65 acres per family. The rest remained in trust for future generations.

With families clustered within a mile of one another, the physical settings of New England towns were conducive to traditional reciprocity. They also fostered an atmosphere of mutual watchfulness that Puritans hoped would promote godly order. For the enforcement of such order, they relied on the women of each town as well as male magistrates.

Although women's public roles had been sharply curtailed following the Antinomian crisis, women—especially female saints—remained a social force in their communities. With their husbands and older sons attending the family's fields and business, women remained at home in the tightly knit neighborhoods at the center of each town. Neighboring women exchanged not only goods—say, a pound of butter for a section of spun wool—but advice and news of other neighbors as

Anne Hutchinson vs. John Winthrop

The following excerpt from the transcript of the trial of Anne Hutchinson, held in Boston in 1637, consists of an exchange between her and Governor John Winthrop regarding meetings of women that she held in her home. It reveals the differences between her views and those of the colony's male political and religious leaders on the proper role and place of women in church affairs.

WINTHROP: *Why do you keep such a meeting at your house as you do every week upon a set day?*

HUTCHINSON: *It is lawful for me to do so, as it is all your practices, and can you find a warrant for yourself and condemn me for the same thing? The ground of my taking it up was, when I first came to this land, because I did not go to such meetings, ... it was ... reported that I did not allow of such meetings but held them unlawful and therefore ... they said I was proud and did despise all*

ordinances. *Upon that a friend came unto me and told me of it and I to prevent such aspersions took it up, but it was in practice before I came. Therefore I was not the first.*

WINTHROP: *By what warrant do you continue such a course?*

HUTCHINSON: *I conceive there lies a clear rule in Titus that the elder women should instruct the younger and then I must have a time wherein I must do it....*

WINTHROP: *You know that there is no rule that crosses another, but this rule crosses that in the Corinthians. But you must take it in this sense that elder women must instruct the younger about their business and to love their husbands and not to make them to clash.*

HUTCHINSON: *Will it please you to answer me this and to give me a rule for then I will willingly submit to any truth. If any come to my house to be instructed in the ways of God what rule have I to put*

well. They also gathered at the bedside when one of them gave birth, an occasion supervised by a midwife and entirely closed to men. In these settings, women confided in one another, creating a "community of women" within each town that helped enforce morals and protect the poor and vulnerable. In 1663, Mary Rolfe of Newbury, Massachusetts, was sexually harassed by a high-ranking gentleman while her fisherman husband was at sea. Rolfe confided in her mother, who in turn consulted with a neighboring woman of influence before filing formal charges. Clearly influenced by the town's women, a male jury convicted the gentleman of attempted adultery. When a gentlewoman, Patience Dennison, charged her maidservant with repeatedly stealing food and clothing, another woman testified that the maid had given the provisions to a poor young wife, whose family was thereby saved from perishing. The servant was cleared while her mistress gained a lifelong reputation for stinginess.

Puritans defined matrimony as a contract rather than a religious sacrament, and justices of the peace rather than ministers married New England couples. As a civil institution, a marriage could be dissolved in cases of desertion, bigamy, adultery, or physical cruelty. By permitting divorce, the colonies diverged from practices in England, where Anglican authorities rarely annulled marriages and civil divorces *them away? ... Do you think it not lawful for me to teach women and why do you call me to teach the court?*

WINTHROP: *We do not call you to teach the court but to lay open yourself....*

WINTHROP: *Your course is not to be suffered for. Besides that we find such a course as this to be greatly prejudicial to the state. Besides the occasion that it is to seduce many honest persons that are called to those meetings and your opinions being known to be different from the word of God, may seduce many simple souls that resort unto you. Besides that the occasion which hath come of late hath come from none but such as have frequented your meetings, so that now they are flown off from magistrates and ministers and since they have come to you. And besides that it will not well stand with the commonwealth that families should be neglected for so many neighbors and dames and so much time spent. We see no rule of God for this. We see not that any should have authority to set up any other exercises besides what authority hath already set up and so what hurt comes of this you will be guilty of and we for suffering you.*

HUTCHINSON: *Sir, I do not believe that to be so.*

WINTHROP: *Well, we see how it is. We must therefore put it away from you or restrain you from maintaining this course.*

HUTCHINSON: *If you have a rule for it from God's word you may.*

WINTHROP: *We are your judges, and not you ours and we must compel you to it.*

Questions

1. On what grounds do Hutchinson and Winthrop base their respective arguments?
2. In what ways does the transcript reflect the emotions behind these arguments?

Go to www.cengagebrain.com for additional primary sources on this period.

required a special act of Parliament. Still, New Englanders saw divorce as a remedy fit only for extremely wronged spouses, such as the Plymouth woman who discovered that her husband was also married to women in Boston, Barbados, and England. Massachusetts courts allowed just twenty-seven divorces before 1692.

Despite their greater legal protections, New England wives suffered the same legal disabilities as all Englishwomen. An English wife had no property rights independent of her husband unless he consented to a prenuptial agreement leaving her in control of property she already owned. Only if a husband had no other heirs or so stipulated in a will could a widow claim more than the third of the estate reserved by law for her lifetime use.

In contrast to the Chesapeake, New England benefited from a remarkably benign disease environment. Most families owned farms and produced the foods needed to ensure an adequate diet, thereby improving resistance to disease and lowering death rates associated with childbirth. Malaria and other tropical diseases did not thrive in New England's frozen winters. New Englanders seldom traveled outside their own towns, so communicable diseases rarely spread inland from Boston and other ports.

Consequently, New Englanders lived longer and raised larger families than their contemporaries in England and in other colonial regions. Life expectancy for men reached sixty-five, and women lived nearly that long. More than 80 percent of all infants survived long enough to get married. The fifty-eight men and women who founded Andover, Massachusetts, for example, had 247 children; by the fourth generation, the families of their descendants numbered two thousand (including spouses who married in from other families). Because most settlers came as members of family groups, the population was evenly divided between males and females from the beginning. This balance permitted rapid population growth without heavy immigration.

Most colonists had little or no cash, relying instead on the labor of their large, healthy families to sustain them and secure their futures. Married men managed the family's crops and livestock, conducted most of its business transactions, and represented it in town government. Their wives bore, nursed, and reared their children and were in charge of work in the house, barn, and garden; they prepared food and made clothing. Women also did charitable work and played other roles in their communities, as already discussed.

More than in England and the other colonies, the sons of New England's founding generation depended on their parents to provide them with farmland. With eventual landownership guaranteed and few other opportunities available, sons delayed marriage and worked in their fathers' fields until receiving their own land, usually after age twenty-five. Because the average family raised three or four boys to adulthood, parents could depend on thirty to forty years of sons' labor.

While daughters performed equally vital labor, their future lay with another family—the one into which they would marry. Being young, with many childbearing years ahead of them, enhanced their value to that family. Thus first-generation women, on average, were only twenty-one when they married.

Economic and Religious Tensions

Despite a short growing season and rocky soil, most New Englanders managed to feed large families and keep ahead of their debts, but few became wealthy from farming. Others turned lumbering, fishing, fur trading, shipbuilding, and rum distilling into major industries. As its economy became more diversified, New England prospered. But the colonists grew more worldly, and their values began to shift.

The most fundamental threat to Winthrop's city upon a hill was that colonists would abandon the ideal of a close-knit community to pursue self-interest. Other colonies—most pointedly, Virginia—displayed the acquisitive impulses transforming England, but in New England, as one writer put it, "religion and profit jump together." While hoping for prosperity, Puritans believed there were limits to legitimate commercial behavior. Government leaders tried to regulate prices so that consumers would not suffer from the chronic shortage of manufactured goods that afflicted New England. In 1635, when the Massachusetts General Court forbade pricing any item more than 5 percent above its cost, Robert Keayne of Boston and other merchants objected. These men argued that they had to sell some goods at higher rates to offset their losses from other sales, shipwrecked cargoes, and inflation. In 1639, after selling nails at 25 percent to 33 percent above cost, Keayne was fined heavily in court and was forced to make a humiliating apology before his congregation.

Controversies between the Puritan clergy and rural elites on one hand, and urban merchants on the other, were part of a struggle for New England's soul. Some merchants favored less rigid variants of Calvinism. Merchants figured among the followers of both Roger Williams and Anne Hutchinson. Another merchant returned to England after Massachusetts authorities burned an allegedly heretical tract he had written. In all these conflicts, political and religious leaders sought to minimize merchants' influence on public opinion.

Other social and economic changes further undermined Winthrop's vision. After about 1660, farmers eager to expand their agricultural output and provide land for their sons voted themselves larger amounts of land and insisted that their scattered parcels be consolidated. For example, Dedham, Massachusetts, which distributed only three thousand acres from 1636 to 1656, allocated five times as much in the next dozen years. Rather than continue living closely together, many farmers built homes on their outlying tracts. The dispersal of settlers away from town centers generated friction between townspeople settled near the meetinghouse and "out-livers," whose distance from the town center limited their influence over town affairs. Although groups of outlivers often formed new towns, John Winthrop's vision of a closely-knit society was slowly giving way to the more individualistic society that the original immigrants had fled in England.

As New England slowly prospered, England fell into chaos. The efforts of Charles I to impose taxes without Parliament's consent sparked a civil war in 1642. Alienated by years of religious harassment, Puritans gained control of the successful revolt and beheaded Charles in 1649. Puritan Oliver Cromwell's consolidation of power raised orthodox New Englanders' hopes that England would establish a truly reformed church. But Cromwell supported religious toleration and favored Rhode Island's Roger Williams over other New Englanders. After Cromwell died, chaos returned to England until a provisional government proclaimed the **Restoration** of the monarchy and crowned King Charles II (ruled 1660–1685). Charles sought to undermine Puritan rule, especially in Massachusetts (covered in Chapter 4), putting its leaders increasingly on the defensive. Contrary to Winthrop's vision, "the eyes of all people" were no longer (if ever they had been) fixed on New England.

The erosion of Winthrop's social vision was accompanied by the decline of the religious vision embodied in the New England Way. This decline was reflected most vividly in a crisis over church membership. The crisis arose because many first-generation Puritans' children were not joining congregations. By 1650, for example, fewer than half of Boston's adults belonged to its church. The principal reason was the children's reluctance to undergo public grilling on their conversion experience. Most children must have witnessed at least one ordeal like Sarah Fiske's. For more than a year, Fiske answered petty charges of speaking uncharitably about her relatives—especially her husband—and then was admitted to the Wenham, Massachusetts, congregation only after publicly denouncing herself as worse "than any toad."

Because Puritan ministers baptized only babies born to saints, the unwillingness of the second generation to provide a conversion relation meant that most third-generation children would remain unbaptized. Unless a solution was found, saints' numbers would dwindle and Puritan rule would end. In 1662, a meeting of clergy proposed a compromise that would permit the children of baptized adults, including nonsaints, to receive baptism. Derisively termed the "halfway" covenant by its opponents, the proposal would allow the founders' descendants to transmit potential church membership to their grandchildren, leaving their adult children "halfway" members who could not take communion or vote in church affairs. Congregations divided bitterly over limiting membership to pure saints or compromising purity to maintain Puritan power in New England. In the end, most opted for worldly power over spiritual purity.

The crisis in church membership signaled a weakening of the New England Way. Most second-generation adults remained in "halfway" status for life, and the saints became a shrinking minority as the third and fourth generations matured. Sainthood tended to flow in certain families, and soon there were more women than men among the elect. But because women could not vote in church affairs, religious authority stayed in male hands. Nevertheless, ministers publicly recognized women's role in upholding piety and the church itself.

Expansion and Native Americans   New England's first colonists met with little sustained resistance from Native Americans, whose numbers were drastically reduced by the ravages of disease. After one epidemic killed about 90 percent of New England's coastal Indians (see Chapter 2), smallpox inflicted comparable casualties on Indians throughout the Northeast in 1633–1634. Having dwindled from twenty thousand in 1600 to a few dozen survivors by the mid-1630s, the coastal Massachusett and Pawtucket Indians were pressed to sell most of their land to the English. During the 1640s, Massachusetts Bay passed laws prohibiting them from practicing their own religion and authorizing missionaries to convert them to Christianity. Thereafter, they ceded more land to the colonists and moved into "praying towns" like Natick, a reservation established by the colony. In the praying towns, Puritan missionary John Eliot hoped to teach the Native Americans Christianity and English "civilization."

However, English expansion inland aroused Native American resistance. Beginning in 1633, settlers moved into the Connecticut River Valley and in 1635 organized the new colony of Connecticut. Friction quickly developed with the Pequot Indians, who controlled the trade in furs and wampum with New Netherland. After tensions escalated into violence, Massachusetts and Connecticut took coordinated military action in 1637, thereby beginning the **Pequot War**. Having gained the support of the Mohegan and Narragansett Indians, they waged a ruthless campaign. In a predawn attack, English troops surrounded and set fire to a Pequot village at Mystic, Connecticut, and then cut down all who tried to escape. Several hundred Pequots, mostly women and children, were killed. Although their Narragansett allies protested that "it is too furious, and slays too many men," the English found a cause for celebration in the grisly massacre. Wrote Plymouth's Governor William Bradford,

> It was a fearful sight to see them [the Pequots] thus frying in the fire and the streams of blood quenching the same, and horrible was the stink and scent thereof; but the victory seemed a sweet sacrifice, and they [the English] gave the praise to God, who had wrought so wonderfully for them, thus to enclose their enemies in their hands and give them so speedy a victory over so proud and insulting an enemy.

By late 1637, Pequot resistance was crushed, with the survivors taken by pro-English Indians as captives or by the English as slaves. The Pequots' lands were awarded to the colonists of Connecticut and New Haven.

As settlements grew and colonists prospered, the numbers and conditions of Native Americans in New England declined. Although Indians began to recover from the initial epidemics by midcentury, the settlers brought new diseases such as diphtheria, measles, and tuberculosis as well as new outbreaks of smallpox, which took heavy tolls. New England's Indian population fell from 125,000 in 1600 to 10,000 in 1675.

Native Americans felt the English presence in other ways. The fur trade, which initially benefited interior Natives, soon became a liability. Once Indians began hunting for trade instead of just for their own needs, they quickly depleted the region's beavers and other fur-bearing animals. Because English traders shrewdly advanced trade goods on credit to Indian hunters before the hunting season, the lack of pelts pushed many Natives into debt. Traders thereupon began taking Indian land as collateral and selling it to settlers. The expansion of English settlement often separated Native villages from one another and from hunting, gathering, and fishing areas.

English expansion put new pressures on Native peoples and the land. As early as 1642, Miantonomi, a Narragansett sachem (chief), warned neighboring Indians,

These English having gotten our land, they with scythes cut down the grass, and with axes fell the trees; their cows and horses eat the grass, and their hogs spoil our clam banks, and we shall all be starved.

Within a generation, Miantonomi's fears were being borne out. By clearing away trees for fields and for use as fuel and building material, colonial farmers altered an entire ecosystem. Deer were no longer attracted, and the wild plants upon which Native Americans depended for food and medicine ceased to grow. The soil became drier and flooding more frequent in the face of this deforestation. The settlers' domestic livestock, according to English custom, ranged freely. Pigs damaged Indian cornfields (until the Natives adopted the alien practice of fencing their fields) along with shellfish-gathering sites. Settlers replaced the native grasses, which English cattle and horses quickly devoured, with English varieties.

With their leaders powerless to halt the alarming decline of their population, land, and food sources, many Indians became demoralized. In their despair, some turned to alcohol, increasingly available during the 1660s despite colonial efforts to suppress its sale to Native Americans. Interpreting the crisis as one of belief, other Natives responded to an expanded initiative by Puritan missionaries to convert them to Christianity. By 1675, about 2,300 Indians inhabited thirty praying towns in eastern Massachusetts, Plymouth, and offshore islands. Regularly visited by supervising missionaries, each praying town had its own Native American magistrate, usually a sachem, and some congregations had Indian preachers.

Although the missionaries struggled to convert the Indians to "civilization" (meaning English culture and lifestyles) as well as Christianity, most praying Indians integrated the new faith with their Native cultural identities.

Anglo-Indian conflict became acute during the 1670s because of pressures imposed on unwilling Indians to sell more land and to accept missionaries and the legal authority of colonial courts. Tension ran especially high in Plymouth colony where Metacom, or "King Philip," the son of the colony's onetime ally Massasoit (see Chapter 2), was now the leading Wampanoag sachem. The English had engulfed the Wampanoags, persuaded many of them to renounce their loyalty to Metacom, and forced several humiliating concessions on the sachem.

In 1675, Plymouth hanged three Wampanoags for killing a Christian Indian and threatened to arrest Metacom. The resulting tensions ignited the conflict known as **King Philip's War.**

Eventually, two-thirds of the colonies' Native Americans rallied around Metacom. Unlike Indians in the Pequot War, they were familiar with guns and were as well armed as the colonists. Indian raiders attacked fifty-two of New England's ninety towns (entirely destroying twelve), burned twelve hundred houses, slaughtered eight thousand head of cattle, and killed twenty-five hundred colonists (5 percent).

The tide turned against Metacom's forces in 1676 after the Mohawk Iroquois of New York and many local Indians joined the English against him. The colonists and their Native American allies scattered their enemies and destroyed their food supplies. About five thousand Indians starved or fell in battle, including Metacom himself, and others fled to New York and Canada. After crushing the uprising, the English sold hundreds of captives into West Indian slavery, including Metacom's wife and child.

King Philip's War reduced southern New England's Indian population by about 40 percent and eliminated organized resistance to white expansion. It also deepened English hostility toward all Native Americans, even those who had supported the colonies. In Massachusetts, ten praying towns were disbanded, and Native peoples restricted to the remaining four; all Indian courts were dismantled; and English "guardians" were appointed to supervise the reservations. In the face of poverty and discrimination, remaining Indians struggled to survive and maintain their communities.

Salem Witchcraft, 1691–1693   Nowhere in New England did the conflicts dividing white New Englanders converge more forcefully than in Salem, Massachusetts, the region's second largest port. Trade made Salem prosperous but also destroyed the relatively equal society of first-generation fishermen and farmers. Salem's divisions were especially sharp in the precinct of Salem Village (now Danvers), an economically stagnant district located north of Salem Town. Residents of the village's eastern section farmed richer soils and benefited from Salem Town's commercial expansion, whereas those in the less fertile western half did not share in this prosperity and had lost the political influence they once held in Salem.

In late 1691, several Salem Village girls encouraged an enslaved African woman, Tituba, to tell them their fortunes and talk about sorcery. When the girls later began behaving strangely, villagers assumed they were victims of witchcraft. Pressed to identify their tormenters, the girls named two local white women and Tituba.

So far, the incident was not unusual. Witchcraft beliefs remained strong in seventeenth-century Europe and its colonies. Witches were people (usually women) whose pride, envy, discontent, or greed supposedly led them to sign a pact with the devil. Thereafter, they allegedly used *maleficium* (the devil's supernatural power of evil) to torment neighbors and others by causing illness, destroying property, or—as with the girls in Salem Village—inhabiting or "possessing" their victims' bodies and minds. Witches also supposedly displayed aggressive, unfeminine behavior. In most earlier witchcraft accusations in New England, there was only one defendant and the case never went to trial. The few trials proceeded with little fanfare. Events in Salem Village, on the other hand, led to a colony-wide panic.

By April 1692, the girls had denounced two locally prominent women and had identified the village's former minister as a wizard (male witch). Fears of witchcraft soon overrode doubts about the girls' credibility and led local judges to sweep aside normal procedural safeguards. In particular, the judges ignored the law's ban on "spectral evidence"—testimony that a spirit resembling the accused had been seen tormenting a victim. Thereafter, accusations multiplied until the jails overflowed with 342 accused witches.

Images of Witchcraft
Most seventeenth-century Europeans and colonists feared that, at any time, Satan and those in his grip (witches) could attack and harm them with the power of evil.

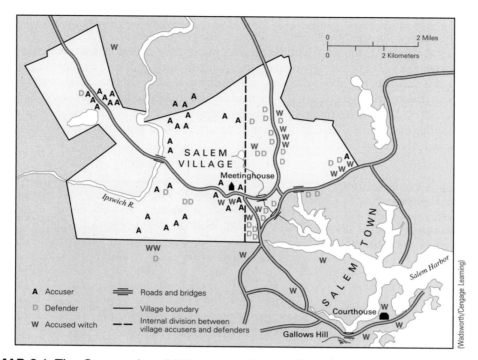

MAP 3.1 The Geography of Witchcraft: Salem Village, 1692

Most of those who leveled accusations of witchcraft lived in western Salem Village while those they targeted, along with those who defended the accused, lived in the eastern village or in Salem Town.

Source: Adapted from Paul Boyer and Stephen Nissenbaum, Salem Possessed: The Social Origins of Witchcraft *(Cambridge, Mass.: Harvard University Press, 1974).*

The pattern of hysteria in Salem Village reflected that community's internal divisions. Most accusations originated in the village's poorer western division and were directed largely at wealthier families in the eastern village or in Salem Town (see Map 3.1).

Other patterns were also apparent. Two-thirds of all "possessed" accusers were females aged eleven to twenty, and more than half had lost one or both parents in Anglo-Indian conflicts in Maine. Having fled to Massachusetts, most were now servants in other families' households. These young women gained momentary power and prominence by voicing the anxieties and hostilities of others in their community and by virtually dictating the course of events in and around Salem for several months.

Accusers and witnesses most frequently named as witches middle-aged wives and widows—women who had avoided the poverty and uncertainty they themselves faced. A disproportionate number of accused women had inherited, or stood to inherit, property beyond the one-third of a husband's estate normally bequeathed to widows. In other words, the accused tended to be women who had or soon might have more economic power and independence than many men. For New

Englanders who felt the need to limit both female independence and economic individualism, witches symbolized the dangers awaiting those who disregarded such limits.

The number of persons facing trial multiplied quickly. Those found guilty desperately tried to stave off death by implicating others. As the pandemonium spread beyond Salem, fear dissolved ties of friendship and family. A minister heard himself condemned by his own granddaughter. A seven-year-old girl helped send her mother to the gallows. Fifty persons saved themselves by confessing. Twenty others who refused to confess falsely or to betray other innocents went to their graves. Shortly before she was hanged, a victim named Mary Easty begged the court to come to its senses: "I petition your honors not for my own life, for I know I must die...[but] if it be possible, that no more innocent blood be shed."

By late 1692, most Massachusetts ministers came to doubt that justice was being done. They objected that spectral evidence, crucial in most convictions, was suspect because the devil could manipulate it. Backed by the clergy (and alarmed by an accusation against his wife), Governor William Phips forbade further imprisonments for witchcraft in October—by which time over a hundred individuals were in jail and twice that many stood accused. Shortly thereafter, he suspended all trials, and in early 1693 he pardoned all those convicted or suspected of witchcraft.

Along with the revocation of Massachusetts' charter (discussed in Chapter 4), the witchcraft hysteria ended what was left of "Puritan" New England. Colonists reaching maturity thereafter would instead become "Yankees" who shrewdly pursued material gain. True to their Puritan roots, they would retain their forceful convictions and self-discipline, giving New England a distinctive regional identity that would endure.

THE SPREAD OF SLAVERY: THE CARIBBEAN AND CAROLINA

As the Chesapeake and New England flourished, an even larger wave of settlement swept the West Indies. Between 1630 and 1642, more than half of the eighty thousand English who emigrated to the Americas went to the Caribbean. Beginning in the 1640s, English planters began using slave labor to produce sugar on large plantations. After 1670, many English islanders moved to the new mainland colony of Carolina, thereby facilitating the spread of large-scale plantation slavery to North America.

Sugar and Slaves: The West Indies   As on the North American mainland, the Netherlands, France, and England entered the colonial race in the West Indies during the early seventeenth century and expanded thereafter. Challenging Spain's monopoly, each nation seized islands in the region, but it was the English who became the most powerful and prosperous during the 1600s.

The tobacco boom that powered Virginia's economy until 1630 led early English settlers on the island of Barbados to cultivate that plant. But with most colonists farming small plots, few realized spectacular profits.

During the 1640s, an even greater boom—in sugar—revolutionized the islands' economy and society. Dutch planters in Brazil (where the Netherlands had captured some territory) showed English West Indian planters how to raise and process sugar cane, which the Dutch then marketed (see Technology and Culture in Chapter 2). Turning spectacular profits, sugar production quickly moved beyond Barbados to other English islands.

Because sugar production required three times as many workers per acre as tobacco, West Indian planters increasingly purchased enslaved Africans from Dutch traders to do fieldwork and used English indentured servants as overseers and skilled artisans.

Sugar planters preferred black slaves to white servants because slaves could be driven harder and cost less to maintain. Whereas most servants ended their indentures after four years, slaves toiled until death. Although slaves initially cost two to four times more than servants, they proved a more economical long-term investment. In this way, the profit motive and the racism that emerged with the "new slavery" (see Chapter 2) reinforced one another.

By 1670, the sugar revolution had transformed the English West Indies into a predominantly slave society. Thereafter, the number of enslaved Africans rose from approximately 40,000 to 130,000 in 1713 while the white population remained stable at about 33,000.

Three victorious wars with the Dutch and enactment of the Navigation Acts (covered in Chapter 4) enabled English merchants and shippers to monopolize the trade in sugar and slaves from the 1660s onward. The profits from this trade were the principal factor in England's becoming the wealthiest nation in the Atlantic world by 1700.

Declining demand for white labor in the West Indies diverted the flow of English immigration from the islands to mainland North America and so contributed to population growth there. Furthermore, because land was priced beyond the reach of most whites, perhaps thirty thousand people left the islands from 1655 to 1700. Most whites who quit the West Indies migrated to the mainland colonies, especially Carolina.

Rice and Slaves: Carolina   In 1663, King Charles II bestowed the swampy coast between Virginia and Spanish Florida on several English supporters, making it the first of several Restoration colonies. The grateful proprietors named their colony Carolina in honor of Charles (*Carolus* in Latin).

One of the proprietors, Anthony Ashley Cooper, and his young secretary, future philosopher John Locke (further discussed in Chapter 4), drew up a plan for Carolina's settlement and government. Their Fundamental Constitutions provided for a nobility that would hold two-fifths of all land while controlling the upper house of the legislature and the judiciary. Ordinary Carolinians with smaller landholdings were expected to defer to this nobility, although they would enjoy religious toleration and English common law, and could elect an assembly. To induce settlement, the proprietors offered a headright of one hundred fifty acres to planters for each arriving family member or slave as well as one hundred acres to each servant who completed a term of indenture.

Uninterested in moving themselves, the proprietors arranged for settlers from Barbados to get their colony started. Accordingly, in 1670, two hundred white

Barbadians and their slaves landed near modern-day Charleston, "in the very chops of the Spanish." The settlement called Charles Town formed the colony's nucleus.

Until the 1680s, most settlers were from Barbados, with smaller numbers from other colonies and some French Huguenots (Calvinists). Obtaining all the land they needed, the colonists saw little reason to obey absentee lords' plans drawn up for them across the Atlantic. Southern Carolinians raised livestock and exported Indian slaves (as discussed shortly), while colonists in northern Carolina produced tobacco, lumber, and pitch, giving local people the name "tarheels." At first, these activities did not produce enough profit to warrant maintaining many slaves, so self-sufficient white families predominated in the area.

But some southern Carolinians, particularly those from Barbados, sought a staple crop that could make them rich. By the early eighteenth century, they found it in rice. Because rice, like sugar, enormously enriched a few men with capital to invest in costly dams, dikes, and slaves, it remade southern Carolina into a society resembling the one from which Barbadians came. By earning annual profits of 25 percent, rice planters within a generation became the one mainland colonial elite whose wealth rivaled that of the Caribbean sugar planters.

Even when treated humanely, indentured English servants simply did not survive in humid rice paddies swarming with malaria-bearing mosquitoes. The planters' solution was to import an ever-growing force of enslaved Africans. West Africans had developed immunities to malaria and yellow fever—infectious, mosquito-borne diseases that were endemic to their homelands. Enslaved Africans, along with infected slave ships' crews, carried both diseases to North America. (Tragically, the antibody that helps ward off malaria also tends to produce the sickle-cell trait, a genetic condition often fatal to the children who inherit it.) Because a typical Carolina rice planter farming 130 acres needed sixty-five slaves, a great demand for black slave labor resulted. The proportion of enslaved Africans in southern Carolina's population rose from just 17 percent in 1680 to about half by 1700. Thereafter, Carolina would have a black majority.

Rice thrived only within a forty-mile-wide coastal strip extending from Cape Fear to present-day Georgia. Carolinians grimly joked that the malaria-infested rice belt was a paradise in spring, an inferno in summer, and a hospital in the wet, chilly fall. In the worst months, planters' families usually escaped to the relatively cool and more healthful climate of Charles Town and let overseers supervise their slaves during harvests.

Enslavement in Carolina was not confined to Africans. In the 1670s, traders in southern Carolina armed nearby Native Americans and encouraged them to raid rival tribes for slaves. After local supplies of Indian slaves were exhausted, the English-allied Indians captured unarmed Guale, Apalachee, and Timucua Indians at Spanish missions in Florida and traded them to the Carolinians for guns and other European goods. The English in turn sold the enslaved Indians, mostly to planters in the West Indies—where most Indians died quickly because they lacked immunities to European and tropical diseases—but also on the mainland as far north as New England. By the mid-1680s, the Carolinians had extended the trade through alliances with the Yamasees and the Creeks, a powerful confederacy centered in what is now western Georgia and northern Alabama. For three decades, these Indian allies of the English terrorized Indians in Florida with their slave raids.

Between thirty thousand and fifty thousand Native Americans were enslaved in Carolina between 1670 and 1715.

THE MIDDLE COLONIES

Between the Chesapeake and New England, two non-English nations established colonies (see Map 3.2). New Netherland and New Sweden were small commercial outposts, although the Dutch colony eventually flourished and took over New Sweden. But England seized New Netherland from the Dutch in 1664 and carved New York, New Jersey, and Pennsylvania out of the former Dutch territory. These actions together created a fourth English colonial region, the middle colonies.

MAP 3.2 European Colonization in the Middle and North Atlantic, c. 1650

North of Spanish Florida, four European powers competed for territory and trade with Native Americans in the early seventeenth century. Swedish and Dutch colonization was the foundation upon which England's middle colonies were built.

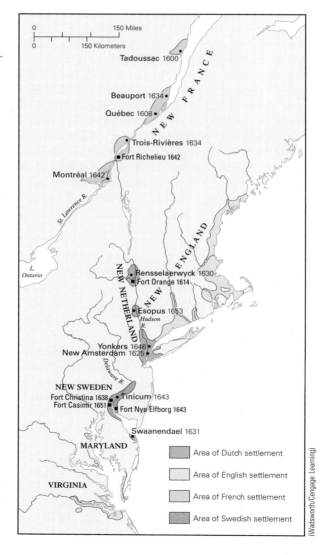

150 Miles
150 Kilometers

Tadoussac 1600
Beauport 1634
Québec 1608
Trois-Rivières 1634
Fort Richelieu 1642
Montréal 1642
St. Lawrence R.
NEW FRANCE
L. Ontario
NEW NETHERLAND
NEW ENGLAND
Rensselaerwyck 1630
Fort Orange 1614
Esopus 1653
Hudson R.
Yonkers 1646
New Amsterdam 1625
Delaware R.
NEW SWEDEN
Fort Christina 1638
Fort Casimir 1651
Tinicum 1643
Fort Nye Elfborg 1643
Swaanendael 1631
MARYLAND
VIRGINIA

Area of Dutch settlement
Area of English settlement
Area of French settlement
Area of Swedish settlement

(Wadsworth/Cengage Learning)

Precursors: New Netherland and New Sweden

New Netherland was North America's first multiethnic colony. Barely half its colonists were Dutch; most of the rest were Germans, French, Scandinavians, and Africans, free as well as enslaved; and eighteen European and African languages were spoken. In 1643, the population included Protestants, Catholics, Jews, and Muslims. But religion counted for little (in 1642, the colony had seventeen taverns but not one place of worship) as did loyalty to Dutch authority. Although the Dutch West India Company—a consortium of merchants—nominally controlled trade in New Netherland, private individuals persisted in illegally trading furs. In 1639, the company bowed to mounting pressure and legalized private fur trading.

Privatization led to a rapid rise in the number of guns reaching New Netherland's Iroquois allies, giving them a distinct advantage over rival Natives. As overhunting depleted local supplies of beaver skins and as smallpox epidemics took their toll, the Iroquois attacked pro-French Indians in Canada, seizing pelts and captives whom they adopted into their families to replace the dead. Between 1648 and 1657, the Iroquois, in a series of bloody "**beaver wars**," dispersed the Hurons and other French allies, incorporating many members of these nations into their own ranks. Then they attacked French settlements along the St. Lawrence. "They come like foxes, they attack like lions, they disappear like birds," wrote a French Jesuit of the Iroquois.

Although the Dutch allied successfully with the inland Iroquois, their relations with nearby coastal Indians paralleled Native-settler relations in England's seaboard colonies. In 1643, all-out war erupted when Governor Willem Kieft ordered the massacre of previously friendly Indians who were protesting settler encroachments on Long Island. By 1645, the Dutch prevailed over these Indians and their allies only with English help and by inflicting additional atrocities. But "Kieft's War," as it became known, helped reduce New Netherland's Indian population from sixteen hundred to seven hundred.

Another European challenger distracted the Dutch as they sought to suppress neighboring Native Americans. In 1638, Sweden had planted a 'small fur-trading colony in the lower Delaware Valley. Trading with the Delaware and Susquehannock Indians, New Sweden diverted many furs from New Netherland. Annoyed, the Dutch colony's governor, Peter Stuyvesant, led seven warships and three hundred troops into New Sweden in 1655. The four hundred residents of the rival colony peacefully accepted Dutch annexation.

Small though they were, the Dutch and Swedish colonies were historically significant. New Netherland had attained a population of nine thousand and featured a wealthy, thriving port city—New Amsterdam—by 1664. Even short-lived New Sweden left a mark—the log cabin, that durable symbol of the American frontier—which Finnish settlers in the Swedish colony first introduced to the continent. Above all, the two colonies bequeathed a social environment characterized by ethnic and religious diversity that would continue in England's middle colonies.

English Conquests: New York and New Jersey

Like Carolina, New York and New Jersey originated as proprietary colonies, awarded by King Charles II to favored upper-class supporters. Here, too, proprietors hoped to create hierarchical societies in which they would profit from settlers' rents. These plans failed in New Jersey, as in Carolina. Only in rural New York did they achieve some success.

Dutch Couple at New Amsterdam *Dutch wealth and enslaved African labor contributed to New Amsterdam's early prosperity.*

In 1664, waging war against the Dutch Republic, Charles II dispatched a naval force to conquer New Netherland. With Dutch forces tied down elsewhere and with Puritan settlers on Long Island supporting England, Stuyvesant and four hundred poorly armed civilians could not defend New Amsterdam. After a peaceful surrender, most of the Dutch remained in the colony on generous terms.

Charles II made his brother James, Duke of York, proprietor of the new province and renamed it New York. When the duke became King James II in 1685, he proclaimed New York a royal colony. Immigration from New England, Britain, and France boosted the population from nine thousand in 1664 to twenty thousand in 1700, of whom just 44 percent were of Dutch descent.

New York's governors rewarded their wealthiest political supporters, both Dutch and English, with large land grants. By 1703, five families held approximately 1.75 million acres in the Hudson River Valley, on which they created manors with rent-paying tenants. Earning an enormous income from their rents over the next half-century the New York **patroons** (the Dutch name for manor lords) formed a landed elite second in wealth only to the Carolina rice planters.

Ambitious plans collided with American realities in New Jersey which also was carved out of New Netherland. Immediately after the conquest of 1664, the Duke of York awarded New Jersey to a group of proprietors. About four thousand

Delaware Indians and a few hundred Dutch and Swedes inhabited the area at the time. From the beginning, New Jersey's proprietors had difficulty controlling their province. By 1672, several thousand New Englanders had settled along the Atlantic shore. After the Puritans rejected their authority, the proprietors sold the region to a group of Quakers who split the territory into the two colonies of West Jersey (1676) and East Jersey (1682).

The Jerseys' Quakers, Anglicans, Puritans, Scottish Presbyterians, Dutch Calvinists, and Swedish Lutherans got along poorly with one another and even worse with the proprietors. Both governments collapsed between 1698 and 1701 as mobs disrupted the courts. In 1702, the disillusioned proprietors surrendered their political powers to the crown, which combined the colonies into a single royal province, New Jersey.

| **Quaker Pennsylvania** | In 1681, Charles II paid off a huge debt by making a supporter's son, **William Penn**, the proprietor of the last unallocated tract of his American domain. Perhaps the most |

distinctive of all English colonial founders, Penn (1644–1718) had two aims in developing Pennsylvania (Penns Woods). First, he wanted to launch a "holy experiment" based on Quaker teachings. Second, "though I desire to extend religious freedom," he explained, "yet I want some recompense for my trouble."

Quakers in late-seventeenth-century England stood well beyond the fringe of respectability. Quakerism appealed strongly to men and women at the bottom of the economic ladder who challenged the social order. George Fox, the movement's originator, had received his inspiration while wandering civil war-torn England and searching for spiritual meaning among distressed common people. Tried on one occasion for blasphemy, he warned the judge to "tremble at the word of the Lord" and was ridiculed as a "quaker." Fox's followers called themselves the Society of Friends, but the name Quaker stuck.

The core of Fox's theology was his belief that the Holy Spirit or "Inner Light" could inspire every soul. Mainstream Christians, by contrast, found any claim of direct, personal communication between God and individuals highly dangerous, as Anne Hutchinson's banishment from Massachusetts Bay in 1637 demonstrated. Friends trusted direct inspiration and disavowed the need for a clergy. In their simple religious services ("meetings"), they sat silently until the Inner Light began prompting participants to speak.

Friends' emphasis on religious individualism and equality extended to the social and political arenas. For example, insisting that individuals deserved recognition for their spiritual state rather than their wealth or status, Quakers refused to tip their hats to their social betters. By wearing their hats in court and refusing to bear arms, moreover, Quakers defied the state's authority. Finally, Quakers accorded women unprecedented equality. The Inner Light, Fox insisted, could "speak in the female as well as the male." Acting on these beliefs, Quakers suffered persecution and occasionally death in England, Massachusetts, and Virginia.

Not all Quakers came from the bottom of society. The movement's emphasis on quiet introspection and its refusal to adopt a formal creed also attracted some well-educated and prosperous individuals disillusioned by the quarreling of rival faiths. The possessor of a great fortune, William Penn was hardly a typical Friend,

but there were significant numbers of merchants among the estimated sixty thous-
and Quakers in the British Isles in the early 1680s. Moreover, their religious self-
discipline carried over into worldly pursuits, ensuring that many humble Quakers
accumulated money and property.

Careful planning gave Pennsylvania the most successful beginning of any European colony in North America. In 1681, Penn sent an advance party to the Delaware Valley, where about five thousand Delaware Indians and one thousand
Swedes and Dutch already lived. Then, after an agonizing voyage in which one-
third of the passengers died, Penn arrived in 1682. Choosing a site for the capital,
he named it Philadelphia—the "City of Brotherly Love." By 1687, some eight thousand settlers had arrived in Pennsylvania—primarily Quakers from the British Isles,
but also Presbyterians, Baptists, Anglicans, and Catholics, as well as Lutherans and
radical sectarians from Germany. Most were attracted by Pennsylvania's religious
toleration as well as its economic promise. As in New England, most immigrants
arrived in family groups rather than as single males, so the population grew rapidly.
In 1698, one Quaker reported that in Pennsylvania one seldom met "any young
Married Woman but hath a Child in her belly, or one upon her lap."

After wavering between authoritarian and more democratic plans, Penn gave
Pennsylvania a government with a strong executive branch (a governor and governor's council) and granted the lower legislative chamber (the assembly) only limited
powers. Friends, forming the majority of the colony's population, dominated this
elected assembly. Penn named Quakers and their supporters as governor, judges,
and sheriffs. Like most elites of the time, he feared "the ambitions of the populace,"
and he intended to check "the rabble" as much as possible. To prevent haphazard
growth and social turmoil in Philadelphia, Penn designed the city with a grid plan,
laying out the streets at right angles and reserving small areas for parks.

Unlike most seaboard colonies, Pennsylvania avoided early hostilities with Native Americans. This was partly because the Native population had been reduced by
epidemics. But it was also a testament to Penn's Quaker tolerance. To the Delaware
Indians, Penn expressed a wish "to live together as Neighbours and Friends," and
he made it the colony's policy to purchase land it wanted for settlement from them.

Land was a key to Pennsylvania's early prosperity. Rich, level lands and a lengthy
growing season enabled immigrants to produce bumper crops. West Indian demand
for the colony's grain rose sharply and by 1700 made Philadelphia a major port.

Like other attempts to base new colonies on preconceived plans or lofty ideals,
Penn's "peaceable kingdom" soon met with resistance. After Penn returned to England
in 1684, an opposition party attacked his efforts to monopolize foreign trade and to
require each landowner pay him a small annual fee. Bitter struggles between Penn's
supporters in the governor's council and opponents in the assembly deadlocked the
government. From 1686 to 1688, the legislature passed no laws, and the council
once ordered the lower house's speaker arrested. During a brief return (1699–1701),
Penn made the legislature a unicameral (one-chamber) assembly and allowed it to
initiate legislation.

Conflict among Quakers also shook Pennsylvania during the 1690s, prompting
some to leave the Friends for the Church of England. Their departure began a major
decline in the Quaker share of Pennsylvania's population. The proportion fell further
once Quakers ceased immigrating in large numbers after 1710.

William Penn met his strongest opposition in the counties on the lower Delaware River, where Swedes and Dutch had taken up the best lands. In 1704, these counties became the separate colony of Delaware, but Penn continued to name their governors.

The middle colonies demonstrated that British America could benefit by encouraging religious toleration and ethnic pluralism. New York and New Jersey successfully integrated New Netherland's Swedish and Dutch population; and neither Pennsylvania, New Jersey, nor Delaware required taxpayers to support an established church.

RIVALS FOR NORTH AMERICA: FRANCE AND SPAIN

In marked contrast to England's compact, densely populated settlements on the Atlantic, France and Spain established far-flung networks of fortified trading posts and missions in North America. Unable to attract large numbers of colonists, they enlisted Native Americans as trading partners and military allies, and the two Catholic nations had far more success than English Protestants in converting Indians to Christianity. By 1700, French and Spanish missionaries, traders, and soldiers—and relatively few settlers—were spreading European influence well beyond the range of England's colonies, to much of Canada and what is now the American Midwest, Southeast, and Southwest.

France Claims a Continent   After briefly losing Canada to England (1629–1632), France resumed and extended its colonization there. Paralleling the early English and Dutch colonies, a privately held company initially assumed responsibility for settling New France. The Company of New France granted extensive tracts to large landlords, who either imported indentured servants or rented out small tracts to prospective farmers. Although some farmers spread along the St. Lawrence River as far inland as Montreal (see Map 3.2), Canada's harsh winters and short growing season sharply limited their numbers.

More successful in New France were commercial traders and missionaries who spread beyond the settlements and relied on stable relations with Indians to succeed. Although the Iroquois defeated France's Native American allies in the beaver wars, French-Indian trade prospered. Indeed, the more lucrative opportunities offered by trade diverted many French men who had initially arrived to take up farming.

The colony also benefited from the substantial efforts of Catholic religious workers, especially Jesuit missionaries and Ursuline nuns. Given a virtual monopoly on missions to Native Americans in 1633, the Jesuits followed the fur trade into the North American interior. Although the missionaries often feuded with the traders, whose morality they condemned, the two groups together spread French influence westward to the Great Lakes, securing the loyalty of the region's Indians in their struggles with the Iroquois. The Ursulines ministered particularly to Native American women and girls nearer Quebec, ensuring that Catholic piety and morality reached all members of Indian families.

The chief minister of France's King Louis XIV (reigned 1661–1715), Jean-Baptiste Colbert, was a forceful proponent of the doctrine of mercantilism (covered in Chapter 4), which held that colonies should provide their home country with raw materials for manufacturing and markets for manufactured goods. Accordingly,

Colbert hoped that New France could increase its output of furs, ship agricultural surpluses to France's new sugar-producing colonies in the West Indies, and export timber to those colonies and for the French navy. To begin realizing these goals, Louis XIV made New France a royal colony in 1663.

With the colony under its direct control, the French government sought to stifle the Iroquois threat to New France's economy. During and after the beaver wars, the Iroquois limited New France's productivity by intercepting convoys of beaver pelts from the interior and taking them to Dutch traders on the Hudson River. In 1666, France dispatched fifteen hundred soldiers to stop Iroquois interference with the fur trade. French troops sacked and burned four Mohawk villages that were well stocked with winter food. After the alarmed Iroquois made a peace that lasted until 1680, New France enormously expanded its fur exports.

Meanwhile, Colbert encouraged French immigration to Canada. Within a decade of the royal takeover, the French population rose from twenty-five hundred to eighty-five hundred. Most were indentured servants who earned wages and received land after three years' work. Others were former soldiers and officers who were given land grants and other incentives to remain in New France and farm while strengthening the colony's defenses. The officers were encouraged to marry among the "king's girls," wealthy female orphans shipped from France with dowries.

The upsurge in French immigration petered out after 1673 as two-thirds of French immigrants returned to their native land. They told tales of disease and other hazards of the transatlantic voyage, of Canada's hard winters, and of wars with the "savage" Iroquois. New France would grow slowly, relying on the natural increase of its small population rather than on newcomers from Europe.

Colbert had encouraged immigration to enhance New France's agricultural productivity. But many French men continued to spurn farming in the St. Lawrence Valley, instead swarming westward in search of furs. By 1670, one-fifth of them were *voyageurs,* or *coureurs de bois*—independent traders unconstrained by government authority. Living in Indian villages and often marrying Native women, the *voyageurs* built an empire for France. From Canadian and Great Lakes Indians, they obtained furs in exchange for European goods, including guns to use against the Iroquois and other rivals. In their commercial interactions, the French and Indians observed Native American norms of reciprocity (see Chapter 1). Their exchanges of goods sealed bonds of friendship and alliance, which served their mutual interests in trade and in war against common enemies.

Alarmed by the rapid expansion of England's colonies and fearing that Spain would link Florida with New Mexico, France boldly sought to dominate the North American heartland. In 1672, fur trader Louis Jolliet and Jesuit missionary Jacques Marquette became the first Europeans known to have reached the upper Mississippi River; they later paddled twelve hundred miles downstream to the Mississippi's junction with the Arkansas River. Ten years later, **Robert Cavelier de La Salle,** an upper-class adventurer, descended the entire Mississippi to the Gulf of Mexico. When he reached the delta, La Salle formally claimed the entire Mississippi basin— half of the present-day continental United States—for Louis XIV, for whom he named it Louisiana.

Having asserted title to this vast empire, the French began settling its southern gateway. In 1698, the first colonizers arrived on the Gulf of Mexico coast. A year later, the French erected a fort near present-day Biloxi, Mississippi. In 1702, they occupied the former Mississippian city of Mabila, where De Soto's expedition had faltered a century and a half earlier (see Chapter 2), founding a trading post, and calling it Mobile. But Louisiana's growth would stall for another decade.

New Mexico: The Pueblo Revolt

Lying at the northerly margin of Spain's empire, New Mexico and Florida remained small and weak through the seventeenth century. With few settlers, they needed ties with friendly Native Americans to obtain land, labor, and security. But Spanish policies made friendly relations hard to come by in both places.

From the beginning, the Spanish sought to rule New Mexico by subordinating the Pueblo Indians to their authority in several ways. First, Franciscan missionaries supervised the Indians' spiritual lives by establishing churches in most of the Indian communities (pueblos) and attempting to force the natives to practice Catholicism. Second, Spanish landowners were awarded *encomiendas* (discussed in Chapter 2), which allowed them to exploit Indian labor and productivity for personal profits. Finally, the Spanish drove a wedge between the Pueblo Indians and their nonfarming neighbors, the Apaches and Navajos. Because the Spanish collected corn as tribute, the Pueblo Indians could no longer trade their surplus crops to their neighbors. Having incorporated corn into their diets, the Apaches and Navajos raided the pueblos for the grain. They also raided the colonists because Spanish slave traders had captured and sold some of their people to work in Mexican silver mines. Several outlying pueblos made common cause with the Apaches, but most Pueblo Indians relied on the Spanish for protection from the raids.

Although local rebellions erupted sporadically, most Pueblo Indians initially accepted Spanish rule and tried to reconcile Catholicism with their own religious traditions. Beginning in the 1660s, however, their crops withered under several consecutive years of sustained drought. Starvation plus deadly epidemic diseases sent the Pueblo population plummeting from about eighty thousand in 1598 to just seventeen thousand in the 1670s. In response, many Christian Indians openly resumed traditional Pueblo ceremonies, hoping to restore the spiritual balance that had brought ample rainfall, good health, and peace before the Spanish arrived. Seeking to suppress this religious revival, Franciscan missionaries entered sacred kivas (underground ceremonial centers), destroyed religious objects, and publicly whipped Native religious leaders and their followers.

Matters came to a head in 1675 when Governor Juan Francisco Treviño ordered soldiers to sack the kivas and arrest Pueblo religious leaders. Three leaders were sentenced to the gallows; a fourth hanged himself; and forty-three others were jailed, whipped, and sold as slaves. In response, armed warriors from several pueblos converged on Santa Fe and demanded the prisoners' release. With most of his soldiers off fighting the Apaches, Governor Treviño complied.

Despite Treviño's concession, there was no cooling of Pueblo resentment against the Spanish. Pueblo leaders began gathering secretly to plan the overthrow of Spanish rule. At the head of this effort was Popé, one of those who had been arrested in 1675.

In August 1680, Popé and his cohorts were ready to act. On the morning of August 10, some Indians from the pueblo of Taos and their Apache allies attacked the homes of the seventy Spanish colonists residing near Taos and killed all but two. Then, with Indians from neighboring pueblos, they proceeded south and joined a massive siege of New Mexico's capital, Santa Fe. Thus began the **Pueblo Revolt** of 1680, the most successful Indian uprising in American history.

At each pueblo, rebels destroyed the churches and religious paraphernalia and killed those missionaries who did not escape. All told, about four hundred colonists were slain. Then the Pueblos "plunge[d] into the rivers and wash[ed] themselves with amole," a native root, to undo their baptisms. As a follower later testified, Popé also called on the Indians "to break and enlarge their cultivated fields, saying now they were as they had been in ancient times, free from the labor they had performed for the religious and the Spaniards."

After the siege of Santa Fe, the Spanish fled from New Mexico. Only in 1692 did a new governor, Diego de Vargas, arrive to "reconquer" New Mexico. Exploiting divisions that had emerged among the Pueblos in the colonists' absence, Vargas used violence and threats of violence to reestablish Spanish rule. Even then, Spain did not effectively quash Pueblo resistance until 1700, and thereafter its control of the province was more limited than before. The Spanish needed Pueblo military support against the Apaches, who now attacked them on horses the colonists had left behind when fleeing the colony. To appease the Pueblos, Spanish authorities abolished the hated *encomienda* and ordered the Franciscans to permit the Pueblos to practice their traditional religion.

(Palace of the Governors, New Mexico History Museum)

Taos Pueblo, New Mexico *Although this photo was taken in 1880, Taos's appearance had changed little during the two centuries since the Pueblo Revolt.*

Pueblos' suspicions of the Spanish lingered after 1700, but they did not again attempt to overthrow them. With the missions and *encomienda* less intrusive, they sustained their cultural identities within, rather than outside, the bounds of colonial rule.

Florida and Texas   The Spanish fared no better in Florida. For most of the seventeenth century, Florida's colonial population numbered only in the hundreds, primarily Spanish soldiers and Franciscan missionaries. Before 1680, the colony faced periodic rebellions from Guale, Timucua, and Apalachee Indians protesting forced labor and Franciscan attempts to impose religious conformity. Thereafter, Creek and other Indian slave raiders allied to the English in Carolina added to the Florida Indians' miseries. While the Spanish, with their small numbers of soldiers and arms looked on helplessly, the invading Indians killed and captured thousands of Florida's Natives and sold them to English slave traders in Carolina. Even before a new round of warfare erupted in Europe at the turn of the century, Spain was ill-prepared to defend its beleaguered North American colonies.

English expansion threatened Florida, while the French establishment of Louisiana defied Spain's hope of one day linking that colony with New Mexico. To counter the French, Spanish authorities in Mexico proclaimed the province of Texas (Tejas) in 1691. But no permanent Spanish settlements appeared there until 1716 (covered in Chapter 4).

CHRONOLOGY
1625–1700

1629	Massachusetts Bay colony founded.
1630–1642	"Great Migration" to New England.
1634	Lord Baltimore establishes Maryland.
1636	Roger Williams founds Providence.
1636–1637	Antinomian crisis in Massachusetts Bay.
1637	Pequot War in Connecticut.
1638	New Sweden established.
1642–1649	English Civil War.
1643–1645	Kieft's War in New Netherland.
1644–1646	Third Anglo-Powhatan War in Virginia.
1648–1657	Iroquois "beaver wars."
1649	Maryland's Act for Religious Toleration. King Charles I executed in England.
1655	New Netherland annexes New Sweden.
1660	Restoration in England; Charles II crowned king.
1661	Maryland defines slavery as a lifelong, inheritable racial status.
1664	English conquer New Netherland; establish New York and New Jersey.

1670	Charles Town, Carolina, founded.
	Virginia defines slavery as a lifelong, inheritable racial status.
1675–1676	King Philip's War in New England.
1676	Bacon's Rebellion in Virginia.
1680	Pueblo Revolt begins in New Mexico.
1681	William Penn founds Pennsylvania.
1682	La Salle claims Louisiana for France.
1690s	End of Royal African Company's monopoly on English slave trade.
1691	Spain establishes Texas.
1692–1700	Spain "reconquers" New Mexico.
1692–1693	Salem witchcraft trials.
1698	First French settlements in Louisiana.

CONCLUSION

In less than a century, from 1625 to 1700, the movements of peoples and goods, across the Atlantic and within the continent, transformed the map of North America. Immigrants and slaves spread far and wide among colonial regions in the Americas. Depending on their circumstances, depopulated Native Americans resisted or accommodated the newcomers.

The English colonies were by far the most populous. By 1700, the combined number of whites and blacks in England's mainland North American colonies was about 250,000, compared with 15,000 for those of France and 4,500 for those of Spain.

Within the English colonies, four distinct regions emerged. After beginning with a labor force consisting primarily of white indentured servants, the tobacco planters of the Chesapeake region replaced them with enslaved Africans. New England's Puritanism grew less utopian and more worldly as the inhabitants gradually reconciled their religious views with the realities of a commercial economy. Slavery had been instituted by English sugar planters in the West Indies, some of whom introduced it in the third North American region, Carolina. Between the Chesapeake and New England, a fourth region, the middle colonies, continued the ethnic pluralism and religious toleration of their Swedish and Dutch predecessors. Middle colonists, including the Quakers, embraced the market economy with far less hesitation than did New England Puritans. While planters or merchants rose to prominence in each English region, most whites continued to live on family farms.

With far fewer colonists, the French and Spanish depended more on Native American allies for their livelihoods and security than the English. Before 1700, most French settlers lived in the St. Lawrence Valley, where a lively commercial-agrarian economy was emerging, though on a far smaller scale than in New England and the middle colonies. Most Spanish colonists not connected to the government, military, or a missionary order resided in the Rio Grande valley in New Mexico. But smaller numbers and geographic isolation would prevent the Southwest from becoming a major center of colonization.

By 1700, clear differences existed between the societies and economies of the three colonial powers in North America. These differences would prove decisive in shaping American history during the century that followed.

4

THE BONDS OF EMPIRE, 1660–1750

REBELLION AND WAR, 1660–1713

The Restoration (1660) of the monarchy did not resolve England's deep-seated political antagonisms. Charles II and James II (ruled 1685–1688) attempted to strengthen the crown at Parliament's expense while attempting to centralize royal authority in the colonies. After England in 1689 overthrew James and replaced him with his daughter, Mary, and her husband, William, Massachusetts, New York, and Maryland carried out their own revolts. Thereafter, both royal authority and representative legislatures became stronger in the colonies.

The overthrow of James, a pro-French Catholic, led directly to a period of warfare between England and France. By the time peace was restored in 1713, the colonists had become closely tied to a new, powerful British empire.

Royal Centralization, 1660–1688
The Restoration monarchs had little use for representative government. Charles II rarely called Parliament into session. James II, Charles's younger brother, hoped to reign as an "absolute" monarch like France's Louis XIV, who never faced an elected legislature. Not surprisingly, the two English kings had little sympathy for American colonial assemblies. Royal intentions of extending direct political control to North America first became evident in New York. The proprietor, the future James II, considered elected legislatures "of dangerous consequence" and forbade New York's assembly (lower legislative chamber) to meet, except briefly between 1682 and 1686.

Puritan-dominated Massachusetts proved most persistent in defending self-government and resisting English authority. The crown insisted that Massachusetts base voting rights on property ownership rather than church membership, that it tolerate Anglicans and Quakers, and that it observe the Navigation Acts (discussed later in this chapter). As early as 1661, the General Court (legislature) defiantly declared Massachusetts exempt from all parliamentary laws and royal decrees except declarations of war. Charles II moved to break the Puritan establishment's power. In 1679, he carved a new royal colony, New Hampshire, out of its territory. Then, in 1684, he declared Massachusetts a royal colony and revoked its charter, the very foundation of the Puritan city upon a hill.

Royal centralization accelerated after James II succeeded Charles. In 1686, the new king consolidated Massachusetts, New Hampshire, Connecticut, Rhode Island, and Plymouth into a single administrative unit, the **Dominion of New England**, with its capital at Boston. He added New York and the Jerseys to the dominion in 1688. With these bold strokes, the legislatures in these colonies ceased to exist, and a single governor, Sir Edmund Andros, headed the new supercolony.

Massachusetts burned with hatred for the dominion and its governor. By "Exercise of an arbitrary Government," preached Salem's minister, "ye wicked walked on Every Side & ye Vilest of men ware [sic] exalted." Andros was indeed arbitrary. He limited towns to a single annual meeting, and strictly enforced religious toleration and the Navigation Acts. "You have no more privileges left you," Andros reportedly told a group of outraged colonists, "than not to be sold for slaves."

Tensions also ran high in New York, where Catholics held prominent political and military posts under James. By 1688, colonists feared these Catholic officials would betray New York to France, England's chief imperial rival. When Andros's local deputy allowed the harbor's forts to deteriorate and downplayed rumors that Native Americans would attack, New Yorkers suspected the worst.

The Glorious Revolution, 1688–1689 Not only colonists but also most English people were alarmed by the direction in which the monarchy was taking the nation. Charles II and James II ignored Parliament, issued decrees allowing Catholics to hold high office and worship openly, and expressed their friendship with France's King Louis XIV, just as Louis was persecuting Protestant Huguenots.

The English tolerated James's Catholicism only because his daughters, Mary and Anne, remained Anglican. But in 1688, James's wife bore a son who would be raised a Catholic and, as a male, precede his sisters to the throne. Aghast at the thought of another Catholic monarch, England's leading political and religious figures invited Mary and her husband, William of Orange (head of state in the Protestant Netherlands), to intervene. When William led a small Dutch army to England in November 1688, most royal troops defected to them, and James II fled to France.

This revolution of 1688, called the **Glorious Revolution**, created a "limited monarchy" as defined by the **English Bill of Rights** (1689). The crown was required to summon Parliament annually, sign all its bills, and respect traditional civil liberties. This circumscribing of monarchial power and vindication of representative government burned deeply into the English political consciousness, and Anglo-Americans never forgot it.

News that James II had fled England electrified New Englanders. On April 18, 1689, well before confirmation of the revolt's success, Boston's militia arrested Andros and his councilors. (The governor tried to flee in women's clothing but was caught after an alert guard spotted a "lady" in army boots.) Massachusetts political leaders acted in the name of William and Mary, risking their necks should James return to power in England.

Although William, now King William III, dismantled the Dominion of New England and permitted Connecticut and Rhode Island to resume electing their own governors, he reined in Massachusetts's independent leanings. He issued a new charter for the colony in 1691, stipulating that the crown would continue to choose the governor. In addition, property ownership, not church membership, became the criterion for voting. Finally, the new charter required Massachusetts to tolerate all Protestants. While Plymouth and Maine remained within Massachusetts, New Hampshire became a separate royal colony. For Puritans already demoralized by the demise of the "New England Way," this was indeed bitter medicine.

New York's counterpart of the Glorious Revolution was **Leisler's Rebellion**. Emboldened by news of Boston's coup, the city's militia—consisting mainly of Dutch and other non-English artisans and shopkeepers—seized the harbor's main fort on May 31, 1689. Militia Captain Jacob Leisler took command of the colony, repaired its rundown defenses, and called elections for an assembly. When English troops arrived at New York in 1691, Leisler, fearing (wrongly) that their commander was loyal to James II, denied them entry to key forts. A skirmish resulted, and Leisler was arrested.

"Hott brain'd" Leisler had jailed many elite New Yorkers for questioning his authority, but now his enemies persuaded the new governor to charge Leisler with treason for firing on royal troops. In the face of popular outrage, a packed jury found Leisler and his son-in-law, Jacob Milborne, guilty. Both men went to the gallows insisting that they were dying "for the king and queen and the Protestant religion."

News of England's Glorious Revolution heartened Maryland's Protestant majority, which had long chafed under Catholic rule. Hoping to prevent a religious uprising, Lord Baltimore sent a messenger from England in early 1689, ordering colonists to obey William and Mary. But the courier died en route, leaving Maryland's Protestants fearful that their Catholic proprietor still supported James II.

Acting on this fear, John Coode and three others organized the **Protestant Association** to secure Maryland for William and Mary. Coode's group seized the capital in July 1689, removed all Catholics from office, and requested a royal governor. They got their wish in 1691, and the Church of England became the established religion in 1692. Catholics, who composed less than one-fourth of the population, lost the right to vote and thereafter could worship only in private. Maryland stayed in royal hands until 1715, when the fourth Lord Baltimore regained his proprietorship after joining the Church of England.

The revolutionary events of 1688–1689 changed the colonies' political climate by reestablishing representative government and ensuring religious freedom for Protestants. Dismantling the Dominion of New England and directing governors to call annual assemblies, William encouraged colonial elites to return to politics. By encouraging the assemblies to work with royal and proprietary governors, he expected elites to identify their interests with those of England. A foundation was thus laid for an empire based on voluntary allegiance rather than submission to raw power imposed from faraway London. The crowning of William and Mary opened a new era in which Americans drew rising confidence from their relationship to the English throne. "As long as they reign," wrote a Bostonian who helped topple Andros, "New England is secure."

A Generation of War, 1689–1713   The Glorious Revolution ushered in a quarter-century of warfare, convulsing both Europe and North America. In 1689, England joined a European coalition against France's Louis XIV, who supported James's claim to the English crown. The resulting War of the League of Augsburg, which Anglo-Americans called **King William's War**, would be the first of several European wars that would be fought in part on North American soil.

With the outbreak of King William's War, New Yorkers and New Englanders launched a two-pronged invasion of New France in 1690, with one prong aimed at Montreal and the other at Quebec. After both invasions failed, the war took the form of cruel but inconclusive border raids against civilians carried out by both English and French troops, and their respective Indian allies.

Having fought against pro-French Indians since 1680, the Five Nations Iroquois Confederacy bore the bloodiest fighting. While their English allies failed to offer adequate support, the Iroquois faced the French as well as virtually all Indians from Maine to the Great Lakes. Although King William's War ended in 1697, the Five Nations staggered until 1700 under additional invasions by pro-French Indians. By then, one-quarter of the Confederacy's two thousand warriors had been killed or taken prisoner or had fled. The total Iroquois population declined 20 percent over twelve years, from eighty-six hundred to fewer than seven thousand. (By comparison, the war cost about thirteen hundred English, Dutch, and French lives.)

By 1700, the Confederacy was divided into pro-English, pro-French, and neutralist factions. Under the impact of war, the neutralists set a new direction for Iroquois diplomacy. In two separate treaties, together called the **Grand Settlement of 1701,** the Five Nations made peace with France and its Indian allies in exchange for access to western furs, and redefined their alliance with Britain to exclude military cooperation. Skillful negotiations brought the exhausted Iroquois far more success than had war by allowing them to keep control of their lands, expand trade with Europeans and Indians, rebuild their decimated population, and avoid more losses in Europe's destructive wars.

In 1702, European war again erupted when England fought France and Spain in the War of the Spanish Succession, called **Queen Anne's War** by England's American colonists. This conflict reinforced Anglo-Americans' awareness of their military weakness. French and Indian raiders from Canada destroyed several towns in Massachusetts and Maine that expanding colonists had recently established on the Indians' homelands. In the Southeast, Spanish forces invaded Carolina and nearly took Charles Town in 1706, while Anglo-American sieges of Quebec and St. Augustine ended as expensive failures.

England's own forces had more success than those of the colonies, seizing Hudson Bay and Acadia (renamed Nova Scotia). England kept these gains in the Treaty of Utrecht (1713).

The most important consequence of the imperial wars for Anglo-Americans was political, not military. The conflicts reinforced colonists' allegiance to post-1689

England as a bastion of Protestantism and political liberty. Recognizing their own military weakness and the extent to which the Royal Navy had protected their shipping, colonists acknowledged their dependence on the newly formed United Kingdom of Great Britain (created by the formal union of England and Scotland in 1707). As a new generation of English colonists matured, war buttressed their loyalty to Great Britain and the crown.

COLONIAL ECONOMIES AND SOCIETIES, 1660–1750

After achieving peace in 1713, Britain, France, and Spain competed economically rather than militarily. Over several decades, England and France had developed maritime empires that successfully seized control of Atlantic commerce from the Dutch. Thereafter, all three powers hoped to expand their American colonies and integrate them into single, imperial economies. Spain and France gained territory but realized few benefits from their mainland colonies north of Mexico. Meanwhile, British North America thrived.

Mercantilist Empires in America   The imperial practices of Britain, France, and Spain were rooted in a set of political-economic assumptions known as **mercantilism**. Mercantilist theory held that each nation's power was measured by its wealth, especially in gold. To secure wealth, a country needed to maximize its sale of goods abroad while minimizing foreign purchases and use of foreign shippers. In pursuit of this goal, mercantilist nations—especially France and England—sought to produce everything they needed without relying on other nations, while obliging other nations to buy from them. Although the home country would do most manufacturing, colonies would supply vital raw materials. If needed, a country would go to war to gain raw materials or markets, or to prevent a rival from doing the same.

Britain's mercantilist policies were articulated above all in a series of **Navigation Acts** governing imperial commerce. Parliament enacted the first Navigation Act in 1651, requiring that trade be carried on in English, including colonial-owned, vessels to replace Dutch shippers with English. After the Restoration, Parliament enacted the Navigation Act of 1660, requiring that certain "enumerated" commodities (discussed shortly) be exported via England or Scotland, and barring imports from arriving in non-English ships. The Navigation Act of 1663 stipulated that imports to the colonies arrive via England rather than directly from another country. Later, the Molasses Act (1733) taxed, at sixpence per gallon, all foreign molasses (produced from sugar cane and imported primarily for distilling rum) entering the mainland colonies. This act was intended less to raise revenue than to serve as a tariff that would protect British West Indian sugar producers at the expense of French rivals.

The Navigation Acts affected the British colonial economy in four major ways. First, they limited all imperial trade to British-owned ships whose crews were at least three-quarters British. The acts classified all colonists, including slaves, as British. This restriction not only contributed to Britain's rise as Europe's foremost shipping nation but also laid the foundations of an American shipbuilding industry and merchant marine. By the 1750s, one-third of all "British" vessels were owned by merchants in New England and the middle colonies. The swift growth of this merchant marine diversified the northern colonial economy and made it more commercial. The expansion of colonial shipping also hastened urbanization by creating a need for centralized docks, warehouses, and repair shops in the colonies. By mid-century Philadelphia, New York City, Boston, and Charles Town had emerged as important transatlantic ports.

The second effect of the Navigation Acts on the colonies lay in their stipulating that "enumerated" exports pass through England or Scotland. The colonies' major "enumerated" exports were sugar (by far the most profitable commodity), tobacco, rice, furs, indigo (a Carolina plant that produced a blue dye), and naval stores (masts, hemp, tar, and turpentine). Parliament never restricted grain, livestock, fish, lumber, or rum, which together made up 60 percent of mainland colonial exports. Parliament further reduced the burdens on exporters of tobacco and rice— the chief mainland commodities affected—with two significant concessions. First, it gave tobacco growers a monopoly over the British market by excluding foreign tobacco, even though this hurt British consumers. (Rice planters enjoyed a natural monopoly because they had no competitors.) Second, it minimized the added cost of landing tobacco and rice in Britain by refunding customs duties when those products were later shipped to other countries. With about 85 percent of all American tobacco and rice eventually sold outside the British Empire, the acts reduced planters' profits by less than 3 percent.

The Navigation Acts' third effect on the colonies was to encourage economic diversification. Parliament used British tax revenues to pay modest bounties to Anglo-Americans producing such items as silk, iron, dyes, hemp, and lumber, and it imposed protective tariffs on imports of these products from other countries. The laws did prohibit Anglo-Americans from competing with British manufacturing of certain products, most notably clothing. However, colonial tailors, hatters, and housewives could continue to make any item of dress in their households or small shops. Manufactured by low-paid labor, British clothing imports generally undersold whatever the colonists could have exported. The colonists were also free to produce iron, and by 1770 they had built 250 ironworks employing thirty thousand men, a work force larger than the entire population of Georgia or of any provincial city.

Finally, the Navigation Acts made the colonies a protected market for low-priced exports from Britain. Steady overseas demand for colonial products spawned a prosperity that enabled white colonists to purchase ever larger amounts not only of clothing but also of dishware, furniture, tea, and a range of other imports from British and other overseas sources. Retail shops sprang up in cities and rural crossroads throughout the colonies, while itinerant peddlers took imported wares into more remote areas of the countryside. One such peddler arrived in Berwick, Maine, in 1721 and sold several kinds of cloth, a "pair of garters," and various "small trifles" before local authorities confiscated his goods because he lacked a license. Other traders traveled to Native American communities to exchange cloth and other commodities for furs. As a result of colonial consumption, the share of British exports bound for North America spurted from just 5 percent in 1700 to almost 40 percent by 1760. Mercantilism had given rise to a "consumer revolution" in British America.

The economic development of the French and Spanish colonies in North America paled beside that of the British. Although the French government had difficulty implementing mercantilist policies, New France did become agriculturally self-sufficient and exported some wheat to the French West Indies. It also exported small amounts of fish and timber to the Caribbean and to France. Although European demand for Canada's chief export—furs—had flattened, the French government expanded the fur trade, even losing money, to retain Native Americans as military allies against Britain. Moreover, France maintained a sizable army in Canada that also drained the royal treasury. French Canadians enjoyed a comfortable if modest standard of living but lacked the private investment, extensive commercial infrastructure, vast consumer market, and manufacturing capacity of their British neighbors.

France's wealthiest colonies were in the West Indies, where French planters, like their English neighbors, imported large numbers of enslaved Africans to produce sugar under appalling conditions. French sugar planters' success was partly a result of their defying mercantilist policies. In St. Domingue, Martinique, and Guadeloupe, many planters built their own sugar refineries and made molasses instead of shipping their raw sugar to refineries in France, as French regulations prescribed. They sold much of their molasses to merchants in Britain's mainland colonies, especially Massachusetts, which similarly ignored British mercantilist laws.

Although Spain had squandered the wealth from gold and silver extracted by the conquistadors and early colonists (see Chapter 2), its economy and that of Latin America revived during the eighteenth century. However, that revival did not extend to the northern borderlands of New Mexico, Texas, and Florida, where colonists conducted little overseas commerce.

Britain's colonies differed fundamentally from those of France and Spain in their respective economies and societies. While mercantilist principles governed all three nations, the monarchy, the nobility, and the Catholic Church controlled most wealth in France and Spain. Most private wealth was inherited and took the form of land. England, on the other hand, had become a mercantile-commercial economy, and a significant portion of its wealth was in the form of capital held by merchants who reinvested it in commercial and shipping enterprises. Moreover, the British government used much of its considerable income from duties, tariffs, and other taxes to enhance commerce. For example, the government strengthened Britain's powerful navy to protect the empire's trade and created the Bank of England in 1694 to ensure a stable money supply and lay the foundation for a network of lending institutions. These benefits extended not only to Britain but also to colonists. Indeed the colonies' per capita income rose 0.6 percent annually from 1650 to 1770, a pace twice that of Britain.

Population Growth and Diversity   Britain's economic advantage over its rivals in North America was reinforced by its sharp demographic edge. In 1700, approximately 250,000 Europeans and Africans resided in England's colonies, compared to only 15,000 in French territory and 4,500 in Spain's possessions. During the first half of the eighteenth century, all three colonial populations at least quadrupled in size—the British to 1,170,000, the French to 60,000, and the Spanish to 19,000—but this only magnified Britain's advantage.

Spanish emigrants could choose from among that nation's many Latin American colonies, most of which offered more opportunities than remote, poorly developed

Florida, Texas, and New Mexico. Reports of Canada's harsh winters and Louisiana's poor economy deterred most potential French colonists. France and Spain attracted few immigrants to North America from outside their own empires. And both limited immigration to Roman Catholics, a restriction that diverted French Huguenots to the English colonies. Meanwhile, England's colonies boasted good farmlands, healthy economies, and a willingness to absorb Europeans of most Protestant denominations. While anti-Catholicism remained strong, small Jewish communities formed in several Anglo-American cities.

Spain regarded its northernmost colonies less as centers of population than as buffers against French and English encroachments on their more valued colonies to the south. While hoping to lure civilian settlers, the Spanish relied heavily on soldiers stationed in *presidios* (forts) for defense plus missionaries who attempted to attract Native Americans to strategically placed missions. Most colonists in Spanish North America came not from Spain itself but from Mexico and other Spanish colonies.

Although boasting more people than the Spanish colonies, New France and Louisiana were also limited. The military played a strong role in Canada, while missionaries and traders enhanced the colony's relations with Native Americans. New France's population growth in the eighteenth century resulted largely from natural increase rather than immigration. Some rural Canadians established new settlements along the Mississippi River in what are now Illinois and Missouri. To boost Louisiana's population, the government sent paupers and criminals, recruited some German refugees, and encouraged large-scale slave imports. By 1732, two-thirds of Louisiana's 5,800 people were black and enslaved.

The British colonies outpaced the population growth of not only their French and Spanish rivals but of Britain itself. White women in the colonies had an average of eight children and forty-two grandchildren, compared to five children and fifteen grandchildren for British women. The ratio of England's population to that of the mainland colonies plummeted from 20 to 1 in 1700 to 3 to 1 in 1775.

Although immigration contributed less to eighteenth-century population growth than did natural increase, it remained important. In the forty years after Queen Anne's War, the British colonies absorbed 350,000 newcomers, approximately 210,000 of whom were non-English Europeans (see Figure 4.1). Rising employment and higher wages in England made voluntary immigration to America less attractive than before. But economic hardship elsewhere in the British Isles and northern Europe supplied a steady stream of immigrants, who contributed to greater ethnic diversity among white North Americans.

One of the largest contingents was made up of 100,000 newcomers from Ireland, two-thirds of them "Scots-Irish" descendants of Scottish Presbyterians who had previously sought economic opportunity in northern Ireland. After 1718, Scots-Irish fled to America to escape rack renting (frequent sharp increases in farm rents), usually moving as complete families.

Meanwhile, from German-speaking regions in central Europe came 125,000 settlers, most of them fleeing wartime devastation and severe land shortages in the Rhine Valley. One-third of German immigrants financed their voyage by indenturing themselves or their children as servants. Most Germans were either Lutherans or Calvinists, but some belonged to small, pacifist religious sects that desired above all to be left alone.

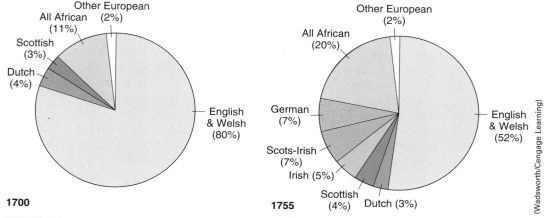

FIGURE 4.1 Distribution of Europeans and Africans within the British Mainland Colonies, 1700–1755

The impact of heavy immigration from 1720 to 1755 can be seen in the reduction of the English and Welsh from four-fifths of the colonial population to a slight majority; in the sudden influx of Germans and Irish (who together comprised a fifth of white colonists by 1755); and in the doubling of the African population.

Source: Thomas L. Purvis, "The European Ancestry of the United States Population," *William & Mary Quarterly,* LXI (1984): 85–101.

Overwhelmingly, the eighteenth-century immigrants were poor. Those who were indentured servants worked from one to four years for an urban or rural master. Servants could be sold or rented out, beaten, granted minimal legal protection, kept from marrying, and sexually harassed. Attempted escape usually meant an extension of their service. But at the end of their terms, most managed to collect "freedom dues," which could help them marry and acquire land.

Few immigrants settled in crowded New England or in the southern tidewater, where land was most scarce and expensive. Philadelphia became immigrants' primary port of entry. So many foreigners went to Pennsylvania that by 1755 the English accounted for only one-third of that colony's population; the rest came mostly from Northern Ireland and Germany. Most of the newcomers settled in central and western Pennsylvania or moved on to the Piedmont region, stretching along the eastern slope of the Appalachians from New York to Carolina. A significant German community developed in upper New York, and thousands of other Germans as well as Scots-Irish fanned southward from Pennsylvania. Others from Germany and Ireland arrived in the second-most popular American gateway, Charles Town. Most moved on to the Carolina Piedmont, where they raised grain, livestock, and tobacco, generally without slaves. After 1750, both streams of immigration merged with an outpouring of Anglo-Americans from the Chesapeake in the rolling, fertile hills of western North Carolina. In 1713, few Anglo-Americans had lived more than fifty miles from the sea, but by 1750 one-third of all colonists resided in the Piedmont.

The least-free white immigrants were English convict laborers. Between 1718 and 1775, about fifty thousand condemned prisoners arrived, mostly in the

Chesapeake colonies. A few of the convicts were murderers; most were guilty of more trivial offenses, like a young Londoner who "got intoxicated with liquor, and in that condition attempted to snatch a handkerchief from the body of a person in the street to him unknown." (English law authorized the death penalty for 160 offenses, including what today would be considered petty theft.) Convicts were sold as servants on arrival. Relatively few committed crimes in America, and most returned to England upon completing their terms.

Many English-descended colonists resented the influx of so many people different from themselves. "These confounded Irish will eat us all up," snorted one Bostonian. Benjamin Franklin spoke for many when he asked,

> Why should Pennsylvania, founded by the English, become a colony of aliens, who will shortly be so numerous as to Germanize us instead of us Anglicizing them, and will never adopt our language or customs any more than they can acquire our complexion?

In the same ungenerous spirit, Franklin objected to the slave trade because it would increase America's black population at the expense of industrious whites, and suggested that the colonists send rattlesnakes to Britain in return for its convict laborers.

Slave Cargo Advertisement, Charles Town, 1769

"Slavers," as the shippers of enslaved Africans were known, sought buyers for their "cargo" upon reaching an American port.

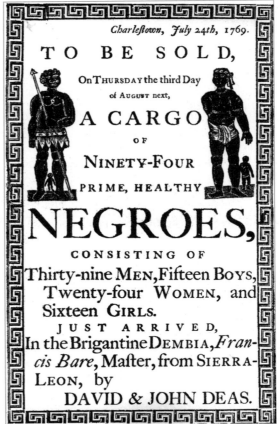

Charlestown, July 24th, 1769.

TO BE SOLD,

On THURSDAY the third Day of AUGUST next,

A CARGO

OF

NINETY-FOUR

PRIME, HEALTHY

NEGROES,

CONSISTING OF

Thirty-nine MEN, Fifteen BOYS, Twenty-four WOMEN, and Sixteen GIRLS.

JUST ARRIVED,

In the Brigantine DEMBIA, *Francis Bare*, Master, from SIERRA-LEON, by

DAVID & JOHN DEAS.

(Courtesy of American Antiquarian Society)

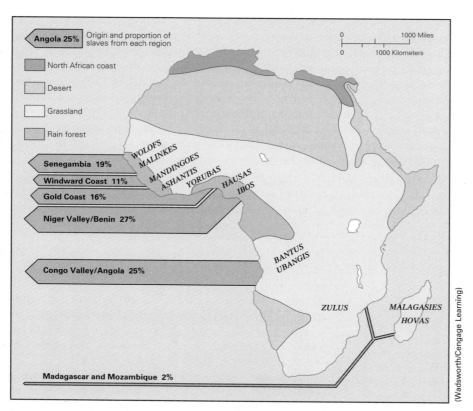

MAP 4.1 African Origins of North American Slaves, 1690–1807

Virtually all slaves brought to English North America came from West Africa, between Senegambia and Angola. Most were captured or bought inland and marched to the coast, where they were sold to African merchants who in turn sold them to European slave traders.

About 40 percent (140,000) of newcomers to the British mainland colonies were African-born slaves who arrived not as passengers but as cargo. All but a few slave ships departed from West African ports with captives from dozens of West and Central African ethnic groups. Most planters deliberately mixed slaves who came from various regions and spoke different languages, to minimize the potential for collective rebellion.

Conditions aboard slave ships during the **Middle Passage,** from Africa to America, were appalling by any standard. Africans were crammed into tight quarters with inadequate sanitary facilities, and many died from disease. A Guinea-born slave, later named Venture Smith, was one of 260 who were on a voyage in 1735. But "smallpox ... broke out on board," Smith recalled, and "when we reached [Barbados], there were found ... not more than two hundred alive."

Slaves who refused to eat or otherwise defied shipboard authority were flogged. Some hurled themselves overboard in a last, desperate act of defiance against those who would profit from their misery. Others acted in groups. Rebellions on one scale or another erupted on about one in ten slave voyages. The rebellions forced shippers to hire full-time guards and install barricades to confine slaves. Shippers then passed the cost on to American buyers.

From 1713 to 1754, five times as many slaves poured onto mainland North America as in all the preceding years. The proportion of blacks in the colonies doubled, rising from 11 percent at the beginning of the century to 20 percent by mid-century. Slavery was primarily a southern institution, but 15 percent of its victims lived north of Maryland, mostly in New York and New Jersey. By 1750, every seventh New Yorker was a slave.

Because slaves were far cheaper in Brazil and the West Indies than farther north, only 5 percent of enslaved Africans arrived in the present-day United States. To economize, rice and tobacco planters purchased African women and protected their investments by minimally maintaining slaves' health. These factors promoted family formation and increased life expectancy far beyond the Caribbean's low levels (see Chapter 3). By 1750, the rate of natural increase for mainland blacks almost equaled that for whites.

Rural White Men and Women

Although most whites benefited from rising living standards in the British colonies, they enjoyed these advantages unevenly. Except for Benjamin Franklin and a few others, most wealthy colonists inherited their fortunes. For other whites, personal success was limited and came through hard work, if at all.

Because most farm families owned just enough acreage for a working farm, they could not provide all their children with land of their own when they married. A young male typically worked from about age sixteen to twenty-three as a field hand for his father or neighbors. After marrying, he often supported his growing family by renting a farm until his early or mid-thirties. In some areas, especially the oldest colonized areas of New England, the continued high birthrates of rural families combined with a shortage of productive land to close off farming opportunities altogether. As a result, many young men turned elsewhere to make their livings—the frontier, the port cities, or the high seas.

Families who did acquire land worked off mortgages slowly because the long-term cash income from a farm (6 percent) about equaled the interest on borrowed money (5 to 8 percent). Only by their late fifties, just as their youngest offspring got ready to leave home, did most colonial parents free themselves of debt.

Remote or poor rural families depended heavily on wives' and daughters' making items that more affluent families could purchase. Besides cooking, cleaning, and washing, wives preserved food, boiled soap, made clothing, and tended the garden, dairy, orchard, poultry house, and pigsty. They also sold dairy products to neighbors or merchants, spun yarn into cloth for tailors, knitted garments for sale, and even sold their own hair for wigs.

Legally, however, white women in the British colonies were constrained (see Chapter 3). A woman's single most autonomous decision was her choice of a husband. Once married, she lost control of her dowry, unless she was a New Yorker subject to Dutch custom, which allowed her somewhat more authority. Women in the French and Spanish colonies retained ownership of, and often augmented, the property they brought to a marriage. Widows did control between 8 and 10 percent of all property in eighteenth-century Anglo-America, and a few—such as Eliza Pinckney of South Carolina—owned and managed large estates.

Colonial Farmers and the Environment

The rapid expansion of Britain's colonies hastened environmental change east of the Appalachians. Eighteenth-century settlers usually had to remove trees to create farm plots. Despite the labor involved, farmers and planters, especially those using slave labor, preferred heavily forested areas where the soil was most fertile. New England farmers also had to clear innumerable heavy rocks, with which they built walls around their fields. Colonists everywhere used timber for buildings and as fuel for heating and cooking. Farmers and planters also sold firewood to the inhabitants of cities and towns. Only six years after Georgia's founding, a colonist noted, there was "no more firewood in Savannah; ... it must be bought from the plantations for which reason firewood is already right expensive."

Removing the trees drove away bears, panthers, wild turkeys, and other forest animals while attracting grass- and seed-eating rabbits, mice, and possums. By removing protection from winds and, in summer, from the sun, deforestation also brought warmer summers and colder winters, further increasing colonists' demand for firewood. By hastening the runoff of spring waters, it led both to heavier flooding and drier streambeds in most areas and, where water could not escape, to more extensive swamps. In turn, less stable temperatures and water levels, along with impediments created by mills and by floating timber downstream, rapidly reduced the fish in colonial waters. Writing in 1766, naturalist John Bartram noted that fish "abounded formerly when the Indians lived much on them & was very numerous," but that "now there is not the 100 [th] or perhaps the 1000th [portion of] fish to be found."

Deforestation dried and hardened the soil, but colonists' crops had even more drastic effects. Native Americans, recognizing the soil-depleting effects of intensive cultivation, rotated their crops regularly, letting fields lie fallow (unplanted) for several years during which vital nutrients replenished the soil. But most colonial farmers did not have enough land to leave some unplanted.

As early as 1637, one New England farmer discovered that his soil "after five or six years [of planting corn] grows barren beyond belief and puts on the face of winter in the time of summer." Chesapeake planters' tobacco yields declined after only three or four years in the same plot. Like farmers elsewhere, they used animal manure to fertilize their food crops but not their tobacco, fearing that manure would spoil the taste for consumers.

Confronting a more serious shortage of land and resources, Europe's well-to-do farmers were already turning their attention to conservation and "scientific" farming. But most colonists ignored such techniques, either because they could not afford to implement them or because they believed that American land, including that still held by Indians, would sustain them and future generations indefinitely.

The Urban Paradox

The cities were British North America's economic paradox. As major ports of entry and exit, they were keys to the colonies' rising prosperity; yet they held only 4 percent of the colonies' population, and a growing percentage of city-dwellers were caught in a downward spiral of declining opportunity.

As colonial prosperity reached new heights after 1740, poverty spread among residents of the major seaports—Philadelphia, New York, Boston, and Charles Town. The cities' poor rolls bulged as poor white men, women (often widowed), and children arrived from Europe and the colonial countryside. High population density and poor sanitation allowed contagious diseases to run rampant, so that half of all city children died before age twenty-one and urban adults lived ten years less on average than country folk.

Changing labor practices also contributed to poverty. Urban artisans traditionally trained apprentices and employed them as journeymen for many years until they could open their own shops. By midcentury, however, employers increasingly kept laborers only as long as business was brisk, releasing them when sales slowed. In 1751, a shrewd Benjamin Franklin recommended this practice to employers as a way to reduce labor costs. Except in Boston, poor whites competed for work with slaves whose masters rented out their labor. Recessions hit more frequently after 1720 and created longer spells of unemployment that made it difficult for many to afford rent, food, and firewood.

Insignificant before 1700, urban poverty became a major problem. By 1730, Boston ceased providing shelter for its growing number of homeless residents. The proportion of residents considered too poor to pay taxes climbed even as the total population leveled (see Figure 4.2). For example, the number of Philadelphia families listed as poor on tax rolls jumped from 3 percent in 1720 to 11 percent by 1760.

Wealth, however, remained highly concentrated. New York's wealthiest 10 percent (mostly merchants) owned about 45 percent of the city's property throughout the eighteenth century. Similar patterns existed in Boston and Philadelphia. Charles Town offered gracious living to wealthy planters who flocked from their plantations to townhouses during the worst months of heat and insect infestation, while shanties on the city's outskirts sheltered a growing crowd of destitute whites. Such trends underscored the polarization of status and wealth in urban America.

Although urban middle-class women performed less manual drudgery than farm women, they managed complex households that often included servants, slaves, and apprentices. While raising poultry and vegetables as well as sewing and knitting, city wives purchased cloth and most of their food in daily trips to public markets. Servants, usually young single women or widows, often helped with cooking, cleaning, and laundering. Urban standards of cleanliness and appearance were higher than in the country. Wives also worked in family businesses or their own shops, which were located in owners' homes.

Less affluent wives and widows had the fewest opportunities of all. They housed boarders rather than servants, and many spun and wove cloth in their homes for local merchants. Poor widows with children looked to the community for relief. Whereas John Winthrop and other Puritans had deemed it a Christian's duty to care for poor dependents (see Chapter 3), affluent Bostonians now scorned the needy. Preaching in 1752, the city's leading minister, Charles Chauncy, lamented "the swarms of children, of both sexes, that are continually strolling and playing about the streets of our metropolis, clothed in rags, and brought up in idleness and ignorance." Another clergyman warned that charity for widows and their children was money "worse than lost."

Slavery   For slaves, the economic progress achieved in colonial America meant only that most masters could afford to keep them healthy. Rarely did masters choose to make their human property comfortable. A visitor to a Virginia plantation from Poland (where peasants lived in dire poverty) recorded this impression of slaves' quality of life:

> We entered some Negroes huts—for their habitations cannot be called houses. They are far more miserable than the poorest of the cottages of our peasants. The husband and wife sleep on a miserable bed, the children on the floor ... a little kitchen furniture amid this misery ... a teakettle and cups ... five or six hens, each with ten or fifteen chickens, walked there. That is the only pleasure allowed to the negroes.

To maintain slaves, masters normally spent just 40 percent of the amount paid for the upkeep of indentured servants. White servants ate two hundred pounds of meat yearly; black slaves consumed fifty pounds. The value of the beer and hard cider given to a typical servant equaled the entire expense of feeding and clothing the average slave. Masters usually provided adult slaves corn and meat but expected them to grow their own vegetables, forage for wild fruits, and perhaps raise poultry.

Blacks worked for a far longer portion of their lives than whites. Slave children entered the fields as part-time helpers after reaching seven and began working full-time between eleven and fourteen. Whereas most white women worked in their homes, barns, and gardens, black females routinely tended tobacco or rice crops, even when pregnant, and often worked outdoors in the winter. Most slaves toiled until they died, although those over sixty were usually spared hard labor.

As the numbers of American-born "creole" slaves grew, sharp differences emerged between them and African-born blacks in the southern colonies. Unlike African-born slaves, creoles spoke a single language, English, and were familiar from birth with their environment and with the ways of slaveowners. As wealthier, longer-established planters diversified economically and developed more elaborate lifestyles (as discussed shortly), they diverted favored creoles toward such services as shoeing horses, repairing and driving carriages, preparing and serving meals, sewing and mending clothing, and caring for planters' children.

Africans and creoles alike proved resourceful at maximizing opportunities within this harsh, confining system. House slaves aggressively demanded that guests tip them for shining shoes and stabling horses. They also sought presents on holidays, as a startled New Jersey visitor to a Virginia plantation discovered early one Christmas morning when slaves demanding gifts of cash roused him from bed.

In the Carolina-Georgia rice country, slaves working under the task system gained some control of about half their waking hours. Under tasking, each slave spent some hours tending rice and food crops, after which his or her plantation duties ended for the day. Thereafter, slaves managed their own crops and sold any surplus, but enjoyed little truly "free time" (see Going to the Source).

The gang system used on tobacco plantations afforded Chesapeake slaves even less relief than those in Carolina. As one white observer noted, Chesapeake blacks labored "from daylight until the dusk of evening and some part of the night, by moon or candlelight, during the winter."

A Planter Describes the Task System

In 1750 Johann Bolzius, a German-born Georgia planter, described how slaves' labor sustained rice plantations on the swampy coastal plain of South Carolina and Georgia under the task system.

The order of planting is the following. 1) The Negroes plant potatoes at the end of March unless the weather is too cold. This keeps all Negroes busy, and they have to loosen the earth as much as they can. The potatoes are cut into several pieces and put into long dug furrows, or mounds.... 2) As soon as one is through with the potatoes, one plants Indian corn. A good Negro man or woman must plant half an acre a day. Holes are merely made in the earth 6 feet from one another, and five or six kernels put into each hole. 3) After the corn the Negroes make furrows for rice planting. A Negro man or woman must account for a quarter acre daily. On the following day the Negroes sow and cover the rice in the furrows, and half an acre is the daily task of a Negro. 4) Now the Negroes start to clean the corn of the grass, and a day's work is half an acre, be he man or woman.... 5) When they are through with that, they plant beans together among the corn. At this time the children must weed out the grass in the potato patches. 6) Thereupon they start for the first time to cultivate the rice and to clean it of grass. A Negro must complete 1/4 acre daily. 7) Now the corn must be cleaned of the grass for the second time, and a little earth put around the stalks like little hills.... Their day's task in this work is half an acre for each. 8) As soon as they are through with the corn, they cultivate the rice a second time. The quality of the land determines their day's work in this. 9) Corn and rice are cultivated for the third and last time. A Negro can take care of an acre and more in this work, and 1/2 an acre of rice.... Afterwards the Negroes are used for all kinds of housework, until the rice is white and ripe for cutting, and the beans are gathered, which grow much more strongly when the corn has been bent down. The rice is cut at the end of August or in September... Towards the middle of August all Negro men of 16 to 60 years must work on the public roads, to start new ones or to improve them, namely for 4 or 5 days, or according to what the government requires, and one has to send along a white man with a rifle or go oneself. At the time when the rice is cut and harvested, the beans are collected too, which task is divided among the Negroes. They gather the rice, thresh it, grind it in wooden mills, and stamp it mornings and evenings. The corn is harvested last. During the 12 days after Christmas they plant peas, garden beans, transplant or prune trees, and plant cabbage. Afterwards the fences are repaired, and new land is prepared for cultivating.

They ["Negroes"] are given as much land as they can handle. On it they plant for themselves corn, potatoes, tobacco, peanuts, water and sugar melons, pumpkins, bottle pumpkins.... They plant for themselves also on Sundays. For if they do not work they make mischief and do damage.... They sell their own crops and buy some necessary things.

Questions

1. What was the role of enslaved Africans in producing wealth and sustenance from the land on rice plantations?

2. In what ways does Bolzius indicate his own racial attitudes?

Go to www.cengagebrain.com for additional primary sources on this period.

Despite the task system's apparent benefits, racial tensions ran high in Carolina. After 1700, as a black majority emerged, whites increasingly used force and fear to control "their" blacks. For example, a 1735 law, noting that many Africans wore "clothes much above the condition of slaves," imposed a dress code limiting slaves' apparel to fabrics worth less than ten shillings per yard and even prohibited the wearing of their owners' cast-off clothes. Of greater concern were large gatherings of slaves uncontrolled by whites. In 1721, Charles Town enacted a 9 P.M. curfew for blacks, while Carolina's assembly placed all local slave patrols under the colonial militia. Slaves responded to such measures with increased instances of arson, theft, flight, and violence.

Violence by slaves peaked in 1739, when the **Stono Rebellion** rocked South Carolina (separated from North Carolina in 1729). It began when twenty Africans seized guns and ammunition from a store at the Stono River Bridge, outside Charles Town. Marching under a makeshift flag and crying "Liberty!" eighty men headed south toward Florida, a well-known refuge for escapees (as discussed below). Along the way, they burned seven plantations and killed twenty whites, but they spared a Scottish innkeeper known for being "a good Man and kind to his slaves." Within a day, mounted militia surrounded the slaves near a riverbank, cut them down mercilessly, and spiked a rebel head on every milepost between that spot and Charles Town. Uprisings elsewhere in the colony required more than a month to suppress, with insurgents generally "put to the most cruel Death." Thereafter, whites enacted a new slave code, essentially in force until the Civil War, which kept South Carolina slaves under constant surveillance. Furthermore, it threatened masters with fines for not disciplining slaves and required legislative approval for manumission (freeing of individual slaves). The Stono Rebellion and its cruel aftermath thus reinforced South Carolina's emergence as a rigid, racist, and fear-ridden society.

Slavery and racial tensions were by no means confined to plantations. By mid-century, enslaved blacks made up 20 percent of New York City's population and formed a majority in Charles Town and Savannah. Southern urban slave owners augmented their incomes by renting out the labor of their slaves, who were cheaper to employ than white workers. Slave artisans worked as coopers, shipwrights, rope makers, and, in a few cases, goldsmiths and cabinetmakers. Some artisans supplemented their work as slaves by earning income of their own. Slaves in northern cities were more often unskilled. Urban slaves in both North and South typically lived apart from their masters in rented quarters alongside free blacks.

Although city life afforded slaves greater freedom of association than did plantations, urban blacks remained the property of others and chafed at racist restrictions. In 1712, rebellious slaves in New York City killed nine whites in a calculated attack. As a result, eighteen blacks were hanged or tortured to death, and six others committed suicide to avoid similar treatment. In 1741, a wave of thefts and fires was attributed on dubious testimony to conspiring New York slaves. Of one hundred fifty-two blacks arrested, thirteen were burned at the stake, seventeen were hanged (along with four whites), and seventy were sent to the West Indies.

| The Rise of Colonial Elites | A few colonists benefited disproportionately from the growing wealth of Britain and its colonies. Most elite colonists inherited their advantages at birth and augmented them by marrying a |

spouse from a similarly wealthy family. Most elite males were large planters or farmers, merchants, or attorneys, clergymen, and other professionals who catered to fellow elites. They constituted British America's upper class, or gentry.

Before 1700, the colonies' class structure was less apparent because elites spent their limited resources buying land, servants, and slaves rather than luxuries. As late as 1715, a traveler noticed that one of Virginia's richest planters, Robert Beverley, owned "nothing in or about his house but just what is necessary, ... [such as] good beds but no curtains and instead of cane chairs he hath stools made of wood."

As British mercantilist trade flourished, higher incomes enabled elite colonists to display their wealth more openly, particularly in their housing. The greater gentry—the richest 2 percent, owning about 15 percent of all property—constructed elaborate showcase mansions that broadcast their elite status. The lesser gentry, or second wealthiest 2 to 10 percent holding about 25 percent of all property, lived in more modest two-story dwellings. In contrast, middle-class farmers commonly inhabited one-story wooden buildings with four small rooms and a loft.

Colonial gentlemen and ladies also exhibited their status by imitating the "refinement" of upper class Europeans. A gentleman was expected to behave with an appropriate degree of responsibility, to display dignity and generosity, and to be a community leader. His wife, a "lady," was to be a skillful household manager and, in the presence of men, a refined yet deferring hostess. Elites wore costly English fashions, drove carriages instead of wagons, and bought expensive chinaware, books, furniture, and musical instruments. They pursued a gracious life by studying foreign languages, learning formal dances, and cultivating polite manners. A few young gentlemen even traveled abroad to get an English education. Thus, elites led colonists' growing taste for British fashions and consumer goods.

COMPETING FOR A CONTINENT, 1713–1750

After a generation of war, Europe's return to peace in 1713 only heightened British, French, and Spanish imperial ambitions in North America. Europeans expanded their territorial claims, intensifying both trade and warfare with Native Americans, and carving out new settlements. Native Americans welcomed some of these developments and resisted others, depending on how they expected their sovereignty and livelihoods to be affected.

France and the American Heartland   To add to its presence in Canada, France sought to strengthen its hold on the Mississippi Valley. In 1718, Louisiana officials established New Orleans as the colony's capital and port. Louisiana's staunchest Indian allies were the Choctaws, through whom the French hoped to counter both the expanding influence of Carolina's traders and the Spanish presence in Florida. But by the 1730s, inroads by the Carolinians had divided the Choctaws into pro-English and pro-French factions.

Life was dismal in Louisiana for whites as well as blacks. A thoroughly corrupt government ran the colony. With tobacco and indigo exports failing to sustain them, Louisiana's settlers and slaves found other means of survival. Like the Native Americans, they hunted, fished, gathered wild plants, and cultivated gardens. In

1727, a priest described how some whites eventually prospered: "A man with his wife or partner clears a little ground, builds himself a house on four piles, covers it with sheets of bark, and plants corn and rice for his provisions; the next year he raises a little more for food, and has also a field of tobacco; if at last he succeeds in having three or four Negroes, then he is out of difficulties."

But many red, white, and black Louisianans depended on exchanges with one another to stay "out of difficulties." Nearby Native Americans provided corn, bear oil, tallow (for candles), and above all deerskins to French merchants in return for blankets, kettles, axes, chickens, hogs, guns, and alcohol. Indian and Spanish traders from west of the Mississippi brought horses and cattle. Familiar with cattle from their homelands, enslaved Africans managed many of Louisiana's herds, and some became rustlers and illicit traders of beef.

French settlers in Upper Louisiana, or Illinois, were somewhat better off, but more than a third of its twenty-six hundred inhabitants were enslaved in 1752. Illinois's principal export was wheat, potentially a more profitable crop than the plantation commodities grown farther south. But Illinois's remote location limited exports and attracted few whites, obliging it to depend on Native American allies to defend it from Indian enemies.

With Canada and the Mississippi Valley secure from European rivals, France sought to counter growing British influence in the Ohio Valley. After the Iroquois declared their neutrality in 1701, many Indian refugees settled in the "Ohio country." Some, such as the Shawnees, returned from elsewhere to reoccupy homelands. Others were newcomers, such as Delawares escaping settler encroachments in Pennsylvania. Hoping to secure commercial and diplomatic ties with these Natives, the French expanded their trade subsidies. Several French posts, most notably Detroit, became sizable towns housing Indians, French, and mixed-ancestry *métis*. But wherever English traders introduced better goods at lower prices, Indians steered a more independent course.

Although generally more effective in Indian diplomacy than the English, the French were not always successful and could be equally violent. They and their Native allies brutally suppressed the Natchez in Louisiana, and for nearly forty years waged war against the Mesquakie (or Fox) Indians in the upper Midwest. The French sold Native Americans captured in these wars as slaves in Louisiana, Illinois, Canada, and the West Indies.

By 1744, French traders were traveling as far west as the Rocky Mountains and were buying buffalo hides and Indian slaves on the Great Plains. These traders and their British competitors spread European-made goods, including guns, to Native Americans throughout central Canada and the Plains. Meanwhile, Indians in the Great Basin and southern Plains were acquiring horses, thousands of which had been left behind by the Spanish when they fled New Mexico during the Pueblo Revolt of 1680. Adopting the horse and gun, Indians such as the Lakota Sioux and Comanches moved to the Plains and built a new, highly mobile way of life based on the pursuit of buffalo. By 1750, France had an immense domain, but one that depended on often-precarious relations with Native Americans.

Native Americans and British Expansion   As in the seventeenth century, British colonial expansion was made possible by the depopulation and dislocation of Native Americans. Epidemic diseases, environmental changes, war, and political pressures on Indians to cede land and to emigrate all combined to make new lands available to white immigrants.

Huron (Wyandotte) Woman *Her cloth dress, glass beads, and iron hoe reflect the influence of French trade on this woman and other Indians of the Great Lakes-Ohio region in the eighteenth century.*

(Mackinac State Historic Park Collections)

Conflict came early to Carolina, where a trade in Indian slaves (see Chapter 3) and imperial war had already produced violence. The **Tuscarora War** (1711–1713) began when Iroquoian-speaking Tuscaroras, provoked by encroaching whites, destroyed New Bern, a nearby settlement of seven hundred Swiss immigrants. Troops from Carolina and Virginia, along with Indian allies, retaliated against the Tuscaroras. By 1713, after about a thousand Tuscaroras (one-fifth of the total population) had been killed or enslaved, the nation surrendered. Most Tuscarora survivors migrated northward to what is now upstate New York and in 1722 became the sixth nation of the Iroquois Confederacy.

After helping defeat the Tuscaroras, Carolina's Indian allies experienced a growing number of abuses, including cheating, violence, and enslavement by English traders and encroachments on their land by settlers. The Yamasees were the most seriously affected. In the **Yamasee War** (1715–1716), they were joined by Catawbas, Creeks, and other disaffected Carolina allies in attacking English trading houses and settlements. Only by enlisting the Cherokee Indians, and allowing four hundred enslaved Africans to bear arms, did Carolina crush the uprising. Yamasees not killed or captured fled to Florida or to Creek towns in the interior.

The defeat of the Yamasees left their Catawba supporters vulnerable to pressures from English on one side and Iroquois on the other. As settlers moved uncomfortably close to some villages, the Catawbas moved inland. Having escaped the settlers, however, the Catawbas faced rising conflict with the Iroquois, who raided them for captives whom they could adopt. To counter the well-armed Iroquois, the Catawbas turned back to Carolina. By ceding land and helping defend Carolina against outside Indians, the Catawbas received guns, food, and clothing. Their relationship with the English allowed the Catawbas to survive and maintain their communities. However, the growing gap in numbers between Catawbas and colonists greatly favored the English in the two peoples' competition for resources.

To the north, the Iroquois Confederacy accommodated English expansion while consolidating its own power among Native Americans. Late in the seventeenth century, the Iroquois and several colonies forged a series of treaties known as the **Covenant Chain**. Under these treaties, the Confederacy helped the colonies subjugate Indians whose lands the English wanted. Under one such agreement, the Iroquois assisted Massachusetts in subjugating that colony's Natives following King Philip's War. Under another, the Susquehannock Indians, after being crushed in Bacon's Rebellion, moved northward from Maryland to a new homeland adjacent to the Iroquois' own. By relocating non-Iroquois on their periphery as well as by inviting the Tuscaroras into their Confederacy, the Iroquois controlled a center of Native American power that was distinct from, but cooperative with, the British. In this way, the Iroquois hoped to deflect English expansion to lands other than their own.

Although not formally belonging to the Covenant Chain, Pennsylvania maintained a similar relationship with the Iroquois. With immigration and commercial success, William Penn's early idealism waned in Pennsylvania, along with his warm ties with the Delaware Indians. Between 1729 and 1734, Penn's sons, now the colony's proprietors, and his former secretary coerced the Delawares into selling more than fifty thousand acres. Then the Penn brothers produced a patently fraudulent "deed," which alleged that the Delawares had agreed in 1686 to sell their land as far westward as a man could walk in a day and a half. After selling much of the land to settlers and speculators in a lottery, the Penns in 1737 hired two men to make the walk. After practicing, the men covered sixty-four miles, meaning that the Delawares, in what became known as the **Walking Purchase,** had to hand over an additional twelve hundred square miles of land and move inland under Iroquois supervision. Settlers began pouring in and, within a generation, the Delawares' former lands were among the most productive in the British Empire.

British Expansion in the South: Georgia

Britain moved to expand southward toward Florida in 1732 when Parliament authorized a new colony, Georgia. Although expecting Georgia to export such expensive commodities as wine and silk, the colony's sponsors intended it as a refuge for bankrupt but honest debtors. A board of trustees was formed to oversee the colony for twenty-one years before turning it over to the crown. During that time, the trustees decreed, Georgia would do without slavery, alcohol, landholdings over five hundred acres, and representative government.

One of the trustees, **James Oglethorpe**, moved to Georgia and dominated it for a decade. Ignoring Spain's claims, Oglethorpe purchased the land for the colony from Creek Indians, with whom he cultivated close ties. Oglethorpe founded the port of Savannah in 1733, and by 1740 twenty-eight hundred colonists had arrived. Almost half the immigrants came from Germany, Switzerland, and Scotland, and most had their overseas passage paid by the government. A small number of Jews were among the early colonists. Along with Pennsylvania, early Georgia was the most inclusive of the British colonies.

Oglethorpe was determined to keep slavery out of Georgia. "They live like cattle," he wrote to the trustees after viewing Charles Town's slave market. "If we allow slaves, we act against the very principles by which we associated together, which was to relieve the distressed." Slavery, he thought, degraded blacks, made whites lazy, and presented the terrible risk of slave revolts, which the Spanish could then exploit. But most of all, he recognized that slavery undermined the economic position of poor whites like those he sought to settle in Georgia.

Oglethorpe's plans failed completely. Few English debtors arrived because Parliament set impossibly stringent conditions for their release from prison. Limitations on settlers' rights to sell or enlarge their holdings, as well as the ban on slavery, also discouraged immigration. Raising exotic export crops proved impractical. Looking to neighboring South Carolina, some Georgians recognized that rice, which required large estates, substantial capital, and many cheap laborers, could flourish in Georgia's lowlands. Under pressure from planters, the trustees lifted limits on the size of landholdings in 1744 and the ban on slavery in 1750. The trustees also authorized a representative assembly in 1750, just two years before turning the colony over to the crown. By 1760, sixty-five hundred whites and thirty-five hundred enslaved blacks were making Georgia profitable.

Spain's Borderlands   While endeavoring to maintain its empire in the face of Native American, French, and British adversaries, Spain spread its language and culture over much of North America. Seeking to recolonize New Mexico after the Pueblo Revolt, Spain awarded grants of approximately twenty-six square miles wherever ten or more families founded a town. As in early New England, settlers built homes on small lots around the church plaza, farmed separate fields nearby, grazed livestock farther away, and shared a community wood lot and pasture.

The livestock-raising ranchos, radiating out for many miles from little clusters of houses, monopolized vast tracts along the Rio Grande and blocked further town settlement. On the ranchos, mounted cattle herders created the way of life later associated with the American cowboy, featuring roping skills, cattle drives, round-ups (rodeos), and livestock branding.

By 1750, New Mexico residents numbered about 14,000, more than half of them Pueblo Indians. Most Pueblos now cooperated with the Spanish, and although many had converted to Catholicism, they also practiced their traditional religion. Like the colonists, the Pueblos were village-dwellers who grew crops and raised livestock, making them equally vulnerable to horse-mounted raiders. Apache raids were now augmented by those of armed and mounted Comanches from the north and east. The raiders sought livestock and European goods as well as captives, often to replace those of their own people who had been seized by Spanish raiders and sent to mine silver in Mexico.

Spain had established Texas to counter growing French influence among the Comanches and other Native Americans on the southern Plains. Colonization began after 1716. Among several outposts, the most prominent center was at San Antonio de Béxar, where two towns, a presidio, and a mission (later known as the Alamo) were

(Florida Museum of Natural History, Fort Mose Exhibition)

Fort Mose *This artist's reconstruction of the free black community at St. Augustine is based on archaeological and documentary evidence.*

clustered. But most Indians in Texas preferred trading with the French to farming, Christianity, and ineffective Spanish protection. Lack of security also deterred immigrants, so that by 1760 only twelve hundred Spaniards inhabited Texas.

Spain's position in Florida was only somewhat less precarious. As early as 1700, thirty-eight hundred English were already in recently founded Carolina, compared to just fifteen hundred Spanish in Florida. This disparity widened thereafter, especially with the founding of Georgia.

Florida found ways to offset its small number of colonists. After the Yamasee War, the Creeks declared their neutrality in conflicts among Europeans. As a result, some Spaniards traded with the Creeks for deerskins, but profits remained limited because Floridians lacked cheap, desirable trade goods.

Florida gained more at English expense through its recruitment of escaped slaves from Carolina. From the time of Carolina's founding, some enslaved Africans had found their way to the Spanish colony. In 1693, Spain's King Charles II ruled that any English-owned slaves arriving in Florida would be freed upon converting to Catholicism. Word of the ruling spread to Carolina, prompting more slaves to flee to Florida. In 1726, Spanish authorities created an all-black militia unit under the command of Francisco Menéndez, a former South Carolina slave, to help defend Florida. In 1738, the colony built a fortified village, Mose, for Menéndez's men and their families adjacent to the capital at St. Augustine.

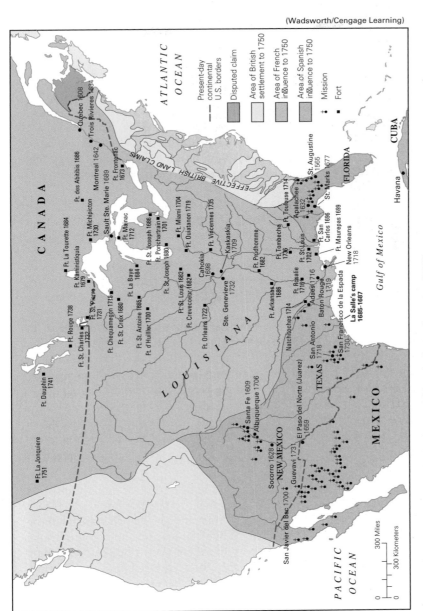

(Wadsworth/Cengage Learning)

MAP 4.2 European Occupation of North America, to 1750

Spanish and French occupation depended on ties with Native Americans. By contrast, British colonists had dispossessed Native peoples and densely settled the eastern seaboard.

By 1750, Spain controlled much of the Southeast and Southwest, while France exercised influence in the Mississippi, Ohio, and Missouri River valleys, as well as around the Great Lakes and in Canada (see Map 4.2). Both empires were spread thin and depended on the support or acquiescence of Native Americans. In contrast, British North America was compact, wealthy, densely populated by whites, and aggressively expansionist.

The Return of War, 1739–1748   After a generation of war ended in 1713, the American colonies enjoyed a generation of peace as well as prosperity. But in 1739, after Spanish authorities cut off the ear of British smuggler Robert Jenkins, Britain declared the "War of Jenkins' Ear." In 1740, James Oglethorpe led a massive British assault on Florida. The English captured Mose but withdrew after Francisco Menéndez's militiamen and other troops recaptured the town. Two years later, Oglethorpe and 650 Georgians repelled 3,000 counterattacking Spanish troops.

The Anglo-Spanish War quickly merged with a larger one in Europe, the War of the Austrian Succession, called **King George's War** in British America (1740–1748). King George's War followed the pattern of earlier imperial conflicts. Few battles involved more than six hundred men, and most were attacks and counterattacks on civilians in the Northeast. Many noncombatants, mostly New Englanders in isolated towns, were killed and others captured. Although prisoners were exchanged at the end of the war, some English women and children elected to remain with their French or Indian captors.

King George's War produced just one major engagement in North America. In 1745, almost four thousand New Englanders besieged and captured the French bastion of Louisbourg, guarding the entrance to the St. Lawrence River. After three more years of inconclusive warfare, Britain signed the Treaty of Aix-la-Chapelle (1748), exchanging Louisbourg for a British outpost in India that the French had seized.

PUBLIC LIFE IN BRITISH AMERICA, 1689–1750

The growing ties between Britain and its colonies included movements of ideas and beliefs as well as of goods and peoples. England's new Bill of Rights was the foundation of government and politics in the colonies. English thinkers initially inspired the intellectual movement known as the Enlightenment, while the English preacher George Whitefield (discussed at the beginning of this chapter) helped transform the practice of Protestantism in British America. While reinforcing the colonies' links with Britain, these developments also led many more colonists than before to participate actively in politics, intellectual discussions, and new religious movements. Taken as a whole, this wider participation signaled the emergence of a broad Anglo-American "public."

Colonial Politics   The most significant political result of the Glorious Revolution was the rise of colonial assemblies as a major political force. Except in Connecticut and Rhode Island, the crown or a proprietor in

England chose each colony's governor. In most colonies, the governor named a council, or upper house of the legislature. The assembly, the legislative lower house, was therefore the only political body whose members were chosen by colonists rather than by English officials. Before 1689, governors and councils took the initiative in drafting laws, and the assemblies followed their lead; but thereafter the assemblies governed more actively.

Anglo-Americans saw their assemblies as comparable to England's House of Commons, which represented the people and defended their liberty against centralized authority, particularly through its exclusive power to originate revenue-raising measures. After Parliament won supremacy over the monarchy through the Bill of Rights, assemblymen insisted that their governors' powers were similarly limited.

The lower houses asserted their prestige and authority by refusing to permit outside meddling in their proceedings, by taking firm control over taxes and budgets, and especially by keeping a tight rein on executive salaries. Although governors had considerable powers (including the right to veto acts, call and dismiss assembly sessions, and schedule elections), they were vulnerable to legislatures' pressure because their income came solely from the assemblies. Using this "power of the purse," assemblies could sometimes force governors to sign laws opposed by the crown.

British policy reinforced the assemblies' growing importance. The Board of Trade, established in 1696 to monitor American developments, could have persuaded the crown to disallow objectionable laws signed by governors. But it rarely exercised this power before midcentury. The resulting political vacuum enabled the colonies to become self-governing in most respects except for trade regulation, restrictions on printing money, and declaring war. Representative government in the colonies originated and was nurtured within the protective environment of the British Empire.

The elite landowners, merchants, and attorneys who monopolized colonial wealth also dominated politics. Most assemblymen ranked among the wealthiest 2 percent of colonists. To placate them, governors invariably appointed other members of the gentry to their councils and to judgeships. Outside New England (where any voter was eligible for office), legal requirements barred 80 percent of white men from running for the assembly, most often by specifying that a candidate own a minimum of a thousand acres. (Farms then averaged 180 acres in the South and 120 acres in the middle colonies.) Even without property qualifications, few ordinary colonists could have afforded to hold elective office. Assemblymen received only living expenses, which might not fully cover the cost of staying at their province's capital, much less compensate a farmer for his absence from home for six to ten weeks a year. As a result, a few wealthy families in each colony dominated the highest political offices. Nine families, for example, provided one-third of Virginia's councilors after 1680. John Adams, a rising young Massachusetts politician, estimated that most towns in his colony chose their representatives from among just three or four families.

By eighteenth-century standards, Anglo-American voting qualifications were liberal, but all provinces barred women and nonwhites from voting. In seven colonies, male voters had to own a minimal amount of land. About 40 percent of free white men—mostly indentured servants and young men—could not meet these requirements. Still, most white males in British North America could vote by age forty, whereas two-thirds of all men in England and nine-tenths in Ireland were never eligible.

In rural areas, voter participation averaged about 45 percent. Most governors called elections when they saw fit, so that elections might lapse for years and suddenly take place on very short notice. Thus voters in isolated areas often had no knowledge of upcoming contests. That polling took place at the county seat discouraged many electors from traveling long distances over poor roads to vote. In several colonies, voters stated their choices orally and publicly, often with the candidates present. This procedure inhibited humbler men from participating or choosing freely if their views differed from those of elites, especially elites they depended on for credit, shipping privileges, or other favors. Finally, most rural elections before 1750 were uncontested. Local elites decided in advance who would "stand" for office. They regarded officeholding as a gentleman's public duty and considered it demeaning to show interest in being chosen, much less to compete or "run" for a position.

Given all these factors, many rural voters were indifferent about politics at the colony level. For example, to avoid paying legislators' expenses at the capital, many smaller Massachusetts towns refused to elect assemblymen. Thirty percent of men elected to South Carolina's assembly neglected to take their seats from 1731 to 1760, twice including a majority of those chosen.

Despite these limitations, rural elections slowly emerged as community events in which many non-elite white men participated. In time, rural voters would follow urban colonists and express themselves more forcefully.

Competitive politics first developed in the northern seaports. Depending on their economic interests and family ties, wealthy colonists aligned themselves with or against royal and proprietary governors. To gain advantage over rivals, some factions courted artisans and shopkeepers whose fortunes had stagnated or declined as the distribution of urban wealth increasingly favored the rich. In courting non-elite voters, they scandalized rival elites who feared that unleashing popular passions could disturb the social order.

New York was the site of the bitterest factional conflicts. In one episode, Governor William Cosby's supporters in 1734 engineered the arrest of newspaper printer John Peter Zenger. The charge was that in printing accusations of corruption against the governor, he had seditiously libeled Cosby. Following a celebrated trial in August 1735, Zenger was acquitted.

Although it neither led to a change in New York's libel law nor greatly enhanced freedom of the press at the time, the Zenger verdict was significant for several reasons. Zenger's brilliant attorney, Andrew Hamilton, effectively employed the growing practice among colonial attorneys of speaking directly to a jury on behalf of a defendant. He persuaded the jury that it alone, without the judges advice, could reject a charge of libel "if you should be of the opinion that there is no falsehood in [Zenger's] papers." Until then, a statement's truth was not, by itself, a sufficient defense against a charge of libel in British and colonial courts of law. Beyond its legal implications, the Zenger trial empowered non-elites as voters, readers, and jurors, and in New York and elsewhere it encouraged broader political discussion and participation beyond a small circle of elites.

The Enlightenment

If property and wealth were keys to political participation and officeholding, literacy and education permitted Anglo-Americans to participate in the transatlantic world of ideas and beliefs. Perhaps 90 percent of New England's adult white men and 40 percent of white women could write well enough to sign documents, thanks to the regions system of primary education. Among white male colonists elsewhere, the literacy rate varied from about 35 percent to more than 50 percent. (In England, by contrast, no more than one-third of all men could read and write.) How regularly most of these people read a book or wrote a letter was another matter.

The best-educated colonists—members of the gentry, well-to-do merchants, educated ministers, and growing numbers of artisans and farmers—embraced a wider world of ideas and information. Though costly, books, newspapers, and writing paper brought the excitement of eighteenth-century European civilization to reading men and women. Scientific advances seemed to explain the laws of nature; human intelligence appeared poised to triumph over ignorance, prejudice, superstition, and irrational tradition. For those who had the time to read and to ponder ideas, an age of optimism and boundless progress was dawning, an age known as the Enlightenment.

Enlightenment ideals combined confidence in human reason with skepticism toward beliefs not founded on science or strict logic. A major source of Enlightenment thought was English physicist Sir Isaac Newton (1642–1727), who in 1687 explained how gravitation ruled the universe. Newton's work appealed to educated Europeans by demonstrating the harmony of natural laws and stimulated others to search for rational principles in medicine, law, psychology, and government.

Before 1750, no American more fully embodied the Enlightenment spirit than **Benjamin Franklin**. Born in Boston in 1706, Franklin migrated to Philadelphia at age seventeen. He brought skill as a printer, considerable ambition, and insatiable intellectual curiosity. In moving to Philadelphia, Franklin put himself in the right place at the right time, for the city was growing much more rapidly than Boston and was attracting merchants and artisans who shared Franklin's zest for learning and new ideas. Franklin organized some of these men into a reading-discussion group called the Junto, and they helped him secure printing contracts. In 1732, he first published *Poor Richard's Almanack,* a collection of maxims and proverbs that made him famous. By age forty-two, Franklin had earned enough money to retire and devote himself to science and public service.

These dual goals—science and public benefit—were intimately related in Franklin's mind, for he believed that all true science would be useful in making everyone's life more comfortable. For example, experimenting with a kite, Franklin demonstrated in 1752 that lightning was electricity, a discovery that led to the lightning rod.

Although some southern planters, such as Thomas Jefferson, later championed progress through science, the Enlightenment's earliest and primary American centers were cities, where the latest European books and ideas circulated and where gentlemen and self-improving artisans met to discuss ideas and conduct experiments. Franklin organized one such group, the American Philosophical Society, in 1743 to encourage "all philosophical experiments that let light into the nature of things, tend to increase the power of man over matter, and multiply the conveniences and pleasures of life." By 1769, this society had blossomed into an intercolonial network of amateur scientists. The societies emulated, and corresponded with, the Royal Society in London, the foremost learned society in the English-speaking world. In this respect, the Enlightenment strengthened the ties between colonial and British elites.

Benjamin Franklin
This earliest known portrait of Franklin dates to about 1740, when he was a rising leader in bustling Philadelphia.

Just as Newton inspired the scientific bent of Enlightenment intellectuals, English philosopher John Locke, in his *Essay Concerning Human Understanding* (1690), led many to embrace "reasonable" or "rational" religion. Locke contended that ideas, including religion, are not inborn but are acquired by toilsome investigation of and reflection upon experience. To most Enlightenment intellectuals, the best argument for the existence of God was the harmony and order of nature, which pointed to a rational Creator. Some individuals, including Franklin and, later, Jefferson and Thomas Paine, carried this argument a step farther by insisting that where the Bible conflicted with reason, one should follow the dictates of reason. Called Deists, they concluded that God, having created a perfect universe, did not thereafter intervene in its workings but rather left it alone to operate according to natural laws.

Most colonists influenced by the Enlightenment described themselves as Christians and attended church. But they feared those Christians who persecuted others in religion's name or who emphasized emotion rather than reason in the practice of piety. Above all, they distrusted zealots and sectarians. Typically, Franklin contributed money to most of the churches in Philadelphia because they encouraged virtue and morality, but he deplored theological hair-splitting.

In 1750, the Enlightenment's greatest contributions to American life still lay in the future. A quarter-century later, Anglo-Americans drew on the Enlightenment's revolutionary ideas as they declared their independence from Britain and created the foundations of a new nation (discussed in Chapters 5 and 6). Meanwhile, a series of religious revivals known as the Great Awakening challenged the Enlightenment's most basic assumptions.

The Great Awakening	Viewing the world as orderly and predictable, rationalists often expressed smug self-satisfaction. Writing his will in 1750, Franklin thanked God for giving him "such a mind,

with moderate passions" and "such a competency of this world's goods as might make a reasonable mind easy." But many Americans lacked such a comfortable competency of goods and lived neither orderly nor predictable lives. Earlier generations of young people coming of age had relied on established authority figures—parents, local leaders, clergy—for wisdom and guidance as they faced the future. But the world had changed by the middle decades of the eighteenth century. Older authorities were of little help when one's economic future was uncertain, when established elites seemed to act out of self-interest, or when one encountered more strangers than familiar faces on a daily basis. The result was a widespread spiritual hunger among ordinary people that neither traditional religion nor Enlightenment philosophy could satisfy.

In 1739, an outpouring of European Protestant revivalism spread to British North America. This "Great Awakening" cut across lines of class, gender, and even race. Above all, the revivals represented an unleashing of anxiety and longing among ordinary people—anxiety about sin, and longing for assurances of salvation. The answers they received were conveyed through the powerful preaching of ministers who appealed to their audiences' emotions rather than to their intellects.

In contrast to rationalists, who stressed the potential for human improvement, revivalist ministers aroused their audiences by depicting the sinfulness of human beings and the need for immediate repentance. Although well read in Enlightenment philosophy and science, the Congregationalist Jonathan Edwards, who led a revival at Northampton, Massachusetts, in 1735, drove home this message with breathtaking clarity. "The God that holds you over the pit of Hell, much as one holds a spider or other loathsome insect over the fire, abhors you," Edwards intoned in a famous sermon, "Sinners in the Hands of an Angry God." "His wrath toward you burns like fire; He looks upon you as worthy of nothing else but to be cast into the fire."

The work of Edwards and other local revivalists was brought together with the arrival from Britain in 1739 of **George Whitefield**. So overpowering was Whitefield that some joked he could make crowds swoon simply by uttering "Mesopotamia." In an age without microphones, crowds exceeding twenty thousand could hear his booming voice clearly, and many wept at his eloquence.

Whitefield's American tour inspired thousands to seek salvation. Most converts were young adults in their late twenties. In Connecticut alone, church membership jumped from 630 in 1740 to 3,217 after Whitefield toured in 1741. Whitefield's allure was so mighty that he even awed potential critics. Hearing him preach in Philadelphia, Benjamin Franklin first vowed to contribute nothing to the collection. But so admirably did Whitefield conclude his sermon, Franklin recalled, "that I empty'd my Pocket wholly into the Collector's Dish, Gold and all."

Divisions over the revivals quickly developed and were often exacerbated by social and economic tensions. For example, after leaving Boston in October 1740, Whitefield invited another preacher, Gilbert Tennent, to follow "in order to blow up the divine flame lately kindled there." Denouncing Boston's established clergymen as "dead Drones" and lashing out at aristocratic fashion, Tennent built a following among the city's poor and downtrodden. Another preacher, James Davenport, spoke daily on the Boston Commons and then led processions of "idle or ignorant persons, and those of the lowest Rank" through the streets. Brought before a grand jury, Davenport was expelled for asserting "that Boston's ministers were leading the people blindfolded to hell."

As Whitefield's exchange with Alexander Garden showed, the lines hardened between the revivalists, known as New Lights, and the rationalist clergy, or Old Lights, who dominated the Anglican, Presbyterian, and Congregational churches. Writing in 1740, Tennent hinted that most Presbyterian ministers lacked saving grace and urged parishioners to abandon them for the New Lights. By sowing seeds of doubt about individual ministers, Tennent undermined one of the foundations of social order. For if the people could not trust their own ministers, whom would they trust?

Old Light rationalists fired back. Charles Chauncy, Boston's leading Congregationalist minister, condemned the revival as an epidemic of the "enthusiasm" that enlightened intellectuals loathed. He even provided a kind of checklist for spotting enthusiasts: "a certain wildness" in their eyes, the "quakings and tremblings" of their limbs, and foaming at the mouth. Put simply, the revival had unleashed "a sort of madness" that overheated imaginations mistook for the experience of divine grace.

The Great Awakening opened unprecedented splits in American Protestantism. In 1741, New and Old Light Presbyterians formed rival branches that did not reunite until 1758, when the revivalists emerged victorious. The Anglicans lost many members to New Light congregations, especially Baptist and New Light Presbyterian. Congregationalists splintered so badly that by 1760, New Lights had seceded from one-third of New England's churches and formed New Light congregations or joined the Baptists.

The secession of New Lights was especially bitter in Massachusetts and Connecticut, where the Congregational church was established by law. Old Lights denied new churches legal status, meaning that New Lights' taxes would go to their former churches. Connecticut passed repressive laws forbidding revivalists to preach or perform marriages, and the colony expelled New Lights from the legislature.

Although New Lights made steady gains until the 1770s, the Great Awakening peaked in New England in 1742. The revival then crested everywhere but in Virginia, where its high point came after 1755 with an upsurge of conversions by Baptists, who also suffered legal harassment. For all the commotion it raised at the time, the Great Awakening's long-term effects exceeded its immediate impact. First, the revival marked a decline in the influence of Quakers, Anglicans, and Congregationalists. In undermining Anglicans and Congregationalists, the Great Awakening contributed to the weakening of officially established denominations. As these churches' importance waned after 1740, the number of Presbyterians and Baptists increased.

The Great Awakening also stimulated the founding of new colleges as both Old and New Lights sought institutions free of one another's influence. In 1746, New Light Presbyterians established the College of New Jersey (Princeton). Then followed King's College (Columbia) for Anglicans in 1754, the College of Rhode

Island (Brown) for Baptists in 1764, and Queen's College (Rutgers) for Dutch Reformed in 1766.

The revivals were also significant because they spread beyond the ranks of white society. The emphasis on piety over intellectual learning as the key to God's grace led some to reach out to Africans and Native Americans. The Great Awakening marked the beginnings of black Protestantism after some slaves and free blacks joined white churches and even preached at revival meetings. New Light Christianity also attracted Native Americans residing within the colonies. A few Christian Indians trained in a special school to become missionaries to other Native Americans, and one, Samson Occom, a Mohegan born in Connecticut, became widely known among whites. Despite these breakthroughs, blacks and Indians still faced considerable religious discrimination, even among New Lights.

The Great Awakening also added to white women's religious prominence. Some New Light churches, mostly Baptist and Congregationalist, granted women the right to speak and vote in church meetings. Like Anne Hutchinson in Puritan New England, some women moved from leading women's prayer and discussion groups to presiding over meetings that included men. One such woman, Sarah Osborn of Newport, Rhode Island, conducted "private praying Societies Male and female" that included black slaves in her home. In 1770, Osborn and her followers won a bitter fight over their congregation's choice of a new minister. While most assertive women were prevented from exercising as much power as Osborn, none was persecuted as Hutchinson had been.

Finally, the revivals blurred denominational differences among Protestants. Although George Whitefield was an Anglican who defied his superior, Garden, and later helped found Methodism, he preached with Presbyterians such as Tennent and Congregationalists like Edwards. By emphasizing the need for salvation over details of doctrine and church governance, revivalism emphasized Protestants' common experiences and promoted the coexistence of denominations.

Historians have disagreed over whether the Great Awakening had political as well as religious effects. Although Tennent and Davenport called the poor "God's people" and flayed the wealthy, they never advocated revolution, and the Awakening did not produce a distinct political ideology. Yet by empowering ordinary people to act publicly on beliefs that countered those in authority, the revivals laid some of the groundwork for political revolutionaries a generation later.

CHRONOLOGY
1660–1750

1651–1663	England enacts first three Navigation Acts.
1660	Restoration of the English monarchy.
1686–1689	Dominion of New England.
1688–1689	Glorious Revolution in England.
1689	English Bill of Rights.
1689–1691	Uprisings in Massachusetts, New York, and Maryland.
1689–1697	King William's War (in Europe, War of the League of Augsburg).

1690	John Locke, *Essay Concerning Human Understanding.*
1693	Spain offers freedom to English-owned slaves escaping to Florida.
1701	Iroquois Grand Settlement with England and France.
1702–1713	Queen Anne's War (in Europe, War of the Spanish Succession).
1711–1713	Tuscarora War in Carolina.
1715–1716	Yamasee War in Carolina.
1716	San Antonio de Béxar founded.
1718	New Orleans founded.
1733	Georgia founded. Molasses Act.
1735	John Peter Zenger acquitted of seditious libel in New York. Jonathan Edwards leads revival in Northampton, Massachusetts.
1737	Walking Purchase of Delaware Indian lands in Pennsylvania.
1739	Great Awakening begins with George Whitefield's arrival in British colonies. Stono Rebellion in South Carolina.
1740–1748	King George's War (in Europe, the War of the Austrian Succession).
1743	Benjamin Franklin founds American Philosophical Society.
1750	Slavery legalized in Georgia.

CONCLUSION

By 1750, Britain's mainland colonies barely resembled those of a century earlier. Mercantilist policies bound an expanded number of colonies to the rising prosperity of the British Empire. A healthy environment for whites, along with encroachments on Native Americans' land, enabled the combined white and black population to grow by more than twenty times—from about fifty thousand to over one million. The political settlement that followed England's Glorious Revolution further bound the colonies to the empire and—at the same time—provided the foundation for representative government in the colonies. Educated Anglo-Americans joined the European intellectual ferment known as the Enlightenment. The Great Awakening, with its European origins and its intercolonial appeal, further signaled the colonies' emergence from provincial isolation. All these developments made British Americans more conscious of their ties to other colonies, to Great Britain, and to the broader Atlantic world.

The achievements of France and Spain on the North American mainland contrasted starkly with those of Britain. More lightly populated by Europeans, their colonies were more dependent on Native Americans for their survival. Despite their mercantilist orientations, neither France nor Spain profited significantly by colonizing mainland North America.

For all of its evident wealth and progress, British America was rife with tensions. In some areas, vast discrepancies in the distribution of wealth and opportunities fostered a rebellious spirit among whites who were less well off. The Enlightenment and the Great Awakening revealed deep-seated religious and ideological divisions. Slave resistance and Anglo-Indian warfare demonstrated the depths of racial antagonisms. The revived imperial warfare of 1739–1748 signaled that the peace that had nurtured prosperity was over and that an Anglo-French showdown was imminent. Buried even deeper were tensions between Britain and its colonies that would only come to the surface after that showdown had concluded.

5

ROADS TO REVOLUTION, 1750–1776

TRIUMPH AND TENSIONS: THE BRITISH EMPIRE, 1750–1763

King George's War ended in 1748 with Britain and France still intent on defeating one another. After a "diplomatic revolution" in which Austria shifted its allegiance from Britain to France, and Britain aligned with Prussia, the Seven Years' War began. This global conflict pitted British and French forces against one another in every continent except Australia. The war resulted in the expulsion of France from mainland North America, leaving the region to a triumphant Britain. Yet even as war wound down, tensions developed within the victorious coalition of Britons, colonists, and Native Americans.

A Fragile Peace, 1750–1754 The tinderbox for Anglo-French conflict in North America was the Ohio valley, claimed by Virginia, Pennsylvania, France, and the Six Nations Iroquois, as well as by the Native Americans who actually lived there.

Traders from Virginia and Pennsylvania were strengthening British influence among Indians in the Ohio valley. Seeking to drive out the traders, the French began building a chain of forts there in 1753. Virginia retaliated by sending troops under a twenty-one-year-old surveyor and speculator, **George Washington**, to persuade or force the French to leave. Fearing that Virginia had designs on their land, Native Americans refused to support Washington, and in 1754 French troops drove the Virginians back to their homes.

While Washington was in Ohio, British officials called a meeting in mid-1754 of delegates from Virginia and colonies to the north to negotiate a treaty with the Six Nations Iroquois. Iroquois support would be vital in any effort to drive the French from the Ohio valley. Seven colonies (but neither Virginia nor New Jersey) sent delegates to the Albany Congress in Albany, New York. Long allied with Britain in the Covenant Chain, the Iroquois were also bound by the Grand Settlement of 1701 to remain neutral in any Anglo-French war. Moreover, the easternmost Mohawk Iroquois were angry because New York settlers were encroaching on their land. Although the delegates obtained expressions of friendship from the Six Nations, Iroquois suspicions of Britain persisted.

The delegates also endorsed a proposal for a colonial confederation, the Albany Plan of Union, largely based on the ideas of Pennsylvania's Benjamin Franklin and Massachusetts's Thomas Hutchinson. The plan called for a Grand Council representing, and funded by, all the colonial assemblies. A crown-appointed executive officer would head the council, which would coordinate military defense and Indian affairs. Although later regarded as a precedent for American unity, the Albany Plan in fact came to nothing because no colonial legislature approved it.

Chief Hendrick (Theyanoguin) of the Mohawk Iroquois

A longtime (but often critical) ally of the British, Hendrick led the Mohawk delegation to the Albany Congress.

(Courtesy of the John Carter Brown Library at Brown University)

The Seven Years' War in America, 1754–1760

Although France and Britain remained at peace in Europe until 1756, Washington's 1754 clash with French troops began the war in North America. In response, the British dispatched General Edward Braddock and a thousand regular troops to North America to seize Fort Duquesne at the headwaters of the Ohio.

Scornful of colonial soldiers and friendly Indians, Braddock expected his disciplined redcoats to make short work of the enemy. On July 9, 1755, about 600 Native Americans and 250 French and Canadians ambushed Braddock's force of 2,200 Britons and Virginians nine miles east of Fort Duquesne. Riddled by three hours of steady fire from an unseen foe, Braddock's troops retreated. Nine hundred British and provincial soldiers, including Braddock, died, compared to just twenty-three French and Indians.

As British colonists absorbed the shock of Braddock's disastrous loss, French-armed Shawnees, Delawares, and Mingos from the upper Ohio valley struck hard at encroaching settlers in western Pennsylvania, Maryland, and Virginia. For three years, these attacks halted English expansion and prevented the three colonies from joining the British war against France.

Confronted by the numerically superior but disorganized Anglo-Americans, the French and their Native American allies—now including the Iroquois—captured Fort Oswego on Lake Ontario in 1756 and Fort William Henry on Lake George in 1757. The French now threatened central New York and western New England (see Map 5.1). In Europe, too, the war began badly for Britain, which by 1757 seemed to be facing defeat on all fronts.

In this dark hour, two developments turned the tide for Britain. First, the Iroquois and most Ohio Indians, angered at French treatment of them and sensing that the French were gaining too decisive an advantage, agreed at a treaty conference at Easton, Pennsylvania, in 1758 to abandon the French. Their subsequent withdrawal from Fort Duquesne enabled the British to capture it and other French forts. Many Native Americans withdrew from the fighting, while others actively joined Britain's cause.

The second decisive development occurred when William Pitt took control of military affairs in the British cabinet and reversed the downward course. Pitt saw himself as the man of the hour. "I know," he declared, "that I can save this country and that no one else can." True to his word, Pitt reinvigorated British patriotism throughout the empire. By the war's end, he was the colonists' most popular hero, the symbol of what Americans and the English could accomplish when united.

Needing British troops in Europe to face France and its allies (which included Spain after 1761), Pitt sought instead to use colonial soldiers on the North American front. He promised the colonies that if they raised the necessary men, Parliament would bear most of the cost of fighting the war. Pitt's offer generated unprecedented Anglo-American support. The colonies provided more than forty thousand troops in 1758–1759, far more soldiers than the crown sent to North America during the entire war.

The impact of Pitt's decision was immediate. Anglo-American troops under General Jeffery Amherst captured Fort Duquesne and Louisbourg in 1758 and drove the French from northern New York the next year. In September 1759, Quebec fell after General James Wolfe defeated the French commander-in-chief, Louis Joseph

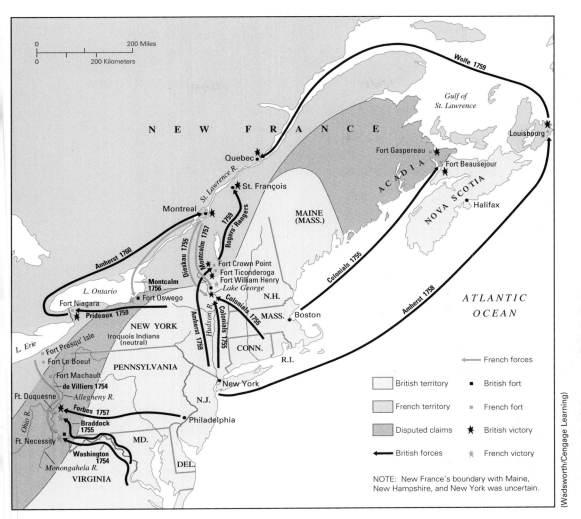

MAP 5.1 The Seven Years' War in North America, 1754–1760

After experiencing major defeats early in the war, Anglo-American forces turned the tide against the French in 1758 by taking Fort Duquesne and Louisbourg. After Canada fell in 1760, the fighting shifted to Spain's Caribbean colonies.

Montcalm, on the Plains of Abraham, where both commanders died in battle. French resistance ended in 1760 when Montreal surrendered.

The End of French North America, 1760–1763

Although the fall of Montreal dashed French hopes of victory in North America, the war continued in Europe and elsewhere. Finally, with defeat inevitable, France in 1762 began negotiating with its enemies. The Seven Years' War officially ended with the signing of the Treaty of Paris in 1763.

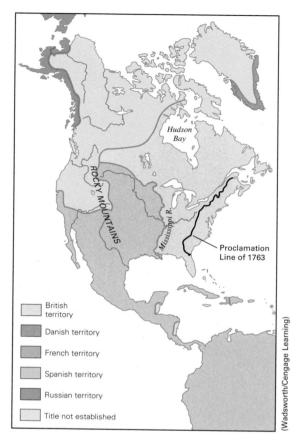

MAP 5.2 European Territorial Claims, 1763

The treaties of San Ildefonso (1762) and Paris (1763) divided France's North American empire between Britain and Spain. Britain in 1763 established direct imperial authority west of the Proclamation Line.

Under terms of the treaty, France gave up all its lands and claims east of the Mississippi (except New Orleans) to Britain. In return for Cuba, seized by the British in 1762, Spain ceded Florida to Britain. Neither France nor Britain wanted the other to control Louisiana, so in the Treaty of San Ildefonso (1762), France ceded the vast territory to Spain. Thus, France's once mighty North American empire was reduced to a few tiny fishing islands off Newfoundland and several prosperous sugar islands in the West Indies. Britain reigned supreme in eastern North America while Spain now claimed the west below Canada (see Map 5.2).

Several thousand French colonists in an area stretching from Quebec to Illinois to Louisiana were suddenly British and Spanish subjects. The most adversely affected Franco-Americans were the Acadians, who had been nominal British subjects since England took over Acadia in 1713 and renamed it Nova Scotia. In 1755, Nova Scotia's government ordered all Acadians to swear loyalty to Britain and not

George III, Studio of A. Ramsay ca. 1767

Although unsure of himself and emotionally little more than a boy upon his accession to the English throne, George III possessed a deep moral sense and a fierce determination to rule as well as to reign.

(Allan Ramsay, Portrait of George III, oil on canvas, 97x63 inches. IMS33.21b Indianapolis Museum of Art, The James E. Roberts Fund)

to bear arms for France. After most refused to take the oath, British soldiers drove them from their homes. About 7,000 of the 18,000 Acadians were forcibly dispersed among Britain's other colonies, while others were sent to France or French colonies. Facing poverty and intense anti-French, anti-Catholic prejudice in the British colonies and seeking to remain together, a majority of the exiles and refugees eventually moved to Louisiana, where their descendants became known as Cajuns.

King George's War and the Seven Years' War produced ironically mixed effects. On one hand, they fused the bonds between the British and the Anglo-Americans. Fighting side by side against the French Catholic enemy, Britons and colonists had further strengthened their common identity. On the other hand, each war also planted seeds of mutual misunderstanding and suspicion.

Anglo-American Friction   During the Seven Years' War, British officers regularly complained about colonial troops, not only their inability to fight but also their tendency to return home—even in the midst of campaigns—when their terms were up or when they were not paid on time. For their part, colonial soldiers complained of British officers who, as one put it, treated their troops "but little better than slaves."

Tensions between British officers and colonial civilians also flared. Officers complained about colonists being unwilling to provide food and shelter while

Anglo-Americans resented the officers' arrogant manners. One general groused that South Carolinians were "extremely pleased to have Soldiers to protect their Plantations but will feel no inconveniences for them." Quakers in the Pennsylvania assembly, acting from pacifist convictions, refused to vote funds to support the war effort, while assemblies in New York and Massachusetts opposed the quartering of British troops on their soil as an encroachment on English liberties. English authorities regarded such actions as affronts to the crown and as undermining Britain's efforts to defend its territories.

Pitt's promise to reimburse the colonial assemblies for their military expenses angered many in Britain, who concluded that the colonists were escaping scot-free from the war's financial burden. Colonists had profited enormously from the war, as military contracts and spending by British troops brought an influx of British currency into the hands of farmers, artisans, and merchants. Some merchants had even traded with the French enemy during wartime. Meanwhile, Britain's national debt nearly doubled during the war, from £72 million to over £132 million. Whereas in 1763 the total debt of all thirteen colonies amounted to £2 million, the interest charges alone on the British debt came to more than £4 million a year. This debt was assumed by British landowners through a land tax and, increasingly, by ordinary consumers through excise duties on such everyday items as beer, tea, salt, and bread.

Colonists felt equally burdened. Those who profited during the war spent their additional income on British imports, the annual value of which doubled during the war. Thus, the war accelerated the Anglo-American "consumer revolution" in which colonists' purchases of British goods fueled Britain's economy, particularly its manufacturing sector. But when peace returned in 1760, the wartime boom in the colonies ended as abruptly as it had begun. To maintain their lifestyles, many colonists went into debt. British creditors obliged their American merchant customers by extending the usual period for remitting payments from six months to a year. Nevertheless, many recently prosperous colonists suddenly found themselves overloaded with debts and, in some cases, bankrupt. As colonial indebtedness to Britain grew, some Americans began to accuse the British of deliberately plotting to "enslave" the colonies.

The ascension to the British throne of King **George III** (ruled 1760–1820) at age twenty-two reinforced Anglo-American tensions. The new king was determined to have a strong influence on government policy, but neither his experience, his temperament, nor his philosophy suited him to the formidable task of building political coalitions and pursuing consistent policies. Until 1774, George III made frequent abrupt changes in government leadership that destabilized politics in Britain and exacerbated relations with the colonies.

Frontier Tensions   Victory over the French spurred new Anglo-Indian conflicts that drove the British debt even higher. With the French gone, Ohio and Great Lakes Indians recognized that they could no longer play the two imperial rivals off against each other. Their fears that the British would treat them as subjects rather than as allies were confirmed when General Jeffery Amherst, Britain's commander in North America, ordered troops occupying former French posts not to distribute food, ammunition (needed for hunting), and other gifts as the French had done. Moreover, squatters from the colonies were moving onto Indian lands and harassing the occupants, and Native Americans feared that the British occupation was intended to support these incursions.

As tensions mounted, a Delaware Indian religious prophet named Neolin reported a vision in which the "Master of Life," or Great Spirit, instructed him to urge Native Americans of all tribes to unify and to take back their land and live on it as they had before Europeans—particularly the British—arrived (see Going to the Source). Drawing on Neolin's message and inspired by Pontiac, an Ottawa, Indians throughout the Ohio-Great Lakes region, unleashed **Pontiac's War**. During the spring and summer of 1763, they sacked eight British forts and besieged four others. But over the next six months, shortages of food and ammunition, a smallpox epidemic at Fort Pitt (triggered when British officers deliberately distributed infected blankets at a peace parley), and a recognition that the French would not return led the Indians to make peace with Britain.

Although not a military victory, Pontiac's War gained some political concessions for Native Americans. Hoping to conciliate the Indians and end the fighting, George III issued the **Proclamation of 1763**, asserting direct British control of land transactions, settlement, trade, and other activities of non-Indians west of a Proclamation Line along the Appalachian crest (see Map 5.2). The government sought to control Anglo-American expansion by asserting its authority over the various (and often competing) colonies claiming western lands. The proclamation recognized existing Indian land titles everywhere west of the "proclamation line" until such time as tribal governments agreed to cede their land to Britain through treaties. Although calming Indian fears, the proclamation angered the colonies by subordinating their western claims to imperial authority and by slowing expansion.

The uprising was also a factor in the British government's decision to leave ten thousand soldiers in France's former forts on the Great Lakes and in the Ohio valley to enforce the Proclamation of 1763. The cost of maintaining this military presence would reach almost a half million pounds a year, fully 6 percent of Britain's peacetime budget. Britons considered it perfectly reasonable for the colonists to help underwrite this expense. Although the troops would help offset the colonies' unfavorable balance of payments with Britain, many Anglo-Americans regarded them as a peacetime "standing army" that threatened their liberty and blocked their expansion onto Indian lands.

IMPERIAL AUTHORITY, COLONIAL OPPOSITION, 1760–1766

After the Seven Years' War, Anglo-American tensions centered on Britain's efforts to finance its suddenly enlarged empire through a series of revenue measures and to enforce these and other measures directly rather than relying on local authorities. Following passage of the Stamp Act, opposition movements arose in the mainland colonies to protest not only the new measures' costs but also what many people considered a dangerous extension of Parliament's power. Opponents came from all segments of colonial society, including poor and working people. The crisis revealed a widening gulf between British and colonial perceptions of the proper relationship between the empire and its colonies.

GOING TO THE SOURCE

Pontiac Recounts a Prophet's Vision

Pontiac was an *ogema* (civil leader) of the Ottawa people. Like many eastern Indians, he distrusted British intentions after the Seven Years War. Speaking to an intertribal audience in spring 1763, Pontiac recounted the vision of the Delaware religious prophet, Neolin. In the following excerpt from that speech (recorded by a French colonist), Pontiac repeats the words spoken to Neolin by the Master of Life. Note how the Master of Life accounts for the absence of wild animals, which others might attribute to commercial overhunting and the environmental effects of European settlement.

I am the Master of Life, whom you desire to know and to whom you would speak. Listen well to what I am going to say to you and all the red brethren. I am He who made heaven and earth, the trees, lakes, rivers, all men, and all that you see, and all that you have seen on earth. Because of this and because I love you, you must do what I say and leave what I hate. I do not like it that you drink until you lose your reason, as you do; or that you fight with each other; or that you take two wives, or run after the wives of others;... I hate that. You must have but one wife, and keep her until death. When you are going to war, you [must] ... join the medicine dance, and believe that I am speaking.... It is ... Manitou to whom you [should] speak. It is a bad spirit who whispers to you nothing but evil, and to whom you listen because you do not know me well. This land, where you live, I have made for you and not for others. How comes it that you suffer the whites on

Writs of Assistance, 1760–1761

Even before the Seven Years' War ended, British authorities attempted to halt American merchants' trade with the French enemy in the West Indies. In 1760, the royal governor of Massachusetts authorized revenue officers to employ a search warrant called a writ of assistance to seize illegally imported goods. The writ permitted customs officials to enter any ship or building (including a merchant's residence) where smuggled goods might be hidden. Because the document required no evidence of probable cause for suspicion, many critics considered it unconstitutional.

Writs of assistance proved effective against smuggling. In quick reaction, some Boston merchants hired lawyer James Otis to challenge the constitutionality of the writs. Before the Massachusetts Supreme Court in 1761, Otis argued that "an act against the Constitution is void"—even one passed by Parliament. But the court, influenced by Chief Justice Thomas Hutchinson, who noted the use of identical writs in England, ruled against the merchants.

Despite losing the case, Otis expressed the fundamental conception of many, both in Britain and in the colonies, of Parliament's role under the British constitution. The British constitution was not a written document but instead a collection of customs and accepted principles that guaranteed certain rights to all citizens. Most British politicians assumed that Parliament's laws were themselves part of the constitution and hence that Parliament could alter the constitution at will. But your lands? Can't you do without them? I know that those whom you call the children of your Great Father supply your wants, but if you were not bad, as you are, you would well do without them. You might live wholly as you did before you knew them. Before those whom you call your brothers came on your lands, did you not live by bow and arrow? You had no need of gun nor powder, nor the rest of their things, and nevertheless you caught animals to live and clothe yourselves with their skins, but when I saw that you went to the bad, I called back the animals into the depths of the woods, so that you had need of your brothers to have your wants supplied and cover you. You have only to become good and do what I want, and I shall send back to you the animals to live on. I do not forbid you, for all that, to suffer among you the children of your father [whites who live peaceably among the Indians]. I love

them, they know me and pray to me, and I give them their necessities and all that they bring to you, but as regards those [whites] who have come to trouble your country, drive them out, make war on them! I love them not, they know me not, they are my enemies and the enemies of your brothers! Send them back to the country which I made for them! There let them remain.

Questions

1. *Why, according to the Master of Life, are Native Americans suffering?*
2. *What does the Master of Life say Indians must do so that the animals will return?*

Go to www.cengagebrain.com for additional primary sources on this period.

Source: Michigan Pioneer and Historical Collections (1886) 8: 270–71.

Otis contended that Parliament possessed no authority to violate the "rights of Englishmen," and he asserted that there were limits "beyond which if Parliaments go, their Acts bind not." Such challenges to parliamentary authority would be renewed once peace was restored.

The Sugar Act, 1764

In 1764, three years after Otis challenged the writs of assistance, Parliament passed the **Sugar Act**. The measure's goal was to raise revenues to help offset Britain's military expenses in North America, and thus ended the exemption of colonial trade from revenue-raising measures. Under the Navigation Acts, English importers, not American producers, paid taxes on colonial products entering Britain, and then passed the cost on to consumers. So little revenue did the Navigation Acts bring in (just £1,800 in 1763) that they did not even pay the cost of their own enforcement.

The Sugar Act amended the Molasses Act of 1733, the last of the Navigation Acts, which taxed foreign (primarily French West Indian) molasses and rum entering the mainland colonies at sixpence per gallon. But colonial merchants had simply continued to import the cheaper French molasses after 1733, bribing customs officials 1½ pence per gallon when it was unloaded. Hoping to end the bribery, Parliament lowered the duty to three-pence per gallon.

The Sugar Act also vastly complicated the requirements for shipping colonial goods. A captain now had to fill out a confusing series of documents to certify his trade as legal, and was required to post expensive bond to ensure his compliance.

Finally, the Sugar Act disregarded many traditional English protections for a fair trial. The law stipulated that smuggling cases be heard in vice-admiralty courts, where a British-appointed judge gave the verdict, rather than in colonial courts, in which juries decided the outcome. Because the Sugar Act (until 1768) awarded vice-admiralty judges 5 percent of any confiscated cargo, judges had a financial incentive to find defendants guilty. Also, customs officials could transfer cases to the vice-admiralty court at Halifax, Nova Scotia, far from any merchant's home port.

The British navy vigorously enforced the Sugar Act. A Boston resident complained in 1764 that "no vessel hardly comes in or goes out but they find some pretense to seize and detain her." That same year, Pennsylvania's chief justice reported that customs officers were extorting fees from small boats carrying lumber across the Delaware River to Philadelphia from New Jersey and seemed likely "to destroy this little River-trade."

Rather than pay the three-pence tax, Americans continued smuggling molasses until 1766. Then, to discourage smuggling, Britain lowered the duty to a penny—less than the customary bribe American shippers paid to get their cargoes past inspectors. The law thereafter raised about £30,000 annually in revenue.

Because the burden of the Sugar Act fell overwhelmingly on Massachusetts, New York, and Pennsylvania, other provinces had little interest in resisting it. The Sugar Act's immediate effect was minor, but it irritated urban merchants and heightened colonists' sensitivities to the new direction of imperial policies.

The Stamp Act Crisis, 1765–1766   The revenue raised by the Sugar Act did little to ease Britain's financial crisis. The national debt continued to rise, and Britons bemoaned the second-highest tax rates in Europe. Particularly irritating was the fact that by 1765 their rates averaged 26 shillings per person, whereas the colonial tax burden varied from ½ to 1½ shillings per inhabitant. Well aware of how lightly the colonists were taxed, British prime minister George Grenville thought they should make a larger contribution to the empire's American expenses.

To raise such revenues, Parliament passed the **Stamp Act** in March 1765. The law obliged colonists to purchase and use special stamped (watermarked) paper for newspapers, customs documents, various licenses, college diplomas, playing cards, and legal forms used for recovering debts, transferring property, and making wills. As with the Sugar Act, violators would face prosecution in vice-admiralty courts, without juries. The prime minister projected yearly revenues of £60,000 to £100,000, which would offset 12 to 20 percent of North American military expenses.

Unlike the Sugar Act, which was an external tax levied on imports, the Stamp Act was an internal tax, or a duty levied directly on property, goods, and government services within the colonies. Whereas external taxes were intended to regulate trade and fell mainly on merchants and ship captains, internal taxes were designed to raise revenue for the crown and affected most people at least occasionally.

To Grenville and his supporters, the new tax seemed a small price for the benefits of empire, especially since Britons had been paying a similar tax since 1695. Nevertheless, some in England, most notably William Pitt, objected to Britain's levying an internal tax on the colonies. They emphasized that the colonists had never been subject to British revenue bills and noted that they already taxed themselves through their own elected assemblies.

Grenville and his followers believed that while Americans did not directly elect members of Parliament, they were "virtually" represented there. The principle of virtual representation held that all members of Parliament stood above the narrow interests of their constituents and each considered the welfare of all subjects when deciding issues. By definition, then, British subjects, including colonists, were not represented by particular individuals but by all members of Parliament.

Grenville and his supporters also denied that colonists were exempt from British taxation because they elected their own assemblies. American assemblies, they alleged, were comparable to British local governments, whose powers did not nullify Parliament's authority over them. But Grenville's position clashed directly with that of colonists who had long maintained that their assemblies exercised legislative powers equivalent to those of the House of Commons in Britain (see Chapter 4).

Many colonists felt that the Stamp Act forced them either to confront the issue of parliamentary taxation head-on or to surrender any claim to meaningful rights of self-government. However highly they regarded Parliament, few colonists imagined that it represented them. They accepted the validity of virtual representation for England and Scotland but denied that it extended to the colonies. Instead, they argued, their self-governance was similar to that of Ireland, whose Parliament alone could tax its people but could not interfere with laws, like the Navigation Acts, passed by the British Parliament. Speaking against the Sugar Act, James Otis had expressed this argument: "by [the British] Constitution, every man in the dominions is a free man: that no parts of His Majesty's dominions can be taxed without consent: that every part has a right to be represented in the supreme or some subordinate legislature." In essence, the colonists assumed that the empire was a loose federation in which their legislatures possessed considerable autonomy, rather than an extended nation governed directly from London.

To many colonists, passage of the Stamp Act demonstrated both Parliament's indifference to their interests and the shallowness of the theory of virtual representation. Provincial assemblies as well as colonial lobbyists in London had urged the act's defeat, but Parliament had dismissed these appeals without a hearing. Parliament "must have thought us Americans all a parcel of Apes and very tame Apes too," concluded Christopher Gadsden of South Carolina, "or they would have never ventured on such a hateful, baneful experiment."

In late May 1765, Patrick Henry, a twenty-nine-year-old Virginia lawyer and planter with a talent for fiery oratory, dramatically conveyed the rising spirit of resistance. Henry urged the Virginia House of Burgesses to adopt seven strongly worded resolutions denying Parliament's power to tax the colonies. In arguing for the resolutions, Henry reportedly stated that "he did not doubt but some good American would stand up in favor of his country." Viewing such language as treasonous, the legislators passed only the mildest four of Henry's resolutions. Garbled accounts of Henry's resolutions and the debates were published in other colonies, and by year's end seven other assemblies had passed resolutions against the act. As in Virginia, the resolutions were grounded in constitutional arguments and avoided Henry's inflammatory language.

Henry's words resonated more loudly outside elite political circles, particularly in Boston. There, in late summer, a group of middle-class artisans and small business owners joined together as the Loyal Nine to fight the Stamp Act. They recognized that the stamp distributors, who alone could accept money for watermarked paper, were the law's weak link. If the public could pressure them into resigning before taxes became due on November 1, the Stamp Act would become inoperable.

It was no accident that Boston set the pace in opposing Parliament. No other port suffered so much from the Sugar Act's trade restrictions. But Boston's misery was compounded by older problems. For several decades, its shipbuilding industry had lost significant ground to New York and Philadelphia, and the output of its rum and sugar producers had fallen by half in just a decade. British impressment (forced recruitment) of Massachusetts fishermen for naval service had undermined the fishing industry. The resulting unemployment led to increased local taxes for poor relief. The taxes, along with a shrinking number of customers, drove many marginal artisans out of business and into the ranks of the poor. Other Bostonians, while remaining employed or in business, struggled in the face of rising prices and taxes. Moreover, the city had not recovered from a great fire in 1760 that had burned 176 warehouses and left every tenth family homeless.

Widespread economic distress produced an explosive situation in Boston. Already resentful of an elite whose fortunes had risen spectacularly while they suffered, many poor and working-class Bostonians blamed British officials and policies for the town's hard times. The crisis was sharpened because they were accustomed to gathering in large crowds that engaged in pointed political expression, both satirical and serious and usually directed against the "better sort."

In response to the Stamp Act, Boston's crowds aimed their traditional forms of protest more directly and forcefully at imperial officials. The morning of August 14 found a likeness of Boston's stamp distributor, Andrew Oliver, swinging from a tree guarded by a menacing crowd organized by the relatively moderate Loyal Nine. By dusk, Oliver had not resigned, so several hundred Bostonians demolished a building of Oliver's. Thereafter, the Loyal Nine withdrew, and the crowd continued on its own. The men surged toward Oliver's house, where they beheaded his effigy and "stamped" it to pieces. They then shattered the windows of his home, smashed his furniture, and even tore out the paneling. When officials tried to disperse the crowd, they were driven off under a barrage of rocks. Surveying his devastated home the next morning, Oliver announced his resignation.

Bitterness against the Stamp Act unleashed spontaneous, contagious violence. Twelve days after Oliver resigned, a crowd demolished the elegant home of Lieutenant Governor and Chief Justice Thomas Hutchinson. Boston's smugglers begrudged Hutchinson for some of his judicial decisions as chief justice while many more citizens saw him as a symbol of the royal policies crippling Boston's economy and their own livelihoods. In their view, wealthy officials "rioted in luxury," with homes and fancy furnishings that cost hundreds of times the annual incomes of most Boston workingmen. They were also reacting to Hutchinson's efforts to stop the destruction of his brother-in-law Andrew Oliver's house. Ironically, Hutchinson privately opposed the Stamp Act.

Thereafter, groups similar to the Loyal Nine calling themselves **Sons of Liberty** began forming throughout the colonies. After the assault on Hutchinson's mansion and an even more violent incident in Newport, Rhode Island, the leaders of the Sons of Liberty sought to prevent more such outbreaks. They recognized that people in the crowds were casting aside their customary deference toward their social "superiors," a development that could broaden to include all elites if not carefully contained. Fearful of alienating wealthy opponents of the Stamp Act, the Sons of Liberty focused their demonstrations strictly against property and invariably left avenues of escape for their victims. Especially fearful that one of their targets might be shot or killed, they forbade their followers to carry weapons.

In October 1765, representatives of nine colonial assemblies met in New York City in a **Stamp Act Congress.** The session was remarkable for the colonies' agreement on and bold articulation of the principle that Parliament lacked authority to levy taxes outside Great Britain and to deny any person a jury trial. "The Ministry never imagined we could or would so generally unite in opposition to their measures," wrote a Connecticut delegate, "nor I confess till I saw the Experiment made did I."

By late 1765, most stamp distributors had resigned or fled, and without the watermarked paper required by law, most royal customs officials and court officers were refusing to perform their duties. In response, legislators compelled the reluctant officials to resume operation by threatening to withhold their pay. At the same time, merchants obtained sailing clearances by insisting they would sue if cargoes spoiled while delayed in port. By late December, the courts and harbors of almost every colony were again functioning.

Thus, colonial elites moved to keep an explosive situation from getting out of hand by supporting the moderate Sons of Liberty over more radical groups, by expressing opposition through the Stamp Act Congress, and by having colonial legislatures restore normal business. Elite leaders feared that chaos could break out, particularly if British troops landed to enforce the Stamp Act. An elite Pennsylvanian, John Dickinson, feared that revolutionary turmoil would lead to "a multitude of Commonwealths, Crimes, and Calamities, Centuries of mutual jealousies, Hatreds, Wars of Devastation, till at last the exhausted provinces shall sink into savagery under the yoke of some fortunate Conqueror."

To force the Stamp Act's repeal, New York's merchants agreed on October 31, 1765, to boycott all British goods, and businessmen in other cities soon followed their example. Because American colonists purchased about 40 percent of England's manufactures, this nonimportation strategy put the English economy in danger of recession. Panicked English businessmen descended on Parliament to warn that continuation of the Stamp Act would stimulate a wave of bankruptcies, massive unemployment, and political unrest.

By early 1766, support was growing in Parliament for repeal of the Stamp Act. William Pitt denounced all efforts to tax the colonies, declaring, "I rejoice that America has resisted." But most members supported repeal only as a matter of practicality, not as a surrender of principle. In March 1766, Parliament revoked the Stamp Act, but only in conjunction with passage of the **Declaratory Act,** which affirmed parliamentary power to legislate for the colonies "in all cases whatsoever."

Because the Declaratory Act was written in general language, Anglo-Americans interpreted it to their own advantage. To them, the measure seemed no more than a parliamentary exercise in saving face to compensate for the Stamp Act's repeal. The House of Commons, however, intended that the colonists take the Declaratory Act literally to mean that they could not claim exemption from any parliamentary statute, including a tax law. The Stamp Act crisis thus ended in a fundamental disagreement between Britain and America over Parliament's authority in the colonies.

Ideology, Religion, and Resistance
The Stamp Act and the conflicts around it revealed a chasm between Britain and its colonies that startled Anglo-Americans. For the first time, some of them critically reconsidered the imperial relationship. To put their concerns into perspective, educated colonists turned to the works of philosophers, historians, and political writers. Many more, both educated and uneducated, looked to religion.

By the 1760s, many colonists were familiar with the political writings of European Enlightenment thinkers, particularly John Locke (see Chapter 4). Locke argued that humans originated in a "state of nature" in which each man enjoyed the "natural rights" of life, liberty, and property. Thereafter, groups of men entered into a "social contract," under which they formed governments for the sole purpose of protecting those individual rights. A government that encroached on natural rights, then, broke its contract with the people. In such cases, people could resist their government, although Locke cautioned against outright rebellion except in the most extreme cases. To many colonial readers, Locke's concept of natural rights appeared to justify opposition to arbitrary legislation by Parliament.

Colonists also read European writers who emphasized excessive concentrations of executive power as tyrannical threats. Some of them developed a set of ideas termed "republican," in which they balanced Locke's emphasis on individual rights with an emphasis on the good of the people as a whole. "Republicans" especially admired the sense of civic duty that motivated citizens of the Roman republic. Like the early Romans, they maintained that a free people had to avoid moral and political corruption, and practice a disinterested "public virtue." An elected leader of a republic, one author noted, would command obedience "more by the virtue of the people, than by the terror of his power."

Among those influenced by republican ideas were a widely read group of English political writers known as oppositionists. According to the oppositionists, Parliament—consisting of the elected representatives of the people—formed the foundation of England's unique political liberties and protected those liberties against the inherent corruption and tyranny of executive power. But recent prime ministers, the oppositionists argued, had exploited the treasury's resources to bribe politicians and voters. Most members of Parliament, in their view, no longer represented the true interests of the people; rather, they had created self-interested "factions" and joined in a "conspiracy against liberty." Often referring to themselves as the "country party," the oppositionists feared that a power-hungry "court party" of unelected officials close to the king was using a corrupted Parliament to gain absolute power for themselves.

Influenced by such ideas, a number of colonists pointed to a diabolical conspiracy behind British policy during the Stamp Act crisis. Joseph Warren of Massachusetts noted that the act "induced some to imagine that the minister designed by this to force the colonies into a rebellion, and from thence to take occasion to treat them with severity, and, by military power, to reduce them to servitude." Over the next decade, a proliferation of pamphlets denounced British efforts to "enslave" the colonies through excessive taxation and the imposition of officials, judges, and a standing army directed from London. In such assaults on liberty and natural rights, some Americans found principled reasons for opposing British policies and actions.

Beginning with the Stamp Act protest, many Protestant clergymen, both Old Lights and New Lights (see Chapter 4), wove resistance to British authority into their sermons, summoning their congregations to protect their God-given liberty. "A just regard to our liberties … is so far from being displeasing to God that it would be ingratitude to him who has given them to us to … tamely give them up," exhorted one New England minister. Most Anglican ministers, whose church was headed by the king, tried to stay neutral or opposed the protest; and pacifist Quakers kept out of the fray. But to large numbers of Congregationalist, Presbyterian, and Baptist clergymen, battling for the Lord and defending liberty were one and the same.

Voicing such a message, clergymen exerted an enormous influence on public opinion. Far more Americans heard sermons than had access to newspapers or pamphlets. Provincial proclamations of days of "fasting and public humiliation"—a traditional means of focusing public attention on an issue and invoking divine aid—inspired sermons on the theme of God's sending the people woes only to strengthen and sustain them until victory. Moreover, protest leaders' calls for boycotting British luxuries fit neatly with traditional pulpit warnings against self-indulgence and wastefulness. Few ordinary Americans escaped the unceasing public reminders that community solidarity against British tyranny and "corruption" meant rejecting sin and obeying God.

RESISTANCE RESUMES, 1766–1770

Although Parliament's repeal of the Stamp Act momentarily quieted colonial protests, its search for new sources of revenue soon revived them. While British leaders condemned the colonists for evading their financial responsibilities and for insubordination, growing numbers of Anglo-Americans became convinced that the Stamp Act had not been an isolated mistake but rather part of a deliberate design to undermine colonial self-governance. In this, they were joined by many in Britain who opposed policies that seemed to threaten Britons and colonists alike.

Opposing the Quartering Act, 1766–1767   Hoping to end disarray in Parliament, George III in August 1766 summoned William Pitt to form a cabinet. Previously sympathetic to the colonies, Pitt might have repaired the Stamp Act's damage, for no Englishman was more respected in America. But after Pitt's health collapsed in March 1767, effective leadership passed to his Chancellor of the Exchequer (treasurer) Charles Townshend.

Just as Townshend took office, a conflict arose with the New York assembly over the Quartering Act, enacted in 1765. This law ordered colonial legislatures to pay for certain goods needed by soldiers stationed within their respective borders. The necessities were inexpensive barracks supplies such as candles, windowpanes, and mattress straw.

Despite its minimal cost, the Quartering Act aroused resentment, for it constituted an indirect tax; that is, although it did not (like the Stamp Act) empower royal officials to collect money directly from the colonists, it obligated assemblies to raise a stated amount of revenue. Such obligations clashed with the assemblies' claimed power to initiate all revenue-raising measures. The law fell lightly or not at all on most colonies; but New York, where more soldiers were stationed than in any other province, refused to comply.

New York's resistance to the Quartering Act produced a torrent of anti-American feeling in Parliament, whose members remained bitter at having had to withdraw the Stamp Act. In response, they passed the New York Suspending Act (1767), which would delay the assembly until it appropriated the funds. The assembly quickly complied before the measure became law.

Although New York's retreat averted further confrontation, the Quartering Act demonstrated that British leaders would not hesitate to defend Parliament's authority through the most drastic of all steps: by interfering with American claims to self-governance.

Crisis over the Townshend Duties, 1767–1770   As Parliament passed the New York Suspending Act, Townshend expanded his efforts to subordinate the colonies to Parliament's authority and raise revenues in America. He sought to tax the colonists by exploiting an oversight in their arguments against the Stamp Act. In confronting the Stamp Act, Americans had emphasized their opposition to internal taxes but had said little about Parliament's right to tax imports as they entered the colonies. Townshend chose to interpret this silence as evidence that the colonists accepted Britain's right to tax their trade—to impose external taxes. Yet not all British politicians were so mistaken. "They will laugh at you," predicted a now wiser George Grenville, "for your distinctions about regulations of trade." Brushing aside Grenville's warnings, Parliament passed the **Revenue Act** (popularly called the Townshend duties) in June and July 1767. The new law taxed glass, paint, lead, paper, and tea imported to the colonies from England.

The Revenue Act differed significantly from what Americans had long seen as a legitimate way of regulating trade through taxation. To the colonists, charging a duty was a lawful way for British authorities to control trade only if that duty excluded foreign goods by making them prohibitively expensive to consumers. The Revenue Act, however, set moderate rates that did not price goods out of the colonial market; clearly, its purpose was to collect money for the treasury. Thus from the colonial standpoint, Townshend's duties were taxes just like the Stamp Act duties.

In reality, the Revenue Act would never yield anything like the income that Townshend anticipated. Of the various items taxed, only tea produced any significant revenue—£20,000 of the £37,000 that the law was expected to yield. And because the measure would serve its purpose only if British tea were affordable to colonial consumers, Townshend eliminated £60,000 worth of import fees paid on tea entering Britain from India before transshipment to America. On balance, the Revenue Act worsened the British treasury's deficit by £23,000. But by 1767, Parliament was less concerned with raising revenues than with asserting its authority over the colonies.

Colonial resistance to the Revenue Act remained weak until December 1767, when John Dickinson published twelve essays entitled *Letters from a Farmer in Pennsylvania*. The essays argued that although Parliament could regulate trade by imposing duties, no tax designed to produce revenue could be considered constitutional unless a people's elected representatives voted for it. Dickinson said nothing that others had not stated or implied during the Stamp Act crisis. Rather, his contribution lay in persuading recent opponents of the Stamp Act that their arguments also applied to the Revenue Act. In early 1768, the Massachusetts assembly condemned the Townshend duties and commissioned Samuel Adams to draft a "circular letter" calling on other colonial legislatures to join it. Adams's letter forthrightly condemned taxation without representation. But it acknowledged Parliament as the "supreme legislative Power over the whole Empire," and it advocated no illegal activities. Three other colonies approved Adams's message and Virginia sent out a more strongly worded circular letter of its own. But most colonial legislatures reacted indifferently. In fact, resistance to the Revenue Act might have disintegrated had the British government not overreacted to the circular letters.

Parliamentary leaders regarded even the mild Massachusetts letter as "little better than an incentive to Rebellion." Following Townshend's sudden death in 1767, Lord Hillsborough, first appointee to the new post of secretary of state for the colonies, took charge of British policy. Hillsborough flatly told the Massachusetts assembly to disown its letter, forbade all colonial assemblies to endorse it, and commanded royal governors to dissolve any legislature that violated his instructions. George III later commented that he never met "a man of less judgment than Lord Hillsborough."

To protest Hillsborough's crude bullying, many legislatures previously indifferent to the Massachusetts circular letter now adopted it enthusiastically. In obedience to Hillsborough, royal governors responded by dismissing legislatures in Massachusetts and elsewhere. These moves played directly into the hands of Samuel Adams, James Otis, and others who sought to ignite widespread public opposition to the Townshend duties.

Although outraged over the Revenue Act, colonial activists needed some effective means of pressuring Parliament for its repeal. One approach, nonimportation, seemed especially promising because it offered an alternative to violence and would distress Britain's economy. In August 1768, Boston's merchants therefore adopted a nonimportation agreement, and the tactic slowly spread southward. "Save your money, and you save your country!" became the watchword of the Sons of Liberty, who began reorganizing after two years of inactivity. The success of nonimportation depended on the compliance of merchants whose livelihood relied on buying and selling imports. In several major communities, including Philadelphia, Baltimore, and Charles Town, merchants continued buying British goods until 1769. Nevertheless, the boycott did significantly limit British imports and mobilized colonists into resuming resistance to British policies.

By 1770, a new British prime minister, Lord North, favored eliminating most of the Townshend duties to prevent the American boycott from widening. But to underscore British authority, he insisted on retaining the tax on tea. Parliament agreed, and in April 1770, giving in for the second time in four years to colonial pressure, it repealed most of the Townshend duties.

Parliament's partial repeal produced a dilemma for American politicians. They considered it intolerable that taxes remained on tea, the most profitable item for the royal treasury. Colonial leaders were unsure whether they should press on with the nonimportation agreement until they achieved total victory, or whether it would suffice to maintain a selective boycott of tea. When the nonimportation movement collapsed in July 1770, colonists resisted external taxation by voluntary agreements not to drink British tea. Through nonconsumption, they succeeded in limiting revenue from tea to about one-sixth the level originally expected. Yet colonial resistance leaders took little satisfaction in having forced Parliament to compromise. The tea duty remained a galling reminder that Parliament refused to retreat from the broadest possible interpretation of the Declaratory Act.

Customs "Racketeering," 1767–1770   Besides taxing colonial imports, Townshend had sought additional means of financing British rule in America. Traditionally, royal governors had depended on colonial legislatures to vote their salaries, and assemblies used this power to influence governors' actions. At Townshend's urging, Parliament authorized paying the salaries of governors and other royal officials in America from revenues raised there, thus freeing officials from the assemblies' control and influence. In effect, by stripping the assemblies of their most potent weapon, the power of the purse, Parliament's action threatened to tip the balance of power away from elected colonial representatives and toward unelected royal officials.

Townshend hoped to raise revenue through stricter enforcement of existing customs laws. Accordingly, he also persuaded Parliament in 1767 to establish the American Board of Customs Commissioners. The law raised the number of port officials, funded a colonial coast guard, and provided money for secret informers. It awarded an informer one-third of the value of all goods and ships appropriated through a conviction for smuggling. That fines could be tripled under certain circumstances provided an even greater incentive to seize illegal cargoes. Smuggling cases were heard in vice-admiralty courts, moreover, where the probability of conviction was extremely high. But the law quickly drew protests because of the way it was enforced and because it assumed those accused to be guilty until or unless they could prove otherwise.

Under the new provisions, revenue agents commonly filed charges for technical violations of the Sugar Act, which gave them a pretext for seizing the entire ship. They most often exploited a provision that declared any cargo illegal that had been loaded or unloaded without a customs officer's written authorization. Customs commissioners also invaded the traditional rights of sailors, who had long supplemented their incomes by making small sales between ports. Anything stored in a sailor's chest had been considered his private property. Under the new policy, crewmen saw their trunks ruthlessly broken open by inspectors who confiscated trading stock worth several months' wages because it was not listed on the captain's loading papers.

Above all, customs commissioners' use of informers provoked retaliation. In 1769, the *Pennsylvania Journal* scorned these agents as "dogs of prey, thirsting after the fortunes of worthy and wealthy men." By betraying the trust of employers, and sometimes of friends, informers aroused hatred in their victims and were roughly handled whenever found.

To merchants and seamen alike, the commissioners had embarked on a program of "customs racketeering" that constituted little more than a system of legalized piracy. Nowhere were customs agents and informers more detested than in Boston, where in June 1768 citizens retaliated against them. The occasion was the seizure, on a technicality, of Boston merchant John Hancock's sloop *Liberty*. Hancock, reportedly North America's richest merchant and a leading opponent of British taxation, had become a chief target of the customs commissioners. Now they fined him £9,000, an amount almost thirteen times greater than the taxes he supposedly evaded on a shipment of Madeira wine. A crowd, "chiefly sturdy boys and Negroes," in Thomas Hutchinson's words, tried to prevent the towing of Hancock's ship and then began assaulting customs agents. Growing to several hundred as it surged through the streets, the mob drove all revenue inspectors from Boston.

Under Lord North, the British government, aware of customs officers' excesses, took steps to dampen colonial protests. Prosecutors dropped the charges against Hancock, fearing that he would appeal a conviction in England, where honest officials might take action against the commissioners responsible for violating his rights. But British officials were conceding nothing to the colonists. For at the same time, they dispatched four thousand troops to Boston, making clear that they would not tolerate further violent defiance of their authority.

"Wilkes and Liberty," 1768–1770   Although wealthy Britons blamed the colonists for their high taxes, others in England found common cause with the Americans. They formed a movement that arose during the 1760s to oppose the domestic and foreign policies of George III and a Parliament dominated by wealthy landowners. Their leader was John Wilkes, a fiery London editor and member of Parliament who acquired notoriety in 1763 when his newspaper regularly and irreverently denounced George III's policies. The government finally arrested Wilkes for seditious libel, but to great popular acclaim, he won his case in court. The government, however, succeeded in shutting down his newspaper and in persuading a majority in the House of Commons to deny Wilkes his seat. After again offending the government with a publication, Wilkes fled to Paris.

Defying a warrant for his arrest, Wilkes returned to England in 1768 and again ran for Parliament. By this time, British policies were sparking widespread protests. Merchants and artisans in London, Bristol, and other cities demanded the dismissal of the "obnoxious" ministers who were "ruining our manufactories by invidiously imposing and establishing the most impolitic and unconstitutional taxations and regulations on your Majesty's colonies." They were joined by (nonvoting) weavers, coal heavers, seamen, and other workers who protested low wages and high prices that stemmed in part from government policies. All these people rallied around the cry "Wilkes and liberty!"

After being elected again to Parliament, Wilkes was arrested. The next day, twenty to forty thousand angry "Wilkesites" gathered on St. George's Fields, outside the prison where he was held. When members of the crowd began throwing stones, soldiers and police responded with gunfire, killing eleven protesters. The "massacre of St. George's Fields" had given the movement some martyrs. Wilkes and an associate were elected twice more and were both times denied their seats by other legislators. Wilkes was besieged by outpourings of popular support from the colonies as well as from Britain. Some Virginians sent him tobacco, and the South Carolina assembly voted to contribute £1,500 to help defray his debts. He maintained a regular correspondence with the Boston Sons of Liberty and, upon his release in April 1770, was hailed in a massive Boston celebration as "the illustrious martyr to Liberty."

Wilkes's cause sharpened the political thinking of government opponents in Britain and the colonies alike. Thousands of English voters signed petitions to Parliament protesting its refusal to seat Wilkes as an affront to the electorate's will. Some of them formed a Society of the Supporters of the Bill of Rights "to defend and maintain the legal, constitutional liberty of the subject." While more "respectable" opponents of the government such as William Pitt and Edmund Burke disdained Wilkes for courting the "mob," his movement emboldened them to speak more forcefully against the government, especially on its policies toward the colonies. Wilkes's movement also provided powerful reinforcement for colonists' challenges to the authority of Parliament and the British government.

John Wilkes, by William Hogarth, 1763 *Detesting Wilkes and all he stood for, Hogarth depicted the radical leader as menacing and untrustworthy.*

(William L. Clements Library, University of Michigan)

Women and Colonial Resistance

Colonial boycotts of British goods provided a unique opportunity for white women to join the resistance to British policies. White women's participation in public affairs had been widening slowly and unevenly in the colonies for several decades. By the 1760s, when colonial protests against British policies began, colonial women such as Sarah Osborn (see Chapter 4) had become well-known religious activists. Calling themselves the Daughters of Liberty, a contingent of upper-class female patriots had played a part in defeating the Stamp Act. Some had attended political rallies during the Stamp Act crisis, and many more had expressed their opposition in discussions and correspondence with family and friends.

Just two years later, women assumed an even more visible role during the Townshend crisis. To protest the Revenue Act's tax on tea, more than three hundred "mistresses of families" in Boston denounced consumption of the beverage in early 1770. In some ways, the threat of nonconsumption was even more effective than that of nonimportation, for women served and drank most of the tea consumed by colonists.

Nonconsumption agreements soon became popular and were extended to include English manufactures, especially clothing. Again women played a vital role, both because they made most household purchases and because it was they who could replace British imports with apparel of their own making. Responding to leaders' pleas that they expand domestic cloth production, women of all social ranks, even those who customarily did not weave their own fabric or sew their own clothing, organized spinning bees. These events attracted intense publicity as evidence of American determination to forgo luxury and idleness for the common defense of liberty. One historian calculates that more than sixteen hundred women participated in spinning bees in New England alone from 1768 to 1770. The colonial cause, noted a New York woman, had enlisted "a fighting army of amazons … armed with spinning wheels."

Spinning bees not only helped undermine the notion that women had no place in public life but also endowed spinning and weaving, previously considered routine household tasks, with special political virtue. "Women might recover to this country the full and free enjoyment of all our rights, properties and privileges," exclaimed the Reverend John Cleaveland of Ipswich, Massachusetts, in 1769, adding that this "is more than the men have been able to do." For many colonists, such logic enlarged the arena of supposed feminine virtues from strictly religious matters to include political issues.

Spinning bees, combined with female support for boycotting tea, dramatically demonstrated that American resistance ran far deeper than the protests of a few male merchants and the largely male crowds in American seaports. Women's participation showed that colonial protests extended into the heart of American households and congregations, and were leading to broader popular participation in politics.

THE DEEPENING CRISIS, 1770–1774

After 1770, the imperial crisis grew more ominous. Colonists and British troops clashed on the streets of Boston. Resistance leaders in the colonies developed means of systematically coordinating their actions and policies. After Bostonians defied a new act of Parliament, the Tea Act, Britain was determined to subordinate the colonies once and for all. Adding to the tensions of the period were several violent conflicts that erupted in the western backcountry.

<table>
<tr><td>

The Boston Massacre, 1770

</td><td>

As noted, in response to the violence provoked by Hancock's case, British authorities had dispatched four thousand troops to Boston in the summer and fall of 1768. Resentful Bosto-

</td></tr>
</table>

nians regarded the redcoats as a standing army that threatened their liberty, as well as a financial burden.

In the presence of so many soldiers, Boston took on the atmosphere of an occupied city and crackled with tension. Armed sentries and resentful civilians traded insults. The overwhelmingly Protestant townspeople were especially angered that many soldiers were Irish Catholics. The poorly paid enlisted men, moreover, were free to seek employment when off-duty. Often agreeing to work for less than local laborers, they generated fierce hostility in a community that was plagued by persistently high unemployment.

Poor Bostonians' deep-seated resentment against British authority erupted on February 22, 1770, when a customs informer shot into a crowd picketing the home of a customs-paying merchant, killing an eleven-year-old boy. While elite Bostonians had disdained the unruly exchanges between soldiers and crowds, the horror at a child's death momentarily united the community. "My Eyes never beheld such a funeral," wrote John Adams. "A vast Number of Boys walked before the Coffin, a vast Number of Women and Men after it.... This Shews there are many more Lives to spend if wanted in the Service of their country."

Although the army had played no part in the shooting, it became a natural target for popular frustration and rage. A week after the boy's funeral, tensions between troops and a crowd led by Crispus Attucks, a seaman of African and Native American descent, and including George Robert Twelves Hewes, erupted at the guard post protecting the customs office. When an officer tried to disperse the civilians, his men endured a steady barrage of flying objects and dares to shoot. A private finally did fire, after having been knocked down by a block of ice, and then shouted, "Fire! Fire!" to his fellow soldiers. The soldiers' volley hit eleven persons, five of whom, including Attucks, died.

The shock that followed the March 5 bloodshed marked the emotional high point of the Townshend crisis. Royal authorities in Massachusetts tried to defuse the situation by isolating all British soldiers on a fortified island in the harbor, and Governor Thomas Hutchinson promised that the soldiers who had fired would be tried. John Adams, an elite patriot who opposed crowd actions, served as their attorney. Adams appealed to the Boston jury by claiming that the soldiers had been provoked by a "motley rabble of saucy boys, negroes and mulattoes, Irish teagues, and outlandish jack tarres," in other words, people not considered "respectable" by the city's elites and middle class. All but two of the soldiers were acquitted, and those found guilty suffered only a branding on their thumbs.

Burning hatreds produced by an intolerable situation underlay the Boston Massacre, as it came to be called in conscious recollection of the St. George's Fields Massacre in London. The shooting of unarmed American civilians by British soldiers and the light punishment given the soldiers forced the colonists to confront the stark possibility that the British government was bent on coercing and suppressing them through naked force. In a play written by Mercy Otis Warren, a character predicted that soon "Murders, blood and carnage/Shall crimson all these streets" as patriots rose to defend their republican liberty against tyrannical authority.

The Committees of Correspondence, 1772–1773   In the fall of 1772, Lord North was preparing to implement Townshend's goal of paying the royal governors' salaries out of customs revenue. The colonists had always viewed efforts to free the governors from financial dependence on the legislatures as a threat to representative government. In response, Samuel Adams persuaded Boston's town meeting to request that every Massachusetts community appoint a committee whose members would be responsible for exchanging information and coordinating measures to defend colonial rights. Of approximately 260 towns, about half immediately established "**committees of correspondence**," and most others did so within a year. The idea soon spread throughout New England.

The committees of correspondence were resistance leaders' first attempt to maintain close and continuing political cooperation over a wide area. By linking almost every interior community to Boston through a network of dedicated activists, the system enabled Adams to send out messages for each local committee to read at its own town meeting, which would then debate the issues and adopt a formal resolution. Involving tens of thousands of colonists to consider evidence that their rights were in danger, the system enabled them to take a personal stand by voting.

Adams's most successful effort to mobilize popular sentiment came in June 1773, when he publicized some letters written by Massachusetts Governor Thomas Hutchinson that Benjamin Franklin had obtained. Massachusetts town meetings discovered through the letters that Hutchinson had advocated "an abridgement of what are called English liberties" and "a great restraint of natural liberty." The publication of Hutchinson's correspondence confirmed many colonists' suspicions of a plot to destroy basic freedoms.

In March 1773, Patrick Henry, Thomas Jefferson, and Richard Henry Lee proposed that Virginia establish committees of correspondence. Within a year, every province but Pennsylvania had followed its example. By early 1774, a communications web linked colonial leaders for the first time since the Stamp Act crisis of 1766.

Conflicts in the Backcountry   Although most of the turbulence between 1763 and 1775 swirled in the eastern seaports, numerous clashes, involving Native Americans, colonists, and colonial governments, erupted in the West. These conflicts were rooted in the rapid population growth that had spurred the migration of whites to the Appalachian backcountry.

Backcountry tensions surfaced soon after the Seven Years' War in western Pennsylvania, where Scots-Irish Presbyterian settlers had fought repeatedly with Native Americans. Settlers near Paxton, Pennsylvania, resented the Quaker-dominated assembly for failing to provide them with adequate military protection and for denying them equal representation in the legislature. They also concluded that all Native Americans, regardless of wartime conduct, were their racial enemies. In December 1763, armed settlers attacked two villages of peaceful Conestoga Indians, killing and scalping men, women, and children. In February 1764, about

200 "Paxton Boys," as they were called, set out for Philadelphia, with plans to kill Christian Indian refugees there. A government delegation headed by Benjamin Franklin met the armed, mounted mob on the outskirts of the city. After Franklin promised that the assembly would consider their grievances, the Paxton Boys returned home.

Land pressures and the lack of adequate revenue from the colonies left the British government utterly helpless in enforcing the Proclamation of 1763. Speculators such as George Washington sought western land because "any person who … neglects the present opportunity of hunting out good Lands will never regain it." Settlers, traders, hunters, and thieves trespassed on Indian land, often responding violently when confronted by the occupants. In the meantime, the British government was unable to maintain garrisons at many of its forts or to enforce violations of laws and treaties. Under such pressure, Britain and its Six Nations Iroquois allies agreed in the Treaty of Fort Stanwix (1768) to grant lands along the Ohio River that were occupied and claimed by Shawnees, Delawares, and Cherokees to the governments of Pennsylvania and Virginia.

The treaty only heightened western tensions, especially in the Ohio country, where settlers agitated to establish a new colony, Kentucky. Growing violence culminated in 1774 in the unprovoked slaughter by colonists of thirteen Shawnees and Mingos, including eight members of the family of Logan, until then a moderate Mingo leader. The outraged Logan led a force of Shawnees and Mingos who retaliated by killing an equal number of white Virginians and then offered to make peace. Repudiating the offer, Virginia mobilized for what became known as Lord Dunmore's War (1774), for the colony's governor. In a decisive battle, the English soundly defeated Logan's people. During the peace conference that followed, Virginia gained uncontested rights to lands south of the Ohio in exchange for its claims on the northern side. But Anglo-Indian resentments persisted, and fighting would resume once Britain and its colonies went to war.

Other western disputes led to conflict among the colonists themselves. Settlers moving west in Massachusetts in the early 1760s found their titles challenged by powerful New York landlords. When two landlords threatened to evict tenant farmers in 1766, the New Englanders joined the tenants in an armed uprising, calling themselves Sons of Liberty after the Stamp Act protesters. In 1769, settlers moving west from New Hampshire also came into conflict with New York. After four years of guerrilla warfare, the New Hampshire settlers, calling themselves the Green Mountain Boys, established an independent government. Unrecognized at the time, it eventually became the state of Vermont. A third group of New England settlers from Connecticut settled in the Wyoming valley of Pennsylvania, where they clashed in 1774 with Pennsylvanians claiming title to the same land.

Expansion also provoked conflicts between backcountry settlers and their colonial governments. In North Carolina, a group known as the Regulators aimed to redress the grievances of westerners who, underrepresented in the colonial assembly, found themselves exploited by eastern officeholders. The Regulator movement climaxed on May 16, 1771, at the battle of Alamance Creek. Leading an army of perhaps thirteen hundred eastern militiamen, North Carolina's royal governor defeated about twenty-five hundred Regulators in a clash that produced almost three hundred casualties. Although the Regulator uprising then disintegrated, it crippled the colony's subsequent ability to resist British authority.

An armed Regulator movement also arose in South Carolina, in this case to counter the government's unwillingness to prosecute bandits who were terrorizing settlers. But the South Carolina government did not dispatch its militia to the back-country for fear that the colony's restive slave population might use the occasion to revolt. Instead, it conceded to the principal demands of the Regulators by establishing four new judicial circuits and allowing jury trials in the newly settled areas.

Although not directly interrelated, these episodes all reflected the tensions generated by an increasingly land hungry white population and its willingness to resort to violence against Native Americans, other colonists, and British officials. As Anglo-American tensions mounted in older settled areas, the western settlers' anxious mood spread.

The Tea Act, 1773   Colonial smuggling and nonconsumption had taken a heavy toll on the British East India Company, which enjoyed a legal monopoly on the sale of tea within Britain's empire. By 1773, with tons of tea rotting in its warehouses, the company was teetering on the brink of bankruptcy. Lord North could not afford to let the company fail. Not only did it pay substantial duties on the tea it shipped to Britain, but it also subsidized British rule in India (as discussed in Chapter 6, Beyond America).

In May 1773, to save the beleaguered East India Company from financial ruin, Parliament passed the **Tea Act**, which eliminated all remaining import duties on tea entering England and thus lowered the selling price to consumers. To lower the price further, the Tea Act also permitted the company to sell its tea directly to consumers rather than through wholesalers. These two concessions reduced the cost of company tea in the colonies well below the price of all smuggled competition. Parliament expected simple economic self-interest to overcome Anglo-American scruples about buying taxed tea.

But the Tea Act alarmed many Americans, above all because it would raise revenue with which the British government would pay royal governors. The law thus threatened to corrupt Americans into accepting the principle of parliamentary taxation by taking advantage of their weakness for a frivolous luxury. Quickly, therefore, the committees of correspondence decided to prevent East India Company cargoes from being landed, either by pressuring the company's agents to refuse acceptance or by intercepting the ships at sea and ordering them home. In Philadelphia, an anonymous "Committee for Tarring and Feathering" warned harbor pilots not to guide any ships carrying tea into port.

In Boston, however, this strategy failed. On November 28, 1773, the first ship came under the jurisdiction of the customs house, where duties would have to be paid on its cargo within twenty days. Otherwise, the cargo would be seized from the captain and the tea claimed by the company's agents and placed on sale. When Samuel Adams, John Hancock, and other popular leaders requested a special clearance for the ship's departure, Thomas Hutchinson refused.

On the evening of December 16, five thousand Bostonians gathered at Old South Church. Samuel Adams informed them of Hutchinson's insistence upon landing the tea and proclaimed that "this meeting can do no more to save the country."

Bostonians Paying the Excise (Tax) Man *In this engraving, a crowd protests the Tea Act by forcing a British tax collector to drink tea.*

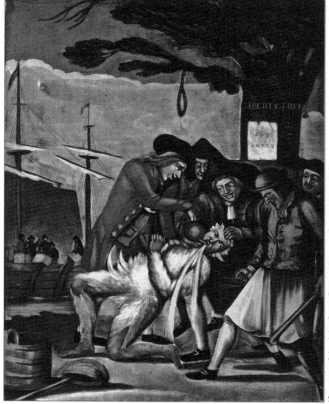

(Courtesy of the John Carter Brown Library at Brown University)

About fifty young men, including George Robert Twelves Hewes, stepped forward and disguised themselves as Mohawk Indians—symbolizing a virtuous, proud, and assertive American identity distinct from that of corrupt Britain. Armed with "tomahawks," they headed for the wharf, followed by most of the crowd.

The disciplined band assaulted no one and damaged nothing but the hated cargo. For almost an hour, thousands of onlookers stood silently transfixed, as if at a religious service, peering through the crisp, cold air of a moonlit night. The only sounds were the steady chop of hatchets breaking open wooden chests and the soft splash of tea—forty-five tons in all—on the water. When Boston's "Tea Party," as it was later called, was finished, the participants left quietly, and the town lapsed into a profound hush.

Toward Independence, 1774–1776

The calm that followed the Boston Tea Party proved to be a calm before the storm. The incident inflamed the British government and Parliament, which now determined once and for all to quash colonial insubordination. Colonial political leaders responded with equal determination to defend self-government and liberty. The empire and its American colonies were on a collision course, leading by spring 1775 to armed clashes. Yet even after blood was shed, colonists hesitated before declaring their independence from Britain. In the meantime, free and enslaved African-Americans pondered how best to realize their own freedom.

Liberty for African-Americans

Throughout the imperial crisis, African-Americans, as a deeply alienated group within society, quickly responded to calls for liberty and equality. In January 1766, when a group of blacks, inspired by anti-Stamp Act protests, had marched through Charles Town, South Carolina, shouting "Liberty!" they were arrested for inciting a rebellion. Thereafter, unrest among slaves—usually in the form of violence or escape—kept pace with that among white rebels. Then in 1772, a court decision in England electrified much of the black population. A Massachusetts slave, James Somerset, had accompanied his master to England, where he ran away but was recaptured. Aided by Quaker abolitionists, Somerset sued for his freedom. Writing for the King's Court, Lord Chief Justice William Mansfield ruled that because Parliament had never explicitly established slavery in England, Somerset must be freed.

Although the decision applied only to Somerset and had no force in the colonies, it inspired African-Americans to pursue their freedom. In January 1773, some of Somerset's fellow Massachusetts blacks filed the first of three petitions to the legislature, arguing that the decision should be extended to the colony. In Virginia and Maryland, dozens of enslaved persons ran away from their masters and sought passage aboard ships bound for England. As Anglo-American tensions mounted in 1774, many slaves, especially in the Chesapeake colonies, looked for war and the arrival of British troops as a means to their liberation. The young Virginia planter James Madison remarked that "if America and Britain come to a hostile rupture, I am afraid an insurrection among the slaves may and will be promoted" by England.

Madison's fears were borne out in November 1775 when Virginia's governor, Lord Dunmore, promised freedom to any able-bodied enslaved man who enlisted in the cause of restoring royal authority. Like Florida's offer of refuge to escaping South Carolina slaves (see Chapter 4), **Lord Dunmore's Proclamation** intended to undermine a planter-dominated society by appealing to slaves' longings for freedom. About one thousand Virginia blacks flocked to Dunmore. Those who fought donned uniforms proclaiming "Liberty to Slaves." Dunmore's proclamation associated British forces with slave liberation in the minds of both blacks and whites in the southern colonies, an association that continued during the war that followed.

The "Intolerable Acts"

Following the Boston Tea Party, Lord North fumed that only "New England fanatics" could imagine themselves oppressed by inexpensive tea. A member of Parliament drew wild applause by declaring that "the town of Boston ought to be knocked about by the ears, and destroy'd." In vain the Americans' supporter, Edmund Burke, pleaded for the one action that could end the crisis. "Leave America ... to tax herself.... Leave the Americans as they anciently stood." The British government, however, swiftly asserted its authority by enacting four "Coercive Acts" that, together with the unrelated Quebec Act, became known to colonists as the "**Intolerable Acts.**"

The first of the Coercive Acts, the Boston Port Bill, became law on April 1, 1774. It ordered the navy to close Boston harbor unless the town arranged to pay for the ruined tea by June 1. Lord North's cabinet deliberately imposed this impossibly short deadline to ensure the harbor's closing, which would lead to serious economic distress.

The second Coercive Act, the Massachusetts Government Act, revoked the Massachusetts charter and restructured the government. The colony's upper house would no longer be elected annually by the assembly but instead be appointed for life by the crown. The governor would independently appoint all judges and sheriffs, while sheriffs would appoint jurymen, who previously had been elected. Finally, towns could hold no more than one meeting a year without the governor's permission. These changes brought Massachusetts into line with other royal colonies.

The third of the new acts, the Administration of Justice Act, which some colonists cynically called the Murder Act, permitted any person charged with murder while enforcing royal authority in Massachusetts (such as the British soldiers indicted for the Boston Massacre) to be tried in England or in other colonies.

Finally, a new Quartering Act went beyond the earlier act of 1765 by allowing the governor to requisition empty private buildings for housing troops.

Americans learned of the Quebec Act along with the previous four statutes and associated it with them. Intended to cement loyalty to Britain among conquered French-Canadian Catholics, the law retained Roman Catholicism as Quebec's established religion. This provision alarmed Protestant Anglo-Americans who widely believed that Catholicism went hand in hand with despotism. Furthermore, the Quebec Act gave Canada's governors sweeping powers but established no legislature. It also permitted property disputes (but not criminal cases) to be decided by French law, which did not use juries. Finally, the law extended Quebec's territorial claims south to the Ohio River and west to the Mississippi, a vast area populated by Native Americans and some French. Although it had been designated off-limits by the Proclamation of 1763, several colonies continued to claim portions of the region.

Along with the appointment of General Thomas Gage, Britain's military commander in North America, as governor of Massachusetts, the "Intolerable Acts" convinced Anglo-Americans that Britain was plotting to abolish traditional English liberties throughout North America. Rebel pamphlets fed fears that Gage would starve Boston into submission and appoint corrupt sheriffs and judges to crush political dissent through rigged trials. By this reasoning, the new Quartering Act would repress any resistance by forcing troops on an unwilling population, and the "Murder Act" would encourage massacres by preventing local juries from convicting soldiers who killed civilians. Once resistance in Massachusetts had been smashed, the Quebec Act would serve as a blueprint for extinguishing representative government throughout the colonies. Parliament would revoke every colony's charter and introduce a government like Quebec's. Elected assemblies, freedom of religion for Protestants, and jury trials would all disappear.

Intended by Parliament simply to punish Massachusetts and particularly that rotten apple in the barrel, Boston—the acts instead pushed most colonies to the brink of rebellion. Repeal of these laws became, in effect, the colonists' nonnegotiable demand. Of the twenty-seven reasons justifying the break with Britain that Americans later cited in the Declaration of Independence, six concerned these statutes.

The First Conti-
nental Congress

In response to the "Intolerable Acts," the extralegal committees of correspondence of every colony but Georgia sent delegates to a **Continental Congress** in Philadelphia. The fifty-six delegates assembled on September 5, 1774, to find a way of defending the colonies' rights in common. Those in attendance included Samuel and John Adams of Massachusetts; John Jay of New York; Joseph Galloway and John Dickinson of Pennsylvania; and Patrick Henry, Richard Henry Lee, and George Washington of Virginia.

The First Continental Congress opened by endorsing a set of statements called the Suffolk Resolves. Recently adopted at a convention of Massachusetts towns, the resolves declared that the colonies owed no obedience to any of the Coercive Acts, that a provisional government should collect all taxes until the former Massachusetts charter was restored, and that defensive measures should be taken in the event of an attack by royal troops. The Continental Congress also voted to boycott all British imports after December 1 and to halt almost all exports to Britain and its West Indian possessions after September 1775 unless a reconciliation had been accomplished. This agreement, the Continental Association, would be enforced by locally elected committees of "observation" or "safety," whose members in effect would be seizing control of American trade from the royal customs service.

Such bold defiance displeased some delegates. Jay, Dickinson, Galloway, and other moderates who dominated the middle-colony contingent feared the internal turmoil that would surely accompany a head-on confrontation with Britain. These "trimmers" (John Adams's scornful phrase) unsuccessfully opposed nonimportation and tried in vain to win endorsement of Galloway's plan for an American legislature that would share the authority to tax and govern the colonies with Parliament.

Finally, however, the delegates summarized their principles and demands in a petition to the king. This document affirmed Parliament's power to regulate imperial commerce, but it argued that all previous parliamentary efforts to impose taxes, enforce laws through admiralty courts, suspend assemblies, and unilaterally revoke charters were unconstitutional. By addressing the king rather than Parliament, Congress was imploring George III to end the crisis by dismissing those ministers responsible for passing the Coercive Acts.

From Resis-
tance to
Rebellion

The divisions within the Continental Congress mirrored those within Anglo-American society at large. Tensions between moderates and radicals ran high, and bonds between Americans formerly united in outlook sometimes snapped. John Adams's onetime friend Jonathan Sewall, for example, charged that the Congress had made the "breach with the parent state a thousand times more irreparable than it was before." Fearing that Congress was enthroning "their High Mightinesses, the MOB," he and like-minded Americans refused to defy the king.

To solidify their defiance, resistance leaders coerced colonists who refused to support them. Thus the elected committees that Congress had created to enforce the Continental Association often became vigilantes, compelling merchants who still traded with Britain to burn their imports and make public apologies, browbeating clergymen who preached pro-British sermons, and pressuring Americans to adopt simpler diets and dress in order to relieve their dependence on British imports.

Additionally, in colony after colony, the committees took on government functions by organizing volunteer military companies and extralegal legislatures. By the spring of 1775, patriots had established provincial "congresses" that paralleled and rivaled the existing assemblies headed by royal governors.

Colonists prepared for the worst by collecting arms and organizing extralegal militia units (locally known as minutemen) whose members could respond instantly to an emergency. On April 19, 1775, Massachusetts's Governor Gage sent seven hundred British soldiers to seize military supplies that colonists had stored at Concord. Two couriers, William Dawes and Paul Revere, rode out to warn nearby towns of the troop movements. At Lexington, about seventy minutemen confronted the soldiers. After a confused skirmish in which eight minutemen died and a single redcoat was wounded, the British pushed on to Concord. There they found few munitions but encountered a growing swarm of armed Yankees. When some minutemen mistakenly thought the town was being burned, they exchanged fire with the British regulars and touched off a running battle that continued for most of the sixteen miles back to Boston. By day's end, the redcoats had suffered 273 casualties, compared to only 92 for the colonists. These engagements awakened the countryside, and by the evening of April 20, some twenty thousand New Englanders were besieging the British garrison in Boston.

Three weeks later, the Second Continental Congress convened in Philadelphia. Most delegates still opposed independence and at Dickinson's urging agreed to send a "loyal message" to George III. Dickinson composed the **Olive Branch Petition** listing three demands: a cease-fire at Boston, repeal of the Coercive Acts, and negotiations to establish guarantees of American rights. Yet while pleading for peace, the delegates also passed measures that Britain could only construe as rebellious. In particular, they voted in May 1775 to establish an "American continental army" and appointed George Washington its commander.

The Olive Branch Petition reached London along with news of the Continental Army's formation and of a battle fought just outside Boston on June 17. In this engagement, British troops attacked colonists entrenched on Breed's Hill and Bunker Hill. Although they succeeded in dislodging the Americans, the British suffered 1,154 casualties out of twenty-two hundred men, compared to a loss of 311 patriots.

After Bunker Hill, many Britons wanted retaliation, not reconciliation. On August 23, George III proclaimed New England in a state of rebellion, and in October he extended that pronouncement to include all the colonies. In December, Parliament likewise declared all the colonies rebellious, outlawing all British trade with them and subjecting their ships to seizure.

Common Sense   Despite the turn of events, many colonists clung to hopes of reconciliation. Even John Adams, who believed in the inevitability of separation, described himself as "fond of reconciliation, if we could reasonably entertain Hopes of it on a constitutional basis."

Through 1775, many colonists clung to the notion that evil ministers rather than the king were forcing unconstitutional measures on them. But with George III having declared the colonies to be in "open and avowed rebellion … for the purpose of establishing an independent empire," Anglo-Americans had no choice but either to submit or to acknowledge their goal of national independence.

Most colonists' sentimental attachment to the king, the last emotional barrier to their accepting independence, finally crumbled in January 1776 with the publication of Thomas Paine's **Common Sense**. A failed corset maker and schoolmaster, Paine immigrated to the colonies from England late in 1774 with a letter of introduction from Benjamin Franklin, a penchant for radical politics, and a gift for writing plain and pungent prose that anyone could understand.

Paine told Americans what they had been unable to bring themselves to say: monarchy was an institution rooted in superstition, dangerous to liberty, and inappropriate to Americans. The king was "the royal brute" and a "hardened, sullen-tempered Pharaoh." Whereas previous writers had maintained that certain corrupt politicians were directing an English conspiracy against American liberty, Paine argued that such a conspiracy was rooted in the very institutions of monarchy and empire. Moreover, he argued, America had no economic need for the British connection. As he put it, "The commerce by which she [America] hath enriched herself are the necessaries of life, and will always have a market while eating is the custom in Europe." In addition, he pointed out the events of the preceding six months had made independence a reality. Finally, Paine linked America's awakening nationalism with the sense of religious mission felt by many when he proclaimed, "We have it in our power to begin the world over again. A situation, similar to the present, hath not happened since the days of Noah until now." America, in Paine's view, would be not only a new nation but a new kind of nation, a model society founded on republican principles and unburdened by the oppressive beliefs and corrupt institutions of the European past.

Printed in both English and German, *Common Sense* sold more than one hundred thousand copies within three months, equal to one for every fourth or fifth adult male, making it a best seller. Readers passed copies from hand to hand and read passages aloud in public gatherings. The *Connecticut Gazette* described Paine's pamphlet as "a landflood that sweeps all before it." *Common Sense* had dissolved lingering allegiance to George III and Great Britain, removing the last psychological barrier to American independence.

Declaring Independence	As Americans absorbed Paine's views, the military conflict between Britain and the colonies escalated, making the possibility of reconciliation even less likely. In May 1775,

irregular troops from Vermont and Massachusetts had captured Fort Ticonderoga and Crown Point on the key route connecting New York and Canada. Six months later, Washington ordered Colonel Henry Knox, the army's senior artillerist, to bring the British artillery seized at Ticonderoga to reinforce the siege of Boston. Knox and his men built crude sleds to haul their fifty-nine cannons through dense forest and rugged, snow-covered mountains. Forty days and three hundred miles after leaving Ticonderoga, Knox and his exhausted troops reported to Washington in January 1776. They had accomplished one of the Revolution's great feats of endurance. The guns from Ticonderoga placed the outnumbered British in a hopeless position and forced them to evacuate Boston on March 17, 1776.

Regrouping and augmenting its forces at Halifax, Nova Scotia, Britain planned an assault on New York to drive a wedge between rebellious New England and the other colonies. Recognizing New York's strategic importance, Washington led most of his troops there in April 1776.

Other military moves reinforced the drift toward all-out war. In June, Congress ordered a two-pronged assault on Canada in which forces under General Philip Schuyler would move northward via Fort Ticonderoga to Montreal while Benedict Arnold would lead a march through the Maine forest to Quebec. Schuyler succeeded but Arnold failed. As Britain poured troops into Canada, the Americans prudently withdrew. At the same time, a British offensive in the southern colonies failed after an unsuccessful attempt to seize Charles Town.

By spring 1776, Paine's pamphlet, reinforced by the growing reality of war, had stimulated dozens of local gatherings—artisan guilds, town meetings, county conventions, and militia musters—to pass resolutions favoring American independence. The groundswell quickly spread to the colonies' extralegal legislatures. New England was already in rebellion, and Rhode Island declared itself independent in May 1776. The middle colonies hesitated to support independence because they feared, correctly, that any war would largely be fought over control of Philadelphia and New York. Following the news in April that North Carolina's congressional delegates were authorized to vote for independence, several southern colonies pressed for separation. Virginia's legislature instructed its delegates to propose independence, which Richard Henry Lee did on June 7. Formally adopting Lee's resolution on July 2, Congress created the United States of America.

The task of drafting a statement to justify the colonies' separation from England fell to a committee of five, including John Adams, Benjamin Franklin, and Thomas Jefferson, with Jefferson as the principal author. Among Congress's revisions to Jefferson's first draft: insertion of the phrase "pursuit of happiness" in place of "property" in the Declaration's most famous sentence, and its deletion of a statement blaming George III for foisting the slave trade on unwilling colonists. The **Declaration of Independence** (reprinted in the Appendix at the back of this volume) never mentioned Parliament by name, for Congress had moved beyond arguments over legislative representation and now wanted to separate America altogether from Britain and its head of state, the king. Jefferson listed twenty-seven "injuries and usurpations" committed by George III against the colonies. And he drew on a familiar line of radical thinking when he added that the king's actions had as their "direct object the establishment of an absolute tyranny over these states."

Like Paine, Jefferson elevated the colonists' grievances from a dispute over English freedoms to a struggle of universal dimensions. In the tradition of Locke and other Enlightenment figures, Jefferson argued that the English government had violated its contract with the colonists, thereby giving them the right to replace it with a government of their own design. And his eloquent emphasis on the equality of all individuals and their natural entitlement to justice, liberty, and self-fulfillment expressed republicans' deepest longing for a government that would rest on neither legal privilege nor exploitation of the majority by the few.

Jefferson addressed the Declaration of Independence as much to Americans uncertain about the wisdom of independence as to world opinion, for even at this late date a significant minority opposed independence or were uncertain whether to endorse it. Above all, he wanted to convince his fellow citizens that social and political progress could no longer be accomplished within the British Empire. But he left unanswered just which Americans were and were not equal to one another and entitled to liberty. All the colonies endorsing the Declaration countenanced, on grounds of racial inequality, the enslavement of blacks and severe restrictions on the rights of free blacks. Moreover, all had property qualifications that prevented many white men from voting. The proclamation that "all men" were created equal accorded with the Anglo-American assumption that women could not and should not function politically or legally as autonomous individuals. And Jefferson's accusation that George III had unleashed "the merciless Indian savages" on innocent colonists seemed to place Native Americans outside the bounds of humanity.

Was the Declaration of Independence a statement that expressed the sentiments of all but a minority of colonists? In a very narrow sense it was, but by framing the Declaration in universal terms, Jefferson and the Continental Congress made it something much greater. The ideas motivating Jefferson and his fellow delegates had moved thousands of ordinary colonists to political action over the preceding eleven years, both on their own behalf and on behalf of the colonies in their quarrel with Britain. For better or worse, the struggle for national independence had hastened, and become intertwined with, a quest for equality and personal independence that, for many Americans, transcended boundaries of class, race, or gender. In their reading, the Declaration never claimed that perfect justice and equal opportunity existed in the United States; rather, it challenged the Revolutionary generation and all who later inherited the nation to bring this ideal closer to reality.

CHRONOLOGY
1750–1776

1754	Albany Congress.
1754–1761	Seven Years' War (in Europe, 1756–1763).
1755	British expel Acadians from Nova Scotia.
1760	George III becomes king of Great Britain. Writs of assistance.
1762	Treaty of San Ildefonso.
1763	Treaty of Paris. Pontiac's War. Proclamation of 1763.
1763–1764	Paxton Boys uprising in Pennsylvania.
1764	Sugar Act.
1765	Stamp Act. African-Americans demand liberty in Charles Town. First Quartering Act.
1766	Stamp Act repealed. Declaratory Act.
1767	Revenue Act (Townshend duties). American Board of Customs Commissioners created.
1768	Massachusetts "circular letters." John Hancock's ship *Liberty* seized by Boston customs commissioner. First Treaty of Fort Stanwix. St. George's Fields Massacre in London.
1770	Townshend duties, except tea tax, repealed. Boston Massacre.

1771	Battle of Alamance Creek in North Carolina.
1772–1774	Committees of correspondence formed.
1772	Somerset decision in England.
1773	Tea Act and Boston Tea Party.
1774	Lord Dunmore's War.
	Coercive Acts and Quebec Act. First Continental Congress.
1775	Battles of Lexington and Concord.
	Lord Dunmore's Proclamation.
	Olive Branch Petition.
	Battles at Breed's Hill and Bunker Hill.
	George III and Parliament declare colonies to be in rebellion.
1776	Thomas Paine, *Common Sense*.
	Declaration of Independence.

CONCLUSION

In 1763, Britain and its North American colonies concluded a stunning victory over France, entirely eliminating that nation's formidable mainland American empire. Colonists proudly joined in hailing Britain as the world's most powerful nation, and they fully expected to reap territorial and economic benefits from the victory. Yet by 1775, colonists and Britons were fighting with one another. The war had exhausted Britain's treasury and led the government to look to the colonies for help in defraying the costs of maintaining its enlarged empire. In attempting to collect more revenue and to centralize imperial authority, English officials confronted the ambitions and attitudes of Americans who felt themselves to be in every way equal to Britons.

The differences between British and American viewpoints sharpened slowly and unevenly between 1760 and 1776. One major turning point was the Stamp Act crisis (1765–1766), when many Americans began questioning Parliament's authority, as opposed to that of their own elected legislatures, to levy taxes in the colonies. Colonists also broadened their protests during the Stamp Act crisis, moving beyond carefully worded petitions to fiery resolutions, crowd actions, an intercolonial congress, and a nonimportation movement. Colonial resistance became even more effective during the crisis over the Townshend duties (1767–1770) because of both increased intercolonial cooperation and support from within Britain. Thereafter, growing numbers of colonists moved from simply denying Parliament's authority to tax them to rejecting virtually any British authority over them.

After 1774, independence was almost inevitable. Yet Americans were the most reluctant of revolutionaries—even after their own state and national legislatures were functioning, their troops had clashed with Britain's, and George III had declared them to be in rebellion. Tom Paine's prose finally persuaded them that they could stand on their own, without the support of Britain's markets, manufactures, or monarch. Thereafter, a grass-roots independence movement began, leading

Congress in July 1776 to proclaim American independence and, thereby, to declare revolutionary war.

Americans by no means followed a single road to revolution. Ambitious elites resented British efforts to curtail colonial autonomy as exercised almost exclusively by members of their own class in the assemblies. They and many more in the middle classes were angered by British policies that made commerce less profitable and consumption more costly. But others, including both western settlers and poor and working city dwellers like George Robert Twelves Hewes, defied conventions demanding that humble people defer to the authority of their social superiors. Sometimes resorting to violence, they directed their wrath toward British officials and colonial elites alike. Many African-Americans, on the other hand, considered Britain as more likely than white colonists, especially slaveholders, to liberate them. And Native Americans recognized that British authority, however limited, provided a measure of protection from land-hungry colonists. These divisions would persist after the eruption of full-scale revolutionary war.

6

SECURING INDEPENDENCE, DEFINING NATIONHOOD 1776–1788

CHAPTER OUTLINE

• The Prospects of War • War and Peace, 1776–1783 • The Revolution and Social Change • Forging New Governments, 1776–1787 • Toward a New Constitution, 1786–1788

THE PROSPECTS OF WAR

The Revolution was both a collective struggle that pitted the independent states against Britain and a civil war among American peoples. American opponents of independence constituted one of several factors working in Britain's favor as war began. Others included Britain's larger population and its superior military resources and preparation. America, on the other hand, was located far from Britain and enjoyed the intense commitment to independence of patriots and the Continental Army, led by the formidable George Washington.

Loyalists and Other British Sympathizers   Even after the Declaration of Independence, some Americans remained opposed to secession from Britain, including about 20 percent of all whites. Although these internal enemies of the Revolution called themselves **loyalists,** they were "Tories" to their patriot, or Whig, opponents. Whigs remarked, only half in jest, that "a tory was a thing with a head in England, a body in America, and a neck that needed stretching."

Loyalists shared many political beliefs with patriots. In particular, most opposed Parliament's claim to tax the colonies. Finding themselves fighting for a cause with which they did not entirely agree, some loyalists would change sides during the war. They probably shared the worry expressed in 1775 by the Reverend Jonathan Boucher, a Maryland loyalist, who preached with two loaded pistols lying on his pulpit cushion: "For my part I equally dread a Victory by either side."

Loyalists disagreed, however, with the patriots' insistence that independence was the only way to preserve the colonists' constitutional rights. The loyalists denounced separation as an illegal act certain to ignite an unnecessary war. Above all, they retained a profound reverence for the crown and believed that if they failed to defend their king, they would sacrifice their personal honor.

The mutual hatred between Whigs and Tories exceeded that of patriots and the British. Each side saw its cause as so sacred that opposition by a fellow American was an unforgivable act of betrayal. Americans inflicted the worst atrocities committed during the war upon each other.

The most important factor in determining loyalist strength in any area was the political power of local Whigs and their success in convincing their neighbors that Britain threatened their liberty. For several years, colonial resistance leaders in New England towns, tidewater Virginia, and coastal South Carolina had vigorously pursued a program of political education and popular mobilization. As a result, probably no more than 5 percent of whites in these areas were committed loyalists in 1776. Where elites and other leaders were divided or indecisive, however, loyalist sentiment flourished. Loyalist strength was greatest in New York and New Jersey, where elites were especially reluctant to declare their allegiance to either side. Those two states eventually furnished about half of the twenty-one thousand Americans who fought as loyalists.

The next most significant factor influencing loyalist military strength was the geographic distribution of recent British immigrants, who remained closely identified with their homeland. Among these newcomers were thousands of British soldiers who had served in the Seven Years' War and stayed on in the colonies, usually in New York, where they could obtain land grants of two hundred acres. An additional 125,000 English, Scots, and Irish landed from 1763 to 1775—the greatest number of Britons to arrive during any dozen years of the colonial era. In New York, Georgia, and the backcountry of North and South Carolina, where native-born Britons were heavily concentrated, the proportion of loyalists among whites probably ranged from 25 percent to 40 percent in 1776. During the war, immigrants from the British Isles would form many Tory units. After the Revolution, foreign-born loyalists were a majority of those whom the British compensated for wartime property losses—including three-quarters of all such claimants from the Carolinas and Georgia.

Quebec's religious and secular elites comprised another significant white minority with pro-British sympathies. After the British had conquered New France in the Seven Years' War, the Quebec Act of 1774 retained Catholicism as the established religion in Quebec and continued partial use of French civil law, measures that reconciled Quebec's provincial leaders to British rule. When Continental forces invaded Quebec in 1775–1776, they found widespread support among nonelite French as well as English Canadians. After British forces repulsed the invasion, Britain's military, supported by local elites, retained control of Canada throughout the war.

The rebels never attempted to win over three other mainland colonies—Nova Scotia and East and West Florida—whose small British populations consisted of recent immigrants and British troops. Nor was independence seriously considered in Britain's thirteen West Indian colonies, which were dominated by absentee plantation

Benedict Arnold, Patriot Turned Loyalist *Arnold was a patriot general who defected to the British. A patriot street parade in Philadelphia in 1780 portrayed him as a two-faced tool of the devil.*

owners who lived in England and depended on selling their sugar exports in the protected British market.

The British cause would draw significant wartime support from nonwhites. Before the war began, African-Americans made clear that they considered their own liberation from slavery a higher priority than the colonies' independence from Britain. After Virginia slaves flocked to Lord Dunmore's ranks, hundreds of South Carolina slaves had escaped and had taken refuge on British ships in Charles Town's harbor. During the war about twenty thousand enslaved African-Americans, mostly from the southern and middle colonies, escaped their owners. Most were recaptured or died, especially from epidemics, but a small minority achieved freedom, often after serving as laborers or soldiers in the Royal Army. Among the slaveholders whose slaves escaped to British protection was Thomas Jefferson. Meanwhile, about five thousand enslaved and free African-Americans, mostly from New England, calculated that supporting the rebels would hasten their own emancipation and equality.

Although Native Americans were deeply divided, most supported the British, either from the beginning or after being pressured by one side or the other to abandon neutrality. In the Ohio country, most Shawnees, Delawares, Mingos, and other Indians continued to resent settlers' incursions, but some sought to remain neutral and a few communities initially supported the Americans. After Pontiac's War, Native Americans in the Great Lakes region had developed improved relations with British agents and now supported Britain's cause.

The most powerful Native American confederacies—the Six Nations Iroquois, the Creeks, and the Cherokees—were badly divided when the war broke out. Among the Six Nations, the central council fire at Onondaga, a symbol of unity since Hiawatha's time, died out. Most Iroquois followed the lead of the Mohawk chief **Joseph Brant** (Thayendagea) in supporting Britain. But the Oneidas and Tuscaroras, influenced by a New England missionary, actively sided with the rebels against other Iroquois. Creeks' allegiances reflected each village's earlier trade ties with either Britain or Spain (the latter leaned toward the colonists). Cherokee ranks were split between anti-American militants who saw an opportunity to drive back settlers and those who thought that Cherokees' best hope was to steer clear of the Anglo-American conflict.

The patriots also had other sources of Indian support. Native Americans in upper New England, easternmost Canada, and the Illinois and Wabash valleys were initially anti-British because of earlier ties with the French, though many of them became alienated from the colonists during the war. In eastern areas long dominated by colonial governments, there were fewer Indians, most of whom supported the American war effort.

The Opposing Sides   Britain entered the war with two major advantages. First, in 1776 the 11 million inhabitants of the British Isles greatly outnumbered the 2.5 million colonists, one-third of whom were either slaves or loyalists. Second, Britain possessed the world's largest navy and one of its best professional armies. Even so, the royal military establishment grew during the war years to a degree that strained Britain's resources. The number of soldiers stationed in North America, the British Isles, and the West Indies more than doubled from 48,000 to 111,000 men, especially after the war became an international conflict (see Beyond America). To meet its manpower needs, the British government hired thirty thousand German mercenaries known as Hessians and enlisted 21,000 loyalists.

Britain's ability to crush the rebellion was further weakened by the decline in its sea power, a result of budget cuts after 1763. Midway through the war, half of the Royal Navy's ships sat in dry dock awaiting major repairs. Although the navy expanded rapidly from 18,000 to 111,000 sailors, it lost 42,000 men to desertion and 20,000 to disease or injuries. In addition, Britain's merchant marine suffered from raids by American privateers. During the war rebel privateers and the fledgling U.S. navy would capture over 2,000 British merchant vessels and 16,000 crewmen.

Britain could ill afford these losses, for it faced a colossal task in trying to supply its troops in America. In fact, it had to import from Britain most of the food consumed by its army, a third of a ton per soldier per year. Seriously overextended, the navy barely kept the army supplied and never effectively blockaded American ports.

Because of the enormous strain that the war imposed, British leaders faced serious problems maintaining their people's support for the conflict. The war more than doubled the national debt, thereby adding to the burdens of a people already paying record taxes. Voters could not be expected to vote against their pocketbooks forever.

The United States faced different but no less severe wartime problems. Besides the fact that many colonists, slaves, and Native Americans favored the British, the patriots faced a formidable military challenge. American men were accustomed to serving as citizen-soldiers in colonial (now state) militias. Although militias often performed well in hit-and-run guerrilla skirmishes, they were not trained to fight pitched battles against professional armies like Britain's. Congress recognized that independence would never be secured if the new nation relied on guerrilla tactics, avoided major battles, and allowed the British to occupy its major population centers. Moreover, potential European allies would recognize that dependence on guerrilla warfare meant the rebels could not drive out the British army.

George Washington, by John Trumbull, 1780 *Washington posed for this portrait at the height of the Revolutionary War, accompanied by his enslaved servant, William Lee.*

For the United States to succeed, the Continental Army would have to supersede the state militias and would need to fight in the standard European fashion. Professional eighteenth-century armies relied on the precisely executed movements of mass formations. Victory often depended on rapid maneuvers to crush an enemy's undefended flank or rear. Attackers needed exceptional skill in close-order drill to fall on an enemy before the enemy could re-form and return fire. Because muskets had a range of less than one hundred yards, armies in battle were never far apart. The troops advanced within musket range of each other, stood upright without cover, and fired volleys at one another until one line weakened from its casualties. Discipline, training, and nerve were essential if soldiers were to stay in ranks while comrades fell beside them. The stronger side then attacked at a quick walk with bayonets drawn and drove off its opponents.

In 1775, Britain possessed a well-trained army with a strong tradition of discipline and bravery under fire. In contrast, the Continental Army lacked an inspirational heritage as well as a deep pool of experienced officers and sergeants who could turn raw recruits into crack units. European officers such as Kósciuszko helped make up for the shortage of leaders. Although the United States mobilized about 220,000 troops, compared to the 162,000 who served the British, most served short terms. Even with bounties (signing bonuses), promises of land after service, and other incentives, the army had difficulty attracting men for the long term. Most whites and blacks who did sign up for multiyear or indefinite lengths of time were poor and landless. Such men joined not out of patriotism but because, as one of them, a jailed debtor named Ezekiel Brown, put it, they had "little or nothing to lose."

The Americans experienced a succession of heartbreaking defeats in the war's early years, and the new nation would have been hard-pressed had it not been for the military contributions of France and Spain in the war's later stages. Yet, to win the war, the Continentals did not have to destroy the British army but only prolong the rebellion until Britain's taxpayers lost patience with the struggle. Until then, American victory would depend on the ability of one man to keep his army fighting. That man was George Washington.

The young Washington's mistakes and defeats in the Ohio valley (see Chapter 5) taught him about the dangers of overconfidence and the need for determination in the face of defeat. He also learned much about American soldiers, especially that they performed best when led by example and treated with respect.

After resigning his commission in 1758, Washington had served in the Virginia House of Burgesses, where his influence grew, not because he thrust himself into every issue but because others respected him and sought his opinion. Having emerged as an early, though not outspoken, opponent of parliamentary taxation, he later sat in the Continental Congress. In the eyes of the many who valued his advice and remembered his military experience, Washington was the logical choice to head the Continental Army.

WAR AND PEACE, 1776–1783

Until mid-1778, the Revolutionary War remained centered in the North, where each side won some important victories. Meanwhile, American forces prevailed over British troops and their Native American allies to gain control of the trans-Appalachian West. The war was finally decided in the South when American and French forces won a stunning victory at Yorktown, Virginia, in 1781. In the peace treaty that followed, Britain finally acknowledged American independence.

Shifting Fortunes in the North, 1776–1778 During the second half of 1776, the two sides focused on New York. Under two brothers—General William Howe and Admiral Richard, Lord Howe—130 British warships carrying 32,000 royal troops landed at New York in the summer of 1776. Defending the city, were 18,000 poorly trained soldiers under George Washington.

By the end of the year, William Howe's men had killed or captured one-quarter of Washington's troops and had forced the survivors to retreat from New York across New Jersey and the Delaware River into Pennsylvania. Thomas Paine aptly described these demoralizing days as "the times that try men's souls."

With the British nearing Philadelphia, Washington decided to seize the offensive before the morale of his army and country collapsed completely. On Christmas night 1776, his troops returned to New Jersey and attacked a Hessian garrison at Trenton, where they captured 918 Germans and lost only four Continentals. Washington's men then attacked twelve hundred British at Princeton on January 3, 1777, and killed or captured one-third of them while sustaining only forty casualties.

The American victories at Trenton and Princeton had several important conse-quences. At a moment when defeat seemed inevitable, they boosted civilian and military morale. In addition, they drove a wedge between New Jersey's five thousand loyalists and the British army. Washington's victories forced the British to remove virtually all their New Jersey garrisons to New York early in 1777. Once the British were gone, New Jersey's militia disarmed known loyalists, jailed their leaders, and kept a constant watch on suspected Tories. Bowing to the inevitable, most remaining loyalists swore allegiance to the Continental Congress. Some even joined the rebels.

After the Battle of Princeton, the Marquis de Lafayette, a young French aristocrat, joined Washington's staff. The twenty-year-old Lafayette was brave, idealistic, and optimistic. Given Lafayette's close connections with the French court, his presence indicated that France might recognize American independence and declare war on Britain. Before recognizing the new nation, however, King Louis XVI wanted proof that the Americans could win a major battle, a feat they had not yet accomplished.

Louis did not have to wait long. In the summer of 1777, the British planned a two-pronged assault intended to crush American resistance in New York State and thereby isolate New England. Pushing off from Montreal, a force of regulars and their Iroquois allies under Lieutenant Colonel Barry St. Leger would march south along Lake Ontario and invade central New York from Fort Oswego in the west. At the same time, General John Burgoyne would lead the main British force south from Quebec through eastern New York and link up with St. Leger near Albany.

Nothing went according to British plans. St. Leger's force of nineteen hundred British and Iroquois advanced one hundred miles and halted to besiege 750 Continentals at Fort Stanwix. Unable to take the post after three weeks, St. Leger retreated in late August 1777.

Burgoyne's campaign appeared more promising after his force of eighty-three hundred British and Hessians recaptured Fort Ticonderoga. But as Burgoyne continued southward, nearly seven thousand American troops under General Horatio Gates prepared to challenge him near Saratoga. In two battles in the fall, the British suffered twelve hundred casualties while failing to dislodge the Americans. Surrounded and hopelessly outnumbered, Burgoyne surrendered on October 17, 1777.

The **Battle of Saratoga** would prove to be the war's turning point. The victory convinced France that the Americans could win the war. In February 1778, France formally recognized the United States. Four months later, it went to war with Britain. Spain declared war on Britain in 1779, but as an ally of France, not the United States, and the Dutch Republic joined them in the last days of 1780 (see Beyond America). Britain faced a coalition of enemies, without allies of its own.

Meanwhile, as Gates and Burgoyne maneuvered in upstate New York, Britain's General Howe landed eighteen thousand troops near Philadelphia. With Washington at their head and Lafayette at his side, sixteen thousand Continentals occupied the imperiled city in late August 1777.

The two armies collided on September 11, 1777, at Brandywine Creek, Pennsylvania. In the face of superior British discipline, most Continental units crumbled, and Congress fled Philadelphia in panic, enabling Howe to occupy the city. Howe again defeated Washington at Germantown on October 4. In one month's bloody fighting, 20 percent of the Continentals were killed, wounded, or captured.

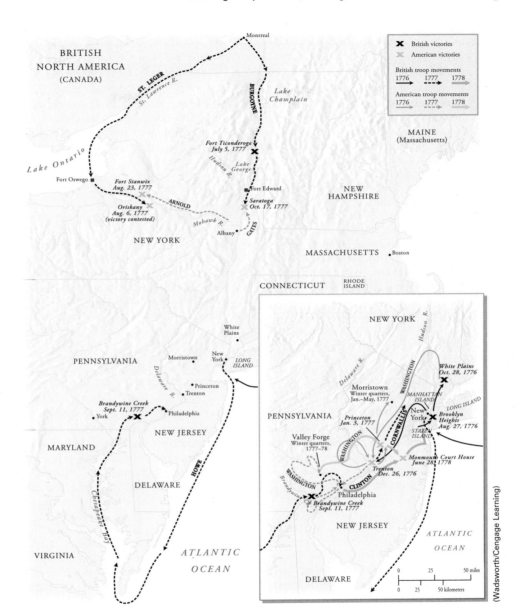

MAP 6.1 Northern Campaigns, 1776–1778

The major revolutionary battles of these years took place in New York, New Jersey, and Pennsylvania. The inset indicates battles in 1776, when the British invaded Long Island and New York City, pushing Washington's troops across New Jersey until they won crucial battles at Trenton and Princeton. The larger map illustrates British offensives in 1777; the 1778 battle at Monmouth Court House appears on the inset.

BEYOND AMERICA – GLOBAL INTERACTIONS

The American Revolution as an International War

Originating as a conflict between Britain and its colonies in mainland North America, the American Revolution turned into an international war that extended to Europe, the West Indies, South America, Africa, and Asia. The widening of the war contributed directly to America's struggle for independence from Britain.

Britain and France had emerged as rival maritime empires nearly a century earlier and had fought four major wars. Most recently, in the Seven Years' War (1754–1763), the balance of power between them shifted dramatically when France lost all its possessions in mainland North America and India.

The war left both nations facing enormous debts and populations that were heavily but inequitably taxed, especially in France. Britain also sought to finance and administer its suddenly enlarged empire. The East India Company, which functioned as both colonial government in India and monopolistic trade company throughout Asia, was financially troubled. Its local officials in India pursued personal profits, it had accumulated an enormous surplus of tea from China, and American colonists refused to buy its tea. To enhance Company revenues, Parliament passed the Tea Act (1773), which lowered the price of tea by lifting import duties and by allowing Company agents to sell directly to colonial consumers, bypassing American merchants. When, in the Boston Tea Party, radical protesters destroyed Company tea to prevent its unloading, British officials no longer doubted that Americans were disloyal to the empire.

The outbreak of Anglo-American conflict in 1775 provided France with an opportunity to avenge its defeat in the Seven Years' War. France borrowed even more money to supply funds and arms to the rebels and welcomed American ships at its ports. French military volunteers, most notably the Marquis de Lafayette, joined the American cause. France also sped up the rebuilding of its army and navy, achieving naval equality with Britain by 1778. Spain, an ally of France and rival of Britain for nearly a century, also contributed arms and other supplies to the rebels. Imported weapons and ammunition were a critical factor in the American victory at Saratoga in October 1777.

As a result of Saratoga, France in February 1778 formally recognized American independence, allied with the United States against Britain, and renounced all territorial claims in mainland North America. After declaring war on Britain in June, France dispatched warships and troops to the West Indies, forcing Britain to evacuate Philadelphia and divert five thousand troops from North America to defend its sugar colonies. Over the next year, British troops seized France's military stronghold at St. Lucia while French forces captured the British colonies of St. Vincent, Grenada, and Dominica.

Spain, eager to reclaim Gibraltar from Britain, joined the war in 1779 as an ally of France but not of the Americans. (Spain feared that an independent United States would threaten Louisiana.) Spain and France then planned a massive invasion of England. Although they failed to launch the invasion, Britain as a precaution kept half its war fleet nearby and five thousand troops in Ireland, thereby spreading its forces even more thinly.

The Americans gained another ally when the Netherlands abandoned its alliance with Britain. Since the outbreak of the Revolution, Dutch merchants and Dutch West Indian planters had traded with the Americans. Many Dutch also linked their republican aspirations with those of the United States while resenting British domination of its trade and foreign policy. After the British in 1780 seized a

Dutch convoy bound for France, the Netherlands declared war on Britain. British forces in 1781 captured most Dutch possessions in the West Indies and adjacent South American mainland.

Like the Netherlands, most European countries bristled under British naval domination and feared that Britain would interfere with their trade. To prevent such an outcome, Empress Catherine II ("the Great") in 1780 declared Russia's "armed neutrality." She asserted Russia's right as a neutral country to trade commodities with any nation, threatened to retaliate against any belligerent attempting to search Russian ships, and called on other countries to join a League of Armed Neutrality. Sweden, Denmark, the Netherlands, Prussia, Portugal, Turkey, and several smaller nations joined the League. Recognizing its diplomatic isolation, Britain left League members alone (except the Netherlands) lest it find itself fighting even more enemies.

In 1781, a formidable French fleet commanded by Admiral François de Grasse sailed from France via the West Indies to Chesapeake Bay. Arriving in August, the fleet landed several thousand French troops. The French troops joined Continental forces under George Washington in besieging Lord Cornwallis's base at Yorktown while the fleet prevented any British from slipping out. The Franco-American trap forced Cornwallis to surrender in October.

Although the victory at Yorktown ensured America's independence, it did not end the international war. In 1782, Spain attempted, unsuccessfully, to seize Gibraltar. Meanwhile, de Grasse had returned to the Caribbean. Although failing to recapture St. Lucia, he seized St. Kitts after five weeks of fierce British resistance. As he prepared a massive French-Spanish invasion of Jamaica, British forces cornered his fleet in an inter-island passage called the Saintes and captured four ships and de Grasse himself. Elsewhere, France sought to regain territory it had lost to Britain in

the Seven Years' War. In 1779, its forces seized Senegal in West Africa. The most powerful state in India, Mysore, had long resisted the British East India Company and, before 1763, had favored France. In 1780, the ruler of Mysore, Hyder Ali, joined four other Indian rulers (usually rivals of one another) in calling for "the expulsion of the English nation from India." Although the alliance failed to act, Hyder Ali led Mysore's forces in a standoff with British troops for two years. In 1782, a French naval fleet arrived to aid Mysore, threatening Britain's presence in South India.

By then, however, the war's protagonists were discussing terms of peace. The result of their negotiations was the Treaty of Paris (1783), under which America became independent; Britain and France returned all territories seized from one another in the Caribbean (except for one French-held island), India, and Senegal; and Britain returned a port at Ceylon (now Sri Lanka) to the Netherlands.

The American Revolution left a volatile mix in the North Atlantic. In achieving independence, the United States accelerated the appeal of republican ideals that were fomenting popular discontent with monarchies across Europe. Ironically, by supporting the birth of a revolutionary republic, the French monarchy added to France's already crushing debts, thereby hastening its own downfall and the advent of an even more radical revolution in its own country. The French Revolution would in turn generate a new cycle of global warfare lasting until 1815.

Questions for Analysis

1. *What impact did other countries have on the struggle between Britain and its American colonies?*

2. *How did the results of the war in mainland North America compare with the outcome elsewhere?*

While the British army wintered comfortably in Philadelphia, the Continentals huddled eighteen miles away in the bleak hills of Valley Forge. Joseph Plumb Martin, a seventeen-year-old Massachusetts recruit, recorded the troops' condition in his diary: "The greatest part were not only shirtless and barefoot but destitute of all other clothing, especially blankets." However, he concluded, "we had engaged in the defense of our injured country and were willing nay, we were determined, to persevere as long as such hardships were not altogether intolerable." Shortages of provisions, especially food, would continue to undermine morale and, on some occasions, discipline among American forces.

The army also lacked training. At Saratoga, the Americans' overwhelming numbers more than their skill had forced Burgoyne to surrender. Indeed, when Washington's men had met Howe's forces on equal terms, they lost badly.

The Continental Army received a desperately needed boost in February 1778, when a German soldier of fortune, Friedrich von Steuben, arrived at Valley Forge. The short, squat Steuben did not look like a soldier, but this earthy German instinctively liked Americans and became immensely popular. He had a talent for motivating men (sometimes by staging humorous tantrums featuring a barrage of German, English, and French swearing); but more important, he possessed administrative genius. In a mere four months, General Steuben almost single-handedly turned the army into a formidable fighting force.

British officials decided to evacuate Philadelphia in June 1778 so as to free up several thousand troops for action against France in the West Indies. General Henry Clinton, the new commander-in-chief in North America, led the troops northward for New York. The Continental Army got its first opportunity to demonstrate Steuben's training when it caught up with Clinton's rear guard at Monmouth, New Jersey, on June 28, 1778. The battle raged for six hours in one-hundred-degree heat until Clinton broke off contact. Expecting to renew the fight at daybreak, the Americans slept on their arms, but Clinton's army slipped away before then. The British would never again win easily, except when they faced more militiamen than Continentals.

The Battle of Monmouth ended the contest for the North. Clinton occupied New York, which the Royal Navy made safe from attack. Washington kept his army nearby to watch Clinton, while the Whig militia hunted down the last few Tory guerrillas and extinguished loyalism.

The War in the West, 1776–1782

A different kind of war developed west of the Appalachians, consisting of small-scale skirmishes rather than major battles involving thousands of troops. Long-standing tensions between Native peoples and land-hungry settlers continued to simmer. In one sense, the warfare between them only continued an older frontier struggle. Despite its smaller scale, the war in the West was fierce, and the stakes—for the new nation, for the British, and for Indians in the region—were enormous.

The war in the West erupted in 1776 when Cherokees began attacking settlers from North Carolina and nearby colonies who had encroached on their homelands. After suffering heavy losses, the colonies recovered and organized retaliatory expeditions. Within a year, these expeditions had burned most Cherokee towns, forcing

Joseph Brant, by Gilbert Stuart, 1786 *The youthful Mohawk leader was a staunch ally of the British during the Revolutionary War, and thereafter resisted U.S. expansion in the Northwest.*

the Cherokees to sign treaties that ceded most of their land in South Carolina and substantial tracts in North Carolina and Tennessee.

The intense fighting lasted longer in the Northwest. Largely independent of American and British coordination, Ohio Indians and white settlers fought for two years in Kentucky, with neither side gaining a clear advantage. But after British troops occupied French settlements in what is now Illinois and Indiana, Colonel George Rogers Clark led 175 Kentucky militiamen north of the Ohio River. After capturing and losing Vincennes, Clark retook the French town for good in February 1779. With the British unable to offer assistance, their Native American allies were vulnerable. In May, John Bowman led a second Kentucky unit in a campaign that destroyed most Shawnee villages, and in August a move northward from Pittsburgh by Daniel Brodhead inflicted similar damage on the Delawares and Mingos.

Although these raids depleted their populations and food supplies, most Ohio Indians resisted the Americans until the war's end.

Meanwhile, pro-British Iroquois, led by the gifted Mohawk leader Joseph Brant, devastated the Pennsylvania and New York frontiers in 1778, killing about seven hundred settlers. In 1779, American General John Sullivan retaliated by invading Iroquois country with thirty-seven hundred Continental troops, along with several hundred Tuscaroras and Oneidas who had broken with the other Iroquois nations. Sullivan fought just one battle, near present-day Elmira, New York, in which his artillery routed Brant's warriors. Then he burned two dozen Iroquois villages and destroyed a million bushels of corn, causing most Iroquois to flee without food into Canada. Untold hundreds starved during the next winter, when more than sixty inches of snow fell.

In 1780, Brant's thousand warriors took revenge on the Tuscaroras and Oneidas, and then laid waste to Pennsylvania and New York for two years. But this final whirlwind masked reality: Sullivan's campaign had devastated the pro-British Iroquois.

Fighting continued in the West until 1782. Despite their intensity, the western campaigns did not determine the outcome of the war itself. Nevertheless, they would have a significant impact on the future shape of the United States.

Victory in the South, 1778–1781

In 1778, the war's focus shifted to the South. By securing southern ports, Britain expected to acquire the flexibility needed to move its forces back and forth between the West Indies—where they faced French and Spanish opposition— and the mainland, as necessity dictated. In addition, the South looked like a relatively easy target. General Clinton expected to seize key southern ports and, with the aid of loyalist militiamen, move back toward the North, pacifying one region after another.

The plan unfolded smoothly at first. In the spring of 1778, British troops from East Florida took control of Georgia. After a two-year delay caused by political bickering at home, Clinton sailed from New York with nine thousand troops and forced the surrender of Charles Town, South Carolina, and its thirty-four-hundred-man garrison on May 12, 1780. However, the British quickly found that there were fewer loyalists than they had expected.

Southern loyalism had suffered several serious blows since the war began. When the Cherokees had attacked the Carolina frontier in 1776, they killed whites indiscriminately. Numerous Tories had switched sides, joining the rebel militia to defend their homes. The arrival of British troops sparked a renewed exodus of enslaved Africans from their plantations. About one-third of Georgia's blacks and one-fourth of South Carolina's fled to British lines or to British-held Florida in quest of freedom. Although British officials attempted to return runaway slaves to loyalist masters, they met with limited success. Planters feared that loss of control over their human property would lead to a black uprising. Despite British efforts to placate them, many white loyalists abandoned the British and welcomed the rebels' return to power in 1782. Those who remained loyalists, embittered by countless instances of harsh treatment under patriot rule, took revenge. Patriots struck back whenever possible, perpetuating an ongoing cycle of revenge, retribution, and retaliation among whites.

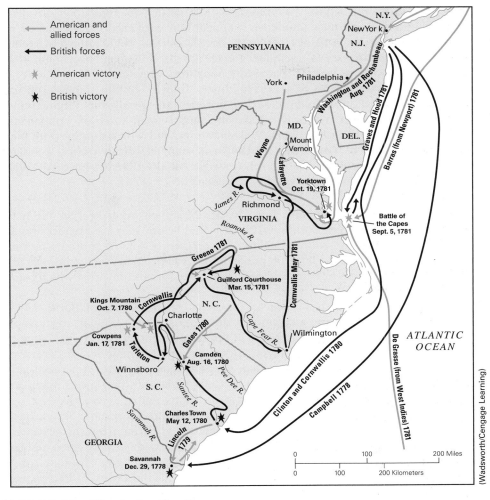

MAP 6.2 The War in the South

The southern war—after the British invasion of Georgia in late 1778—was characterized by a series of British thrusts into the interior, leading to battles with American defenders in both North and South Carolina. Finally, after promising beginnings, Cornwallis's foray into Virginia ended with disaster at Yorktown in October 1781.

Meanwhile, Horatio Gates took command of American forces in the South. With only a small force of Continentals at his disposal, Gates had to rely on poorly trained militiamen. In August 1780, Lord Charles Cornwallis inflicted a crushing defeat on Gates at Camden, South Carolina. Fleeing after firing a single volley, Gates's militia left his badly outnumbered Continentals to be overrun. Camden was the worst rebel defeat of the war.

Washington and Congress responded by relieving Gates of command and sending General Nathanael Greene to confront Cornwallis. Greene subsequently fought and lost three major battles between March and September 1781. "We fight, get beat, rise, and fight again," he wrote back to Washington. Still, Greene won the campaign, for he gave the Whig militia the protection they needed to hunt down loyalists, stretched British supply lines until they snapped, and weakened Cornwallis by inflicting much heavier casualties than the British general could afford. Greene's dogged resistance forced Cornwallis to leave the Carolina backcountry in American hands and to lead his battered troops into Virginia.

Cornwallis established a base at Yorktown, Virginia. Britain's undoing began on August 30, 1781, when a French fleet dropped anchor off the Virginia coast and landed troops near Yorktown. Lafayette and a small force of Continentals from nearby joined the French while Washington arrived with his army from New York. In the **Battle of Yorktown,** six thousand trapped British troops stood off eighty-eight hundred Americans and seventy-eight hundred French for three weeks before surrendering with military honors on October 19, 1781.

Peace at Last, 1782–1783   "Oh God!" Lord North exclaimed upon hearing the news from Yorktown. "It's all over." Cornwallis's surrender drained the will of England's overtaxed people to continue fighting and forced Britain to negotiate for peace. John Adams, Benjamin Franklin, and John Jay were America's principal delegates to the peace talks in Paris, which began in June 1782.

Military realities largely influenced the terms of the **Treaty of Paris** (1783). Britain recognized American independence and agreed to withdraw all royal troops from the new nation's soil. The British had little choice but to award the Confederation all lands east of the Mississippi. Although the vast majority of Americans were clustered near the eastern seaboard, twenty thousand Anglo-Americans now lived west of the Appalachians. Moreover, Clark's victories had given Americans control of the Northwest, while Spain had kept Britain out of the Southwest.

On the whole, the settlement was highly favorable to the United States, but it left some disputes unresolved. Under a separate treaty, Britain returned East and West Florida to Spain, but the boundaries designated by this treaty were ambiguous. Spain interpreted the treaty to mean that it regained the same Florida territory that it had ceded to Britain in 1763 (see Chapter 5). But the Treaty of Paris named the thirty-first parallel as Florida's northern border, well south of the area claimed by Spain. Spain and the United States would dispute the northern boundary of Florida until 1795 (as discussed later in this chapter and in Chapter 7).

The Treaty of Paris failed to prevent several future disputes between Britain and America. Not bound by the treaty, which extended only to national governments, state governments refused to compensate loyalists for their property losses and erected barriers against British creditors' attempts to collect prewar debts. In retaliation, the British refused to honor treaty pledges to abandon forts in the Northwest and to return American-owned slaves under their control.

Notably missing in the Treaty of Paris was any reference to Native Americans, most of whom had supported the British to avert the alternative—an independent American nation whose citizens would covet their lands. In effect, the treaty left Native peoples to deal with the Confederation on their own, without any provision for their status or treatment. Joseph Brant and other Native American leaders were outraged. Not surprisingly, most Indians did not acknowledge the new nation's claims to sovereignty over their territory.

The Treaty of Paris ratified American independence, but winning independence had exacted a heavy price. At least 5 percent of all free males between the ages of sixteen and forty-five—white, black, and Native American—died fighting the British. Only the Civil War produced a higher ratio of casualties to the nation's population. Furthermore, the war drove perhaps one of every six loyalists, several thousand slaves, and several thousand Native Americans into exile. Whites, blacks, and Indians moved to Canada, and whites moved to Britain and the West Indies. After finding that both the land and inhabitants in Nova Scotia were inhospitable, many blacks moved from there to the new British colony of Sierra Leone in West Africa. Perhaps as much as 20 percent of New York's white population fled. When the British evacuated Savannah in 1782, 15 percent of Georgia's whites accompanied them. Most whites who departed were recent British immigrants. Finally, although the war secured American independence, it did not address two important issues: what kind of society America would become and what sort of government the new nation would possess. But the war had a profound effect on both questions.

THE REVOLUTION AND SOCIAL CHANGE

As Chapter 5 explained, during the decade preceding the Revolution, nonelite colonists had become more politically active than previously. After 1776, the principles articulated in the Declaration of Independence and dislocations caused by the war forced questions of class, gender, and race into public discussion. As a result, popular attitudes regarding the rights of nonelite white men and of white women, and the future of slavery, shifted somewhat. Although the resulting changes were not substantive, the discussions ensured that these issues would continue to be debated in the United States. For Native Americans, however, the Revolution was a definite step backward.

Egalitarianism among White Men   For much of the eighteenth century, members of the colonial gentry emphasized their social position by conspicuously consuming expensive English imports. By the late 1760s, however, many elite politicians began wearing homespun rather than imported English clothes to win popular political approval during the colonial boycott of British goods. When Virginia planters organized minutemen companies in 1775, they put aside their expensive officers' uniforms and dressed in buckskin or homespun hunting shirts of a sort that even the poorest farmer could afford. By 1776, the anti-British movement had persuaded many elites to maintain the appearance, if not the substance, of equality with common people.

Then came war, which accelerated the trend by pressuring the gentry, who held officers' rank, to show respect to the ordinary men serving under them. Indeed, the soldiers demanded to be treated with consideration, especially in light of the ringing words of the Declaration of Independence, "All men are created equal." The soldiers would follow commands, but not if they were addressed as inferiors.

A few officers, among them General Israel Putnam of Connecticut, went out of their way to show that they felt no superiority to their troops. While inspecting a regiment digging fortifications around Boston in 1776, Putnam saw a large stone nearby and told a soldier to throw it onto the outer wall. The individual protested,

"Sir, I am a corporal." "Oh," replied Putnam, "I ask your pardon, sir." The general then dismounted his horse and hurled the rock himself, to the immense delight of the troops working there.

Unlike Putnam, many officers insisted that soldiers remain disciplined and subordinate under all circumstances. In May 1780—more than two years after the terrible winter at Valley Forge—Continental Army troops in New Jersey were again, in Joseph Plumb Martin's words, "starved and naked." "The men were now exasperated beyond endurance," Martin continued. "They could not stand it any longer." After a day of exercising with their arms, Martin's regiment defied orders to disarm and return to its quarters, instead urging two nearby regiments to join in protesting the lack of provisions. A colonel, who "considered himself the soldier's friend," was wounded when trying to prevent his men from getting their weapons. After several officers seized one defiant soldier, his comrades pointed their rifles at the officers until they released the soldier. Other officers tried without success to order the men to disarm and finally gave up. The soldiers' willingness to defy their superiors paid off. Within a few days, more provisions arrived and, as Martin put it, "we had no great cause for complaint for some time."

After returning to civilian life, the soldiers retained their sense of self-esteem and insisted on respectful treatment by elites. As these feelings of personal pride gradually translated into political behavior and beliefs, many candidates took care not to scorn the common people. The war thus subtly democratized Americans' political assumptions.

Many elites who considered themselves republicans did not welcome the apparent trend toward democracy. These men continued to insist that each social class had its own particular virtues and that a chief virtue of the lower classes was deference to those possessing the wealth and education necessary to govern. Writing to a friend in 1776, John Adams expressed alarm that "a jealousy or an Envy taking Place among the Multitude" would exclude "Men of Learning ... from the public Councils and from Military Command." "A popular government is the worse Curse," he concluded, "despotism is better."

Nevertheless, most Revolutionary-generation Americans came to insist that virtue and sacrifice defined a citizen's worth independently of his wealth. Voters still elected the wealthy to office, but not if they flaunted their money or were condescending toward common people. The new emphasis on equality did not extend to propertyless males, women, and nonwhites, but it undermined the tendency to believe that wealth or distinguished family background conferred a special claim to public office.

Although many whites became more egalitarian in their attitudes, the Revolution left the actual distribution of wealth in the nation unchanged. The war had been directed at British imperial rule and not at the structure of American society. The exodus of loyalists did not affect the class structure because the 3 percent who fled the United States represented a cross-section of society and equally well-to-do Whig gentlemen usually bought up their confiscated estates. Overall, the American upper class seems to have owned about as much of the national wealth in 1783 as it did in 1776.

White Women in Wartime

White women's support of colonial resistance before the Revolution (see Chapter 5) broadened into an even wider range of activities during the war. Female "camp followers," many of them soldiers' wives, served military units on both sides by cooking, laundering, and nursing the wounded. A few female patriots, such as Massachusetts's Deborah Sampson, disguised themselves as men and joined in the fighting. But most women remained at home, where they managed families, households, farms, and businesses on their own.

Even traditional female roles took on new meaning in the absence of male household heads. After her civilian husband was seized by loyalists and turned over to the British on Long Island, Mary Silliman of Fairfield, Connecticut, tended to her four children (and bore a fifth), oversaw several servants and slaves, ran a commercial farm that had to be evacuated when the British attacked Fairfield, and launched repeated appeals for her husband's release. Despite often enormous struggles, such experiences boosted white women's confidence in their abilities to think and act on matters traditionally reserved for men. "I have the vanity," wrote another Connecticut woman, Mary Fish, to a female friend, "to think I have in some measure acted the *heroine* as well as my dear Husband the Hero."

As in all wars, women's public roles and visibility were heightened during the Revolution. Some women interpreted their public activities in militant terms. In 1779, as the Continental Army struggled to feed and clothe itself, Esther de Berdte Reed and Sally Franklin Bache (Benjamin Franklin's daughter) organized a campaign among Philadelphia women to raise money for the troops. Not content to see their movement's role as secondary, they compared it to those of Joan of Arc and other female heroes who had saved their people, and proclaimed that American women were "born for liberty" and would never "bear the irons of a tyrannic Government."

The most direct wartime challenge to established gender relations came from **Abigail Adams.** "In the new Code of Laws which I suppose it will be necessary for you to make," Adams wrote to her husband John in 1776, "I desire that you would Remember the Ladies." Otherwise, she continued, "we are determined to foment a Rebellion and will not hold ourselves bound by any Laws in which we have no voice, or Representation." Abigail made clear that, besides participating in boycotts and spinning bees, women recognized that colonists' arguments against arbitrary British rule also applied to gender relations. Despite his high regard for his wife's intellect, John dismissed her plea as yet another effort to extend rights and power to those who were unworthy. The assumption that women were naturally dependent—either as children subordinate to their parents or as wives to their husbands—continued to dominate discussions of the female role. For that reason, married women's property remained, in Abigail's bitter words, "subject to the control and disposal of our partners, to whom the law have given a sovereign authority."

A Revolution for African-Americans   The wartime situation of African-Americans contradicted the ideals of equality and justice for which Americans were fighting. About a half million blacks—20 percent of the total population—inhabited the United States in 1776, all but about twenty-five thousand of whom were enslaved. Even those who were free could not vote, lived under curfews and other galling restrictions, and lacked the guarantees of equal justice held by the poorest white criminal. Free blacks could expect no more than grudging toleration, and few slaves ever gained their freedom.

The early fighting in New England drew several hundred blacks into militia and Continental units. Some slaves, among them Jehu Grant of Rhode Island, ran off and posed as free persons. Grant later recalled that "when I saw liberty poles and the people all engaged for the support of freedom,... I could not but like and be pleased with such a thing." But pressure from white southern politicians led Washington to ban blacks from serving on November 12, 1775, ironically just five days after Lord Dunmore's proclamation invited enslaved Virginians to join the British.

Most wartime opportunities for African-American men grew out of the army's need for personnel rather than a white commitment to equal justice. Just six weeks after barring all black enlistments, Washington decided to admit free blacks to the army. Two years later, he agreed to Rhode Island's plea that it be allowed to raise a nonwhite regiment. Slaves could enlist and would be freed, in return for which the state paid their masters about $2,400 in today's currency. The regiment of African-Americans and Native Americans distinguished itself in several battles, including at Yorktown.

As desperate as he was for additional troops, Washington firmly opposed arming enslaved African-Americans. In 1779, as British troops poured from Georgia into South Carolina, Congress urged the two states to arm three thousand slaves. As in Rhode Island, the slaves would be freed and their masters compensated. But fearing that such an action would "render slavery more irksome to those who remain in it," Washington vetoed the plan.

Until the mid-eighteenth century, few Europeans and white Americans had criticized slavery at all. But in the decade before the Revolution, American opposition to slavery had swelled, especially as resistance leaders increasingly compared the colonies' relationship with Britain to that between slaves and a master.

Given Quakers' beliefs in human equality, it is not surprising that the earliest organized initiatives against slavery originated among Quakers. The yearly meeting of the New England Friends abolished slavery among its members in 1770, and yearly meetings in New York and Philadelphia followed suit in 1776. By 1779, Quaker slave owners had freed 80 percent of their slaves.

Although the Quakers aimed mainly to abolish slave-holding within their own ranks, some activists, most notably Anthony Benezet and John Woolman, broadened their condemnations to include slavery everywhere. Discussions of liberty, equality, and natural rights, particularly in the Declaration of Independence, also spurred antislavery sentiments. Between 1777 and 1784, Vermont, Pennsylvania, Massachusetts, Rhode Island, and Connecticut began phasing out slavery. New York did not do so until 1799, and New Jersey until 1804. New Hampshire, unmoved by petitions like that written in 1779 by Portsmouth slaves demanding liberty "to dispose of our lives, freedom, and property," never freed its slaves; but by 1810 none remained in the state.

Rather than immediately abolishing slavery, the northern states took steps that weakened the institution, paving the way for its eventual demise. Most state abolition laws provided for gradual emancipation, typically declaring all children born of a slave woman after a certain date—often July 4—free. (They still had to work, without pay, for their mother's master up to age twenty-eight.) Furthermore, northern politicians did not press for decisive action against slavery in the South. They argued that the Confederation, already deeply in debt as a result of the war, could not finance abolition in the South, and feared that any attempt to do so without compensation would drive that region into secession.

Yet even in the South, where it was most firmly entrenched, slavery troubled some whites. When one of his slaves ran off to join the British and later was recaptured, James Madison of Virginia concluded that it would be hypocritical to punish the runaway "merely for coveting that liberty for which we have paid the price of so much blood." Still, Madison did not free the slave, and no state south of Pennsylvania abolished slavery. Nevertheless, all states except South Carolina and Georgia ended slave imports and all but North Carolina passed laws making it easy for masters to manumit (set free) slaves. The number of free blacks in Virginia and Maryland rose from about four thousand in 1775 to nearly twenty-one thousand, or about 5 percent of all African-Americans there, by 1790.

These "free persons of color" faced the future as destitute, second-class citizens. Most had purchased their freedom by spending small cash savings earned in off-hours and were past their physical prime. Once free, they found whites reluctant to hire them or to pay equal wages. Black ship carpenters in Charleston (formerly Charles Town), South Carolina, for example, earned one-third less than their white coworkers in 1783. Under such circumstances, most free blacks remained poor laborers, domestic servants, and tenant farmers.

One of the most prominent free blacks to emerge during the Revolutionary period was Boston's **Prince Hall.** Born a slave, Hall received his freedom in 1770 and immediately took a leading role among Boston blacks protesting slavery. During the war, he formed a separate African-American Masonic lodge, beginning a movement that spread to other northern cities and became an important source of community support for black Americans. In 1786, Hall petitioned the Massachusetts legislature for support of a plan that would enable interested blacks "to return to Africa, our native country ... where we shall live among our equals and be more comfortable and happy than we can be in our present situation." Hall's request was unsuccessful, but later activists would revive his call for blacks to "return to Africa."

The most widely recognized African-American among whites was the Boston poet and slave Phillis Wheatley. Wheatley drew on Revolutionary ideals in considering her people's status. Several of her poems explicitly linked the liberty sought by white Americans with a plea for the liberty of slaves, including one that was autobiographical:

> I, young in life, by seeming cruel fate
> Was snatch'd from Afric's fancy'ed happy seat:
> Such, such my case. And can I then but pray
> Others may never feel tyrannic sway?

Most states granted some civil rights to free blacks during and after the Revolution. Free blacks had not participated in colonial elections, but those who were male and met the property qualification gained this privilege in a few states during the 1780s. Most northern states repealed or stopped enforcing curfews and other colonial laws restricting free African-Americans' freedom of movement. These same states generally changed their laws to guarantee free blacks equal treatment in court hearings.

Phillis Wheatley, African-American Poet *Wheatley was America's best-known poet at the time of the Revolution. Despite her fame, she remained a slave and died in poverty in 1784.*

(Library of Congress)

The Revolution neither ended slavery nor brought equality to free blacks, but it did begin a process by which slavery eventually might have been extinguished. In half the nation, the end of human bondage seemed to be in sight. Many white southerners viewed slavery as a necessary evil rather than as a positive good. Slavery had begun to crack, and free blacks had made some gains. But events in the 1790s would reverse the tentative move toward egalitarianism (as discussed in Chapter 7).

Native Americans and the Revolution   Whereas Revolutionary ideology held out at least an abstract hope for white women, blacks, and others seeking liberty and equal rights within American society, it made no provision for Native Americans wishing to remain independent of European-Americans. Regardless of which side they had fought on—or whether they had fought at all—Native Americans suffered worse than any group during the war. During the three decades encompassed by the Seven Years' War and the Revolution (1754–1783), the Native population east of the Mississippi declined by about half, and many Indian communities were uprooted. Moreover, in an overwhelmingly agrarian society like the United States, the Revolution's implicit promise of equal economic opportunity for all male citizens set the stage for territorial expansion onto Native American landholdings. Even where Indians retained their land, newly arrived whites posed dangers in the form of deadly diseases, farming practices inimical to Indian subsistence (see Chapter 3), and alcohol.

Despite these threats, most Native Americans continued to incorporate useful aspects of European culture into their own. For several centuries, Indians in eastern North America had selectively adopted European-made goods, domestic animals, and even Christianity into their lives. Many Indians, especially those no longer resisting American expansion, participated in the American economy by working for wages or by selling food, crafts, or other products. But Native Americans never gave up their older ways altogether; rather, they combined elements of the old and the new.

Although flexible on matters of culture, Native Americans did insist on retaining control of their homelands and their ways of life. Unable to do so, Samson Occom (see Chapter 4) and several hundred disillusioned Christian Indians from New England in 1784 established the new community of Brothertown on land granted them by the Oneida Iroquois in upstate New York. In a similar spirit, the Chickasaws of the Mississippi valley addressed Congress in 1783. While asking "from whare and whome we are to be supplied with necessaries," they also requested that the Confederation "put a stop to any encroachments on our lands, without our consent, and silence those [white] People who ... inflame and exasperate our Young Men."

In the Revolution's aftermath, it appeared doubtful that the new nation would concede even this much to Native Americans.

FORGING NEW GOVERNMENTS, 1776–1787

In establishing new political institutions, revolutionary Americans endeavored to guarantee liberty at the state level by minimizing executive power and by subjecting all officeholders to frequent scrutiny by voters. In turn, the new national government was subordinate, under the Articles of Confederation, to the thirteen states. Only after several years did elites, fearing that excessive decentralization and democracy were weakening the states, push through more hierarchical frames of government. Meanwhile, challenges facing the Confederation made clear to many elites the need for more centralized authority at the national level as well.

From Colonies to States   Before 1776, colonists had regarded their popularly elected assemblies as the bulwark of their liberties against encroachments by governors wielding executive power. Thereafter, the legislatures retained that role even when voters, rather than the British crown, chose governors.

In keeping with colonial practice, eleven states maintained bicameral (two-chamber) legislatures. Colonial legislatures had consisted of an elected lower house (or assembly) and an upper house (or council) appointed by the governor or chosen by the assembly (see Chapter 4). These two-part legislatures mirrored Parliament's division into the House of Commons and House of Lords, symbolizing the assumption that a government should have separate representation by the upper class and the common people.

Despite participation by people from all classes in the struggle against Britain, few questioned the long standing practice of setting property requirements for voters and elected officials. In the prevailing view, the ownership of property, especially land, gave voters a direct stake in the outcome of elections. Whereas propertyless men might vote to please landlords, creditors, or employers, sell their votes, or be fooled by a demagogue, property owners supposedly had the financial means and the education to vote freely and responsibly. Nine of the thirteen states slightly reduced property requirements for voting, but none abolished such qualifications entirely.

Another colonial practice that persisted beyond independence was the equal (or nearly equal) division of legislative seats among all counties or towns, regardless of differences in population. As a result, a minority of voters usually elected a majority of assemblymen. Only the most radical constitution, Pennsylvania's, sought to avoid such outcomes by attempting to ensure that election districts would be roughly equal in population.

Despite the holdover of certain colonial-era practices, the state constitutions in other respects departed radically from the past. Above all, they were written documents that usually required popular ratification and could be amended only by the voters. In short, Americans jettisoned the British conception of a constitution as a body of customary arrangements and practices, insisting instead that constitutions were written compacts that defined and limited the powers of rulers. Moreover, as a final check on government power, the Revolutionary constitutions spelled out citizens' fundamental rights. By 1784, all state constitutions included explicit bills of rights that outlined certain freedoms that lay beyond the control of any government.

The earliest state constitutions strengthened legislatures at governors' expense. In most states, the governor became an elected official, and elections themselves occurred far more frequently. Whereas most colonial elections had been called at the governor's pleasure, after 1776 all states scheduled annual elections except South Carolina, which held them every two years. In most states, the power of appointments was transferred from the governor to the legislature. Legislatures usually appointed judges and could reduce their salaries, and legislatures could impeach both judges and governors (try them for wrongdoing). By relieving governors of most appointive powers, denying them the right to veto laws, and making them subject to impeachment, the constitutions gave governors little to do except chair councils that made militia appointments and supervised financial business. Pennsylvania went further, simply eliminating the office of governor.

As the new state constitutions weakened the executive branch and vested more power in the legislatures, they also made the legislatures more responsive to the will of the voters. Nowhere could the governor appoint the upper chamber. Eight constitutions written before 1780 allowed voters to select both houses of the legislature; one (Maryland) used a popularly chosen "electoral college" for its upper house; and the remaining "senates" were filled by vote of their assemblies. Pennsylvania and Georgia abolished the upper house altogether. States' weakening of the executive branch and enhancement of legislative and popular authority reflected Americans' fears of centralized authority, rooted in bitter memories of royal governors who had acted arbitrarily.

Despite their high regard for popularly elected legislatures, Revolutionary leaders described themselves as republicans rather than democrats. These words had different connotations in the eighteenth century than they do today. To many elites, democracy suggested mob rule or, at least, the concentration of power in the hands of an uneducated multitude. In contrast, republicanism presumed that government would be entrusted to virtuous leaders elected for their superior talents and commitment to the public good. For most republicans, the ideal government would delicately balance the interests of different classes to prevent any one group from gaining absolute power. A few, including John Adams, thought that a republic could include a hereditary aristocracy or even a monarchy if needed to counterbalance democratic tendencies. But having rid themselves of one king, even most elites did not wish to enthrone another.

In the first flush of revolutionary enthusiasm, elites had to content themselves with state governments dominated by popularly elected legislatures. Gradually, however, wealthier landowners, bankers, merchants, and lawyers reasserted their desires for centralized authority and the political prerogatives of wealth. In Massachusetts, where voters had thus far resisted having a constitution at all, an elite-dominated convention in 1780 pushed through a constitution largely authored by John Adams. The document stipulated stiff property qualifications for voting and holding office, state senate districts that were apportioned according to property values, and a governor with considerable powers in making appointments and vetoing legislative measures. The Massachusetts constitution signaled a general trend. Georgia and Pennsylvania substituted bicameral for unicameral legislatures by 1790. Other states raised property qualifications for members of the upper chamber in a bid to encourage the "senatorial element" and to make room for men of "Wisdom, remarkable integrity, or that Weight which arises from property."

Formalizing a Confederation, 1776–1781

As in their revolt against Britain and their early state constitutions, Americans' first national government reflected widespread fears of centralized authority and its potential for corruption and tyranny. It also reflected their strong attachments to their states (the former colonies) and the states' elected legislatures, as opposed to the newly declared nation.

In 1776, John Dickinson, who had stayed in the Continental Congress despite having refused to sign the Declaration of Independence, drafted a proposal for a national constitution. Congress adopted a weakened version of Dickinson's proposal, called the **Articles of Confederation,** and sent it to the states for ratification in 1777. But only in February 1781—six months before the American victory at Yorktown—did the last state, Maryland, agree to ratification.

The Articles of Confederation explicitly reserved to each state—and not to the national government—"its sovereignty, freedom and independence." The "United States of America" was no more than "a firm league of friendship" among sovereign states, much like today's European Union. As John Adams later explained, Congress never thought of "consolidating this vast Continent under one national Government" but instead erected "a Confederacy of States, each of which must have a separate government."

Under the Articles, the national government consisted of a single-chamber Congress, elected by the state legislatures, in which each state had one vote. Congress could request funds from the states but could not enact any tax without every state's approval, and could not regulate interstate or overseas commerce. The approval of seven states was required to pass minor legislation; nine states had to approve declarations of war, treaties, and the coining and borrowing of money. Besides for taxes, unanimous approval was required to ratify and amend the Articles. The Articles did not provide for an independent executive branch. Rather, congressional committees oversaw financial, diplomatic, military, and Indian affairs, and resolved interstate disputes. Nor was there a judicial system by which the national government could compel allegiance to its laws. The Articles did eliminate all barriers to interstate travel and trade, and guaranteed that all states would recognize one another's judicial decisions.

Finance, Trade, and the Economy, 1781–1786   Aside from finishing the war on the battlefield, the greatest challenge facing the Confederation was putting the nation on a sound financial footing. The war cost a staggering $160 million, a sum that exceeded by 2,400 percent the taxes raised to pay for the Seven Years' War. Yet even this was not enough; to finance the war fully, the government had borrowed funds from abroad and printed its own paper money, called Continentals. Lack of public faith in the government destroyed 98 percent of the value of the Continentals from 1776 to 1781, an inflationary disaster that gave rise to the expression "not worth a Continental."

Seeking to overcome the national government's financial weakness, Congress in 1781 appointed a wealthy Philadelphia merchant, Robert Morris, as Superintendent of Finance. Morris proposed that the states authorize the collection of a national import duty of 5 percent, which would finance the congressional budget and guarantee interest payments on the war debt. Because the Articles required that every state approve any national tax, the import duty failed because Rhode Island alone rejected it.

Meanwhile, seeing themselves as sovereign, most states had assumed some responsibility for the war debt and begun compensating veterans and creditors within their borders. But Morris and other nationally-minded elites insisted that the United States needed sources of revenue independent of the states to attract capital and to establish a strong national government. Hoping to panic the country into seeing things their way, Morris and New York congressman Alexander Hamilton engineered a dangerous gamble known later as the Newburgh Conspiracy. In 1783, the two men secretly persuaded some army officers, then encamped at Newburgh, New York, to threaten a coup d'état unless the treasury obtained the taxation authority needed to raise their pay, which was months in arrears. But George Washington, learning of the conspiracy before it was carried out, ended the plot by delivering a speech that appealed to his officers' honor and left them unwilling to proceed. Although Morris may not have intended for a coup to actually occur, his willingness to take such a risk demonstrated the new nation's perilous financial straits and the vulnerability of its political institutions.

When peace came in 1783, Congress sent another tax measure to the states, but once again a single legislature, this time New York's, blocked it. From then on, the states steadily decreased their contributions to Congress. By the late 1780s, the states had fallen behind nearly 80 percent in providing the funds that Congress requested to operate the government and honor the national debt.

Nor did the Confederation succeed in prying trade concessions from Britain. The continuation after the war of British trade prohibitions contributed to an economic depression that gripped New England beginning in 1784. A short growing season and poor soil kept yields so low, even in the best of times, that farmers barely produced enough grain for local consumption. New Englanders also faced both high taxes to repay the money borrowed to finance the Revolution and a tightening of credit that spawned countless lawsuits against debtors. Economic depression and overpopulation only aggravated the region's miseries.

The mid-Atlantic states, on the other hand, were less dependent on British-controlled markets for their exports. As famine stalked Europe, farmers in Pennsylvania and New York prospered from climbing export prices. By 1788, the region had largely recovered from the Revolution's ravages.

Southern planters faced frustration at the failure of their principal crops, tobacco and rice, to return to prewar export levels. Whereas nearly two-thirds of American exports originated in the South in 1770, less than half were produced by southern states in 1790. In an effort to stay afloat, many Chesapeake tobacco planters shifted to wheat, while others began growing hemp. But these changes had little effect on the region's exports and, because wheat and hemp required fewer laborers than tobacco, left slave owners with a large amount of underemployed, restless "human property."

The Confederation and the West

Another formidable challenge confronting the Confederation was the postwar settlement and administration of American territory outside the states. White American squatters and speculators were already encroaching on these lands, and Native Americans were determined to keep them out. Britain and Spain supported the Indian nations in the hope of strengthening their own positions between the Appalachians and the Mississippi. Congress hoped to impose order on the process of settling these lands and to gain revenue through selling individual tracts.

After the states surrendered claims to more than 160 million acres north of the Ohio River, (see Map 6.3), Congress established procedures for surveying this land in the **Ordinance of 1785** (see Map 6.4). Subsequently, in the **Northwest Ordinance** (1787), Congress defined the steps for the creation and admission of new states. This law designated the area north of the Ohio River as the Northwest Territory and provided for its later division into states. It forbade slavery while the region remained a territory, although the citizens could legalize the institution after statehood.

The Northwest Ordinance outlined three stages for admitting states into the Union. First, during the initial years of settlement, Congress would appoint a territorial governor and judges. Second, as soon as five thousand adult males lived in a territory, voters would approve a territorial constitution and elect a legislature. Third, when the total population reached sixty thousand, voters would ratify a state constitution, which Congress would have to approve before granting statehood.

The most significant achievements of the Confederation, the Ordinance of 1785 and the Northwest Ordinance had lasting effects. Besides laying out procedures for settling and establishing governments in the Northwest, they later served as models for organizing territories farther west. The Northwest Ordinance also established a significant precedent for banning slavery from certain territories.

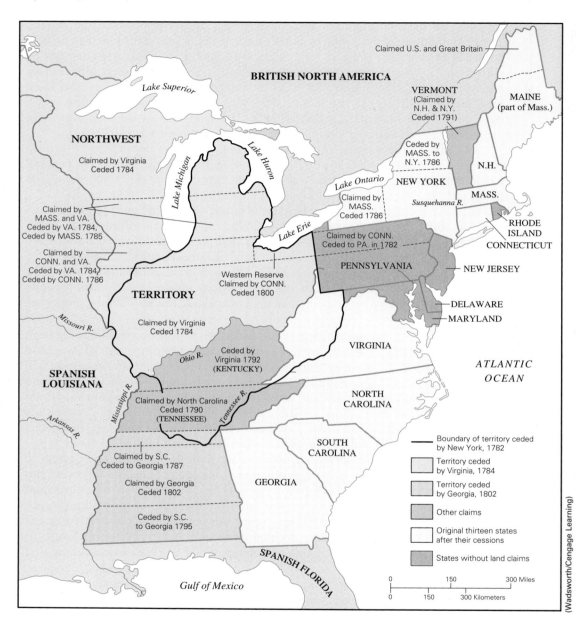

MAP 6.3 State Claims to Western Lands, and State Cessions to the Federal Government, 1782–1802

Eastern states' surrender of land claims paved the way for new state governments in the West.

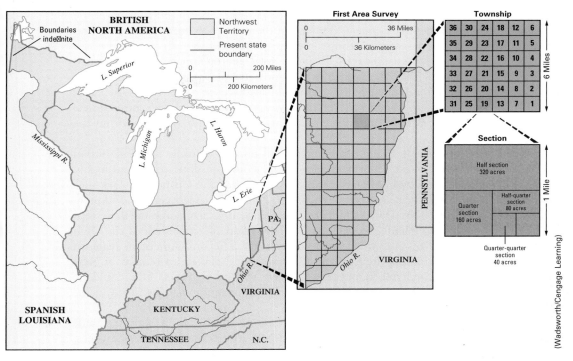

MAP 6.4 The Northwest Territory, 1785–1787

The Ordinance of 1785 provided for surveying land into townships of thirty-six sections, each support-ing four families on 160-acre plots. In 1787, the Northwest Ordinance stipulated that states ultimately be created in the region.

The Northwest Territory seemed to offer enough land to guarantee property to American citizens for centuries. This fact satisfied republicans like Thomas Jefferson who feared that the rapidly growing white population would quickly exhaust avail-able land east of the Appalachians and so create a large class of landless poor who could not vote. Such a development would undermine the equality of opportunity among whites that expansionist republicans thought essential for a healthy nation.

The realization of these expansionist dreams was by no means inevitable. Most "available" territory from the Appalachians to the Mississippi River belonged to those peoples whom the Declaration of Independence had condemned as "merciless Indian savages." Divided into more than eighty tribes and numbering perhaps 150,000 people in 1789, Native Americans were struggling to preserve their own independence. At postwar treaty negotiations, they repeatedly heard Confederation commissioners scornfully declare, "You are a subdued people ... we claim the country by conquest."

Under threats of continued warfare with the United States, some northwestern Indian leaders gave in to American pressure. The Iroquois, who had suffered heavily during the war, lost about half their land in New York and Pennsylvania in the second Treaty of Fort Stanwix (1784). In the treaties of Fort McIntosh (1785) and Fort Finney (1786), Delaware and Shawnee leaders, respectively, were obliged to recognize American sovereignty over their lands. But upon hearing of the treaties, most tribal members angrily repudiated them on the grounds that they had never authorized their negotiators to give up territory.

Native Americans' resistance to Confederation encroachments also stemmed from their confidence that the British would provide the arms and ammunition they needed to defy the United States. As noted in discussing the Treaty of Paris, the British had refused to abandon seven northwestern forts within U.S. boundaries. With Indian support, Britain hoped eventually to reclaim lands that lay within the Northwest Territory.

The Mohawk Joseph Brant emerged as the initial inspiration behind Indian resistance in the Northwest. Courageous in battle, skillful in diplomacy, and highly educated (he had translated an Anglican prayer book and the Gospel of Mark into Mohawk), Brant became a celebrity when he visited King George in London in 1785. At British-held Fort Detroit in 1786, he helped organize some northwestern Indians into a military alliance to exclude Confederation citizens north of the Ohio River. But Brant and his followers, who had relocated beyond American reach in Canada, could not win support from Iroquois who had chosen to remain in New York, where they now lived in peace with their white neighbors. Nor could he count on the support of the Ohio Indians, whom the Iroquois had betrayed in the past (as discussed in Chapters 4 and 5).

Seizing on disunity within Indian ranks, western settlers organized militia raids into the Northwest Territory. These raids gradually forced the Miamis, Shawnees, and Delawares to evacuate southern Indiana and Ohio. The Indians' withdrawal northward, toward the Great Lakes, tempted whites to make their first settlements north of the Ohio River. In spring 1788, about fifty New Englanders sailed down the river in a bulletproof barge named the *Mayflower* and founded the town of Marietta. Later that year, other newcomers established a second community on the site of modern-day Cincinnati. By then, another phase in the long-running contest for the Ohio valley was nearing a decisive stage (as discussed in Chapter 7).

The Confederation confronted similar challenges in the Southeast, where Spain and its Indian allies took steps to keep American settlers off their lands. The Spanish found a brilliant ally in the Creek leader **Alexander McGillivray.** In some fraudulent treaties, two Creeks had surrendered extensive territory to Georgia that McGillivray intended to regain. McGillivray negotiated a secret treaty in which Spain promised weapons so that the Creeks could protect themselves "from the Bears and other fierce Animals." Attacking in 1786, the Creeks shrewdly expelled only those whites occupying disputed lands and then offered Georgia a cease-fire. Eager to avoid approving taxes for a costly war, Georgia politicians let the Creeks keep the land.

Spain also sought to prevent American infiltration by denying western settlers permission to ship their crops down the Mississippi River to New Orleans. As noted earlier, Spain had negotiated a separate treaty with Britain and had not signed the Peace of Paris, by which Britain promised the United States export rights down the Mississippi. In 1784, the Spanish closed New Orleans to American commerce. Spain and the United States negotiated the Jay-Gardoqui Treaty (1786), which opened Spanish markets to American merchants and renounced Spanish claims to disputed lands—at the cost, however, of postponing American exporters' access to New Orleans for another twenty years. Westerners and southerners charged that the treaty sacrificed their interests to benefit northern commerce, and Congress rejected it.

Unable to prevent American settlers from occupying territory it claimed in the Southeast, Spain sought to win the newcomers' allegiance by bribes and offers of citizenship. Noting that Congress seemed ready to accept the permanent closing of New Orleans in return for Spanish concessions elsewhere, many settlers began talking openly of secession. As young Andrew Jackson (the future U.S. general and president) concluded in 1789, making some arrangements with the Spanish seemed "the only immediate way to obtain peace with the Savage [Indians]." Although only a few settlers actually conspired with Spain against the United States, the incident revealed the new nation's weak authority in newly settled areas.

TOWARD A NEW CONSTITUTION, 1786–1788

The Jay-Gardoqui Treaty revealed deep-seated tensions beneath the surface appearance of American national unity. Despite the nation's general prosperity outside New England, a growing minority was dissatisfied with the Confederation for various reasons. Bondholders, merchants, and shippers wanted a central government powerful enough to secure trading privileges for them abroad and to strengthen America's standing in the Atlantic economy. Land speculators and western settlers sought a government that would pursue a more activist policy against Spain, Britain, and Native Americans in the West, and prevent citizens there from defecting. Urban artisans hoped for a national government that could impose uniformly high tariffs and thereby protect them from foreign competition. Meanwhile, wealthy elites decried state governments that refused to clamp down on debtors and delinquent taxpayers, many of whom were organizing resistance movements.

Impatience turned to anxiety in 1786 after Massachusetts farmers threatened to seize a federal arsenal and march on Boston. A national convention called to consider amendments to the Articles instead proposed a radical new frame of government, the Constitution. In 1788, the states ratified the Constitution, setting a bold new course for America.

Shays's Rebellion, 1786–1787 The depression that had begun in 1784 persisted in New England, which had never recovered from the loss of its prime export market in the British West Indies. With farmers already squeezed financially, the state legislature, dominated by commercially minded elites, voted early in 1786 to pay off its Revolutionary debt in three years. This ill-considered policy necessitated a huge tax hike. Meanwhile, the state's unfavorable balance of payments with Britain had produced a shortage of specie (gold and silver coin) because British creditors refused any other currency. Fearing a flood of worthless paper notes, Massachusetts bankers and merchants insisted that they, too, be paid in specie, while the state mandated the same for payment of taxes. Lowest in this cycle of debt were thousands of small family farmers.

The plight of small farmers was especially severe in western Massachusetts, where agriculture was least profitable. Facing demands that they pay their debts and taxes in hard currency, which few of them had, farmers held public meetings.

As in similar meetings more than a decade earlier, the farmers—most of whom were Revolutionary War veterans—discussed "the Suppressing of tyrannical government," referring this time to the Massachusetts government rather than the British. Reminiscent of pre-Revolutionary backcountry "regulators" (see Chapter 5), farmers led by Daniel Shays in 1786 shut down the courts in five counties. Then in January 1787, they marched on a federal arsenal at Springfield, Massachusetts. But troops, funded by Boston elites to quell the uprising, reached the arsenal first and beat back the rebels. Thereafter, the troops scattered or routed bands of insurgents. Although the movement was defeated militarily, sympathizers of Shays won control of the Massachusetts legislature in elections later that year, and cut taxes and secured a pardon for their leader.

The Shaysites had limited objectives, were dispersed with relatively little bloodshed, and never seriously threatened anarchy. But their uprising, and similar but smaller movements in other states, became the rallying cry for advocates of a stronger central government. By threatening to seize weapons from a federal arsenal, the Shaysites unintentionally enabled nationalists to argue that the United States had become vulnerable to "mobocracy." Writing to a fellow wartime general, Henry Knox, for news from Massachusetts, an anxious George Washington worried that "there are combustibles in every state, which a spark might set fire to," destroying the Republic.

Instead of igniting an uprising from below, as Washington feared, Shays's Rebellion sparked elite nationalists into action from above. Shortly before the outbreak of the rebellion, delegates from five states had assembled at Annapolis, Maryland. They had intended to discuss means of promoting interstate commerce but instead called for a general convention to propose amendments to the Articles of Confederation. Accepting their suggestion, Congress asked the states to appoint delegations to meet in Philadelphia.

The Philadelphia Convention, 1787   In May 1787, fifty-five delegates from every state but Rhode Island began gathering at the Pennsylvania State House in Philadelphia, later known as Independence Hall. Among them were established figures like George Washington and Benjamin Franklin, as well as talented newcomers such as Alexander Hamilton and James Madison. Most were wealthy and in their thirties or forties, and nineteen owned slaves. More than half had legal training.

The convention immediately closed its sessions to the press and the public, kept no official journal, and even monitored the aged and talkative Franklin at dinner parties lest he disclose details of its discussions. Although these measures opened the convention to charges of being undemocratic and conspiratorial, the delegates preferred secrecy to minimize public pressure on their debates.

The delegates shared a "continental" or "nationalist" perspective, instilled through their extended involvement with the national government. Thirty-nine had sat in Congress, where they had seen the Confederation's limitations firsthand. In the postwar years, they had become convinced that unless the national government was freed from the control of state legislatures, the country would disintegrate. Although the legislatures had instructed them to consider amendments to the Articles, most were prepared to replace the Articles altogether with a new constitution that gave more power to the national government.

The first debate among the delegates concerned the conflicting interests of large and small states. **James Madison** of Virginia boldly called for the establishment of a strong central government rather than a federation of states. Madison's **Virginia Plan** gave Congress virtually unrestricted powers to legislate, levy taxes, veto state laws, and authorize military force against the states. As one delegate immediately saw, the Virginia Plan was designed "to abolish the State Govern[men]ts altogether." The Virginia Plan specified a bicameral legislature and fixed representation in both houses of Congress proportionally to each state's population. The voters would elect the lower house, which would then choose delegates to the upper chamber from nominations submitted by the legislatures. Both houses would jointly name the country's president and judges.

Madison's scheme aroused immediate opposition, however, especially his call for state representation according to population—a provision highly favorable to his own Virginia. On June 15, William Paterson of New Jersey offered a counter-proposal, the so-called **New Jersey Plan,** which recommended a single-chamber congress in which each state had an equal vote, as under the Articles.

The two plans exposed the convention's great stumbling block: the question of representation. The Virginia Plan would have given the four largest states a majority in both houses. Under the New Jersey Plan, the seven smallest states, which included just 25 percent of all Americans, could have controlled Congress. By July 2, the convention had arrived "at a full stop," as one delegate put it. Finally, a "grand committee," consisting of one delegate from each state, proposed the Great (or Connecticut) Compromise, whereby each state would have an equal vote in the upper house while representation in the lower house would be based on population. Although Madison and the Virginians doggedly opposed this compromise, it passed on July 17.

Despite their differences over representation, Paterson's and Madison's proposals alike would have strengthened the national government at the states' expense. No less than Madison, Paterson wished to empower Congress to raise taxes, regulate interstate commerce, and use military force against the states. The New Jersey Plan, in fact, defined congressional laws and treaties as the "supreme law of the land" and would also have established courts to force reluctant states to accept these measures. But other delegates were wary of undermining the sovereignty of the states altogether. Only after a good deal of bargaining did they reconcile their differences.

As finally approved on September 17, 1787, the **Constitution of the United States** (reprinted in the Appendix) was an extraordinary document, and not merely because it reconciled the conflicting interests of large and small states. In contrast to the Articles of Confederation, the Constitution provided for a vigorous national authority that superseded that of the states in several significant ways. Although it did not incorporate Madison's proposal to give Congress a veto over state laws, it followed the New Jersey Plan by asserting in "the supremacy clause" that all acts and treaties of the United States were "the supreme law of the land." The Constitution vested in Congress the authority to lay and collect taxes, to regulate interstate commerce, and to conduct diplomacy. States could no longer coin money, interfere with contracts and debts, or tax interstate commerce. All state officials had to swear to uphold the Constitution, even against acts of their own states. The national government could use military force against any state. Beyond these powers, the Constitution empowered Congress to enact "all laws which shall be necessary and proper" for the national government to fulfill its constitutional responsibilities. These provisions added up to a complete abandonment of the principle on which the Articles had rested: that the United States was a federation of sovereign states, with ultimate authority concentrated in their legislatures.

To allay the concerns of more moderate delegates, the Constitution's framers devised two means of restraining the power of the new central government. First, in keeping with republican political theory and the state constitutions, they established a **separation of powers** among the national government's three distinct branches—executive, legislative, and judicial; and second, they designed a system of **checks and balances** to prevent any one branch from dominating the other two. In the bicameral Congress, states' equal representation in the Senate was offset by proportional representation, by population, in the House; and each chamber could block measures approved by the other. Furthermore, where the state constitutions had deliberately weakened the executive, the Constitution gave the president the power to veto acts of Congress; but to prevent abuse of the veto, Congress could override the president by a two-thirds majority in each house. The president could conduct diplomacy, but the Senate had to ratify treaties. The president appointed a cabinet, but only with Senate approval. The president and any presidential appointee could be removed from office by a joint vote of Congress, but only for "high crimes," not for political disagreements.

To further ensure the independence of each branch, the Constitution provided that the members of one branch would not choose those of another, except for judges, whose independence would be protected because they were appointed for life by the president with the "advice and consent" of the Senate. For example, the president was to be selected by electors, whom the states would select as their legislatures saw fit. The number of electors in each state would equal the number of its senators and representatives. In the event of a deadlock among the electors, the House of Representatives, with one vote per state, would choose the president. The state legislatures would elect the members of the Senate, whereas members of the House of Representatives would be chosen by direct popular vote.

In addition to checks and balances, the founders devised a system of shared power and dual lawmaking by the national and state governments—**"federalism"**—in order to place limits on central authority. Not only did the state legislatures have a key role in electing the president and senators, but the Constitution could be amended by the votes of three-fourths of the states. Thus, the convention departed sharply from Madison's plan to establish a "consolidated" national government entirely independent of, and superior to, the states.

A key assumption behind federalism was that the national government would limit its activities to foreign affairs, national defense, regulating interstate commerce, and coining money. Most other political matters would be left to the states. Regarding slavery in particular, each state retained full authority.

The dilemma confronting the Philadelphia convention centered not on whether slavery would be allowed but only on the much narrower question of whether slaves should be counted as persons when it came to determining a state's representation at the national level. For most legal purposes, slaves were regarded not as persons but rather as the chattel property of their owners, meaning that they were on a par with other living property such as horses and cattle. But southern states saw their large numbers of slaves as a means of augmenting their numbers in the House of Representatives and in the electoral meetings ("colleges") that would elect the nation's presidents. So strengthened, they hoped to prevent northerners from ever abolishing slavery.

Representing states that had begun ending slavery, northern delegates opposed giving southern states a political advantage by allowing them to count people who had no civil or political rights. As Madison—himself a slave owner—observed, "it seemed now to be pretty well understood that the real difference of interests lay, not between the large & small [states] but between the N. & South." But after Georgia and South Carolina threatened to secede if their demands were not met, northerners agreed to the **"three-fifths clause,"** allowing three-fifths of all slaves to be counted for congressional representation and, thereby, in the electoral college.

The Constitution also reinforced slavery in other ways. Most notably, it forbade citizens of any state, even those that had abolished slavery, to prevent the return of escaped slaves to another state. The Constitution limited slavery only to the extent of prohibiting Congress from banning the importation of slaves before 1808, and by maintaining Congress's earlier ban on slavery in the Northwest Territory.

Although leaving much authority to the states, the Constitution established a national government whose sovereignty, unlike under the Articles of Confederation, clearly superseded that of the states. Having thus strengthened national authority, the convention had to face the issue of ratification. For two reasons, it seemed unwise to submit the Constitution to state legislatures for ratification. First, the delegates realized that the state legislatures would reject the Constitution, which shrank their power relative to the national government. Second, most of them rejected the idea—implicit in ratification by state legislatures—that the states were the foundation of the new government. The opening words of the Constitution, "We the People of the United States," underlined the delegates' conviction that the government had to be based on the consent of the American people themselves, "the fountain of all power" in Madison's words, and not of the states.

In the end, the Philadelphia convention provided for the Constitution's ratification by special state conventions composed of delegates elected by the voters. Approval by nine such conventions would put the new government in operation. Because any state refusing to ratify the Constitution would legally remain under the Articles, the possibility existed that the country would divide into two nations.

Under the Constitution, the Framers expected the nation's elites to continue exercising political leadership. Seeking to rein in the democratic currents set in motion by the Revolution, they curtailed what they considered the excessive power of popularly elected state legislatures. And while they located sovereignty in the people rather than in the states, they provided for an electoral college that would actually elect the president. The Framers did provide for one crucial democratic element in the new government, the House of Representatives. Moreover, by making the Constitution flexible and amendable (though not easily amendable), and by dividing political power among competing branches of government, the Framers made it possible for the national government to be slowly democratized, in ways unforeseen in 1787.

The Struggle over Ratification, 1787–1788

The Constitution's supporters began the campaign for ratification without significant popular support. Expecting the Philadelphia convention to offer some amendments to the Articles of Confederation, most Americans hesitated to replace the entire system of government. Undaunted, the Constitution's friends moved decisively to marshal political support. In a clever stroke, they called themselves "Federalists," a term implying that the Constitution would more nearly balance the relationship between the national and state governments, and thereby undermined the arguments of those hostile to a centralized national government.

The Constitution's opponents became known as "Antifederalists." This negative-sounding title probably hurt them, for it did not convey the crux of their argument against the Constitution—that it was not "federalist" at all since it failed to balance the power of the national and state governments. By augmenting national authority, Antifederalists maintained, the Constitution would ultimately doom the states and the people's liberty.

The Antifederalist arguments reflected Anglo-Americans' long-standing suspicion of centralized executive power, reiterated by Americans from the time of the Stamp Act crisis, through the Revolution, to the framing of the first state constitutions and the Articles of Confederation. Patrick Henry feared that a president "of ambition and abilities" could, as commander in chief, use the army to "render himself absolute," while another Antifederalist feared that the national government would "fall into the hands of the few and the great." Compared to a distant national government, Antifederalists argued, state governments were far more responsive to the popular will. They acknowledged that the Framers had guarded against tyranny by preserving limited state powers and devising a system of checks and balances, but doubted that these devices would succeed. The proposed constitution, concluded one Antifederalist, "nullified and declared void" the constitutions and laws of the states except where they did not contradict federal mandates. Moreover, for all its checks and balances, opponents noted, the Constitution provided no guarantees that the new government would protect the liberties of individuals.

Although the Antifederalists advanced some formidable arguments, they confronted a number of disadvantages in publicizing their cause. While Antifederalist ranks included some prominent figures, none had the stature of George Washington or Benjamin Franklin. As state and local leaders, the Antifederalists lacked their opponents' contacts and experience at the national level, acquired through service as Continental Army officers, diplomats, or members of Congress. Moreover, most American newspapers were pro-Constitution and did not hesitate to bias their reporting in favor of ratification.

The Federalists' advantages in funds and political organizing proved decisive. The Antifederalists failed to create a sense of urgency among their supporters, assuming incorrectly that a large majority would rally to them. Only one-quarter of the voters turned out to elect delegates to the state ratifying conventions, and most had been mobilized by Federalists.

The Constitution became the law of the land when the ninth state, New Hampshire, ratified it on June 21, 1788. Federalist delegates prevailed in seven of the first nine state conventions by margins of at least two-thirds. Such lopsided votes reflected the Federalists' organizational skills and aggressiveness rather than the degree of popular support for the Constitution. The Constitution's advocates rammed through approval in some states "before it can be digested or deliberately considered," in the words of a Pennsylvania Antifederalist.

But unless Virginia and New York—two of the largest states—ratified, the new government would be fatally weakened. In both states (and elsewhere), Antifederalist sentiment ran high among small farmers, who saw the Constitution as a scheme favoring city dwellers and moneyed interests. Prominent Antifederalists in these two states included New York governor George Clinton and Virginia's Patrick Henry, Richard Henry Lee, George Mason, and future president James Monroe.

At Virginia's convention, Federalists won crucial support from the representatives of the Allegheny counties—modern West Virginia—who wanted a strong national government capable of ending Indian raids from north of the Ohio River. Western Virginians' votes, combined with James Madison's leadership among tidewater planters, proved too much for Henry's spellbinding oratory. On June 25, the Virginia delegates ratified by a narrow 53 percent majority.

The struggle was even closer and more hotly contested in New York. Antifederalists had solid control of the state convention and would probably have voted down the Constitution, but then news arrived that New Hampshire (the ninth state) and powerful Virginia had approved. Federalist leaders Alexander Hamilton and John Jay spread rumors that if the convention failed to ratify, pro-Federalist New York City and adjacent counties would secede from the state and join the Union alone, leaving upstate New York landlocked. When several Antifederalist delegates took alarm at this threat and switched sides, on July 26 New York ratified by a 30 to 27 vote.

So the Antifederalists went down in defeat, and they did not survive as a political movement. Yet their influence was lasting. At their insistence, the Virginia, New York, and Massachusetts conventions approved the Constitution with the accompanying request that it be amended to include a bill of rights protecting Americans' basic freedoms. Moreover, Antifederalists' concerns for the sovereignty of states under the Constitution's federal framework would be echoed in the bitter political debates that roiled the new government during its first decade and long thereafter.

Antifederalists' objections in New York also stimulated a response in the form of one of the great classics of political thought, **The Federalist,** a series of eighty-five newspaper essays penned by Alexander Hamilton, James Madison, and John Jay. The Federalist Papers, as they are commonly termed, had little influence on voting in the New York convention. Rather, their importance lay in articulating arguments defending the Constitution and addressing Americans' wide-ranging concerns about the powers and limits of the new federal government, thereby shaping a new political philosophy. The Constitution, insisted *The Federalist's* authors, had a twofold purpose: first, to defend the rights of political minorities against majority tyranny; and second, to prevent a stubborn minority from blocking well-considered measures that the majority believed necessary for the national interest. Critics, argued *The Federalist,* had no reason to fear that the Constitution would allow a single economic or regional interest to dominate. "Extend the sphere," Madison insisted in *Federalist* No. 10, "and … you make it less probable [than in a small republic] that a majority of the whole will have a common motive to invade the rights of other citizens, … [or will be able to] act in unison with each other." The country's very size and diversity would neutralize the attempts of factions to push unwise laws through Congress.

Madison's analysis was far too optimistic, however. As the Antifederalists predicted, the Constitution afforded enormous scope for special interests to influence the government. The great challenge for Madison's generation would be how to maintain a government that would provide equal benefits to all and at the same time accord special privileges to none.

CHRONOLOGY
1776–1788

1776	British force American troops from New York City.
1777	Congress approves Articles of Confederation. American victory at Saratoga.
1777–1778	British troops occupy Philadelphia. Continental Army winters at Valley Forge.
1778	France formally recognizes the United States; declares war on Britain.
1779	Spain declares war on Britain. John Sullivan leads American raids in Iroquois country.
1780	British seize Charles Town.
1781	Articles of Confederation ratified. Battle of Yorktown; British General Cornwallis surrenders.
1783	Treaty of Paris.
1784	Spain closes New Orleans to American trade. Economic depression begins in New England. Second Treaty of Fort Stanwix.
1785	Ordinance of 1785. Treaty of Fort McIntosh.
1786	Congress rejects Jay-Gardoqui Treaty. Treaty of Fort Finney. Joseph Brant organizes Indian resistance to U.S. expansion.
1786–1787	Shays's Rebellion in Massachusetts.
1787	Northwest Ordinance. Philadelphia convention frames federal Constitution.
1787–1788	Alexander Hamilton, James Madison, and John Jay, *The Federalist*.
1788	Constitution ratified.

CONCLUSION

The entry of North Carolina into the Union in late 1789 and of Rhode Island in May 1790 marked the final triumph of an uncertain nationalism. Among whites, blacks, and Native Americans alike, the American Revolution was a civil war as well as a war of national independence. So long as the war involved only Britain and America, it cost both sides heavily in casualties and finances without producing a conclusive result. Once other nations joined the anti-British cause, making the Revolution an international war, the tide turned. Now fatally overextended, Britain was defeated by American-French forces at Yorktown and obliged to surrender.

Winning the war proved to be only the first step in establishing a new American nation. Forming new governments at the state and national levels was just as challenging. The early state constitutions and the Articles of Confederation reflected the concerns of most white Americans to limit sharply the political power of elected officials, particularly executives. Over time, elites favoring stronger executive power gained support from others in altering several state constitutions and, most decisively, in replacing the Articles of Confederation with the new federal Constitution. The Constitution definitely limited democracy; but by locating sovereignty in the people it created a legal and institutional framework within which Americans could struggle to attain democracy. In that way, its conception was a fundamental moment in the history of America's enduring vision.

7

LAUNCHING THE NEW REPUBLIC, 1788–1800

CHAPTER OUTLINE

• Constitutional Government Takes Shape, 1788–1796 • Hamilton's Domestic Policies, 1789–1794 • The United States in a Wider World, 1789–1796 • Parties and Politics, 1793–1800 • Economic and Social Change

CONSTITUTIONAL GOVERNMENT TAKES SHAPE, 1788–1796

Although the Constitution had replaced the Articles of Confederation as the law of the land, its effectiveness had yet to be tested. Given the social and political divisions among Americans, the successful establishment of a national government was anything but guaranteed. Would Americans accept the results of a national election? Would the legislative, executive, and judicial branches of the new government function effectively? Would Congress and the states amend the Constitution with a Bill of Rights, as even many of its proponents advocated?

Implementing Government   The first step in implementing the new government was the election of a president and Congress. The first elections under the Constitution, in fall 1788, resulted in a Federalist sweep. Antifederalists won just two of twenty seats in the Senate and five of fifty-nine in the House of Representatives. An electoral college met in each state on February 9, 1789, with each elector voting for two presidential candidates. Although unaware of deliberations in other states, every elector designated George Washington as one of their choices. Having gotten the second-most votes, John Adams became the vice president. (The Twelfth Amendment would later supersede this procedure for choosing the president and vice president, as discussed in Chapter 8).

There was nothing surprising about the unanimity of Washington's victory. His leadership during the Revolutionary War and the constitutional convention earned him a reputation as a national hero whose abilities and integrity far surpassed those of his peers. Because of his exalted stature, Washington was able to calm Americans' fears of unlimited executive power.

Traveling slowly over the nation's miserable roads, the men entrusted with launching the federal experiment began assembling in New York, the new national capital, in March 1789. Because so few members were on hand, Congress opened its session a month late. George Washington did not arrive until April 23 and took his oath of office a week later.

The Constitution required the president to obtain the Senate's "advice and consent" to his nominees to head executive departments. Otherwise, Congress was free to determine the organization and accountability of what became known as the cabinet. The first cabinet, established by Congress, consisted of five departments, headed by the secretaries of state, treasury, and war and by the attorney general and postmaster general. Vice President John Adams's tie-breaking vote defeated a proposal that would have forbidden the president from dismissing cabinet officers without Senate approval. This outcome strengthened the president's authority to make and carry out policy independently of congressional oversight, beyond what the Constitution required.

The Federal Judiciary and the Bill of Rights   The Constitution authorized Congress to establish federal courts below the level of the Supreme Court, but provided no plan for their structure. Many citizens feared that federal courts would ride roughshod over each state's distinctive blend of judicial procedures.

With the **Judiciary Act** of 1789, Congress quieted popular apprehensions by establishing in each state a federal district court that operated according to local procedures. As the Constitution stipulated, the Supreme Court exercised final jurisdiction. Congress had struck a compromise between nationalists and states' rights advocates, one that respected state traditions while offering wide access to federal justice.

The Constitution offered some protection of citizens' individual rights. It barred Congress from passing ex post facto laws (criminalizing previously legal actions and then punishing those who had engaged in them) and bills of attainder (proclaiming a person's guilt and stipulating punishment without a trial). Nevertheless, the absence of a comprehensive bill of rights had prompted several delegates at Philadelphia to refuse to sign the Constitution and had been a condition of ratification in several states. James Madison, who had been elected to the House of Representatives, led the drafting of the ten amendments that became known as the **Bill of Rights**.

The First Amendment guaranteed the most fundamental freedoms of expression—religion, speech, press, and political activity—against federal interference. The Second Amendment ensured that "a well-regulated militia" would preserve the nation's security by guaranteeing "the right of the people to bear arms." Along with the Third Amendment, it sought to protect citizens from what eighteenth-century Britons and Americans alike considered the most sinister embodiment of tyrannical power: standing armies. The Fourth through Eighth Amendments limited the police powers of the state by guaranteeing individuals' fair treatment in legal and judicial proceedings. The Ninth and Tenth Amendments reserved to the people or to the states powers not allocated to the federal government under the Constitution, but Madison headed off proposals to limit federal power more explicitly. In general, the Bill of Rights imposed no serious check on the Framers' nationalist objectives. The ten amendments were submitted to the states and ratified by December 1791.

HAMILTON'S DOMESTIC POLICIES, 1789–1794

President Washington left his secretary of the treasury, **Alexander Hamilton**, in charge of setting the administration's domestic priorities. Hamilton quickly emerged as an imaginative and dynamic statesman with a sweeping program for strengthening the federal government and promoting national economic development. While Hamilton succeeded in pushing his proposals through Congress, the controversies surrounding them undermined popular support for Federalist policies.

Establishing the Nation's Credit   In Hamilton's mind, the most immediate danger facing the United States concerned the possibility of war with Britain, Spain, or both. The republic could finance a major war only by borrowing heavily, but because Congress under the Confederation had not assumed responsibility for the Revolutionary War debt, the nation's credit was weakened abroad and at home.

Responding to a request from Congress, Hamilton in January 1790 issued the first of two **Reports on the Public Credit**. It outlined a plan to strengthen the country's credit, enable it to defer paying its debt, and entice wealthy investors to place their capital at its service. The report listed $54 million in U.S. debt, $42 million of which was owed to Americans, and the rest to Europeans. Hamilton estimated that on top of the national debt, the states had debts of $25 million, some of which the United States had promised to reimburse.

Hamilton recommended first that the federal government "fund" the $54 million national debt by selling an equal sum in new government bonds. Purchasers of these securities would choose from several combinations of federal "stock" and western lands. Those who wished could retain their original bonds and earn 4 percent interest. All these options would reduce interest payments on the debt from the full 6 percent set by the Confederation Congress. Hamilton knew that creditors would not object to this reduction because their investments would now be more valuable and more secure. His report also proposed that the federal government pay off the $25 million in state debts remaining from the Revolution in the same manner.

Hamilton exhorted the government to use the money earned by selling federal lands in the West to pay off the $12 million owed to Europeans as quickly as possible. In his Second Report on the Public Credit, submitted to Congress in December 1790, he argued that the Treasury could accumulate the interest owed on the remaining $42 million by collecting customs duties on imports and an excise tax (a tax on products made, sold, or transported within a nation's borders) on whiskey. In addition, Hamilton proposed that money owed to American citizens should be made a permanent debt. That is, he urged that the government not attempt to repay the $42 million principal but instead keep paying interest to bondholders. Under Hamilton's plan, the only burden on taxpayers would be the small annual cost of interest. The government could uphold the national credit at minimal expense, without ever paying off the debt itself.

Hamilton advocated a perpetual debt as a lasting means of uniting the economic fortunes of the nation's creditors to the United States. In an age when financial investments were notoriously risky, the federal government would protect the savings of wealthy bondholders through conservative policies while offering an interest rate competitive with the Bank of England's. The guarantee of future interest payments would unite the interests of the moneyed class with those of the government. Few other investments would entail so little risk.

Hamilton's recommendations provoked immediate controversy. Although no one in Congress doubted that they would enhance the country's fiscal reputation, many objected that those least deserving of reward would gain the most. The original owners of more than three-fifths of the debt certificates issued by the Continental Congress were Revolutionary patriots of modest means who had long before sold their certificates for a fraction of their promised value, usually out of dire financial need. Foreseeing that the government would fund the debt, wealthy speculators had bought the certificates and now stood to reap huge gains at the expense of the original owners, even collecting interest that had accrued before they purchased the certificates. "That the case of those who parted with their securities from necessity is a hard one, cannot be denied," Hamilton admitted. But making exceptions, he argued, would be even worse.

To Hamilton's surprise, Madison—his longtime ally—emerged as a leading opponent of funding. Facing opposition to the plan in his home state of Virginia, Madison tried but failed to obtain compensation for original owners who had sold their certificates. Congress rejected his proposal primarily on the grounds that it would weaken the nation's credit.

Opposition to Hamilton's proposal that the federal government assume states' war debts also ran high. Only Massachusetts, Connecticut, and South Carolina had failed to make effective provisions for satisfying their creditors. The issue stirred the fiercest indignation in the South, which except for South Carolina had paid off 83 percent of its debt. Madison and others maintained that to allow residents of the laggard states to escape heavy taxes while others had liquidated theirs at great expense was to reward irresponsibility.

Southern hostility almost defeated assumption. In the end, however, Hamilton saved his proposal by enlisting Secretary of State Thomas Jefferson's help. Jefferson and other Virginians favored moving the capital to the Potomac River, hoping to make Virginia a national crossroads and thus preserve its position as the largest, most influential state. In return for the northern votes necessary to transfer the capital, Hamilton secured enough Virginians' support to win the battle for assumption. The capital would move in the following year to Philadelphia and remain there until a new capital city was built. Despite this concession, the debate over state debts confirmed many white southerners' suspicions that northern financial and commercial interests would benefit from Hamilton's policies at southerners' expense.

Congressional enactment in 1790 of Hamilton's recommendations dramatically reversed the nation's fiscal standing. European investors grew so enthusiastic about U.S. bonds that by 1792 some securities were selling at 10 percent above face value.

Creating a National Bank

Having significantly expanded the stock of capital available for investment, Hamilton intended to direct that money toward projects that would diversify the national economy through a federally chartered bank. Accordingly, in December 1790 he presented Congress with the **Report on a National Bank**.

The proposed Bank of the United States would raise $10 million through a public stock offering. Private investors could purchase shares by paying for three-quarters of their value in government bonds. In this way, the bank would capture a significant portion of the recently funded debt and make it available for loans; it would also receive a steady flow of interest payments from the Treasury. Under these circumstances, shareholders were positioned to profit handsomely.

Hamilton argued that the bank would cost the taxpayers nothing and greatly benefit the nation. It would provide a safe place for the federal government to deposit tax revenues, make inexpensive loans to the government when taxes fell short, and help relieve the scarcity of hard cash by issuing paper notes that would circulate as money. Furthermore, it would possess authority to regulate the business practices of state banks and would provide much needed credit to expand the economy.

Hamilton's critics denounced his proposal for a national bank, interpreting it as a dangerous scheme that would give a small, elite group special power to influence the government. These critics believed that the Bank of England had undermined the integrity of government in Britain. Shareholders of the new bank could just as easily become the tools of unscrupulous politicians. Jefferson openly opposed Hamilton, claiming that the bank would be "a machine for the corruption of the legislature [Congress]." Another Virginian, John Taylor, predicted that the bank would take over the country, which would thereafter, he quipped, be known as the United States of the Bank.

Madison led the opposition to the bank in Congress, arguing that it was unconstitutional. Unless Congress closely followed the Constitution, he argued, the central government might oppress the states and trample on individual liberties, just as Parliament had done to the colonies. Strictly limiting federal power seemed the surest way of preventing the United States from degenerating into a corrupt despotism.

Congress approved the bank by only a thin margin. Uncertain of the bank's constitutionality, Washington turned to both Jefferson and Hamilton for advice before signing the measure into law. Like many southern planters whose investments in slaves left them short of capital and often in debt, Jefferson distrusted banking. Moreover, his fear of concentrated economic and political power led him, like Madison, to favor a "strict interpretation" of the Constitution. "To take a single step beyond the boundaries thus specifically drawn around the powers of Congress is to take possession of a boundless field of power no longer susceptible of any definition," warned Jefferson.

Hamilton fought back, urging Washington to sign the bill. Because the Constitution authorized Congress to enact all measures "necessary and proper" (Article I,

Section 8), Hamilton contended, it could execute such measures. The only unconstitutional activities of the national government, he concluded, were those expressly prohibited. In the end, the president accepted Hamilton's argument for a "loose interpretation" of the Constitution. In February 1791, the Bank of the United States obtained a charter guaranteeing its existence for twenty years. Washington's acceptance of the principle of loose interpretation was an important victory for those advocating an active, assertive national government. But the split between Jefferson and Hamilton, and Washington's siding with the latter, signaled a deepening political divide within the administration.

Emerging Partisanship   Hamilton's attempt to build political support for Federalist policies by appealing to economic self-interest was successful but also divisive. His arrangements for rescuing the nation's credit provided enormous gains for speculators, merchants, and other investors in the port cities who by 1790 held most of the Revolutionary debt. As holders of bank stock, these groups had yet another reason to favor centralized national authority. Assumption of the state debts liberated New England, New Jersey, and South Carolina taxpayers from a crushing burden, enabling Federalists to dominate politics in these places. Hamilton's efforts to promote industry, commerce, and shipping also struck a responsive chord among northeastern entrepreneurs.

Opposition to Hamilton's program was strongest in sections of the country where it offered few benefits. Outside of Charleston, South Carolina, few southerners or westerners retained Revolutionary certificates in 1790, invested in the Bank of the United States, or borrowed from it. Resentment against a national economic program whose main beneficiaries seemed to be eastern "monied men" and New Englanders who refused to pay their debts gradually united westerners, southerners, and some mid-Atlantic citizens into a political coalition that challenged the Federalists and called for a return to the "true principles" of republicanism.

With Hamilton having presented his measures as "Federalist," Jefferson, Madison, and their supporters began referring to themselves as "republicans." In this way, they implied that Hamilton's schemes to centralize the national government threatened liberty. Having separated from the Federalists, Jefferson and Madison drew support from former Antifederalists whose ranks had been fatally weakened after the election of 1788. In 1791, they supported the establishment in Philadelphia of an opposition newspaper, *The National Gazette*, whose editor, Philip Freneau, had been an ardent Antifederalist. For the year preceding the election of 1792, Freneau attacked Hamilton relentlessly, accusing him of trying to create an aristocracy and monarchy in America. Hamilton responded vigorously to the attacks through his own column in Philadelphia's Federalist newspaper, *The Gazette of the United States*. Using pseudonyms, he also wrote columns in which he attacked Jefferson as an enemy of President Washington.

Although political partisanship intensified as the election approached, there was no organized political campaigning. For one thing, most voters believed that organized factions or parties were inherently corrupt and threatened liberty. The Constitution's framers had neither wanted nor planned for political parties. Indeed, in *Federalist* No. 10, James Madison had argued that the Constitution would prevent the rise of national political factions. For another thing, George Washington, by appearing to be above the partisan disputes, remained supremely popular.

Meeting in 1792, the electoral college was again unanimous in choosing Washington to be president. John Adams was reelected vice president but by a closer vote than in 1788, receiving 77 votes compared to 50 for George Clinton, the Antifederalist governor of New York.

The Whiskey Rebellion   Hamilton's program not only sparked an angry congressional debate but also helped ignite a civil insurrection in 1794 called the **Whiskey Rebellion.** Reflecting serious regional and class tensions, this popular uprising was the young republic's first serious crisis.

As part of his financial program, Hamilton had recommended an excise tax on domestically produced whiskey. He insisted that such a tax would not only help in financing the national debt but would improve morals by inducing Americans to drink less liquor. Though Congress enacted the tax, some members doubted that Americans (who on average annually consumed six gallons of hard liquor per adult) would submit tamely to limitations on their drinking. James Jackson of Georgia, for example, warned the administration that his constituents "have long been in the habit of getting drunk and that they will get drunk in defiance of … all the excise duties which Congress might be weak or wicked enough to pass."

The validity of such doubts became apparent in September 1791 when a crowd tarred and feathered an excise agent near Pittsburgh. Western Pennsylvanians found the new tax especially burdensome. Unable to export crops through New Orleans, most farmers distilled their rye or corn into alcohol, which could be carried across the Appalachians at a fraction of the price charged for bulkier grain. Hamilton's excise equaled 25 percent of whiskey's retail value, enough to wipe out a farmer's profit.

(Granger Collection)

Whiskey Rebellion, 1794 *Rebels in Washington County, Pennsylvania, tar and feather a federal tax collector.*

The law also stipulated that trials for evading the tax be conducted in federal courts. Any western Pennsylvanian indicted for noncompliance would have to travel three hundred miles to Philadelphia. Besides facing a jury of unsympathetic easterners, the accused would have to bear the cost of the long journey and lost earnings while at court, in addition to fines and other penalties if found guilty. Moreover, Treasury officials rarely enforced the law rigorously outside western Pennsylvania. For all these reasons, western Pennsylvanians complained that the whiskey excise was excessively burdensome.

In a scene reminiscent of Revolutionary-era popular protests, large-scale resistance erupted in July 1794. One hundred western Pennsylvanians attacked a U.S. marshal serving sixty delinquent taxpayers with summonses to appear in court at Philadelphia. A crowd of five hundred burned the chief revenue officer's house after a shootout with federal soldiers. Roving bands torched buildings, assaulted tax collectors, harassed government supporters, and flew a flag symbolizing an independent country they hoped to create from six western counties.

Echoing elites' denunciations of earlier protests, Hamilton condemned the rebellion as lawlessness. He noted that Congress had reduced the tax rate per gallon in 1792 and had recently voted to allow state judges in western Pennsylvania to hear trials. As during Shays's Rebellion, Washington concluded that failure to respond strongly to the uprising would encourage outbreaks in other western areas.

Washington accordingly mustered nearly thirteen thousand militiamen from Pennsylvania and neighboring states to march west under his command. Opposition evaporated once the troops reached the Appalachians, and the president left Hamilton in charge of making arrests. Of about 150 suspects seized, Hamilton sent twenty in irons to Philadelphia. Two men received death sentences, but Washington eventually pardoned them both, noting that one was a "simpleton" and the other "insane."

The Whiskey Rebellion resulted in severe limits on public opposition to federal policies. In the early 1790s, many Americans still believed it was legitimate to protest unpopular laws using the same tactics with which they had blocked parliamentary measures like the Stamp Act. Indeed, western Pennsylvanians had justified their resistance with exactly such reasoning. By firmly suppressing the first major challenge to national authority, Washington served notice that citizens who resorted to violent or other extralegal means of political action would feel the full force of federal authority. In this way, he gave voice and substance to elites' fears of "mobocracy," now resurfacing in reaction to the French Revolution (discussed shortly).

THE UNITED STATES IN A WIDER WORLD, 1789–1796

By 1793, disagreements over foreign affairs had emerged as the primary source of friction in American public life. The political divisions created by Hamilton's financial program hardened into ideologically oriented factions that argued vehemently over whether the country's foreign policy should favor industrial and overseas mercantile interests or those of farmers, planters, small businesses, and artisans. Moreover, having ratified its Constitution in the year the French Revolution began (1789), the new nation entered the international arena as European tensions were once again exploding. The rapid spread of pro-French revolutionary ideas and organizations alarmed Europe's monarchs and aristocrats. Perceiving a threat to their social orders as well as their territorial interests, most European nations declared war on France by early 1793. For most of the next twenty-two years—until Napoleon's final defeat in 1815—Europe and the Atlantic world remained in a state of war.

While most Americans hoped that their nation could avoid this latest European conflict, the interests or values of many citizens led them to be partial toward either Britain, France, or Spain. Thus, differences over foreign policy fused with differences over domestic affairs, further intensifying partisanship in American politics.

Spanish Power in Western North America   Stimulated by having won Louisiana from France in 1762 (see Chapter 5), Spain enjoyed a brief revival of its North American fortunes in the late eighteenth century. Strengthened by new presidios and additional troops north of the Rio Grande, Spain sought to force nomadic Apaches, Navajos, and Comanches to end their damaging raids on Spanish colonists and allied Indians and to submit to Spanish authority. This effort succeeded, but only up to a point. The Apaches and Navajos moved farther from Spanish settlements, but primarily to avoid Indian enemies rather than Spanish attacks. Ironically, colonists in New Mexico and Texas depended on the Comanches as sources of some European goods, which the Comanches obtained through trade networks extending to Louisiana and to American territory east of the Mississippi. By 1800, nomadic Indians had agreed to cease their raids in New Mexico and Texas, but whether the truce would become a permanent peace depended on whether Spain could strengthen and broaden its imperial position in North America.

Spain's efforts in New Mexico and Texas were part of its larger effort to counter rivals for North American territory and influence. The first challenge arose in the Pacific Ocean, where Spain had enjoyed an unchallenged monopoly for more than two centuries until Russian traders entered Alaska.

Perceiving Russia's move into Alaska as a threat, Spain expanded northward on the Pacific coast from Mexico. In 1769, it established the province of **Alta California**, the present American state of California (see Map 7.1). Efforts to encourage large-scale Mexican immigration to Alta California failed, leaving the colony to be sustained by a chain of religious missions, several presidios, and a few large ranchos (ranches). Seeking support against inland adversaries, coastal California Indians welcomed the Spanish at first. But the Franciscan missionaries sought to convert them to Catholicism while imposing harsh disciplinary measures and putting them to work in vineyards and in other enterprises. Meanwhile, Spanish colonists' spreading of epidemic and venereal diseases among natives precipitated a decline in the Native American population from about seventy-two thousand in 1770 to about eighteen thousand by 1830.

Between New Mexico and California, Spain attempted to make alliances with Indians in the area later known as Arizona. In this way, Spain hoped to dominate North America between the Pacific and the Mississippi River. But resistance from the Hopi, Quechan (Yuma), and other Native Americans thwarted these hopes. Fortunately for Spain, Arizona had not yet attracted the interest of other imperial powers.

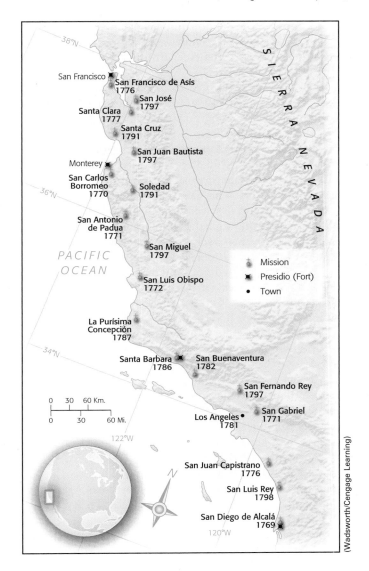

MAP 7.1 Spanish Settlements in Alta California, 1800

While the United States was struggling to win its independence, Spain was establishing a new colony on the Pacific coast.

Challenging American Expansion, 1789–1792

Between the Appalachians and the Mississippi River, Spain, Britain, the United States, and numerous Indian nations jockeyed for advantage in a region that all considered central to their interests and that Native Americans regarded as homelands.

Realizing that the United States was in no position to dictate developments immediately in the West, President Washington pursued a course of patient diplomacy that was intended "to preserve the country in peace if I can, and to be prepared for war if I cannot." The prospect of peace improved in 1789 when Spain unexpectedly opened New Orleans to American commerce, although exports remained subject to a 15 percent duty.

Thereafter, Spanish officials continued to bribe well-known political figures in Tennessee and Kentucky, among them a former general on Washington's staff, James Wilkinson. Thomas Scott, a congressman from western Pennsylvania, meanwhile schemed with the British. Between 1791 and 1796, the federal government anxiously admitted Vermont, Kentucky, and Tennessee to the Union, partly in the hope of strengthening their residents' flickering loyalty to the United States.

Washington also tried to weaken Spanish influence by neutralizing Spain's most important ally, the Creek Indians. The Creeks numbered more than twenty thousand, including perhaps five thousand warriors, and they bore a fierce hostility toward Georgian settlers, whom they called Ecunnaunuxulgee, or "the greedy people who want our lands." In 1790, the Creek leader Alexander McGillivray signed the Treaty of New York with the United States. The treaty permitted American settlers to remain on lands in the Georgia piedmont fought over since 1786 (see Chapter 6), but in other respects preserved Creek territory against U.S. expansion. Washington insisted that Georgia restore to the Creeks' allies, the Chickasaws and Choctaws, the vast area along the Mississippi River known as the Yazoo Tract, which Georgia claimed had begun selling off to white land speculators (as discussed in Chapter 8).

Washington and his secretary of war, Henry Knox, adopted a harsher policy toward Native Americans who resisted efforts by American citizens to occupy the Ohio valley. In 1790, the first U.S. military effort collapsed when a coalition of tribes chased General Josiah Harmar and 1,500 troops from the Maumee River. A second campaign failed in November 1791, when one thousand Shawnee warriors surrounded an encampment of fourteen hundred soldiers led by General Arthur St. Clair. More than six hundred soldiers were killed and several hundred wounded before the survivors could flee for safety.

With Native Americans having twice humiliated U.S. forces in the Northwest Territory, Washington's western policy was in shambles. Matters worsened in 1792 when Spain persuaded the Creeks to renounce the Treaty of New York and resume hostilities. The damage done to U.S. prestige by these setbacks convinced many Americans that the combined strength of Britain, Spain, and the Native Americans could be counterbalanced only by an alliance with France.

France and Factional Politics, 1793   One of the most momentous events in world history, the French Revolution began in 1789. The French were inspired by America's revolution, and Americans were initially sympathetic as France abolished nobles' privileges, wrote a constitution, bravely repelled foreign invaders, and proclaimed itself a republic. But the Revolution took a radical turn in 1793 when France declared an international revolutionary war of all peoples against all kings and began a "Reign of Terror," executing not only the king but dissenting revolutionaries.

Americans grew bitterly divided in their attitudes toward the French Revolution and over how the United States should respond to it. While republicans such as

Jefferson supported it as an assault on monarchy and tyranny, Federalists like Hamilton denounced France as a "mobocracy" and supported Britain in resisting French efforts to export revolution.

White southern slave owners were among France's fiercest supporters. In 1793, a slave uprising in the Caribbean colony of Saint Domingue became a revolution against French rule. Thousands of terrified French planters fled to the United States, recounting how British invaders had supported the uprising. Inspired by the American and French revolutions, enslaved blacks had fought with determination and inflicted heavy casualties on French colonists. Recalling British courting of their own slaves during the American Revolution, southern whites concluded that the British had intentionally sparked the bloodbath and would do the same in the South.

Many northerners, on the other hand, were more repelled by the bloodshed in revolutionary France. The revolution was "an open hell," thundered Massachusetts's Fisher Ames, "still ringing with agonies and blasphemies, still smoking with sufferings and crimes." New England Protestants detested the French for worshiping Reason instead of God. Less religious Federalists condemned French leaders as evil radicals who incited the poor against the rich.

Northern and southern reactions to the French Revolution also diverged for economic reasons. Merchants, shippers, and ordinary sailors in New England, Philadelphia, and New York (which conducted most of the country's foreign trade) feared that an alliance with France would provoke British retaliation against American commerce. They argued that the United States could win valuable concessions by demonstrating friendly intentions toward Britain and noted that some influential members of Parliament leaned toward liberalizing trade with the United States.

Southern elites, on the other hand, viewed Americans' reliance on British commerce as a menace to national self-determination and wished to divert most U.S. trade to France. Jefferson and Madison advocated reducing British imports through the imposition of steep duties. Federalist opponents countered that Britain, which sold more manufactured goods to the United States than to any other country, would not stand idly by under such circumstances. If Congress adopted a discriminatory tariff, Hamilton predicted in 1792, "there would be, in less than six months, an open war between the United States and Great Britain."

Enthusiasm for a pro-French foreign policy intensified in the southern and western states after France went to war against Spain and Great Britain in 1793. Increasingly, western settlers and speculators hoped for a French victory that, they reasoned, would induce Britain and Spain to cease blocking U.S. expansion. The United States could then insist on free navigation of the Mississippi, force the evacuation of British garrisons, and end both nations' support of Native American resistance.

After declaring war on Britain and Spain, France actively tried to embroil the United States in the conflict. The French dispatched Edmond Genet as minister to the United States with orders to mobilize republican sentiment in support of France, enlist American mercenaries to conquer Spanish territories and attack British shipping, and strengthen the French-American alliance. Responding to France's aggressive diplomacy, President Washington issued a proclamation of American neutrality on April 22, 1793.

Citizen Edmond Genet *After the French diplomat actively recruited American citizens to the French cause, the French government recalled him at the request of the United States.*

(Granger Collection)

Defying Washington's proclamation, **Citizen Genet** (as he was known in French Revolutionary style) recruited volunteers for his American Foreign Legion. Making generals of George Rogers Clark of Kentucky and Elisha Clarke of Georgia, Genet directed them to seize Spanish garrisons at New Orleans and St. Augustine. Genet also contracted with American privateers. By the summer of 1793, almost a thousand Americans were at sea in a dozen ships flying the French flag. These privateers seized more than eighty British vessels and towed them to U.S. ports, where French consuls sold the ships and cargoes at auction. Refusing Secretary of State Jefferson's patient requests that he desist, Genet threatened to urge Americans to defy their own government.

Diplomacy and War, 1793–1796   Although the Washington administration swiftly closed U.S. harbors to Genet's buccaneers and demanded that France recall him, Genet's exploits provoked an Anglo-American crisis. George III's ministers decided that only a massive show of force would deter American support for France. Accordingly, on November 6, 1793, Britain's Privy Council ordered the Royal Navy to confiscate foreign ships trading with the French in the West Indies. The council purposely delayed publishing these instructions until after most American ships sailing to the Caribbean had left port, so that their captains would not know that they were entering a war zone. The British then seized more than 250 American vessels.

The Royal Navy added a second galling indignity—the impressment (forced enlistment) of crewmen from U.S. ships. Thousands of British sailors had previously fled to the U.S. merchant marine, where they hoped to find an easier life than under the tough, poorly paying British system. In late 1793, British naval officers began routinely inspecting American crews for British subjects, whom they then impressed as the king's sailors. Overzealous commanders sometimes broke royal orders by taking U.S. citizens, and in any case the British did not recognize former subjects' right to adopt American citizenship. Impressment scratched a raw nerve in most Americans, who argued that their government's willingness to defend its citizens from such abuse was a critical test of national character.

Meanwhile, Britain, Spain, and many Native Americans continued to challenge the United States for control of territory west of the Appalachians. During a large intertribal council in February 1794, the Shawnees and other Ohio Indians welcomed an inflammatory speech by Canada's royal governor denying U.S. claims north of the Ohio River and urging destruction of every American settlement in the Northwest. Soon British troops were building an eighth garrison on U.S. soil, Fort Miami, near present-day Toledo. Spanish troops also encroached on territory claimed by the United States by building Fort San Fernando in 1794 at what is now Memphis, Tennessee.

Hoping to halt the drift toward war, Washington launched three desperate initiatives in 1794. He authorized General Anthony Wayne to negotiate a treaty with the Shawnees and their Ohio valley allies, sent Chief Justice John Jay to Great Britain, and dispatched Thomas Pinckney to Spain.

Having twice defeated federal armies, the Shawnees and their allies scoffed at Washington's peace offer. "Mad Anthony" Wayne then led thirty-five hundred U.S. troops deep into Shawnee homelands, building forts and ruthlessly burning every village within his reach. On August 20, 1794, his troops routed four hundred Shawnees at the Battle of Fallen Timbers just two miles from Fort Miami. As Indians fled toward the fort, the British closed its gates, denying entry to their allies. Wayne's army then built an imposing stronghold to challenge British authority in the Northwest, appropriately named Fort Defiance. Indian morale plummeted, because of the American victory and their own losses but also because of Britain's betrayal.

In August 1795, Wayne compelled the Shawnees and eleven other tribes to sign the **Treaty of Greenville,** which opened most of modern-day Ohio and a portion of Indiana to American settlement. But aside from the older leaders who were pressured to sign the treaty, most Shawnees knew that U.S. designs on Indian land in the Northwest had not been satisfied and would soon resurface (as discussed in Chapter 8).

Wayne's victory at Fallen Timbers helped John Jay, in **Jay's Treaty,** win a British promise to withdraw troops from American soil by June 1796. Jay also managed to gain access to British West Indian markets for small American ships, but only by bargaining away U.S. rights to load cargoes of sugar, molasses, and coffee from French colonies during wartime.

Aside from fellow Federalists, few Americans interpreted Jay's Treaty as preserving peace with honor. The treaty left Britain free to violate American neutrality and to restrict U.S. trade with France. Opponents condemned the treaty's failure to end impressment and predicted that Great Britain would thereafter force even more Americans into the Royal Navy. Slave owners were resentful that Jay had not obtained compensation for slaves taken away by the British army during the Revolution. After the Senate barely ratified the treaty in 1795, Jay nervously joked that he could find his way across the country at night by the fires of rallies burning him in effigy.

Despite its unpopularity, Jay's Treaty prevented war with Britain and finally ended British occupation of U.S. territory. The treaty also helped stimulate an enormous expansion of American trade. Upon its ratification, Britain permitted Americans to trade with its West Indian colonies and with India. Within a few years, American exports to the British Empire shot up 300 percent.

On the heels of Jay's controversial treaty came an unqualified diplomatic triumph engineered by Thomas Pinckney. Ratified in 1796, the **Treaty of San Lorenzo** with Spain (also called Pinckney's Treaty) won westerners the right of unrestricted, duty-free access to world markets via the Mississippi River. Spain also agreed to recognize the thirty-first parallel as the United States' southern boundary, to dismantle its fortifications on American soil, and to discourage Native American attacks against western settlers.

By 1796, the Washington administration could claim to have successfully extended American authority throughout the trans-Appalachian West, opened the Mississippi for western exports, enabled northeastern shippers to regain British markets, and kept the nation out of a dangerous European war. As the popular outcry over Jay's Treaty demonstrated, however, the nation's foreign policy left Americans much more deeply divided in 1796 than they had been in 1789.

PARTIES AND POLITICS, 1793–1800

By the time Washington was reelected, the controversies over domestic and foreign policy had led to the formation of two distinct political factions. During the president's second term, these factions became formal political parties, Federalists and Republicans, which advanced their members' interests, ambitions, and ideals. Thereafter, the two parties waged a bitter battle, culminating in the election of 1800.

Ideological Confrontation, 1793–1794   Conflicting attitudes about events in France, federal power, and democracy accelerated the polarization of American politics. Linking the French Revolution and the Whiskey Rebellion, Federalists trembled at the thought of guillotines and "mob rule." They were also horrified by the sight of artisans in Philadelphia and New York bandying the French revolutionary slogan "Liberty, Equality, Fraternity" and rallying around pro-French politicians such as Jefferson. Citizen Genet had openly encouraged opposition to the Washington administration, and had found hundreds of Americans willing to fight for France. Federalists worried that all of this was just the tip of a revolutionary iceberg.

By the mid-1790s, Federalists' worst fears of democracy seemed to have been confirmed. The people, they believed, were undependable and vulnerable to rabble rousers such as Genet. For Federalists, democracy meant "government by the passions of the multitude." They argued that, as in colonial times, ordinary voters should not be presented with choices over policy, but should vote simply on the basis of the personal merits of elite candidates. Elected officials, they maintained, should rule in the people's name but be independent of direct popular influence.

Republicans offered a very different perspective on government and politics. They stressed the corruption inherent in a powerful government dominated by a highly visible few, and insisted that liberty would be safe only if power were widely diffused among white male property owners.

It might at first glance seem contradictory for southern slave owners to support a radical ideology like republicanism, with its emphasis on liberty and equality. A few southern republicans advocated abolishing slavery gradually, but most did not trouble themselves over their ownership of human beings. Although expressed in universal terms, the liberty and equality they advocated were intended for white men only.

Political ambition drove men like Jefferson and Madison to rouse ordinary voters' concerns about civic affairs. The widespread awe in which Washington was held inhibited open criticism of him and his policies. If, however, his fellow Federalists could be held accountable to the public, they would think twice before enacting measures opposed by the majority; or if they persisted in advocating misguided policies, they would ultimately be removed from office. Such reasoning led Jefferson, a wealthy landowner and large slave holder, to say, "I am not among those who fear the people; they and not the rich, are our dependence for continued freedom."

Jefferson's frustration at being overruled at every turn by Hamilton and Washington finally prompted his resignation from the cabinet in 1793, and thereafter not even the president could halt the widening political split. Each side portrayed itself as the guardian of republican virtue and attacked the other as an illegitimate "cabal" or "faction."

In 1793–1794, opponents of Federalist policies began organizing Democratic societies. The societies formed primarily in seaboard cities but also in the rural South and West. Their members included planters, small farmers and merchants, artisans, distillers, and sailors; conspicuously absent were big businessmen, the clergy, the poor, nonwhites, and women.

The Republican Party, 1794–1796   In 1794, party development reached a decisive stage after Washington openly identified himself with Federalist policies. Republicans attacked the Federalists' pro-British leanings in many local elections and won a slight majority in the House of Representatives. The election signaled the Republicans' transformation from a coalition of officeholders and local societies to a broad-based party capable of coordinating local political campaigns throughout the nation.

Federalists and Republicans alike used the press to mold public opinion. In the 1790s, American journalism came of age as the number of newspapers rose from 92 to 242, mostly in New England and the mid-Atlantic states. By 1800, newspapers had about 140,000 paid subscribers (roughly one-fifth of eligible voters), and their secondhand readership probably exceeded 300,000. Newspapers of both camps did not hesitate to engage in fear-mongering and character assassination. Federalists accused Republicans of plotting a reign of terror and of conspiring to turn the nation over to France. Republicans charged Federalists with favoring a hereditary aristocracy and even a royal dynasty that would form when John Adams's daughter married George III. Despite the extreme rhetoric, newspaper warfare stimulated many citizens to become politically active.

Washington grew impatient with the nation's growing polarization into openly hostile parties, and he deeply resented Republican charges that he secretly supported alleged Federalist plots to establish a monarchy. "By God," Jefferson reported him swearing, "he [Washington] would rather be in his grave than in his present situation ... he had rather be on his farm than to be made emperor of the world." Lonely and surrounded by mediocre advisers after Hamilton returned to private life, Washington decided in the spring of 1796 to retire after two terms. Washington recalled Hamilton to write his Farewell Address.

The heart of Washington's message was a vigorous condemnation of political parties. Partisan alignments, he insisted, endangered the republic's survival, especially if they became entangled in disputes over foreign policy. Washington warned that the country's safety depended on citizens' avoiding "excessive partiality for one nation and excessive dislike of another." Otherwise, "real patriots" would be overwhelmed by demagogues championing foreign causes and paid by foreign governments. Aside from scrupulously fulfilling its existing treaty obligations and maintaining its foreign commerce, the United States must avoid "political connection" with Europe and its wars. If the United States gathered its strength under "an efficient government," it could defy any foreign challenge; but if it became sucked into Europe's quarrels, violence, and corruption, the republican experiment was doomed. Washington and Hamilton had skillfully turned republicanism's fear of corruption against their Republican critics. They had also evoked a vision of an America virtuously isolated from foreign intrigue and power politics, which would remain a potent inspiration for long afterward.

Washington left the presidency in 1797 and died in 1799. Like many later presidents, he went out amid a barrage of partisan criticism.

The Election of 1796

With the **election of 1796** approaching, the Republicans cultivated a large, loyal body of voters. Their efforts to marshal popular support marked the first time since the Constitution was ratified that political elites had effectively mobilized nonelites to participate in politics. The Republicans' constituency included the Democratic societies, workingmen's clubs, and immigrant-aid associations.

Immigrants became prime targets for Republican recruiters. During the 1790s, the United States absorbed about twenty thousand French refugees from Saint Domingue and more than sixty thousand Irish, many of whom had been exiled for opposing British rule. Although potential immigrant voters made up less than 2 percent of the electorate, the Irish could make a difference in closely-divided Pennsylvania and New York.

In 1796, the presidential candidates were the Federalist vice president John Adams and the Republicans' Jefferson. Republicans expected to win as many southern electoral votes and congressional seats as the Federalists counted on in New England, New Jersey, and South Carolina. The crucial "swing" states were Pennsylvania and New York, where the Republicans fought hard to win the large immigrant vote with their pro-French and anti-British rhetoric. In the end, the Republicans took Pennsylvania but not New York, so that Jefferson lost the presidency by just three electoral votes. As the second-highest vote-getter in the electoral college, he became vice president. The Federalists narrowly regained control of the House and maintained their firm grip on the Senate.

Adams's intellect and devotion to principle have rarely been equaled among American presidents. But the new president was more comfortable with ideas than with people, especially nonelites. He inspired trust and often admiration but could not command personal loyalty or inspire the public. Adams's stubborn personality and disdain for ordinary people left him ill-suited to govern, and he ultimately proved unable to unify the country.

The French Crisis, 1798–1799

Even before the election, the French had recognized that Jay's Treaty was a Federalist-sponsored attempt to assist Britain in its war against France. On learning of Jefferson's defeat, France began seizing American ships carrying goods to British ports and within a year had plundered more than three hundred vessels. The French also directed that every American captured on a British naval ship (even those involuntarily impressed) should be hanged.

Hoping to avoid war, Adams sent a peace commission to Paris. But the French foreign minister, Charles de Talleyrand, refused to meet the delegation, instead promising through three unnamed agents ("X, Y, and Z") that talks could begin after he received $250,000 and France obtained a loan of $12 million. Americans were outraged at this barefaced demand for a bribe, which became known as the XYZ Affair. "Millions for defense, not one cent for tribute" became a popular slogan as the 1798 congressional elections began.

The XYZ Affair discredited the Republicans' foreign policy views, but the party's leaders compounded the damage by refusing to condemn French aggression and opposing Adams's call for military preparations. The Republicans tried to excuse French behavior, whereas the Federalists rode a wave of militant patriotism. In the 1798 elections, Jefferson's supporters were routed almost everywhere, even in the South.

Congress responded to the XYZ Affair by arming fifty-four ships to protect American commerce. During an undeclared Franco-American naval conflict in the Caribbean known as the Quasi-War (1798–1800), U.S. forces seized ninety-three French privateers while losing just one vessel. The British navy meanwhile extended the protection of its convoys to America's merchant marine. By early 1799, the French remained a nuisance but were no longer a serious threat at sea.

Meanwhile, the Federalist-dominated Congress quadrupled the size of the regular army to twelve thousand men in 1798, with ten thousand more troops in reserve. Yet the risk of a land war with France was minimal. In reality, the Federalists wanted a military force ready in the event of a civil war, for the crisis had produced near-hysteria among them about conspiracies being hatched by French and Irish revolutionaries flooding into the United States.

The Alien and Sedition Acts, 1798

The most heated controversies of the late 1790s arose from the Federalists' insistence that the threat of war with France required strict laws to protect national security. In 1798, the Federalist-dominated Congress accordingly passed four measures known collectively as the **Alien and Sedition Acts**. Adams neither requested nor particularly wanted these laws, but he deferred to Federalist congressional leaders and signed them.

The least controversial of the laws, the Alien Enemies Act, outlined procedures for determining whether citizens of a hostile country posed a threat to the United States as spies or saboteurs. If so, they were to be deported or jailed. The law established fundamental principles for protecting national security and respecting the rights of enemy citizens. It was to operate only if Congress declared war and thus was not used until the War of 1812 (discussed in Chapter 8).

Second, the Alien Friends Act, a temporary statute, authorized the president to expel any foreign residents whose activities he considered dangerous. The law did not require proof of guilt, on the assumption that spies would hide or destroy evidence of their crime. Republicans maintained that the law's real purpose was to deport immigrants critical of Federalist policies.

Republicans also denounced the third law, the Naturalization Act. This measure increased the residency requirement for U.S. citizenship from five to fourteen years (the last five continuously in one state), with the purpose of reducing Irish voting.

Finally came the Sedition Act, the only one of these measures enforceable against U.S. citizens. Although its alleged purpose was to punish attempts to encourage the violation of federal laws or to overthrow the government, the act defined criminal activity so broadly that it blurred any distinction between sedition and legitimate political discussion. For example, it prohibited an individual or group from opposing "any measure or measures of the United States"—wording that could be interpreted to ban any criticism of the party in power. Another clause made it illegal to speak, write, or print any statement about the president that would bring him "into contempt or disrepute." Under such restrictions, a newspaper editor could face imprisonment for criticizing an action by Adams. The Federalist *Gazette of the United States* expressed the twisted logic of the Sedition Act perfectly: "It is patriotism to write in favor of our government—it is sedition to write against it." However one regarded it, the Sedition Act interfered with free speech. Ingeniously, the Federalists wrote the law to expire in 1801, so that it could not be turned against them if they lost the next election, while leaving them free to heap abuse on Vice President Jefferson (who did not participate in the making of government policy).

A principal target of Federalist repression was the opposition press. Four of the five largest Republican newspapers were charged with sedition just as the election campaign of 1800 was getting under way. The attorney general used the Alien Friends Act to threaten Irish journalist John Daly Burk with expulsion (Burk went underground instead), and Scottish editor, Thomas Callender, went to prison for criticizing the president.

Federalist leaders never intended to fill the jails with Republican martyrs. Rather, they hoped to use a few highly visible prosecutions to silence Republican journalists and candidates during the election of 1800. The attorney general charged seventeen persons with sedition and won ten convictions. Among the victims was Republican congressman Matthew Lyon of Vermont ("Ragged Matt, the democrat," to the Federalists), who spent four months in prison for publishing a blast against Adams.

In 1788, opponents of the Constitution had warned that giving the national government extensive powers would eventually endanger freedom. Ten years later, their prediction seemed to have come true. Shocked Republicans realized that because the Federalists controlled all three branches of the government, neither the Bill of Rights nor the system of checks and balances reliably protected individual liberties. In this context, they advanced the doctrine of states' rights as a means of preventing the national government from violating basic freedoms.

Recognizing that opponents of federal power would never prevail in the Supreme Court, which was still dominated by Federalists, Madison and Jefferson anonymously wrote manifestos on states' rights known as the **Virginia and Kentucky Resolutions**, adopted respectively by the legislatures of those states in 1798. Repudiating his position at the constitutional convention (see Chapter 6), Madison in the Virginia Resolutions declared that state legislatures had never surrendered their right to judge the constitutionality of federal actions and that they retained an authority called *interposition*, which enabled them to protect the liberties of their citizens. Jefferson's resolution for Kentucky went further by declaring that ultimate sovereignty rested with the states, which empowered them to "nullify" federal laws to which they objected. Although Kentucky's legislature deleted the term "nullify" before approving the resolution in 1799, the intention of both resolutions was to invalidate any federal law in a state that had deemed the law unconstitutional. Although the resolutions were intended as nonviolent protests, they challenged the jurisdiction of federal courts and could have enabled state militias to march into a federal courtroom to halt proceedings at bayonet point.

No other state endorsed these resolutions (ten expressed disapproval), but their passage demonstrated the great potential for disunion in the late 1790s. So did several near-violent confrontations between Federalist and Republican crowds in Philadelphia and New York City. A minor insurrection, the Fries Rebellion, broke out in 1799 when crowds of Pennsylvania German farmers released prisoners jailed for refusing to pay taxes needed to fund the national army's expansion. But the uprising collapsed when federal troops intervened.

The nation's leaders increasingly acted as if a crisis were imminent. Vice President Jefferson hinted that events might push the southern states into secession from the Union, while President Adams hid guns in his home. After passing through Richmond and learning that state officials were purchasing thousands of muskets for the militia, an alarmed Supreme Court justice wrote in January 1799 that "the General Assembly of Virginia are pursuing steps which will lead directly to civil war." A tense atmosphere hung over the Republic as the election of 1800 neared.

The Election of 1800   In the election campaign, the two parties again rallied around the Federalist Adams and the Republican Jefferson. The leadership of moderates in both parties helped to ensure that the nation survived the **election of 1800** without a civil war. Jefferson and Madison discouraged radical activity that might provoke intervention by the national army, while Adams rejected demands by extreme "High Federalists" that he ensure victory by deliberately sparking an insurrection or asking Congress to declare war on France.

"Nothing but an open war can save us," argued one High Federalist cabinet officer. But when Adams suddenly learned in 1799 that France wanted peace, he proposed a special diplomatic mission. "Surprise, indignation, grief & disgust followed each other in quick succession," said a Federalist senator on hearing the news. Adams obtained Senate approval for his envoys only by threatening to resign and so make Jefferson president. Outraged High Federalists tried to dump Adams, but their ill-considered maneuver rallied most New Englanders around the stubborn, upright president.

Adams's envoys did not achieve a settlement with France until 1800, but his pursuit of peace with France prevented the Federalists from exploiting charges of Republican sympathy for the enemy. Without the immediate threat of war, moreover, voters grew resentful that in only two years, taxes had soared 33 percent to support an army that had done nothing except chase Pennsylvania farmers. As the danger of war receded, voters gave the Federalists less credit for standing up to France and more blame for adding $10 million to the national debt.

While High Federalists spitefully withheld the backing that Adams needed to win, Republicans redoubled their efforts to elect Jefferson. As a result of Republicans' mobilization of voters, popular interest in politics rose sharply. Voter turnout in 1800 leaped to more than double that of 1788, rising from about 15 percent to almost 40 percent; in hotly contested Pennsylvania and New York, more than half the eligible voters participated.

Adams lost the presidency by just eight electoral votes out of 138. But Adams's loss did not ensure Jefferson's election. Because all 73 Republican electors voted for both Jefferson and his running mate, New York's Aaron Burr, the electoral college deadlocked in a tie between them. Even more seriously than in 1796, the Constitution's failure to anticipate organized, rival parties affected the outcome of the electoral college's vote. The choice of president devolved upon the House of Representatives, where thirty-five ballots over six days produced no result. Aware that Republican voters and electors wanted Jefferson to be president, the wily Burr cast about for Federalist support. But after Hamilton—Burr's bitter rival in New York politics—declared his preference for Jefferson as "by far not so dangerous a man," a Federalist representative abandoned Burr and gave Jefferson the presidency by history's narrowest margin.

ECONOMIC AND SOCIAL CHANGE

During the nation's first twelve years under the Constitution, the spread of economic production for markets, even by family farms, transformed the lives of many Americans. These transformations marked the United States' first small steps toward industrial capitalism.

Meanwhile, some Americans rethought questions of gender and race in American society during the 1790s. Even so, legal and political barriers to gender and racial equality actually became more entrenched.

Producing for Markets

For centuries most economic production in European societies and their colonial offshoots took place in household settings. At the core of each household was a patriarchal nuclear family—the male head, his wife, and their unmarried children. Many households included additional people—relatives; boarders; apprentices and journeymen in artisan shops; servants and slaves in well-off urban households; and slaves, "hired hands," and tenant farmers in rural settings. (Even slaves living in separate "quarters" on large plantations labored in enterprises centered on planters' households.) Unlike in our modern world, before the nineteenth century most people except mariners worked at what was temporarily or permanently "home." The notion of "going to work" would have struck them as odd.

Although households varied greatly in the late eighteenth century, most were on small farms and consisted of only an owner and his family. By 1800, such farm families typically included seven children whose labor contributed to production. While husbands and older sons worked in fields away from the house, wives, daughters, and young sons maintained the barns and gardens near the house. Wives, of course, bore and reared the children as well. As in the colonial period, most farm families produced food and other products largely for their own consumption, adding small surpluses for bartering with neighbors or local merchants.

After the American Revolution, households in the most densely populated regions of the Northeast began to change. Relatively prosperous farm families, particularly in the mid-Atlantic states, increasingly directed their surplus production to meet the growing demands of urban customers for produce, meat, and dairy products. These families often turned to agricultural experts, whose advice their parents and grandparents had usually spurned. Accordingly, men introduced clover into their pastures, expanded acreage devoted to hay, and built barns to shelter their cows in cold weather and to store the hay. A federal census in 1798 revealed that about half the farms in eastern Pennsylvania had barns, usually of logs or framed but occasionally of stone. Consequently, dairy production rose as mid-Atlantic farmwomen, or "dairymaids," by 1800 milked an average of six animals twice a day, with each "milch cow" producing about two gallons per day during the summer. Farmwomen turned much of the milk into butter for sale to urban consumers.

Poorer farm families, especially in New England, found less lucrative ways to produce for commercial markets. Small plots of land on New England's thin, rocky soil no longer supported large families, leading young people to look elsewhere for a living. While many young men and young couples moved west, unmarried daughters more frequently remained at home, where they helped satisfy a growing demand for ready-made clothing. After the Revolution, enterprising merchants began catering to urban consumers as well as southern slave owners seeking to clothe their slaves as cheaply as possible. Making regular circuits through rural areas, the merchants supplied cloth for sewing to mothers and daughters in farm households. A few weeks later, they would return and pay the women in cash for their handiwork.

A comparable transition began in some artisans' households. The shoemakers of Lynn, Massachusetts, had expanded their production during the Revolution when filling orders from the Continental Army. After the war, some more successful artisans began supplying leather to rural families beyond Lynn, paying them for the finished product. In this way, they filled an annual demand that rose from 189,000 pairs in 1789 to 400,000 in 1800.

Numerous other enterprises likewise emerged, employing men as well as women to satisfy demands that self-contained households could never have met on their own. For example, a traveler passing through Middleborough, Massachusetts, observed,

> In the winter season, the inhabitants...are principally employed in making nails, of which they send large quantities to market. This business is a profitable addition to their husbandry; and fills up a part of the year, in which, otherwise, many of them would find little employment.

Behind the new industries was an ambitious, aggressive class of businessmen, most of whom had begun as merchants and now invested their profits in factories, ships, government bonds, and banks. Such entrepreneurs stimulated a flurry of innovative business ventures that pointed toward the future. The country's first private banks were founded in the 1780s in Philadelphia, Boston, and New York. Philadelphia merchants created the Pennsylvania Society for the Encouragement of Manufactures and the Useful Arts in 1787. This organization promoted the immigration of English artisans familiar with the latest industrial technology, including Samuel Slater, a pioneer of American industrialization who helped establish a cotton-spinning mill at Pawtucket, Rhode Island, in 1790 (see Chapter 9). In 1791, investors from New York and Philadelphia, with Hamilton's enthusiastic endorsement, started the Society for the Encouragement of Useful Manufactures, which attempted to demonstrate the potential of large-scale industrial enterprises by building a factory town at Paterson, New Jersey. That same year, New York merchants and insurance underwriters organized America's first formal association for trading government bonds, out of which the New York Stock Exchange evolved.

For many Americans, the choice between manufacturing and farming was moral as well as economic. Hamilton's aggressive support of entrepreneurship and industrialization was consistent with his larger vision for America and contradicted that of Jefferson. As outlined in his Report on the Subject of Manufactures (1791), Hamilton admired efficiently run factories in which a few managers supervised large numbers of workers. Manufacturing would provide employment opportunities, promote emigration, and expand the applications of technology. It would also offer "greater scope for the talents and dispositions [of] men," afford "a more ample and various field for enterprise," and create "a more certain and steady demand for the surplus produce of the soil." Jefferson, on the other hand, idealized white, landowning family farmers as bulwarks of republican liberty and virtue. "Those who labour in the earth are the chosen people," he wrote in 1784, whereas the dependency of European factory workers "begets subservience and venality, suffocates the germ of virtue, and prepares fit tools for the designs of ambition." For Hamilton, capital, technology, and managerial discipline were the surest roads to national order and wealth. Jefferson, putting more trust in white male citizens, envisioned land as the key to prosperity and liberty for all. The argument over the relative merits of these two ideals would remain a constant in American politics and culture until the twentieth century.

White Women in   Alongside the growing importance of women's economic
the Republic   roles, whites' discussions of republicanism raised questions
of women's rights and equality. Yet women did not gain
political rights, except in New Jersey. That state's 1776 constitution, by not specifying gender and race, left a loophole that enabled white female and black property owners to vote, which many began to do. More women voted during the
1790s, when New Jersey adopted laws that stipulated "he or she" when referring to
voters. In a hotly contested legislative race in 1797, seventy-five women voters
nearly gave the victory to a Federalist candidate. His victorious Republican opponent, John Condict, would get his revenge in 1807 by successfully advocating a
bill to disenfranchise women (along with free blacks).

Social change and republican ideology together fostered several formidable
challenges to traditional attitudes toward women's rights. American republicans increasingly recognized the right of a woman to choose her husband—a striking departure from the continued practice among some elites whereby fathers approved or
even arranged marriages. Thus in 1790, on the occasion of his daughter Martha's
marriage, Jefferson wrote to a friend that, following "the usage of my country, I
scrupulously suppressed my wishes, [so] that my daughter might indulge her sentiments freely."

Outside elite circles, such independence was even more apparent. Especially in
the Northeast, daughters increasingly got pregnant by preferred partners, thus forcing their fathers to consent to their marrying to avoid a public scandal. In Hallo-
well, Maine, in May 1792, for example, Mary Brown's father objected to her
marrying John Chamberlain. In December, he finally consented and the couple
wed—just two days before Mary gave birth. By becoming pregnant, northeastern
women secured economic support in a region where an exodus of young, unmarried men was leaving a growing number of women single.

White women also had fewer children overall than had their mothers and
grandmothers. In Sturbridge, Massachusetts, women in the mid-eighteenth century
averaged nearly nine children per marriage, compared with six in the first decade of
the nineteenth century. Whereas 40 percent of Quaker women had nine or more
children before 1770, only 14 percent bore that many thereafter. Such statistics
testify to declining farm sizes and urbanization, both of which were incentives for
having fewer children. But they also indicate that some women were finding relief
from the near-constant state of pregnancy and nursing that had consumed their
grandmothers.

As white women's roles expanded, so too did republican notions of male-
female relations. "I object to the word 'obey' in the marriage-service," wrote a
female author calling herself Matrimonial Republican, "…The obedience between
man and wife is, or ought to be mutual." Lack of mutuality was one reason for a
rising number of divorce petitions from women, from fewer than fourteen per year
in Connecticut before the Revolution, to forty-five in 1795.

A few women also challenged the sexual double standard that allowed men to
indulge in extramarital affairs while their female partners, single or married, were
condemned. Writing in 1784, an author calling herself "Daphne" pointed out how
a woman whose illicit affair was exposed was "forever deprive[d]…of all that ren-
ders life valuable," while "the base [male] betrayer is suffered to triumph in the

Advocating Women's Rights, 1792 *In this illustration from an American magazine for women, the "Genius of the Ladies Magazine" and the "Genius of Emulation" present Liberty with a petition based on British feminist Mary Wollstonecraft's* Vindication of the Rights of Woman.

success of his unmanly arts, and to pass unpunished even by a frown." Daphne called on her "sister Americans" to "stand by and support the dignity of our own sex" by publicly condemning seducers rather than their victims.

Gradually, the subordination of women, which most whites had always taken for granted, became the subject of debate. In "On the Equality of the Sexes" (1790), essayist and poet Judith Sargent Murray contended that the genders had equal intellectual ability and deserved equal education. Murray hoped that "sensible and informed" women would improve their minds rather than rush into marriage (as she had at eighteen).

Like many of her contemporaries, Murray supported the idea of **"republican motherhood."** Advocates of republican motherhood emphasized the importance of educating white women in the values of liberty and independence to strengthen virtue in the new nation. It was the republican duty of mothers to inculcate these values in their sons—the nation's future leaders—as well as their daughters. John Adams reminded his daughter that she was part of "a young generation, coming up in America ... [and] will be responsible for a great share of the duty and opportunity of educating a rising family, from whom much will be expected." Before the 1780s, only a few women had acquired an advanced education through private tutors. Thereafter, urban elites broadened such opportunities by founding numerous private schools, or academies, for girls. Massachusetts also established an important precedent in 1789 when it forbade any town to exclude girls from its elementary schools.

Although the great struggle for female political equality would not begin until the next century, assertions that women were intellectually and morally men's peers, and that republican mothers played a vital public role, provoked additional calls for equality beyond those voiced by Abigail Adams and a few other women during the Revolution (see Chapter 6). In 1793, Priscilla Mason, a student at a female academy, blamed "*Man*, despotic man" for shutting women out of the church, the courts, and government. In her graduation speech, she urged that a women's senate be established by Congress to evoke "all that is human—all that is *divine* in the soul of woman." Mason pointed out that while women could be virtuous wives and mothers, the world outside their homes still offered them few opportunities to apply their education. And neither she nor anyone else at the time challenged prohibitions against married women's ownership of property.

Land and Culture: Native Americans

Native Americans occupied the most tenuous position in American society. By 1800, Indians east of the Mississippi had suffered severe losses of population, territory (see Map 7.2), and political and cultural self-determination. Thousands of deaths had resulted from battle, famine, and disease during successive wars since the 1750s and from poverty, losses of land, and discrimination during peacetime. From 1775 to 1800, the Cherokee population declined from sixteen thousand to ten thousand, and Iroquois numbers fell from about nine thousand to four thousand. During the same period, Native Americans lost more land than the area inhabited by whites in 1775. Settlers, liquor dealers, and criminals trespassed on Indian lands, often defrauding, stealing, or inflicting violence on Native Americans and provoking them to retaliate. Indians who sold land or worked for whites were often paid in the unfamiliar medium of cash and then found little to spend it on in their isolated communities except alcohol.

While employing military force against Native Americans who resisted U.S. authority, Washington and Secretary of War Knox recognized that American citizens' actions often contributed to Indians' resentment. Accordingly, they pursued a policy similar to Britain's under the Proclamation of 1763 (see Chapter 5) in which the federal government sought to regulate relations between Indians and non-Indians. Congress enacted the new policy gradually in a series of **Indian Trade and Intercourse Acts** (1790–1796). (Thereafter, Congress periodically renewed and amended the legislation until making it permanent in 1834.) To halt fraudulent land cessions, the acts prohibited transfers of tribal lands to outsiders except as authorized in formal treaties or by Congress. Other provisions regulated the conduct

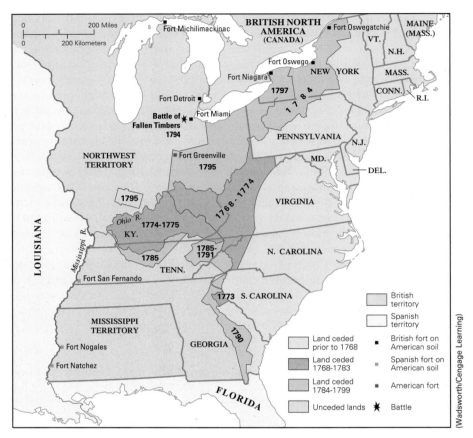

MAP 7.2 Indian Land Cessions, 1768–1799

During the last third of the eighteenth century, Native Americans were forced to give up extensive homelands throughout the eastern backcountry and farther west in the Ohio and Tennessee River valleys.

of non-Indians on lands still under tribal control. To regulate intercultural trade and reduce abuses, the acts required that traders be licensed by the federal government. (But until 1802, the law did not prohibit the sale of liquor on Indian lands.) The law also defined murder and other abuses committed by non-Indians against Indians on tribal lands as federal offenses. Finally, the legislation authorized the federal government to establish programs that would "promote civilization" among Native Americans as a replacement for traditional culture. By "civilization," Knox and his supporters meant Anglo-American culture, particularly private property and a strictly agricultural way of life, with men replacing women in the fields. By abandoning communal landownership and seasonal migrations for hunting, gathering, and fishing, they argued, Indians would no longer need most of the land they were trying to protect, thereby making it available for whites. But before 1800, the "civilization" program was offered to relatively few Native Americans, and the Indian Trade and Intercourse Acts went largely unenforced.

Among the most devastated Native Americans in the 1790s were the Seneca Iroquois of western New York and Pennsylvania. Most surviving Iroquois had moved to Canada after the Revolution, and those like the Seneca who stayed behind were pressured to sell, or were simply defrauded of, most of their land, leaving them isolated from one another on tiny reservations. Unable to hunt, trade, or wage mourning wars, Seneca men frequently resorted to heavy drinking, often becoming violent. All too typical were the tragedies that beset Mary Jemison, born a half-century earlier to white settlers but a Seneca since her wartime capture and adoption at age ten. Jemison saw one of her sons murder his two brothers in alcohol-related episodes before meeting a similar fate himself.

In 1799, a Seneca prophet, **Handsome Lake**, emerged and led his people in a remarkable spiritual revival. Severely ill, alcoholic, and near death, he experienced a series of visions, which Iroquois and many other Native American societies interpreted as prophetic messages. As in the visions of the Iroquois prophet Hiawatha in the fourteenth century, spiritual guides appeared to Handsome Lake and instructed him in

Red Jacket, Seneca Iroquois Chief (CA. 1750–1830) *Red Jacket was an eloquent defender of Seneca traditions against the efforts of both Christian missionaries and Handsome Lake to change Seneca religion and culture.*

(Gilcrease Museum, Tulsa, Oklahoma)

his own recovery and in that of his people. Invoking Iroquois religious traditions, Handsome Lake preached against alcoholism and sought to revive unity and self-confidence among the Seneca. But whereas many Indian visionary prophets rejected all white ways, Handsome Lake welcomed civilization, as introduced by Quaker missionaries (who did not attempt to convert Native Americans) supported by federal aid. In particular, he urged a radical shift in gender roles, with Seneca men displacing women not only in farming but also as heads of their families. At the same time, he insisted that men treat their wives respectfully and without violence.

The most traditional Senecas rejected Handsome Lake's message that Native men should work like white farmers. While many Seneca men welcomed the change, women often resisted because they stood to lose their control of farming and their considerable political influence. Some of Handsome Lake's supporters accused women who rejected his teachings of witchcraft, and even killed a few of them. The violence soon ceased and Handsome Lake's followers formed their own church, complete with traditional Iroquois religious ceremonies. The Seneca case would prove to be unique; after 1800, missionaries would expect Native Americans to convert to Christianity as well as adopt "civilization."

African-American Struggles

The Republic's first years marked the high tide of African-Americans' Revolutionary-era success in bettering their lot. Blacks and even many whites recognized that the ideals of liberty and equality were inconsistent with slavery. By 1790, 8 percent of all African-Americans had been freed from slavery. Ten years later, 11 percent were free (see Figure 7.1). Various state reforms meanwhile attempted to improve the conditions of those who remained enslaved. In 1791, for example, the North Carolina legislature declared that the former "distinction of criminality between the murder of a white person and one who is equally an human creature, but merely of a different complexion, is disgraceful to humanity" and authorized the execution of whites who murdered slaves. Although more for economic than humanitarian reasons, by 1794 most states had outlawed the Atlantic slave trade.

Hesitant measures to ensure free blacks' legal equality also appeared in the 1780s and early 1790s. Most states dropped restrictions on African-Americans' freedom of movement and protected their property. By 1796, all but three of the sixteen states either permitted free blacks to vote or did not specifically exclude them. But by then a countertrend was reversing many of the Revolutionary-era advances. Before the 1790s ended, abolitionist sentiment ebbed among whites, slavery became more entrenched, and free blacks faced new obstacles to equality.

Federal law led the way in restricting the rights of blacks and other nonwhites. When Congress passed the first Naturalization Act (1790), it limited eligibility for U.S. citizenship to "free white aliens." The federal militia law of 1792 required whites to enroll in local units but allowed states to exclude free blacks, which state governments increasingly did. The navy and the marine corps forbade nonwhite enlistments in 1798. Delaware stripped free, property-owning black males of the vote in 1792, and by 1807 Maryland, Kentucky, and New Jersey had followed suit. Free black men continued to vote and to serve in some militia units after 1800 (including in the slave states of North Carolina and Tennessee), but the number of settings in which they were treated as the equals of whites dropped sharply.

State	Total Number of Free Blacks	Free Blacks as a Percentage of Total Black Population
Massachusetts	7,378	100%
Vermont	557	100%
New Hampshire	855	99%
Rhode Island	3,304	90%
Pennsylvania	14,564	89%
Connecticut	5,300	85%
Delaware	8,268	57%
New York	10,374	33%
New Jersey	4,402	26%
Maryland	19,587	16%
Virginia	20,124	6%
North Carolina	7,043	5%
South Carolina	3,185	2%
Georgia	1,019	2%
Kentucky	741	2%
Tennessee	309	2%
UNITED STATES	108,395*	11%

(Wadsworth/Cengage Learning)

* Total includes figures from the District of Columbia, Mississippi Territory, and Northwest Territory. These areas are not shown on the chart.

FIGURE 7.1 Number and Percentage of Free Blacks, by State, 1800

Within a generation of the Declaration of Independence, a large free black population emerged that included every ninth African-American. In the North, only in New Jersey and New York did most blacks remain slaves. Almost half of all free blacks lived in the South. Every sixth black in Maryland was free by 1800.

Source: U.S. Bureau of the Census.

Despite these disadvantages, some free blacks became landowners or skilled artisans, and a few gained recognition among whites. Among the best known was Benjamin Banneker of Maryland, a self-taught mathematician and astronomer. In 1789, Banneker was one of three surveyors who laid out the new national capital in Washington, D.C., and after 1791 he published a series of widely read almanacs. Sending a copy of one to Thomas Jefferson, Banneker chided the future president for holding views of black inferiority that contradicted his words in the Declaration of Independence (see Going to the Source). In a brief reply, Jefferson expressed hope that blacks' physical and mental condition would be raised "as far as the imbecility of their present existence … will admit." (At the time, "imbecility" referred to non-mental as well as mental limitations.) The two men's exchange was published a year later.

In the face of growing constrictions on their freedom and opportunities, free African-Americans in the North turned to one another for support. Self-help among African-Americans flowed especially through religious channels. During the 1780s, two free black Christians, Richard Allen and Absalom Jones, formed the

GOING TO THE SOURCE

Benjamin Banneker to Thomas Jefferson

The following excerpt is from a letter that Benjamin Banneker wrote to Thomas Jefferson, dated August 19, 1791. Banneker issued the most forceful challenge of the time to Jefferson's positions on race and slavery.

Sir, I freely and cheerfully acknowledge, that I am of the African race, and in that color which is natural to them of the deepest dye; and it is under a sense of the most profound gratitude to the Supreme Ruler of the Universe, that I now confess to you, that I am not under that state of tyrannical thralldom, and inhuman captivity, to which too many of my brethren are doomed, but that I have abundantly tasted of the fruition of those blessings, which proceed from that free and unequalled liberty with which you are favored; and which, I hope, you will willingly allow you have mercifully received, from the immediate hand of that Being, from whom proceedeth every good and perfect Gift.

Sir, suffer me to recall to your mind that time, in which the arms and tyranny of the British crown were exerted, with every powerful effort, in order to reduce you to a state of servitude: look back, I entreat you, on the variety of dangers to which you were exposed; reflect on that time, in which every human aid appeared unavailable, and in which even hope and fortitude wore the aspect of inability to the conflict, and you cannot but be led to a serious and grateful sense of your miraculous and providential preservation; you cannot but acknowledge, that the present freedom and tranquility which you enjoy you have mercifully received, and that it is the peculiar blessing of Heaven.

This, Sir, was a time when you clearly saw into the injustice of a state of slavery, and in which you had just apprehensions of the horrors of its condition. It was now that your abhorrence thereof was so excited, that you publicly held forth this true and invaluable doctrine, which is worthy to be recorded and remembered in all succeeding ages: "We hold these truths

Free African Society of Philadelphia, a community organization whose members pooled their scarce resources to assist one another and other blacks in need. After the white-dominated Methodist church they attended restricted black worshipers to the gallery, Allen, Jones, and most other black members withdrew and formed a separate congregation. Comparable developments in other northern communities eventually resulted in the formation of a new denomination, the African Methodist Episcopal Church (discussed in Chapter 9).

In 1793, Philadelphia experienced a yellow fever epidemic in which about four thousand residents died. As most affluent whites fled, Allen and Jones organized a relief effort in which African-Americans, at great personal risk, tended to the sick and buried the dead of both races. But their only reward was a vicious publicity campaign wrongly accusing blacks of profiting at whites' expense. Allen and Jones vigorously defended the black community against these charges while condemning slavery and racism.

Another revealing indication of whites' changing racial attitudes occurred in 1793 with passage of the **Fugitive Slave Law**. This law required judges to award possession of an escaped slave upon any formal request by a master or his representative. Accused runaways not only were denied a jury trial but also were sometimes refused permission to present evidence of their freedom. Slaves' legal status as property disqualified them from claiming these constitutional privileges, but the Fugitive Slave to be self-evident, that all men are created equal; that they are endowed by their Creator with certain unalienable rights, and that among these are, life, liberty, and the pursuit of happiness." Here was a time, in which your tender feelings for yourselves had engaged you thus to declare, you were then impressed with proper ideas of the great violation of liberty, and the free possession of those blessings, to which you were entitled by nature; but, Sir, how pitiable is it to reflect, that although you were so fully convinced of the benevolence of the Father of Mankind, and of his equal and impartial distribution of these rights and privileges, which he hath conferred upon them, that you should at the same time counteract his mercies, in detaining by fraud and violence so numerous a part of my brethren, under groaning captivity and cruel oppression, that you should at the same time be found guilty of that most criminal act, which you professedly detested in others, with respect to yourselves.

I suppose that your knowledge of the situation of my brethren, is too extensive to need a recital here; neither shall I presume to prescribe methods by which they may be relieved, otherwise than by recommending to you and all others, to wean yourselves from those narrow prejudices which you have imbibed with respect to them, and as Job [a figure in the Bible] proposed to his friends, "put your soul in their souls' stead;" thus shall your hearts be enlarged with kindness and benevolence towards them; and thus shall you need neither the direction of myself or others, in what manner to proceed herein.

Source: American Multiculturalism Series. Unit One. Documenting the African American Experience, Special Collections, University of Virginia Library.

Questions

1. *How does Banneker use Jefferson's words in the Declaration of Independence in his argument with Jefferson?*

2. *How does Banneker characterize Jefferson's ownership of slaves?*

Go to www.cengagebrain.com for additional primary sources on this period.

Law denied free blacks the legal protections that the Bill of Rights guaranteed them as citizens. Congress nevertheless passed this measure without serious opposition. The law marked a striking departure from the atmosphere of the 1780s, when state governments had moved toward granting free blacks legal equality with whites.

The slave revolution on Saint Domingue (which victorious blacks would rename Haiti in 1802) heightened slave owners' fears of violent retaliation by blacks. In August 1800, such fears were kindled when a slave insurrection broke out near Richmond, Virginia's capital. Amid the election campaign that year, in which Federalists and Republicans accused one another of endangering liberty and hinted at violence, a slave named Gabriel calculated that the split among whites afforded blacks an opportunity to gain their freedom. Having secretly assembled weapons, he and several other African Americans organized a march on Richmond by more than a thousand slaves. The plot of **Gabriel's Rebellion** was leaked on the eve of the march. Obtaining confessions from some participants, the authorities rounded up the rest and executed thirty-five of them, including Gabriel. "I have nothing more to offer than what General Washington would have had to offer, had he been taken by the British officers and put to trial by them," said one rebel before his execution. "I have ventured my life in endeavoring to obtain the liberty of my countrymen, and I am a willing sacrifice to their cause." In the end, Gabriel's Rebellion only confirmed whites' anxieties that Haiti's revolution could be replayed on American soil.

A technological development also strengthened slavery. During the 1790s, demand in the British textile industry stimulated the cultivation of cotton in coastal South Carolina and Georgia. The soil and climate were ideal for growing long-staple cotton, a variety whose fibers could be separated easily from its seed by squeezing it through rollers. In the South's upland and interior regions, however, the only cotton that would thrive was the short-staple variety, whose seed stuck so tenaciously to the fibers that rollers crushed the seeds and ruined the fibers. It was as if growers had discovered gold only to find that they could not mine it. But in 1793, a New Englander, Eli Whitney, invented a cotton gin that successfully separated the fibers of short-staple cotton from the seed. Quickly copied and improved upon by others, Whitney's invention removed a major obstacle to the spread of cotton cultivation. It gave a new lease on life to plantation slavery and undermined the doubts of those who considered slavery economically outmoded.

By 1800, free blacks had suffered noticeable erosion of their post-Revolutionary gains, and southern slaves were farther from freedom than a decade earlier. Two vignettes poignantly communicate the plight of African-Americans. By arrangement with her late husband, Martha Washington freed the family's slaves a year after George died. But many of the freed blacks remained impoverished and dependent on the Washington estate because Virginia law prohibited the education of blacks and otherwise denied them opportunities to realize their freedom. Meanwhile, across the Potomac at the site surveyed by Benjamin Banneker, enslaved blacks were performing most of the labor on the new national capital that would bear the first president's name. African-Americans were manifestly losing ground.

CHRONOLOGY
1788–1800

1788	First election under the Constitution.
1789	First Congress convenes in New York.
	George Washington inaugurated as first president.
	Judiciary Act.
	French Revolution begins.
1790	Alexander Hamilton submits Reports on Public Credit and National Bank to Congress.
	Treaty of New York.
	Judith Sargent Murray, "On the Equality of the Sexes."
	First Indian Trade and Intercourse Act.
1791	Bank of the United States established with twenty-year charter.
	Bill of Rights ratified. *National Gazette* established.
	Slave uprising begins in Saint Domingue.
	Society for the Encouragement of Useful Manufactures founded.
1792	Washington reelected president.

1793	Fugitive Slave Law. France at war with Britain and Spain. Citizen Genet arrives in United States. First Democratic societies established.
1794	Whiskey Rebellion. Battle of Fallen Timbers.
1795	Treaty of Greenville. Jay's Treaty.
1796	Treaty of San Lorenzo. Washington's Farewell Address. John Adams elected president.
1798	XYZ Affair. Alien and Sedition Acts. Eleventh Amendment to the Constitution ratified.
1798–1799	Virginia and Kentucky Resolutions.
1798–1800	Quasi-War between United States and France.
1799	Russia establishes colony in Alaska. Fries Rebellion in Pennsylvania. Handsome Lake begins reform movement among Senecas.
1800	Gabriel's Rebellion in Virginia. Thomas Jefferson elected president.

8

AMERICA AT WAR AND PEACE, 1801–1824

CHAPTER OUTLINE

• The Age of Jefferson • The Gathering Storm • The War of 1812 • The Awakening of American Nationalism

---

THE AGE OF JEFFERSON

Narrowly elected in 1800, Jefferson saw his popularity rise during his first term when he moved quickly to scale down government expenditures. Increasingly confident of popular support, he worked to loosen the Federalists' grip on appointive federal offices, especially in the judiciary. His purchase of Louisiana against Federalist opposition added to his popularity. In all of these moves, Jefferson was guided not merely by political calculation, but also by his philosophy of government—eventually known as Jeffersonianism.

Jefferson and Jeffersonianism A man of extraordinary attainments, Jefferson was fluent in French, read Latin and Greek, and studied several Native American languages. He served for more than twenty years as president of America's foremost scientific association, the American Philosophical Society. A student of architecture, he designed his own mansion in Virginia, Monticello. Gadgets fascinated him. He invented a device for duplicating his letters, of which he wrote over twenty thousand, and he improved the design for a revolving book stand, which enabled him to consult up to five books at once. His public career was luminous: principal author of the Declaration of Independence, governor of Virginia, ambassador to France, secretary of state under Washington, and vice president under John Adams.

Yet he was, and remains, a controversial figure. His critics, pointing to his doubts about some Christian doctrines and his early support for the French

Revolution, portrayed him as an infidel and radical. Federalists alleged that he kept a slave mistress, and in 1802 James Callender, a former supporter furious about not receiving a government job he wanted, wrote a newspaper account naming her as Sally Hemings, a house slave at Monticello. Drawing on the DNA of Sally's male descendents and linking the timing of Jefferson's visits to Monticello with the start of Sally's pregnancies, most scholars now view it as very likely that Jefferson, a widower, was the father of at least one of her four surviving children.

Callender's story did Jefferson little damage in Virginia, because Jefferson had acted according to the rules of white Virginia gentlemen by never acknowledging any of Sally's children as his own. Although he freed two of her children (the other two ran away), he never freed Sally, the daughter of Jefferson's own father-in-law and so light-skinned that she could pass for white, nor did he ever mention her in his vast correspondence. Yet the story of Sally fed the charge that Jefferson was a hypocrite, for throughout his career he condemned the very "race-mixing" to which he appears to have contributed.

Jefferson did not believe that blacks and whites could live permanently side by side in American society. As the black population grew, he feared a race war so vicious that it could be suppressed only by a dictator. This view was consistent with his conviction that the real threat to republics rose less from hostile neighbors than from within. He believed that the French had turned to a dictator, Napoleon Bonaparte, to save them from the chaos of their own revolution. Only by colonizing blacks in Africa, an idea embodied in the American Colonization Society (1816), could America avert a similar fate, he believed.

Jefferson worried that high taxes, standing armies, and corruption could destroy American liberty by turning government into the master rather than servant of the people. To prevent tyranny, he advocated that state governments retain considerable authority. In a vast republic, he reasoned, state governments would be more responsive to the popular will than would the government in Washington.

He also believed that popular liberty required popular virtue. For republican theorists like Jefferson, virtue consisted of a decision to place the public good ahead of one's private interests and to exercise vigilance to keep governments from growing out of control. To Jefferson, the most vigilant and virtuous people were educated farmers who were accustomed to act and think with sturdy independence. Jefferson regarded cities as breeding grounds for mobs and as menaces to liberty. Men who relied on merchants or factory owners for their jobs could have their votes influenced, unlike farmers who worked their own land. When the people "get piled upon one another in large cities, as in Europe," he wrote, "they will become corrupt as in Europe."

Jefferson's "Revolution"

Jefferson described his election as a revolution. But the revolution he sought was to restore the liberty and tranquility that (he thought) the United States had enjoyed in its early years and to reverse what he saw as a drift into despotism. The $10 million growth in the national debt under the Federalists alarmed Jefferson and his secretary of the treasury, Albert Gallatin. They rejected Hamilton's idea that a national debt would strengthen the government by giving creditors a stake in its health. Just paying the interest on the debt would require taxes, which would suck money from industrious farmers—the backbone of the Republic. The money would then fall into the hands of creditors, parasites who leeched off interest payments. Increased tax revenues might also tempt the government to establish a standing army, always a threat to liberty.

Jefferson and Gallatin secured the repeal of many taxes, and they slashed expenditures by closing some embassies overseas and reducing the army, which declined from an authorized strength of over 14,000 in 1798 to 3,287 in 1802. A lull in the war between Britain and France that had threatened American shipping in the 1790s persuaded Jefferson that minimal military preparedness was a sound policy: "We can now proceed without risks in demolishing useless structures of expense, lightening the burdens of our constituents, and fortifying the principles of free government." This may have been wishful thinking, but it rested on a sound economic calculation, for the vast territory of the United States could not be secured from attack without astronomical expense.

Jefferson and the Judiciary   Jefferson hoped to conciliate the moderate Federalists, but conflicts over the judiciary derailed this objective. Washington and Adams had appointed only Federalists to the bench, including the new chief justice, **John Marshall.** Still bitter about the zeal of federal courts in enforcing the Alien and Sedition Acts, Jefferson saw the Federalist-sponsored Judiciary Act of 1801 as the last straw. By reducing the number of Supreme Court justices from six to five, the act threatened to strip him of an early opportunity to appoint a justice. At the same time, the act created sixteen new federal judgeships, which outgoing president John Adams had filled by last-minute ("midnight") appointments of Federalists. To Jefferson, this was proof that the Federalists intended to use the judiciary as a stronghold from which "all the works of Republicanism are to be beaten down and erased." In 1802, he won congressional repeal of the Judiciary Act of 1801.

Jefferson's troubles with the judiciary were not over. On his last day in office, Adams had appointed a Federalist, William Marbury, as justice of the peace in the District of Columbia but failed to deliver Marbury's commission before midnight. When Jefferson's secretary of state, James Madison, refused to send him notice of the appointment, Marbury petitioned the Supreme Court to issue a writ compelling delivery. In **Marbury v. Madison** (1803), Chief Justice John Marshall wrote the unanimous opinion. Marshall ruled that, although Madison should have delivered Marbury's commission, he was under no legal obligation to do so because part of the Judiciary Act of 1789 that had granted the Court the authority to issue such a writ as unconstitutional.

For the first time, the Supreme Court had asserted its authority to void an act of Congress on the grounds that it was "repugnant" to the Constitution. Jefferson did not reject this principle, known as the doctrine of judicial review and destined to become highly influential, but he was enraged that Marshall had used part of his decision to lecture Madison on his moral duty (as opposed to his legal obligation) to deliver Marbury's commission. This gratuitous lecture, which was really directed at Jefferson as Madison's superior, struck Jefferson as another example of Federalist partisanship.

While the *Marbury* decision was brewing, the Republicans took the offensive against the judiciary by moving to impeach (charge with wrongdoing) two Federalist judges, John Pickering and Samuel Chase. Pickering, an insane alcoholic, was quickly removed from office, but Chase presented difficulties. He was a partisan Federalist notorious for jailing several Republican editors under the Sedition Act of 1798. Nonetheless, the Constitution specified that judges could be impeached only for treason, bribery, and "high Crimes and Misdemeanors." Was impeachment appropriate because a judge was excessively partisan? Moderate Republicans came to doubt it, and partly for that reason, the Senate narrowly failed to convict Chase.

Chase's acquittal ended Jefferson's skirmishes with the judiciary. Unlike his radical followers, Jefferson objected neither to judicial review nor to an appointed judiciary; he merely challenged Federalist use of judicial power for political goals. Yet there was always a gray area between law and politics. To Federalists there was no conflict between protecting the Constitution and advancing their party's cause. But nor did the Federalists attempt to use their control of the federal judiciary to undo Jefferson's "revolution" of 1800. The Marshall court, for example, upheld the constitutionality of the repeal of the Judiciary Act of 1801. For his part, Jefferson never proposed to impeach Marshall.

Extending the Land: The Louisiana Purchase, 1803   Jefferson's goal of avoiding foreign entanglements would remain beyond reach as long as European powers had large landholdings in North America. Spain owned East Florida and the vast Louisiana Territory, including New Orleans, and it claimed West Florida (now the southern portions of Alabama and Mississippi). In 1800, a weakened Spain returned Louisiana to France which, under Napoleon Bonaparte, was fast emerging as Europe's strongest military power. Jefferson was appalled.

The president had long imagined the inevitable expansion of the free and virtuous American people would create an "empire of liberty." Spain was no obstacle, but Jefferson knew that Bonaparte's capacity for mischief was boundless. Bonaparte was sure of his destiny as a conqueror, and he dreamed of recreating a French New World empire bordering the Caribbean and the Gulf of Mexico. The island of Saint Domingue (modern Haiti and the Dominican Republic) would be the fulcrum of the empire, and Louisiana would be its breadbasket. Before this dream could become a reality, however, the French would have to subdue Saint Domingue, where by 1800 a bloody slave revolution had resulted in a takeover of the government by the former slave Toussaint L'Ouverture (see Chapter 7). Bonaparte dispatched an army to reassert French control and reestablish slavery, but yellow fever and fierce resistance by former slaves doomed the French force.

In the short run, Jefferson worried most about New Orleans, the only port for the $3 million in annual produce of farmers along the Ohio and Mississippi river system. The Spanish had temporarily granted Americans the right to park their produce there while awaiting transfer to seagoing vessels. But in 1802, the Spanish colonial administrator in New Orleans issued an order revoking this right. The order had originated in Spain, but most Americans assumed it had come from Bonaparte who, although he now owned Louisiana, had yet to take possession of it. An alarmed Jefferson described New Orleans as the "one single spot" on the globe whose possessor "is our natural and habitual enemy." "The day that France takes possession of N. Orleans," he added, "we must marry ourselves to the British fleet and nation."

The combination of France's failure to subdue Saint Domingue and the termination of American rights to deposit produce in New Orleans led to the American purchase of Louisiana. Jefferson dispatched James Monroe and Robert R. Livingston to Paris to buy New Orleans from France. Meanwhile, Bonaparte had concluded that his Caribbean empire was not worth the cost. In addition, he planned to resume war in Europe and needed cash. So he decided to sell *all* of Louisiana. The American commissioners and the French government settled on a price of $15 million. Thus, the United States gained an immense, uncharted territory between the Mississippi River and the Rocky Mountains (see Map 8.1). No one knew its exact size. Bonaparte's minister merely observed that the bargain was noble. But the **Louisiana Purchase** virtually doubled the area of the United States at a cost, omitting interest, of thirteen and one-half cents an acre.

Jefferson found himself caught between his ideals and reality. No provision of the Constitution explicitly authorized the government to acquire new territory. Jefferson believed in strict construction—the doctrine that the Constitution should be interpreted according to its letter—but he recognized that doubling the size of the Republic would guarantee land for American farmers, the backbone of the nation and the true guardians of liberty. Strict construction was not an end in itself but a means to promote republican liberty. If that end could be achieved in some way other than by strict construction, so be it. Jefferson was also alert to practical considerations. Most Federalists opposed the Louisiana Purchase because it would decrease the relative importance of their strongholds on the eastern seaboard. As the leader of the Republican Party, Jefferson saw no reason to hand the Federalists an issue by dallying over ratification of the treaty to reconcile constitutional issues.

The Election of 1804

Jefferson's acquisition of Louisiana left the Federalists dispirited and without a popular national issue. As the election of 1804 approached, the main threat to Jefferson was not the Federalist Party but his own vice president, Aaron Burr. In 1800, Burr had tried to take advantage of a tie in the Electoral College to gain the presidency, a betrayal in the eyes of most Republicans who assumed he had been nominated for the vice presidency. The adoption in 1804 of the Twelfth Amendment, which required separate and distinct ballots in the Electoral College for the presidential and the vice-presidential candidates, clarified the electoral process, but did not end Burr's conniving. He had spent much of his vice presidency in intrigues with the Federalists. The Republicans dumped him from their ticket in 1804 in favor of George Clinton. In the election, the Federalist nominees Charles C. Pinckney and Rufus King carried only two states, failing to hold even Massachusetts. Jefferson's overwhelming victory brought his first term to a fitting close. Between 1801 and 1804, the United States had doubled its territory and started to pay off its debt.

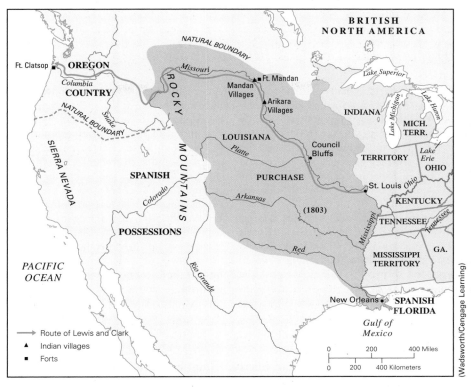

MAP 8.1 The Louisiana Purchase and the Exploration of the West

The explorations of Lewis and Clark demonstrated the vast extent of the area purchased from France.

Exploring the Land: The Lewis and Clark Expedition

Louisiana dazzled Jefferson' imagination. Americans knew virtually nothing about the immense territory, not even its western boundary. A case could be made for the Pacific Ocean, but Spain claimed part of the Pacific coast. Jefferson was content to claim that Louisiana extended at least to the mountains west of the Mississippi, which few citizens of the United States had ever seen. Thus, the Louisiana Purchase was both a bargain and a surprise package.

Even before the acquisition of Louisiana, Jefferson had planned an exploratory expedition; picked its leader, his personal secretary and fellow Virginian Lieutenant Meriwether Lewis; and sent him to Philadelphia for a crash course in sciences such as zoology, astronomy, and botany that were relevant to exploration. Jefferson instructed Lewis to trace the Missouri River to its source, cross the western highlands, and follow the best water route to the Pacific. Jefferson was genuinely interested in gathering scientific information. His instructions to Lewis cited the need to learn about Indian languages and customs, climate, plants, birds, reptiles, and insects. Above all, Jefferson hoped the **Lewis and Clark expedition** would find a

Going to the Source

Meriwether Lewis's Journal

President Jefferson had instructed Meriwether Lewis and William Clark to trace the Missouri River to its source. Friendly Indians told them that the river originated in great falls in the mountains. Lewis and Clark knew they were near the source, but on June 3, 1805 they came to a fork in the Missouri. Scouting parties briefly followed each fork, but without conclusive results. The right (north) fork, now the Marias River, looked exactly like the Missouri River that Lewis and Clark had followed for a thousand miles, but taking it would have led them to oblivion. Against the opinion of most members of their expedition, Lewis and Clark chose the left (south) fork and two days later came upon great falls, the source of the Missouri. Lewis described the choice in his journal.

This morning early we passed over and formed a camp on the point formed by the junction of the two large rivers....

An interesting question was now to be determined; which of these rivers was the Missouri.... To mistake the stream at this period of the season, two months of the traveling season having now elapsed, and to ascend such stream ... and then be obliged to return and take the other stream would not only loose us the whole of this season but would probably so dishearten the party that it might defeat the expedition altogether.... The no[r]th fork is deeper than the other but it's courant not so swift; it's waters run in the same boiling and roling manner which has uniformly characterized the Missouri throughout it's whole course so far; it's waters are of a whitish brown colour[,] very thick and t[u]rbid, also characteristic of the Missouri; while the South fork is perfectly transparent [and] runs very rappid but with a smooth unriffled surface[,] it's bottom composed of round and flat smooth stones like most rivers issuing

water route across the continent. The potential economic benefits from such a route included diverting the lucrative fur trade from Canadian to American hands and boosting trade with China.

Setting forth from St. Louis in May 1804, Lewis, his second-in-command William Clark, and about fifty others followed the Missouri River and then the Snake and Columbia rivers (see Going to the Source). In the Dakota country, Lewis and Clark hired a French-Canadian fur trader, Toussaint Charbonneau, as a guide and interpreter. Slow-witted and inclined to panic in crises, Charbonneau proved to be a mixed blessing, but his wife, **Sacajawea,** who accompanied him on the trip, made up for his failings. A Shoshone and probably no more than sixteen years old in 1804, Sacajawea had been stolen by a rival tribe and then claimed by Charbonneau. When first encountered by Lewis and Clark, she had just given birth to a son; indeed, the infant's presence helped reassure Native American tribes of the expedition's peaceful intent.

Even with their peaceful intent established, Lewis and Clark faced obstacles. The expedition brought them in contact with numerous tribes, most importantly the powerful Sioux but also Mandans, Hidatsas, and Arikaras, each with a history of warring on other tribes and of carrying on its own internal feuds. Reliant on from a mountainous country. The bed of the N[orth] fork [is] composed of some gravel but principally mud; in short the air & character of this river is so precisely that of the Missouri below that the party with very few exceptions have already pronounced the N[orth] fork to be the Missouri; myself and Capt. C[lark] not quite so precipitate have not yet decided but if we were to give our opinions I believe we should be in the minority, certain it is that the North fork gives the colouring matter and character which is retained from hence to the gulph of Mexico.... Convinced I am that if [the North fork] penetrated the Rocky Mountains to any great extent it's waters would be clearer unless it should run an immence distance indeed after leaving those mountains through those level plains in order to acquire its turbid hue. What astonishes us a little is that the Indians who appeared to be so well acquainted with the geography of this country should not have mentioned this river on [the] [r]ight hand if it not be the Missouri; *the river that scolds all others* as they call it if there is in reality such an one, ought agreeably to their account to have fallen in a considerable distance below, and on the other hand if this right hand or N[orth] fork be the Missouri I am equally astonished at their not mentioning the S[outh] fork which they must have passed to get to those large falls which they mention on the Missouri. Thus have our cogitating faculties been busily employed all day.

Source: Reuben Gold Thwaites, ed., Original Journals of the Lewis and Clark Expedition, 1804–1806, volume 2 [1904] (New York, Arno Press, 1969), 112–115.

Questions

1. *Which fork would you have taken?*
2. *Why did President Jefferson think it was important to American strategic interests that Lewis and Clark find the source of the Missouri river?*

Go to www.cengagebrain.com for additional primary sources on this period.

Indians for guides, packers, and interpreters, Lewis and Clark had to become instant diplomats. Jefferson had told them to assert American sovereignty over the Purchase. This objective led them to distribute medals and uniforms to chiefs ready to support American authority and to stage periodic military parades and displays of their weapons, which included cannons. But no tribe had a single chief; rather, different tribal villages had different chiefs. At times, Lewis and Clark miscalculated, for example, when they treated an Arikara chief as the "grand chief" to the outrage of his rivals. Yet their diplomacy generally was successful, less because they were sophisticated ethnographers than because they avoided violence.

The group finally reached the Pacific Ocean in November 1805 and then returned to St. Louis, but not before collecting a mass of scientific information, including the disturbing fact that more than three hundred miles of mountains separated the Missouri from the Columbia. The expedition also produced a sprinkling of tall tales, many of which Jefferson believed, about gigantic Indians, soil too rich to grow trees, and a mountain composed of salt. Jefferson's political opponents railed that he would soon be reporting the discovery of a molasses-filled lake. For all the ridicule, the expedition's drawings of the geography of the region led to more accurate maps and heightened interest in the West.

THE GATHERING STORM

In gaining control of Louisiana, the United States had benefited from the preoccupation of European powers with their own struggles. But between 1803 and 1814, the renewal of the Napoleonic Wars in Europe turned the United States into a pawn in a chess game played by others and helped make Jefferson's second term far less successful than his first.

Europe was not Jefferson's only problem. He had to deal with a conspiracy to dismantle the United States, the product of the inventive and perverse mind of Aaron Burr, and to face down challenges within his own party, led by John Randolph.

Challenges on the Home Front   Aaron Burr suffered a string of reverses in 1804. After being denied renomination as vice president, he entered into a series of intrigues with a faction of despairing and extreme (or "High") Federalists in New England. Led by Senator Timothy Pickering of Massachusetts, these High Federalists plotted to sever the Union by forming a pro-British Northern Confederacy composed of Nova Scotia (part of British-owned Canada), New England, New York, and even Pennsylvania. Although most Federalists disdained the plot, Pickering and others settled on Burr as their leader and helped him gain the Federalist nomination for the governorship of New York. Alexander Hamilton, who had thwarted Burr's grab for the presidency in 1800 by throwing his weight behind Jefferson, now foiled Burr a second time by allowing publication of his "despicable opinion" of Burr. Defeated in the election for New York's governor, Burr challenged Hamilton to a duel and mortally wounded him at Weehawken, New Jersey, on July 11, 1804.

Indicted in two states for murdering Hamilton, Burr—still vice president—now hatched a scheme so bold that not even his political opponents could believe him capable of such treachery. He allied himself with the unsavory military governor of the Louisiana Territory, General James Wilkinson, who had been on Spain's payroll intermittently as a secret agent since the 1780s. Their plot had several dimensions: they would create an independent confederacy of western states, conquer Mexico, and invade West Florida. The scheming duo presented the plot imaginatively. To westerners, they said it had the covert support of the Jefferson administration; to the British, that it was a way to attack Spanish lands; and to the Spanish, that it would open the way to dividing up the United States.

By the fall of 1806, Burr and about sixty followers were making their way down the Ohio and Mississippi rivers to join Wilkinson at Natchez. In October 1806, Jefferson, who described Burr as a crooked gun that never shot straight, denounced the conspiracy. Wilkinson abandoned the plot and proclaimed himself the most loyal of Jefferson's followers. Burr tried to escape to West Florida but was intercepted. Brought back to Richmond, he was put on trial for treason. Chief Justice Marshall presided at the trial and instructed the jury that the prosecution had to prove actual treasonable acts—an impossible task because the conspiracy had never reached fruition. Jefferson was furious, but Marshall was merely following the clear wording of the Constitution, which deliberately made treason difficult to prove. The jury returned a verdict of not proved, which Marshall entered as "not guilty." Still under indictment for his murder of Hamilton, Burr fled to Europe where he tried to interest Napoleon in making peace with Britain as a prelude to a proposed Anglo-French invasion of the United States and Mexico.

Besides the Burr conspiracy, Jefferson faced a challenge from a group of Republicans led by the president's fellow Virginian, John Randolph, a man of abounding eccentricities and acerbic wit. Like many propertied Americans of the 1770s, Randolph believed that governments always menaced popular liberty. Jefferson had originally shared this view, but he recognized it as an ideology of opposition, not power; once in office, he compromised. In contrast, Randolph remained frozen in the 1770s, denouncing every government action as decline and proclaiming that he would throw all politicians to the dogs except that he had too much respect for dogs.

Randolph turned on Jefferson, most notably, for backing a compromise in the Yazoo land scandal. In 1795, the Georgia legislature had sold the huge Yazoo tract (35 million acres—most of present-day Alabama and Mississippi) for a fraction of its value to land companies that had bribed virtually the entire legislature. The next legislature canceled the sale, but many investors, knowing nothing of the bribery, had already bought land in good faith. In 1803, a federal commission compromised with an award of 5 million acres to Yazoo investors. For Randolph, the compromise was itself a scandal— further evidence of the decay of republican virtue.

The Suppression of American Trade and Impressment   Burr's acquittal and Randolph's taunts shattered the aura of invincibility surrounding Jefferson. Now foreign affairs posed an even sharper challenge. As Britain and France resumed their war in Europe, U.S. merchants prospered by carrying sugar and coffee from the French and Spanish Caribbean colonies to Europe. This trade not only provided Napoleon with supplies but also drove down the price of sugar and coffee from British colonies by adding to the glut of these commodities on the world market. The British concluded that their economic problems stemmed from American prosperity.

For Americans, this boom depended on the re-export trade, which evaded British regulations. According to the British Rule of 1756, any trade closed during peacetime could not be opened during war; if it was, the British would stop it. For example, France usually restricted the sugar trade with Europe to French ships during peacetime and thus could not open it to American ships during war. The U.S. response to the Rule of 1756 was the "broken voyage," by which U.S. ships carried French sugar or coffee to American ports, unloaded it, passed it through customs, and then re-exported it as *American* produce. Britain tolerated this dodge for nearly a decade but in 1805 initiated a policy of total war toward France, including the strangulation of French trade. In 1805, a British court declared broken voyages illegal.

Next came a series of British trade decrees ("Orders in Council,"), which established a blockade of French-controlled ports on the coast of Europe. Napoleon responded with his so-called Continental System, a series of counterproclamations that ships obeying British regulations would be subject to seizure by France.

(William L. Clements Library)

Boarding and Taking of the American Ship *Chesapeake The loss of the frigate Chesapeake to HMS Leopard in 1807 and the dying words of its commander, James Lawrence, inspired the motto "Don't Give Up the Ship," which was emblazoned on the battle flag of Captain Oliver Hazard Perry.*

In effect, this Anglo-French war of decrees outlawed virtually all U.S. trade; if an American ship complied with British regulations, it became a French target, and vice versa.

Both Britain and France seized American ships, but British seizures were far more humiliating to Americans. France was a weaker naval power than Britain; much of the French fleet had been destroyed by the British at the Battle of Trafalgar in October 1805. Accordingly, most of France's seizures of American ships occurred in European ports where American ships had been lured by Napoleon's often inconsistent enforcement of his Continental System. In contrast, British warships hovered just beyond the American coast. The Royal Navy stopped and searched virtually every American vessel off New York, for example. At times, U.S. ships had to line up a few miles from the American coast to be searched by the Royal Navy.

To these provocations the British added **impressment.** For centuries, Royal Navy press gangs had scoured the docks and taverns of British ports and forced ("pressed") civilians into service. As war with France intensified Britain's need for sailors, Britain increasingly extended the practice to seizing alleged Royal Navy deserters on American merchant ships. British sailors had good reason to be discontented with their navy. Discipline on the Royal Navy's "floating hells" was often brutal and the pay low; sailors on American ships made up to five times more than those on British ships. Consequently, the Royal Navy suffered a high rate of desertion to American ships. In 1807, for example, 149 of the 419 sailors on the American warship *Constitution* were British subjects. Although less damaging to the American economy than the seizure of ships, impressment was equally galling. Even American-born seamen, six thousand between 1803 and 1812, were impressed into the Royal Navy. British arrogance peaked in June 1807. A British warship, HMS *Leopard,* patrolling off Virginia, attacked an unsuspecting American frigate, USS *Chesapeake,* and forced it to surrender. The British then boarded the vessel and seized four supposed deserters. One, a genuine deserter, was later hanged; the other three, former Britons, had "deserted" only from impressments and were now American citizens. The so-called *Chesapeake-Leopard* Affair enraged the country. Jefferson remarked that he had not seen so belligerent a spirit in America since 1775.

The Embargo
Act of 1807

Yet while making some preparations for war, Jefferson adopted "peaceable coercion" by suspending trade with Britain and France to gain respect for neutral rights. By far the most controversial legislation of either of Jefferson's terms, the **Embargo Act of 1807** prohibited vessels from leaving American ports for foreign ports. Technically, it prohibited only exports, but its practical effect was to stop imports as well, for few foreign ships would venture into American ports if they had to leave without cargo. Amazed by the boldness of the act, a British newspaper described the embargo as "little short of an absolute secession from the rest of the civilized world."

The embargo did not have the intended effect. Although British sales to the United States dropped 50 percent between 1807 and 1808, the British quickly found new markets in South America, where rebellions against Spanish rule had flared up. Furthermore, the Embargo Act contained some loopholes. For example, it allowed American ships blown off course to put in at European ports if necessary; suddenly, many captains were reporting that adverse winds had forced them across the Atlantic. Treating the embargo as a joke, Napoleon seized any American ships he could lay hands on and then informed the United States that he was only helping to enforce the embargo. The British were less amused, but the embargo confirmed their view that Jefferson was an ineffectual philosopher, an impotent challenger compared with Napoleon.

The United States itself felt the harshest effects of the embargo. Some thirty thousand American seamen found themselves out of work. Hundreds of merchants went into bankruptcy, and jails swelled with debtors. A New York City newspaper noted that the only activity still flourishing in the city was prosecution for debt. Farmers were devastated. Unable to export their produce or sell it at a decent price to hard-pressed urban dwellers, many farmers could not pay their debts. In desperation, one farmer in Schoharie County, New York, sold his cattle, horses, and farm implements, worth eight hundred dollars before the embargo, for fifty-five dollars. Speculators who had purchased land, expecting to sell it later at a higher price, also took a beating because cash-starved farmers stopped buying land. "I live and that is all," wrote one New York speculator. "I am doing no business, cannot sell anybody property, nor collect any money."

The embargo fell hardest on New England, especially Massachusetts, which in 1807 had twice the ship tonnage per capita of any other state and more than a third of the entire nation's ship tonnage in foreign trade. For a state so dependent on foreign trade, the embargo was a calamity. Wits reversed the letters of embargo to form the phrase "O grab me."

The situation was not entirely bleak. The embargo forced a diversion of merchants' capital into manufacturing. Before 1808, the United States had only fifteen mills for fashioning cotton into textiles; by the end of 1809, an additional eighty-seven mills had been constructed (as discussed in Chapter 9). But none of this comforted merchants already ruined or mariners driven to soup kitchens. Nor could New Englanders forget that the source of their misery was a policy initiated by one of the "Virginia lordlings," "Mad Tom" Jefferson, who knew little about New England and who had a dogmatic loathing of cities, the very foundations of New England's prosperity. A Massachusetts poet wrote,

Our ships all in motion once whitened the ocean,
They sailed and returned with a cargo
Now doomed to decay they have fallen a prey
To Jefferson, worms, and embargo

James Madison and the Failure of Peaceable Coercion

Even before the Embargo Act, Jefferson had announced that he would not be a candidate for reelection. With his blessing, the Republican congressional caucus nominated **James Madison** and George Clinton for the presidency and vice presidency. The Federalists countered with Charles C. Pinckney and Rufus King, the same ticket that had made a negligible showing in 1804. In 1808, the Federalists staged a modest comeback, gaining twenty-four congressional seats. Still, Madison won 122 of 175 electoral votes for president, and the Republicans retained control of Congress.

The Federalist revival, modest as it was, rested on two factors. First, Federalist opposition to the Embargo Act gave the party a national issue it had long lacked. Second, younger Federalists had abandoned their elders' gentlemanly disdain for campaigning and deliberately imitated vote-winning techniques such as barbecues and mass meetings that had worked for the Republicans.

To some contemporaries, "Little Jemmy" Madison, five feet, four inches tall, seemed a weak and shadowy figure compared to Jefferson. In fact, Madison's intelligence and capacity for systematic thought matched Jefferson's. He had the added advantage of being married to Dolley Madison. A striking figure in her turbans and colorful dresses, Dolley arranged receptions at the White House in which she charmed Republicans, and even some Federalists, into sympathy with her husband's policies.

Madison continued the embargo with minor changes. Like Jefferson, he reasoned that Britain was "more vulnerable in her commerce than in her armies." The American embargo, however, was coercing no one, and on March 1, 1809, Congress replaced the Embargo Act with the weaker, face-saving Non-Intercourse Act. This act opened trade to all nations except Britain and France and then authorized the president to restore trade with either of those nations if it stopped violating neutral rights. But neither complied. In May 1810, Congress substituted a new measure, Macon's Bill No. 2. This legislation opened trade with Britain and France, and then offered each a clumsy bribe: if either nation repealed its restrictions on neutral shipping, the United States would halt trade with the other.

None of these steps had the desired effect. While Jefferson and Madison lashed out at France and Britain as moral demons ("The one is a den of robbers and the other of pirates," snapped Jefferson), the belligerents saw the world as composed of a few great powers and many weak ones. When great powers went to war, there were no neutrals. Weak nations like the United States should stop babbling about moral ideals and seek the protection of a great power. Neither Napoleon nor the British intended to accommodate the Americans.

As peaceable coercion became a fiasco, Madison came under fire from militant Republicans, known as **war hawks,** who demanded more aggressive policies. Coming mainly from the South and West, regions where "honor" was a sacred word, the militants were infuriated by insults to the American flag. In addition, economic recession between 1808 and 1810 had convinced the firebrands that British policies were wrecking their regions' economies. The election of 1810 brought several war hawks to Congress. Led by thirty-four-year-old Henry Clay of Kentucky, who preferred war to the "putrescent pool of ignominious peace," the war hawks included John C. Calhoun of South Carolina, Richard M. Johnson of Kentucky, and William King of North Carolina, all future vice presidents. Clay was elected Speaker of the House.

Tecumseh and the Prophet

More emotional and pugnaciously nationalistic than Jefferson and Madison, the war hawks called for the expulsion of the British from Canada and the Spanish from the Floridas. Their demands merged with western settlers' fears that the British in Canada were actively recruiting the Indians to halt the march of American settlement. In reality, American policy, not meddling by the British, was the source of bloodshed on the frontier.

In contrast to his views about blacks, Jefferson believed that Indians and whites could live peacefully together if the Indians abandoned their hunting and nomadic ways and took up farming. If they farmed, they would need less land. Jefferson and Madison insisted that the Indians be compensated fairly for ceded land and that only those Indians with a claim to the land they were ceding be allowed to conclude treaties with whites. Reality conflicted with Jefferson's ideals (see Chapter 7). The march of white settlement was steadily shrinking Indian hunting grounds, while some Indians themselves were becoming more willing to sign away land in payment to whites for blankets, guns, and the liquor that transported them into a daze even as their culture collapsed.

In 1809, no American was more eager to acquire Indian lands than William Henry Harrison, the governor of the Indiana Territory. The federal government had just divided Indiana, splitting off the present states of Illinois and Wisconsin into a separate Illinois Territory. Harrison recognized that, shorn of Illinois, Indiana would not achieve statehood unless it could attract more settlers by offering them land currently owned by Indians. Disregarding instructions from Washington to negotiate only with Indians who claimed the land they were ceding, Harrison rounded up a delegation of half-starved Indians, none of whom lived on the rich lands along the Wabash River that he craved. By the Treaty of Fort Wayne in

(Cincinnati Museum Center)

Tecumseh and William Henry Harrison at Vincennes, August 1810 *This portrait of a personal duel between Tecumseh and Indiana governor William Henry Harrison is fanciful. But the confrontation between the two at Vincennes nearly erupted into violence. Tecumseh told Harrison that Indians could never trust whites because "when Jesus Christ came upon the earth you kill'd him and nail'd him on a cross."*

September 1809, these Indians ceded millions of acres along the Wabash at a price of two cents an acre.

This treaty outraged the numerous tribes that had not been party to it. Among the angriest were **Tecumseh,** the Shawnee chief, and his brother, Lalawéthica. Late in 1805, Lalawéthica had had a frightening dream in which he saw drunken Indians tormented for eternity. Overnight, Lalawéthica was transformed from a drunken misfit into a preacher. He gave up liquor and began pleading with Indians to return to their old ways and to avoid contact with whites. He quickly became known as the Prophet. Soon, he would take a new name, **Tenskwatawa,** styling himself the "Open Door" through which all Indians could revitalize their culture. Shawnees listened to his message.

In the meantime, Tecumseh sought to build a coalition of several tribes to stem the tide of white settlement. He insisted that Indian lands belonged collectively to all the tribes and hence could not be sold by splinter groups. Failing to reach a settlement with Tecumseh or the Prophet, Harrison concluded that it was time to attack the Indians. His target was a Shawnee encampment called Prophetstown near the mouth of the Tippecanoe River. With Tecumseh away recruiting southern

Indians to his cause, Tenskwatawa ordered an attack on Harrison's encampment, a mile from Prophetstown, in the predawn hours of November 7, 1811. Outnumbered two to one and short of ammunition, Tenskwatawa's force was beaten off after inflicting heavy casualties.

Although it was a small engagement, the Battle of Tippecanoe had several large effects. It made Harrison a national hero, and the memory of the battle would contribute to his election as president three decades later. It discredited Tenskwatawa, whose conduct during the battle drew criticism from his followers. It elevated Tecumseh into a position of recognized leadership among the western tribes. Finally, it persuaded Tecumseh, who long had distrusted the British as much as the Americans, that alliance with the British was the only way to stop the spread of American settlement.

Congress Votes for War   By spring 1812, President Madison had decided that war with Britain was inevitable. On June 1, he sent his war message to Congress. Meanwhile, an economic depression struck Britain, partly because the American policy of restricting trade with that country had finally started to work. Under pressure from its merchants, Britain suspended the Orders in Council on June 23. But Congress had already passed the declaration of war. Further, Britain's suspension failed to meet Madison's demand that Britain unilaterally pledge to respect the rights of neutrals.

Neither war hawks nor westerners held the key to the vote in favor of war. The West was still too sparsely settled to have many representatives in Congress. Rather, the votes of Republicans in populous states like Pennsylvania, Maryland, and Virginia were the main force propelling the war declaration through Congress. Opposition to war came mostly from the Northeast, with its Federalist strongholds in Massachusetts, Connecticut, and New York. Congressional opposition to war thus revealed a sectional as well as a party split. In general, however, southern Federalists opposed the war declaration, and northern Republicans supported it. In other words, the vote for war followed party lines more closely than sectional lines. Much like James Madison himself, the typical Republican advocate of war had not wanted war in 1810, or even in 1811, but had been led by the accumulation of grievances to demand it in 1812.

In his war message, Madison had listed impressment, the continued presence of British ships in American waters, and British violations of neutral rights as grievances that justified war. None of these complaints fully explains why Americans went to war in 1812 rather than earlier—for example, in 1807 after the *Chesapeake-Leopard* Affair. Madison also listed British incitement of the Indians as a stimulus for war. This grievance contributed to war feeling in the West, but the West had too few American inhabitants to drive the nation into war. A more important underlying cause was the economic recession that affected the South and West after 1808, as well as the conviction, held by John C. Calhoun and others, that British policy was damaging America's economy.

Finally, it was vitally important that Madison rather than Jefferson was president in 1812. Jefferson had believed Britain was motivated primarily by its desire to defeat Napoleon, and that once the war in Europe ended, the provocations would stop. Madison held that Britain's real motive was to strangle American trade once and for all and thereby eliminate the United States as a trading rival. In his war message, he stated flatly that Britain was meddling with American trade not because that trade interfered with Britain's "belligerent rights" but because it "frustrated the monopoly which she covets for her own commerce and navigation."

THE WAR OF 1812

Although American cruisers, notably the Constitution, would win a few sensational duels with British warships, the U.S. Navy could not prevent the British from clamping a naval blockade on the American coast. Canada, which Madison viewed as a key prop of the British Empire, became the principal target. With their vastly larger population and resources, few Americans expected a long or difficult struggle. To Jefferson, the conquest of Canada seemed "a mere matter of marching."

Little justified this optimism. Although many Canadians were immigrants from the United States, to the Americans' surprise they fought to repel the invaders. Many of the best British troops were in Europe fighting Napoleon, but the British enlisted Native Americans—and used fear of these "uncontrollable savages" to force American surrenders. The American state militias were filled with Sunday soldiers who "hollered for water half the time, and whiskey the other." Few militiamen understood the goals of the war. In fact, outside Congress there was not much blood lust in 1812. Opposition to the war ran strong in New England; and even in Kentucky, the home of war hawk Henry Clay, only four hundred answered the first call to arms. For many Americans, local attachments were still stronger than national ones.

On to Canada   From the summer of 1812 to the spring of 1814, the Americans launched a series of unsuccessful attacks on Canada. In July 1812, General William Hull led an American army from Detroit into Canada, quickly returned when Tecumseh cut his supply line, and surrendered Detroit and two thousand men to thirteen hundred British and Indian troops. In the fall of 1812, the British and their Mohawk allies crushed a force of American regulars at the Battle of Queenston, near Niagara Falls, while New York militiamen, contending that they had volunteered only to protect their homes and not to invade Canada, looked on from the New York side of the border. A third American offensive in 1812, a projected attack on Montreal via Lake Champlain, fell apart when the militia again refused to advance into Canada.

Renewed American offensives and subsequent reverses in 1813 convinced the Americans that they could not retake Detroit while the British controlled Lake Erie. During the winter of 1812–1813, Captain Oliver H. Perry constructed a little fleet of vessels; on September 10, 1813, he destroyed a British squadron at Put-in-Bay on the western end of the lake. "We have met the enemy, and they are ours," Perry triumphantly reported. The British then pulled out of Detroit, but American forces under General William Henry Harrison overtook and defeated a combined British and Indian force at the Battle of the Thames on October 5, where

Tecumseh died. These victories by Perry and Harrison cheered Americans, but efforts to invade Canada continued to falter. In June 1814, American troops crossed into Canada on the Niagara front but withdrew after fighting two bloody but inconclusive battles at Chippewa (July 5) and Lundy's Lane (July 25).

The British Offensive

With fresh reinforcements from Europe, where Napoleon had abdicated as emperor after his disastrous invasion of Russia, the British took the offensive in the summer of 1814. General Sir George Prevost led a force of ten thousand British veterans in an offensive meant to split the New England states, where opposition to the war was strong, from the rest of the country. The British advanced down Lake Champlain until meeting the well-entrenched American forces at Plattsburgh. After his fleet met defeat on September 11, Prevost abandoned the campaign.

Ironically, the British achieved a far more spectacular success in an operation originally designed as a diversion from their main thrust down Lake Champlain. In 1814, a British army landed near Washington and met a larger American force, composed mainly of militia, at Bladensburg, Maryland, on August 24. The Battle of Bladensburg quickly became the "Bladensburg races" as the American militia fled, almost without firing a shot. The British then descended on Washington. Madison,

First Lady Dolley Madison by Rembrandt Peale, Circa 1809 *As the attractive young wife of Secretary of State James Madison, Dolley Madison acted virtually as the nation's First Lady during the administration of Jefferson, a widower. Friendly, tactful, and blessed with an unfailing memory for names and events, she added to her reputation as an elegant hostess after her husband became president.*

(© Bettmann/Corbis)

who had witnessed the Bladensburg fiasco, escaped into the Virginia hills. His wife, Dolley, pausing only long enough to load her silver, a bed, and a portrait of George Washington onto her carriage, hastened to join her husband, while British troops ate the supper prepared for the Madisons at the presidential mansion. Then they burned the mansion and other public buildings in Washington. A few weeks later, the British attacked Baltimore, but after failing to crack its defenses, they broke off the operation.

The Treaty of Ghent, 1814

In August 1814, negotiations to end the war commenced between British and American commissioners at Ghent, Belgium. News of the American naval victory at Plattsburgh and Prevost's retreat to Canada brought home to the British that after two years of fighting, they controlled neither the Great Lakes nor Lake Champlain. The final **Treaty of Ghent,** signed on Christmas Eve 1814, restored the *status quo ante bellum* (the state of things before the war); neither side gained or lost territory. Several additional issues, including fixing a boundary between the United States and Canada, were referred to joint commissions for future settlement. Nothing was done about impressment, but the end of the war in Europe made neutral rights a dead issue.

Ironically, America's most dramatic victory came on January 8, 1815, two weeks after the treaty had been signed but before word of it had reached America. A British army had descended on New Orleans and attacked the city's defenders. The U.S. troops, commanded by General **Andrew** ("Old Hickory") **Jackson,** legendary as a fierce Indian fighter, shredded the line of advancing redcoats, inflicting more than two thousand casualties while losing only thirteen of their own.

The Hartford Convention

Although it meant nothing in terms of the war, the Battle of New Orleans had a devastating effect on the Federalist party. The Federalist comeback in the election of 1808 had continued into the election of 1812, when their candidate DeWitt Clinton, an antiwar Republican, had lost the electoral vote but carried all of New England except Vermont, as well as New York and New Jersey. American military setbacks in the war intensified Federalist disdain for the Madison administration. He seemed to epitomize over a decade of Republican misrule at Federalist expense. Jefferson's attack on the judiciary had seemed to threaten the rule of law. The Louisiana Purchase, constitutionally dubious, had reduced the relative importance of Federalist New England. Now "Mr. Madison's War" brought fresh misery in the form of the British blockade. A few Federalists began to talk of New England's secession from the Union.

In late 1814, a Federalist convention met in Hartford, Connecticut. Although some advocates of secession were present, moderates took control and passed a series of resolutions summarizing New England's grievances. At the root of these grievances lay the belief that New Englanders were becoming a permanent minority in a nation dominated by southern Republicans who failed to understand New England's commercial interests. The convention proposed to amend the Constitution to abolish the three-fifths clause (which gave the South a disproportionate share of votes in

Congress by allowing it to count slaves as a basis of representation), to require a two-thirds vote of Congress to declare war and admit new states into the Union, to limit the president to a single term, to prohibit the election of two successive presidents from the same state, and to bar embargoes lasting more than sixty days.

News of the Treaty of Ghent and Jackson's victory at New Orleans dashed the Federalists' hopes of gaining broad popular support. The goal of the Hartford Convention had been to assert states' rights rather than disunion, but to many the proceedings smelled of a traitorous plot. The restoration of peace, moreover, stripped the Federalists of the primary grievance that had fueled the convention. In the election of 1816, Republican James Monroe, Madison's hand-picked successor and a fellow Virginian, swept the nation over negligible Federalist opposition. He would win reelection in 1820 with only a single dissenting electoral vote. As a force in national politics, the Federalists were finished.

THE AWAKENING OF AMERICAN NATIONALISM

The United States emerged from the War of 1812 bruised but intact. In its first major war since the Revolution, the Republic had demonstrated not only that it could fight on even terms against a major power but also that republics could fight wars without turning to despotism. The war produced more than its share of symbols of American nationalism. Whitewash cleared the smoke damage to the presidential mansion; thereafter, it became known as the White House. The British attack on Fort McHenry, guarding Baltimore, prompted a young observer, Francis Scott Key, to compose "The Star-Spangled Banner."

The Battle of New Orleans boosted Andrew Jackson onto the stage of national politics and became a source of legends about American military prowess. It appears to most contemporary scholars that the British lost because as they advanced within range of Jackson's riflemen and cannon, they unaccountably paused and became sitting ducks. But in the wake of the battle, Americans spun a different tale. The legend arose that Jackson owed his victory not to Pakenham's blundering tactics but to hawk-eyed Kentucky frontiersmen whose rifles picked off the British with unerring accuracy. In fact, many frontiersmen in Jackson's army had not carried rifles; even if they had, gunpowder smoke would have obscured the enemy. But none of this mattered at the time. Just as Americans preferred militia to professional soldiers, they chose to believe that their greatest victory of the war had been the handiwork of amateurs.

Madison's Nationalism and the Era of Good Feelings, 1817–1824
The War of 1812 had three major political consequences. First, it eliminated the Federalists as a national political force. Second, it went a long way toward convincing the Republicans that the nation and its liberties were strong and resilient. Third, with the Federalists no longer a force, and with fears about the fragility of republics fading, Republicans increasingly embraced doctrines long associated with the Federalists.

In a message to Congress in December 1815, Madison called for federal support for internal improvements such as roads and canals, tariff protection for the new industries that had sprung up during the embargo, and the creation of a new national bank. (The charter of the first Bank of the United States had expired in 1811.) In Congress, another Republican, Henry Clay of Kentucky, proposed similar measures, which he called the American System, with the aim of making the young nation economically self-sufficient and free from dependence on Europe. In 1816, Congress chartered the Second Bank of the United States and enacted a moderate tariff. Federal support for internal improvements proved to be a thornier problem. Madison favored federal aid in principle but believed that a constitutional amendment was necessary to authorize it. Accordingly, just before leaving office in 1817, he vetoed an internal-improvements bill.

As Republicans adopted positions they had once disdained, an **"Era of Good Feelings"** dawned on American politics. A Boston newspaper, impressed by the warm reception accorded President James Monroe while touring New England, coined the phrase in 1817. It has stuck as a description of Monroe's two administrations from 1817 to 1825.

But the good feelings were paper-thin. Madison's 1817 veto of the internal-improvements bill revealed the persistence of disagreements about the role of the federal government under the Constitution. Furthermore, the continuation of slavery was arousing sectional animosities that a journalist's phrase about good feelings could not dispel. Not surprisingly, the postwar consensus began to unravel almost as soon as Americans recognized its existence.

John Marshall and the Supreme Court   In 1819, Jefferson's old antagonist John Marshall, who was still chief justice, issued two opinions that stunned Republicans. In the first case, *Dartmouth College v. Woodward* Marshall concluded that the college's original charter, granted to its trustees by George III in 1769, was a contract. Since the Constitution specifically forbade states to interfere with contracts, an effort by New Hampshire to turn Dartmouth into a state university was unconstitutional. The implications of Marshall's ruling were far-reaching for businesses as well as colleges. In effect, Marshall said that once a state had chartered a college or a business, it surrendered both its power to alter the charter and, in large measure, its authority to regulate the beneficiary.

A few weeks later, the chief justice handed down an even more momentous decision in *McCulloch v. Maryland.* The issue here was whether the state of Maryland had the power to tax a national corporation, specifically the Baltimore branch of the Second Bank of the United States, a national corporation chartered by Congress. Speaking for a unanimous Court, Marshall concentrated on two issues. First, did Congress have the power to charter a national bank? Nothing in the Constitution, Marshall conceded, explicitly granted this power. But the broad sweep of enumerated powers, he reasoned, implied the power to charter a bank. Marshall was clearly engaging in a broad, or "loose," rather than strict, construction (interpretation) of the Constitution. The second issue was whether a state could tax an agency of the federal government that lay within its borders. Marshall argued that any power of the national government, enumerated or implied, was supreme within its sphere. States could not interfere with the exercise of federal powers. Maryland's tax was such an interference, since "the power to tax involves the power to destroy," and was plainly unconstitutional.

James Monroe by Samuel F.B. Morse *The last member of the generation active in the Revolution to occupy the presidency, Monroe was loyal to Jefferson's principles but sought to rise above partisanship. His two terms (1817–1825) became known as the Era of Good Feeling.*

Marshall's decision in the *McCulloch* case dismayed many Republicans. Although Madison and Monroe had supported the establishment of the Second Bank of the United States, the bank had made itself unpopular by tightening its loan policies during the summer of 1818. This contraction of credit triggered the Panic of 1819, a severe depression that gave rise to considerable distress throughout the country, especially among western farmers. At a time when the bank was widely blamed for the panic, Marshall's ruling stirred controversy by placing the bank beyond the regulatory power of any state government. His decision, indeed, was as much an attack on state sovereignty as it was a defense of the bank. The Constitution, Marshall argued, was the creation not of state governments but of the people of all the states, and thus was more fundamental than state laws. His reasoning assailed the Republican theory, best expressed in the Virginia and Kentucky

Resolutions of 1798–1799 (see Chapter 7), that the Union was essentially a compact among states, which were more immediately responsive to the people's will than the federal government. Republicans regarded the compact theory of the Union as a guarantor of popular liberty. As they saw it, Marshall's *McCulloch* decision, along with his decision in the *Dartmouth College* case, stripped state governments of the power to impose the will of their people on corporations.

The Missouri Compromise, 1820–1821   The fragility of the Era of Good Feelings became even more apparent in the two-year-long controversy over statehood for Missouri. Carved from the Louisiana Purchase, Missouri attracted slaveholders. In 1819, when the House of Representatives was considering a bill to admit Missouri as a state, 16 percent of the territory's inhabitants were slaves. Then a New York Republican offered an amendment that prohibited the further introduction of slaves and provided for the emancipation, at age twenty-five, of all slave offspring born after Missouri's admission as a state. Following rancorous debate, the House accepted the amendment, and the Senate rejected it. Both chambers voted along sectional lines.

Prior to 1819, slavery had not been the primary source of the nation's sectional divisions. For example, Federalists' opposition to the embargo and the War of 1812 had sprung from their fear that the dominant Republicans were sacrificing New England's commercial interests to those of the South and West—not from hostility to slavery. The Missouri question, which Jefferson compared to "a fire bell in the night, [which] awakened me and filled me with terror," now thrust slavery into the center of long-standing sectional divisions.

In 1819, the Union had eleven free and eleven slave states. The admission of Missouri as a slave state would upset this balance to the advantage of the South. Equally important, Missouri was on the same latitude as the free states of Ohio, Indiana, and Illinois, and northerners worried that admitting Missouri as a slave state would set a precedent for the extension of slavery into the northern part of the Purchase. Finally, the disintegration of the Federalists as a national force reduced the need for unity among Republicans, and they increasingly heeded sectional pressures more than calls for party loyalty.

Virtually every issue that was to wrack the Union during the next forty years was present in the controversy over Missouri: southern charges that the North was conspiring to destroy the Union and end slavery; accusations by northerners that southerners were conspiring to extend the institution. Southerners openly proclaimed that antislavery northerners were kindling fires that only "seas of blood" could extinguish. Such threats of civil war persuaded some northern congressmen who had originally supported the restriction of slavery in Missouri to back down. A series of congressional agreements known collectively as the **Missouri Compromise** resolved the crisis.

To balance the number of free and slave states, Congress in 1820 admitted Maine as a free state and Missouri as a slave state; to forestall a further crisis, it also prohibited slavery in the remainder of the Louisiana Purchase north of 36°30'—the southern boundary of Missouri (see Map 8.2). But compromise did not come easily. The individual components of the eventual compromise passed by close and ominously sectional votes.

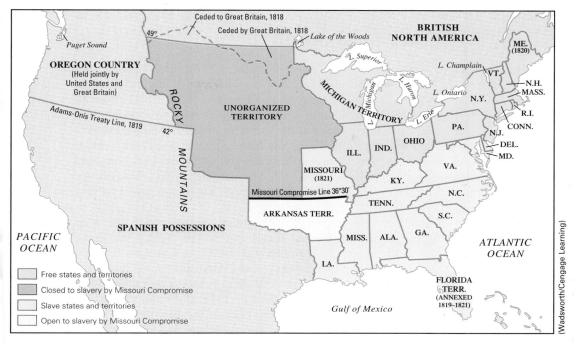

The map shows ceded territories and state classifications. Labels include: Ceded to Great Britain, 1818; Ceded by Great Britain, 1818; Lake of the Woods; BRITISH NORTH AMERICA; ME. (1820); Puget Sound; 49°; L. Superior; L. Champlain; VT.; OREGON COUNTRY (Held jointly by United States and Great Britain); MICHIGAN TERRITORY; L. Michigan; L. Huron; L. Ontario; N.H.; MASS.; N.Y.; ROCKY MOUNTAINS; UNORGANIZED TERRITORY; L. Erie; R.I.; Adams-Onís Treaty Line, 1819; 42°; PA.; CONN.; N.J.; OHIO; DEL.; ILL.; IND.; MD.; MISSOURI (1821); VA.; Missouri Compromise Line 36°30'; KY.; ARKANSAS TERR.; TENN.; N.C.; SPANISH POSSESSIONS; PACIFIC OCEAN; MISS.; ALA.; GA.; S.C.; ATLANTIC OCEAN; LA.; FLORIDA TERR. (ANNEXED 1819–1821); Gulf of Mexico; (Wadsworth/Cengage Learning)

Legend:
Free states and territories
Closed to slavery by Missouri Compromise
Slave states and territories
Open to slavery by Missouri Compromise

MAP 8.2 The Missouri Compromise, 1820–1821

The Missouri Compromise temporarily quelled controversy over slavery by admitting Maine as a free state and Missouri as a slave state, and by prohibiting slavery in the remainder of the Louisiana Purchase north of 36°30'.

No sooner had the compromise been forged than it nearly fell apart. As a prelude to statehood, Missourians drafted a constitution that prohibited free blacks, whom some eastern states viewed as citizens, from entering their territory. This provision clashed with the federal Constitution's provision that citizens of one state were entitled to the same rights as citizens of other states. Balking at Missourians' exclusion of free blacks, antislavery northerners barred Missouri's admission into the Union until 1821, when Henry Clay engineered a new agreement. This second Missouri Compromise prohibited Missouri from discriminating against citizens of other states but left open the issue of whether free blacks were citizens.

The Missouri Compromise was widely viewed as a southern victory. The South had gained admission of Missouri, whose acceptance of slavery was controversial, while the North had merely gained Maine, whose rejection of slavery inspired no controversy. Yet the South had conceded to freedom a vast block of territory north of 36°30'. Although much of this territory was unorganized Indian country that some viewed as unfit for white habitation, seven states eventually would be formed out of it. Also, the Missouri Compromise reinforced the principle, originally set down by the Northwest Ordinance of 1787, that Congress had the right to prohibit slavery in some territories. Southerners had implicitly accepted the argument that slaves were not like other forms of property that could be moved from place to place at will.

Foreign Policy under Monroe   American foreign policy between 1816 and 1824 reflected more consensus than conflict. The end of the Napoleonic Wars and the signing of the Treaty of Ghent had removed most of the foreign-policy disagreements between Federalists and Republicans. Moreover, Monroe was fortunate to have as his secretary of state an extraordinary diplomat, **John Quincy Adams.** The son of the last Federalist president, Adams had been the only Federalist in the Senate to support the Louisiana Purchase, and he later became an ardent Republican. An austere and scholarly man whose library equaled his house in monetary value, Adams was a tough negotiator and a fervent nationalist.

As secretary of state, Adams moved quickly to strengthen the peace with Great Britain. During his tenure, the United States and Britain signed the Rush-Bagot Treaty of 1817, which effectively demilitarized the Great Lakes by severely restricting the number of ships the two powers could maintain there. Next, the British-American Convention of 1818 restored to Americans the same fishing rights off Newfoundland they had enjoyed before the War of 1812 and fixed the boundary between the United States and Canada from the Lake of the Woods west to the Rockies. Beyond the Rockies, the vast country known as Oregon was declared "free and open" to both American and British citizens. As a result of these two agreements, the United States had a secure border with British-controlled Canada for the first time since independence, and a claim to the Pacific.

The nation now turned its attention to dealing with Spain, which still owned East Florida and claimed West Florida. No one was certain whether the Louisiana Purchase included West Florida. Acting as if it did, the United States in 1812 had simply added a slice of West Florida to the state of Louisiana and another slice to the Mississippi Territory. Using the pretext that it was a base for Seminole Indian raids and a refuge for fugitive slaves, Andrew Jackson, now the military commander in the South, invaded East Florida in 1818. He hanged two British subjects and captured Spanish forts. Jackson had acted without explicit orders, but Adams supported the raid, guessing correctly that it would panic the Spanish into further concessions.

In 1819, Spain agreed to the **Adams-Onis (Transcontinental) Treaty.** By its terms, Spain ceded East Florida to the United States, renounced its claims to West Florida, and agreed to a southern border of the United States west of the Mississippi, by which the United States conceded that Texas was not part of the Louisiana Purchase, while Spain agreed to a northern limit to its claims to the West Coast (see Map 8.2) It thereby left the United States free to pursue its interests in Oregon.

The Monroe Doctrine, 1823   John Quincy Adams had long believed that God and nature had ordained that the United States would eventually span the entire continent of North America. Throughout his negotiations leading up to the Adams-Onís Treaty, he made it clear to Spain that, if the Spanish did not concede some of their territory in North America, the United

States might seize all of it, including Texas and even Mexico. Yet Spain was concerned with larger issues than American encroachment. Its primary objective was to suppress the revolutions against Spanish rule that had broken out in South America. To accomplish this goal, Spain sought support from the European monarchs who had organized the Holy Alliance in 1815. The brainchild of the tsar of Russia, the Holy Alliance aimed to quash revolutions everywhere in the name of Christian and monarchist principles. Britain, whose trading interests in South America were hampered by Spanish restrictions, refused to join the Holy Alliance. British foreign minister George Canning proposed that the United States and Britain issue a joint statement opposing any European interference in South America, while pledging that neither would annex any part of Spain's old empire in the New World.

While sharing Cannings opposition to European intervention in the New World, Adams preferred that the United States make a declaration of policy on its own rather than "come in as a cock-boat in the wake of the British man-of-war." Adams flatly rejected Cannings insistence on a joint pledge never to annex Spain's former territories, for Adams wanted the freedom to annex Texas or Cuba, should their inhabitants one day "solicit a union with us."

This was the background of the **Monroe Doctrine,** as President Monroe's message to Congress on December 2, 1823, later came to be called. The message, written largely by Adams, announced three key principles: that unless American interests were involved, U.S. policy was to abstain from European wars; that the "American continents" were not "subjects for future colonization by any European power"; and that the United States would construe any attempt at European colonization in the New World as an "unfriendly act."

Europeans widely derided the Monroe Doctrine as an empty pronouncement. Fear of the British navy, not the Monroe Doctrine, prevented the Holy Alliance from intervening in South America. With hindsight, however, the Europeans might have taken the doctrine more seriously, for it had important implications. First, by pledging itself not to interfere in European wars, the United States was excluding the possibility that it would support revolutionary movements in Europe. For example, Adams opposed U.S. recognition of Greek patriots fighting for independence from the Ottoman Turks. Second, by keeping open its options to annex territory in the Americas, the United States was using the Monroe Doctrine to claim a preeminent position in the New World.

CHRONOLOGY
1801–1824

1801	Thomas Jefferson's inauguration.
1801–1805	Tripolitan War.
1802	Repeal of the Judiciary Act of 1801. Yazoo land compromise.
1803	*Marbury* v. *Madison.*
	Conclusion of the Louisiana Purchase.
1804	Impeachment of Justice Samuel Chase.
	Aaron Burr kills Alexander Hamilton in a duel.
	Jefferson elected to a second term.

1804–1806	Lewis and Clark expedition.
1805	British court declares the broken voyage illegal.
1807	*Chesapeake* Affair. Embargo Act passed.
1808	James Madison elected president.
1809	Non-Intercourse Act passed. Embargo Act repealed.
1810	Macon's Bill No.2.
1811	Battle of Tippecanoe.
1812	United States declares war on Britain. Madison reelected to a second term. General William Hull surrenders at Detroit. Battle of Queenston.
1813	Battle of the Thames.
1814	British burn Washington, D.C. Hartford Convention. Treaty of Ghent signed.
1815	Battle of New Orleans. Algerine War.
1816	James Monroe elected president. Second Bank of the United States chartered.
1817	Rush-Bagot Treaty.
1818	British-American Convention of 1818 sets U.S.–Canada border in West. Andrew Jackson invades East Florida.
1819	Adams-Onis (Transcontinental) Treaty. *Dartmouth College* v. *Woodward*. *McCulloch* v. *Maryland*.
1820	Monroe elected to a second term.
1820–1821	Missouri Compromise.
1823	Monroe Doctrine.

Conclusion

A newcomer among nations, the United States commanded little international respect in 1801, much more by 1824. During the intervening years, it fought two wars against the Barbary pirates and one against Britain. It doubled its size with the Louisiana Purchase, gained possession of the Floridas, and staked a claim to the Pacific Coast. The vision and leadership of Jefferson, Madison, and John Quincy Adams contributed to American successes. Jefferson's purchase of the Louisiana Territory in 1803 reflected his view that American liberty depended on the perpetuation of agriculture, and it would bring new states, dominated by Republicans, into the Union. As the Federalist Party waned, Jefferson had to face down challenges from within his own party, notably from the mischief of Aaron Burr and from die-hard old Republicans like John Randolph, who charged that Jefferson was abandoning pure Republican doctrines.

The outbreak of war between Napoleon's France and Britain, and the threat it posed to American neutrality, preoccupied Jefferson's second term and both terms of his successor, James Madison. The failure of the embargo and peaceable coercion to force Europeans to respect American neutrality led the United States into war with Britain in 1812. The War of 1812 and its aftermath exemplified how events in Europe sometimes worked to the Americans' advantage. Although the United States failed to achieve its main war goal, forcing Britain to principled acceptance of neutral rights, Napoleon's downfall and the end of hostilities in Europe made the issue irrelevant. In addition, the war destroyed the Federalists, who committed political suicide at the Hartford Convention. It also led Madison to jettison part of Jefferson's legacy by calling for a new national bank, federal support for internal improvements, and protective tariffs. The Transcontinental Treaty of 1819 and the Monroe Doctrine's bold pronouncement that European powers must not meddle in the affairs of the Western Hemisphere expressed America's increasingly assertive nationalism.

Conflict was never far below the surface of the apparent consensus. In the absence of Federalist opposition, Republicans began to fragment into sectional factions, most notably in the conflict over Missouri's admission to the Union as a slave state.

9

THE TRANSFORMATION OF AMERICAN SOCIETY 1815–1840

WESTWARD EXPANSION

In 1790, the vast majority of the non-Indian population of the United States, nearly 4 million people, lived east of the Appalachian Mountains and within a few hundred miles of the Atlantic Ocean. But by 1840, one-third of the non-Indian population of just over 17 million were living between the Appalachians and the Mississippi River, the area that Americans of the time referred to as the West but that historians call the **Old Northwest** and **Old Southwest**.

Only a few Americans moved west to seek adventure, and these few usually headed into the half-known region west of the Rocky Mountains, the present Far West. Most migrants desired and expected a better version of the life they had known in the East: more land and more bountiful crops. Several factors nurtured this expectation: the growing power of the federal government; its often ruthless removal of the Indians from the path of white settlement; and a boom in the prices of agricultural commodities after the War of 1812.

The Sweep West   Americans moved west in a series of bursts. Americans leapfrogged the Appalachians after 1791 to bring four new states into the Union by 1803: Vermont, Kentucky, Tennessee, and Ohio. The second burst occurred between 1816 and 1821, when six states entered the Union: Indiana, Mississippi, Illinois, Alabama, Maine, and Missouri. Even as Indiana and Illinois were gaining statehood, settlers were pouring farther west into Michigan. Ohio's population jumped from 45,000 in 1800 to 581,000 by 1820 and 1,519,000 by 1840; Michigan's from 5,000 in 1810 to 212,000 by 1840.

Seeking security, pioneers usually migrated as families rather than as individuals. To reach markets with their produce, most settlers clustered near the navigable rivers of the West, especially the magnificent water system created by the Ohio and Mississippi Rivers. Only with the spread of canals in the 1820s and 1830s, and later of railroads, did westerners feel free to venture far from rivers.

Western Society and Customs   Migrants to the West brought with them values and customs peculiar to the regions of the East they had left behind. For example, migrants to the Old Northwest who hailed from New England or upstate New York settled the northern areas of Ohio, Indiana, and Illinois, where they primarily grew wheat, supplemented by dairying and fruit orchards. These "Yankees" valued public schools, usually lived in houses made of sod, stone, or clapboard, and were quick to form towns. In 1836, a group of farmers from nearby towns met at Castleton, Vermont, listened to a minister intone from the Bible, "And Moses sent them to spy out the land of Canaan," and soon established the town of Vermontville in Michigan. In contrast, emigrants from the Upland South to the Old Northwest, called "Butternuts" from the color of their homespun clothing, settled the southern parts of Ohio, Indiana, and Illinois, where they raised corn and hogs. Coming from less densely populated regions of the East than the Yankees, Butternuts tended to live in log cabins on isolated farmsteads. Some Butternuts like Abraham Lincoln's father Thomas Lincoln, who moved with his family from Kentucky to Indiana in 1816, were antislavery, but many were proslavery. Little love was lost between antislavery Yankees and proslavery Butternuts. In 1824, an attempt to legalize slavery in Illinois was only narrowly defeated at the polls.

Regardless of their origins, most westerners craved sociability. Rural families joined with their neighbors in group sports and festivities. Men met for games that, with a few exceptions like marbles (popular among all ages), were tests of strength or agility. These included wrestling, weight lifting, pole jumping (for distance rather than height), and a variant of the modern hammer toss. Some of these games were brutal. In gander pulling, horseback riders competed to pull the head off a male duck whose neck had been stripped of feathers and greased. Women usually combined work and play in quilting and sewing parties, carpet tackings, and even chicken and goose pluckings. Social activities brought the genders together. Group corn huskings usually ended with dances; and in a variety of "hoedowns" and "frolics," even westerners who in principle might disapprove of dancing promenaded to singing and a fiddler's tune.

The West developed a character of its own. Before 1840, few westerners could afford elegant living. Arriving on the Michigan frontier from New York City in 1835, the well-bred Caroline Kirkland quickly discovered that her neighbors thought they had a right to borrow anything she owned with no more than a blunt declaration that "you've got plenty." "For my own part," Caroline related, "I have lent my broom, my thread, my tape, my spoons, my cat, my thimble, my scissors, my shawl, my shoes, and have been asked for my comb and brushes." Their relative lack of refinement made westerners easy targets for easterners' contemptuous jibes.

Westerners responded that at least they were honest democrats, not soft would-be aristocrats. Pretension got short shrift. On one occasion, a traveler who hung up a blanket in a tavern to shield his bed from public gaze had it promptly ripped down. On another, a woman who improvised a screen behind which to retire in a crowded room was dismissed as "stuck up." A politician who rode to a public meeting in a buggy instead of on horseback lost votes.

The Far West   Exploration carried some Americans even farther west. Exploring the Spanish Southwest in 1806, Zebulon Pike sighted the Colorado peak that was later named after him. In 1811, in the wake of the Lewis and Clark expedition, New York merchant John Jacob Astor founded the fur-trading post of Astoria at the mouth of the Columbia River in the Oregon Country. In the 1820s and 1830s, fur traders also operated along the Missouri River from St. Louis to the Rocky Mountains and beyond. At first, whites relied on Native Americans to bring them furs, but during the 1820s white trappers or "mountain men"—among them, Kit Carson, Jedediah Smith, and the mulatto Jim Beckwourth—gathered furs on their own while performing astounding feats of survival in harsh surroundings.

Jedediah Smith was representative of these men. Born in the Susquehanna Valley of New York in 1799, Smith moved west with his family to Pennsylvania and Illinois and signed on with an expedition bound for the upper Missouri River in 1822. In the course of this and subsequent explorations, he was almost killed by a grizzly bear in the Black Hills of South Dakota, learned from the Native Americans to trap beaver and kill buffalo, crossed the Mojave Desert into California, explored California's San Joaquin Valley, and hiked back across the Sierras and the primeval Great Basin to the Great Salt Lake, a trip so forbidding that even Native Americans avoided it. The exploits of Smith and the other mountain men were popularized in biographies, and they became legends in their own day.

The Federal Government and the West   Of the various causes of expansion to the Mississippi from 1790 to 1840, the one that operated most generally and uniformly throughout the period was the growing strength of the federal government. Even before the Constitution's ratification, several states had ceded their western land claims to the national government, thereby creating the bountiful public domain. The Land Ordinance of 1785 had provided for the survey and sale of these lands, and the Northwest Ordinance of 1787 had established procedures for transforming them into states. The Louisiana Purchase of 1803 brought the entire Mississippi River under American control, and the Transcontinental Treaty of 1819 wiped out the last vestiges of Spanish power east of the Mississippi.

The federal government directly stimulated settlement of the West by promising land to men who enlisted during the War of 1812. With 6 million acres allotted to these so-called military bounties, many former soldiers and their families pulled up roots and settled in the West. To facilitate westward migration, Congress authorized funds in 1816 for the extension of the National Road, a highway begun in 1811 that reached Wheeling, Virginia, on the Ohio River in 1818 and Vandalia, Illinois, by

1838. Soon settlers thronged the road. "Old America seems to be breaking up," a traveler on the National Road wrote in 1817. "We are seldom out of sight, as we travel on this grand track towards the Ohio, of family groups before and behind us."

The same government strength that aided whites brought misery to the Indians. Virtually all the foreign-policy successes during the Jefferson, Madison, and Monroe administrations worked to Native Americans' disadvantage. In the wake of the Louisiana Purchase, Lewis and Clark bluntly told the Indians that they must "shut their ears to the counsels of bad birds" and listen henceforth only to the "Great Father" in Washington. The outcome of the War of 1812 also worked against the Native Americans; indeed, the Indians were the only real losers of the war. Early in the negotiations leading to the Treaty of Ghent, the British had insisted on the creation of an Indian buffer state between the United States and Canada in the Old Northwest. But the British eventually dropped the demand and essentially abandoned the Indians to the Americans.

The Removal of the Indians   Westward-moving white settlers found sizable numbers of Native Americans in their paths, particularly in the South, home to the so-called **Five Civilized Tribes:** the Cherokees, Choctaws, Creeks, Chickasaws, and Seminoles. Years of commercial dealings and intermarriage with whites had created in these tribes, especially the Cherokees, an influential minority of mixed-bloods who embraced Christianity, practiced agriculture, built gristmills, and even owned slaves. One of their chiefs, Sequoyah, devised a written form of their language; other Cherokees published a bilingual newspaper, the *Cherokee Phoenix*.

The "civilization" of the southern Indians impressed New England missionaries more than southern whites, who viewed the Civilized Tribes with contempt and their land with envy. Presidents James Monroe and John Quincy Adams had concluded several treaties with Indian tribes providing for their voluntary removal to public lands west of the Mississippi River. Although some assimilated mixed-bloods sold their tribal lands to the government, other mixed-bloods resisted because their prosperity depended on trade with close-by whites. In addition, full-bloods, the majority even in the "civilized" tribes, clung to their land and customs. They wanted to remain near the burial grounds of their ancestors and condemned mixed-bloods who bartered away tribal lands to whites. When the Creek mixed-blood chief William McIntosh sold all Creek lands in Georgia and two-thirds of Creek lands in Alabama to the government in the Treaty of Indian Springs (1825), a Creek tribal council executed him.

During the 1820s, whites in Alabama, Georgia, and Mississippi intensified pressure on the Indians by surveying tribal lands and squatting on them. Southern legislatures, loath to restrain white settlers, moved to expropriate Indian lands unless the Indians moved west. State laws extended state jurisdiction over the tribes, which effectively outlawed tribal government, and excluded Indians from serving as witnesses in court cases involving whites, which made it difficult for Indians to collect debts owed them by whites.

These measures delighted President Andrew Jackson. Reared on the frontier and sharing its contempt for Indians, Jackson believed it was ridiculous to treat the Indians as independent nations; rather, they should be subject to the laws of the states where they lived. This position spelled doom for the Indians, who could not vote or hold state office. In 1834, Cherokee chief John Ross got a taste of what state jurisdiction meant; Georgia, without consulting him, put his house up as a prize in the state lottery.

In 1830, Jackson secured passage of the **Indian Removal Act,** which authorized him to exchange public lands in the West for Indian territories in the East and appropriated $500,000 to cover the expenses of removal. But the real costs of removal, human and monetary, were vastly greater. During Jackson's eight years in office, the federal government forced Indians to exchange 100 million acres of their lands for 32 million acres of public lands. In the late 1820s and early 1830s, the Choctaws, Creeks, and Chickasaws started their "voluntary" removal to the West. In 1836, Creeks who clung to their homes were forcibly removed, many in chains. Most Seminoles were removed from Florida, but only after a bitter war between 1835 and 1842 that cost the federal government $20 million.

Ironically, the Cherokees, often considered the "most civilized" tribe, suffered the worst fate. In 1827, the Cherokees proclaimed themselves an independent republic within Georgia and petitioned the U.S. Supreme Court for an injunction to halt Georgia's attempt to claim state jurisdiction over their "nation." In the case of *Cherokee Nation v. Georgia* (1831), Chief Justice John Marshall denied the Cherokees' claim to status as a republic within Georgia; rather, they were a "domestic dependent nation," a kind of ward of the United States. Marshall added that prolonged occupancy had given the Cherokees a claim to their lands within Georgia. A year later, he clarified the Cherokees' legal position in *Worcester v. Georgia* by holding that they were a "distinct" political community entitled to federal protection from Georgia's claims.

(Trail of Tears" by Robert Lindneaux. Woolaroc Museum, Bartlesville, OK)

***Trail of Tears,* by Robert Lindneux** *Forced by Andrew Jackson's removal policy to give up its lands east of the Mississippi and migrate to an area in present-day Oklahoma, the Cherokee people suffered disease, hunger, and exhaustion on what they remembered as "the Trail of Tears."*

Reportedly sneering, "John Marshall has made his decision; now let him enforce it," President Jackson ignored it. Next, federal agents persuaded some minor Cherokee chiefs to sign the Treaty of New Echota (1835), which ceded all Cherokee lands in the United States for $5.6 million and free passage west. Congress ratified this treaty (by one vote), but the vast majority of Cherokees denounced it. In 1839, a Cherokee party took revenge by murdering its three principal signers, including a former editor of the *Cherokee Phoenix*.

The end of the story was simple and tragic. In 1838, the Cherokees were forcibly removed to the new Indian Territory in what is now Oklahoma. They traveled west along what became known as the **"Trail of Tears"** (see Map 9.1). A young man who would become a colonel in the Confederate Army participated in the forced removal. He later recollected: "I fought through the civil war and have seen men shot to pieces and slaughtered by the thousands, but the Cherokees removal was the cruelest work I ever knew." Perhaps as many as eight thousand Cherokees, more than one-third of the entire nation, died during and just after the removal.

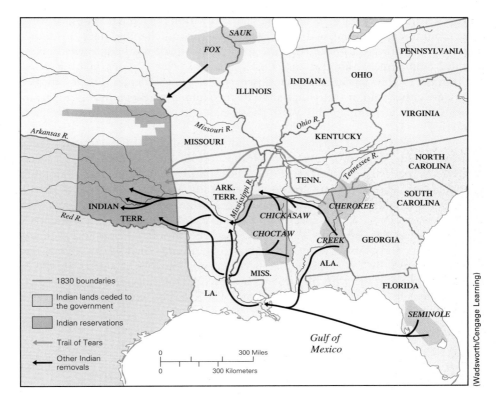

MAP 9.1 The Removal of the Native Americans to the West, 1820–1840

The so-called Trail of Tears, followed by the Cherokees, was one of several routes along which various tribes migrated on their forced removal to reservations west of the Mississippi.

Indians living in the Northwest Territory fared no better. A series of treaties extinguished their land titles, and most moved west of the Mississippi. The removal of the northwestern Indians was notable for two uprisings. The first, led by Red Bird, a Winnebago chief, began in 1827 but was quickly crushed. The second, led by a Sac and Fox chief, Black Hawk, raged along the Illinois frontier until 1832, when federal troops and Illinois militia virtually annihilated Black Hawk's followers. Black Hawk's downfall persuaded the other Old Northwest tribes to cede their lands. Between 1832 and 1837, the United States acquired nearly 190 million acres of Indian land in the Northwest for $70 million in gifts and annual payments.

Working the Land: The Agricultural Boom After the War of 1812, the rising prices of agricultural commodities such as wheat, corn, and cotton sharpened white land hunger. Several factors accounted for the skyrocketing farm prices. During the Napoleonic Wars, the United States had quickly captured former British markets in the West Indies and former Spanish markets in South America. With the conclusion of the wars, American farmers found brisk demand for their wheat and corn in Britain and France, both exhausted by two decades of warfare. In addition, demand within the United States for western farm commodities intensified after 1815 as the quickening pace of industrialization and urbanization in the East spurred a shift of workers toward nonagricultural employment. Finally, the West's splendid river systems made it possible for farmers to ship wheat and corn downriver to New Orleans. There, wheat and corn were either sold or transshipped to the beckoning markets. Just as government policies made farming in the West possible, high prices for foodstuffs made it attractive.

As the prospect of raising wheat and corn pulled farmers toward the Old Northwest, Eli Whitney's invention of the cotton gin in 1793 (see Chapter 7) cleared the path for settlement of the Old Southwest, particularly the states of Alabama and Mississippi. As cotton clothing came into fashion around 1815, the British textile industry provided seemingly bottomless demand for raw cotton. With its warm climate, wet springs and summers, and relatively dry autumns, the Old Southwest was especially suited to cotton cultivation. The explosive thrust of small farmers and planters from the seaboard South into the Old Southwest resembled a gold rush. By 1817, "Alabama fever" gripped the South; settlers bid the price of good land up to thirty to fifty dollars an acre. Accounting for less than a quarter of all American exports between 1802 and 1807, cotton comprised just over half by 1830, and nearly two-thirds by 1836.

THE GROWTH OF THE MARKET ECONOMY

Many farmers traditionally had grown only enough food to feed their families (subsistence agriculture). With agricultural commodities like wheat and cotton commanding high prices, a growing number of farmers added a cash crop (called commercial agriculture, or the **market economy**). In the South, slaves increasingly became a valuable commodity; the sale of slaves from declining agricultural states in the Southeast to planters and farmers migrating to Alabama and Mississippi grew into a huge business after 1815. "Virginia," an observer stated in 1832, "is, in fact, a *negro* raising State for other States; she produces enough for her own supply and six thousand a year for sale."

The unprecedented scale of commercial agriculture after 1815 exposed farmers to new risks. Farmers had no control over prices in distant markets. Furthermore, the often long interval between harvesting a cash crop and selling it forced farmers to borrow money to sustain their families. Thus the market economy forced farmers into short-term debt in the hope of long-term profit.

In addition, many western farmers had to borrow money to buy their land. The roots of this indebtedness for land lay in the federal government's inability to devise an effective policy for transferring the public domain directly into the hands of small farmers.

Federal Land Policy   Partisan and sectional pressures buffeted federal land policy like a kite in a March wind. The result was a succession of land laws passed between 1796 and 1820, each of which sought to undo the damage caused by its predecessors.

At the root of early federal land policy lay a preference for the orderly settlement of the public domain. To this end, the Ordinance of 1785 divided public lands into sections of 640 acres (see Chapter 6). The architects of the ordinance did not expect that ordinary farmers could afford such large lots; rather, they assumed that farmers who shared ties based on religion or region of origin would band together to purchase sections. This outcome would ensure that compatible settlers would live on adjoining lots in what amounted to rural neighborhoods, and it would make the task of government much easier than if settlers were to live in isolation on widely scattered homesteads.

Political developments in the 1790s undermined the expectations of the ordinance's framers. Federalists, with their political bases in the east, were reluctant to encourage western settlement, but at the same time they were eager to raise revenue for the federal government from land sales. They reconciled their conflicting goals by encouraging the sale of huge tracts of land to wealthy speculators who waited for its value to rise and then sold off parcels to farmers. For example, in the 1790s the Holland Land Company, composed mainly of Dutch investors, bought up much of western New York and western Pennsylvania. A federal land law passed in 1796 reflected Federalist aims by maintaining the minimum purchase at 640 acres at a minimum price of two dollars an acre, and by allowing only a year for complete payment. Few small farmers could afford to buy that much land at that price.

Sure that the small farmer was the backbone of the republic, Jefferson and the Republicans took a different tack. The land law of 1800 dropped the minimum purchase to 320 acres at a minimum of $2 an acre and allowed up to four years for full payment. By 1832, the minimum purchase had shrunk to 40 acres and the price to $1.25 an acre.

Although Congress steadily liberalized land policy, speculators always remained one step ahead. Long before 1832, speculators were selling forty-acre lots to farmers. Farmers preferred small lots (and rarely bought more than 160 acres) because the farms they purchased typically were forested. A new landowner could clear no more than ten to twelve acres of trees a year. All land in the public domain was sold at auction, usually for much more than the price set by law. With agricultural prices soaring, speculators assumed that land would continue to rise in value and accordingly were willing to bid high on new land, which they resold to farmers at hefty profits.

The growing availability of credit after the War of 1812 fed speculation. The chartering of the Second Bank of the United States in 1816 had the dual effect of increasing the amount of money in circulation and stimulating the chartering of private banks within individual states (state banks). Between 1812 and 1817, the value of all bank notes in circulation soared from $45 million to $100 million. Stockholders and officers saw banks as agencies that could lend them money for land speculation. The result was an orgy of land speculation; by 1819, the dollar value of sales of public land was over 1,000 percent greater than the average between 1800 and 1814.

The Speculator and the Squatter

Nevertheless, most of the public domain eventually found its way into the hands of small farmers. Because speculators gained nothing by holding land for prolonged periods, they were only too happy to sell it when the price was right. In addition, a familiar frontier type, the squatter, exerted a restraining influence on the speculator.

Even before the creation of the public domain, **squatters** had helped themselves to western land. George Washington himself had been unable to drive squatters off lands he owned in the West. Squatters were an independent and proud lot, scornful of their fellow citizens who were "softened by Ease, enervated by Affluence and Luxurious Plenty, & unaccustomed to Fatigues, Hardships, Difficulties or dangers." Disdaining land speculators above all, squatters formed claims associations to police land auctions and prevent speculators from bidding up the price of land. Squatters also pressured Congress to allow them preemption rights—that is, the right to purchase at the minimum price the land they had already settled on and improved. Seeking to undo the damaging effects of its own laws, Congress responded by passing special preemption laws for squatters in specific areas and finally, in 1841, acknowledged a general right of preemption.

Preemption laws were of no use to farmers who arrived after speculators had already bought up land. Having spent their small savings on livestock, seed, and tools, these settlers had to buy land from speculators on credit at interest rates that ranged as high as 40 percent. Many western farmers, drowning in debt, had to skimp on subsistence crops while expanding cash crops in the hope of paying off their creditors.

Countless farmers who had carried basically conservative expectations to the West quickly became economic adventurers. Forced to raise cash crops in a hurry, many worked their acreage to exhaustion and thus had to keep moving in search of new land. The phrase "the moving frontier" refers not only to the obvious fact that the line of settlement shifted farther west with each passing decade, but also to the fact that the same people kept moving. The experience of Abraham Lincoln's parents, who migrated from the East through several farms in Kentucky and then to Indiana, was representative of the westward trek.

**The Panic of
1819**

The land boom collapsed in the financial **Panic of 1819.** The state banks' loose practices contributed mightily to the panic. State banks issued their own bank notes, which were promises to pay the bearer ("redeem") a certain amount of specie (gold or silver coinage) on demand. State banks had long issued far more bank notes than they could redeem, and these notes had fueled the land boom after 1815. Farmers also borrowed to buy more land and plant more crops, depending on sales to Europe to enable them to repay loans. After 1817, however, the combination of bumper crops in Europe and a recession in Britain trimmed foreign demand for U.S. wheat, flour, and cotton at the very time when American farmers were becoming more dependent on exports to pay their debts.

In the summer of 1818, reacting to the flood of state bank notes, the Bank of the United States began to insist that state banks redeem in specie their notes that were held by the Bank of the United States. Because the Bank of the United States had more branches than any state bank, notes of state banks often were presented by their holders to branches of the Bank of the United States for redemption. Whenever the Bank of the United States redeemed a state bank note in specie, it became a creditor of the state bank. To pay their debts to the Bank of the United States, the state banks had no choice but to force farmers and land speculators to repay loans. The result was a cascade of economic catastrophes.

The biggest losers were the land speculators. Land that had once sold for as much as sixty-nine dollars an acre dropped to two dollars an acre. Land prices fell because the credit squeeze drove down the market prices of staples like wheat, corn, cotton, and tobacco. Cotton, which sold for thirty-two cents a pound in 1818, sank as low as seventeen cents a pound in 1820. Since farmers could not get much cash for their crops, they could not pay the debts that they owed on land. Since speculators could not collect money owed them by farmers, the value of land they still held for sale collapsed.

The Panic left a bitter taste about banks, particularly the Bank of the United States, which was widely blamed for the hard times. The Panic also demonstrated how dependent farmers had become on distant markets. This in turn accelerated the search for better, cheaper ways to get crops to market.

TRAVERSING THE LAND: THE TRANSPORTATION REVOLUTION

The transportation system linking Americans in 1820 had severe weaknesses. The great rivers west of the Appalachians flowed north to south and hence could not by themselves connect western farmers to eastern markets. Roads were expensive to maintain, and horse-drawn wagons had limited capacity. Consequently, after 1820 attention and investment shifted to improving transportation on waterways, thus initiating the **transportation revolution.**

**Steamboats,
Canals, and
Railroads**

In 1807, Robert R. Livingston and Robert Fulton introduced the steamboat *Clermont* on the Hudson River. They soon gained a monopoly from the New York legislature to run a New York–New Jersey ferry service. Spectacular profits lured competitors, who secured a license from Congress and then filed suit to break the

Livingston-Fulton monopoly. After a long court battle, the Supreme Court decided against the monopoly in 1824 in the famous case of **Gibbons v. Ogden.** Speaking for a unanimous court, Chief Justice John Marshall ruled that Congress's constitutional power to regulate interstate commerce applied to navigation and thus had to prevail over New York's power to license the Livingston-Fulton monopoly. In the aftermath of this decision, other state-granted monopolies collapsed, and steamboat traffic increased rapidly. The number of steamboats operating on western rivers jumped from seventeen in 1817 to 727 by 1855.

Steamboats assumed a vital role along the Mississippi-Ohio River system. It took a keelboat (a covered flatboat pushed by oars or poles) three or four months to complete the 1,350-mile voyage from New Orleans to Louisville; in 1817, a steamboat could make the trip in twenty-five days. The development of long, shallow hulls permitted the navigation of the Mississippi-Ohio system even when hot, dry summers lowered the river level. Steamboats became more ornate as well as practical. To compete for passengers, they began to offer luxurious cabins and lounges, called saloons. The saloon of the *Eclipse,* a Mississippi River steamboat, was the length of a football field and featured skylights, chandeliers, a ceiling criss-crossed with Gothic arches, and velvet-upholstered mahogany furniture.

While steamboats proved their value, canals replaced roads and turnpikes as the focus of popular enthusiasm and investment. Although the cost of canal construction was mind-boggling—Jefferson dismissed the idea as little short of

(Library of Congress)

Steamship Ben Campbell at Landing, 1852 *By the time the steamship Ben Campbell was built around 1852, steamboats had gotten a lot faster.*

madness—canals offered the prospect of connecting the Mississippi-Ohio River system with the Great Lakes, and the Great Lakes with eastern markets.

Constructed between 1817 and 1825, New York's **Erie Canal,** connecting the Hudson River with Lake Erie, enabled produce from Ohio to reach New York City by a continuous stretch of waterways (see Map 9.2). Completion of the Erie Canal

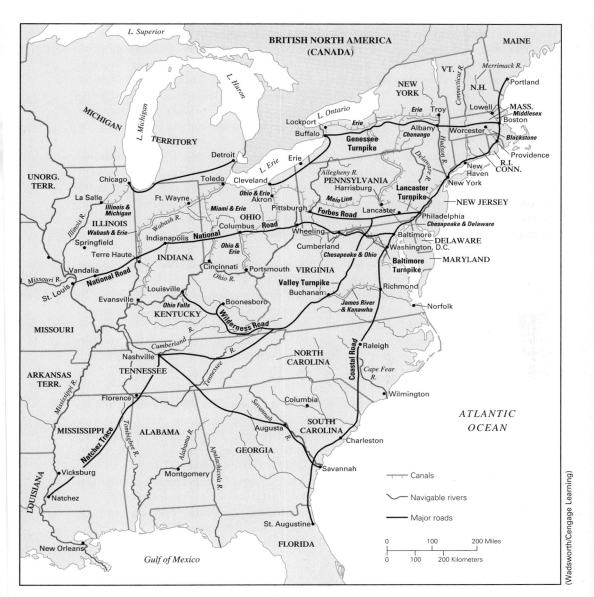

(Wadsworth/Cengage Learning)

MAP 9.2 Major Rivers, Roads, and Canals, 1825–1860

Railroads and canals increasingly tied the economy of the Midwest to that of the Northeast.

started a canal boom during the late 1820s and 1830s. Ohio constructed a network of canals that allowed its farmers to send their wheat by water to Lake Erie. After transport across Lake Erie, the wheat would be milled into flour in Rochester, New York, then shipped on the Erie Canal to Albany and down the Hudson River to New York City. Throughout the nation, canals reduced shipping costs from twenty to thirty cents a ton per mile in 1815 to two to three cents a ton per mile by 1830.

When another economic depression hit in the late 1830s, states found themselves overcommitted to costly canal projects and ultimately scrapped many. As the canal boom was ending, the railroad, an entirely new form of transportation, was being introduced. In 1825, the world's first commercial railroad began operation in England, and by 1840 some three thousand miles of track had been laid in America, about the same as the total canal mileage in 1840. During the 1830s, investment in American railroads exceeded that in canals. Cities like Baltimore and Boston, which lacked major inland waterway connections, turned to railroads to enlarge their share of the western market.

Cheaper to build, faster, and able to reach more places, railroads had obvious advantages over canals. But railroads' potential was only slowly realized. Most early railroads ran between cities in the East, rather than from east to west, and carried more passengers than freight. Not until 1849 did freight revenues exceed passenger revenues, and not until 1850 was the East Coast connected by rail to the Great Lakes.

Two factors explain the relatively slow spread of interregional railroads. First, unlike canals, which were built by state governments, most railroads were constructed by private corporations seeking quick profits. To minimize their original investment, railroad companies commonly resorted to cost-cutting measures such as covering wooden rails with iron bars. As a result, although relatively cheap to build, American railroads needed constant repairs. In contrast, although expensive to construct, canals needed relatively little maintenance and were kept in operation for decades after railroads appeared. Second, it remained much cheaper to ship bulky commodities such as iron ore, coal, and nonperishable agricultural produce by canal.

The Growth of the Cities   The transportation revolution speeded the growth of towns and cities. Canals and railroads vastly increased opportunities for city businesses: banks to lend money, insurers to cover risks of transport, warehouses and brokers to store and sell goods. In relative terms, the most rapid urbanization in American history occurred between 1820 and 1860. The Erie Canal turned New York City into the nation's largest city; its population rose from 124,000 in 1820 to 800,000 by 1860. An even more revealing change was the transformation of sleepy villages of a few hundred people into thriving towns of several thousand. For example, the Erie Canal turned Rochester, New York, home to a few hundred villagers in 1817, into the Flour City with nine thousand residents by 1830.

City and town growth occurred with dramatic suddenness, especially in the West. Pittsburgh, Cincinnati, and St. Louis were little more than hamlets in 1800. Military activities in the Old Northwest during the War of 1812 stimulated the growth of Pittsburgh and Cincinnati, and St. Louis acquired some importance as a fur-trading center. Then, between 1815 and 1819, the agricultural boom and the introduction of the steamboat transformed all three places from outposts with transient populations of hunters, traders, and soldiers into bustling cities. Cincinnati's population nearly quadrupled between 1810 and 1820, then doubled in the 1820s.

All the prominent western cities were river ports: Pittsburgh, Cincinnati, and Louisville on the Ohio; St. Louis and New Orleans on the Mississippi. Except for Pittsburgh, all were essentially commercial hubs rather than manufacturing centers and were flooded by individuals eager to make money. In 1819, land speculators in St. Louis were bidding as much as a thousand dollars an acre for lots that had sold for thirty dollars an acre in 1815. Waterfronts endowed with natural beauty were swiftly overrun by stores and docks.

The transportation revolution acted like a fickle god, selecting some cities for growth while sentencing others to relative decline. The completion of the Erie Canal shifted the center of western economic activity toward the Great Lakes. The result was a gradual decline in the importance of river cities such as Cincinnati and Louisville and a rise in the importance of lake cities such as Buffalo, Cleveland, Detroit, Chicago, and Milwaukee. In 1830, nearly 75 percent of all western city-dwellers lived in the river ports of New Orleans, Louisville, Cincinnati, and Pittsburgh; by 1840 the proportion had dropped to 20 percent.

INDUSTRIAL BEGINNINGS

Industrialization gave an added boost to the growth of cities and towns. The United States lagged a generation behind Britain in building factories. Eager to keep the lead, Britain banned the emigration of its skilled mechanics. Samuel Slater therefore passed himself off as a farm laborer to come to the United States in 1789 and help design and build the country's first cotton mill, at Pawtucket, Rhode Island, the following year. Slater's work force quickly grew from nine to one hundred, and his mills multiplied. From these beginnings, the pace of industrialization quickened in the 1810s and 1820s, especially in cotton textiles and shoes.

Industrialization varied widely from region to region. There was very little in the South, where planters preferred to invest in land and slaves rather than machines. In contrast, New England's poor soil stimulated investment in factories instead of agriculture. Industrialization itself was a gradual process, with several distinct components. It always involved the subdivision of tasks, with each worker now fabricating only a part of the final product. Often, but not always, it led to the gathering of workers in large factories. Finally, high-speed machines replaced skilled handwork. In some industries, these elements arrived simultaneously, but more often their timing was spread out over several years.

Industrialization changed lives. Most workers in the early factories were recruited from farms. On farms, men and women had worked hard from sunrise to sunset, but they had set their own pace and taken breaks after completing tasks. Factory workers, operating machines that ran continuously, encountered the new discipline of industrial time, regulated by clocks rather than tasks and signaled by the ringing of bells. Industrialization also changed the lives of those outside of factories by encouraging specialization. During the colonial era, most farm families had made their own clothes and often their shoes. With industrialization, they concentrated on farming, while purchasing factory-made clothes and shoes.

**Causes of
Industrialization**
A host of factors stimulated industrialization. Merchants barred from foreign trade by the Embargo Act of 1807 redirected their capital into factories. The Era of Good Feelings saw general agreement that the United States needed tariffs, and protected from foreign competition, New England's output of cloth spun from cotton rose from 4 million yards in 1817 to 323 million yards by 1840. America also possessed an environmental advantage in its many cascading rivers that flowed from the Appalachian Mountains to the Atlantic Ocean and provided abundant waterpower for mills. The transportation revolution gave manufacturers easier access to markets in the South and West.

Industrialization also sprang from tensions in the rural economy, especially in New England, where in the late eighteenth century population grew beyond the land available to support it. Farm families adopted new strategies to survive. For example, a farmer would decide to grow flax, which his wife and daughters would make into linen for sale; or he would choose to plant broomcorn (used for making broom whisks), and he and his sons would spend the winter months making brooms for local sale. In time, he would form a partnership with other broom makers to manufacture brooms on a larger scale and for more-distant markets. At some point, he would cease to be a farmer; instead, he would purchase his broomcorn from farmers and, with hired help, concentrate on manufacturing brooms. By now, he had built extensive contacts with merchants, who would provide him with broom handles and twine and purchase and sell all the brooms he could make.

The comparatively high wages paid unskilled laborers in the United States spurred the search for labor-saving machines. Britain had a head start in developing the technology relevant to industrialization, and in some instances, Americans simply copied British designs. Ostensibly on vacation, a wealthy Boston merchant, Francis Cabot Lowell, used his visit to England in 1811 to charm information about British textile machinery out of his hosts; later he engaged an American mechanic to construct machines from drawings he had made each night in his hotel room. The United States also benefited from the fact that, unlike Britain, America had no craft organizations (called guilds) that tied artisans to a single trade. As a result, American artisans freely experimented with machines outside their crafts. In the 1790s, Oliver Evans, a wagon-maker from Delaware, built an automated flour mill that required only a single supervisor to watch as the grain poured in on one side and was discharged from the other as flour.

Even in the absence of new technology, Americans searched for new methods of production to cut costs. After inventing the cotton gin, **Eli Whitney** won a government contract in 1798 to produce ten thousand muskets by 1800. Whitney's idea was to meet this seemingly impossible deadline by using unskilled workers to make interchangeable parts that could be used in any of his factory's muskets. Whitney promised much more than he could deliver (as discussed in Chapter 11), and he missed his deadline by nearly a decade. But his idea captured the imagination of prominent Americans, including Thomas Jefferson.

**Textile Towns in
New England**
New England became America's first industrial region. The trade wars leading up to the War of 1812 had devastated its commercial economy and stimulated capital investment in

manufacturing. The region's swift rivers were ideal sources of waterpower for mills. The westward migration of many of New England's young men left a surplus of young women, who supplied cheap industrial labor.

Cotton textiles led the way. In 1813, a group of Boston merchants, known as the Boston Associates and including Francis Cabot Lowell, incorporated the Boston Manufacturing Company. With ten times the capital of any previous American cotton mill, this company quickly built textile mills in the Massachusetts towns of Waltham and Lowell. By 1836, the Boston Associates controlled eight companies employing more than six thousand workers.

The **Waltham and Lowell textile mills** differed in two ways from the earlier Rhode Island mills established by Samuel Slater. Slater's mills performed only two of the operations needed to turn raw cotton into clothing: carding (separating batches of cotton into fine strands) and spinning these strands into yarn. In what was essentially cottage manufacturing, he contracted the weaving to women working in their homes. Unlike Slater's mills, the Waltham and Lowell mills turned out finished fabrics that required only one additional step, stitching into clothes. In addition, the Waltham and Lowell mills upset the traditional order of New England society. Slater had sought to preserve tradition not only by contracting weaving to farm families but also by hiring entire families for carding and spinning in his mill complexes. Men raised crops on nearby company lands, while women and children

Mill Girl Around 1850

This girl mostly likely worked in a Massachusetts textile mill, at either Lowell or Waltham. Her swollen and rough hands suggest that she was a "warper," one of the jobs usually given to children. Warpers were responsible for constantly straightening out the strands of cotton or wool as they entered the loom.

(Jack Naylor Collection/Picture Research Consultants and Archives)

tended the machines inside. In contrast, 80 percent of the workers in Waltham and Lowell, places that had not even existed in the eighteenth century, were young unmarried women who had been lured from farms by the promise of wages. Mary Paul, a Vermont teenager, settled her doubts about leaving home for Lowell by concluding that "I ... must work where I can get more pay."

In place of traditional family discipline, the workers ("operatives") experienced new restraints. They had to live either in company boardinghouses or in licensed private dwellings, attend church on the Sabbath, observe a 10:00 P.M. curfew, and accept the company's "moral police." Regulations were designed to give the mills a good reputation so that New England farm daughters would continue to be attracted to factory work.

Mill conditions were far from attractive. To provide the humidity necessary to keep the threads from snapping, overseers nailed factory windows shut and sprayed the air with water. Operatives also had to contend with flying dust and the deafening roar of the machines. Keener competition and a worsening economy in the late 1830s led mill owners to reduce wages and speed up work schedules. The system's impersonality intensified the harshness of the work environment.

Each of the major groups that contributed to the system lived in a self-contained world. The Boston Associates raised capital but rarely visited the factories. Their agents, all men, gave orders to the operatives, mainly women. Some eight hundred Lowell mill women quit work in 1834 to protest a wage reduction. Two years later, there another "turnout" involved fifteen hundred to two thousand women. These were the largest strikes in American history to that date, noteworthy as strikes not only of employees against employers but also of women against men.

The Waltham and Lowell mills were much larger than most factories; as late as 1860, the average industrial establishment employed only eight workers. Outside of textiles, many industries continued to depend on industrial **"outwork."** For example, more than fifty thousand New England farmwomen earned wages in their homes during the 1830s by making hats out of straw and palm leaves provided by merchants. Similarly, before the introduction of the sewing machine led to the concentration of all aspects of shoe manufacture in large factories in the 1850s, women often sewed parts of shoes at home and sent the piecework to factories for finishing.

Artisans and Workers in Mid-Atlantic Cities   New York City and Philadelphia also became industrial centers dependent on outwork. Lured by the prospect of distant markets, some urban artisans and merchants started to scour the country for orders for consumer goods. They hired unskilled workers, often women, to work in small shops or homes fashioning parts of shoes or saddles or dresses. A New York reporter wrote,

> We have been in some fifty cellars in different parts of the city, each inhabited by a shoemaker and his family. The floor is made of rough plank laid loosely down, and the ceiling is not quite so high as a tall man. The walls are dark and damp and ... the miserable room is lighted only by ... the little light that struggles from the steep and rotting stairs. In this apartment often lives the man and his work-bench, the wife, and five or six children of all ages; and perhaps a palsied grandfather or grandmother and often both.... Here they work, here they cook, they eat, they sleep, they pray.

New York and Philadelphia were home to artisans with proud craft traditions and independence. Those with highly marketable skills like cutting leather or clothing patterns continued to earn good wages. Others grew rich by turning themselves into businessmen who spent less time making products than making trips to obtain orders. But artisans lacking the capital to become businessmen found themselves on the downslide in the face of competition from cheap, unskilled labor.

In the late 1820s, skilled male artisans in New York, Philadelphia, and other cities began to form trade unions and workingmen's political parties to protect their interests. Disdaining association with unskilled workers, most of these groups initially sought to restore privileges and working conditions that artisans had once enjoyed rather than to act as leaders of unskilled workers. But the steady deterioration of working conditions in the early 1830s tended to throw skilled and unskilled workers into the same boat. When coal haulers in Philadelphia struck for a ten-hour day in 1835, they were quickly joined by carpenters, cigar makers, shoemakers, leather workers, and other artisans in the United States' first general strike. With so many workers facing a declining economic position by the 1830s, many white Americans wondered whether their nation was truly a land of equality.

EQUALITY AND INEQUALITY

That one (white) man was as good as another became the national creed in antebellum America. For example, servants insisted on being viewed as neighbors invited to assist in running the household rather than as permanent subordinates. Merchants, held in disdain in Europe by the nobility, refused in America to bow to anyone. Politicians never lost an opportunity to celebrate artisans and farmers as the equal of lawyers and bankers. A French visitor observed that the wealthiest Americans pretended to respect equality by riding in public in ordinary rather than luxurious carriages.

The market and transportation revolutions, however, were placing new pressure on the ideal of equality between 1815 and 1840. At the same time that improved transportation enabled some eastern farmers to migrate to the richer soils of the West, it became difficult for those left behind to compete with the cheaper grain carried east by canals and railroads. Many eastern farmers now had to move to cities to take whatever work they could find, often as casual day laborers on the docks or in small workshops.

Urban Inequality: The Rich and the Poor
The gap between the rich and poor widened in the first half of the nineteenth century. In cities, a small fraction of the people owned a huge share of the wealth. For example, in New York City, the richest 4 percent owned nearly half the wealth in 1828 and more than two-thirds by 1845. Splendid residences and social clubs set the rich apart. In 1828, over half of the five hundred wealthiest families in New York City lived on just eight of its more than 250 streets. By the late 1820s, the city had a club so exclusive that it was called simply The Club.

Although commentators celebrated the self-made man's rise from "rags to riches," few actually fit this pattern. Less than 5 percent of the wealthy had started life poor; almost 90 percent of well-off people had been born rich. The usual way to wealth was to inherit it, marry into more, and then invest wisely. Occasional rags-to-riches stories like that of John Jacob Astor and his fur-trading empire sustained the myth, but it was mainly a myth.

At the opposite end of the social ladder were the poor. By today's standards, most antebellum Americans were poor. They lived close to the edge of misery and depended heavily on their children's labor to meet expenses. For example, Harriet Hanson Robinson's widowed mother ran a boarding house in Lowell where she shopped, cooked, and did the laundry for forty-five people each day; before entering the mills, Harriet washed the dishes. But when antebellum Americans spoke of poverty, they were not thinking of the hardships that affected most people. Instead, they were referring to "pauperism," a state of dependency or inability to fend for oneself that affected some people. Epidemics of yellow fever and cholera could devastate families. A frozen canal, river, or harbor spelled unemployment for boatmen and dock workers, and for workers in factories that depended on waterpower. The absence of health insurance and old-age pensions condemned many infirm and aged people to pauperism.

Contemporaries usually classified all such people as the "deserving" poor and contrasted them with the "undeserving" poor, such as indolent loafers and drunkards whose poverty was seen as self-willed. Most moralists assumed that since pauperism resulted either from circumstances beyond anyone's control, such as old age and disease, or from voluntary decisions to squander money on liquor, it would not pass from generation to generation.

This assumption was comforting but also misleading. A class of people who could not escape poverty was emerging in the major cities during the first half of the nineteenth century. One source was immigration. As early as 1801, a New York newspaper called attention to the arrival of boatloads of immigrants with large families, without money or health, and "expiring from the want of sustenance."

The poorest white immigrants were from Ireland, where English landlords had evicted peasants from the land and converted it to commercial use in the eighteenth century. Severed from the land, the Irish increasingly became a nation of wanderers, scrounging for wages wherever they could. "The poor Irishman," it was said, "the wheelbarrow is his country." By the early 1830s, the great majority of canal workers in the North were Irish immigrants. Without the backbreaking labor of the Irish, the Erie Canal would never have been built. Other Irish congregated in New York's infamous Five Points district. Starting with the conversion of a brewery into housing for hundreds of people in 1837, Five Points became the worst slum in America.

The Irish were not only poor but were also Catholics, a faith despised by the Protestant majority in the United States. In short, they were different and had little claim on the kindly impulses of most Protestants. But even the Protestant poor came in for rough treatment in the years between 1815 and 1840. The more that Americans convinced themselves that success was within everyone's grasp, the less they accepted the traditional doctrine that poverty was ordained by God, and the more they were inclined to hold the poor responsible for their own misery. Ironically, even as many Americans blamed the poor for being poor, they practiced discrimination that kept some groups mired in enduring poverty. Nowhere was this more true than in the case of northern free blacks.

Free Blacks in the North

Prejudice against blacks was deeply ingrained in white society throughout the nation. Although slavery had largely disappeared in the North by 1820, laws restricted black voting rights. In New York State, for example, a constitutional revision of 1821 eliminated property requirements for white voters but kept them for blacks. Rhode Island banned blacks from voting in 1822; Pennsylvania did the same in 1837. Throughout the half-century after 1800, blacks could vote on equal terms with whites in only one of the nation's major cities, Boston.

Laws frequently barred free blacks from migrating to other states and cities. Missouri's original constitution authorized the state legislature to prevent blacks from entering the state "under any pretext whatsoever." Municipal ordinances often barred free blacks from public conveyances and facilities and either excluded them from public schools or forced them into segregated schools. Segregation was the rule in northern jails, almshouses, and hospitals.

Of all restrictions on free blacks, the most damaging was the social pressure that forced them into the least-skilled and lowest-paying occupations throughout the northern cities. Recollecting his youthful days in Providence, Rhode Island, in the early 1830s, the free black William J. Brown wrote: "To drive carriages, carry a market basket after the boss, and brush his boots, or saw wood and run errands was as high as a colored man could rise." Although a few free blacks became successful entrepreneurs and grew moderately wealthy, urban free blacks were only half as likely as city-dwellers in general to own real estate.

One important black response to discrimination was to establish their own churches. White churches confined blacks to separate benches or galleries. When black worshipers mistakenly sat in a gallery designated for whites at a Methodist church in Philadelphia, they were ejected from the church. Their leader, former slave and future bishop **Richard Allen,** related, "we all went out of the church in a body, and they were no longer plagued by us." Allen initiated the organization of the **African Methodist Episcopal Church,** the first black-run Protestant denomination, in 1816. By 1822, the A.M.E. Church had active congregations in Washington, D.C., Pittsburgh, New York City, and throughout the mid-Atlantic states. Its members campaigned against slavery, in part by refusing to purchase produce grown by slaves.

Just as northern African-Americans formed their own churches, free blacks gradually acquired some control over the education of their children. The 1820s and 1830s witnessed an explosion of black self-help societies like New York City's Phoenixonian Literary Society, devoted to encouraging black education and run by such black leaders as Samuel Cornish and Henry Garnett.

The "Middling Classes"

The majority of antebellum Americans lived neither in splendid wealth nor in grinding poverty. Most belonged to what men and women of the time called the middling classes. Even though the rich owned an increasing proportion of all wealth, most people's standard of living rose between 1800 and 1860, particularly between 1840 and 1860 when per capita income grew at an annual rate of around 1.5 percent.

Americans applied the term *middling classes* to families headed by professionals, small merchants and manufacturers, landowning farmers, and self-employed artisans. Commentators portrayed these people as living stable and secure lives. In reality, life in the middle often was unpredictable. The increasingly commercial economy of antebellum America created greater opportunities for success and for failure. An enterprising import merchant, Alan Melville, the father of novelist Herman Melville, did well until the late 1820s, when his business sagged. By 1830, he was "destitute of resources and without a shilling." Despite loans of $3500, Melville's downward spiral continued. In 1832 he died, broken in spirit and nearly insane.

In the emerging market economy, even such seemingly crisp occupational descriptions as farmer and artisan often proved misleading. Asa G. Sheldon, born in Massachusetts in 1788, described himself in his autobiography as a farmer, offered advice on growing corn and cranberries, and gave speeches about the glories of farming. Although Sheldon undoubtedly knew a great deal about farming, he actually spent very little time tilling the soil. In 1812, he began to transport hops from New England to brewers in New York City, and he soon extended this business to Philadelphia and Baltimore. He invested his profits in land, but rather than farm the land, he made money selling its timber. When a business setback forced him to sell his property, he was soon back in operation "through the disinterested kindness of friends" who lent him money with which he purchased carts and oxen. These he used to get contracts for filling in swamps in Boston and for clearing and grading land for railroads. From all this and from the backbreaking labor of the Irish immigrants he hired to do the shoveling, Sheldon the "farmer" grew prosperous.

The emerging market economy also transformed the lives of artisans. During the colonial period, artisans had formed a proud and cohesive group whose members often attained the goal of self-employment. They owned their own tools, made their own products on order from customers, and boarded their apprentices and journeymen in their homes. By 1840, in contrast, artisans had entered a new world of economic relationships. This was true even of crafts like carpentry that did not experience any industrial or technological change. Town and city growth in the wake of the transportation revolution created a demand for housing. Some carpenters, usually those with access to capital, became contractors. They took orders for more houses than they could build themselves and hired large numbers of journeymen to do the construction work. Likewise, some shoemakers spent less time crafting shoes than making trips to obtain orders, then hired workers to fashion parts of shoes. In effect, the old class of artisans was splitting into two new groupings. On one side were artisans who had become entrepreneurs; on the other, journeymen with little prospect of self-employment.

An additional characteristic of the middling classes, one they shared with the poor, was a high degree of transience, or spatial mobility. The transportation revolution made it easier for Americans to purchase services as well as goods and spurred many young men to abandon farming for the professions. For example, the number of medical schools rose from one in 1765 to twenty in 1830 and sixty-five in 1860. Frequently, the new men who crowded into medicine and into the ministry and law were forced into incessant motion. Physicians rode from town to town looking for patients. The itinerant clergyman riding an old nag to visit the faithful or conduct revivals became a familiar figure in newly settled areas. Even well-established lawyers and judges spent part of each year riding from one county courthouse to another, bunking (usually two to a bed) in rough country inns.

Transience affected the lives of most Americans. Farmers exhausted their land by intensively cultivating cash crops and then moved on. City dwellers moved frequently as they changed jobs—public transportation lagged far behind the spread of cities. A survey by the Boston police on Saturday, September 6, 1851, when Boston's population was 145,000, showed that from 6:30 A.M. to 7:30 P.M., 41,729 people entered the city and 42,313 left. At a time when there were few suburbs, it is safe to say that these people were not commuters. Most likely, they were moving in search of work, as much a necessity for many in the middling classes as for the poor.

THE REVOLUTION IN SOCIAL RELATIONSHIPS

Following the War of 1812, the growth of interregional trade, commercial agriculture, and manufacturing disrupted traditional social relationships and forged new ones. Two broad changes took place. First, more Americans questioned authority, even that of their parents, and embraced individualism; once the term had meant nothing more than selfishness, but now it connoted positive qualities such as self-reliance and the ability of each person to judge his or her own best interests. Ordinary Americans might still agree with the opinions of their leaders, but only after they had thought matters through on their own. Those with superior wealth, education, or social position could no longer expect the automatic deference of the common people.

Second, even as Americans widely proclaimed themselves a nation of self-reliant individualists and questioned the traditional basis of authority, they sought to construct new foundations for authority. For example, middle-class men and women came to embrace the idea that women possessed a "separate sphere" of authority in the home. In addition, individuals increasingly joined with others in these years to form voluntary associations to influence the direction of society.

The Attack on the Professions   Intense criticism of lawyers, physicians, and ministers exemplified the assault on traditional authority. As a writer put it in 1836, "Everywhere the disposition is found among those who live in the valleys to ask those who live on the hills, 'How came we here and you there?'"

Some complained that lawyers needlessly prolonged and confused court cases so that they could charge high fees. Between 1800 and 1840, during a wave of religious revivals known as the Second Great Awakening (covered in Chapter 10), some revivalists blasted the clergy for creating complicated theologies that ordinary men and women could not comprehend, for drinking expensive wines, and for fleecing the people. One religious revivalist, Elias Smith, extended the criticism to physicians, whom he accused of inventing Latin and Greek names for diseases to disguise their own ignorance of how to cure them.

These jabs at the learned professions peaked between 1820 and 1850. Samuel Thomson, a farmer's son with little formal education, led a successful movement to eliminate all barriers to entry into the medical profession, including educational requirements. By 1845, every state had repealed laws that required licenses and education to practice medicine. Meanwhile, relations between ministers and their parishioners grew tense and acrimonious. In colonial New England, ministers had usually served a single parish for life, but by the 1830s a rapid turnover of ministers was becoming the norm as finicky parishioners commonly dismissed clergymen whose theology displeased them. Ministers themselves were becoming more ambitious—more inclined to leave small, poor congregations for large, wealthy ones.

The increasing commercialization of the economy led to both more professionals and more attacks on them. The newly minted lawyers and doctors had neither deep roots in the towns they served nor convincing claims to social superiority. "Men dropped down into their places as from clouds," one critic wrote. "Nobody knew who or what they were, except as they claimed." A horse doctor one day would the next day hang up his sign as "Physician and Surgeon" and "fire at random a box of his pills into your bowels, with a vague chance of hitting some disease unknown to him, but with a better prospect of killing the patient, whom or whose administrator he charged some ten dollars a trial for his marksmanship."

The questioning of authority was particularly sharp on the frontier. Easterners sneered that every man they met was a "judge," "general," "colonel," or "squire." In a society in which everyone was new, such titles were easily adopted and just as easily challenged. Where neither law nor custom sanctioned claims of superiority, would-be gentlemen substituted an exaggerated sense of personal honor. Obsessed with their fragile status, many reacted testily to the slightest insult. Dueling became a widespread frontier practice. At a Kentucky militia parade in 1819, an officer's dog jogged onto the field and sat at his master's knee. Enraged by this breach of military decorum, another officer ran the dog through with his sword. A week later, both officers met with pistols at ten paces. One was killed; the other maimed for life.

The Challenge to Family Authority   In contrast to adults' public philosophical attacks on the learned professions, children engaged in a quiet questioning of parental authority. The era's economic change forced young people to choose between staying at home to help their parents or venturing out on their own. Writing to her parents in Vermont shortly before taking a job in a Lowell textile mill, eighteen-year-old Sally Rice quickly got to the point. "I must of course have something of my own before many more years have passed over my head and where is that something coming from if I go home and earn nothing. I have but one life to live and I want to enjoy myself as I can while I live."

A similar desire for independence tempted young men to leave home at earlier ages than in the past. Although the great migration to the West was primarily a movement of entire families, movement from farms to towns and cities within regions was frequently spearheaded by restless and single young people. Two young men in Virginia put it succinctly. "All the promise of life seemed to us to be at the other end of the rainbow—somewhere else—anywhere else but on the farm .... And so all our youthful plans had as their chief object the getting away from the farm."

Courtship and marriage patterns also changed. Many young people who no longer depended on their parents for land insisted on privacy in courting and wanted to decide for themselves when and whom to marry. Whereas seventeenth-century Puritans had advised young people to choose marriage partners whom they could learn to love, by the early 1800s young men and women viewed romantic love as indispensable to a successful marriage. "In affairs of love," a young lawyer in

Maine wrote, "young people's hearts are generally much wiser than old people's heads."

One sign of young people's growing control over courtship and marriage was the declining likelihood that the young women of a family would marry in their exact birth order. Traditionally, fathers had wanted their daughters to marry in the order of their birth to avoid planting the suspicion that something was wrong with one or more of them. Toward the end of the eighteenth century, however, daughters were making their own marital decisions, and the practice ceased to be customary. Another mark of the times was the growing number of long engagements. Having made the decision to marry, some young women were reluctant to tie the knot, fearing that marriage would snuff out their independence. For example, New Yorkers Caroline and William Kirkland were engaged for seven years before their marriage in 1828. Equally striking was the increasing number of young women who chose not to marry. **Catharine Beecher,** a leading author and the daughter of the prominent minister Lyman Beecher, broke off her engagement to a young man during the 1820s despite her father's pressure to marry him. She later renewed the engagement, but after her fiancé's death in a shipwreck, she remained single for the rest of her life.

Signs that young people were living in a world of their own alarmed moralists, who flooded the country with books of advice stressing the same message: newly independent young people should develop self-control and "character." The self-made adult began with the self-made youth.

Wives and Husbands	Relations between spouses, too, were changing. Young men and women who had grown accustomed to making decisions on their own as teenagers were more likely than their ances-

tors to approach wedlock as a compact between equals. Of course, wives remained unequal to their husbands in many ways. With few exceptions, the law did not allow married women to own property. But relations between wives and husbands were changing during the 1820s and 1830s toward a form of equality.

One source of the change, zealously advocated by Catharine Beecher, lay in the doctrine of **separate spheres.** Traditionally, women had been viewed as subordinate to men in all spheres of life. Now middle-class men and women developed a kind of separate-but-equal doctrine that portrayed men as superior in making money and governing the world, and women as superior for their moral influence on family members.

One of the most important duties assigned to the sphere of women was raising children. During the eighteenth century, church sermons reminded fathers of their duty to govern the family; by the 1830s, child-rearing manuals were addressed to mothers rather than fathers. "How entire and perfect is this dominion over the un-formed character of your infant," the popular writer Lydia Sigourney proclaimed in her *Letters to Mothers* (1838). Advice books instructed mothers to discipline their children by loving them and withdrawing affection when they misbehaved rather than by using corporal punishment. A whipped child might become more obedient but would remain sullen and bitter; gentler methods would penetrate the child's heart, making the child want to do the right thing.

The idea of a separate women's sphere blended with a related image of the family and home as refuges secluded from a society marked by commotion and disorder. The popular culture of the 1830s and 1840s painted an alluring portrait of the pleasures of home life through songs like "Home, Sweet Home" and poems such as Henry Wadsworth Longfellow's "The Children's Hour" and Clement Moore's "A Visit from St. Nicholas." The publication of Moore's poem coincided with the growing popularity of Christmas as a holiday season in which family members gathered to exchange warm affection. Even the physical appearance of houses changed. The prominent architect Andrew Jackson Downing published plans for peaceful single-family homes that he hoped would offset the "spirit of unrest" and the feverish pace of American life. He wrote of the ideal home, "There should be something to love. There must be nooks about it, where one would love to linger; windows, where one can enjoy the quiet landscape at his leisure; cozy rooms, where all fireside joys are invited to dwell."

Downing deserves high marks as a prophet, because one of the motives that impelled many Americans to flee cities for suburbs in the twentieth century was the desire to own their own homes. In the 1820s and 1830s, this ideal was beyond the reach of most people—not only blacks, immigrants, and sweatshop workers, but also most members of the middle class. In the countryside, although middle-class farmers still managed productive households, these were anything but tranquil; wives milked cows and bled hogs, and children fetched wood, drove cows to pasture, and chased blackbirds from cornfields. In the cities, middle-class families often had to sacrifice their privacy by taking in boarders to supplement family income.

Despite their distortions, the doctrine of separate spheres and the image of the home as a refuge intersected with reality at some points. The rising number of urban families headed by lawyers and merchants (who worked away from home) gave mothers time to spend on child rearing. Above all, married women found that they could capitalize on these notions to gain new power within their families. A subtle implication of the doctrine of separate spheres was that women should have control not only over the discipline of children but also over the more fundamental issue of how many children they would bear.

In 1800, the United States had one of the highest birthrates ever recorded. The average American woman bore 7.04 children. It is safe to say that married women had become pregnant as often as possible. In the prevailing farm economy, children carried out essential tasks and, as time passed, took care of their aging parents. Most parents had assumed that the more children, the better. The spread of a commercial economy raised troublesome questions about children's economic value. Unlike a farmer, a merchant or lawyer could not put his children to work at the age of seven or eight. The average woman was bearing only 5.02 children by 1850, and 3.98 by 1900. The birthrate remained high among blacks and many immigrant groups, but it fell drastically among native-born whites, particularly in towns and cities.

For the most part, the decline in the birthrate was accomplished by abstinence from sexual intercourse, by *coitus interruptus* (withdrawal before ejaculation), or by abortion. By the 1840s, abortionists advertised remedies for "female irregularities," a common euphemism for unwanted pregnancies. There were no foolproof birth-control devices, and as much misinformation as information circulated about techniques of birth control. Nonetheless, interest in birth-control devices was intensifying. In 1832, Charles Knowlton, a Massachusetts physician, described the procedure for vaginal douching in his book *Fruits of Philosophy*. Although Knowlton was frequently prosecuted and once

(Courtesy Childs Gallery, Boston)

The Country Parson Disturbed at Breakfast *This young couple's decision to wed seems to have been on the spur of the moment. As young men and women became more independent of parental control, they gave their impulses freer play.*

jailed for obscenity, efforts to suppress his ideas publicized them even more. By 1865, popular tracts had familiarized Americans with a wide range of birth-control methods, including the condom and the diaphragm. The decision to limit family size was usually reached jointly by wives and husbands. Economic and ideological considerations blended together. Husbands could note that the economic value of children was declining; wives, that having fewer children would give them more time to nurture each one and thereby carry out domestic duties.

Supporters of the ideal of separate spheres did not advocate full legal equality for women. Indeed, the idea of separate spheres was an explicit alternative to legal equality. But in addition to enhancing women's power within marriage, it allowed some women a measure of independence from the home. For example, it sanctioned the travels of Catharine Beecher, a leading advocate of separate spheres, to lecture women on better ways to raise children and manage their households.

Horizontal Allegiances and the Rise of Voluntary Associations

As some forms of authority were weakening, Americans devised new ways for individuals to extend their influence over others. The pre-Civil War period witnessed the widespread substitution of **horizontal allegiances** for **vertical allegiances**. In vertical allegiances, authority flows from the top down. Subordinates identify their interests with those of their superiors rather than with others in the same subordinate role. The traditional

Tocqueville on American Democracy

In 1831, Alexis de Tocqueville, a twenty-five-year-old French aristocrat, arrived in the United States. Officially, Tocqueville and his traveling companion, Gustave de Beaumont, came to study American prisons. But Tocqueville's real interest lay in investigating American "democracy;" his two-volume *Democracy in America* (1835, 1840) is widely considered the keenest analysis of the United States ever written by a foreigner.

Tocqueville associated democracy with government by the people and an increasing "equality of condition." Constant political turmoil battered progress toward equality in Europe. In contrast, the United States, founded as a republic, had enjoyed a half-century of political stability; no one was proposing to change its form of government.

Tocqueville knew that some white Americans were rich and others poor, and that many blacks were enslaved. Still, there was more equality of condition in America than in France. Above all, American citizens *thought* they were equal to each other. They were unaccustomed to giving, or taking, orders. That these people could build so many roads, canals, factories, model towns, churches, schools, and whatnot, Tocqueville believed, was because of their penchant for "public associations in civil life."

Americans of all ages, all conditions, and all dispositions constantly form associations. They have not only commercial and manufacturing companies, in which all take part, but associations of a thousand other kinds, religious, moral, serious, futile, general or restricted, enormous or diminutive. The Americans make associations to give entertainments, to found seminaries, to build inns, to construct churches, to diffuse books, to send missionaries to the antipodes; in this manner, they found hospitals, prisons, and schools. If it is proposed to inculcate some truth or to foster some feeling by the encouragement of a great example, they form a society. Wherever at the head of some new undertaking you see the government in France or a man of rank in England, in the United States you

---

patriarchal family was an example of a vertical allegiance: the wife and children looked up to the father for leadership. Another example occurred in the small eighteenth-century workshop, where apprentices and journeymen took direction from the master craftsman and even lived in the craftsman's house, subject to his authority.

Although vertical relationships did not disappear, they became less important in people's lives. Increasingly, relationships were more likely to be marked by horizontal allegiances that linked those in a similar position. For example, in large textile mills, operatives discovered they had more in common with one another than with their managers and overseers. Similarly, married women formed maternal associations to exchange advice about child rearing. Young men formed debating societies to sharpen their wits and to bring themselves to the attention of influential older men. Maternal and debating societies exemplified the American zeal for **voluntary associations**—associations that arose apart from government and sought to accomplish some goal of value to their members. **Alexis de Tocqueville,**

will be sure to find an association .... The English often perform great things singly, whereas the Americans form associations for the smallest undertakings. It is evident that the former people consider association as a powerful means they have of acting....

Aristocratic communities always contain, among a multitude of persons who by themselves are powerless, a small number of powerful and wealthy citizens, each of whom can achieve great undertakings single-handed. In aristocratic societies, men do not need to combine in order to act, because they are strong held together. Every wealthy and powerful citizen constitutes the head of a permanent and compulsory association, composed of all those who are dependent on him or whom he makes subservient to the execution of his designs.

Among democratic nations, on the contrary, all the citizens are independent and feeble; they can hardly do anything by themselves, and none of them can oblige his fellow men to lend him their assistance. They all, therefore, become powerless if they do not learn voluntarily to help one another. If men living in democratic countries had no right and no inclination to associate for political purposes, their independence would be in great jeopardy, but they might long preserve their wealth and their cultivation: whereas if they never acquired the habit of forming associations in ordinary life, civilization itself would be endangered. A people among whom individuals lost the power of achieving great things single-handed, without acquiring the means of producing them by united exertions, would soon relapse into barbarism.

Source: Alexis de Tocqueville, Democracy in America [1840] (vol. 2, New York, Vintage, 1972), 106–107.

Questions

1. *List some examples from this chapter of the sort of organizations that Tocqueville would have viewed as "public associations in civil life."*
2. *What did Tocqueville mean when he said that in democratic nations all citizens are "independent and feeble?"*

Go to www.cengagebrain.com for additional primary sources on this period.

a brilliant French observer, described them as "public associations in civil life" (see Going to the Source).

Voluntary associations encouraged sociability. As transients and newcomers flocked into towns and cities, they tended to join others with similar characteristics, experiences, or interests. Gender was the basis of many voluntary societies. Of twenty-six religious and charitable associations in Utica, New York, in 1832, for instance, one-third were exclusively for women. Race was still another basis for voluntary associations. Although their names did not indicate it, Boston's Thompson Literary and Debating Society and its Philomathean Adelphic Union for the Promotion of Literature and Science were organizations for free blacks.

Voluntary associations also enhanced their members' public influence. At a time when state legislatures had little interest in regulating the sale of alcoholic beverages, men and women joined in temperance societies to promote voluntary abstinence. To combat prostitution, women formed moral-reform societies, which sought to shame men into chastity by publishing the names of brothel patrons in newspapers. Aiming to suppress an ancient vice, moral-reform societies also tended to enhance women's power over men. Just as strikes in Lowell in the 1830s were a form of collective action by working women, moral-reform societies represented collective action by middle-class women to increase their influence in society. Here, as elsewhere, the tendency of the times was to forge new forms of horizontal allegiance between like-minded Americans.

CHRONOLOGY
1815–1840

1790	Samuel Slater opens his first Rhode Island mill for the production of cotton yarn.
1793	Eli Whitney invents the cotton gin.
1807	Robert R. Livingston and Robert Fulton introduce the steamboat *Clermont* on the Hudson River.
1811	Construction of the National Road begins at Cumberland, Maryland.
1813	Incorporation of the Boston Manufacturing Company.
1816	Second Bank of the United States chartered.
1817–1825	Construction of the Erie Canal started. Mississippi enters the Union.
1819	Economic panic, ushering in four-year depression. Alabama enters the Union.
1820–1850	Growth of female moral-reform societies.
1820s	Expansion of New England textile mills.
1824	*Gibbons* v. *Ogden.*
1828	Baltimore and Ohio Railroad chartered.
1830	Indian Removal Act passed by Congress.
1831	*Cherokee Nation* v. *Georgia.* Alexis de Tocqueville begins visit to the United States to study American penitentiaries.
1832	*Worcester* v. *Georgia.*
1834	First strike at the Lowell mills.
1835	Treaty of New Echota.
1837	Economic panic begins a depression that lasts until 1843.
1838	The Trail of Tears.
1840	System of production by interchangeable parts perfected.

Conclusion

European demand for American cotton and other agricultural products, federal policies that eased the sale of public lands and encouraged the removal of Indians from the path of white settlement, and the availability of loose-lending banks and paper money all contributed to the flow of population into the area between the Appalachians and the Mississippi River after 1815. The collapse of the boom in 1819 reminded farmers of how dependent they had become on distant markets and prompted improvements in transportation during the 1820s and 1830s. The introduction of steamboats, the building of canals, and the gradual spread of railroads— the transportation revolution—encouraged a turn to commercial occupations and the growth of towns and cities. Now able to reach distant consumers, merchants plunged capital into manufacturing enterprises. Ranging from the great textile mills of Lowell and Waltham to rural cottages that performed outwork to urban sweatshops, early industrialization laid the foundations for America's emergence a half-century later as a major industrial power.

The changes associated with the market economy and early industrialization carved new avenues to prosperity for some—and to penury for others. They challenged traditional hierarchies and created new forms of social alignment based on voluntary associations. By joining voluntary associations based on shared interests or opinions, footloose Americans forged new identities that paralleled and often supplanted older allegiances to their parents or places of birth.

10

Democratic Politics, Religious Revival, and Reform, 1824–1840

THE RISE OF DEMOCRATIC POLITICS, 1824–1832

In 1824, Andrew Jackson and Martin Van Buren, who would guide the Democratic Party in the 1830s, and Henry Clay and John Quincy Adams, who would become that decade's leading Whigs, all belonged to the Republican Party of Thomas Jefferson. But the Republican Party was coming apart under pressures generated by industrialization in New England, the spread of cotton cultivation in the South, and westward expansion. These forces would split Jefferson's Party into two new parties. In general, Republicans who retained Jefferson's preference for states' rights became Democrats; Republicans who believed that the national government should actively encourage economic development, the so-called National Republicans, became Whigs.

Whatever their differences, all politicians in the 1820s and 1830s had to adapt to the increasingly democratic view of politics as a forum for expressing the will of the common people. Gentlemen could still be elected to office, but their political success now depended less on their education and wealth than on their ability to win the battle over public opinion.

Democratic Ferment   **Political democratization** took several forms. Beginning in the West, one state after another abolished the requirement that voters own property. Written ballots replaced the custom of voting aloud, which had enabled elites to influence their subordinates at the polls. Formerly appointive offices became elective. Though the Electoral College survived, the choice of presidential electors by state legislatures gave way to direct election by the voters. In 1800, a supporter of Thomas Jefferson could only vote for the men who would vote for the men who would vote for Jefferson. By 1824, however, only six state legislatures continued to choose presidential electors, and by 1832, only one.

The fierce battles between the Republicans and the Federalists beginning in the 1790s had taught both parties how to court voters. At grand party-run barbecues from Maine to Maryland, potential voters happily washed down free clams and oysters with free beer and whiskey. Republicans sought to expand suffrage in the North, and Federalists did the same in the South, each in the hope of becoming the majority party in that section. Democratization was also advanced by the transportation and communications revolutions that enabled the creation of a politically informed public.

Political democratization had its limitations. In 1820, both Federalists and Republicans were still organized from the top down. To nominate candidates, both parties relied on the caucus (a conference of party members in the legislature) rather than on popularly elected nominating conventions. Women and free blacks remained disfranchised. Nevertheless, open opposition to the "common people" (meaning adult white males) was becoming a formula for political suicide. The people, one Federalist complained, "have become too saucy and are really beginning to fancy themselves equal to their betters."

The Election of 1824 and the Adams Presidency

In 1824, sectional tensions ended the Era of Good Feelings when five Republican candidates vied for the presidency. John Quincy Adams emerged as New England's favorite. South Carolina's brilliant John C. Calhoun competed with Georgia's William Crawford for southern support. Out of the West marched the ambitious **Henry Clay** of Kentucky, confident that his American System of protective tariffs and federally supported internal improvements would win votes from both eastern manufacturing interests and western agriculturalists.

The fifth candidate was Andrew Jackson of Tennessee. Already popular on the frontier and in the South, he quickly won support from opponents of the American System in Pennsylvania and northern states. As the only presidential candidate in the election of 1824 not linked to the Monroe administration, Jackson had gained popularity after the Panic of 1819, which, as Calhoun commented, had left people with "a general mass of disaffection to the Government" and "looking out anywhere for a leader." To Thomas Jefferson, however, Jackson was "one of the most unfit men I know of for such a place" as the presidency.

When the Republican caucus met, three-fourths of Congressional Republicans refused to attend, and Crawford was selected as presidential candidate. But his weak prospects evaporated when he suffered a paralyzing stroke. Calhoun assessed Jackson's support and prudently decided to run unopposed for the vice presidency.

In the election, Jackson won more popular and electoral votes than any other candidate but failed to gain the majority required by the Constitution. So the election was thrown into the House of Representatives, whose members had to choose a president from the top three candidates—Jackson, Adams, and Crawford. Hoping to forge an alliance between the West and Northeast for a future presidential bid, Clay threw his support to New Englander John Quincy Adams, who won the election. "The Judah of the West," commented Jackson bitterly, "has closed the contract and will receive the thirty pieces of silver." When the new president appointed Clay his secretary of state, Jackson's supporters accused Adams of stealing victory by entering a "corrupt bargain" with Clay, an allegation that formed a dark cloud over Adams's presidency.

The guiding principle of the Adams presidency was improvement, both social and personal. "The spirit of improvement is abroad upon the earth," he wrote. In his eyes, the American republic was the culmination of human progress, and he intended to further that progress through a broad-gauged program for American development. In his First Annual Message to Congress, he laid out his plans to improve public education, expand communications and commerce, and launch an ambitious program of federal internal improvements. In foreign policy, he proposed that the U.S. participate in the first pan-American conference as a way to promote commerce with Latin America. Condemning what he called "the baneful weed of party strife," Adams sought to remain aloof from partisan politics, leaving most of Monroe's officeholders in place, and even appointing his own opponents to high office.

But Adams's ambitions met with growing political opposition. Strict constructionists opposed internal improvements on constitutional grounds. Southerners protested U.S. participation in the pan-American conference because it required association with regimes that had abolished slavery, including the black republic of Haiti, created by slave revolutionaries. And "the baneful weed of party strife" swirled around his presidency. At the midterm congressional elections of 1826 and 1827, Adams's opponents took control of both houses of Congress. While Adams continued to practice a time-honored politics of courting regional leaders so they would deliver the votes of their followings, his opponents—most important, Martin Van Buren of New York—were inventing a new grass-roots politics based on organization and partisan loyalty. John Quincy Adams's outdated notion of the president as a custodian of the public good, as well as his distaste for partisan politics, helped guarantee him a single-term presidency.

The Rise of Andrew Jackson and the Election of 1828

As President Adams's popularity declined, Andrew Jackson's rose. While seasoned politicians distrusted his notoriously hot temper and his penchant for duels, Jackson was still a popular hero for his victory over the British in the Battle of New Orleans. And because he had fought in the American Revolution as a boy, Jackson seemed to many Americans a living link to a more virtuous past.

The presidential campaign of 1828 began almost as soon as Adams was inaugurated. Jackson's supporters began to put together a modern political machine based on local committees and state conventions, partisan newspapers and public rallies. Two years before the election of 1828, towns and villages across the United States were buzzing with political activity and debate between "Adams men," or

National Republicans, and "Jackson men," or Democratic Republicans. But few Americans realized that a new political system was being born. The man most alert to the transformation was Martin Van Buren, whose political savvy would make him vice president during Jackson's second term, and then president.

Van Buren exemplified a new breed of politician. A tavern keeper's son, he began his political career at the county level. As governor, he built a powerful political machine, the Albany Regency, composed mainly of men like himself from the lower and middling ranks. His archrival, DeWitt Clinton, was everything Van Buren was not—tall, handsome, and aristocratic. But Van Buren's geniality put ordinary people at ease. More important, he had an uncanny ability to anticipate which way the political winds would blow, an ability that would earn him the nickname "Little Magician."

The election of 1824 convinced Van Buren of the need for two-party competition. Without the discipline imposed by an opposition party, the Republicans had splintered into sectional pieces, and the final selection was decided by self-interested leaders in Congress. It would be better, Van Buren decided, to organize the spectrum of political opinions into two opposing groups. Then the parties would compete, and a clear winner would emerge. Jackson's strong showing in the election persuaded Van Buren that "Old Hickory" could lead a new political party. In the election of 1828, this party, soon to be called the **Democratic Party,** ran Jackson for president and Calhoun for vice president. Its opponents, the National Republicans, rallied behind Adams and his running mate, treasury secretary Richard Rush. The second American party system was beginning to take shape.

The 1828 campaign was a vicious, mudslinging affair. The National Republicans called Jackson a murderer for killing several men in duels and military executions. They charged him with adultery for living with Rachel Robards when she was still married to another man. "Ought a convicted adulteress and her paramour husband," the Adams men taunted, "be placed in the highest office of this free and Christian land?" Jackson's supporters responded by accusing Adams of wearing silk underwear, spending public funds on a billiard table for the White House, and offering a beautiful American prostitute to the Russian tsar.

Although both sides slung mud, Jackson's men had better aim. Charges by Adams's supporters that Jackson was an illiterate backwoodsman backfired, increasing his popularity by casting him as a common man. Jackson's supporters explained that the people's choice was between "the democracy of the country, on the one hand, and a lordly purse-proud aristocracy on the other." Jackson's mind, they boasted, was unclouded by learning, his morals were simple and true, and his will was fiercely resolute. Adams, they sneered, was an aristocrat, a scholar whose learning obscured the truth, a writer not a fighter. Though Jackson was actually a wealthy slaveholder, people wanted to see in him the idealized common man: uncorrupt, natural, and plain.

Jackson won the election with more than twice the electoral vote of Adams (see Map 10.1). Yet the popular vote was much closer, and reflected the sectional bases of the new parties. Adams's voter support in New England was twice that of Jackson's, while Jackson received double his opponent's vote in the South and nearly triple in the Southwest.

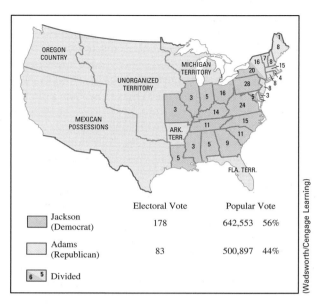

	Electoral Vote	Popular Vote	
Jackson (Democrat)	178	642,553	56%
Adams (Republican)	83	500,897	44%
Divided			

(Wadsworth/Cengage Learning)

MAP 10.1 The Election of 1828

Jackson in Office   As a vocal opponent to corruption and privilege, President Jackson made the federal civil service his first target. Many officeholders, he believed, regarded their jobs as entitlements. Jackson, by contrast, supported "rotation in office" so that as many common people as possible would have a chance to work for the government. Jackson did not invent rotation, but he applied it more thoroughly than his predecessors by firing nearly half the higher civil service, especially postmasters and customs officers.

Although Jackson defended these dismissals on democratic grounds, he also had a partisan motive. The firings were concentrated in the Northeast, stronghold of his defeated presidential opponent—though President Adams had actually left most of his predecessor Monroe's officeholders in place. Among Jackson's new appointments was his supporter Samuel Swartwout. As the chief customs officer for the port of New York, Swartwout embarrassed Jackson by running off with millions of dollars of customs receipts. Critics dubbed the practice of basing appointments on party loyalty the **"spoils system."**

Jackson's positions on internal improvements and tariffs sparked even more intense controversy. He did not oppose all federal aid for internal improvements. But Jackson suspected that public officials used such aid to win political support by handing out favors. To end such corruption, he flatly rejected federal support for roads within states. In 1830, when a bill came before him that would have provided federal money for a road between Maysville and Lexington, Kentucky, Jackson vetoed it on the grounds of its "purely local character."

The tariff issue tested Jackson's support even in the South, where the Indian Removal Act of 1830 (see Chapter 9) enhanced his popularity. In 1828, while Adams was still president, some of Jackson's supporters in Congress had helped pass a high protective tariff that strongly favored western agriculture and New England manufacturing over the South, which had few industries to protect and would now face higher prices for manufactured goods. Taking for granted southern support in the coming election, Jackson's supporters had calculated that southerners would blame the Adams administration for this "Tariff of Abominations." Instead, they leveled their fury at Jackson.

Nullification   The tariff of 1828 opened a major rift between Jackson and his vice president, John C. Calhoun, which would shake the foundations of the Republic. Early in his career, Calhoun had been an ardent nationalist. He entered Congress in 1811 as a war hawk, supported the protectionist tariff of 1816, and dismissed strict construction of the Constitution as philosophical nonsense. During the late 1820s, however, Calhoun the nationalist became Calhoun the states' rights sectionalist. The reasons for his shift were complex. He had supported the tariff of 1816 to encourage fledgling industries and provide revenue for military preparedness. By 1826, however, national defense was no longer a priority, and the infant industries of 1816 had grown into troublesome adolescents demanding even higher tariffs.

Calhoun also burned with ambition to be president. Jackson had stated that he would serve for only one term, and Calhoun planned to succeed him. But to become president, the one-time protectionist had to maintain the support of the South, which was growing opposed to tariffs. Calhoun's own home state of South Carolina, suffering economically from the migration of cotton cultivation into Alabama and Mississippi, blamed its troubles on tariffs. Tariffs, according to Calhoun's constituents, not only drove up the price of manufactured goods; they also threatened to damage the American market for British textiles and thus reduce British demand for southern cotton. The more New England industrialized, the more protectionist its Congressmen became. And the more the South came to rely on King Cotton, the more vigorously Southerners opposed the tariff.

Opposition to tariffs in the South was not just economic. Many Southerners feared that if the federal government could pass tariff laws favoring one section over another, it could also pass laws meddling with slavery. Because Jackson himself was a slaveholder, the fear of federal interference with slavery was perhaps far-fetched. But South Carolinians had especially strong reasons for concern. Theirs was one of only two states in which blacks comprised a majority of the population. In 1831, they became alarmed over a slave revolt led by Nat Turner in Virginia. That same year in Massachusetts, William Lloyd Garrison launched an abolitionist newspaper called *The Liberator*. These developments convinced many South Carolinians that a line had to be drawn against tariffs and possible future interference with slavery.

Calhoun opposed the tariff on constitutional grounds. He embraced the view, set forth in the Virginia and Kentucky Resolutions of 1798–1799, that the Union was a compact by which the states had conferred limited and specified powers on the federal government. Although the Constitution did empower Congress to levy tariffs, Calhoun insisted that only tariffs that raised revenue for such common purposes as defense were constitutional. Because the tariff of 1828 was set so high that it deterred foreigners from shipping their products to the United States, it could raise little revenue and was thus, he argued, unconstitutional. In 1828, Calhoun anonymously wrote the *South Carolina Exposition and Protest,* arguing that aggrieved states had the right to nullify the law within their borders.

Like Calhoun, Jackson was strong-willed and proud. Unlike Calhoun, he was already president and the leader of a national party that included supporters in such protariff states as Pennsylvania. To retain key northern support while soothing the South, Jackson devised two policies.

The first was to distribute surplus federal revenue to the states. In the years before federal income taxes, tariffs on foreign imports were a major source of federal revenue. Jackson hoped these funds, fairly distributed among the states, would remove the taint of sectional injustice from the tariff, while forcing the federal government to restrict its own spending. Second, Jackson hoped to reduce tariffs from the sky-high levels of 1828. Calhoun, reluctant to break openly with Jackson, muffled his protest, hoping that Jackson would lower the tariff and thus protect Calhoun's presidential hopes. In 1832, Congress did pass slightly reduced tariff rates, but these did not satisfy South Carolinians.

Meanwhile, two personal issues further damaged relations between Calhoun and Jackson. In 1829, Jackson's secretary of war, John H. Eaton, had married the widowed daughter of a Washington tavern keeper. By her own account, Peggy O'Neale Timberlake was "frivolous, wayward, [and] passionate." While still married to a naval officer away on duty, Peggy had openly flirted with Eaton, a boarder at her father's tavern. After her husband died and she married Eaton, the newlyweds were snubbed socially by Calhoun's wife and his friends in the cabinet. Jackson, who blamed his wife's recent death on the campaign mudslinging against her, befriended the Eatons. The Calhouns, he decided, had snubbed the Eatons to discredit Jackson and advance Calhoun's presidential aspirations.

To make matters worse, in 1830 Jackson received conclusive evidence supporting his long-time suspicion that in 1818, then-secretary of war Calhoun had urged that Jackson be punished for his unauthorized raid into Spanish Florida. This confirmation combined with the Eaton affair to convince Jackson that he had to "destroy [Calhoun] regardless of what injury it might do me or my administration." At a Jefferson Day dinner in April 1830, when Jackson proposed the toast, "Our Union: It must be preserved," Calhoun pointedly responded, "The Union next to Liberty the most dear. May we always remember that it can only be preserved by distributing equally the benefits and burdens of the Union."

The stage was now set for the **nullification crisis,** a direct clash between the president and vice president. In 1831, Calhoun acknowledged authorship of the *South Carolina Exposition and Protest.* In November 1832, a South Carolina convention nullified the tariffs of 1828 and 1832 and forbade the collection of customs duties within the state. Jackson reacted quickly. He labeled nullification an "abominable doctrine" that would reduce the government to anarchy, and berated the nullifiers as "unprincipled men who would rather rule in hell, than be subordinate in heaven." Jackson even sent weapons to loyal Unionists in South Carolina. In December 1832, he issued a proclamation that, while promising South Carolinians

Andrew Jackson, by Ralph Earl *Jackson during the nullification crisis, looking serene in the uniform of a major-general and determined to face down the greatest challenge to his presidency.*

(Memphis Brooks Museum of Art, Memphis, TN, Memphis Park Commission Purchase)

further tariff reductions, condemned nullification as itself unconstitutional. The Constitution, he emphasized, had established "a single nation," not a league of states.

The crisis eased in March 1833 when Jackson signed into law two measures, called by one historian "the olive branch and the sword." The olive branch was the Compromise Tariff of 1833, which provided for a gradual reduction of duties between 1833 and 1842. The sword was the Force Bill, authorizing the president to use arms to collect customs duties in South Carolina. Although South Carolina promptly nullified the Force Bill, it construed the Compromise Tariff as a concession and rescinded its nullification of the tariffs of 1828 and 1832.

Like most of the accommodations by which the Union lurched from one sectional crisis to the next in the decades before the Civil War, the Compromise of 1833 mixed partisanship with statesmanship. The moving spirit behind this compromise was Kentucky senator Henry Clay. Clay, who had long favored high tariffs, supported tariff reduction because he feared that without some concessions to South Carolina, the Force Bill would produce civil war. He also feared that without compromise, the basic principle of protective tariffs would be destroyed. Clay preferred to take responsibility for lowering tariffs himself, rather than pass the responsibility to the Jacksonians.

For their part, the nullifiers defiantly toasted "Andrew Jackson: On the soil of South Carolina he received an humble birthplace. May he not find in it a traitor's grave!" Although recognizing that South Carolina had failed to gain broad southern support for nullification and that they would have to bow to pressure, the nullifiers preferred that Clay, not Jackson, be the hero of the hour. So they supported Clay's Compromise Tariff. Everywhere Americans hailed Clay as the Great Compromiser. Even Martin Van Buren acknowledged that Clay had "saved the country."

The Bank Veto and the Election of 1832   Andrew Jackson recognized that the gap between rich and poor was widening during the 1820s and 1830s (see Chapter 9). He did not object to wealth acquired by hard work. But he disapproved of the wealthy growing wealthier by securing favors or "privileges" from corrupt legislatures. In addition, his own disastrous financial speculations early in his career had left him with a deep suspicion of all banks, paper money, and monopolies. The Bank of the United States was guilty on every count.

The **second Bank of the United States** had received a twenty-year charter from Congress in 1816. As a creditor to state banks, with the option of demanding repayment in specie (gold or silver coinage), the Bank of the United States held the power to restrain the state banks from excessive printing and lending of money. Such power provoked hostility. Many Americans blamed the bank for precipitating the Panic of 1819. Further, as the official depository for federal revenue, the bank's capital of $35 million was more than double the annual expenditures of the federal government. Yet this powerful institution was only distantly controlled by the government. Its stockholders were private citizens. Although chartered by Congress, the bank was located in Philadelphia. Its directors enjoyed considerable independence, and its president, the aristocratic Nicholas Biddle, viewed himself as a public servant, duty-bound to keep the bank above politics.

Encouraged by Henry Clay, who hoped that supporting the bank would help carry him to the White House in 1832, Biddle secured congressional passage of a bill to recharter the bank. Jackson vetoed it, denouncing the bank as a private and privileged monopoly that drained the West of specie, eluded state taxation, and made "the rich richer and the potent more powerful." Failing to persuade Congress to override Jackson's veto, Clay pinned his hopes on gaining the presidency himself.

By 1832, Jackson had made his views on major issues clear. He was simultaneously a staunch defender of states' rights and a staunch Unionist. Although he cherished the Union, he believed the states were too diverse to accept strong direction from Washington. The safest course was to allow the states considerable freedom so they would remain content within the Union and reject dangerous doctrines like nullification.

Breaking his earlier promises to retire, Jackson again ran for the presidency in 1832, with Martin Van Buren as his running mate. Henry Clay ran on the National Republican ticket, touting his American System of protective tariffs, national banking, and federal support for internal improvements. Jackson won. Secure in office for another four years, he was ready to finish dismantling the Bank of the United States.

THE BANK CONTROVERSY AND THE SECOND PARTY SYSTEM, 1833–1840

Jackson's veto of the recharter ignited a searing controversy. His efforts to destroy the Bank of the United States gave rise to the opposition Whig Party, stimulated popular interest in politics, and contributed to the severe economic downturn, known as the Panic of 1837, that would greet his successor, Martin Van Buren. By 1840, the Whig and Democratic parties had divided fundamentally over the bank.

In part, tempers flared over banking because the U.S. government issued no official paper currency. Instead, money took the form of notes (promises to redeem in specie) dispensed by banks. These IOUs fueled economic development by making it easier for businesses and farmers to acquire loans for building factories or buying land. But when notes depreciated because of public doubts about a bank's solvency, wage earners who had been paid in paper rather than specie suffered. Further, paper money encouraged economic speculation. Farmers who bought land on credit in the expectation of rising values could be left mired in debt when agricultural prices dropped. Would the United States embrace swift economic development at the price of allowing some speculators to languish, while others got rich quickly? Or would the nation opt for more modest growth based on "honest" manual work and frugality? Between 1833 and 1840 these questions dominated American politics.

The War on the Bank   Jackson could have allowed the bank to die quietly when its charter ran out in 1836. But Jackson and some of his followers feared the bank's power too much to wait. When Biddle, anticipating further attacks, began to call in the bank's loans and contract credit during the winter of 1832–1833, Jacksonians saw their darkest fears confirmed. The bank, Jackson assured Van Buren, "is trying to kill me, but I will kill it." Jackson then began to remove federal deposits from the Bank of the United States and place them in state banks, called "pet banks" by their critics because they were usually selected for loyalty to the Democratic Party.

But Jackson's redistribution of federal deposits backfired. He himself opposed paper money and easy credit, which encouraged ordinary Americans to undertake risky get-rich-quick schemes. But as state banks became depositories for federal revenue, they were able to print more paper money and extend more loans to farmers and speculators eager to buy public lands in the West. Government land sales rose from $6 million in 1834 to $25 million in 1836. Jackson's policy was producing exactly the kind of economy he wanted to suppress.

Jackson had hoped to limit the number of state banks that would receive federal deposits. But all demanded a piece of the action, and the number of state-bank depositories grew to twenty-three by the end of 1833. Jackson was caught between crosswinds. Some Democrats resented the Bank of the United States because it periodically contracted credit and restricted lending by state banks. Western Democrats, in particular, had long viewed the Cincinnati branch of the Bank of the United States as inadequate to supply their credit needs. Advocating "soft" or paper money, these Democrats in 1836 pressured a reluctant Jackson to sign the Deposit Act, which increased the number of deposit banks and loosened federal control over them. But Jackson continued to believe that paper money sapped "public virtue" and "robbed honest labour of its earnings to make knaves rich, powerful and dangerous." Seeking to reverse the damaging effects of the Deposit Act, Jackson issued a proclamation in 1836 called the Specie Circular, which provided that only specie could be accepted in payment for public lands.

Prior to the depression of 1837, most Democrats favored soft money. The hard-money (specie) view was advocated within Jackson's inner circle and by a faction of the New York Democratic Party called the Locofocos. The Locofocos grew out of several different "workingmen's" parties that called for free public education, the abolition of imprisonment for debt, and a ten-hour workday. Most of these parties proved short-lived, but in New York the "workies" were gradually absorbed by the Democratic Party. A mixture of intellectuals, small artisans, and journeymen, they worried about inflation, demanded payment in specie, and distrusted banks and paper money. In 1835, a faction of workingmen broke away from Tammany Hall, the main Democratic Party organization in New York City, and met in a hall whose candles were lit by a newfangled invention called the "locofoco," or match. Thereafter, these radical workingmen were called Locofocos.

The Rise of Whig Opposition   During Jackson's second term, the opposition National Republican Party gave way to the new **Whig Party.** Jackson's magnetic personality had swept him to victory in 1828 and 1832. But his opposition to federal aid for internal improvements and protective tariffs, to the Bank of the United States and nullification, prompted his opponents to align with the new Whig Party.

Jackson's crushing of nullification drove some southerners into the Whig Party simply because they opposed Jackson. His war on the Bank of the United States produced similar results. Jackson's policy of redistributing federal deposits pleased some southerners but dismayed others who did not need cheaper and easier credit. The president's suspicion of federal aid for internal improvements also alienated some southerners who feared that the South would lag behind the North unless it initiated improvements. Because so much southern capital was tied up in slavery, southerners looked to the federal government for funding, and when rebuffed, they drifted into the Whig Party. Despite these defections, the South remained the Democrats' strongest base. But the Whigs were making significant inroads, particularly in market towns and among planters with close ties to southern bankers and merchants.

Meanwhile, Northern social reformers were strengthening the opposition to Jackson. These reformers wanted to improve American society by ending slavery and liquor consumption, improving public education, and elevating public morality. Most reformers found Whig philosophy more compatible with their goals than Democratic ideas. Democrats believed that government should not impose a uniform standard of conduct on a diverse society. By contrast, the Whigs' commitment to Clay's American System implied an acceptance of government intervention to improve society—morally as well as economically. Reformers also indirectly stimulated Whig support from native-born Protestant workers. The reformers, overwhelmingly Protestant, distrusted immigrants, especially Irish Catholics, who viewed drinking as a normal recreation and opposed public schools because they promoted Protestantism. The rise of reform drove the Irish into the Democratic Party. By the same token, reform activities won Whig support from many native-born Protestant workers who were contemptuous of the Irish.

No source of Whig strength, however, was more remarkable than Anti-Masonry. Freemasonry had long provided prominent men, including George Washington, with fraternal fellowship based in exotic rituals. What sparked the Anti-Masonic crusade was the abduction and disappearance in 1826 of William Morgan, a Mason who had threatened to expose the order's secrets. Every effort to solve the mystery of Morgan's disappearance failed when local officials who were themselves Masons obstructed the investigation. Throughout the Northeast, the public became increasingly aroused against the perceived evils of the Masonic order. Rumors spread that Masonry was a powerful, anti-Christian conspiracy to suppress popular liberty and provide a safe haven for wealthy drunkards. Anti-Masonry brought many northeastern small farmers and artisans into the Whig Party.

By 1836, the Whigs had become a national party with widespread appeal. In both the North and South, they attracted those with close ties to the market economy—commercial farmers, planters, merchants, and bankers. In the North, they picked up additional support from reformers, evangelical clergymen (especially Presbyterians and Congregationalists), Anti-Masons, and manufacturers. In the South, they appealed to some former nullificationists including, briefly, Calhoun himself. Everywhere the Whigs attacked Jackson as "King Andrew I"; and they named their party after that of the American patriots who opposed King George III in 1776.

The Election of 1836

Jackson's popularity was a tough act to follow. In 1836, the Democrats ran Martin Van Buren for president. Party leaders reminded voters that Van Buren was Jackson's chosen favorite, and that the Democratic Party itself was the real heir to Jackson, because it perfectly embodied the popular will. The less cohesive Whigs produced three candidates: William Henry Harrison of Ohio, Daniel Webster of Massachusetts, and W.P. Mangum of North Carolina. A fourth candidate, Democrat Hugh Lawson White of Tennessee, also ran against Van Buren, whom he distrusted, then defected to the Whigs after the election.

Democrats responded to this proliferation of Van Buren opponents by accusing the Whigs of a plot to divide the vote so that no candidate would receive the required majority in the Electoral College. The election would then be thrown into the House of Representatives, where once again, as in 1824, damaging bargains would be struck. In reality, the Whigs were simply divided, and Van Buren won a clear majority. But there were signs of trouble ahead for the Democrats. The popular vote was close. In the South, where four years earlier the Democrats had won two-thirds of the votes, they now won barely half.

The Panic of 1837

Jackson left office and returned to Nashville in a burst of glory. But the public's mood quickly darkened, for no sooner was Van Buren in office than a severe depression, called the **Panic of 1837,** struck.

In the speculative boom of 1835 and 1836, the total number of banks doubled, the value of bank notes in circulation nearly tripled, and commodity and land prices soared. Encouraged by easy money and high commodity prices, states made new commitments to build canals. Then in May 1837, prices began to tumble, and bank after bank suspended specie payments. After a short rally, the economy crashed again in 1839. The Bank of the United States, which had continued to operate as a state bank with a Pennsylvania charter, failed. Nicholas Biddle was charged with fraud and theft. Once again, banks throughout the nation suspended specie payments.

The ensuing depression was far more severe than the economic downturn of 1819. Those lucky enough to find work saw their wage rates drop by roughly one-third. In despair, many workers turned to the teachings of William Miller, a New England religious enthusiast convinced that the end of the world was imminent. Dressed in black coats and stovepipe hats, Miller's followers roamed urban sidewalks and rural villages in search of converts. Many sold their possessions and purchased white robes to ascend into heaven on October 22, 1843, the day the world was supposed to end. By then, the worst of the depression was over; but at its depths, the economic slump made despairing people receptive to Miller's predictions.

"Little Magician" Martin Van Buren needed all his political skills to confront the depression that was damaging not only ordinary citizens but the Democratic Party itself. Whigs dubbed him "Martin Van Ruin," and in 1838 succeeded in sweeping the governorship and most legislative seats in Van Buren's own New York. To seize the initiative, Van Buren called for the creation of an independent Treasury. The idea was simple: the federal government, instead of depositing its money in banks, which would use it as the basis for speculative loans, would hold onto its revenues and keep them from the grasp of corporations. When Van Buren finally signed the Independent Treasury Bill into law on July 4, 1840, his supporters hailed it as America's second Declaration of Independence.

The independent Treasury reflected the deep Jacksonian suspicion of an alliance between government and banking. But the Independent Treasury Act failed to address the banking issue on the state level, where newly chartered state banks—over nine hundred of them by 1840—lent money to farmers and businessmen. The Whigs, who blamed the depression on Jackson's Specie Circular rather than on the banks, continued to encourage bank charters as a way to spur economic development. In contrast, growing numbers of Democrats blamed the depression on banks and paper money, and swung toward the hard-money stance long favored by Jackson and his inner circle. In Louisiana and Arkansas, Democrats prohibited banks altogether, and elsewhere they imposed severe restrictions—banning, for example, the issuing of paper money in small denominations. After 1837, the Democrats became an antibank, hard-money party.

Log Cabins, Hard Cider, and a Maturing Second Party System

Despite the depression, the Democrats renominated Van Buren for president. The Whigs avoided their mistake of 1836 by settling on a single candidate, Ohio's William Henry Harrison, and ran former Senator John Tyler of Virginia as vice president. Harrison, who at age sixty-seven was barely eking out a living as a farmer, was picked because he had few enemies. Early in the campaign, the Democrats made a fatal mistake by ridiculing Harrison as "Old Granny," a man who desired only to spend his declining years sipping cider in a log cabin. Unwittingly, the Democrats had handed their opponents the most famous campaign symbol in American history. The Whigs immediately praised Harrison as a rugged frontiersman, the hero of the Battle of Tippecanoe, and a defender of all western settlers living in log cabins.

Refusing to publish a platform, the Whigs ran a "hurrah" campaign, trumpeting "Tippecanoe and Tyler too." They used log cabins for headquarters, sang log-cabin songs, passed around log-cabin cider, and called their newspaper *Log Cabin*. Van Buren, they charged, was a soft aristocrat who lived in "regal splendor," drinking fine wines from silver goblets while people went hungry in the streets. Harrison, by contrast, was content to drink hard cider from a plain mug. Just twelve years after Jackson's triumph over the "purse-proud aristocrat" Adams, the Whigs were effectively using Democratic tactics against the Democratic candidate.

The election results gave Harrison a clear victory. Van Buren carried only seven states, even failing to hold his home state of New York. The depression would probably have made it impossible for any Democrat to have triumphed in 1840, but Van Buren had other problems. Unlike Harrison and Jackson, he wore no halo of military glory. He also ran a surprisingly old-fashioned campaign. While Van Buren was writing encouraging letters to key supporters, Harrison was breaking with tradition to travel by railroad around the country. Van Buren, the master politician, was beaten at his own game.

In addition to electioneering tactics like log cabins and hard cider, the 1840 election ushered in a significant long-term trend in voting. Between 1836 and 1840, the popular vote expanded by 60 percent, the greatest proportional jump between consecutive elections in American history. Since 1828, the total number of votes cast in presidential elections had risen from 1.2 million to 2.4 million. Neither reduced suffrage requirements nor population growth was the main cause of this increase. Rather, it resulted from a jump in voter turnout. In 1828, 1832, and 1836, the proportion of white males who voted had fluctuated between 55 percent and 58 percent. In 1840, it shot to 80 percent.

Both severe economic depression and the noisy log-cabin campaign brought voters to the polls in 1840. Yet voter turnout remained high even after prosperity returned during the following decade. The second party system, which had been developing slowly since 1828, reached a high plateau in 1840 and remained there for more than a decade. Politicians increasingly presented clear alternatives to voters. The gradual hardening of the line dividing the two parties stimulated enduring popular interest in politics.

Another major current feeding partisan political passions in American life was reform. Yet the social and moral reform movements that burst onto the national scene in the 1830s originated not in politics, but in religion.

THE RISE OF POPULAR RELIGION

In *Democracy in America*, Alexis de Tocqueville pointed out an important difference between his country and the United States. "In France I had almost always seen the spirit of religion and the spirit of freedom pursuing courses diametrically opposed to each other; but in America I found that they were intimately united, and that they reigned in common over the same country." From this observation, Tocqueville drew a startling conclusion: religion was "the foremost of the political institutions" of the United States.

In calling religion a political institution, Tocqueville did not mean that Americans gave special political privileges to any particular denomination. He meant that in America, religion and democracy were compatible rather than antagonistic: religion reinforced American democracy, even as American democracy informed religious practice. Just as Americans expected their politicians to address the common man, they insisted that ministers preach to ordinary people. The most successful ministers were those who used plain words to move the heart, not those who tried to dazzle their listeners with theological complexities. Increasingly, too, Americans demanded theological doctrines that put individuals in charge of their own religious destiny. They moved away from the Calvinist creed that God had selected some people for salvation and others for damnation, and toward the belief that anyone could attain heaven.

Americans were democratizing heaven itself. The harmony between religious and democratic impulses owed much to a series of religious revivals known as the Second Great Awakening.

The Second Great Awakening

The **Second Great Awakening** ignited in Connecticut during the 1790s and swept one region after another during the half-century that followed. At first, educated Congregationalists and Presbyterians such as Yale president Timothy Dwight had dominated the revivals. But as they spread to frontier states like Tennessee and Kentucky, revivals underwent striking changes that were typified by the rise of camp meetings. These were gigantic, prolonged revivals in which members of several denominations gathered into sprawling open-air camps to hear revivalists proclaim that the Second Coming of Jesus was near and the time for repentance was now.

The most famous camp meeting occurred at Cane Ridge, Kentucky, in August 1801, when a huge crowd assembled to hear thunderous sermons, sing hymns, and experience the influx of divine grace. One eyewitness described the meeting:

> At night, the whole scene was awfully sublime. The ranges of tents, the fires, reflecting light amidst the branches of the towering trees; the candles and lamps illuminating the encampment; hundreds moving to and fro, with lights or torches, like Gideon's army; the preaching, praying, singing, and shouting, all heard at once, rushing from different parts of the ground, like the sound of many waters, was enough to swallow up all the powers of contemplation.

Among the more extreme features of frontier revivals was the "exercises" in which men and women rolled around like logs, jerked their heads furiously, and barked like dogs. Critics blasted the frontier frenzy for encouraging more lust than spirituality and complained that "more souls were begot [meaning conceived] than saved." The early frontier revivals fundamentally challenged traditional religious customs. The most successful revivalists were not college graduates but ordinary farmers and artisans who had themselves experienced powerful religious conversions and regarded learned ministers with contempt for their dry expositions of orthodox theology.

No religious denomination proved more successful on the frontier than the Methodists. With fewer than seventy thousand members in 1800, the Methodists became America's largest Protestant denomination by 1844, claiming over a million members. In contrast to New England Congregationalists and Presbyterians, Methodists emphasized that religion was primarily a matter of the heart rather than the head. The frontier Methodists disdained "settled" ministers tied to fixed parishes. They preferred itinerant circuit riders—young, often unmarried men who traveled from place to place on horseback and preached in houses, open fields, and wherever listeners gathered. As circuit rider Peter Cartwright explained, it was his mission to "carry the gospel to destitute souls that had, by their removal into some new country, been deprived of the means of grace."

Although the frontier revivals disrupted religious custom, they also promoted social and moral order on the frontier. After Methodist circuit riders left an area, their converts formed weekly "classes" which served as the grassroots structure for Methodist churches. The classes established a Methodist code of behavior, called the Discipline, which reinforced family and community values amidst the social disorder of frontier life. Class members not only worshiped together, they provided mutual religious and moral encouragement, and reprimanded one another for drunkenness, fighting, fornication, gossiping, and even sharp business practices.

Eastern Revivals   By the 1820s, the Second Great Awakening had begun to shift eastward. The fires of revival blazed hottest in an area of western New York that came to be known as the "Burned-Over District." This region was filling with descendants of Puritans who hungered for religious experience and with enterprising people drawn by the hope of wealth after the completion of the Erie Canal. The Burned-Over District offered a fertile field for both high expectations and bitter discontent.

The man who harnessed these social forces to religion was **Charles G. Finney.** In 1821, while studying to become a lawyer, Finney experienced a powerful religious conversion. When a church deacon arrived at his office to remind him that he had retained Finney's legal services for a trial that morning, Finney replied, "I have a retainer from the Lord Jesus Christ to plead his cause, and I cannot plead yours." He became a Presbyterian minister and conducted dozens of revivals in towns along the canal, as well as in New York City and Boston. But his greatest "harvest" of souls was gathered in the thriving canal city of Rochester in 1830–1831.

The Rochester revival had several features that justify Finney's reputation as the "father of modern revivalism." First, it was a citywide revival in which all denominations participated. Finney was a pioneer of cooperation among Protestant denominations. Second, in Rochester and elsewhere, Finney introduced new devices for speeding conversions, such as the "anxious seat," where those ready for conversion were led so they could be made objects of special prayer, and the "protracted meeting," which went on nightly for up to a week.

Lorenzo Dow and The Jerking Exercise *Lorenzo Dow (1777–1834) was a spellbinding Methodist revivalist who preached throughout the United States early in the Second Great Awakening. His unkempt appearance, harsh voice, and jerky physical movements earned him a reputation for eccentricity. But his success in winning souls demonstrated the democratic appeal of revivalism.*

(Caricature of Fundamentalist Prayer-Meeting 1840 by Lossing-Barrett/Picture Research Consultants & Archives)

Finney's emphasis on special techniques distinguished him from eighteenth-century revivalists, such as Jonathan Edwards. Whereas Edwards had portrayed revivals as the miraculous work of divine grace, Finney understood them to be human creations. Although a Presbyterian, Finney flatly rejected the Calvinist doctrine of innate depravity—the belief that humans had an inborn, irresistible inclination to sin. Sin, according to Finney, was a voluntary act, and sinners could will themselves out of sin just as readily as they had chosen it. They even exercised the power to lead perfect lives free of all sin, on the model of Christ. Finney's converts left his meetings convinced that all their past guilt had been washed away and they were beginning a new life. "I have been born again," a young convert wrote. "I am three days old when I write this letter."

Originally controversial, Finney's ideas came to dominate "evangelical" Protestantism—forms of Protestantism that focused on the need for an emotional conversion experience. He was successful because he told nineteenth-century Americans what they wanted to hear: that their destinies were in their own hands. A society that celebrated the self-made man embraced Finney's assertion that, even in religion, people could make of themselves what they chose. As a frontier revivalist with a relatively dignified style, Finney had an appeal that extended to merchants, lawyers, and small manufacturers in the towns and cities of the Northeast.

More than most revivalists, Finney recognized that revivals seldom succeeded without the active participation of women. During the Second Great Awakening, female converts outnumbered male converts by about two to one. Finney encouraged women to give public testimonies of their religious experiences, and often succeeded in converting men by first converting their wives and daughters. After a visit from Finney, Melania Smith, the religiously inactive wife of a Rochester physician, greeted her husband with a blunt reminder of "the woe which is denounced against the families which call not on the Name of the Lord." Dr. Smith soon joined one of Rochester's Presbyterian churches.

Critics of Revivals: The Unitarians   The revivals drew criticism. Some people openly doubted that revivals produced permanent changes in behavior. Critics condemned them for encouraging "such extravagant and incoherent expressions, and such enthusiastic fervor, as puts common sense and modesty to the blush."

One small but influential group of critics was the Unitarians. Their basic doctrine—that Jesus was not divine, but rather a human model for the moral life—had gained quiet acceptance among religious rationalists during the eighteenth-century Enlightenment. Only in the early nineteenth century did Unitarianism emerge as a separate denomination. In New England, hundreds of Congregational churches were divided by the withdrawal of Unitarians, and ensuing legal battles over which group—Congregationalists or Unitarians—could occupy church property. Although Unitarianism won relatively few converts outside New England, its tendency to attract the wealthy and educated gave Unitarians influence beyond their numbers.

Unitarians criticized revivals as uncouth emotional exhibitions. They argued that moral goodness should be cultivated, not through a dramatic conversion experience, but through a gradual process of "character building" in which believers modeled their behavior on that of Jesus. Yet both Unitarians and revivalists rejected the Calvinist emphasis on innate depravity and shared the belief that human behavior could be changed for the better. William Ellery Channing, the Unitarian leader who most influenced Dorothea Dix, claimed that all Christianity had but one purpose: "the perfection of human nature, the elevation of men into nobler beings."

The Rise of Mormonism   The Unitarians' assertion that Jesus was not divine challenged a fundamental doctrine of orthodox Christianity. Yet Unitarianism proved far less controversial than another new denomination of the 1820s and 1830s—the Church of Jesus Christ of Latter-day Saints, or **Mormons.** Its founder, Joseph Smith, grew to manhood in one of those families that seemed to be in constant motion to and fro, but never up. His ne'er-do-well father moved his family nearly twenty times in ten years before settling in Palmyra, New York, in the heart of the Burned-Over District. As a boy, Smith dreamed of finding buried treasure and wrestled with religious uncertainty created by the conflicting claims of the Methodists, Presbyterians, and Baptists who surrounded him. Who was right and who was wrong, he wondered, or were they "all wrong together"?

Smith's religious perplexity was common in the Burned-Over District, but his path to resolving the confusion was unique. An angel named Moroni, he reported, led him to a buried book of revelation and special seer stones to help with its translation, which he completed in 1827. The Book of Mormon tells the story of an ancient Hebrew prophet, Lehi, whose descendants came to America and created a prosperous civilization to await Jesus as its savior. Jesus had actually appeared and performed miracles in the New World, but the American descendants of Lehi had departed from the Lord's ways. As punishment, God had cursed some with dark skin—thus creating the American Indians who, by the time of Columbus's arrival, had forgotten their history. Mormonism—one of the few major religions to originate in the United States—placed America at the center of religious history (see Going to the Source).

Smith quickly gathered followers. For some believers, the Book of Mormon resolved the turmoil created by conflicting Protestant interpretations of the Bible. But Smith's claim to a new revelation guaranteed a hostile response from many American Protestants, who believed he had undermined the authority of their Scripture. To escape persecution, and move closer to the Indians whose conversion was one of their goals, Smith and his followers began relocating west from New York. In Illinois, they built a model city called Nauvoo and a magnificent temple supported by thirty huge pillars (see Map 10.2). But in 1844, a group of dissident Mormons accused Smith and his inner circle of practicing plural marriage. When Smith destroyed the group's newspaper press, militias moved in to restore law and order. They arrested Smith and his brother Hirum and threw them into jail in Carthage, Illinois, where a lynch mob killed them both. One of Joseph's plural wives wrote, "Never, since the Son of God was slain/Has blood so noble flow'd from human vein."

Joseph Smith had once hoped that Americans would fully embrace Mormonism. But ongoing persecution had gradually convinced the Mormons' prophet that their survival lay in separation from American society. In removing from the larger society of "Gentiles," the Mormons mirrored the efforts of many other religious communities during the 1830s and 40s. One in particular, the Shakers, has held an enduring fascination for Americans.

The Shakers   The Shakers were founded by Mother Ann Lee, the illiterate daughter of an English blacksmith, who emigrated to America in 1774. Mother Ann's followers believed she was the second incarnation of God: as Jesus had been the Son of God, she was God's Daughter. Called "Shakers" for their convulsive religious dancing at worship services, the group established tightly knit agricultural-artisan communities, whose purpose was the

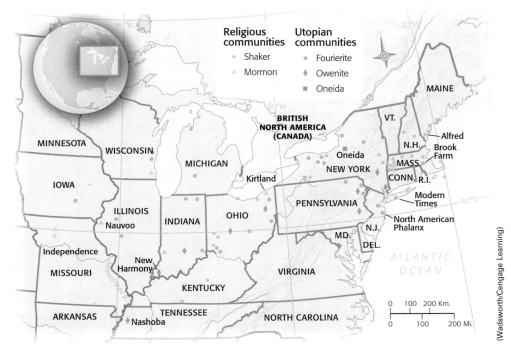

MAP 10.2 Religious and Utopian Communities, 1800–1845

The desire to construct a perfect society gave rise to hundreds of utopian communities between 1800 and 1845. Some, like the Shaker and Mormon communities, arose from religious motives. Others, as discussed later in this chapter, were more secular in origin, attempting to allay the selfish excesses of social and economic competition.

pursuit of religious perfection. "Hands to work, and hearts to God" was their guiding motto. Shaker artisans produced furniture renowned for its beauty and strength and invented such conveniences as the clothespin and the circular saw.

For all their achievements as artisans, the Shakers were fundamentally other-worldly. Mother Ann, who had lost four infant children, had a religious vision in which God expelled Adam and Eve from the Garden of Eden for their sin of sexual intercourse. Shaker communities practiced celibacy and carefully separated the sleeping and working quarters of men and women to discourage contact between them. To maintain their membership, Shakers relied on new converts and the adoption of orphans, and at their peak in the 1830s and 1840s they numbered about six thousand members in eight states. As part of their pursuit of religious perfection, they practiced a form of Christian socialism, pooling their land and implements to create remarkably prosperous villages. A British visitor observed that "the earth does not show more flourishing fields, gardens, and orchards than theirs."

The Mormon Land of Promise

Joseph Smith presented the Book of Mormon as a record of ancient American Christians, translated from golden plates that had been buried near Palmyra, New York. In this passage, Nephi recorded a prophecy by his father Lehi regarding the land of promise, the place where Lehi and his children had recently arrived from Jerusalem (ca. 600 BCE). Though Joseph Smith did not explicitly identify the location of this "promised land," these revelations were understood by Mormons to have particular application to the United States and to the Americas more widely.

And he also spake unto them concerning the land of promise, which they had obtained: how merciful the Lord had been in warning us that we should flee out of the land of Jerusalem. For, Behold, said he, I have seen a vision, in which I know that Jerusalem is destroyed; and had we remained in Jerusalem, we should also have perished. But, said he, notwithstanding our afflictions, we have obtained a land of promise, a land which is choice above all other lands; a land which the Lord God hath covenanted with me should be a land for the inheritance of my seed. Yea, the Lord hath covenanted this land unto me, and to my children forever; and also all those who should be led out of other countries, by the hand of the Lord. Wherefore, I, Lehi, prophesy according to the workings of the spirit which is in me, that there shall none come into this land, save they shall be brought by the hand of the Lord. Wherefore, this land is consecrated unto him whom he shall bring. And if it so be that they shall serve him according to the commandments which he hath given, it shall be a land of liberty unto them; wherefore, they shall never be brought down into captivity; if so, it shall be because of iniquity: for if iniquity shall abound, cursed shall be the

While the Shakers chose to separate themselves from the competitive individualism of the larger society, the message of most evangelical Protestants, including Charles G. Finney, was that religion and economic self-advancement were compatible. Most revivalists taught that the pursuit of wealth was acceptable as long as people were honest, temperate, and bound by conscience. But many of them recognized that the world was in serious need of improvement, and they believed that converts had a religious responsibility to pursue moral and social reform.

THE AGE OF REFORM

The heart of religious revival was the democratic belief that individual men and women could take charge of their own spiritual destinies, and strive toward perfection. For many converts, similar expectations applied to the society around them. Saved souls, they believed, could band together to stamp out the many evils that plagued the American republic. Like John Quincy Adams, they embraced "the spirit of improvement," forming a wide range of voluntary associations land for their sakes; but unto the righteous it shall be blessed forever. And behold, it is wisdom that this land should be kept as yet from the knowledge of other nations: for behold, many nations would overrun the land, that there would be no place for an inheritance. Wherefore, I, Lehi, have obtained a promise, that inasmuch as they which the Lord God shall bring out of the land of Jerusalem shall keep his commandments, they shall prosper upon the face of this land; and they shall be kept from all other nations, that they may possess this land unto themselves. And if it so be that they shall keep his commandments, they shall be blessed upon the face of this land, and there shall be none to molest them, nor to take away the land of their inheritance; and they shall dwell safely forever. But behold, when the time cometh that they shall dwindle in unbelief, after they have received so great blessings from the hand of the Lord ... behold, the judgments of him that is just, shall rest upon them; yea, he will bring other nations unto them, and he will give unto them power, and he will take away from them the lands of their possessions; and he will cause them to be scattered and smitten.

Source: The Book of Mormon   by Joseph Smith, Junior, Author and Proprietor [because copyright law wasn't yet applicable to translations]. Palmyra [New York]: Printed by E.B. Grandin, for the Author. 1830 Excerpt from The Second Book of Nephi, Chapter I, pp. 59–61.

Questions

1. *What are the major elements of the ancient American history recorded in The Book of Mormon?*

2. *How, in your view, might this historical treatment of America as "promised land" have appealed to the thousands of people who flocked to the new Mormon religion in the antebellum period?*

Go to www.cengagebrain.com for additional primary sources on this period.

whose purpose was to improve society. The abolition of slavery, the rights of women, temperance, the humane treatment of criminals and the insane, and public education were high on reformers' agendas. Carrying the moralism of revival into their reform activities, they tended to view all social problems as clashes between good and evil and to assume that God was on their side.

Not all reformers were converts of revival. Many school reformers and women's rights advocates were religious liberals—either hostile or indifferent to revivals. Dorothea Dix's work on behalf of the mentally ill drew more power from her involvement in Boston Unitarianism than from the Methodism of her early childhood. Abolitionists openly criticized the churches for condoning slavery and often separated themselves from denominational bodies that refused to condemn the institution. But by portraying slaveholding as a sin that called for immediate repentance, even religiously liberal abolitionists borrowed their language and their psychological appeal from revivalism. Whatever a reformer's personal relationship to the revivals of the Second Great Awakening, the Age of Reform drew much of its fuel from that evangelical movement.

The War on Liquor

Early nineteenth-century Americans were very heavy drinkers. In 1825, the average adult male drank about seven gallons of alcohol annually (mostly whiskey and hard cider), in contrast to less than two gallons in our own time (mostly beer and wine). One reason for this heavy consumption was the state of western agriculture. Before the transportation revolution, western farmers could not make a profit by shipping grain in bulk to eastern markets. But they could profit by condensing their corn and rye into a distilled liquor called whiskey, which poured out of the west in large quantities. Drunkenness pervaded all social classes and occupations. The relatively new habit of binge-drinking generated the medical diagnosis of delirium tremens. Other problems generated by heavy drinking included domestic violence, disease, and economic failure.

Before 1825, temperance reformers advocated moderation in consuming alcohol. But in that year, Connecticut revivalist Lyman Beecher delivered six widely acclaimed lectures that condemned all use of alcoholic beverages. A year later, evangelical Protestants created the **American Temperance Society,** the first national temperance organization, which followed Beecher's lead in demanding total abstinence. By 1834, some five thousand state and local temperance societies were affiliated with the American Temperance Society. Although usually led by men, their membership was between one-third and one-half women, who, along with their children, endured the bulk of drink-induced domestic violence and poverty.

The primary strategy of the American Temperance Society was to use "moral suasion" to persuade people to "take the pledge"—the promise never to consume any alcoholic beverage. To that end, temperance reformers flooded the country with tracts denouncing the "amazing evil" of strong drink, paid reformed drunkards to deliver public lectures, and produced temperance plays. They even formed a children's organization called the "Cold Water Army." Its small members pledged, "We, Cold Water Girls and Boys,/Freely renounce the treacherous joys/ Of Brandy, Whiskey, Rum and Gin;/The Serpent's lure to death and sin."

Among the main targets of evangelical temperance reformers were the laboring classes. In the small workshops of the pre-industrial era, passing the jug every few hours throughout the workday was a time-honored practice. But early factories demanded a more disciplined, sober work force, so industrial employers were quick to embrace temperance reform. In East Dudley, Massachusetts, three manufacturers refused to sell liquor in their factory stores, calculating that any profits from the sale would be wiped out by lost work time and "the scenes of riot and wickedness thus produced." Industrial employers in Rochester, New York, invited Charles G. Finney to preach up a revival in their city as part of an effort to convince their workers to abstain from alcohol.

Workers themselves initially showed little interest in temperance. But after the Panic of 1837, some grew convinced that their economic survival depended on a commitment to sobriety. In 1840, in Baltimore, they formed the Washington Temperance Society, and a branch for women called the Martha Washingtonians. Drawing more mechanics (workingmen) than ministers or manufacturers, the Washington Societies offered mutual self-help. Many members were themselves reformed drunkards, like Boston baker Charles Woodman, who blamed his business collapse on his return to his "old habit" of excessive drinking. Men like Woodman reasoned that, while the forces of economic dislocation were beyond their control, their own sobriety lay within their control. Take care of temperance, one Washingtonian assured his Baltimore audience, and the Lord will take care of the economy.

Despite the early resistance of working-class drinkers to middle-class temperance reform, the Washingtonians' debt to religious revivalism was actually greater than that of the American Temperance Society. Washingtonians viewed drinking as sinful and held "experience meetings" in which members testified to their "salvation" from liquor and their "regeneration" through total abstinence or "teetotalism" (an emphatic form of the word *total).* Martha Washingtonians pledged to smell their husbands' breath each night, and paraded with banners that read "Teetotal or No Husband." The Washington Societies spread farther and faster than any other antebellum temperance organization.

As the temperance movement won new supporters, some crusaders began to demand legal prohibition—the banning of liquor traffic at the local and state level. In 1838, Massachusetts prohibited the sale of distilled spirits in amounts less than fifteen gallons, thereby restricting small purchases by individual drinkers. In 1851, Maine banned the manufacture and sale of all intoxicating beverages. Prohibition was controversial, even within the movement. But taken together, the two central strategies of the temperance movement—moral suasion and legal prohibition—scored remarkable success. Per capita consumption of distilled spirits, which had risen steadily between 1800 and 1830, began to fall during the 1830s. By the 1840s, consumption had dropped to less than half its peak rate in the 1820s.

Public-School Reform

In the early nineteenth century, the typical American school was a rural one-room schoolhouse. Here students ranging in age from three to twenty or older sat on benches learning to read and count, but little more, and spending only a few months in school each year. Their teachers were typically recent college graduates who took teaching jobs just to tide them over until they entered other professions. Students never forgot the primitive conditions and harsh discipline of these schools, especially the floggings until "the youngster vomited or wet his breeches."

Expecting little more than basic literacy-training for their children, rural parents were generally content with these schools. But reformers found them unacceptable. They wanted schools to equip students for an increasingly competitive industrial economy. **Horace Mann,** the first secretary of the Massachusetts board of education, created in 1837, set out to achieve this goal through several different strategies: shifting the burden of school financial support from parents to the state, extending the school term to as many as ten months each year, standardizing textbooks, dividing students into grades based on their age and achievements, and compelling attendance. Within Mann's educational vision, school should occupy the bulk of every child's time and energy.

School reformers sought to spread industrial values as well as combat ignorance. Requiring students to arrive on time would teach punctuality, and matching students against their peers would stimulate competitiveness. Assigned textbooks would teach such lessons as "Idleness is the nest in which mischief lays its eggs." The McGuffey readers, which sold 50 million copies between 1836 and 1870, preached industry, honesty, sobriety, and patriotism.

Success did not come easily. Educational reformers faced challenges from farmers who were satisfied with the district schools and reluctant to remove their children from the fields for most of the year. Urban Catholics, led by New York City's Bishop John Hughes, pointed out that the textbooks used in public schools were anti-Catholic and anti-Irish. In both rural and urban areas, the laboring poor opposed compulsory education because their family economy depended on children's wage-earning.

Yet school reformers prevailed, at least in the North, in part because their opponents failed to unify (schooling in the South is discussed in Chapter 12). Reformers also enlisted influential allies. Urban workingmen's parties were converted to the cause by the prospect of free, tax-supported schools. Industrial employers were won over by the promise that public schools would help create a disciplined work force. Women were drawn by the recognition that dividing students into different grade levels would improve their own opportunities to become teachers. It was generally assumed that women were incapable of controlling one-room schools whose pupils included rambunctious young men. But few people doubted a woman's ability to manage a class of eight-year-olds. Educational reformer Catharine Beecher (Lyman's daughter) accurately predicted that school reform would open the teaching profession to women. By 1900, about 70 percent of the nation's schoolteachers were women.

School reform also appealed to native-born Americans alarmed by the influx of immigrant foreigners. The public school was coming to be seen as the best mechanism for creating a common American culture out of an increasingly diverse society. As one reformer observed, "We must decompose and cleanse the impurities which rush into our midst" through the "one infallible filter—the SCHOOL." Very few educational reformers, however, called for the integration of black and white children. When black children did enter public schools, they encountered open hostility and sometimes violence.

Abolition

Antislavery sentiment flourished in the Revolutionary era, encouraging northern states to establish emancipation schemes within their borders. But opposition to slavery declined in the first two decades of the nineteenth century. The American Colonization Society (founded in 1816) did propose a limited plan for emancipation, under which slaveholders would be compensated for voluntarily freeing their slaves, and free blacks would be "colonized" in Liberia in West Africa. But colonization expressed little moral outrage against slavery, and actually enlisted some slaveholders who opposed emancipation but wanted free blacks removed from their vicinity. And colonization had virtually no hope of succeeding. Owing to the South's growing dependence on slavery, even compensated manumission was unacceptable to most slaveholders. In addition, the Society never had enough funds to buy freedom for significant numbers of slaves. Between 1820 and 1830—a period when the slave population nearly doubled in size—only 1,400 blacks migrated to Liberia, and most of them were already free blacks, rather than recently enslaved people who had been manumitted by colonizationists.

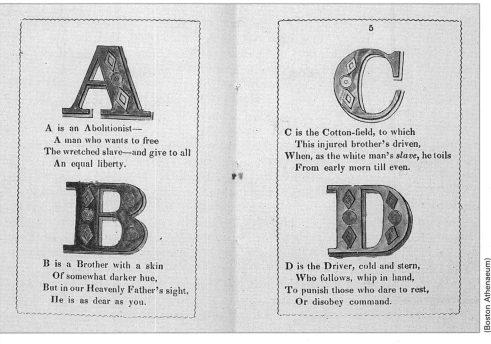

The Antislavery Alphabet *Abolitionists tried to enlist what they viewed as the natural purity of children to their cause by producing antislavery toys, games, and even alphabet books.*

Most African-Americans opposed colonization. As native-born Americans, they asked, how could they be sent back to a continent they had never known? "We are natives of this country," one black pastor proclaimed. "We only ask that we be treated as well as foreigners." In opposition to colonization, blacks formed their own abolition societies. David Walker, a North Carolina-born free black who owned a used-clothing store in Boston, smuggled antislavery tracts into the South by stuffing them into the pockets of clothes he shipped there. In 1829, Walker published an *Appeal ... to the Colored Citizens of the World*, urging slaves to rise up and murder their masters if slavery were not abolished. He warned whites that "your DESTRUCTION is at hand, and will be speedily consummated unless you REPENT." In 1830, black leaders began holding annual conventions devoted to abolishing slavery in the South and repealing discriminatory black codes in the North.

Some white abolitionists also began to move toward more radical positions. In 1821, the Quaker Benjamin Lundy began a newspaper, the *Genius of Universal Emancipation,* which proposed that no new slave states be admitted to the Union, the internal slave trade be outlawed, and the three-fifths clause of the Constitution repealed, and that Congress abolish slavery wherever it had the authority to do so.

In 1828, Lundy hired a young New Englander, **William Lloyd Garrison,** as his assistant editor. With his premature baldness and steel-rimmed glasses, Garrison looked more like a schoolmaster than a revolutionary. But in 1831, when he launched his own newspaper, *The Liberator,* he quickly established himself as the most prominent and provocative white abolitionist. "I am in earnest," Garrison wrote. "I will not equivocate—I will not excuse—I will not retreat a single inch— AND I WILL BE HEARD." He filled the pages of *The Liberator* with stories of slaves beaten to death or burned alive by their masters, and appealed to the humanity of his readers to abolish the institution.

In 1833, Garrison gathered with about sixty delegates, black and white, men and women, to form the American Antislavery Society. His battle cry was "immediate emancipation" without compensation to slaveholders. Free blacks, he insisted, should not be shipped to Africa, but granted full equality with whites. He pointedly greeted slaves as "a Man and a Brother," "a Woman and a Sister." But even Garrison did not think that all slaves could be freed at the stroke of a pen. "Immediate emancipation" meant that all Americans had to acknowledge that slavery was intolerable and must be destroyed. Garrison quickly gained support from the growing ranks of black abolitionists, who made up three-fourths of his newspaper subscribers in the early years. One black barber in Pittsburgh sent Garrison sixty dollars to support *The Liberator*.

Fugitive slaves played a central role in the abolitionist movement. The foremost of these was Frederick Douglass, who escaped from slavery in Maryland in 1838, and spoke out against slavery in his powerful autobiography, his newspaper the *North Star,* and his public lectures. Douglass could rivet an audience with an opening line. "I appear before the immense assembly this evening as a thief and a robber," he proclaimed. "I stole this head, these limbs, this body from my master, and ran off with them." Other fugitive slaves—including William Wells Brown and Harriet Tubman—served the cause by publicizing the horrors of slavery, telling tales of brutal treatment and families separated by sale.

Relations between black and white abolitionists were not always harmonious. Many white abolitionists supported legal but not social equality for blacks. They favored lighter-skinned Negroes and sometimes excluded black abolitionists from their meetings. Yet the racial prejudice of white abolitionists was mild compared to that of most whites, some of whom transferred their hatred of blacks to abolitionists. Mobs led by local elites attacked the homes and businesses of black and white abolitionists, destroyed their printing presses, and disrupted their meetings. In 1834, an anti-abolitionist mob destroyed forty-five homes in Philadelphia's black community. In 1835, a Boston mob dragged Garrison through town with a hanging noose around his neck. And in 1837, a mob in Alton, Illinois, destroyed the printing press of antislavery editor Elijah P. Lovejoy, then shot him dead and dragged his mutilated corpse through the streets.

Abolitionists, like temperance reformers, drew on the language of revivals and condemned slavery as sin. But Protestant churches did not rally behind abolition as they rallied behind temperance. The Rev. Lyman Beecher roared against the evils of strong drink but merely whispered about those of slavery. In 1834, he tried to suppress abolitionists at Cincinnati's Lane Theological Seminary where he was president. In response, a student named Theodore Dwight Weld, who was a follower of Charles G. Finney, led the "Lane rebels" out of Beecher's seminary to the more radical Oberlin College.

Issues of strategy and tactics divided abolitionists during the 1830s. Some believed that the legal and political arena presented the best opportunities for ending slavery. But Garrison and his followers were beginning to reject all participation not only in party politics, but in government itself. In 1838, they founded the New England Non-Resistance Society, based on Garrison's radical new doctrine of non-resistance. According to that doctrine, the fundamental evil of slavery was its reliance on force, the opposite of Christian love. And just like slavery, government itself ultimately rested on coercion; even laws passed by elected legislatures required police enforcement. True Christians, Garrison concluded, should refuse to vote, hold office, or have anything to do with government.

The second major issue dividing abolitionists was the role of women in the movement. From the outset, women had actively participated in antislavery societies, but in separate female auxiliaries. Then in 1837, **Angelina and Sarah Grimké,** daughters of a South Carolina slaveholder, undertook an antislavery lecture tour of New England, speaking in public before mixed audiences of men and women. Such conduct, said critics, was indelicate; women should obey men, not lecture them. The Grimkés responded in 1838 by writing two classics of American feminism: Sarah Grimké's *Letters on the Condition of Women and the Equality of the Sexes,* and Angelina Grimké's *Letters to Catharine E. Beecher* (who opposed female equality). Some abolitionists dismissed their efforts: women's grievances, said poet John Greenleaf Whittier, were "paltry" compared to the "great and dreadful wrongs of the slave." Even Angelina's husband, "Lane Rebel" Theodore Dwight Weld, thought women's rights should be subordinated to antislavery.

In 1840, the issues of nonresistance and women's rights split the American Antislavery Society. The precipitating event was the election of Abby Kelley to a previously all-male committee. In the battle that followed, Garrison, a strong supporter of women's rights, won control of the organization, and his anti-feminist opponents—including wealthy New York philanthropists Arthur and Lewis Tappan and former slaveholder James G. Birney of Alabama—walked out. Some of them flocked to the new Liberty Party, which nominated Birney for president in 1840 on a platform that called on Congress to abolish slavery in the District of Columbia, end the interstate slave trade, and stop admitting new slave states to the Union. Others followed Lewis Tappan into the new American and Foreign Anti-Slavery Society.

But the break-up of the American Anti-Slavery Society did not significantly damage the larger movement. By 1840, there were more than fifteen hundred local antislavery societies circulating abolitionist tracts, newspapers, and even chocolates wrapped in antislavery messages. Local societies pursued a grassroots campaign to flood Congress with petitions calling for an end to slavery in the District of Columbia. When exasperated southerners in 1836 adopted a "gag rule" automatically tabling these petitions without discussion, they triggered a debate that shifted public attention from abolitionism to the constitutional rights of free expression and Congressional petition—a debate that further served the antislavery cause. And the split between moderates and radicals within the antislavery ranks helped the movement by giving northerners a choice between different levels and strategies of commitment.

Women's Rights   When Sarah and Angelina Grimké took up the cause of women's rights in 1838, they were not merely defending their right to participate in the antislavery movement. They were responding to perceived similarities between the conditions of slaves and women. Garrison himself stressed the special degradation and sexual vulnerability of women under slavery, denouncing the slaveholding South as one vast brothel. Early issues of *The Liberator* contained a "Ladies' Department" illustrated with a kneeling slave woman imploring, "Am I Not a Woman and a Sister?" When abolitionists such as Philadelphia Quaker **Lucretia Mott,** Lucy Stone, and Abby Kelley embraced women's rights, they were acknowledging a sisterhood in oppression with female slaves.

In the early nineteenth century, American women were prohibited from voting or holding public office and denied access to higher education and the professions. Married women had no legal identity apart from their husbands: they could not own property or control their own earnings, sue or be sued, or enter a contract. Divorced women could not gain custody of their children. And in the midst of many humanitarian efforts to eradicate violence—including movements against dueling and war, military flogging, and capital punishment—domestic violence went virtually unchallenged, except as a side issue within the temperance movement. According to the popular idea of separate spheres, women's place was in the home, and even in their proper sphere their legal rights were severely limited.

But reform movements provided middle-class women with unprecedented opportunities to work in public without openly defying the dictate that their proper sphere was the home. When women left their homes to distribute religious tracts, battle intemperance, or work for peace, they could claim they were transforming wretched homes into nurseries of happiness. It was a tricky argument to make: justifying reform activities on behalf of family protection could undercut women's demands for legal equality. But the experiences acquired in a range of reform activities provided invaluable skills for women to take up the cause of their own rights. And the women's rights movement, at its most radical, openly challenged gender-based double standards. "Men and women," Sarah Grimké wrote, "are CREATED EQUAL! They are both moral and accountable beings, and whatever is right for man to do, is right for woman."

Although feminism first emerged within abolitionism, the discrimination encountered by women in the antislavery movement drove them to make women's rights a separate cause. In the 1840s, Lucy Stone became the first abolitionist to give a lecture devoted entirely to women's rights. When Lucretia Mott arrived at the World's Anti-Slavery Convention in London in 1840, and was seated in a screened-off section for women, her own allegiance to women's rights was sealed. So was that of **Elizabeth Cady Stanton,** who attended the London meeting with her abolitionist husband on their honeymoon. In 1848, Mott and Stanton together organized the **Seneca Falls Convention** for women's rights at Seneca Falls, New York. That convention's Declaration of Sentiments, modeled on the Declaration of Independence, began with the assertion that "all men and women are created equal." The convention passed twelve resolutions, eleven of them unanimously, and the twelfth, women's right to vote, over a minority opposition. After the Civil War, however, woman suffrage became the main demand of women's rights advocates.

Women's rights advocates won a few notable victories. In 1860, Stanton's lobbying helped secure passage of a New York law allowing married women to own property—not the first such law, but the most comprehensive to that date. But women's rights had less impact than many other reforms including temperance, school reform, and abolitionism. Women would not secure the national right to vote until 1920, fifty-five years after the Thirteenth Amendment abolished slavery. Nineteenth-century feminists had to content themselves with piecemeal gains. The cause of women's rights suffered from its association with abolitionism and met resistance from advocates of women's separate sphere (see Chapter 9). Nevertheless, women made important strides toward equality.

Penitentiaries and Asylums   Beginning in the 1820s, reformers began to combat poverty, crime, and insanity by establishing new model institutions based on innovative theories about the roots of deviancy. As urban poverty and crime grew increasingly visible, investigators concluded that

Sojourner Truth, 1864 *Born into slavery in New York, the woman who named herself Sojourner Truth became a religious perfectionist, a powerful evangelical preacher, and one of the most influential abolitionists and feminists of her time. In the 1860s, she sold photographic portraits of herself printed on small cards, explaining, "I sell the shadow to support the substance."*

(Library of Congress)

such problems arose not from innate sinfulness, but from poor home environments, especially a failure of parental discipline. Both religious and secular reformers believed that human nature could be improved through placement in the proper moral environment. The reformers' model of the proper moral environment for paupers, criminals, and the mentally ill was the asylum, an institution that would remove deviants from corrupting influences by placing them in a controlled, orderly environment, and provide them with moral supervision and disciplined work.

Unitarian minister William Ellery Channing hoped that "The study of the causes of crime may lead us to its cure." The colonial jail had been merely a temporary holding cell for offenders awaiting trial; early American criminals were punished by flogging, branding, or hanging rather than extended prison terms. By contrast, the nineteenth-century penitentiary was an asylum designed to lead criminals to "penitential" reformation by isolating them and encouraging them to contemplate their guilt for designated terms of incarceration. Two different models for the penitentiary emerged in the antebellum era. New York's "Auburn system" forbade prisoners to speak or look at one another as they worked together by day, and confined them in individual, windowless cells by night. Under the more extreme "Pennsylvania" or "separate system," each prisoner was confined day and night in a single cell with a walled courtyard for exercise, deprived of human contact within the prison, and permitted no news or visits from the outside.

Antebellum reformers also designed special asylums for the poor and the mentally ill. The prevailing colonial practice of poor relief was "outdoor relief," supporting the poor by placing them in other people's households. The new "indoor relief" confined the infirm poor in almshouses, and the able-bodied poor in workhouses. Once again, reformers believed that removing the poor from their demoralizing surroundings and subjecting them to institutional regimentation and disciplined labor would transform them into virtuous, productive citizens. A parallel movement shaped new approaches to treating the mentally ill, as illuminated in the work of humanitarian reformer Dorothea Dix. Instead of imprisoning the insane in jails and sheds, she argued, society should house them in orderly hospitals where they should receive proper medical and moral care.

Penitentiaries, almshouses and workhouses, and insane asylums all reflected the same optimistic belief that the solution for deviancy lay in proper moral environments. From one point of view, such efforts were humanitarian: they confined criminals rather than flogging them, offered relief to the poor, and provided shelter and medical care to the homeless insane. But from another point of view, the asylum reformers were practicing extreme forms of social control. Convinced that criminals, the poor, and the insane required regimentation, they confined them in prison-like conditions, policed their social interaction, and controlled their every move. The idealism behind the new asylums was genuine, but utopian intentions did not protect asylum inmates from the sufferings of incarceration and regimentation.

**Utopian
Communities**
The reformist belief in the possibility of human perfection assumed purest expression in the **utopian communities** that first began to surface in the 1820s, and flourished during the next few decades (see Map 10.2). Among the hundreds of utopian experiments

undertaken in the antebellum period, most aimed at offering alternatives to the selfish excesses of social and economic competition. Modern Times on Long Island and the North American Phalanx at Red Bank, New Jersey, were influenced by the ideas of Frenchman Charles Fourier, who sought to eradicate the evils of economic competition by establishing a harmonious society whose members all pursued "attractive" labor.

In 1825, British industrialist Robert Owen founded the New Harmony community in Indiana. As a successful Scottish mill-owner, Owen had substantially improved his workers' living conditions and educational opportunities. If social arrangements could be perfected, he believed, then vice and misery would disappear, because human character was formed entirely by environment. Owen proposed to create small, planned communities—"Villages of Unity and Mutual Cooperation"—where occupational, religious, and political groups would live together in perfect balance. Upon founding New Harmony, Owen confidently predicted that northerners would embrace its principles within two years. Instead, the community became a magnet for idlers and fanatics, and failed within two years. But Owen's ideas survived the wreckage of New Harmony. His insistence that human character was formed by environment and that cooperation was superior to competition had an enduring impact on urban workers, who took up his cause of educational reform in the years to come.

Experimental communities multiplied rapidly during the economic crises of the late 1830s and 1840s. Brook Farm, near Boston, was the creation of a group of religious philosophers called transcendentalists, who sought to revitalize Christianity by proclaiming the infinite spiritual capacities of ordinary men and women. Convinced that the competitive commercial life of the cities was unnatural, and committed (if only briefly) to balancing mental and manual labor in their own personal lives, Brook Farmers spent their days milking cows and mowing hay, and their evenings contemplating philosophy. This utopian community attracted several renowned writers, including Ralph Waldo Emerson and Nathaniel Hawthorne, and its literary magazine, *The Dial,* became an important forum for transcendentalist ideas about philosophy, art, and literature (as discussed further in Chapter 11). But its life-span was brief.

The most controversial utopian experiment was the Oneida Community, established in 1848 in New York by John Humphrey Noyes. A convert of Charles Finney, Noyes too became a theological perfectionist. At Oneida, he advocated a form of Christian communism that challenged conventional notions of religion and property, gender roles, even dress and child rearing. The Oneidans renounced private property, put men to work in kitchens, and adopted the radical new bloomer costume for women. But what most upset their critics was the application of communism to marriage. In place of conventional marriage, which Noyes regarded as profoundly selfish, he advocated "complex marriage," in which every member of the community was married to every other member of the other sex. Oneida did not promote sexual free-for-all: couplings were arranged through an intermediary, in part to track paternity. Contemporaries dismissed Noyes as a licentious crackpot. Yet Oneida achieved considerable economic prosperity and was attracting new members long after other, less radical utopias had failed.

Despite the ridicule of many of their contemporaries, utopian communities exemplified the idealism and hopefulness that permeated nearly all reform movements in the antebellum period.

CHRONOLOGY
1824–1840

1824	John Quincy Adams elected president by the House of Representatives.
1826	American Temperance Society organized.
1828	Andrew Jackson elected president. "Tariff of Abominations." John Calhoun anonymously writes *South Carolina Exposition and Protest*.
1830	Jackson's Maysville Road Bill veto. Indian Removal Act.
1830–1831	Charles G. Finney's Rochester revival.
1831	William Lloyd Garrison starts *The Liberator*.
1832	Jackson vetoes recharter of the Bank of the United States. Jackson reelected president. South Carolina Nullification Proclamation.
1833	Force Bill. Compromise Tariff. American Anti-Slavery Society founded. South Carolina nullifies the Force Bill.
1834	Whig Party organized.
1836	Specie Circular. Martin Van Buren elected president.
1837	Horace Mann becomes secretary of the Massachusetts Board of Education. Elijah Lovejoy murdered by proslavery mob. Grimké sisters set out on lecture tour of New England.
1837–1843	Economic depression.
1838	Garrison's New England Non-Resistance Society founded. Sarah Grimké's *Letters on the Condition of Women and the Equality of the Sexes* and Angelina Grimké's *Letters to Catharine E. Beecher*.
1840	Independent Treasury Act passed. William Henry Harrison elected president. First Washington Temperance Society Started.
1841	Dorothea Dix begins exposé of prison conditions. Brook Farm community founded.
1848	Seneca Falls convention.

CONCLUSION

The voices of the common people resounded through politics during the 1820s and 1830s. As voting barriers such as property requirements collapsed, and the wheels of party machines began to turn, the surface harmony of the Era of Good Feelings gave way to the raucous huzzahs of mass politics. Similar developments transformed American religion. Revivals swelled the numbers of Methodists and Baptists, who did not require an educated ministry, while Presbyterians and Congregationalists, who insisted on an educated clergy, experienced relative decline. Calvinist clergymen found their doctrine of human depravity undermined by the revivalists' insistence that men and women hold the capacity to remake and even perfect themselves.

The louder the people spoke, the more divided they became. The cries of "foul" that had greeted the highly contested election of 1824 later catapulted Andrew Jackson into office as the embodiment of the popular will. But Jackson's dictatorial manner and his stands on internal improvements, tariffs, nullification, and banking provoked opposition and contributed to the emergence of the Whigs and the second party system. The Panic of 1837 deepened party divisions by pushing Democrats toward a hard-money, antibank position. Similarly, religious revivals, which aimed to unite Americans in a religion of the heart, drew criticism for emotional excess and spawned controversial new religious groups such as the Mormons.

Seeded in part by religious revivals, a variety of reform movements sprouted in the 1820s and 1830s. Some reforms, such as women's rights and the abolition of slavery, promised legal equality for groups excluded from political participation. Others, such as temperance, education, prison reform, and utopian communitarianism, sought the radical improvement of human nature through a combination of individual and institutional efforts. Yet for all their optimism about improving human nature, reformers betrayed profound anxieties about the direction of American society. Many of them proved willing to coerce people into change by such measures as prohibiting liquor sales, requiring school attendance, and placing prisoners in solitary confinement. While disdaining politics as corrupt, many reformers enlisted strategies and tactics similar to those of politics, blasting liquor and slavery with the same fervor that Jacksonians directed at banks and monopolies, and stirring up public opinion in support of their causes. Mass democracy, their actions suggested, tended to politicize everything in its path.

11

TECHNOLOGY, CULTURE, AND
EVERYDAY LIFE 1840–1860

TECHNOLOGY AND ECONOMIC GROWTH

Widely hailed as democratic, technology drew praise from all sides. Conservative statesman Daniel Webster praised machines for doing the work of people without consuming food or clothing. Radical labor organizer Sarah Bagley, a textile worker, traced the improvement of society to new technology. American schoolboys, reported a Swedish tourist to the United States in 1849–1851, constantly drew pictures on their slates of steamboats, engines, and other forms of "locomotive machinery."

The technological improvements that transformed life in antebellum America included the steam engine, the cotton gin, the reaper, the sewing machine, and the telegraph. Some of these originated in Europe, but Americans had a flair for investing in others' inventions and perfecting their own. Improvements in Eli Whitney's cotton gin between 1793 and 1860, for example, increased eightfold the amount of cotton that could be cleaned in a day. Of course, technology did not benefit everyone. The cotton gin entrenched slavery by intensifying southern dependence on cotton. Machine manufacture undercut the position of artisans by rendering many traditional skills obsolete. But by improving transportation and increasing productivity, technology lowered commodity prices and raised living standards for substantial numbers of Americans between 1840 and 1860.

Agricultural Advancement   After 1830, American settlers were edging westward from the woodlands of Ohio and Kentucky into parts of Indiana, Michigan, Illinois, and Missouri, where the flat grasslands of the prairie alternated with forests. Prairie soil, though richly fertile, was

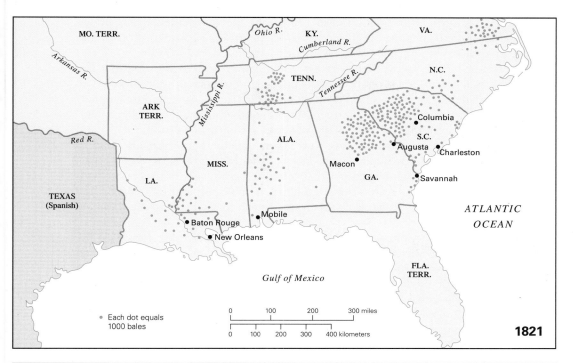

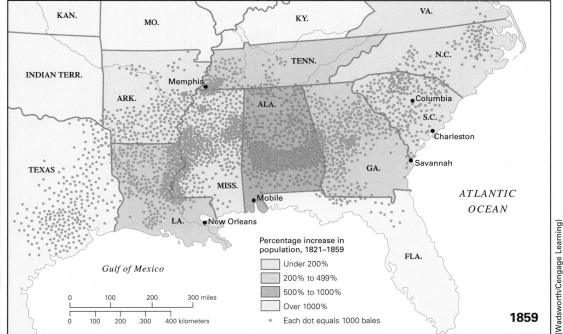

MAP 11.1 Cotton Production in the South

These two maps reveal the rapid westward expansion of cotton production and its importance to the antebellum South.

root-matted and difficult to break. But in 1837, John Deere invented a steel-tipped plow that cut in half the labor required to till for planting. Timber for houses and fencing was available in nearby woods, and settlements spread rapidly.

Wheat became to midwestern farmers what cotton was to the South. "The wheat crop is the great crop of the North-west," an agricultural journal noted in 1850. "It pays debts, buys groceries, clothing and lands, and answers more emphatically the purposes of trade among farmers than any other crop." Technological advances sped the harvesting as well as the planting of wheat. The traditional hand sickle consumed huge amounts of time and labor, and the cut wheat also had to be picked up and bound by hand. But in 1834, Cyrus McCormick of Virginia patented a horse-drawn mechanical reaper that harvested grain seven times faster with half the work force. In 1847, he opened a factory in Chicago, and by 1860 he had sold 80,000 reapers. The mechanical reaper guaranteed that wheat would dominate the midwestern prairies.

Ironically, just as a Connecticut Yankee named Eli Whitney had stimulated the southern economy by inventing the cotton gin, a proslavery southerner named Cyrus McCormick would help the North win the Civil War. The North provided the main market for the **McCormick reaper** and its many competitors; the South, with its reliance on unpaid slave labor, had little incentive to invest in labor-saving agricultural machinery. During the Civil War, McCormick sold more than a quarter of a million reapers, and thus helped keep northern agricultural production high at a time when labor shortages caused by troop mobilization might otherwise have slashed production.

Even as Americans were mechanizing agriculture, they tended to farm wastefully, preferring to seek "virgin" soil rather than improve "worn out" soil. But some eastern farmers, confronted by competition from the West, began to experiment with improved agricultural techniques. In Orange County, New York, dairy farmers fed their cows the best clover and bluegrass and undertook cleaner dairy processing. The result was a superior butter that commanded more than double the price of ordinary butter. Other eastern farmers turned to soil improvement. By fertilizing their fields with plaster left over from canal construction, Virginia wheat growers raised their average yield from six bushels per acre in 1800 to fifteen bushels by the 1850s. American cotton planters in the Southeast began to import guano (sea bird droppings) from Peru to fertilize their fields in an effort to compete successfully with the fertile soil of the Old Southwest.

Technology and Industrial Progress   Industrial advances between 1840 and 1860 owed an immense debt to the development of effective machine tools, power-driven machines that cut and shaped metal to precise specifications. In the early 1800s, Eli Whitney's plan to manufacture muskets by using interchangeable parts actually awaited the development of the machine tools essential to the system. After 1830, American manufacturers began to import machine-tool technology from Britain. By the 1840s, machine tools had greatly reduced the need to hand file parts to make them fit, and they were applied to the manufacture of firearms, clocks, and sewing machines. After mid-century, Europeans began to call this system of manufacturing interchangeable parts the

"American System of Manufacturing" and to import machine tools manufactured in the United States. After touring American factories in 1854, a British engineer concluded that Americans "universally and willingly" resorted to machines as a substitute for manual labor.

The American manufacturing system had several distinct advantages. Traditionally, damage to any part of a mechanical contrivance had rendered the whole thing useless, because no new part would fit. The perfection of interchangeable parts made replacement parts possible. In addition, improved machine tools enabled entrepreneurs to push inventions into mass production with a speed that attracted investors. Sophisticated machine tools, according to one manufacturer, increased production "by confining a worker to one particular limb of a pistol until he had made two thousand."

After the transmission of the first telegraph message in 1844, Americans also seized enthusiastically on the telegraph's promise to eliminate the constraints of time and space. The speed with which Americans formed telegraph companies and the ease with which they strung their lines stunned a British engineer, who noted in 1854 that "no private interests can oppose the passage of a line through any property." Boston developed an elaborate system of telegraph stations that could alert fire companies throughout the city to a blaze in any neighborhood. By 1852, more than fifteen thousand miles of telegraph lines connected cities as distant as Quebec, New Orleans, and St. Louis. (Chapter 13, Technology and Culture, further discusses the telegraph.)

The Railroad Boom

Even more than the telegraph, the railroad dramatized the democratic promise of technology. In 1790, even European royalty could travel no faster than fourteen miles an hour—by horse. By 1850, ordinary Americans could travel three times as fast—by train.

Americans loved railroads, reported one Frenchman, "as a lover loves his mistress." Their love of early railroad travel had a great deal to overcome. Sparks from locomotives showered passengers riding in open cars, and discouraged passengers in closed coaches from opening the windows. (Frontier hero Davy Crockett was an exception: he explained that "I can only judge of the speed by putting my head out to spit, which I did, and overtook it so quick, that it hit me smack in the face.") In the absence of brakes, passengers on trains often had to get off to help stop them. Trains rarely ran at night because they lacked lights. Before the introduction of standard time zones in 1883, scheduling was a nightmare and delays were frequent. Individual railroads used different gauge track, making frequent train changes necessary; even in the 1850s, a journey from Charleston to Philadelphia required eight transfers.

Yet nothing slowed the advance of railroads or cured Americans' mania for them. In 1851, the editor of the *American Railroad Journal* wrote that in the previous twenty years, the locomotive had become "the great agent of civilization and progress, the most powerful instrument for good the world has yet reached." Between 1840 and 1860, the size of the rail network and the power and convenience of trains underwent a stunning transformation. Railroads extended track mileage from three thousand to thirty thousand miles; closed coaches replaced open cars;

(National Gallery of Art, Washington, D.C., Gift of Mrs. Huttleston Rogers 1945.4.1)

George Innes, The Lackawanna Valley, ca. 1856. *This landscape painting was commissioned by the Delaware, Lackawanna, and Western Railroad to celebrate the railroad's growth—specifically, the construction of the line's first roundhouse, just outside Scranton, Pennsylvania. But the tree stumps littering the foreground suggest the painter's concerns over the impact of industrial progress on the American landscape.*

kerosene lamps made night travel possible; and increasingly powerful engines enabled trains to climb steep hills. Fifty thousand miles of telegraph wire enabled dispatchers to communicate with trains en route and thus reduce delays. By 1860, the United States had more track than all the rest of the world combined.

Railroads represented the second major phase of the transportation revolution. Canals remained in use—the Erie Canal did not reach its peak volume until 1880—but the railroads gradually overtook them, first in passengers and then in freight. By 1860, the value of goods transported by railroads greatly surpassed that carried by canals.

By 1860, railroads had spread like vast spider webs east of the Mississippi River. They transformed southern cities like Atlanta and Chattanooga into thriving commercial hubs. Most important, the railroads linked the East and the Midwest. The New York Central and the Erie Railroads joined New York City to Buffalo; the Pennsylvania Railroad connected Philadelphia to Pittsburgh; and the Baltimore and Ohio linked Baltimore to Wheeling, Virginia (now West Virginia). Simultaneously, intense construction in Ohio, Indiana, and Illinois created trunk lines that tied these routes to cities farther west. By 1860, rail lines ran from Buffalo to Chicago, from Pittsburgh to Fort Wayne, and from Wheeling to St. Louis (see Map 11.2).

The dramatic growth of Chicago illustrates the impact of expanding rail links. In 1849, Chicago was just a village of a few hundred people with virtually no rail service. By 1860, it had become a city of one hundred thousand served by eleven railroads. Farmers in the Upper Midwest, who had once shipped their grain, livestock, and dairy products down the Mississippi River to New Orleans, could now send products directly east by railroad. Chicago thus supplanted New Orleans as the main commercial hub of the continental interior.

Rail lines stimulated the settlement of the Midwest. By 1860 Illinois, Indiana, and Wisconsin had replaced Ohio, Pennsylvania, and New York as the leading wheat-growing states. Railroads increased the value of farmland and promoted additional settlement. In turn, population growth triggered industrial development in cities such as Chicago, Davenport, and Minneapolis because the new settlers needed lumber for fences and houses, and gristmills to grind wheat into flour.

Railroads also encouraged the growth of small towns along their routes. The Illinois Central, which had more track than any other railroad in 1855, made money not only from its traffic but from real estate speculation. Purchasing land for stations along its path, the Illinois Central then laid out towns around the stations. In 1854 Manteno,

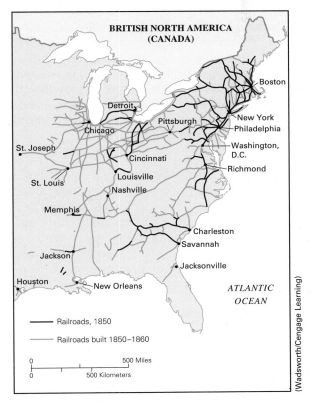

MAP 11.2 Railroad Growth, 1850–1860

Rail ties between the East and the Midwest greatly increased during the railroad "boom" of the 1850s.

Illinois was a vacant crossroads; after it became a railroad stop, it grew, by 1860, into a bustling town with hotels, lumberyards, grain elevators, and gristmills. (The Illinois Central even dictated the naming of streets. Those running east and west were named after trees, while those running north and south were numbered.) By the Civil War, few thought of the railroad-linked Midwest as a frontier region.

As the nation's first big business, the railroads transformed the way business was conducted. During the early 1830s railroads, like canals, depended on state funding. With the onset of depression in the late 1830s, however, state governments scrapped many railroad projects. Convinced that railroads burdened them with high taxes and blasted hopes, voters in several states amended their constitutions to bar state funding for railroads and canals. Federal aid would not become widely available until the Civil War, and local and county governments could not keep up with the funding needed for the dramatic expansion of the railroad network in the 1850s. Aware of the economic benefits of railroads, people living near them had long purchased government-issued railroad securities and railroad stock. But the large railroads of the 1850s needed more capital than small investors could generate.

Gradually, the center of railroad financing shifted to New York City, where the railroad boom of the 1850s helped make Wall Street the nation's greatest capital market. The securities of all the leading railroads were traded on the floor of the **New York Stock Exchange**. Railroad expansion also turned New York City into the center of modern investment firms. Investment firms evaluated the securities of railroads in Toledo or Davenport or Chattanooga, then found purchasers for these securities in New York and Philadelphia, Paris and London, and Hamburg. Controlling the flow of funds to railroads, investment bankers began to exert influence over the railroads' internal affairs. A Wall Street analyst noted that railroad men seeking financing "must remember that money is power, and that the [financier] can dictate to a great extent his own terms."

Rising Prosperity

Technological advances also improved the lives of consumers by reducing prices on many commodities. For example, clocks that had cost $50 to fabricate by hand in 1800 could be produced by machine for fifty cents in 1850. At the same time, the widening use of steam power contributed to a 25 percent rise in the average worker's real income (actual purchasing power) between 1840 and 1860. Earlier factories, which relied on water power, had to shut down when rivers or streams froze. With the spread of steam engines, factories stayed open longer and thus increased workers' annual wages. Textile workers were among those who benefited: although their hourly wages showed little gain, their average annual wages rose from $163 in 1830 to $201 by 1859.

The growth of towns and cities also contributed to an increase in incomes. Farmers living in sparsely settled areas experienced the same seasonal fluctuations as early factory workers. "A year in some farming states such as Pennsylvania," a traveler commented in 1823, "is only of eight months duration, four months being lost to the laborer, who is turned away as a useless animal." Densely populated towns and cities, by contrast, offered more opportunities for year-round work. The urban dockworker thrown out of work by frozen waterways might find employment as a hotel porter or an unskilled indoor laborer.

Towns and cities also provided women and children with new opportunities for paid work—as opposed to the unpaid labor they had long performed on farms. The wages of children between the ages of ten and eighteen came to play an integral role in the family economy. Family heads who earned more than six hundred dollars a year could afford to keep their children in school, but many breadwinners made less than three hundred dollars a year. Despite declines in commodity prices, most families lived close to the margin. Budgets of working-class families in New York City and Philadelphia during the early 1850s reveal annual expenditures of five hundred to six hundred dollars, with more than 40 percent spent on food, 25 to 30 percent on rent, and most of the remainder on clothing and fuel. Such a family needed the wages of the children and sometimes the wife, as well as the male head of the household.

The quality of life in urban wage-earning families was not necessarily superior to life in farming communities. A farmer who owned land, livestock, and a house did not have to worry about paying rent or buying fuel and rarely ran short of food. Still, to purchase, clear, and stock a farm could cost as much as five hundred dollars and promised no financial return for a few years. The majority of agricultural workers did not own farms and were exposed to seasonal fluctuations in demand for labor. In many respects, urban wage earners were better off than agricultural workers.

The economic advantages of urban living help explain why so many Americans were moving to cities. During the 1840s and 1850s, American cities provided their residents with an unprecedented range of comforts and conveniences.

THE QUALITY OF LIFE

"Think of the numberless contrivances and inventions for our comfort and luxury," exclaimed poet Walt Whitman, "and you will bless your star that Fate has cast your lot in the year of Our Lord 1857." Improvements in the quality of life affected such mundane activities as eating, drinking, and washing. The patent office in Washington was flooded with sketches of reclining seats, washing machines, mechanical street sweepers, and fly traps. Machine-made furniture began to transform the interiors of houses. Stoves revolutionized heating and cooking.

Yet change occurred unevenly. Technology enabled the middle class to enjoy luxuries formerly reserved for the rich but widened the distance between the middle class and the poor. As middle-class homes became increasingly lavish, the urban poor lived in cramped tenements. Some critical elements such as medicine lagged behind. Nevertheless, the benefits of progress impressed Americans more than its limitations.

Dwellings During the early 1800s, the randomly sited wood frame houses that had dotted colonial cities began to yield to more orderly brick row houses. Row houses, which were practical responses to rising land values (as much as 750 percent in Manhattan between 1785 and 1815), drew criticism for their "extreme uniformity." But they were not all alike. Middle-class row houses, with their cast iron balconies, curved staircases, and beautifully finished interiors, were larger and more elaborate than working-class row houses and less likely to be subdivided for occupancy by several families. The worst of the subdivided row houses were called tenements and often inhabited by Irish immigrants and free blacks.

Home furnishings also revealed the widening gap between the prosperous and the poor. Middle- and upper-class families decorated their houses with fine furniture in the ornate, rococo style, along with wool carpeting, wallpaper, pianos, pictures, and gilt-framed mirrors. The mass-production of furniture reduced prices and tended to level taste between the middle and upper classes, while still setting those classes off from everyone else. Some members of the middle class took pains to decorate the public areas of their houses, especially the parlor, as lavishly as possible, in an effort to impress visitors, while furnishing the rest of the house sparsely.

In rural areas, the quality of housing depended largely on the age of the settlement. In new settlements, the standard dwelling was a rude log cabin with planked floors, clay chimneys, and windows covered by oiled paper or cloth. As rural communities matured, log cabins gave way to insulated balloon-frame houses of two or more rooms. Instead of thick posts and beams laboriously fitted together, a balloon-frame house had a skeleton of two-by-fours spaced at eighteen-inch intervals. The balloon-frame was lighter and stronger than the older post-and-beam method, and it required no technical knowledge of joinery. The simplicity and cheapness of such houses endeared them to western builders.

Conveniences and Inconveniences

By today's standards, everyday life in the 1840s and 1850s was primitive. But contemporaries were struck by how much better it was becoming. In urban areas, coal-burning stoves were rapidly displacing open hearths for heating and cooking. Stoves made it possible to cook several dishes at once and thus helped diversify the American diet, while railroads brought in fresh vegetables which a century earlier had been absent from even elite dinner tables.

Contemporaries were also grateful for the new urban waterworks—systems of pipes and aqueducts that brought fresh water from rivers or reservoirs to street hydrants. In the 1840s, New York City completed the Croton aqueduct, which carried water into the city from reservoirs to the north. By 1860, sixty-eight public water systems operated in the United States.

Despite these improvements, home comforts remained limited. Coal burned longer and hotter than wood, but left a dirty residue that polluted the air, and faulty stoves could emit carbon monoxide. One architect called stoves "the national curse," "secret poisoners" that were "more insidious" than "slavery, socialism, Mormonism … tobacco, patent medicines, or coffee." The American diet continued to be affected by seasonal fluctuations. Only the rich could afford fruit out of season, since they alone could afford the sugar to preserve it. Home iceboxes were rare before 1860, so salt remained the most widely used preservative. One reason antebellum Americans ate more pork than beef was that salt pork didn't taste quite as bad as salt beef.

Although public waterworks were among the most impressive engineering feats of the age, their impact is easily exaggerated. Only a fraction of the urban population lived near water hydrants, so most houses still had no running water. Taking a

Family Group *This daguerreotype, taken about 1852, reveals the domestic details so essential to claiming middle-class social status: curtains, a wall hanging, a piano with scrolled legs, a family pet, ladies engaged in music and reading, and a young man staring into space—perhaps pondering how to pay for it all.*

(George Eastman House)

bath still required heating the water, pot by pot, on a stove. A New England physician reported that not one in five of his patients took even one bath a year.

Infrequent bathing added pungent body odors to the many strong smells of urban life. In the absence of municipal sanitation, street cleaning was done by private contractors with a reputation for slack performance. Hogs were allowed to roam freely and scavenge (and hogs that turned down the wrong street often landed in the dinner pots of the poor). Mounds of stable manure and outdoor privies added to the stench. Flush toilets were rare, and sewer systems lagged behind water-supply systems. Boston—which boasted more flush toilets than most other cities—had only five thousand for a population of 178,000 in 1860. Conveniences like running water and flush toilets became one more way for progress to set off the upper and middle classes from the poor. Conveniences also sharpened gender differences. In her popular *Treatise on Domestic Economy* (1841), Catharine Beecher told women that technological progress made it their duty to make every house a "glorious temple" by keeping floors swept and furniture polished. Skeptical of this trend toward fastidiousness, another writer cautioned women in 1857 against "ultra-housewifery."

Disease and Medicine   Despite their improving standard of living, Americans remained vulnerable to disease. **Epidemics** swept through cities and felled thousands. Yellow fever and cholera together killed one-fifth of New Orleans's population in 1832–1833, and cholera alone carried off 10 percent of the St. Louis population in 1849. Life expectancy for newborns in New York and Philadelphia during the 1830s and 1840s averaged only twenty-four years.

The transportation revolution actually increased the peril from epidemics by helping them spread from one community to the next. The cholera epidemic of 1832, which was the first truly national epidemic, followed transportation networks out of New York City: one disease route ran up the Hudson River across the Erie Canal to Ohio and down the Ohio and Mississippi Rivers to New Orleans; the other route followed shipping lines up and down the East Coast.

The failure of physicians to explain epidemic diseases reinforced hostility toward their profession. No one understood that bacteria caused cholera and yellow fever. Physicians clashed over whether epidemic diseases were spread by human touch or by "miasmas," gases arising from rotten vegetation or dead animals. Neither theory worked. Quarantines failed to prevent the spread of epidemics (an argument against the contagion theory), and many residents of swampy areas contracted neither yellow fever nor cholera (a refutation of the miasma theory). Understandably, municipal leaders declined to delegate more than advisory powers to boards of health, which were dominated by physicians.

Although epidemic disease baffled physicians, surgery made major progress with the discovery of anesthesia. Prior to 1840, young people sometimes entertained themselves at parties by inhaling nitrous oxide or "laughing gas," which suppressed pain and produced giddiness. Samuel Colt himself had exhibited laughing gas as a showman of popular science. But few recognized its surgical possibilities. Then in 1842, Crawford Long, a Georgia physician who had attended laughing-gas frolics in his youth, employed sulfuric ether (a liquid with the same properties as nitrous oxide) during a surgical operation. Dr. Long failed to follow up on his discovery, but four years later William T. G. Morton, a Boston dentist, successfully administered sulfuric ether during an operation at Massachusetts General Hospital. Within a few years, ether came into wide surgical use.

The discovery of anesthesia improved the public image of surgeons, long viewed as brutes who tortured their patients. It also permitted longer and more careful operations. Nevertheless, physicians' ignorance of the importance of clean hands and sterilized instruments continued to harm patients. In 1843, Boston physician and poet Oliver Wendell Holmes, Sr. published a paper blaming the spread of puerperal (childbed) fever on the failure of obstetricians to disinfect their hands between one delivery and the next. But doctors only gradually accepted the importance of disinfection. Operations remained as dangerous as the diseases or wounds they tried to heal. The mortality rate for amputations hovered around 40 percent.

Popular Health Movements   Suspicious of orthodox medicine, antebellum Americans turned to a variety of alternative therapies and regimens that promised longer and healthier lives. One popular treatment was hydropathy, or the "water cure," which arrived from Europe during the 1840s. By the mid-1850s, the United States had twenty-seven hydropathic sanatoriums, which used cold baths and wet packs to provide "an abundance of water of dewy softness and crystal transparency, to cleanse, renovate, and rejuvenate the disease-worn and dilapidated system." The water cure held a special attraction for women: hydropathy promised to relieve the pain associated with childbirth and menstruation, and sanatoriums proved to be congenial gathering places for middle-class women.

In contrast to the relatively expensive water cure, Sylvester Graham, a former temperance reformer, propounded a health system that anyone could afford. In response to the 1832 cholera epidemic, Graham urged Americans to eat vegetables, fruits, and whole-grain bread (called Graham bread), and abstain from meat, spices, coffee, and tea as well as alcohol. Soon he added to his list of forbidden indulgences "sexual excess"—which for married couples meant having intercourse more than once a month. Many of Graham's disciples were moral and social reformers. Grahamites had a special table at the Brook Farm community. One of Graham's followers ran the student dining room at Oberlin College until angry parents and hungry students drove him out. Like other reformers, Grahamites traced the evils of American society to unnatural cravings. Just as temperance reformers blamed the craving for alcohol and abolitionists, the craving for illicit power, Graham blamed the craving for meat, stimulants, and sex.

Graham was dismissed by Ralph Waldo Emerson as "the prophet of bran bread and pumpkins," and he was mobbed on three occasions—once by butchers and commercial bakers whose businesses were threatened by his reform principles. But Graham's doctrines attracted a broad audience. Boarding houses began to set Grahamite tables in their dining rooms. Graham's books sold well, and his public lectures were thronged. His regime addressed the popular desire for better health at a time when orthodox medicine seemed to do more damage than good.

Phrenology   The belief that each person was master of his or her own destiny underlay not only evangelical religion and popular health movements but also the scientific fad of **phrenology**. Phrenology rested on the idea that the human mind comprised thirty-seven distinct faculties, or "organs," each located in a different part of the brain. Because the degree of each organ's development determined skull shape, phrenologists believed, a person's character could be determined through an examination of the bumps and depressions of the skull.

In the United States two brothers, Orson and Lorenzo Fowler, became the chief promoters of phrenology in the 1840s. Orson originally planned to be a Protestant missionary, but instead became a missionary for phrenology, opening a publishing house in New York City (Fowler and Wells) that mass-marketed books on the subject. When criticized for godlessness, the Fowlers pointed to a huge organ called "Veneration" to prove that people were naturally religious. When criticized for pessimistic determinism, they replied that exercise could improve every desirable mental organ. Lorenzo proudly reported that several of his own skull bumps had been grown. As Orson liked to say, "Self-Made, or Never-Made."

Americans were drawn to the practicality of phrenology. In a mobile, individualistic society, it promised practitioners a quick way to assess other people. Some merchants used phrenological charts to pick suitable clerks, and some women asked their fiancés to undergo phrenological analysis before the wedding. Easily understood and practiced, and filled with the promise of universal improvement, phrenology was ideal for antebellum Americans. Just as they had invented machines to better their lives, they invented "sciences" that promised personal improvement.

DEMOCRATIC PASTIMES

Between 1830 and 1860, technology transformed leisure by making Americans more dependent on recreations that were manufactured and sold. People purchased entertainment in the form of cheap newspapers and novels as well as affordable tickets to plays, museums, and lectures.

Just as the Boston Associates adopted new technology to produce textiles, imaginative entrepreneurs adapted technology to making and selling entertainment. Men like James Gordon Bennett, one of the founders of the penny press in America, and P. T. Barnum, the greatest showman of the nineteenth century, amassed fortunes by making the public want whatever they had to sell.

Technology also encouraged individuals to become spectators rather than creators of their own amusements. Americans had long found ways to enjoy themselves. Even New England Puritans had indulged in games and sports. After 1830, however, the burden of providing entertainment began to shift from ordinary people to entrepreneurs who supplied ways to entertain the public. Mass entertainment was commercial entertainment, and commercial entertainment encouraged the passivity of those who consumed it.

Newspapers   In 1830, the typical American newspaper was only four pages long. Its front and back pages were devoted to advertisements, and the two middle pages contained editorials, details of ship arrivals and cargoes, reprints of political speeches, and notices of political events. Fortunately, such papers relied financially not on circulation, but on subsidies from the political groups with which they allied. They could profit without offering the exciting news stories and eye-catching illustrations that later generations of newspaper readers would take for granted.

The 1830s witnessed the beginnings of a stunning transformation in the American newspaper. Technological innovation increased both the supply of paper and the speed of production. The new steam-driven cylindrical presses led to a tenfold increase in the number of printed pages that could be produced in an hour. Enterprising journalists, among them the Scottish-born James Gordon Bennett, responded by introducing the

penny press, which would rely on mass circulation to turn a profit. In 1833, the *New York Sun* became America's first penny newspaper, and Bennett's *New York Herald* followed in 1835. By June 1835, the combined daily circulation of New York's three penny papers reached forty-four thousand, almost twenty thousand higher than the combined circulation of the city's eleven dailies before 1833. From 1830 to 1840, the combined daily circulation of American newspapers rose from roughly seventy-eight thousand to 300,000 and the number of weekly newspapers more than doubled.

The penny press also revolutionized the marketing and contents of newspapers. Whereas six-cent papers had been purchased at the printer's office, penny papers were hawked by newsboys on busy street corners. The penny papers subordinated political and commercial coverage to human-interest stories of robberies, murders, rapes, and abandoned children. They dispatched reporters to police courts and printed transcripts of sensational trials, such as that of Richard Robinson for the hatchet-murder of the beautiful prostitute Helen Jewett in a New York brothel in 1836. Charles Dickens parodied such coverage by naming one fictional American newspaper the *New York Stabber*.

But despite such limitations, as sociologist Michael Schudson observes, "The penny press invented the modern concept of 'news.'" Penny newspapers also invented modern news reporting, employing their own correspondents and using the telegraph to speed the communications process. The best penny papers, including Bennett's *New York Herald* and Horace Greeley's *New York Tribune*, pioneered modern financial and political reporting. From its inception, the *Herald* contained a daily "money article" that analyzed financial events. As Bennett observed, "The spirit, pith, and philosophy of commercial affairs is what men of business want." Snooping reporters from the *Tribune* outraged Washington politicians. In 1848, *Tribune* correspondents were temporarily barred from the House of Representatives for reporting that an Ohio Congressman ate his lunch of sausage and bread each day in the House chamber, picked his teeth with a jackknife, and wiped his greasy hands on his clothing.

The Theater

Theaters, like newspapers, increasingly appealed to a mass audience. Antebellum theaters were large (sometimes seating twenty-five hundred to four thousand people) and drew all social classes. With seat prices ranging from twelve to fifty cents, the typical theater audience included lawyers and merchants and their wives, artisans and clerks, sailors, apprentices, African-Americans, and prostitutes. Prostitutes usually sat in the top gallery, called the third tier, "that dark, horrible, guilty" place. Their presence in theaters was taken for granted, though the public sometimes grumbled when they left the third tier to solicit customers in the more expensive seats.

Theater audiences, according to critics, were notoriously ill-behaved. The lower orders of patrons cracked peanuts, spat tobacco, got drunk, and talked loudly throughout the performance. They stamped their feet, hooted at villains, and threw garbage at characters or performances they disliked. Contributing to such rowdiness was the animosity between the fan bases of different theatrical stars. In 1849, a long-running feud between the leading American actor Edwin Forrest and popular

British actor William Macready culminated in the Astor Place riot in New York City, which left twenty-two people dead. The Astor Place riot demonstrated the broad popularity of the theater. Forrest's supporters included Irish workers who loathed the British and appealed to "working men" to rally against the "aristocrat" Macready. Macready, who projected a polished and intellectual image, attracted the better-educated classes. Had not a range of classes patronized the theater, the deadly riot would probably never have occurred.

The most popular plays were emotionally charged melodramas in which virtue was rewarded, vice punished, and the hero won the beautiful heroine. Melodramas offered theater-goers such sensational features as volcanic eruptions, staged battles, even live horses on stage. Yet the single most popular dramatist in the antebellum theater was William Shakespeare. In 1835, Philadelphians witnessed sixty-five performances of Shakespeare's plays. Americans who never read a line of Shakespeare grew familiar with Othello, Juliet, and King Lear. Theatrical managers adapted Shakespeare to a popular audience. They highlighted sword fights and assassinations, cut some speeches, and occasionally substituted happy endings for sad ones. And they entertained audiences between acts with jugglers and acrobats, impersonations of Tecumseh or Aaron Burr, or the exhibition of a three-year-old child who weighed one hundred pounds.

Minstrel Shows   A stock character in antebellum plays was the Yankee or "Brother Jonathan" figure who helped audiences form an image of the ideal American as a rustic but clever patriot who was more than a match for city slickers and decadent aristocrats. In a different way, the popular minstrel shows of the 1840s and 1850s forged enduring racial stereotypes that buttressed white Americans' sense of superiority by diminishing black Americans.

Minstrel shows featured white performers in burnt-cork blackface who entertained their audiences with songs, dances, and humorous sketches that pretended to mimic black culture. But while minstrelsy did borrow a few elements of African-American culture, most of its contents were white inventions, such as Stephen Foster's song "Massa's in the Cold Ground," which made its first appearance in a minstrel show. The shows' images of African-Americans both expressed and reinforced the prejudices of the working-class whites who dominated the audience. Minstrel troupes depicted blacks as stupid, clumsy, and absurdly musical, and parodied Africanness by naming their performances the "Nubian Jungle Dance" and the "African Fling." At a time of intensifying political conflict over slavery, minstrel shows used stock characters to capture white expectations about black behavior. These included Uncle Ned, the tattered and docile slave, and Zip Coon, the arrogant urban freeman who paraded around in high hat and long-tailed coat and lived off his girlfriends.

By the 1850s, major cities from New York to San Francisco had several minstrel theaters. Touring professionals and local amateurs brought minstrelsy to small towns and villages. Author Mark Twain recalled how minstrelsy had burst upon Hannibal, Missouri, in the early 1840s as "a glad and stunning surprise." Minstrel troupes even entertained a succession of presidents in the antebellum White House.

P. T. Barnum

P. T. Barnum was the father of mass entertainment in the United States who well understood how to turn the public's demand for entertainment into profit. As a young man in Bethel, Connecticut, he started a newspaper, the *Herald of Freedom*, which assailed wrongdoing in high places; and throughout his life, he thought of himself as a public benefactor who gave people what they wanted. Yet honesty was never his strong suit. As a small-town grocer in Connecticut, he regularly cheated his customers on the dubious premise that they were trying to cheat him. Barnum, in short, was a Yankee hustler and idealist rolled into one.

After moving to New York City in 1834, Barnum launched his career as an entertainment entrepreneur. He got his start exhibiting a black woman named Joice Heth, whom he billed as the 169-year-old former slave nurse of George Washington. In fact, she was probably around eighty, but Barnum neither knew nor cared, so long as people paid to see her. When audiences began to dwindle, Barnum sent an anonymous letter to a newspaper saying that "Joice Heth is not a human being [but] an automaton, made up of whalebone, india-rubber, and numberless springs." In response, hundreds of people who had already paid to see Heth returned to determine whether she was machine or living woman. Suspicions of fraud, Barnum knew, only sold more tickets. He was playing a game with the public, and the public played right back.

In 1841, Barnum purchased a run-down museum in New York City, rechristened it the American Museum, and opened a new chapter in the history of popular entertainment. Earlier museums had exhibited stuffed birds and animals, rock specimens, and portraits of famous people—largely for educational purposes. Barnum's goal, by contrast, was to draw paying customers by stimulating public curiosity. Visitors to the American Museum could see ventriloquists, magicians, albinos, a 25-inch-tall five-year-old whom Barnum named General Tom Thumb, and the "Feejee Mermaid," billed by Barnum as "positively asserted by its owner to have been taken alive in the Feejee Islands." By 1850, the American Museum had become the best-known museum in the nation.

Blessed with a genius for publicity, Barnum recognized that newspapers could invent news as well as report it. One of his favorite tactics was to puff his own exhibits by writing letters to newspapers (under various names) reporting that the scientific world was agog over some astonishing natural curiosity that the public could see for itself at the American Museum. But Barnum's success rested on more than clever publicity. To secure his museum a reputation for providing safe family entertainment, he provided regular lectures on the evils of alcohol and the benefits of Christian religion. By marketing his museum as family entertainment, Barnum helped break down barriers that had long divided the pastimes of husbands from those of their wives.

Finally, Barnum successfully tapped the public's insatiable curiosity about natural wonders. In 1835, the editor of the *New York Sun* had boosted his circulation by claiming that a famous astronomer had discovered pelicans and winged men on the moon. At a time when each passing year brought new technological wonders, the public was ready to believe in anything, even the Feejee Mermaid.

THE QUEST FOR NATIONALITY IN LITERATURE AND ART

In the early nineteenth century, Europeans took little notice of American literature. "Who ever reads an American book?" taunted one British critic. Americans

P. T. Barnum and Tom Thumb *When P. T. Barnum posed with his protégée—whose real name was Charles Sherwood Stratton— sometime around 1850, the twelve-year-old 'human curiosity' stood a little over two feet in height. Barnum and Stratton enjoyed a long partnership which brought considerable wealth to both of them.*

(National Portrait Gallery, Smithsonian Institution/Art Resource, NY)

responded by pointing to Washington Irving, author of "Rip Van Winkle" and "The Legend of Sleepy Hollow." Irving's readers showered him with praise, even naming hotels and steamboats after him, but they had to concede that Irving had done much of his best writing while living in England.

After 1820, the United States experienced a flowering of literature called the **American Renaissance**. Its leading figures included James Fenimore Cooper, Ralph Waldo Emerson, Henry David Thoreau, Margaret Fuller, Walt Whitman, Nathaniel Hawthorne, Herman Melville, and Edgar Allan Poe. In 1800, American authors accounted for a negligible proportion of the output of American publishers. By 1830, 40 percent of the books published in the United States were written by Americans; by 1850, that number had increased to 75 percent.

American writers often sought to depict the national features of the United States—its land and its people—in their work. The quest for a distinctively American culture especially shaped the writings of Cooper, Emerson, and Whitman. It also revealed itself in the majestic paintings of the so-called Hudson River school—the first homegrown American movement in painting—and in the landscape architecture of Frederick Law Olmsted, designer of New York's Central Park.

Roots of the American Renaissance

Two broad developments, one economic and the other philosophical, contributed to the cultural efflorescence of the American Renaissance. First, the transportation revolution created a national market for books, especially fiction. Initially, this market worked to the advantage of British authors, especially Sir Walter Scott. With the publication of *Waverley* (1814), a historical novel set in Britain, Scott's star began its spectacular ascent on the American horizon. American readers gobbled up his books; they named more than a dozen towns Waverley; and advertisements for his novels bore the simple caption, "By the author of *Waverley*." Scott's success demonstrated that the public wanted to read fiction and prompted Americans like James Fenimore Cooper to write fiction for the market.

Second, the American Renaissance reflected the rise of a philosophical movement known as romanticism. In contrast to eighteenth-century classicism, which had regarded standards of beauty as universal, romanticism insisted that literature reveal the longings of the individual author's soul. Classicists saw the ideal author as an educated gentleman who wrote to display his learning—especially of ancient Greek and Roman civilization. Romantics valued the emotional expressiveness of literature and its truthfulness to its creator's inner feelings.

The emergence of a national market for books and the influence of romanticism combined to make American literature more democratic. The conventions of classicism viewed literature as a pastime of gentlemen who wrote poetry and essays primarily for one another, and never for profit. In contrast, romanticists accepted the production of books for a national market, and elevated the importance of fiction over poetry and essays. Reading and writing novels did not require knowledge of Latin and Greek or a familiarity with ancient history and mythology; it rested instead on shared human feelings and experiences. Significantly, many of the best-selling novels of the antebellum period—for example, Harriet Beecher Stowe's *Uncle Tom's Cabin*—were written by women. And one response to Stowe's work was the novel written by an African-American woman: the semi-autobiographical *Our Nig; Or, Sketches from the Life of a Free Black* (1859), now regarded as a major work of American literature.

In addition, fiction had a subversive quality that contributed to its popularity. Authors could create unconventional characters, situations, and outcomes. Whereas essays usually developed unmistakable conclusions, novels left more room for interpretation by the reader. A novel might well have a lesson to teach, but the reader's interest was likely to be aroused less by the moral of the story than by the development of characters and plot.

Cooper, Emerson, Thoreau, Fuller, and Whitman

James Fenimore Cooper was the first important figure in this literary upsurge. He introduced an enduringly influential American fictional character, the frontiersman Natty Bumppo ("Leatherstocking"). In *The Pioneers* (1823), Natty is an old man settled on the shores of Lake Otsego in upstate New York. A spokesman for nature against the relentless advance of civilization, Natty blames farmers for wantonly destroying game and turning the majestic forests into wastelands littered with tree stumps. Natty immediately became a popular figure, and in subsequent novels such as *The Last of the Mohicans* (1826), *The Pathfinder* (1840), and *The Deerslayer*

(1841), Cooper unfolded the frontier hero's earlier life for a reading public eager for what we'd now call the prequel.

Ralph Waldo Emerson (who actually disliked fiction) emerged in the late 1830s as the most influential spokesman for American literary nationalism. As the leading light of the movement known as transcendentalism, an American expression of romanticism, Emerson believed that our ideas of God and freedom are not learned, but inborn. Knowledge, like sight, involves an instantaneous and direct perception of truth. So learned people, Emerson concluded, enjoyed no special advantage in pursuing truth. All persons can glimpse the truth by simply trusting the promptings of their hearts.

This basic premise of transcendentalism posed the exciting possibility that the United States, a young and democratic society, could produce as noble a literature and art as Old World cultures. "Our day of dependence, our long apprenticeship to the learning of other lands draws to a close," Emerson announced in his address "The American Scholar" (1837). The time had come for Americans to trust themselves. Let "the single man plant himself indomitably on his instincts and there abide," he proclaimed, and "the huge world will come around to him."

Emerson's literary nationalism was expressed mainly in his essays, which explored broad themes—"Beauty," "Wealth," and "Representative Men"—in vivid, fresh language. For example, he praised independent thinking by saying the scholar should not "quit his belief that a popgun is a popgun, though the ancient and honorable of the earth affirm it to be the crack of doom." A contemporary said listening to Emerson was like trying to see the sun in a fog; one could see light but never the sun itself. Believing that knowledge reflected God's voice within each individual and that truth was intuitive, Emerson did not present systematic arguments backed by evidence to prove his point. Rather, he relied on a sequence of vivid if unconnected assertions whose truth the reader was supposed to see instantly. (One reader complained that she might have understood Emerson better if she had stood on her head.)

From his home in Concord, Massachusetts Emerson exercised a magnetic attraction for young intellectuals who were social misfits, including **Henry David Thoreau**. A crucial difference, however, separated the two men. Though intellectually adventurous, Emerson was not adventurous in action. By contrast, Thoreau fully lived his ideas. When war with Mexico broke out, he went to jail rather than pay his poll tax, refusing to support a war he regarded as part of a southern conspiracy to extend slavery. This experience led Thoreau to write his abidingly influential essay on "Civil Disobedience" (1849), in which he defended a citizen's right to disobey unjust laws.

On July 4, 1845, in a personal declaration of independence, Thoreau moved a few miles from Concord Center to the woods near Walden Pond. He spent two years there living in a small cabin he constructed on land owned by Emerson and providing for his own wants as simply as possible. His purpose in retreating to Walden was to write an account of a canoe trip he took with his brother in 1839—later published as *A Week on the Concord and Merrimack Rivers*. But he wrote a more important book, *Walden* (1854), described by a contemporary as "the logbook of his woodland cruise." Thoreau filled it with day-to-day descriptions of hawks and the pond, his invention of raisin bread, and his trapping of the woodchucks that ravaged his vegetable garden. But *Walden* had a larger transcendentalist message. Thoreau's retreat taught him that anyone could satisfy his material wants with only a few weeks' work each year and preserve the remainder of his time for examining life's purpose. The problem with

Americans, he said, was that they turned themselves into "mere machines" to acquire pointless wealth. For Thoreau, material and moral progress were not as intimately related as most Americans liked to think (see Going to the Source).

Among the most remarkable figures in Emerson's circle was **Margaret Fuller,** whose status as an intellectual woman distanced her from conventional society. Disappointed that his first child was not a boy, Fuller's father, a prominent Massachusetts politician, determined to give Margaret the sort of education young men acquired at Harvard. First drilled in Latin and Greek, she then turned to the German romantics and English literary classics. Her exposure to Emerson's ideas during a stay at Concord in 1836 pushed her toward transcendentalism, with its vindication of the free life of the spirit over formal doctrines and its insistence on the need for each person to discover truth on her own.

Ingeniously, Fuller managed to turn transcendentalism into a profession. Between 1839 and 1844, she conducted "Conversations" for fee-paying participants drawn from Boston's elite. Transcendentalism also influenced her feminist classic, *Woman in the Nineteenth Century* (1845). Breaking with the prevailing notion of separate spheres for men and women, Fuller contended that no woman could achieve the intellectual fulfillment promoted by Emerson unless she devoted herself to developing her mental abilities without fear of being called "masculine." Fuller asserted that "What Woman needs is not as a woman to act or rule, but as a nature to grow, as an intellect to discern, as a soul to live freely and unimpeded, to unfold such powers as were given to her when we left our common home."

One of Emerson's qualities was an ability to sympathize with such dissimilar people as the prickly Thoreau, the scholarly Fuller, and the outgoing and earthy **Walt Whitman.** The self-educated Whitman had left school at age eleven and worked his way up from printer's apprentice to journalist and then editor for various newspapers in Brooklyn, Manhattan, and New Orleans. A familiar figure at Democratic Party functions, he marched in party parades and put his pen to the service of its antislavery wing.

Journalism and politics, in addition to his own rough-and-tumble life, gave Whitman an intimate knowledge of ordinary Americans. The more he came to know them, the more he loved them. Reading Emerson nurtured his own belief that America would be the cradle of a new man in whom natural virtue would flourish untainted by European corruption—a man like Andrew Jackson, that "massive, yet most sweet and plain character." The threads of Whitman's early life and career came together in his major work *Leaves of Grass*, a book of poems first published in 1855 and reissued with additions in subsequent years.

Leaves of Grass shattered poetic conventions. Whitman wrote in free verse, meaning that most of his poems had neither rhyme nor meter. His poems were passionate and earthy at a time when delicacy reigned in the literary world. To the dismay of critics, he wrote of "the scent of these armpits finer than prayer" and "winds whose soft-tickling genitals rub against me." Whitman also introduced himself into his poems, most explicitly in "Song of Walt Whitman" (later retitled "Song of Myself"). He wrote of himself because he viewed himself—crude and plain, self-taught and passionately democratic—as the personification of the American people:

> Comrade of raftsmen and coalmen, comrade of all who shake hands and welcome to drink and meat, A learner with the simplest, a teacher of the thought-fullest.

Henry David Thoreau, "Walking" (1862)

In the early 1850s, Henry David Thoreau (1817–1862) developed two new lectures for the lyceum circuit, titled "The Wild" and "Walking." He later merged them into the single essay "Walking" that was published one month after his death. "Walking," a companion essay to his most famous work *Walden*, expressed his views on natural wildness, the American West, and the need for an American literature rooted in nature. Thoreau's line, "in Wildness is the preservation of the World," has become a touchstone of modern environmentalism.

"I wish to speak a word for Nature, for absolute freedom and wildness, as contrasted with a freedom and culture merely civil—to regard man as an inhabitant, or a part and parcel of Nature, rather than a member of society. I wish to make an extreme statement, if so I may make an emphatic one, for there are enough champions of civilization: the

minister and the school committee and every one of you will take care of that....

Nowadays almost all man's improvements, so called, as the building of houses and the cutting down of the forest and of all large trees, simply deform the landscape, and make it more and more tame and cheap....

We go eastward to realize history and study the works of art and literature, retracing the steps of the race; we go westward as into the future, with a spirit of enterprise and adventure. The Atlantic is a Lethean stream*, in our passage over which we have had an opportunity to forget the Old World and its institutions....

The West of which I speak is but another name for the Wild; and what I have been preparing to say is, that in Wildness is the preservation of the World. Every tree sends its fibers forth in search of the Wild. The cities import it at any price. Men plow and sail for it. From the forest and wilderness come

By 1860, Whitman had acquired a considerable reputation as a poet. Nevertheless, the small original edition of *Leaves* was ignored or even ridiculed as a "heterogeneous mass of bombast, egotism, vulgarity, and nonsense." One reviewer suggested that it was the work of an escaped lunatic. But within two weeks of its publication, Emerson, who had never met Whitman, wrote, "I find it the most extraordinary piece of wit and wisdom that America has yet contributed." Emerson had long called for the appearance of "the poet of America" and his transcendental intuition told him that Whitman was that poet.

Hawthorne, Melville, and Poe

Two major contributors to the American Renaissance—**Nathaniel Hawthorne** and **Herman Melville**—were best known for writing fiction, and a third, **Edgar Allan Poe**, wrote both fiction and poetry. None heeded Emerson's call for a literature that would comprehend the everyday experiences of ordinary Americans—what Emerson called "the meal in the firkin [bucket]; the milk in the pan; the ballad in the street." Hawthorne set *The Scarlet Letter* (1850) in Puritan New England; *The House of the Seven Gables* (1851) in a mansion haunted by the tonics and barks which brace mankind. Our ancestors were savages. The story of Romulus and Remus being suckled by a wolf is not a meaningless fable.** The founders of every state which has risen to eminence have drawn their nourishment and vigor from a similar wild source. It was because the children of the Empire were not suckled by the wolf that they were conquered and displaced by the children of the northern forests who were....

Where is the literature which gives expression to Nature? He would be a poet who could impress the winds and streams into his service, to speak for him; who nailed words to their primitive senses, as farmers drive down stakes in the spring, which the frost has heaved; who derived his words as often as he used them—transplanted them to his page with earth adhering to their roots; whose words were so true and fresh and natural that they would appear to expand like the buds at the approach of spring, though they lay half smothered between two musty leaves in a library—aye, to bloom and bear fruit

there, after their kind, annually, for the faithful reader, in sympathy with surrounding Nature."

Source: Henry David Thoreau, "Walking," *Atlantic Monthly*, vol. 9, no. 56 (June 1862): [657]–674.

Questions

1. *What were Thoreau's views on the ideal relationship between Nature and civilization, and between Nature and the individual? What sorts of "improvements" in his lifetime do you think were shaping his ideas?*

2. *How was Thoreau responding to Emerson's call for a distinctively American literature?*

Go to www.cengagebrain.com for additional primary sources on this period.

*In the underworld of Greek mythology, Lethe was the river of forgetfulness.

**Romulus and Remus, the mythical founders of Ancient Rome, were abandoned as infants in the wilderness but saved by a wolf who fed and protected them.

memories of the colonial past; and *The Marble Faun* (1859) in Rome. Poe chose Europe as the setting for several of his short stories—including "The Murders in the Rue Morgue" (1841) and "The Cask of Amontillado" (1846). Melville's seagoing novels *Typee* (1846) and *Omoo* (1847) took place among exotic South Sea islands, and his masterpiece *Moby-Dick* (1851) was set on a whaling ship at sea. If the only surviving documents from the 1840s and 1850s were its major novels, historians would face an impossible task in trying to understand daily life in antebellum America.

The unusual settings favored by these three writers reflected their view that American life lacked the stuff of great fiction. Hawthorne bemoaned the difficulty of writing about a country "where there is no shadow, no antiquity, no mystery, no picturesque and gloomy wrong, nor anything but a commonplace prosperity in broad and simple daylight." In addition, all three writers were more interested in probing the depths of human psychology than the intricacies of social relationships. Their preoccupation with the mental states of their characters grew out of their underlying pessimism about the human condition. Whereas Emerson, Fuller, and Whitman were inclined to believe that social conflicts could be resolved if people would follow the promptings of their better selves, Hawthorne, Poe, and Melville saw individuals as bundles of dark, internal conflicts that might never be resolved.

The pessimism of these dark romantics led them to create characters obsessed by pride and guilt, and driven by a desire for revenge or an unnatural quest for perfection. Their stories were played out on the margins of society, where they were free to explore the complexities of human motivation without dealing with the jarring intrusions of everyday life. For example, in *The Scarlet Letter*, Hawthorne turned to the Puritan past to examine the psychological and moral consequences of adultery. So intensely did Hawthorne focus on the moral dilemmas of his central characters, Hester Prynne and the Rev. Arthur Dimmesdale, that he conveyed little sense of the social life of the Puritan village surrounding them. Melville, who dedicated *Moby-Dick* to Hawthorne, shared the latter's dark imagination. Captain Ahab's relentless and futile pursuit of the white whale that had cost him his leg fails to fill the chasm in his soul and brings death to all his mates except the novel's narrator, Ishmael. Poe also channeled his pessimism—and possibly his madness—into dark romantic achievements. In perhaps his finest short story, "The Fall of the House of Usher" (1839), he employed the Gothic setting of a nightmarish, crumbling mansion to convey the moral agony of a decaying, incestuous family.

Hawthorne, Melville, and Poe deliberately ignored Emerson's call to write about the everyday experiences of Americans. Nor did they follow Cooper's lead by creating distinctively American heroes. Yet each contributed to an indisputably American literature. Ironically, their conviction that the lives of ordinary Americans provided inadequate materials for fiction led them to create a uniquely American fiction marked less by the description of ordinary life than by the analysis of psychological states. In this way, they fulfilled a prediction made by Alexis de Tocqueville that writers in democratic nations, while rejecting many of the traditional sources of fiction, would explore abstract and universal questions of human nature.

Literature in the Marketplace   Even with the decline of the gentleman classicist, the suspicion that commercialism corrupted art did not disappear during the American Renaissance. The reclusive poet Emily Dickinson lived all of her fifty-six years on the same street in Amherst, Massachusetts ("I do not go from home," she said), writing exquisite poems that examined, in her words, every splinter in the groove of the brain. Dickinson refused to publish her work. But in an age that offered few university professorships or artists' fellowships, writers were tempted and often compelled to write for profit. Poe, a notoriously heavy drinker always pressed for cash, scratched out a meager living writing short stories for popular magazines. Thoreau, despite his reputation for aloof self-reliance, craved public recognition. Only after trying and failing to market his poems in 1843 did he turn to the detailed accounts of nature that won him a readership.

Emerson, too, wanted to reach a broader public. After abandoning his first vocation as a Unitarian minister, he reached for a new sort of audience and a new source of income: the lyceum. Lyceums—local organizations for sponsoring lectures—spread throughout the northern tier of states after the late 1820s to meet popular demands for entertainment and self-improvement. Most of Emerson's published essays originated as lyceum lectures given throughout the Northeast and Midwest, including some sixty speeches in Ohio alone between 1850 and 1867. Thanks to newly built

Nathaniel Hawthorne *This photograph shows Hawthorne in 1850, when* The Scarlet Letter *was published.* The House of the Seven Gables *was published the following year.*

railroads and the cheap newspapers that publicized lyceum programs, other speakers followed in Emerson's path. Thoreau presented a digest of *Walden* as a lyceum lecture before the book was published. One stalwart of the lyceum circuit said that he lectured in exchange for "F-A-M-E—Fifty and My Expenses." As Herman Melville pledged, "If they will pay my expenses and give a reasonable fee, I am ready to lecture in Labrador or on the Isle of Desolation off Patagonia."

As the Grimke sisters had discovered, the age offered women few opportunities for public speaking, and most lyceum lecturers were men. But women were tapping into the growing market for literature. Fiction-writing became the most lucrative occupation open to women before the Civil War. Novelist Susan Warner's *The Wide, Wide World*, published in 1850, went through fourteen editions by 1852. Maria Cummins's *The Lamplighter*, published in 1854, sold forty thousand copies in eight weeks. Harriet Beecher Stowe's *Uncle Tom's Cabin*, published in 1852, exceeded all previous sales by selling 100,000 copies in just five months. Nathaniel Hawthorne, whose own works sold modestly, bitterly condemned what he called the "d—d mob of scribbling women" who were outselling and outearning him.

Warner and others benefited from advances in printing technology that significantly reduced the price of books. Before 1830, Sir Walter Scott's novels had been issued in three-volume sets that retailed for as much as thirty dollars. As canals and railroads began to carry new books to crossroads stores across the land, publishers in New York and Philadelphia vied to fill the stores' shelves with inexpensive novels. By the 1840s, cheap paperbacks costing as little as seven cents were flooding the market. Those who did not purchase books could read fiction in "story newspapers" such as the weekly *New York Ledger*, which was devoted mainly to serializing novels; the *Ledger's* subscribers numbered four hundred thousand in 1860. In addition, the spread of public schools and academies contributed to higher literacy and a widening audience for fiction, especially among women.

The most popular form of fiction in the 1840s and 1850s was the sentimental or domestic novel, written mostly by women for women. The typical plot centers on a young girl who is either a poor and friendless orphan, or a wealthy heiress accustomed to financial and emotional support suddenly faced with the necessity of making her own way in the world. In either case, the girl's situation awakens her to inner resources that she hadn't previously recognized, and instills in her a new sense of her value and strength. The moral of Susan Warner's *The Wide, Wide World* (1850) was that women had what it took to clean up the messes left by men.

Another popular genre in the antebellum reading market was sensationalist fiction, which drew on such dark romantic themes as criminality, mystery, and horror, but took them to extremes unknown in the works of Hawthorne, Melville, or even Poe. The bestselling novel in America before *Uncle Tom's Cabin* was George Lippard's *The Quaker City; or The Monks of Monk Hall, A Romance of Philadelphia Life, Mystery, and Crime*, published in 1845. Based loosely on a real Philadelphia murder, it told the story of Monk Hall, a six-story structure (three floors above ground, three below) filled with secret passageways and trapdoors, where outwardly respectable Philadelphians gathered nightly to carouse, consume drugs, and rape young virgins. Works such as this tapped into the market for sensationalism created in part by the penny press.

So authors such as Hawthorne, Poe, and Melville had to compete with the popular culture of the story newspapers, sentimental fiction, and sensationalism. The philosopher Emerson shared the lecture circuit with the showman P. T. Barnum. Poe sneered that the public's judgment of a writer's merits was nearly always wrong. By and large, however, the major writers of the American Renaissance (with the exception of Melville, whose critical acclaim was delayed to the twentieth century) were not overlooked by their society. Emerson's lectures were highly successful, Hawthorne's *The Scarlet Letter* enjoyed respectable sales, and Poe's "The Raven" (1844) was extremely popular. But the writers most likely to achieve commercial success were those who best met certain popular expectations, such as moral and spiritual uplift, horror and mystery, or love stories and happy endings.

American Land-scape Painting   At the same time as American writers were trying to create a distinctly American literature, American painters were searching for a national style in art. European neoclassicists had devoted much attention to the dramas and glories of the ancient and medieval past, painting historical scenes and portraits that celebrated the antiquity of their civilizations. In the absence of such traditions, American artists turned to landscape painting. But just as Hawthorne had complained about the lack of shadow and antiquity in American society, American painters lamented that the American landscape had no "poetry of decay" in the form of ruined castles and crumbling temples. In the absence of the evocative ruins that dotted European landscapes, American painters strove to capture the natural grandeur of their own land.

The center of American landscape painting in the nineteenth century was the **Hudson River School**, which flourished from the 1820s to the 1870s. Numbering more than fifty painters, it was best represented by Thomas Cole, Asher Durand, and Frederick Church. None was exclusively a landscapist. Some of Cole's most popular paintings were allegories, including *The Course of Empire*, a sequence of five canvases depicting the rise and fall of an ancient city and clearly implying that luxury doomed republican virtue. Nor did these artists paint only the Hudson River. Cole's student Frederick Church, who was internationally the best known of the three, painted the Andes Mountains during an extended trip to South America in 1853. After the Civil War, the German-born Albert Bierstadt adapted Hudson River school conventions to his monumental canvases of the Rocky Mountains.

But American landscape artists did paint countless scenes of the region around the Hudson River. The works of Washington Irving and the opening of the Erie Canal in 1825 sparked artistic interest in the Hudson. The special contribution to American art made by the Hudson River painters was to emphasize emotional effect over illustrative accuracy. Thomas Cole's dramatic use of rich colors, towering peaks, deep chasms, and massive gnarled trees prompted poet William Cullen Bryant to compare them to "acts of religion." Similar motifs marked Frederick Church's paintings of the Andes Mountains, which used erupting volcanoes and thunderstorms to evoke dread and a sense of majesty.

After 1830, the writings of Emerson and Thoreau along with the paintings of the Hudson River School popularized a new view of nature. Intent on cultivating land, the pioneers of Kentucky and Ohio had deforested a vast area. One traveler complained that Americans would rather view a wheat field or a cabbage patch than a virgin forest. But Romantic writers and artists glorified pristine nature; "in wildness is the preservation of the world," Thoreau wrote. Their outlook blended with growing popular fears that, as one contemporary wrote in 1847, "The axe of civilization is busy with our old forests." As the "wild and picturesque haunts of the Red Man" became "the abodes of commerce and the seats of civilization," this writer concluded, "it behooves our artists to rescue from its grasp the little that is left before it is too late." Cole and other landscape painters often used the motif of the felled tree to express their concern about the encroachments of civilization on American nature.

Like Cole, the painter **George Catlin** also tried to preserve a vanishing America, but his main concern was the native peoples of the land. Observing an Indian delegation passing through Philadelphia in 1824, Catlin resolved that his life's work would be to paint as many Native Americans as possible in their pure and "savage" state. Journeying up the Missouri River in 1832 he sketched at a feverish pace, and in 1837 exhibited his "Indian gallery," oil paintings and sketches of faces and customs from nearly fifty tribes. Catlin viewed the Indian as a noble savage whose mind, in his words, was "a beautiful blank." His paintings, though intended to preserve what nineteenth-century Euro-Americans called the "vanishing Indian," actually encouraged viewers to believe that Indians were doomed to extinction by the encroachment of civilization—an attitude that quietly justified further white expansion and conquest.

By the 1830s, sprawling urban growth was prompting the development of little enclaves of nature to provide spiritual refreshment to harried city-dwellers. Starting with Mount Auburn Cemetery near Boston in 1831, "rural" cemeteries with names such as "Harmony Grove" and "Greenwood" sprang up near major cities, offering curving tree-lined lanes and artificial ponds for the enjoyment of strolling city-dwellers. Designed for the living rather than the dead, they quickly became tourist attractions. In a related development, in 1858 New York City chose a plan drawn by landscape architect **Frederick Law Olmsted** and Calvert Vaux for its proposed Central Park. Olmsted and Vaux wanted the park to look as much like the countryside as possible, showing nothing of the surrounding city. Bordering trees were planted to screen out buildings, drainage pipes were dug to create lakes, and four sunken thoroughfares were constructed to carry traffic unobtrusively across the park. The effect was to make Central Park "picturesque," meaning that its man-made woods, meadows, and lake should remind visitors of natural landscapes they had seen in pictures. Thus nature was made to mirror art.

CHRONOLOGY
1840–1860

1820	Washington Irving, *The Sketch Book*.
1823	Philadelphia completes the first urban water-supply system. James Fenimore Cooper, *The Pioneers*.
1826	Cooper, *The Last of the Mohicans*.
1831	Mount Auburn Cemetery opens.
1832	A cholera epidemic strikes the United States.
1833	The *New York Sun*, the first penny newspaper, is established.
1834	Cyrus McCormick patents the mechanical reaper.
1835	James Gordon Bennett establishes the *New York Herald*.
1837	Ralph Waldo Emerson, "The American Scholar."
1841	P.T. Barnum opens the American Museum. Edgar Allan Poe, "The Murders in the Rue Morgue."
1844	First telegraph message transmitted.
1846	W.T.G. Morton successfully uses anesthesia. Elias Howe, Jr., patents the sewing machine.
1849	Second major cholera epidemic. Astor Place theater riot leaves twenty dead.
1850	Nathaniel Hawthorne, *The Scarlet Letter*.
1851	Hawthorne, *The House of the Seven Gables*. Herman Melville, *Moby-Dick*. Erie Railroad completes its line to the West.

1853   Ten small railroads are consolidated into the New York Central Railroad.

1854   Henry David Thoreau, *Walden.*

1855   Walt Whitman, *Leaves of Grass.*

1856   Pennsylvania Railroad completes Chicago link.

1857   Baltimore-St. Louis rail service completed.

1858   Frederick Law Olmsted is appointed architect in chief for Central Park.

CONCLUSION

Technological advances transformed the lives of millions of Americans between 1840 and 1860. The mechanical reaper increased wheat production and enabled agriculture to keep pace with the growing population. The development of machine tools, first in gun manufacture and then in the production of sewing machines, made possible Eli Whitney's system of interchangeable parts and made a range of luxuries affordable for the middle class. Steam power reduced the vulnerability of factories to the vagaries of the weather, extended the employment season, and increased productivity and workers' incomes. The spread of railroads and the invention of the telegraph overcame barriers of space and time.

Many of these developments unified Americans. Railroad tracks threaded the nation together. The telegraph speeded communication and made it possible for Americans in widely scattered areas to read the same news and fiction in their newspapers. The advances in printing that gave birth to the penny press and cheap fiction contributed to a widening of the reading public. Theater audiences from New York to San Francisco attended the same minstrel shows. Advocates of progress hailed these developments as instruments of ever-expanding happiness. By reducing commodity prices and bringing one-time luxuries within the financial reach of the middle class, technology narrowed the social distance between the middle and upper classes.

Progress, however, carried a price. At the same time that technology was closing the gap between the middle and upper classes, it was widening the gap between those classes and the poor. Progress also posed moral and spiritual challenges. Transcendentalists such as Emerson and Thoreau warned that Americans were growing ever more materialistic and endangering their intuitive access to inborn truth. Novelists Hawthorne and Melville challenged the easy confidence that technology and democracy could liberate Americans from the dilemmas of the human condition. And romantic writers and artists alike feared that the march of progress threatened to devour unspoiled nature. In different ways, Cooper, Emerson, and Thoreau treated the heightened conflict between nature and civilization as a distinctive feature of the American experience. The quest for their own national culture forced Americans to ponder the costs as well as the benefits of technological progress.

12

THE OLD SOUTH AND SLAVERY, 1830–1860

CHAPTER OUTLINE

• King Cotton • The Social Groups of the White South • Social Relations in the White South • Life Under Slavery • The Emergence of African-American Culture

---

KING COTTON

In 1790, the South was essentially stagnant. Tobacco, its primary cash crop, had lost economic vitality even as it had depleted the once-rich southern soils. The growing of alternative cash crops, such as rice and cotton, was confined to coastal areas. Three out of four southerners still lived along the Atlantic seaboard, specifically in the Chesapeake and the Carolinas. One of three resided in Virginia alone.

The contrast between that South and the dynamic South of 1850 was stunning. By 1850, southerners had moved south and west. Now, only one of every seven southerners lived in Virginia, and cotton reigned as king, shaping this new South. The growth of the British textile industry had created a huge demand for cotton, while Indian removal (see Chapter 9) had made way for southern expansion into the **"Cotton Kingdom,"** a broad swath of territory that stretched from South Carolina, Georgia, and northern Florida in the east through Alabama, Mississippi, central and western Tennessee, and Louisiana, and from there on to Arkansas and Texas (See Map 12.1).

The Lure of Cotton To a British traveler, it seemed that all southerners could talk about was cotton. "Every flow of wind from the shore wafted off the smell of that useful plant; at every dock or wharf we encountered it in huge piles or pyramids of bales, and our decks were soon choked with it. All day, and almost all night long, the captain, pilot, crew, and passengers were talking of nothing else."

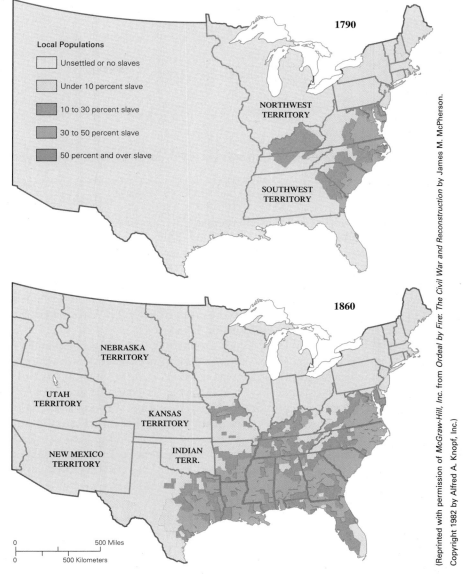

Local Populations

☐ Unsettled or no slaves

☐ Under 10 percent slave

☐ 10 to 30 percent slave

☐ 30 to 50 percent slave

☐ 50 percent and over slave

1790

NORTHWEST
TERRITORY

SOUTHWEST
TERRITORY

1860

NEBRASKA
TERRITORY

UTAH
TERRITORY

KANSAS
TERRITORY

NEW MEXICO
TERRITORY

INDIAN
TERR.

0   500 Miles

0   500 Kilometers

(Reprinted with permission of McGraw-Hill, Inc. from *Ordeal by Fire: The Civil War and Reconstruction* by James M. McPherson. Copyright 1982 by Alfred A. Knopf, Inc.)

MAP 12.1 Distribution of Slaves, 1790 and 1860

In 1790 the majority of slaves resided along the southeastern seaboard. By 1860, however, slavery had spread throughout the South, and slaves were most heavily concentrated in the Deep South states.

A warm climate, wet springs and summers, and relatively dry autumns made the Lower South ideal for cultivating cotton. A cotton farmer needed neither slaves nor cotton gins nor the capital required for sugar cultivation. Perhaps fifty percent of the farmers in the "Cotton Belt" owned no slaves, and to process their harvest

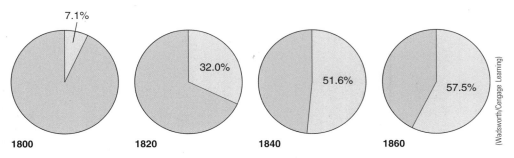

FIGURE 12.1 Value of Cotton Exports as a Percentage of All U.S. Exports, 1800–1860

By 1840 cotton accounted for more than half of all U.S. exports.

they could turn to widely available commercial gins. Cotton promised to make poor men prosperous and rich men kings (see Figure 12.1).

Yet large-scale cotton growing and slavery grew together as the southern slave population nearly doubled between 1810 and 1830 (see Figure 12.2). Three-fourths of all slaves worked in the cotton economy in 1830. Owning slaves made it possible to harvest vast tracts of cotton speedily, a crucial advantage because a sudden rainstorm at harvest time could pelt cotton to the ground and soil it. Slaveholding planters could increase their cotton acreage and hence their profits.

Cotton was also compatible with corn production. Corn could be planted earlier or later than cotton and harvested before or after. Since the cost of owning a slave was the same whether or not he or she was working, corn production enabled slaveholders to shift slave labor between corn and cotton. By 1860, the acreage devoted to corn in the Old South exceeded that devoted to cotton. Economically, corn and cotton gave the South the best of two worlds. Intense demand in Britain and New England kept cotton prices high and money flowed into the South. Because of southern self-sufficiency in growing corn and raising hogs that thrived on the corn (in 1860 the region had two-thirds of the nation's hogs), money did not drain away to pay for food. In 1860, the twelve wealthiest counties in the United States were all in the South.

Ties Between the Lower and Upper South

Two giant cash crops, sugar and cotton, dominated agriculture in the Lower South. The Upper South, a region of tobacco, vegetable, hemp, and wheat growers, depended far less on the great cash crops. Yet the Upper South identified with the Lower South rather than with the agricultural regions of the free states.

A range of social, political, and economic factors promoted this unity. First, many settlers in the Lower South had come from the Upper South. Second, all white southerners benefited from the three-fifths clause of the Constitution, which enabled them to count slaves as a basis for congressional representation. Third, all southerners were stung by abolitionist criticisms of slavery, which drew no distinction between the Upper and Lower South. Economic ties also linked the South. The profitability of cotton and sugar increased the value of slaves throughout the entire region and encouraged the internal slave trade from the Upper to the Lower South. Without the sale of its slaves to the Lower South, an observer wrote, "Virginia will be a desert".

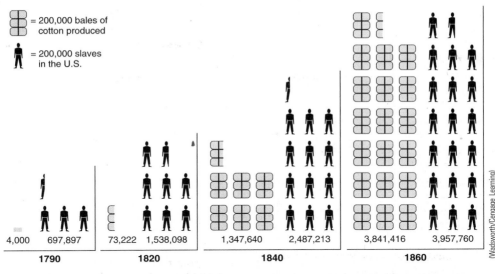

= 200,000 bales of cotton produced

= 200,000 slaves in the U.S.

| 4,000 | 697,897 | 73,222 | 1,538,098 | 1,347,640 | 2,487,213 | 3,841,416 | 3,957,760 |

| 1790 | 1820 | 1840 | 1860 |

(Wadsworth/Cengage Learning)

FIGURE 12.2 Growth of Cotton Production and the Slave Population, 1790–1860

Cotton and slavery rose together in the Old South.

The North and South Diverge   The changes responsible for the dynamic growth of the South widened the distance between it and the North. The South remained predominantly rural at a time when the North became more and more urban. In 1860, the proportion of the South's population living in urban areas was only one-third that of New England and the mid-Atlantic states, down from one-half in 1820.

Lack of industry kept the South rural; by 1860, it had one-third of the U.S. population but accounted for only one-tenth of the nation's manufacturing. The industrial output of the entire South in 1850 was less than one-third that of Massachusetts alone.

A few southerners advocated industrialization to reduce the South's dependency on northern manufactured products. After touring northern textile mills, South Carolina's William Gregg established a company town for textiles at Graniteville in 1845. By 1860, Richmond boasted the nation's fourth-largest producer of iron products, the **Tredegar Iron Works**. But these were exceptions.

Compared to factories in the North, most southern factories were small, produced for nearby markets, and were closely tied to agriculture. The leading northern factories turned hides into tanned leather and leather into shoes, or cotton into threads and threads into suits. In contrast, southern factories, only a step removed from agriculture, turned grain into flour, corn into meal, and logs into lumber.

Slavery posed a major obstacle to southern industrialization, but not because slaves were unfit for factories. The Tredegar Iron Works employed slaves in skilled positions. But industrial slavery troubled southerners. Away from the strict supervision of plantations, slaves sometimes behaved as if they were free, shifting jobs, working overtime, and even negotiating better working conditions. A Virginia planter who rented slaves to an iron manufacturer complained that they "got the habit of roaming about and *taking care of themselves*." But the chief brake on southern industrialization was money, not labor. To raise the capital needed to build factories, southerners would have to sell slaves. They had little incentive to do so. Cash crops like cotton and sugar were proven winners, whereas the benefits of industrialization were remote and doubtful. As long as southerners believed that an economy founded on cash crops would remain profitable, they had little reason to leap into the uncertainties of industrialization.

In education as in industry, the South also lagged behind the North. White southerners rejected compulsory education and were reluctant to tax property to support schools. They abhorred the thought of educating slaves, so much so that southern lawmakers made it a crime to teach slaves to read. Some public aid flowed to state universities, but for most whites the only available schools were private. White illiteracy remained high in the South even as it declined in the North. For example, nearly 60 percent of the North Carolinians who enlisted in the U.S. army before the Civil War were illiterate, compared to 30 percent for northern enlistees.

Agricultural, self-sufficient, and independent, the middling and poor whites of the South remained unconvinced of the need for public education. They had little dependency on the printed word, few complex economic transactions, and infrequent dealings with urban people. Planters did not need an educated white work force; they already had a black one that they were determined to keep illiterate lest it acquire ideas of freedom.

Because the South diverged so sharply from the North, outsiders often dismissed it as backward. Increasingly, northerners associated the spread of cities and factories with progress. Finding few cities and factories in the South, they concluded that the region was a stranger to progress as well. A northern journalist wrote of white southerners in the 1850s that "[t]hey work little, and that little, badly; they earn little, they sell little; they buy little, and they have little—very little—of the common comforts and consolations of civilized life." Visitors to the South sometimes thought that they were traveling backward in time. "It seems as if everything had stopped growing, and was growing backwards," novelist Harriet Beecher Stowe wrote of the region.

Yet the white South did not lack progressive features. In 1840, per capita income in the white South was only slightly below the national average, and by 1860 it exceeded the national average. Like northerners, white southerners were restless, eager to make money, skillful at managing complex commercial enterprises, and, when they chose, capable of becoming successful industrialists. Thus the white South was not economically backward—it was merely different. Cotton was a wonderful crop, and southerners could hardly be blamed for making it their ruler. As a southern senator wrote in 1858, "You dare not make war upon cotton; no power on earth dares to make war upon it. Cotton is king."

THE SOCIAL GROUPS OF THE WHITE SOUTH

Considerable diversity existed within and between the South's slaveholding and nonslaveholding classes. Some slaveholders owned hundreds of slaves, and lived lavishly, but most lived more modestly. In 1860, one-quarter of all white families in the South owned slaves. Of these, nearly half owned fewer than five slaves, and nearly three-quarters had fewer than ten slaves. Only 12 percent owned twenty or more slaves, and only 1 percent had a hundred or more. Large slaveholders clearly were a minority within a minority. Nonslaveholders also formed a diverse group. Most owned farms and drew on the labor of family members, but others squatted on land in the so-called pine barrens or piney woods and scratched out livelihoods by raising livestock, hunting and fishing, and planting a few acres of corn, oats, or sweet potatoes.

Planters (those owning twenty or more slaves), small slaveholders, yeomen (family farmers), and pine barrens folk composed the South's four main white groups. Lawyers, physicians, merchants, and artisans did not fall into any of these groups, but they tended to identify their interests with one or another of the agricultural groups. Rural artisans and merchants had extensive dealings with yeomen. Urban merchants and lawyers depended on the planters and adopted their viewpoint on most issues. Similarly, slave traders relied on the plantation economy for their livelihood. Nathan Bedford Forrest, the uneducated son of a humble Tennessee blacksmith, made a fortune as a slave trader in Natchez, Mississippi. When the Civil War broke out, Forrest enlisted in the Confederate army as a private and rose swiftly to become the South's greatest cavalry general. Plantation slavery directed Forrest's allegiances as surely as it did those of planters like Jefferson Davis, the Confederacy's president.

Planters and Plantation Mistresses	With porticoed mansion and fields teeming with slaves, the plantation still stands at the center of the popular image of the Old South. This romanticized view is not entirely misleading, for the South contained plantations that travelers

found "superb beyond description." Whether devoted to cotton, tobacco, rice, or sugar, **plantation agriculture** was characterized by a high degree of division of labor. In the 1850s, Bellmead, a tobacco plantation on Virginia's James River, was virtually an agricultural equivalent of a factory village. Its more than one hundred slaves were classified into the domestic staff (butlers, waiters, seamstresses, laundresses, maids, and gardeners), the pasture staff (shepherds, cowherds, and hog drivers),outdoor artisans (stonemasons and carpenters), indoor artisans (blacksmiths, carpenters, shoemakers, spinners, and weavers), and field hands. Such a division of labor was inconceivable without abundant slaves and land. With such resources, it is not surprising that large plantations could generate incomes that contemporaries viewed as immense (twenty to thirty thousand dollars a year).

During the first flush of settlement in the Piedmont and trans-Appalachian South in the eighteenth century, most well-off planters had been content to live in simple log cabins. In contrast, between 1810 and 1860, elite planters often vied with one another to build stately mansions. Some, like Lyman Hardy of Mississippi, hired architects. Hardy's Auburn, built in 1812 near Natchez, featured Ionic columns and a portico thirty-one feet long and twelve feet deep. But the wealth of most planters, especially in states like Alabama and Mississippi, consisted primarily in the value of their slaves rather than in expensive furniture or silver plate. A field

(The Gibbes Museum of Art, Carolina Art Association, Gift of Alicia Hopton Middleton)

Charlotte Helen and Her Nurse Lydia, 1857 *Ten days after Charlotte's birth, which occurred when the family sought refuge on Sullivan's Island, South Carolina, during a yellow fever epidemic, a terrible storm swamped the beaches. Lydia refused the aid of a soldier, trusting no one but herself, and waded through the swirling waters to carry the newborn Charlotte Helen to safety.*

hand was worth as much as $1700 in the 1850s. Planters could convert their wealth into cash for purchasing luxuries only by selling slaves. A planter who sold his slaves ceased to be a planter and relinquished the South's most prestigious social status. Not surprisingly, most planters clung to large-scale slaveholding, even if it meant scrimping on their lifestyles. A northern journalist observed that in the Southwest, men worth millions lived as if they were not worth hundreds.

In their constant worry about profit, planters enjoyed neither repose nor security. High fixed costs—housing and feeding slaves, maintaining cotton gins, hiring overseers—led them to search for more and better land, higher efficiency, and greater self-sufficiency. Because cotton prices fluctuated seasonally, planters often assigned their cotton to commercial agents in cities, who held the cotton until the price was right. The agents extended credit so that planters could pay their bills until the cotton was sold. Indebtedness became part of the plantation economy and intensified the planters' quest for profitability. Psychological strains compounded economic worries. Frequent moves disrupted circles of friends and relatives, especially as migration to the Old Southwest (Alabama, Mississippi, and eastern Texas), which carried families into progressively less settled, more desolate areas. Until 1850, this area was still the frontier.

Migration to the Southwest often deeply unsettled plantation women. They found themselves in frontier regions, surrounded by slaves and bereft of the companionship of white social peers. "I am sad tonight, sickness preys on my frame," wrote a bride who moved to Mississippi in 1833. "I am alone and more than 150 miles from any near relative in the wild woods of an Indian nation." At times, wives lacked even their husbands' companionship. Plantation agriculture kept men on the road, scouting new land for purchase, supervising outlying holdings, and transacting business in New Orleans or Memphis.

Planters and their wives found various ways to cope with their isolation. Hiring overseers to supervise their plantations, many spent long periods in cities. In 1850, fully one-half the planters in the Mississippi Delta were absentees living in or near Natchez or New Orleans rather than on their plantations. Most planters acted as their own overseers, however, and dealt with harsh living conditions by opening their homes to visitors. The responsibility for such hospitality fell heavily on wives, who might have to entertain as many as fifteen people for breakfast and attend to the needs of visitors who stayed for days. Plantation wives bore the burdens of raising their children, supervising house slaves, making clothes and carpets, looking after smokehouses and dairies, planting gardens, and keeping accounts. On the frequent occasions when their husbands were away on business or holding political office, their wives, along with their overseers, ran their plantations.

Among the greatest sorrows of some plantation mistresses was the presence of mulatto children, who stood as daily reminders of their husbands' infidelities. Mary Boykin Chesnut, an astute Charleston woman and famous diarist, commented, "Any lady is ready to tell you who is the father of all the mulatto children in everybody's household but her own. These, she seems to think, drop from clouds." Insisting on sexual purity for white women, southern men followed a looser standard for themselves. After the death of his wife, the brother of the abolitionist sisters Sarah and Angelina Grimké fathered three mulatto children. The gentlemanly code usually tolerated such transgressions as long as they were not paraded in public— and, at times, even if they were. Richard M. Johnson of Kentucky, the man who allegedly killed Tecumseh during the War of 1812, was elected vice president of the United States in 1836 despite having lived openly for years with his black mistress.

The isolation, drudgery, and humiliation that planters' wives experienced turned very few against the system. When the Civil War came, they supported the Confederacy as enthusiastically as any group. However much they might hate living as white islands in a sea of slaves, they recognized no less than their husbands that their wealth and position depended on slavery.

The Small Slaveholders   In 1860, 88 percent of all slaveholders owned fewer than twenty slaves, and most of these possessed fewer than ten. One out of every five slaveholders was employed outside of agriculture, as a lawyer, physician, merchant, or artisan.

Small slaveholders experienced conflicting loyalties and ambitions. In the upland regions, where yeomen (nonslaveholding family farmers) were the dominant group, small slaveholders rarely aspired to become large planters. In contrast, in the low country and delta regions, where planters formed the dominant group, small slaveholders often aspired to planter status. In these planter-dominated areas, someone with ten slaves could realistically look forward to owning thirty. The deltas were thus filled with ambitious and acquisitive individuals who linked success to owning more slaves. Whether one owned ten slaves or fifty, the logic of slaveholding was much the same. The investment in slaves could be justified only by setting them to work on profitable crops. Profitable crops demanded, in turn, more and better land. Much like the planters, the small slaveholders of the low country and delta areas were restless and footloose.

The social structure of the deltas was fluid. In the early antebellum period, large planters had been reluctant to risk transporting their hundreds of valuable slaves into a still-turbulent region. It was the small slaveholders who led the initial westward push into the Cotton Belt in the 1810s and 1820s. Gradually, large planters moved westward, buying up the land that the small slave owners had developed and turning the region from Vicksburg to Natchez into large plantations. Small slaveholders took the profits from selling their land, bought more slaves, and moved on. They gradually transformed the region from Vicksburg to Tuscaloosa, Alabama, into a belt of medium-sized farms with a dozen or so slaves on each.

The Yeomen   Nonslaveholding family farmers, or yeomen, comprised the largest single group of southern whites. Most were landowners. Landholding yeomen, because they owned no slaves of their own, frequently hired slaves at harvest time to help in the fields. Where the land was poor, as in eastern Tennessee, the landowning yeomen were typically subsistence farmers, but most grew some crops for the market. Whether they engaged in subsistence or commercial agriculture, they controlled landholdings far more modest than those of the planters—more likely in the range of fifty to two hundred acres than five hundred or more acres.

Yeomen could be found anywhere in the South, but they tended to congregate in the upland regions. In the seaboard South, they populated the Piedmont region of Georgia, South Carolina, North Carolina, and Virginia; in the Southwest, they usually lived in the hilly upcountry, far from the rich alluvial soil of the deltas. A minority of yeomen did not own land. Typically young, these men resided with and worked for landowners to whom they were related.

The leading characteristic of the yeomen was the value that they attached to self-sufficiency. As nonslaveholders, they were not carried along by the logic that impelled slaveholders to acquire more land and plant more cash crops. Although most yeomen raised cash crops, they devoted much of their acreage to subsistence crops like corn, sweet potatoes, and oats. The ideal of the planters was profit with modest self-sufficiency; that of the yeomen, self-sufficiency with modest profit.

Yeomen dwelling in the low country and delta regions dominated by planters often were dismissed as "poor white trash." But in the upland areas that they dominated, yeomen were highly respected. Upland slaveholders tended to own only a few slaves; like the yeomen, they were essentially family farmers.

In contrast to the far-flung commercial transactions of the planters, who depended on distant commercial agents to market their crops, the economic transactions of yeomen usually occurred within the neighborhood of their farms. Yeomen often exchanged their cotton, wheat, or tobacco for goods and services from local artisans and merchants. In some areas, they sold their surplus corn to the herdsmen and drovers who made a living in the South's upland regions by specializing in raising hogs. Along the French Broad River in eastern Tennessee, some twenty to thirty thousand hogs were fattened for market each year; at peak season, a traveler would see a thousand hogs a mile. When driven to market, the hogs were quartered at night in huge stock stands, veritable hog "hotels," and fed with corn supplied by the local yeomen.

The People of the Pine Barrens

One of the most controversial groups in the Old South was the independent whites of the wooded pine barrens. Making up about 10 percent of southern whites, they usually squated on the land, put up crude cabins, cleared some acreage on which they planted corn between tree stumps, and grazed hogs and cattle in the woods. They neither raised cash crops nor engaged in the daily routine of orderly work that characterized family farmers. With their ramshackle houses and handful of stump-strewn acres, they appeared lazy and shiftless.

Antislavery northerners cited the **pine barrens people** as proof that slavery degraded poor whites, but southerners shot back that while the pine barrens people were poor, they could at least feed themselves, unlike the paupers of northern cities. In general, the people of the pine barrens were self-reliant and fiercely independent. Pine barrens men were reluctant to hire themselves out as laborers to do "slave" tasks, and the women refused to become servants.

Neither victimized nor oppressed, these people generally lived in the pine barrens by choice. The grandson of a farmer who had migrated from Emanuel County, Georgia, to the Mississippi pine barrens explained his grandfather's decision: "The turpentine smell, the moan of the winds through the pine trees, and nobody within fifty miles of him, [were] too captivating…to be resisted, and he rested there."

SOCIAL RELATIONS IN THE WHITE SOUTH

Northerners often charged that slavery twisted the entire social structure of the South out of shape. The enslavement of blacks, they alleged, robbed lower-class whites of the incentive to work, reduced them to shiftless misery, and rendered the South a throwback in an otherwise progressive age. The behavior of individual southerners also struck northerners as running to extremes. One minute, southerners were hospitable and gracious; the next, savagely violent. "The Americans of the

South," Alexis de Tocqueville asserted, "are brave, comparatively ignorant, hospitable, generous, easy to irritate, violent in their resentments, without industry or the spirit of enterprise." The practice of dueling intensified in the Old South at a time when it was dying in the North.

In reality, a curious mix of aristocratic and democratic, premodern and modern features marked social relations in the white South. Although it contained considerable class inequality, property ownership was widespread. Rich planters occupied seats in state legislatures out of proportion to their numbers in the population, but they did not necessarily get their way, nor did their political agenda always differ from that of other whites.

Conflict and Consensus in the White South   Planters tangled with yeomen on several issues in the Old South. With their extensive economic dealings and need for credit, planters and their urban commercial allies inclined toward the Whig party, which generally was more sympathetic to banking and economic development. Cherishing their self-sufficiency and economically independent, the yeomen tended to be Democrats.

The occasions for conflict between these groups were minimal, however, and an underlying political unity reigned. Especially in the Lower South, each of the four main social groups—planters, small slaveholders, yeomen, and pine barrens people—tended to cluster in different regions. The delta areas that planters dominated contained relatively small numbers of yeomen. In other regions, small slave-owning families with ten to fifteen slaves predominated. In the upland areas far from the deltas, the yeomen congregated. The people of the pine barrens lived in a world of their own. There was more geographical intermingling of groups in the Upper South than in the Lower, but throughout the South each group attained a degree of independence from the others. With widespread landownership and relatively few factories, the Old South was not a place where whites worked for other whites, and this tended to minimize friction.

In addition, the white South's political structure was sufficiently democratic to prevent any one social group from gaining exclusive control over politics. In both the Upper and the Lower South, the majority of state legislators were planters. Yet these same planters owed their election to the popular vote. The white South was affected by the same democratic currents that swept northern politics between 1815 and 1860, and the newer states of the South had usually entered the Union with democratic constitutions that included universal white manhood suffrage—the right of all adult white males to vote.

Although yeomen often voted for planters, the nonslaveholders did not issue their elected representatives a blank check to govern as they pleased. During the 1830s and 1840s, Whig planters who favored banks faced intense and often successful opposition from Democratic yeomen. These yeomen blamed banks for the Panic of 1837 and pressured southern legislatures to restrict bank operations. On banking issues, nonslaveholders got their way often enough to nurture their belief that they ultimately controlled politics and that slaveholders could not block their goals.

Conflict over
Slavery

Nevertheless, considerable potential for conflict existed between the slaveholders and nonslaveholders. The white
carpenter who complained in 1849 that "unjust, oppressive,
and degrading" competition from slave labor depressed his wages surely had a point.
Between 1830 and 1860, slaveholders gained an increasing proportion of the South's
wealth while declining as a proportion of its white population. The size of the
slaveholding class shrank from 36 percent of the white population in 1831 to 31 percent
in 1850 and to 25 percent in 1860. A Louisiana editor warned in 1858 that "the
present tendency of supply and demand is to concentrate all the slaves in the hands of
the few, and thus excite the envy rather than cultivate the sympathy of the people."
Some southerners began to support the idea of Congress's reopening the African
slave trade to increase the supply of slaves, bring down their price, and give more
whites a stake in the institution.

As the proposed **Virginia emancipation legislation** in 1831–1832 attests,
slaveholders had good reasons for uncertainty over the allegiance of nonslaveholders to the "peculiar institution" of slavery. The publication in 1857 of Hinton
R. Helper's *The Impending Crisis of the South*, which called on nonslaveholders
to abolish slavery in their own interest, revealed the persistence of a degree of
white opposition to slavery. On balance, however, slavery did not create profound
and lasting divisions between the South's slaveholders and nonslaveholders.
Although antagonism to slavery flourished in parts of Virginia up to 1860, proposals for emancipation dropped from the state's political agenda after 1832. In
Kentucky, calls for emancipation were revived in 1849 in a popular referendum.
But the pro-emancipation forces went down to crushing defeat. Thereafter, the
continuation of slavery ceased to be a political issue in Kentucky and elsewhere in
the South.

The rise and fall of pro-emancipation sentiment in the South raises a key question. Since the majority of white southerners were not slaveholders, why did they
not attack the institution more consistently? To look ahead, why did so many of
them fight ferociously during the Civil War in defense of an institution in which
they appeared not to have had any real stake?

There are various answers to these questions. First, some nonslaveholders
hoped to become slaveholders. Second, most simply accepted the racial assumptions
upon which slavery rested. Whether slaveholders or nonslaveholders, white southerners dreaded the likelihood that emancipation might encourage "impudent"
blacks to entertain ideas of social equality with whites. Blacks might demand the
right to sit next to whites in railroad cars and even make advances to white
women. "Now suppose they [the slaves] was free," a white southerner told a northern journalist in the 1850s; "you see they'd all think themselves just as good as we;
of course they would if they was free. Now just suppose you had a family of children, how would you like to hev a niggar steppin' up to your darter?" Slavery, in
short, appealed to whites as a legal, time-honored, and foolproof way to enforce the
social subordination of blacks.

Finally, no one knew where the slaves, if freed, would go or what they would
do. Colonizing freed blacks in Africa was unrealistic, southerners concluded, but
they also believed that without colonization emancipation would lead to a race
war. In 1860, Georgia's governor sent a blunt message to his constituents, many

of them nonslaveholders: "So soon as the slaves were at liberty thousands of them would leave the cotton and rice fields…and make their way to the healthier climate of the mountain region [where] we should have them plundering and stealing, robbing and killing." There was no mistaking the conclusion. Emancipation would not merely deprive slaveholders of their property; it would also jeopardize the lives of nonslaveholders.

The Proslavery Argument   Between 1830 and 1860, southern writers constructed a defense of slavery as a positive good rather than a necessary evil (see Going to the Source). Southerners answered northern attacks on slavery as a backward institution by pointing out that the slave society of ancient Athens had produced Plato and Aristotle and that Roman slaveholders had laid the basis of Western civilization. A Virginian, **George Fitzhugh**, launched another line of attack by contrasting the plight of northern factory workers, "wage slaves" who were callously discarded by their bosses when they were too old or too sick to work, with the southern slaves, who were fed and clothed even when old and ill because they were the property of conscientious masters.

Many proslavery treatises were aimed less at northerners than at skeptics among the South's nonslaveholding yeomanry. Southern clergymen, who wrote roughly half of all proslavery tracts, invoked the Bible, especially St. Paul's order that slaves obey their masters. Too, proslavery writers warned southerners that the real intention of abolitionists, many of whom advocated equal rights for women, was to destroy the family as much as slavery by undermining the "natural" submission of children to parents, wives to husbands, and slaves to masters.

As southerners closed ranks behind slavery, they increasingly suppressed open discussion of the institution within the South. In the 1830s, southerners seized and burned abolitionist literature mailed to the South. In Kentucky, abolitionist editor Cassius Marcellus Clay positioned two cannons and a powder keg to protect his press, but in 1845 a mob dismantled it anyway. By 1860, any southerner found with a copy of *The Impending Crisis* had reason to fear for his life.

The rise of the proslavery argument coincided with a shift in the position of the southern churches on slavery. During the 1790s and early 1800s, some Protestant ministers had assailed slavery as immoral. By the 1830s, however, most members of the southern clergy had convinced themselves that slavery was not only compatible with Christianity but also necessary for the proper exercise of the Christian religion. Slavery, they proclaimed, provided the opportunity to display Christian responsibility toward one's inferiors, and it helped blacks develop Christian virtues like humility and self-control. Southerners increasingly attacked antislavery evangelicals in the North for disrupting the "superior" social arrangement of the South. In 1837, southerners and conservative northerners had combined to drive the antislavery New School Presbyterians out of that denomination's main body. In 1844, the Methodist Episcopal Church split into northern and southern wings. In 1845, Baptists formed a separate Southern Convention. In effect, southern evangelicals seceded from national church denominations long before the South seceded from the Union.

Violence, Honor, and Dueling in the Old South

Throughout the colonial and antebellum periods, violence deeply colored the daily lives of white southerners. In the 1760s, a minister described backcountry Virginians "biting one anothers Lips and Noses off, and gowging one another— that is, thrusting out anothers Eyes, and kicking one another on the Cods [genitals], to the Great damage of many a Poor Woman." In the 1840s, a New York newspaper described a fight between two raftsmen on the Mississippi that started when one accidentally bumped the other into shallow water. When it was over, one raftsman was dead. The other gloated, "I can lick a steamboat. My fingernails is related to a sawmill on my mother's side…and the brass buttons on my coat have all been boiled in poison."

Gouging out eyes became a specialty of sorts among poor whites. On one occasion, a South Carolina judge entered his court to find a plaintiff, a juror, and two witnesses all missing one eye. Stories of eye gouging and ear biting lost nothing in the telling and became part of the folklore of the Old South. Mike Fink, a legendary southern fighter and hunter, boasted that he was so mean that, in infancy, he refused his mother's milk and cried out for a bottle of whiskey. Yet beneath the folklore lay the reality of violence that gave the South a murder rate as much as ten times higher than that of the North.

At the root of most violence in the white South lay intensified feelings of personal pride that reflected the inescapable presence of slaves. Every day of their lives, white southerners saw slaves degraded, insulted, and powerless to resist. This experience had a searing impact on whites, for it encouraged them to react violently to even trivial insults to demonstrate that they had nothing in common with the slaves.

Among gentlemen, this exaggerated pride took the form of a distinctive **southern code of honor**, with honor defined as an extraordinary sensitivity to one's reputation, a belief that one's self-esteem depends on the judgment of others. In the antebellum North, moralists celebrated a rival ideal, character—the quality that enabled an individual to behave in a steady fashion regardless of how others acted toward him or her. A person possessed of character acted out of the prompting of conscience. In contrast, in the honor culture of the Old South, the slightest insult, as long as it was perceived as intentional, could become the basis for a duel.

Formalized by British and French officers during the Revolutionary War, dueling gained a secure niche in the Old South as a means by which gentlemen dealt with affronts to their honor. To outsiders, the incidents that sparked duels seemed trivial: a casual remark accidentally overheard, a harmless brushing against someone at a public event, even a hostile glance. Yet dueling did not necessarily terminate in violence. Gentlemen viewed dueling as a refined alternative to the random violence of lower-class life. The code of dueling did not dictate that the insulted party leap at his antagonist's throat or draw his pistol at the perceived moment of insult. Rather, he was to remain cool, bide his time, settle on a choice of weapons, and agree to a meeting place. In the interval, negotiations between friends of the parties sought to clear up the "misunderstanding" that had evoked the challenge. In this way, most confrontations ended peaceably rather than on the field of honor at dawn.

Although dueling was as much a way of settling disputes peaceably as of ending them violently, the ritual could easily terminate in a death or maiming.

GOING TO THE SOURCE

Daniel R. Hundley Defends the South

Daniel R. Hundley (1832–1899) was a well-educated Alabama lawyer who had spent time in the North on business and who in 1860 defended the South's civilization, including slavery, against the attacks by northerners.

No matter what be the Southern Gentleman's avocation, his dearest affections usually centre in the country. He longs to live as his fathers lived before him, in both the Old World and the New, and he ever turns with unfeigned delight from the bustle of cities, the hollow ceremonies of courts, the turmoil of politics, the glories and dangers of the battle-field, or the wearisome treadmill of professional routine, to the quiet and peaceful scenes of country life....Indeed, with all classes in the South the home feeling is much stronger than it is in the North; for the bane of hotel life and the curse of boarding-houses have not as yet extended their pernicious influences to our Southern States, or at best in a very small degree. Nearly every citizen is a landowner, and therefore feels an interest in the permanency of his country's institutions. This is one reason why the South has ever been the ready advocate of war, whenever the rights of the nation have been trampled upon, or the national flag insulted. But if the patriotic feeling is strongest in the breast of even the poorest citizen, whose home is a log-cabin and whose sole patrimony consists of less than a dozen acres of land, how must it be intensified in the bosoms of those whose plantations spread out into all magnificence of old-country manors....

Certainly, in some portions of the South the Southern Gentleman does not live in very grand style—his house is not always showy, nor his furniture elegant, nor his pleasure-grounds in the best keeping—but he is always hospitable, gentlemanly, courteous, and more anxious to please than to be pleased....

And tell us honestly; have you ever witnessed in the miserable tenant-houses of your own toiling poor after the day's weary labors are done, such evidences of

Dueling did not allow the resolution of grievances by the courts, a form of redress that would have guaranteed a peaceful outcome. As a way of settling personal disputes that involved honor, recourse to the law struck many southerners as cowardly and shameless. Andrew Jackson's mother told the future president, "The law affords no remedy that can satisfy the feelings of a true man."

In addition, dueling rested on the assumption that a gentleman could recognize another gentleman and hence would know when to respond to a challenge. Nothing in the code of dueling compelled a gentleman to duel someone beneath his status because such a person's opinion of a gentleman hardly mattered. An insolent porter who insulted a gentleman might get a whipping but did not merit a challenge to a duel. Yet it was often difficult to determine who was a gentleman. The Old South teemed with pretentious would-be gentlemen. A clerk in a country store in Arkansas in the 1850s found it remarkable that ordinary farmers who hung around the store talked of their honor and that the store's proprietor, a German Jew, kept a dueling pistol.

light-heartedness and physical comfort? And do you suppose, O noble champion of Equal Rights; you, sir, who turn aside with a curse from the ragged starveling on your own doorsteps to clamor that the poor slave shall be freed, but afterward refuse to sit with the freedman in the house of God, or in the theatres, or in public conveyances…do you suppose that your love for the sooty African equals that of his vilified master. If you do so delude yourself, the more's the pity; for despite what you or any other person may think to the contrary, the Southern Gentleman entertains more real love for his "human chattel" than all hare-brained abolitionists the world ever saw. His love is not theoretical but practical….

Hence, the ceaseless clamor of the so-called civilized world—of those peoples whose bread comes through the sweat of the African's brow, and whose commercial prosperity is due to the products of slave-labor—passes by the Southern Gentleman as the ideal wind which he heeds not. Yea, let them clamor, let them denounce, let them misrepresent and vilify to their heart's content,…still never will one single Southern Gentleman be influenced by the very disinterested outcry. He knows that this is not the first time a successful burglar has joined in the general shout, "Stop thief!" "Stop thief!"

Source: D.R. Hundley, *Social Relation in Our Southern States* (New York, 1860), 55–62.

Questions

1. *Hundley was writing to persuade the majority of northerners, who were neither abolitionists nor even necessarily convinced that slavery was a moral evil, that their criticisms of the slave South were wrong. Judging from what he said, what sort of negative views about the South did these people hold?*
2. *Were Hundley's arguments likely to change northern minds? Explain your answer.*

Go to www.cengagebrain.com for additional primary sources on this period.

The Southern Evangelicals and White Values

With its emphasis on the personal redress of grievances and its inclination toward violence, the ideal of honor potentially conflicted with the values preached by the southern evangelical churches, notably the Baptists, Methodists, and Presbyterians. These evangelical denominations were on the rise even before the Great Kentucky Revival of 1800–1801 (see Chapter 10) and continued to grow in the wake of the revival. For example, the Methodists grew from forty-eight thousand southern members in 1801 to eighty thousand by 1807. All of the evangelical denominations stressed humility and self-restraint, virtues sharply contrasting with the entire culture of show and display that buttressed the extravagance and violence of the Old South.

Evangelical values were changing by the 1830s. Methodists and Baptists increasingly attracted well-to-do converts, and they began to open colleges such as Randolph Macon (Methodist, 1830), and Wake Forest (Baptist, 1830). As evangelicals became more respectable, they no longer allowed white women to exhort in churches. They encouraged urban blacks to form their own churches rather than to exhort in racially mixed churches. With these developments, some members of the gentry embraced evangelical virtues. By the 1860s, the South contained many Christian gentlemen like the Bible-quoting Presbyterian general Thomas J. "Stonewall" Jackson, fierce in a righteous war but a sworn opponent of strong drink, the gaming table, and the duel.

LIFE UNDER SLAVERY

As they fashioned the proslavery argument, southern clergymen emphasized the Christian responsibility of masters toward their slaves. "Give your servants that which is just and equal," a Baptist minister advised in 1854, "knowing that you also have a Master in heaven." Some masters were benevolent, and many more liked to think they were benevolent. But masters bought slaves to make a profit on their labor, not to practice charity toward them. Kind masters might complain about cruel overseers, but the masters hired and paid the overseers to get as much work as possible out of blacks. When the master of one plantation chastised his overseer for "barbarity," the latter replied, "Do you not remember what you told me the time you employed me that [if] I failed to make you good crops I would have to leave?" Indeed, kindness was a double-edged sword, for the benevolent master came to expect grateful affection from his slaves and then interpreted that affection as loyalty to the institution of slavery. In fact, blacks felt little, if any, loyalty to slavery. When northern troops descended upon plantations during the Civil War, masters were dismayed to find many of their most trusted slaves deserting to Union lines.

The kindness or cruelty of masters was important, but three other factors primarily determined slaves' experience: the kind of agriculture in which they worked, whether they resided in rural or urban areas, and what century they lived in. The experiences of slaves working on cotton plantations in the 1830s differed drastically from those of slaves in 1700, for reasons unrelated to the kindness or brutality of masters.

The Maturing of the Plantation System   Slavery changed significantly between 1700 and 1830. In 1700, the typical slave was a young man in his twenties who had recently arrived aboard a slave ship from Africa or the Caribbean and worked in the company of other recent arrivals on isolated small farms. Drawn from different African regions and cultures, few such slaves spoke the same language. Because slave ships contained twice as many men as women, and because slaves were widely scattered, blacks had difficulty finding partners and creating a semblance of family life. Furthermore, as a result of severe malnutrition, black women who had been brought to North America on slave ships bore relatively few children. Without importation, the number of slaves in North America would have declined between 1710 and 1730.

In contrast, by 1830 the typical North American slave was as likely to be female as male, had been born in America, spoke English, and worked in the company of numerous other slaves on a plantation. The key to the change lay in the rise

niggar selling   Charleston S.C. 4th March 1833 "The Land of the free & the home of the brave"

(National Archives of Canada)

The Land of the Free and the Home of the Brave, by Henry Byam Martin, 1833 *White southerners could not escape the fact that much of the Western world loathed their "peculiar institution." In 1833, when a Canadian sketched this Charleston slave auction, Britain was about to abolish slavery in the West Indies.*

of plantation agriculture in the Chesapeake and South Carolina during the eighteenth century. Plantation slaves had an easier time finding mates than those on the remote farms of the early 1700s. As the ratio between slave men and women fell into balance, marriages occurred with increasing frequency between slaves on the same or nearby plantations. The native-born slave population rose after 1730 and soared after 1750. Importation of African slaves gradually declined after 1760, and in 1808 Congress banned it.

Work and Discipline of Plantation Slaves   In 1850, the typical slave worked on a large farm or plantation with at least ten fellow bond servants. Almost three-quarters of all slaves that year were owned by masters with ten or more slaves, and slightly over one-half lived in units of twenty or more slaves. In smaller units, slaves usually worked under the **task system**. Each slave had a daily or weekly quota of tasks to complete. On large cotton and sugar plantations, slaves would occasionally work under the task system, but more closely supervised and regimented **gang labor** prevailed.

The day of antebellum plantation slaves usually began an hour before sunrise with the sounding of a horn or bell. After a sparse breakfast, slaves marched to the fields. A traveler in Mississippi described a procession of slaves on their way to work. "First came, led by an old driver carrying a whip, forty of the largest and strongest women I ever saw together; they were all in a simple uniform dress of bluish check stuff, the skirts reaching little below the knee; their legs and feet were bare; they carried themselves loftily, each having a hoe over the shoulder, and walking with a free, powerful swing." Then came the plow hands, "thirty strong, mostly men, but few of them women....A lean and vigilant white overseer, on a brisk pony, brought up the rear."

As this account indicates, slave men and women worked side by side in the fields. Female slaves who did not labor in the fields toiled at other tasks. A former slave, John Curry, described how his mother milked cows, cared for the children whose mothers worked in the fields, cooked for field hands, did the ironing and washing for her master's household, and took care of her own seven children. Plantations never lacked tasks for slaves of either gender. As former slave Solomon Northup noted, "ploughing, planting, picking cotton, gathering the corn, and pulling and burning stalks, occupies the whole of the four seasons of the year. Drawing and cutting wood, pressing cotton, fattening and killing hogs, are but incidental labors."

Regardless of the season, the slave's day stretched from dawn to dusk. Touring the South in the 1850s, Frederick Law Olmsted prided himself on rising early and riding late but added, "I always found the negroes in the field when I first looked out, and generally had to wait for the negroes to come from the field to have my horse fed when I stopped for the night." When darkness made fieldwork impossible, slaves transported cotton bales to the gin house, gathered up wood for supper fires, and fed the mules. When the day's labor finally ended, they slept in log cabins on wooden planks.

Although virtually all antebellum Americans worked long hours, no others experienced the same combination of long hours and harsh discipline that slave field hands endured. Northern factory workers did not have to put up with drivers who, like one described by Olmsted, walked among the slaves with a whip, "which he often cracked at them, sometimes allowing the lash to fall lightly upon their shoulders." The lash did not always fall lightly. The annals of American slavery contain stories of repulsive brutality. Drivers sometimes forced pregnant slave women to lie in depressions in the ground while enduring the whip on their backs, a practice that supposedly protected the fetus while abusing the mother.

The disciplining and punishment of slaves were often left to white overseers and black drivers rather than to masters. "Dat was de meanest devil dat ever lived on the Lord's green earth," a former Mississippi slave said of his driver. The barbaric discipline meted out by their subordinates twinged the conscience of many masters, but most justified it as their Christian duty to ensure the slaves' proper "submissiveness." The black abolitionist **Frederick Douglass**, once a slave, recalled that his worst master had been converted at a Methodist camp meeting. "If religion had any effect on his character at all," Douglass related, "it made him more cruel and hateful in all his ways."

Despite the relentless, often vicious discipline, some slaves advanced—not to freedom but to semiskilled or skilled indoor work. Some became blacksmiths, carpenters, or gin operators, and others served as cooks, butlers, and dining room attendants. These house slaves became legendary for their arrogant disdain of field hands and poor whites. The legend often distorted the reality, for house slaves were as subject to discipline as field slaves. "I liked the field work better than I did the house work," a female slave recalled. "We could talk and do anything we wanted to, just so we picked the cotton." Such sentiments were typical, but skilled slave artisans and house servants were greatly valued and treated accordingly; they occupied higher rungs than field hands on the social ladder of slavery.

The Slave Family   Masters thought of slaves as naturally promiscuous and flattered themselves into thinking that they alone held slave marriages together. Slaveowners had powerful incentives to encourage slave marriages: to bring new slaves into the world and to discourage slaves from running away. Some masters baked wedding cakes for slaves and even arbitrated marital disputes. Still, the keenest challenge to the slave family came not from the slaves themselves but from slavery. The law did not recognize or protect slave families. Although some slaveholders were reluctant to break slave marriages by sale, economic hardships might force their hand. The reality, one historian has calculated, was that in a lifetime, on average, a slave would witness the sale of eleven family members.

Naturally, the commonplace buying and selling severely disrupted slaves' attempts to create a stable family life. Poignant testimony to the effects of sale on slave families, and to the desire of slaves to remain near their families, was provided by an advertisement for a runaway in North Carolina in 1851. The advertisement described the fugitive as presumed to be "lurking in the neighborhood of E.D. Walker's, at Moore's Creek, who owns most of his relatives, or Nathan Bonham's who owns his mother; or, perhaps, near Fletcher Bell's, at Long Creek, who owns his father." Small wonder that a slave preacher pronounced a slave couple married "until death or distance do you part."

Aside from disruption by sale, slave families experienced separations and degradations from other sources. The marriage of a slave woman gave her no protection against the sexual demands of a master nor, indeed, of any white. The slave children of white masters became targets of the wrath of white mistresses at times. Sarah Wilson, the daughter of a slave and her white master, remembered that as a child, she was "picked on" by her mistress until the master ordered his wife to let Sarah alone because she "got big, big blood in her." Slave women who worked in the fields were usually separated from their children by day; young sons and daughters often were cared for by the aged or by the mothers of other children. When slave women took husbands from nearby (rather than their own) plantations, the children usually stayed with the mother. Hannah Chapman remembered that her father tried to visit his family under cover of darkness "because he missed us and us longed for him." But if his master found him, "us would track him the nex' day by de blood stains."

Despite enormous obstacles, the relationships within slave families often were intimate and, where possible, long-lasting. In the absence of legal protection, slaves developed their own standards of family morality. A southern white woman observed that slaves "did not consider it wrong for a girl to have a child before she married, but afterwards were extremely severe upon anything like infidelity on her part." When given the opportunity, slaves sought to solemnize their marriages before clergymen. White clergymen who accompanied the Union army into Mississippi and Louisiana in the closing years of the Civil War conducted thousands of marriage rites for slaves who had long viewed themselves as married and desired a formal ceremony and registration.

On balance, slave families differed profoundly from white families. Even on large plantations where roughly equal numbers of black men and women made marriage a theoretical possibility, planters, including George Washington, often divided their holdings into several dispersed farms and distributed their slaves among them without regard to marriage ties. Conditions on small farms and new plantations discouraged the formation of families, and everywhere spouses were vulnerable to being sold as payment for the master's debts. Slave adults were more likely than whites never to marry or to marry late, and slave children were more likely to live with a single parent (usually the mother) or with neither parent.

In white families, the parent-child bond overrode all others; slaves, in contrast, emphasized ties between children and their grandparents, uncles, and aunts as well as their parents. Such broad kinship ties marked the West African cultures from which many slaves had originally been brought to America, and they were reinforced by the separations between children and one or both parents that routinely occurred under slavery. Frederick Douglass never knew his father and saw his mother infrequently, but he vividly remembered his grandmother, "a good nurse, and a capital hand at making nets for catching shad and herring."

In addition, slaves often created "fictive" kin networks; in the absence of uncles and aunts, they simply called friends their uncles, aunts, brothers, or sisters. In effect, slaves invested non-kin relations with symbolic kin functions. In this way, they helped protect themselves against the involuntary disruption of family ties by forced sale and established a broader community of obligation. When plantation slaves greeted each other as "brudder," they were not making a statement about actual kinship but about kindred obligations they felt for each other. Apologists for slavery liked to argue that a "community of interests" bound masters and slaves together. In truth, the real community of interests was the one that slaves developed among themselves to survive.

The Longevity, Diet, and Health of Slaves   Of the 10 to 12 million Africans imported to the New World between the fifteenth and nineteenth centuries, only some 550,000 (about 5 percent) had come to North America, whereas 3.5 million (nearly 33 percent) had been taken to Brazil. Yet by 1825, 36 percent of all slaves in the Western Hemisphere lived in the United States, and only 31 percent in Brazil. The reason for this difference is that slaves in the United States reproduced faster and lived longer than those in Brazil and elsewhere in the Western Hemisphere.

Several factors account for this difference. First, the gender ratio among slaves equalized more rapidly in North America, encouraging earlier and longer marriages and more children. Second, because growing corn and raising livestock were compatible with cotton cultivation, the Old South produced plenty of food. The normal ration for a slave was a peck of cornmeal and three to four pounds of fatty pork a week. Slaves often supplemented this nutritionally unbalanced diet with vegetables grown in small plots that masters allowed them to farm and with fish and game. In the barren winter months, slaves ate less than in the summer; in this respect, how-ever, they did not differ much from most whites.

As for disease, slaves had greater immunities to both malaria and yellow fever than did whites, but they suffered more from cholera, dysentery, and diarrhea. In the absence of privies, slaves usually relieved themselves behind bushes; urine and feces washed into the sources of drinking water and caused many diseases. Yet slaves developed some remedies that, though commonly ridiculed by whites, were effective against stomach ailments. For example, slaves ate white clay to relieve dys-entery and diarrhea; we know now that kaolin, an ingredient of white clay, is a remedy for these ailments.

Although slave remedies often were more effective than those of white physi-cians, slaves experienced higher mortality rates than whites. The very young suf-fered most; infant mortality among slaves was double that of whites, and one in three African-American children died before the age of ten. Plantations in the disease-ridden lowlands had the worst mortality rates, but overworked field hands often miscarried or gave birth to weakened infants even in healthier regions. Mas-ters allowed pregnant women to rest, but rarely enough. "Labor is conducive to health," a Mississippi planter told a northern journalist; "a healthy woman will rear [the] most children."

Away from the Plantation: Slaves in Town and Free Blacks   Greater freedom from supervision and greater opportunities awaited slaves who worked off plantations and farms. In towns and cities slaves were in steady demand to drive wagons, to work as stevedores on the docks, to man river barges, and to toil in mining and lumbering. In 1860, lumbering employed sixteen thousand workers, most of them slaves who cut trees, hauled them to sawmills, and fashioned them into useful lumber. In sawmills, black engineers fired and fixed the steam engines that provided power. In iron-ore ranges and ironworks, slaves not only served as laborers but occasionally supervised less-skilled white workers. Black women and children constituted the main labor force in the South's fledgling textile mills.

Slave or free, blacks found it easier to pursue skilled occupations in southern cities than in northern ones, partly because southern cities attracted few immi-grants to compete for work, and partly because the profitability of southern cash crops long had pulled white laborers out of towns and cities, and left behind opportunities for blacks, slave or free, to acquire craft skills. Slaves who worked in factories, mining, or lumbering usually were hired from their owners rather than owned by their employers. If working conditions threatened to harm their slaves, masters would refuse to provide employers with more. Consequently, working conditions for slaves off plantations usually stayed at a tolerable level. Watching workers load cotton onto a steamboat, Frederick Law Olmsted was amazed to see slaves sent to the top of the bank to roll the bales down to Irish-men who stowed them on the ship. Asking the reason for this arrangement, Olmsted was told, "The niggers are worth too much to be risked here; if the Pad-dies [Irish] are knocked overboard, or get their backs broke, nobody loses anything."

Even more likely than southern blacks in general to live in cities were **free blacks**. In 1860, one-third of the free blacks in the Upper South and more than half in the Lower South were urban. The relatively specialized economies of the cities provided free people of color with opportunities to become carpenters, barrel makers, barbers, and even small traders. A visitor to an antebellum southern market would find that most of the meat, fish, vegetables, and fruit had been prepared for sale by free blacks. Urban free blacks formed their own fraternal orders and churches; a church run by free blacks often was the largest house of worship in a southern city. In New Orleans, free blacks had their own literary journals and opera. In Natchez, a free black barber, William Tiler Johnson, invested the profits of his shop in real estate, acquired stores that he rented out, purchased slaves and a plantation, and even hired a white overseer.

As Johnson's career suggests, some free blacks were highly successful. But free blacks were always vulnerable in southern society and became more so as the antebellum period wore on. Until 1820, masters with doubts about the rightness of slavery frequently manumitted (freed) their black mistresses and mulatto children, and some freed their entire work forces. After 1810, however, fewer and fewer southern whites set slaves free. Although free blacks continued to increase in absolute numbers (a little more than a quarter-million free people of color

A Barber's Shop at Richmond, Virginia, 1861 *Free blacks dominated the barber's trade in Richmond on the eve of the Civil War. As meeting places for men, barber shops supplied newspapers and political discussion. Black barbers were politically informed and prosperous. As was the custom at the time, barbers also performed medical procedures like drawing blood.*

(Valentine Museum, Cook Collection)

dwelled in the South in 1860), the rate of growth of the free-black population slowed radically. In the wake of the Nat Turner rebellion in 1831, laws restricting the liberties of free blacks were tightened. During the mid-1830s, for example, most southern states made it a felony to teach blacks to read and write. Every southern state forbade free blacks to enter, and in 1859 Arkansas ordered all free blacks to leave.

So although a free-black culture flowered in cities like New Orleans and Natchez, that culture did not reflect the conditions under which most free blacks lived. Free blacks were tolerated in New Orleans, in part because there were not too many of them. A much higher percentage of blacks were free in the Upper South than in the Lower South. Furthermore, although a disproportionate number of free blacks lived in cities, the majority lived in rural areas, where whites lumped them together with slaves. Even a successful free black like William Tiler Johnson could never dine or drink with whites. When Johnson attended the theater, he sat in the colored gallery.

The position of free blacks in the Old South held many contradictions. So did their minds. As the offspring, or the descendants of offspring, of mixed liaisons, a disproportionate number of free blacks had light brown skin. Some of them were as color-conscious as whites and looked down on "darky" field hands and coal-black laborers. Yet as whites' discrimination against free people of color intensified during the late antebellum period, many free blacks realized that whatever future they had was as blacks, not as whites. Feelings of racial solidarity increased in the 1850s, and after the Civil War, the leaders of the freed slaves were usually blacks who had been free before the war.

Slave Resistance

Ever-present fears of slave insurrections haunted the Old South. In the delta areas of the Lower South where blacks outnumbered whites, slaves experienced continuous forced labor on plantations and communicated their bitterness to each other in the slave quarters. Free blacks in the cities could have provided leadership for rebellions. Rumors of slave conspiracies flew around the southern white community, and all whites shuddered at the memory of the massive black insurrection that had destroyed French rule in Saint Domingue in the 1790s.

Yet Nat Turner's 1831 insurrection in Virginia was the only slave rebellion that resulted in the deaths of whites. A larger but more obscure uprising occurred in Louisiana in 1811 when some two hundred slaves sought to march on New Orleans. Other, better known, slave insurrections were merely conspiracies that never materialized. In 1800, Virginia slave Gabriel Prosser's planned uprising was betrayed by other slaves, and Gabriel and his followers were executed. That same year, a South Carolina slave, **Denmark Vesey**, won fifteen hundred dollars in a lottery and bought his freedom. Purchasing a carpentry shop in Charleston and becoming a preacher at that city's African Methodist Episcopal Church, Vesey built a cadre of black followers, including a slave of the governor of South Carolina and a black conjurer named Gullah Jack. In 1822, they devised a plan to attack Charleston and seize all the city's arms and ammunition, but other slaves informed authorities, and the conspirators were executed.

For several reasons, the Old South experienced far fewer rebellions than the Caribbean region or South America. Although slaves formed a majority in South Carolina and a few other states, they did not constitute a large majority in any state. In contrast to the Caribbean, an area of absentee landlords and sparse white population, the white presence in the Old South was formidable, and the whites had all the guns and soldiers. The rumors of slave conspiracies that periodically swept the white South demonstrated to blacks the promptness with which whites could muster forces and mount slave patrols. The development of family ties among slaves made them reluctant to risk death and leave their children parentless. Finally, blacks who ran away or plotted rebellions had no allies. By the 1820s, southern Indians routinely captured runaway slaves and exchanged them for rewards; some Indians even owned slaves.

Short of rebellion, slaves could try to escape to freedom in the North. Perhaps the most ingenious, Henry Brown, induced a friend to ship him from Richmond to Philadelphia in a box and won immediate fame as "Box" Brown. Some light mulattos passed as whites on the journey north. More often, fugitive slaves borrowed, stole, or forged passes from plantations or obtained papers describing themselves as free. Frederick Douglass borrowed a sailor's papers in making his escape from Baltimore to New York City in 1838. Some former slaves, among them **Harriet Tubman** and Josiah Henson, made repeated trips back to the South to help other slaves escape. These sundry methods of escape fed the legend of the **"Underground Railroad,"** supposedly an organized network of safe houses owned by white abolitionists who spirited blacks to freedom in the North and Canada. In reality, fugitive slaves owed little to abolitionists. Some white sympathizers in border states offered refuge, but these houses were better known to watchful slave catchers than to most blacks.

Escape to freedom was a dream rather than an alternative for most blacks. Out of millions of slaves, probably fewer than a thousand escaped to the North. Often, slaves ran away from masters not to escape to freedom but to visit spouses or avoid punishment. Most runaways remained in the South; some sought only to return to kinder former masters. During the eighteenth century, African slaves had often run away in groups to the interior and sought to create self-sufficient colonies or villages of the sort they had known in Africa. But by the time the United States acquired Florida, long a haven for runaways, few uninhabited places remained in the South to which slaves could flee.

Despite poor prospects for permanent escape, slaves could disappear for prolonged periods into the free-black communities of southern cities. Slaves enjoyed a fair degree of practical freedom to drive wagons to market and to come and go when they were off plantations. Slaves who were hired out or sent to a city might overstay their leave and even pass themselves off as free. This kind of practical freedom did not change slavery's underlying oppressiveness, but it did give slaves a sense of having certain rights, and it helped deflect slave resistance into forms that were essentially furtive rather than open and violent. Theft was so common that planters learned to keep their tools, smokehouses, closets, and trunks under lock and key. Overworked field hands might leave valuable tools out to rust, or feign illness, or simply refuse to work. As an institution, slavery was vulnerable to such tactics; unlike free laborers, slaves could not be fired for negligence or malingering.

Frederick Law Olmsted found slaveholders in the 1850s afraid to inflict punishment on slaves "lest the slave should abscond, or take a sulky fit and not work, or poison some of the family, or set fire to the dwelling, or have recourse to any other mode of avenging himself."

Olmsted's reference to arson and poisoning reminds us that not all furtive resistance was peaceful. Arson and poisoning, both common in African culture as forms of vengeance, were widespread in the Old South, and the fear of each was even more so. Masters afflicted by dysentery and similar ailments never knew for sure that they had not been poisoned.

Arson, poisoning, work stoppages, and negligence were alternatives to violent rebellion. Yet these furtive forms of resistance differed from rebellion. The goal of rebellion was freedom from slavery. The goal of furtive resistance was to make slavery bearable. The kind of resistance slaves usually practiced sought to establish customs and rules that would govern the conduct of masters as well as that of slaves without challenging the institution of slavery as such. Most slaves would have preferred freedom but settled for less. "White folks do as they please," an ex-slave said, "and the darkies do as they can."

THE EMERGENCE OF AFRICAN-AMERICAN CULTURE

A distinctive culture emerged among blacks in the slave quarters of antebellum plantations. This culture drew on both African and American sources, but it was more than a mixture of the two. Enslaved blacks gave a distinctive twist to the American as well as African components of their culture.

The Language of Slaves

Before slaves could develop a common culture, they needed a common language. During the colonial period, African-born slaves, speaking a variety of languages, had developed a "pidgin"—that is, a language with no native speakers but in which people with different native languages can communicate. Many African-born slaves spoke English pidgin poorly, but their American-born descendants used it as their primary language.

Like all pidgins, English pidgin was a simplified language. Slaves usually dropped the verb *to be* (which had no equivalent in African tongues) and either ignored or confused genders. Instead of saying "Mary is in the cabin," they said, "Mary, he in cabin." To negate, they substituted *no* for *not*, saying, "He no wicked." Pidgin English contained several African words. Some, like *banjo*, became part of standard English; others, like *goober* (peanut), became part of southern white slang. Although many whites ridiculed pidgin and black house servants struggled to speak standard English, pidgin proved indispensable for communication among slaves.

African-American Religion

Religion played an equally important part in forging African-American culture. The majority of slaves transported from Africa worshiped in one of many native African religions. Most of these religions drew little distinction between the spiritual and material worlds—storms, illnesses, and earthquakes were all assumed to stem from supernatural forces. But Africans differed from each other in their specific beliefs, and the majority of slaves brought to America in the seventeenth and eighteenth centuries were young men who may not have absorbed much of this religious heritage before their enslavement.

For these reasons, African religions did not unify blacks in America. Yet remnants of African religion remained, in part because whites undertook few efforts before the 1790s to convert slaves to Christianity. Dimly remembered African beliefs such as the reverence for water may have predisposed slaves to accept Christianity when they were finally urged to do so, because water has a symbolic significance for Christians, too, in the sacrament of baptism. The Christianity preached to slaves by Methodist and Baptist revivalists during the late eighteenth and nineteenth centuries, moreover, resembled African religions in that it also drew few distinctions between the sacred and the secular. Just as Africans believed that a crop-destroying drought or a plague resulted from supernatural forces, the early revivalists knew in their hearts that every drunkard who fell off his horse and every Sabbath-breaker struck by lightning had experienced a deliberate and direct punishment from God.

By the 1790s, blacks formed about a quarter of the membership of the Methodist and Baptist denominations. That converted slaves played major roles in the slave rebellions led by Gabriel Prosser, Denmark Vesey, and Nat Turner actually stimulated Protestant missionaries to intensify their efforts to convert slaves. Missionaries pointed to the self-taught Turner to prove that slaves would hear about Christianity in any event and that organized efforts to convert blacks were the only way to ensure that slaves learned correct versions of Christianity, which emphasized obedience rather than insurgence. Georgia missionary and slaveholder Charles Colcock Jones reassuringly told white planters of the venerable black preacher who, upon receiving some abolitionist tracts in the mail, promptly turned them over to the white authorities for destruction. A Christian slave, the argument ran, would be a better slave. For whites, the clincher was the split of the Methodists, Baptists, and Presbyterians into northern and southern wings by the mid-1840s. Now, they argued, it had finally become safe to convert slaves, for the churches had rid themselves of their antislavery wings. Between 1845 and 1860, the number of black Baptists doubled.

The experiences of Christianized blacks in the Old South illustrate the contradictions of life under slavery. Urban blacks often had their own churches, but in the rural South, slaves worshiped in the same churches as whites. Although the slaves sat in segregated sections, they heard the same sermons and sang the same hymns as whites. Some black preachers actually developed followings among whites, and Christian masters were sometimes rebuked by biracial churches for abusing Christian slaves in the same congregation. The churches were, in fact, the most interracial institutions in the Old South. Yet none of this meant that Christianity was an acceptable route to black liberation. Ministers went out of their way to remind slaves that spiritual equality was not the same as civil equality. The effort to convert slaves gained momentum only to the extent that it was certain that Christianity would not change the basic inequality of southern society.

Although they listened to the same sermons as whites, slaves did not necessarily draw the same conclusions. It was impossible to Christianize the slaves without telling them about the Chosen People, the ancient Jews whom Moses led from captivity in Pharaoh's Egypt into the Promised Land of Israel. Inevitably, slaves drew parallels between their own condition and the Jews' captivity. Like the Jews, blacks concluded, they themselves were "de people of de Lord." If they kept the faith, then, like the Jews, they too would reach the Promised Land. The themes of the Chosen People and the Promised Land ran through the sacred songs, or "spirituals," that blacks sang, to the point where Moses and Jesus almost merged:

> *Gwine to write to Massa Jesus,*
> *To send some Valiant Soldier*
> *To turn back Pharaoh's army,*
> *Hallelu!*

Forever Free sculpture by Mary Edmonia Lewis *Mary Edmonia Lewis's **Forever Free** (1867) commemorated the abolition of slavery.*

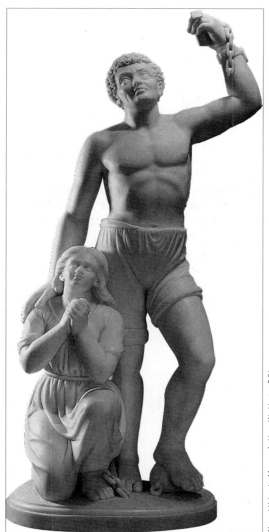

(Howard University Museum Archives, Washington, D.C.)

A listener could interpret a phrase like "the Promised Land" in several ways; it could refer to Israel, to heaven, or to freedom. From the perspective of whites, the only permissible interpretations were Israel and heaven, but some blacks, like Denmark Vesey, thought of freedom as well. The ease with which slaves constructed alternative interpretations of the Bible also reflected that many plantations contained black preachers, slaves trained by white ministers to spread Christianity among blacks. When in the presence of masters or white ministers, these black preachers usually just repeated the familiar biblical command, "Obey your master." Often, however, slaves met for services apart from whites, usually on Sunday evenings but during the week as well. Then the message changed. A black preacher in Texas related how his master would say, "tell them niggers iffen they obeys the master they goes to Heaven." The minister quickly added, "I knowed there's something better for them, but I daren't tell them 'cept on the sly. That I done lots. I tells 'em iffen they keep praying, the Lord will set 'em free."

Some slaves privately interpreted Christianity as a religion of liberation, but most recognized that their prospects for freedom were slight. Generally, Christianity neither turned slaves into revolutionaries nor made them model slaves. It did, however, provide slaves with a view of slavery different from their masters' outlook. Masters argued that slavery was a divinely ordained institution, but Christianity told slaves that it was really an affliction, a terrible and unjust institution that God had allowed to test their faith. For having endured slavery, he would reward blacks. For having created it, he would punish masters.

Black Music and Dance

Compared to the prevailing cultural patterns among elite whites, the culture of blacks in the Old South was extremely expressive. In religious services, blacks shouted "Amen" and let their bodily movements reflect their feelings long after white religious observances, some of which had once been similarly expressive, had grown sober and sedate. Frederick Law Olmsted recorded how, during a slave service in New Orleans during the 1850s, parishioners "in indescribable expression of ecstasy" exclaimed every few moments: "Glory! oh yes! yes!—sweet Lord! sweet Lord!"

Slaves also expressed their feelings in music and dance. Drawing on their African musical heritage, which used hand clapping to mark rhythm, American slaves made rhythmical hand clapping—called patting juba—an indispensable accompaniment to dancing because southern law forbade them to own "drums, horns, or other loud instruments, which may call together or give sign or notice to one another of their wicked designs and intentions." Slaves also played an African instrument, the banjo, and beat tin buckets as a substitute for drums. Whatever instrument they played, their music was tied to bodily movement. Sometimes, slaves imitated white dances like the minuet, but in a way that ridiculed the high manners of their masters. More often, they expressed themselves in a dance African in origin, emphasizing shuffling steps and bodily contortions rather than the erect precision of whites' dances.

Whether at work or at prayer, slaves liked to sing. Work songs describing slave experiences usually consisted of a leader's chant and a choral response:

I love old Virginny
So ho! boys! so ho! I love to shuck corn
So ho! boys! so ho!
Now's picking cotton time
So ho! boys! so ho!

Masters encouraged such songs, believing that singing induced the slaves to work harder and that the innocent content of most work songs proved the slaves were happy. Recalling his own past, Frederick Douglass came closer to the truth when he observed that "slaves sing most when they are most unhappy. The songs of the slave represent the sorrows of his heart; and he is relieved by them, only as an aching heart is relieved by its tears."

Blacks also sang religious songs, later known as **spirituals**. By 1820, blacks at camp meetings had improvised what one white described as "short scraps of disjointed affirmations, pledges, or prayers lengthened out with long repetition choruses." Whites usually took a dim view of spirituals and tried to make slaves sing traditional hymns instead of the "hallelujah songs of their own composing." But slaves clung to their spirituals, which promised, "We will soon be free, when the Lord will call us home," and they sang,

In that morning, true believers,
In that morning,
We will sit aside of Jesus
In that morning,
If you should go fore I go,
In that morning,
You will sit aside of Jesus
In that morning,
True believers, where your
tickets
In that morning,
Master Jesus got your tickets
In that morning.

CHRONOLOGY

1830–1860

1790s	Methodists and Baptists start to make major strides in converting slaves to Christianity.
1793	Eli Whitney invents the cotton gin.
1800	Gabriel Prosser leads a slave rebellion in Virginia.
1808	Congress prohibits external slave trade.

1812	Louisiana, the first state formed out of the Louisiana Purchase, is admitted to the Union.
1816–1819	Boom in cotton prices stimulates settlement of the Old Southwest.
1819–1820	Missouri Compromise.
1822	Denmark Vesey's conspiracy uncovered in South Carolina.
1831	William Lloyd Garrison starts *The Liberator*. Nat Turner rebellion in Virginia.
1832	Virginia legislature narrowly defeats a proposal for gradual emancipation. Virginia's Thomas R. Dew writes an influential defense of slavery.
1835	Arkansas admitted to the Union.
1837	Economic panic begins, lowering cotton prices.
1844–1845	Methodist Episcopal and Baptist Churches split into northern and southern wings over slavery.
1845	Florida and Texas admitted to the Union.
1849	Sugar production in Louisiana reaches its peak.
1849–1860	Period of high cotton prices.
1857	Hinton R. Helper, *The Impending Crisis of the South*.
1859	John Brown's raid on Harpers Ferry.
1860	South Carolina secedes from the Union.

CONCLUSION

The cotton gin revitalized southern agriculture and spurred a redistribution of the South's population, slave and free, from Virginia and other southeastern states to southwestern states like Alabama and Mississippi. As the Old South became more dependent on cotton, it also became more reliant on slave labor.

Slavery left a deep imprint on social relations among the Old South's major white social groups: the planters, the small slaveholders, the yeomen, and the people of the pine barrens. The presence of slaves fed the exaggerated notions of personal honor that made white southerners so violent. Although there was always potential for conflict between slaveholders and nonslaveholders, slavery gave a distinctive unity to the Old South. Most whites did not own any slaves, but the vast majority concluded that their region's prosperity, their ascendancy over blacks, and perhaps even their safety depended on perpetuating slavery. Slavery also shaped the North's perception of the South. Whether northerners believed that the federal government should tamper with slavery or not, they grew convinced that slavery had cut the South off from progress and had turned it into a region of "sterile lands and bankrupt estates."

In contrast, to most white southerners the North, and especially the industrial Northeast, appeared to be the region that deviated from the march of progress. In their eyes, most Americans—indeed, most people throughout the world—practiced agriculture, and agriculture rendered the South a more comfortable place than factories rendered the North. In reaction to northern assaults on slavery, southerners portrayed the institution as a time-honored and benevolent response to the natural inequality of the black and white races. Southerners pointed to the slaves' adequate nutrition, their embrace of Christianity, the affection of some slaves for their masters, and even their work songs as evidence of their contentment.

These white perceptions of the culture that developed in the slave quarters with the maturing of plantation agriculture were misguided. In reality, few if any slaves accepted slavery. Although slaves rebelled infrequently and had little chance for permanent escape, they often engaged in covert resistance to their bondage. They embraced Christianity, but they understood it differently from whites. Whereas whites heard in the Christian gospel the need to make slaves submissive, slaves learned of the gross injustice of human bondage and the promise of eventual deliverance.

13

IMMIGRATION, EXPANSION, AND SECTIONAL CONFLICT 1840–1848

CHAPTER OUTLINE

• Newcomers and Natives • The West and Beyond • The Politics
of Expansion, 1840–1846 • The Mexican-American War and Its
Aftermath, 1846–1848

NEWCOMERS AND NATIVES

Between 1815 and 1860, 5 million European immigrants landed in the United
States (see Figure 13.1). Of these, 4.2 million arrived between 1840 and 1860,
3 million of whom crowded in from 1845 to 1854, the largest immigration relative
to population (then around 20 million) in American history. The Irish led the way
as the most numerous immigrants between 1840 and 1860, with the Germans running a close second. Smaller contingents continued to immigrate to the United
States from England, Scotland, and Wales, and a growing number came from
Norway, Sweden, Switzerland, and Holland. But by 1860, three-fourths of the
foreign-born were either Irish or German.

Expectations   A desire for religious freedom drew some immigrants to the
and Realities   United States. Mormon missionaries actively recruited con-
                            verts in the slums of English factory towns. But a far larger
number of Europeans sailed for America to better their economic condition. Travelers'
accounts and letters from relatives described America as a utopia for poor people.
German peasants learned they could purchase a large farm in America for the price of
renting a small one in Germany. Britons were told that enough good peaches and
apples were left rotting in the orchards of Ohio to sink the British fleet.

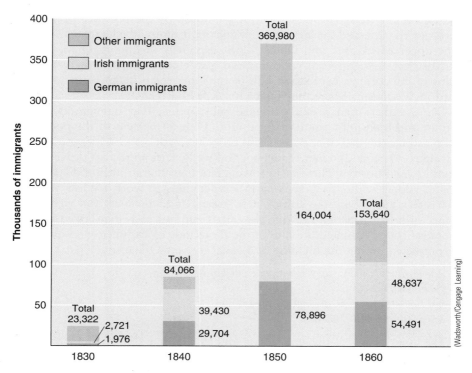

FIGURE 13.1 German, Irish, and Total Immigration, 1830–1860

Irish and German immigrants led the more than tenfold growth of immigration between 1830 and 1860. *Source:* U.S. Bureau of the Census, *Historical Statistics of the United States, Colonial Times to 1970,* Bicentennial Edition I (Washington, D.C., 1975.)

Hoping for the best, emigrants often encountered the worst. Their problems began at ports of embarkation. Because ships sailed irregularly, many spent precious savings in waterfront slums while awaiting departure. Squalid cargo ships carried most of the emigrants, who endured quarters almost as crowded as on slave ships.

For many emigrants, the greatest shock came when they landed. "The folks aboard ship formed great plans for their future, all of which vanished quickly after landing," wrote a young German from Frankfurt in 1840. Immigrants quickly discovered that farming in America differed radically from European farming. Unlike the compact farming villages of Europe, American agricultural areas featured scattered farms. Although meeting occasionally for revivals or militia musters, American farmers lived in relative isolation, and they possessed an individualistic psychology that led them to speculate in land and to move frequently.

Clear patterns emerged amid the shocks and dislocations of immigration. Most of the Irish settlers before 1840 departed from Liverpool on sailing ships that carried English manufactures to eastern Canada and New England in return for timber. On arrival in America, few of these Irish had the capital to become farmers, so they crowded into the urban areas of New England, New York, Pennsylvania, and New Jersey, where they could more easily find jobs. In contrast, German emigrants usually left from continental ports on ships engaged in the cotton trade with

New Orleans. Deterred from settling in the South by the presence of slavery, the oppressive climate, and the lack of economic opportunity, the Germans congregated in the upper Mississippi and Ohio valleys, especially in Illinois, Ohio, Wisconsin, and Missouri. Geographical concentration also characterized most of the smaller groups of immigrants. More than half of the Norwegian immigrants, for example, settled in Wisconsin, where they typically became farmers.

Cities, rather than farms, attracted most antebellum immigrants. By 1860, **German and Irish immigrants** formed more than 60 percent of the population of St. Louis; nearly half the population of New York City, Chicago, Cincinnati, Milwaukee, Detroit, and San Francisco; and well over a third that of New Orleans, Baltimore, and Boston. These fast-growing cities created an intense demand for the labor of people with strong backs and a willingness to work for low wages. Irish construction gangs built the houses, new streets, and aqueducts that were changing the face of urban America and dug the canals and railroads that linked these cities. A popular song recounted the fate of the thousands of Irishmen who died of cholera contracted during the building of a canal in New Orleans:

Ten thousand Micks, they swung their picks,
To build the New Canal
But the choleray was stronger 'n they.
An' twice it killed them awl.

The cities provided the sort of community life that seemed lacking in farming settlements. Immigrant societies like the Friendly Sons of St. Patrick took root in cities and combined with associations like the Hibernian Society for the Relief of Emigrants from Ireland to welcome the newcomers.

The Germans   In 1860, there was no German nation, only a collection of principalities and small kingdoms. German immigrants thought of themselves as Bavarians, Westphalians, or Saxons rather than as Germans. Moreover, the German immigrants included Catholics, Protestants, and Jews as well as a sprinkling of freethinkers who denounced the ritual, clergy, and doctrines of all religions. Although few in number, these critics were vehement in their attacks on the established churches. A pious Milwaukee Lutheran complained in 1860 that he could not drink a glass of beer in a saloon "without being angered by anti-Christian remarks or raillery against preachers."

German immigrants spanned a wide spectrum of social classes and occupations. Most were farmers, but a sizable minority were professionals, artisans, and tradespeople. Heinrich Steinweg, an obscure piano maker from Lower Saxony, arrived in New York City in 1851, anglicized his name to Henry Steinway, and in 1853 opened the firm of Steinway and Sons, which quickly achieved international acclaim for the quality of its pianos. Levi Strauss, a Jewish tailor from Bavaria, migrated to the United States in 1847. On hearing of the discovery of gold in California in 1848, Strauss gathered rolls of cloth and sailed for San Francisco. When a miner told him of the need for durable work trousers, Strauss fashioned a pair of overalls from canvas. To meet a quickly skyrocketing demand, he opened a factory in San Francisco; his cheap overalls, later known as blue jeans or Levi's, made him rich and famous.

For all their differences, the Germans were bound together by their common language, which strongly induced recent immigrants to the United States to congregate in German neighborhoods. Even prosperous Germans bent on climbing the social ladder usually did so within their ethnic communities. Germans formed their own militia and fire companies, sponsored parochial schools in which German was the language of instruction, started German-language newspapers, and organized their own balls and singing groups. The range of voluntary associations among Germans was almost as broad as among native-born Americans.

Other factors beyond their common language brought unity to the German immigrants. Ironically, the Germans' diversity also promoted their solidarity. For example, because they supplied their own doctors, lawyers, teachers, journalists, merchants, artisans, and clergy, the Germans had little need to go outside their own neighborhoods. Native-born Americans simultaneously admired Germans' industriousness and resented German self-sufficiency, which they interpreted as clannishness. German refugee Moritz Busch complained that "the great mass of Anglo-Americans" held the Germans in contempt. The Germans responded by becoming more clannish. Their psychological separateness made it difficult for the Germans to be as politically influential as the Irish immigrants.

The Irish   Between 1815 and the mid-1820s, most Irish immigrants were Protestants, small landowners, and merchants in search of better economic opportunity. Many were drawn by enthusiastic veterans of the War of 1812, who had reported that America was a paradise filled with fertile land and abundant game, a place where "all a man wanted was a gun and sufficient ammunition to be able to live like a prince." From the mid-1820s to the mid-1840s, Irish immigrants became poorer and more frequently Catholic, primarily comprising tenant farmers whom Protestant landowners had evicted as "superfluous."

Protestant or Catholic, rich or poor, nearly one million Irish immigrants entered the United States between 1815 and 1844. Then, between 1845 and the early 1850s, blight destroyed harvest after harvest of Ireland's potatoes, virtually the only food of the peasantry, and created one of the most devastating famines in history. The Great Famine killed a million people. One landlord characterized the surviving tenants on his estate as no more than "famished and ghastly skeletons." To escape the ravages of famine, 1.8 million Irish migrated to the United States in the decade after 1845.

Overwhelmingly poor and Catholic, these newest Irish immigrants usually entered the work force at or near the bottom. The popular image of Paddy with his pickax and Bridget the maid contained a good deal of truth. Irish men dug canals and railroad beds. Compared to other immigrant women, a high proportion of Irish women entered the work force, if not as maids then often as textile workers. By the 1840s, Irish women were displacing native-born women in the textile mills of Lowell and Waltham. Poverty drove Irish women to work at an early age, and the outdoor, all-season work performed by their husbands turned many of them into working widows. Winifred Rooney became a nursemaid at the age of seven and an errand girl at eleven. She then learned needlework, a skill that helped her support her family after her husband's early death. Because the Irish usually married late, almost half the Irish immigrants were single, adult women, many of whom never married. For Irish women to become self-supporting was only natural.

Most Irish people lived a harsh existence. One immigrant described the life of the average Irish laborer in America as "despicable, humiliating, [and] slavish"; there was "no love for him—no protection of life—[he] can be shot down, run through, kicked, cuffed, spat upon—and no redress, but a response of 'served the damn son of an Irish b—right, damn him.'" Yet some Irish struggled up the social ladder. In Philadelphia, which had a more varied industrial base than Boston, Irish men made their way into iron foundries, where some became foremen and supervisors. Other Irish rose into the middle class by opening grocery and liquor stores.

Irish immigrants often conflicted with two quite different groups. The poorer Irish who dug canals and cellars, worked on the docks, took in laundry, and served white families competed directly with equally poor free blacks. This competition stirred up Irish animosity toward blacks and a hatred of abolitionists. At the same time, the Irish who secured skilled or semiskilled jobs clashed with native-born white workers.

Anti-Catholicism, Nativism, and Labor Protest　The surge of Irish immigration revived anti-Catholic fever, long a latent impulse among American Protestants. For example, in 1834 a mob, fueled by rumors that a Catholic convent in Charlestown, Massachusetts, contained dungeons and torture chambers, burned the building to the ground. In 1835, the combative evangelical Protestant Lyman Beecher issued *A Plea for the West*, a tract in which he warned faithful Protestants of an alleged Catholic conspiracy to send immigrants to the West in sufficient numbers to dominate the region. A year later, the publication of Maria Monk's best-selling *Awful Disclosures of the Hotel Dieu Nunnery in Montreal* rekindled anti-Catholic hysteria. Although Maria Monk was actually a prostitute who had never lived in a convent, she professed to be a former nun. In her book, she described how the mother superior forced nuns to submit to the lustful advances of priests who entered the convent by a subterranean passage.

As Catholic immigration swelled in the 1840s, Protestants mounted a political counterattack. It took the form of nativist (anti-immigrant) societies with names like the American Republican party and the United Order of Americans. Although usually started as secret or semisecret fraternal orders, most of these societies developed political offshoots. One, the Order of the Star-Spangled Banner, would evolve by 1854 into the "Know-Nothing," or American, party and would become a major political force in the 1850s.

During the 1840s, however, nativist parties enjoyed only brief moments in the sun. These occurred mainly during flare-ups over local issues, such as whether students in predominantly Catholic neighborhoods should be allowed to use the Catholic Douay rather than Protestant King James version of the Bible for the scriptural readings that began each school day. In 1844, after the American Republican party won some offices in Philadelphia, fiery Protestant orators mounted soapboxes to denounce "popery," and Protestant mobs descended on Catholic neighborhoods. Before the militia quelled these "Bible Riots," thirty buildings lay in charred ruins, and at least sixteen people had been killed.

Nativism fed on an explosive mixture of fears and discontents. Protestants thought that their doctrine that each individual could interpret the Bible was more democratic than Catholicism, which made doctrine the province of the pope and bishops. In addition, at a time when the wages of native-born artisans and journeymen were depressed by the subdivision of tasks and by the aftermath of the Panic of 1837 (see Chapter 10), many Protestant workers concluded that Catholic immigrants, often desperately poor and willing to work for anything, were threats to their jobs.

Demand for land reform joined nativism as a proposed solution to workers' economic woes. Land reformers argued that workers' true interests could never be reconciled with an economic order in which factory workers sold their labor for wages and became "wage slaves." In 1844, the English-born radical George Henry Evans organized the National Reform Association and rallied supporters with the slogan "Vote Yourself a Farm." Evans advanced neo-Jeffersonian plans for the establishment of "rural republican townships" composed of 160-acre plots for workers. Land reform offered little to factory operatives and wage-earning journeymen who completely lacked economic independence. In an age when a horse cost the average worker three months' pay and most factory workers dreaded "the horrors of wilderness life," the idea of solving industrial problems by resettling workers on farms seemed a pipe dream.

Labor unions appealed to workers left cold by the promises of land reformers. For example, desperately poor Irish immigrants, refugees from an agricultural society, believed they could gain more by unions and strikes than by plowing and planting. Even women workers organized unions in these years. The leader of a seamstresses' union proclaimed, "Too long have we been bound down by tyrant employers."

Probably the most important development for workers in the 1840s was a state court decision. In **Commonwealth v. Hunt** (1842), the Massachusetts Supreme Judicial Court ruled that labor unions were not illegal monopolies that restrained trade. But because less than 1 percent of the work force belonged to labor unions in the 1840s, this decision initially had little impact. Massachusetts employers brushed aside the *Commonwealth* decision, firing union agitators and replacing them with cheap immigrant labor. "Hundreds of honest laborers," a labor paper reported in 1848, "have been dismissed from employment in the manufactories of New England because they have been suspected of knowing their rights and daring to assert them." This repression effectively blunted demands for a ten-hour workday in an era when the twelve- or fourteen-hour day was typical.

Ethnic and religious tensions also split the working class during the 1830s and 1840s. Friction between native-born and immigrant workers inevitably became intertwined with the political divisions of the second party system.

Immigrant Politics   Few immigrants had ever cast a vote in an election prior to their arrival in America, and even fewer were refugees from political persecution. Political upheavals had erupted in Austria and several German states in the turbulent year of 1848 (the so-called Revolutions of 1848), but among the million German immigrants to the United States, only about ten thousand were political refugees, or "Forty-Eighters."

Once they had settled in the United States, however, many immigrants became politically active. They quickly found that urban political organizations would help them to find lodging and job, in return for votes. Both the Irish and the Germans identified overwhelmingly with the Democratic Party. An obituary of 1837 that described a New Yorker as a "warm-hearted Irishman and an unflinching Democrat" could have been written of millions of other Irish. Similarly, the Germans became stalwart supporters of the Democrats in cities like Milwaukee and St. Louis.

Immigrants' fears about jobs partly explain their widespread support of the Democrats. Former president Andrew Jackson had given the Democratic Party an anti-aristocratic coloration, making the Democrats seem more sympathetic than the

Whigs to the common people. In addition, antislavery was linked to the Whig party, and the Irish loathed abolitionism because they feared that freed slaves would become their economic competitors. Moreover, the Whigs' moral and religious values seemed to threaten those of the Irish and Germans. Hearty-drinking Irish and German immigrants shunned temperance-crusading Whigs, many of whom were also rabid anti-Catholics. Even public-school reform, championed by the Whigs, was seen as a menace to the Catholicism of Irish children and as a threat to German language and culture.

Although liquor regulations and school laws were city or state concerns rather than federal responsibilities, the Democratic Party schooled immigrants in broad, national principles. It taught them to venerate George Washington, to revere Thomas Jefferson and Andrew Jackson, and to view "monied capitalists" as parasites who would tremble when the people spoke. It introduced immigrants to Democratic newspapers, Democratic picnics, and Democratic parades. The Democrats, by identifying their party with all that they thought best about the United States, helped give immigrants a sense of themselves as Americans. By the same token, the Democratic Party introduced immigrants to national issues. It redirected political loyalties that often had been forged on local issues into the arena of national politics. During the 1830s, the party had persuaded immigrants that national measures like the Bank of the United States and the tariff, seemingly remote from their daily lives, were vital to them. Now, in the 1840s, the Democrats would try to convince immigrants that national expansion likewise advanced their interests.

THE WEST AND BEYOND

As late as 1840, Americans who referred to the West still meant the area between the Appalachian Mountains and the Mississippi River or just beyond. West of that lay the inhospitable Great Plains, a semiarid plateau with few trees. Winds sucked the moisture from the soil. Bands of nomadic Indians—including the Pawnees, Kiowas, and Sioux—roamed this territory and gained sustenance mainly from the buffalo. They ate its meat, wore its fur, and covered their dwellings with its hide. Aside from some well-watered sections of northern Missouri and eastern Kansas and Nebraska, the Great Plains presented would-be farmers with massive obstacles.

The formidable barrier of the Great Plains did not stop settlement of the West in the long run. Temporarily, however, it shifted public interest toward the verdant region lying beyond the Rockies, the Far West (see Map 13.1).

The Far West   By the Transcontinental (or Adams-Onís) Treaty of 1819, the United States had given up its claims to Texas west of the Sabine River and in return had received Spanish claims to the **Oregon country** north of California. Two years later, Mexico won its independence from Spain and took over all North American territory previously claimed by Spain. Then in 1824 and 1825, Russia abandoned its claims to Oregon south of 54°40' (the southern boundary of Alaska). In 1827, the United States and Britain, each of which had claims to Oregon based on discovery and exploration, revived an agreement (originally signed in 1818) for joint occupation of the territory between 42° and 54°40'—a colossal area that contemporaries could describe no more precisely than the "North West Coast of America, Westward of the Stony [Rocky] Mountains"

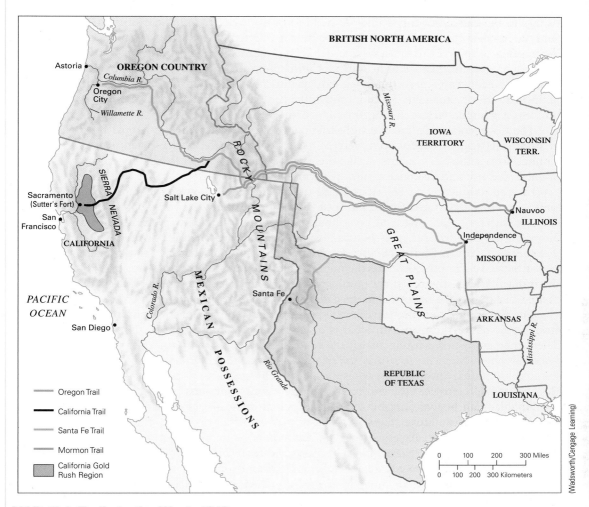

MAP 13.1 Trails to the West, 1840

By 1840, several trails carried pioneers from Missouri and Illinois to the West.

and that included all of modern Oregon, Washington, and Idaho as well as parts of present-day Wyoming, Montana, and Canada.

Despite these agreements and treaties, the vast Far West remained a remote and shadowy frontier during the 1820s. By 1820, the American line of settlement had reached only to Missouri, well over two thousand miles (counting detours for mountains) from the West Coast. El Paso on the Rio Grande and Taos in New Mexico lay, respectively, twelve hundred and fifteen hundred miles north of Mexico City. Britain, of course, was many thousands of miles from Oregon.

Far Western Trade

After sailing around South America and up the Pacific, early merchants had established American and British outposts on the West Coast. Between the late 1790s and the 1820s, for example, Boston merchants had built a thriving trade, exchanging eastern goods for western sea otter fur, cattle, hides, and tallow (rendered from cattle fat and used for making soap and candles). Between 1826 and 1828 alone, Boston traders took more than 6 million cattle hides out of California; in the otherwise undeveloped California economy, these hides, called "California bank-notes," served as the main medium of exchange. During the 1820s, the British Hudson's Bay Company developed a similar trade in Oregon and northern California.

The California trade created little friction with Mexico. Hispanic people born in California (called **Californios**) were as eager to buy as the traders were to sell. Traders who settled in California, like the Swiss-born John Sutter, learned to speak Spanish and became assimilated into Mexican culture.

Farther south, trading links developed during the 1820s between St. Louis and Santa Fe along the famed **Santa Fe Trail**. Each spring, midwesterners loaded their wagons with tools, clothing, and household sundries and rumbled westward to Santa Fe, where they traded their merchandise for mules and New Mexican silver. Mexico welcomed this trade. By the 1830s, more than half the goods entering New Mexico by the Santa Fe Trail trickled into the mineral-rich interior provinces of Mexico, with the result that the Mexican silver peso, which midwestern traders brought back with them, quickly became the principal medium of exchange in Missouri.

The profitability of the beaver trade also prompted Americans to venture west from St. Louis to trap beaver in what is today western Colorado and eastern Utah. There they competed with agents of the Hudson's Bay Company. In 1825, on the Green River in Mexican territory, the St. Louis-based trader William Ashley inaugurated an annual encampment where traders exchanged beaver pelts for supplies, thereby saving themselves the trip to St. Louis. Although silk hats had become more fashionable than beaver hats by 1854, over a half-million beaver pelts were auctioned off in London alone that year.

For the most part, American traders and trappers operating on the northern Mexican frontier in the 1820s and 1830s posed more of a threat to the beaver than to Mexico's provinces. The Mexican people of California and New Mexico depended on the American trade for manufactured goods, and Mexican officials in both provinces relied on customs duties to support their governments. In New Mexico, the government often had to await the arrival of the annual caravan of traders from St. Louis before it could pay its officials and soldiers.

Although the relations between Mexicans and Americans were mutually beneficial during the 1820s, the potential for conflict was always present. Spanish-speaking, Roman Catholic, and accustomed to a more hierarchical society, the Mexicans formed a striking contrast to the largely Protestant, individualistic Americans. Further, American traders returned with glowing reports of the climate and fertility of Mexico's northern provinces. By the 1820s, American settlers were already moving into eastern Texas. At the same time, the ties that bound the central government of Mexico to its northern frontier provinces were starting to fray.

Mexican Government in the Far West

Spain, and later Mexico, recognized that the key to controlling the frontier provinces lay in promoting their settlement by civilized Hispanic people—Spaniards, Mexicans, and Indians who had embraced Catholicism and agriculture. The key instruments of Spain's expansion on the frontier had long been the Spanish missions. Paid by the government, the Franciscan priests who staffed the missions endeavored to convert Native Americans and settle them as farmers on mission lands. To protect the missions, the Spanish often had constructed forts, or presidios, near them. San Francisco was the site of a mission and a presidio founded in 1776, and did not develop as a town until the 1830s.

Dealt a blow by the successful struggle for Mexican independence, Spain's system of missions began to decline in the late 1820s. The Mexican government gradually "secularized" the missions by distributing their lands to ambitious government officials and private ranchers who turned the mission Indians into forced laborers. As many Native Americans fled the missions, returned to their nomadic ways, and joined with Indians who had always resisted the missions, lawlessness surged on the Mexican frontier, and few Mexicans ventured into the undeveloped territory.

To bring in settlers and to gain protection against Indian attacks, in 1824 the Mexican government began to encourage Americans to settle in the eastern part of the Mexican state known as Coahuila-Texas by bestowing generous land grants on agents known as *empresarios* to recruit American settlers. Initially, most Americans, like the *empresario* Stephen F. Austin, were content to live in Texas as naturalized Mexican citizens. But trouble brewed quickly. Most of the American settlers were southern farmers, often slaveholders. Having emancipated its own slaves in 1829, Mexico closed Texas to further American immigration in 1830 and forbade the introduction of more slaves. But the Americans, white and black, kept coming, and in 1834 Austin secured repeal of the 1830 prohibition on American immigration. Two years later, Mexican general Manuel Mier y Téran ran a sword through his heart in despair over Mexico's inability to stem and control the American advance. By 1836, Texas contained some thirty thousand white Americans, five thousand black slaves, and four thousand Mexicans.

As American immigration swelled, Mexican politics (which Austin compared to the country's volcanic geology) grew increasingly unstable. In 1834, Mexican president Antonio López de Santa Anna instituted a policy of restricting the powers of the regimes in Coahuila-Texas and other Mexican states. His actions ignited a series of rebellions in those regions, the most important of which became known as the Texas Revolution.

Texas Revolution, 1836   Santa Anna's brutality in crushing most of the rebellions alarmed the initially moderate Austin and others. When Santa Anna invaded Texas in the fall of 1835, Austin cast his lot with the more radical Americans who wanted independence. Santa Anna's army initially met with success. In February 1836, his force of four thousand men laid siege to San Antonio, whose two hundred defenders, including some *Tejanos*, retreated into an abandoned mission, the **Alamo**. On March 6, four days after Texas had declared its independence, the defenders of the Alamo were overwhelmed by Mexican troops. Most were killed in the final assault. A few, including the famed frontiersman Davy Crockett, surrendered. Crockett then was executed on Santa Anna's orders. A few weeks later, Mexican troops massacred some 350 prisoners taken from an American settlement at Goliad.

Meanwhile, the Texans had formed an army, with **Sam Houston** at its head. A giant man who wore leopard-skin vests, Houston retreated east to pick up recruits

(Daughters of the Republic of Texas Library, Gift of the Yanaguana Society)

Entirro de un Angel **(Funeral of an Angel), by Theodore Gentilz** *Protestant Americans who ventured into Texas came upon a Hispanic culture unlike anything they had seen. Here a San Antonio procession follows the coffin of a baptized infant, who, in Catholic belief, will become an angel in heaven.*

(mostly Americans who crossed the border to fight Santa Anna). Once reinforced, Houston turned and surprised the complacent Mexicans at San Jacinto, just east of what is now the city of Houston. Shouting "Remember the Alamo," Houston's army of eight hundred tore through the Mexican lines, killing nearly half of Santa Anna's men in fifteen minutes and taking Santa Anna himself prisoner. Houston then forced Santa Anna to sign a treaty (which the Mexican government never ratified) recognizing the independence of Texas.

American Settlements in California, New Mexico, and Oregon   Before 1840, California and New Mexico, both less accessible than Texas, exerted no more than a mild attraction for American settlers. Only a few hundred Americans resided in New Mexico in 1840 and perhaps four hundred in California. A contemporary observed that the Americans living in California and New Mexico "are scattered throughout the whole Mexican population, and most of them have Spanish wives. ...They live in every respect like the Spanish."

Yet the beginnings of change were already evident. During the 1840s, Americans streamed into the Sacramento Valley, welcomed by California's Hispanic population as a way to encourage economic development and lured by favorable reports of the region. One tongue-in-cheek story told of a 250-year-old man who had to leave the idyllic region in order to die. For these land-hungry settlers, no sacrifice seemed too great if it led to California.

To the north, Oregon's abundant farmland beckoned settlers from the Mississippi valley. During the 1830s, missionaries like the Methodist Jason Lee moved into Oregon's Willamette valley, and by 1840 the area contained some five hundred Americans. Enthusiastic reports sent back by Lee piqued interest about Oregon. An orator in Missouri described Oregon as a "pioneer's paradise" where "the pigs are running around under the great acorn trees, round and fat and already cooked, with knives and forks sticking in them so that you can cut off a slice whenever you are hungry." To some, Oregon seemed even more attractive than California, especially because the joint American-British occupation seemed to herald better prospects for eventual U.S. annexation than California's.

The Overland Trails   Whether bound for California or Oregon, the emigrants faced a four-month journey across terrain little known in reality but vividly depicted in fiction as an Indian killing ground. Assuming that they would have to fight their way across the Plains, settlers prepared for the trip by buying enough guns for an army from merchants in the rival jump-off towns of Independence and St. Joseph, Missouri. In reality, the pioneers were more likely to shoot themselves or each other by accident than to be shot by the usually cooperative Indians, and much more likely to be scalped by the inflated prices charged by merchants in Independence or "St. Joe."

Once embarked, the emigrants faced new hardships and hazards: kicks from mules, oxen that collapsed from thirst, overloaded wagons that broke down. Trails were difficult to follow—at least until they became littered by the debris of broken wagons and by the bleached bones of oxen. Guidebooks to help emigrants chart their course were more like guessbooks. The Donner party, which set out from Illinois in 1846, lost so much time following the advice of one such book that its members became snowbound in the High Sierras and reached California only after its survivors had turned to cannibalism.

Emigrants responded to the challenges of the overland trails by close coopera-tion with one another, traveling in huge wagon trains rather than alone. Men yoked and unyoked the wagons, drove the wagons and stock, and hunted. Women packed and unpacked the wagons each day, milked the cows brought along to stock the new farms in the West, cooked, and assisted with the childbirths that occurred on the trail at about the same frequency as in the nation as a whole.

Between 1840 and 1848, an estimated 11,500 emigrants followed an overland trail to Oregon, and some 2,700 reached California. Such numbers made a differ-ence, for the British did not settle Oregon at all, and the Mexican population in California was small and scattered. By 1845, California clung to Mexico by the thinnest of threads. The territory's Hispanic population, the *Californios*, felt little allegiance to Mexico, which they contemptuously referred to as the "other shore." Some *Californios* wanted independence from Mexico; others looked to the day when California might become a protectorate of Britain or perhaps even France. But these *Californios*, with their shaky allegiances, now faced a growing number of American settlers with definite political allegiances.

THE POLITICS OF EXPANSION, 1840–1846

Westward expansion raised the question of whether the United States should annex the independent Texas republic. In the mid-1840s, the Texas-annexation issue generated the kind of political passions that banking questions had ignited in the 1830s, and became entangled with equally unsettling issues relating to California, New Mexico, and Oregon. Between 1846 and 1848, a war with Mexico and a dramatic confrontation with Britain settled all these questions on terms favorable to the United States.

At the start of the 1840s, western issues received little attention in a nation concerned with issues relating to economic recovery—notably, banking, the tariff, and internal improvements. Only after politicians failed to address the economic issues coherently did opportunistic leaders thrust issues relating to expansion to the top of the political agenda.

The Whig Ascendancy   The election of 1840 brought Whig candidate William Henry Harrison to the presidency and installed Whig majorities in both houses of Congress. The Whigs had proposed to replace Van Buren's darling, the Independent Treasury (see Chapter 10), with a national "fiscal agent," which, like the defunct Bank of the United States, would be a private corporation chartered by Congress and charged with regulating the currency. The Whigs also favored a revised tariff that would increase government revenues but remain low enough to permit the importation of foreign goods. According to the Whig plan, the states would then receive tariff-generated revenues for internal improvements.

The Whig agenda might have breezed into law. But Harrison died after only one month in office, and his successor, Vice President **John Tyler**, an upper-crust Virginian put on the ticket in 1840 for his southern appeal, assumed the presidency. A former Democrat, Tyler had broken with Jackson over nullification, but he favored the Democratic philosophy of states' rights. As president, he repeatedly vetoed Whig proposals, including a bill to create a new national bank.

Tyler also played havoc with Whig tariff policy. The Compromise Tariff of 1833 had provided for a gradual scaling down of tariff duties, until none was to exceed 20 percent by 1842. Amid the depression of the early 1840s, however, the provision for a 20 percent maximum tariff appeared too low to generate revenue. Without revenue, the Whigs would have no money to distribute among the states for internal improvements and no program with national appeal. In response, the Whig congressional majority passed two bills in the summer of 1842 that simultaneously postponed the final reduction of tariffs to 20 percent and ordered distribution to the states to proceed. Tyler promptly vetoed both bills. Tyler's mounting vetoes infuriated Whig leadership. "Again has the imbecile, into whose hands accident has placed the power, vetoed a bill passed by a majority of those legally authorized to pass it," screamed the *Daily Richmond Whig*. Some Whigs talked of impeaching Tyler. Finally, in August, needing revenue to run the government, Tyler signed a new bill that maintained some tariffs above 20 percent but abandoned distribution to the states.

Tyler's erratic course confounded and disrupted his party. By maintaining some tariffs above 20 percent, the tariff of 1842 satisfied northern manufacturers, but by abandoning distribution, it infuriated many southerners and westerners. In the congressional elections of 1842, the Whigs paid a heavy price for failing to enact their program. Although retaining a slim majority in the Senate, they lost control of the House to the Democrats. Now the nation had one party in control of the Senate, its rival in control of the House, and a president who appeared to belong to neither party.

Tyler and the Annexation of Texas   Although disowned by his party, Tyler ardently desired a second term as president. Domestic issues offered him little hope of building a popular following, but foreign policy was another matter. In 1842, Tyler's secretary of state, Daniel Webster, concluded a treaty with Great Britain, represented by Lord Ashburton, that settled a long-festering dispute over the boundary between Maine and the Canadian province of New Brunswick. Awarding more than half of the disputed territory to the United States, the Webster-Ashburton Treaty was popular in the North. Tyler reasoned that if he could now arrange for the **annexation of Texas**, he would build a national following.

The issue of slavery, however, clouded every discussion of Texas. Antislavery northerners viewed proposals to annex Texas as part of an elaborate southern conspiracy to extend slavery, because Texas would certainly enter the Union as a slave state. In fact, some southerners dreamed of creating four or five slave states from Texas's vast area.

Nevertheless, in the summer of 1843, Tyler launched a propaganda campaign for Texas annexation. He alleged that Britain had designs on Texas, which Americans would be prudent to forestall. Tyler's campaign was fed by reports from his unofficial agent in London, Duff Green, a protégé of John C. Calhoun and a man whom John Quincy Adams contemptuously dismissed as an "ambassador of slavery." Green assured Tyler that, as a prelude to undermining slavery in the United States, the British would pressure Mexico to recognize the independence of Texas in return for the abolition of slavery there. Calhoun, who became Tyler's secretary of state early in 1844, embroidered these reports with fanciful theories about British plans to use abolition as a way to destroy rice, sugar, and cotton production in the United States and gain for itself a monopoly on all three staples.

In the spring of 1844, Calhoun and Tyler submitted for Senate ratification a treaty annexing Texas to the United States. Among the supporting documents accompanying the treaty was a letter from Calhoun to the British minister in Washington, defending slavery as beneficial to blacks, the only way to protect them from "vice and pauperism." Abolitionists now had evidence that the annexation of Texas was linked to a conspiracy to extend slavery. Both Martin Van Buren, the leading northern Democrat, and Henry Clay, the most powerful Whig, came out against immediate annexation on the grounds that annexation would provoke the kind of sectional conflict that each had sought to bury, and the treaty went down to crushing defeat in the Senate. However decisive it appeared, however, this vote only postponed the final decision on annexation to the upcoming election of 1844.

The Election of 1844   Tyler's ineptitude turned the presidential campaign into a free-for-all. The president lacked a base in either party, and after testing the waters as an independent, he was forced to drop out of the race.

Henry Clay had a secure grip on the Whig nomination. Martin Van Buren appeared to have an equally firm grasp on the Democratic nomination, but the issue of Texas annexation split his party. Trying to appease all shades of opinion within his party, Van Buren stated that he would abide by whatever Congress might decide on the annexation issue. Van Buren's attempt to evade the issue succeeded only in alienating the modest number of northern annexationists, led by Michigan's former governor Lewis Cass, and the much larger group of southern annexationists. At the Democratic convention, Van Buren and Cass effectively blocked each other's nomination. The resulting deadlock was broken by the nomination of **James K. Polk** of Tennessee, the first "dark-horse" presidential nominee in American history and a supporter of immediate annexation (see Technology and Culture).

Jeering "Who is James K. Polk?" the Whigs derided the nomination. Polk was little known outside the South, and he had lost successive elections for the governorship of Tennessee. Yet Polk persuaded many northerners that annexation of Texas would benefit them. Conjuring an imaginative scenario, Polk and his supporters argued that if Britain succeeded in abolishing slavery in Texas, slavery would not be able to move westward; racial tensions in existing slave states would intensify; and the chances of a race war, which might spill over into the North, would increase. However far-fetched, this argument played effectively on northern racial phobias and helped Polk detach annexation from Calhoun's narrow, prosouthern defense of it.

In contrast to the Democrats, whose position was clear, Clay kept muddying the waters. First he told his followers he had nothing against annexation as long as it would not disrupt sectional harmony. In September 1844, he came out against annexation. Clay's shifts on annexation alienated his southern supporters and prompted a small but influential body of northern antislavery Whigs to desert to the Liberty party, which had been organized in 1840. Devoted to the abolition of slavery by political action, the Liberty party nominated Ohio's James G. Birney for the presidency.

Annexation was not the sole issue of the campaign. The Whigs infuriated Catholic immigrant voters by nominating Theodore Frelinghuysen as Clay's running mate. A supporter of temperance and other Protestant causes, Frelinghuysen confirmed the image of the Whigs as the orthodox Protestant party and roused the largely Catholic foreign-born voters to turn out in large numbers for the Democrats.

On the eve of the election in New York City, so many Irish marched to the courthouse to be qualified for voting that the windows had to be left open for people to get in and out. "Ireland has reconquered the country which England lost," an embittered Whig moaned. Polk won the electoral vote 170 to 105, but his margin in the popular vote was only 38,000 out of 2.6 million votes cast, and he lost his own state of Tennessee by 113 votes. A shift of six thousand votes in New York, where the immigrant vote and Whig defections to the Liberty party had hurt Clay, would have given Clay the state and the presidency.

Manifest Destiny, 1845

The election of 1844 demonstrated that the annexation of Texas had more national support than Clay had realized. The surging popular sentiment for expansion that made the underdog Polk rather than Clay the man of the hour reflected a growing conviction among the people that America's natural destiny was to expand into Texas and all the way to the Pacific Ocean.

James K. Polk

Lacking charm, Polk bored even his friends, but few presidents could match his record of acquiring land for the United States.

(James K. Polk Memorial Association, Columbia, Tennessee)

Expansionists emphasized extending the "area of freedom" and talked of "repelling the contaminating proximity of monarchies upon the soil that we have consecrated to the rights of man." For young Americans like Walt Whitman, such restless expansionism knew few limits. "The more we reflect upon annexation as involving a part of Mexico, the more do doubts and obstacles resolve themselves away," Whitman wrote. "Then there is California, on the way to which lovely tract lies Santa Fe; how long a time will elapse before they shine as two new stars in our mighty firmament?"

Americans awaited only a phrase to capture this ebullient spirit. In 1845, John L. O'Sullivan, a New York Democratic journalist, supplied that phrase when he wrote of "our **manifest destiny** to overspread and to possess the whole of the continent which Providence has given us for the development of the great experiment of liberty and federated self-government entrusted to us."

Advocates of Manifest Destiny used lofty language and invoked God and Nature to sanction expansion. Inasmuch as most proponents of Manifest Destiny were Democrats who favored annexing Texas, northern Whigs frequently dismissed Manifest Destiny as a smoke screen aimed at concealing the evil intent of expanding slavery. In reality, many expansionists were neither supporters of slavery nor zealous annexationists. Most had their eyes not on Texas but on Oregon and

California. Despite their flowery phrases, these expansionists rested their case on hard material calculations. Blaming the post-1837 depression on the failure of the United States to acquire markets for its agricultural surplus, they saw the acquisition of Oregon and California as solutions. A Missouri Democrat observed that "the ports of Asia are as convenient to Oregon as the ports of Europe are to the eastern slope of our confederacy, with an infinitely better ocean for navigation." An Alabama Democrat praised California's "safe and capacious harbors," which, he assured, "invite to their bosoms the rich commerce of the East."

Expansionists desired more than profitable trade routes, however. At the heart of their thinking lay an impulse to preserve the predominantly agricultural character of the American people and thereby to safeguard democracy. Fundamentally, most expansionists were Jeffersonians. They equated cities and factories with class strife. After a tour of New England mill towns in 1842, John L. O'Sullivan warned Americans that should they fail to encourage alternatives to factories, the United States would sink to the level of Britain, a nation that the ardent Democratic expansionist James Gordon Bennett described as a land of "bloated wealth" and "terrible misery."

Most Democratic expansionists linked the acquisition of new territory to their party's policies of low tariffs and decentralized banking. Where tariffs and banks tended to "favor and foster the factory system," expansion would provide farmers with land and with access to foreign markets for their produce. The acquisition of California and Oregon would provide enough land and harbors to sustain not only the 20 million Americans of 1845 but the 100 million that some expansionists projected for 1900 and the 250 million that O'Sullivan predicted for 1945.

Trumpeted by the penny press, this message made sense to the laboring poor of America's cities, many of them Irish immigrants. Expansion would open economic opportunities for the common people and thwart British plans to free American slaves, whom the poor viewed as potential competitors for scarce jobs.

Expansionism drew ideas from Thomas Jefferson, John Quincy Adams, and other leaders of the early Republic who had proclaimed the American people's right to displace both "uncivilized" and European people from the path of their westward movement. Early expansionists, however, had feared that overexpansion might create an ungovernable empire. Jefferson, for example, had proposed an indefinite restriction on the settlement of Louisiana. In contrast, the expansionists of the 1840s, citing the virtues of the telegraph and the railroad, believed that the problem of distance had been "literally annihilated" (see Technology and Culture).

Polk and Oregon   The growing spirit of Manifest Destiny escalated the issue of Oregon. To soften northern criticism of the still-pending annexation of Texas, the Democrats had included in their 1844 platform the assertion that American title "to the whole of the Territory of Oregon is clear and unquestionable." Taken literally, this statement, which Polk later repeated, pressed an unprecedented American claim to the entire Oregon Territory between California and 54°40', the southern boundary of Alaska.

Polk's objectives in Oregon were more subtle than his language. He knew that the United States could never obtain all of Oregon without a war with Britain, and he wanted to avoid that. He proposed to use the threat of hostilities to persuade the British to accept what they had repeatedly rejected in the past—a division of

Oregon at the forty-ninth parallel. Such a division, extending the existing boundary between the United States and Canada from the Rockies to the Pacific, would give the United States both the excellent deep-water harbors of Puget Sound and the southern tip of British-controlled Vancouver Island. For their part, the British had long held out for a division along the Columbia River, which entered the Pacific Ocean far south of the forty-ninth parallel (see Map 13.2).

Polk's position aroused American support for acquiring the whole territory. Mass meetings adopted such resolutions as "We are all for Oregon, and *all* Oregon in the West" and "The Whole or None!" Furthermore, each passing year brought new American settlers into Oregon. John Quincy Adams, no supporter of the annexation of Texas or the 54°40' boundary for Oregon, believed that the American settlements gave the United States a far more reasonable claim to Oregon than mere exploration and discovery gave the British. The United States, not Britain, Adams preached, was the nation bound "to make the wilderness blossom as the rose, to establish laws, to increase, multiply, and subdue the earth," all "at the first behest of God Almighty."

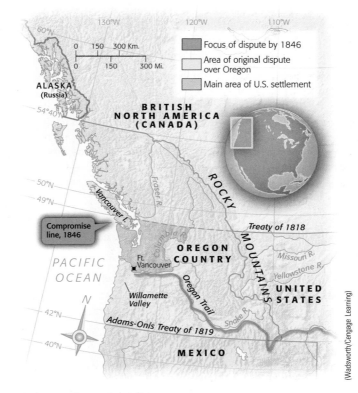

MAP 13.2 Oregon Boundary Dispute

Although demanding that Britain cede the entire Oregon Territory south of 54°40', the United States settled for a compromise at the forty-ninth parallel.

TECHNOLOGY & CULTURE

The Telegraph

In 1837, Samuel F.B. Morse was a forty-six-year-old art professor at New York University trying to get over some disappointments. His talent as a painter was widely recognized, but he was passed over when Congress selected four artists to paint scenes for the rotunda of the Capitol in Washington. He was also well known as a nativist who fiercely opposed Catholic immigration and who had written anti-Catholic tracts. Nativism was on the rise in the 1830s, when more than half a million immigrants arrived in New York City alone. That many of these were Catholics alarmed Morse, who, as an art student in Europe, had been attracted by Italy's beauty but repelled by what he saw as the submissiveness of its people to the pope. In 1836, he had run for mayor of New York City on the ticket of an anti-Catholic nativist party, only to finish last in a field of four.

Since 1832, Morse had been developing one other interest: sending information by electrical currents on wires. That even a crude battery could transmit a shock to a person holding an iron wire had long been known. Benjamin Franklin's kite experiments nearly a century earlier had shown that lightning was a form of electricity. If messages could be sent at the speed of lightning, close to 200,000 miles a second, then the era of instant messaging was at hand.

Fearing needlessly that inventors in France were about to beat him to the punch, Morse moved quickly. He constructed a crude telegraph, which consisted of a battery and a transmitter that sent electrical impulses to an electromagnetic receiver. Once energized, the receiver moved an arm and recorded coded signals on a band of paper. Short impulses appeared as dots, longer ones as dashes. In manifold combinations, these dots and dashes stood for different letters of the alphabet and became known as Morse Code.

With the help of physicists, he improved his device and successfully demonstrated it in a university lecture hall in September 1837. Next, eager to show the public that electrical messaging over long distances was practical, he teamed with Samuel Colt, the inventor of the revolving pistol (see Chapter 11). Colt, whose gun company had gone bankrupt, wanted to persuade Congress that an electrical current could detonate gunpowder. If so, it would be possible to lay mines in the nation's harbors and explode them when hostile warships approached. Morse recognized that if electrical impulses could be transmitted through water, telegraph cables could cross the nation's innumerable rivers. In 1842, before an audience estimated at forty thousand—including the secretary of war—Colt and Morse ran an electrical cable from one ship in New York harbor to another, aptly named the *Volta*, which had been stripped and mined. The current triggered the mines. "Bang! bang! bang!," reported the *Herald*, "combusti-blowup eruption ... 1,705,901 pieces."

Six months later, Congress approved a grant of $30,000 to build a telegraph line from Washington to Baltimore. Construction went slowly. Morse's plan to bury the cable had to be abandoned because of insulation problems, forcing a resort to lines in the air from wooden post to wooden post. But by May 1844, twenty-two miles had been completed, just in time for news of the Whig national convention, meeting in Baltimore, to be carried by train to Annapolis Junction and then transmitted by wire to dignitaries assembled in the chamber of the Supreme Court in Washington.

Within a few weeks, the line had been completed to Baltimore, where the

Democratic national convention was also meeting. Morse asked a friend to send a message of her choice to Baltimore, and she chose (from the Bible) "What hath God wrought?" History books have made this one of the most memorable quotations in American history, but contemporaries were more interested in the next question: "Have you any news?" Much was at stake. The Whig nominee, Henry Clay, had come out against the annexation of Texas. Martin Van Buren, the likely Democratic nominee, had tried to evade the issue. But southern opponents of Van Buren had put in a new rule, requiring a two-thirds majority for nomination. This rule stopped the Van Buren steamroller and eventually led to the nomination of the dark horse, James K. Polk. No less important than the news of Polk's upset victory was its delivery as breaking news. Here was real excitement. "Mr. Brewster is speaking in favor of [James] Buchanan; ... Mr. Brewster says his delegation will go for V[an] B[uren] but if VB's friends desert him, the delegation will go for Buchanan;" and then "Illinois goes for Polk ... Mich[igan] goes for Polk ... Polk is unanimously nom[inated.]"

At first, newspaper editors worried that the telegraph would put them out of business. Since news would arrive instantly, no editor could beat his rivals to a story. Soon they saw their error. With the telegraph, stories could be put out in installments that recorded each new development. Were a story really spicy, newspapers could put out several editions a day. Further, the construction of telegraph lines was just starting, with much of the capital coming from newspaper publishers. By 1848, a line ran from Boston all the way to New York City. As yet, no line connected Boston with Halifax in Canada, where steamers from Europe first docked. Newspapers were potentially the most valuable cargo carried by these steamers, for they contained news of prices of European commodity markets. A New Yorker who speculated in wheat futures and who became the first to learn that wheat was up (or down) on the Brussels exchange could make an overnight fortune. Rival newspaper editors hired riders and fast horses to speed news of commodity prices from Halifax to Boston, but they were no match for the ingenious Daniel Craig, who successfully trained carrier pigeons to carry information about European prices over the same route. Craig was so successful that he was hired by the newly formed Associated Press, a consortium of New York City editors who pooled their resources to gain access to news before it reached the telegraph.

In the five years after the opening of the Baltimore-Washington line, the United States expanded to include Texas, the vast Oregon territory, and all or part of the present states of California, Utah, Nevada, New Mexico, Arizona, Wyoming, and Colorado. Morse, who long had feared that European monarchs were conspiring with the pope to infiltrate Catholic immigrants into the sparsely settled West, was confident that his invention would make it possible to protect American liberty against "Catholic plots." The nation would become a lightning-bound network of communities within instant reach of each other. Should European despots threaten invasion, the whole nation could be activated in a moment. Ironically, European monarchs would pose less of a threat than Americans themselves to the safety of the Republic, which would implode in civil war in 1861.

Questions for Analysis

1. *What obstacles had to be overcome before Morse's invention came into wide use?*

2. *What role did newspapers play in overcoming these obstacles?*

In April 1846, Polk forced the issue by notifying Britain that the United States was terminating joint British-American occupation of Oregon. In effect, his message was that Britain could either go to war over American claims to 54°40'—or negotiate. Britain chose to negotiate. Although the British raged against "that ill-regulated, overbearing, and aggressive spirit of American democracy," they had too many domestic and foreign problems to welcome a war over what Lord Aberdeen, the British foreign secretary, dismissed as "a few miles of pine swamp." The ensuing treaty provided for a division at the forty-ninth parallel, with some modifications. Britain retained all of Vancouver Island as well as navigation rights on the Columbia River. On June 15, 1846, the Senate ratified the treaty, stipulating that Britain's navigation rights on the Columbia were merely temporary.

The Mexican-American War and Its Aftermath, 1846–1848

Between 1846 and 1848, the United States successfully fought a war with Mexico that led Mexico to renounce all claims to Texas and to cede its provinces of New Mexico and California to the United States. Many Americans rejoiced in the stunning victory. But some recognized that deep divisions over the status of slavery in New Mexico and California boded ill for their nation's future.

The Origins of the Mexican-American War
While Polk was challenging Britain over Oregon, the United States and Mexico moved toward war. The impending conflict had both remote and immediate causes. One long-standing grievance lay in the failure of the Mexican government to pay some $2 million in debts owed to American citizens. Bitter memories of the Alamo and the Goliad massacre reinforced American loathing of Mexico. Above all, the issue of Texas poisoned relations between the two nations. Mexico still hoped to regain Texas or at least to keep it independent of the United States. Beset by internal strife—Mexico's presidency changed hands twenty times between 1829 and 1844—Mexico feared that, once in control of Texas, the "Colossus of the North" might seize other provinces, perhaps even Mexico itself, and treat Mexicans much as it treated its slaves.

Polk's election increased the strength of the pro-annexationists, for his campaign had persuaded many northerners that enfolding Texas would bring national benefits. In February 1845, both houses of Congress responded to popular sentiment by passing a resolution annexing Texas. Texans, however, balked, in part because some feared that union with the United States would provoke a Mexican invasion and war on Texas soil.

Confronted by Texan timidity and Mexican belligerence, Polk moved on two fronts. To sweeten the pot for the Texans, he supported their claim that the Rio Grande constituted Texas's southern boundary, despite Mexico's contention that the Nueces River, a hundred miles north of the Rio Grande, bounded Texas. The area between the Nueces and the Rio Grande was largely uninhabited, but the stakes were high. Although only a hundred miles south of the Nueces at its mouth on the Gulf of Mexico, the Rio Grande meandered west and then north for nearly two thousand miles and encompassed a huge territory, including part of modern New Mexico. The Texas that Polk proposed to annex thus encompassed far more land than the Texas that had gained independence from Mexico in 1836. On July 4, 1845, reassured by Polk's largesse, a Texas convention overwhelmingly voted to accept annexation. In response to Mexican war preparations, Polk then made a second move, ordering American troops under General **Zachary Taylor** to the edge of the disputed territory. Taylor took up a position at Corpus Christi, a tiny Texas outpost situated just south of the Nueces and hence in territory still claimed by Mexico.

One reason for Polk's insistence on the Rio Grande boundary for Texas was to provoke a war with Mexico, Then, the United States could seize California and for its fine harbors of San Diego and San Francisco. In fact, Polk had entered the White House with the firm intention of extending American control over California. By the summer of 1845, his followers were openly proclaiming that, if Mexico went to war with the United States over Texas, "the road to California will be open to us." Reports from American agents persuaded Polk that California might be acquired by the same methods as Texas: revolution followed by annexation.

Continued turmoil in Mexico further complicated the situation. In early 1845, a new Mexican government agreed to negotiate with the United States, and Polk, locked into a war of words with Britain over Oregon, decided to give negotiations a chance. In November 1845, he dispatched John Slidell to Mexico City with instructions to gain Mexican recognition of the annexation of Texas with the Rio Grande border. In exchange, the United States government would assume the debt owed by Mexico to American citizens. Polk also authorized Slidell to offer up to $25 million for California and New Mexico. But by the time Slidell reached Mexico City, the government there had become too weak to make concessions to the United States, and its head, General José Herrera, refused to receive Slidell. Polk then ordered Taylor to move southward to the Rio Grande, hoping to provoke a Mexican attack and unite the American people behind war.

The Mexican government dawdled. Polk was about to send a war message to Congress when word finally arrived that Mexican forces had crossed the Rio Grande and ambushed two companies of Taylor's troops. Now the pro-war press had its martyrs. *American blood has been shed on American soil!* one of Polk's followers proclaimed. On May 11, Polk informed Congress that war "exists by the act of Mexico herself" and called for $10 million to fight the war.

Polk's disarming assertion that the United States was already at war provoked furious opposition in Congress, where antislavery Whigs protested the president's high-handedness. For one thing, the Mexican attack on Taylor's troops had occurred on land never before claimed by the United States. By announcing that war already existed, moreover, Polk seemed to be undercutting Congress's power to declare war and using a mere border incident as a pretext to acquire more slave territory. The pro-Whig *New York Tribune* warned its readers that Polk was "precipitating you into a fathomless abyss of crime and calamity." Antislavery poet James Russell Lowell of Massachusetts wrote of the Polk Democrats,

> *They just want this Californy*
> *So's to lug new slave-states in*
> *To abuse ye, an' to scorn ye,*
> *An' to plunder ye like sin.*

But Polk had maneuvered the Whigs into a corner. Few Whigs could forget that the Federalists' opposition to the War of 1812 had wrecked the Federalist Party, and few wanted to appear unpatriotic by refusing to support Taylor's beleaguered troops. Swallowing their outrage, most Whigs backed appropriations for war against Mexico.

Polk's single-minded pursuit of his goals had prevailed. A humorless, austere man who banned dancing and liquor at White House receptions, Polk inspired little personal warmth. But he had clear objectives and pursued them unflinchingly. At every point, he had encountered opposition on the home front: from Whigs who saw him as a reckless adventurer; from northerners of both parties opposed to any expansion of slavery; and from John C. Calhoun, who despised Polk for his high-handedness and fretted that a war with Britain would strip the South of its market for cotton. Yet Polk triumphed over all opposition, in part because of his opponents' fragmentation, in part because of expansion's popular appeal, and in part because of the weakness of his foreign antagonists. Reluctant to fight over Oregon, Britain had negotiated. Too weak to negotiate, Mexico chose to fight over territory that it had already lost (Texas) and for territories over which its hold was feeble (California and New Mexico).

The Mexican-American War   Most European observers expected Mexico to win the war. Its regular army was four times the size of the American forces, and it was fighting on home ground. The United States, having botched its one previous attempt to invade a foreign nation, Canada in 1812, now had to sustain offensive operations in an area remote from American settlements. American expansionists, however, hardly expected the Mexicans to fight at all. Racism and arrogance persuaded many Americans that the Mexicans, degraded by their mixed Spanish and Indian population, were "as sure to melt away at the approach of [American] energy and enterprise as snow before a southern sun."

In fact, the Mexicans fought bravely and stubbornly, although unsuccessfully. In May 1846, Taylor, "Old Rough and Ready," routed the Mexican army in Texas and pursued it across the Rio Grande, eventually capturing the major city of Monterrey. War enthusiasm surged in the United States. Recruiting posters blared, "Here's to old Zach! Glorious Times! Roast Beef, Ice Cream, and Three Months' Advance." Taylor's conspicuously ordinary manner—he went into battle wearing a straw hat and a plain brown coat—endeared him to the public, which kicked up its heels in celebration to the "Rough and Ready Polka" and the "General Taylor Quick Step."

After taking Monterrey, Taylor, starved for supplies, halted and granted Mexico an eight-week armistice. Eager to undercut Taylor's popularity—the Whigs were already touting him as a presidential candidate—Polk stripped him of half his forces and reassigned them to General Winfield Scott. Scott was to mount an amphibious attack on Vera Cruz and proceed to Mexico City, following the path of Cortés and his conquistadors. Events outstripped Polk's scheme, however, when Taylor defeated a far larger Mexican army at the Battle of Buena Vista, on February 22–23, 1847.

While Taylor was winning fame in northern Mexico, and before Scott had launched his attack on Vera Cruz, American forces farther north were dealing decisive blows to the remnants of Mexican rule in New Mexico and California. In the spring of 1846, Colonel Stephen Kearny marched an army from Fort Leavenworth, Kansas, toward Santa Fe. Reaching New Mexico, Kearny took the territory by a combination of bluff, bluster, and perhaps bribery, without firing a shot. The Mexican governor, following his own advice that "it is better to be thought brave than to be so," fled at Kearny's approach. After suppressing a brief rebellion by Mexicans and Indians, Kearny sent a detachment of his army south into Mexico. There, having marched fifteen hundred miles from Fort Leavenworth, these troops joined Taylor in time for the Battle of Buena Vista.

California also fell easily into American hands. In 1845, Polk had ordered the Pacific Squadron under Commodore John D. Sloat to occupy California's ports in the event of war with Mexico. To ensure victory, Polk also dispatched a courier overland with secret orders for one of the most colorful and important actors in the conquest of California, John C. Frémont. A Georgia-born adventurer, Frémont had married Jesse Benton, the daughter of powerful Senator Thomas Hart Benton of Missouri. Benton used his influence to have accounts of Frémont's explorations in the Northwest (mainly written by Jesse Benton Frémont) published as government documents. All of this earned glory for Frémont as "the Great Pathfinder." Finally overtaken by Polk's courier in Oregon, Frémont was dispatched to California to "watch over the interests of the United States." In June 1846, he rounded up a small force of American settlers, seized the village of Sonoma, and proclaimed the independent "Bear Flag Republic." The combined efforts of Frémont, Sloat, his successor David Stockton, and Stephen Kearny (who arrived in California after capturing New Mexico) quickly established American control over California.

The final and most important campaign of the war saw the conquest of Mexico City itself. In March 1847, Winfield Scott landed near Vera Cruz and quickly pounded that city into submission. Moving inland, Scott encountered Santa Anna at the seemingly impregnable pass of Cerro Gordo, but a young captain in Scott's

(Library of Congress)

Battle of Buena Vista *On February 23, 1847 an American army led by Major General Zachary Taylor defeated a larger Mexican force under Antonio López de Santa Anna. Lt. Col. Henry Clay, Jr., the son of Henry Clay, was killed in the battle. The battle was Taylor's last. He returned to the U.S. to pursue the political career that led him to the presidency.*

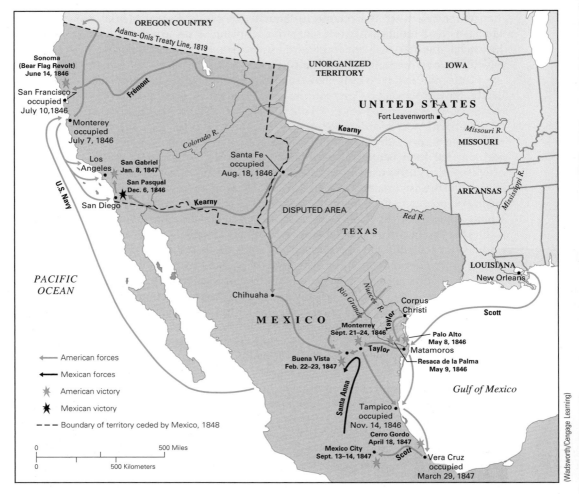

MAP 13.3 Major Battles of the Mexican-American War

The Mexican War's decisive campaign began with General Winfield Scott's capture of Vera Cruz and ended with his conquest of Mexico City.

command, Robert E. Lee, helped find a trail that led around the Mexican flank to a small peak overlooking the pass. There Scott planted howitzers and, on April 18, stormed the pass and routed the Mexicans. Scott now moved directly on Mexico City. Taking the key fortresses of Churubusco and Chapultepec (where another young captain, Ulysses S. Grant, was cited for bravery), Scott took the city on September 13, 1847 (see Map 13.3).

Although the Mexican army outnumbered the Americans in virtually every battle, they could not match the superior artillery or the logistics and organization of the "barbarians of the North." The Americans died like flies from yellow fever, and they carried into battle the agonies of venereal disease, which they picked up (and left) in many of the Mexican towns they took. But the Americans benefited from the unprecedented quality of their weapons, supplies, and organization.

By the **Treaty of Guadalupe Hidalgo** (February 2, 1848), Mexico ceded Texas with the Rio Grande boundary, New Mexico, and California to the United States. In return, the United States assumed the claims of American citizens against the Mexican government and paid Mexico $15 million. Although the United States gained the present states of California, Nevada, New Mexico, Utah, most of Arizona, and parts of Colorado and Wyoming, some rabid expansionists in the Senate denounced the treaty because it failed to include all of Mexico. But the acquisition of California ultimately satisfied Polk. Few senators, moreover, wanted to annex the mixed Spanish and Indian population of Mexico. A writer in the *Democratic Review* expressed the prevailing view that "the annexation of the country [Mexico] to the United States would be a calamity," for it would incorporate into the United States "ignorant and indolent half-civilized Indians," not to mention "free negroes and mulattoes" left over from the British slave trade. The virulent racism of American leaders allowed the Mexicans to retain part of their nation. On March 10, 1848, the Senate ratified the treaty by a vote of 38 to 10.

The War's Effects on Sectional Conflict

Despite wartime patriotic enthusiasm, sectional conflict sharpened between 1846 and 1848. Territorial expansion sparked the Polk administration's major battles. To Polk, it mattered little whether new territories were slave or free. Expansion would serve the nation's interests by dispersing population and retaining its agricultural and democratic character. Focusing attention on slavery in the territories struck him as "not only unwise but wicked." The Missouri Compromise, prohibiting slavery north of 36°30', impressed him as a simple and permanent solution to the problem of territorial slavery.

But many northerners were coming to see slavery in the territories as a profoundly disruptive issue that neither could nor should be solved simply by extending the 36°30' line westward. Amounting to a small minority, abolitionists, who opposed any extension of slavery on moral grounds, posed a minor threat to Polk. More important were northern Democrats who feared that expansion of slavery into California and New Mexico (parts of each lay south of 36°30') would deter free laborers from settling those territories. These Democrats argued that competition with slaves degraded free labor, that the westward extension of slavery would check the westward migration of free labor, and that such a barrier would aggravate the social problems already beginning to plague the East: class strife, social stratification, and labor protest.

The Wilmot Proviso

A young Democratic congressman from Pennsylvania, David Wilmot, became the spokesman for these disaffected northern Democrats. In August 1846, he introduced an amendment to an appropriations bill. This amendment, known as the **Wilmot Proviso**, stipulated that slavery be prohibited in any territory acquired by the war with Mexico. Neither an abolitionist nor a critic of Polk on tariff policy, Wilmot spoke for those loyal Democrats who had supported the annexation of Texas on the assumption that Texas would be the last slave state. Wilmot's intention was not to split his party along sectional lines but instead to hold Polk to what Wilmot and other northern Democrats took as an implicit understanding: Texas for the slaveholders, California and New Mexico for free labor.

With strong northern support, the proviso passed in the House but stalled in the Senate. Polk refused to endorse it, and most southern Democrats opposed any barrier to the expansion of slavery south of the Missouri Compromise line. They believed that the westward extension of slavery would reduce the concentration of slaves in the older regions of the South and thus lessen the chances of a slave revolt.

The proviso raised unsettling constitutional issues. Calhoun and fellow southerners contended that since slaves were property, the Constitution protected slaveholders' right to carry their slaves wherever they chose. This position led to the conclusion (drawn explicitly by Calhoun) that the Missouri Compromise of 1820, prohibiting slavery in the territories north of 36°30', was unconstitutional. On the other side were many northerners who cited the Northwest Ordinance of 1787, the Missouri Compromise, and the Constitution itself, which gave Congress the power to "make all needful rules and regulations respecting the territory or other property belonging to the United States," as justification for congressional legislation on slavery in the territories. With the election of 1848 approaching, politicians of both sides, eager to hold their parties together and avert civil war, frantically searched for a middle ground.

The Election of 1848   The Whigs watched in dismay as prosperity returned under Polk's program of an independent treasury and low tariffs. Never before had Clay's American System seemed so irrelevant. But the Wilmot Proviso gave the Whigs a political windfall; originating in the Democratic Party, it enabled the Whigs to portray themselves as the South's only dependable friends.

These considerations inclined the majority of Whigs toward Zachary Taylor. As a Louisiana slaveholder, he had obvious appeal to the South. As a political newcomer, he had no loyalty to the discredited American System. As a war hero, he had broad national appeal. Nominating Taylor as their presidential candidate in 1848, the Whigs presented him as an ideal man "without regard to creeds or principles" and ran him without any platform.

The Democrats faced a greater challenge because David Wilmot was one of their own. They could not ignore the issue of slavery in the territories, but if they embraced the positions of either Wilmot or Calhoun, the party would split along sectional lines. When Polk declined to run for reelection, the Democrats nominated Lewis Cass of Michigan, who solved their dilemma by announcing the doctrine of "squatter sovereignty," or popular sovereignty as it was later called. Cass argued that Congress should let the question of slavery in the territories be decided by the settlers. Squatter sovereignty appealed to many because of its arresting simplicity and vagueness. It neatly dodged the divisive issue of whether Congress had the power to prohibit territorial slavery. In fact, few Democrats wanted a definitive answer to this question. As long as the doctrine remained ambiguous, northern and southern Democrats alike could interpret it to their respective benefit.

In the campaign, both parties tried to ignore the issue of territorial slavery, but neither succeeded. A faction of the Democratic Party in New York that favored the Wilmot Proviso, called the Barnburners, broke away from the party, linked up with former Liberty party abolitionists, and courted antislavery "Conscience" Whigs to create the **Free-Soil party**. Declaring their dedication to "Free Trade, Free Labor, Free Speech, and Free Men," the Free-Soilers nominated Martin Van Buren on a platform opposing any extension of slavery.

"Union" Woodcut, by Thomas W. Strong, 1848 *This 1848 campaign poster for Zachary Taylor reminded Americans of his military victories, unmilitary bearing (note the civilian dress and straw hat), and deliberately vague promises. As president, Taylor finally took a stand on the issue of slavery in the Mexican cession, but his position angered the South.*

(Library of Congress)

Zachary Taylor benefited from Democratic disunity over the Wilmot Proviso and from his war-hero stature. He captured a majority of electoral votes in both North and South. Although failing to carry any state, the Free-Soil party ran well enough in the North to demonstrate the grass-roots popularity of opposition to slavery extension. Defections to the Free-Soilers, for example, probably cost the Whigs Ohio. By showing that opposition to the spread of slavery had far greater appeal than the staunch abolitionism of the old Liberty party, the Free-Soilers sent the Whigs and Democrats a message that they would be unable to ignore in future elections.

The California Gold Rush   When Wilmot announced his proviso, the issue of slavery in the Far West was more abstract than practical because Mexico had yet to cede any territory and relatively few Americans resided in either California or New Mexico. Nine days before the signing of the Treaty of Guadalupe Hidalgo, however, an American carpenter discovered gold in the foothills of California's Sierra Nevada range. The **California gold rush** began within a few months. A San Francisco newspaper complained that "the whole country from San Francisco to Los Angeles, and from the shore to the base of the Sierra Nevada, resounds with the sordid cry to *gold*, GOLD, GOLD! while the field is left half-planted, the house half-built, and everything neglected but the manufacture of shovels and pickaxes."

By December 1848, pamphlets with titles like *The Emigrant's Guide to the Gold Mines* had hit the streets of New York City. Arriving by sea and by land, gold-rushers drove up the population of California from around fifteen thousand in the summer of 1848 to nearly 250,000 by 1852. Miners came from every corner of the world. A female journalist reported walking through a mining camp in the Sierras and hearing English, Italian, French, Spanish, German, and Hawaiian. Conflicts over claims quickly led to violent clashes between Americans and Hispanics (mostly Mexicans, Chileans, and Peruvians). Americans especially resented the Chinese who flooded into California in the 1850s, most as contract laborers for wealthy Chinese merchants, and who struck Americans as slave laborers. Yet rampant prejudice against the Chinese did not stop some American businessmen from hiring them as contract workers for the American mining combinations that were forming in the 1850s.

Within a decade, the gold rush turned the sleepy Hispanic town of Yerba Buena, with 150 people in 1846, into "a pandemonium of a city" of 50,000 known as San Francisco. No other U.S. city contained people from more parts of the world. Many of the immigrants were Irish convicts who arrived by way of Australia, to which they had been exiled for their crimes. All the ethnic and racial tensions of the gold fields were evident in the city. A young clergyman confessed that he carried a harmless-looking cane, which "will be found to contain a sword two-and-a-half feet long." In 1851, San Francisco's merchants organized the first of several Committees of Vigilance, which patrolled the streets, deported undesirables, and tried and hanged alleged thieves and murderers.

With the gold rush, the issue of slavery in the Far West became practical as well as abstract, and immediate rather than remote. The newcomers attracted to California in 1849 included free blacks and slaves brought by planters from the South. White prospectors loathed the thought of competing with either of these groups and wanted to drive all blacks, along with California's Indians, out of the gold fields. Tensions also intensified between the gold-rushers and the *Californios*, whose extensive (if often vaguely worded) land holdings were protected by the terms of the Treaty of Guadalupe Hidalgo. Spawned by disputed claims and prejudice, violence mounted, and demands grew for a strong civilian government to replace the ineffective military government in place in California since the war. Polk began to fear that without a satisfactory congressional solution to the slavery issue, Californians might organize a government independent of the United States. The gold rush thus guaranteed that the question of slavery in the Mexican cession would be the first item on the agenda for Polk's successor and, indeed, for the nation.

CHRONOLOGY

1840–1848

1822	Stephen F. Austin founds the first American community in Texas.
1830	Mexico closes Texas to further American immigration.
1835	Santa Anna invades Texas.
1836	Texas declares its independence from Mexico. Fall of the Alamo. Goliad massacre. Battle of San Jacinto.
1840	William Henry Harrison elected president.
1841	Harrison dies; John Tyler becomes president.

1842	Webster-Ashburton Treaty.
1844	James K. Polk elected president.
1845	Congress votes joint resolution to annex Texas.
	Mexico rejects Slidell mission.
1846	The United States declares war on Mexico.
	John C. Frémont proclaims the Bear Flag Republic in California.
	Congress votes to accept a settlement of the Oregon boundary issue with Britain.
	Tariff of 1846.
	Wilmot Proviso introduced.
1847	Mexico City falls to Scott.
	Lewis Cass's principle of "squatter sovereignty."
1848	Gold discovered in California.
	Treaty of Guadalupe Hidalgo.
	Taylor elected president.

CONCLUSION

The massive immigration of the 1840s changed the face of American politics. Angered by Whig nativism and anti-Catholicism, the new German and Irish immigrants swelled the ranks of the Democratic Party. Meanwhile, the Whigs were unraveling. The untimely death of President Harrison brought John Tyler, a Democrat in Whig's clothing, to the White House. Tyler's vetoes of key Whig measures left the Whig party in disarray. In combination, these developments led to the surprise election of James K. Polk, a Democrat and ardent expansionist, in 1844.

Wrapped in the language of Manifest Destiny, westward expansion appealed to Americans for many reasons. It fit their belief that settlers had more right to the American continent than the Europeans (who based their claims on centuries-old explorations), the lethargic and Catholic Mexicans, and the nomadic Indians. Expansion promised trade routes to the Pacific, more land for farming, and, in the case of Texas, more slave states. Polk simultaneously rode the wave of national sentiment for Manifest Destiny and gave it direction by annexing Texas, provoking a crisis with Britain over Oregon, and leading the United States into a war with Mexico. Initially, Polk succeeded in uniting broad swaths of public opinion behind expansion. Polk and his followers ingeniously argued that national expansion was in the interests of northern working-class voters, many of them immigrants. By encouraging the spread of slavery to the Southwest, the argument went, the annexation of Texas would reduce the chances of a race war in the Southeast that might spill over into the North.

Yet even as war with Mexico was commencing, cracks in Polk's coalition were starting to show. The Wilmot Proviso exposed deep sectional divisions that had only been papered over by the ideal of Manifest Destiny and that would explode in the secession of Free-Soil Democrats in 1848. Victorious over Mexico and enriched by the discovery of gold in California, Americans counted the blessings of expansion but began to fear its costs.

14

FROM COMPROMISE TO SECESSION, 1850–1861

CHAPTER OUTLINE

• The Compromise of 1850 • The Collapse of the Second Party System, 1853–1856 • The Crisis of the Union, 1857–1860 • The Collapse of the Union, 1860–1861

THE COMPROMISE OF 1850

Ralph Waldo Emerson's grim prediction that an American victory in the Mexican-American War would be like swallowing arsenic proved disturbingly accurate. When the war ended in 1848, the United States contained an equal number of free and slave states (fifteen each), but the vast territory acquired by the war threatened to upset this balance. Any solution to the question of slavery in the Mexican cession ensured controversy. The doctrine of **free soil,** which insisted that Congress prohibit slavery in the territories, horrified southerners. The idea of extending the Missouri Compromise line of 36°30′ to the Pacific angered free-soilers because it would allow slavery in New Mexico and southern California, while it angered southern proslavery extremists because it conceded that Congress could bar slavery in some territories. A third solution, **popular sovereignty,** which promised to ease the slavery extension issue out of national politics by allowing each territory to decide the question for itself, pleased neither free-soilers nor proslavery extremists.

As the rhetoric escalated, events plunged the nation into crisis. Utah and then California, both acquired from Mexico, sought admission to the Union as free states. Texas, admitted as a slave state in 1845, aggravated matters by claiming the eastern half of New Mexico, where the Mexican government had abolished slavery.

By 1850, these territorial issues had become intertwined with two other concerns. Northerners increasingly attacked slavery in the District of Columbia, within the shadow of the Capitol; southerners complained about lax enforcement of the Fugitive Slave Act of 1793. Any broad compromise would have to take both troublesome matters into account.

Zachary Taylor's Strategy

President Zachary Taylor believed that the South must not kindle the issue of slavery in the territories because neither New Mexico nor California was suited to slavery. In 1849, Taylor asserted that "the people of the North need have no apprehension of the further extension of slavery."

Taylor's position differed significantly from the thinking behind the still controversial Wilmot Proviso, which insisted that Congress bar slavery from territories ceded by Mexico. Taylor's plan, in contrast, left the decision to new states. He prompted California to apply for admission as a free state, bypassing the territorial stage, and he strongly hinted that New Mexico do the same. Taylor's strategy appeared to guarantee a quick, practical solution to the problem of slavery extension. It would give the North two new free states. At the same time, it would acknowledge a position upon which all southerners agreed: a state could bar or permit slavery as it chose.

But southerners rejected Taylor's plan. It would effectively ban slavery in the Mexican cession, and it rested on the shaky assumption that slavery could never take root in California or New Mexico. Both areas already contained slaves, who could be employed profitably in mining gold and silver. "California is by nature," a southerner proclaimed, "peculiarly a slaveholding State." Calhoun trembled at the thought of adding more free states. "If this scheme excluding slavery from California and New Mexico should be carried out—if we are to be reduced to a mere handful ... wo, wo, I say to this Union." Disillusioned with Taylor, nine southern states agreed to send delegations to a southern convention that was scheduled to meet in Nashville in June 1850.

Henry Clay Proposes a Compromise

Taylor might have been able to contain mounting southern opposition if he had held a secure position in the Whig party. But such leading Whigs as Daniel Webster of Massachusetts and Henry Clay of Kentucky, each of whom had presidential aspirations, never reconciled themselves to Taylor, a political novice. Early in 1850, Clay boldly challenged Taylor's leadership by forging a set of compromise proposals to resolve the range of contentious issues. Clay proposed (1) the admission of California as a free state; (2) the division of the remainder of the Mexican cession into two territories, New Mexico and Utah (formerly Deseret), without federal restrictions on slavery; (3) the settlement of the Texas-New Mexico boundary dispute on terms favorable to New Mexico; (4) as an incentive for Texas, an agreement that the federal government would assume the considerable public debt of Texas; (5) the continuance of slavery in the District of Columbia but the abolition of the slave trade there; and (6) a more effective fugitive slave law.

Clay rolled all of these proposals into a single "omnibus" bill, which he hoped to steer through Congress. The debates over the omnibus during the late winter and early spring of 1850 witnessed the last major appearances on the public stage of Clay, Webster, and Calhoun—the trio of distinguished senators whose lives had mirrored every public event of note since the War of 1812. Clay played the role of the conciliator, as he had during the controversy over Missouri in 1820 and again during the nullification crisis in the early 1830s. Warning the South against secession, he assured the North that nature would check the spread of slavery more effectively than a thousand Wilmot Provisos. Gaunt and gloomy, a dying Calhoun listened as another senator read his address for him, a repetition of what he had been saying for years: the North's growing power, enhanced by protective tariffs and by the Missouri Compromise's exclusion of slaveholders from the northern part of the Louisiana Purchase, had created an imbalance between the sections. Only a decision by the North to treat the South as an equal could now save the Union. Three days later, Daniel Webster, who believed that slavery, "like the cotton-plant, is confined to certain parallels of climate," delivered his memorable "Seventh of March" speech. Speaking not "as a Massachusetts man, nor as a Northern man, but as an American," Webster chided the North for trying to "reenact the will of God" by legally excluding slavery from the Mexican cession and declared himself a forthright proponent of compromise.

However eloquent, the conciliatory voices of Clay and Webster made few converts. Strident voices countered these attempts at conciliation. The antislavery New York Whig William Seward, for example, enraged southerners by talking of a **"higher law"** than the Constitution—namely, the will of God against the extension of slavery. Clay's compromise faltered as Clay broke with President Taylor, who attacked Clay as a glory-hunter.

As the Union faced its worst crisis since 1789, a series of events in the summer of 1850 eased the way toward a resolution. When the Nashville convention assembled in June, the nine of fifteen slave states that sent delegates were primarily in the Lower South. Despite the reckless pronouncements of the "fire-eaters" (extreme advocates of "southern rights"), moderates dominated. Then Zachary Taylor, after eating and drinking too much at an Independence Day celebration, fell ill with gastroenteritis and died on July 9. His successor, Vice President Millard Fillmore of New York, supported Clay's compromise. Finally, Illinois Democrat **Stephen A. Douglas** took over the floor leadership from the exhausted Clay. Recognizing that Clay's "omnibus" lacked majority support in Congress, Douglas chopped it into a series of separate measures and sought to secure passage of each bill individually. To secure support from Democrats, he included the principle of popular sovereignty in the bills organizing New Mexico and Utah. By summer's end, Congress had passed each component of the Compromise of 1850: statehood for California; territorial status for Utah and New Mexico, allowing popular sovereignty; resolution of the Texas–New Mexico boundary disagreement; federal assumption of the Texas debt; abolition of the slave trade in the District of Columbia; and a new fugitive slave law (see Map 14.1).

Assessing the Compromise   President Fillmore hailed the compromise as a "final settlement" of sectional divisions, and Clay's reputation for conciliation reached new heights. Yet the compromise did not bridge the underlying differences between the two sections. Far from leaping forward to save the Union, Congress had backed into the Compromise of 1850; the majority of congressmen in one or another section opposed virtually all of the specific bills that made up the compromise. Most southerners, for example, voted against the admission of California and the abolition of the slave trade in the District of Columbia; the majority of northerners opposed the Fugitive Slave Act and the organization of New Mexico and Utah without a forthright congressional prohibition of slavery. These measures passed only because the minority of congressmen who genuinely desired compromise combined with the majority in either the North or the South who favored each specific bill.

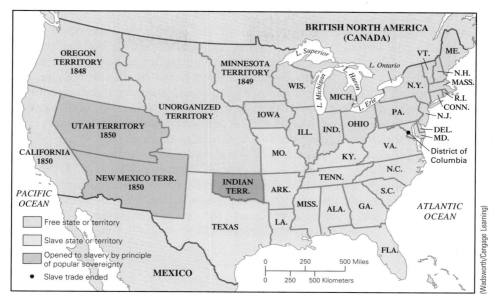

MAP 14.1 The Compromise of 1850

The Compromise of 1850 admitted California as a free state. Utah and New Mexico were left open to slavery or freedom on the principle of popular sovereignty.

Each section both gained and lost from the Compromise of 1850. The North won California as a free state, New Mexico and Utah as likely future free states, a favorable settlement of the Texas–New Mexico boundary (most of the disputed area was awarded to New Mexico, a probable free state), and the abolition of the slave trade in the District of Columbia. The South's benefits were cloudier. By stipulating popular sovereignty for New Mexico and Utah, the compromise, to most southerners' relief, had buried the Wilmot Proviso's insistence that Congress formally prohibit slavery in these territories. But to southerners' dismay, the compromise left open the question of whether Congress could prohibit slavery in territories outside of the Mexican cession.

The one clear advantage gained by the South, a more stringent fugitive slave law, quickly proved a mixed blessing. Because few slaves had been taken into the Mexican cession, the question of slavery there had a hypothetical quality. However, the new fugitive slave law authorized real southerners to pursue real fugitives on northern soil. Here was a concrete issue to which the average northerner, who may never have seen a slave and who cared little about slavery a thousand miles away, would respond with fury.

Enforcement of the Fugitive Slave Act

Northern moderates accepted the **Fugitive Slave Act** as the price of saving the Union. But the law contained features distasteful to moderates and outrageous to staunchly antislavery northerners. It denied alleged fugitives the right of trial by jury, did not allow them to testify in their own behalf, permitted their return to slavery merely on the testimony of the claimant, and enabled court-appointed commissioners to collect ten dollars if they ruled for the slaveholder but only five dollars if they ruled for the fugitive. In authorizing federal marshals to raise posses to pursue fugitives on northern soil, the law threatened to turn the North into "one vast hunting ground." In addition, the law targeted all runaways, putting at risk fugitives who had lived in the North for thirty years or more. Above all, the law brought home to northerners the uncomfortable truth that the continuation of slavery depended on their complicity. By legalizing the activities of slave-catchers on northern soil, the law reminded northerners that slavery was a national problem, not merely a peculiar southern institution.

Antislavery northerners assailed the law as the "vilest monument of infamy of the nineteenth century." "Let the President ... drench our land of freedom in blood," proclaimed Ohio Whig congressman Joshua Giddings, "but he will never make us obey that law." His support for the law turned Senator Daniel Webster of Massachusetts into a villain in the eyes of the very people who for years had revered him as the "godlike Daniel." The abolitionist poet John Greenleaf Whittier wrote of his fallen idol,

> All else is gone; from those giant eyes
> The soul has fled:
> When faith is lost, when honor dies,
> The man is dead

Efforts to catch and return fugitive slaves inflamed feelings in both the North and the South. In 1854, a Boston mob, aroused by antislavery speeches, broke into a courthouse and killed a guard in an abortive effort to rescue the fugitive slave Anthony Burns. Determined to prove that the law could be enforced "even in Boston," President Franklin Pierce sent a detachment of federal troops to escort Burns to the harbor, where a ship carried him back to slavery. No witness would ever forget the scene. As five platoons of troops marched with Burns to the ship, some fifty thousand people lined the streets. As the procession passed, one Bostonian hung from his window a black coffin bearing the words "THE FUNERAL OF LIBERTY." Another draped an American flag upside down as a symbol that "my country is eternally disgraced by this day's proceedings." The Burns incident shattered the complacency of conservative supporters of the Compromise of 1850. "We went to bed one night old fashioned conservative Compromise Union Whigs," the textile manufacturer Amos A. Lawrence wrote, "and waked up stark mad Abolitionists." A Boston committee later successfully purchased Burns's freedom, but other fugitives had worse fates. Margaret Garner, about to be captured and sent back to Kentucky as a slave, slit her daughter's throat and tried to kill her other children rather than witness their return to slavery.

In response to the Fugitive Slave Act, "vigilance" committees spirited endangered blacks to Canada. Lawyers dragged out legal proceedings to raise slave-catchers' expenses, and nine northern states passed **personal-liberty laws.** By such techniques as forbidding the use of state jails to incarcerate alleged fugitives, these laws aimed to preclude state officials from enforcing the law.

The frequent cold stares, obstructive legal tactics, and occasional violence encountered by slaveholders who ventured north to capture runaway slaves helped demonstrate to southerners that opposition to slavery boiled just beneath the surface of northern opinion. In the eyes of most southerners, the South had gained little more

For decades, the second party system had kept the conflict over slavery in check by giving Americans other issues—banking, internal improvements, tariffs, and temperance—to argue about. By the 1850s, the debate over slavery extension was pushing such issues into the background and exposing raw divisions in each party. Of the two parties, the Whigs had the larger, more aggressive free-soil wing, and hence they were more vulnerable than the Democrats to disruption. When Stephen A. Douglas put forth a proposal in 1854 to organize the vast Nebraska territory without restrictions on slavery, he ignited a firestorm that consumed the Whig party.

The Kansas-Nebraska Act   Signed by President Pierce at the end of May 1854, the **Kansas-Nebraska Act** shattered the already weakened second party system and triggered renewed sectional strife. The origins of the act lay in the seemingly uncontroversial desire of farm families to establish homesteads west of Iowa and Missouri. Bills to organize this area to extinguish Indian land titles and to provide a basis of government also had the backing of railroad enthusiasts, who dreamed of a rail line linking the Midwest to the Pacific.

In January 1854, Senator Stephen A. Douglas of Illinois proposed a bill to organize Nebraska as a territory. An ardent expansionist, Douglas had formed his political ideology in the heady atmosphere of Manifest Destiny during the 1840s. Although he preferred a railroad from his hometown of Chicago to San Francisco, Douglas dwelled on the national benefits that would attend construction of a railroad from anywhere in the Midwest to the Pacific. Such a railroad would enhance the importance of the Midwest, which could then hold the balance of power between the older sections of the North and South, and guide the nation toward unity rather than disruption. In addition, westward expansion through Nebraska with the aid of a railroad struck Douglas as an issue, comparable to Manifest Destiny, around which the splintering factions of the Democratic Party would unite.

Two sources of potential conflict loomed. First, some southerners advocated a rival route for the Pacific railroad that would start at either New Orleans or Memphis. Second, Nebraska lay within the Louisiana Purchase and north of the Missouri Compromise line of 36°30′, a region closed to slavery. Under Douglas's bill, the South would lose the Pacific rail route *and* face the possibility of more free territory in the Union. To placate southerners and win their votes, Douglas made two concessions. He stated publicly that the Nebraska bill "superseded" the Missouri Compromise and rendered it "void." Next, he agreed to a division of Nebraska into two territories: Nebraska to the west of Iowa, and Kansas to the west of Missouri. Because Missouri was a slave state, most congressmen assumed that the division aimed to secure Kansas for slavery and Nebraska for free soil.

The modifications of Douglas's original bill set off a storm of protest. Congress quickly tabled the Pacific railroad (which, in the turn of events, would not be built until after the Civil War) and focused on the issue of slavery extension. Antislavery northerners assailed the bill as "an atrocious plot" to violate the "sacred pledge" of the Missouri Compromise and to turn Kansas into a "dreary region of despotism, inhabited by masters and slaves." Their rage electrified southerners, many of whom initially had reacted indifferently to the Nebraska bill. Some southerners had opposed an explicit repeal of the Missouri Compromise, from fear of stimulating sectional discord; others doubted that Kansas would attract many slaveholders. But the furious assault of antislavery northerners united the South behind the Kansas-Nebraska bill by turning the issue into one of sectional pride as much as slavery extension.

Despite the uproar, Douglas successfully guided the Kansas-Nebraska bill through the Senate, where it passed by a vote of 37 to 14. In the House of Representatives, where the bill passed by little more than a whisker, 113 to 100, the true dimensions of the conflict became apparent. Not a single northern Whig representative in the House voted for the bill, whereas the northern Democrats divided evenly, 44 to 44.

The Surge of Free Soil   Amid the clamor over his bill, Douglas ruefully observed that he could now travel to Chicago by the light of his own burning effigies. Neither a fool nor a political novice, he was the victim of a political bombshell—free soil—that exploded under his feet.

Support for free soil united northerners who agreed on little else. Some free-soilers opposed slavery on moral grounds and rejected racist legislation, but others were racists who opposed allowing any African-Americans, slave or free, into the West. An abolitionist traced the free-soil convictions of many westerners to a "perfect, if not supreme" hatred of blacks. Racist free-soilers in Iowa and Illinois secured laws prohibiting settlement by black people.

One opinion shared by free-soilers of all persuasions was that slavery impeded whites' progress. Because a slave worked for nothing, the argument ran, no free laborer could compete with a slave. A territory might contain only a handful of slaves or none at all, but as long as Congress refused to prohibit slavery in the territories, the institution would gain a foothold and free laborers would flee. Wherever slavery appeared, a free-soiler proclaimed, "labor loses its dignity; industry sickens; education finds no schools; religion finds no churches; and the whole land of slavery is impoverished." Free-soilers also blasted the idea that slavery had natural limits. One warned that "slavery is as certain to invade New Mexico and Utah as the sun is to rise"; others predicted that if slavery gained a toehold in Kansas, it would soon invade Minnesota.

To free-soilers, the Kansas-Nebraska Act, with its erasure of the Missouri Compromise, was the last straw, for it revealed, one wrote, "a continuous movement by slaveholders to spread slavery over the entire North." For a Whig congressman from Massachusetts who had voted for the Compromise of 1850 and opposed abolitionists, the Kansas-Nebraska Act, "that most wanton and wicked act, so obviously designed to promote the extension of slavery," was too much to bear. "I now advocate the freedom of Kansas under all circumstances, and the prohibition of slavery in all territories now free."

The Ebbing of Manifest Destiny   The uproar over the Kansas-Nebraska Act embarrassed the Pierce administration. It also doomed Manifest Destiny, the one issue that had held the Democrats together in the 1840s.

Franklin Pierce had come to office championing Manifest Destiny, but increasing sectional rivalries sidetracked his efforts. In 1853, his emissary James Gadsden negotiated the purchase from Mexico of a strip of land south of the Gila River (now southern Arizona and part of southern New Mexico), an acquisition favored by advocates of a southern railroad route to the Pacific. Fierce opposition to the

Gadsden Purchase revealed mounting free-soilers' suspicion of expansion, and the Senate approved the treaty only after slashing nine thousand square miles from the parcel. The sectional rivalries beginning to engulf the Nebraska bill clearly threatened any proposal to gain new territory.

Cuba provided even more vivid proof of the change in public attitudes about expansion. In 1854, a former Mississippi governor, John A. Quitman, planned a filibuster (an unofficial military expedition) to seize Cuba from Spain. Eager to acquire Cuba, Pierce may have encouraged Quitman, but Pierce forced Quitman to scuttle the expedition when faced with intense opposition from antislavery northerners who saw filibusters as just another manifestation of the **Slave Power**—the conspiracy of slaveholders and their northern dupes to grab more territory for slavery.

Pierce still hoped to purchase Cuba, but events quickly slipped out of his control. In October 1854, the American ambassadors to Great Britain, France, and Spain, two of them southerners, met in Belgium and issued the unofficial Ostend Manifesto, calling on the United States to acquire Cuba by any means, including force. Beset by the storm over the Kansas-Nebraska Act and the furor over Quitman's proposed filibuster, Pierce rejected the mandate.

Despite Pierce's disavowal of the Ostend Manifesto, the idea of expansion into the Caribbean continued to attract southerners, including the Tennessee-born adventurer William Walker. Slightly built and so unassuming that he usually spoke with his hands in his pockets, Walker seemed an unlikely soldier of fortune. Yet between 1853 and 1860, the year a firing squad in Honduras executed him, Walker led a succession of filibustering expeditions into Central America. Taking advantage of civil chaos in Nicaragua, he made himself the chief political force there, reinstituted slavery, and talked of making Nicaragua a U.S. colony.

For all the proclamations and intrigues that surrounded the movement for southern expansion, its strength and goals remained open to question. With few exceptions, the adventurers were shady characters whom southern politicians might admire but on whom they could never depend. Some southerners were against expansion, among them Louisiana sugar planters who opposed acquiring Cuba because Cuban sugar would compete with their product. But expansionists stirred enough commotion to worry antislavery northerners that the South was conspiring to establish a Caribbean slave empire. Like a card in a poker game, the threat of expansion southward was all the more menacing for not being played. As long as the debate on the extension of slavery focused on the continental United States, prospects for expansion were limited. However, adding Caribbean territory to the pot changed all calculations.

The Whigs Disintegrate, 1854–1855

While straining Democratic unity, the Kansas-Nebraska Act wrecked the Whig party. In the law's immediate aftermath, most northern Whigs hoped to blame the Democrats for the act and to entice free-soil Democrats to their side. In the state and congressional elections of 1854, the Democrats were decisively defeated. But the Whig party failed to benefit from the backlash against the Democrats. However furious at Douglas for initiating the act, free-soil Democrats could not forget that the southern Whigs had supported Douglas. In addition, the northern Whigs themselves were deeply divided between antislavery "Conscience" Whigs, led by

Senator William Seward of New York, and conservatives, led by former president Millard Fillmore. The conservatives believed that the Whig party had to adhere to the Compromise of 1850 to maintain itself as a national party.

Divisions within the Whig party repelled antislavery Democrats from affiliating with it and prompted many antislavery Whigs to look for an alternative party. By 1856, the new Republican Party would become the home for most of these northern refugees from the traditional parties; but in 1854 and 1855, when the Republican Party was only starting to organize, the American, or Know-Nothing, party emerged as the principal alternative.

The Rise and Fall of the Know-Nothings, 1853–1856

One of a number of nativist societies that mushroomed in opposition to the massive immigration of the 1840s, the **Know-Nothings** originated in the secret Order of the Star-Spangled Banner. The party's popular name, Know-Nothing, derived from the standard response of its members to inquiries about its activities: "I know nothing." The Know-Nothings' core purpose was to rid the United States of immigrant and Catholic political influence. To this end, they pressured the existing parties to nominate and appoint only native-born Protestants to office and advocated an extension of the naturalization period before immigrants could vote.

Throughout the 1840s, nativists usually voted Whig, but their allegiance to the Whigs started to buckle during Winfield Scott's campaign for the presidency in 1852. In an attempt to revitalize his party, which was badly split over slavery, Scott had courted the traditionally Democratic Catholic vote. But Scott's tactic backfired. Most Catholics voted for Franklin Pierce. Nativists, meanwhile, felt betrayed by their party, and after Scott's defeat, many gravitated toward the Know-Nothings. The Kansas-Nebraska Act cemented their allegiance to the Know-Nothings, who in the North opposed both the extension of slavery and Catholicism. An obsessive fear of conspiracies unified the Know-Nothings. They simultaneously denounced a papal conspiracy against the American republic and a Slave Power conspiracy spreading its tentacles throughout the United States. The Know-Nothings' surge was truly stunning. In 1854, they captured the governorship, all the congressional seats, and almost all the seats in the state legislature in Massachusetts.

After rising spectacularly between 1853 and 1855, the star of Know-Nothingism plummeted and gradually disappeared below the horizon after 1856. The Know-Nothings proved as vulnerable as the Whigs to sectional conflicts over slavery. Although primarily a force in the North, the Know-Nothings had a southern wing, comprised mainly of former Whigs who loathed both the antislavery northerners who were abandoning the Whig party and the southern Democrats, whom they viewed as disunionist firebrands. In 1855, these southern Know-Nothings combined with northern conservatives to make acceptance of the Kansas-Nebraska Act part of the Know-Nothing platform, and thus they blurred the attraction of Know-Nothingism to those northern voters who were more antislavery than anti-Catholic.

One such Whig refugee, Illinois congressman Abraham Lincoln, asked pointedly: "How can anyone who abhors the oppression of negroes be in favor of degrading classes of white people?" "We began by declaring," Lincoln continued, "that 'all men are created equal.' We now practically read it 'all men are created equal except negroes.' When the Know-Nothings get control, it will read 'all men are created equal, except Negroes and foreigners and Catholics.'" Finally, even most Know-Nothings eventually came to conclude that, as one observer put it, "neither the Pope nor the foreigners ever can govern the country or endanger its liberties, but the slavebreeders and slavetraders do govern it, and threaten to put an end to all government but theirs." Consequently, the Know-Nothings proved vulnerable to the challenge posed by the emerging Republican Party, which did not officially embrace nativism and which had no southern wing to blunt its antislavery message.

The Republican Party and the Crisis in Kansas, 1855–1856

Born in the chaotic aftermath of the Kansas-Nebraska Act, the **Republican Party** sprang up in several northern states in 1854 and 1855. With the Know-Nothings' demise after 1856, the Republicans would become the main opposition to the Democratic Party. But few in 1855 would have predicted this. While united by opposition to the Kansas-Nebraska Act, the Republicans held various shades of opinion in uneasy balance. At one extreme were conservatives who merely wanted to restore the Missouri Compromise; at the other was a small faction of former Liberty Party abolitionists; and the middle held a sizable body of free-soilers.

Faced with these diverse constituencies, Republican leaders became political jugglers. To maintain internal harmony, the party's leaders avoided potentially divisive national issues such as the tariff and banking. Even so, Republican leaders recognized that they and the Know-Nothings were competing for many of the same voters. Believing that addiction to alcohol and submission to the pope were forms of enslavement, these voters often were protemperance, anti-Catholic, *and* antislavery.

The Republicans had clearer antislavery credentials than the Know-Nothings, but this fact alone did not guarantee that voters would respond more to antislavery than to anti-Catholicism or temperance. The Republicans needed a development that would make voters worry more about the Slave Power than about rum or Catholicism. Violence in Kansas, which quickly became known as Bleeding Kansas, united the party around its free-soil center, intensified antislavery feelings, and boosted Republican fortunes.

In the wake of the Kansas-Nebraska Act, Boston-based abolitionists had organized the New England Emigrant Aid Company to send antislavery settlers into Kansas. The abolitionists' aim was to stifle efforts to turn Kansas into a slave state. But antislavery New Englanders arrived slowly in Kansas; the bulk of the territory's early settlers came from Missouri or elsewhere in the Midwest. Very few of these early settlers opposed slavery on moral grounds. Some, in fact, favored slavery; others wanted to keep all blacks, whether slave or free, out of Kansas.

Despite most settlers' racist leanings and utter hatred of abolitionists, Kansas became a battleground between proslavery and antislavery forces. In March 1855, thousands of proslavery Missourian "border ruffians," led by Senator David R. Atchison, crossed into Kansas to vote illegally in the first election for a territorial legislature. Drawing and cocking their revolvers, they quickly silenced any judges who questioned their right to vote in Kansas. These proslavery advocates probably would have won an honest election because they would have been supported by the votes both of slaveholders and of nonslaveholders horrified at rumors that abolitionists planned to use Kansas as a colony for fugitive slaves. But by stealing the election, the proslavery forces committed a grave tactical blunder. A cloud of fraudulence thereafter hung over the proslavery legislature subsequently established at Lecompton, Kansas. "There is not a proslavery man of my acquaintance in Kansas," wrote the wife of an antislavery farmer, "who does not acknowledge that the Bogus Legislature was the result of a gigantic and well planned fraud, that the elections were carried by an invading mob from Missouri." This legislature then further darkened its image by passing a succession of outrageous laws, limiting officeholding to individuals who would swear allegiance to slavery, punishing the harboring of fugitive slaves by ten years' imprisonment, and making the circulation of abolitionist literature a capital offense.

The territorial legislature's actions set off a chain reaction. Free-staters, including many settlers enraged by the proceedings at Lecompton, organized a rival government at Topeka in the summer and fall of 1855. In response, the Lecompton government in May 1856 dispatched a posse to Lawrence, where free-staters, heeding the advice of antislavery minister Henry Ward Beecher that rifles would do more than Bibles to enforce morality in Kansas, had taken up arms and dubbed their guns "Beecher's Bibles." Bearing banners emblazoned "southern rights" and "let yankees tremble and abolitionists fall," the proslavery posse tore through Lawrence, burning several buildings and destroying two free-state presses. There were no deaths, but Republicans immediately dubbed the incident "the sack of Lawrence."

The next move was made by John Brown. The sack of Lawrence convinced Brown that God now beckoned him "to break the jaws of the wicked." In late May, Brown led seven men, including his four sons and his son-in-law, toward the Pottawatomie Creek near Lawrence. Setting upon five men associated with the Lecompton government, they shot one to death and hacked the others to pieces with broadswords. Brown's "Pottawatomie massacre" struck terror into the hearts of southerners and completed the transformation of Bleeding Kansas into a battleground between the South and the North.

Popular sovereignty had failed in Kansas. Instead of resolving the issue of slavery extension, popular sovereignty merely institutionalized the division over slavery by creating rival governments in Lecompton and Topeka. The Pierce administration then shot itself in the foot by denouncing the Topeka government and recognizing only its Lecompton rival. Pierce had forced northern Democrats into the awkward position of appearing to ally with the South in support of the "Bogus Legislature" at Lecompton.

Nor did popular sovereignty keep the slavery issue out of national politics. On the day before the sack of Lawrence, Republican senator **Charles Sumner** of Massachusetts delivered a bombastic and wrathful speech, "The Crime Against Kansas," in which he verbally whipped most of the U.S. Senate for complicity in slavery. Sumner singled out Senator Andrew Butler of South Carolina for making "the harlot, slavery" his mistress and for the "loose expectoration" of his speech (a nasty reference to the aging Butler's tendency to drool). Two days later, a relative of Butler, Democratic representative Preston Brooks of South Carolina, strode into the Senate chamber, found Sumner at his desk, and struck him repeatedly with a cane. The hollow cane broke after five or six blows, but Sumner required stitches, experienced shock, and did not return to the Senate for three years. Brooks became an instant hero in the South, and

(Kansas State Historical Society)

Admit Me Free Flag *In 1856 this flag was used at a rally at Pittsburgh, Pennsylvania, for Republican presidential nominee John C. Frémont. The oversized 34th star and the words "Admit Me Free" in the upper left part of the flag are in support of Kansas's admittance as a free state.*

the fragments of his weapon were "begged as sacred relics." A new cane, presented to Brooks by the city of Charleston, bore the inscription "Hit him again."

Now Bleeding Kansas and Bleeding Sumner united the North. The sack of Lawrence, Pierce's recognition of the proslavery Lecompton government, and Brooks's actions seemed to clinch the Republican argument that an aggressive "slaveocracy" held white northerners in contempt. Abolitionists remained unpopular in northern opinion, but southerners were becoming even less popular. Northern migrants to Kansas coined a name reflecting their feelings about southerners: "the pukes." By denouncing the Slave Power more than slavery itself, Republican propagandists sidestepped the issue of slavery's morality, which divided their followers, and focused on portraying southern planters as arrogant aristocrats and the natural enemies of the laboring people of the North.

The Election of 1856

The election of 1856 revealed the scope of the political realignments of the preceding few years. In this, its first presidential contest, the Republican Party nominated John C. Frémont, the famed "pathfinder" who had played a key role in the conquest of California during the Mexican War. The Republicans then maneuvered the northern Know-Nothings into endorsing Frémont. The southern Know-Nothings picked the last Whig president, Millard Fillmore, as their candidate, and the Democrats dumped the battered Pierce for James Buchanan of Pennsylvania. A four-term congressman and long an aspirant to the presidency, Buchanan finally secured his party's nomination because he had the good luck to be out of the country (as minister to Great Britain) during the furor over the Kansas-Nebraska

Act. As a signer of the Ostend Manifesto, he was popular in the South: virtually all of his close friends in Washington were southerners.

The campaign quickly turned into two separate races—Frémont versus Buchanan in the free states and Fillmore versus Buchanan in the slave states. In the North, the candidates divided clearly over slavery extension; Frémont's platform called for congressional prohibition of slavery in the territories, whereas Buchanan pledged congressional "noninterference." In the South, Fillmore appealed to traditionally Whig voters and called for moderation in the face of secessionist threats. But by nominating a well-known moderate in Buchanan, the Democrats undercut some of Fillmore's appeal. Although Fillmore garnered more than 40 percent of the popular vote in ten of the slave states, he carried only Maryland. In the North, Frémont outpolled Buchanan in the popular vote and won eleven of the sixteen free states; if Frémont had carried Pennsylvania and either Illinois, Indiana, or New Jersey, he would have won the election. As it turned out, Buchanan, the only truly national candidate in the race, secured the presidency.

The election yielded three clear conclusions. First, the American party was finished as a major national force. Having worked for the Republican Frémont, most northern Know-Nothings now joined that party, and southern Know-Nothings gave up on their party and sought new political affiliations. Second, although in existence scarcely more than a year, lacking any base in the South, and running a political novice, the Republican Party did very well. A purely sectional party had come within reach of capturing the presidency. Finally, as long as the Democrats could unite behind a single national candidate, they would be hard to defeat. To achieve such unity, however, the Democrats would have to find more James Buchanans—"doughface" moderates who would be acceptable to southerners and who would not drive even more northerners into Republican arms.

THE CRISIS OF THE UNION, 1857–1860

No one ever accused James Buchanan of impulsiveness or fanaticism. Although a moderate eager to avoid controversy, he presided over one of the most controversy-ridden administrations in American history. Trouble arose first over the famed *Dred Scott* decision of the Supreme Court, then over the proslavery Lecompton constitution in Kansas, next following the raid by John Brown on Harpers Ferry, and finally concerning secession itself.

The forces driving the nation apart were already spinning out of control by 1856. By the time of Buchanan's inauguration, southerners who looked north saw creeping abolitionism in the guise of free soil, whereas northerners who looked south saw an insatiable Slave Power. Once these images had taken hold in the minds of the American people, politicians like James Buchanan had little room to maneuver.

The Dred Scott Case, 1857   Pledged to congressional "non-interference" with slavery in the territories, Buchanan had long looked to the courts for a nonpartisan resolution of the vexing issue of slavery extension. A case that appeared to promise such a solution had been wending its way through the courts for years; and on March 6, 1857, two days after Buchanan's inauguration, the Supreme Court handed down its decision in **Dred Scott v. Sandford.**

During the 1830s, Dred Scott, a slave, had been taken by his master from the slave state of Missouri into Illinois and the Wisconsin Territory, areas respectively closed to slavery by the Northwest Ordinance of 1787 and the Missouri Compromise. After his master's death, Scott sued for his freedom on the grounds of his residence in free territory. In 1856, the case finally reached the Supreme Court.

The Court faced two key questions. Did Scott's residence in free territory during the 1830s make him free? Regardless of the answer to this question, did Scott, again enslaved in Missouri, have a right to sue in the federal courts? The Court could have resolved the case on narrow grounds by answering the second question in the negative, but Buchanan wanted a far-reaching decision that would deal with the broad issue of slavery in the territories.

In the end, Buchanan got the broad ruling that he sought, but one so controversial that it settled little. In the most important of six separate majority opinions, Chief Justice Roger B. Taney, a seventy-nine-year-old Marylander whom Andrew Jackson had appointed to succeed John Marshall in 1835, began with the narrow conclusion that Scott, a slave, could not sue for his freedom. Then the thunder started. No black, whether a slave or a free person descended from a slave, could become a citizen of the United States, Taney continued. Next Taney whipped the thunderheads into a tornado. Even if Scott had been a legal plaintiff, Taney ruled, his residence in free territory years earlier did not make him free, because the Missouri Compromise, whose provisions prohibited slavery in the Wisconsin Territory, was itself unconstitutional. The compromise, declared Taney, violated the Fifth Amendment's protection of property (including slaves).

Contrary to Buchanan's hopes, the decision touched off a new blast of controversy over slavery in the territories. The antislavery press flayed it as a "willful perversion" filled with "gross historical falsehoods." Taney's ruling gave Republicans more evidence that a fiendish Slave Power conspiracy gripped the nation. Although the Kansas-Nebraska Act had effectively repealed the Missouri Compromise, the Court's majority now rejected even the principle behind the compromise, the idea that Congress could prohibit slavery in the territories. Five of the six justices who rejected this principle were from slave states. The Slave Power, a northern paper bellowed, "has marched over and annihilated the boundaries of the states. We are now one great homogenous slaveholding community."

Like Stephen Douglas after the Kansas-Nebraska Act, President Buchanan now appeared to be a northern dupe of the "slaveocracy." Republicans restrained themselves from open defiance of the decision only by insisting that it did not bind the nation; Taney's comments on the constitutionality of the Missouri Compromise, they contended, amounted merely to *obiter dicta*, opinions superfluous to settling the case.

Reactions to the decision underscored the fact that by 1857 no "judicious" or nonpartisan solution to slavery extension was possible. Anyone who still doubted this needed only to read the fast-breaking news from Kansas.

The Lecompton Constitution, 1857

In Kansas, the free-state government at Topeka and the officially recognized proslavery government at Lecompton viewed each other with profound distrust. Buchanan's plan for Kansas looked simple: an elected territorial convention would draw up a constitution that would either permit or prohibit slavery; Buchanan would submit the constitution to Congress; Congress would then admit Kansas as a state.

Unfortunately, the plan exploded in Buchanan's face. Popular sovereignty, the essence of Buchanan's plan, demanded fair play, a scarce commodity in Kansas. The territory's history of fraudulent elections left both sides reluctant to commit their fortunes to the polls. An election for a constitutional convention took place in June 1857, but free-staters, by now a majority in Kansas, boycotted the election on the grounds that the proslavery side would rig it. Dominated by proslavery delegates, a constitutional convention then met and drew up a frame of government, the **Lecompton constitution,** that protected the rights of those slaveholders already living in Kansas to their slave property and provided for a referendum in which voters could decide whether to allow in more slaves.

The Lecompton constitution created a dilemma for Buchanan. A supporter of popular sovereignty, he had gone on record in favor of letting the voters in Kansas decide the slavery issue. Now he was confronted by a constitution drawn up by a convention that had been elected by less than 10 percent of the eligible voters, by plans for a referendum that would not allow voters to remove slaves already in Kansas, and by the prospect that the proslavery side would conduct the referendum no more honestly than it had other ballots. Yet Buchanan had compelling reasons to accept the Lecompton constitution as the basis for the admission of Kansas as a state. The South, which had provided him with 112 of his 174 electoral votes in 1856, supported the constitution. Buchanan knew, moreover, that only about two hundred slaves resided in Kansas, and he believed that the prospects for slavery in the remaining territories were slight. The contention over slavery in Kansas struck him as another example of how extremists could turn minor issues into major ones. To accept the constitution and speed the admission of Kansas as either a free state or a slave state seemed the best way to pull the rug from beneath the extremists and quiet the ruckus in Kansas. Accordingly, in December 1857, Buchanan endorsed the Lecompton constitution.

Stephen A. Douglas and other northern Democrats broke with Buchanan. To them, the Lecompton constitution, in allowing voters to decide only whether more slaves could enter Kansas, violated the spirit of popular sovereignty. "I care not whether [slavery] is voted down or voted up," Douglas declared. But to refuse to allow a vote on the constitution itself, with its protection of existing slave property, smacked of a "system of trickery and jugglery to defeat the fair expression of the will of the people."

Even as Douglas broke with Buchanan, events in Kansas took a new turn. A few months after electing delegates to the convention that drew up the Lecompton constitution, Kansans had gone to the polls to elect a territorial legislature. So flagrant was the fraud in this election—one village with thirty eligible voters returned more than sixteen hundred proslavery votes—that the governor disallowed enough proslavery returns to give free-staters a majority in the legislature. This territorial legislature then called for a referendum on the Lecompton constitution and thus slavery itself. Whereas the Kansas constitutional convention had restricted the choice of voters to the narrow issue of the future introduction of slaves, the territorial legislature sought a referendum that would allow Kansans to vote against the protection of existing slave property as well.

In December 1857, the referendum called earlier by the constitutional convention was held. Boycotted by free-staters, the constitution with slavery passed overwhelmingly. Two weeks later, in the election called by the territorial legislature, the proslavery side abstained, and the constitution went down to crushing defeat. Buchanan tried to ignore this second election, but when he attempted to bring Kansas into the Union under the Lecompton constitution, Congress blocked him and forced yet another referendum. This time, Kansans were given the choice between accepting or rejecting the entire constitution, with the proviso that rejection would delay statehood. Despite the proviso, Kansans overwhelmingly voted down the constitution.

Buchanan simultaneously had failed to tranquilize Kansas and alienated northerners in his own party. His support for the Lecompton constitution confirmed the suspicion of northern Democrats that the southern Slave Power pulled all the important strings in their party. Douglas became the hero of the hour for northern Democrats. "The bone and sinew of the Northern Democracy are with you," a New Yorker wrote to Douglas. Yet Douglas himself could take little comfort from the Lecompton fiasco, as his cherished formula of popular sovereignty increasingly looked like a prescription for civil strife rather than harmony.

The Lincoln-Douglas Debates, 1858   Despite the acclaim he gained in the North for his stand against the Lecompton constitution, Douglas faced a stiff challenge in Illinois for reelection to the United States Senate. Of his Republican opponent, Abraham Lincoln, Douglas said: "I shall have my hands full. He is the strong man of his party—full of wit, facts, dates—and the best stump speaker with his droll ways and dry jokes, in the West."

Physically as well as ideologically, the two men formed a striking contrast. Tall (6′4″) and gangling, **Abraham Lincoln** once described himself as "a piece of floating driftwood." Energy, ambition, and a passion for self-education had carried him from the Kentucky log cabin in which he was born in 1809 through a youth filled with various occupations (farm laborer, surveyor, rail-splitter, flatboatman, and storekeeper) into law and politics in his adopted Illinois. There he had capitalized on westerners' support for internal improvements to gain election to Congress in 1846 as a Whig. Having opposed the Mexican-American War and the Kansas-Nebraska Act, he joined the Republican Party in 1856.

Douglas was fully a foot shorter than the towering Lincoln. But his compact frame contained astonishing energy. Born in New England, Douglas appealed primarily to the small farmers of southern origin who populated the Illinois flatlands. To these and others, he was the "little giant," the personification of the Democratic Party in the West. The campaign quickly became more than just another Senate race, for it pitted the Republican Party's rising star against the Senate's leading Democrat and, thanks to the railroad and the telegraph, received unprecedented national attention.

Although some Republicans extolled Douglas's stand against the Lecompton constitution, to Lincoln nothing had changed. Douglas was still Douglas, the author of the infamous Kansas-Nebraska Act and a man who cared not whether slavery was voted up or down as long as the vote was honest. Opening his campaign with the "House Divided" speech ("this nation cannot exist permanently half slave and half free"), Lincoln reminded his Republican followers of the gulf that still separated his doctrine of free soil from Douglas's popular sovereignty. Douglas dismissed the house-divided doctrine as an invitation to secession. What mattered to him was not slavery, which he viewed as merely an extreme way to subordinate a supposedly inferior race, but the continued expansion of white settlement. Like Lincoln, he wanted to keep slavery out of the path of white settlement. But unlike his rival, Douglas believed popular sovereignty was the surest way to attain this goal without disrupting the Union.

The high point of the campaign came in a series of seven debates held from August to October 1858. The Lincoln-Douglas debates mixed political drama with the atmosphere of a festival. At the debate in Galesburg, for example, dozens of horse-drawn floats descended on the town from nearby farming communities. One bore thirty-two girls dressed in white, one for each state, and a thirty-third who dressed in black with the label "Kansas" and carried a banner proclaiming "they won't let me in."

Douglas used the debates to portray Lincoln as a virtual abolitionist and advocate of racial equality. Both charges were calculated to doom Lincoln in the eyes of the intensely racist Illinois voters. In response, Lincoln affirmed that Congress had no constitutional authority to abolish slavery in the South, and in one debate he asserted bluntly that "I am not, nor ever have been in favor of bringing about the social and political equality of the white, and black man." However, fending off charges of extremism was getting Lincoln nowhere; so in order to seize the initiative, he tried to maneuver Douglas into a corner.

In view of the *Dred Scott* decision, Lincoln asked in the debate at Freeport, could the people of a territory lawfully exclude slavery? In essence, Lincoln was asking Douglas to reconcile popular sovereignty with the *Dred Scott* decision. Lincoln had long contended that the Court's decision rendered popular sovereignty

Stephen A. Douglas
Douglas's politics were founded on his unflinching conviction that most Americans favored national expansion and would support popular sovereignty as the fastest and least controversial way to achieve it. Douglas's self-assurance blinded him to rising northern sentiment for free soil.

(National Portrait Gallery, Smithsonian Institution, Washington, D.C./Art Resource, NY)

Abraham Lincoln
Clean-shaven at the time of his famous debates with Douglas, Lincoln would soon grow a beard to give himself a more distinguished appearance.

(Library of Congress)

as thin as soup boiled from the shadow of a pigeon that had starved to death. If, as the Supreme Court's ruling affirmed, Congress had no authority to exclude slavery from a territory, then it seemingly followed that a territorial legislature created by Congress also lacked power to do so. To no one's surprise, Douglas replied that notwithstanding the *Dred Scott* decision, the voters of a territory could effectively exclude slavery simply by refusing to enact laws that gave legal protection to slave property.

Douglas's "Freeport doctrine" salvaged popular sovereignty but did nothing for his reputation among southerners, who preferred the guarantees of the *Dred Scott* ruling to the uncertainties of popular sovereignty. Whereas Douglas's stand against the Lecompton constitution had already tattered his reputation in the South ("he is already dead there," Lincoln affirmed), his Freeport doctrine stiffened southern opposition to his presidential ambitions.

Lincoln faced the problem throughout the debates that free soil and popular sovereignty, although distinguishable in theory, had much the same practical effect. Neither Lincoln nor Douglas doubted that popular sovereignty, if fairly applied, would keep slavery out of the territories. In the closing debates, to keep the initiative and sharpen their differences, Lincoln shifted toward attacks on slavery as "a moral, social, and political evil." He argued that Douglas's view of slavery as merely an eccentric and unsavory southern custom would dull the nation's conscience and facilitate the legalization of slavery everywhere. But Lincoln compromised his own position by rejecting both abolition and equality for blacks.

Neither man scored a clear victory in argument, and the senatorial election itself settled no major issues. Douglas's supporters captured a majority of the seats in the state legislature, which at the time was responsible for electing U.S. senators. But despite the racist leanings of most Illinois voters, Republican candidates for the state legislature won a slightly larger share of the popular vote than did their Democratic rivals. Moreover, in its larger significance, the contest solidified the sectional split in the national Democratic Party and made Lincoln famous in the North and infamous in the South.

The Legacy of Harpers Ferry

Although Lincoln rejected abolitionism, he called free soil a step toward the "ultimate extinction" of slavery. Similarly, New York Republican senator William H. Seward spoke of an "irrepressible conflict" between slavery and freedom. Predictably, many white southerners ignored the distinction between free soil and abolition, and concluded that Republicans and abolitionists were joined in an unholy alliance against slavery. To many in the South, the North seemed to be controlled by demented leaders bent on civil war. One southern defender of slavery equated the doctrines of the abolitionists with those of "Socialists, of Free Love and Free Lands, Free Churches, Free Women and Free Negroes-of No-Marriage, No-Religion, No-Private Property, No-Law and No-Government."

Nothing did more to freeze this southern image of the North than the evidence of northern complicity in John Brown's raid on the federal arsenal at Harpers Ferry, Virginia, on October 16, 1859. Brown and his followers were quickly overpowered; Brown himself was tried, convicted, and hanged. Lincoln and Seward condemned the raid. But some northerners turned Brown into a martyr; Ralph Waldo Emerson exulted that Brown's execution would "make the gallows as glorious as the cross." Further, captured correspondence disclosed that Brown had received financial support from northern abolitionists. His objective, to inspire an armed slave insurrection, rekindled the deepest fears of white southerners.

In the wake of Brown's raid, rumors flew around the South, and vigilantes turned out to battle conspiracies that existed only in their minds. Volunteers, for example, mobilized to defend northeastern Texas against thousands of abolitionists supposedly on their way to pillage Dallas and its environs. In other incidents, vigilantes rounded up thousands of slaves, tortured some into confessing to nonexistent plots, and then lynched them. The hysteria fed by such rumors played into the hands of the extremists known as fire-eaters, who encouraged the witch hunt by spreading tales of slave conspiracies in the press so that southern voters would turn to them as alone able to "stem the current of Abolition."

More and more southerners concluded that the Republican Party itself directed abolitionism and deserved blame for Brown's raid. After all, had not influential Republicans spoken of an "irrepressible conflict" between slavery and freedom? The Tennessee legislature reflected southern views when it passed resolutions declaring that the Harpers Ferry raid was "the natural fruit of this treasonable 'irrepressible conflict' doctrine put forth by the great head of the Black Republican party and echoed by his subordinates."

The South Contemplates Secession   A pamphlet published in 1860 embodied in its title the growing conviction of southerners that *The South Alone Should Govern the South*. Southerners reached this conclusion gradually and often reluctantly. In 1850, few southerners could have conceived of transferring their allegiance from the United States to some new nation. Relatively insulated from the main tide of immigration, southerners thought of themselves as the most American of Americans. But the events of the 1850s persuaded many southerners that the North had deserted the true principles of the Union. Southerners interpreted northern resistance to the Fugitive Slave Act and to slavery in Kansas as either illegal or unconstitutional, and they viewed headline-grabbing phrases such as "irrepressible conflict" and "a higher law" as virtual declarations of war on the South. To southerners, it was the North, not the South, that had grown peculiar.

Viewed as a practical tactic to secure concrete goals, secession did not make a great deal of sense. Some southerners contended that secession would make it easier for the South to acquire more territory for slavery in the Caribbean; yet the South was scarcely united in desiring additional slave territory in Mexico, Cuba, or Central America. States like Alabama, Mississippi, and Texas contained vast tracts of unsettled land that could be converted to cotton cultivation far more easily than the Caribbean. Other southerners continued to complain that the North blocked the access of slaveholders to territories in the continental United States. But if the South were to secede, the remaining continental territories would belong exclusively to the North, which could then legislate for them as it chose. Nor would secession stop future John Browns from infiltrating the South to provoke slave insurrections.

Yet to dwell on the impracticality of secession as a choice for the South is to miss the point. Talk of secession was less a tactic with clear goals than an expression of the South's outrage at what southerners viewed as the irresponsible and unconstitutional course that the Republicans were taking in the North. It was not merely that Republican attacks on slavery sowed the seeds of slave uprisings. More fundamentally, southerners believed that the North was treating the South as its inferior, as no more than a slave. "Talk of Negro slavery," exclaimed southern proslavery philosopher George Fitzhugh, "is not half so humiliating and disgraceful as the slavery of the South to the North." Having persuaded themselves that slavery made it possible for them to enjoy unprecedented freedom and equality, white southerners took great pride in their homeland. They bitterly dismissed Republican portrayals of the South as a region of arrogant planters and degraded white common folk. Submission to the Republicans, declared Democratic senator Jefferson Davis of Mississippi, "would be intolerable to a proud people."

THE COLLAPSE OF THE UNION, 1860–1861

As long as the pliant James Buchanan occupied the White House, southerners did no more than talk about secession. Once aware that Buchanan had declined to seek reelection, however, they approached the election of 1860 with anxiety. Although not all voters realized it, when they cast their ballots in 1860 they were deciding not just the outcome of an election but the fate of the Union. Lincoln's election initiated the process by which the southern states abandoned the United States for a new nation, the Confederate States of America. Initially, the Confederacy consisted only of states in the Lower South. As the Upper South hesitated to embrace secession, moderates searched frantically for a compromise that would save the Union. But they searched in vain. The time for compromise had passed.

The Election of 1860

As a single-issue, free-soil party, the Republicans had done well in the election of 1856. To win in 1860, however, they would have to broaden their appeal in the North, particularly in states like Pennsylvania and Illinois, which they had lost in 1856. To do so, Republican leaders had concluded, they needed to forge an economic program to complement their advocacy of free soil.

A severe economic slump following the so-called Panic of 1857 furnished the Republicans with a fitting opening. The depression shattered more than a decade of American prosperity and thrust economic concerns to the fore. In response, in the late 1850s the Republicans developed an economic program based on support for a protective tariff (popular in Pennsylvania) and on two issues favored in the Midwest, federal aid for internal improvements and the granting to settlers of free 160-acre homesteads out of publicly owned land. By proposing to make these homesteads available to immigrants who were not yet citizens, the Republicans went far in shedding the nativist image that lingered from their early association with the Know-Nothings. Carl Schurz, an 1848 German political refugee who had campaigned for Lincoln against Douglas in 1858, now labored mightily to bring his antislavery countrymen over to the Republican Party.

The Republicans' desire to broaden their appeal also influenced their choice of a candidate. At their convention in Chicago, they nominated Abraham Lincoln over the early front-runner, William H. Seward of New York. Although better known than Lincoln, Seward failed to convince his party that he could carry the key states of Pennsylvania, Illinois, Indiana, and New Jersey. Lincoln held the advantage not only of hailing from Illinois but also of projecting a more moderate image than Seward on the slavery issue. Seward's penchant for controversial phrases like "irrepressible conflict" and "higher law" had given him a radical image. Lincoln, in contrast, had repeatedly affirmed that Congress had no constitutional right to interfere with slavery in the South and had explicitly rejected the "higher law" doctrine. The Republicans now needed only to widen their northern appeal.

The Democrats, still claiming to be a national party, had to bridge their own sectional differences. The *Dred Scott* decision and the conflict over the Lecompton constitution had weakened the northern Democrats and strengthened southern Democrats. While Douglas still desperately defended popular sovereignty, southern Democrats stretched *Dred Scott* to conclude that Congress now had to protect slavery in the territories.

The Democrats' internal turmoil boiled over at their Charleston convention in 1860. Failing to force acceptance of a platform guaranteeing federal protection of slavery in the territories, the delegates from the Lower South stalked out. The convention adjourned to Baltimore, where a new fight broke out over the question of seating hastily elected pro-Douglas slates of delegates from the Lower South states that had seceded from the Charleston convention. The decision to seat these pro-Douglas slates led to a walkout by delegates from Virginia and other states in the Upper South. The remaining delegates nominated Douglas; the seceders marched off to another hall in Baltimore and nominated Buchanan's vice president, John C. Breckinridge of Kentucky, on a platform calling for the congressional protection of slavery in the territories. Unable to rally behind a single nominee, the divided Democrats thus ran two candidates, Douglas and Breckinridge. The disruption of the Democratic Party was now complete.

The South still contained an appreciable number of moderates, often former Whigs who had joined with the Know-Nothings behind Fillmore in 1856. In 1860, these moderates, aided by former northern Whigs who opposed both Lincoln and Douglas, forged the new Constitutional Union Party and nominated John Bell, a Tennessee slaveholder who had opposed both the Kansas-Nebraska Act and the Lecompton constitution. Calling for the preservation of the Union, the new party took no stand on the divisive issue of slavery extension.

With four candidates in the field, voters faced a relatively clear choice. Lincoln conceded that the South had a constitutional right to preserve slavery but demanded that Congress prohibit its extension. At the other extreme, Breckinridge insisted that Congress had to protect slavery in any territory that contained slaves. This left the middle ground to Bell and Douglas, the latter still committed to popular sovereignty but in search of a verbal formula that might reconcile it with the *Dred Scott* decision. Lincoln won a clear majority of the electoral vote, 180 to 123 for his three opponents combined. Although Lincoln gained only 39 percent of the popular vote, his popular votes were concentrated in the North, the majority section, and were sufficient to carry every free state. Douglas ran a respectable second to Lincoln in the popular vote but a dismal last in the electoral vote. As the only candidate to campaign in both sections, Douglas suffered from the scattered nature of his votes and carried only Missouri. Bell won Virginia, Kentucky, and Tennessee, and Breckinridge captured Maryland and the Lower South (see Map 14.2).

The Movement for Secession   Lincoln's election struck most of the white South as a calculated northern insult. The North, a South Carolina planter told a visitor from England, "has got so far toward being abolitionized as to elect a man avowedly hostile to our institutions."

Few southerners believed Lincoln would fulfill his promise to protect slavery in the South, and most feared he would act as a mere front man for more John

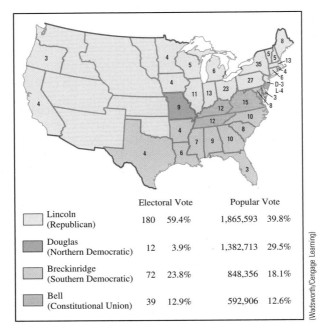

	Electoral Vote		Popular Vote	
Lincoln (Republican)	180	59.4%	1,865,593	39.8%
Douglas (Northern Democratic)	12	3.9%	1,382,713	29.5%
Breckinridge (Southern Democratic)	72	23.8%	848,356	18.1%
Bell (Constitutional Union)	39	12.9%	592,906	12.6%

(Wadsworth/Cengage Learning)

MAP 14.2 The Election of 1860

Having given the nation four of its first five presidents, the South confronted permanent minority status after the election of 1860. Despite receiving no votes in the South, Lincoln won the electoral vote easily. Even had the Democrats united behind a single candidate, Lincoln would have won the election.

Browns. "Now that the black radical Republicans have the power I suppose they will Brown us all," a South Carolinian lamented (see Going to the Source). An uneducated Mississippian residing in Illinois expressed his reaction to the election more bluntly:

> It seems the north wants the south to raise cotton and sugar rice tobacco for the northern states, also to pay taxes and fight her battles and get territory for the purpose of the north to send her greasy Dutch and free niggers into the territory to get rid of them. At any rate that was what elected old Abe President. Some professed conservative Republicans Think and say that Lincoln will be conservative also but sir my opinion is that Lincoln will deceive them. [He] will undoubtedly please the abolitionists for at his election they nearly all went into fits with Joy.

Some southerners had threatened secession at the prospect of Lincoln's election. Now the moment of decision had arrived. On December 20, 1860, a South Carolina convention voted unanimously for secession; in short order Alabama, Mississippi, Florida, Georgia, Louisiana, and Texas followed. On February 4, delegates from these seven states met in Montgomery, Alabama, and established the **Confederate States of America**.

Despite the abruptness of southern withdrawal from the Union, the movement for secession was laced with uncertainty. Many southerners had resisted calls for

Lincoln at Cooper Union

Abraham Lincoln's Cooper Union speech, delivered in New York City on February 27, 1860, elevated him into the national spotlight. On the basis of his own extensive research, he established that in later votes in Congress, a clear majority of the thirty-nine signers of the Constitution demonstrated their view that the federal government had the power to restrict slavery in the territories. So much for the South's insistence that it was the true heir to the Founding generation. Lincoln then continued as follows.

Will they [southerners] be satisfied if the Territories be unconditionally surrendered to them? We know they will not. In all their present complaints against us, the Territories are scarcely mentioned. Invasions and insurrections are the rage now [a reference to John Brown's raid]. Will it satisfy them if in the future we have nothing to do with invasions and insurrections? We know it will not. We so know because we know we never had anything to do with invasions and insurrections; and yet this total abstaining does not exempt us from the charge and the denunciation.

The question recurs, what will satisfy them? Simply this: we must not only let them alone, but we must somehow convince them that we do let them alone. This, we know by experience, is no easy task. We have been trying to convince them from the very beginning of our organization [the Republican party], but with no success. In all our platforms and speeches we have constantly protested our purpose to let them alone; but this has had no tendency to convince them....

These natural, and apparently adequate means all failing, what will convince them?

This, and this only: cease to call slavery *wrong* and join them in calling it *right*. And this must be done thoroughly—done in *acts* as well as *words*. Silence will not be tolerated ... We must arrest and return their fugitive slaves with greedy pleasure. We must pull down our free state constitutions. The whole atmosphere must be disinfected of all taint of opposition to slavery, before they will cease to believe that all their troubles proceed from us.

I am quite aware they do not state their case in precisely this way. Most of them would probably say to us, "Let us alone, do nothing to us, and say what you please about slavery." But we do let them alone —have never disturbed them—so that, after all, it is what we say, which dissatisfies them. They will continue to accuse us of doing, until we cease saying ... Holding, as they do, that slavery is morally right, and socially elevating, they cannot cease to demand a full national recognition of it, as a legal right, and a social blessing.

Source: Appears in LINCOLN AT COOPER UNION: The Speech that Made Abraham Lincoln President by Harold Holzer (New York: Simon & Schuster, 2004).

Questions

1. Lincoln's mainly Republican audience included some prominent Democrats. What image of the Republican party was he trying to counter?

2. Was Lincoln trying to conciliate the South, or unify the North? Explain your answer.

Go to www.cengagebrain.com for additional primary sources on this period.

immediate secession. Even after Lincoln's election, fire-eating secessionists had met fierce opposition in the Lower South from so-called cooperationists, who called upon the South to act in unison or not at all. Many cooperationists had hoped to delay secession to wring concessions from the North that might remove the need for secession. Jefferson Davis, inaugurated in February 1861 as president of the Confederacy, was a reluctant secessionist who remained in the United States Senate two weeks after his own state of Mississippi had seceded. Even zealous advocates of secession had a hard time reconciling themselves to secession and believing that they were no longer citizens of the United States. "How do you feel now, dear Mother," a Georgian wrote, "that *we* are in a foreign land?"

At first, the Upper South states of Virginia, North Carolina, Tennessee, and Arkansas flatly rejected secession (see Map 14.3). In contrast to the Lower South, which had a guaranteed export market for its cotton, the Upper South depended heavily on economic ties to the North that would be severed by secession. Furthermore, with proportionately far fewer slaves than the Lower South, the states of the Upper South doubted the loyalty of their sizable nonslaveholding populations to the idea of secession. Virginia, for example, had every reason to question the allegiance to secession of its nonslaveholding western counties, which would soon break away to

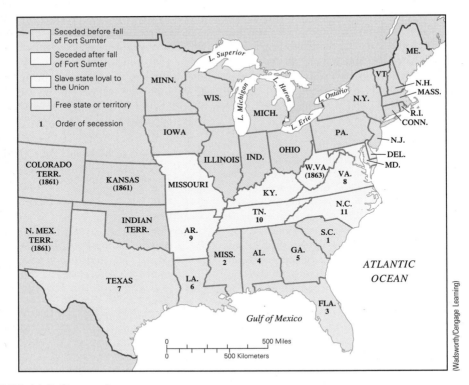

MAP 14.3 Secession

Four key states—Virginia, Arkansas, Tennessee, and North Carolina—did not secede until after the fall of Fort Sumter. The border slave states of Maryland, Delaware, Kentucky, and Missouri stayed in the Union.

form Unionist West Virginia. Few in the Upper South could forget the raw nerve touched by the publication in 1857 of Hinton R. Helper's *The Impending Crisis of the South*. A nonslaveholding North Carolinian, Helper had described slavery as a curse upon poor white southerners and thereby questioned one of the most sacred southern doctrines, the idea that slavery rendered all whites equal. If secession were to spark a war between the states, moreover, the Upper South appeared to be the likeliest battleground. Whatever the exact weight assignable to each of these factors, one point is clear: the secession movement that South Carolina so boldly started in December 1860 seemed to be falling apart by March 1861.

The Search for Compromise

The lack of southern unity confirmed the view of most Republicans that the secessionists were more bluster than substance. Seward described secession as the work of "a relatively few hotheads," and Lincoln believed that the loyal majority of southerners would soon wrest control from the fire-eating minority.

This perception stiffened Republican resolve to resist compromise. Moderate John J. Crittenden of Kentucky proposed compensation for owners of runaway slaves, repeal of northern personal-liberty laws, a constitutional amendment to prohibit the federal government from interfering with slavery in the southern states, and another amendment to restore the Missouri Compromise line for the remaining territories and protect slavery below it. But in the face of steadfast Republican opposition, the Crittenden plan collapsed.

Lincoln's faith in a "loyal majority" of southerners exaggerated both their numbers and their devotion to the Union. Many southern opponents of the fire-eating secessionists were sitting on the fence and hoping for major concessions from the North; their allegiance to the Union thus was conditional. Lincoln can be faulted for misreading southern opinion, but even if his assessment had been accurate, it is unlikely that he would have accepted the Crittenden plan. The sticking point was the proposed extension of the Missouri Compromise line. To Republicans this was a surrender, not a compromise, because it hinged on the abandonment of free soil, the founding principle of their party. In addition, Lincoln well knew that some southerners still talked of seizing more territory for slavery in the Caribbean. In proposing to extend the 36°30' line, the Crittenden plan specifically referred to territories "hereafter acquired." Lincoln feared it would be only a matter of time "till we shall have to take Cuba as a condition upon which they [the seceding states] will stay in the Union."

Beyond these considerations, the precipitous secession of the Lower South changed the question that Lincoln faced. The issue was no longer slavery extension but secession. The Lower South had left the Union in the face of losing a fair election. For Lincoln to have caved in to such pressure would have violated majority rule, the principle upon which the nation, not just his party, had been founded.

The Coming of War

By the time Lincoln took office in March 1861, little more than a spark was needed to ignite a war. William Seward, whom Lincoln had appointed secretary of state, now became obsessed with the idea of conciliating the Lower South in order to hold the Upper

South in the Union. In addition to advising the evacuation of federal forces from **Fort Sumter,** Seward proposed a scheme to reunify the nation by provoking a war with France and Spain. But Lincoln brushed aside Seward's advice. Instead, the president informed the governor of South Carolina of his intention to supply Fort Sumter with much-needed provisions, but not with men and ammunition. To gain the dubious military advantage of attacking Fort Sumter before the arrival of relief ships, Confederate batteries began to bombard the fort shortly before dawn on April 12. The next day, the fort's garrison surrendered.

Lincoln's appeal for seventy-five thousand volunteers from the loyal states to suppress the rebellion pushed citizens of the Upper South off the fence upon which they had perched for three months. "I am a Union man," one southerner wrote, "but when they [the Lincoln administration] send men south it will change my notions. I can do nothing against my own people." In quick succession, Virginia, North Carolina, Arkansas, and Tennessee leagued with the Confederacy. After acknowledging that "I am one of those dull creatures that cannot see the good of secession," Robert E. Lee resigned from the army rather than lead federal troops against his native Virginia.

The North, too, was ready for a fight, less to abolish slavery than to punish secession. Worn out from his efforts to find a peaceable solution to the issue of slavery extension, and with only a short time to live, Stephen Douglas assaulted "the new system of resistance by the sword and bayonet to the results of the ballot-box" and affirmed: "I deprecate war, but if it must come I am with my country, under all circumstances, and in every contingency."

CHRONOLOGY
1850–1861

1848	Zachary Taylor elected president.
1849	California seeks admission to the Union as a free state.
1850	Nashville convention assembles to discuss the South's grievances. Compromise of 1850.
1852	Harriet Beecher Stowe, *Uncle Tom's Cabin.* Franklin Pierce elected president.
1853	Gadsden Purchase.
1854	Ostend Manifesto. Kansas-Nebraska Act. William Walker leads filibustering expedition into Nicaragua.
1854–1855	Know-Nothing and Republican parties emerge.
1855	Proslavery forces steal the election for a territorial legislature in Kansas. Proslavery Kansans establish a government in Lecompton. Free-soil government established in Topeka, Kansas.
1856	"The sack of Lawrence." John Brown's Pottawatomie massacre. James Buchanan elected president.

1857	*Dred Scott* decision.
	President Buchanan endorses the Lecompton constitution in Kansas.
	Panic of 1857.
1858	Congress refuses to admit Kansas to the Union under the Lecompton constitution.
	Lincoln-Douglas debates.
1859	John Brown's raid on Harpers Ferry.
1860	Abraham Lincoln elected president.
	South Carolina secedes from the Union.
1861	The remaining Lower South states secede.
	Confederate States of America established.
	Crittenden compromise plan collapses.
	Lincoln takes office.
	Firing on Fort Sumter; Civil War begins.
	Upper South secedes.

Conclusion

The expectation of most American political leaders that the Compromise of 1850 would finally resolve the vexing issue of slavery extension had a surface plausibility. In neither 1850 nor 1860 did the great majority of Americans favor the abolition of slavery in the southern states. Rather, they divided over slavery in the territories, an issue seemingly settled by the Compromise. Stephen A. Douglas, its leading architect and a man who assumed he always had his finger on the popular pulse, was sure that slavery had reached its natural limits, that popular sovereignty would keep it out of the territories, and that the furor over slavery extension would die down.

Douglas believed that only a few hotheads had kept the slavery extension issue alive. He was wrong. The differences between northerners and southerners over slavery extension were grounded on different understandings of liberty, which to northerners meant their freedom to pursue self-interest without competition from slaves, and to southerners their freedom to dispose of their legally acquired property, slaves, as they chose. The Compromise, which had barely scraped through Congress, soon unraveled. Enforcement of the Fugitive Slave Act brought to the surface widespread northern resentment of slaveholders, people who seemingly lived off the work of others, and a determination to exclude the possibility of slavery in the territories. Southern support for Douglas's Kansas-Nebraska bill, with its repeal of the Missouri Compromise and its apparent invitation to southerners to bring slaves into Kansas, persuaded many northerners that the South harbored the design of extending slavery. For their part, southerners, already angered by northern defiance of the Fugitive Slave Act, interpreted northern outrage against Douglas's bill as further evidence of the North's disrespect for the rule of law.

By the mid-1850s, the sectional division was spinning out of the control of politicians. Deep divisions between the Whigs' free-soil northern wing and their proslavery southern wing led to the party's collapse in the wake of the Kansas-Nebraska Act. Divisions between northern and southern Democrats would be papered over as long as the Democratic Party could unite behind Douglas's formula of popular sovereignty. But popular sovereignty failed its test in Kansas. The outbreak of civil strife in Kansas pushed former northern Whigs and many northern Democrats toward the new, purely sectional, Republicans, a party whose very existence southerners interpreted as a mark of northern contempt for them.

The South was not yet ready for secession. Before it took that drastic step, it had to convince itself that the North's real design was not merely to restrict the extension of slavery but to destroy slavery and, with it, the South itself. Northern hostility to the *Dred Scott* decision and sympathy for John Brown struck southerners as proof of just such an intent.

As an expression of principled outrage, secession capped a decade in which each side had clothed itself in principles that were deeply embedded in the nation's political heritage. Both sides subscribed to the rule of law, which each accused the other of deserting. In the end, war broke out between siblings who, although they claimed the same heritage and inheritance, had become virtual strangers to each other.

15

CRUCIBLE OF FREEDOM: CIVIL WAR, 1861–1865

MOBILIZING FOR WAR

North and South alike were unprepared for war. In April 1861, the Union had only a small army of sixteen thousand men scattered all over the country, mostly in the West. One-third of Union army officers had resigned to join the Confederacy. The nation's new president, Abraham Lincoln, struck many observers as a yokel. That such a government could marshal its people for war seemed doubtful. The federal government had levied no direct taxes for decades and had never imposed a draft. The Confederacy, even less prepared, had no tax structure, no navy, only two tiny gunpowder factories, and poorly equipped, unconnected railroad lines.

During the first two years of war, both sides would have to overcome these deficiencies, raise and supply large armies, and finance the war's heavy costs. In each region, mobilization expanded the powers of government to an extent that few had anticipated.

Recruitment and Conscription The Civil War armies were the largest organizations ever created in America; by the war's end, over 2 million men served in the Union army and 800,000 in the Confederate army. In the first flush of enthusiasm, volunteers rushed to the colors. "We will be held responsible before God if we don't do our part," declared a New Jersey recruit. "I go for wiping them out," a Virginian told his governor.

At first, raising armies depended on local efforts rather than on national or even state direction. Citizens opened hometown recruiting offices, held rallies, and signed up volunteers; regiments usually consisted of soldiers from the same locale. Southern cavalrymen provided their own horses, and uniforms everywhere depended mainly on local option. In both armies, the troops themselves elected officers up to the rank of colonel.

This informal and democratic way of raising and organizing soldiers could not long withstand the stress of war. As early as July 1861, the Union began examinations for officers. Also, as casualties mounted, military demand soon exceeded the supply of volunteers. The Confederacy felt the pinch first and in April 1862 enacted the first **conscription** law in American history. It required all able-bodied white men aged eighteen to thirty-five to serve in the military for three years. Subsequent amendments made the age limits seventeen and fifty.

The Confederacy's Conscription Act antagonized southerners. Opponents charged that the draft was a despotic assault on state sovereignty and that the law would "do away with all the patriotism we have." Exemptions for many occupations, from religious ministry to shoemaking, aggrieved the nonexempt. So did a loophole, closed in 1863, that allowed the well-off to hire substitutes. One amendment, the so-called 20-Negro law, exempted an owner or overseer of twenty or more slaves from service. Although southerners widely feared loss of control over slaves if all able-bodied white men were away in the army, the 20-Negro law led to complaints about "a rich man's war but a poor man's fight."

Despite opposition, the Confederate draft became increasingly hard to evade; this stimulated volunteering. Only one soldier in five was a draftee, but 70 to 80 percent of eligible white southerners served in the Confederate army. An 1864 law that required all soldiers then in the army to serve for the duration of the war ensured that a high proportion of Confederate soldiers would be battle-hardened veterans.

Once the army was raised, it needed supplies. At first, the South relied on arms and ammunition imported from Europe, weapons confiscated from federal arsenals, and guns captured on the battlefield. These stopgap measures bought time to develop an industrial base. By 1862, southerners had a competent head of ordnance (weaponry), Josiah Gorgas. The Confederacy assigned ordnance contracts to privately owned factories like the Tredegar Iron Works in Richmond, provided loans to establish new factories, and created government-owned industries like the giant Augusta Powder Works in Georgia. The South lost few, if any, battles for want of munitions.

Supplying troops with clothing and food proved more difficult. Southern soldiers frequently lacked shoes; during the South's invasion of Maryland in 1862, thousands of Confederate soldiers remained behind because they could not march barefoot on Maryland's gravel-surfaced roads. Late in the war, Robert E. Lee's Army of Northern Virginia ran out of food but never out of ammunition. Southern supply problems had several sources: railroads that fell into disrepair or were captured, an economy that relied more heavily on producing tobacco and cotton than growing food, and Union invasions early in the war that overran the livestock and grain-raising districts of central Tennessee and Virginia. Close to desperation, the Confederate Congress in 1863 passed the Impressment Act, an unpopular law that authorized army officers to take food from reluctant farmers at prescribed prices and to impress slaves into labor for the army, a provision that provoked yet more resentment.

The industrial North had fewer supply problems. But recruitment was another matter. When the initial tide of enthusiasm for enlistment ebbed, Congress followed the Confederacy's example and turned to conscription with the Enrollment Act of March 1863; every able-bodied white male citizen aged twenty to forty-five now faced the draft.

Like the Confederate conscription law of 1862, the Enrollment Act granted exemptions, although only to high government officials, ministers, and men who were the sole support of widows, orphans, or indigent parents. It also offered two means of escaping the draft: substitution, or paying another man who would serve instead; and commutation, paying a $300 fee to the government. Enrollment districts often competed for volunteers by offering cash payments (bounties); dishonest "bounty jumpers" repeatedly deserted after collecting payments. Democrats charged that conscription violated individual liberties and states' rights. Ordinary citizens resented the commutation and substitution provision and leveled their own "poor man's fight" charges. Still, as in the Confederacy, the law stimulated volunteering. Only 8 percent of Union soldiers were draftees or substitutes.

Financing the War   The recruitment and supply of huge armies lay far beyond the capacity of American public finance at the start of the war. In the 1840s and 1850s, the federal government met its meager revenue needs from tariff duties and income from public land sales. During the war, however, annual federal expenditures gradually rose, and the need for new sources of revenue became urgent. Yet neither Union nor Confederacy initially wished to impose taxes, to which Americans were unaccustomed.

Both sides therefore turned to war bonds; that is, to loans from citizens to be repaid by future generations. Patriotic southerners quickly bought up the Confederacy's first bond issue ($15 million) in 1861. That same year, a financial wizard, Philadelphia banker Jay Cooke, urged the northern public to buy a much larger bond issue ($150 million). But bonds had to be paid for in gold or silver coin (specie), which was in short supply. Soaking up most of its available specie, the South's first bond issue threatened to be its last. In the North, many hoarded their gold rather than spend it on bonds.

Grasping the limits of taxes and of bond issues, both sides began to print paper money. Early in 1862, Lincoln signed into law the **Legal Tender Act,** which authorized the issue of $150 million of so-called greenbacks. Christopher Memminger, the Confederacy's treasury secretary, and Salmon P. Chase, his Union counterpart, shared a distrust of paper money, but as funds dwindled each came around to the idea. The availability of paper money made it easier to pay soldiers, levy taxes, and sell war bonds. Yet doubts about paper money lingered. Unlike gold and silver, which had established market values, the value of paper money depended mainly on public confidence in the government that issued it. To bolster that confidence, Union officials made the greenbacks legal tender (that is, acceptable in payment of most public and private debts).

In contrast, the Confederacy never made its paper money legal tender; suspicions arose that the southern government lacked confidence in it. To compound the problem, the Confederacy raised less than 5 percent of its wartime revenue from taxes (compared to 21 percent in the North). The Confederacy did enact a comprehensive tax measure in 1863, but Union invasions and the South's relatively undeveloped system of internal transportation made tax collection a hit-or-miss proposition.

Confidence in the South's paper money quickly evaporated, and the value of Confederate paper in relation to gold plunged. The Confederate response—printing more paper money, a billion dollars by 1865—merely accelerated southern inflation. Whereas prices in the North rose about 80 percent during the war, the Confederacy suffered an inflation rate of over 9,000 percent. What cost a southerner one dollar in 1861 cost forty-six dollars by 1864.

By raising taxes, floating bonds, and printing paper money, both North and South broke with the hard-money, minimal-government traditions of American public finance. For the most part, these changes were unanticipated and often reluctant adaptations to wartime conditions. But in the North, Republicans took advantage of the southern Democrats' departure from Congress to push through one measure that they and their Whig predecessors had long advocated, a system of national banking. Passed in February 1863 over Democratic opposition, the **National Bank Act** established criteria by which a bank could obtain a federal charter and issue national bank notes (notes backed by the federal government). It also gave private bankers an incentive to purchase war bonds. The North's ability to revolutionize its public finance system reflected both long experience with complex financial transactions and political cohesion in wartime.

Political Leadership in Wartime	The Civil War pitted rival political systems as well as armies and economies against each other. The South entered the war with several apparent political advantages. Lincoln's call for

militiamen to suppress the rebellion had transformed Southern waverers into tenacious secessionists. "Never was a people more united or more determined," a New Orleans woman wrote in the spring of 1861. Southerners also claimed a strong leader. A former secretary of war and U.S. senator from Mississippi, President **Jefferson Davis** of the Confederacy possessed experience, honesty, courage, and what one officer described as "a jaw sawed in *steel*."

In contrast, the Union's list of political liabilities seemed long. Loyal but contentious, northern Democrats disliked conscription, the National Bank Act, and abolition of slavery. Among Republicans, Lincoln had trouble commanding respect. Unlike Davis, he had served in neither the cabinet nor the Senate; his informal western manners dismayed easterners. Northern setbacks early in the war convinced most Republicans in Congress that Lincoln was ineffectual. Criticism of Lincoln sprang from **Radical Republicans,** a group that included Secretary of the Treasury Salmon P. Chase, Senator Charles Sumner of Massachusetts, and Representative Thaddeus Stevens of Pennsylvania. On some issues, the Radicals cooperated with Lincoln. But they assailed him early in the war for failing to make emancipation a war goal and later for being too eager to readmit the conquered rebel states into the Union.

Lincoln's distinctive style of leadership at once encouraged and disarmed opposition among Republicans. Self-contained until ready to act, he met complaints with homespun anecdotes that caught opponents off guard. The Radicals often saw Lincoln as a prisoner of the party's conservative wing; conservatives complained he was too close to the Radicals. But Lincoln's cautious reserve left open his lines of communication with both wings of the party and fragmented his opposition. He also co-opted some of his critics, including Chase, by bringing them into his cabinet.

In contrast, Jefferson Davis had a knack for making enemies. A West Pointer, he would rather have led the army than the government. His cabinet endured frequent resignations; the Confederacy had five secretaries of war in four years. Davis's relations with his vice president, Alexander Stephens of Georgia, verged on disastrous. A wisp of a man, Stephens weighed less than a hundred pounds, but he compensated for his slight physique with an acidic tongue. Leaving Richmond, the Confederate capital, in 1862, Stephens spent most of the war in Georgia, where he sniped at Davis as "weak and vacillating, timid, petulant, peevish, obstinate."

The clash between Davis and Stephens also involved an ideological division, a rift, in fact, like that at the heart of the Confederacy. The Confederate Constitution, drafted in February 1861, explicitly guaranteed state sovereignty and prohibited the Confederate Congress from enacting protective tariffs or supporting internal improvements (measures long opposed by southern voters). For Stephens and other influential Confederates—among them the governors of Georgia and North Carolina—the Confederacy existed not only to protect slavery but, equally important, to enshrine the doctrine of states' rights. In contrast, Davis's main objective was to secure the independence of the South from the North, if necessary at the expense of states' rights.

This difference between Davis and Stephens somewhat resembled the discord between Lincoln and northern Democrats. Like Davis, Lincoln believed that victory demanded a strong central government; like Stephens, northern Democrats resisted governmental centralization. But Lincoln could control his foes more skillfully than Davis because, by temperament, he was more suited to conciliation and also because the nature of party politics in the two sections differed.

In the South, the Democrats and the remaining Whigs agreed to suspend party rivalries for the duration of the war. Although intended to promote southern unity, this decision actually encouraged disunity. Without the organization that party rivalry provided, southern politics disintegrated along personal and factional lines. Lacking a party system to back him, Davis could not mobilize votes to pass measures that he favored nor depend on the support of party loyalists.

In contrast, in the Union, northern Democrats' organized opposition to Lincoln tended to unify the Republicans. After Democrats in 1862 won control of five states (including Lincoln's Illinois), Republican leaders learned a lesson: no matter how much they disdained Lincoln, they had to rally behind him or risk losing office. Ultimately, the Union developed more political cohesion than the Confederacy, not because it had fewer divisions but because it managed its divisions more effectively.

Securing the Union's Borders   Even before large-scale fighting began, Lincoln moved to safeguard Washington, which was bordered by two slave states (Virginia and Maryland) and filled with Confederate sympathizers. A week after Fort Sumter, a Baltimore mob attacked a Massachusetts regiment bound for Washington, but enough troops slipped through to protect the capital. Lincoln then dispatched federal troops to Maryland, where he suspended the writ of *habeas corpus* (a court order requiring that the detainer of a prisoner bring that person to court and show cause for his or her detention); federal troops could now arrest prosecession Marylanders without formally charging them with specific offenses. Cowed by Lincoln's bold moves, the legislatures of Maryland and Delaware (another border slave state) rejected secession.

Next, Lincoln authorized the arming of Union sympathizers in Kentucky, a slave state with a Unionist legislature, a secessionist governor, and a thin chance of staying neutral. Lincoln also stationed troops under General Ulysses S. Grant just across the Ohio River from Kentucky, in Illinois. When a Confederate army invaded Kentucky early in 1862, Grant's soldiers drove it out. Officially, at least, Kentucky became the third slave state to declare for the Union. The fourth, Missouri, faced four years of fighting between Union and Confederate troops, and between bands of guerrillas and bushwhackers, a name for Confederate guerrillas who lurked in the underbrush. These included William Quantrill, a rebel desperado, and his murderous apprentices, Frank and Jesse James. Despite savage combat and the divided loyalties of its people, Missouri never left the Union. West Virginia, admitted to the Union in 1863, would become the last of five border states, or slave states that remained in the Union. (West Virginia was established in 1861, when thirty-five counties in the mainly nonslaveholding region of Virginia west of the Shenandoah Valley refused to follow the state's leaders into secession.)

By holding the first four border slave states—Maryland, Delaware, Kentucky, and Missouri—in the Union, Lincoln kept open his routes to the free states and gained access to the river systems in Kentucky and Missouri that led into the heart of the Confederacy. Lincoln's firmness, particularly in Maryland, scotched charges that he was weak-willed. The crisis also forced the president to exercise long-dormant powers. In the case *Ex parte* Merryman (1861), Chief Justice Roger B. Taney ruled that Lincoln had exceeded his authority in suspending the writ of *habeas corpus* in Maryland. The president, citing the Constitution's authorization of the writ's suspension in "Cases of Rebellion" (Article I, Section 9), insisted that he, rather than Congress, would determine whether a rebellion existed; he ignored Taney's ruling.

IN BATTLE, 1861–1862

The Civil War was the first war to rely extensively on railroads, the telegraph, mass-produced weapons, joint army-navy tactics, iron-plated warships, rifled guns and artillery, and trench warfare. All of this lends some justification to its description as the first modern war. But to the participants, slogging through muddy swamps and laden with equipment, the war hardly seemed modern. In many ways, the soldiers had the more accurate perspective, for the new weapons did not always work, and both sides employed tactics that were more traditional than modern.

Armies, Weapons, and Strategies   Compared to the Confederacy's 9 million people, one-third of them slaves, the Union had 22 million people in 1861 (see Figure 15.1). The North also had 3.5 times as many white men of military age, 90 percent of all U.S. industrial capacity, and two-thirds of its railroad track. Yet the Union faced a daunting challenge: to force the South back into the Union. The South, in contrast, fought merely for its independence. To subdue the Confederacy, the North would have to sustain offensive operations over a vast area.

Measured against this challenge, the Union's advantages in population and technology shrank. The North had more men, but needed to defend long supply lines and occupy captured areas; consequently, it could commit a smaller proportion to frontline duty. The South, which relied on slaves for labor, could assign a higher proportion of white men to combat. The North required, and possessed, superior railroads, though it had to move troops and supplies huge distances, and guerrillas could easily sabotage northern lines; the South could shift troops relatively short distances within its defensive arc without using railroads. Finally, southerners had an edge in soldiers' morale, for Confederate troops battled on home ground. "No people ever warred for independence," a southern general acknowledged, "with more relative advantages than the Confederates."

The Civil War witnessed experiments with various newly developed weapons, including the submarine, the repeating rifle, and the multibarreled Gatling gun, the forerunner of the machine gun. More important was the perfection in the 1850s of a bullet whose powder would not clog a rifle's spiraled internal grooves after a few shots. Like the smoothbore muskets that both armies had employed at the start of the war, most improved rifles had to be reloaded after each shot. But the smoothbore had an effective range of only eighty yards; the Springfield or Enfield rifles widely employed by 1863 could hit targets accurately at up to four hundred yards.

The rifle's development challenged long-accepted military tactics, which stressed the mass infantry charge against an opponent's weakest point. Pre-war military manuals assumed that defenders armed with muskets would fire only a round or two before being overwhelmed. Armed with rifles, however, a defending force could fire several rounds before closing with the enemy. Attackers would now

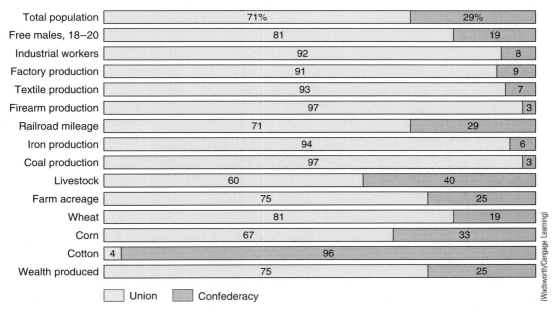

Union | Confederacy

FIGURE 15.1 Comparative Population and Economic Resources of the Union and the Confederacy, 1861

At the start of the war, the Union enjoyed huge advantages in population, industry, railroad mileage, and wealth, and—as it would soon prove—a superior ability to mobilize its vast resources. The Confederacy, however, enjoyed the many advantages of fighting a defensive war.

rarely get close enough to thrust bayonets; fewer than 1 percent of the casualties in the Civil War resulted from bayonet wounds.

Thus, the rifle produced some changes in tactics. Both sides came to grasp the value of trenches, which provided defenders protection against withering rifle fire. By 1865, trenches pockmarked the landscape in Virginia and Georgia. Also, growing use of the rifle forced generals to rely less on cavalry. Traditionally, cavalry had ranked among the most prestigious components of an army, in part because cavalry charges were effective and in part because the cavalry helped maintain class distinctions within the army. More accurate rifles reduced cavalry effectiveness by increasing the firepower of foot soldiers. Thus both sides relegated cavalry to reconnaissance missions and raids on supply trains.

Still, the introduction of the rifle did not totally invalidate traditional tactics. On the contrary, historians now contend, high casualties reflected the long duration of battles rather than the new efficacy of rifles. The attacking army still stood an excellent chance of success if it achieved surprise the South's lush forests provided abundant opportunities for an army to sneak up on its foe. For example, at the Battle of Shiloh in 1862, Confederate attackers surprised and almost defeated a larger Union army despite the rumpus created by green rebel troops en route to the battle, many of whom fired their rifles into the air to see if they would work.

Lack of any element of surprise could doom an attacking army. At the Battle of Fredericksburg in December 1862, Confederate troops inflicted appalling casualties on Union forces attacking uphill over open terrain, and at Gettysburg in July 1863, Union riflemen and artillery shredded charging southerners. But generals might still achieve partial surprise by hitting an enemy before it had concentrated its troops; in fact, this is what the North tried to do at Fredericksburg. Because surprise often proved effective, most generals continued to believe their best chance of success lay in striking an unwary or weakened enemy with all the troops they could muster rather than in relying on guerrilla or trench warfare.

Much like previous wars, the Civil War was fought basically in a succession of battles during which exposed infantry traded volleys, charged, and countercharged. Whichever side withdrew from the field usually was considered the loser, though it frequently sustained lighter casualties than the supposed victor. Both sides had trouble exploiting their victories. As a rule, the beaten army moved back a few miles from the field to lick its wounds; the winners stayed in place to lick theirs. Politicians on both sides raged at generals for not pursuing a beaten foe, but it was difficult for a mangled victor to gather horses, mules, supply trains, and exhausted soldiers for a new attack. Not surprisingly, for much of the war, generals on both sides concluded that the best defense was a good offense.

To the extent that the North had a long-range strategy in 1861, it lay in the so-called **Anaconda plan**. Devised by a hero of the Mexican-American War, General Winfield Scott, the plan called for the Union to blockade the southern coastline and to thrust, like a snake, down the Mississippi River. Sealing off and severing the Confederacy, Scott expected, would make the South recognize the futility of secession and end the war quickly. However, although Lincoln quickly ordered a blockade of the southern coast, the North lacked the troops and naval flotillas to seize the Mississippi in 1861. So while the Mississippi remained an objective, northern strategy did not unfold according to a specific blueprint like the Anaconda plan.

Early in the war, the pressing need to secure the border slave states, particularly Kentucky and Missouri, dictated Union strategy west of the Appalachian Mountains. Once in control of Kentucky, northern troops plunged southward into Tennessee. The Appalachians tended to seal this western theater off from the eastern theater, where major clashes of 1861 occurred.

Stalemate in the East

The Confederacy's decision in May 1861 to move its capital from Montgomery, Alabama, to Richmond, Virginia, shaped Union strategy. "Forward to Richmond" became the Union's first war cry. Before they could reach Richmond, one hundred miles southwest of Washington, Union troops had to dislodge a Confederate army brazenly encamped at Manassas Junction, Virginia, only twenty-five miles from the Union capital (see Map 15.1). Lincoln ordered General Irvin McDowell to attack his former West Point classmate, Confederate general P.G.T. Beauregard. In the resulting **First Battle of Bull Run** (or First Manassas), amateur armies clashed in bloody chaos under a blistering July sun. Well-dressed, picnicking Washington dignitaries witnessed the carnage, as Beauregard routed the larger Union army.

After Bull Run, Lincoln replaced McDowell with General George B. McClellan as commander of the Army of the Potomac, the Union's main fighting force in the East. Another West Pointer, McClellan had served with distinction in the Mexican-American War. A master of administration and training, he could turn a ragtag mob into a disciplined fighting force. His soldiers adored him, but Lincoln quickly became disenchanted. Lincoln believed the key to a Union victory lay in simultaneous, coordinated attacks on several fronts so that the North could exploit its advantage in manpower and resources. McClellan, a proslavery Democrat, hoped for a relatively bloodless Southern defeat, followed by readmission of the Confederate states with slavery intact.

"Scott's Great Snake," 1861 *General Winfield Scott's scheme to surround the South and await a seizure of power by southern Unionists drew scorn from critics who called it the Anaconda plan. In this lithograph, the "great snake" prepares to push down the Mississippi, seal off the Confederacy, and crush it.*

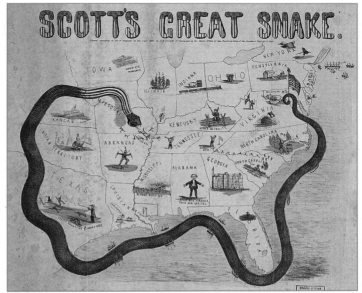

(Library of Congress)

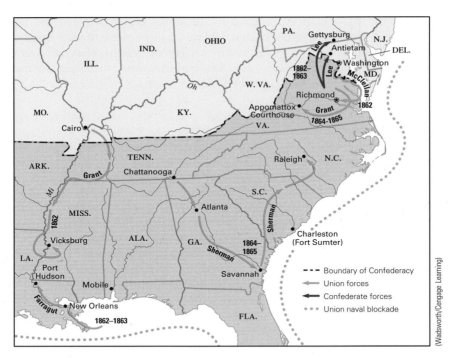

MAP 15.1 The War in the East, 1861–1862

Union advances on Richmond were turned back at Fredericksburg and the Seven Days' Battles, and the Confederacy's invasion of Union territory was stopped at Antietam.

In the spring of 1862, McClellan got a chance to implement his strategy. After Bull Run, the Confederates had pulled back to block the Union onslaught against Richmond. Rather than directly attack the Confederate army, McClellan decided to move his army by water to the tip of the peninsula formed by the York and James Rivers and then move northwestward up the peninsula to Richmond. McClellan's plan had several advantages. Depending on water transport rather than on railroads exposed to Confederate cavalry, the McClellan strategy reduced the vulnerability of northern supply lines. Approaching Richmond from the southeast, it threatened the South's supply lines. By aiming for the Confederate capital rather than for the Confederate army stationed to its northeast, McClellan hoped to maneuver the southern troops into a futile attack on his army.

At first, the massive Peninsula Campaign unfolded smoothly. Three hundred ships transported seventy thousand men and huge stores of supplies to the tip of the peninsula. Reinforcements swelled McClellan's army to one hundred thousand. By late May, McClellan was within five miles of Richmond. But then he hesitated. Overestimating Confederate strength, he refused to launch a final attack without further reinforcements, which were turned back by Confederate general Thomas "Stonewall" Jackson in the Shenandoah Valley.

While McClellan delayed, General **Robert E. Lee** took command of the Confederacy's Army of Northern Virginia. A foe of secession and so courteous that at times he seemed too gentle, Lee possessed the qualities that McClellan most lacked: boldness and a willingness to accept casualties. Seizing the initiative, Lee attacked McClellan in late June 1862. The ensuing Seven Days' Battles, fought in the forests east of Richmond, cost the South nearly twice as many men as the North and ended in a virtual slaughter of Confederates. Unnerved by mounting casualties, McClellan sent increasingly panicky reports to Washington. Lincoln, who cared little for McClellan's peninsula strategy, ordered McClellan to call off the campaign and return to Washington.

With McClellan off the scene, Lee and his lieutenant, Stonewall Jackson, boldly struck north and, at the Second Battle of Bull Run (Second Manassas), routed a Union army under General John Pope. Lee's next stroke was even bolder. Crossing the Potomac River in early September 1862, he invaded western Maryland, where the forthcoming harvest could feed his troops. Lee could now threaten Washington, indirectly relieve pressure on Richmond, improve the prospects of peace candidates in the North's fall elections, and possibly induce Britain and France to recognize Confederate independence. But McClellan met Lee at the **Battle of Antietam** (or Sharpsburg) on September 17. A tactical draw, Antietam proved a strategic victory for the North: Lee subsequently canceled his invasion and retreated south of the Potomac.

Heartened by Northern success, Lincoln then issued the Emancipation Proclamation, a war measure that freed all slaves under rebel control. The toll of 24,000 casualties at Antietam, however, made it the bloodiest day of the entire war. One part of the battlefield, a Union veteran recalled, contained so many bodies that a man could have walked through it without stepping on the ground.

Complaining that McClellan had "the slows," Lincoln faulted his commander for not pursuing Lee after Antietam. McClellan's replacement, General Ambrose Burnside, thought himself unfit for high command. He was right. In December 1862, Burnside led 122,000 federal troops against 78,500 Confederates at the Battle of Fredericksburg. Burnside captured the town of Fredericksburg, northeast of Richmond, but then sacrificed his army in futile charges up the heights west of the town. Even Lee shuddered at the carnage. "It is well that war is so terrible, or we should grow too fond of it," he told an aide. Richmond remained, in the words of a southern song, "a hard road to travel." The war in the East had become a stalemate.

The War in the West

The Union fared better in the West. There, the war ranged over a vast terrain that provided access to rivers leading directly into the South. The West also spawned new leadership: In the war's first year, an obscure Union general, **Ulysses S. Grant,** won attention. A West Point graduate, Grant had fought in the Mexican-American War and retired from the army in 1854 with a reputation for heavy drinking. He then failed in farming and business. When the Civil War began, he gained an army commission through political pressure.

In 1861–1862, Grant retained control of two border states, Missouri and Kentucky. Moving into Tennessee, he captured two strategic forts, Fort Henry on the Tennessee River and Fort Donelson on the Cumberland. Grant then headed south to attack Corinth, Mississippi, a major railroad junction.

In early April 1862, to defend Corinth, Confederates under generals Albert Sidney Johnston and P. G. T. Beauregard surprised Grant's army, encamped near a church named Shiloh twenty miles north of the town, in southern Tennessee. Hoping to whip Grant before Union reinforcements arrived, Confederates exploded from the woods near Shiloh before breakfast and almost drove the federals into the Tennessee River. Beauregard cabled Richmond with news of Confederate triumph. But Grant and his lieutenant, **William T. Sherman**—a West Point graduate and Mexican-American war veteran who had most recently run a southern military academy—steadied the Union line. Union reinforcements arrived at night, and a federal counterattack drove the Confederates from the field the next day. Although Antietam would soon erase the distinction, the **Battle of Shiloh** was the bloodiest in American history to that date. Of the seventy-seven thousand men engaged, twenty-three thousand were killed or wounded, including Confederate general Albert Sidney Johnston, who bled to death from a leg wound. Defeated at Shiloh, the Confederates soon evacuated Corinth.

To attack Grant at Shiloh, the Confederacy had stripped the defenses of its largest city, New Orleans. A combined Union land-sea force under General Benjamin Butler, a Massachusetts politician, and Admiral David G. Farragut, a Tennessean loyal to the Union, seized the opportunity. Farragut took New Orleans in late April and soon conquered Baton Rouge and Natchez as well. Meanwhile, another Union flotilla moved down the Mississippi and captured Memphis in June. Now the North controlled the entire river, except for a two-hundred-mile stretch between Port Hudson, Louisiana, and Vicksburg, Mississippi.

Union and Confederate forces also clashed in 1862 in the trans-Mississippi West. On the banks of the Rio Grande, Union volunteers, joined by Mexican-American companies, drove a Confederate army from Texas out of New Mexico. A thousand miles to the east, in northern Arkansas and western Missouri, armies vied to secure the Missouri River, a crucial waterway that flowed into the Mississippi. In Pea Ridge, Arkansas, in March 1862, forewarned northern troops scattered a Confederate force of sixteen thousand that included three Cherokee regiments. (Indian units fought on both sides in Missouri, where guerrilla combat raged until the war's end.)

These Union victories changed the nature of the trans-Mississippi war. As the rebel threat faded, regiments of western volunteers that had mobilized to crush Confederates turned to fighting Indians. Conflict between Union forces and Native Americans erupted in Minnesota, Arizona, Nevada, Colorado, and New Mexico, where California volunteers and the New Mexico cavalry, led by Colonel Kit Carson, overwhelmed the Apaches and Navajos. After 1865, federal troops moved west to complete the rout of the Indians that had begun in the Civil War.

The Soldiers' War   Civil War soldiers were typically volunteers from farms and small towns who joined companies of recruits from their locales. Many who enrolled in 1861 and 1862—those who served at Shiloh and Antietam—reenlisted when their terms expired and became the backbones of their respective armies. Local loyalties spurred enrollment, especially in the South; so did ideals of honor and valor. Soldiers on both sides envisioned military life as a transforming experience in which citizens became warriors and boys became men. Exultant after a victory, an Alabama volunteer told his father, "With your first shot you become a new man." Thousands of underage volunteers, that is, boys under eighteen, also served in the war; so did at least 250 women disguised as men.

Recruits were meshed into regiments and then sent to camps of instruction. Training was meager, and much of army life tedious and uncomfortable. Food was one complaint. Union troops ate beans, bacon, salt pork, pickled beef, and a staple called hardtack, square flour-and-water biscuits that were almost impossible to crack with a blow. Confederate diets featured bacon and cornmeal, and as a southern soldier summed it up, "Our rations is small." Rebel armies often ran out of food, blankets, clothes, socks, and shoes. On both sides, crowded military camps—plagued by poor sanitation and infested with lice, fleas, ticks, flies, and rodents—ensured soaring disease rates and widespread grievances. A sergeant from New York, only partly in jest, described his lot as "laying around in the dirt and mud, living on hardtack, facing death in bullets and shells, eat up by wood-ticks and body-lice."

Dreams of military glory swiftly faded. For most soldiers, Civil War battles meant inuring themselves to the stench of death. "Soldier," a Confederate chaplain told his troops in 1863, "your business is to die." Soldiers rapidly grasped the value of caution in combat. According to a northern volunteer, "The consuming passion is to get out of the way." Others described the zeal aroused by combat. "[Y]ou know that every shot you fire into them sends some one to eternity," a New Jersey

A Union Soldier *Sarah Rosetta Wakeman, alias Private Lyons Wakeman, served in the Union army disguised as a man. She joined the 153rd Regiment, New York State Volunteers.*

(Courtesy of Jackson K. Doane)

artilleryman recalled, "but still you are a prompted by a terrible desire to kill all you can." The deadly cost of battle fell most heavily on the infantry, in which at least three out of four soldiers served. Although repeating rifles had three or four times the range of the old smoothbore muskets, a combination of inexperience, inadequate training, and barriers of terrain curbed their impact. Instead, masses of soldiers faced one another at close range for long periods, exchanging fire until one side or the other gave up and fell back. The high casualty figures at Shiloh and Antietam reflected not advanced technology but the armies' inability to use it effectively. "Our victories … seem to settle nothing," a southern officer wrote in 1862. "It is only so many killed or wounded, leaving the war of blood to go on." Armies gained efficiency in battle through experience, and only late in the war.

In their voluminous letters home (Civil War armies were the most literate armies that had ever existed), volunteers discussed their motives as soldiers. Some Confederates enlisted to defend slavery, which they paired with liberty. "I choose to fight for southern rights and southern liberty" against the "vandals of the North" who were "determined to destroy slavery," a Kentucky Confederate announced. "A stand must be made for African slavery or it is forever lost," wrote a South Carolinian. A small minority of northern soldiers voiced antislavery sentiments early in the war: "I have no heart in this war if the slaves cannot go free," a soldier from Wisconsin declared. Few Union recruits, however, initially shared this antipathy to slavery, and some voiced the opposite view. "I don't want to fire another shot for the negroes and I wish all the abolitionists were in hell," a New York soldier declared. But as war went on, northern soldiers accepted the need to free the slaves, sometimes for humanitarian reasons. "Since I am down here I have learned and seen more of what the horrors of slavery was than I ever knew before," an Ohio officer wrote from Louisiana. Others had more practical goals. By the summer of 1862, Union soldiers in the South had become agents of liberation; many who once had damned the "abolitionist war" now endorsed emancipation as part of the Union war effort. As an Indiana soldier declared, "Every negro we get strengthens us and weakens the rebels."

Ironclads and Cruisers: The Naval War

By plunging its navy into the Confederacy like a dagger, the Union exploited a clear-cut advantage. The North began the war with over forty active warships against none for the South, and by 1865 the United States had the largest navy in the world. Steamships could penetrate the South's excellent river system from any direction.

Yet the Union navy faced an extraordinary challenge: to blockade the South's thirty-five hundred miles of coast. Early in the war, small, sleek Confederate blockade-runners darted with impunity in and out of southern harbors. The North gradually tightened the blockade by outfitting tugs, whalers, excursion steamers, and ferries as well as frigates to patrol southern coasts. The proportion of Confederate blockade-runners that made it through dropped from 90 percent early in the war to 50 percent by 1865. Northern seizure of rebel ports and coastal areas diminished the South's foreign trade even more. In daring amphibious assaults of 1861 and 1862, the Union captured the excellent harbor of Port Royal, South Carolina, the coastal islands off South Carolina, and most of North Carolina's river outlets. Naval patrols and amphibious operations reduced the South's ocean trade to one-third its prewar level.

Despite meager resources, the South strove to offset the North's naval advantage. Early in the war, the Confederacy raised the scuttled Union frigate *Merrimac*, sheathed its sides with an armor of ironplate, rechristened it *Virginia*, and dispatched it to attack wooden Union ships in Hampton Roads, Virginia. The *Merrimac* destroyed two northern warships but met its match in the hastily built Union ironclad the *Monitor*. In the first engagement of ironclads in history, the two ships fought an indecisive battle on March 9, 1862. The South constructed other ironclads and even the first submarine, which dragged a mine through water to sink a Union ship off Charleston in 1864; the "fish" failed to resurface and went down with its prey. But the South never built enough ironclads to over come Northern supremacy in home waters. Nor did Confederate success on the high seas—where wooden, steam-driven commerce raiders wreaked havoc on the Union's merchant marine—tip the balance of war in the South's favor: the North, unlike its foe, did not depend on imports for war materials. The South would lose the naval war.

| The Diplomatic War | While armies and navies clashed in 1861–1862, conflict developed on a third front, diplomacy. At the war's start, the Confederacy sought European recognition of its independence. |

Southern confidence ran high. Planning to establish a colonial empire in Mexico, Napoleon III of France welcomed a permanent division of the United States. The French and British upper classes seemed sympathetic to the South and eager for the downfall of the brash Yankee republic. Furthermore, influential southerners contended, an embargo of cotton exports would bring Britain to its knees. Britain, dependent on the South for four-fifths of its cotton, they reasoned, would break the Union blockade and provoke war with the North rather than endure an embargo.

Leaving nothing to chance, the Confederacy in 1861 dispatched emissaries James Mason to Britain and John Slidell to France to lobby for recognition of an independent South. But their ship, the *Trent*, fell into Union hands, and when the pair ended up in Boston as prisoners, British tempers exploded. Considering one war at a time enough, President Lincoln released Mason and Slidell. But settling the *Trent* affair did not eliminate friction between the United States and Britain. Union diplomats protested the construction in British shipyards of two Confederate commerce raiders, the *Florida* and the *Alabama*. In 1863, the U.S. minister to London, Charles Francis Adams (the son of former president John Quincy Adams), threatened war if two British-built ironclads commissioned by the Confederacy, the so-called Laird rams, were turned over to the South. Britain capitulated to Adams's protests and purchased the rams for its own navy.

On balance, the South fell far short of its diplomatic objectives. Although recognizing the Confederacy as a belligerent, neither Britain nor France ever recognized it as a nation. Basically, the Confederacy overestimated the power of its vaunted **"cotton diplomacy."** Southern threats to Britain about an embargo of cotton exports failed: Planters conducted business as usual by raising cotton and trying to slip it through the blockade. Still, the South's share of the British cotton market slumped from 77 percent in 1860 to only 10 percent in 1865. Forces beyond Southern control had weakened British demand. Bumper cotton crops in the late 1850s had glutted the British market by the start of the war and Britain had found new suppliers in Egypt and India. Gradually, too, the North's tightened blockade restricted southern exports.

(Library of Congress)

Sailors on the *Monitor* *Union sailors on the deck of the USS* Monitor *in 1862. Typically, when photographers arrived, crew members posed near the turret by themselves, apart from officers.*

The South also exaggerated Britain's stake in helping the Confederacy. As a naval power that had frequently blockaded its own enemies, Britain's diplomatic interest lay in supporting the Union blockade in principle; from Britain's standpoint, to help the South break the blockade would set a precedent that could easily boomerang. Finally, although France and Britain often considered recognizing the Confederacy, the timing never seemed quite right. Union success at Antietam in 1862 and Lincoln's subsequent issuance of the **Emancipation Proclamation** dampened Europe's enthusiasm for recognition at a crucial juncture. By transforming the war into a struggle to end slavery, the Emancipation Proclamation stirred pro-Union feeling in antislavery Britain, particularly among liberals and the working class. The proclamation, declared Henry Adams (diplomat Charles Francis Adams's son) from London, "has done more for us here than all of our former victories and all our diplomacy."

EMANCIPATION TRANSFORMS THE WAR, 1863

"I hear old John Brown knocking on the lid of his coffin and shouting 'Let me out! Let me out!'" abolitionist Henry Stanton wrote to his wife after the fall of Fort Sumter. "The Doom of Slavery is at hand." In 1861, this prediction seemed wildly premature. In his inaugural that year, Lincoln had stated bluntly, "I have no purpose, directly or indirectly, to interfere with the institution of slavery in the states where it exists." Yet in two years, the North's priorities shifted. A mix of necessity and conviction thrust emancipation to the forefront of northern war goals.

The rise of emancipation as a war goal reflected the changing character of the war. As the struggle dragged on, demands intensified in the North for the prosecution of "total war"—a war that would shatter the social and economic foundations of the Confederacy. Even northerners who saw no moral value in abolishing slavery started to recognize the military value of emancipation as a tactic to cripple the South.

From Confiscation to Emancipation   Union policy on emancipation developed in stages. As soon as northern troops began to invade the South, questions arose about the disposition of captured rebel property, including slaves. Slaves who fled behind the Union lines were sometimes considered "contraband"—enemy property liable to seizure—and were put to work for the Union army. Some commanders viewed this practice as a useful tool of war; others did not, and the Lincoln administration was evasive. To establish an official policy, Congress in August 1861 passed the first Confiscation Act, which authorized the seizure of all property used in military aid of the rebellion, including slaves. Under this act, slaves who had been employed directly by the Confederate armed forces and who later fled to freedom became "captives of war." But nothing in the act actually freed these individuals, nor did the law apply to fugitive slaves who had not worked for the Confederate military.

Several factors underlay the Union's cautious approach to the confiscation of rebel property. Officially maintaining that the South could not legally secede, Lincoln argued that southerners were still entitled to the Constitution's protection of property. The president also had practical reasons to walk softly. He did not want to alienate slaveholders in the border states or proslavery Democrats in the North. If the Union tampered with slavery, these Democrats feared, southern blacks might come north and compete with white workers. Aware of such fears, Lincoln assured Congress in December 1861 that the war would not become a "remorseless revolutionary struggle."

From the start of the war, however, Radical Republicans pushed Lincoln to adopt a policy of emancipation. Radicals agreed with black abolitionist Frederick Douglass that "to fight against slaveholders without fighting against slavery, is but a half-hearted business." Each Union defeat, moreover, reminded northerners that the Confederacy, with a slave labor force in place, could commit a higher proportion of its white men to battle. The idea of emancipation as a military measure thus gained increasing favor in the North, and in July 1862 Congress passed the second Confiscation Act. This law authorized the seizure of the property of all persons in rebellion and stipulated that slaves who came within Union lines "shall be forever free." The law also authorized the president to employ blacks as soldiers.

Nevertheless, Lincoln continued to stall, even as pressure for emancipation rose. "My paramount object in this struggle is to save the Union, and is not either to save or destroy slavery," Lincoln told antislavery journalist Horace Greeley. "If I could save the Union with out freeing *any* slave, I would do it; and if I could save it by freeing *all* the slaves, I would do it; and if I could do it by freeing some and leaving others alone, I would also do that." Yet Lincoln had always loathed slavery, and by the spring of 1862, he had accepted the Radical position that the war must lead to its abolition. He hesitated principally because he did not want to be stampeded by

Congress into a measure that might disrupt northern unity; he was also reluctant to press the issue while Union armies reeled in defeat. After failing to persuade the Union slave states to emancipate slaves in return for federal compensation, Lincoln drafted a proclamation of emancipation, circulated it within his cabinet, and waited for a right moment to announce it. Finally, after the Union victory in September 1862 at Antietam, Lincoln issued the preliminary Emancipation Proclamation, which declared all slaves under rebel control free as of January 1, 1863. Announcing the plan in advance softened the surprise, tested public opinion, and gave the states still in rebellion an opportunity to preserve slavery by returning to the Union—an opportunity that none, however, took. The final Emancipation Proclamation, issued on January 1, 1863, declared "forever free" all slaves in areas in rebellion.

The proclamation had limited practical impact. Applying only to rebellious areas where the Union had no authority, it exempted the Union slave states and those parts of the Confederacy then under Union control (Tennessee, West Virginia, southern Louisiana, and sections of Virginia). Moreover, it mainly restated what the second Confiscation Act had already stipulated: if rebels' slaves fell into Union hands, those slaves would be free. Yet the proclamation was a brilliant political stroke. By issuing it as a military measure in his role as commander-in-chief, Lincoln pacified northern conservatives. Its aim, he stressed, was to injure the Confederacy, threaten its property, heighten its dread, sap its morale, and hasten its demise. By issuing the proclamation himself, Lincoln stole the initiative from the Radicals in Congress and mobilized support for the Union among European liberals far more dramatically than could any act of Congress. Furthermore, the proclamation pushed the border states toward emancipation: by the end of the war, Maryland and Missouri would abolish slavery. Finally, it increased slaves' incentives to escape as northern troops approached. Fulfilling the worst of Confederate fears, it enabled blacks to join the Union army.

The Emancipation Proclamation did not end slavery everywhere or free "*all* the slaves." But it changed the war. From 1863 on, the war for the Union would also be a war against slavery.

Crossing Union Lines   The attacks and counterattacks of opposing armies turned many slaves into pawns of war. Some slaves became free when Union soldiers overran their areas. Others fled their plantations as federal troops approached to take refuge behind Union lines. A few were freed by northern assaults, only to be re-enslaved by Confederate counterthrusts. One North Carolina slave celebrated liberation on twelve occasions, as often as Union soldiers marched through his locale. By 1865, about half a million slaves were in Union hands.

In the first year of the war, when the Union had not yet established a policy toward "contrabands" (fugitive slaves), masters could retrieve them from the Union army. After 1862, however, slaves who crossed Union lines were considered free. Many freedmen served in army camps as cooks, teamsters, and laborers. Some worked for pay on abandoned plantations or were leased out to planters who swore allegiance to the Union. In camps or outside them, freedmen had cause to question the value of liberation. Deductions for clothing, rations, and medicine ate up most of their earnings. Labor contracts often tied them to their employers for long periods. Moreover, freedmen encountered fierce prejudice among Yankee soldiers, many of whom feared that emancipation would propel postwar blacks north.

The best solution to the "question of what to do with the darkies," wrote one northern soldier, "would be to shoot them."

But this was not the whole story. Fugitive slaves who aided the Union army as spies and scouts helped to break down ingrained bigotry. "The sooner we get rid of our foolish prejudice the better for us," a Massachusetts soldier wrote. Before the war's end, northern missionary groups and freedmen's aid societies sent agents south to work among freed slaves, distribute relief, and organize schools. In March 1865, just before hostilities ceased, Congress created the **Freedmen's Bureau,** an agency responsible for the relief, education, and employment of former slaves. The Freedmen's Bureau law also stipulated that forty acres of abandoned or confiscated land could be leased to each freedman or southern Unionist, with an option to buy after three years. This was the first and only time that Congress provided for the redistribution of confiscated Confederate property.

Black Soldiers in the Union Army   In the war's first year, the Union had rejected African-American soldiers. After the second Confiscation Act, Union generals formed black regiments in occupied New Orleans and on the Sea Islands off the coasts of South Carolina and Georgia. Only after the Emancipation Proclamation did large-scale enlistment begin. Prominent African-Americans such as Frederick Douglass worked as recruiting agents in northern cities. Douglass linked black military service to black claims as citizens. "Once let the black man get ... an eagle on his button, and a musket on his shoulder and bullets in his pocket, and there is no power on earth which can deny that he has earned the right to citizenship." Union drafts now included blacks, and freedmen in refugee camps throughout the occupied South enlisted. By the war's end, 186,000 African-Americans had served in the Union army, one-tenth of all Union soldiers. Fully half came from the Confederate states (see Going to the Source).

White Union soldiers often objected to black recruits on racial grounds. But some, including Colonel Thomas Wentworth Higginson, a liberal minister and former John Brown supporter who led a black regiment, welcomed black soldiers. "Nobody knows anything about these men who has not seen them in battle," Higginson exulted after a successful raid in Florida in 1863. "There is a fierce energy about them beyond anything of which I have ever read, except it be the French Zouaves [French troops in North Africa]." Even Union soldiers who held blacks in contempt came to approve of "anything that will kill a rebel." All blacks served in separate regiments under white officers. Colonel Robert Gould Shaw of the 54th Massachusetts Infantry, an elite black regiment, died in combat—as did half his troops—in an attack on Fort Wagner in Charleston harbor in July 1863.

Black soldiers suffered a far higher mortality rate than white troops. Typically assigned to labor detachments or garrison duty, blacks were less likely than whites to be killed in action but more likely to die of illness in bacteria-ridden garrisons. The Confederacy refused to treat captured black soldiers as prisoners of war, a policy that prevented their exchange for Southern prisoners. Instead, Jefferson Davis ordered all blacks taken in battle to be sent back to the states from which they came, to be re-enslaved or executed. In a notorious incident, when Confederate troops under General Nathan Bedford Forrest captured Fort Pillow, Tennessee, in 1864, they massacred many black soldiers who had surrendered—an act that provoked outcries but no retaliation from the North.

GOING TO THE SOURCE

A Union Commander Praises Black Troops

Thomas Wentworth Higginson (1823–1911) of Massachusetts—liberal minister, abolitionist, supporter of John Brown, and mentor of poet Emily Dickinson—accepted an offer in 1862 to command the First South Carolina Volunteers, the Union's first African-American regiment. Higginson led his troops, all former slaves, on skirmishes in Georgia and Florida; the regiment also took part in a larger Union attack in South Carolina. Looking back on his war experience, Higginson praised the admirable traits of his troops. He also stressed the strategic significance of African-American soldiers (and their commanders).

I often asked myself why it was that, with this capacity of daring and endurance, they had not kept the land in a perpetual flame of insurrection; why, especially since the opening of the war, they had kept so still. The answer was to be found in the peculiar temperament of the [race], in their religious faith, and in the habit of patience that centuries had fortified. . . .

It always seemed to me that, had I been a slave, my life would have been one long scheme of insurrection. But I learned to respect the patient self-control of those who had waited till the course of events should open a better way. When it came, they accepted it. Insurrection on their part would at once have divided the Northern sentiment; and a large part of our army would have joined with the Southern army to hunt them down. By their waiting till we needed them, their freedom was secured.

Two things chiefly surprised me in their feeling toward their former masters—the absence of affection and the absence of revenge. . . . I never heard one speak of the masters except as natural enemies. Yet they were perfectly discriminating as to individuals; many of them claimed to have kind owners, and some expressed gratitude toward them for particular favors received. It was not the individuals,

Well into the war, African-American soldiers faced inequities in pay. White soldiers earned $13 a month plus a $3.50 clothing allowance; black privates received only $10 a month, with clothing deducted. "We have come out like men and we Expected to be Treated as men but we have bin Treated more Like Dogs then men," a black soldier complained to Secretary of War Edwin Stanton. In June 1864, Congress belatedly equalized the earnings of black and white soldiers.

Although fraught with hardships and inequities, military service became a symbol of citizenship for blacks. It proved that "black men can give blows as well as take them," Frederick Douglass declared. "Liberty won by white men would lose half its lustre." Above all, the use of black soldiers, especially former slaves, struck a telling blow against the Confederacy. "They will make good soldiers," General Grant wrote to Lincoln in 1863, "and taking them from the enemy weakens him in the same proportion they strengthen us."

Slavery in Wartime   Anxious white southerners on the home front felt perched on a volcano. "We should be practically helpless should the negroes rise," declared a Louisiana planter's daughter, "since there are so few men left at home." When Mary Boykin Chesnut of South Carolina but the ownership, of which they complained. That they saw to be a wrong which no special kindnesses could right. On this, as on all points connected with slavery, they understood the matter as clearly as [William Lloyd] Garrison or [Wendell] Phillips.... After all, personal experience is the best logician....

No doubt there were reasons why this particular war was an especially favorable test of the [black] soldiers. They had more to fight for than the whites. Besides the flag and the Union, they had home and wife and child. They fought with ropes around their necks, and when orders were issued that the officers of [black] troops should be put to death on capture, they took a grim satisfaction. It helped their *esprit de corps* immensely....

We who served with the black troops have this peculiar satisfaction, that, whatever dignity or sacredness the memories of the war may have to others, they have more to us.... [T]he peculiar privilege of associating with an outcast race, of training it to defend its rights ... this was our special meed [task]. The vacillating policy of the Government sometimes filled other officers with doubt and shame; until the Negro had justice, they were but defending liberty with one hand and crushing it with the other. From this inconsistency we were free. Whatever the Government did, we at least were working in the right direction.... We had touched the pivot of the war.... Till the blacks were armed, there was no guarantee of their freedom. It was their demeanor under arms that shamed the nation into recognizing them as men.

Questions

1. *In what ways did Higginson's stance as an abolitionist affect his view of his troops?*
2. *Why (to Higginson) was the role of African-American soldiers especially significant ("the pivot of the war")?*

Go to www.cengagebrain.com for additional primary sources on this period.

Source: Thomas Wentworth Higginson, *Army Life in a Black Regiment* [1870] (New York: Penguin Books, 1997), 192–193, 194–195, 205–206.

learned of her cousin's murder in bed by two trusted house slaves, she became almost frantic. "The murder," Chesnut wrote, "has clearly driven us all wild." To control 3 million slaves, white southerners tightened slave patrols, moved entire plantations to relative safety from Union troops in Texas or in upland regions of the coastal South, and spread fear among slaves. "The whites would tell the colored people not to go to the Yankees, for they would harness them to carts ... in place of horses," reported Susie King Taylor, a black fugitive from Savannah.

Some slaves remained faithful to their owners and helped hide family treasures from marauding Union soldiers. Others wavered between loyalty and hunger for freedom: one slave accompanied his master to war, rescued him when he was wounded, and then escaped on his master's horse. Given a choice between freedom and bondage, slaves usually chose freedom. Few slaves helped the North as dramatically as Robert Smalls, a hired-out slave boatman who turned over a Confederate steamer to the Union navy, but most who had a chance to flee to Union lines did so. The idea of freedom was irresistible. On learning of his freedom from a Union soldier, a Virginia coachman dressed in his master's clothes, "put on his best watch and chain, took his stick, and ... told him [the master] that he might for the future drive his own coach."

Most slaves, however, lacked means of escape and remained under their owners' nominal control. Despite fears of southern whites, no general uprising of slaves occurred; the Confederacy continued to impress thousands of slaves to toil in war plants, army camps, and field hospitals. But even slaves with no chance of flight were alert to the opportunity that war provided and swiftly tested the limits of enforced labor. As a Savannah mistress noted as early as 1861, the slaves "show a very different face from what they have had heretofore." Moreover, wartime conditions reduced slave productivity. With most white men off at war, the master-slave relationship weakened. White women and boys on plantations complained of their difficulty in controlling slaves, who commonly refused to work, labored inefficiently, or destroyed property. A Texas wife contended that her slaves were "trying all they can, it seems to me, to aggravate me" by neglecting the stock, breaking plows, and tearing down fences. "You may give your Negroes away," she finally wrote despairingly to her husband in 1864.

Whether southern slaves fled to freedom or merely stopped working, they acted effectively to defy slavery, liberate themselves from its regulations, and undermine the plantation system. Thus southern slavery disintegrated even as the Confederacy fought to preserve it. Hard-pressed by Union armies and short of manpower, the Confederate Congress in 1864 considered the drastic step of impressing slaves into its army as soldiers in exchange for their freedom at the war's end. Robert E. Lee favored the policy on the grounds that if the Confederacy did not arm its slaves, the Union would. Others were adamantly opposed. "If slaves will make good soldiers," a Georgia general argued, "our whole theory of slavery is wrong." Originally against arming slaves, Jefferson Davis changed his mind in 1865. In March 1865, the Confederate Congress narrowly passed a bill to arm three hundred thousand slave soldiers, although it omitted any mention of emancipation. Since the war ended a few weeks later, however, the plan was never put into effect.

Although the Confederacy's decision to arm the slaves came too late to affect the war, debate over arming them hurt southern morale. By then, the South's military position had started to deteriorate.

The Turning Point of 1863   In the summer and fall of 1863, Union fortunes dramatically improved in every theater of war. Yet the year began badly. The Northern slide, which had started with Burnside's defeat at Fredericksburg, Virginia, in December 1862, persisted into the spring of 1863. Burnside's successor, General Joseph "Fighting Joe" Hooker, a windbag fond of issuing pompous proclamations to his troops, suffered a crushing defeat in May 1863 at Chancellorsville, Virginia, where he was routed by Lee and Stonewall Jackson. Chancellorsville proved costly for the South—Confederate sentries accidentally killed Stonewall Jackson—but it humiliated the North; Hooker had twice as many men as Lee. Reports from the West brought no better news. Repulsed at Shiloh in western Tennessee, the Confederates still had a powerful army in central Tennessee under General Braxton Bragg. Furthermore, despite repeated efforts, Grant was unable to take Vicksburg; the two-hundred-mile stretch of the Mississippi between Vicksburg and Port Hudson remained in rebel hands.

Union fortunes rose after Chancellorsville when Lee decided to invade the North. Lee needed supplies that war-wracked Virginia could no longer provide; he also hoped to draw Northern troops from besieged Vicksburg to the eastern theater. Lee envisioned a major Confederate victory on northern soil that would increase the sway of pro-peace Democrats and gain European recognition of the Confederacy. Moving his seventy-five thousand men down the Shenandoah Valley, Lee pressed forward into southern Pennsylvania. Lincoln, rejecting Hooker's plan to attack an unprotected Richmond, replaced Hooker with the more reliable George G. Meade.

Early in July 1863, Lee's offensive ground to a halt at a Pennsylvania road junction, Gettysburg (see Map 15.2). Confederates foraging for shoes in the town stumbled into some Union cavalry. Soon both sides called for reinforcements, and the war's greatest battle, the **Battle of Gettysburg,** began. On July 1, Meade's troops installed themselves in hills south of town along a line that resembled a fishhook: the shank ran along Cemetery Ridge and a northern hook encircled Culp's Hill. By the end of the first day, Meade's army outnumbered the Confederates ninety thousand to seventy-five thousand. On July 2, Lee rejected advice to plant his army in a defensive stance between Meade's forces and Washington and instead attacked the Union flanks, with some success. But because Confederate assaults were uncoordinated,

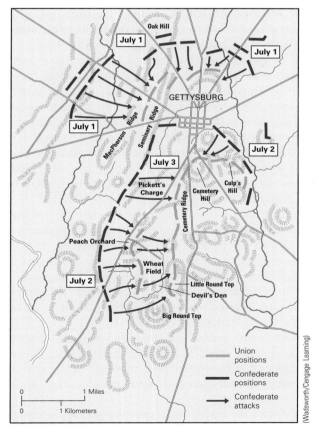

MAP 15.2 Gettysburg, 1863

The failure of Pickett's charge against the Union center on July 3 was the decisive action in the war's greatest battle.

and some southern generals disregarded orders and struck where they chose, the Union moved in reinforcements and regained its earlier losses.

By the afternoon of July 3, believing that the Union flanks had been weakened, Lee attacked Cemetery Ridge in the center of the North's defensive line. After southern cannon shelled the line, a massive infantry force of fifteen thousand Confederates, Pickett's charge, moved in. But as Confederate cannon sank into the ground and fired too high, Union fire wiped out the rebel charge; rifled weapons proved their deadly effectiveness. At day's end, Confederate bodies littered the field. More than half of Pickett's troops were dead, wounded, or captured. When Lee withdrew to Virginia on July 4, he had lost seventeen generals and over one-third of his army. Total Union and Confederate casualties numbered almost fifty thousand. Although Meade failed to pursue and destroy the retreating rebels, he had halted Lee's foray into the North; the Union rejoiced.

Almost simultaneously, the North won a strategic victory in the West, at the **Battle of Vicksburg;** here, Grant finally pierced Vicksburg's defenses. Situated on a bluff on the east bank of the Mississippi, Vicksburg was protected on the west by the river and on the north by hills, forests, and swamps. It could be attacked only over a thin strip of dry land to its east and south. Positioned to the north of Vicksburg, Grant moved his troops far to the west of the city and down to a point on the river south of Vicksburg. Meanwhile, Union gunboats and supply ships ran past the Confederate batteries overlooking the river at Vicksburg (sustaining considerable damage) to transport Grant's army across to the east bank. Grant then swung in a large semicircle, first northeastward to capture Jackson, the capital of Mississippi, and then westward back to Vicksburg. After a six-week siege, in which famished soldiers and civilians in Vicksburg survived by eating mules and even rats, General John C. Pemberton surrendered his thirty-thousand-man garrison to Grant on July 4, the day after Pickett's charge at Gettysburg. Port Hudson, the last Confederate holdout on the Mississippi, soon surrendered to another Union army. "The Father of Waters flows unvexed to the sea," Lincoln declared.

A second crucial Union victory in the West soon followed. General William S. Rosecrans fought and maneuvered Braxton Bragg's Confederate army out of central Tennessee and into Chattanooga, in the southeastern tip of the state. Forced to evacuate Chattanooga, Bragg defeated the pursuing Rosecrans at the bloody Battle of Chickamauga (September 19–20, 1863) and drove him back into Chattanooga. The arrival of Grant and reinforcements from the Army of the Potomac broke Bragg's siege of Chattanooga in November. With Chattanooga secure, the way lay open for a Union strike into Georgia.

Union successes in the second half of 1863 stiffened Northern will to keep fighting and plunged some rebel leaders into despair. Hearing of Vicksburg's fall, Confederate ordnance chief Josiah Gorgas lamented, "Yesterday we rode the pinnacle of success—today absolute ruin seems our portion. The Confederacy totters to its destruction."

Totter it might, but the South was far from beaten. Although the outcome at Gettysburg quashed southerners' hopes for victory on northern soil, Lee could still defend Virginia. The loss of Vicksburg and the Mississippi cut the Confederacy in half but the rebel states west of the river—Arkansas, Louisiana, and Texas— could still provide soldiers. Even with the loss of Chattanooga, the Confederacy retained most of the Carolinas, Georgia, Florida, and Mississippi. Few thought the fate of the Confederacy had been sealed.

WAR AND SOCIETY, NORTH AND SOUTH

Extending beyond battlefields, the Civil War engulfed two economies and societies. By 1863, stark contrasts emerged: superior resources enabled the Union to meet wartime demand as the imperiled Confederacy could not. But both regions experienced labor shortages and inflation; both confronted problems of disunity and dissent. In both societies, war impinged on everyday life. Families were disrupted and dislocated, especially in the South. Women on both sides assumed new roles at home, in the workplace, and in relief efforts.

The War's Economic Impact: The North

War affected the Union's economy unevenly. Some industries fared poorly: deprived of raw cotton, the cotton-textile industry went into a tailspin. But industries directly linked to the war effort, such as the manufacture of arms, shoes, and clothing, profited from huge government contracts; the Union army needed a million uniforms a year. Railroads flourished. Some privately owned lines, which had overbuilt before the war, doubled their volume of traffic. In 1862, the federal government itself went into the railroad business; it established the United States Military Railroads (USMRR) to carry troops and supplies to the front. By 1865, the USMRR was the world's largest railroad.

Republicans in Congress, now a big majority, actively promoted business growth. Overriding Democratic foes, they hiked the tariff in 1862 and again in 1864 to protect domestic industries. The Republican-sponsored Pacific Railroad Act of 1862 provided for the development of a transcontinental railroad, an idea that had foundered before the war on feuds over which route such a railroad should follow. With the South out of the picture and unable to demand a southern route, Congress chose a northern route from Omaha to San Francisco. Chartering the Union Pacific and Central Railroad corporations, Congress gave each large land grants and generous loans: more than 60 million acres and $20 million. Issuance of greenbacks and the creation of national banking rules brought a measure of uniformity to the nation's financial system.

Republicans designed these measures to benefit all social classes, and partially succeeded. The **Homestead Act,** passed in 1862, embodied the party's ideal of "free soil, free labor, free men." It granted 160 acres of public land to settlers after five years of residence on the land. By 1865, twenty thousand homesteaders occupied new land in the West under the Homestead Act. Republicans also sponsored the **Morrill Land Grant Act** of 1862, which gave the states proceeds of public lands to fund the start of universities that offered "such branches of learning as are related to agriculture and mechanic arts." The law spurred the growth of large state universities, mainly in the Midwest and West, including Michigan State, Iowa State, and Purdue, among many others.

In general, however, the war benefited wealthy citizens more than others. Corrupt contractors grew rich by selling the government substandard merchandise such as the notorious "shoddy" clothing made from compressed rags, which quickly disintegrated. Speculators made millions in the gold market. Because the price of gold in relation to greenbacks rose whenever public confidence in the government fell, gold speculators gained from Union defeats. Businessmen with access to scarce commodities also reaped astounding profits. Manpower shortages stimulated wartime demand for the mechanical reaper that Cyrus McCormick had patented in 1834. Paid for reapers in greenbacks, which he distrusted, McCormick at once reinvested them in pig iron and watched in glee as wartime demand almost doubled its price.

Ordinary Americans suffered. Higher protective tariffs, wartime excise taxes, and inflation bloated the prices of finished goods, while wages lagged 20 percent or more behind cost increases. Lagging wages became severe as boys and women replaced army-bound men in government offices and factories. For women employees, entry into government jobs—even at half the pay of male clerks—represented a major advance. But employers' access to low-paid labor undercut the bargaining power of men who remained in the work force.

Many workers decried low wages, and some, such as cigar makers and locomotive engineers, formed national unions, a process that would accelerate after the war. Employers denounced worker complaints as unpatriotic hindrances to the war effort, and in 1864, the government diverted troops from combat to put down protests in war industries from New York to the Midwest.

The War's Economic Impact: The South

The war shattered the South's economy. Indeed, if both regions are considered together, the war retarded *American* economic growth. For example, American commodity output, which had registered huge increases of 51 percent and 62 percent in the 1840s and 1850s respectively, rose only 22 percent in the 1860s. This modest gain depended wholly on the North, for in the 1860s commodity output in the South actually *declined* 39 percent.

Multiple factors offset the South's substantial wartime industrial growth. War wrecked the South's railroads; invading Union troops tore up tracks, twisted rails, and burned railroad cars. Cotton production, once the foundation of southern prosperity, sank from more than 4 million bales in 1861 to three hundred thousand bales in 1865; Union invasions took their toll on production, particularly in Tennessee and Louisiana.

Union invaders also occupied the South's food-growing regions, and in areas under Confederate control, the manpower drain cut yields per acre of crops like wheat and corn; scarcities abounded. Agricultural shortages compounded severe inflation. By 1863, salt selling for $1.25 a sack in New York City cost $60 in the Confederacy. Food riots erupted in 1863 in Mobile, Atlanta, and Richmond; in Richmond ironworkers' wives paraded to demand lower food prices.

Part of the blame for Southern food shortages rested with planters. Despite government pleas to grow more food, many planters continued to raise cotton, with far-reaching consequences. To feed hungry armies, the Confederacy had to impress food from civilians, a policy that evoked resentment and spurred military desertions. Food-impressment agents usually concentrated on the easiest targets—farms run by the wives of active soldiers. "I don't want you to stop fighting them Yankees," wrote the wife of an Alabama soldier, "but try and get off and come home and fix us all up some and then you can go back." By the end of 1864, half of the Confederacy's soldiers were absent from their units.

The manpower drain that hampered food production reshaped the lives of southern white women. With three out of four white men in the military over the course of the war, Confederate women found their locales transformed. "There is a vacant chair in every house," mourned a Kentucky Confederate girl. Left in charge of farms and plantations, women faced new challenges and chronic shortages. As manufactured goods became scarce, southern homemakers wove cloth and devised replacements for goods no longer attainable, including inks, dyes, coffee, shoes, and wax candles. The war's proximity made many Confederate women into refugees. Property destruction or even the threat of Union invasions drove families away from their homes; those with slave property to preserve, in particular, sought to flee before Union forces arrived. Areas remote from military action, especially Texas, were favored destinations. Disorienting and disheartening, the refugee experience sapped morale. "I will never feel like myself again," a Georgia woman who had escaped from the path of Union troops wrote to her husband in 1864.

In one respect, the persistence of cotton growing helped the South: cotton became the basis for the Confederacy's flourishing trade with the enemy. The U.S. Congress virtually legalized this trade in July 1861 by allowing northern commerce with southerners loyal to the Union. In practice, of course, it proved impossible to tell loyalists from rebels; northern traders happily swapped bacon, salt, blankets, and other products for southern cotton. By 1864, traffic through the lines provided enough food for Lee's Army of Northern Virginia. A northern congressman lamented that the Union's policy was "to feed an army and fight it at the same time."

Trading with the enemy alleviated Southern food shortages but damaged morale. The prospect of traffic with Yankees gave planters an incentive to keep growing cotton, and fattened middlemen. "Oh! the extortioners," complained a Confederate war office clerk in Richmond. "Our patriotism is mainly in the army and among the ladies of the South. The avarice and cupidity of men at home could only be exceeded by ravenous wolves."

Dealing with Dissent

Both wartime governments faced mounting dissent and disloyalty. Among Confederates, dissent took two basic forms. First, a vocal group of states' rights activists, notably Vice President Alexander Stephens and governors Zebulon Vance of North Carolina and Joseph Brown of Georgia, persistently attacked Jefferson Davis's government as despotic. Second, pro-Union sentiment flourished among a segment of Confederate common people, particularly those in the Appalachian Mountain region that ran from western North Carolina through Tennessee into northern Georgia and Alabama. Nonslaveholding small farmers who predominated here saw Confederate rebellion as a slave owners' conspiracy. Resentful of such measures as the 20-Negro exemption from conscription, they voiced reluctance to fight for what a North Carolinian called "an adored trinity," of cotton, slaves, and "chivalry." "All they want," an Alabama farmer complained of the planters, "is to get you pupt up and to fight for their infurnal Negroes and after you do there fighting you may kiss there hine parts for o they care."

On the whole, the Confederate government responded mildly to popular disaffection. In 1862, the Confederate Congress gave Jefferson Davis the power to suspend the writ of *habeas corpus*, but Davis used his power only sparingly.

Lincoln faced similar challenges in the North, where the Democratic minority opposed both emancipation and wartime growth of centralized power. Although "War Democrats" conceded that war was necessary to preserve the Union, "Peace Democrats" (called "Copperheads" by their opponents, to suggest resemblance to a species of easily concealed poisonous snakes) demanded a truce and a peace conference. They charged that administration war policy would "exterminate the South," make reconciliation impossible, and spark "terrible social change and revolution."

Strongest in the border states, the Midwest, and the northeastern cities, the Democrats mobilized support among farmers of southern background in the Ohio Valley and urban workers, especially recent immigrants, who feared job loss to free blacks. In 1863, this volatile brew of antagonisms exploded into antidraft protests in several cities. Most violent were the **New York City Draft Riots** in July. Enraged by the first drawing of names under the Enrollment Act and by a longshoremen's strike in which blacks had been used as strikebreakers, mobs of Irish working class men and women roamed the streets for four days until suppressed by federal troops. The city's Irish loathed the idea of being drafted to fight a war on behalf of the slaves who, once free, might migrate north to compete for jobs, and they resented the provision of the draft law that allowed the rich to purchase substitutes. The rioters lynched at least a dozen blacks, injured hundreds more, and burned draft offices, the homes of wealthy Republicans, and the Colored Orphan Asylum.

President Lincoln's dispatch of federal troops to quash these riots typified his forceful response to dissent. Lincoln imposed martial law with far less hesitancy than Davis. After suspending the writ of *habeas corpus* in Maryland in 1861, he barred it nationwide in 1863 and authorized the arrest of rebels, draft resisters, and those engaged in "any disloyal practice." The responses of Davis and Lincoln to dissent underscored the differences between the two regions' wartime political systems. As we have seen, Davis lacked the institutionalization of dissent provided by party conflict and had to tread warily, lest his foes brand him a despot. In contrast, Lincoln and other Republicans used dissent to rally patriotic fervor against the Democrats.

Forceful as he was, Lincoln did not unleash a reign of terror against dissent. In general, the North preserved freedom of the press, speech, and assembly. Of some fifteen thousand civilians arrested during the war, most were quickly released. A few cases aroused concern. In 1864, a military commission sentenced an Indiana man to be hanged for an alleged plot to free Confederate prisoners. The Supreme Court reversed his conviction two years later; it ruled that civilians could not be tried by military courts when the civil courts were open (*Ex parte* Milligan, 1866). Of more concern were arrests of politicians, notably Clement L. Vallandigham, an Ohio Peace Democrat. Courting arrest, Vallandigham challenged the administration, denounced the suspension of *habeas corpus*, proposed an armistice, and in 1863 was sentenced to jail for the war's duration by a military commission. When Ohio Democrats then nominated him for governor, Lincoln changed the sentence to banishment. Escorted to enemy lines in Tennessee, Vallandigham was left in the hands of bewildered Confederates and eventually fled to Canada. The Supreme Court refused to review his case.

The Medical War   Wartime patriotism impelled civilians North and South, especially women, to work tirelessly to aid soldiers. The **United States Sanitary Commission,** formed early in the war by civilians to help the Union's medical bureau, depended on women volunteers.

Described by one woman as a "great artery that bears the people's love to the army," the commission raised funds at "sanitary fairs," bought and distributed supplies, ran special kitchens to supplement army rations, tracked down the missing, and inspected army camps. The volunteers' exploits became legendary. One poor widow, Mary Ann "Mother" Bickerdyke, served sick and wounded Union soldiers. When a doctor asked by what authority she demanded supplies, she shot back: "From the Lord God Almighty. Do you have anything that ranks higher than that?"

Women also reached out to the battlefront as nurses. Some thirty-two hundred women nurses served the Union and the Confederacy. Famous for her tireless campaigns on behalf of the insane, Dorothea Dix became head of the Union's nursing corps. Clara Barton, an obscure clerk in the U.S. Patent Office, found ingenious ways to channel medicine to the sick and wounded. Learning of Union movements before Antietam, Barton showed up at the battlefield on the eve of the clash with a wagonload of supplies. When army surgeons ran out of bandages and started to dress wounds with corn husks, she raced forward with lint and bandages. After the war, in 1881, she would found the American Red Cross.

The Confederacy, too, had legendary nurses. One, Sally Tompkins, was commissioned a captain for her hospital work; another, Belle Boyd, a nurse and spy, once dashed through a field, waving her bonnet, to give Stonewall Jackson information. Danger stalked nurses in hospitals far from the front. Author Louisa May Alcott, a nurse at the Union Hotel Hospital in Washington, D.C., contracted typhoid. Wherever they worked, nurses witnessed haunting sights. "About the amputating table," one reported, "lay large piles of human flesh ... the stiffened membranes seemed to be clutching oftentimes at our clothing."

Pioneered by British reformer Florence Nightingale in the 1850s, nursing was a new vocation for women and to critics, a brazen departure from women's proper sphere. Male doctors were unsure how to react to women in the wards. Some saw the potential for mischief, but others viewed women nurses as potentially useful. The miasma theory of disease (see Chapter 11) won wide respect among physicians and stimulated valuable sanitary measures. In partial consequence, the ratio of disease to battle deaths was much lower in the Civil War than in the Mexican-American War. Still, for every soldier killed during the Civil War, two died of disease. "These Big Battles is not as Bad as the fever," a North Carolina soldier wrote. Scientific investigations that would lead to the germ theory of disease were only starting in the 1860s. Arm and leg wounds frequently led to gangrene or tetanus, and typhoid, malaria, diarrhea, and dysentery raged through army camps.

Prison camps posed a special problem. Prisoner exchanges between North and South, at first common, collapsed by midwar, partly because the South refused to exchange black prisoners and partly because the North gradually concluded that exchanges benefited the manpower-short Confederacy more than the Union. As a result, the two sides had far more prisoners than either could handle; prisoners on both sides suffered. Miserable conditions plagued southern camps. Squalor and insufficient rations turned the Confederate prison camp at Andersonville, Georgia, into a virtual death camp; three thousand prisoners a month (out of a total of thirty-two thousand) were dying there by August 1864. After the war an outraged northern public secured the execution of Andersonville's commandant. Deterioration of the southern economy contributed massively to the wretched state of southern prison camps. Union camps, though not much better, had lower fatality rates.

The War and
Women's Rights
Nurses and Sanitary Commission workers were not the only women to serve society in wartime. North and south, thousands of women took over jobs vacated by men in offices and mills. Home industry revived at all levels of society. In rural areas, where manpower dwindled, women often plowed, planted, and harvested. "Women were in the field everywhere," an Illinois woman recalled. "No rebuffs could chill their zeal; no reverses repress their ardor."

Few women worked more effectively for their region's cause than Philadelphia-born Anna E. Dickinson. After losing her job in the federal mint (for denouncing General George McClellan as a traitor), Dickinson threw herself into hospital volunteer work and public lecturing. Her lecture "Hospital Life," about soldiers' suffering, won attention among Republican politicians. In 1863, hard-pressed by the Democrats, they invited Dickinson, then scarcely twenty-one, to campaign for Republicans in New Hampshire and Connecticut. Articulate and poised, Dickinson captivated her listeners. Soon Republican candidates who had dismissed the offer of aid from a woman begged her to campaign for them.

(Massachusetts Commandery Military Order of the Loyal Legion and the U.S. Army Military History Institute)

Andersonville Prison *Started in early 1864, the overcrowded Andersonville prison in southwest Georgia provided no shelter for its inmates, who built tentlike structures out of blankets, sticks, or whatever they could find. Exposure, disease, and poor sanitation contributed to a mortality rate almost double that in other Confederate prison camps. The prisoners in this unusual image, made by a Confederate photographer, barely had room to stand.*

Northern women's rights advocates hoped that the war would yield equality for women as well as freedom for slaves. Not only should a grateful North reward women for their wartime services, these women reasoned, but it should recognize the link between black rights and women's rights. In 1863, Elizabeth Cady Stanton and Susan B. Anthony organized the **Woman's National Loyal League.** The league gathered four hundred thousand signatures on a petition calling for a constitutional amendment to abolish slavery; its founders used the organization to promote woman suffrage as well.

Despite high expectations, the war brought women little closer to economic or political equality. Women in offices and factories continued to earn less than men. Sanitary Commission workers and most wartime nurses, as volunteers, earned nothing. Nor did the war alter the prevailing definition of woman's sphere. In 1860, that sphere already included charitable and benevolent activities; in wartime the scope of benevolence grew to embrace care for the wounded. Yet men continued to dominate the medical profession. The keenest disappointment of women's rights advocates lay in their failure to capitalize on rising abolitionist sentiment to secure the vote for women. Northern politicians saw little value in woman suffrage. The *New York Herald*, which supported the Loyal League's attack on slavery, dismissed its call for woman suffrage as "nonsense and tomfoolery." Stanton wrote bitterly, a few years later, "Women's cause is in deep water."

THE UNION VICTORIOUS, 1864–1865

Despite successes at Gettysburg and Vicksburg in 1863, the Union stood no closer to taking Richmond at the start of 1864 than in 1861; most of the Lower South still remained under Confederate control. Union invasion had taken a toll on the South, but inability to destroy the main Confederate armies eroded the Union's will to attack. War weariness strengthened Northern Democrats and jeopardized Lincoln's prospects for reelection.

The year 1864 was crucial for the North. While Grant dueled with Lee in the East, a Union army under William T. Sherman attacked from Tennessee and captured Atlanta in early September. Atlanta's fall boosted northern morale and helped to reelect Lincoln. The curtain now rose on the last act of war: after taking Atlanta, Sherman marched across Georgia and on into South Carolina; in Virginia, Grant backed Lee into trenches around Petersburg and Richmond and brought on the Confederacy's collapse.

The Eastern Theater in 1864   Early in 1864, Lincoln made Grant commander of all Union armies and promoted him to lieutenant general. At first glance, the stony-faced, cigar-puffing Grant seemed an unlikely candidate for so exalted a rank, held previously only by George Washington. Grant's only distinguishing characteristics were his ever-present cigars and a penchant for whittling sticks into chips. But Grant's success in the West had made him the Union's most popular general. With his promotion, Grant moved his headquarters to the Army of the Potomac in the East and mapped a strategy for final victory.

Like Lincoln, Grant believed that the Union had to coordinate its attacks on all fronts in order to exploit its numerical advantage and prevent the South from shifting troops between eastern and western theaters. Accordingly, Grant planned a sustained offensive against Lee in the East while sending Sherman to attack in Georgia. Sherman's mission was to break up the Confederate army and "to get into the interior of the enemy's country ... inflicting all the damage you can."

The war's pace quickened dramatically. In early May 1864, Grant led 118,000 men against Lee's sixty-four thousand in a forested area near Fredericksburg, Virginia, called the Wilderness. Checked by Lee in a series of bloody engagements (the Battle of the Wilderness, May 5–7), Grant then suffered new reverses at Spotsylvania on May 12 and Cold Harbor on June 3. These engagements were fierce; at Cold Harbor, Grant lost seven thousand men in a single hour. Oliver Wendell Holmes, Jr., a Union lieutenant and later a Supreme Court justice, wrote home how "immense the butcher's bill has been." Instead of recoiling, Grant persisted; he forced Lee to pull back to the trenches guarding Petersburg and Richmond.

Once entrenched, Lee could no longer swing around to the Union rear, cut Yankee supply lines, or as at Chancellorsville, surprise the Union's main force. Lee dispatched General Jubal A. Early on raids down the Shenandoah Valley, which served Confederates as a granary and an indirect way to menace Washington. Grant countered by ordering General Philip Sheridan to march through the valley from the north and "lay it waste." By September 1864, Sheridan controlled the Shenandoah Valley.

While Grant and Lee grappled in the Wilderness, Sherman led ninety-eight thousand men into Georgia. Opposing him with fifty-three thousand Confederate troops (soon reinforced to sixty-five thousand), General Joseph Johnston retreated toward Atlanta. Johnston planned to conserve strength for a final defense of Atlanta while forcing Sherman to extend his supply lines. Dismayed by Johnston's defensive strategy, Jefferson Davis replaced him with the adventurous John B. Hood. Hood, who had lost the use of an arm at Gettysburg and a leg at Chickamauga, had to be strapped to his saddle; but for all his disabilities, he liked to take risks. In a prewar poker game, he had bet $2,500 with "nary a pair in his hand." Hood gave Davis what he wanted, a series of attacks on Sherman's army. But Sherman pressed forward against Hood's depleted army. Unable to defend Atlanta's supply lines, Hood evacuated the city, which Sherman took on September 2, 1864.

The Election of 1864   Atlanta's fall came at a timely moment for Lincoln, who faced a tough reelection campaign. Lincoln had secured the Republican renomination with difficulty. Radical Republicans, who had flayed Lincoln for delay in declaring emancipation a war goal, now spurned his plans to restore the occupied parts of the Confederacy to the Union. The Radicals insisted that only Congress, not the president, could set requirements for readmission of conquered areas; they found Lincoln's standards too lenient and endorsed treasury secretary Salmon P. Chase for the nomination. Democrats, meanwhile, had never forgiven Lincoln for making emancipation a war goal. Peace Democrats now demanded an immediate armistice, followed by negotiations between North and South.

Facing formidable challenges, Lincoln benefited from both his own resourcefulness and his foes' problems. Chase's challenge failed, and by the time of the Republican convention in July, Lincoln's managers held control. To isolate the Peace Democrats and attract prowar Democrats, Republicans formed a temporary organization, the National Union party, and replaced Lincoln's vice president, Hannibal

Hamlin, with a prowar southern Unionist, Democratic Senator Andrew Johnson of Tennessee. This tactic helped exploit the widening split among the Democrats, who nominated George B. McClellan, former commander of the Army of the Potomac. But McClellan, saddled with a Copperhead platform, spent much of his campaign distancing himself from his party's peace-without-victory plank.

Despite disarray among Democrats, as late as August 1864, Lincoln seriously doubted his reelection. Leaving little to chance, he arranged for furloughs so that Union soldiers, most of whom supported him, could vote in states lacking absentee ballots. But the timely fall of Atlanta aided him even more; it punctured the northern antiwar movement and saved Lincoln's presidency. With 55 percent of the popular vote and 212 out of 233 electoral votes, Lincoln swept to victory.

The convention that nominated Lincoln had endorsed a constitutional amendment to abolish slavery, which Congress passed early in 1865. The **Thirteenth Amendment** would be ratified by the end of the year.

Sherman's March Through Georgia

Meanwhile, Sherman gave the South a new lesson in total war. After evacuating Atlanta, Hood led his Confederate army north toward Tennessee in the hope of luring Sherman out of Georgia. Refusing to chase Hood around Tennessee, Sherman proposed to abandon his supply lines, march his army across Georgia to Savannah, and live off the countryside. He would break the South's will to fight, terrify its people, and "make war so terrible ... that generations would pass before they could appeal again to it."

Sherman began by burning much of Atlanta and forcing most of its civilian population to leave. This harsh measure relieved him of the need to feed and garrison the city. Then, sending enough troops north to stop Hood in Tennessee, he led the bulk of his army, sixty-two thousand men, on a 285-mile trek to Savannah. Soon thousands of slaves followed the army. "Dar's de man dat rules the world," a slave cried on seeing Sherman.

Sherman's four columns of infantry, augmented by cavalry screens, moved on a front sixty miles wide and at a pace of ten miles a day. They destroyed everything that could aid southern resistance—arsenals, munitions plants, cotton gins, cotton stores, crops, livestock, and railroads. Ripping up tracks, Union soldiers heated rails in giant fires and twisted them into "Sherman neckties." Although told not to destroy civilian property, foragers ransacked and sometimes demolished homes. Indeed, havoc seemed a vital part of Sherman's strategy. By the time he reached Savannah, he estimated that his army had destroyed about a hundred million dollars' worth of property.

After taking Savannah in December 1864, Sherman's army wheeled north toward South Carolina, the first state to secede and, in Sherman's view, one "that deserves all that seems in store for her." His columns advanced unimpeded to Columbia, South Carolina's capital, where looters, slaves, and soldiers of both sides razed much of the city. Sherman then headed for North Carolina. By spring 1865, his army had left behind over four hundred miles of ruin. Other Union armies moved into Alabama and Georgia and took thousands of prisoners. Northern forces had penetrated the entire Confederacy, except for Texas and Florida, and crushed its wealth. "War is cruelty and you cannot refine it," Sherman wrote. "Those who brought war into our country deserve all the curses and maledictions a people can pour out."

New Hope Church, Georgia *General Sherman's campaign through Georgia and South Carolina in 1864 turned parts of the landscape into rubble. This scene of devastation in Georgia, captured by northern photographer George N. Barnard in 1866, suggests the impact of war on the southern environment.*

(Library of Congress)

Toward Appomattox   While Sherman headed north, Grant renewed his assault on the entrenched Army of Northern Virginia. His objective was Petersburg, a railroad hub south of Richmond (see Map 15.3). Although Grant had previously failed to overwhelm Confederate defenses in front of Petersburg, the devastation wrought by Sherman's army crippled Confederate morale: rebel desertions reached epidemic proportions. Late in March 1865 Grant, reinforced by Sheridan, swung his forces around the western flank of Petersburg's defenders. Lee could not stop him. On April 2, Sheridan smashed the rebel flank at the Battle of Five Forks. A courier bore the grim news to Jefferson Davis, attending church in Richmond: "General Lee telegraphs that he can hold his position no longer."

Davis left his pew, gathered his government, and fled the city. In the morning of April 3, Union troops entered Richmond, pulled down the Confederate flag, and ran up the Stars and Stripes over the capitol. Explosions set by retreating Confederates left the city "a sea of flames." Fires damaged the Tredegar Iron Works. Union troops liberated the town jail, which housed slaves awaiting sale, and its rejoicing inmates poured into the streets. On April 4, Lincoln toured the city and, for a few minutes, sat at Jefferson Davis's desk.

Lee made a last-ditch effort to escape Grant and reach Lynchburg, sixty miles west of Petersburg. He planned to use rail connections there to join General Joseph Johnston's army, which Sherman had pushed into North Carolina. But Grant and Sheridan choked off Lee's escape route, and on April 9 Lee bowed to the inevitable. He asked for terms of surrender and met Grant in a private home in the village of **Appomattox Court House,** Virginia, east of Lynchburg. While stunned troops gathered outside, Lee appeared in full dress uniform, with a sword. Grant entered in his customary disarray, smoking a cigar. The final surrender occurred four days later: Lee's troops laid down their arms between federal ranks. "On our part," wrote a Union officer, "not a sound of trumpet … nor roll of drum; not a cheer … but an awed stillness rather." Grant paroled Lee's twenty-six thousand men and sent them home with their horses and mules "to work their little farms." Remnants of Confederate resistance collapsed within a month. Johnston surrendered to Sherman on April 18, and Davis was captured in Georgia on May 10.

Grant returned to a jubilant Washington, and on April 14 turned down a theater date with the Lincolns. That night at Ford's Theater, an unemployed pro-Confederate

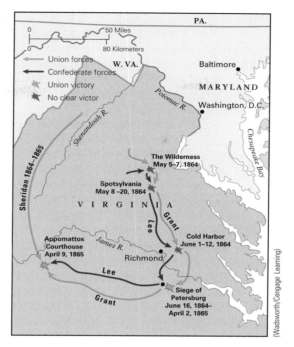

MAP 15.3 The Final Virginia Campaign, 1864–1865

Refusing to abandon his campaign in the face of enormous casualties, Grant finally pushed Lee into defensive fortifications around Petersburg, whose fall doomed Richmond. When Lee tried to escape to the west, Grant cut him off and forced his surrender. *(Library of Congress)*

actor, John Wilkes Booth, entered Lincoln's box and shot him in the head. Waving a knife, Booth leaped onstage shouting the Virginia state motto, *"Sic semper tyrannis"* ("Such is always the fate of tyrants") and then fled, despite a broken leg. That same night, a Booth accomplice stabbed Secretary of State Seward, who later recovered; a third conspirator, assigned to Vice President Johnson, failed to attack. Union troops hunted down Booth in Virginia within two weeks and shot him to death. Of eight accused accomplices, four were hanged and the rest imprisoned. On April 15, Lincoln died, and Andrew Johnson became president. Six days later, Lincoln's funeral train departed on a mournful journey from Washington to Springfield, Illinois, with crowds of thousands gathering at stations to weep as it passed.

The Impact of the War   The Civil War took a larger human toll than any other war in American history. The 620,000 soldiers who lost their lives nearly equaled the number of American soldiers killed in all the nation's earlier and later wars combined. The death count stood at 360,000 Union soldiers and 260,000 Confederates. Most families suffered losses. Vivid reminders of the price of Union remained for many years; armless and legless veterans gathered at regimental reunions; and monuments to the dead arose on village greens. Soldiers' widows collected pensions well into the twentieth century.

The war's costs were staggering, but war did not ruin the national economy, only the southern part of it. Vast Confederate losses, about 60 percent of southern wealth, were offset by northern advances. At the war's end, the North had almost all of the nation's wealth and capacity for production. Spurring economic modernization, the war provided a friendly climate for industrial development and capital investment. No longer the largest slave-owning power in the world, the United States would now become a major industrial nation.

The war had political as well as economic ramifications. It created a "more perfect Union" in place of the prewar federation of states. The doctrine of states' rights did not disappear, but talk of secession stopped; states would never again exercise their antebellum range of powers. The national banking system, created in 1863, gradually supplanted state banks. Greenbacks provided a national currency. The federal government had exercised powers that many in 1860 doubted it possessed. By ending slavery and imposing an income tax, it asserted power over kinds of private property once thought untouchable.

Finally, the Civil War fulfilled abolitionist prophecies as well as Unionist goals. Freeing 3.5 million slaves and expediting efforts by slaves to liberate themselves, the war produced the very sort of radical upheaval in southern society that Lincoln had originally said it would not induce.

CHRONOLOGY
1861–1865

1861   President Abraham Lincoln calls for volunteers to suppress the rebellion (April).
Virginia, Arkansas, Tennessee, and North Carolina join the Confederacy (April–May).
Lincoln imposes a naval blockade on the South (April).
U.S. Sanitary Commission formed (June).
First Battle of Bull Run (July).
First Confiscation Act (August).

1862   Legal Tender Act (February).
George B. McClellan's Peninsula Campaign (March–July).
Battle of Shiloh (April).
Confederate Congress passes the Conscription Act (April).
David G. Farragut captures New Orleans (April).
Homestead Act (May).
Seven Days' Battles (June–July).
Pacific Railroad Act (July).
Morrill Land Grant Act (July).
Second Confiscation Act (July).
Battle of Antietam (September).
Preliminary Emancipation Proclamation (September).
Battle of Fredericksburg (December).

1863   Emancipation Proclamation issued (January).
Lincoln suspends writ of *habeas corpus* nationwide (January).
National Bank Act (February).
Congress passes the Enrollment Act (March).

Battle of Chancellorsville (May).
Woman's National Loyal League formed (May).
Battle of Gettysburg (July).
Surrender of Vicksburg (July).
New York City draft riots (July).
Battle of Chickamauga (September).

1864   Ulysses S. Grant given command of all Union armies (March).
Battle of the Wilderness (May).
Battle of Spotsylvania (May).
Battle of Cold Harbor (June).
Surrender of Atlanta (September).
Lincoln reelected (November).
William T. Sherman's march to the sea (November–December).

1865   Congress passes the Thirteenth Amendment (January).
Sherman moves through South Carolina (January–March).
Grant takes Richmond (April).
Robert E. Lee surrenders at Appomattox (April).
Lincoln dies (April).
Joseph Johnston surrenders to Sherman (April).

CONCLUSION

When war began in April 1861, both sides were unprepared, but each had distinct strengths. The Union held vast advantages of manpower and resources, including most of the nation's industrial strength and two-thirds of its railroads. The North, however, faced a stiff challenge. To achieve its goal of forcing the rebel states back into the Union, it had to conquer large pieces of southern territory, cripple the South's resources, and destroy its armies. The Union's challenge was the Confederacy's asset. To sustain Confederate independence, the South had to fight a defensive war, far less costly in men and materiel. It had to prevent Union conquest of its territory, preserve its armies from annihilation, and hold out long enough to convince the North that further effort would be pointless. Moreover, southerners expected to fight on home ground and to enjoy an advantage in morale. Thus, though its resources were fewer, the Confederacy's task was less daunting.

The start of war challenged governments, North and South, in similar ways: both sides had to raise armies and funds. Within two years, both Union and Confederacy had drafted troops, imposed taxes, and printed paper money. As war dragged on, both regions faced political and economic problems. Leaders on each side confronted disunity and dissent. Northern Democrats assailed President Lincoln; in the South, states' rights supporters defied the authority of the Confederate government. The North's two-party system and the skills of its political leaders proved to be assets that the Confederacy lacked. Economically, too, the North held an edge. Both regions endured labor shortages and inflation. But the Union with its far greater resources more handily met the demands of war. In the North, Republicans in Congress enacted innovative laws that enhanced federal might, such as the National Banking Act, Pacific Railroad Act, and Homestead Act. The beleaguered South, in contrast, coped with food shortages and economic dislocation. Loss of southern manpower to the army also took a toll; slavery began to disintegrate as a labor system during the war. By 1864, even the Confederate Congress considered measures to free at least some slaves.

Significantly, war itself pressed the North to bring slavery to an end. To deprive the South of resources, the Union began to seize rebel property, including slaves, in 1861. Step by step, Union policy shifted toward emancipation. The second Confiscation Act in 1862 freed slaves who fled behind Union lines. Finally, seizing the initiative from Radical Republicans, Lincoln announced a crucial policy change. A war measure, the Emancipation Proclamation of January 1, 1863, served many purposes. The edict freed only slaves behind Confederate lines, those beyond the reach of the Union army. But it won foreign support, outflanked the Radicals, and confounded the Confederates. It also empowered Union soldiers to liberate slaves, enabled former slaves to serve in the Union army, and vastly strengthened the Union's hand. "Crippling the institution of slavery," as a Union officer declared, meant "striking a blow at the heart of the rebellion." Most important, the proclamation changed the nature of the war. After January 1, 1863, the war to save the Union was also a war to end slavery. Emancipation took effect mainly at the war's end and became permanent with the ratification of the Thirteenth Amendment in 1865. The proclamation of 1863 was a pivotal turning point in the war.

Historians have long debated the causes of Union victory. They have weighed many factors, including the North's imposing strengths, or what Robert E. Lee called its "overwhelming numbers and resources." Recently, two competing interpretations have held sway. One focuses on southern shortcomings. Did the South, in the end, lose the will to win? Did the economic dislocations of war undercut southern morale? Were there defects of Confederate nationalism that could not be overcome? Some historians point to internal weaknesses in the Confederacy as a major cause of Union triumph. Other historians stress the utterly unpredictable nature of the conflict. In their view, the two sides were fairly equally matched, and the war was a cliffhanger; that is, the North might have crushed the South much earlier or, alternatively, not at all. The North won the war, these historians contend, because it won a series of crucial contests on the battlefield, including the battles of Antietam, Vicksburg, Gettysburg, and Atlanta, any one of which could have gone the other way. The factors that determined the military outcome of the war continue to be a source of contention.

The impact of the Civil War is more clear-cut than the precise cause of Union triumph. The war gave a massive boost to the northern economy. It left in its wake a stronger national government, with a national banking system, a national currency, and an enfeebled version of states' rights. It confirmed the triumph of the Republican Party, with its commitment to competition, free labor, and industry. Finally, it left a nation of free people, including the millions of African-Americans who had once been slaves. Emancipation and a new sense of nationalism were the war's major legacies. The nation now turned its attention to the restoration of the conquered South to the Union and to deciding the future of the former slaves.

16

THE CRISES OF RECONSTRUCTION, 1865–1877

CHAPTER OUTLINE

• Reconstruction Politics, 1865–1868 • Reconstruction Governments •
The Impact of Emancipation • New Concerns in the North, 1868–1876 •
Reconstruction Abandoned, 1876–1877

RECONSTRUCTION POLITICS, 1865–1868

At the end of the Civil War, President Johnson might have exiled, imprisoned, or executed Confederate leaders and imposed martial law indefinitely. Demobilized Confederate soldiers might have continued armed resistance to federal occupation forces. Freed slaves might have taken revenge on former owners and other white southerners. But none of this occurred. Instead, intense *political* conflict dominated the immediate postwar years. National politics produced new constitutional amendments, a presidential impeachment, and some of the most ambitious domestic legislation ever enacted by Congress, the Reconstruction Acts of 1867–1868. The major outcome of Reconstruction politics was the enfranchisement of black men, a development that few—black or white—had expected when Lee surrendered.

In 1865, only a small group of politicians supported black suffrage. All were Radical Republicans, a minority faction that had emerged during the war. Led by Senator **Charles Sumner** of Massachusetts and Congressman **Thaddeus Stevens** of Pennsylvania, the Radicals had clamored for the abolition of slavery and a demanding reconstruction policy. But the Radicals, outnumbered in Congress by other Republicans and opposed by the Democratic minority, faced long odds. Still, they managed to win broad Republican support for parts of their Reconstruction program, including black male enfranchisement. Just as civil war had led to emancipation, a goal once supported by only a minority of Americans, so Reconstruction policy became bound to black suffrage, a momentous change that originally had only narrow political backing.

Lincoln's Plan   Conflict over Reconstruction began even before the war ended. In December 1863, President Lincoln issued the Proclamation of Amnesty and Reconstruction, which enabled southern states to rejoin the Union if at least 10 percent of those who had cast ballots in the election of 1860 would take an oath of allegiance to the Union and accept emancipation. This minority could then create a loyal state government. Lincoln's plan excluded some southerners from oath-taking, such as Confederate officials and military officers. Such persons would have to apply for presidential pardons. Also excluded were blacks, who had not been voters in 1860. Lincoln hoped to undermine the Confederacy by establishing pro-Union governments within it and to build a southern Republican party.

Radical Republicans in Congress, however, envisioned a slower readmission process that would bar even more ex-Confederates from political life. The Wade-Davis bill, passed by Congress in July 1864, provided that a military governor would rule each former Confederate state; after at least half the eligible voters took an oath of allegiance to the Union, delegates could be elected to a state convention that would repeal secession and abolish slavery. To qualify as a voter or delegate, a southerner would have to take a second, "ironclad" oath, swearing that he had never voluntarily supported the Confederacy. Like the 10 percent plan, the congressional plan did not provide for black suffrage, a measure then supported by only some Radicals. Unlike Lincoln's plan, however, the Wade-Davis scheme would have delayed the readmission process almost indefinitely.

Claiming he did not want to bind himself to any single restoration policy, Lincoln pocket-vetoed the Wade-Davis bill (failed to sign the bill within ten days of the adjournment of Congress). The bill's sponsors, Senator Benjamin Wade of Ohio and Congressman Henry Winter Davis of Maryland, blasted Lincoln's act. By the war's end, the president and Congress had reached an impasse. Arkansas, Louisiana, Tennessee, and parts of Virginia under Union army control moved toward readmission under variants of Lincoln's plan. But Congress refused to seat their delegates, as it had a right to do. What Lincoln's ultimate policy would have been remains unknown. But after his assassination, on April 14, 1865, Radical Republicans turned with hope toward his successor, **Andrew Johnson** of Tennessee.

Presidential   The only southern senator to remain in Congress when his
Reconstruction   state seceded, Andrew Johnson had served as military governor
Under Johnson   of Tennessee from 1862 to 1864. Defying the Confederate stand, he had declared that "treason is a crime and must be made odious." Above all, Johnson had long sought the destruction of the planter aristocracy. A self-educated man of humble North Carolina origins, Johnson had moved to Greenville, Tennessee, in 1826. He had entered politics in the 1830s as a spokesman for non-slave-owning whites and rose rapidly from local official to congressman to governor to senator. Once the owner of eight slaves, Johnson reversed his position on slavery during the war. When emancipation became Union policy, he supported it. But Johnson neither adopted abolitionist ideals nor challenged racist sentiments. He hoped mainly that the fall of slavery would injure southern aristocrats. Johnson, in short, had his own political agenda, which, as Republicans would soon learn, did not duplicate theirs. Moreover, he was a lifelong Democrat who had been added to the Republican, or National Union, ticket in 1864 to broaden its appeal and who had become president by accident.

In May 1865, with Congress out of session, Johnson shocked Republicans by announcing in two proclamations his own program to bring back into the Union the seven southern states still without reconstruction governments—Alabama, Florida, Georgia, Mississippi, North Carolina, South Carolina, and Texas. Almost all southerners who took an oath of allegiance would receive a pardon and amnesty; all their property except slaves would be restored. Oath takers could elect delegates to state conventions, which would provide for regular elections. Each state convention, Johnson later added, would have to proclaim the illegality of secession, repudiate state debts incurred when the state belonged to the Confederacy, and ratify the Thirteenth Amendment, which abolished slavery. (Proposed by an enthusiastic wartime Congress early in 1865, the amendment would be ratified in December of that year.) As under Lincoln's plan, Confederate civil and military officers would still be disqualified, as would well-off ex-Confederates—those with taxable property worth $20,000 or more. This purge of the plantation aristocracy, Johnson said, would benefit "humble men, the peasantry and yeomen of the South, who have been decoyed … into rebellion." Poorer whites would now be in control.

Presidential Reconstruction took effect in the summer of 1865, but with unforeseen consequences. Disqualified Southerners applied in droves for pardons, which Johnson handed out liberally—some thirteen thousand of them. Johnson also dropped plans to punish treason. By the end of 1865, all seven states had created new civil governments that in effect restored the status quo from before the war. Confederate army officers and large planters assumed state offices. Former Confederate generals and officials—including Alexander Stephens of Georgia, the former Confederate vice president—won election to Congress. Some states refused to ratify the Thirteenth Amendment or to repudiate their Confederate debts.

Most infuriating to Radical Republicans, all seven states took steps to ensure a landless, dependent black labor force: they passed **"black codes"** to replace the slave codes, state laws that had regulated slavery. Because Johnson's plan assured the ratification of the Thirteenth Amendment, all states guaranteed the freedmen some basic rights—to marry, own property, make contracts, and testify in court against other blacks—but the codes harshly restricted freedmen's behavior. Some established racial segregation in public places; most prohibited racial intermarriage, jury service by blacks, and court testimony by blacks against whites. All codes included provisions that effectively barred former slaves from leaving the plantations. South Carolina required special licenses for blacks who wished to enter nonagricultural employment. Mississippi prohibited blacks from buying and selling farmland. Most states required annual contracts between landowners and black agricultural workers; blacks without contracts risked arrest as vagrants and involuntary servitude.

The black codes left freedmen no longer slaves but not really liberated either. In practice, many clauses in the codes never took effect: the Union army and the Freedmen's Bureau (a federal agency that assisted former slaves) suspended the enforcement of racially discriminatory provisions of the new laws. But the black codes revealed white southern intentions. They showed what "home rule" would have been like without federal interference.

Many northerners denounced what they saw as southern defiance. "What can be hatched from such an egg but another rebellion?" asked a Boston newspaper. Republicans in Congress agreed. When Congress convened in December 1865, it refused to seat delegates of ex-Confederate states. Establishing the Joint

(House-Senate) Committee on Reconstruction, Republicans prepared to dismantle the black codes and lock ex-Confederates out of power.

Congress versus Johnson   Southern blacks' status now became the major issue in Congress. Radical Republicans like Congressman Thaddeus Stevens—who hoped to impose black suffrage on the former Confederacy and delay southern readmission—were still a minority in Congress. Conservative Republicans, who favored Johnson's plan, formed a minority too, as did the Democrats, who also supported the president. Moderate Republicans, the largest congressional bloc, agreed with Radicals that Johnson's plan was too feeble, but they wanted to avoid a dispute with the president. None of the four congressional blocs could claim the two-thirds majority needed to overturn a presidential veto. But ineptly, Johnson alienated a majority of moderates and pushed them into the Radicals' arms.

Two proposals to invalidate the black codes, drafted by a moderate Republican, Senator Lyman Trumbull of Illinois, won wide Republican support. Congress first voted to continue the Freedmen's Bureau, started in March 1865, whose term was ending. This federal agency, headed by former Union general O.O. Howard and staffed mainly by army officers, provided relief, rations, and medical care; built schools for freed blacks; put them to work on abandoned or confiscated lands; and tried to protect their rights as laborers. Congress extended the bureau's life for three years and gave it new power to run special military courts, to settle labor disputes, and to invalidate labor contracts forced on freedmen by the black codes. In February 1866, Johnson vetoed the Freedmen's Bureau bill. The Constitution, he declared, did not sanction military trials of civilians in peacetime, nor did it support a system to care for "indigent persons."

In March 1866, Congress passed a second measure proposed by Trumbull, a bill that made blacks U.S. citizens with the same civil rights as other citizens and authorized federal intervention in the states to ensure black rights in court. Johnson vetoed the civil rights bill also. He argued that it would "operate in favor of the colored and against the white race." In April, Congress overrode his veto; the **Civil Rights Act of 1866** was the first major law ever passed over a presidential veto. In July, Congress enacted the Supplementary Freedmen's Bureau Act over Johnson's veto as well. Johnson's vetoes puzzled many Republicans because the new laws did not undercut presidential Reconstruction. The president insisted, however, that both bills were illegitimate because southerners had been shut out of the Congress that passed them. His stance won support in the South and from northern Democrats. But the president had alienated moderate Republicans, who now joined Radicals to oppose him. Johnson had lost "every friend he has," one moderate declared.

Some historians view Andrew Johnson as a political incompetent who, at this crucial juncture, bungled both his readmission scheme and his political future. Others contend he was merely trying to forge a centrist coalition. In either case, Johnson underestimated the possibility of Republican unity. Once united, the Republicans took their next step: the passage of a constitutional amendment to prevent the Supreme Court from invalidating the new Civil Rights Act and block Democrats in Congress from repealing it.

The Fourteenth Amendment, 1866

In April 1866, Congress adopted the **Fourteenth Amendment,** which had been proposed by the Joint Committee on Reconstruction. To protect blacks' rights, the amendment declared in its first clause that all persons born or naturalized in the United States were citizens of the nation and of their states and that no state could abridge their rights without due process of law or deny them equal protection of the law. This section nullified the *Dred Scott* decision of 1857, which had declared that blacks were not citizens. Second, the amendment guaranteed that if a state denied suffrage to any of its male citizens, its representation in Congress would be proportionally reduced. This clause did not guarantee black suffrage, but it threatened to deprive southern states of some legislators if black men were denied the vote. This was the first time that the word *male* was written into the Constitution; to the women's rights advocates, woman suffrage seemed a yet more distant prospect. Third, the amendment disqualified from state and national office *all* prewar office-holders—civil and military, state and federal—who had supported the Confederacy, unless Congress removed their disqualifications by a two-thirds vote. In so providing, Congress intended to invalidate Johnson's wholesale distribution of amnesties and pardons. Finally, the amendment repudiated the Confederate debt and maintained the validity of the federal debt.

The most ambitious step Congress had yet taken, the Fourteenth Amendment revealed growing Republican receptivity to Radical demands, including black male enfranchisement. The amendment's passage created a firestorm. Abolitionists decried the second clause as a "swindle" because it did not explicitly ensure black suffrage. Southerners and northern Democrats condemned the third clause as vengeful. Southern legislatures, except for Tennessee's, refused to ratify the amendment, and President Johnson denounced it. His defiance solidified the new alliance between moderate and Radical Republicans, and turned the congressional elections of 1866 into a referendum on the Fourteenth Amendment.

Over the summer, Johnson set off on a whistlestop train tour from Washington to St. Louis and Chicago and back. But this innovative campaign tactic—the "swing around the circle," as Johnson called it—failed. Humorless and defensive, the president made fresh enemies and doomed his hope of sinking the Fourteenth Amendment, which Moderate and Radical Republicans defended.

Republicans carried the congressional elections of 1866 in a landslide, winning almost two-thirds of the House and four-fifths of the Senate. They had secured a mandate for the Fourteenth Amendment and their own Reconstruction program, even if the president vetoed every part of it.

Congressional Reconstruction, 1866–1867

Congressional debate over reconstructing the South began in December 1866 and lasted three months. Radical Republican leaders called for black suffrage, federal support for public schools, confiscation of Confederate estates, and an extended period of military occupation in the South. Moderate Republicans accepted parts of the plan. In February 1867, after complex legislative maneuvers, Congress passed the **Reconstruction Act of 1867.** Johnson vetoed the law, and on March 2, Congress passed it over his veto. Later that year and in 1868, Congress passed three further Reconstruction acts, all enacted over presidential vetoes, to refine and enforce the first.

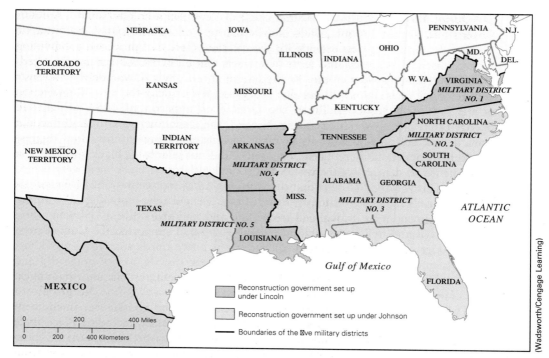

MAP 16.1 The Reconstruction of the South

The Reconstruction Act of 1867 divided the former Confederate states, except Tennessee, into five military districts and set forth the steps by which new state governments could be created.

The Reconstruction Act of 1867 invalidated the state governments formed under the Lincoln and Johnson plans. Only Tennessee, which had ratified the Fourteenth Amendment and had been readmitted to the Union, escaped further reconstruction. The new law divided the other ten former Confederate states into five temporary military districts, each run by a Union general (see Map 16.1). Voters—all black men, plus those white men who had not been disqualified by the Fourteenth Amendment—could elect delegates to a state convention that would write a new state constitution granting black suffrage. When eligible voters ratified the new constitution, elections could be held for state officers. Once Congress approved the state constitution, once the state legislature ratified the Fourteenth Amendment, and once the amendment became part of the federal Constitution, Congress would readmit the state into the Union.

The Reconstruction Act of 1867 was far more radical than the Johnson program because it enfranchised blacks and disfranchised many ex-Confederates. It fulfilled a central goal of the Radical Republicans: to delay the readmission of former Confederate states until Republican governments could be established and thereby prevent an immediate rebel resurgence. But the new law was not as harsh toward ex-Confederates as it might have been. It provided for only temporary military rule; it did not prosecute Confederate leaders for treason, permanently bar them from politics, or provide for confiscation or redistribution of property.

During the congressional debates, Radical Republican congressman Thaddeus Stevens had argued for the confiscation of large Confederate estates to "humble the proud traitors" and to provide for former slaves. He had proposed subdividing such confiscated property into forty-acre tracts to be distributed among the freedmen and selling the rest, some 90 percent of it, to pay off war debts. Stevens's land-reform bill won Radical support but never made progress; most Republicans held property rights sacred. Tampering with such rights in the South, they feared, would jeopardize those rights in the North. Moreover, Stevens's proposal would alienate southern ex-Whigs, antagonize other white southerners, and thereby endanger the rest of Reconstruction. Thus land reform never came about. The "radical" Reconstruction acts were a compromise.

Congressional Reconstruction took effect in the spring of 1867, but Johnson, as Commander in Chief, impeded its enforcement by replacing pro-Radical military officers with conservative ones. Republicans seethed. More suspicious than ever, congressional moderates and Radicals again joined forces to block Johnson from further obstructing Reconstruction.

The Impeachment Crisis, 1867–1868   In March 1867, Republicans in Congress passed two laws to curb presidential power. The **Tenure of Office Act** prohibited the president from removing civil officers without Senate consent. Cabinet members, the law stated, were to hold office "during the term of the president by whom they may have been appointed" and could be fired only with the Senate's approval. The goal was to bar Johnson from dismissing Secretary of War Edwin M. Stanton, a Radical ally. The other law, a rider to an army appropriations bill, barred the president from issuing military orders except through the commanding general, Ulysses S. Grant, who could not be removed without the Senate's consent.

The Radicals' enmity toward Johnson, however, went further: they began to seek grounds on which to impeach him. The House Judiciary Committee, aided by private detectives, could at first find no valid charges against Johnson. But Johnson again rescued his foes by providing the charges they needed.

In August 1867, with Congress out of session, Johnson suspended Secretary of War Stanton and replaced him with General Grant. In early 1868, the reconvened Senate refused to approve Stanton's suspension, and Grant, sensing the Republican mood, vacated the office. Johnson then removed Stanton and replaced him with another general. Johnson's defiance forced Republican moderates, who had at first resisted impeachment, into yet another alliance with the Radicals: the president had "thrown down the gauntlet," a moderate charged. The House approved eleven charges of impeachment, nine based on violation of the Tenure of Office Act. The other charges accused Johnson of being "unmindful of the high duties of office," seeking to disgrace Congress, and not enforcing the Reconstruction acts.

Johnson's trial in the Senate, which began in March 1868, riveted public attention for eleven weeks. Seven congressmen, including leading Radical Republicans, served as prosecutors or "managers." Johnson's lawyers maintained that he was merely seeking a court test by violating the Tenure of Office Act, which he thought was unconstitutional. They also contended, somewhat inconsistently, that the law did not protect Secretary Stanton, an appointee of Lincoln, not Johnson. Finally, they asserted, Johnson was guilty of no crime indictable in a regular court.

The congressional "managers" countered that impeachment was a political process, not a criminal trial, and that Johnson's "abuse of discretionary power" constituted an impeachable offense. Although Senate opinion split along party lines, some Republicans wavered, fearful that removal of a president would destroy the balance of power among the three branches of the federal government. They also distrusted Radical Republican Benjamin Wade, the president pro tempore of the Senate, who, because there was no vice president, would become president if Johnson were thrown out.

Late in May 1868, the Senate voted against Johnson 35 to 19, one vote short of the two-thirds majority needed for conviction. Despite intense pressure, seven Republicans had risked political suicide and sided with the twelve Senate Democrats against removal. In so doing, they set a precedent: their vote discouraged impeachment on political grounds for decades to come. But the anti-Johnson forces had also achieved their goal: Andrew Johnson had no future as president. Serving out the rest of his term, Johnson returned to Tennessee, where he was reelected to the Senate five years later. Republicans in Congress, meanwhile, pursued their last major Reconstruction objective: to guarantee black male suffrage.

The Fifteenth Amendment and the Question of Woman Suffrage, 1869–1870

Black suffrage was the linchpin of congressional Reconstruction. Only with the black vote could Republicans secure control of the ex-Confederate states. The Reconstruction Act of 1867 had forced southern states to enfranchise black men in order to reenter the Union, but much of the North rejected black suffrage. Congressional Republicans therefore had two aims. The **Fifteenth Amendment,** proposed by Congress in 1869, sought to protect black suffrage in the South against future repeal by Congress or the states, and to enfranchise northern and border-state blacks, who would presumably vote Republican. The amendment prohibited the denial of suffrage by the states to any citizen on account of "race, color, or previous condition of servitude."

Democrats argued that the proposed amendment violated states' rights by denying each state leverage over who would vote. But Democrats did not control enough states to defeat the amendment, and it was ratified in 1870. Four ex-Confederate states—Mississippi, Virginia, Georgia, and Texas—that had delayed the Reconstruction process were therefore forced to approve the Fifteenth Amendment, as well as the Fourteenth, in order to rejoin the Union. Some southerners appreciated the new amendment's omissions: as a Richmond newspaper pointed out, it had "loopholes through which a coach and four horses can be driven." What were these loopholes? The Fifteenth Amendment neither guaranteed black office holding nor prohibited voting restrictions such as property requirements and literacy tests. Such restrictions might be used—and ultimately were used—to deny blacks the vote.

The debate over black suffrage drew new participants into the political fray. In 1866, when Congress debated the Fourteenth Amendment, women's rights advocates tried to join forces with abolitionist allies to promote both black suffrage and woman suffrage. Most Radical Republicans, however, did not want to be saddled with the woman-suffrage plank; they feared it would impede their primary goal, black enfranchisement.

This defection provoked disputes among women's rights advocates. Some argued that black suffrage would pave the way for the women's vote and that black men deserved priority. "If the elective franchise is not extended to the

Anthony and Stanton, CA. 1870

Women's rights advocates Susan B. Anthony (left) and Elizabeth Cady Stanton began to promote woman suffrage when the issue of black suffrage arose in 1866. They subsequently assailed the proposed Fifteenth Amendment for excluding women. By the end of the 1860s, activists had formed two competing suffragist organizations.

(Schlesinger Library, Radcliffe Institute, Harvard University/The Bridgeman Art Library)

Negro, he is dead," explained Frederick Douglass, a longtime women's rights supporter. "Woman has a thousand ways by which she can attach herself to the ruling power of the land that we have not." But women's rights leaders Elizabeth Cady Stanton and **Susan B. Anthony** disagreed. In their view, the Fourteenth Amendment had disabled women by including the word *male*, and the Fifteenth Amendment failed to remedy this injustice. Instead, Stanton contended, the Fifteenth Amendment established an "aristocracy of sex" and increased women's disadvantages.

The battle over black suffrage and the Fifteenth Amendment split women's rights advocates into two rival suffrage associations, formed in 1869. The Boston-based American Woman Suffrage Association, endorsed by reformers such as Julia Ward Howe and Lucy Stone, retained an alliance with male abolitionists and campaigned for woman suffrage in the states. The New York-based and more radical National Woman Suffrage Association, led by Stanton and Anthony, condemned its former male allies and promoted a federal woman suffrage amendment.

Throughout the 1870s, the rival woman suffrage associations vied for constituents. In 1869 and 1870, independent of the suffrage movement, two territories, Wyoming and Utah, enfranchised women. But suffragists failed to sway legislators elsewhere. When Susan B. Anthony mobilized about seventy women to vote nationwide in 1872, she was indicted, convicted, and fined. One woman who tried to vote, Missouri suffragist Virginia Minor, brought suit with her husband against the registrar who had excluded her. The Minors claimed that the Fourteenth Amendment enfranchised women. In *Minor v. Happersett* (1875), however, the Supreme Court declared that a state could constitutionally deny women the vote. Divided and rebuffed, woman suffrage advocates braced for a long struggle.

By 1870, when the Fifteenth Amendment was ratified, Congress could look back on five years of achievement. Since the start of 1865, three constitutional amendments had broadened the scope of American democracy: The Thirteenth Amendment abolished slavery, the Fourteenth expanded civil rights, and the Fifteenth prohibited the denial of suffrage on the basis of race. Congress had also readmitted the former Confederate states into the Union. But after 1868, congressional momentum slowed, and the theater of action shifted to the South, where tumultuous change occurred.

RECONSTRUCTION GOVERNMENTS

During the unstable years of presidential Reconstruction, 1865–1867, the southern states had to create new governments, revive the war-torn economy, and face the impact of emancipation. Crises abounded. War costs had devastated southern wealth, cities and factories lay in rubble, plantation labor systems disintegrated, and racial tensions flared. Beginning in 1865, freedmen organized black conventions, political meetings at which they protested ill treatment and demanded equal rights. A climate of violence prevailed. Race riots erupted in major southern cities, such as Memphis in May 1866 and New Orleans two months later. Even when Congress imposed military rule, ex-Confederates did not feel defeated. "Having reached bottom, there is hope now that we may rise again," a South Carolina planter wrote in his diary.

Congressional Reconstruction, supervised by federal troops, took effect in the spring of 1867. The Johnson regimes were dismantled, state constitutional conventions met, and voters elected new state governments, which Republicans dominated. In 1868, most former Confederate states rejoined the Union, and two years later, the last four states—Virginia, Mississippi, Georgia, and Texas—followed.

But Republican rule was very brief, lasting less than a decade in all southern states, far less in most of them, and on average under five years. Opposition from southern Democrats, the landowning elite, thousands of vigilantes, and, indeed, most white voters proved insurmountable. Still, the governments formed under congressional Reconstruction were unique, because black men, including exslaves, participated in them. In no other society where slaves had been liberated—neither Haiti, where slaves had revolted in the 1790s, nor the British Caribbean islands, where Parliament had ended slavery in 1833—had freedmen gained democratic political rights.

A New Electorate   The Reconstruction laws of 1867–1868 transformed the southern electorate by temporarily disfranchising 10 to 15 percent of potential white voters and by enfranchising more than seven hundred thousand freedmen. Outnumbering white voters by one hundred thousand, blacks held voting majorities in five states.

The new electorate provided a base for the Republican Party, which had never existed in the South. To scornful Democrats, southern Republicans comprised three types of scoundrels: northern "carpetbaggers," who had allegedly come south seeking wealth and power (with so few possessions that they could be stuffed into traveling bags made of carpet material); southern "scalawags," predominantly poor and ignorant whites, who sought to profit from Republican rule; and hordes of uneducated freedmen, who were ready prey for Republican manipulators. Although the "carpetbag" and "scalawag" labels were derogatory and the stereotypes they conveyed inaccurate, they remain in use as a form of shorthand. Crossing class and racial lines, the hastily established Republican Party was in fact a loose coalition of diverse factions with often contradictory goals.

To northerners who moved south after the Civil War, the former Confederacy was an undeveloped region, ripe with possibility. The carpetbaggers' ranks included many former Union soldiers who hoped to buy land, open factories, build railroads, or simply enjoy the warmer climate. Albion Tourgee, a young lawyer who had served with the New York and Ohio volunteers, for example, relocated in North Carolina after the war to improve his health; there he worked as a journalist, politician, and Republican judge. Perhaps no more than twenty thousand northern migrants like Tourgee—including veterans, missionaries, teachers, and Freedmen's Bureau agents—headed south immediately after the war, and many soon returned north. But those who remained held almost one out of three state offices and wielded disproportionate political power.

Scalawags, white southerners who supported the Republicans, included some entrepreneurs who applauded party policies such as the national banking system and high protective tariffs as well as some prosperous planters, former Whigs who had opposed secession. Their numbers included a few prominent politicians, among them James Orr of South Carolina and Mississippi's governor James Alcorn, who became Republicans in order to retain influence and limit Republican radicalism. Most scalawags, however, were small farmers from the mountain regions of North Carolina, Georgia, Alabama, and Arkansas. Former Unionists who had owned no slaves and felt no loyalty toward the landowning elite, they sought to improve their economic position. Unlike carpetbaggers, they lacked commitment to black rights or black suffrage; most came from regions with few blacks and cared little whether blacks voted or not. Scalawags held the most political offices during Reconstruction, but they proved the least stable element of the southern Republican coalition: eventually, many drifted back to the Democratic fold.

Freedmen, the backbone of southern Republicanism, provided eight out of ten Republican votes. Republican rule lasted longest in states with the largest black populations—South Carolina, Mississippi, Alabama, and Louisiana. Introduced to politics in the black conventions of 1865–1867, the freedmen sought land, education, civil rights, and political equality, and remained loyal Republicans. As an elderly freedman announced at a Georgia political convention in 1867, "We know our friends." Although Reconstruction governments depended on African-American votes, freedmen held at most one in five political offices. Blacks served in all southern legislatures but constituted a majority only in the legislature of South Carolina, whose population was more than 60 percent black. In the House of Representatives, a mere 6 percent of southern members were black, and almost half of these came from South Carolina. No blacks became governor, and only two—Hiram Revels and Blanche K. Bruce, both of Mississippi—served in the U.S. Senate. (Still, the same number of African-Americans served in the Senate throughout the entire twentieth century.)

Black officeholders on the state level formed a political elite. They often differed from black voters in background, education, and wealth. A disproportionate number were literate blacks who had been free before the Civil War. In the South Carolina legislature, most black members, unlike their constituents, came from large towns and cities; many had spent time in the North; and some were well-off property owners or even former slave owners. Color differences were evident, too: 43 percent of South Carolina's black state legislators were mulattos (mixed race), compared to only 7 percent of the state's black population.

Black officials and black voters often had different priorities. Most freedmen cared mainly about their economic future, especially about acquiring land; black officeholders cared most about attaining equal rights. Still, both groups shared high expectations and prized enfranchisement. "We'd walk fifteen miles in wartime to find out about the battle," a Georgia freedman declared. "We can walk fifteen miles and more to find how to vote."

Republican Rule   Large numbers of blacks participated in American government for the first time in the state constitutional conventions
of 1867–1868. The South Carolina convention had a black majority, and in Louisiana half the delegates were freedmen. The conventions forged democratic changes
in their state constitutions. Delegates abolished property qualifications for office
holding, made many appointive offices elective, and redistricted state legislatures
more equitably. All states established universal manhood suffrage.

But no state instituted land reform. When proposals for land confiscation and redistribution arose at the state conventions, they fell to defeat, as they had in Congress.
Hoping to attract northern investment to the reconstructed South, southern Republicans
hesitated to threaten property rights or to adopt land-reform measures that northern
Republicans had rejected. South Carolina did set up a commission to buy land and
make it available to freedmen, and several states changed their tax structures to force
uncultivated land onto the market, but in no case was ex-Confederate land confiscated.

Once civil power shifted from the federal army to the new state governments,
Republican regimes began ambitious programs of public works. They built
roads, bridges, and public buildings; approved railroad bonds; and funded institutions to care for orphans, the insane, and the disabled. They also expanded state
bureaucracies, raised pay for state employees, and formed state militia, in which
blacks were often heavily represented. Finally, they created public-school systems,
almost nonexistent in the South until then.

These changes cost millions, and taxes skyrocketed. State legislatures increased
poll taxes or "head" taxes (levies on individuals); enacted luxury, sales, and occupation taxes; and imposed new property taxes. Before the war southern states had
taxed property in slaves but had barely taxed landed property. Now state governments assessed even small farmers' holdings; propertied planters felt overburdened.
Although northern tax rates still exceeded southern rates, southern landowners
resented the new levies. In their view, Reconstruction punished the propertied,
already beset by labor problems and falling land values, in order to finance the
vast expenditures of Republican legislators.

To Reconstruction's foes, Republican rule was wasteful and corrupt, the "most
stupendous system of organized robbery in history." A state like Mississippi, which
had an honest government, provided little basis for such charges. But critics could
justifiably point to Louisiana, where the governor pocketed thousands of dollars of
state funds and corruption permeated all government transactions (as indeed it had
before the war). Or they could cite South Carolina, where bribery ran rampant.
Besides government officials who took bribes, postwar profiteers included the railroad promoters who doled them out. Not all were Republicans. Nor did the Republican regimes in the South hold a monopoly on corruption. After the war, bribery
pervaded government transactions North and South, and far more money changed
hands in the North. But critics assailed Republican rule for additional reasons.

Counterattacks   Ex-Confederates spoke with dread about black enfranchisement and the "horror of Negro domination." As soon as con-
gressional Reconstruction took effect, former Confederates campaigned to undermine it.
Democratic newspapers assailed delegates to North Carolina's constitutional convention as an "Ethiopian minstrelsy" and called Louisiana's constitution "the work
of ignorant Negroes cooperating with a gang of white adventurers."

Democrats delayed mobilization until southern states were readmitted to the Union, and then swung into action. At first, they sought to win black votes; but when that failed, they tried other tactics. In 1868–1869, Georgia Democrats challenged the eligibility of black legislators and expelled them from office. In response, the federal government reestablished military rule in Georgia, but determined Democrats still undercut Republican power. In every southern state, they contested elections, backed dissident Republican factions, elected some Democratic legislators, and lured scalawags away from the Republican Party.

Vigilante efforts to reduce black votes bolstered the Democrats' campaigns to win white ones. Antagonism toward free blacks, long a motif in southern life, resurged after the war. In 1865, Freedmen's Bureau agents itemized outrages against blacks, including shooting, murder, rape, arson, and "inhuman beating." Vigilante groups sprang up spontaneously in all parts of the former Confederacy under names like moderators, regulators, and, in Louisiana, Knights of the White Camelia. One group rose to dominance. In the spring of 1866, six young Confederate war veterans in Tennessee formed a social club, the **Ku Klux Klan,** distinguished by elaborate rituals, hooded costumes, and secret passwords. By the election of 1868, when black men could first vote, Klan dens had spread to all southern states. Klansmen embarked on night raids to intimidate black voters. No longer a social club, the Ku Klux Klan was now a terrorist movement and a violent arm of the Democratic Party.

The Klan sought to suppress black voting, reestablish white supremacy, and topple Reconstruction governments. Its members attacked Freedmen's Bureau officials, white Republicans, black militia units, economically successful blacks, and black voters. Concentrated in areas where black and white populations were most evenly balanced and racial tensions greatest, Klan dens adapted their tactics and timing to local conditions. In Mississippi, the Klan targeted black schools; in Alabama, it concentrated on Republican officeholders. In Arkansas, terror reigned in 1868; in Georgia and Florida, Klan strength surged in 1870. Some Democrats denounced Klan members as "cutthroats and riff-raff." But Klansmen included prominent ex-Confederates, among them General Nathan Bedford Forrest, the leader of the 1864 Fort Pillow massacre, in which Confederate troops who captured a Union garrison in Tennessee murdered black soldiers who had surrendered. Vigilantism united southern whites of different social classes and drew on Confederate veterans' energy. In areas where the Klan was inactive, other vigilante groups took its place.

Republican legislatures passed laws to outlaw vigilantism, but as state militia could not enforce them, state officials sought federal help. Between May 1870 and February 1871, Congress passed three **Enforcement Acts,** each progressively more stringent. The First Enforcement Act protected black voters, but witnesses to violations were afraid to testify against vigilantes, and local juries refused to convict them. The Second Enforcement Act provided for federal supervision of southern elections, and the Third Enforcement Act, or Ku Klux Klan Act, strengthened punishments for those who prevented blacks from voting. It also empowered the president to use federal troops to enforce the law and to suspend the writ of *habeas corpus* in areas that he declared in insurrection. (The writ of *habeas corpus* is a court order requiring that the detainer of a prisoner bring that person to court and show cause for his or her detention.) The Ku Klux Klan Act generated thousands of arrests; most terrorists, however, escaped conviction.

By 1872, the federal government had effectively suppressed the Klan, but vigilantism had served its purpose. Only a large military presence in the South could

(Tennessee State Archives/Picture Research Consultants & Archives)

The Ku Klux Klan *Disguised in long white robes and hoods, Ku Klux Klansmen sometimes claimed to be the ghosts of Confederate soldiers. The Klan, which spread rapidly after 1867, sought to end Republican rule, restore white supremacy, and obliterate, in one southern editor's words, "the preposterous and wicked dogma of Negro equality."*

have protected black rights, and the government in Washington never provided it. Instead, federal power in the former Confederacy diminished. President Grant steadily reduced troop levels in the South; Congress allowed the Freedmen's Bureau to die in 1869; and the Enforcement acts became dead letters. White southerners, a Georgia politician told congressional investigators in 1871, could not discard "a feeling of bitterness, a feeling that the Negro is a sort of instinctual enemy of ours." The battle over Reconstruction was in essence a battle over the implications of emancipation, and it had begun as soon as the war ended.

The Impact of Emancipation

"The master he says we are all free," a South Carolina slave declared in 1865. "But it don't mean we is white. And it don't mean we is equal." Emancipated slaves faced daunting handicaps. They had no property, tools, or capital; possessed meager skills; and more than 95 percent were illiterate. Still, the exhilaration of freedom was overwhelming, as slaves realized, "Now I am for myself" and "All that I make is my own." Emancipation gave them the right to their own labor and a new sense of autonomy. Under Reconstruction, they sought to cast off white control and shed the vestiges of slavery.

Confronting Freedom

For former slaves, liberty meant mobility. Some moved out of slave quarters and set up dwellings elsewhere on their plantations; others left their plantations entirely. Landowners found that one freed slave after another vanished, with house servants and artisans leading the way. "I have never in my life met with such ingratitude," one South Carolina mistress exclaimed when a former slave ran off. Field workers, who had less contact with whites, were more likely to stay behind. Still, flight remained tempting. "The moment they see an opportunity to improve themselves, they will move on," diarist Mary Chesnut observed.

Emancipation stirred waves of migration within the former Confederacy. Some freed slaves left the Upper South for the Deep South and the Southwest—Florida, Mississippi, Arkansas, and Texas—where planters desperately needed labor and paid higher wages. More left the countryside for towns and cities. Urban black populations sometimes doubled or tripled after emancipation; the number of blacks in small rural towns grew as well. Many migrants eventually returned to their old locales, but they tended to settle on neighboring plantations rather than with former owners. Freedom was the major goal. "I's wants to be a free man ... and nobody say nuffin to me, nor order me roun,'" an Alabama freedman told a northern journalist.

Efforts to find lost family members prompted much movement. "They had a passion, not so much for wandering as for getting together," a Freedmen's Bureau official commented. Parents sought children who had been sold; husbands and wives who had been separated by sale, or who lived on different plantations, reunited; and families reclaimed youngsters from masters' homes. The Freedmen's Bureau helped former slaves get information about missing relatives and travel to find them. Bureau agents also tried to resolve conflicts that arose when spouses who had been separated under slavery married other people.

Reunification efforts often failed. Some fugitive slaves had died during the war or were untraceable. Other exslaves had formed new relationships and could not revive old ones. Still, success stories abounded. Once reunited, freed blacks quickly legalized unions formed under slavery, sometimes in mass ceremonies of up to seventy couples. Legal marriage affected family life. Men asserted themselves as household heads; wives of able-bodied men often withdrew from the labor force to care for homes and families. "When I married my wife, I married her to wait on me and she has got all she can do right here for me and the children," a Tennessee freedman explained.

Black women's desire for domestic life caused labor shortages. Before the war, at least half of field workers had been women; in 1866, a southern journal claimed, men performed almost all the field labor. Still, by Reconstruction's end, many black women had returned to agricultural work as part of sharecropper families. Others took paid work in cities, as laundresses, cooks, and domestic servants. (White women often sought employment, too, for the war had incapacitated many white breadwinners, reduced the supply of future husbands, and left families impoverished.) However, former slaves continued to view stable, independent domestic life, especially the right to bring up their own children, as a major blessing of freedom. In 1870, eight out of ten black families in the cotton-producing South were two-parent families, about the same proportion as among whites.

African-American Institutions

Freed blacks' desire for independence also fostered growth of black churches. In the late 1860s, some freedmen congregated at churches operated by northern missionaries; others withdrew from white-run churches and formed their own. The African Methodist Episcopal church, founded by Philadelphia blacks in the 1790s, gained thousands of new southern members. Negro Baptist churches sprouted everywhere, often growing out of plantation "praise meetings," religious gatherings organized by slaves.

Black churches offered a fervent, participatory experience. They also provided relief, raised funds for schools, and supported Republican policies. Black ministers assumed leading political roles, first in the black conventions of 1865–1866 and later in Reconstruction governments. After southern Democrats excluded most freedmen from political life at Reconstruction's end, ministers remained the main pillars of authority in black communities.

Black schools played a crucial role for freedmen, too; exslaves eagerly sought literacy for themselves and above all for their children. At emancipation, blacks organized their own schools, which the Freedmen's Bureau soon supervised. Northern philanthropic societies paid the wages of instructors, about half of them women. In 1869, the bureau reported more than four thousand black schools in the former Confederacy. Within three years, each southern state had a public school system, at least in principle, generally with separate schools for blacks and whites. Advanced schools for blacks

(Archival and Museum Collection, Hampton University)

Hampton Institute *Founded in 1868, Hampton Institute in southeastern Virginia welcomed newly freed African-Americans to vocational programs in agriculture, teacher training, and homemaking. These students, photographed at the school's entrance around 1870, were among Hampton's first classes.*

opened to train tradespeople, teachers, and ministers. The Freedmen's Bureau and northern organizations like the American Missionary Association helped found Howard, Atlanta, and Fisk universities (1866–1867) and Hampton Institute (1868).

However, black education remained limited. Few rural blacks could reach freedmen's schools located in towns. Underfunded black public schools, similarly inaccessible to most rural black children, held classes only for short seasons and sometimes drew vigilante attacks. At the end of Reconstruction, more than 80 percent of the black population was still illiterate, though literacy rose steadily among youngsters.

School segregation and other forms of racial separation were taken for granted. Some black codes of 1865–1866 had segregated public-transportation and public accommodations. Even after the invalidation of the codes, the custom of segregation continued on streetcars, steamboats, and trains as well as in churches, theaters, inns, and restaurants. In 1870, Senator Charles Sumner of Massachusetts began promoting a bill to desegregate schools, transportation facilities, juries, and public accommodations. After Sumner's death in 1874, Congress honored him by a new law, the **Civil Rights Act of 1875,** which included his proposals, save for the controversial school-integration provision. But in 1883, in the *Civil Rights Cases*, the Supreme Court invalidated the law; the Fourteenth Amendment did not prohibit discrimination by individuals, the Court ruled, only that perpetrated by the state.

White southerners rejected the prospect of racial integration, which they insisted would lead to racial amalgamation. "If we have social equality, we shall have intermarriage," one white southerner contended, "and if we have intermarriage, we shall degenerate." Urban blacks sometimes challenged segregation practices; black legislators promoted bills to desegregate public transit; and some black officeholders decried all forms of racial separatism. "The sooner we as a people forget our sable complexion," said a Mobile official, "the better it will be for us as a race." But most freed blacks were less interested in "social equality," in the sense of interracial mingling, than in black liberty and community. The new postwar elite—teachers, ministers, and politicians—served black constituencies and therefore had a vested interest in separate black institutions. Rural blacks, too, widely preferred all-black institutions. They had little desire to mix with whites. On the contrary, they sought freedom from white control. Above all, they wanted to secure personal independence by acquiring land.

Land, Labor, and Sharecropping   "The sole ambition of the freedman," a New Englander wrote from South Carolina in 1865, "appears to be to become the owner of a little piece of land, there to erect a humble home, and to dwell in peace and security, at his own free will and pleasure." Indeed, to freed blacks everywhere, landownership signified economic independence; "forty acres and a mule" (a phrase that originated in 1864 when Union general William T. Sherman set aside land on the South Carolina Sea Islands for black settlement) promised emancipation from plantation labor, white domination, and cotton, the "slave crop."

But freedmen's visions of landownership failed to materialize, for, as we have seen, neither Congress nor the southern states imposed large-scale land reform. Some freedmen obtained land with the help of the Union army or the Freedmen's Bureau, and black soldiers sometimes pooled resources to buy land, as on the Sea Islands of South Carolina and Georgia. In 1866, Congress passed the Southern Homestead Act, which set aside 44 million acres of public land in five southern

states for freedmen and loyal whites. This acreage contained poor soil, and few former slaves had the resources to survive even until their first harvest. About four
thousand blacks resettled on homesteads under the law, but most were unable to
establish farms (poor whites fared little better.) By Reconstruction's end, only a
small minority of former slaves owned working farms. In Georgia in 1876, for
instance, blacks controlled a mere 1.3 percent of total acreage. Without large-scale
land reform, obstacles to black landownership remained overwhelming.

What were these obstacles? First, most freedmen lacked the capital to buy land
and the equipment needed to work it. Furthermore, white southerners generally
opposed selling land to blacks. Most important, planters sought to preserve a black
labor force. Freedmen, they insisted, would work only under coercion, and not at all
if the possibility of landownership arose. As soon as the war ended, the white South
took steps to ensure that black labor would remain available on plantations.

During presidential Reconstruction, southern state legislatures tried to curb black
mobility and preserve a captive labor force through the black codes. Under labor
contracts in effect in 1865–1866, freedmen received wages, housing, food, and clothing in exchange for field work. With cash scarce, wages usually took the form of a
very small share of the crop, often one-eighth or less, divided among the entire plantation work force. Freedmen's Bureau agents promoted the new labor system; they
saw black wage labor as an interim arrangement that would lead to economic independence. "You must begin at the bottom of the ladder and climb up," Freedmen's
Bureau head O.O. Howard exhorted a group of Louisiana freedmen in 1865.

But freedmen disliked the new wage system, especially the use of gang labor,
which resembled the work pattern under slavery. Planters had complaints, too. In
some regions the black labor force had shrunk to half its prewar size or less, due to
the migration of freedmen and to black women's withdrawal from fieldwork. Once
united in defense of slavery, planters now competed for black workers. But the freedmen, whom planters often scorned as lazy or inefficient, did not intend to work as
long or as hard as they had labored under slavery. One planter claimed that workers
accomplished only "two-fifths of what they did under the old system." As productivity fell, so did land values. Plummeting cotton prices and poor harvests compounded
planters' woes. By 1867, an agricultural impasse had been reached: landowners
lacked labor, and freedmen lacked land. But free blacks, unlike slaves, had the right
to enter into contracts—or to refuse to do so—and thereby gained some leverage.

Planters and freedmen began experimenting with new labor schemes, including
the division of plantations into small tenancies (see Map 16.2). **Sharecropping**, the
most widespread arrangement, evolved as a compromise. Under the sharecropping
system, landowners subdivided large plantations into farms of thirty to fifty acres,
which they rented to freedmen under annual leases for a share of the crop, usually
half. Freedmen preferred sharecropping to wage labor because it represented a step
toward independence. Household heads could use the labor of family members.
Moreover, a half-share of the crop far exceeded the fraction that freedmen had
received as wages under the black codes. Planters often spoke of sharecropping as
a concession, but they benefited, too. They retained power over tenants, because
annual leases did not have to be renewed; they could expel undesirable tenants at
the end of the year. Planters also shared the risk of planting with tenants: if a
crop failed, both suffered the loss. Most important, planters retained control of
their land and in some cases extended their holdings. The most productive land,

therefore, remained in the hands of a small group of owners, as before the war. Sharecropping forced planters to relinquish daily control over the labor of freedmen but helped to preserve the planter elite (see Going to the Source).

Sharecropping arrangements varied widely. On sugar and rice plantations, the wage system continued; strong markets for those crops enabled planters to pay workers in cash—cash that cotton planters lacked. Some freedmen remained independent renters. Some landowners leased areas to white tenants, who then subcontracted with black labor. But by the end of the 1860s, sharecropping prevailed in the cotton South, and continued to expand. A severe depression in 1873 drove many black renters into sharecropping. Thousands of independent white farmers became sharecroppers as well. Stung by wartime losses and by the dismal postwar economy, they sank into debt and lost their land to creditors. Many backcountry residents, no longer able to get by on subsistence farming, shifted to cash crops like cotton and suffered the same fate. At Reconstruction's end, one-third of white farmers in Mississippi, for instance, were sharecroppers.

By 1880, 80 percent of the land in the cotton-producing states had been subdivided into tenancies, most of it farmed by sharecroppers, white and black. Indeed, white sharecroppers now outnumbered black ones, although a higher proportion of southern blacks, about 75 percent, were involved in the system. Changes in marketing and finance, meanwhile, made the sharecroppers' lot increasingly precarious.

Toward a Crop-Lien Economy   Before the Civil War, planters had depended on factors, or middlemen, who sold them supplies, extended credit, and marketed their crops through urban merchants. These long-distance credit arrangements were backed by the high value and liquidity of slave property. When slavery ended, the factorage system collapsed. The postwar South, with hundreds of thousands of tenants and sharecroppers, needed a far more localized credit network.

Into the gap stepped the rural merchants (often themselves planters), who advanced supplies to tenants and sharecroppers on credit and sold their crops to wholesalers or textile manufacturers. Because renters had no property to use as collateral, the merchants secured their loans with a lien, or claim, on each farmer's next crop. Exorbitant interest rates of 50 percent or more quickly forced many tenants and sharecroppers into a cycle of indebtedness. Owing part of the crop to a landowner for rent, a sharecropper also owed a rural merchant a large sum (perhaps amounting to the rest of his crop, or more) for supplies. Illiterate tenants who lost track of their financial arrangements often fell prey to unscrupulous merchants. "A man that didn't know how to count would always lose," an Arkansas freedman later explained. Once a tenant's debts or alleged debts exceeded the value of his crop, he was tied to the land, to cotton, and to sharecropping.

By Reconstruction's end, sharecropping and crop liens had transformed southern agriculture. They bound the region to staple production and prevented crop diversification. Despite plunging cotton prices, creditors—landowners and merchants—insisted that tenants raise only easily marketable cash crops. Short of capital, planters could no longer invest in new equipment or improve their land by crop rotation and contour plowing. Soil depletion, land erosion, and agricultural backwardness soon locked much of the South into a cycle of poverty.

Trapped in perpetual debt, tenant farmers became the chief victims of the new agricultural order. Raising cotton for distant markets, for prices over which they

Sharecroppers During Reconstruction *By the end of the 1870s, about three out of four African-Americans in the cotton-producing states had become sharecroppers. Here, sharecroppers pick cotton in Aiken, South Carolina.*

(© Collection of the New York Historical Society)

had no control, remained the only survival route open to poor farmers, regardless of race. But low income from cotton locked them into sharecropping and crop liens, from which escape was difficult. African-American tenants saw their political rights dwindle, too. As one southern regime after another returned to Democratic control, freedmen could look for protection to neither state governments nor the federal government; northern politicians were preoccupied with their own problems.

NEW CONCERNS IN THE NORTH, 1868–1876

The nomination of Ulysses S. Grant for president in 1868 launched a chaotic era in national politics. Grant's two terms in office saw political scandals, a party revolt, massive depression, and steady retreat from Reconstruction policies. By the mid-1870s, northern voters cared more about the economic climate, unemployment, labor unrest, and currency problems than about the "southern question." Responsive to the shift in popular mood, Republicans became eager to end sectional conflict and turned their backs on the freedmen of the South.

Grantism   Republicans had good reason to bypass party leaders and nominate the popular Grant. A war hero, Grant was endorsed by Union veterans and widely admired throughout the North. To oppose Grant, the Democrats nominated New York governor Horatio Seymour, arch-critic of the Lincoln administration in wartime and now a foe of Reconstruction. Grant ran on personal popularity more than issues. Although he carried all but eight states, the popular vote was close; in the South, newly enfranchised freedmen provided Grant's margin of victory.

A strong leader in war, Grant proved a passive president. Although he lacked Johnson's instinct for disaster, he had little political skill. Many of his cabinet appointees were mediocre if not unscrupulous; scandals plagued his administration. In 1869, financier Jay Gould and his partner Jim Fisk tried to corner the gold market with the help of Grant's brother-in-law, a New York speculator. When gold prices tumbled, investors were ruined and Grant's reputation suffered. Then, before the president's first term ended, his vice president, Schuyler Colfax, was found to be linked to the Crédit Mobilier, a fraudulent scheme to skim off the profits of the Union Pacific Railroad. Discredited, Colfax was dropped from the Grant ticket in 1872.

More trouble lay ahead. Grant's private secretary, Orville Babcock, was unmasked in 1875 after taking money from the "whiskey ring," distillers who bribed federal agents to avoid paying millions in taxes. In 1876, voters learned that Grant's secretary of war, William E. Belknap, had taken bribes to sell lucrative Indian trading posts in Oklahoma. Impeached and disgraced, Belknap resigned.

Although uninvolved in the scandals, Grant defended his subordinates. To his critics, "Grantism" came to stand for fraud, bribery, and political corruption—evils that spread far beyond Washington. In Pennsylvania, for example, the Standard Oil Company and the Pennsylvania Railroad controlled the legislature. Urban politics also provided rich opportunities for graft and swindles. The New York City press revealed in 1872 that Democratic boss William M. Tweed, the leader of Tammany Hall, led a ring that had looted the city treasury and collected at millions in kickbacks and payoffs. When Mark Twain and coauthor Charles Dudley Warner published their satiric novel *The Gilded Age* (1873), readers recognized the book's speculators, self-promoters, and opportunists as familiar types in public life. (The term "Gilded Age" was subsequently used to refer to the decades from the 1870s to the 1890s.)

Grant had some success in foreign policy. In 1872, his administration engineered the settlement of the *Alabama* claims with Britain. To compensate for damage done by Confederate-owned but British-built ships, an international tribunal awarded the United States $15.5 million. But Grant's administration faltered when it tried to add non-adjacent territory to the United States. In 1867, Johnson's secretary of state, William H. Seward, had negotiated a treaty in which the United States bought Alaska from Russia at the bargain price of $7.2 million. Although the press mocked "Seward's Ice Box," the purchase kindled expansionists' hopes. In 1870, Grant decided to annex the eastern half of the Caribbean island of Santo Domingo (today called the Dominican Republic); the territory had been passed back and forth since the late eighteenth century among France, Spain, and Haiti. Annexation, Grant believed, would promote Caribbean trade and provide a haven for persecuted southern blacks. American speculators anticipated windfalls from land sales, commerce, and mining. But Congress disliked Grant's plan. Senator Charles Sumner denounced it as an imperialist "dance of blood." The Senate rejected the annexation treaty and further diminished Grant's reputation.

As the election of 1872 approached, dissident Republicans expressed fears that "Grantism" at home and abroad would ruin the party. The dissidents took action. Led by a combination of former Radicals and other Republicans left out of Grant's "Great Barbecue" (a disparaging reference to profiteers who feasted at the public trough), the president's critics formed their own party, the **Liberal Republicans.**

The Liberals' Revolt

The Liberal Republican revolt split the Republican Party and undermined support for Republican southern policy. (The label "liberal" at the time meant support for economic doctrines

Going to the Source

The Barrow Plantation

David Crenshaw Barrow (1852–1929), who grew up on his family's 2,000-acre plantation in Oglethorpe County, Georgia, described in an 1881 article the changes that occurred there after the Civil War, as former slaves became tenant farmers. His father, landowner David C. Barrow, Sr., once a slaveholder, now rented out plots of land to tenant families, with a total of 162 members, who raised cotton and other crops. The younger Barrow in 1881 taught mathematics at the University of Georgia; he later served for many years as chancellor. His article, aimed at a national audience, seeks to assure northern readers that postwar changes in southern labor worked "thoroughly well."

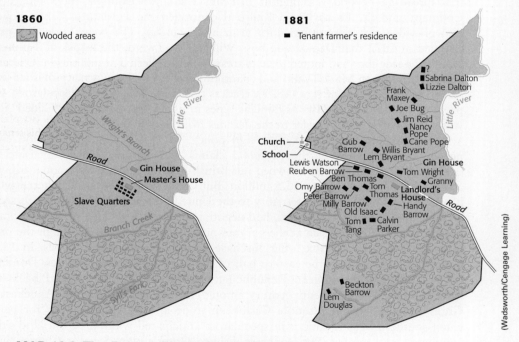

MAP 16.2 The Barrow Plantation, 1860 and 1881

The transformation of the Barrow plantation illustrates the striking changes in southern agriculture during Reconstruction. Before the Civil War, about 135 slaves worked on the plantation; after the war, the former slaves who remained signed labor contracts with owner David C. Barrow, Sr. Supervised by a hired foreman, the freedmen grew cotton for wages in competing squads, but disliked the new arrangement. In the late 1860s, Barrow subdivided his land into tenancies and freedmen moved their households from the old slave quarter to family farms. Among Barrow plantation tenants in 1881, one out of four families was named Barrow.

"In Georgia, the Negro has adapted himself to his new circumstances, and freedom fits him as if it had been cut out and made for him....

One of the first planters in Middle Georgia to divide his plantations into farms was Mr. Barrow of Oglethorpe. The plantation upon which he now lives ...with the exception of a single acre, [used by tenants] for church and school purposes, is the same size it was before the war. Here, however, the similarity ceases. Before the war everything on the place was under the absolute rule of an overseer (Mr. Barrow living then on another place).... [A]ll the Negro houses were close together, forming "the quarter." The house in which the overseer lived was close to the quarter.... This all has been so changed that the place would now hardly be recognized by one who had not seen it during the past sixteen years.

The transformation has been so gradual that almost imperceptibly a radical change has been effected. For several years after the war, the force on the plantation was divided into two squads.... Each of these squads was under the control of a foreman.... [T]he laborers were paid a portion of the crop as their wages, which did much toward making them feel interested in it....

This was the first change made, and for several years it produced good results. After a while, however, even the liberal control of the foremen grew irksome, each man feeling the very natural desire to be his own "boss" and farm to himself. As a consequence of this feeling, the two squads split into smaller and then still smaller squads, still working for part of the crop ... [But this system proved unsatisfactory].

[T]he present arrangement ... while it had difficulties in inception, has been found to work thoroughly well. Under it our colored farmers are tenants, who are responsible only for damage to the farms they work and for the prompt payment of their rent. [They] farm on a small scale, only two of them having more than one mule.... [T]he location of the houses caused considerable inconvenience and so it was determined to scatter them....

The labor of the farm is performed by the man, who usually does the plowing, and his wife and children, who do the hoeing, under his direction.... [T]heir landlord interferes only far enough to see that sufficient cotton is made to pay the rent.... The usual quantity of land planted is between twenty-five and thirty acres, about half of which is in cotton and the rest in corn and [vegetable] patches....

The slight supervision which is exercised over these tenants may surprise those ignorant of how completely the relations between the races at the South have changed. Mr. Barrow lives on his plantation, and yet there are some of his tenants' farms which he does not visit as often as once a month....

[The tenants] have become suited to their new estate, and it to them. I do not know of a single Negro who has swelled the number of the "exodus.""

Questions

1. What changes in labor arrangements occurred on the Barrow plantation in the sixteen years after the Civil War? What remained the same?

2. Do you think Barrow's role as a member of landowning family shaped his account of postwar changes? If so, how?

Go to www.cengagebrain.com for additional primary sources on this period.

Source: David Crenshaw Barrow, "A Georgia Plantation," Scribner's Monthly XXI (April 1881) pp. 830–836.

(Brown Brothers and Harper's Weekly, 1871)

Boss Tweed *Thomas Nast's cartoons in* Harper's Weekly *helped topple New York Democratic boss William M. Tweed, who, with his associates, embodied corruption on a large scale. The Tweed Ring had granted lucrative franchises to companies they controlled, padded construction bills, practiced graft and extortion, and exploited every opportunity to plunder the city's funds.*

such as free trade, the gold standard, and the law of supply and demand.) Denouncing "Grantism" and "spoilsmen" (political hacks who gained party office), Liberals demanded civil service reform to bring the "best men" into government. Rejecting the "regular" Republicans' high-tariff policy, they espoused free trade. Most important, Liberals condemned "bayonet rule" in the South. Even some once-Radical Republicans claimed that Reconstruction had achieved its goal: blacks had been enfranchised and could now manage for themselves. Corruption in government, North and South, posed greater danger than Confederate resurgence, Liberals claimed. In the South, they said, corrupt Republican regimes remained in power because the "best men"— the most capable politicians—were ex-Confederates barred from office holding.

For president, the new party nominated *New York Tribune* editor Horace Greeley, who had inconsistently supported both a stringent reconstruction policy and leniency toward former rebels. The Democrats endorsed Greeley as well; their campaign slogan was "Anything to Beat Grant." Horace Greeley campaigned so diligently that he worked himself to death making speeches from the back of a train, and died a few weeks after the election.

Grant, who won 56 percent of the popular vote, carried all the northern states and most of the sixteen southern and border states. But division among Republicans affected Reconstruction. To deprive the Liberals of a campaign issue, Grant

Republicans in Congress, the "regulars," passed the Amnesty Act, which allowed all but a few hundred ex-Confederate officials to hold office. A flood of private amnesty acts followed. In Grant's second term, Republican desires to discard the "southern question" mounted as depression gripped the nation.

The Panic of 1873   The postwar years brought accelerated industrialization, rapid economic growth, and frantic speculation. Investors rushed to profit from rising prices, new markets, high tariffs, and seemingly boundless opportunities. Railroads led the speculative boom. In May 1869, railroad executives drove a golden spike into the ground at Promontory Point, Utah, joining the Union Pacific and Central Pacific lines. By 1873, almost four hundred railroad corporations crisscrossed the Northeast, consuming tons of coal and miles of steel rail from the mines and mills of Pennsylvania and neighboring states. Transforming the economy, the railroad boom led entrepreneurs to over-speculate, with drastic results.

Philadelphia banker Jay Cooke, who had helped finance the Union effort with his wartime bond campaign, had taken over a new transcontinental line, the Northern Pacific, in 1869. Northern Pacific securities sold briskly for several years, but in 1873 the line's construction costs outran bond sales. In September, Cooke defaulted on his obligations, and his bank, the largest in the nation, shut down. A financial panic began; other firms collapsed, as did the stock market. The Panic of 1873 triggered a five-year depression. Banks closed, farm prices plummeted, steel furnaces stood idle, and one out of four railroads failed. Within two years, eighteen thousand businesses went bankrupt; 3 million were unemployed by 1878. Wage cuts struck those still employed; labor protests mounted; and industrial violence spread. The depression of the 1870s revealed that conflicts born of industrialization had replaced sectional divisions.

The depression also fed a dispute over currency that had begun in 1865. During the Civil War, Americans had used greenbacks, a paper currency not backed by a specific weight in gold. To stabilize the postwar currency, "sound money" supporters demanded withdrawal of greenbacks from circulation. Their opponents, "easy money" advocates, such as farmers and manufacturers dependent on easy credit, wanted an expanding currency, that is, more greenbacks. Once depression began, demands for such "easy money" rose. The issue divided both major parties and was compounded by another one: how to repay the federal debt.

In wartime, the Union government had borrowed what were then astronomical sums, mainly by selling war bonds. Bondholders wanted repayment in coin, gold or silver, even though many had paid for bonds in greenbacks. To pacify bondholders, Senator John Sherman of Ohio and other Republicans pressed for the Public Credit Act of 1869, which promised repayment in coin. With investors reassured, Sherman guided legislation through Congress that swapped the old short-term bonds for new ones payable over the next generation. In 1872, another bill in effect defined "coin" as "gold coin" by dropping the silver dollar from the official coinage. Through a feat of compromise, which placated investors and debtors, Sherman preserved the public credit, the currency, and Republican unity. His Specie Resumption Act of 1875 promised to put the nation on the gold standard in 1879.

But Sherman's measures did not satisfy the Democrats, who gained control of the House in 1875. Many Democrats and some Republicans demanded restoration of the silver dollar in order to expand the currency and relieve the depression. These "free-silver" advocates secured passage of the Bland-Allison Act of 1878, which partially restored silver coinage by requiring the Treasury to buy several million dollars worth of silver each month and turn it into coin. In 1876, other expansionists formed the **Greenback Party,** which adopted the debtors' cause and fought to keep greenbacks in circulation, though with little success. As the depression receded in 1879, the clamor for "easy money" subsided, only to resurge in the 1890s. The controversial "money question" of the 1870s, never resolved, gave politicians and voters another reason to forget about the South.

Reconstruction and the Constitution

The Supreme Court of the 1870s also played a role in weakening northern support for Reconstruction. In wartime, few cases of note had reached the Court. After the war, however, constitutional questions arose.

First, would the Court support congressional laws to protect freedmen's rights? The decision in *Ex parte* Milligan (1866) suggested not. In *Milligan*, the Court declared that a military commission established by the president or Congress could not try civilians in areas remote from war where the civil courts were functioning. Thus special military courts to enforce the Supplementary Freedmen's Bureau Act were doomed. Second, would the Court sabotage the congressional Reconstruction plan, as Republicans feared? In *Texas v. White* (1869), the Court ruled that although the Union was indissoluble and secession was legally impossible, the process of Reconstruction was still constitutional. It was grounded in Congress's power to ensure each state a republican form of government and to recognize the legitimate government in any state.

But in the 1870s, the Court backed away from Reconstruction. In the **slaughterhouse cases** of 1873, the Supreme Court chipped away at the Fourteenth Amendment. The cases involved a business monopoly, not freedmen's rights, but provided an opportunity to interpret the amendment narrowly. In 1869, the Louisiana legislature had granted a monopoly over the New Orleans slaughterhouse business to one firm and closed down all other slaughterhouses in the interest of public health. The excluded butchers brought suit. The state had deprived them of their lawful occupation without due process of law, they claimed; such action violated the Fourteenth Amendment, which guaranteed that no state could "abridge the privileges or immunities" of U.S. citizens. The Supreme Court upheld the Louisiana legislature by issuing a doctrine of "dual citizenship." The Fourteenth Amendment, declared the Court, protected only the rights of *national* citizenship, such as the right of interstate travel, but not those rights that fell to citizens through *state* citizenship. The *Slaughterhouse* decision vitiated the intent of the Fourteenth Amendment—to secure freedmen's rights against state encroachment.

The Supreme Court again backed away from Reconstruction in two cases in 1876 involving the Enforcement Act of 1870, enacted to protect black suffrage. In *United States v. Reese* and *United States v. Cruikshank*, the Supreme Court undercut the act's effectiveness. Continuing its retreat from Reconstruction, the Supreme Court in 1883 invalidated both the Civil Rights Act of 1875 and the Ku Klux Klan Act of 1871. These decisions cumulatively dismantled the Reconstruction policies that Republicans had sponsored after the war and confirmed rising northern sentiment that Reconstruction's egalitarian goals could not be enforced.

Republicans in Retreat

The Republicans did not reject Reconstruction suddenly but rather disengaged from it gradually, a process that began with Grant's election to the presidency in 1868. Not an architect of Reconstruction policy, Grant defended it. But he believed in decentralized government and hesitated to assert federal authority in local and state affairs.

In the 1870s, as northern military force shrank in the South, Republican idealism waned in the North. The Liberal Republican revolt of 1872 eroded what remained of radicalism. Among "regular" Republicans, who backed Grant, many held ambivalent views. Commercial and industrial interests now dominated both wings of the party, and few Republicans wished to rekindle sectional strife. After the Democrats won the House in 1874, support for Reconstruction became a political liability.

By 1875, the Radical Republicans, so prominent in the 1860s, had vanished. Chase, Stevens, and Sumner were dead. Other Radicals had lost office or conviction. "Waving the Bloody Shirt"—defaming Democratic opponents by reviving wartime animosity—now seemed counterproductive. Republican leaders reported that voters were "sick of carpetbag government" and tiring of both the "southern question" and the "Negro question." It seemed pointless to continue the unpopular and expensive policy of military intervention in the South to prop up Republican regimes that even President Grant found corrupt. Finally, few Republicans shared the egalitarian spirit that had animated Stevens and Sumner. Politics aside, Republican leaders and voters generally agreed with southern Democrats that blacks, although worthy of freedom, were inferior to whites. To insist on black equality would be thankless, divisive, politically suicidal—and would quash any hope of reunion between the regions. The Republicans' retreat from Reconstruction set the stage for its demise in 1877.

RECONSTRUCTION ABANDONED, 1876–1877

"We are in a very hot political contest just now," a Mississippi planter wrote to his daughter in 1875, "with a good prospect of turning out the carpetbag thieves by whom we have been robbed for the past six to ten years." Similar contests raged through the South in the 1870s, as the white resentment grew and Democratic influence surged. By the end of 1872, the Democrats had regained power in Tennessee, Virginia, Georgia, and North Carolina. Within three years, they won control in Texas, Alabama, Arkansas, and Mississippi. By 1876, Republican rule survived in only three states—South Carolina, Florida, and Louisiana. Democratic victories in state elections of 1876 and political bargaining in Washington in 1877 abruptly ended what little remained of Reconstruction.

"Redeeming" the South   Republican collapse in the South accelerated after 1872. Congressional amnesty enabled ex-Confederate officials to regain office; divisions among the Republicans weakened their party's grip on the southern electorate; and attrition diminished Republican ranks. Carpetbaggers returned North or became Democrats. Scalawags deserted in even larger numbers. Tired of northern interference and finding "home rule" by Democrats a possibility, Scalawags concluded that staying Republican meant going down with a sinking ship. Scalawag defections ruined Republican prospects. Unable to win new white votes or retain the old ones, the always-fragile Republican coalition crumbled.

Meanwhile, Democrats mobilized once-apathetic white voters. The resurrected southern Democratic party was divided: businessmen who envisioned an industrialized "New South" opposed an agrarian faction called the Bourbons—the old planter elite. But Democrats shared one goal: to oust Republicans from office. Tactics varied by state. Alabama Democrats won by promising to cut taxes and by getting out the white vote. In Louisiana, the "White League," a vigilante organization formed in 1874, undermined Republicans. Intimidation also proved effective in Mississippi, where violent incidents—like the 1874 slaughter in Vicksburg of about three hundred blacks by rampaging whites—terrorized black voters. In 1875, the "Mississippi plan" took effect: local Democratic clubs armed their members, who dispersed Republican meetings, patrolled voter-registration places, and marched through black areas. "The Republicans are paralyzed through fear and will not act," the anguished carpetbag governor of Mississippi wrote to his wife. "Why should I fight a hopeless battle?" In 1876, South Carolina's "Rifle Clubs" and "Red Shirts," armed groups that threatened Republicans, continued the scare tactics that had worked so well in Mississippi.

Intimidation did not completely squelch black voting, but Democrats deprived Republicans of enough black votes to win state elections. In some counties, they encouraged freedmen to vote Democratic at supervised polls where voters publicly placed a card with a party label in a box. In other instances, economic pressure impeded black suffrage. Labor contracts included clauses barring attendance at political meetings; planters used eviction threats to keep sharecroppers in line. Together, intimidation and economic pressure succeeded.

"Redemption," the word Democrats used to describe their return to power, brought sweeping changes. Some states called constitutional conventions to reverse Republican policies. All cut back expenses, wiped out social programs, lowered taxes, and revised their tax systems to relieve landowners of large burdens. State courts limited the rights of tenants and sharecroppers. Most important, the Democrats, or "redeemers," used the law to ensure a stable black labor force. Legislatures restored vagrancy laws, revised crop-lien statutes to make landowners' claims superior to those of merchants, and rewrote criminal law. Local ordinances in heavily black counties often restricted hunting, fishing, gun carrying, and ownership of dogs and thereby curtailed freedmen's everyday activities. States passed severe laws against trespassing and theft; stealing livestock or wrongly taking part of a crop became grand larceny with a penalty of up to five years at hard labor. By Reconstruction's end, black convict labor was commonplace.

For the freedmen, whose aspirations rose under Republican rule, redemption was devastating. The new laws, Tennessee blacks contended at an 1875 convention, would impose "a condition of servitude scarcely less degrading than that endured before the late civil war." In the late 1870s, as the political climate grew more oppressive, an "exodus" movement spread through Mississippi, Tennessee, Texas, and Louisiana. Some African-Americans became homesteaders in Kansas. After an outbreak of "Kansas fever" in 1879, four thousand **exodusters** from Mississippi and Louisiana joined about ten thousand who had reached Kansas earlier in the decade. But the vast majority of freedmen, devoid of resources, had no migration options or escape route. Mass movement of southern blacks to the North and Midwest would not gain momentum until the twentieth century.

The Election of 1876   By the autumn of 1876, with redemption almost complete, both parties sought to discard the heritage of animosity left by the war and Reconstruction. Republicans nominated Rutherford B. Hayes, three times Ohio's governor, for president. Untainted by the Grant-era scandals and popular with all factions in his party, Hayes presented himself as a "moderate" on southern policy. He favored "home rule" in the South and a guarantee of civil and political rights for all—two contradictory goals. The Democrats nominated Governor

Samuel J. Tilden of New York, a millionaire corporate lawyer and political reformer, known for his assaults on the Tweed Ring that had plundered New York City's treasury. Both candidates favored sound money, endorsed civil-service reform, and decried corruption, an irony since the 1876 election would be extremely corrupt.

Tilden won the popular vote by a 3 percent margin and seemed destined to capture the 185 electoral votes needed for victory (see Map 16.3). But the Republicans challenged the pro-Tilden returns from South Carolina, Florida, and Louisiana. If they could deprive the Democrats of these nineteen electoral votes, Hayes would triumph. The Democrats, who needed only one of the disputed electoral votes for victory, challenged (on a technicality) the validity of Oregon's single electoral vote, which the Republicans had won. Twenty electoral votes, therefore, were in contention. But Republicans still controlled the electoral machinery in the three unredeemed southern states, where they threw out enough Democratic ballots to declare Hayes the winner.

The nation now faced an unprecedented dilemma. Each party claimed victory in the contested states, and each accused the other of fraud. In fact, both sets of southern results involved fraud: the Republicans had discarded legitimate Democratic ballots, and the Democrats had illegally prevented freedmen from voting. In January 1877, Congress created a special electoral commission—seven Democrats, seven Republicans, and one independent—to decide which party would get the contested electoral votes. When the independent resigned, Congress replaced him with a Republican, and the commission gave Hayes the election by a vote of 8 to 7.

Congress now had to certify the new electoral vote. But Democrats controlled the House, and some threatened to obstruct debate and delay approval of the electoral

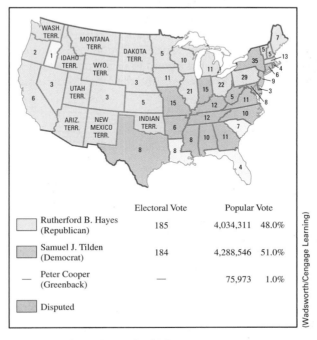

		Electoral Vote	Popular Vote	
▢	Rutherford B. Hayes (Republican)	185	4,034,311	48.0%
▨	Samuel J. Tilden (Democrat)	184	4,288,546	51.0%
—	Peter Cooper (Greenback)	—	75,973	1.0%
▨	Disputed			

(Wadsworth/Cengage Learning)

MAP 16.3 The Disputed Election of 1876

Congress resolved the contested electoral vote of 1876 in favor of Republican Rutherford B. Hayes.

vote. Had they done so, the nation would have lacked a president on inauguration day, March 4. Room for compromise remained, for many southern Democrats accepted Hayes's election: former scalawags with commercial interests still favored Republican financial policies; railroad investors expected Republican support for a southern transcontinental line. Other southerners did not mind conceding the presidency as long as the new Republican administration would leave the South alone. Republican leaders, although sure of eventual triumph, were willing to bargain as well, for candidate Hayes desired not merely victory but southern approval.

Informal negotiations ensued, at which politicians exchanged promises. Ohio Republicans and southern Democrats, who met at a Washington hotel, agreed that if Hayes won the election, he would remove federal troops from South Carolina and Louisiana, and Democrats could gain control of those states. In other bargaining sessions, southern politicians asked for federal patronage, federal aid to railroads, and federal support for internal improvements. In return, they promised to drop the filibuster, to accept Hayes as president, and to treat freedmen fairly. With the threatened filibuster broken, Congress ratified Hayes's election. Once in office, Hayes fulfilled some of the promises his Republican colleagues had made. He appointed a former Confederate as postmaster general and ordered federal troops who guarded the South Carolina and Louisiana statehouses back to their barracks. Federal soldiers remained in the South after 1877 but no longer served a political function. Democrats, meanwhile, took over state governments in Louisiana, South Carolina, and Florida. When Republican rule toppled in these states, the era of Reconstruction finally ended.

But some of the bargains struck in the **Compromise of 1877,** such as Democratic promises to treat southern blacks fairly, were forgotten, as were Hayes's pledges to ensure freedmen's rights. "When you turned us loose, you turned us loose to the sky, to the storm, to the whirlwind, and worst of all … to the wrath of our infuriated masters," Frederick Douglass had charged at the Republican convention in 1876. "The question now is, do you mean to make good to us the promises in your Constitution?" The answer provided by the 1876 election and the 1877 compromises was "No."

CHRONOLOGY
1865–1877

1863	President Abraham Lincoln issues Proclamation of Amnesty and Reconstruction.
1864	Wade-Davis bill passed by Congress and pocket-vetoed by Lincoln.
1865	Freedmen's Bureau established.
	Civil War ends.
	Lincoln assassinated.
	Andrew Johnson becomes president.
	Johnson issues Proclamation of Amnesty and Reconstruction.
	Ex-Confederate states hold constitutional conventions (May–December).
	Black conventions begin in the ex-Confederate states.
	Thirteenth Amendment added to the Constitution.
	Presidential Reconstruction completed.
1866	Congress enacts the Civil Rights Act of 1866 and the Supplementary Freedmen's Bureau Act over Johnson's vetoes.

Ku Klux Klan founded in Tennessee.
Tennessee readmitted to the Union.
Race riots in southern cities.
Republicans win congressional elections.

1867 Reconstruction Act of 1867.
William Seward negotiates the purchase of Alaska.
Constitutional conventions meet in the ex-Confederate states.
Howard University founded.

1868 President Johnson is impeached, tried, and acquitted.
Omnibus Act.
Fourteenth Amendment added to the Constitution.
Ulysses S. Grant elected president.

1869 Transcontinental railroad completed.

1870 Congress readmits the four remaining southern states to the Union.
Fifteenth Amendment added to the Constitution.
Enforcement Act of 1870.

1871 Second Enforcement Act.
Ku Klux Klan Act.

1872 Liberal Republican party formed.
Amnesty Act.
Alabama claims settled.
Grant reelected president.

1873 Panic of 1873 begins (September–October), setting off a five-year depression.

1874 Democrats gain control of the House of Representatives.

1875 Civil Rights Act of 1875. Specie Resumption Act.

1876 Disputed presidential election: Rutherford B. Hayes versus Samuel J. Tilden.

1877 Electoral commission decides election in favor of Hayes.
The last Republican-controlled governments overthrown in Florida, Louisiana, and South Carolina.

1879 "Exodus" movement spreads through several southern states.

CONCLUSION

Between 1865 and 1877, the nation experienced a series of crises. In Washington, conflict between President Johnson and Congress led to a stringent Republican plan for restoring the South, a plan that included the radical provision of black male enfranchisement. President Johnson ineptly abetted the triumph of his foes by his defiant stance, which drove moderate Republicans into an alliance against him with Radical Republicans. In the ex-Confederate states, Republicans took over and reorganized state governments. A new electorate, in which recently freed African-Americans were prominent, endorsed Republican policies. Rebuilding the South cost millions, and state expenditures soared. Objections to taxes, resentment of black suffrage, and fear of "Negro domination" spurred counterattacks on African-Americans by former Confederates.

Emancipation reshaped black communities where former slaves sought new identities as free people. African-Americans reconstituted their families; created black institutions, such as churches and schools; and participated in government for the first time in American history. They also took part in the transformation of southern agriculture. By Reconstruction's end, a new labor system, sharecropping, replaced slavery. Begun as a compromise between freedmen and landowners, sharecropping soon trapped African-Americans and other tenant farmers in a cycle of debt; black political rights waned as well as Republicans lost control of the southern states.

The North, meanwhile, hurtled headlong into an era of industrial growth, labor unrest, and financial crises. The political scandals of the Grant administration and the impact of depression after the Panic of 1873 diverted northern attention from the South. By the mid-1870s, northern politicians were ready to discard the Reconstruction policies that Congress had imposed a decade before. Simultaneously, the southern states returned to Democratic rule, as Republican regimes toppled one by one. Reconstruction's final collapse in 1877 reflected not only a waning of northern resolve but a successful ex-Confederate campaign of violence, intimidation, and protest that had started in the 1860s.

Reconstruction's end gratified both political parties. Although unable to retain a southern constituency, the Republican Party no longer faced the unpopular "southern question." The Democrats, now empowered in the former Confederacy, remained entrenched there for over a century. To be sure, the South was tied to sharecropping and economic backwardness as securely as it had once been tied to slavery. But "home rule" was firmly in place. Reconstruction's end also signified a triumph for nationalism and reunion. As the nation applauded reconciliation of South and North, Reconstruction's reputation sank. Looking back on the 1860s and 1870s, most late-nineteenth-century Americans dismissed the congressional effort to reconstruct the South as a fiasco—a tragic interlude of "radical rule" or "black reconstruction" fashioned by carpetbaggers, scalawags, and Radical Republicans.

With the hindsight of a century, historians continued to regard Reconstruction as a failure, though of a different kind. No longer viewed as a misguided scheme that collapsed because of radical excess, Reconstruction is now widely seen as a democratic experiment that did not go far enough. Historians cite two main causes. First, Congress did not promote freedmen's independence through land reform; without property of their own, southern blacks lacked the economic power to defend their interests as free citizens. Property ownership, however, does not necessarily ensure political rights nor invariably provide economic security. Considering the depressed state of postwar southern agriculture, the freedmen's fate as independent farmers would likely have been perilous. Thus the land-reform question remains a subject of debate. A second cause of Reconstruction's collapse evokes less dispute: the federal government neglected to back congressional Reconstruction with military force. Given the choice between protecting blacks' rights at whatever cost and promoting reunion, the government opted for reunion. As a result, the nation's adjustment to the consequences of emancipation would continue into the twentieth century.

The Reconstruction era left some significant legacies, including the Fourteenth and Fifteenth amendments. Although neither amendment would be used to protect minority rights for almost a century, they remain monuments to the democratic zeal that swept Congress in the 1860s. The aspirations and achievements of Reconstruction also left an indelible mark on black citizens. After Reconstruction, many Americans turned to their economic futures—to railroads, factories, and mills, and to the exploitation of the country's bountiful natural resources.

17

THE TRANSFORMATION OF THE TRANS-MISSISSIPPI WEST, 1860–1900

CHAPTER OUTLINE

- Native Americans and the Trans-Mississippi West • Settling the West
- Southwestern Borderlands • Exploiting the Western Landscape
- The West of Life and Legend

NATIVE AMERICANS AND THE TRANS-MISSISSIPPI WEST

No aspect of the transformation of the West was more visible and dramatic than the destruction of traditional Indian ways of life. Even before the newcomers poured onto the Great Plains at midcentury, Indian life in the trans-Mississippi West had changed considerably. In the Southwest, the Navajos had gradually given up migratory life in favor of settled agriculture. To the north, the Cheyenne and the Lakota Sioux, pushed out of the Great Lakes region by white settlement, had moved onto the Great Plains and had driven their enemies, the Pawnees and the Crows, farther west. These and other nomadic warrior tribes, dispersed in small bands, had followed the bison herds.

When whites invaded their territory at midcentury, these Indians protested and resisted. Caught between a stampede of miners and settlers who took their land and the federal government that sought to force them onto reservations, Native Americans fought back. By the 1890s, confinement on reservations had become the fate of almost every Indian nation. Undaunted, Native Americans struggled to preserve their customs and rebuild their numbers.

The Plains Indians   The Indians of the Great Plains inhabited three major subregions. The northern Plains, from the Dakotas and Montana southward to Nebraska, were home to large tribes, most notably the Lakota, as well as Flatheads, Blackfeet, Assiniboins, northern Cheyennes,

Arapahos, Crows, Hidatsas, and Mandans. Some of these were allies, but others were bitter enemies frequently at war. In the Central Plains, the so-called Five Civilized Tribes, driven there from the Southeast in the 1830s, pursued an agricultural life in the Indian Territory (present-day Oklahoma). Farther west, the Pawnees of Nebraska maintained the older, more settled tradition characteristic of Plains river valley culture before the introduction of horses. On the southern Plains of western Kansas, Colorado, eastern New Mexico, and Texas, the Comanches, Kiowas, Cheyennes, southern Arapahos, and Apaches maintained a migratory life appropriate to the arid environment.

Considerable diversity flourished among the Plains peoples, and customs varied even within subdivisions of the same tribe. For example, the easternmost branch of the great Sioux Nation, the Dakota Sioux of Minnesota who inhabited the wooded edge of the prairie, led a semisedentary life based on small-scale agriculture and bison hunting. In contrast, many Plains tribes—not only the Lakota Sioux, but also the Blackfeet, Crows, and Cheyennes—using horses obtained from the Spanish, roamed the High Plains to the west, and followed the bison migrations.

For all the **Plains Indians,** life revolved around extended family ties and tribal cooperation. Children were raised without physical punishment and were taught to treat each adult clan member with the respect accorded to relatives. Families and clans joined forces to hunt and farm, and reached decisions by consensus.

Sioux religion, which provided the cement for village and camp life, was complex. The Lakota Sioux thought of life as a series of circles. Living within the daily cycles of the sun and moon, Lakotas were born into a circle of relatives, which broadened to the band, the tribe, the Sioux Nation, and on to animals and plants. The Lakotas also believed in a hierarchy of spirits whose help could be invoked in ceremonies like the Sun Dance. To gain access to spiritual power, or to fulfill vows made on behalf of their relatives' well-being, young men would "sacrifice" themselves by forgoing food and water, dancing until exhausted, and suffering self-torture. For example, some suspended themselves from poles or cut pieces of their flesh and placed them at the foot of the Sun Dance pole. Painter George Catlin, who recorded Great Plains Indian life before the Civil War, described such a ceremony: "Several of them, seeing me making sketches, beckoned me to look at their faces, which I watched through all this horrid operation, without being able to detect anything but the pleasantest smiles as they looked me in the eye, while I could hear the knife rip through the flesh."

On the semiarid High Plains, where rainfall averaged less than twenty inches a year, both the bison and the Native peoples adapted to the environment. The huge bison herds, which at their peak contained an estimated 30 million animals, broke into small groups in the winter and dispersed into river valleys. In the summer, they returned to the High Plains to mate and feed on the nutritious short grasses. Like the bison, the Indians dispersed across the landscape to minimize their impact on the land, wintering in the river valleys and returning to the High Plains in summer. When their horses consumed the grasses near their camps, they moved. Hunting bison not only supplied the Native peoples with food, clothing, and tipi covers, but also created a valuable trading commodity, buffalo robes. To benefit from this trade, Indians themselves, as the nineteenth century progressed, increased their harvest of animals.

(Detroit Public Library, Burton Historical Collection)

Buffalo Skulls at the Michigan Carbon Works, 1895 *Once the vast herds of bison had been decimated, resourceful entrepreneurs, such as those pictured here, collected the skulls and sold them for industrial use. In all, nearly 2 million tons of bones were processed.*

The movement of miners and settlers onto the eastern High Plains in the 1850s eroded the habitat and threatened the Native American way of life. Pioneers occupied the river valley sites, where the buffalo had wintered, and exhausted the grasses. In the 1860s, the whites began systematically to hunt the animals, often with Indian help, to supply eastern markets with carriage robes and industrial belting. **William F. "Buffalo Bill" Cody,** a famous scout, killed thousands of bison in 1867–1868 to feed railroad construction crews. Army commanders also encouraged the slaughter of buffalo to undermine Indian resistance. Inconceivable carnage resulted. Between 1872 and 1875, hunters killed 9 million buffalo, taking only the skin and leaving the carcasses to rot. By the 1880s, the once-thundering herds had been reduced to a few thousand animals, and the Native American way of life dependent on the buffalo had been ruined.

The Assault on Nomadic Indian Life

In the 1850s, Indians faced the onslaught of thousands of pioneers lured by the discovery of gold and silver in the Rocky Mountains. The federal government's response was to reexamine its Indian policies. Abandoning the previous position, which had treated much of the West as a vast Indian reserve, the federal government sought to introduce a system of smaller tribal reservations where the Indians were to be concentrated, by force if necessary.

Some Native Americans, like the Pueblos of the Southwest (who had adapted to Spanish colonial life), the Crows of Montana, and the Hidatsas of North Dakota, adjusted peacefully. Others, among them the Navajos of Arizona and New Mexico and the eastern Dakota Sioux, opposed the new policy to no avail. By 1860, eight western reservations had been established.

Significant segments of the remaining tribes on the Great Plains, more than a hundred thousand people, fought against removal. Between 1860 and 1890, the western Sioux, Cheyennes, Arapahos, Kiowas, and Comanches on the Great Plains; the Nez Percés and Bannocks in the northern Rockies; and the Apaches in the Southwest—faced the U.S. army in a series of final battles for the West (see Map 17.1).

Misunderstandings, unfulfilled promises, brutality, and butchery marked the conflict. Near Sand Creek, Colorado, in 1864, soldiers from the local militia destroyed Cheyenne and Arapaho camps. The Indians retaliated with a flurry of attacks on travelers. The governor, in a panic, authorized Colorado's white citizenry

(Wadsworth/Cengage Learning)

MAP 17.1 Major Indian Battles in the West

Although they were never recognized as such in the popular press, the battles between the Native Americans and the U.S. army on the Great Plains amounted to an undeclared war.

to seek out and kill hostile Indians on sight. He then activated a regiment of troops under Colonel John M. Chivington, a Methodist minister. At dawn on November 29, under orders to "remember the murdered women and children on the Platte [River]," Chivington's troops massacred a peaceful band of Indians, including terrified women and children, camped at Sand Creek.

This massacre and others rekindled public debate over federal Indian policy. In response, in 1867 Congress sent a peace commission to end the fighting, and set aside two large land reserves, one north of Nebraska, the other south of Kansas. There, it was hoped, the tribes would take up farming and convert to Christianity. Behind the federal government's persuasion lay the threat of force. Any Native Americans who refused to relocate, warned Commissioner of Indian Affairs Ely S. Parker, himself a Seneca Indian, "would be subject wholly to the control and supervision of military authorities, [and]…treated as friendly or hostile as circumstances might justify."

At first, the plan appeared to work. Representatives of sixty-eight thousand southern Kiowas, Comanches, Cheyennes, and Arapahos signed the Medicine Lodge Treaty of 1867 and pledged to live in present-day Oklahoma. The following year, scattered bands of Sioux, representing nearly fifty-four thousand northern Plains Indians, signed the **Fort Laramie Treaty** and agreed to move to reservations on the so-called Great Sioux Reserve in the western part of what is now South Dakota in return for money and provisions.

But Indian dissatisfaction with the treaties ran deep. As a Sioux chief, Spotted Tail, told the commissioners, "We do not want to live like the white man….The Great Spirit gave us hunting grounds, gave us the buffalo, the elk, the deer, and the antelope. Our fathers have taught us to hunt and live on the Plains, and we are contented." Rejecting the new system, many bands of Indians refused to move to the reservations or to remain on them once there.

In August 1868, war parties of defiant Cheyennes, Arapahos, and Sioux raided settlements in Kansas and Colorado, burning homes and killing whites. In retaliation, army troops attacked Indians, even peaceful ones, who refused confinement. That autumn Lieutenant Colonel George Armstrong Custer's raiding party struck a sleeping Cheyenne village, killing more than a hundred warriors, shooting more than eight hundred horses, and taking fifty-three women and children prisoner. Other hostile Cheyennes and Arapahos were pursued, captured, and returned to the reservations.

In 1869, spurred on by Christian reformers, Congress established a Board of Indian Commissioners drawn from the major Protestant denominations to reform abuses on the reservations. But the new and inexperienced church-appointed Indian agents quickly encountered problems. Indians left the reservations in large numbers and agents were unable to restrain scheming whites who fraudulently purchased reservation lands from those who remained. Frustrated by the manipulation of Indian treaties and irritated by the ineptness of the Indian agents, Congress in 1871 abolished treaty making and replaced treaties with executive orders and acts of Congress. In the 1880s, the federal government ignored the churches' nominations for Indian agents and made its own appointments.

Caught in the sticky web of an ambiguous and deceptive federal policy, defiant Native Americans struck back in the 1870s. On the southern Plains, Kiowa,

Comanche, and Cheyenne raids in the Texas Panhandle in 1874 set off the so-called Red River War. In a fierce winter campaign, regular army troops slaughtered a hundred Cheyenne fugitives near the Sappa River in Kansas. The exile of seventy-four "ringleaders" to reservations in Florida thus ended Native American independence on the southern Plains. In the Southwest, in present-day Arizona and New Mexico, the Apaches fought an intermittent guerrilla war until their leader, Geronimo, surrendered in 1886.

Custer's Last Stand, 1876   Of all the acts of Indian resistance against the new reservation policy, none aroused more passion or caused more bloodshed than the battles waged by the western Sioux tribes in the Dakotas, Montana, and Wyoming. The 1868 Treaty of Fort Laramie had set aside the Great Sioux Reserve "in perpetuity." But not all the Sioux bands had signed the treaty.

By 1873, Chief Red Cloud's Oglala band and Chief Spotted Tail's Brulé band had managed to remain on their traditional lands. To protect their hunting grounds, they raided encroaching non-Indian settlements in Nebraska and Wyoming, intimidated federal agents and harassed anyone who ventured onto their lands.

Nontreaty Sioux found a powerful leader in the Lakota Sioux chief and holy man **Sitting Bull.** Broad-shouldered and powerfully built, Sitting Bull led by example and had considerable fighting experience. "You are fools," he told the reservation Indians, "to make yourselves slaves to a piece of fat bacon, some hard-tack, and a little sugar and coffee."

Pressured by would-be settlers and developers, General William Tecumseh Sherman in 1874 sent a force under Colonel George Armstrong Custer into the Black Hills of South Dakota, near the western edge of the Great Sioux Reserve. Lean and mustachioed, the thirty-four-year-old Custer had been a celebrity since his days as an impetuous young Civil War officer.

Custer's mission was to extract concessions from the Sioux. In November 1875, negotiations to buy the Black Hills had broken down because the Indians' asking price was deemed too high. Custer now sought to drive the Indians out of the Black Hills. Indians still outside the reservations after January 31, 1876, the government announced, would be hunted down and taken in by force.

In June 1876, leading 600 troops of the Seventh Cavalry, Custer proceeded to the Little Bighorn River area of present-day Montana, a hub of Indian resistance. On the morning of June 25, underestimating the Indian enemy and unwisely dividing his force, Custer, with 209 men, recklessly advanced against Cheyenne and Sioux warriors led by Chief Sitting Bull, who had encamped along the Little Bighorn. Custer and his outnumbered troops were wiped out.

Americans reeled from this unexpected Indian victory. Newspaper columnists groped to assess the meaning of "Custer's last stand." Some questioned the wisdom of current federal policy toward the Indians. Others worried that an outraged public would demand retaliation. Most, however, endorsed the federal government's determination to quash the Native American rebellion. "It is inconsistent with our civilization and with common sense," trumpeted a writer in the *New York Herald*, "to allow the Indian to roam over a country as fine as that around the Black Hills, preventing its development in order that he may shoot game and scalp his neighbors. That can never be."

Defeat at Little Bighorn made the army more determined. In Montana, troops harassed various Sioux bands for more than five years, attacking Indian camps in the dead of winter and destroying all supplies. Even Sitting Bull, who had led his band to Canada to escape the army, surrendered in 1881 for lack of provisions. The slaughter of the buffalo had wiped out his tribe's major food source.

Similar measures were used elsewhere in the West. Chief Dull Knife led some 150 survivors, including men, women, and children, north in September 1878 to join the Sioux. But the army chased them down and imprisoned them in Fort Robinson, Nebraska. When the army denied their request to stay nearer to their traditional northern lands, tribal leaders refused to cooperate. The post commander then withheld all food, water, and fuel. On a frigid night in January 1879, Dull Knife and his followers, in a desperate escape attempt, shot the guards and broke for freedom. Soldiers chased the Indians and gunned down half of them in the snow, including women and children as well as Dull Knife himself. The *Atlanta Constitution* condemned the incident as "a dastardly outrage upon humanity and a lasting disgrace to our boasted civilization." Although sporadic Indian resistance continued until the end of the century, these brutal tactics had sapped the Indians' will to resist.

"Saving" the Indians

A growing number of Americans were outraged by the federal government's flagrant violation of its Indian treaties. The Women's National Indian Rights Association, founded in 1883, and other groups took up the cause. **Helen Hunt Jackson** published *A Century of Dishonor* in 1881 to rally public opinion against the government's record of broken treaty obligations. "It makes little difference…where one opens the record of the history of the Indians," she wrote; "every page and every year has its dark stain."

To encourage Indians to abandon nomadic life, reformers like Jackson advocated the creation of Indian boarding schools, much like those established for emancipated slaves. Richard Henry Pratt, a retired military officer, opened such a school in Carlisle, Pennsylvania, in 1879. Pratt believed that the Indians' customs and languages had halted their progress toward white civilization. His motto therefore became "Kill the Indian and save the man." Modeled after Carlisle, other Indian boarding schools taught farming, carpentry, dressmaking, and nursing.

Despite the reformers' best efforts, the attempt to stamp out Indian identity in the boarding schools often backfired. Forming friendships with Indians from many different tribes, boarding school students forged their own sense of Indian identity. As Mitch Walking Elk, a Cheyenne-Arapaho-Hopi student at the Phoenix Indian School, put it, "They put me in the boarding school and they cut off all my hair, gave me an education, but the Apache's still in there."

In addition to their advocacy of boarding schools, well intentioned humanitarians concluded that the Indians' interests would be best served by breaking up the reservations, ending recognition of tribal governments, and gradually giving them the rights of citizens. In short, they proposed to eliminate the "Indian problem" by eliminating the Indians as a culturally distinct entity. Inspired by this vision, they supported the **Dawes Severalty Act,** passed in 1887.

The Dawes Act sought to turn Indians into landowners and farmers. The law emphasized severalty, or the treatment of Indians as individuals rather than as tribal members, and called for the distribution of 160 acres of reservation land for farming, or 320 acres for grazing, to each head of an Indian family who accepted the law's provisions. The remaining reservation lands were to be sold to speculators and settlers. To prevent unscrupulous people taking the lands granted to individual Indians, the government would hold each tribal member's property in trust for twenty-five years and make them U.S. citizens.

The Dawes Act did not specify a timetable for the breakup of the reservations. Few allotments were made to the Indians until the 1890s. The act proved to be a boon to speculators, who evaded its safeguards and obtained the Indians' best land. Much of what remained in Indian hands was too dry and gravelly for farming. In the twentieth century, ironically, periodic droughts and the fragile, arid High Plains landscape would push many white farmers back off the land.

Although some Native Americans who received land under the Dawes Act prospered enough to expand their holdings, countless others struggled just to survive. Hunting restrictions on the former reservation lands prevented many Indians from supplementing their limited farm yields. Alcoholism, a continuing problem exacerbated by the prevalence of whiskey as a trade item (and by the boredom that resulted from the disruption of hunting and other traditional pursuits), became more prevalent as Native Americans strove to adapt to the constraints of reservation life.

The Ghost Dance and the End of Indian Resistance on the Great Plains, 1890

Living conditions for the Sioux worsened in the late 1880s. The federal government reduced their meat rations and restricted hunting. When disease killed a third of their cattle, they became desperate. The Sioux, who still numbered almost twenty-five thousand, turned to Wovoka, a new visionary prophet popular among the Great Basin Indians in Nevada.

Wovoka foresaw a catastrophic event that would bring the return of dead relatives, the restoration of the bison herds, and the renewal of traditional life. Some versions of his vision included the destruction of European-Americans and their removal from Indian lands. To bring on this new day, the prophet preached a return to traditional ethics, and taught his followers a cycle of ritual songs and dance steps known as the **Ghost Dance.**

In the fall of 1890, as the Ghost Dance movement spread among the Sioux in the Dakota Territory, Indian officials grew alarmed. The local reservation agent decided that Chief Sitting Bull, whose cabin on the reservation had become a rallying point for the Ghost Dance movement, must be arrested. On a freezing, drizzly December morning, he dispatched Indian policemen from the agency to take Sitting Bull into custody. When the chief was pulled from his cabin, shots rang out, and Sitting Bull was mortally wounded. As bullets whizzed by, Sitting Bull's horse began to perform the tricks it remembered from its days in the Wild West show. Observers were terrified, convinced that the spirit of the dead chief had entered his horse.

Two weeks later, one of the bloodiest episodes of Indian–white strife on the Plains occurred. On December 29, as the Seventh Cavalry was rounding up 340 starving and freezing Sioux at **Wounded Knee,** South Dakota, a shot was fired. The soldiers responded with cannon fire. Within minutes three hundred Indians, including seven infants, were slaughtered. Three days later, a baby who had miraculously survived was found wrapped in a blanket under the snow. She wore a buckskin cap on which a beadwork American flag had been embroidered. Brigadier General L.W. Colby, who adopted the baby, named her Marguerite, but the Indians called her Lost Bird.

As the frozen corpses at Wounded Knee were dumped into mass graves, a generation of Indian–white conflict on the Great Plains shuddered to a close. Lost Bird, with her poignantly patriotic beadwork cap, highlights the irony of the Plains Indians' response to white expansion. Many Natives did try to adapt to non-Indian ways, and some succeeded fully. Goodbird, the son of Buffalo Bird Woman, became a Congregational minister, a prosperous farmer, and a leader of the Hidatsa tribe. He carefully blended his traditional Indian religious beliefs with Christianity. Others struggled with poverty. Driven onto reservations, many Indians became dependent on governmental support. By 1900, the Plains Indian population had shrunk from nearly a quarter-million to just over a hundred thousand. Nevertheless, the population began to increase slowly after 1900. Against overwhelming odds, the pride, religious traditions, and cultural identities of the Plains Indians survived all efforts at eradication.

Unlike the nomadic western Sioux, the more settled Navajos of the Southwest adjusted more successfully to the reservation system, preserving traditional ways

(Denver Public Library, Western History Division)

Wounded Knee, Pine Ridge Reservation, South Dakota, 1890 *Thrown into an open trench, the frozen bodies of the Sioux slaughtered at Wounded Knee were a grim reminder that the U.S. Army would brook no opposition to its control of Indian reservations.*

and adapting to their new locations. By 1900, the Navajos had tripled their reservation land, dramatically increased their numbers and their herds, and carved out for themselves a distinct place in Arizona and New Mexico.

In the name of civilization and progress, whites after the Civil War had forced Indians off their lands in an effort that involved a mixture of sincere (if misguided) benevolence, coercion wrapped in an aura of legality, and outbursts of naked violence. Many Americans felt only contempt for Indians and greed for their land. Others had tried to uplift and Christianize the natives. Both groups, however, were blind to the value of Native American life and traditions. And both were unsuccessful in their attempts to shatter proud peoples and their ancient cultures.

SETTLING THE WEST

The successive defeats of the Native Americans and their removal to reservations opened a vast territory for settlement. In the 1840s, when nearly a quarter-million Americans had trudged overland to Oregon and California, they had typically endured a six- to eight-month trip in ox-drawn wagons. After 1870, railroad expansion made the trip faster and considerably easier. In the next three decades, more land was parceled out into farms than in the previous 250 years of American history combined, and agricultural production doubled.

The First Transcontinental Railroad   Passed in 1862, the Pacific Railroad Act authorized the construction of a new transcontinental link. The act provided grants of land and other subsidies to the railroads for each mile of track laid, which made them the largest landholders in the West. More than any other factor, the expansion of these railroads accelerated the transformation of everyday life west of the Mississippi.

Building the railroad took backbreaking work. Searching for inexpensive labor, the railroads turned to immigrants. The Central Pacific employed Chinese workers to chip and blast rail bed out of solid rock in the Sierra Nevada. The railroad preferred the Chinese because they worked hard for low wages, did not drink, and furnished their own food and tents. Nearly twelve thousand Chinese graded the roadbed while Irish, Mexican-American, and black workers put down the track.

On May 10, 1869, Americans celebrated the completion of the first railroad spanning North America. As the two sets of tracks—the Union Pacific's, stretching westward from Omaha, Nebraska, and the Central Pacific's, reaching eastward from Sacramento, California—met at Promontory Point, Utah, beaming officials drove in a final ceremonial golden spike. The nation's vast midsection was now far more accessible than it had ever been.

The railroads sped up western development. In the battles against Native Americans, the army shipped horses and men west in the dead of winter to attack the Indians when they were most vulnerable. From the same trains, hunters gained quick access to the bison ranges and increased their harvest of the animals. Once Indian resistance had been broken, the railroads hastened the arrival of new settlers and later shipped their cattle and grain to eastern urban markets. Railroads even supplied special detectives to support local police in towns along their lines.

Settlers and the Railroad   During the decade after the passage of the Pacific Railroad Act, Congress awarded the railroads 170 million acres, worth over half a billion dollars. By 1893, Minnesota and Washington had also deeded to railroad companies a quarter of their state lands. As mighty landowners, the railroads had a unique opportunity to shape settlement in the region—and to reap enormous profits.

The railroads set up land sales offices and sent agents to the East Coast to recruit settlers. While the agents glorified the West as a new Garden of Eden, the land bureaus offered prospective buyers long-term loans and free transportation. Acknowledging that life on the Great Plains could be lonely, the promoters advised young men to bring their wives (because "maidens are scarce") and to emigrate as entire families and with friends.

One unintended consequence of these land promotions was to make land available to single women, or "girl homesteaders" as they were known at the time. In Wyoming, single women made up more than 18 percent of the claimants. Women filed 10 to 20 percent of the claims in Colorado, sometimes as individuals and sometimes to add to family holdings.

In addition to the millions of American migrants, the railroads helped bring nearly 2.2 million foreign-born settlers to the trans-Mississippi West between 1870 and 1900. Some agents recruited whole villages of Germans to relocate to the North Dakota plains. Irish laborers hired to lay track could be found in every town along the rail lines. By 1905, the Santa Fe Railroad alone had transported sixty thousand Russian Mennonites to the fertile Kansas plains where black pioneers called exodusters had preceded them in the 1870s (see Chapter 16).

The railroads influenced agriculture as well. To ensure repayment of money owed to them, the railroads urged farmers to specialize in cash crops—wheat on the northern Plains, corn in Iowa and Kansas, cotton in Texas. Although these crops initially brought in high revenues, many farmers grew dependent on income from a single crop and became vulnerable to fluctuating market forces.

Homesteading on the Great Plains   Liberalized land laws pulled settlers westward. The 1862 Homestead Act reflected the Republican Party's belief that free land would promote economic opportunity. It offered 160 acres of land to anyone who would pay a ten-dollar registration fee, live on the land for five years, and cultivate it. Although nearly four hundred thousand families claimed land under its provisions between 1860 and 1900, the law did not function as Congress had envisioned. Unscrupulous speculators filed false claims for the choicest locations, and railroads acquired huge landholdings. Only one acre in every nine went to the pioneers for whom it was intended.

The 160-acre limit specified by the Homestead Act created a second problem. On the rich soils of Iowa or in the fertile lands in Oregon, and Washington, a 160-acre farm was ample, but in the drier areas west of the hundredth meridian, a farmer needed more land. In 1873, to rectify this problem, Congress passed the Timber Culture Act, which gave homesteaders an additional 160 acres if they planted trees on 40 acres. Congress enacted the Desert Land Act in 1877, which made 640 acres available at $1.25 an acre, and the Timber and Stone Act of

1878, which permitted the purchase of up to 160 acres of forest land for $2.50 an acre. However, these measures were abused by grasping speculators, lumber-company representatives, and cattle ranchers. Yet, even though families did not receive as much land as Congress had intended, federal laws kept alive the dream of the West as a place for new beginnings.

In addition to problems caused by insufficient rainfall in many regions, almost all settlers faced difficult psychological adjustments to frontier life. The first years of settlement were the most difficult. Toiling to build a house, plant the first crop, and dig a well, the pioneers put in an average of sixty-eight hours of backbreaking work a week in isolated surroundings. Howard Ruede, a Pennsylvania printer who migrated to Kansas to farm, wrote home in 1877 complaining about the mosquitoes and bedbugs infesting his house, which was cut out of thick grass sod and dug into the ground. He and countless others saw their shining vision of idyllic farm life quickly dim. For blacks who emigrated from the South to Kansas and other parts of the Plains after the Civil War, prejudice compounded the burdens of adjusting to a different life.

Many women found adaptation to Plains frontier life especially difficult. At least initially, some were enchanted by the landscape. But far more were struck by the "horrible tribes of Mosquitoes"; the violent drenching summer thunderstorms with hailstones as "big as hen's eggs" and blinding winter blizzards; and the crude sod huts that served as their early homes because of the scarcity of timber. One woman burst into tears upon first seeing her new sod house. The young bride angrily informed her husband that her father had built a better house for his hogs.

The high transience rate on the Great Plains in these years reflected the difficulty that newcomers faced in adjusting. Nearly half of those who staked homestead claims in Kansas between 1862 and 1890 gave up and moved on. However, in places like Minnesota and the Pacific Northwest that were populated by Germans, Norwegians, and other immigrants with a tradition of family prosperity tied to continuous landownership, the persistence rate (or percentage of people staying for a decade or more) could be considerably higher.

Many who weathered the lean early years came to identify deeply with the land. Within a decade, the typical Plains family that had "stuck it out" had moved into a new wood-framed house and had fixed up the front parlor. Women worked particularly hard on these farms and took pride in their accomplishments. "Just done the chores," wrote one woman to a friend. "I went fence mending and getting out cattle...and came in after sundown. I fed my White Leghorns [chickens] and then sat on the step to read over your letter. I forgot my wet feet and shoes full of gravel and giggled joyously."

New Farms, New Markets   Farmers on the Plains took advantage of advances in farm mechanization and the development of improved strains of wheat and corn to boost production dramatically. Efficient steel plows; specially designed wheat planters; and improved grain binders, threshers, and windmills enabled the typical Great Plains farmer of the late nineteenth century to increase the land's yield tenfold.

Barbed wire, patented in 1874, was another crucial invention that permitted farmers to keep roving livestock out of their crops. But fencing the land touched off violent clashes between farmers and cattle ranchers, who demanded the right to let their herds roam freely until the roundup. Generally the farmers won.

The invention of labor-saving machinery together with increased demand for wheat, milk, and other farm products created the impression that farming was entering a period of unparalleled prosperity. But few fully understood the perils of pursuing agriculture as a livelihood. The cost of the land, horses, machinery, and seed needed to start up a farm could exceed twelve hundred dollars, far more than the annual earnings of the average industrial worker. Faced with substantial mortgage payments, many farmers had to specialize in a crop such as wheat or corn that would fetch high prices. This specialization made them dependent on the railroads for shipping and put them at the mercy of the international grain market's shifting prices.

Far from being an independent producer, the western grain grower was a player in a complex world market economy. High demand could bring prosperity, but when world overproduction forced grain prices down, the heavily indebted grower faced ruin. Confronted with these realities, many Plains farmers quickly abandoned the illusion of frontier independence and easy wealth.

Unpredictable rainfall and weather conditions further exacerbated homesteaders' difficulties west of the hundredth meridian, where rainfall averaged less than twenty inches a year. Farmers compensated through "dry farming"—plowing deeply to stimulate the capillary action of the soils and harrowing lightly to raise a covering of dirt that would retain precious moisture after a rainfall. They also built windmills and diverted creeks for irrigation. But the onset of unusually dry years in the 1870s, together with grasshopper infestations and the major economic depression that struck the United States between 1873 and 1878 (see Chapter 16), made the plight of some midwesterners desperate.

Building a Society and Achieving Statehood

Despite the hardships, many remote farm settlements blossomed into thriving communities. Churches and Sunday schools became humming centers of social activity as well as of worship. Neighbors readily lent a hand to the farmer whose barn had burned or whose family was sick. Cooperation was a practical necessity and a form of insurance in a rugged environment where everyone was vulnerable to instant misfortune or even disaster.

When the population increased, local boosters lobbied to turn the territory into a state. Achieving statehood required the residents of the territory to petition Congress to pass an enabling act and then to elect delegates for a state constitutional convention. Once the state constitution had been drawn up and ratified by popular vote, the territory applied to Congress for admission as a state.

Under these procedures, Kansas entered the Union in 1861, followed by Nevada in 1864, Nebraska in 1867, and Colorado in 1876. Not until 1889 did North Dakota, South Dakota, Montana, and Washington gain statehood. Wyoming and Idaho followed the next year, and Utah in 1896. Oklahoma's admission in 1907 and Arizona's and New Mexico's in 1912 completed the process of creating states in the trans-Mississippi West (see Map 17.2).

Although generally socially conservative, the new state governments supported woman suffrage. As territories became states, pioneer women battled for the vote.

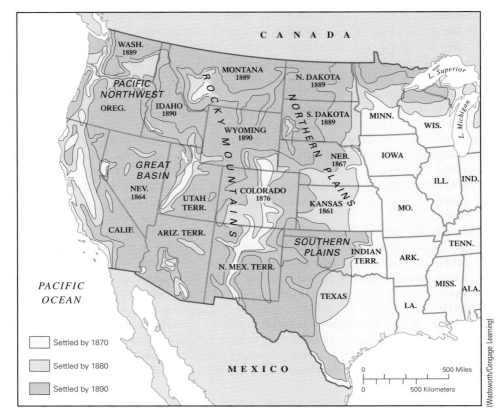

MAP 17.2 The Settlement of the Trans-Mississippi West, 1860–1890

The West was not settled by a movement of peoples gradually creeping westward from the East. Rather, settlers first occupied California and the Midwest and then filled up the nation's vast interior.

Seven western states held referenda on this issue between 1870 and 1910. Success came first in the Wyoming Territory, where men outnumbered women 6 to 1. The tiny legislature enfranchised women in 1869 in the hope that it would attract women, families, and economic growth. The Utah Territory followed in 1870 and reaffirmed its support for woman suffrage when it became a state. Nebraska in 1867 and Colorado in 1876 permitted women to vote in school elections. Although these successes were significant, by 1910 only four states—Idaho, Wyoming, Utah, and Colorado—had granted women full voting rights.

The Spread of Mormonism   In 1847, members of the Church of Jesus Christ of Latter-day Saints known as Mormons had escaped persecution by moving to the Great Salt Lake Valley. Led by Brigham Young, their prophet-president, and a Council of Twelve Apostles, they sought to create the independent country of Deseret. Their faith emphasized self-sufficiency and commitment to family. In the next two decades, recruitment in Great Britain and the Scandinavian countries boosted their numbers to more than 100,000. These Mormon communities increasingly conflicted with non-Mormons and with the U.S. government, which disapproved of the church's involvement in politics, its communal business practices, and its support of polygamy or plural marriage.

The Mormons sought at first to be economically independent. In 1869, they developed their own railroad branches connecting Salt Lake City and Ogden to the Central Pacific Railroad and set up Zion's Cooperative Mercantile Institution to control wholesale and retail activities. They asked all Mormons to abstain from coffee, tea, and alcohol, and established their own People's Party to mobilize the Mormon vote.

But a series of federal acts and court decisions, starting with the Morrill Anti-Bigamy Act in 1862, challenged the authority of their church and their practice of polygamy. In *United States v. Reynolds* (1879), the Supreme Court declared plural marriages unlawful and held that freedom of religion did not protect religious practices. Then, in 1887, the **Edmunds-Tucker Act** dissolved the church corporation, limited the church's assets to $50,000, abolished women's right to vote, and put its properties and funds into receivership (control by the courts).

In response, in 1890 the church president publicly announced the official end of polygamy. A year later, the Mormons dissolved their People's Party. The church supported the application for statehood, which was granted in 1896. Confiscated church properties were returned, voting rights were restored, and jailed polygamists were pardoned, but the balance between sacred and secular had permanently shifted. Mormon settlements would continue in the twentieth century to draw new members and influence development in western communities.

SOUTHWESTERN BORDERLANDS

The annexation of Texas in 1845 and the Treaty of Guadalupe Hidalgo that had ended the Mexican-American War in 1848 ceded to the United States an immense territory, part of which became Texas, California, Arizona, and New Mexico. At the time, Mexicans had controlled vast expanses of the Southwest, maintaining their own churches, large ranching operations, and trade with the Indians. Although the United States had pledged to protect the property of Mexicans who remained on American soil, over the next three decades American ranchers and settlers forced much of the Spanish-speaking population off the land. Mexicans who stayed in the region adapted to the new Anglo society with varying degrees of success.

In Texas, the struggle for independence from Mexico had left a legacy of bitterness and misunderstanding. After 1848, Texas cotton planters confiscated Mexican lands and began a racist campaign that labeled Mexicans as nonwhite. Angered by their loss of land and discriminatory treatment, Mexican bandits retaliated by raiding American communities. Tensions peaked in 1859 when Juan Cortina, a Mexican rancher, attacked the Anglo border community of Brownsville, Texas, and freed all the prisoners in jail. Cortina battled the U.S. army for years until the Mexican government, fearing a U.S. invasion, imprisoned him in 1875.

Mexican-Americans in California in the 1850s and 1860s faced similar pressures. A cycle of flood and drought, together with a slumping cattle industry, had ruined many of the large southern California ranches owned by the *californios*, Spanish-speaking descendants of the original Spanish settlers. The collapse of the ranch economy forced many of them to retreat into segregated urban neighborhoods called barrios. Spanish-surnamed citizens made up nearly half the 2,640 residents of Santa Barbara, California, in 1870; ten years later, after an influx of new settlers, they comprised barely a quarter of the population.

In many western states, Mexicans, Native Americans, and Chinese experienced similar patterns of racial discrimination, manipulation, and exclusion. At first, the number of new "Anglos" was small. As the number of whites increased, they identified minority racial, cultural, and language differences as marks of inferiority. White state legislators passed laws that made ownership of property difficult for non-Anglos. Relegated to a migratory labor force, non-Anglos were tagged as shiftless and irresponsible. Yet their labor made possible increased prosperity for the farmers, railroads, and households that hired them.

The cultural adaptation of Spanish-speaking Americans to Anglo society initially unfolded more smoothly in Arizona and New Mexico, where Spanish settlement had been sparse and a small class of wealthy Mexican landowners had long dominated a poor, illiterate peasantry. Moreover, since the 1820s, well-to-do Mexicans in Tucson, Arizona, had educated their children in the United States and formed trading partnerships and business alliances with Americans. One of the most successful was Estevan Ochoa, who began a long-distance freight business in 1859 with a U.S. partner and then expanded it into a lucrative merchandising, mining, and sheep-raising operation.

The success of men such as Ochoa, who became mayor of Tucson, helped moderate American settlers' antagonistic attitudes. So, too, did the work of popular writers like Helen Hunt Jackson, who sentimentalized the colonial Spanish past. Jackson's 1884 romance *Ramona*, a tale of the doomed love of a Hispanicized mixed-blood (Irish-Indian) woman set on a California ranch overwhelmed by the onrushing tide of Anglo civilization, was enormously popular. Jackson's novel also appealed to upper-class Mexican-Americans known as *Nuevomexicanos* who traced their lineage back to the Spanish conquest.

Still, conflicts over property persisted in Arizona and New Mexico. In the 1880s, Mexican-American ranchers organized themselves into a self-protection vigilante group called Las Gorras Blancas (the **White Caps**). In 1888, they tore up railroad tracks and attacked both Anglo newcomers and those upper-class Hispanics who had fenced acreage previously considered public grazing land. But this vigilante action did not stop the Anglo-dominated corporate ranchers from steadily increasing their land holdings. In towns and cities, discrimination limited the economic opportunities for Mexican-American businessmen and the Spanish-speaking population as a whole became more impoverished. Even in Tucson, where the Mexican-American elite enjoyed considerable economic and political success, 80 percent of the Mexican-Americans in the work force were laborers in 1880, taking jobs as butchers, barbers, cowboys, and railroad workers.

As increasing numbers of Mexican-American men were forced to search for seasonal migrant work, women took responsibility for holding families and communities together. Women managed the households when their husbands were away and fostered group identification by maintaining traditional customs, kinship ties, and allegiance to the Catholic Church. They tended garden plots and traded food, soap, and produce with other women, generally stabilizing the community in times of drought or persecution by Anglos.

Violence and discrimination against Spanish-speaking citizens of the Southwest escalated in the 1890s, a time of rising racism in the United States. Rioters in Beeville and Laredo, Texas, in 1894 and 1899 attacked and beat up Mexican-Americans. Whites increasingly labeled Mexican-Americans as violent and lazy. For Spanish-speaking citizens, the battle for fair treatment and respect would continue into the twentieth century.

EXPLOITING THE WESTERN LANDSCAPE

The displacement of Mexican-American and Native peoples from their lands opened the way for the exploitation of the natural environment in the trans-Mississippi West. Between 1860 and 1900, a generation of Americans sought to strike it rich by joining the ranks of those convinced of the region's boundless opportunity. Although the mining, ranching, and farming "bonanzas" promised unheard-of wealth, they set in motion a boom-and-bust economy in which some succeeded but others went bankrupt or barely survived.

The Mining Frontier   In the half-century that began with the California gold rush in 1849, a series of mining booms swept from the Southwest northward into Canada and Alaska. In 1853, Henry Comstock, an illiterate prospector, stumbled on the rich **Comstock Lode** along Nevada's Carson River. Later in the same decade, prospectors swarmed into the Rocky Mountains and uncovered deep veins of gold and silver near present-day Denver. Over the next five decades, gold was discovered in Idaho, Montana, Wyoming, South Dakota, and, in 1896, in the Canadian Klondike. Although the popular press clearly exaggerated reports of miners scooping up gold by the panful, by 1900 more than a billion dollars' worth of gold had been mined in California alone.

The early discoveries of "placer" gold, panned from streams, attracted a young male population thirsting for wealth and reinforced the myth of mining country as "a poor man's paradise". In contrast to the Great Plains, where ethnic groups recreated their own ethnic enclaves, western mining camps became ethnic melting pots. In the California census of 1860, more than thirty-three thousand Irish and thirty-four thousand Chinese had staked out early claims.

Although a few prospectors became fabulously wealthy, the experience of Henry Comstock, who sold out one claim for eleven thousand dollars and another for two mules, was more typical. Because the larger gold and silver deposits lay embedded in veins of quartz deep within the earth, extracting them required huge investments in expensive equipment. Deep shafts had to be blasted into the rock. Once lifted to the surface, the rock had to be crushed and flushed with mercury or cyanide to collect the silver, which was then smelted into ingots. No sooner had the major discoveries been made, therefore, than large mining companies backed by eastern or British capital bought them out and took them over.

Life in the new mining towns was vibrant but unpredictable. During the heyday of the Comstock Lode in the 1860s and 1870s, Virginia City, Nevada, erupted in an orgy of speculation and building. Started as a shantytown in 1859, it swelled by 1873 into a thriving metropolis of twenty thousand people complete with elaborate mansions, a six-story hotel, an opera house, 131 saloons, 4 banks, and uncounted brothels. Men outnumbered women three to one. Money quickly earned was even more rapidly lost.

The boom-and-bust cycle evident in Virginia City was repeated in towns across the West. Mark Twain captured the thrill of the mining "stampedes" in *Roughing It* (1872). "Every few days," wrote Twain, "news would come of the discovery of a brand-new mining region: immediately the papers would teem with accounts of its richness, and away the surplus population would scamper to take possession. By the time I was fairly inoculated with the disease, 'Esmeralda' had just had a run and 'Humboldt' was beginning to shriek for attention. 'Humboldt! Humboldt!' was the new cry, and straightway Humboldt, the newest of the new, the richest of the rich, the most marvelous of the marvelous discoveries in silver-land, was occupying two columns of the public prints to 'Esmeralda's' one."

The gold rush mania also spurred the growth of settlement in Alaska. Small strikes there in 1869, two years after the United States had purchased the territory from Russia, brought the first prospectors. More miners arrived in the 1880s. But it was the discovery of gold in the Canadian Klondike in 1897 that brought thousands of prospectors into the area and eventually enabled Alaska to establish its own territorial government in 1912.

Word of new ore deposits like the ones in Alaska lured transient populations salivating to get rich. Miners typically earned about $2,000 a year at a time when teachers made $450 to $650 and domestic help $250 to $350. But the work was extremely dangerous. One journalist commented that "no premature explosion of blasts, crushing in of timbers, caving of earth or rock—no accident of any kind is so much feared…or is more terrible than a great fire in a large mine. It is hell.…" One out of eighty miners died annually in the 1870s. Most prospectors earned only enough to go elsewhere, perhaps buy some land, and try again. Nevertheless, the production of millions of ounces of gold and silver stimulated the economy, lured new foreign investors, and helped usher the United States into the mainstream of the world economy.

Progress came at a high cost to the environment. Hydraulic mining, which used water cannons to dislodge minerals, polluted rivers, turned creeks brown, and flushed millions of tons of silt into valleys. The scarred landscape that remained was littered with rock and gravel filled with traces of mercury and cyanide, and nothing would grow on it. Smelters spewed dense smoke containing lead, arsenic, and other carcinogenic chemicals, often making those who lived nearby sick. The devastation is still evident today.

Cowboys and the Cattle Frontier

The feverish growth of open-range cattle ranching paralleled the expansion of the mining frontier during the 1860s and 1870s. In this case, astute businessmen and railroad entrepreneurs, eager to fund their new investments in miles of track, promoted cattle herding as the new route to fame and fortune. The cowboy, once scorned as a ne'er-do-well and drifter, was now glorified as a man of rough-hewn integrity and self-reliant strength.

In 1868, Joseph G. McCoy, a young cattle dealer from Springfield, Illinois, shrewdly combined organizational and promotional skills to turn the cattle industry into a new money-maker. With the forced relocation of the Plains Indians onto reservations and the extension of the railroads into Kansas after the Civil War, McCoy realized that cattle dealers could now amass enormous fortunes by raising steers cheaply in Texas and bringing them north for shipment to eastern urban markets.

(Library of Congress)

Nat Love *Although Nat Love, pictured here with his Winchester rifle, personified the rugged, tough cowboy, when the railroads undercut the cattle-drive business, Love became a Pullman sleeping car porter. In 1907 he published his memoires detailing his colorful career.*

McCoy built a new stockyard in Abilene, Kansas. By guaranteeing to transport his steers in railcars to hungry eastern markets, he obtained a five-dollar kickback from the railroads on each cattle car shipped. To make the overland cattle drives from Texas to Abilene easier, McCoy also helped survey and shorten the Chisholm Trail in Kansas. Finally, in a clever feat of showmanship, he organized the first Wild West show, sending four Texas cowboys to St. Louis and Chicago, where they staged roping and riding exhibitions that attracted exuberant crowds. At the end of his first year in business, thirty-five thousand steers were sold in Abilene; the following year the number more than doubled.

The great **cattle drives** of the 1860s and 1870s turned into a bonanza for herd owners. Steers purchased in Texas at nine dollars a head could be sold in Abilene, after deducting four dollars in trail expenses, for twenty-eight dollars. A herd of two thousand head could thus bring a tidy thirty-thousand-dollar profit. But the cattlemen, like the grain growers farther north on the Great Plains, lived at the mercy of high interest rates and an unstable market. During the financial panic of 1873, cattle drovers fell into bankruptcy by the hundreds.

Little of the money made by the large-scale cattle ranchers found its way into the pockets of the cowboys themselves. The typical cowpunchers who drove herds through the dirt and dust from southern Texas to Abilene earned a mere thirty dollars a month, about the same as common laborers. They also braved the gangs of cattle thieves that operated along the trails. The most notorious of the cattle rustlers, William H. Bonney, better known as Billy the Kid, may have murdered as many as eleven men before he was killed by a sheriff in 1881 at the age of twenty-one. The long hours, low pay, and hazardous work discouraged older ranch hands from applying. Most cowboys were men in their teens and twenties who worked for a year or two and then pursued different livelihoods.

Of the estimated 35,000 to 55,000 men who rode the trails in these years, nearly one-fifth were black or Mexican. Barred by discrimination from many other trades, blacks enjoyed the freedom of life on the trail. Although they were excluded from the position of trail boss, they distinguished themselves as resourceful and shrewd cowpunchers. **Nat Love,** the son of Tennessee slaves, left for Kansas after the Civil War to work for Texas cattle companies. As chief brander, he moved through Texas and Arizona "dancing, drinking, and shooting up the town." On July 4, 1876, when the Black Hills gold rush was in full swing, Love delivered three thousand head of cattle to a point near the hills and rode into Deadwood to celebrate. Local miners and gamblers had raised prize money for roping and shooting contests, and Nat Love won both, as well as a new title, Deadwood Dick.

Close relationships sometimes developed between black and white cowboys. Shortly before Charles Goodnight, a white pioneer trailblazer, died in 1929, he recalled of the black cowboy Bose Ikard, a former slave, that "he was my detective, banker, and everything else in Colorado, New Mexico, and the other wild country I was in. The nearest and only bank was at Denver, and when we carried money I gave it to Bose." Goodnight revealed much about the economic situation of blacks on the Plains, however, when he added that "a thief would...never think of looking in a Negro's bed for money."

The cattle bonanza, which peaked between 1880 and 1885, produced more than 4.5 million head of cattle for eastern markets (see Beyond America). Prices began to sag as early as 1882, however, and many ranchers plunged heavily into debt. In 1885 and 1886, two of the coldest and snowiest winters on record combined with summer droughts and Texas fever to destroy nearly 90 percent of the cattle in some regions, pushing thousands of ranchers into bankruptcy. The cattle industry lived on, but railroad expansion brought the days of the open range and the great cattle drives to an end. As had the mining frontier, the cattle frontier left behind memories of individual daring, towering fortunes for some, and hard times for many.

Cattle Towns and Prostitutes   One legacy of the cattle boom was the growth of cities like Abilene, Kansas, which shipped steers to Chicago and eastern markets. Like other cattle towns, Abilene went through an early period of violence that saw cowboys pulling down the walls of the jail as it was being built. But the town quickly established a police force to maintain law and order. City ordinances forbade carrying firearms and regulated saloons, gambling, and prostitution. James B. "Wild Bill" Hickok served as town marshal in 1871. Dime novelists described him as "a veritable terror to bad men on the border," but during his term as Abilene's lawman, Hickok killed just two men, one of them by mistake. Transient, unruly types certainly gave a distinctive flavor to cattle towns like Abilene, Wichita, and Dodge City, but the overall homicide rates there were not unusually high.

If cattle towns were neither as violent nor as lawless as legend would have it, they did still experience a lively business in prostitution, as did most cities at this time. Given the large numbers of unattached young men and numerous saloons (Abilene, in the 1870s, with a permanent population of five hundred, had 32 drinking establishments), prostitution thrived. Prostitutes came from all social classes and from as far away as China, Ireland, Germany, and Mexico. Some became prostitutes as an escape from domestic violence or because of economic hardship. Others, like the Chinese, were forced into the trade. All prostitutes risked venereal disease, physical abuse, and drug and alcohol addiction.

As western towns became more settled, the numbers of women in other occupations increased. Some found work as cooks or laundresses on ranches. Others married merchants, doctors, and businessmen. Although few of the first generation rode the range, their daughters became increasingly involved in the everyday work of ranching and became proficient riders themselves.

Bonanza Farms   Like the gold rushes and cattle bonanzas, the wheat boom of the 1870s and 1880s started small but rapidly attracted large capital investments that produced the nation's first agribusinesses. The boom in the Dakota Territory began during the Panic of 1873, when the Northern Pacific Railroad began exchanging land for its depreciated bonds. Speculators purchased more than three hundred thousand acres in the fertile Red River valley of North Dakota for between fifty cents and a dollar an acre.

Operating singly or in groups, the speculators established factory-like tenthousand-acre farms, each run by a hired manager, and invested heavily in labor and equipment. On the Cass-Cheney-Dalrymple farm near Fargo, North Dakota, fifty or sixty plows rumbled across the flat landscape on a typical spring day.

BEYOND AMERICA — GLOBAL INTERACTIONS

Cattle-Raising in the Americas

Nineteenth-century dime novels and Wild West Shows celebrated cowboys as quintessentially American—independent, self-reliant, tough, and occasionally violent. Driving herds of cattle north from Texas to Kansas, the cowboys, who rode the open range from the end of the Civil War through the mid-1880s, appeared to be the unique product of the American West. From a more global perspective, however, North-American cowboys shared much in common with the Mexican *vaqueros* and Argentinian *gauchos*. Like their counterparts in Latin and South America, they drew on a long tradition of cattle herding that had begun centuries earlier in Africa, England, and Spain.

Spanish conquistadors and English colonists brought to the New World their practice of raising beef cattle on the open range rather than in fixed enclosures. In sixteenth-century Mexico, African slaves often joined mixed-bloods of Spanish and Indian ancestry to brand and tend cattle. On the rich grasslands of Argentina, horsemen first hunted wild cattle that had escaped earlier settlements. Later, after the Indians were driven off the open range, these horsemen, now called *gauchos*, tended cattle on large ranches.

Gauchos and cowboys were colorful characters, usually young men, often from lower-class backgrounds. The English naturalist, Charles Darwin, visiting Argentina in 1833, described them as "generally tall and handsome, but with a proud and dissolute expression of countenance. They frequently wear their mustaches, and long black hair curling down their backs. With their brightly-colored garments, great spurs clanking about their heels, and knives stuck as daggers (and often so used) at their waists, they look a very different race of men from what might be expected from their name of Gauchos, or simple countrymen." Like cowboys, they busted broncos, taming the wild horses to accept riders, and rounded up strays. They also hunted wild ostriches, whose feathers fetched high prices in Europe. As in North America, some gauchos became bandits, which added to their romantic appeal.

Gauchos and cowboys, like other cattle herders around the world, whether Russian Cossacks, South African Dutch farmers, or Canadian cowhands, were often skilled horsemen. American cowboys drew on both Anglo and Hispanic traditions. Unlike the gauchos in Argentina who used *bolas*, an Indian invention of three balls connected by rawhide thongs, to entangle a steer's feet and immobilize it, American cowboys used the Hispanic *lariat to* rope the necks of their cattle and place them in a corral. Like British herders who used dogs, American cowboys taught their horses to maneuver quickly and sharply to keep the herd in

Northern Pacific president George W. Cass, who had invested fifty thousand dollars for land and equipment, paid all his expenses plus the cost of the ten thousand acres with his first harvest alone.

The publicity generated by the tremendous success of a few large investors like Cass led to an unprecedented wheat boom in the Red River valley in 1880. Eastern banking syndicates and small farmers alike rushed to buy land. North Dakota's population tripled in the 1880s. Wheat production skyrocketed to almost 29 million bushels by the end of the decade. But the profits soon evaporated. By 1890, some Red River valley farmers were destitute.

line or to cut out a steer to be branded. Like their counterparts in Canada, they organized rodeos to show off their riding and lassoing skills.

Although horses were universally used to herd cattle throughout the Americas, each open-range cattle-raising region had its own distinctive features. In California, where the open-range cattle boom peaked in the decade after 1848, Hispanic cowhands used rawhide lassos, which they looped around the saddle horn to immobilize steers, and wore the Spanish great-rowel spurs over soft shoes. Since Anglo-Texans adapted British cattle-herding practices that used abrupt turns to cut a steer from the herd, they modified the traditional Spanish saddle by adding a second belt to hold it more securely on the horse, and adopted the pointed-toe, high-heeled riding boot to hold it in the stirrup during these tight turns. Cattle-raisers on the Great Plains, while following many Texas cowboy practices, added river irrigation to grow hay fields to help tide their herds over the harsh winters. Canadian cattlemen, in contrast, employed acculturated Indians as cowhands and sometimes followed British practices and used collie dogs as well as horses to help herd cattle.

By the end of the nineteenth century, the cattle booms in both North and South America that depended on open-range grazing practices had passed. By maximizing herd size and fertility, cattlemen had inadvertently destroyed perennial grasses, damaged the landscape, and in some cases caused desertification. Farmers and sheep-raisers competed for grazing land and fenced off access to many ranges. At the same time, the extension of railroad lines made it possible to ship cattle directly from ranches to urban areas, a practice that fundamentally changed the livestock industry. In both North and South America, large-scale ranchers took control of cattle-raising and kept wages low. British investment syndicates, for example, purchased large ranches in Texas and Wyoming where they raised immense herds for eastern urban markets.

Not surprisingly, the idealization and romanticization of the cowboy that occurred after open-range grazing had disappeared in North America produced similar celebrations of gauchos and *vaqueros* in Argentina and Mexico. In all three areas, the reality was different. The colorful cowhands who had stirred the popular imagination as symbols of a freer, more independent way of life had been reduced to seasonal laborers with little chance of advancement.

Questions for Analysis

1. *What traditions shaped open-range ranching in the Americas?*
2. *What was the popular mythic image of the cowboy, the vaquero, and the gaucho?*
3. *What was the environmental impact of open-range grazing?*

The wheat boom collapsed for a variety of reasons. Overproduction, high investment costs, too little or too much rain, excessive reliance on one crop, and depressed grain prices on the international market all undercut farmers' earnings. Large-scale farmers who had invested in hopes of getting rich felt lucky just to survive. Oliver Dalrymple lamented in 1889 that "it seems as if the time has come when there is no money in wheat raising."

Large-scale farms proved most successful in California's Central Valley. Using canals and other irrigation systems to water their crops, farmers by the mid-1880s were growing higher-priced specialty crops and had created new cooperative marketing associations for cherries, apricots, grapes, and oranges. By 1900, led by California citrus growers, who used the "Sunkist" trademark for their oranges, large-scale agribusinesses in California were shipping a variety of fruits and vegetables in refrigerated train cars to midwestern and eastern markets.

The Oklahoma Land Rush, 1889   As farmers in the Dakotas and Minnesota were enduring poor harvests and falling prices, would-be homesteaders greedily eyed the Indian Territory, as present-day Oklahoma was then known. The federal government, considering much of this land virtually worthless, had reserved it for the Five Civilized Tribes since the 1830s. These tribes (except for some Cherokees) had sided with the Confederacy during the Civil War. Although Washington had already punished them by settling other tribes on lands in the western part of the territory, land-hungry whites demanded even more land.

In 1889, over the Native Americans' protests, Congress transferred to the federally owned public domain nearly 2 million acres in the central part of the Oklahoma Territory that had not been specifically assigned to any Indian tribe. At noon on April 22, 1889, thousands of men stampeded into the new lands to stake out homesteads. (Other settlers, the so-called Sooners, had illegally arrived earlier and were already plowing the fields.) Before nightfall tent communities had risen at Oklahoma City and Guthrie near stations on the Santa Fe Railroad. Nine weeks later, six thousand homestead claims had been filed. In the next decade, the Dawes Severalty Act broke up the Indian reservations into individual allotments and opened the surplus to non-Indian settlement. The **Curtis Act** in 1898 dissolved the Indian Territory and abolished tribal governments.

The Oklahoma land rush demonstrated the continuing power of the frontier myth, which tied "free" land to the ideal of economic opportunity. Most Oklahoma farmers survived because they had obtained fertile land in an area where the normal rainfall was thirty inches, ten inches more than in the semiarid regions farther west. Still, within two generations a combination of exploitative farming, poor land management, and sporadic drought would place Oklahoma at the desolate center of the dust bowl in the 1930s (covered in Chapter 24).

THE WEST OF LIFE AND LEGEND

In 1893, four years after the last major tract of western Indian land, the Oklahoma Territory, was opened to non-Indian settlement, a young Wisconsin historian, Frederick Jackson Turner, delivered a lecture entitled "The Significance of the Frontier in American History." "[T]he frontier has gone," declared Turner, "and with its going has closed the first period of American history." Although Turner's assertion that the frontier was closed was based on a Census Bureau announcement, it was inaccurate (more western land would be settled in the twentieth century than in the nineteenth). But his linking of economic opportunity with the transformation of the trans-Mississippi West caught the popular imagination and launched a new school of historical inquiry into the effects of the frontier on U.S. history.

Scholars now recognize that many parts of Turner's "frontier thesis," particularly its ethnocentric omission of Native Americans' claims to the land, were inaccurate. Yet his idealized view of the West did reflect ideas popular among his contemporaries in the 1890s. A legendary West had taken deep root in the American imagination. In the nineteenth century, this mythic West was a product of novels, songs, and paintings. In the twentieth century, it would be perpetuated by movies, radio programs, and television shows. The legend merits attention, for its evolution is fascinating and its influence has been far-reaching.

The American Adam and the Dime-Novel Hero

Late-nineteenth-century writers presented the frontiersman as a kind of mythic American Adam—simple, virtuous, and innocent—untainted by a corrupt social order. For example, at the end of Mark Twain's *Huckleberry Finn*, Huck rejects the constraints of settled society as represented by Aunt Sally and heads west with the declaration, "I reckon I got to light out for the territory ahead of the rest, because Aunt Sally she's going to adopt me and sivilize me, and I can't stand it. I been there before." In this version of the legend, the West is a place of adventure where one can escape from society and its pressures.

But even as this conception of the myth was being popularized, another powerful theme had emerged as well. The authors of the dime novels of the 1860s and 1870s offered the image of the western frontiersman as a new masculine ideal, the tough guy who fights for truth and honor. In *Buffalo Bill: King of the Border Men* (1869), a dime novel loosely based on real-life William F. "Buffalo Bill" Cody, Edward Judson (who published under the name Ned Buntline) created an idealized hero who is a powerful moral force as he drives off treacherous Indians and rounds up villainous cattle rustlers.

Cody himself, playing upon the public fascination with cowboys, organized his own **Wild West Show** in 1883. In the show, which toured the East Coast and Europe, cowboys engaged in mock battles with Indians, reinforcing the dime-novel image of the West as an arena of moral encounter where virtue always triumphed.

Revitalizing the Frontier Legend

Eastern writers and artists eagerly embraced both versions of the myth—the West as a place of escape from society and the West as a stage on which the moral conflicts confronting society were played out. Three young members of the eastern establishment, Theodore Roosevelt, Frederic Remington, and Owen Wister, spent much time in the West in the 1880s, and each was intensely affected by the adventure.

Each man found precisely what he was looking for. The frontier that Roosevelt glorified in such books as *The Winning of the West* (four volumes, 1889–1896), and that Remington portrayed in his statues and paintings, was a stark physical and moral environment that stripped away all social artifice and tested each individual's character. Drawing on a popular version of English scientist Charles Darwin's evolutionary theory, which characterized life as a struggle in which only the fittest survived, Roosevelt and Remington exalted the disappearing frontier as the proving ground for a new kind of virile manhood and the last outpost of an honest and true social order.

This version of the frontier myth reached its apogee in **Owen Wister's** popular novel *The Virginian* (1902). In Wister's tale, the elemental environment of the Great Plains produces individuals like his unnamed cowboy hero, "the Virginian," an honest, strong, and compassionate man, quick to help the weak and fight the wicked. The Virginian sums up his own moral code in describing his view of God's justice: "He plays a square game with us." For Wister, as for Roosevelt and Remington, the cowboy was the Christian knight on the Plains, indifferent to material gain as he pursued justice and attacked evil.

Needless to say, the western myth was far removed from the reality of the West. Critics delighted in pointing out that not one scene in *The Virginian* showed the hard physical labor of the cattle range. The idealized version of the West also glossed over the darker underside of frontier expansion—the brutalities of Indian warfare, the racist discrimination against Mexican-Americans and blacks, the risks of commercial agriculture and cattle-raising, and the boom-and-bust mentality rooted in the exploitation of natural resources.

Further, the myth obscured the complex links between the settlement of the frontier and the emergence of the United States as a major industrialized nation increasingly tied to a global economy. Eastern and foreign capitalists controlled large-scale mining, cattle, and agricultural operations in the West. The technical know-how of industrial America underlay the marvels of western agricultural productivity. Without the railroad, that quintessential symbol of the new industrial order, the transformation of the West would have been far slower.

Beginning a National Parks Movement	Despite its one-sided and idealized vision, Owen Wister's celebration of the western experience reinforced a growing recognition that many unique features of the western landscape were being threatened by overeager entrepreneurs.

One important byproduct of the western legend was a surge of public support for creating national parks and the beginning of an organized conservation movement.

Those who went west in the 1860s and 1870s to map its rugged terrain were often awed by the natural beauty of the landscape. Major **John Wesley Powell,** the one-armed veteran of the Civil War who charted the Colorado River through the Grand Canyon in 1869, waxed euphoric about its towering rock formations and powerful cataracts. "The river turns sharply to the east, and seems enclosed by a wall, set with a million brilliant gems ... On coming nearer, we find fountains bursting from the rock, high overhead, and the spray in the sunshine forms the gems which bedeck the way."

In his important study, *Report on the Lands of the Arid Regions of the United States* (1878), Powell argued that settlers needed to readjust their expectations about the use of water in the dry terrain west of the hundredth meridian. He urged Congress to establish governmental control of watersheds, irrigation, and public lands, a request that went largely unheeded.

Around the time Powell was educating Congress about the arid nature of the far West, a group of adventurers led by General Henry D. Washburn visited the hot springs and geysers near the Yellowstone River in northwestern Wyoming and eastern Montana. They were stunned by what they saw. Wrote one of the party,

"[A]mid the canyon and falls, the boiling springs and sulphur mountain, and, above all, the mud volcano and the geysers of the Yellowstone, your memory becomes filled and clogged with objects new in experience, wonderful in extent, and possessing unlimited grandeur and beauty." Overwhelmed by the view, the Washburn explorers abandoned their plan to claim the area for the Northern Pacific Railroad and instead petitioned Congress to protect it from settlement, occupancy, and sale. Congress responded in 1872 by creating **Yellowstone National Park** to "provide for the preservation...for all time, [of] mineral deposits, natural curiosities, or wonders within said park...in their natural condition." In doing so, they excluded the Native Americans who had long considered the area a prime hunting range.

These first steps to conserve a few of the West's unique natural sites reflected the beginning of a changed awareness of the environment. In his influential study *Man and Nature* in 1864, **George Perkins Marsh,** an architect and politician from Vermont, attacked the view that nature existed to be tamed and conquered. Cautioning Americans to curb their destructive use of the landscape, he warned the public to change its ways. "Man," he wrote, "is everywhere a disturbing agent. Wherever he plants his foot, the harmonies of nature are turned to discords."

Marsh's plea for conservation found its most eloquent support in the work of **John Muir,** a Scottish immigrant who had grown up in Wisconsin. In 1869, Muir traveled to San Francisco and quickly fell in love with the redwood forests. For the next forty years, he tramped the rugged mountains of the West and campaigned for their preservation. A romantic at heart, he struggled to experience the wilderness at its most elemental level. Once trekking high in the Rockies during a summer storm, he climbed the tallest pine he could find and swayed back and forth in the raging wind.

Muir became the late nineteenth century's most articulate publicist for wilderness protection. "Climb the mountains and get their good tidings," he advised city dwellers. "Nature's peace will flow into you as the sunshine into the trees." Muir's spirited campaign to protect the wilderness contributed strongly to the establishment of Yosemite National Park in 1890. Two years later, he became president of the Sierra Club, an organization created to encourage the enjoyment and protection of the wilderness in the mountain regions of the Pacific coast.

The precedent established by the creation of Yellowstone National Park remained ambiguous well into the twentieth century. Other parks that preserved the high rugged landforms of the West were often chosen because Congress viewed the sites as worthless for other purposes. Awareness of the need for biological conservation would not emerge until later in the twentieth century (as discussed in Chapter 21).

Ironically, despite the crusades of Muir, Powell, and Marsh to educate the public about conservation, the campaign for wilderness preservation reaffirmed the image of the West as a unique region whose magnificent landscape produced tough individuals of superior ability. Overlooking the senseless violence and ruthless exploitation of the land, contemporary writers, historians, and publicists proclaimed that the settlement of the final frontier marked a new stage in the history of civilization, and they kept alive the legend of the western frontier as a seedbed of American virtues.

CHRONOLOGY
1860–1900

1862	Homestead Act. Morrill Anti-Bigamy Act. Pacific Railroad Act.
1864	Nevada admitted to the Union. Massacre of Cheyennes at Sand Creek, Colorado. George Perkins Marsh, *Man and Nature*.
1867	Joseph McCoy organizes cattle drives to Abilene, Kansas. New Indian policy of smaller reservations adopted. Medicine Lodge Treaty. Purchase of Alaska.
1868	Fort Laramie Treaty.
1869	Board of Indian Commissioners established to reform Indian reservation life. Wyoming gives women the vote.
1872	Yellowstone National Park established.
1873	Panic allows speculators to purchase thousands of acres in the Red River valley of North Dakota cheaply. Timber Culture Act. Biggest strike on Nevada's Comstock Lode.
1874	Invention of barbed wire. Gold discovered in the Black Hills of South Dakota. Red River War.
1875	John Wesley Powell, *The Exploration of the Colorado River*.
1876	Colorado admitted to the Union, gives women the right to vote in school elections. Little Bighorn massacre.
1877	Desert Land Act.
1878	Timber and Stone Act. John Wesley Powell, *Report on the Lands of the Arid Regions of the United States*.
1879	*United States* v. *Reynolds*.
1881	Helen Hunt Jackson, *A Century of Dishonor*.
1883	Women's National Indian Rights Association founded. William ("Buffalo Bill") Cody organizes Wild West Show.
1884	Helen Hunt Jackson, *Ramona*.
1886	Severe drought on the Plains destroys cattle and grain.
1887	Dawes Severalty Act. Edmunds-Tucker Act.
1888	White Caps raid ranches in northern New Mexico.
1889	Oklahoma Territory opened for settlement.

1890	Ghost Dance movement spreads to the Black Hills.
	Massacre of Teton Sioux at Wounded Knee, South Dakota.
1892	John Muir organizes Sierra Club.
1898	Curtis Act.

CONCLUSION

The image of the mythic West has long obscured the transformation of people and landscape that took place there in the second half of the nineteenth century. Precisely because industrialization, urbanization, and immigration were altering the rest of the nation in unsettling ways (covered in Chapters 18 and 19), many Americans embraced the legend of the West as a visionary, uncomplicated, untainted Eden of social simplicity and moral clarity. The mythic West represented what the entire society had once been like (or so Americans chose to believe), before the advent of cities, factories, and masses of immigrants.

But the mythic view of the frontier West obscured the dark side of expansion onto the Great Plains and beyond. Under the banner of economic opportunity and individual achievement, nineteenth-century Americans used the army to subdue the Indians, undermine their traditional way of life, and drive them onto reservations. They also ruthlessly exploited the region's vast natural resources. In less than three decades, they killed off the enormous buffalo herds, tore up the prairie sod, and littered parts of the landscape with mining debris.

Despite the promise of the Homestead Act, which offered 160 acres of free land to those who would settle on it for five years, much of the best land in the West had been given to railroads to encourage their expansion. Speculators purchased other prime locations. Homesteaders were often forced to settle on poorer-quality tracts in areas where rainfall was marginal. In many places, large business enterprises in mining, ranching, and agribusiness, financed by eastern and European bankers, shoved aside the small entrepreneur and took control of the choicest natural resources.

Nevertheless, the settlement of the vast continental interior did reinforce the popular image of the United States as a land of unprecedented economic opportunity and as a seedbed for democracy. The founding of new towns, the creation of new territorial and state governments, and the interaction of peoples of different races and ethnicities tested these ideas and, with time, forced their rethinking. The exclusion of blacks, Indians, and Spanish-speaking Americans belied the voiced commitment to an open society, but the increasing willingness to give women the vote in many of the new western states would spread within the next two decades.

Although the persisting mythic view of the West hid the more ruthless and destructive features of western expansionism, settling the interior territories and exploiting their extensive physical resources gave birth to the conservation movement and a reassessment of traditional American views of the environment. By the turn of the century, the West's thriving farms, ranches, mines, and cities would help make the United States into one of the world's most prosperous nations.

18

THE RISE OF INDUSTRIAL AMERICA, 1865–1900

CHAPTER OUTLINE

• The Rise of Corporate America • Stimulating Economic Growth • The New South • Factories and the Work Force • Labor Unions and Industrial Conflict

---

THE RISE OF CORPORATE AMERICA

In the early nineteenth century, the corporate form of business organization had been used to raise large amounts of start-up capital for transportation enterprises such as turnpikes and canals. By selling stocks and bonds to raise money, the corporation separated the company's managers, who guided its day-to-day operation, from its owners. After the Civil War, American business leaders pioneered new forms of corporate organization that combined innovative technologies, creative management structures, and limited liability should the enterprise fail. The rise of the giant corporation is a story of risk-taking and innovation as well as of conspiracy and corruption.

The Character of Industrial Change   Six features dominated the world of large-scale manufacturing after the Civil War: (1) the exploitation of immense coal deposits as a source of cheap energy; (2) the rapid spread of technological innovation in transportation, communication, and factory systems; (3) the demand for workers who could be carefully controlled; (4) the constant pressure on firms to compete tooth-and-nail by cutting costs and prices, eliminating rivals, and creating monopolies; (5) the relentless drop in prices (a stark contrast to the inflation of other eras); and (6) the failure of the money supply to keep pace with productivity, a development that drove up interest rates and restricted the availability of credit.

All six factors were closely related. The great coal deposits in Pennsylvania, West Virginia, and Kentucky provided cheap energy to fuel railroad and factory growth. New technologies stimulated productivity and catalyzed breathtaking industrial expansion. Technological innovation enabled manufacturers to cut costs and hire cheap unskilled labor. Cost cutting enabled firms to undersell one another, destroy weaker competitors, and consolidate themselves into more efficient and more ruthless firms. At least until the mid-1890s, cheap energy, cost reduction, new technology, and fierce competition forced down overall price levels.

But almost everyone struggled terribly during the depression years, when the government did nothing to relieve distress. "The sufferings of the working classes are daily increasing," wrote a Philadelphia worker in 1874. "Famine has broken into the home of many of us, and is at the door of all." Above all, business leaders' unflagging drive to reduce costs both created colossal fortunes at the top of the economic ladder and forced millions of wage earners to live near the subsistence level.

Out of the new industrial system poured clouds of haze and soot, as well as the first tantalizing trickle of what would become an avalanche of consumer goods. In turn, mounting demands for consumer goods stimulated heavy industry's production of capital goods—machines to boost farm and factory output even further. Together with the railroads, the corporations that manufactured capital goods, refined petroleum, and made steel became driving forces in the nation's economic growth (see Figure 18.1).

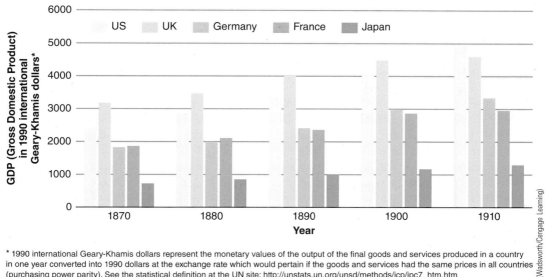

* 1990 international Geary-Khamis dollars represent the monetary values of the output of the final goods and services produced in a country in one year converted into 1990 dollars at the exchange rate which would pertain if the goods and services had the same prices in all countries (purchasing power parity). See the statistical definition at the UN site: http://unstats.un.org/unsd/methods/icp/ipc7_htm.htm

(Wadsworth/Cengage Learning)

FIGURE 18.1 Late Nineteenth-Century Economic Growth in Global Perspective

Railroad   Competition among the capitalists who headed American
Innovations   heavy industry was most intense among the nation's rail-
                            roads. By 1900, 193,000 miles of railroad track crisscrossed
the United States—more than in all of Europe including Russia. These rail lines connected every state in the Union, opened up an immense new internal market, and
pioneered new forms of large-scale corporate enterprise. They created national distribution and marketing systems, and perfected new organizational and management structures.

Railroad entrepreneurs such as Collis P. Huntington of the Central Pacific Railroad, **Jay Gould** of the Union Pacific, and James J. Hill of the Northern Pacific
faced enormous financial and organizational problems. To raise the staggering
sums necessary for laying track and building engines, railroads obtained generous
land and loan subsidies from federal, state, and local governments (see Chapter
17). Even so, they had to borrow heavily by selling stocks and bonds to the public.
Bond holders earned a fixed rate of interest; stockholders received dividends only
when the company earned a profit. By 1900, the yearly interest repayments
required by the combined debt of all U.S. railroads (which stood at an astounding
$5.1 billion—nearly five times that of the federal government) cut heavily into their
earnings.

In addition to raising large amounts of capital, the railroads created new systems for collecting and using information. To coordinate the complex flow of cars
across the country, they relied on the magnetic telegraph, invented in 1837. To improve efficiency, they set up clearly defined, hierarchical organizational structures
and divided their lines into separate divisions, each with its own superintendent.
Elaborate accounting systems documented the cost of every operation for each division, from coal consumption to the repair of engines and cars. Using these reports,
railroad officials could set rates and accurately predict profits as early as the 1860s,
a time when most businesses had no idea of their total profit until they closed their
books at year's end. Railroad management innovations thus became a model for
many other businesses seeking a national market.

Consolidating   The expansion and consolidation of railroading reflected both
the Railroad   the ingenuity and the dishonesty flourishing on the corporate
Industry   management scene. Despite their organizational innovations,
                            the industry remained chaotic in the 1870s. Hundreds of
small companies used different standards for track width and engine size. Financed
by large eastern and British banks, Huntington, Gould, and others devoured these
smaller lines to create large, integrated track networks. In the Northeast, four
major trunk lines were completed. West of the Mississippi, five great companies controlled most of the track by 1893.

Huntington, Gould, and the other corporate leaders who reorganized and expanded the railroad industry in the 1870s and 1880s often were depicted by their
contemporaries as villains and robber barons who manipulated stock markets to
line their own pockets. Newspaper publisher Joseph Pulitzer called Jay Gould, the
short, secretive president of the Union Pacific, "one of the most sinister figures that
have ever flitted batlike across the vision of the American people." Recent historians,

however, have pointed out that the great industrialists were a diverse group. Some were indeed corrupt pirates; others managed their companies with daring and innovation. Indeed, some of their ideas were startling in their originality and inventiveness.

The massive railroad systems created by these entrepreneurs became the largest business enterprises in the world. As they consolidated small railroads into a few interlocking systems, these masterminds standardized all basic equipment and facilities, from engines and cars to automatic couplers, air brakes, and signal systems. In 1883, independently of the federal government, the railroads corrected scheduling problems by dividing the country into four time zones. In May 1886, all railroads shifted simultaneously to the new standard 4'8½" gauge track. Finally, cooperative billing arrangements enabled the railroads to ship cars from other roads at uniform rates nationwide.

But the systemization and consolidation of the railroads had its costs. Heavy indebtedness, overextended systems, and crooked business practices forced the railroads to compete recklessly with each other for traffic. They cut rates for large shippers, showered free passes on politicians, and granted substantial rebates and kickbacks to favored clients. None of these tactics, however, shored up the railroads' precarious financial position. Ruthless competition and fraudulent business practices drove some overbuilt lines into bankruptcy.

Stung by exorbitant rates and secret kickbacks, farmers and small business owners turned to state governments for help. In the 1870s, midwestern state legislatures responded by outlawing rate discrimination. Initially upheld by the Supreme Court, these and other decisions were negated in the 1880s when the Court ruled that states could not regulate interstate commerce. In response in 1887, Congress passed the **Interstate Commerce Act**. A five-member Interstate Commerce Commission (ICC) was established to oversee the practices of interstate railroads. The law banned monopolistic activity like pooling, rebates, and discriminatory short-distance rates.

The railroads challenged the commission's rulings in the federal courts. Of the sixteen cases brought to the Supreme Court before 1905, the justices found in favor of the railroads in all but one, essentially nullifying the ICC's regulatory clout. The Hepburn Act (covered in Chapter 21), passed in 1906, strengthened the ICC by finally empowering it to set rates.

The railroads' vicious competition weakened in 1893 when a national depression forced a number of roads into the hands of **J. Pierpont Morgan** and other investment bankers. Morgan, a massively built man with piercing eyes and a commanding presence, took over the weakened systems, reorganized their administration, refinanced their debts, and built intersystem alliances. By 1906, under the bankers' centralized management, seven giant networks controlled two-thirds of the nation's rail mileage.

Applying the Lessons of the Railroads to Steel	The close connections between railroad expansion, which absorbed millions of tons of steel for tracks, and the growth of corporate organization and management are well illustrated in the career of **Andrew Carnegie**. Born in Scotland, Carnegie immigrated to America in 1848 at the age of twelve.

His first job as a bobbin boy in a Pittsburgh textile mill paid only $1.20 a week. The following year, Carnegie became a Western Union messenger boy. Taking over when the telegraph operators wanted a break, he soon became the city's fastest telegraph operator. Because he had to decode the messages for every major business in Pittsburgh, Carnegie gained an insider's view of their operations.

Carnegie's big break came in 1852 when Tom Scott, superintendent of the Pennsylvania Railroad's western division, hired him as his secretary and personal telegrapher. Later promoted to division chief, Carnegie cut costs while more than doubling the road's mileage. Having invested his earnings in the railroads, by 1868 Carnegie was earning more than $56,000 a year from his investments, a substantial fortune in that era.

In the early 1870s, Carnegie decided to build his own steel mill. His connections within the railroad industry ensured his success. Carnegie's mill produced high grade steel using a new technology named after its English inventor, Henry Bessemer, which shot a blast of air through an enormous crucible of molten iron to burn off carbon and impurities. Combining this new technology with the cost-analysis approach learned from his railroad experience, Carnegie became the first steelmaker to know the actual production cost of each ton of steel.

Carnegie's philosophy was deceptively simple: "Watch the costs, and the profits will take care of themselves." Using rigorous cost accounting and limiting wage increases to his workers, he lowered his production costs and prices below those of his competitors. When these tactics did not drive them out of business, he asked for favors from his railroad-president friends and gave "commissions" to railroad purchasing agents to win business.

As output climbed, Carnegie discovered the benefits of **vertical integration**, that is, controlling all aspects of manufacturing, from extracting raw materials to selling the finished product. In Carnegie's case, this control embraced every stage from the mining and smelting of ore to the selling of steel rails. Carnegie Steel thus became the classic example of how sophisticated new technology could be combined with innovative management (and brutally low wages) to create a mass-production system that could dramatically increase production and slash consumer prices (see Figure 18.2).

The management of daily operations by his close associates left Carnegie free to pursue philanthropic activities. While still in his early thirties, Carnegie donated money to charitable projects. In his lifetime, he gave more than $300 million to libraries, universities, and international-peace causes.

By 1900, Carnegie Steel, employing twenty thousand people, had become the world's largest industrial corporation. Carnegie's competitors, worried about his domination of the market, decided to buy him out. In 1901, J. Pierpont Morgan purchased Carnegie's companies and set up the United States Steel Corporation, the first business capitalized at more than $1 billion. The corporation, made up of two hundred member companies employing 168,000 people, marked a new scale in industrial enterprise.

A systematic self-publicist, Carnegie portrayed his success as the result of self-discipline and hard work. The full story was more complex. Carnegie did not mention his uncanny ability to see the larger picture, his cleverness in hiring talented associates who would drive themselves (and the company's factory workers) mercilessly, his ingenuity in transferring organizational systems and cost accounting

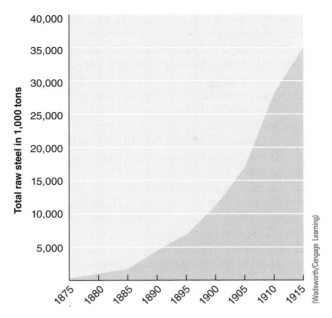

(Wadsworth/Cengage Learning)

FIGURE 18.2 Iron and Steel Production, 1875–1915

New technologies, improved plant organization, economies of scale, and the vertical integration of production brought a dramatic spurt in iron and steel production. Note: short ton = 2,000 pounds.

Source: Historical Statistics of the United States.

methods from railroads to steel, and his callousness in keeping wages as low as possible. To a public unaware of corporate management techniques, however, Carnegie's success gave credence to the idea that anyone might rise from rags to riches.

The Trust: Creating New Forms of Corporate Organization

Between 1870 and 1900, the same fierce competition that had stimulated consolidation in the railroad and steel industries also swept the oil, salt, sugar, tobacco, and meat-packing industries. Like steel, these highly competitive businesses required large capital investments. Entrepreneurs in each industry therefore raced to reduce costs, lower prices, and drive their rivals out of the market.

The evolution of the oil industry illustrates the process by which new corporate structures evolved. After Edwin L. Drake drilled the first successful petroleum (or "crude-oil") well in 1859 near Titusville, Pennsylvania, competitors rushed into the business. Petroleum was distilled into oil, which soon replaced animal tallow as the major lubricant, and into kerosene, which became the leading fuel for household and public lighting.

By the 1870s, the landscape near Pittsburgh and Cleveland, the sites of the first discoveries, was littered with rickety drilling rigs, assorted collection tanks, and ramshackle refineries. Oil spills were a constant problem. "So much oil is produced," reported one Pennsylvania newspaper in 1861, "that it is impossible to care for it, and thousands of barrels are running into the creek; the surface of the river is covered with oil for miles."

In this rush for riches, **John D. Rockefeller**, a young Cleveland merchant, gradually achieved dominance. Like Andrew Carnegie, the solemn Rockefeller had a passion for cost cutting and efficiency. In one case, he insisted a manager find 750 missing barrel stoppers. He realized that in a mass-production enterprise, small changes could save thousands of dollars.

Rockefeller resembled Carnegie, too, in his ability to understand the inner workings of an entire industry and the benefits of vertical integration. The firm that controlled the shipment of oil between the well and the refinery and between the refinery and the retailers, he realized, could dominate the industry. In 1872, he purchased his own tanker cars and obtained not only a 10 percent rebate from the railroads for hauling his oil but also a kickback on his competitors' shipments. When new pipeline technology became available, Rockefeller set up his own massive interregional pipeline network.

Like Carnegie, Rockefeller aggressively forced out his competitors. If local refineries rejected his offers to buy them out, he priced his products below cost and strangled their businesses. When rival firms teamed up against him, Rockefeller set up a pool—an agreement among several companies—that established production quotas and fixed prices. By 1879, Rockefeller had seized control of 90 percent of the country's oil-refining capacity.

Worried about competition, Rockefeller in 1882 decided to eliminate it by establishing a new form of corporate organization, the **Standard Oil Trust**. In place of the "pool" or verbal agreement among companies to control prices and markets, which lacked legal status, the trust created an umbrella corporation that ran them all. To implement his trust, Rockefeller and his associates persuaded the stockholders of forty companies to exchange their stock for trust certificates. Under this arrangement, stockholders retained their share of the trust's profits while enabling the trust to control production. Within three years, the Standard Oil Trust had consolidated crude-oil buying throughout its member firms and slashed the number of refineries in half. In this way, Rockefeller integrated the petroleum industry both vertically, by controlling every function from production to local retailing, and horizontally, by merging the competing oil companies into one giant system.

While Standard Oil justified its trust organization by pointing to the public usefulness of inexpensive heating and cooking fuels, other monopolies did not provide such benefits. James B. "Buck" Duke's American Tobacco trust, for example, targeted youths with trading cards and prizes to persuade them to smoke cigarettes. For addictive products such as cigarettes, targeting children became a means for ensuring continuous use. To gain access to even bigger markets, Duke purchased controlling interests in tobacco companies in England and Japan.

Taking a leaf from Duke and Rockefeller's book, companies in the copper, sugar, whiskey, lead, and other industries established their own trust arrangements. By limiting the number of competitors, the trusts created an *oligopoly*, the market condition that exists when a small number of sellers can greatly influence prices. But their unscrupulous tactics, semimonopolistic control, and sky-high earnings provoked a public outcry. Both major political parties denounced them in the presidential election of 1888.

Fearful that the trusts would stamp out all competition, Congress, under the leadership of Senator John Sherman of Ohio, passed the **Sherman Anti-Trust Act** in 1890. The Sherman Act outlawed trusts and any other monopolies that fixed prices in restraint of trade and slapped violators with fines of up to $5,000 and a year in jail. But the act failed to define clearly either *trust* or *restraint of trade*. The government prosecuted only eighteen antitrust suits between 1890 and 1904. When Standard Oil's structure was challenged in 1892, its lawyers simply reorganized the trust as an enormous holding company. Unlike a trust, which literally owned other businesses, a holding company simply owned a controlling share of the stock of one or more firms. The new board of directors for Standard Oil (New Jersey), the new holding company, made more money than ever.

The Supreme Court further hamstrung congressional antitrust efforts by interpreting the Sherman Act in ways sympathetic to big business. In 1895, for example, the federal government brought suit against the sugar trust in *United States* v. *E C. Knight Company*. It argued that the Knight firm, which controlled more than 90 percent of all U.S. sugar refining, operated in illegal restraint of trade. Asserting that manufacturing was not interstate commerce and ignoring the company's vast distribution network that enabled it to dominate the market, the Court threw out the suit. Thus vindicated, corporate mergers and consolidations surged ahead at the turn of the century. By 1900, these mammoth firms accounted for nearly two-fifths of the capital invested in the nation's manufacturing sector.

STIMULATING ECONOMIC GROWTH

Large-scale corporate enterprise did not alone account for the colossal growth of the U.S. economy in the late nineteenth-century. Other factors proved equally important, including new inventions, specialty production, and innovations in advertising and marketing. In fact, the resourcefulness of small enterprises, which combined innovative technology with new methods of advertising and merchandising, enabled many sectors of the economy to grow dramatically by adapting quickly to changing fashions and consumer preferences.

The Triumph of Technology   New inventions not only streamlined the manufacture of traditional products but also stimulated consumer demand by creating entirely new product lines. The development of a safe, practical way to generate electricity, for example, made possible a vast number of electrical motors, household appliances, and lighting systems.

Many of the major inventions that stimulated industrial output and underlay mass production in these years were largely hidden from public view. Few Americans had heard of the improved technologies that facilitated bottle making and glassmaking, canning, flour milling, match production, and petroleum refining. Fewer still knew much about the refrigerated railcars that enabled Gustavus Swift's company to slaughter beef in Chicago and ship it east.

The inventions people did see were the ones that changed the patterns of everyday life: the sewing machine, mass-produced by the Singer Sewing Machine Company beginning in the 1860s; the telephone, developed by Alexander Graham Bell in 1876; and the light bulb, perfected by **Thomas A. Edison** in 1879.

TECHNOLOGY & CULTURE

Electricity

Of all the technological achievements of the nineteenth century, none seemed more inspiring or mysterious than the ability to generate electricity. Using Alessandro Volta's discovery that chemical reactions in batteries produced a weak electric current, Samuel F.B. Morse had used batteries to power his telegraph in 1837. Alexander Graham Bell followed suit with his telephone in 1876. But higher voltages were needed to run lighting systems and motors. Michael Faraday in England and Joseph Henry in America discovered in 1831 that a rotating magnet surrounded by a conducting wire would produce a continuous flow of electric current. After the Civil War, American inventors used this discovery to develop powerful generators to run incandescent lights (1879), to power motors to run trolley cars (1888), and to drive machines in factories. For many Americans, the ability to harness electricity marked the subjugation of nature and indicated the progress of American civilization.

Nowhere did the knowledge of electricity seem more impressive than its promise to reveal the secrets of the human body. X-rays, discovered in 1895 by the German physicist Wilhelm Roentgen and developed into a practical hospital machine a year later by Thomas Edison, enabled doctors to see inside the body. Physicians discovered that the workings of the nervous system and the brain itself depended on electrical impulses. In short, electrical science, given the breadth of its applications and its power to provide insights into nature, seemed close to being the embodiment of supernatural power. It was no accident that Edison was known as the "wizard of Menlo Park," where his research laboratory was located.

The spread of electric lighting illustrates how technological advances pushed innovation. Thomas Edison's vision went far beyond the development of a practical light bulb. He conceived of an interrelated system of power plants, transmission lines, and light fixtures, all to be produced by companies he had established. Edison's system of direct current lighting (DC—which flowed in only one direction in the wires) required that users be located near power plants. But in 1886, George Westinghouse set up a competing company that used the Italian inventor Nikola Tesla's discovery that alternating current (AC—which cycled back and forth within the wires) could send high voltage electricity efficiently over long distances. Competition between the two systems was finally resolved in 1896 when Edison's successor company, General Electric, agreed to share its patents with the Westinghouse Company. With electric current now standardized as 110 volts AC at 60 Hertz (60 cycles per second), dozens of other inventors developed electric motors, spotlights, electric signs, water pumps, elevators, and household appliances—all drawing power from the same power grid. Only twenty years after the first power station had been built, electrification had started to transform everyday life.

By 1898, when the city of London had sixty-two different utilities that produced thirty-two different voltage levels, American companies had created a unified national electrical system with standardized voltages, and the United States

These new inventions eased household drudgery and reshaped social interactions. The sewing machine, which relieved the tedium of sewing apparel by hand, expanded personal wardrobes. The spread of telephones—by 1900, the Bell Telephone Company had installed almost eight hundred thousand in the United States—not only had established itself as a world leader in electrical technology. The remarkable achievements of the American electrical industry resulted from a combination of factors. Skilled inventors such as Edison, Westinghouse, and Frank Sprague, who developed electric motors for trolley and subway cars, were critical. But the efforts might never have made it out of the laboratories without financiers, such as J.P. Morgan and Henry Villard, who funded the enormous investment in electric generators, power plants, and transmission lines. A third factor was the independence of large corporations like General Electric and Westinghouse, which were able to operate nationally and avoid conflicting state regulations. Operating as regional monopolies, these corporations standardized voltage, alternating current, and electrical fixtures nationwide. Finally, the pooling of patents was crucial. The American patent system, by granting inventors property rights in their inventions and by publicly identifying how the discoveries worked, stimulated technological innovation in general.

At first, electricity was very expensive, and the general public could not afford the cost of wiring homes. Still, even confined to the public sphere, the establishment of a national electrical system was one of the greatest technological innovations of the century. Electric streetcars and subways, public lighting systems, and electric elevators transformed urban America, allowing the construction of skyscrapers and the quick transportation of millions of people. The electrification of factories extended the workday into the night and made work safer. In the following decades, electrification made possible the invention of lighting systems, fans, washing machines, and a host of other devices to ease the drudgery of everyday life.

In the twentieth century, some shortcomings in Americans' love affair with electricity became obvious. In the early years, urban electrification accentuated the differences between city and country life. After World War II, massive power failures showed that the centralization of power distribution systems, first constructed as private monopolies between 1880 and 1932, made them vulnerable to failure when a subsystem problem cascaded throughout the network. The private ownership of power companies, now called utility companies, has enabled them at times to inflate energy prices for their own profit. Most electrical power in the United States today is produced from coal, a nonrenewable resource that also produces acid rain and air pollution. Nevertheless, the creation of a national system of electrical power generation paved the way for remarkable innovations—from lighting to televisions and computers—that remain today closely tied to America's sense of progress and material advancement.

Questions for Analysis

1. *Why did the early electrical inventions seem to mark the subjugation of nature?*
2. *What technological breakthroughs paved the way for the widespread use of electricity for street lighting and transportation?*
3. *Why did the standardization and consolidation of the electric industry take place more quickly in the United States than in England?*

transformed communication but also undermined social conventions for polite behavior that had been premised on face-to-face or written exchanges. The light bulb, by freeing people from dependence on daylight, made it possible to shop after work.

In the eyes of many, Thomas A. Edison epitomized the inventive impulse and the capacity for creating new consumer products. Born in 1847 in Milan, Ohio, Edison, like Andrew Carnegie, had little formal education and worked in the telegraphic industry. A born salesman and self-promoter, Edison shared Carnegie's vision of a large, interconnected industrial system resting on a foundation of technological innovation (see Technology and Culture).

Edison's first major invention, a stock-quotation printer, in 1868 earned enough money to finance Edison's first "invention factory" in Newark, New Jersey, a research facility he moved to nearby Menlo Park in 1876. Assembling a staff that included university-trained scientists, Edison boastfully predicted "a minor invention every ten days, and a big one every six months."

Buoyed by the success and popularity of his invention in 1877 of a phonograph, or "sound writer" (*phono*: "sound"; *graph*: "writer"), Edison set out to develop a new filament for incandescent light bulbs. Characteristically, he announced his plans for an electricity-generation process before he perfected his inventions and then worked feverishly, testing hundreds of materials before he found a carbon filament that would glow dependably in a vacuum.

Edison realized that practical electrical lighting had to be part of a complete system containing generators, voltage regulators, electric meters, and insulated wiring and that the system needed to be easy to install and repair. It also had to be cheaper and more convenient than kerosene or natural gas lighting, its main competitors. In 1882, having built this system with the support of banker J. Pierpont Morgan, the Edison Illuminating Company opened a power plant in the heart of New York City's financial district, furnishing lighting for eighty-five buildings.

In the following years, Edison and his researchers pumped out invention after invention, including the mimeograph machine, the microphone, the motion picture camera and film, and the storage battery. By the time of his death in 1931, he had patented 1,093 inventions and amassed an estate worth more than $6 million. Yet Edison's greatest achievement remained his laboratory at Menlo Park. A model for the industrial research labs later established by Kodak, General Electric, and Du Pont, Edison's laboratory demonstrated that the systematic use of science in support of industrial technology paid large dividends. Invention had become big business.

Specialized Production

Along with inventors, manufacturers of custom and specialized products such as machinery, jewelry, furniture, and women's clothes dramatically expanded economic output. Using skilled labor, these companies crafted one-of-a-kind or small batches of articles that ranged in size from large steam engines and machine tools to silverware, furniture, and custom-made dresses. Keenly attuned to innovations in technology and design, they constantly created new products tailored to the needs of individual buyers.

Small dressmaking shops were typical of flexible specialization displayed by small batch processors. Until the turn of the twentieth century, when ready-to-wear clothes came to dominate the market, most women's apparel was custom produced in small shops run by female proprietors. Unlike the tenement sweatshops that produced men's shirts and pants, dressmakers and milliners (a term derived from fancy goods vendors in sixteenth-and seventeenth-century Milan, Italy) paid good wages to highly skilled seamstresses. The small size of the shops together with the skill of the workers enabled them to shift styles quickly to follow the latest fashions.

Thus, alongside of the increasingly rationalized and bureaucratic big businesses like steel and oil in the late nineteenth century, American productivity was also stimulated by small producers who provided a variety of goods that supplemented the bulk-manufactured staples of everyday life.

Advertising and Marketing   As small and large factories alike spewed out an amazing array of new products, business leaders often discovered that their output exceeded what the market could absorb. This was particularly true for mass-produced consumer goods such as matches, flour, soap, and canned foods. Not surprisingly, these industries were trailblazers in developing advertising and marketing techniques. Strategies for whetting consumer demand and for differentiating one product from another represented a critical component of industrial expansion in the post–Civil War era.

The growth of the flour industry illustrates both the spread of mass production and the emergence of new marketing concepts. In the 1870s, the nation's flour mills adopted new continuous-process machines that graded, cleaned, hulled, ground, and packaged the product in one rapid operation. Since they now produced more flour than they could sell, the companies developed new products such as cake mixes and breakfast cereals and sold them using easy-to-remember brand names like Quaker Oats.

Through the use of brand names, trademarks, guarantees, slogans, endorsements, and other gimmicks, manufacturers built demand for their products and won enduring consumer loyalty. Americans bought Ivory Soap, first made in 1879 by Procter and Gamble of Cincinnati, because of the absurdly precise but impressive pledge that it was "99 and 44/100ths percent pure."

Other manufacturers won consumer loyalty through the development of unique products. In the 1880s, George Eastman developed a paper-based photographic film as an alternative to the fragile glass plates then in use and sold this film loaded into an inexpensive camera. Consumers returned the camera to his Rochester factory where, for a charge of ten dollars, the film was developed and printed, the camera reloaded, and everything shipped back. In marketing a new technology, Eastman had revolutionized an industry and democratized a visual medium previously confined to a few.

Social and Environmental Costs and Benefits   By 1900, the chaos of early industrial competition, when thousands of companies had struggled to enter a national market, had given way to the most productive economy in the world, supported by a legion of small, specialized companies and dominated by a few enormous ones. An industrial transformation that had originated in railroading and expanded to steel and petroleum had spread to every nook and cranny of American business and raised the United States to a position of world leadership.

The vast expansion of economic output brought social benefits in the form of labor-saving products, lower prices, and advances in transportation and communications. The benefits and liabilities sometimes seemed inextricably interconnected. The sewing machine, for example, created thousands of new factory jobs, made

COBB, DETROIT

(Library of Congress)

Baseball Trading Card *To encourage boys and young men to smoke cigarettes, the American Tobacco Company included in the cigarette package collectable cards with pictures of baseball heroes such as Ty Cobb.*

Industrial Pollution
Although some Americans celebrated factory smoke as a sign of industrial growth, those who lived downwind, such as the longshoreman in this Thomas Nast cartoon, often suffered from respiratory diseases and other ailments. For him as well as for other Americans, the price of industrial progress often was pollution.

available a wider variety of clothing, and eased the lives of millions of housewives. At the same time, it encouraged avaricious entrepreneurs to operate sweatshops in which the immigrant poor—often vulnerable young women—toiled long hours for pitifully low wages (discussed further in Chapter 21).

For those who fell by the wayside in this era of spectacular economic growth, the cost could be measured in bankrupted companies and shattered dreams. John D. Rockefeller put things with characteristic bluntness when he said he wanted "only the big ones, only those who have already proved they can do a big business" in the Standard Oil Trust. "As for the others, unfortunately they will have to die."

The cost was high, too, for millions of American workers, immigrant and native-born alike. The vast expansion of new products was built on the backs of an army of laborers who were paid subsistence wages and who could be fired on a moment's notice when hard times or new technologies made them expendable.

Industrial growth often devastated the environment as well. Rivers fouled by oil or chemical waste, skies filled with clouds of soot, and a landscape littered with reeking garbage and toxic materials bore mute witness to the relentless drive for efficiency and profit.

Whatever the final balance sheet of social gains and costs, one thing was clear: the United States had muscled its way onto the world stage as an industrial titan. The ambition and drive of countless inventors, financiers, managerial innovators, and marketing wizards had combined to lay the groundwork for a new social and economic order in the twentieth century.

THE NEW SOUTH

The South entered the industrial era far more slowly than the Northeast. As late as 1900, total southern cotton-mill output, for example, remained little more than half that of the mills within a thirty-mile radius of Providence, Rhode Island. Moreover, the South's $509 average per capita income was less than half that of northerners.

The reasons for the South's late economic blossoming are not hard to discern. The Civil War's physical devastation, racism, the scarcity of southern towns and cities, lack of capital, illiteracy, northern control of financial markets and patents, and a low rate of technological innovation crippled efforts by southern business leaders to promote industrialization. Economic progress was also impeded by the myth of the Lost Cause, which, through its nostalgic portrayal of pre–Civil War society, perpetuated an image of the South as traditional and unchanging. As a result, southern industrialization inched forward haltingly and was shaped in distinctive ways.

Obstacles to Economic Development   Much of the South's difficulty in industrializing arose from its lack of capital and the devastation of the Civil War. So many southern banks failed during the Civil War that by 1865 the South, with more than a quarter of the nation's population, possessed just 2 percent of its banks. The federal government policies added to the banking problem by requiring anyone wishing to start a bank to have $50,000 in capital. Few southerners could meet this standard.

With banks in short supply, country merchants and storekeepers became bankers by default, lending supplies rather than cash to local farmers in return for a lien, or mortgage, on their crops (see Chapter 16). The burden of paying these liens trapped farmers on their own land and created a shortage of the labor needed for industrial expansion.

The shift from planting corn to specializing in either cotton or tobacco made small southern farmers particularly vulnerable to the fluctuations of commercial agriculture. When the price of cotton tumbled in national and international markets from eleven cents per pound in 1875 to less than five cents in 1894, well under the cost of production, many southern farmers grew desperate.

The South's chronic shortage of funds affected the economy in indirect ways as well, by limiting the resources available for education. During Reconstruction, northern philanthropists together with the Freedmen's Bureau, the American Missionary Association, and other relief agencies had begun a modest expansion of public schooling for both blacks and whites. But Georgia and many other southern states operated segregated schools and refused to tax property for school support until 1889. As a result, school attendance remained low, severely limiting the number of educated people able to staff technical and managerial positions in business and industry.

Southern states, like those in the North, often contributed the modest funds they had to war veterans' pensions. In this way, southern state governments built a white patronage system for Confederate veterans and helped reinforce southerners' idealization of the old Confederacy—the South's Lost Cause. As late as 1911, veterans' pensions in Georgia ate up 22 percent of the state's entire budget, leaving little for economic or educational development.

The New South Creed and Southern Industrialization   Despite these obstacles, energetic southern newspaper editors such as **Henry W. Grady** of the *Atlanta Constitution* and Henry Watterson of the *Louisville Courier Journal* championed the doctrine that became known as the New South creed. The South's rich coal and timber resources and cheap labor, they proclaimed in their papers, made it a natural site for industrial development.

The movement to industrialize the South gained momentum in the 1880s. To attract northern capital, southern states offered tax exemptions for new businesses, set up industrial and agricultural expositions, and leased prison convicts to serve as cheap labor. Florida, Texas, and other states gave huge tracts of lands to railroads, whose expansion in turn stimulated the birth of new towns and villages. Other states sold forest and mineral rights on nearly 6 million acres of federal lands to speculators, mostly from the North, who significantly expanded the production of iron, sulfur, coal, and lumber.

Following the lead of their northern counterparts, the southern iron and steel industries expanded as well. Birmingham, Alabama, founded in 1871 in a region blessed with rich deposits of coal, limestone, and iron ore, grew in less than three decades to a bustling city with noisy railroad yards and roaring blast furnaces. By 1900, it was the nation's largest pig-iron shipper. In these same years, Chattanooga, Tennessee, housed nine furnaces, seventeen foundries, and numerous machine shops.

As large-scale recruiters of black workers, the southern iron and steel mills contributed to the migration of blacks to the cities. By 1900, 20 percent of the southern black population was urban. Many urban blacks toiled as domestics or in similar menial capacities, but others entered the industrial work force. Southern industry reflected the patterns of racial segregation in southern life. Tobacco companies used black workers, particularly women, to clean the tobacco leaves while white women, at a different location, ran the machines that made cigarettes. The burgeoning textile mills were lilywhite. In the iron and steel industry, blacks, who comprised 60 percent of the unskilled work force by 1900, had practically no chance of advancement. Nevertheless, in a rare reversal of the usual pattern, southern blacks in the iron and steel industry had a higher skill level and on average earned more than did southern white textile workers.

Black miners were also recruited by the West Virginia coal industry that lured them with free transportation, high wages, and company housing. The coal boom at first forced companies to pay similar wages to blacks and whites, and they initially joined biracial labor unions. But the depression of 1893 weakened the unions and workers became increasingly confined to separate jobs.

Southern segregation, while restricting black employment in many ways, opened up new opportunities for black barbers, doctors, and businessmen to work with black customers. Nevertheless, economic opportunities for blacks remained severely limited. In lumbering, which was the South's largest industry, large numbers of blacks worked in the turpentine industry, collecting sap from trees. In good times, wages could be better than those offered to farm laborers, but during economic downturns workers were laid off or confined to work camps by vagrancy laws and armed guards.

The Southern   Unlike the urban-based southern iron and steel industry, the tex-
Mill Economy   tile mills that mushroomed in the southern countryside in the
1880s often became catalysts for the formation of new towns and villages. In these mill towns, country ways and values suffused the new industrial workplace.

The cotton-mill economy grew largely in the Piedmont, the highland country stretching from central Virginia to northern Georgia and Alabama. The Piedmont had long been the South's backcountry, a land of subsistence farming and limited roads. But postwar railroad construction sparked a period of intense town building and textile-mill expansion. By 1920, the South was the nation's leading textile-mill center. Augusta, Georgia, with 2,800 mill workers, became known as the Lowell of the South, named after the mill town in Massachusetts where industrialization had flourished earlier. The expansion of the textile industry nurtured promoters' visions of a new, more prosperous, industrialized South.

Sharecroppers and tenant farmers at first hailed the new cotton mills as a way out of rural poverty. But appearances were deceptive. The chief cotton-mill promoters were drawn from the same ranks of merchants, lawyers, doctors, and bankers who had profited from the commercialization of southern agriculture (and from the misfortunes of poor black and white tenant farmers and sharecroppers trapped in the new system). Cotton-mill entrepreneurs shamelessly exploited their workers, paying just seven to eleven cents an hour, 30 percent to 50 percent less than what comparable mill workers in New England were paid.

The mills dominated most Piedmont textile communities. The mill operator not only built and owned the workers' housing and the company store but also supported the village church, financed the local elementary school, and pried into the morals and behavior of the mill hands. To prevent workers from moving from one mill to another, the mill owner usually paid them just once a month, often in scrip—a certificate redeemable only in goods from the company store. Since few families had enough money to get through a month, they often overspent and fell behind in their payments. The charges were deducted from workers' wages the following month. In this way, the mill drew workers and their families into a cycle of indebtedness very much like that faced by sharecroppers and tenant farmers.

To help make ends meet, mill workers kept their own garden patches and raised chickens, cows, and pigs. Southern mill hands thus brought communal farm values, long associated with large farm families and nurtured through cooperative planting and harvesting, into the mills themselves. Although they had to adapt to machine-paced work and received barely enough pay to live on, the working poor in the mill districts, like their prewar counterparts in the North, eased the shift from rural to village-industrial life by embracing a cooperative country ethic.

As northern cotton mills did before the Civil War, southern textile companies exploited the cheap rural labor around them, settling transplanted farm people in paternalistic company-run villages. Using these tactics, the industry underwent a period of steady growth.

The Southern   Industrialization progressed at a slower rate in the South
Industrial Lag   than in the North and depended on outside financing, tech-
                      nology, and expertise. The late-nineteenth-century southern economy remained essentially in a colonial status, dominated by northern industries and financial syndicates. U.S. Steel, for example, controlled the Birmingham foundries and in 1900 priced Birmingham steel according to the "Pittsburgh plus" formula based on the price of Pittsburgh steel, plus the freight costs of shipping from Pittsburgh. As a result, southerners paid higher prices for steel than northerners, despite cheaper production costs.

An array of factors thus combined to retard industrialization in the South. Banking regulations requiring large reserves, scarce capital, wartime debts, lack of industrial experience, a segregated labor force, discrimination against blacks, and control by profit-hungry northern enterprises all hampered the region's economic development. Dragged down by a poorly educated white population and by a largely unskilled black population, southern industry languished. Not until after the turn of the century did southern industry undergo the restructuring and consolidation that had occurred in northern business enterprise two decades earlier.

As in the North, industrialization brought significant environmental damage, including polluted rivers and streams, decimated forests, grimy coal-mining towns, and soot-infested steel-making cities. Although Henry Grady's vision of a New South may have inspired many southerners to work toward industrialization, economic growth in the South, limited as it was by outside forces, progressed in its own distinctly regional way.

FACTORIES AND THE WORK FORCE

Industrialization proceeded unevenly nationwide, and most late-nineteenth-century Americans still worked in small shops. But as the century unfolded, large factories with armies of workers sprang onto the industrial scene in more and more locales. The pattern of change was evident. Between 1860 and 1900, the number of industrial workers jumped from 885,000 to 3.2 million, and the trend toward large-scale production became unmistakable.

From Workshop   The transition to a factory economy came not as an earth-
to Factory   quake but rather as a series of seismic jolts varying in
                     strength and duration. Whether they occurred quickly or slowly, however, the changes in factory production had a profound impact on artisans and unskilled laborers alike, for they involved a fundamental restructuring of work habits and a new emphasis on workplace discipline. The impact of these changes can be seen by examining the boot and shoe industry. As late as the

1840s, most shoes were custom-made by skilled artisans who worked in small, independent shops. Shoemakers were aristocrats in the world of labor. Taught in an apprentice system, they took pride in their work and controlled the quality of their products.

A distinctive working-class culture subdivided along ethnic lines evolved among these shoemakers. Foreign-born English, German, and Irish workers set up ethnic trade organizations and joined affiliated benevolent associations. Bound together by religious and ethnic ties, they observed weddings and funerals according to old-country traditions, relaxed together at the local saloon after work, and helped one another weather accidents or sicknesses.

As early as the 1850s, even before the widespread use of machinery, changes in the ready-made shoe trade had eroded the status of skilled labor. The manufacturing process was broken down into a sequence of repetitive, easily mastered tasks. Thus, instead of crafting a pair of shoes from start to finish, each team member specialized in only one part of the process, such as attaching the heel or polishing the leather.

In the 1880s, shoe factories became larger and more mechanized, and traditional skills largely vanished. Shoe companies replaced skilled operatives with lower-paid, less-skilled women and children. By 1890, women made up more than 35 percent of the work force. Like the laborer whose machine nailed heels on forty-eight hundred shoes a day, even "skilled" workers in the new factories specializing in consumer goods found themselves performing numbingly repetitive tasks.

The Hardships of Industrial Labor

The expansion of the factory system spawned an unprecedented demand for unskilled labor. By the 1880s, nearly one-third of the 750,000 workers employed in the railroad and steel industries, for example, were common laborers.

In the construction trades and the garment-making industries, unskilled laborers were hired under the so-called contract system by a subcontractor who took responsibility for employee relations. These common workers were seasonal help, hired in times of need and laid off in slack periods. The steel industry employed them to shovel ore in the yards and to move ingots inside the mills. The foremen drove the gangs hard; in the Pittsburgh area, the workers called the foremen "pushers."

Notoriously transient, unskilled laborers drifted from city to city and from industry to industry. In the late 1870s, unskilled laborers earned $1.30 a day while bricklayers and blacksmiths earned more than $3. Only unskilled southern mill workers, whose wages averaged a meager eighty-four cents a day, earned less.

Unskilled and skilled workers alike worked up to twelve-hour shifts and faced grave hazards to their health and safety. Children were the most vulnerable. In the coal mines and cotton mills, child laborers typically entered the work force at age eight or nine. In the cotton mills, children could be injured by the unprotected pulley belts that powered the machines or develop brown lung disease, a crippling illness caused by breathing in cotton dust. In the coal industry, where children were commonly employed to remove pieces of slate from the conveyor belts, the cloud of

(Library of Congress)

Textile Workers *Young children like this one often were used in the textile mills because their small fingers could tie together broken threads more easily than those of adults.*

coal dust that swirled around them gave them black lung disease—a disorder that leads to emphysema and heart failure.

For adult workers, the railroad industry was one of the most perilous. In 1889, the first year the Interstate Commerce Commission compiled reliable statistics, almost two thousand rail workers were killed on the job and more than twenty thousand injured.

Disabled workers and widows received minimal financial aid from employers. Until the 1890s, the courts considered employer negligence one of the normal risks borne by employees. Railroad and factory owners fought the adoption of state safety and health standards on the grounds that the cost would be excessive. For sickness and accident benefits, workers joined fraternal organizations and ethnic clubs, part of whose monthly dues benefited those in need. But in most cases, the amounts set aside were too low to be of much help. When a worker was killed or maimed in an accident, the family had to rely on relatives or friends for support.

Immigrant Labor   As we shall see in more detail in Chapter 19, factory owners turned to unskilled immigrants for the muscle they needed in dangerous and undesirable jobs. Poverty-stricken French Canadians filled the most menial positions in northeastern textile mills. On the West Coast, Chinese immigrants performed the dirtiest and most physically demanding jobs in mining, canning, and railroad construction.

Writing home in the 1890s, eastern European immigrants described the hazardous and draining work in the steel mills. "Wherever the heat is most insupportable, the flames most scorching, the smoke and soot most choking, there we are certain to find compatriots bent and wasted in toil," reported one Hungarian. Yet those immigrants disposed to live frugally in a boardinghouse and to work an eighty-four-hour week could save fifteen dollars a month, far more than they could have earned in their homeland.

Although most immigrants worked hard, few adjusted easily to the fast pace of the factory. Factory operations were relentless, dictated by the unvarying speed of the machines. A brochure used by the International Harvester Corporation to teach English to its Polish workers promoted the "proper" values. Lesson I read:

> I hear the whistle. I must hurry.
> I hear the five minute whistle.
> It is time to go into the shop.
> I take my check from the gate board and hang it on the department board.
> I change my clothes and get ready to work.
> The starting whistle blows.
> I eat my lunch.
> It is forbidden to eat until then.
> The whistle blows at five minutes of starting time.
> I get ready to go to work.
> I work until the whistle blows to quit.
> I leave my place nice and clean.
> I put all my clothes in the locker.
> I must go home.

As this "lesson" reveals, factory work tied the immigrants to a rigid timetable very different from the pace of farm life.

When immigrant workers resisted the tempo of factory work, drank on the job, or took unexcused absences, employers used a variety of tactics to enforce discipline. Some sponsored temperance societies and Sunday schools to teach punctuality and sobriety. Others cut wages and put workers on the piecework system, paying them only for the items produced. Employers sometimes also provided low-cost housing to gain leverage against work stoppages; if workers went on strike, the boss could simply evict them.

In the case of immigrants from southern Europe whose skin colors were often darker than northern Europeans', employers asserted that the workers were non-white and thus did not deserve the same compensation as native-born Americans. Because the concept of "whiteness" in the United States bestowed a sense of privilege and the automatic extension of the rights of citizenship, Irish, Greek, Italian, Jewish, and a host of other immigrants, although of the Caucasian race, were also considered nonwhite. Rather than a fixed category based on biological differences, the concept of race was thus used to justify the harsh treatment of foreign-born labor.

Women and Work in Industrial America

Women's work experiences, like those of men, were shaped by marital status, social class, and race. Upper-class white married women widely accepted an ideology of "separate spheres" (as discussed in Chapter 19) and remained at home, raised children, and looked after the household. The well-to-do hired maids and cooks to ease their burdens.

Working-class married women, in contrast, often had to contribute to the financial support of the family. In fact, working for wages at home by sewing, button-making, taking in boarders, or doing laundry had predated industrialization. In the late nineteenth century, unscrupulous urban entrepreneurs exploited this captive work force. In the clothing industry, manufacturers hired out finishing tasks to lower-class married women and their children, who labored long hours in crowded apartments.

Young, working-class single women often viewed factory work as an opportunity. In 1870, 13 percent of all women worked outside the home, the majority as cooks, maids, cleaning ladies, and laundresses. But most working women intensely disliked the long hours, low pay, and social stigma of being a "servant." When jobs in industry expanded in the last quarter of the century, growing numbers of single white women abandoned domestic employment for better-paying work in the textile, food-processing, and garment industries. Discrimination barred black working women from following this path. Between 1870 and 1900, the number of women of all races working outside the home nearly tripled. By the turn of the century, women made up 17 percent of the country's labor force.

A variety of factors propelled the rise in the employment of single women. Changes in agriculture prompted many young farmwomen to seek employment in the industrial sector (discussed further in Chapter 19), and immigrant parents often sent their daughters to the factories to supplement meager family incomes. Plant managers welcomed young immigrant women as a ready source of inexpensive unskilled labor. But factory owners treated them as temporary help and kept their wages low. In 1890, young women operating sewing machines earned as little as four dollars for seventy hours of work while their male counterparts made eight.

Despite their paltry wages, long hours, and often unpleasant working conditions, many young women relished earning their own income and joined the work force in increasing numbers. Although the financial support these working women contributed to their families was significant, few working women were paid enough to provide homes for themselves. Rather than fostering their independence, industrial work tied them more deeply to a family economy that depended on their earnings.

When the typewriter and the telephone came into general use in the 1890s, office work provided new employment opportunities, and women with high school educations moved into clerical and secretarial jobs earlier filled by men. They were attracted by the clean, safe working conditions and relatively good pay. First-rate typists could earn six to eight dollars a week, which compared favorably with factory wages. Office work carried higher prestige and generally was steadier than work in the factory or shop.

Despite the growing number of women workers, the late-nineteenth-century popular press portrayed women's work outside the home as temporary. Few people even considered the possibility that a woman could attain local or even national prominence in the emerging corporate order.

Hard Work and the Gospel of Success

Although women generally were excluded from the equation, influential opinion molders in these years preached that any man could achieve success in the new industrial era. In *Ragged Dick* (1867) and scores of later tales, **Horatio Alger**, a Unitarian minister turned dime novelist, recounted the adventures of poor but honest lads who rose through initiative and self-discipline. The career of Andrew Carnegie was often offered as proof that the United States remained the land of opportunity and "rags to riches."

Some critics did not accept this belief. In an 1871 essay, Mark Twain chided the public for its naïveté and suggested that business success was more likely to come to those who lied and cheated. In testimony given in 1883 before a Senate committee investigating labor conditions, a New Yorker named Thomas B. McGuire dolefully recounted how he had been forced out of the horse-cart business by larger, better financed concerns. Declared McGuire, "I live in a tenement house, three stories up, where the water comes in through the roof, and I cannot better myself.... Why? Simply because this present system ... is all for the privileged classes, nothing for the man who produces the wealth." Only with starting capital of $10,000—then a large sum—said McGuire, could the independent entrepreneur hope to compete with the large companies.

What are the facts? Carnegie's rise from abject poverty to colossal wealth was the rare exception, as studies of nearly two hundred of the largest corporations reveal. Ninety-five percent of the industrial leaders came from middle- and upper-class backgrounds. The best chance for native-born working-class Americans to get ahead was to master a skill and to rise to the top in a small company. Although only a few reaped immense fortunes, many improved their standard of living.

The different fates of immigrant workers in San Francisco show the possibilities and perils of moving up within the working class. In the 1860s, the Irish-born Donahue brothers grew wealthy from the Union Iron Works they had founded, where six hundred men built heavy equipment for the mining industry. In contrast, the nearly fifteen thousand Chinese workers who returned to the city after the Central Pacific's rail line was completed in 1869 were consigned by prejudice to work in cigar, textile, and other light-industry factories. Even successful Chinese entrepreneurs faced discrimination. When a Chinese merchant, Mr. Yung, refused to sell out to the wealthy Charles Crocker, a dry-goods merchant turned railroad entrepreneur who was building a mansion on Nob Hill, Crocker built a thirty-foot-high "spite fence" around Yung's house so that it would be completely sealed from view.

Thus, while some skilled workers became owners of their own companies, the opportunities for advancement for unskilled immigrant workers were considerably more limited. Some did move to semiskilled or skilled positions. Yet most immigrants, particularly the Irish, Italians, and Chinese, moved far more slowly than the sons of middle- and upper-class Americans who began with greater educational advantages and family financial backing. The upward mobility possible for such unskilled workers was generally mobility within the working class. Immigrants who got ahead in the late nineteenth century went from rags to respectability, not rags to riches.

One positive economic trend in these years was the rise in real wages, representing gains in actual buying power. Average real wages climbed 31 percent for unskilled workers and 74 percent for skilled workers between 1860 and 1900. Overall gains in purchasing power, however, often were undercut by injuries and unemployment during slack times or economic slumps. The position of unskilled immigrant laborers was particularly shaky. Even during a prosperous year like 1890, one out of every five nonagricultural workers was unemployed at least one month of the year. During the depressions of the 1870s and 1890s, wage cuts, extended layoffs, and irregular employment pushed those at the bottom of the industrial work force to the brink of starvation.

Thus, the overall picture of late-nineteenth-century economic mobility is complex. At the top of the scale, a mere 10 percent of American families owned 73 percent of the nation's wealth in 1890, while less than half of industrial laborers earned more than the five-hundred dollar poverty line annually. In between the very rich and the very poor, skilled immigrants and small shopkeepers improved their economic position significantly. So although the standard of living for millions of Americans rose, the gap between the poor and the well-off remained a yawning abyss.

LABOR UNIONS AND INDUSTRIAL CONFLICT

Aware that the growth of large corporations gave industrial leaders unprecedented power to control the workplace, labor leaders searched for ways to create broad-based, national organizations that could protect their members. But this drive to create a nationwide labor movement faced many problems. Employers deliberately accentuated ethnic and racial divisions within the work force to hamper unionizing efforts. Skilled crafts workers, moreover, felt little kinship with low-paid common laborers. Divided into different trades, they often saw little reason to work together. Thus, unionization efforts moved forward slowly and experienced setbacks.

Two groups, the National Labor Union and the Knights of Labor, struggled to build a mass labor movement that would unite skilled and unskilled workers regardless of their specialties. After impressive initial growth, however, both efforts collapsed. Far more effective was the American Federation of Labor (AFL), which represented skilled workers in powerful independent craft unions. The AFL survived and grew, but it represented only a small portion of the total labor force.

With unions weak, labor unrest during economic downturns reached crisis proportions. When pay rates were cut or working conditions became intolerable, laborers walked off the job without union authorization. These actions, called **wildcat strikes** often exploded into violence. The labor crisis of the 1890s, with its strikes and bloodshed, would reshape the legal environment, increase the demand for state regulation, and eventually contribute to a movement for progressive reform.

Organizing Workers   From the eighteenth century on, skilled workers had organized local trade unions to fight wage reductions and provide benefits for their members in times of illness or accident. But the effectiveness of these organizations was limited. The challenge that labor leaders faced in the postwar period was how to boost the unions' clout. Some believed this goal could be achieved by forming one big association that would transcend craft lines and pull in the mass of unskilled workers.

Inspired by this vision of a nationwide labor association, William H. Sylvis, president of the Iron Molders' International Union, an organization of iron-foundry workers, in 1866 called a convention in Baltimore to form a new organization, the **National Labor Union** (NLU). Reflecting the pre–Civil War idealism, the NLU endorsed the eight-hour-day movement, which insisted that labor deserved eight hours for work, eight hours for sleep, and eight hours for personal affairs. Leaders also called for an end to convict labor, for the establishment of a federal department of labor, and for currency and banking reform. To push wage scales higher, they endorsed immigration restriction, especially of Chinese migrants, whom native-born workers blamed for undercutting prevailing wage levels. The NLU under Sylvis's leadership supported the cause of working women and elected a woman as one of its national officers. It urged black workers to organize as well, though in racially separate unions.

When Sylvis's own union failed to win a strike in 1867 to improve wages, Sylvis turned to national political reform. He invited a number of reformers to the 1868 NLU convention, including woman suffrage advocates Susan B. Anthony and Elizabeth Cady Stanton, who, according to a reporter, made "no mean impression on the bearded delegates." But when Sylvis suddenly died in 1869, the NLU faded quickly. After a brief incarnation in 1872 as the National Labor Reform party, it vanished from the scene.

The dream of a labor movement that combined skilled and unskilled workers lived on in a new organization, the Noble and Holy Order of the **Knights of Labor**, founded in 1869. Led by Uriah H. Stephens, head of the Garment Cutters of Philadelphia, the Knights welcomed all wage earners or former wage earners. The Knights demanded equal pay for women, an end to child labor and convict labor, and the cooperative employer employee ownership of factories, mines, and other businesses. At a time when no federal income tax existed, they called for a progressive tax on all earnings, graduated so that higher-income earners would pay more.

The Knights grew slowly at first. But membership rocketed in the 1880s after the eloquent Terence V. Powderly replaced Stephens as the organization's head. In the early 1880s, the Knights of Labor reflected both its idealistic origins and Powderly's collaborative vision. Powderly opposed strikes, which he considered "a relic of barbarism," and organized producer and consumer cooperatives. A teetotaler, he also urged temperance upon the membership. Powderly advocated the admission of blacks into local Knights of Labor assemblies, although he recognized the strength of racism and allowed southern local assemblies to be segregated. Under his leadership the Knights welcomed women members; by 1886, women organizers had recruited thousands of workers, and women made up an estimated 10 percent of the union's membership.

Powderly supported restrictions on immigration and a total ban on Chinese immigration. He echoed the popular perception of Chinese laborers as "servile" and "dependent," a stereotype that made white workers seem "manly" and "independent." In 1877, San Francisco workers demonstrating for an eight-hour workday, destroyed twenty-five Chinese-run laundries and terrorized the local Chinese population. In 1880, both major party platforms included anti-Chinese immigration plans. Two years later, Congress passed the Chinese Exclusion Act, placing a ten-year moratorium on Chinese immigration. The ban was extended in 1902 and not repealed until 1943.

Powderly's greatest triumph came in 1885. In that year, Jay Gould tried to get rid of the Knights of Labor on his Wabash railroad by firing active union members, Powderly and his executive board instructed all Knights on the Wabash line to walk off the job and those on other lines to refuse to handle Wabash cars. This action crippled the Wabash's operations. To the nation's amazement, Gould met with Powderly and canceled his campaign against the Knights of Labor. "The Wabash victory is with the Knights," declared a St. Louis newspaper; "no such victory has ever before been secured in this or any other country."

Membership in the Knights of Labor soared. By 1886, more than seven hundred thousand workers were organized in nearly six thousand locals. Turning to political action that fall, the Knights mounted campaigns in nearly two hundred towns and cities nationwide, electing several mayors and judges (Powderly himself had served as mayor of Scranton since 1878). They secured passage of state laws banning convict labor and federal laws against the importation of foreign contract labor. Business executives warned that the Knights could cripple the economy and take over the country if they chose.

But the organization's strength soon waned. Workers became disillusioned when a series of unauthorized strikes failed in 1886. By the late 1880s, the Knights of Labor was a shadow of its former self. Nevertheless, the organization had awakened in thousands of workers a sense of group solidarity and potential strength. Powderly, who survived to 1924, remained proud of his role "in forcing to the forefront the cause of misunderstood and downtrodden humanity."

As the Knights of Labor declined, another national labor organization, pursuing more immediate and practical goals, was gaining strength. The skilled craft unions had long been uncomfortable with labor organizations like the Knights that welcomed skilled and unskilled alike. They were also concerned that the Knights' broad reform goals would undercut their own commitment to better wages and protecting the interests of their particular crafts. The break came in May 1886 when the craft unions left the Knights of Labor to form the **American Federation of Labor** (AFL).

The AFL replaced the Knights' grand visions with practical tactics aimed at bread-and-butter issues. **Samuel Gompers**, the immigrant cigar maker who became head of the AFL in 1886 and led it until his death in 1924, believed in "trade unionism, pure and simple." For Gompers, higher wages were the necessary base to enable working class families to live decently, with respect and dignity. The stocky, mustachioed labor leader argued that labor, to stand up to the corporations, would have to harness the bargaining power of skilled workers,

Ethnic and Racial Hatred *Conservative business owners used racist advertising such as this trade card stigmatizing Chinese laundry workers to promote their own products and to associate their company with patriotism.*

(Library of Congress)

whom employers could not easily replace, and concentrate on the practical goals of raising wages and reducing hours.

A master tactician, Gompers believed the trend toward large-scale industrial organization necessitated a comparable degree of organization by labor. He also recognized, however, that the skilled craft unions that made up the AFL retained a strong sense of independence. To persuade crafts workers from the various trades to join forces without violating their sense of craft autonomy, Gompers organized the AFL as a federation of trade unions, each retaining control of its own members but all linked by an executive council that coordinated strategy during boycotts and strike actions. "We want to make the trade union movement under the AFL as distinct as the billows, yet one as the sea," he told a national convention.

Focusing the federation's efforts on short-term improvements in wages and hours, Gompers at first sidestepped divisive political issues. The new organization's platform did, however, demand an eight-hour workday, employers' liability for workers' injuries, and mine safety laws. Although women participated in many craft unions, the AFL did little to recruit women workers after 1894 because Gompers and others believed that women workers undercut men's wages. By 1904, under Gompers's careful tutelage, the AFL had grown to more than 1.6 million strong.

Although the unions held up an ideal toward which many might strive, labor organizations before 1900 remained weak. Less than 5 percent of the work force joined union ranks. Split between skilled artisans and common laborers, separated along ethnic and religious lines, and divided over tactics, the unions battled with only occasional effectiveness against the growing power of corporate enterprise. Lacking financial resources, they typically watched from the sidelines when unorganized workers launched wildcat strikes that sometimes turned violent.

Strikes and Labor Unrest Americans lived with a high level of violence from the nation's beginnings, and the nineteenth century—with its international and civil wars, urban riots, and Indian-white conflict—was no exception. Terrible labor clashes toward the end of the century were part of this continuing pattern, but they nevertheless shocked and dismayed contemporaries. From 1881 to 1905, close to thirty-seven thousand strikes erupted, in which nearly 7 million workers participated.

The first major wave of strikes began in 1873 when a Wall Street crash triggered a stock-market panic and a major depression. Six thousand businesses closed the following year, and many more cut wages and laid off workers. Striking Pennsylvania coal miners were fired and evicted from their homes. The tension turned deadly in 1877 during a wildcat railroad strike. Ignited by wage reductions on the Baltimore and Ohio Railroad in July, the strike exploded up and down the railroad lines, spreading to New York, Pittsburgh, St. Louis, Kansas City, Chicago, and San Francisco. Rioters in Pittsburgh torched Union Depot. By the time newly installed president Rutherford B. Hayes had called out the troops and quelled the strike two weeks later, nearly one hundred people had died, and two-thirds of the nation's railroads stood idle.

The railroad strike stunned middle-class America. The religious press responded hysterically. "If the club of the policeman, knocking out the brains of the rioter, will answer, then well and good," declared one Congregationalist journal, "[but if not] then bullets and bayonets … constitute the one remedy." The same middle-class Americans who worried about Jay Gould and the corporate abuse of power grew terrified of mob violence.

Employers capitalized on the public hysteria to crack down on labor. Many required their workers to sign "yellow dog" contracts in which they promised not to strike or join a union. Some hired Pinkerton agents, a private police force, to defend their factories and, when necessary, turned to the federal government and the U.S. army to suppress labor unrest.

Although the economy recovered, more strikes and violence followed in the 1880s. On May 1, 1886, 340,000 workers walked off their jobs in support of the campaign for an eight-hour workday. Three days later, Chicago police shot and killed four strikers at the McCormick Harvester plant. At a protest rally the next evening in the city's Haymarket Square, someone threw a bomb, killing or fatally wounding seven policemen. In response, the police fired wildly into the crowd and killed four demonstrators.

Public reaction was immediate. Business leaders and middle-class citizens lashed out at labor activists and particularly at the sponsors of the Haymarket meeting, most of whom were associated with a German-language anarchist newspaper that advocated the violent overthrow of capitalism. Eight men were arrested. Although no evidence connected them directly to the bomb throwing, all were convicted of murder, and four were executed. One committed suicide in prison. In Haymarket's aftermath, still more Americans became convinced that the nation was in the grip of a deadly foreign conspiracy, and animosity toward labor unions intensified.

Confrontations between capital and labor became particularly violent in the West. When the Mine Owners' Protective Association cut wages at work sites along Idaho's Coeur d'Alene River in 1892, the miners, who were skilled dynamiters, blew up a mill and captured the guards sent to defend it. Mine owners responded by mustering the Idaho National Guard to round up the men and cripple their union.

Back east that same year, armed conflict broke out during the **Homestead Strike** at the Carnegie Steel Company plant in Homestead, Pennsylvania. To destroy the union, managers had cut wages and locked out the workers. When workers fired on the armed men from the Pinkerton Detective Agency who came to protect the plant, a battle broke out. Seven union members and three Pinkertons died. A week later the governor sent National Guardsmen to restore order. The union crushed, the mills resumed full operation a month later.

The most systematic use of troops to smash union power came in 1894 during a strike against the Pullman Palace Car Company. In 1880 George Pullman, a manufacturer of elegant dining and sleeping cars for the nation's railroads, had constructed a factory and town, called Pullman, ten miles south of Chicago. The carefully planned community provided solid brick houses for the workers, beautiful parks and playgrounds, and even its own sewage-treatment plant. Pullman also closely policed workers' activities, outlawed saloons, and insisted that his properties turn a profit.

When the depression of 1893 hit, Pullman slashed workers' wages without reducing their rents. In reaction thousands of workers joined the newly formed American Railway Union and went on strike. They were led by a fiery young organizer, **Eugene V. Debs**, who vowed "to strip the mask of hypocrisy from the pretended philanthropist and show him to the world as an oppressor of labor." Union members working for the nation's largest railroads refused to switch Pullman cars, paralyzing rail traffic in and out of Chicago, one of the nation's premier rail hubs.

In response, the General Managers' Association, an organization of top railroad executives, set out to break the union. The General Managers imported strikebreakers from among jobless easterners and asked U.S. attorney general Richard Olney, who sat on the board of directors of three major railroad networks, for a federal injunction (court order) against the strikers for allegedly refusing to move railroad cars carrying U.S. mail.

In fact, union members had volunteered to switch mail cars onto any trains that did not carry Pullman cars, and it was the railroads' managers who were delaying the mail by refusing to send their trains without the full complement of cars. Nevertheless, Olney, supported by President Grover Cleveland and citing the Sherman Anti-Trust Act, secured an injunction against the leaders of the American Railway Union for restraint of commerce. When the union refused to order its members back to work, Debs was arrested, and federal troops poured in. During the ensuing riot, workers burned seven hundred freight cars, thirteen people died, and fifty-three were wounded. By July 18, the strike had been crushed.

By playing upon a popular identification of strikers with anarchism and violence, crafty corporate leaders persuaded state and federal officials to cripple organized labor's ability to bargain with business. When the Supreme Court (in the 1895 case *In re Debs*) upheld Debs's prison sentence and legalized the use of injunctions against labor unions, the judicial system gave business a potent new weapon with which to restrain labor organizers.

Yet organizers persisted. In 1897, the feisty Irish-born Mary Harris Jones, known as Mother Jones, persuaded coal miners in Pennsylvania to join the United Mine Workers of America, a union founded seven years earlier. She staged parades of children, invited workers' wives to stockpile food, and dramatized the importance of militant mothers fighting for their families. Her efforts were successful. Wage reductions were restored because no large companies dominated the industry and the owners needed to restore production.

Despite the achievements of the United Mine Workers, whose members had climbed to three hundred thousand by 1900, the successive attempts by the National Labor Union, Knights of Labor, American Federation of Labor, and American Railway Union to build a national working class labor movement achieved only limited success. Aggressive employer associations and conservative state and local officials hamstrung their efforts. In sharp contrast to Great Britain and Germany, where state officials often mediated disputes between labor and capital, federal and state officials in the United States increasingly sided with manufacturers. Ineffective in the political arena, blocked by state officials, divided by ethnic differences, harassed by employers, and frustrated by court decisions, American unions failed to expand their base of support. Post–Civil War labor turmoil had sapped the vitality of organized labor and given it a negative public image that it would not shed until the 1930s.

Social Thinkers Probe for Alternatives   Widespread industrial violence was particularly unsettling when examined in the context of working-class poverty. In 1879, after observing three men rummaging through garbage to find food, the poet and journalist Walt Whitman wrote, "If the United States, like the countries of the Old World, are also to grow vast crops of poor, desperate, dissatisfied, nomadic, miserably-waged populations, such as we see looming upon us of late years … then our republican experiment, notwithstanding all its surface-successes, is at heart an unhealthy failure." Whitman's bleak speculation was part of a general public debate over the social meaning of the new industrial order. At stake was a larger issue: should government become the mechanism for helping the poor and regulating big business?

Defenders of capitalism preached the laissez-faire ("hands-off") argument, insisting that government should never attempt to control business. They buttressed their case by citing Scottish economist Adam Smith, who had argued in *The Wealth of Nations* (1776) that self-interest acted as an "invisible hand" in the marketplace, automatically regulating the supply of and demand for goods and services. In "The

Gospel of Wealth," an influential essay published in 1889, Andrew Carnegie justified laissez-faire by applying the evolutionary theories of British social scientist Herbert Spencer to human society. "The law of competition," Carnegie argued, "may be sometimes hard for the individual, [but] it is best for the race, because it insures the survival of the fittest in every department."

Tough-minded Yale professor **William Graham Sumner** shared Carnegie's disapproval of government interference. His combative book *What Social Classes Owe to Each Other* (1883) applied the evolutionary theories of British naturalist Charles Darwin to human society. In an early statement of what became known as **Social Darwinism**, Sumner asserted that inexorable natural laws controlled the social order: "A drunkard in the gutter is just where he ought to be.... The law of survival of the fittest was not made by man, and it cannot be abrogated by man. We can only, by interfering with it, produce the survival of the unfittest." The state, declared Sumner, owed its citizens nothing but law, order, and basic political rights.

Sumner's argument did not go unchallenged. In *Dynamic Sociology* (1883), Lester Frank Ward, a geologist, argued that contrary to Sumner's claim, the supposed "laws" of nature could be circumvented by human will. Just as scientists had applied their knowledge to breeding superior livestock, government experts could use the power of the state to regulate big business, protect society's weaker members, and prevent the heedless exploitation of natural resources.

Other social theorists offered more utopian solutions to the problems of poverty and social unrest. Henry George, a self-taught San Francisco newspaper editor and economic theorist, proposed to solve the nation's uneven distribution of wealth through what he called the single tax. In *Progress and Poverty* (1879), he noted that speculators reaped huge profits from the rising price of land that they neither developed nor improved. By taxing this "unearned increment," the government could obtain the funds necessary to ameliorate the misery caused by industrialization. The result would bring the benefits of socialism—a state controlled economic system that distributed resources according to need—without socialism's great disadvantage, the stifling of individual initiative. George's program was so popular that he lectured around the country and only narrowly missed being elected mayor of New York in 1886.

The vision of a harmonious industrialized society was vividly expressed in the utopian novel *Looking Backward* (1888) by Massachusetts newspaper editor Edward Bellamy. Cast as a glimpse into the future, Bellamy's novel tells of Julian West, who falls asleep in 1888 and awakens in the year 2000 to find a nation without poverty or strife. In this future world, West learns, a completely centralized, state-run economy and a new religion of solidarity have combined to create a society in which everyone works for the common welfare. Bellamy's vision of a conflict-free society where all share equally in industrialization's benefits so inspired middle-class Americans fearful of corporate power and working-class violence that nearly five hundred local Bellamyite organizations, called Nationalist clubs, sprang up to try to turn his dream into reality.

Ward, George, and Bellamy did not deny the benefits of the existing industrial order; they simply sought to humanize it. These utopian reformers envisioned a harmonious society whose members all worked together.

Marxist socialists advanced a different view. Elaborated by German philosopher and radical agitator Karl Marx (1818–1883) in *Das Kapital* (1867) and other works, **Marxism** rested on the labor theory of value: a proposition (which Adam Smith had also accepted) that the labor required to produce a commodity was the only true measure of that commodity's value. Any profit made by the capitalist employer was "surplus value" appropriated from the exploited workers. As competition among capitalists increased, Marx predicted, wages would decline to starvation levels, and more and more capitalists would be driven out of business. Society would be divided between a shrinking bourgeoisie (capitalists, merchants, and middle-class professionals) and an impoverished proletariat (the workers). The proletariat would then revolt and seize control of the state and of the economy. Although Marx viewed class struggle as the essence of modern history, his eyes were also fixed on the shining vision of the communist millennium that the revolution would eventually usher in—a classless utopia in which the state would "wither away" and all exploitation would cease. To lead the working class in its showdown with capitalism, Marx and his collaborator Friedrich Engels helped found socialist parties in Europe, whose strength grew steadily, beginning in the 1870s.

Despite Marx's keen interest in the United States, Marxism proved to have little appeal in late-nineteenth-century America other than for a tiny group of primarily German-born immigrants. The Marxist oriented Socialist Labor party (1877) had attracted only about fifteen hundred members by 1890. More alarming to the public at large was the handful of anarchists, again mostly immigrants, who rejected Marxist discipline and preached the destruction of capitalism, the violent overthrow of the state, and the immediate introduction of a stateless utopia. In 1892 Alexander Berkman, a Russian immigrant anarchist, attempted to assassinate Henry Clay Frick, the manager of Andrew Carnegie's Homestead Steel Works. Entering Frick's office with a pistol, Berkman shot him in the neck and then tried to stab him. A carpenter working in Frick's office overpowered the assailant. Rather than igniting a workers' insurrection that would usher in a new social order as he had hoped, Berkman came away with a long prison sentence. His act confirmed the business stereotype of "labor agitators" as lawless and violent.

CHRONOLOGY
1865–1900

1859	First oil well drilled in Titusville, Pennsylvania.
1866	National Labor Union founded.
1869	Transcontinental railroad completed.
	Knights of Labor organized.
1870	John D. Rockefeller establishes Standard Oil Company.
1873	Panic of 1873 triggers a depression lasting until 1879.
1876	Alexander Graham Bell patents the telephone.
1877	Edison invents phonograph.
	Railway workers stage first nationwide strike.

1879	Henry George, *Progress and Poverty*.
	Edison perfects incandescent lamp.
1882	Standard Oil Trust established.
	Edison opens first electric power station in New York City.
	Chinese Exclusion Act.
1883	William Graham Sumner, *What Social Classes Owe to Each Other*.
	Lester Frank Ward, *Dynamic Sociology*.
1886	American Federation of Labor (AFL) formed.
	Haymarket riot in Chicago.
1887	Interstate Commerce Act establishes Interstate Commerce Commission.
1888	Edward Bellamy, *Looking Backward*.
1889	Andrew Carnegie, "The Gospel of Wealth."
1890	Sherman Anti-Trust Act.
	United Mine Workers formed.
1892	Standard Oil of New Jersey and General Electric formed.
	Homestead Strike.
	Columbian Exposition in Chicago.
	Miners strike at Coeur d'Alene, Idaho.
1893	Panic of 1893 triggers a depression lasting until 1897.
1894	Pullman Palace Car workers strike.
1901	J. Pierpont Morgan organizes United States Steel.

CONCLUSION

By 1900, industrialization had propelled the United States into the forefront of the world's major powers, lowered the cost of goods through mass production, generated thousands of jobs, and produced a wide range of new consumer products. Using accounting systems first developed by the railroads and sophisticated new technologies, national corporations had pioneered innovative systems for distributing and marketing their goods. In the steel and oil industries, Andrew Carnegie and John D. Rockefeller had vertically integrated their companies, controlling production from the raw materials to the finished product. Through systematic cost cutting and ruthless underselling of their competitors, they had gained control of most of their industry and lowered prices.

Despite these advantages, most Americans recognized that industrialization's cost was high. The rise of the giant corporations had been achieved through savage competition, exploited workers, shady business practices, polluted factory sites, and the collapse of an economic order built on craft skills. In the South in particular, the devastation of the Civil War and the control of banking and raw materials by northern capitalists encouraged industrialists to adopt a paternalistic, family-oriented approach in the cotton mills and to pay exceedingly low wages.

Outbursts of labor violence, the growth of urban slums, and grinding poverty showed starkly that all was not well in industrial America. Although the Knights of Labor and the American Federation of Labor attempted to organize workers nationally, the labor movement could not control spontaneous wildcat strikes and violence. In response, company owners appealed to government authorities to arrest strikers, obtain court injunctions against union actions, and cripple the ability of labor leaders to expand their organizations.

As a result, Americans remained profoundly ambivalent about the new industrial order. Caught between their desire for the higher standard of living that industrialization made possible and their fears of capitalist power and social chaos, Americans of the 1880s and 1890s sought strategies that would preserve the benefits while eliminating corruption. Efforts to regulate railroads at the state level and such national measures as the Interstate Commerce Act and the Sherman Anti-Trust Act, as well as the fervor with which the ideas of a utopian theorist like Edward Bellamy were embraced, represented early manifestations of this impulse. In the Progressive Era of the early twentieth century, Americans would redouble their efforts to formulate political and social responses to the nation's economic transformation after the Civil War.

19

IMMIGRATION, URBANIZATION, AND EVERYDAY LIFE, 1860–1900

CHAPTER OUTLINE

• The New American City • Middle- and Upper-Class Society and Culture • Reforming the Working Class • Working-Class Leisure in the Immigrant City • Cultures in Conflict

---

THE NEW AMERICAN CITY

Everyday life was transformed most visibly in cities. During the late nineteenth century, American cities grew spectacularly. Between 1870 and 1900, New Orleans's population increased by nearly fifty percent, Buffalo's tripled, and Chicago's increased more than fivefold. At the start of the new century, Philadelphia, New York, and Chicago all had more than a million residents, and 40 percent of all Americans lived in cities. (In the census, cities were defined as having more than twenty-five hundred inhabitants.) In 1900, New York's 3.4 million inhabitants almost equaled the nation's entire 1850 urban population.

This spectacular urban growth, fueled by migration from the countryside and the arrival of nearly 11 million immigrants between 1870 and 1900, stimulated economic development. Like the frontier, the city symbolized opportunity for all comers.

The city's unprecedented scale and diversity threatened traditional expectations about community life and social stability. Rural America had been a place of face-to-face personal relations. In contrast, the city was a seething caldron where immigrant groups contended with one another and with native-born Americans for jobs, power, and influence. Moreover, the same rapid growth that energized manufacturing and production strained city services, generated terrible housing and sanitation problems, and accentuated class differences.

Native-born Americans complained about the noise, stench, and congestion of this transformed cityscape. They fretted about the newcomers' squalid tenements, fondness for drink, and strange customs. When native-born reformers set about cleaning up the city, they sought not only to improve the physical environment but also to destroy the distinctive customs that made immigrant culture different from their own. The late nineteenth century thus witnessed an intense struggle to control the city and benefit from its economic and cultural potential. The stakes were high, for America was increasingly becoming an urban nation.

Migrants and Immigrants   The concentration of industries in urban settings produced demands for thousands of new workers. The promise of good wages and a broad range of jobs (labeled by historians as "pull factors") drew men and women from the countryside. So great was the migration from rural areas, especially New England, that some farm communities vanished from the map.

Young farmwomen led the exodus to the cities. With the growing mechanization of farming in the late nineteenth century, farming was increasingly male work. Rising sales of factory-produced goods through nationally distributed mail-order catalogs reduced the need for rural women's labor. So young farmwomen flocked to the cities, where they competed for jobs with immigrant, black, and city-born white women.

From 1860 to 1890, the prospect of a better life also attracted nearly 10 million northern European immigrants to American cities. Their numbers included nearly 3 million Germans, 2 million English, Scottish, and Welsh immigrants, and almost 1.5 million Irish. By 1900 more than eight hundred thousand French-Canadians had entered the New England mills, and close to a million Scandinavian newcomers had put down roots in the rich farmlands of Wisconsin and Minnesota. On the West Coast, despite the Chinese Exclusion Act of 1882 (see Chapter 18), more than eighty-one thousand Chinese remained in California and nearby states in 1900.

In the 1890s, these earlier immigrants from northern and western Europe were joined by swelling numbers of **"new immigrants"**—Italians, Slavs, Greeks, and Jews from southern and eastern Europe, Armenians from the Middle East, and in Hawaii, Japanese from Asia. In the next three decades, these new immigrants, many from peasant backgrounds, would boost America's foreign-born population by more than 18 million (see Map 19.1).

The overwhelming majority of immigrants settled in cities in the northeastern and north-central states, with the Irish predominating in New England and the Germans in the Midwest. The effect of their numbers was staggering. In 1890, New York City (including Brooklyn, still a legally separate municipality) contained twice as many Irish as Dublin, as many Germans as Hamburg, half as many Italians as Naples, and 2½ times the Jewish population of Warsaw. That same year four out of five people living in New York had been born abroad or were children of foreign-born parents.

Overpopulation, crop failure, famine, religious persecution, violence, or industrial depression drove some of these immigrants from their homelands. (Historians call these reasons for immigration "push factors.") At the same time, the promise of

(Wadsworth/Cengage Learning)

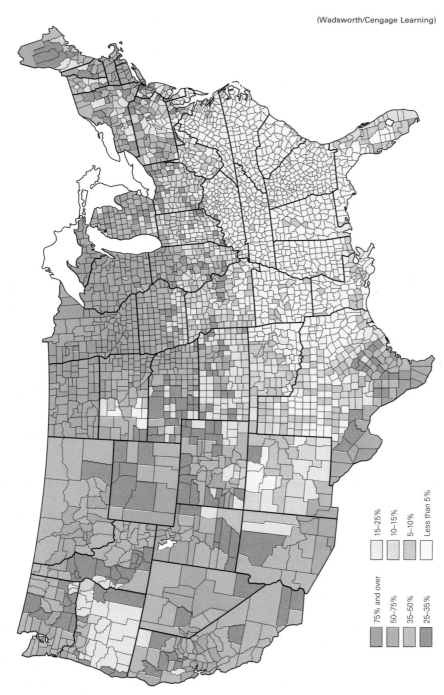

MAP 19.1 Percent of Foreign-born Whites and Native Whites of Foreign or Mixed Parentage in Total Population, by Counties, 1910

As this map indicates, new immigrants rarely settled in the South.

Source: D. W. Meinig, The Shaping of America—A Geographical Perspective of 500 Years of History. Yale University Press, Volume 3.

75% and over

50–75%

35–50%

25–35%

15–25%

10–15%

5–10%

Less than 5%

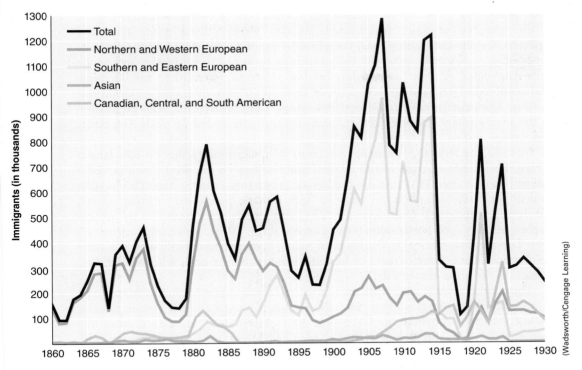

FIGURE 19.1 The Changing Face of U.S. Immigration, 1860–1930

Between 1865 and 1895, the majority of newcomers to America hailed from northern and western Europe. But the early twentieth century witnessed a surge of immigration from southern and eastern Europe.

high wages (a "pull factor") lured more than one hundred thousand Japanese laborers to Hawaii in the 1890s to work on sugar plantations.

A large number of immigrants were single young men. Birger Osland, an eighteen-year-old Norwegian, explained his reasons for leaving to a friend: "as I now probably have a foundation upon which I can build my own further education, I have come to feel that the most sensible thing I can do is to emigrate to America." Although significant numbers of young men remained in the United States after they had become successful, large numbers, especially Italians and Chinese, returned home as well.

Single women were less likely to come on their own, but Irish women often did so and sent their earnings back home. Most commonly, wives and children waited in the old country until the family breadwinner had secured a job and saved enough money to pay for their passage to America. They then endured a cramped steamship journey noted for its poor food, lack of privacy, and rudimentary sanitary facilities. Immigrants arrived tired, fearful, and in some cases sick.

Further complications awaited the travelers when they reached their destination, most often New York City or San Francisco. Customs officials inspected the newcomers for physical handicaps and contagious diseases. After 1892, those with "loathsome" infections such as leprosy, trachoma (a contagious viral disease of the eye), or sexually transmitted diseases were refused admittance and deported. Immigrants who passed the physical examination then had their names recorded. If a customs inspector had difficulty pronouncing a foreign name, he often Anglicized it. One German Jew became flustered when asked for his name and mumbled, "Schon vergessen [already forgotten]," meaning that he could not recall it. The inspector, who did not understand German, wrote "Sean Ferguson" on the man's roster. In this manner, many immigrants ended up with American-ized names.

In 1892, the federal government built a new immigration facility on **Ellis Island** in New York harbor. Angel Island in San Francisco Bay on the West Coast served a similar purpose after 1910. At the immigrant processing centers, America's newest residents exchanged foreign currency for U.S. dollars, purchased railroad tickets, and arranged lodgings. Outside the facility, immigrants were hounded by tavern-keepers, peddlers, and porters who tried to exploit them. "When you land in America," wrote one Swedish resident to friends back home, "you will find many who will offer their services, but beware of them because there are so many rascals who make it their business to cheat the immigrants."

Those who arrived with sufficient cash, including many German artisans and Scandinavian farmers, commonly traveled west to Chicago and the rolling prairies beyond. Most of the Irish, and later the Italians remained in eastern cities like Boston, New York, and Philadelphia. The Irish and Italians who did go west typically made the trip in stages, moving from job to job on the railroad and canal systems.

Adjusting to an Urban Society   In the cities, immigrants clustered together with compatriots, often friends or relatives from their original town, to ease the stress of adjusting to a new life. (Historians call this tendency "chain migration.") If a map of New York City's streets and neighborhoods were colored in by nationality, Jacob Riis observed in 1890, it "would show more stripes than on the skin of a zebra, and more colors than any rainbow." Between the West Side Irish and the East Side German neighborhoods, the streets of Manhattan teemed with Poles, Hungarians, Russians, Italians, and Chinese.

Within the cities, some immigrant groups adjusted more easily than others. Skilled workers and those familiar with Anglo-American customs had relatively few problems. Ethnic groups that formed a substantial percentage of a city's population also had a major advantage. The Irish, for example, who by the 1880s made up nearly 16 percent of New York's population, 8 percent of Chicago's, and 17 percent of Boston's, facilitated Irish immigrants' entry into the American mainstream by dominating Democratic Party politics and controlling the hierarchy of the Catholic church in all three cities. Because of their success, upwardly mobile Irish became known as "lace curtain" Irish, a reference to their adoption of middle-class ideals.

The domination of urban institutions by one immigrant group, however, often made adjustment to American society more difficult for others. In cities like Milwaukee, Germans excluded Poles from desirable jobs. Elsewhere, English and German dominance of the building trades enabled those nationalities to limit the numbers of Italians hired.

The experience of being discriminated against helped create a new common ethnic identity for many groups. Groups of immigrants forged a new sense of ethnic distinctiveness as Irish-Americans, German-Americans, or Jewish-Americans that helped them compete for political power and move into mainstream society.

Not all immigrants intended to remain in the United States. Expecting only a brief stay, some made little effort to learn English or understand American customs. Of the Italians who immigrated to New York before 1914, nearly 50 percent went back to Italy. Although the rate of return migration was greatest among Chinese and Italians, significant numbers of other nationalities eventually returned to their homelands as well.

As the number of foreigners in U.S. cities ballooned toward the turn of the century, all immigrant groups faced increasing hostility from white native-born Americans who disliked the newcomers' social customs and worried about their growing influence. Fearing the loss of the privileges and status that were associated with their white skin color, native-born whites often stigmatized immigrants as racially different and inferior. Only gradually, and with much effort, did Irish, Jews, Slavs, and Italians come to be considered "white."

Slums and Ghettos	Every major city had its share of rundown, overcrowded slum neighborhoods. Generally clustered within walking distance of manufacturing districts, slums developed when

landlords subdivided long, narrow buildings with few windows, called tenements, and packed in many residents. The poorer the renters, the worse the slum. Slums became ghettos when laws, prejudice, and community pressure prevented the tenement inhabitants from renting elsewhere. During the 1890s Italians in New York, blacks in Philadelphia and Chicago, Mexican-Americans in Los Angeles, and Chinese in San Francisco increasingly became locked in segregated ghettos.

Life in the slums was particularly difficult for children. Whooping cough (pertussis), measles, and scarlet fever took a fearful toll, and infant mortality was high. In one immigrant ward in Chicago in 1900, 20 percent of infants died in their first year of life.

Because tenements often bordered industrial districts, residents had to put up with the noise, pollution, and foul odors of tanneries, foundries, factories, and packing houses. Coal-fired steam engines and apartment house furnaces produced vast quantities of soot and dust that tinged the atmosphere a hazy gray and coated buildings with a grimy patina.

Most immigrants stayed in the shabbiest tenements only until they could afford better housing. Blacks, in contrast, were trapped in segregated districts. Driven out of the skilled trades and excluded from most factory work, blacks took menial jobs whose low pay left them little income for housing (see Chapter 18). Racist city-dwellers used high rents, real-estate covenants (agreements not to rent or sell to blacks), and neighborhood pressure to exclude them from areas inhabited by whites. Because the numbers of northern urban blacks in 1890 remained relatively small—for example, they composed only 1.2 percent of Cleveland's population and 1.3 percent of Chicago's—they could not overcome whites' concerted campaigns to shut them out. Instead, wealthy black entrepreneurs established their

TECHNOLOGY & CULTURE

Flush Toilets and the Invention of the Nineteenth–Century Bathroom

The development of a system of indoor plumbing was typical of the technological breakthroughs that simplified everyday life in the late nineteenth century. In the 1860s, only about 5 percent of American houses had running water. Most Americans used chamber pots or outhouses that emptied into slimy, smelly cesspools. Two decades later, indoor plumbing standards had been established in most major U.S. cities, and wealthier urban Americans used flush toilets connected to municipal sewer systems.

The driving force for change came from outbreaks of cholera, typhoid, and yellow fever, diseases spread by polluted water, that periodically terrorized American cities. Building on the discovery of germs by Louis Pasteur and Robert Koch, sanitary reformers established stringent metropolitan health laws, created state boards of health, and mandated the licensing of plumbers and the inspection of their work. By the turn of the century,

George E. Waring, Jr., a prominent sanitary engineer, could confidently declare that "Plumbing, as we know it, is essentially and almost exclusively an American Institution."

The decision to adopt a water-based system for the removal of human wastes depended on a series of inventions. First, municipal water systems had to be built with reservoirs, pumps, and water towers to provide water to the pipes that supplied buildings. A sewage system of interconnected pipes was also necessary to remove and process wastes. Machines to manufacture lead, cast-iron, and glazed stoneware pipes had to be created, as did a uniform system of pipe threads and melted lead joints to create a reliable standardized system for connecting them. Finally, a porcelain toilet with a built-in gas trap was needed because the bacteria in feces produce methane or sewer gas. (A trap is a U-shaped joint in which the water at the low part of the U prevents

own churches and charitable organizations in the black neighborhoods where they lived.

Fashionable Avenues and Suburbs

The same cities that harbored slums, filth, suffering, and violence also boasted of neighborhoods of dazzling opulence with the latest lighting and plumbing technologies (see Technology & Culture). The wealthy built monumental residences along thoroughfares radiating from the city centers, among them Commonwealth Avenue in Boston, Euclid Avenue in Cleveland, and Summit Avenue in St. Paul.

In the 1870s and 1880s, city-dwellers began moving to nearby suburbs. Promoters of the suburban ideal contrasted the rolling lawns and stately houses on the city's periphery with the teeming streets, noisy saloons, and mounds of garbage and horse excrement downtown. Soon, many major cities could boast of their own stylish suburbs.

gas from seeping back into the bathroom. The gas vents through a pipe in the roof.)

Despite its usefulness, the new technology was not rapidly adopted. In 1890, only 24 percent of American dwellings had running water. As late as 1897, over 90 percent of the families in tenements had no baths and had to wash in hallway sinks or courtyard hydrants. By 1920, 80 percent of American houses, particularly those in rural areas, still lacked indoor flush toilets. The reason was simple: indoor plumbing was expensive and depended on the availability of water and sewer systems. Adding indoor plumbing increased the price of a new house by 20 percent.

Advertisers did their best to increase demand. They skillfully used the findings of science to advocate new standards of cleanliness or "hygiene," as it was called, which they associated with upper-class principles of respectability and decorum. Bathing and hand washing were touted as symbols of upper-class refinement.

Indoor plumbing not only reinforced higher standards for personal hygiene; it also enmeshed the homeowner in a web of local and state regulations. As sewage and water systems expanded to cover larger constituencies, political control moved from local to state and sometimes national arenas. Once largely independent, the homeowner now had to deal with water and power companies that often functioned regionally.

The adoption of strict sanitation systems and the use of indoor plumbing did achieve their intended result: they dramatically reduced the spread of disease. But the advances had unintended consequences. Indoor plumbing encouraged the phenomenal waste of water. A single faulty toilet could easily leak a hundred gallons of water a day. Not until the 1990s with the development of new low-water-usage toilets, which could save between 18,000 and 26,400 gallons of water a year, would new standards be established to reduce the use of water, an increasingly precious natural resource.

Questions for Analysis

- *Why does the successful introduction of new technologies often involve a system of inventions rather than a single invention?*

Middle-class city-dwellers followed the precedents set by the wealthy. Skilled artisans, shopkeepers, clerks, accountants, and sales personnel moved either to new developments at the city's edge or to outlying suburban communities (although those at the lower fringe of the middle class typically rented apartments in neighborhoods closer to the city center). Lawyers, doctors, small businessmen, and other professionals moved farther out along the main thoroughfares served by the street railway, where they purchased homes on large lots.

In time, a pattern of informal residential segregation by income took shape in the cities and suburbs. Built up for families of a particular income level, certain neighborhoods and suburbs developed remarkably similar standards for lot size and house design. Two-story houses with front porches, set back thirty feet from the sidewalk, became the norm in many neighborhoods. Commuters who rode the new street railways out from the city center could identify the social class of the suburban dwellers along the way as readily as a geologist might distinguish different strata on a washed-out riverbank.

By 1900, whirring trolley cars and hissing steam powered trains had burst the boundaries of the compact midcentury city. As they expanded, cities often annexed contingent suburbs. Within this enlarged city, sharp dissimilarities in building height and neighborhood quality set off business sectors from fashionable residential avenues and differentiated squalid manufacturing districts from parklike suburban subdivisions. Musing about urban America in 1902, James F. Muirhead, a popular Scottish guidebook author, wrote that New York and other U.S. cities reminded him of "a lady in a ball costume, with diamonds in her ears, and her toes out at her boots." To Muirhead, urban America had become a "land of contrasts" in which the separation of various social groups and the increasingly dissimilar living conditions for rich and poor had heightened ethnic, racial, and class divisions. Along with the physical change in American cities, in short, had come a new awareness of class and cultural disparities.

MIDDLE- AND UPPER-CLASS SOCIETY AND CULTURE

Spared the struggle for survival that confronted most Americans after the Civil War, society's middle and upper ranks faced a different challenge: how to rationalize their enjoyment of the products of the emerging consumer society. To justify the position of society's wealthier members, ministers such as Brooklyn preacher Henry Ward Beecher and advice-book writers appealed to **Victorian morality,** a set of social ideas embraced by the privileged classes of England and America during the long reign (1837–1901) of Britain's Queen Victoria.

E. L. Godkin, the editor of *The Nation*, Phillips Brooks, minister to Boston's Trinity Church, and other proponents of Victorian morality argued that the financial success of the middle and upper classes arose from their superior talent, intelligence, morality, and self-control. They also extended the antebellum ideal of separate spheres by arguing that women were the driving force for moral improvement. While men were expected to engage in self-disciplined, "manly" dedication to the new industrial order, women would provide the gentle, elevating influence that would lead society in its upward march. A network of institutions, from elegant department stores and hotels to elite colleges and universities, reinforced the privileged position of these groups.

Manners and Morals   Several fundamental assumptions shaped the Victorian worldview. First, human nature was malleable: people could improve themselves. Second, work had social value: working hard not only developed self-discipline but also helped advance the progress of the nation. Finally, good manners and the cultivation of literature and art ennobled society. Although these genteel assumptions were sometimes ignored, they were held up as universal standards.

Victorian morality stressed the importance of manners and social rituals. Middle-and upper-class families in the 1870s and 1880s increasingly defined their own social standing in terms not only of income but also of behavior. Good manners, including knowledge of dining and entertaining etiquette, and good posture became important marks of status.

In her popular advice book, *The American Woman's Home* (1869), Catharine Beecher (the sister of Henry Ward Beecher) displayed the typical Victorian self-consciousness about proper manners. The following dinner-table behaviors, she said, should be avoided by those of "good breeding":

> *Reaching over another person's plate; standing up to reach distant articles, instead of asking to have them passed ... using the table-cloth instead of napkins; eating fast, and in a noisy manner; putting large pieces in the mouth; ... [and] picking the teeth at the table.*

For Beecher and other molders of manners, meals became important rituals that differentiated the social classes. The elaborate china and silver that wealthy families exclusively possessed also provided telltale clues to a family's level of refinement and sophistication.

The Victorian code—with its emphasis on morals, manners, and proper behavior—thus heightened the sense of class differences and created visible distinctions among social groups. Victorian Americans made bold claims about their interest in helping others improve themselves. More often than not, however, their self-righteous, intensely moralistic outlook simply widened the gap that income disparities had already opened.

The Cult of Domesticity

Victorian views on morality and culture, coupled with the need to make decisions about a mountain of domestic products, had a subtle but important effect on middle-class expectations about women's role within the home. From the 1840s on, architects, clergymen, and other promoters of the so-called cult of domesticity had idealized the home as "the woman's sphere." They praised the home as a protected retreat where women could express their maternal gifts, including sensitivity toward children and an aptitude for religion. "The home is the wife's province," asserted one writer; "it is her natural field of labor ... to govern and direct its interior management."

During the 1880s and 1890s, Victorian advocates of the cult of domesticity added a new obligation to foster an artistic environment that would nurture her family's cultural improvement. Houses became statements of cultural aspiration with front parlors cluttered with artwork and curiosities. Excluded from the world of business and commerce, many middle- and upper-class women directed their energies to decorating their homes, seeking to make the home, as one advice book suggested, "a place of repose, a refuge from the excitement and distractions of outside ..., provided with every attainable means of rest and recreation."

Not all middle-class women pursued this domestic ideal. For some, housework and family responsibilities overwhelmed the concern for artistic accomplishment. For others, the artistic ideal was not to their taste. Sixteen-year-old Mary Putnam complained privately to a friend that she played the piano because of "an abstract general idea ... of a father coming home regularly tired at night (from the plow, I believe the usual legend runs), and being solaced by the brilliant yet touching performance of a sweet only daughter upon the piano." She then confessed that she detested the piano. In the 1880s and 1890s, as middle- and upper-class women sought other outlets for their creative energies in settlement-house work, social reform, and women's club activities, the older domestic ideal began to unravel.

Department Stores   Although Victorian social thought justified the privileges of the well-to-do, many people found it difficult to shake the thriftiness of their early years and accept the new preoccupation with accumulation and display. To lure these consumers, merchandisers in the 1880s stressed the high quality and low cost of the objects they sold, encouraging Americans to loosen their purse strings and enjoy prosperity without reservations. This argument particularly appealed to women who, to provide for their families, now had to shop for soap, canned foods, and other products formerly made at home.

Department stores set the standard for consumption. In the final quarter of the nineteenth century, Rowland H. Macy in New York, John Wanamaker in Philadelphia, and Marshall Field in Chicago built giant department stores that transformed the shopping experience for their middle- and upper-class patrons. The stores advertised "rock-bottom" prices and engaged in price wars. To avoid keeping their stock too long, they held giant end-of-the-season sales at drastically marked-down prices.

Department stores made shopping an exciting activity. Rapid turnover of merchandise created a sense of constant novelty. With stained-glass skylights, marble staircases, sparkling chandeliers, and plush carpets, the large urban department store functioned as a workplace for the lower classes and as a social club for comfortably fixed women. For those who could afford it, shopping became an adventure, a form of entertainment, and a way to affirm their place in society.

The Transformation of Higher Education   At a time when relatively few Americans had even a high school education and only 4 percent of the nation's eighteen- to twenty-one-year-olds were enrolled in institutions of higher learning, colleges and universities represented another stronghold of the business and professional elite.

Wealthy capitalists gained status and a measure of immortality by endowing colleges and universities. Leland Stanford and his wife, Jane Lathrop Stanford, launched Stanford University in 1885 with a bequest of $24 million; John D. Rockefeller donated $34 million to the University of Chicago in 1891. Industrialists and businessmen dominated the boards of trustees of most educational institutions.

Not only the classroom experience but also social contacts and athletic activities—especially football—prepared affluent young men for later responsibilities in business and the professions. Adapted by American college students in the 1860s from English rugby, football became an elite sport played by college teams. But the game, initially played without pads or helmets, was marred by violence. In 1905, eighteen students died of playing-field injuries. Many college presidents dismissed football as a dangerous waste of time and money. In 1873, when the University of Michigan challenged Cornell to a game in Ann Arbor, Cornell's president Andrew D. White huffily telegraphed back, "I will not permit thirty men to travel four hundred miles merely to agitate a bag of wind."

But eager alumni and coaches strongly defended the new sport. Some—among them Henry Lee Higginson, the Civil War veteran and Boston banker who gave Harvard "Soldiers' Field" stadium as a memorial to those who had died in battle—praised football as a character-building sport. Others, including famed Yale coach

Walter Camp, insisted that football could function as a surrogate frontier experience in an increasingly urbanized society. By 1900, collegiate football had become a popular fall ritual, and team captains were campus heroes.

More than 150 new colleges and universities were founded between 1880 and 1900, and enrollments more than doubled. While wealthy capitalists endowed some institutions, others, such as the state universities in the South and Midwest, were financed largely through public funds generated from public land sales under the Morrill Land Grant Act (1862). Many colleges were also founded and funded by religious denominations.

Following the precedent set by Oberlin College in 1836, coeducational private colleges and public universities in the Midwest enrolled increasing numbers of women. In the East, Columbia, Brown, and Harvard universities admitted women to the affiliated but separate institutions of Barnard (1889), Pembroke (1891), and Radcliffe (1894), respectively. Some colleges—Mount Holyoke (1837), Vassar (1865), Wellesley and Smith (1875), and Bryn Mawr (1884)—were founded solely for women. The generation of women educated at female institutions in the late nineteenth century developed the self-confidence to break with the Victorian ideal of passive womanhood and to compete with men by displaying strength, aggressiveness, and intelligence—popularly considered male attributes. Nationally, the percentage of colleges admitting women jumped from 30 percent to 71 percent between 1880 and 1900. By the turn of the century, women made up more than one-third of the total college-student population.

At the university level, innovative presidents such as Cornell's Andrew D. White and Harvard's Charles W. Eliot, influenced by new discoveries in science and medicine, sought to change the focus of higher education. In the 1850s, most physicians had attended medical school for only two sixteen-week terms. They typically received their degrees without ever having visited a hospital or examined a patient. The Civil War exposed the abysmal state of American medical knowledge. Twice as many soldiers died from infections as from wounds. Doctors were so poorly trained and ignorant about sanitation that they often infected soldiers' injuries when they probed wounds with hands wiped on pus-stained aprons. "The ignorance and general incompetency of the average graduate of American medical schools, at the time when he receives the degree which turns him loose upon the community," wrote Eliot in 1870, "is something horrible to contemplate."

In the 1880s and 1890s, leading medical professors, many of whom had studied in France and Germany, began restructuring American medical education. Using the experimental method developed by German scientists, they insisted that all medical students be trained in biology, chemistry, and physics, including working in a laboratory. Although medical school reform improved health care in some areas, it also effectively shut out African-American and poor women who could not afford the tuition. New educational and professional standards, similarly, were established for architects, engineers, and lawyers.

These changes were part of a larger transformation in higher education, the rise of a new kind of institution, the **research university.** Unlike the best of the mid-nineteenth-century colleges, which focused on teaching Latin and Greek, theology, logic, and mathematics, the new research universities offered courses in a wide variety of subject areas, established professional schools, and encouraged faculty

Chemistry Class, Smith College, 1889

Thanks to their education in science at colleges and universities, increasing numbers of women in the 1890s became physicians. Nevertheless, most medical schools refused to appoint women doctors to their teaching staffs.

(Sophia Smith Collection, Smith College)

members to pursue basic research. At Cornell University, President Andrew D. White's objective was to create an environment "where any person can find instruction in any study." At Cornell, the University of Wisconsin at Madison, Johns Hopkins, Harvard, and other institutions, this new conception of higher education laid the groundwork for the central role that America's universities would play in the intellectual, cultural, and scientific life of the twentieth century.

REFORMING THE WORKING CLASS

The contrast between the affluent world of the college educated middle and upper classes and the gritty lives of the working class was most graphically on display in the nation's growing urban centers, where immigrant newcomers reshaped political and social institutions to meet their own needs. If fancy department stores and elegant hotels furnished new social spaces for the middle and upper classes, saloons became the poor man's club, and dance halls became single women's home away from home. While the rich and the wellborn looked suspiciously at lower-class recreational activities and sought to force the poor to change their ways, working-class Americans, the immigrant newcomers in particular, fought to preserve their own distinctive way of life. Indeed, the late nineteenth century witnessed an ongoing battle to eradicate social drinking and curb lower-class recreational activities.

Battling Poverty   Stunned by the levels of poverty and suffering in the expanding industrial cities, middle-class city leaders sought comprehensive solutions for relieving poverty. Jacob Riis and the first generation of reformers believed that immigrants' lack of self-discipline and their unsanitary living conditions caused their problems. Consequently, Riis and his peers focused on moral improvement and exposing squalid tenement housing. Only later would Jane Addams, Florence Kelley, and other settlement-house workers examine the crippling impact of low wages and dangerous working conditions. Although many reformers genuinely sympathized with the suffering of the lower classes, the humanitarians often turned their campaigns to help the destitute into missions to Americanize the immigrants and eliminate customs that they perceived as offensive and self-destructive.

Poverty-relief workers first targeted their efforts at the young, who were thought to be most malleable. Energized by the religious revivals of the 1830s and 1840s, Protestant reformers started charitable societies to help transient youths and abandoned street children. In 1843, Robert M. Hartley, a former employee of the New York Temperance Society, organized the New York Association for Improving the Condition of the Poor to help poor families.

Hartley's voluntaristic approach was supplemented by the more coercive tactics of Charles Loring Brace, who founded the New York Children's Aid Society in 1853. Brace admired "these little traders of the city … battling for a hard living in the snow and mud of the street" but worried that they might join the city's "dangerous classes." Brace established dormitories, reading rooms, and workshops where the boys could learn practical skills; he also swept orphaned children off the streets, shipped them to the country, and placed them with families to work as farm hands.

Where Brace's Children's Aid Society gave adolescents an alternative to living in the slums, the Young Men's Christian Association (YMCA), founded in England in 1841 and exported to America ten years later, provided housing and wholesome recreation for country boys who had migrated to the city. The Young Women's Christian Association (YWCA) similarly provided housing and a day nursery for young women and their children. Both organizations subjected their members to curfews and expelled them for drinking and other forbidden behavior.

By 1900, more than fifteen hundred YMCAs and YWCAs served as havens for nearly a quarter-million young men and women. But YMCA and YWCA leaders reached only a small portion of the young adult population. Although charity workers made some progress in their efforts to aid youth, the strategy was too narrowly focused to stem the rising tide of urban problems.

New Approaches to Social Reform The inability of the Children's Aid Society, YMCA, YWCA, and other relief organizations to cope with the explosive growth of the urban poor in the 1870s and 1880s convinced reformers to search for new allies in the fight against poverty. One effective agency was the **Salvation Army.** A church established along pseudomilitary lines in England in 1865 by Methodist minister "General" William Booth, the Salvation Army sent uniformed volunteers to the United States in 1880 to provide food, shelter, and temporary employment for families. Its members ran soup kitchens and day nurseries and dispatched its "slum brigades" to carry the message of morality to the immigrant poor. The army's strategy was simple. Attract the poor with marching bands and lively preaching; follow up with offers of food, assistance, and employment; and then teach them the solid middle-class virtues of temperance, hard work, and self-discipline.

(Chicago Historical Society)

Garbage Box, First Ward, Chicago, CA. **1900** *Lacking space for recreation, immigrant children played atop garbage boxes in crowded alleys. Concerned for their health, Jane Addams wrote that "this slaughter of the innocents, this infliction of suffering on the newborn, is so gratuitous and so unfair, that it is only a question of time until an outraged sense of justice shall be aroused on behalf of these children."*

The New York Charity Organization Society (COS), founded in 1882 by **Josephine Shaw Lowell,** implemented a similar approach to poor relief. To make aid to the poor more efficient, Lowell and the COS leaders divided New York City into districts, compiled files on all aid recipients, and sent "friendly visitors," who were trained, salaried women, into the tenements to counsel families on how to improve their lives. Convinced that moral deficiencies lay at the root of poverty and that the "promiscuous charity" of overlapping church welfare agencies undermined the desire to work, the COS tried to foster self-sufficiency in its charges. In 1891, Lowell helped found the Consumers' League of New York, which encouraged women to buy only from manufacturers who paid fair wages and maintained decent working conditions.

Although the COS did coordinate relief efforts and developed helpful statistics on the extent of poverty, critics justly accused the society of seeking more to control the poor than to alleviate their suffering. One of the manuals, for example, stressed the importance of introducing "messy housekeepers" to the "pleasures of a cheery, well-ordered home." Unable to see slum problems from the vantage point of the poor, they failed, for the most part, in their underlying objective: to convert the poor to their own standards of morality and decorum.

The Moral-Purity Campaign

While Josephine Shaw Lowell and other like-minded social disciplinarians worked to eradicate urban poverty, other reformers pushed for tougher measures against sin and immorality. In 1872, **Anthony Comstock,** a pious young dry-goods clerk, founded the New York Society for the Suppression of Vice. The organization demanded that municipal authorities close down gambling and lottery operations and censor obscene publications.

Nothing symbolized the contested terrain between middle- and lower-class culture better than the fight over prostitution. Considered socially degenerate by some and a source of recreation by others, prostitution both exploited women and offered them a steady income and a measure of personal freedom. After the Civil War, the number of brothels expanded rapidly. In the 1880s, saloons, tenements, and cabarets hired prostitutes of their own. Even though immigrant women do not appear to have made up the majority of big-city prostitutes, reformers often labeled them as the major source of the problem.

In 1892, brothels, along with gambling dens and saloons, became targets for the reform efforts of New York Presbyterian minister Charles Parkhurst. Blaming the "slimy, oozy soil of Tammany Hall" (the Democratic organization that dominated New York City politics, discussed in the next chapter) and the New York City police—"the dirtiest, crookedest, and ugliest lot of men ever combined in semi-military array outside of Japan and Turkey"—for the city's rampant evils, he organized the City Vigilance League to clean up the city. Two years later a nonpartisan Committee of Seventy elected a new mayor who pressured city officials to enforce the laws against prostitution, gambling, and Sunday liquor sales.

The purity campaign lasted scarcely three years. The reform coalition quickly fell apart. New York City's population was too large, and its ethnic constituencies too diverse, for middle- and upper-class reformers to curb all the illegal activities flourishing within the sprawling metropolis.

The Social Gospel

In the 1870s and 1880s, a handful of Protestant ministers who served upper-class congregations and were appalled by slum conditions took a different approach to helping impoverished city dwellers. These ministers argued that the rich and the wellborn had a Christian responsibility to do something about urban poverty.

William S. Rainsford, the Irish-born minister of New York City's Saint George's Episcopal Church, pioneered the development of the so-called institutional church movement. Large downtown churches in once-elite districts that had been overrun by immigrants would provide their new neighbors with social services as well as a place to worship. With the financial help of J. Pierpont Morgan, a warden of his church, Rainsford organized a boys' club, built church recreational facilities for the destitute on the Lower East Side, and established an industrial training program.

Other Protestant ministers, led by Washington Gladden, a Congregational clergyman in Columbus, Ohio, launched the **Social Gospel** movement in the 1870s. Gladden insisted that true Christianity commits men and women to fight social injustice wherever it exists. Thus, in response to the wave of violent strikes in 1877, he urged church leaders to mediate the conflict between business and labor. Their attempt to do so was unsuccessful.

If Gladden set the tone for the Social Gospel, Walter Rauschenbusch, a minister at a German Baptist church in New York's notorious "Hell's Kitchen" neighborhood, articulated the movement's central philosophy. Educated in Germany, Rauschenbusch argued that a truly Christian society would unite all churches, reorganize the industrial system, and work for international peace. Rauschenbusch's appeal for Christian unity led to the formation of the Federal Council of Churches in 1908, but his other goals were never achieved. Although the Social Gospel attracted only a handful of Protestants, their earnest voices blended with a growing chorus of critics bemoaning the nation's urban woes.

The Settlement-House Movement   In the 1880s, a younger generation of charity workers led by **Jane Addams** developed a new weapon against destitution: the settlement house. Like the Social Gospelers, these reformers recognized that the hardships of slum life were often beyond the individual's control. Living in the poor neighborhoods where they worked, they could see firsthand "the struggle for existence, which is so much harsher among people near the edge of pauperism."

The youngest daughter of a successful Illinois businessman, Jane Addams purchased a dilapidated mansion on Chicago's south side in 1889 and opened it as Hull House. Putting the middle-class ideal of true womanhood into action, Addams turned Hull House into a social center for immigrants. She invited them to plays; sponsored art projects; held classes in English, civics, cooking, and dressmaking; and encouraged them to preserve their traditional crafts. She set up a kindergarten, a laundry, an employment bureau, and a day nursery for working mothers. Hull House also sponsored recreational and athletic programs and dispensed legal aid and health care.

In the hope of upgrading the filthy and overcrowded housing in its environs, Addams and her coworkers conducted surveys of city housing conditions and pressured politicians to enforce sanitation regulations. For a time, demonstrating her principle of direct engagement with the lives of the poor, Addams even served as garbage inspector for her local ward.

By 1895, at least fifty settlement houses had opened in cities around the nation. Settlement-house leaders trained a generation of young college students, mostly women, many of whom would later serve as state and local government officials. **Florence Kelley,** for example, who had worked at Hull House, became the chief factory inspector for Illinois in 1893. For Kelley as for other female settlement workers, settlement houses functioned as a supportive sisterhood of reform. Many settlement-house veterans would later draw on their experience to play an influential role in the regulatory movements of the Progressive Era (covered in Chapter 21). Through their sympathetic attitudes toward the immigrants and their systematic publication of data about slum conditions, settlement-house workers gave Americans renewed hope that urban problems could be overcome.

In their attempt to promote class cooperation and social harmony, however, settlement houses had mixed success. Although many immigrants appreciated the settlement houses' resources and activities, they believed that the reformers had little interest in helping them gain political power. Settlement-house workers did tend to overlook immigrant organizations and their leaders. In 1894, Hull House attracted two thousand visitors per week, but this was only a fraction of the more than seventy thousand people who lived within six blocks of the building. "They're like the rest," complained one immigrant, "a bunch of people planning for us and deciding what is good for us without consulting us or taking us into their confidence."

WORKING-CLASS LEISURE IN THE IMMIGRANT CITY

In colonial America, preachers had warned against leisure and idleness as temptations to sin. In the rural culture of the early nineteenth century, the unremitting routines of farm labor left little time for relaxation. Family picnics, horse races, county fairs, revival meetings, and Fourth of July and Christmas celebrations had provided occasional permissible diversions. But most Americans continued to view leisure activities skeptically. Henry Clay Work's popular song "My Grandfather's Clock" (1876), which praised the ancient timepiece for "wasting no time" and working "ninety years, without slumbering," bore witness to the tenacity of this deep-seated reverence for work and suspicion of play.

As urban populations shot up after the Civil War, striking new patterns of leisure and amusement emerged, most notably among the urban working class. After spending long hours in factories, in mills, behind department-store counters, or as domestic servants in the homes of the wealthy, working-class Americans craved relaxation and diversion. They thronged the streets, patronized saloons and dance halls, cheered at boxing matches and baseball games, and organized group picnics and holiday celebrations. As amusement parks, vaudeville theaters, sporting clubs, and racetracks provided further outlets for workers' need for entertainment, leisure became a big business catering to a mass public rather than to a wealthy elite.

For millions of working-class Americans, leisure time took on increasing importance as factory work became routinized and impersonal. Although many recreational activities involved both men and women, others attracted one gender in particular. Saloons offered an intensely male environment where patrons could share good stories, discuss and bet on sporting events, and momentarily put aside pressures of job and family. Young working women preferred to share confidences with friends in informal social clubs, tried out new fashions in street promenading, and found excitement in neighborhood dance halls and amusement parks.

Streets, Saloons, and Boxing Matches   No segment of the population had a greater need for amusement and recreation than the urban working class. Hours of tedious, highly disciplined, and physically exhausting labor left workers tired and thirsting for excitement and escape from their cramped housing quarters. In 1889, a banner carried by a carpenters' union summed up their wishes: "EIGHT HOURS FOR WORK, EIGHT HOURS FOR REST, AND EIGHT HOURS FOR WHAT WE WILL."

City streets provided recreation that anyone could afford. Relaxing after a day's work, shop girls and laborers clustered on busy corners, watching shouting pushcart peddlers and listening to organ grinders and street musicians play familiar melodies. For a penny or a nickel, they could buy bagels, baked potatoes, soda, and other foods and drinks. In the summer, when the heat and humidity in tenement apartments reached unbearable levels, the streets became a hive of neighborhood social life. One immigrant fondly recalled his boyhood on the streets of New York's Lower East Side: "Something was always happening, and our attention was continually being shifted from one excitement to another."

The streets were open to all, but other leisure institutions drew mainly a male clientele. For example, in cities with a strong German immigrant presence like Baltimore, Milwaukee, and Cincinnati, gymnastic clubs (called *Turnverein*) and singing societies (*Gesangverein*) provided both companionship and the opportunity to perpetuate old-world cultural traditions.

For workmen of all ethnic backgrounds, saloons offered companionship, conviviality, and five-cent beer, often with a free lunch thrown in. New York City had an estimated ten thousand saloons by 1900 and Denver nearly five hundred. As neighborhood gathering places, saloons reinforced group identity and became centers for immigrant politics. Saloonkeepers, who often doubled as local ward bosses and turned out the vote in their neighborhoods, performed small services for their patrons, including finding jobs and writing letters for illiterate immigrants. Sports memorabilia and pictures of prominent prizefighters adorned saloon walls. With their rich mahogany bars, etched glass, shiny brass rails, and elegant mirrors, saloons provided patrons with a taste of high-toned luxury. Although working-class women rarely joined their husbands at the saloon, they might send a son or daughter to the corner pub to fetch a "growler"—a large tin pail of beer.

The conventions of saloon culture thus stood in marked contrast to both the socially isolating routines of factory labor and the increasingly private and family-centered social life of the middle class. Nevertheless, it would be a mistake to view the old-time saloon through a haze of sentimental nostalgia. Prostitution and crime flourished in the rougher saloons. Moreover, drunken husbands sometimes beat their wives and children, squandered their limited income, and lost their jobs. The pervasiveness of alcoholism was devastating. Temperance reformers, in their attack on saloons, targeted a widespread social problem.

The Rise of Professional Sports   Contrary to the prevailing myth, schoolboy Abner Doubleday did not invent baseball in Cooperstown, New York, in 1839. As an English game called rounders, the pastime had existed in one form or another since the seventeenth century. If Americans did not create baseball, they did turn it into a major professional sport. In 1845, the first organized baseball team, the New York Knickerbockers, was formed. In the 1860s, rules were codified and the sport assumed its modern form. Overhand pitches replaced underhand tosses. Fielders wore gloves, games were standardized at nine innings, and bases were spaced ninety feet apart.

In that same decade, promoters organized professional clubs and began to charge admission and compete for players. The Cincinnati Red Stockings, the first team to put its players under contract for the whole season, gained fame in 1869 by touring the country and ending the season with fifty-seven wins and no losses. Team owners organized the National League in 1876, took control from the players by requiring them to sign contracts that barred them from playing for rival organizations, and limited each city to one professional team. Soon the owners were filling

FOR THE HEAVY-WEIGHT CHAMPIONSHIP OF THE WORLD.

John Lawrence Sullivan, the Champion, and James J. Corbett, the Adonis of the Fistic Arena. Who Are to Battle September 7th Next For a Purse and Stakes of $25,000 and the Big Fellow's Title.

Published by Arthur T. Lumley, New York Illustrated News.

(From the Collections of The Henry Ford)

World's Heavyweight Boxing Championship, 1892 *In dethroning ring champion John L. Sullivan, "Gentleman Jim" Corbett demonstrated that speed and finesse were more than a match for brute strength.*

baseball parks with crowds of ten to twelve thousand fans and earning enormous profits. By the 1890s, baseball had become big business.

Although baseball attracted a national following from all social levels, the working class particularly took the sport to heart. The most profitable teams were those in major industrial cities with a large working-class population. Workers avidly followed their team's progress. Many saloons reported scores on blackboards and an estimated 50 percent of players worked in saloons in the off season or became saloon owners when they retired from the game.

If baseball helped build solidarity among some ethnic groups, it also fostered discrimination against blacks. Although at least fifty-five blacks played on integrated teams between 1883 and 1898, the refusal of the Chicago White Stockings in 1887 to play a team with George Stovey, a star black pitcher, marked a turning point. That same year, Colored baseball clubs opened in six cities. Increasingly thereafter, blacks were banned from playing on professional teams.

Newspapers thrived on baseball. Joseph Pulitzer introduced the first separate sports page when he bought the *New York World* in 1883, and much of the sporting news in the *World* and other papers was devoted to baseball. Fans who cheered the hometown team provided cities with a shared sports loyalty that reduced ethnic, class, and religious differences, but drinking and gambling continued to plague the game.

Although no organized sport attracted as large a following as baseball, horse racing and boxing contests drew big crowds of spectators and bettors. Louisville's Kentucky Derby became an important social event for the rich, but professional boxing aroused more passionate devotion among laborers. Bare-knuckled prize-fighting became a testing ground where men could demonstrate their toughness and physical prowess.

For many working-class Americans, heavyweight fighter **John L. Sullivan,** "the Boston Strong Boy" personified these traits. Of Irish immigrant stock, Sullivan began boxing in 1877 at the age of nineteen. His first professional fight came in 1880 when he knocked out John Donaldson, "the Champion of the West," in a Cincinnati beer hall. With his massive physique, handlebar mustache, and arrogant swagger, Sullivan was enormously popular among immigrants. Barnstorming across the country, he vanquished a succession of local strongmen, invariably wearing his trademark green tights with an American flag wrapped around his middle. Yet, Sullivan refused to fight blacks, supposedly in deference to the wishes of his fans. This policy conveniently allowed him to avoid facing the finest boxer of the 1880s, the Australian black, Peter Jackson.

Sullivan loved drink and high living, and by the end of the eighties he was sadly out of shape. But when the editor of the *Police Gazette,* a sensational tabloid, designed a new heavyweight championship belt—allegedly containing two hundred ounces of silver and encrusted with diamonds and pure gold—and awarded it to Sullivan's rival Jake Kilrain, the champion had to defend himself. The two met on a sweltering, hundred-degree day in New Orleans in July 1889 for the last bare-knuckles championship match. After seventy-five short but grueling rounds, Kilrain's managers threw in the towel. Newspapers around the nation banner-headlined the story. Contemptuously returning the championship belt to the *Police Gazette* after having had it appraised at $175, Sullivan went on the road to star in a melodrama written specifically for him. Playing the role of a blacksmith, he (in the words of a recent historian of bare-knuckles boxing) "pounded an anvil, beat a bully, and mutilated his lines." But his fans did not care; he was one of them, and they adored him. As one admirer wrote,

> His colors are the Stars and Stripes,
> He also wears the green,
> And he's the grandest slugger that
> The ring has ever seen.

Vaudeville, Amusement Parks, and Dance Halls

In contrast to the male preserve of saloons and prizefights, the world of vaudeville, amusement parks, and neighborhood dance halls welcomed all comers regardless of gender. Some of them proved particularly congenial to working-class women.

Vaudeville evolved out of antebellum minstrel shows that featured white singers made up as blacks. The shows typically opened with a trained animal routine or a dance number, followed by a musical interlude. Comic skits then ridiculed the trials of urban life, satirizing police and municipal ineptitude, poking fun at immigrant accents, and mining a rich vein of broad ethnic humor and stereotypes. Blackface skits were sometimes included. After a highbrow operatic aria and acts by ventrilo-quists, pantomimes, and magicians, the program ended with a "flash" finale such as flying-trapeze artists swinging against a black background. By the 1880s, vaudeville was drawing larger crowds than any other form of theater.

The white working class's fascination with vaudeville's blackface acts has been the subject of considerable recent scrutiny by historians. Some have interpreted it as a way for the white working class to mock middle-class ideals. By pretending to act like the popular stereotypes of blacks, white working-class youths could challenge traditional family structures, the virtue of sexual self-denial, and adult expectations about working hard. In this view popular culture was making fun of the ideals of thrift and propriety being promoted in marketplace and domestic ideology. Other historians have argued that blackface buffoonery, with its grotesque, demeaning caricatures of African-Americans, reinforced prejudice against blacks and restricted their escape from lower-class status. Paradoxically, therefore, the popularity of blackface vaudeville acts reinforced white racial solidarity and strengthened the expanding wall separating whites and African-Americans.

Where vaudeville offered psychological escape from the stresses of working-class life, amusement parks provided physical escape. New York's Coney Island, a section of Brooklyn's oceanfront evolved into a resort for the masses in the 1870s. At Coney Island, young couples went dancing, rode through the dark Tunnel of Love, sped down the dizzying roller coaster in Steeplechase Park, or watched belly dancers in the carnival sideshows. Customers were encouraged to surrender to the spirit of play, forget the demands of the industrial world, and lose themselves in fantasy.

By the end of the nineteenth century, New York City had well over three hundred thousand female wage earners, most of them young, unmarried women working as seamstresses, laundresses, typists, domestic servants, and department-store clerks. For this army of low-paid young working women and their counterparts in other cit-ies, amusement parks exerted a powerful lure. Here they could meet friends, spend time with young men beyond the watchful eyes of their parents, show off their new dresses, and try out the latest dance steps. As a twenty-year-old German immigrant woman who worked as a servant in a wealthy household observed, *I have heard some of the high people with whom I have been living say that Coney Island is not tony. The trouble is that these high people don't know how to dance. I have to laugh when I see them at their balls and parties. If only I could get out on the floor and show them how—they would be astonished.*

For such women, the brightly decorated dance pavilion, the exciting music, and the spell of a warm summer night could seem a magical release from the drudgery of daily life.

Ragtime

Nothing could illustrate more sharply the differences between middle- and working-class culture than the contrasting styles of popular music they favored. The middle class preferred hymns or songs that con-veyed a moral lesson. The working class delighted in ragtime, which originated in the 1880s with black musicians in the saloons and brothels of the South and Midwest and was played strictly for entertainment.

Ragtime developed out of the rich tradition of sacred and secular songs through which African-Americans had long eased the burdens of their lives. Like spirituals, ragtime used syncopated rhythms and complex harmonies, but it blended these with marching-band musical structures to create a distinctive style. A favorite of "honky-tonk" piano players, ragtime was introduced to the broader public in the 1890s and became a national sensation.

The reasons for the sudden ragtime craze were complex. Inventive, playful, with catchy syncopations and an infectious rhythm in the bass clef, the music displayed an originality that had an appeal all its own. Part of ragtime's popularity also came from its origin in brothels and its association with blacks, who were widely stereotyped in the 1890s as sexual, sensual, and uninhibited by the rigid Victorian social conventions that restricted whites. The "wild" and complex rhythms of ragtime were widely interpreted to be a freer and more "natural" expression of elemental feelings about love and sex.

Ragtime's great popularity proved a mixed blessing for blacks. It testified to the achievements of brilliant composers like Scott Joplin, helped break down the barriers faced by blacks in the music industry, and contributed to a spreading rebellion against the repressiveness of Victorian standards. But ragtime simply confirmed some whites' stereotype of blacks as primitive and sensual, a bias that underlay the racism of the period and helped justify segregation and discrimination.

CULTURES IN CONFLICT

Even within the elite and middle classes, Victorian morality and genteel cultural standards were never totally accepted. As the century ended, increasing numbers of people questioned these beliefs. Women stood at the center of the era's cultural turbulence. Thwarted by a restrictive code of feminine propriety, they made their dissatisfactions heard. The rise of women's clubs, the growth of women's colleges, and even the 1890s bicycle fad testified to the emergence of what some began to call the "new woman."

At the same time, a widening chasm divided the well-to-do from urban working-class immigrants. In no period of American history have class conflicts—cultural as well as economic—been more open and raw. As middle-class leaders nervously eyed the sometimes disorderly culture of city streets, saloons, boxing clubs, dance halls, and amusement parks, they saw a challenge to their own cultural and social values. Some middle-class reformers promoted the public school as a way to impose middle-class values on the urban masses. Others battled urban "vice" and "immorality." But ultimately it was the polite mores of the middle class, not urban working-class culture, that proved more vulnerable. By 1900, the Victorian social and moral ethos was crumbling on every front.

The Genteel Tradition and Its Critics
What was this genteel culture that aroused such opposition? In the 1870s and 1880s, a group of upper-class writers and magazine editors, led by Harvard art history professor Charles Eliot Norton and New York editors Richard Watson Gilder of *The Century* magazine and E. L. Godkin of *The Nation*, codified Victorian

standards for literature and the arts. They campaigned to improve American taste in interior furnishings, textiles, ceramics, wallpaper, and books. By fashioning rigorous criteria for excellence in writing and design, they hoped to create a coherent national artistic culture.

In the 1880s Norton, Godkin, and Gilder, joined by the editors of other high-brow periodicals such as the *Atlantic Monthly* and *North American Review,* set up new guidelines for serious literature. They lectured the middle class about the value of high culture and the insights to be gained from painting and music. They censored their own publications to remove all sexual allusions, disrespectful treatments of Christianity, and unhappy endings. Expanding their combined circulation to nearly two hundred thousand copies, Godkin and the other editors of "quality" periodicals created an important forum for serious writing. Novelists Henry James, who published virtually all of his work in the *Atlantic,* and William Dean Howells, who served as editor of the same magazine, helped lead this elite literary establishment. James believed that "it is art that makes life .... [There is] no substitute whatever for [its] force and beauty...."

This interest in art for art's sake paralleled a broader crusade called the "aesthetic movement," led in England by William Morris, Oscar Wilde, and other art critics, who sought to bring art into every facet of life. In America, Candace Wheeler and other reformers made its influence felt through the work of architects, jewelers, and interior decorators.

Although the magazines initially provided an important forum for new writers, their editors' elitism and desire to control the nation's literary standards soon aroused opposition. Samuel Langhorne Clemens, better known as **Mark Twain,** spoke for many young writers when he declared that he was through with "literature and all that bosh." Attacking aristocratic literary conventions, Twain and other authors who shared his concerns explored new forms of fiction and worked to broaden its appeal to the general public.

These efforts to chart new directions for American literature rested on fundamental changes taking place in the publishing industry. To compete with elite periodicals costing twenty-five to thirty-five cents, new magazines like *Ladies' Home Journal, Cosmopolitan,* and *McClure's* lowered their prices to a dime or fifteen cents and tripled or quadrupled their circulation. Supporting themselves through advertising, these magazines encouraged new trends in fiction while mass-marketing new products. Their editors sought writers who could provide accurate depictions of the "whirlpool of real life" and create a new civic consciousness to heal the class divisions of American society.

Some of these authors have been called regionalists because they captured the distinctive dialect and details of local life in their environs. In *The Country of the Pointed Firs* (1896), for example, Sarah Orne Jewett wrote of the New England village life that she knew in South Berwick, Maine. Others, most notably William Dean Howells, have been called realists because of their focus on the truthful depiction of the commonplace and the everyday, especially in urban areas. Still others have been categorized as naturalists because their novels and stories deny free will and stress the ways in which life's outcomes are determined by economic and psychological forces. Stephen Crane's *Maggie: A Girl of the Streets* (1892), a bleak story of an innocent girl's exploitation and ultimate suicide in an urban slum,

Mark Twain *Twain not only broke from highbred literary standards but also created unique personal style through his studied poses and distinctive attire.*

generally is considered the first naturalistic American novel. Yet in practice, these categories are imprecise and often overlap. What many of these writers shared was a skepticism about literary conventions and an intense desire to understand the society around them and portray it in words.

The careers of Mark Twain and Theodore Dreiser highlight the changes in the publishing industry and the evolution of new forms of writing. Both authors grew up in the Midwest, outside the East Coast literary establishment. Twain was born near Hannibal, Missouri, in 1835, and Dreiser in Terre Haute, Indiana, in 1871. As young men, both worked as newspaper reporters and traveled widely. Both learned from direct and sometimes bitter experience about the greed, speculation, and fraud that figured centrally in Gilded Age life.

Of the two, Twain more incessantly sought a mass-market audience. With his drooping mustache, white hair, and white suits, Twain turned himself into a media personality, lecturing from coast to coast, founding his own publishing house, and using door-to-door salesmen to sell his books. The name Mark Twain became his trademark, identifying him to readers as a literary celebrity much as the labels Coca-Cola and Ivory Soap won instant consumer recognition. Although Dreiser possessed neither Twain's flamboyant personality nor his instinct for salesmanship, he, too, learned to crank out articles.

Drawing on their own experiences, Twain and Dreiser wrote about the human impact of the wrenching social changes taking place around them: the flow of people to the cities and the relentless scramble for power, wealth, and fame. In *The Adventures of Huckleberry Finn* (1884), Twain tells a story of two runaways, the rebellious Huck and the slave Jim, drifting down the Mississippi in search of freedom. Their physical journey, which contrasts idyllic life on the raft with the tawdry, fraudulent world of small riverfront towns, is a journey of identity that brings with it a deeper understanding of contemporary American society.

Dreiser's *Sister Carrie* (1900) also tells of a journey. In this case, the main character, Carrie Meeber, an innocent girl on her way from her Wisconsin farm home to Chicago, is seduced by a traveling salesman and then moves in with the married proprietor of a fancy saloon. Driven by her desire for expensive department-store clothes and lavish entertainment, Carrie is an opportunist incapable of feeling guilt. She follows her married lover to New York, knowing that he has stolen the receipts from his saloon, abandons him when his money runs out, and pursues her own career in the theater.

Twain and Dreiser broke decisively with the genteel tradition's emphasis on manners and decorum. *Century* magazine readers complained that *Huckleberry Finn* was coarse and "destitute of a single redeeming quality." The publisher of *Sister Carrie* was so repelled by Dreiser's novel that he printed only a thousand copies (to fulfill the legal terms of his contract) and then stored them in a warehouse, refusing to promote them.

Growing numbers of scholars and critics similarly challenged the self-serving certitudes of Victorian mores, including assumptions that moral worth and economic standing were closely linked and that the status quo of the 1870s and 1880s represented a social order decreed by God and nature alike. Whereas Henry George, Lester Ward, and Edward Bellamy elaborated their visions of a cooperative and harmonious society (see Chapter 18), economist Thorstein Veblen in *The Theory of the Leisure Class* (1899) offered a caustic critique of the lifestyles of the new capitalist elite. Raised in a Norwegian farm community in Minnesota, Veblen looked at the captains of industry and their families with a jaundiced eye, documenting their "conspicuous consumption" of expensive products and lamenting the widening gap between "those who worked without profit" and "those who profited without working."

Within the new discipline of sociology, Annie MacLean exposed the exploitation of department-store clerks, Walter Wyckoff uncovered the hand-to-mouth existence of unskilled laborers, and W. E. B. Du Bois documented the suffering and hardships faced by blacks in Philadelphia. The publication of these social scientists' writings, coupled with the economic depression and seething labor agitation of the 1890s, made it increasingly difficult for turn-of-the-century middle-class Americans to accept the smug, self-satisfied belief in progress and gentility that had been a hallmark of the Victorian outlook.

Modernism in Architecture and Painting The challenge to the genteel tradition also found strong support among architects and painters. By the 1890s Chicago architects William Holabird, John Wellborn Root, and others had tired of copying European designs. Breaking with established architects such as Richard Morris Hunt, the designer of French châteaux for New York's Fifth Avenue, these Chicago architects followed the lead of Louis Sullivan, who argued that a building's form should follow its function. In their view, banks should look like the financial institutions they were, not like Greek temples. Striving to create functional American design standards, the Chicago architects looked for inspiration to the future—to **modernism**—not to the past.

The Chicago architect **Frank Lloyd Wright** designed "prairie-school" houses that represented a typical modernist break with past styles. Wright scorned the three-story Victorian house with its large attic and basement. His designs, which featured broad, sheltering roofs and horizontal silhouettes, used interconnecting rooms to create a sense of spaciousness.

The call of modernism, with its rejection of Victorian refinement, influenced late-nineteenth-century American painting as well. The watercolors of Winslow Homer, a magazine illustrator during the Civil War, revealed nature as brutally tough and unsentimental. In Homer's grim, elemental seascapes, lone men struggle against massive waves that constantly threaten to overwhelm them. Thomas Eakins's canvases of swimmers, boxers, and rowers (such as his well-known *Champion Single Sculls,* painted in 1871) similarly captured moments of vigorous physical exertion in everyday life. While Mary Cassatt shared Eakins's interest in everyday life, she often took as her subject the bond between mother and child, as in her painting *The Bath* (ca. 1891). After studying at the Pennsylvania Academy of Fine Arts, she moved to Paris in 1874, where she worked closely with French Impressionist painters such as Monet and Degas.

The revolt by architects and painters against Victorian standards was symptomatic of a larger shift in middle-class thought. This shift resulted from fundamental economic changes that had spawned a far more complex social environment than that of the past. As Protestant minister Josiah Strong perceptively observed in 1898, the transition from muscle to mechanical power had "separated, as by an impassable gulf, the simple, homespun, individualistic world of the ... past, from the complex, closely associated life of the present." The increasingly evident gap between rural or small-town life—a world of quiet parlors and flickering kerosene lamps—and life in the big, glittering, electrified cities of iron and glass made nineteenth-century Americans acutely aware of differences in upbringing and wealth. Given the disparities between rich and poor, between rural and urban, and between native-born Americans and recent immigrants, it is no wonder that pious Victorian platitudes about proper manners and graceful arts seemed out of touch with the new social realities.

Distrusting the idealistic Victorian assumptions about social progress, middle-class journalists, novelists, artists, and politicians nevertheless remained divided over how to replace them. Not until the Progressive Era would social reformers draw on a new expertise in social research and an enlarged conception of the federal government's regulatory power to break sharply with their Victorian predecessors' social outlook.

From Victorian Lady to New Woman

Although middle-class women figured importantly in the revolt against Victorian refinement, their role was complex and ambiguous. Dissatisfaction with the cult of domesticity did not necessarily lead to open rebellion. Many women, although chafing against the constraints of deference and the assumption that they should limit their activities to the home, remained committed to playing a nurturing role within the family. In fact, early advocates of a "widened sphere" for women often fused the traditional Victorian ideal of womanhood with a firm commitment to political action.

The career of temperance leader **Frances Willard** illustrates how the cult of domesticity, with its celebration of special female virtues, could evolve into a broader view of women's social and political responsibilities. Like many of her contemporaries, Willard believed that women were compassionate and nurturing by nature. She was also convinced that drinking encouraged thriftlessness and profoundly threatened family life. Resigning as dean of women and professor of English at Northwestern University in 1874, Willard devoted her energies full-time to the temperance cause. Five years later she was elected president of the newly formed Woman's Christian Temperance Union (WCTU).

Willard took the traditional belief that women had unique moral virtues and transformed it into a rationale for political action. The domestication of politics, she asserted, would protect the family and improve public morality. Choosing as the union's badge a bow of white ribbon, symbolizing the purity of the home, she launched a crusade in 1880 to win the franchise for women so that they could vote to outlaw liquor. Willard soon expanded WCTU activities to include welfare work, prison reform, labor arbitration, and public health. Under her leadership the WCTU, with a membership of nearly 150,000 by 1890, became the nation's first mass organization of women. Through it, women gained experience as lobbyists, organizers, and lecturers, in the process undercutting the assumption of "separate spheres."

An expanding network of women's clubs offered another means by which middle- and upper-class women could hone their skills in civic affairs, public speaking, and intellectual analysis. In the 1870s, many well-to-do women met weekly to study topics of mutual interest. These clubwomen soon became involved in social-welfare projects, public library expansion, and tenement reform. By 1892, the General Federation of Women's Clubs, an umbrella organization established that year, boasted 495 affiliates and a hundred thousand members. Middle-class black women, excluded from many white clubs, formed their own National Association of Colored Women's Clubs in 1900.

While older women eroded the Victorian constraints placed on them by social conventions by joining women's clubs, younger women challenged social conventions by joining the bicycling craze that swept urban America at the turn of the century. The fascination with bicycle riding developed as part of a new interest in health and physical fitness. Middle- and upper-class Americans explored various ways to improve their vigor. Some used health products such as cod liver oil and sarsaparilla for "weak blood." Others played basketball, invented in 1891 by a physical education instructor at Springfield College in Massachusetts to keep students in shape during the winter months. But bicycling, which could be done individually or in groups, quickly became the most popular sport for those who wished to combine exercise with recreation.

Bicycles of various designs had been manufactured since the 1870s, but bicycling did not become a national craze until the invention in the 1880s of the so-called safety bicycle, with smaller wheels, ball-bearing axles, and air-filled tires. By the 1890s, over a million Americans owned bicycles.

Bicycling especially appealed to young women who had chafed under the restrictive Victorian attitudes about female exercise, which held that proper young ladies must never sweat and that the female body must be fully covered at all times. Pedaling along in a shirtwaist or "split" skirt, a woman bicyclist made an implicit feminist statement suggesting that she had broken with genteel conventions and wanted to explore new activities beyond the traditional sphere.

Changing attitudes about femininity and women's proper role also found expression in gradually shifting ideas about marriage. Charlotte Perkins Gilman, a suffrage advocate and speaker for women's rights, asserted that women would make an effective contribution to society only when they won economic independence from men through work outside the home (see Chapter 21). One very tangible indicator of women's changing relationship to men was the substantial rise in the divorce rate between 1880 and 1900. In 1880, one in every twenty-one marriages ended in divorce. By 1900, the rate had climbed to one in twelve. Women who brought suit for divorce increasingly cited their husbands' failure to act responsibly and to respect their autonomy. Accepting such arguments, courts frequently awarded the wife alimony, a monetary settlement payable by the ex-husband to support her and their children.

Women writers generally welcomed the new female commitment to independence and self-sufficiency. In the short stories of Mary Wilkins Freeman, for example, women's expanding role is implicitly compared to the frontier ideal of freedom. Feminist **Kate Chopin** pushed the debate to the extreme by having Edna Pontellier, the married heroine of her controversial 1899 novel *The Awakening*, violate social conventions. First Edna falls in love with another man; then she takes her own life when his ideas about women prove as narrow and traditional as those of her husband.

Despite the efforts of these and other champions of the new woman, attitudes changed slowly. The enlarged conception of women's role in society exerted its greatest influence on college-educated, middle-class women who had leisure time and could reasonably hope for success in journalism, social work, or nursing. For female immigrant factory workers and for shop girls who worked sixty hours a week to try to make ends meet, however, the ideal remained a more distant goal. Although many women were seeking more independence and control over their lives, most still viewed the home as their primary responsibility.

Public Education as an Arena of Class Conflict   While the debate over women's proper role remained largely confined to the middle class, a very different controversy, over the scope and function of public education, engaged Americans of all socioeconomic levels. This debate starkly highlighted the class and cultural divisions in late-nineteenth-century society. From the 1870s on, viewing the public schools as an instrument for indoctrinating and controlling the lower ranks of society, middle-class educators and civic leaders campaigned to expand public schooling and bring it under centralized control. Not surprisingly, the reformers' efforts aroused considerable opposition from ethnic and religious groups whose outlook and interests differed sharply from theirs.

Thanks to the crusade for universal public education started by Horace Mann and other antebellum educational reformers, most states had public school systems by the Civil War, and more than half the nation's children were receiving some formal education. But most attended school for only three or four years, and few went on to high school.

Concerned that many Americans lacked sufficient knowledge to participate wisely in public affairs or function effectively in the labor force, reformers such as William Torrey Harris worked to increase the number of years that children spent in school. First as superintendent of the St. Louis public schools in the 1870s and later as the federal commissioner of education, Harris urged teachers to instill in their students a sense of order, decorum, self-discipline, and civic loyalty. Believing that modern industrial society depended on citizens' conforming to the timetables of the factory and the train, he envisioned the schools as models of punctuality and precise scheduling: "The pupil must have his lessons ready at the appointed time, must rise at the tap of the bell, move to the line, return; in short, go through all the evolutions with equal precision."

To achieve these goals and to wrest control of the schools from neighborhood leaders and ward politicians, reform-minded educators like Harris elaborated a philosophy of public education stressing punctuality, centralized administration, compulsory-attendance laws, and a tenure system to insulate teachers from political favoritism and parental pressure. By 1900, thirty-one states required school attendance of all children from eight to fourteen years of age.

The steamroller methods used by Harris and likeminded administrators to systematize public education quickly prompted protests. New York pediatrician Joseph Mayer Rice, who toured thirty-six cities and interviewed twelve hundred teachers in 1892, scornfully criticized an educational establishment that stressed singsong memorization and prisonlike discipline.

Rice's biting attack on public education overlooked the real advances in reading and mathematics made in the previous two decades. Nationally, despite the influx of immigrants, the illiteracy rate in English for individuals ten years and older dropped from 17 percent in 1880 to 13 percent in 1890, largely because of the expansion of urban educational facilities. American high schools were also coeducational, and girls made up the majority of the students by 1900. But Rice was on target in assailing many teachers' rigid emphasis on silence, docility, and unquestioning obedience to the rules. When a Chicago school inspector found a thirteen-year-old boy huddled in the basement of a stockyard building and ordered him back to school, the weeping boy blurted out, "[T]hey hits ye if yer don't learn, and they hits ye if ye whisper, and they hits ye if ye have string in yer pocket, and they hits ye if yer seat squeaks, and they hits ye if ye don't stan' up in time, and they hits ye if yer late, and they hits ye if ye ferget the page."

By the 1880s, several different groups found themselves in opposition to centralized urban public school bureaucracies. Although many working-class families valued education, those who depended on their children's meager wages for survival resisted the attempt to force their sons and daughters to attend school past the elementary grades. Although some immigrant families made great sacrifices to enable their children to get an education, many withdrew their offspring from school as soon as they had learned the rudiments of reading and writing, and sent them to work.

Furthermore, Catholic immigrants objected to the overwhelmingly Protestant orientation of the public schools. Distressed by the use of the King James translation of the Bible and by the schools' failure to observe saints' days, Catholics set up separate parochial school systems. In response, Republican politicians, resentful of Catholic immigrants' overwhelming preference for the Democratic Party, tried unsuccessfully to pass a constitutional amendment cutting off all public aid to church-related schools in 1875. Catholics in turn denounced federal aid to public schools as intended "to suppress Catholic education, gradually extinguish Catholicity in this country, and to form one homogeneous American people after the New England Evangelical type."

At the other end of the social scale, upper-class parents who did not wish to send their children to immigrant-thronged public schools enrolled their daughters in female seminaries such as Chatham Hall in Chatham, Virginia, and their sons in private academies and boarding schools like St. Paul's in Concord, New Hampshire. The proliferation of private and parochial schools, together with the controversies over compulsory education, school funding, and classroom decorum, reveals the extent to which public education had become mired in ethnic and class differences. Unlike Germany and Japan, which created national education systems in the late nineteenth century, the United States, reflecting its social heterogeneity, maintained a system of locally run public and private institutions that allowed each segment of society to retain some influence over the schools attended by its own children. Amid the disputes, school enrollments dramatically expanded. In 1870, fewer than seventy-two thousand students were attending the nation's 1,026 high schools. By 1900, the number of high schools had jumped to more than five thousand and the number of students to more than half a million.

CHRONOLOGY
1860–1900

1865	Vassar College founded.
1869	First intercollegiate football game.
1872	Anthony Comstock founds New York Society for the Suppression of Vice.
1873	John Wanamaker opens his Philadelphia department store.
1875	Smith and Wellesley colleges founded.
1876	National League of baseball organized.
1880	William Booth's followers establish an American branch of the Salvation Army.
1881	Josephine Shaw Lowell founds New York Charity Organization Society (COS).

1884 Mark Twain, *Huckleberry Finn.*

1885 Stanford University founded.

1889 Jane Addams and Ellen Gates Starr open Hull House.

1891 University of Chicago founded.
Basketball invented at Springfield College, Massachusetts.

1892 Ellis Island Immigration Center opened.
General Federation of Women's Clubs organized.

1895 Coney Island amusement parks open in Brooklyn, New York.

1899 Scott Joplin, "Maple Leaf Rag."
Kate Chopin, *The Awakening.*
Thorstein Veblen, *The Theory of the Leisure Class.*

1900 Theodore Dreiser, *Sister Carrie.*
National Association of Colored Women's Clubs organized.

1910 Angel Island Immigration Center opens in San Francisco.

Conclusion

By the 1890s, class conflict was evident in practically every area of city life, from mealtime manners to popular entertainment and recreation. As new immigrants flooded the tenements and spilled out onto neighborhood streets, it became impossible for native-born Americans to ignore their strange religious and social customs. Ethnic differences were compounded by class differences. Often poor and from peasant or working-class backgrounds, the immigrants from southern and eastern Europe took unskilled jobs and worked for subsistence-level wages. The slums and tenements in which they lived had high rates of disease. Middle- and upper-class Americans often responded by moving to fashionable avenues or suburbs and by stigmatizing them as nonwhite and racially inferior.

To distinguish themselves from these newcomers, native-born Americans stressed their commitment to Victorian morality, with its emphasis on manners, decorum, and self-control. Although never fully accepted even among the well-to-do, these Victorian ideals were meant to apply new standards for society. Lavish department stores and artistically designed houses reflected the middle- and upper-class faith that the consumption of material goods indicated good taste.

To raise standards, the prosperous classes expanded the number of high schools and created a new research university system for training educators, lawyers, doctors, and other professionals. As defenders of the new Victorian morality, educated middle- and upper-class women were expected to become the protectors of the home. Some members of the upper classes also tried to address the problems of poverty and congestion in the inner city. While Jacob Riis, Jane Addams, and other reformers worked to improve overcrowded housing and dangerous working conditions, Anthony Comstock and less sympathetic reformers attacked immigrant values and cultures in an effort to uplift and Americanize them.

Nowhere was the conflict between the social classes more evident than in the controversy over leisure entertainment. Caught up in the material benefits of a prospering industrial society, middle- and upper-class Americans battled against what they deemed "indecent" lower-class behavior in all its forms, from dancing to ragtime, gambling, and prizefighting to playing baseball on Sunday and visiting bawdy boardwalk sideshows. Even public parks became arenas of class conflict. Whereas the elite favored large, impeccably groomed urban parks that would serve as models of orderliness and propriety, working people fought for parks where they could picnic, play ball, drink beer, and escape the stifling heat of tenement apartments.

Although the well-to-do classes often appeared to have the upper hand in these clashes, significant disagreements about moral standards surfaced early within their own ranks. Critics, among them Charlotte Perkins Gilman, faulted middle-class society for its obsession with polite manners, empty social rituals, and restrictions on the occupations open to women.

By 1900, the contest for power between the elite classes and the largely immigrant working class was heading toward a partial resolution. As Victorian morality eroded, undermined by dissension from within and opposition from without, new standards emerged that blended elements of earlier positions. For example, new rules regulated behavior in the boxing ring and on the baseball field. Still, it was immigrant heroes who captured the popular imagination. The elite vision of sport as a vehicle for instilling self-discipline and self-control was transformed into a new commitment to sports as spectacle and entertainment. Sports had become big business and an important part of the new consumerism.

Similar patterns of compromise and change took place in other arenas. Vaudeville houses, attacked by the affluent for their risqué performances, evolved into the nation's first movie theaters. Ragtime music, with its syncopated rhythms, gave rise to jazz. In short, the dashing, disreputable, and raucous working-class culture of the late-nineteenth-century city can be seen as the seedbed of twentieth-century mass culture. And everywhere popular culture became increasingly dominated by commercial interests that capitalized on the disposable income created by the nation's explosive urban growth.

20

POLITICS AND EXPANSION IN AN INDUSTRIALIZING AGE, 1877–1900

CHAPTER OUTLINE

• Party Politics in an Era of Upheaval, 1877–1884 • Politics of Privilege, Politics of Exclusion, 1884–1892 • The 1890s: Politics in a Depression Decade • Expansionist Stirrings and War with Spain, 1878–1901

PARTY POLITICS IN AN ERA OF UPHEAVAL, 1877–1884

Between 1877 and 1894, four presidents squeezed into office by the narrowest of margins; control of the House of Representatives changed hands five times; and seven new western states were admitted into the Union. Competition between political parties was intense. No one party could muster a working majority.

To meet these challenges, party leaders sought desperately to cement the loyalty of their followers. While the Democrats rebuilt their strength in the South, Republicans struggled to maintain the loyalties of the working class and to increase their support from business. At the municipal level, political machines worked to attract loyalty among immigrants and other newcomers in the rapidly expanding cities.

Contested Political Visions

In the late nineteenth century, more than 80 percent of eligible white males often voted, and in hard-fought elections, the percentage rose to 95 percent. Voter participation a century later would equal scarcely half that level.

Higher voter turnout resulted in part from the attempts of the major parties to navigate the stormy economy created by postwar industrial and geographic expansion, the influx of millions of immigrants, and the explosive growth of cities. As voter turnout shot up, however, political parties sidestepped many of the issues created by industrialization, such as taxation of corporations, support for those injured in factory accidents, and poverty relief. Nor was the American labor movement, unlike its counterpart in Europe, able to organize itself effectively as a political force. Except for the Interstate Commerce Act of 1887 and the largely symbolic Sherman Anti-Trust Act of 1890, Washington generally ignored the social consequences of industrialization and focused instead on encouraging economic growth.

How can we explain this refusal to address economic concerns and, at the same time, account for the enormous popular support for parties? The answer lies in the political ideology of the period and the three major symbolic and economic issues that preoccupied lawmakers nationally: the tariff, the money supply, and civil-service reform.

Political parties in the late nineteenth century energized voters not only by appealing to economic self interest, as was evident in support for industrialization and pensions for Civil War veterans and their widows, but also by linking their programs to deeply held beliefs about the nature of the family and the proper role of government. Republicans justified their support for the tariff and defended their commitment to Union widows' pensions as a protection for the family home. Democrats countered, using metaphors of the seduction and rape of white women by outsiders and labeling Republican programs as classic examples of the perils of using excessive government force. High tariffs imperiled the family and threatened economic disaster. With respect to both parties, men, in particular, associated loyalty to party with a sense of masculinity.

Despite their differences over the tariff and monetary policy, neither Republicans nor Democrats believed that the national government had any right to regulate corporations or to protect the social welfare of workers. Neither party therefore courted the labor union vote. Many members of both parties embraced the doctrine of **laissez-faire**—the belief that unregulated competition represented the best path to progress. According to this view, the federal government should promote economic development but not regulate industry.

Rather than looking to Washington, people turned to local or state authorities. On the Great Plains, angry farmers demanded that their state legislatures regulate railroad rates. In the cities, immigrant groups, organized by political bosses, battled for control of municipal governments and local contracts. In response, native-born reformers attempted to oust the organizations in power and clean up corruption. Meanwhile, city and state governments vied with each other for control. Cities often could not change their system of government, alter their tax structure, or regulate municipal utilities without state approval. When Chicago wanted to issue permits to street popcorn vendors, for example, the Illinois legislature had to pass a special act.

Both parties, in the North and the South, practiced fraud by rigging elections, throwing out opposition votes, and paying for "floaters" who moved from precinct to precinct to vote. Each also expressed moral outrage at the other's illegal behavior.

By linking economic policy to family values, both parties reinforced the appeal of their platforms and encouraged the participation of women in the political process. Although most women could not vote, they played an active role in politics. Frances Willard and her followers in the Woman's Christian Temperance Union (WCTU), for example, helped create a Prohibition and Home Protection Party in the 1880s. A decade later, western women Populists won full suffrage in Colorado, Idaho, and Utah.

**Patterns of
Party Strength**   In the 1870s and 1880s, each party had its own ideological appeal and centers of regional strength. The Democrats ruled the South, southern sections of border states like Ohio, and northern cities with large immigrant populations. They campaigned for minimal government expenditures, opposed tariff increases, and generally attacked what they considered to be "governmental interference in the economy." In addition, Democrats staunchly defended their immigrant followers. On the state and local levels, they fiercely opposed prohibition, supported parochial schools, and rejected requirements that immigrant children attend only those schools that taught in English.

The Republicans reigned in rural and small town New England, Pennsylvania, and the upper Midwest and drew support from the **Grand Army of the Republic (GAR),** a social and political lobbying organization of northern Civil War veterans. They often "waved the bloody shirt," reminding voters that their party had led the nation during the Civil War. "The Democratic Party," wrote one Republican, "may be described as a common sewer and loathsome receptacle, into which is emptied every element of treason North and South." To emphasize their patriotism, the Republicans ran a series of former Union army generals for president and voted generous veterans' benefits.

State and local party leaders managed campaigns. They chose the candidates, raised money, organized rallies, and—if their candidate won—distributed public jobs to party workers. Bosses like the former saloonkeepers "Big Jim" Pendergast of Kansas City, a Democrat, and George B. Cox of Cincinnati, a Republican, turned out the vote by taking care of constituents, handing out municipal jobs, and financing campaigns with "contributions" extracted from city employees.

Although issues of governmental authority dominated on the federal level, family tradition, ethnic ties, religious affiliation, and local issues often determined an individual's vote. Outside the South, ethnicity and religion were the most reliable predictors of party affiliation. Catholics, especially Irish Catholics, and Americans of German ancestry tended to vote Democratic. Old-stock Protestant northerners, in contrast, voted Republican. Among immigrant groups, most British-born Protestants and 80 percent of Swedish and Norwegian Lutherans voted Republican, as did African-Americans, North and South. Although intolerant of racial differences, the Democrats were generally more accepting of religious diversity than were the Republicans.

Political battles often centered on cultural differences, most notably, prohibition. Irish whiskey drinkers, German beer drinkers, and Italian wine drinkers were equally outraged by antiliquor legislation. State and local prohibition proposals always aroused passionate voter interest.

**Political Bosses
and Machine
Politics**   The swelling numbers of urban dwellers gave rise to a new kind of politician, the "boss," who listened to his urban constituents and lobbied on their behalf. The boss presided over the city's "machine"—an unofficial political organization designed to keep a particular party or faction in office. Whether officially serving as mayor or not, the boss, assisted by local ward or precinct captains, wielded enormous influence in city government. Often a former saloonkeeper or labor leader, the boss knew his constituents well.

For better or worse, the **political machine** was America's unique contribution to municipal government in an era of pell-mell urban growth. Typified by Tammany Hall, the Democratic organization that dominated New York City politics from the 1830s to the 1930s, machines emerged in Baltimore, Philadelphia, Atlanta, San Francisco, and a host of other cities after the Civil War.

By the turn of the century, many cities had experienced machine rule. Working through the local ward captains to turn out voters, the machine rode herd on the tangle of municipal bureaucracies, controlling who was hired for the police and fire departments. It rewarded its friends and punished its enemies through its control of taxes, licenses, and inspections. The machine gave tax breaks to favored contractors in return for large payoffs and slipped them insider information about upcoming street and sewer projects.

At the neighborhood level, the ward boss often acted as a welfare agent, helping the needy and protecting the troubled. To spend three dollars to pay a fine for a juvenile offense meant a lot to the poor, but it was small change to a boss who raked in millions from public-utility contracts and land deals. While the machine helped alleviate some suffering, it entangled urban social services with corrupt politics and often prevented city government from responding to the real problems of the city's neediest inhabitants.

Under New York City's boss **William "Magear" Tweed,** the Tammany Hall machine revealed the slimy depths to which extortion and contract padding could sink. Between 1869 and 1871, Tweed gave $50, 000 to the poor and $2,250,000 to schools, orphanages, and hospitals. In these same years, his machine dispensed sixty thousand patronage positions and pumped up the city's debt by $70 million through graft.

By the turn of the century, the bosses were facing well organized assaults on their power, led by an urban elite whose members sought to restore "good government." In this atmosphere, the bosses increasingly forged alliances with civic organizations and reform leagues. The results, although never entirely satisfactory to anyone involved, paved the way for new sewage and transportation systems, expanded parklands, and improved public services—a record of considerable accomplishment, given the magnitude of the problems created by urban growth.

Regulating the Money Supply

In the 1870s, politicians confronted a tough problem: how to create a money supply adequate for a growing economy without producing inflation. Americans' almost superstitious reverence for gold and silver created problems of its own. Many believed that only gold or silver, or certificates exchangeable for these metals, were trustworthy. Reflecting this notion, all the federally issued currency in circulation in 1860 consisted of gold or silver coins or U.S. Treasury notes redeemable for gold or silver. (Currency from some sixteen hundred state banks was also in circulation, worsening a chaotic monetary situation.) During the Civil War, the federal government issued "greenbacks," paper money not backed by gold or silver.

Bankers and creditors also believed that economic stability required a strictly limited currency supply. Debtors, in contrast, favored expanding the money supply to make it easier for them to pay off their debts. The monetary debate thus focused on a specific question: Should the Civil War paper "greenbacks" currently in circulation be retained or eliminated, leaving only a currency backed by gold? The hard times associated with the Panic of 1873 sharpened this dispute.

The Greenback party (founded 1877) advocated an expanded money supply, and other measures to benefit workers and farmers. In the 1878 midterm elections, with the support of labor organizations angered by the government's hostility in the labor unrest of 1877, Greenback candidates won fourteen seats in Congress.

As prosperity returned and the Greenback party faded, the debate became focused on the even longer lasting controversy over the coinage of silver. In 1873, Congress instructed the U.S. mint to cease making silver coins. Silver had been "demonetized." But new discoveries in Nevada (see Chapter 17) vastly increased the silver supply, and debtor groups now demanded that the government resume the coinage of silver.

Enthusiastically backed by the silver-mine owners, silver forces won a partial victory in 1878, when Congress required the treasury to buy and mint up to $4 million worth of silver each month. But the treasury, dominated by monetary conservatives, sabotaged the law's intent by refusing to circulate the silver dollars that it minted.

Frustrated silver advocates tried a new approach in the **Sherman Silver Purchase Act** of 1890. This measure instructed the treasury to buy 4.5 million ounces of silver monthly and issue treasury notes, redeemable in gold or silver, equivalent to the cost of these purchases. The monetary supply slightly increased but the government paid far less for its monthly purchases and therefore issued fewer treasury notes. The controversy over silver dragged on.

Civil-Service Reform

For decades, successful candidates in national, state, and local elections had rewarded supporters with jobs ranging from cabinet seats to lowly municipal posts. Defenders called this system rotation in office and claimed that it was a democratic means of filling government positions. Critics called it the spoils system after the old expression, "To the victor belong the spoils."

For years, a small but influential group of upper-class reformers, including Missouri senator Carl Schurz and editor E. L. Godkin of the *Nation*, had campaigned for a professional civil service based on merit. Well-educated and wealthy, these reformers favored a civil service staffed by "gentlemen." The reformers had a point. A professional civil service was needed as government grew more complex.

Elected through the compromise that ended Reconstruction (see Chapter 16), Republican president Rutherford B. Hayes cautiously embraced the civil-service cause. In 1877, he launched an investigation of the corruption-riddled New York City customs office and fired two high officials. One, Chester A. Arthur, had played a key role in passing out jobs.

When Congressman James A. Garfield won the 1880 Republican presidential nomination, the delegates, to appease the opposing New York faction, chose Chester A. Arthur, the loyalist Hayes had recently fired, as Garfield's running mate. Since Garfield enjoyed excellent health, the choice of the totally unqualified Arthur seemed safe.

The Democrats nominated a career army officer from Pennsylvania, Winfield Scott Hancock, and the Greenbackers gave the nod to Congressman James B. Weaver of Iowa. Garfield's managers stressed his Civil War record and his log-cabin birth. By a razor-thin margin, Garfield edged out Hancock; Weaver trailed far behind.

"Where Is the Difference?" 1894 *By equating criminal payoffs to the police with corporate contributions to senators, this cartoon in* Puck *magazine suggests that corruption pervades society and needs to be stopped.*

Garfield's assassination in 1881 by the crazed office-seeker Charles Guiteau brought to the White House Vice President Arthur, the very symbol of patronage corruption, and gave a powerful emotional thrust to the reform cause. Civil-service reformers portrayed the fallen president as a spoils-system martyr. In 1883, Congress enacted a civil-service law introduced by Senator George Pendleton of Ohio (Garfield's home state) and drafted by the Civil Service Reform League that had been created two years earlier. The **Pendleton Civil Service Act** set up a commission to prepare competitive examinations and establish standards of merit for a variety of federal jobs; it also forbade political candidates to solicit contributions from government workers.

Although the Pendleton Act initially covered only about 12 percent of federal employees, subsequent presidents gradually expanded the number of positions. By the 1890s, the act had opened up new positions for women, who now held nearly a third of the jobs as federal clerks in government agencies. The creation of a professional civil service thus helped bring the federal government in step with the modernizing trends transforming society.

As for Chester A. Arthur, his performance surprised those who had expected him to be an utter disaster. Arthur supported civil-service reform and proved quite independent. Fed up with the feuding Republicans, in 1882 the voters gave the Democrats a strong majority in the House of Representatives. In 1884, for the first time since 1856, they would put a Democrat in the White House: Grover Cleveland.

POLITICS OF PRIVILEGE, POLITICS OF EXCLUSION, 1884–1892

The stalemate between the two major parties in their battle to establish the standards for economic growth continued under President Cleveland, a Democrat, and President Harrison, a Republican. Both Presidents challenged powerful interests and faced stiff opposition. Cleveland alienated strong lobbies by calling for cuts in the tariff and in veterans' pensions. In 1888, business and veterans' groups rallied to defeat Cleveland and elect Benjamin Harrison of Indiana, a former Civil War general, in one of the most corrupt campaigns in American history. Harrison alienated voters by passing a high tariff and an expanded pension law that increased the number of pensioners by 43 percent.

Responding to major party fraud and inattention to the needs of rural Americans, farmers mounted protests and began to organize. While the Grange and Farmers' Alliance movements condemned the monopolistic practices of grain and cotton buyers in the post-Reconstruction South, the white majority consolidated their political power by denying the region's black citizens their most basic rights.

A Democrat in the White House: Grover Cleveland, 1885–1889   At a tumultuous Chicago convention in 1884, the Republicans nominated their best-known leader, James G. Blaine. A gifted orator, Blaine spoke for the younger, more dynamic wing of the Republican Party eager to promote economic development and reinvigorate foreign policy.

But Blaine had been stained by the revelation that he, as Speaker of the House, had offered political favors to a railroad company in exchange for stock. For reformers, Blaine epitomized the hated patronage system. To E. L. Godkin, he "wallowed in spoils like a rhinoceros in an African pool."

Sensing Blaine's vulnerability, the Democrats chose a sharply contrasting nominee, Grover Cleveland of New York. In a meteoric rise from reform mayor of Buffalo to governor, Cleveland had fought the bosses and spoils men. The shrewdness of the Democrats' choice became apparent when Godkin, Carl Schurz, and other Republican reformers bolted to Cleveland. They were promptly nicknamed **Mugwumps,** an Algonquian term for a renegade chief.

Unfortunately, Cleveland as a youth had fathered an illegitimate child. Although he admitted the indiscretion, Republicans still jeered at rallies: "Ma, Ma, where's my pa?" Cleveland also faced opposition from Tammany Hall, the New York City Democratic machine that he had fought as governor. If Tammany's immigrant voters stayed home on election day, Cleveland could lose his own state. But in October a New York City clergyman denounced the Democrats as the party of "Rum, Romanism, and Rebellion." Blaine failed to immediately repudiate the remark. The Cleveland campaign managers widely publicized this triple insult to Catholics, to patriotic Democrats, and to drinkers. This blunder and the Mugwumps' defection allowed Cleveland to carry New York State by twelve hundred votes, and with it the election.

Once in office, Cleveland embraced the belief that government must not meddle in the economy and opposed any public regulation of corporations. He also rejected providing any governmental help for those in need. Vetoing a bill that would have given seeds to drought stricken farmers in Texas, he warned that people should not expect the government to solve their problems.

One public matter did arouse Cleveland's energies: the tariff. Since it brought in revenue in the era before a federal income tax, the tariff functioned as a protection for special interests and a source of government income. But which imported goods should be subject to duties, and how much? Opinions differed radically. Producers of such commodities as coal, hides, timber, and wool demanded tariff protection against foreign competition as did many manufacturers. Other businesses, however, while seeking protection for their finished products, wanted low tariffs on the raw materials they required. Massachusetts shoe manufacturers, for example, urged high duties on imported shoes but low duties on imported hides. Most farmers, by contrast, hated all tariffs for making it hard to sell American farm products abroad.

Cleveland's call for lower tariffs arose from his concern that high tariffs created huge federal budget surpluses, which tempted legislators to distribute the money in the form of veterans' pensions or expensive public-works programs in their home districts, commonly called pork-barrel projects. With his horror of paternalistic government, Cleveland viewed the budget surplus as a corrupting influence. Although the Democratic campaign of 1888 gave little attention to the issue, Cleveland's talk of lowering the tariff angered many corporate leaders.

Cleveland stirred up another hornet's nest by opposing the routine payment of veterans' disability pensions. No one opposed pensions for the deserving, but fraudulent claims had proliferated. Unlike his predecessors, Cleveland investigated these claims and rejected many of them. He also vetoed a bill that would have pensioned all disabled veterans whether or not their injuries occurred in military service. The pension list should be an honor roll, he stressed, not a refuge for fraud.

Big Business Strikes Back; Benjamin Harrison, 1889–1893

By 1888, some influential interest groups had concluded that Cleveland must go. The Republicans turned to Benjamin Harrison of Indiana. A corporation lawyer and former senator, Harrison was so aloof that some ridiculed him as the human iceberg. To avoid alienating voters, his campaign managers brought delegations to Indianapolis and hammered at the tariff issue. Harrison warned that only a high tariff would ensure business prosperity, decent wages for workers, and a healthy home market for farmers.

The Republicans amassed a $4 million campaign fund from worried business leaders to purchase posters, buttons, and votes. Despite voter fraud, Cleveland received almost a hundred thousand more votes than Harrison. But Harrison carried the key states of Indiana and New York and won the Electoral College vote. The Republicans held the Senate and regained the House. Once in office, Harrison swiftly rewarded his supporters. He appointed as commissioner of pensions a GAR official who, on taking office, declared "God help the surplus!" The pension rolls soon ballooned from 676,000 to nearly a million. This massive pension system (which was coupled with medical care in a network of veterans' hospitals) became America's first large-scale public welfare program. In 1890, the triumphant Republicans also enacted the McKinley Tariff, which pushed rates to an all-time high.

Rarely has the federal government been so subservient to entrenched economic interests and so out of touch with the plight of the disadvantaged as during the

1880s. But inaction bred discontent. In the election of 1890, the Democrats gained sixty-six congressional seats and won control of the House of Representatives. Farmers, too, turned to politics and swung into action.

Agrarian Protest and the Rise of the People's Party Great Plains farming had long been a risky venture. Between 1873 and 1877, terrible grasshopper infestations had consumed nearly half the Midwestern wheat crop. As production rose, prices fell. Wheat tumbled from $2.95 a bushel in 1866 to $1.06 in 1880 (see Figure 20.1). Farmers who had borrowed heavily to finance homesteads went bankrupt or barely survived. One struggling Minnesota farmer wrote the governor in 1874, "[W]e can see nothing but starvation in the future if relief does not come."

Midwestern farmers in 1867, under the leadership of Oliver H. Kelley, a Department of Agriculture clerk, formed the **Grange,** or "Patrons of Husbandry." In the next decade, membership soared to more than 1.5 million. Offering information, emotional support, and fellowship, the Grange urged farmers to "buy less and produce more, in order to make our farms more self-sustaining." They negotiated special discounts with farm-machinery dealers and set up "cash-only" cooperative stores and grain-storage elevators to cut out the "middlemen"—the bankers, grain brokers, and merchants who made money at the farmers' expense.

Grangers focused their wrath on railroads, which routinely gave discounts to large shippers, bribed state legislators, and charged higher rates for short runs than for long hauls. Stung by these practices, Grangers in Illinois, Wisconsin, Minnesota,

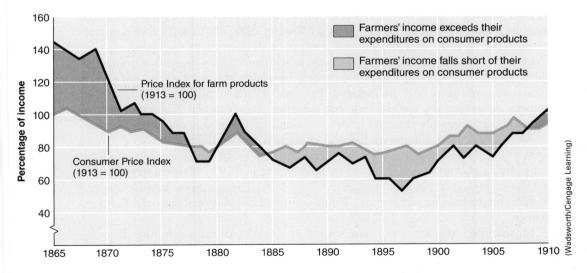

FIGURE 20.1 Consumer Prices and Farm-Product Prices, 1865–1913

From 1865 to 1895, the prices that farmers received for their crops gradually declined. Even when they increased after 1895, farmers had difficulty making ends meet. As cycles of drought and debt battered Great Plains wheat growers, a Kansas farmer wrote, "At the age of 52, after a long life of toil, economy, and self-denial, I find myself and family virtually paupers."

and Iowa lobbied state legislatures in 1874 to pass laws fixing maximum rates for freight shipments.

The railroads appealed these "Granger laws" to the Supreme Court, but in *Munn v. Illinois* (1877) the Court rejected the railroads' appeal and upheld an Illinois law setting maximum grain storage rates. The regulation of grain elevators, declared the Court's majority, was legitimate under the federal Constitution's acknowledgment of the right of states to exercise police powers. When the Court in *Wabash v. Illinois* (1886) modified this position by prohibiting states from regulating interstate railroad rates, Congress passed the Interstate Commerce Act (1887), reaffirming the federal government's power to oversee railroad activities and establishing a new agency, the Interstate Commerce Commission (ICC), to do just that. Although the commission failed to curb the railroads' monopolistic practices, it did establish the principle of federal regulation of interstate transportation.

Despite promising beginnings, the Grange movement soon faltered. In 1878, the railroads, which had lost their battle on the national level, lobbied state legislatures and won repeal of most of the state-regulation laws. The cash-only cooperative stores closed because most farmers had little cash. The Grange ideal of financial independence from banks and merchants proved unrealistic because conditions on the Plains made it impossible to farm without borrowing money. When the prices of corn, wheat, and cotton briefly revived after 1878, many farmers deserted the movement. The Grange lived on as a social and educational institution, but it had lost its appeal because it was unable to improve its members' financial position.

The problems that drove farmers to form the Grange prompted Southern and Midwestern farmers to form the alliance movement. The **Farmers' Alliance** began in Texas in the 1870s as small planters, trapped by the crop lien system, mortgaged future harvests to cover current expenses. Mired in debt, about a third of southern farmers gave up their land and became tenants or sharecroppers by 1900.

In 1887, Texan Charles W. Macune, a self-trained lawyer and a physician, assumed leadership of the Alliance movement. By 1889, Macune had merged several regional organizations into the National Farmers' Alliance and Industrial Union, or Southern Alliance. A parallel black organization, the National Colored Farmers' Alliance, had meanwhile emerged in Arkansas and spread to other southern states.

As they attended alliance rallies and picnics, read the alliance newspaper, and listened to alliance speakers, hard-hit farm families became increasingly aware of their political potential. An Arkansas member wrote in 1889, "Reform never begins with the leaders, it comes from the people." By 1890, the Southern Alliance claimed 3 million members. An additional 1.2 million joined the National Colored Farmers' Alliance.

Meanwhile, Alliance fever had spread to the Great Plains. In the drought-plagued years of 1880 and 1881, alliances sprang up in Kansas, Nebraska, Iowa, and Minnesota. Membership grew when insects destroyed much of the wheat crop and increases in world production drove down prices for agricultural products. Under these conditions, many settlers returned East. "In God we trusted, in Kansas we busted," some scrawled on their wagons. Western Kansas lost 50 percent of its population between 1888 and 1892. Others hung on, and the Northwestern Alliance grew rapidly. By 1890, the Kansas Alliance claimed 130,000 members, followed closely by alliances in Nebraska, the Dakotas, and Minnesota. What had begun as a desperate attempt to save their farms had now turned into a massive political campaign to change the American political and economic system.

Alliance members at first tried to create a biracial movement. Southern Alliance leaders Tom Watson of Georgia and Leonidas Polk of North Carolina urged southern farmers, black and white, to act together. For a time, this message of racial cooperation in the interest of reform offered promise. But Alliance members also shared the "separate but equal" philosophy of their "New South" counterparts that combined progressive reform with the separation of races (see Chapter 18).

Women joined the alliance leadership as well. Mary E. Lease, a Wichita lawyer, burst on the scene in 1890 as a fiery alliance orator. Other women, veterans of the Granger or prohibition cause, founded the National Women's Alliance (NWA) in 1891. Declared the NWA, "Put 1,000 women lecturers in the field and revolution is here." By no coincidence, a strong feminist strain pervades Ignatius Donnelly's *The Golden Bottle* (1892), a novel portraying the agrarian reformers' social vision (see Going to the Source).

As the movement swelled, the opposition turned nasty. When Jerry Simpson, an Alliance rancher from Kansas, mentioned the silk stockings of a conservative politician in his district and noted that he had no such finery, a hostile newspaper editor labeled him "Sockless Jerry" Simpson, the nickname he carried to his grave. When Mary Lease advised Kansas to "raise less corn and more hell," another editor sneered: "[Kansas] has started to raise hell, as Mrs. Lease advised, and [the state] seems to have an overproduction. But that doesn't matter. Kansas never did believe in diversified crops."

All this activity helped shape a new political agenda. In 1889, the Southern and Northwestern Alliances loosely merged and lined up candidates in the 1890 midterm elections. Alliance candidates focused on government action on behalf of farmers and workers, including tariff reduction, a graduated income tax, public ownership of the railroads, federal funding for irrigation research, a ban on landownership by aliens, and "the free and unlimited coinage of silver."

The 1890 elections revealed the strength of agrarian protest. Southern Democrats who endorsed alliance goals won four governorships and control of eight state legislatures. On the Great Plains, alliance-endorsed candidates controlled the Kansas and Nebraska legislatures and gained the balance of power in Minnesota and South Dakota. Three alliance-backed senators, together with some fifty congressmen (including Watson and Simpson), went to Washington as angry winds from the hinterlands buffeted the political system.

Regional differences, which threatened to divide the movement, were soon overcome by shared economic grievance. Southern Alliance leaders who initially opposed endorsing a third party, fearing it would weaken the southern Democratic Party, the bastion of white supremacy, eventually adopted the third-party idea. In February 1892, alliance leaders organized the People's Party of the United States, generally called the **Populist Party.** At the party convention in Omaha, Nebraska, that August, cheering delegates nominated for president the former Civil War general and Greenback nominee James B. Weaver of Iowa. Courting the South, they chose as Weaver's running mate the Virginian James Field, who had lost a leg fighting for the Confederacy.

The Populist platform called for the direct popular election of senators and other electoral reforms. It also endorsed a **subtreasury plan** devised by alliance leader Charles Macune by which farmers could store their nonperishable commodities in government warehouses, receive low-interest loans using the crops as collateral, and then sell the stored commodities when market prices rose. Their model was the postal service, an efficient, centralized, large-scale organization that worked for the public good. Ignatius Donnelly's ringing preamble pronounced the nation on "the verge of moral, political, and material ruin" and called for a return of the government "to the hands of 'the plain people' with which class it originated."

African-Americans After Reconstruction   As the Populists organized, a group of citizens with profound grievances suffered renewed oppression. With the end of Reconstruction in 1877 and the restoration of power to white elites (see Chapter 16), southern white opinion demanded an end to the hated "Negro rule," and local Democratic Party officials pursued this objective. Suppressing the black vote became a major goal. Intimidation, terror, and vote fraud kept blacks from the polls or forced them to vote Democratic. Mississippi amended its state constitution in 1890 to exclude most black voters, and other southern states soon followed suit.

Because the Fifteenth Amendment (1870) guaranteed all male citizens' right to vote, white southerners used indirect means such as literacy tests (a test of the ability to read), poll taxes (a tax paid to vote), and property requirements (which restricted the right to vote to those who owned property) to disfranchise blacks. To protect illiterate whites, the so-called grandfather clause exempted from these electoral requirements anyone with an ancestor who had voted in 1860. Although black disfranchisement proceeded erratically over the South, by the early twentieth century it was essentially complete.

Disfranchisement was only one part of the system of white supremacy. In a parallel development, state after state passed laws imposing strict racial segregation in many realms of life (to be discussed in Chapter 21). African-American caterers, barbers, bricklayers, and other artisans lost their white clientele. Blacks who went to prison—sometimes for minor offenses—faced the convict-lease system, which cotton planters, railroad builders, and other employers used to "lease" prison gangs and force them to work under slave-labor conditions.

The convict-lease system enforced the racial hierarchy and played an important economic role as industrialization and agricultural change came to the South. The system brought income to hard-pressed state governments and provided factories, railroads, and large-scale farms with predictable, controllable, cheap labor. The system also intimidated free laborers and discouraged foreign immigrants from going South. Thousands died under this brutal convict-labor system, which continued into the early decades of the twentieth century.

Lynching became the ultimate enforcer of southern white supremacy. Through the 1880s and 1890s, about a hundred blacks were lynched annually in the United States, mainly in the South. The stated reasons, often the rape of a white woman, frequently arose from rumor and unsubstantiated accusations. The charge of "attempted rape," as the black journalist Ida B. Wells pointed out to a national audience, could cover a wide range of behaviors unacceptable to whites, such as questioning authority or talking back.

The lynch mob demonstrated whites' absolute power. In the South, more than 80 percent of the lynchings involved black victims. Lynchings most commonly occurred in the Cotton Belt, and they tended to rise at times of economic distress. By no coincidence, lynching peaked in 1892 as many poor blacks embraced the Farmers' Alliance movement and rallied to the Populist Party banner. Fifteen black Populists were killed in Georgia alone, it has been estimated, during that year's bitter campaign.

The relationship between southern agrarian protest and white racism was complex. Some Populists, like Georgia's Tom Watson, sought to build an interracial movement. Watson denounced lynching and the convict-lease system. When a black Populist leader pursued by a lynch mob took refuge in his house during the 1892 campaign, Watson summoned two thousand armed white Populists to defend him. But most white Populists clung to racism. The white ruling elite, eager to drive a wedge in the protest movement, inflamed lower-class white racism.

On balance, the rise of southern agrarian protest deepened racial hatred and ultimately worsened blacks' situation. Meanwhile, the federal government stood aside. A generation of northern politicians paid lip service to egalitarian principles but failed to apply them to African-Americans.

The Supreme Court similarly abandoned African-Americans. The Court ripped gaping holes in the Fourteenth Amendment (1868), which granted blacks citizenship and the equal protection of the law, and in the Civil Rights Act of 1875, which outlawed racial discrimination on juries, in public places, and on railroads and streetcars. In the *Civil Rights Cases* (1883), the Court declared the Civil Rights Act of 1875 unconstitutional. The Fourteenth Amendment protected citizens only from governmental infringement of their civil rights, the justices ruled, not from acts by private citizens such as railroad conductors. In *Plessy v. Ferguson* **(1896),** the justices upheld a Louisiana law requiring segregated railroad cars. Racial segregation was constitutional, the Court held, if equal facilities were made available to each race. With the Supreme Court's blessing, the South segregated its public school system, ignoring the caveat that such separate facilities must be equal. White children studied in nicer buildings, used newer equipment, and were taught by better-paid teachers. Not until 1954 did the Court overturn the "separate but equal" doctrine. Rounding out their dismal record, in 1898 the justices upheld the poll tax and literacy tests by which southern states had disfranchised blacks.

Few northerners protested the South's white supremacist society. Until the North condemned lynching outright, declared the aged abolitionist Frederick Douglass in 1892, "it will remain equally involved with the South in this common crime." The restoration of sectional harmony, in short, came at a high price: acquiescence by the North in the utter debasement of the South's African-American citizenry. Further, the separatist principle endorsed in *Plessy* had a pervasive impact, affecting blacks nationwide, Mexicans in Texas, Asians in California, and other groups.

Blacks responded to their plight in various ways. The nation's foremost black leader from the 1890s to his death in 1915 was **Booker T. Washington.** Born in slavery in Virginia in 1856, Washington attended a freedman's school in Hampton,

GOING TO THE SOURCE

Women in Politics

In this article, written for the *Arena* magazine in 1892, Annie L. Diggs, a Populist orator and editor from Kansas, identifies twenty-five prominent women speakers and editors who played important roles nationally in the Farmers' Alliance and the Populist Party. In 1892, the Populists in Kansas elected the governor and a majority in the state senate only to be stymied by a Republican majority in the state house.

"Farm life for women is a treadmill.... The worn and weary treadmillers are anxious, troubled.... Instead of mythologic lore, they read "Seven Financial Conspiracies," "Looking Backward," "Progress and Poverty." Alas! Of this last word they know much and fear more – fear for their children's future. The [women] ... turn with all the fierceness of their primal mother-nature to protect their younglings from devouring, devastating plutocracy.

The great political victory of the people of Kansas would not have been won without the help of the women of the Alliance. Women who never dreamed of becoming public speakers grew eloquent in their zeal and fervor....

Before this question of the salvation of the imperiled homes of the nation, all other questions, whether of "prohibition" or "suffrage" pale into relative inconsequence. For where shall temperance or high thought of franchise be taught to children, by whose breath the world is saved, if sacred hearth fires shall go out? The overtopping, all-embracing moral question of the age is this for which the Alliance came. Upon such great ethical foundations is the labor movement today building itself. How could women do otherwise than be in it?

Easily first among Kansas women who rose to prominence as a platform speaker for the political party which grew out of the Alliance is Mrs. Mary E. Lease....

Virginia, and in 1881 organized a black state vocational school in Alabama that eventually became Tuskegee University. Although Washington secretly contributed to lawyers who challenged segregation, he publicly urged accommodation to a racist society. In a widely publicized address in Atlanta in 1895, he insisted that the first task of America's blacks must be to acquire useful skills such as farming and carpentry. Once blacks proved their economic value, he predicted, racism would fade; meanwhile, they must patiently accept their lot. This was a position later challenged by W. E. B. Du Bois (covered in Chapter 21). Washington lectured widely, and his autobiography, *Up from Slavery* (1901), recounted his rise from poverty thanks to honesty, hard work, and kindly patrons—themes familiar to a generation reared on Horatio Alger's self-help books.

Other blacks responded resourcefully to racism. Black churches provided emotional support, as did black fraternal lodges like the Knights of Pythias. Some African-Americans started businesses to serve their community. Two black-owned banks, in Richmond and Washington, D.C., were chartered in 1888. The North Carolina Mutual Insurance Company, organized in 1898 by John Merrick, a prosperous Durham barber, evolved into a major enterprise. Bishop Henry M. Turner

Seldom, if ever, was a woman so vilified and so misrepresented by malignant newspaper attacks. A woman of other quality would have sunk under the avalanche. She was quite competent to cope with all that was visited upon her. Indeed, the abuse did her much service. The people loved her for the enemies she made.

Already the story of the wondrous part she has played in the people's struggle for justice has reached other countries. . . .

In the to-be-written history of this great epoch, Mrs. Mary E. Lease will have a most conspicuous place.

Consider this Kansas record, oh supercilious sneerer at "strong-minded" women. Most of these women have opened their mouths and spake before many people.... All these heretical things they have done, and yet are the womanliest, gentlest of women, the best of homekeepers, the loyalist of wives, the carefulest of mothers. . . .

Thus splendidly do the *facts* about women in politics refute the frivolous *theories* of timorous or hostile objectors. The women prominent as active, responsible

factors in the political arena are those who are characterized by strong common sense, high ideals, and lofty patriotism. When such as these cast ballot throughout the nation,

> *"Then shall their voice of sovereign choice
> Swell the deep bass of duty done,*
>
> *And strike the key of time to be
> When God and man shall speak as one."*

Questions

1. *How does Diggs justify women's participation in politics?*
2. *What roles do traditional ideas about women's responsibilities play in her argument?*
3. *What ideals shaped Populist religiosity?*

Go to www.cengagebrain.com for additional primary sources on this period.

Source: Annie L. Diggs, "The Women in the Alliance Movement," *The Arena*, July 1892, No. XXXII, pp. 160–180.

of the African Methodist Episcopal church urged blacks to return to Africa and build a great Christian nation.

Meanwhile, African-American protest never wholly died out. Frederick Douglass urged that blacks press for full equality. Blacks should meet violence with violence, insisted militant New York black leader T. Thomas Fortune. But for others, the solution was to leave the South. In 1879, several thousand moved to Kansas (see Chapter 16). Some ten thousand migrated to Chicago between 1870 and 1890. Blacks who moved north, however, soon found that public opinion sanctioned many forms of de facto discrimination.

The rise of the so-called solid South, firmly established on racist foundations, had important political implications. For one thing, it made a mockery of the two-party system in the South. For years, the only meaningful election south of the Potomac was the Democratic primary. Only in the 1960s, in the wake of sweeping social and economic changes, would a genuine two-party system emerge there. The large bloc of southern Democrats selected to Congress each year, accumulating seniority and power, exerted a great and often reactionary influence on public policy. Finally, southern Democrats wielded enormous clout in the national party.

Lynching at Clanton, Alabama, August 1891 *Reprinted in Ida B. Wells's* A Red Record, *this photograph is typical of many taken where the white audience faces the camera near the body of the victim. Such photographs were meant to intimidate any blacks who challenged white supremacy.*

(Chicago Historical Society)

No Democratic contender for national office who was unacceptable to them stood a chance.

Above all, the caste system that evolved in the post-Reconstruction South shaped the consciousness of those caught up in it, white and black alike. White novelist Lillian Smith described her girlhood in turn-of-the-century Florida and Georgia: "From the day I was born, I began to learn my lessons.... I learned it is possible to be a Christian and a white southerner simultaneously; to be a gentle-woman and an arrogant callous creature at the same moment; to pray at night and ride a Jim Crow car the next morning; ... to glow when the word democracy was used, and to practice slavery from morning to night."

THE 1890s: POLITICS IN A DEPRESSION DECADE

Discontent with the major parties, which had smoldered during the 1870s and 1880s, burst into flames in the 1890s. As banks failed and railroads went bankrupt, the nation slid into a grinding depression. The crises of the 1890s laid bare the paralysis of the federal government—dominated by a business elite—when confronted by the new social realities of factories, urban slums, immigrant workers, and desperate farmers. In response, irate farmers, laborers, and their supporters joined a new party, the Populists, to change the system. But in 1896, in the aftermath of the massive depression, the Republicans built a coalition strong enough to control Congress and the presidency for the next fifteen years.

1892: Populists Challenge the Status Quo   In July 1892, the same month that the Populists adopted their party platform, thirteen people died in a gun battle between strikers and strikebreakers at the Homestead steel plant near Pittsburgh, and President Harrison sent federal troops to Coeur d'Alene, Idaho, where a silver-mine strike had turned violent. Events seemed to justify the platform's warnings of chaos ahead.

Ignoring the escalating unrest, both major parties launched campaigns for the White House that replayed the1888 contest. The Republicans renominated Harrison. The Democrats turned again to Grover Cleveland, who in four years out of office had made clear his growing conservatism and his opposition to the Populists. But this time Cleveland won by more than 360,000 votes, a decisive margin in this era of close elections. A public reaction against labor violence and the McKinley Tariff hurt Harrison, while Cleveland's support for the gold standard won business support.

Meanwhile, a solid showing by Populist candidates sparked great hopes for the future. James B. Weaver got more than a million votes—8.5 percent of the total—and the Populists elected five senators, ten congressmen, and three governors. The new party carried Kansas and registered some appeal in the West and in Georgia, Alabama, and Texas, where the alliance movement had taken deep root. But the party's strength was spotty. It made no dent in New England, the urban East, or the traditionally Republican farm regions of the Midwest. It even failed to show broad strength in the upper Great Plains. "Beaten! Whipped! Smashed!" moaned Minnesota Populist Ignatius Donnelly in his diary.

Throughout most of the South, racism, ingrained Democratic loyalty, distaste for a ticket headed by a former Union general, and widespread voter fraud kept the Populist vote under 25 percent. This failure killed the prospects for interracial agrarian reform. After 1892, as Populism began to revive in the South and Midwest, many southern politicians seeking to appeal to poor whites—including a disillusioned Tom Watson—stayed within the Democratic fold and laced their populism with racism.

Capitalism in Crisis: The Depression of 1893–1897   Cleveland soon confronted a major crisis, an economic collapse in the railroad industry that quickly spread. The first hint of trouble flared up in February 1893 when the Philadelphia and Reading Railroad failed. This bankruptcy came at a time of weakened confidence in the gold standard, the government's pledge to redeem paper money for gold on demand.

Confidence had ebbed when, in response to the collapse of a leading London investment bank in 1890, British investors had sold millions of dollars' worth of stock in American railroads and converted their dollars to gold, draining U.S. gold reserves. Moreover, Congress's lavish veterans' benefits during the Harrison administration had reduced government resources just as tariff revenues were dropping because of the high McKinley Tariff. Finally, the 1890 Sherman Silver Purchase Act's requirement that the government pay for its monthly silver purchases with treasury certificates redeemable for either silver or gold had further drained gold reserves.

Between January 1892 and March 1893, when Cleveland took office, the gold reserve had fallen sharply to around $100 million, the minimum considered necessary to support the dollar. This decline alarmed those who viewed the gold standard as the only sure evidence of the government's financial stability.

The collapse of a railroad thus triggered the **Panic of 1893.** Fear fed on itself as alarmed investors converted their stock holdings to gold. Stock prices fell in May and June; gold reserves sank; by the end of the year, seventy-four railroads and more than fifteen thousand commercial institutions, including six hundred banks, had failed. Just as the railroad boom had spurred the industrial prosperity of the 1880s, so had the railroad crisis of the early 1890s battered the entire economy. The Panic of 1893 started a full-scale depression and set off four years of hard times.

The crisis took a heavy human toll. Industrial unemployment soared into the 20 to 25 percent range, leaving millions of factory workers with no money to feed their families and heat their homes. Recent immigrants faced disaster. Jobless men tramped the streets and rode freight trains from city to city seeking work.

The unusually harsh winters of 1893 and 1894 made matters worse. In New York City, where the crisis quickly swamped local relief agencies, a minister reported actual starvation. Rural America, already hard-hit by declining agricultural prices, faced ruin. Farm prices dropped by more than 20 percent between 1890 and 1896. Corn plummeted from fifty cents to twenty-one cents a bushel; wheat, from eighty-four cents to fifty-one cents. Cotton sold for five cents a pound in 1894.

Some desperate Americans turned to protest. In Chicago, workers at the Pullman factory reacted to successive wage cuts by walking off the job in June 1894 (see Chapter 18). In Massillon, Ohio, self-taught monetary expert Jacob Coxey proposed as a solution to unemployment a $500 million public-works program funded with paper money not backed by gold but simply designated "legal tender" (just as it is today). A man of action as well as ideas, Coxey organized a march on Washington to lobby for his scheme. Thousands joined him en route, and several hundred reached Washington in late April 1894. Police arrested Coxey and other leaders when they attempted to enter the Capitol grounds, and his "army" broke up. Although some considered Coxey eccentric, his proposal closely resembled programs that the government would adopt during the depression of the 1930s.

As unrest intensified, fear clutched middle-class Americans. A church magazine demanded that troops put "a pitiless stop" to outbreaks of unrest. To some observers, a bloody upheaval seemed imminent.

Business Leaders Respond   In the face of suffering and turmoil, Cleveland refused to intervene. Boom-and-bust economic cycles were inevitable, he insisted. The government could do nothing. Missing the larger picture, Cleveland focused on a single issue: the gold standard. In August 1893 he persuaded Congress to repeal the Sherman Silver Purchase Act, which he blamed for the run on gold.

Nevertheless, the gold drain continued. In early 1895, with the gold reserve down to $41 million, Cleveland turned to Wall Street. Bankers J. P. Morgan and August Belmont agreed to lend the government $62 million in exchange for U.S. bonds at a special discount. With this loan, the government purchased gold to replenish its reserve. Meanwhile, Morgan and Belmont resold the bonds for a substantial profit. This deal with the bankers did help restore confidence in the government's economic stability but it confirmed radicals' suspicions of an unholy alliance between Washington and Wall Street.

As the battle over the tariff made clear, corporate interests held the whip hand. Although Cleveland favored tariff reform, the Congress of 1893–1895—despite its Democratic majorities—generally yielded to high-tariff lobbyists. The Wilson-Gorman Tariff of 1894 lowered duties somewhat, but made so many concessions to protectionist interests that Cleveland disgustedly allowed it to become law without his signature.

Hinting at changes ahead, the Wilson-Gorman Tariff imposed a modest income tax of 2 percent on all income over $4,000 (about $40,000 in purchasing power today). But in *Pollock v. Farmers' Loan & Trust Co.* (1895), the Supreme Court narrowly ruled the law unconstitutional, arguing that the federal government could impose such a direct tax on personal property only if it were apportioned according to the population of each state. Whether one looked at the executive, the legislature, or the judiciary, Washington's subordination to financial interests seemed absolute.

Cleveland's policies split the Democratic Party. Farm leaders and silver Democrats condemned his opposition to the Sherman Silver Purchase Act. This split in the Democratic ranks affected the elections of 1894 and 1896 and reshaped politics as the century ended.

The depression also helped reorient social thought. Middle-class charitable workers, long convinced that individual character flaws caused poverty, now realized—as socialists proclaimed and as the poor well knew—that even sober and hardworking people could succumb to economic forces beyond their control. Laissez-faire ideology weakened too, as many depression-worn Americans adopted a broadened view of the government's role in dealing with the social consequences of industrialization. The depression, in short, not only brought suffering; it also taught lessons.

Silver Advocates Capture the Democratic Party   Republican gains in the 1894 midterm election revealed the depth of revulsion against Cleveland and the Democrats, who were blamed for the hard times. The Republicans gained control of Congress and several key states. Populist candidates won nearly 1.5 million votes, 40 percent more than their 1892 total. Most Populist gains occurred in the South.

The serious economic divisions that split Americans in the mid-1890s focused on a symbolic issue: free silver. Cleveland's rigid defense of the gold standard forced his opponents into an equally exaggerated obsession with silver, obscuring the genuine issues that divided rich and poor, creditor and debtor, and farmer and city dweller. Conservatives tirelessly upheld the gold standard while agrarian radicals, urged on and sometimes financed by western silver-mine owners, extolled silver as a universal cure-all.

Each side had a point. Gold advocates recognized that a nation's paper money must be based on more than a government's ability to run printing presses and that uncontrolled inflation could be catastrophic. The silver advocates knew from experience how tight-money policies depressed prices and devastated farmers. Unfortunately, these underlying realities were rarely expressed clearly.

At the 1896 Democratic convention in Chicago, western and southern delegates adopted a platform including a demand for the free and unlimited coinage of silver at the ratio to gold of sixteen to one, in effect repudiating the Cleveland administration. **William Jennings Bryan** of Nebraska, an ardent advocate of free silver, captured the nomination. Only thirty-six years old, the young lawyer had already served two terms in Congress championing western agrarian interests.

Joining Christian imagery with economic analysis, Bryan delivered his major convention speech in the debate over the platform. With his booming voice carrying his words to the upper gallery of the convention hall, Bryan praised farmers as the nation's bedrock. The wildly cheering delegates had identified their candidate even before he reached his rousing conclusion—"You shall not press down upon the brow of labor this crown of thorns, you shall not crucify mankind upon a cross of gold!"

The silverites' capture of the Democratic Party presented a dilemma to the Populists. They, too, advocated free silver, but only as one reform among many. To back Bryan would be to abandon the broad Populist program. Furthermore, fusion with the Democrats could destroy their influence as a third party. Yet the Populist leaders recognized that a separate Populist ticket would likely siphon votes from Bryan and ensure a Republican victory. Reluctantly, the Populists endorsed Bryan, while preserving a shred of independence (and confusing voters) by naming their own vice-presidential candidate, Tom Watson of Georgia. The Populists were learning the difficulty of organizing an independent political movement in a nation wedded to the two-party system.

The Republicans, meanwhile, had nominated former governor William McKinley, who as an Ohio congressman had given his name to the McKinley Tariff of 1890. The Republican platform embraced the high protective tariff and endorsed the gold standard.

1896: Republicans Triumphant

Bryan tried to sustain the momentum of the Chicago convention. Crisscrossing the nation by train, he delivered his free-silver campaign speech to hundreds of audiences in twenty-nine states. One skeptical editor compared him to Nebraska's notoriously shallow Platte River: six inches deep and a mile wide at the mouth.

McKinley's campaign was shrewdly managed by Mark Hanna, a Cleveland industrialist. Dignified and aloof, McKinley could not match Bryan's popular touch. Accordingly, Hanna built the campaign not around the candidate but around posters, pamphlets, and newspaper editorials. These publications warned of the dangers of free silver, caricatured Bryan as a rabid radical, and portrayed McKinley and the gold standard as twin pillars of prosperity.

Drawing on a war chest possibly as large as $7 million, Hanna spent lavishly. J. P. Morgan and John D. Rockefeller together contributed half a million dollars, far

Women Bryan Supporters *Although women could not vote in national elections in the 1890s, they actively participated in political campaigns. These women worked to turn out the vote for William Jennings Bryan.*

more than Bryan's total campaign contributions. Like Benjamin Harrison in 1888, McKinley stayed home in Canton, Ohio, emerging from time to time to read speeches to visiting delegations. Carefully orchestrated by Hanna, McKinley's deceptively bucolic "front-porch" campaign involved elaborate organization. All told, 750,000 people trekked to Canton that summer.

On election day, McKinley beat Bryan by over six hundred thousand votes (see Map 20.1). He swept the Northeast and the Midwest and even carried three farm states beyond the Mississippi—Iowa, Minnesota, and North Dakota—as well as California and Oregon. Bryan's strength was limited to the South and the sparsely settled Great Plains and mountain states. The Republicans retained control of Congress.

Why did Bryan lose despite the depression and the protest spirit abroad in the land? Certainly, Republicans' cash reserves, influence on the East Coast press, and scare tactics played a role. But Bryan's candidacy carried its own liabilities. His core constituency, while passionately loyal, was limited. Seduced by free silver and Bryan's oratory, the Democrats had upheld a platform and a candidate with little appeal for factory workers, the urban middle class, or the settled family farmers of the midwestern corn belt. Urban voters, realizing that higher farm prices, a major free-silver goal, also meant higher food prices, went heavily for McKinley. Bryan's weakness in urban America reflected cultural differences as well. To urban Catholics and Jews, this moralistic, teetotaling Nebraskan thundering like a Protestant revival preacher seemed utterly alien.

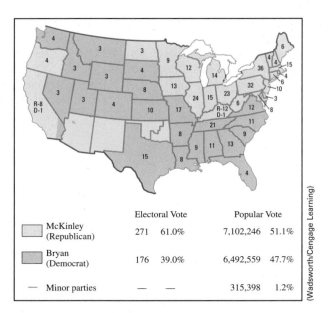

		Electoral Vote		Popular Vote	
	McKinley (Republican)	271	61.0%	7,102,246	51.1%
	Bryan (Democrat)	176	39.0%	6,492,559	47.7%
—	Minor parties	—	—	315,398	1.2%

(Wadsworth/Cengage Learning)

MAP 20.1 The Election of 1896

Republicans won the election by carrying the urban vote.

The McKinley administration quickly translated its conservative platform into law. The Dingley Tariff (1897) pushed rates to all-time high levels, and the Currency Act of 1900 officially committed the United States to the gold standard. With returning prosperity, rising farm prices after 1897, and the discovery of gold in Alaska and elsewhere, these measures aroused little protest. Bryan won renomination in 1900, but the fervor of 1896 was missing. The Republican campaign theme of prosperity easily won McKinley a second term.

The elections of 1894 and 1896 produced a Republican majority that, except for Woodrow Wilson's two presidential terms (1913–1921), would dominate national politics until the election of Franklin D. Roosevelt in 1932. Bryan's defeat and the Republicans' emergence as the party of prosperity killed the Populist Party and drove the Democrats back to their regional base in the South. But although populism collapsed, a new reform movement called progressivism was emerging. Many of the Populists' reform proposals would be enacted into law in the progressive years.

EXPANSIONIST STIRRINGS AND WAR WITH SPAIN, 1878–1901

The same corporate elite that dominated late-nineteenth century domestic politics influenced U.S. foreign policy as well, contributing to surging expansionist pressures. Not only business leaders but politicians, statesmen, and editorial writers insisted that national greatness required that America match Europe's imperial expansion. Fanned by sensationalistic newspaper coverage of a Cuban struggle for independence and by elite calls for greater American international assertiveness, war between the United States and Spain broke out in 1898.

Roots of Expansionist Sentiment

Ever since the first European settlers colonized North America's Atlantic coast, the newcomers had been an expansionist people. By the 1840s, the push westward had acquired a name: Manifest Destiny. Directed inward after 1865 toward the settlement of the trans-Mississippi West (see Chapter 17), this impulse turned outward in the 1880s as Americans followed the example set by Great Britain, France, Belgium, Italy, Germany, and Japan, which were busily collecting colonies from North Africa to the Pacific islands. National greatness, it appeared, demanded an empire.

Many business leaders believed that continued domestic prosperity required overseas markets. As American industrial capacity expanded, foreign markets offered a safety valve for potentially explosive pressures in the U.S. economy. Secretary of State James Blaine warned in 1890 that U.S. productivity was outrunning "the demands of the home market" and insisted that American business must look abroad.

Advocates of a stronger navy further fueled the expansionist mood. In *The Influence of Sea Power upon History* (1890), **Alfred Thayer Mahan** equated sea power with national greatness and urged a U.S. naval buildup. Since a strong navy required bases abroad, Mahan and other naval advocates supported the movement to acquire foreign territories, especially Pacific islands with good harbors. Military strategy, in this case and others, often masked the desire for access to new markets.

Religious leaders proclaimed America's mission to spread Christianity. This expansionist argument sometimes took on a racist tinge. As Josiah Strong put it in his 1885 work *Our Country*, "God is training the Anglo-Saxon race for its mission"—a mission of Christianizing and civilizing the world's "weaker races".

A group of Republican expansionists, led by Senator Henry Cabot Lodge of Massachusetts, diplomat John Hay, and Theodore Roosevelt of New York, preached imperial greatness and military might. "I should welcome almost any war," declared Roosevelt in 1897; ". . . this country needs one." Advocates of expansionism, like Roosevelt and Lodge, built upon the Social Darwinist rhetoric of the day and argued that war, as a vehicle for natural selection, would test and refurbish American manhood, restore chivalry and honor, and create a new generation of civic-minded Americans. This gendered appeal to renew American masculinity both counterbalanced concerns about women's political activism and helped forge the disparate arguments for expansionism into a simpler, more visceral plea for international engagement that had a broad appeal.

A series of diplomatic skirmishes between 1885 and 1895 revealed the newly assertive American mood and paved the way for the war that Roosevelt desired. In the mid-1880s, quarrels between the United States and Great Britain over fishing rights in the North Atlantic and in the Bering Sea off Alaska reawakened Americans' latent anti-British feelings as well as the old dream of acquiring Canada. A poem published in the *Detroit News* (adapted from an English music-hall song) supplied the nickname that critics would apply to the promoters of expansion—jingoists:

> *We do not want to fight,*
> *But, by jingo, if we do,*
> *We'll scoop in all the fishing grounds*
> *And the whole dominion too!*

The fishing-rights dispute was resolved in 1898, but by then attention had shifted to Latin America. In 1891, as civil war raged in Chile, U.S. officials seized a Chilean vessel that was attempting to buy guns in San Diego. Soon after, a mob in Valparaiso, Chile, killed two unarmed sailors on shore leave. President Harrison practically called for war. Only when Chile apologized and paid an indemnity was the incident closed.

Another Latin American conflict arose from a boundary dispute between Venezuela and British Guiana in 1895. The disagreement worsened after gold was discovered in the contested territory. When the British rejected a U.S. arbitration offer and condescendingly insisted that America's revered Monroe Doctrine had no standing in international law, a livid Grover Cleveland asked Congress to set up a commission to settle the disputed boundary even without Britain's approval. As patriotic fervor pulsed through the nation, the British in 1897 accepted the commission's findings.

Pacific Expansion   Meanwhile, the U.S. navy focused on the Samoan Islands in the South Pacific, where it sought access to the port of Pago Pago as a refueling station. Britain and Germany had ambitions in Samoa as well, and in March 1889 the United States and Germany narrowly avoided a naval clash when a hurricane wrecked both fleets. Secretary of State Blaine's wife wrote to one of their children, "Your father is now looking up Samoa on the map." Once he found it, negotiations began, and the United States, Great Britain, and Germany established a three-way "protectorate" over the islands.

Attention had by that time shifted to the Hawaiian Islands, which had both strategic and economic significance for the United States (see Map 20.2). New England trading vessels had visited **Hawai'i** as early as the 1790s, and Yankee missionaries had come in the 1820s. By the 1860s American-owned sugar plantations worked by Chinese and Japanese laborers dotted the islands. Under an 1887 treaty (negotiated after the planters had forcibly imposed a new constitution on Hawai'i's native ruler, Kala-kaua), the United States built a naval base at Pearl Harbor, near Honolulu. American economic dominance and the influx of foreigners angered Hawaiians. In 1891, they welcomed Liliuokalani, a strong-willed woman hostile to Americans, to the Hawaiian throne.

Meanwhile, in 1890, the framers of the McKinley Tariff, pressured by domestic sugar growers, eliminated the duty-free status enjoyed by Hawaiian sugar. In January 1893, facing ruin as Hawai'i's wholesale sugar prices plunged 40 percent, the planters deposed Queen Liliuokalani, proclaimed the independent Republic of Hawai'i, and requested U.S. annexation. The U.S. State Department's representative in Hawai'i cabled Washington, "The Hawaiian pear is now fully ripe, and this is the golden hour for the United States to pluck it." But the grab for Hawai'i troubled Grover Cleveland, who sent a representative to investigate the situation. This representative's report questioned whether the Hawaiian people actually desired annexation.

Cleveland's scruples infuriated expansionists. When William McKinley succeeded Cleveland in 1897, the acquisition of Hawai'i was pushed forward by sugar companies that had similar investments in Cuba. In 1898 Congress proclaimed Hawai'i an American territory. Sixty-one years later, it joined the Union as the fiftieth state.

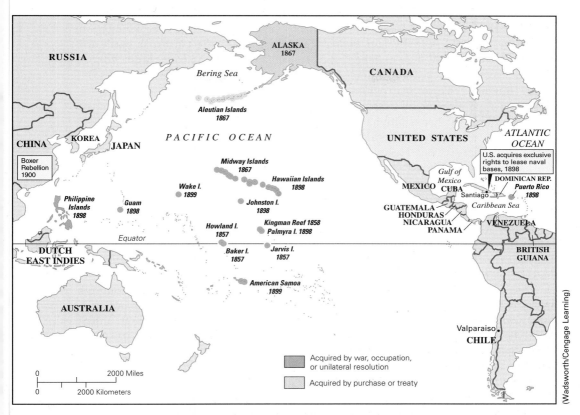

MAP 20.2 U.S. Territorial Expansion in the Late Nineteenth Century

The major U.S. territorial expansion abroad came in a short burst of activity in the late 1890s, when newspapers and some politicians urged Americans to acquire strategic ports and coaling stations abroad.

Crisis over Cuba Many of the same expansionists who had argued for the annexation of Hawai'i turned their attention in 1898 to the Spanish colony of Cuba, ninety miles off Florida, where in 1895 an anti-Spanish rebellion had broken out. This revolt, organized by the Cuban writer José Martí and other Cuban exiles in New York City, won little support from U.S. business, which had $50 million invested in Cuba and annually imported $100 million worth of sugar and other products from the island. Nor did the rebels initially secure the backing of Washington, which urged Spain to grant Cuba a degree of autonomy.

But the rebels' cause aroused popular sympathy in the United States. This support increased with revelations that the Spanish commander in Cuba, Valeriano Weyler, was herding vast numbers of Cubans into squalid camps. Malnutrition and disease turned these camps into hellholes in which perhaps two hundred thousand Cubans died.

Fueling American anger was the sensationalized reporting of two competing New York City newspapers, William Randolph Hearst's *Journal* and Joseph

Pulitzer's *World*. The *Journal*'s color comic strip, "The Yellow Kid," provided a name for Hearst's debased editorial approach: yellow journalism. The Hungarian immigrant Pulitzer normally had higher standards, but in the cutthroat battle for readers, Pulitzer's *World* matched the *Journal*'s sensationalism. Both editors exploited the Cuban crisis. Headlines turned rumor into fact, and feature stories detailed "Butcher" Weyler's atrocities. When a young Cuban woman was jailed for resisting a rape attempt by a Spanish officer, a Hearst reporter helped the woman escape and brought her triumphantly to New York.

In 1897, a new, more liberal Spanish government sought a peaceful resolution of the Cuban crisis. But Hearst and Pulitzer continued to inflame the public. On February 8, 1898, Hearst's *Journal* published a private letter by Spain's minister to the United States that described McKinley as "weak" and "a bidder for the admiration of the crowd." Irritation over this incident turned to outrage when on February 15 an explosion sank the U.S. battleship *Maine* in Havana harbor and killed 266 crewmen. Scholarly opinion about what caused the explosion is still divided, but a careful review of the evidence in 1998 concluded that a mine most likely set off the ammunition explosion that sank the ship. Newspaper headlines at the time blamed the same cause and war spirit flared high.

Despite further Spanish concessions, McKinley sent a war message to Congress on April 11, and legislators enacted a joint resolution recognizing Cuba's independence and authorizing force to expel the Spanish. The Teller Amendment, introduced by Senator Henry M. Teller of Colorado, renounced any U.S. interest in "sovereignty, jurisdiction, or control" in Cuba and pledged that America would leave the island alone once independence was assured.

The Spanish-American War, 1898   The war with Spain involved only a few days of actual combat. The first action came on May 1, 1898, when a U.S. fleet commanded by George Dewey steamed into Manila Bay in the Philippines and destroyed or captured all ten Spanish ships anchored there, at the cost of 1 American and 381 Spanish lives. In mid-August, U.S. troops occupied the capital, Manila.

In Cuba, the fighting centered on the military stronghold of Santiago on the southeastern coast. On May 19, a Spanish battle fleet of seven aging vessels sailed into the Santiago harbor, where five U.S. battleships and two cruisers blockaded them. On July 1, in the war's only significant land action, American troops seized three strongly defended Spanish garrisons overlooking Santiago on El Caney Hill, Kettleman's Hill, and San Juan Hill. Leading the volunteer "Rough Riders" unit in the capture of San Juan Hill was Theodore Roosevelt, who became a war hero. Emphasizing his toughness and sense of honor, Roosevelt would later use his war experience to reaffirm the aptitude of men like himself for political leadership.

On July 3, the Spanish attempted to break through the American blockade to the open sea. The U.S. navy fired and sank their archaic vessels. Spain lost 474 men in this gallant but doomed defense. Americans might have found a cautionary lesson in this sorry end to four hundred years of Spanish rule in the New World, but few had time for somber musings. The *Washington Post* observed, "A new consciousness seems to have come upon us—the consciousness of strength—and with it a new appetite, the yearning to show our strength. . . ." Secretary of State John Hay was more succinct. It had been, he wrote Roosevelt, "a splendid little war."

Many who served in Cuba found the war far from splendid. Ill-trained and poorly equipped, the troops went into summer combat wearing heavy woolen uniforms. The army also lacked adequate medical support. When **Clara Barton,** president of the American Association for Red Cross, visited Santiago, she found wounded soldiers lying in the rain, unable to eat the hardtack rations. Under her leadership, 1,000 trained nurses worked with the medical corps. Despite the efforts of these nurses and doctors, 379 American soldiers died in combat and more than 5,000 succumbed to food poisoning, yellow fever, malaria, and other diseases during and after the war.

Several thousand black troops fought in Cuba. Some, such as the Twenty-fourth Infantry and Tenth Cavalry, were seasoned regular army "buffalo soldiers" transferred from bases in the West. Others were volunteers from various states. At assembly points in Georgia, and then at the embarkation port of Tampa, Florida, these troops encountered the racism of a Jim Crow society. Tampa restaurants and bars refused them service; Tampa whites disparaged them. On June 6, after weeks of racist treatment, some black troops exploded in riotous rage, storming into restaurants, bars, and other establishments that had barred them. White troops from Georgia restored order. Although white and black troops sailed to Cuba on the same transport ships (actually, hastily converted freighters), the ships themselves were segregated, with black troops often confined to the lowest quarters in the stifling heat, denied permission to mingle on deck with the other units, and in other ways discriminated against.

(National Archives)

African-American Soldiers of the Tenth U.S. Cavalry in Cuba, July 1898
These men posed shortly after the capture of San Juan Hill. Black troops, known as buffalo soldiers, played an important role in the Spanish-American War, but they were subject to harassment and discrimination.

Despite the racism, African-Americans served with distinction once they reached Cuba. Black troops played key roles in the taking of both San Juan Hill and El Caney Hill. Of the total U.S. troops involved in the latter action, some 15 percent were black.

The Spanish sought an armistice on July 17. In the peace treaty signed that December in Paris, Spain recognized Cuba's independence and, after a U.S. payment of $20 million, ceded the Philippines, Puerto Rico, and the Pacific island of Guam to the United States. Americans now possessed an island empire stretching from the Caribbean to the Pacific.

From 1898 to 1902, the U.S. army governed Cuba under the command of General Leonard Wood. Wood's administration improved public health, education, and sanitation but nevertheless violated the spirit of the 1898 Teller Amendment. The troops eventually withdrew, though under conditions that limited Cuban sovereignty. The 1901 **Platt Amendment,** attached to an army appropriations bill offered by a Connecticut senator at the request of the War Department, authorized American withdrawal only after Cuba agreed not to make any treaty with a foreign power limiting its independence and not to borrow beyond its means. The United States also reserved the right to intervene in Cuba when it saw fit and to maintain a naval base there, a policy resented by the Cubans. With U.S. troops still occupying the island, the Cuban constitutional convention of 1901 accepted the Platt Amendment, which remained in force until 1934. Under its terms the United States established a naval base at Guantánamo Bay, near Santiago de Cuba, which it still maintains. U.S. investments in Cuba, some $50 million in 1898, soared to half a billion dollars by 1920.

Critics of Empire   Some Americans, who had opposed imperialism for more than a decade, were dismayed by the victories of the expansionists in Cuba and the Philippines. Although few in number, the critics, like the Mugwumps who had challenged the spoils system, were influential. Indeed, some of them, like Carl Schurz and E. L. Godkin, were former Mugwumps. Other anti-imperialists included William Jennings Bryan, settlement-house founder Jane Addams, novelist Mark Twain, and Harvard philosopher William James. Steel king Andrew Carnegie gave thousands of dollars to the cause. In 1898, these critics of empire formed the **Anti-Imperialist League.**

For the United States to rule other peoples, the anti-imperialists believed, was to violate the principles of the Declaration of Independence and the Constitution. As one of them wrote, "Dewey took Manila with the loss of one man—and all our institutions." The military fever that accompanied expansionism also dismayed the anti-imperialists. Some labor leaders feared that imperial expansion would lead to competition from cheap foreign labor and products.

In February 1899, the anti-imperialists failed by one vote to prevent Senate ratification of the peace treaty with Spain. McKinley's overwhelming reelection victory in 1900 and the defeat of expansionist critic William Jennings Bryan eroded the anti-imperialists' cause. Nevertheless, at a time of jingoistic rhetoric and militaristic posturing, they had upheld an older and more traditional vision of America.

Guerrilla War in the Philippines, 1898–1902
Events in the Philippines confirmed the worst fears of the anti-imperialists. When the war ended, President McKinley was faced with the urgent problem of what to do about this group of Pacific islands that had a population of more than 5 million people. At the war's outset, few Americans knew that the Philippines belonged to Spain or even where they were. Without a map, McKinley later confessed, "I could not have told where those darn islands were within two thousand miles."

But the victory over Spain whetted the appetite for expansion. To the U.S. business community, the Philippines offered a steppingstone to the China market. McKinley, reflecting the prevailing mood as always, reasoned that the Filipinos were unready for self-government and would be gobbled up if set adrift in a world of imperial rivalries. McKinley further persuaded himself that American rule would enormously benefit the Filipinos, whom he called "our little brown brothers." A devout Methodist, he explained that America's mission was "to educate the Filipinos, and to uplift and civilize and Christianize them, and by God's grace do the very best we could by them." (In fact, most Filipinos were already Catholic, a legacy of centuries of Spanish rule.) Having prayerfully reached his decision, McKinley instructed the American peace negotiators in Paris to insist on U.S. acquisition of the Philippines.

"Uplifting" the Filipinos required a struggle. In 1896 young **Emilio Aguinaldo** had organized a Filipino independence movement to drive out Spain. In 1898, with arms supplied by George Dewey, Aguinaldo's forces had captured most of Luzon, the Philippines' main island. When the Spanish surrendered, Aguinaldo proclaimed Filipino independence and drafted a democratic constitution. Feeling betrayed when the peace treaty ceded his country to the United States, Aguinaldo ordered his rebel force to attack Manila, the American base of operations. Seventy thousand more U.S. troops were shipped to the Philippines, and by the end of 1899 the initial Filipino resistance had been crushed.

These hostilities became the opening phase of a long guerrilla conflict. Before it ended, over 125,000 American men had served in the Philippines, and four thousand had been killed. As many as twenty thousand Filipino independence fighters died. As in the later Vietnam and Iraq Wars, casualties and suffering ravaged the civilian population as well. Historians estimate that at least 200,000 civilians died in the conflict. Aguinaldo was captured in March 1901, but large-scale guerrilla fighting continued through the summer of 1902.

In 1902, a special Senate committee heard testimony from veterans of the Philippines war about the execution of prisoners, the torture of suspects, and the burning of villages. The humanitarian mood of 1898, when Americans had rushed to save Cuba from the cruel Spaniards, seemed remote indeed. In retrospect, the American troops' ambivalent attitudes about the peoples of the Philippines, while deplorable, are not hard to understand. Despite America's self-image as a beacon of liberty and a savior of the world's peoples, many Americans in the 1880s and 1890s had been deeply troubled by the new immigrants from southern and eastern Europe and had expressed concerns over "backward" and "useless" races. As American nationalism was reformulated in this cauldron of immigration, imperialism, and the "winning of the West," racist attitudes about Native peoples and foreigners intermixed with rhetorical pleas for supervision and stewardship. In the process, as was evident in the treatment of American Indians (see Chapter 17), well-meaning paternalism often degenerated into deadly domination.

The subjugation of the Philippines followed years of expansionism that proclaimed America's debut on the world stage and underscored the global reach of U.S. capitalism. Nevertheless, most Americans remained ambivalent about the acquisition of territory. While anti-imperialist Mark Twain could acidly condemn "the Blessings of Civilization Trust," labor leader Samuel Gompers warned that "an inundation of Mongolians" might steal jobs from white labor. From the debate over the annexation of Hawai'i in 1898 to the end of the war against Philippine independence in 1902, white Americans recoiled from making these "barbarian peoples" a part of the United States. Not fit to manage their own affairs, Cuban, Puerto Rican, Hawaiian, and Filipino peoples were placed in a protective status that denied their independence and kept them under U.S. control.

To stabilize relations in the Philippines, Congress passed the Philippine Government Act in 1902, which vested authority in a governor general to be appointed by the president. The act also provided for an elected Filipino assembly and promised eventual self-government. Progress toward this goal inched forward, with intervals of semi military rule. In 1946, nearly half a century after Admiral Dewey's guns had boomed in Manila Bay, independence finally came to the Philippines.

CHRONOLOGY
1877–1902

1869	Boss William M. Tweed gains control of New York's Tammany Hall political machine.
1878	Congress requires U.S. Treasury to purchase silver.
1880	James Garfield elected president.
1881	Assassination of Garfield; Chester A. Arthur becomes president.
1883	Pendleton Civil Service Act.
1884	Grover Cleveland elected president.
1886	*Wabash v. Illinois.*
1887	Interstate Commerce Act.
1888	Benjamin Harrison elected president.
1889	National Farmers' Alliance formed.
1890	Sherman Silver Purchase Act. Sherman Anti-Trust Act. McKinley Tariff pushes tariffs to all-time high.
1893	Panic of 1893; depression of 1893–1897 begins. Repeal of the Sherman Silver Purchase Act.
1894	Coxey's "army" marches on Washington. Pullman strike. Wilson-Gorman Tariff.

1895	Supreme Court declares federal income tax unconstitutional.
1896	Free-silver forces capture Democratic Party and nominate William Jennings Bryan.
	William McKinley elected president.
1898	Acquisition of Hawai'i.
	Spanish-American War.
1898–1902	Guerrilla uprising in Philippines.
1900	Currency Act officially places United States on gold standard.
1901	Platt Amendment retains U.S. role in Cuba.
	Regular Army Nursing Corps founded.
1902	Philippine Government Act.

CONCLUSION

By 1900 immigration, the settlement of the frontier West, and rapid industrial expansion had pushed America to the forefront of the world economy and had sparked a major realignment in American politics. After nearly two decades of hard-fought elections in which political control had seesawed back and forth between the major parties, the Republicans now held power.

It had been difficult to achieve political dominance. The dynamic growth of the American economy together with rapid urbanization and a massive influx of immigrants had initially strained the political process. As the parties struggled to define their vision of the proper role of government in stimulating economic development, they were forced to deal with ethnic, cultural, and racial issues that included prohibition, church schools, and segregation. All this was further complicated by the Democratic Party's attempt to throw off the limits imposed by Reconstruction and gain political control of the South.

On the national level, both parties built a loyal following by linking their positions to deeply held beliefs about the family and the proper role of government. Republicans justified their support for the tariff and soldiers' pensions in terms of patriotic protection of the family. Democrats countered that a high-tariff policy was indicative of precisely the kind of excessive governmental force that would destroy family life. On the local level, both parties secured loyal voters by stressing ethnic and cultural issues. Democrats, often as political bosses and urban machines, courted the new immigrants, while Republicans catered to rural and small-town native-born Americans in the Northeast and Midwest. Political bosses gave immigrants a foothold in the political process but their participation often came at the high cost of inflated contracts and corruption that siphoned millions of dollars from the public treasury.

In the competition for new voters, the needs of rural Americans were often overlooked. Caught between declining prices for grain and cotton, and high railroad and bank rates, farmers struggled to survive. Their precarious position was further strained by years of drought, insect infestation, and overspecialization in one crop. In desperation, farmers turned first to the Grange and Farmers' Alliance movements and then to the Populist Party for help. In the South, after first courting black farmers, members of the Farmers' Alliance and later the Populists joined with Democrats to disfranchise black voters. Using lynching and intimidation, Democrats seized control of southern politics.

In the face of these threats, the Republican Party in 1896 raised huge sums from big business to turn back the Populist challenge and take control of national politics. The fusion of the Populists and Democrats behind William Jennings Bryan and the silver issue created problems of its own. Although he carried the South and almost all the Midwest, the teetotaling Bryan had little appeal for urban workers and the middle class who believed that a monetary policy based on free silver promised only inflation and higher prices. McKinley won by playing down moral reforms such as prohibition and emphasizing patriotism and fiscal responsibility. Republicans won over the urban-industrial core of the nation—the Northeast and much of the Midwest. They would control the House of Representatives for twenty-eight out of the thirty-six years from 1894 to 1930.

McKinley's administration was drawn by events in Cuba and jingoistic advocates within his own party into the Spanish-American War and the subsequent acquisition of Hawai'i, Samoa, Guam, the Philippines, and Cuba. Although the Republicans preferred the term "expansionism" to "imperialism," the move to acquire new bases for access to global markets fit the party's probusiness stance. But expansion into the Pacific created its own obstacles when the United States became involved in a guerrilla war with Philippine nationalists. Facing mounting criticism at home, the expansionists adopted the Teller and Platt Amendments, which foreshadowed eventual disengagement from the acquisition of foreign territory.

Notwithstanding these foreign interventions, the fundamental question of late-nineteenth century American politics persisted: could a government designed for the needs of a small agrarian society serve an industrialized nation of factories and immigrant-crowded cities? The answer was by no means clear. Although issues such as patronage, the tariff, veterans' benefits, and monetary policy had enabled the industrial system to grow dramatically, the needs of farmers, workers, and immigrant Americans had largely been ignored. The Republicans successfully carried the field in 1896, but Populists and other critics who argued that government should play an assertive role in solving social and economic problems would help shape the political environment of the progressive movement.

21

THE PROGRESSIVE ERA, 1900–1917

CHAPTER OUTLINE

• Progressives and Their Ideas • Grassroots Progressivism •
Progressivism and Social Control • Blacks, Women, and Workers
Organize • National Progressivism, Phase I: Roosevelt and Taft,
1901–1913 • National Progressivism, Phase II: Woodrow Wilson,
1913–1917

PROGRESSIVES AND THEIR IDEAS

As the twentieth century dawned, groups across the nation grappled with the problems of the new urban-industrial order. Workers protested unsafe and exhausting jobs. Experts investigated social conditions. Women's clubs embraced reform. Intellectuals challenged the ideological foundations of a business-dominated social order, and journalists exposed municipal corruption and industrialism's human toll. Throughout America, activists worked to make government more democratic, improve conditions in cities and factories, and curb corporate power.

Historians have grouped all these efforts under a single label: "the progressive movement." In fact, "progressivism" was less a single movement than a spirit of discontent with the status quo and an exciting sense of new social possibilities. International in scope, this spirit found many outlets and addressed many issues.

The Many Faces of Progressivism   Who were the progressives, and what reforms did they pursue? To answer this, we must examine the social changes of the era. Along with immigration, a growing middle class transformed U.S. cities. From the men and women of this class—mostly white, native-born Protestants—came many of the progressive movement's leaders and supporters.

From 1900 to 1920, the white-collar work force jumped from 5.1 million to 10.5 million—more than double the growth rate of the labor force as a whole. This burgeoning white-collar class included corporate executives and small-business owners; secretaries, accountants, and sales clerks; civil engineers and people in advertising; and professionals such as lawyers, physicians, and teachers. New professional groups arose, from the American Association of University Professors (1915) to the American Association of Advertising Agencies (1917). For many middle-class Americans, membership in a national professional society provided a sense of identity that might earlier have come from neighborhood, church, or political party. Ambitious, well educated, and valuing social stability, the members of this new middle class were eager to make their influence felt.

For middle-class women, the city offered both opportunities and frustrations. Young unmarried women often became schoolteachers, secretaries, typists, clerks, and telephone operators. The number of women in such white-collar jobs, as well as the ranks of college-educated women, more than tripled from 1900 to 1920.

But for middle-class married women caring for homes and children, city life could bring stress and loneliness. The divorce rate rose from one in twelve marriages in 1900 to one in nine by 1916. As we shall see, middle-class women joined female white-collar workers and college graduates in leading a revived women's movement. Cultural commentators wrote nervously of the "New Woman."

This urban middle class rallied to the banner of reform. The initial reform impetus came not from political parties but from women's clubs, settlement houses, and groups with names like the Playground Association of America, the National Child Labor Committee, and the American League for Civic Improvement. In this era of organizations, the reform movement, too, drew strength from organized interest groups.

But the native-born middle class was not alone in promoting reform. On issues affecting factory workers and slum dwellers, the urban-immigrant political machines—and workers themselves—often took the initiative. After the 1911 Triangle fire, New York's machine politicians joined with middle-class reformers and union officials to investigate the disaster and push for protective legislation. Some corporate leaders promoted business regulations that served their interests.

What, then, was progressivism? Fundamentally, it was a broad-based response to industrialization and its social byproducts: immigration, urban growth, growing corporate power, and widening class divisions. In contrast to populism, it enlisted many more citydwellers, journalists, academics, and social theorists. Finally, most progressives were *reformers,* not radicals. They wished to make the new urban-industrial order more humane, not overturn it entirely.

But what specific remedies were required? Reaching different answers to this key question, progressive reformers embraced causes that sometimes overlapped, sometimes diverged. Many demanded stricter business regulation, from local transit companies to the almighty trusts. Others focused on protecting workers and the urban poor. Still others championed reform of municipal government. Some, fearful of urban disorder, favored immigration restriction or social-control strategies to regulate city-dwellers' behavior. All this contributed to the mosaic of progressive reform.

Progressives believed that most social problems could be solved through study and organized effort. They respected science and expert knowledge. Since scientific and technological expertise had produced the new industrial order, such expertise could surely also correct the social problems spawned by industrialism. Progressives marshaled research data, surveys, and statistics to support their various causes.

Some historians have portrayed progressivism as an organizational stage that all modernizing societies pass through. This perspective is useful, provided we remember that it was not an automatic process unfolding independently of human will. Persistent journalists, activist workers, and passionate reformers all played a role. Human emotion—whether indignation over child labor, suspicion of corporate power, or raw political ambition—drove the movement forward.

Intellectuals Offer New Social Views   A group of innovative social thinkers provided progressivism's underlying ideas. As we have seen, some Gilded Age intellectuals had argued that Charles Darwin's theory of evolution justified unrestrained economic competition. In the 1880s and 1890s, sociologist Lester Ward, utopian novelist Edward Bellamy, and leaders of the Social Gospel movement had all attacked this harsh version of Social Darwinism (see Chapters 18 and 19). This attack intensified after 1900.

Economist Thorstein Veblen, a Norwegian-American from Minnesota, satirized America's newly rich capitalists in *The Theory of the Leisure Class* (1899). Dissecting their lifestyle the way an anthropologist might study an exotic tribe, he argued that they built mansions, threw elaborate parties, and otherwise engaged in "conspicuous consumption" to flaunt their wealth and assert their claims to superiority.

The Harvard philosopher William James argued in *Pragmatism* (1907) that truth emerges not from abstract theorizing but from the experience of coping with life's realities through practical action. James's philosophy of pragmatism deepened reformers' skepticism toward the older generation's entrenched ideas and strengthened their belief in the necessity of social change.

Herbert Croly, the son of reform-minded New York journalists, shared this faith that new ideas could transform society. In *The Promise of American Life* (1909), Croly called for an activist government of the kind advocated by Alexander Hamilton, the first secretary of the treasury. But rather than serving the interests of the business class, as Hamilton had proposed, he argued that government should promote the welfare of all. In 1914, Croly founded the *New Republic* magazine to promote progressive ideas.

The settlement-house leader Jane Addams also helped shape the ideology of the Progressive Era. In *Democracy and Social Ethics* (1902) and other books, Addams rejected the claim that unrestrained competition offered the best path to social progress. Instead, she argued, in a complex industrial society, each individual's well-being depends on the well-being of all. Addams urged middle-class Americans to recognize their common interests with the laboring masses, and to demand better conditions in factories and immigrant slums. Teaching by example, Addams made her Chicago social settlement, Hull House, a center of social activism and legislative-reform initiatives.

With public-school enrollment growing from about 7 million in 1870 to more than 23 million in 1920, the educational reformer John Dewey saw schools as potent engines of social change. In his model school at the University of Chicago, Dewey encouraged pupils to work collaboratively and to interact with one another. The ideal school, he said in *Democracy and Education* (1916), would be an "embryonic community" where children would learn to live as members of a social group.

(Library of Congress)

Women Enter the Labor Force *Young female workers take an exercise break at the National Cash Register Company in Dayton, Ohio around 1900. From schools and hospitals to corporate offices and crowded sweatshops, women poured into the workforce in the early twentieth century.*

Oliver Wendell Holmes, Jr., a law professor, focused on changing judicial thinking. In *The Common Law* (1881), Holmes had criticized judges who interpreted the law rigidly to protect corporate interests and had insisted that law must evolve as society changes. In a phrase much quoted by progressives, he had declared, "The life of the law has not been logic; it has been experience." Appointed to the United States Supreme Court in 1902, Holmes often dissented from the conservative Court majority. As the new social thinking took hold, the courts slowly grew more open to reform legislation.

Novelists, Journalists, and Artists Spotlight Social Problems   While reform-minded intellectuals reoriented American social thought, novelists and journalists chronicled corporate wrongdoing, municipal corruption, slum conditions, and industrial abuses.

In his novel *The Octopus* (1901), Frank Norris of San Francisco portrayed the struggle between California railroad barons and the state's wheat growers. Though writing fiction, Norris accurately described the railroad owners' bribery, intimidation, rate manipulation, and other tactics.

Theodore Dreiser's novel *The Financier* (1912) featured a hard-driving business tycoon utterly lacking a social conscience. Dreiser modeled his story on the scandal-ridden career of an actual railway financier. Like Veblen's *Theory of the Leisure Class*, such works encouraged skepticism toward the industrial elite and stimulated pressures for tougher business regulation.

Mass magazines such as *McClure's* and *Collier's* stirred reform energies with articles exposing urban political corruption and corporate wrongdoing. President Theodore Roosevelt criticized the authors as **"muckrakers"** publicizing the worst in American life, but the label became a badge of honor. Journalist Lincoln Steffens began the exposé vogue in 1902 with a *McClure's* article documenting municipal corruption in St. Louis.

To gather material, some journalists worked as factory laborers or lived in slum tenements. One described her experiences working in a Massachusetts shoe factory where the caustic dyes rotted workers' fingernails. The British immigrant John Spargo researched his 1906 book about child labor, *The Bitter Cry of the Children,* by visiting mines in Pennsylvania and West Virginia and attempting to do the work that young boys performed for ten hours a day, picking out slate and other refuse from coal in cramped workspaces filled with choking coal dust.

The muckrakers awakened middle-class readers to conditions in industrial America. Some magazine exposés later appeared in book form, including Lincoln Steffens's *The Shame of the Cities* (1904), Ida Tarbell's damning *History of the Standard Oil Company* (1904), and David Graham Phillips's *The Treason of the Senate* (1906).

Artists and photographers played a role as well. A group of New York painters dubbed the Ashcan School portrayed the harshness as well as the vitality of slum life. The photographer Lewis Hine, working for the National Child Labor Committee, captured haunting images of child workers with stunted bodies and worn expressions.

GRASSROOTS PROGRESSIVISM

Middle-class citizens did more than read about the problems of urban-industrial America. They observed these problems firsthand in their own communities. In fact, the progressive movement began with grass-roots campaigns to end urban political corruption, regulate corporate behavior, and improve conditions in factories and slums. Eventually, these local efforts came together in a powerful national movement.

Reforming Local Politics   Beginning in the 1890s, middle-class reformers battled corrupt city governments that provided services and jobs to immigrants, but often at the price of graft and rigged elections (see Chapter 19). In New York City, Protestant clergy battled Tammany Hall, the city's entrenched Democratic organization. In Detroit, the reform mayor Hazen Pingree (served 1890–1897) brought honesty to city hall, lowered transit fares, and provided public baths and other services. Pingree once slapped a health quarantine on a brothel, holding hostage a well-known business leader until he promised to back Pingree's reforms.

In San Francisco, a courageous newspaper editor led a 1907 crusade against the city's corrupt boss. When the original prosecutor was gunned down in court, attorney Hiram Johnson took his place, winning convictions against the boss and his cronies. Full of reform zeal—one observer called him "a volcano in perpetual eruption"—Johnson rode his newly won fame to the California governorship and the U.S. Senate.

In Toledo, Ohio, a colorful figure named Samuel M. ("Golden Rule") Jones led the reform crusade. A businessman converted to the Social Gospel, Jones introduced profit sharing in his factory, and as mayor he established playgrounds, free kindergartens, and lodging houses for homeless transients.

Urban political reformers soon began to probe the roots of municipal misgovernment, including the private monopolies that ran municipal water, gas, electricity, and transit systems. Reformers passed laws regulating the rates these utilities could charge and curbing their political influence. (Some even advocated public ownership of these companies.)

Reflecting the Progressive Era's regard for expertise and efficiency, some municipal reformers advocated substituting professional city managers for mayors, and councils chosen in citywide elections for aldermen elected on a ward-by-ward basis. Dayton, Ohio, adopted a city-manager system after a ruinous flood in 1913. Supposedly above politics, these experts were expected to run the city like an efficient business.

Municipal reform attracted different groups, depending on the issue. The native-born middle class, led by clergymen, editors, and other opinion molders, provided the initial impetus and core support. Business interests often pushed for citywide elections and the city-manager system, since these changes reduced immigrants' political clout and increased the influence of the corporate elite. Reforms that promised improved services or better conditions for ordinary city-dwellers won support from immigrants and political bosses who realized that the old, informal system of patronage could no longer meet constituents' needs.

The electoral-reform movement soon spread to the state level. By 1910, for example, all states had replaced the old system of voting, involving preprinted ballots bearing the names of specific candidates, with the secret ballot, which made it harder to rig elections. The direct primary, introduced in Wisconsin in 1903, enabled rank-and-file voters rather than party bosses to select their parties' candidates for public office.

Hoping to trim the political power of corporate interests, some western states inaugurated the *initiative, referendum,* and *recall.* By an initiative, voters can instruct the legislature to consider a specific bill. In a referendum, citizens can actually enact a law or express their views on a proposed measure. By a recall petition, voters can remove a public official from office if they muster enough signatures.

While these reforms aimed to democratize voting, party leaders and interest groups soon learned to manipulate the new electoral machinery. Ironically, the new procedures may have weakened party loyalty and reduced voter interest. Voter-participation rates dropped steeply in these years, while political activity by organized interest groups increased.

Regulating
Business,
Protecting
Workers

The corporate consolidation that produced giants like Carnegie Steel and Standard Oil (see Chapter 18) continued after 1900. The United States Steel Company created by J. P. Morgan in 1901 controlled 80 percent of all U.S. steel production. A year later, Morgan combined six competing companies into the International Harvester Company, which dominated the farm-implement business. The General Motors Company, formed in 1908 by William C. Durant with backing from the DuPont Corporation, brought various independent automobile manufacturers, from the inexpensive Chevrolet to the luxury Cadillac, under one corporate umbrella.

Many workers benefited from this corporate growth. Industrial workers' average annual real wages (defined in terms of actual purchasing power) rose from $487 in 1900 to $687 by 1915. In railroading and other unionized industries, wages climbed still higher. But even with the cost of living far lower than today, such wages barely supported a family and provided little cushion for emergencies.

To survive, entire families went to work. Two-thirds of young immigrant women entered the labor force in the early 1900s, working as factory help or domestics or in small business establishments.

Even children worked. In 1910, the nonfarm labor force included some 1.6 million children aged ten to fifteen employed in factories, mills, tenement sweatshops, and street trades such as shoe shining and newspaper vending. The total may have been higher, since many "women workers" listed in the census were in fact young girls. One investigator found a girl of five working nights in a South Carolina textile mill.

Work was long and hazardous. Despite the eight-hour movement of the 1880s, in 1900 the average worker still toiled 9½ hours a day. Some southern textile mills required workdays of 12 or 13 hours. In one typical year (1907), 4,534 railroad workers and more than 3,000 miners were killed on the job. Few workers enjoyed vacations or retirement benefits.

Workers accustomed to the rhythms of farm labor faced the discipline of the factory. Efficiency experts used time-and-motion studies to increase production. In *Principles of Scientific Management* (1911), Frederick W. Taylor explained how to increase output by standardizing job routines and rewarding the fastest workers. "Efficiency" became a popular catchword, but workers resented the pressures to speed up.

Americans concerned about the social implications of industrialization deplored unregulated corporate power and the hazards facing industrial workers. The drive to regulate big business, inherited from the populists, became an important component of progressivism. Since corporations had benefited from government policies such as high protective tariffs and railroad subsidies, reformers reasoned, they should also be subject to government regulation.

Wisconsin, under Governor **Robert** ("Fighting Bob") **La Follette**, took the lead in regulating railroads, mines, and other businesses. As a Republican congressman, La Follette had feuded with the state's conservative party leadership, and in 1900 he won the governorship as an independent. Challenging powerful corporate interests, La Follette and his administration adopted the direct-primary system, set up a railroad regulatory commission, increased corporate taxes, and limited campaign spending. Reflecting progressivism's faith in experts, La Follette consulted reform-minded professors at the University of Wisconsin and set up a legislative reference library to help lawmakers draft bills. La Follette's reforms gained national attention as the "Wisconsin Idea."

If electoral reform and corporate regulation represented the brain of progressivism, the impulse to improve conditions for workers represented its heart. This movement, too, began at the local and state level. By 1907, for example, thirty states had outlawed child labor. A 1903 Oregon law limited women in industry to a ten-hour workday.

Campaigns for industrial safety and better working conditions won support from political bosses in the immigrant cities. State senator Robert F. Wagner, a leader of New York City's Democratic organization, headed the Triangle-fire investigation. Thanks to his committee's efforts, New York passed fifty-six worker-protection laws, including required fire-safety inspections. By 1914, twenty-five states had made employers liable for job-related injuries or deaths.

Florence Kelley of Hull House, the daughter of a conservative Republican congressman, spearheaded the drive to remedy industrial abuses. In 1893, after investigating conditions in factories and sweatshops, Kelley persuaded the Illinois legislature to outlaw child labor and limit working hours for women. In 1899, she became head of the National Consumers' League, which mobilized consumer pressure for improved factory conditions. Campaigning for a federal child-labor law, Kelley asked, "Why are ... wild game in the national parks, buffalo, [and] migratory birds all found suitable for federal protection, but not children?"

Like many progressive reforms, the crusade for workplace safety relied on expert research. The bacteriologist Alice Hamilton, a pioneer in the new field of "industrial hygiene," reported on lead poisoning among industrial workers in 1910. Later, as an investigator for the U.S. Bureau of Labor, Hamilton publicized other work-related medical hazards.

Workers themselves, who well understood the hazards of their jobs, provided further pressure for reform. For example, when the granite industry introduced new power drills that created a fine dust that workers inhaled, the *Granite Cutters' Journal* called them "widow makers." Sure enough, investigators soon linked the dust to a deadly lung disease, silicosis.

Making Cities More Livable
By 1920, the U.S. urban population passed the 50 percent mark, and sixty-eight cities boasted more than a hundred thousand inhabitants. New York City grew by 2.2 million from 1900 to 1920, Chicago by 1 million. America had become an urban nation.

Political corruption was only one of many urban problems. As manufacturing and businesses grew, a tide of immigrants and native-born newcomers engulfed the cities. Many cities became congested human warehouses, lacking adequate parks, public-health resources, recreational facilities, and basic municipal services. As the reform spirit spread, the urban crisis loomed large.

Extending the achievements of Frederick Law Olmsted and others (see Chapter 19), reformers campaigned for parks, boulevards, and street lights; opposed unsightly billboards and overhead electrical wires; and advocated city planning and beautification

(Bettmann/Corbis)

The Price of Industrialization *Smoke and pollutants pour from a Pittsburgh steel mill in 1890. "Hell with the lid off" was one observer's description of the city in these years.*

projects. Daniel Burnham, chief architect of the 1893 Chicago world's fair, led a successful 1906 effort to revive a plan for Washington, D.C., first proposed in 1791. He also developed plans for Cleveland, San Francisco, and other cities.

Burnham's 1909 *Plan of Chicago* offered a vision of a city both more efficient and more beautiful. He recommended wide boulevards; lakefront parks and museums; statuary and fountains; and a majestic domed city hall and vast civic plaza. Chicago spent more than $300 million on projects reflecting his ideas. Many urban planners shared Burnham's faith that more beautiful cities and imposing public buildings would produce orderly, law-abiding citizens.

The municipal reform impulse also included such practical goals as decent housing and better garbage collection and street cleaning. Providing a model for other cities and states, the New York legislature imposed strict health and safety regulations on tenements in 1911.

With the discovery in the 1880s that germs cause cholera, typhoid fever, and other diseases, municipal hygiene became a high priority. Reformers distributed public-health information; promoted school vaccination programs; and called for safer water and sewer systems and the regulation of food and milk suppliers. When Mary Mallon, an Irish-immigrant cook in New York, was found to be a healthy carrier of the typhoid bacillus in 1907, she was confined by the city health authorities and demonized in the press as "Typhoid Mary."

These efforts bore fruit. From 1900 to 1920, U.S. infant mortality (defined as death in the first year of life), as well as death rates from tuberculosis, typhoid fever, and other infectious or communicable diseases, all fell sharply.

Urban reformers shared the era's heightened environmental consciousness (see Chapter 17). Factory chimneys belching smoke had once inspired pride, but by the early 1900s physicians had linked factory smoke to respiratory problems, and civic reformers were deploring the soot and smoke spewing from coal-fueled factory steam boilers.

The antismoke campaign combined expertise with activism. Civil engineers formed the Smoke Prevention Association in 1906, and researchers at the University of Pittsburgh—one of the nation's smokiest cities with its steel mills—documented the hazards and costs of air pollution. Chicago merchant Marshall Field declared that the "soot tax" he paid to clean his buildings' exteriors exceeded his real-estate taxes. As women's clubs and other civic groups embraced the cause, many cities passed smoke-abatement laws.

Success proved elusive, however, as railroads and corporations fought back in the courts. With coal still providing 70 percent of the nation's energy as late as 1920, cities remained smoky. Not until years later, with the shift to other energy sources, did municipal air pollution significantly diminish.

PROGRESSIVISM AND SOCIAL CONTROL

Progressives' belief in research, legislation, and aroused public opinion sprang from their confidence that they knew what was best for society. While municipal corruption, unsafe factories, and corporate abuses captured their attention, so, too, did issues of personal behavior, particularly immigrant behavior. The problems they addressed deserved attention, but their moralistic rhetoric and coercive remedies also betrayed an impulse to impose their own moral standards by force of law.

Urban Amuse-ments; Urban Moral Control   Despite the slums, dangerous factories, and other problems, early-twentieth-century cities also offered fun and diversion with their department stores, vaudeville, music halls, and amusement parks (see Chapter 19). While some vaudeville owners sought respectability, bawdy routines full of sexual innuendo delighted working-class audiences.

Amusement parks offered families escape from tenements, and gave female workers an opportunity to socialize with friends, meet young men, and show off new outfits. New York City's amusement park, Coney Island, a subway ride from the city, attracted several million visitors a year by 1914.

With electrification, streetcar rides and evening strolls on well-lit downtown streets became leisure activities in themselves. Orville and Wilbur Wright's successful airplane flight in 1903, and the introduction of Henry Ford's Model T in 1908, transforming the automobile from a toy of the rich to a vehicle for the masses, foretold exciting changes ahead, with cities central to the action.

Jaunty music-hall songs added to the vibrancy of city life. The blues, rooted in the chants of southern black sharecroppers, reached a broader public with such songs as W. C. Handy's classic "St. Louis Blues" (1914). Ragtime, another import from the black South (see Chapter 19), enjoyed great popularity in early-twentieth-century urban America. Both the black composer Scott Joplin, with such works as "Maple Leaf Rag" (1899), and the white composer Irving Berlin, with his hit tune "Alexander's Rag-Time Band" (1911), contributed to this vogue.

These years also brought a new entertainment medium—the movies. Initially a part of vaudeville shows, movies soon migrated to five-cent halls called "nickelodeons" in immigrant neighborhoods. At first featuring brief comic sequences like *The Sneeze* or *The Kiss*, movies began to tell stories with *The Great Train Robbery* (1903). *A Fool There Was* (1914), with its daring line, "Kiss me, my fool!," made Theda Bara (really Theodosia Goodman of Cincinnati) the first female star. The British music-hall performer Charlie Chaplin immigrated to America and appeared in some sixty short comedies between 1914 and 1917. Like amusement parks, the movies allowed immigrant youth briefly to escape parental supervision. As a New York garment worker recalled, "The one place I was allowed to go by myself was the movies. My parents wouldn't let me go anywhere else."

The diversions that eased city life for the poor struck some middle-class reformers as moral traps as dangerous as the physical hazards of the factory. Fearful of immorality and disorder, reformers campaigned to regulate amusement parks, dance halls, movies, and the darkened nickelodeons, which they saw as potential dens of vice. Several states and cities set up film censorship boards, and the Supreme Court upheld such measures in 1915.

Building on the moral-purity crusade of the Woman's Christian Temperance Union (WCTU) and other groups (see Chapter 19), reformers also targeted prostitution, a major urban problem. Male procurers lured young women into prostitution and then took a share of their income. Women's paltry wages for factory work or domestic service made this more-lucrative occupation tempting. Why "get up at 6:30 ... and work in a close stuffy room ... until dark for $6 or $7 a week," reasoned one prostitute, when an afternoon with a man could bring in more.

Adopting the usual progressive approach, investigators gathered statistics on what they called "the social evil." The American Social Hygiene Association (1914), financed by John D. Rockefeller, Jr., sponsored research on sexually transmitted diseases, paid for "vice investigations" in major cities, and drafted antiprostitution laws.

As prostitution came to symbolize urban America's larger moral dangers, a "white slave" hysteria took hold. Novels, films, and magazine articles warned of kidnapped farm girls forced into urban brothels. The Mann Act (1910) made it illegal to transport a woman across a state line "for immoral purposes." Amid much fanfare, reformers shut down the red-light districts of New Orleans, Chicago, and other cities.

Racism, anti-immigrant prejudice, and anxieties about changing sexual mores all fueled the antiprostitution crusade. Authorities employed the new legislation to pry into private sexual behavior. Blackmailers entrapped men into Mann Act violations. In 1913, the African-American boxer Jack Johnson, the heavyweight champion, was convicted under the Mann Act for crossing a state line with a (white) woman for "immoral purposes." Johnson went abroad to escape imprisonment.

Battling Alcohol and Drugs   Temperance had long been part of America's reform agenda, but reformers' objectives changed in the Progressive Era. Earlier campaigns had urged individuals to give up drink. By contrast, the **Anti-Saloon League** (ASL), founded in 1895, called for a total ban on the sale of alcoholic beverages. In typical Progressive fashion, full-time professionals ran the ASL, with Protestant ministers staffing state committees. ASL publications offered statistics documenting alcohol's role in many social problems. As churches and temperance groups worked for prohibition at the municipal, county, and state levels, the ASL moved to its larger goal: national prohibition.

Alcohol abuse did indeed contribute to domestic violence, health problems, and workplace injuries. But like the antiprostitution crusade, the prohibition campaign became a symbolic battleground pitting native-born citizens against immigrants. The ASL, while raising legitimate issues, also embodied Protestant America's impulse to control the immigrant city.

Reformers also targeted drug abuse—and for good reason. Physicians, patent-medicine peddlers, and legitimate drug companies freely prescribed or sold opium (derived from poppies) and its derivatives morphine and heroin. Cocaine, extracted from coca leaves, was an ingredient of Coca-Cola until about 1900.

Amid mounting reform pressure, Congress in 1914 passed the Harrison Act, banning the distribution of heroin, morphine, cocaine, and other addictive drugs except by licensed physicians or pharmacists. Like progressives' environmental concerns, this campaign anticipated an issue that remains important today. But this reform, too, had racist undertones. Antidrug crusaders luridly described Chinese "opium dens" (places where this addictive narcotic was smoked) and warned that "drug-crazed Negroes" imperiled white womanhood.

Immigration Restriction and Eugenics   While many new city-dwellers came from farms and small towns, immigration remained the main source of urban growth. More than 17 million newcomers arrived from 1900 to 1917 (many passing through New York's immigration center, Ellis Island), and most settled in cities (see Figure 21.1). As in the 1890s (see Chapter 19), the influx came mainly from southern and eastern Europe, but more than two hundred thousand Japanese arrived between 1900 and 1920. An estimated forty thousand Chinese entered in these years, despite the 1882 Chinese Exclusion Act (see Chapter 18), which remained in force until 1943. Thousands of Mexicans came as well, many seeking railroad work.

The dismay that middle-class Americans felt about urban slum conditions stimulated support not only for protective legislation, but also for immigration restriction. If the immigrant city bred social problems, some concluded, immigrants

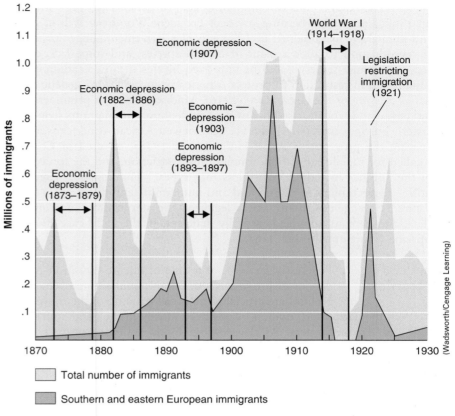

Total number of immigrants

Southern and eastern European immigrants

FIGURE 21.1 Immigration to the United States, 1870–1930

With the end of the depression of the 1890s, immigrants from southern and eastern Europe filled American cities, spurring an immigration-restriction movement, urban moral-purity campaigns, and efforts to improve the physical and social conditions of immigrant life.

Source: Statistical History of the United States from Colonial Times to the Present (Stamford, Conn.: Fairfield Publishers, 1965); and report presented by Senator William P. Dillingham, Senate document 742, 61st Congress, 3rd session, December 5, 1910: Abstracts of Reports to the Immigration Commission.

should be excluded. Prominent Bostonians formed the Immigration Restriction League in 1894. The American Federation of Labor, fearing job competition, also endorsed restriction.

Like most Progressive Era reformers, immigration-restriction advocates tried to document their case. A 1911 congressional report allegedly proved the new immigrants' innate degeneracy. One prominent sociologist described the newcomers as "low-browed, big-faced persons of obviously low mentality."

Led by Massachusetts senator Henry Cabot Lodge, Congress passed literacy-test bills in 1896, 1913, and 1915, only to see them vetoed. These measures would have excluded immigrants over sixteen years old who could not read either English or their native language, thus discriminating against persons lacking formal education. In 1917, Lodge's bill became law over President Woodrow Wilson's veto.

Anti-immigrant fears helped fuel the eugenics movement. Eugenics is the control of reproduction to alter a plant or animal species, and some U.S. eugenicists believed that human society could be improved by this means. Leading eugenicists urged immigration restriction to protect America from "inferior" genetic stock.

In *The Passing of the Great Race* (1916), Madison Grant, a prominent progressive and eugenics advocate, used bogus data to denounce immigrants from southern and eastern Europe, especially Jews. He also viewed African-Americans as inferior. Anticipating the program of Adolf Hitler in the 1930s (covered in Chapter 25), Grant called for racial segregation, immigration restriction, and the forced sterilization of the "unfit," including "worthless race types." The vogue of eugenics gave "scientific" respectability to racism and anti-immigrant sentiment.

Inspired by eugenics, many states legalized the sterilization of criminals, sex offenders, and persons adjudged mentally deficient. In the 1927 case *Buck v. Bell,* the Supreme Court upheld such laws.

Racism and Progressivism	Progressivism arose at a time of intense racism in America as well of major African-American population movements. These realities are crucial to an understanding of the movement.

In 1900, the nation's 10 million blacks lived mostly in the rural South as sharecroppers and tenant farmers. As devastating floods and the cotton boll weevil, which spread from Mexico in the 1890s, worsened their lot, many southern blacks left the land. By 1910, over 20 percent of blacks lived in cities, mostly in the South, but many in the North. Black men in the cities took jobs in factories, docks, and railroads or became carpenters, plasterers, or bricklayers. Many black women became domestic servants, seamstresses, or workers in laundries and tobacco factories. By 1910, 54 percent of America's black women held jobs.

Across the South, legally enforced racism peaked after 1900. Local "Jim Crow" laws segregated streetcars, schools, parks, and even cemeteries. The facilities for blacks, including the schools, were invariably inferior. Many southern cities imposed residential segregation by law until the Supreme Court restricted it in 1917. Most labor unions excluded black workers. Disfranchised and trapped in a cycle of poverty, poor education, and discrimination, southern blacks faced bleak prospects.

Fleeing such conditions, two hundred thousand blacks migrated north between 1890 and 1910. Wartime job opportunities drew still more in 1917–1918 (as discussed in Chapter 22), and by 1920, 1.4 million African-Americans lived in the North, mostly in cities. Here, too, racism worsened after 1890 as hard times and immigration heightened social tensions. (Immigrants, competing with blacks for jobs and housing, sometimes exhibited intense racial prejudice.) Segregation, though not imposed by law, was enforced by custom and sometimes by violence. Blacks lived in run-down "colored districts," attended dilapidated schools, and worked at the lowest-paying jobs.

Their ballots—usually cast for the party of Lincoln—brought little political influence. The only black politicians tolerated by Republican party leaders distributed low-level patronage jobs and otherwise kept silent. African-Americans in the segregated army faced hostility from white soldiers and from nearby civilians.

Even the movies preached racism. D. W. Griffith's *The Birth of a Nation* (1915) disparaged blacks and glorified the Ku Klux Klan.

Smoldering racism sometimes exploded in violence. Antiblack rioters in Atlanta in 1906 murdered twenty-five blacks and burned many black homes. From 1900 to 1920, an average of about seventy-five lynchings occurred yearly. Blacks whose assertive behavior or economic aspirations angered whites were especially vulnerable to lynch mobs. Some lynchings involved incredible sadism, with large crowds on hand, victims' bodies mutilated, and graphic photo postcards sold later. Authorities rarely intervened. At a 1916 lynching in Texas, the mayor warned the mob not to damage the hanging tree, on city property.

In such trying times, African Americans developed strong institutions. Black churches proved a bulwark of support. Working African-American mothers, drawing on strategies dating to slavery days, relied on relatives and neighbors for child care. A handful of black higher-education institutions carried on against heavy odds. John Hope, who became president of Atlanta's Morehouse College in 1906, assembled a distinguished faculty, championed African-American education, and fought segregation. His sister Jane (Hope) Lyons was dean of women at Spelman College, another black institution in Atlanta.

The urban black community included black-owned insurance companies and banks, and a small elite of entrepreneurs, teachers, and ministers. Although major-league baseball excluded blacks, a thriving Negro League attracted many African-American fans.

In this racist age, progressives compiled a mixed racial record. Lillian Wald, director of a New York City settlement house, protested racial injustice. Muckraker Ray Stannard Baker documented racism in *Following the Color Line* (1908). Settlement-house worker Mary White Ovington helped found the National Association for the Advancement of Colored People (discussed in the next section) and wrote *Half a Man* (1911), about racism's psychological toll.

But most progressives kept silent as blacks enduring lynching, disfranchisement, and discrimination. Viewing African-Americans, like immigrants, not as potential allies but as part of the problem, white progressives generally supported or tolerated segregated schools and housing; restrictions on black voting rights; strict moral oversight of black communities; and, at best, paternalistic efforts to "uplift" this supposedly backward and childlike people. Viciously racist southern politicians like Mississippi governor James K. Vardaman and South Carolina senator Ben Tillman also supported progressive reforms. Southern woman-suffrage leaders argued that enfranchising women would strengthen white supremacy.

At the national level, President Theodore Roosevelt's racial record was marginally better than that of other politicians in this racist age. He appointed a black to head the Charleston customs house despite white opposition, and closed a Mississippi post office rather than yield to demands to dismiss the black postmistress. In a symbolically important gesture, he dined with Booker T. Washington at the White House. In 1906, however, he approved the dishonorable discharge of an entire regiment of black soldiers in Brownsville, Texas, because some members of the unit, goaded by racist taunts, had killed a local civilian. The "Brownsville Incident" incensed African Americans. (In 1972, after most of the men were dead, Congress reversed the dishonorable discharges.)

Under President Woodrow Wilson, racism became rampant in Washington. A southerner, Wilson displayed at best a patronizing attitude toward blacks, praised the racist movie *The Birth of a Nation,* and allowed southerners in his cabinet and in Congress to impose rigid segregation on all levels of the government.

BLACKS, WOMEN, AND WORKERS ORGANIZE

The organizational strategy so central to progressivism generally also proved useful for groups facing discrimination or exploitation. African-Americans, middle-class women, and wage workers all organized to address their grievances and improve their situation.

African-American Leaders Organize Against Racism   With racism on the rise, Booker T. Washington's self-help message (see Chapter 20) seemed increasingly unrealistic, particularly to northern blacks. Washington's themes would appeal to later generations of African-Americans, but in the early twentieth century, blacks confronting segregation, lynching, and blatant racism tired of his cautious approach. In 1902, William Monroe Trotter, editor of the *Boston Guardian,* a black newspaper, called Washington's go-slow policies "a fatal blow ... to the Negro's political rights and liberty."

Another opponent was the black activist **Ida Wells-Barnett**. Moving to Chicago from Memphis in 1892 after a white mob destroyed her offices, Wells-Barnett mounted a national antilynching campaign, in contrast to Booker T. Washington's public silence on the subject. Documenting the grim facts in *A Red Record* (1895), she toured the United States and Great Britain lecturing against lynching and other racial abuses.

Booker T. Washington's principal black critic was **W. E. B. Du Bois** (1868–1963). After earning a Ph.D. in history from Harvard in 1895, Du Bois taught at Ohio's Wilberforce College, the University of Pennsylvania, and Atlanta University. In *The Souls of Black Folk* (1903), Du Bois rejected Washington's call for patience and his exclusive emphasis on manual skills. Instead, Du Bois demanded full racial equality, including equal educational opportunities, and urged resistance to all forms of racism.

In 1905, under Du Bois's leadership, blacks committed to battling racism held a conference at Niagara Falls. For the next few years, participants in the "Niagara Movement" met annually. Meanwhile, white reformers led by newspaper publisher Oswald Garrison Villard, grandson of abolitionist William Lloyd Garrison, had also grown dissatisfied with Washington's cautiousness. In 1909, Villard and his allies joined with Du Bois and other blacks from the Niagara Movement to form the **National Association for the Advancement of Colored People** (NAACP). This new organization called for sustained activism, including legal challenges, to achieve political equality for blacks and full integration into American life. Attracting the urban black middle class, the NAACP by 1914 had six thousand members in fifty branches.

(Schomburg Center for Research in Black Culture, New York Public Library/Art Resource, NY; Special Collections and Archives, W.E.B. Du Bois Library, University of Massachusetts Amherst)

A New Black Leadership *Ida Wells-Barnett, Chicago-based crusader against lynching, and W. E. B. Du Bois, outspoken critic of Booker T. Washington and author of the classic* The Souls of Black Folk. *The challenge, wrote Du Bois, was to find a way "to be both a Negro and an American."*

Revival of the Woman-Suffrage Movement

As late as 1910, women could vote in only four western states: Wyoming, Utah, Colorado, and Idaho. But women's active role in progressive reform movements revitalized the suffrage cause. A vigorous suffrage movement in Great Britain reverberated in America as well. Like progressivism itself, this revived campaign had grass roots origins. A 1915 suffrage campaign in New York State, though unsuccessful, underscored the new momentum.

Developments in California illustrate both the movement's new momentum and its limitations. In the early 1900s, California's women's clubs shifted from their earlier focus on cultural and domestic themes to become a potent force for reform, addressing city-government and public-school issues. In the process, many women activists became convinced that full citizenship meant the right to vote. While working with labor leaders and male progressives, the woman-suffrage strategists also insisted on the unique role of "organized womanhood" in building a better society. Success came in 1911 when California voters approved woman suffrage.

But "organized womanhood" in California had its limits. Elite and middle-class women, mainly based in Los Angeles and San Francisco, led the campaign. Working-class and farm women played a small role, while African-American, Mexican-American, and Asian-American women were almost totally excluded.

New leaders translated the momentum in New York, California, and other states into a revitalized national movement. In 1900, **Carrie Chapman Catt** of Iowa succeeded Susan B. Anthony as president of the National American Woman

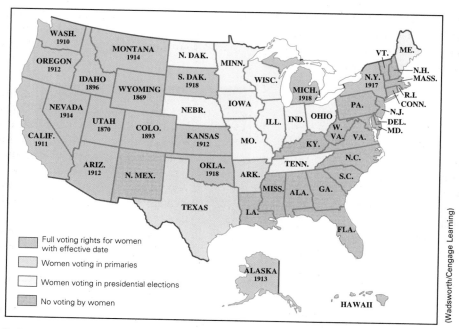

MAP 21.1 Woman Suffrage Before the Nineteenth Amendment

Beginning with Wyoming in 1869, woman suffrage made steady gains in western states before 1920. Farther east, key victories came in New York (1917) and Michigan (1918). But much of the East remained an anti-woman-suffrage bastion throughout the period.

Suffrage Association (NAWSA). Under Catt, NAWSA adopted the so-called Winning Plan: grass-roots organization with tight central coordination, focused on state-level campaigns.

Adopting techniques from the new urban consumer culture, suffragists ran newspaper ads; put up posters; waved banners with catchy slogans; organized parades in open cars; arranged photo opportunities for the media; and distributed fans and other items emblazoned with the suffrage message. Gradually, state after state fell into the suffrage column (see Map 21.1).

As in California (and like progressive organizations generally), NAWSA's membership remained largely white, native-born, and middle class. Few black, immigrant, or working-class women joined. Some upper-class women opposed the reform. Women already enjoyed behind-the-scenes influence, they argued; invading the male realm of electoral politics would tarnish their moral and spiritual role.

Not all suffragists accepted Catt's strategy. Alice Paul, influenced by the British suffragists' militant tactics, rejected NAWSA's state-by-state approach. In 1913, Paul founded the Congressional Union for Woman Suffrage, renamed the National Woman's Party in 1916, to pressure Congress to enact a woman-suffrage constitutional amendment. Targeting "the party in power"—in this case, the Democrats—Paul and her followers in the 1916 election opposed President Woodrow Wilson and congressional Democrats who had failed to endorse a suffrage amendment. In 1917–1918, with the United States at war, the suffrage cause prevailed in New York and Michigan (see Map 21.1) and advanced toward final success (further discussed in Chapter 22).

Enlarging "Woman's Sphere"

The suffrage cause did not exhaust women's energies in the Progressive Era. Women's clubs, settlement-house residents, and individual activists liked Florence Kelley, Alice Hamilton, and Ida Wells-Barnett promoted an array of reforms. These included the campaigns to bring playgrounds and day nurseries to the slums, abolish child labor, and ban unsafe foods and quack remedies. As Jane Addams observed, women's concern for their own families' welfare could also draw them into political activism in an industrial age when hazards came from outside the home as well as inside.

Cultural assumptions about "woman's sphere" weakened as women invaded many fronts. Katherine Bement Davis served as New York City's commissioner of corrections. Emma Goldman crisscrossed the country lecturing on politics, feminism, and modern drama while coediting a radical monthly, *Mother Earth*. A vanguard of women in higher education included the chemist Ellen Richards of the Massachusetts Institute of Technology and Marion Talbot, first dean of women at the University of Chicago.

In *Women and Economics* (1898) and other works, Charlotte Perkins Gilman explored the cultural roots of gender roles and linked women's subordinate status to their economic dependence on men. Confining women to the domestic sphere, Gilman argued, was an evolutionary throwback that had become outdated and inefficient. She advocated gender equality in the workplace; the collectivization of cooking and other domestic tasks; and state-run child-care centers. In the utopian novel *Herland* (1915), Gilman wittily critiqued patriarchal assumptions by injecting three naïve young men into an exclusively female society.

Some Progressive Era reformers challenged laws banning the distribution of contraceptives and birth-control information. Although countless women, particularly the poor, suffered exhaustion and ill health from frequent pregnancies, artificial contraception was widely denounced as immoral. In 1914, **Margaret Sanger** of New York, whose mother had died after bearing eleven children, began her crusade for birth control, a term she coined. When her journal *The Woman Rebel* faced prosecution on obscenity charges, Sanger fled to England. Returning in 1916, she opened the nation's first birth-control clinic in Brooklyn; launched *The Birth Control Review;* and founded the American Birth Control League, forerunner of today's Planned Parenthood Federation.

Meanwhile, another New Yorker, Mary Ware Dennett, had also emerged as an advocate of birth control and sex education. While Sanger championed direct action to promote the cause, Dennett urged lobbying efforts to change the law. Sanger insisted that only physicians should supply contraceptives; Dennett argued for widespread distribution. These differences, plus personal rivalries, produced divisions in the movement.

The birth-control and sex-education movements stand as important legacies of progressivism. At the time, however, conservatives and religious leaders bitterly opposed them. Dennett's frank 1919 informational pamphlet for youth, *The Sex Side of Life,* was long banned as obscene. Not until 1965 did the Supreme Court fully legalize the dissemination of contraceptive materials and information.

Workers Orga-
nize; Socialism
Advances
In this age of organization, labor unions continued to expand. In 1900–1920, the American Federation of Labor (AFL) grew from 625,000 to 4 million members. This still represented only about 20 percent of the industrial work force. With recent immigrants hungry for jobs, union activities posed risks. The boss could always fire an "agitator" and hire a newcomer. Judicial hostility also retarded unionization. In the 1908 *Danbury Hatters* case, for example, the Supreme Court ruled that boycotts in support of strikes were a "conspiracy in restraint of trade," and thus a violation of the Sherman Anti-Trust Act. The AFL's strength remained in the traditional skilled trades, not in the factories, mills, and sweatshops where most immigrants and women worked.

A few unions did try to reach these laborers. The International Ladies' Garment Workers' Union (ILGWU), founded in 1900 by immigrant workers in New York City's needle trades, conducted successful strikes in 1909 and after the 1911 Triangle fire. The 1909 strike began when young Clara Lemlich jumped up as speechmaking droned on at a union meeting and passionately called for a strike. Some picketers lost their jobs or endured police beatings, but the strikers did win higher wages and improved working conditions.

Another union that targeted the most exploited workers was the **Industrial Workers of the World** (IWW), nicknamed the Wobblies, founded in Chicago in 1905. The IWW's leader was William "Big Bill" Haywood, a Utah-born miner who in 1905 was acquitted of complicity in the assassination of an antilabor former governor of Idaho. IWW membership peaked at around thirty thousand, mostly western miners, lumbermen, fruit pickers, and itinerant laborers. It captured the imagination of young cultural rebels in New York City's Greenwich Village, where Haywood, a compelling orator, often visited.

The IWW led strikes of Nevada gold miners; Minnesota iron miners; and timber workers in Louisiana, Texas, and the Northwest. Its victory in a bitter 1912 textile strike in Massachusetts owed much to Elizabeth Gurley Flynn, a fiery Irish-American orator who publicized the cause by sending strikers' children to sympathizers in New York City for temporary care. With an exaggerated reputation for violence, the IWW faced government harassment, especially during World War I, and by 1920 its strength was broken.

Other workers, along with some middle-class Americans, turned to socialism. All socialists advocated an end to capitalism and public ownership of factories, utilities, railroads, and communications systems, but they differed on how to achieve these goals. The revolutionary ideology of German social theorist Karl Marx won a few converts, but the vision of democratic socialism achieved at the ballot box proved more appealing. In 1900 democratic socialists formed the Socialist Party of America (SPA). Members included Morris Hillquit, a New York City labor organizer; Victor Berger, leader of Milwaukee's German socialists; and **Eugene V. Debs**, the Indiana labor leader. Debs, a popular orator, ran for president five times between 1900 and 1920. Many Greenwich Village cultural rebels embraced socialism and supported the radical magazine *The Masses,* founded in 1911.

Socialism's high-water mark came around 1912 when SPA membership stood at 118,000. Debs won more than 900,000 votes for president that year (about 6 percent of the total), and the Socialists elected a congressman (Berger) and many municipal officials. The party published over three hundred newspapers, including foreign-languages papers targeting immigrants.

NATIONAL PROGRESSIVISM, PHASE I: ROOSEVELT AND TAFT, 1901–1913

By around 1905, local and state reform activities were coalescing into a national movement. In 1906 Wisconsin governor Robert La Follette was elected a U.S. senator. Five years earlier, progressivism had found its first national leader, **Theodore Roosevelt**, nicknamed "TR."

Self-righteous, jingoistic, verbose—but also brilliant, politically savvy, and endlessly interesting—Roosevelt became president in 1901 and made the White House a cauldron of activism. Orchestrating public opinion, Roosevelt pursued his goals— labor mediation, consumer protection, corporate regulation, natural-resource conservation, and engagement abroad.

TR's activist approach permanently enlarged the powers of the presidency. His handpicked successor, William Howard Taft, proved politically inept, however, and controversy marked his administration. With the Republicans divided, the Democrat Woodrow Wilson, espousing a somewhat different reform vision, won the presidency in 1912.

Roosevelt's Path to the White House   On September 6, 1901, in Buffalo, anarchist Leon Czolgosz shot William McKinley. At first recovery seemed likely, and Vice President Theodore Roosevelt continued a hiking trip in New York's Adirondack Mountains. But on September 14, McKinley died. At age forty-two, Theodore Roosevelt became president.

Many Republican leaders shuddered at the thought of what one called "that damned cowboy" in the White House. Roosevelt did, indeed, display traits associated with the West. The son of an aristocratic New York family of Dutch origins, he overcame a sickly childhood through bodybuilding exercises and summers in Wyoming to become a model of physical fitness. When his young wife died in 1884, he stoically carried on. Two years on a Dakota ranch deepened his enthusiasm for what he termed "the strenuous life."

Although his social peers scorned politics, Roosevelt served as a state assemblyman, New York City police commissioner, and a U.S. civil-service commissioner. In 1898, fresh from his Cuban exploits, he was elected New York's governor. Two years later, the state's Republican boss, eager to be rid of him, arranged for Roosevelt's nomination as vice president.

As with everything he did, TR found the presidency energizing. "I have been President emphatically ...," he boasted. "I believe in a strong executive." He enjoyed public life and loved the limelight. "When Theodore attends a wedding he wants to be the bride," his daughter observed, "and when he attends a funeral he wants to be the corpse." With his toothy grin, machine-gun speech, and amazing energy, he dominated the political landscape. When he refused to shoot a bear cub on a hunting trip, a shrewd toy maker marketed a cuddly new product, the Teddy Bear.

Labor Disputes, Trustbusting, Railroad Regulation   Events soon tested the new president's political skills. In May 1902, the United Mine Workers Union (UMW) called a strike to gain not only higher wages and shorter hours but also recognition as a union. The mine owners resisted, and in October, with winter looming, TR acted. Summoning the two sides to the White House and threatening to seize the mines, he forced them to accept arbitration. The arbitration commission granted the miners a 10 percent wage increase and reduced their working day from ten to nine hours.

TR's approach to labor disputes differed from that of his predecessors, who typically sided with management, sometimes using troops as strikebreakers. Though not consistently prolabor, he defended workers' right to organize. When a mine owner insisted that the miners' welfare should be left to those "whom God in his infinite wisdom has given control of the [country's] property interests," Roosevelt derided such "arrogant stupidity."

With his elite background, TR neither feared nor much liked business tycoons. The prospect of spending time with "big-money men," he once wrote, "fills me with frank horror." While believing that corporations contributed to national greatness, he also embraced the progressive conviction that they must be regulated. A strict moralist, he held corporations, like individuals, to a high standard.

Yet as a political realist, Roosevelt also understood that many Washington politicians abhorred his views—among them Senator Nelson Aldrich of Rhode Island, a wily defender of business interests. Roosevelt's progressive impulses thus remained in tension with his grasp of power realities in capitalist America.

Another test came when J. P. Morgan in 1901 formed the United States Steel Company, the nation's first billion-dollar business. As public distrust of big corporations deepened, TR dashed to the head of the parade. His 1902 State of the Union message called for breaking up business monopolies, or "trustbusting." Roosevelt's attorney general soon sued the Northern Securities Company, a giant holding company recently created by Morgan and other tycoons to control railroading in the Northwest, for violating the Sherman Anti-Trust Act. On a speaking tour in the summer of 1902, TR called for a "square deal" for all Americans and denounced special treatment for capitalists. "We don't wish to destroy corporations," he said, "but we do wish to make them ... serve the public good." In 1904, a divided Supreme Court ordered the Northern Securities Company dissolved.

The Roosevelt administration filed over forty antitrust lawsuits. In two key rulings in 1911, the Supreme Court ordered the breakup of the Standard Oil Company and the reorganization of the American Tobacco Company to make it less monopolistic.

As the 1904 election neared, Roosevelt made peace with Morgan and other business magnates. The GOP convention that nominated Roosevelt adopted a probusiness platform, stimulating $2 million in corporate contributions. The Democrats, meanwhile, eager to erase the taint of radicalism lingering from the 1890s, embraced the gold standard and nominated a conservative New York judge.

Winning easily, Roosevelt turned to a major goal: railroad regulation. He now saw corporate regulation as more effective than trust-busting, and this shift underlay the 1906 **Hepburn Act**. This law empowered the Interstate Commerce Commission to set maximum railroad rates and to examine railroads' financial records. It also curtailed the railroads' practice of distributing free passes to ministers and other shapers of public opinion.

The Hepburn Act displayed TR's political skills. In a key compromise with Senator Aldrich and other conservatives, he agreed to delay tariff reform in return for railroad regulation. Although failing to fully satisfy reformers, the Hepburn Act did expand the government's regulatory powers.

Consumer Protection   Of all progressive reforms, the campaign against unsafe food, drugs, and medicine proved especially popular. Upton Sinclair's *The Jungle* (1906) graphically described conditions in some meatpacking plants. Wrote Sinclair in one vivid passage, "[A] man could run his hand over these piles of meat and sweep off handfuls of dried dung of rats. These rats were nuisances, and the packers would put poisoned bread out for them, they would die, and then rats, bread, and meat would go into the hoppers together." (The socialist Sinclair also detailed the exploitation of immigrant workers, but this message proved less potent. "I aimed at the nation's heart, but hit it in the stomach," he later lamented.) As women's organizations and consumer groups rallied public opinion, an Agriculture Department chemist, Harvey W. Wiley, helped shape the proposed legislation. Other muckrakers exposed useless or dangerous patent medicines laced with cocaine, opium, or alcohol. One tonic "for treatment of the alcohol habit" contained 26.5 percent alcohol. Peddlers of these nostrums freely claimed that they could cure cancer, grow hair, and restore sexual vigor.

Sensing the public mood, Roosevelt supported the **Pure Food and Drug Act** and the Meat Inspection Act, both passed in 1906. The former outlawed the sale of adulterated foods or drugs and required accurate ingredient labels; the latter imposed strict sanitary rules on meatpackers and set up a federal meat-inspection system. Reputable food processors, meatpackers, and medicinal companies, eager to regain public confidence, supported these measures.

Environmentalism Progressive-Style   Environmental concerns loomed large for Theodore Roosevelt. Describing conservation in his first State of the Union message as America's "most vital internal question," he highlighted an issue that still reverberates.

By 1900, decades of expansion and urban-industrial growth had taken a heavy toll on the land. In the West, mining and timber interests, farmers, ranchers, sheep growers, and preservationists advanced competing land-use claims. While business interests and boosters preached exploitation of the West's resources, and agricultural groups sought government aid for irrigation projects, John Muir's Sierra Club (founded in San Francisco in 1892) urged wilderness preservation. Under a

John Muir on America's Parks and Forests

John Muir (1838–1914), born in Scotland and reared in Wisconsin, founded the Sierra Club, an early environmental organization, in San Francisco in 1892. Intimately familiar with America's wilderness areas through his travels and camping trips, Muir became an eloquent advocate for their preservation. The extracts below are from a series of articles he first published in *The Atlantic Monthly,* and then gathered in book form in 1901.

The tendency nowadays to wander in wildernesses is delightful to see. Thousands of tired, nerve-shaken, over-civilized people are beginning to find out that going to the mountains is going home; that wildness is a necessity; and that mountain parks and [forest] reservations are useful not only as fountains of timber and irrigating rivers, but as fountains of life.... This is fine and natural and full of promise. So also is the growing interest in the care and preservation of forests and wild place in general, and in the half wild parks and gardens of towns.... Few in

these hot, dim, strenuous times are quite sane or free; choked with care like clocks full of dust, laboriously doing so much good and making so much money,—or so little,—they are no longer good for themselves....

But the continent's outer beauty is fast passing away, especially the plant part of it, the most destructible and most universally charming of all.

Only thirty years ago, the great Central Valley of California ... was one bed of golden and purple flowers. Now it is ploughed and pastured out of existence, gone forever.... [T]he noble forests [of the Sierra mountains] ... are sadly hacked and trampled, ... the ground, once divinely beautiful, is desolate and repulsive, like a face ravaged by disease. This is true also of many other Pacific Coast and Rocky Mountain valleys and forests. The same fate, sooner or later, is awaiting them all, unless awakening public opinion comes forward to stop it....

The forests of America, however slighted by man, must have been a great

law passed in 1891, Presidents Harrison and Cleveland had set aside some 35 million acres of public lands as national forests.

In the early twentieth century, amid spreading cities and factories, a wilderness vogue swept America. Popular writers evoked the tang of the campfire and the lure of the primitive. Summer camps, as well as the Boy Scouts (founded in 1910) and Girl Scouts (1912), gave city children a taste of wilderness living. Socially prominent easterners embraced the cause (see Going to the Source).

Between the wilderness enthusiasts and the developers stood government experts like Gifford Pinchot who saw the public domain as a resource to be managed wisely. Appointed by TR in 1905 to head the new U.S. Forest Service, Pinchot stressed not preservation but conservation—the planned use of forest lands for public and commercial purposes.

Wilderness advocates welcomed Pinchot's opposition to mindless exploitation, but worried that the multiple-use approach would despoil wilderness areas. "[T]rees are for human use," conceded a Sierra Club member, but added that these uses included "the spiritual wealth of us all, as well as ... the material wealth of some."

delight to God; for they were the best He ever planted. The whole continent was a garden, and from the beginning it seemed to be favored above all the other wild parks and gardens of the globe.... American forests! the glory of the world!... [F]rom the east to the west, from the north to the south, they are rich beyond thought, immortal, immeasurable....

So they appeared a few centuries ago.... The Indians with stone axes could do them no more harm than could gnawing beavers and browsing moose.... But when the steel axe of the white man rang out on the startled air their doom was sealed.... [Here Muir discusses late-19th century legislation that permitted unregulated logging and pasturing on western lands, with little government oversight or management.]

Land commissioners and Secretaries of the Interior have repeatedly called attention to this ruinous state of affairs, and asked Congress to enact the requisite legislation for reasonable reform. But, busied with tariffs, etc., Congress has given no heed to these or other appeals, and our forests, the most valuable and the most destructible of all the natural resources of the country, are being robbed and burned more rapidly than ever....

Any fool can destroy trees. They cannot run away; and ... [f]ew that fell trees plant them.... Through all the ... eventful centuries ... God has cared for these trees, saved them from drought, disease, avalanches, and a thousand straining, leveling tempests and floods; but he cannot save them from fools—only Uncle Sam can do that.

Questions

1. *In Muir's view, what benefits can the citizens of urban-industrial America gain from the nation's parks, forests, and wilderness areas?*

2. *Do you agree with Muir that preserving wilderness areas should be left entirely to the federal government? Why, or why not?*

Go to www.cengagebrain.com for additional primary sources on this period.

Source: John Muir, *Our National Parks* (Boston: Houghton Mifflin, 1901), 1–2, 5–6, 331, 334–335, 344, 364–365.

At heart Roosevelt was a preservationist. In 1903, he spent a blissful few days camping in Yosemite National Park with John Muir. He once compared "the destruction of a species" to the loss of "all the works of some great writer." But TR the politician backed the conservationists' call for planned development. He supported the **National Reclamation Act** (1902), which designated the money from public-land sales for water management in arid western regions, and set up the Reclamation Service to construct dams and irrigation projects.

This measure (also known as the Newlands Act for its sponsor, a Nevada congressman) ranks with the Northwest Ordinance of 1787 for promoting the settlement and productivity of a vast continental region—this one between the Rockies and the Pacific. Arizona's Roosevelt Dam spurred the growth of Phoenix; dams and waterways in Idaho's Snake River valley stimulated the production of potatoes and other commodities on hitherto barren acres. The law required farmers who benefited from these projects to repay the construction costs, creating a federal fund for further projects. The Newlands Act and other measures of these years transformed the West from a series of isolated "island settlements" into a thriving, interconnected region.

The competition for scarce water resources in the West sparked bitter political battles. The Los Angeles basin, for example, with 40 percent of California's population in 1900, found itself with only 2 percent of the state's surface water. In 1907, the city derailed a Reclamation Service project intended for the farmers of California's Owens Valley, more than 230 miles to the north, and diverted the precious water to Los Angeles.

Meanwhile, President Roosevelt, embracing Pinchot's multiple-use land-management program, set aside 200 million acres of public land (85 million of them in Alaska) as national forests, mineral reserves, and waterpower sites. But the national-forest provisions provoked corporate opposition, and in 1907 Congress revoked the president's authority to create national forests in six timber-rich western states. Before signing the bill, Roosevelt designated 16 million more acres in the six states as national forests. TR also created fifty-three wildlife reserves, sixteen national monuments, and five new national parks. Congress established the National Park Service in 1916 to manage them.

In 1908, Gifford Pinchot organized a White House conservation conference for the nation's governors. There, experts discussed the utilitarian benefits of resource management. John Muir and other wilderness preservationists were not invited. But the struggle between wilderness purists and multiple-use advocates went on. Rallying support through magazine articles, preservationist groups and women's organizations saved a large grove of California's giant redwoods and a lovely stretch of the Maine coastline from logging.

The Sierra Club lost a battle to save the Hetch Hetchy Valley in Yosemite National Park when Congress in 1913 approved a dam on the Tuolumne River to provide water and hydroelectric power for San Francisco, 150 miles away. (Other opponents of the dam were less interested in preserving Hetch Hetchy as a wilderness than in developing it for tourism.) While the preservationists lost this battle, the controversy focused attention on environmental issues, as Americans for the first time weighed the aesthetic implications of a major public-works project.

Taft in the White House, 1909–1913   Roosevelt had pledged not to seek a third term, and as the 1908 election approached, the Republican Party's most conservative leaders regained control. They nominated TR's choice, Secretary of War **William Howard Taft**, for president but selected a conservative vice-presidential nominee and adopted a deeply conservative platform. The Democrats, meanwhile, nominated William Jennings Bryan for a third time. The Democratic platform called for a lower tariff, denounced the trusts, and embraced the cause of labor.

With Roosevelt's endorsement, Taft coasted to victory. But Bryan bested the Democrats' 1904 vote total by 1.3 million, and progressive Republican state candidates outran the national ticket. Overall, the outcome suggested a lull in the reform movement, not its end.

Republican conservatives welcomed Roosevelt's departure to hunt big game in Africa. Quipped Senator Aldrich, "Let every lion do its duty." But even an ocean away, TR's presence remained vivid. "When I am addressed as 'Mr. President,'" Taft wrote him, "I turn to see whether you are not at my elbow."

Taft, from a prominent Ohio political family, differed from TR in many respects. Whereas TR kept in fighting trim, Taft was obese. Roosevelt had installed a boxing ring in the White House; Taft preferred golf. TR loved speechmaking and battling evildoers; Taft disliked controversy. His happiest days would come later, as chief justice of the United States.

Pledged to support TR's program, Taft backed the Mann-Elkins Act (1910), which beefed up the Interstate Commerce Commission's regulatory authority and extended it to telephone and telegraph companies. Taft's administration actually prosecuted more antitrust cases than had Roosevelt's, but with little publicity. To the public, TR remained the mighty trustbuster.

The reform spotlight, meanwhile, shifted to Congress, where a group of reform-minded Republicans, nicknamed the Insurgents, including Senators La Follette and Albert Beveridge of Indiana and Congressman George Norris of Nebraska, had challenged their party's conservative congressional leadership. In 1909, the Insurgents and Taft fought a bruising battle over the tariff. Taft first backed the Insurgents' call for a lower tariff. But when high-tariff advocates in Congress pushed through a measure raising duties on hundreds of items, Taft not only signed it but praised it extravagantly, infuriating the Insurgents.

The Insurgents next set their sights on House Speaker Joseph G. Cannon of Illinois, a reactionary Republican who prevented most reform bills from even reaching a vote. In March 1910, the Insurgents joined with the Democrats to trim Cannon's power by removing him from the pivotal Rules Committee. This directly challenged Taft, who supported Cannon.

The so-called Ballinger-Pinchot controversy widened the rift. Taft's interior secretary, Richard Ballinger, was a Seattle lawyer who favored unregulated private development of natural resources. In one of several decisions galling to conservationists, Ballinger in 1909 approved the sale of several million acres of coal-rich public lands in Alaska to a Seattle business consortium that promptly resold it to J. P. Morgan and other financiers. When an Interior Department official protested, he was fired. In true muckraking style, he went public, blasting Ballinger in a *Collier's* magazine article. When Gifford Pinchot of the Forest Service also criticized Ballinger, he too got the ax. TR's supporters seethed.

Upon Roosevelt's return to America in June 1910, Pinchot met the boat. Openly breaking with Taft, Roosevelt campaigned for Insurgent candidates in that year's midterm elections. In a speech that alarmed conservatives, he endorsed the radical idea of reversing by popular vote judicial rulings that struck down reform laws favored by progressives. Borrowing a term from Herbert Croly's *The Promise of American Life,* TR proposed a "New Nationalism" that would powerfully engage the federal government in reform.

The Democrats captured the House in 1910, a coalition of Democrats and Insurgent Republicans controlled the Senate, and TR increasingly sounded like a presidential candidate.

The Four-Way Election of 1912   In February 1912, Roosevelt announced his candidacy for the Republican nomination. But Taft wanted a second term. Roosevelt generally walloped Taft in the Republican state primaries and conventions. Taft controlled the party machinery, however, and the

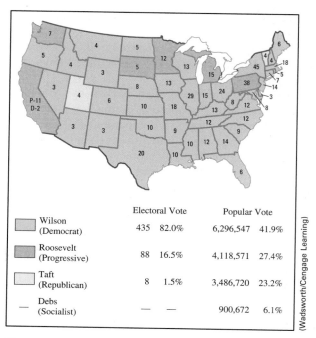

	Electoral Vote		Popular Vote	
Wilson (Democrat)	435	82.0%	6,296,547	41.9%
Roosevelt (Progressive)	88	16.5%	4,118,571	27.4%
Taft (Republican)	8	1.5%	3,486,720	23.2%
Debs (Socialist)	—	—	900,672	6.1%

(Wadsworth/Cengage Learning)

MAP 21.2 The Election of 1912

Republican convention in Chicago disqualified many of Roosevelt's hard-won delegates. Outraged, TR's backers walked out and formed the **Progressive Party**. What had been a general term for a broad reform movement now became the official name of a political party. Riding an emotional high, the cheering delegates nominated their hero, with California senator Hiram Johnson as his running mate.

"I feel fit as a bull moose," Roosevelt trumpeted, giving his organization its nickname, the Bull Moose Party. The convention platform endorsed most reform causes of the day, including lower tariffs, woman suffrage, business regulation, the abolition of child labor, the eight-hour workday, workers' compensation, the direct primary, and the popular election of senators. The new party attracted a diverse following, united mainly by affection for Roosevelt.

Meanwhile, the reform spirit had also infused the Democratic Party. In New Jersey in 1910, voters had elected a political novice, **Woodrow Wilson**, as governor. A "Wilson for President" boom soon arose, and at the Democratic convention in Baltimore, Wilson won the nomination, defeating several established party leaders.

In the campaign, Taft more or less gave up, satisfied to have kept his party safe for conservatism. The Socialist candidate Eugene Debs proposed an end to capitalism and a socialized economic order. TR preached his New Nationalism: corporations must be regulated in the public interest, the welfare of workers and consumers safeguarded, and the environment protected.

Wilson, by contrast, called his political vision the "New Freedom." Warning that corporations were choking off opportunity for ordinary Americans, he nostalgically evoked an era of small government, small businesses, and free competition. "The history of liberty," he said, "is the history of the limitation of governmental power, not the increase of it."

Roosevelt outpolled Taft by 630,000 votes, but the Republicans' split proved costly (see Map 21.2). Wilson easily won the presidency, and the Democrats took both houses of Congress. More than 900,000 voters opted for Debs and socialism.

The 1912 election linked the Democrats firmly with reform (except on the issue of race)—a link that Franklin D. Roosevelt would strengthen in the 1930s. TR's third-party campaign demonstrated the continued appeal of reform among many grass-roots Republicans.

NATIONAL PROGRESSIVISM, PHASE II: WOODROW WILSON, 1913–1917

The son and grandson of Presbyterian ministers, Wilson grew up in Virginia and Georgia in a churchly atmosphere that shaped his oratorical style and moral outlook. Despite a learning disability (probably dyslexia), he graduated from Princeton and earned a Ph.D. in political science from Johns Hopkins University. Joining Princeton's faculty, he became its president in 1902. A rigid unwillingness to compromise cost him faculty support, and in 1910 Wilson resigned to enter politics. Three years later, he was president of the United States.

Impressive in bearing, with piercing gray eyes, Wilson was an eloquent orator. But the idealism that inspired people could also alienate them. At his best, he excelled at political dealmaking. "He can walk on dead leaves and make no more noise than a tiger," declared one awed politician. But under pressure, he could retreat into a fortress of absolute certitude. As president, all these facets of his personality would come into play.

The progressive movement gained fresh momentum in Wilson's first term. Under his leadership, Congress enacted an array of reform measures. Despite the nostalgia for simpler times in his campaign rhetoric, he proved ready to address the problems of the new corporate order.

Tariff and Banking Reform   Lowering tariff rates—long a goal of southern and agrarian Democrats—headed Wilson's agenda. Many progressives agreed that high protective tariffs increased corporate profits at the public's expense. Breaking a precedent dating from Thomas Jefferson's presidency, Wilson appeared personally before Congress in April 1913 to read his tariff message. A low-tariff bill quickly passed the House but bogged down in the Senate. Showing his flair for drama, Wilson denounced the lobbyists flooding into Washington. His censure led to a Senate investigation of lobbyists and of senators who profited from high tariffs. Stung by the publicity, the Senate slashed tariff rates even more than the House had done. The Underwood-Simmons Tariff reduced rates an average of 15 percent.

Wilson again addressed Congress in June, this time calling for banking and currency reform. The nation's banking system clearly needed overhauling. Totally decentralized, it lacked a strong central institution, a "lender of last resort" to help banks survive fiscal crises. A financial panic in 1907, when many banks had failed, remained a vivid memory.

No consensus existed on specifics, however. Many reformers wanted a publicly controlled central banking system. But the nation's bankers, whose Senate spokesman was Nelson Aldrich, favored a privately controlled central bank similar to the Bank of England. The large banks of New York City advocated a strong central bank, preferably privately owned, so they could better compete with London banks in international finance. Others, including influential Virginia congressman Carter Glass, opposed any central banking authority, public or private.

No banking expert, Wilson did insist that the monetary system ultimately be publicly controlled. As the bargaining unfolded, Wilson's behind-the-scenes role proved crucial. The result was the **Federal Reserve Act** (1913). This compromise measure created twelve regional Federal Reserve banks under mixed public/private control. Each could issue U.S. dollars, called Federal Reserve notes, to the banks in its district to make loans to corporations and individual borrowers. Overall control of the system was shared by the heads of the twelve regional banks and the members of a Washington-based Federal Reserve Board, appointed by the president for fourteen-year terms.

The Federal Reserve Act stands as Wilson's greatest legislative achievement. Initially, the Federal Reserve Board's authority was diffuse, but eventually "the Fed" grew into the strong central monetary institution it remains today, setting interest rates and adopting fiscal policies to prevent financial panics, promote economic growth, and combat inflation.

Regulating Business; Aiding Workers and Farmers

In 1914, Wilson and Congress turned to that perennial progressive cause, business regulation. The two laws that resulted sought a common goal, but embodied different approaches.

The Federal Trade Commission Act took an administrative approach. This law created a new "watchdog" agency, the **Federal Trade Commission** (FTC), with power to investigate violations of federal regulations, require regular reports from corporations, and issue cease-and-desist orders (subject to judicial review) when it found unfair methods of competition.

The Clayton Antitrust Act, by contrast, took a legal approach. It listed corporate activities that could lead to federal lawsuits. The Sherman Act of 1890, although outlawing business practices in restraint of trade, had been vague about details. The Clayton Act spelled out specific illegal practices, such as selling at a loss to undercut competitors.

Because Wilson appointed some conservatives with big-business links to the FTC, this agency initially proved ineffective. But under the Clayton Act, the Wilson administration filed antitrust suits against nearly a hundred corporations.

Leading a party long identified with workers, Wilson supported labor unions and workers' right to organize. He also endorsed a Clayton Act clause exempting strikes, boycotts, and picketing from the antitrust laws' prohibition of actions in restraint of trade.

In 1916 (an election year), Wilson and congressional Democrats enacted three important worker-protection laws. The Keating-Owen Act barred from interstate commerce products manufactured by child labor. (This law was declared unconstitutional in 1918, as was a similar law enacted in 1919.) The Adamson Act established an eight-hour day for interstate railway workers. The Workmen's Compensation Act provided accident and injury protection to federal workers. As we have seen, however, Wilson's sympathies for the underdog stopped at the color line.

Other 1916 laws helped farmers. The Federal Farm Loan Act and the Federal Warehouse Act enabled farmers, using land or crops as collateral, to get low-interest federal loans. The Federal Highway Act, providing funds for highway programs, benefited not only the new automobile industry but also farmers plagued by bad roads.

Progressivism and the Constitution

The probusiness bias of the courts weakened a bit in the Progressive Era. In *Muller v. Oregon* (1908), the Supreme Court upheld an Oregon law limiting female laundry and factory workers to a ten-hour workday. Defending this law's constitutionality, Boston attorney **Louis Brandeis** not only cited legal precedent, but offered economic, medical, and sociological evidence documenting the ways long hours harmed women workers. While making an exception based on gender, the Court continued to hold (as it had in the 1905 case *Lochner v. New York*) that in general such worker-protection laws violated the due-process clause of the Fourteenth Amendment. Nevertheless, *Muller v. Oregon* marked an advance in making the legal system more responsive to new social realities.

In 1916, Woodrow Wilson nominated Brandeis to the Supreme Court. Disapproving of Brandeis's innovative approach to the law, the conservative American Bar Association protested, as did Republican congressional leaders and other prominent conservative voices. Anti-Semites opposed Brandeis because he was a Jew. But Wilson stood firm, and Brandeis won Senate confirmation.

These years also produced four Constitutional amendments, the first since 1870. The Sixteenth (ratified in 1913) empowered Congress to tax incomes, thus ending a long legal battle. A Civil War income tax had been phased out in 1872. Congress had again imposed an income tax as part of an 1894 tariff act, but the Supreme Court had promptly denounced it as "communistic" and ruled it unconstitutional. With the constitutional issue resolved, Congress in 1913 imposed a graduated federal income tax with a maximum rate of 7 percent on incomes over five hundred thousand dollars. Income-tax revenues helped pay for the government's expanded regulatory duties under various progressive reform measures.

The Seventeenth Amendment (1913) provided for the direct election of U.S. senators by the voters, rather than their selection by state legislatures, as described in Article I of the Constitution. This reform, earlier advocated by the Populists, sought to make the Senate less subject to corporate influence and more responsive to the popular will.

The Eighteenth Amendment (1919) prohibited the manufacture, sale, or importation of "intoxicating liquors." The Nineteenth (1920) granted women the vote. This remarkable wave of amendments underscored the Progressive Movement's profound impact on the political landscape.

1916: Wilson Edges Out Hughes

As Wilson won renomination in 1916, the Republicans turned to Charles Evans Hughes, a Supreme Court justice and former New York governor. Progressive Party loyalists again courted Theodore Roosevelt. But TR, now obsessed with the war in Europe (covered in the next chapter), told them to endorse Hughes, which they did, effectively removing the Progressive Party from the contest.

With the Republicans more or less reunited, the election was extremely close. War-related issues loomed large. Wilson won the popular vote, but the Electoral College outcome remained in doubt for several weeks as the California tally see-sawed back and forth. Ultimately, Wilson carried the state by fewer than four thousand votes and, with it, the election.

The progressive movement lost momentum as attention turned from reform to war. Final success for the prohibition and woman-suffrage campaigns came in 1919–1920, and Congress enacted a few reform measures in the 1920s. But, overall, the movement faded as America marched to war in 1917.

CHRONOLOGY
1900–1920

1900	International Ladies' Garment Workers' Union (ILGWU) founded. Socialist Party of America organized. Theodore Dreiser, *Sister Carrie*. Carrie Chapman Catt becomes president of the National American Woman Suffrage Association (NAWSA).
1901	Assassination of McKinley; Theodore Roosevelt becomes president. J.P. Morgan forms United States Steel Company.
1902	Jane Addams, *Democracy and Social Ethics*.
1903	W. E. B. Du Bois, *The Souls of Black Folk*. Wright brothers' flight.
1904	Theodore Roosevelt elected president in his own right. Lincoln Steffens, *The Shame of the Cities*.
1905	Industrial Workers of the World (IWW) organized.
1906	Upton Sinclair, *The Jungle*.
1907	William James, *Pragmatism*.
1908	William Howard Taft elected president. Model T Ford introduced.
1909	Ballinger-Pinchot controversy. National Association for the Advancement of Colored People (NAACP) founded. Herbert Croly, *The Promise of American Life*. Daniel Burnham, Plan of Chicago.
1910	Insurgents curb power of House Speaker Joseph Cannon.
1911	Triangle Shirtwaist Company fire.

1912   Republican Party split; Progressive (Bull Moose) Party founded.
Woodrow Wilson elected president.
International Opium Treaty.

1913   Sixteenth Amendment (Congress empowered to tax incomes).
Seventeenth Amendment (direct election of U.S. senators).

1914   American Social Hygiene Association founded.
Narcotics Act (Harrison Act).

1915   D. W. Griffith, *The Birth of a Nation.*

1916   John Dewey, *Democracy and Education.*
Margaret Sanger opens nation's first birth-control clinic in Brooklyn, New York.
National Park Service created.
Louis Brandeis appointed to Supreme Court.

1919   Eighteenth Amendment (national prohibition).

1920   Nineteenth Amendment (woman suffrage).

CONCLUSION

What we call the progressive movement began as preachers, novelists, journalists, photographers, and painters highlighted appalling conditions in America's cities and factories. Intellectuals offered ideas for reform through the creative use of government.

At the local and state level, reform-minded politicians, together with a host of reform organizations, worked to combat political corruption, make cities safer and more beautiful, regulate corporations, and improve conditions for workers.

Progressivism had its coercive side. Some reformers concentrated on regulating urban amusements and banning alcohol consumption. Racism and hostility to immigrants are part of the progressive legacy as well.

Progressivism crested as a national movement under presidents Theodore Roosevelt and Woodrow Wilson. These years saw advances in corporate regulation, environmental conservation, banking reform, and consumer and worker protection. Constitutional amendments granted Congress the power to tax incomes and provided for the direct election of senators, woman suffrage, and national prohibition of alcohol—all aspects of the progressive impulse.

Along with specific laws, progressivism's legacy included an enlarged view of government's role in society. Progressives expanded the meaning of democracy and challenged the cynical view of government as a tool of the rich and powerful. They did not seek "big government" for its own sake. Rather, they recognized that in an industrial age of great cities and concentrated corporate power, government, too, must grow to serve the public interest and protect society's more vulnerable members.

This ideal sometimes faltered in practice. Reform laws and regulatory agencies often fell short of their purpose as bureaucratic routine set in. Reforms designed to promote the public good sometimes mainly benefited special interests. Corporations proved adept at manipulating the new regulatory state to their own advantage.

Still, the Progressive Era stands as a time when American politics seriously confronted the social upheavals caused by industrialization. It was also an era when Americans learned to think of government as an arena of possibility where public issues and social problems could be thrashed out. The next great reform movement, the New Deal of the 1930s, would draw on progressivism's legacy.

22

GLOBAL INVOLVEMENTS AND WORLD WAR I, 1902–1920

DEFINING AMERICA'S WORLD ROLE, 1902–1914

The annexation of Hawaii, the Spanish-American War, the occupation of the
Philippines, and other developments in the 1890s (see Chapter 20) signaled America's
growing involvement abroad, especially in Asia and Latin America. These foreign
engagements reflected a desire to assert American power as European nations built
colonial empires, to protect and extend U.S. business investments abroad, and to
impose American standards of good government beyond the nation's borders. This
process of foreign engagement continued after 1900.

America's dealings with Asian and Latin American nations in these years were
shaped by both economic and ideological considerations. U.S. policy makers
wanted to expand corporate America's access to foreign markets and raw materials.
But they also believed that other societies would benefit by adopting the principles
of democracy, individual freedom, and the rule of law. Sometimes economic
motives predominated, sometimes ideological, and often both, as the United States
exerted its power beyond its borders.

The "Open Door":
Competing for
the China Market

As the campaign to suppress the Philippines insurrection
dragged on, American policy makers turned their attention
farther west, to China. Their aim was not territorial but
commercial. Proclaimed Indiana senator Albert J. Beveridge

in 1898, "American factories are making more than the American people can use; American soil is producing more than they can consume …[T]he trade of the world must and shall be ours."

The China market beckoned. Textile producers dreamed of clothing China's millions; investors envisioned railroad construction. As China's 250-year-old Manchu Qing empire faltered, U.S. business people watched carefully. In 1896, a consortium of New York capitalists formed a company to promote trade and railroad investment in China.

But other nations were also eyeing the China market. Some pressured the weak Manchu rulers to give them exclusive trading and development rights in designated regions, or "spheres of influence." In 1896, Russia won both the right to build a railway across the Chinese province of Manchuria and a long-term lease on much of the region. In 1897, Germany secured a ninety-nine-year lease on a Chinese port as well as mining and railroad rights in the adjacent province. The British won concessions as well.

In 1899, U.S. Secretary of State John Hay asked the major European powers to assure American trading rights in China by opening the ports in their spheres of influence to all countries. The nations gave noncommittal answers, but Hay blithely announced their acceptance of the principle of an "Open Door" to American business in China.

Hay's Open Door note showed how commercial considerations were increasingly influencing American foreign policy. It reflected a form of economic expansionism historians have called "informal empire." The U.S. government did not seek Chinese territory, but it did want access to Chinese markets for American businesses.

As Hay pursued this effort, a more urgent threat emerged. For years, antiforeign feeling had simmered in China, fanned by the aged Qing Dynasty empress, who hated the West's growing influence. In 1899, a fanatical antiforeign secret society known as the Harmonious Righteous Fists (called "Boxers" by Western journalists) killed thousands of foreigners and Chinese Christians. In June 1900, the Boxers occupied Beijing (Peking), the Chinese capital, and besieged the foreign legations. The United States contributed twenty-five hundred soldiers to an international army that marched on Beijing, quashed the **Boxer Rebellion**, and rescued the occupants of the threatened legations.

The Boxers' defeat further weakened China's government. Fearing that the regime's collapse would allow European powers to carve up China, Hay issued a second, more important, series of **Open Door notes** in 1900. He reaffirmed the principle of open trade in China for all nations and announced America's determination to preserve China's territorial and administrative integrity. In the 1930s, when Japanese expansionism menaced China, Hay's policy helped shape the American response.

Along with U.S. economic expansion in China came missionary activity. American Protestant missionaries had come to Hawaii as early as the 1820s, and by the late nineteenth century they had reached China. Indeed, by 1900 some five thousand U.S. missionaries were active in China, Africa, India, and elsewhere. While proclaiming their religious message, the missionaries also spread American influence globally and blazed the way for U.S. economic expansion. As a U.S. diplomat in China wrote in 1895: "Missionaries are the pioneers for American trade and commerce…. The missionary, inspired by holy zeal, goes everywhere, and by degrees foreign trade and commerce follow."

The Panama Canal: Hardball Diplomacy

Traders had long dreamed of a canal across the forty-mile-wide ribbon of land joining North and South America, to eliminate the hazardous voyage around South America. In 1879 a French company secured permission from Colombia to build a canal across Panama, then part of Colombia (see Map 22.1). But mismanagement and yellow fever doomed the project, and by 1888 it was bankrupt. Seeking to recoup its losses, the French company offered its assets, including the concession from Colombia, to the United States for $109 million.

America was in an expansionist mood. In 1902, after the French lowered their price to $40 million, Congress authorized President Theodore Roosevelt to accept the offer. The following year, Secretary of State Hay signed an agreement with a Colombian diplomat granting the United States a ninety-nine-year lease on the proposed canal for a down payment of $10 million and an annual fee of $250,000. But the Colombian senate, seeking a better deal, rejected the agreement. An outraged Roosevelt privately denounced the Colombians as "greedy little anthropoids."

Determined to have his canal, Roosevelt found a willing collaborator in Philippe Bunau-Varilla, an official of the bankrupt French company. Dismayed that his company might lose its $40 million, Bunau-Varilla organized a "revolution" in Panama from a New York hotel room. While his wife stitched a flag, he wrote a declaration of independence and a constitution for the new nation. When the "revolution" occurred as scheduled on November 3, 1903, a U.S. warship hovered offshore. Proclaiming Panama's independence, Bunau-Varilla appointed himself its first ambassador to the United States. John Hay quickly recognized the newly hatched nation and signed a treaty with Bunau-Varilla granting the United States a ten-mile-wide strip of land across Panama "in perpetuity" (that is, forever) on the terms earlier rejected by Colombia. Theodore Roosevelt later summed up the episode: "I took the Canal Zone, and let Congress debate, and while the debate goes on, the canal does also."

The U.S. canal builders' first challenge was the yellow fever that had haunted the French. Dr. Walter Reed of the Army Medical Corps led this effort. Earlier, in Cuba, Reed and his research team had used themselves and army volunteers as experimental subjects to prove that mosquitoes breeding in stagnant water spread the yellow fever virus. In Panama, Reed's large-scale drainage project eradicated the disease-bearing mosquito—a remarkable public-health achievement. Construction began in 1906, and in 1914 the first ship sailed through the **Panama Canal**. In 1921, implicitly conceding the dubious methods used to acquire the Canal Zone, the U.S. Senate voted a payment of $25 million to Colombia. But the ill feeling generated by Theodore Roosevelt's actions, combined with other instances of U.S. interventionism, would long shadow U.S.-Latin American relations.

Roosevelt and Taft Assert U.S. Power in Latin America and Asia

While the Panama Canal remains this era's best-known foreign-policy achievement, other episodes underscored Washington's growing readiness to assert U.S. power and protect U.S. business interests in Latin America (see Map 22.1) and Asia. In 1902, German, British, and Italian warships blockaded and bombarded the ports of Venezuela, which had defaulted on its debts to European investors. The standoff ended when President Theodore Roosevelt pressed all sides to settle the dispute through arbitration.

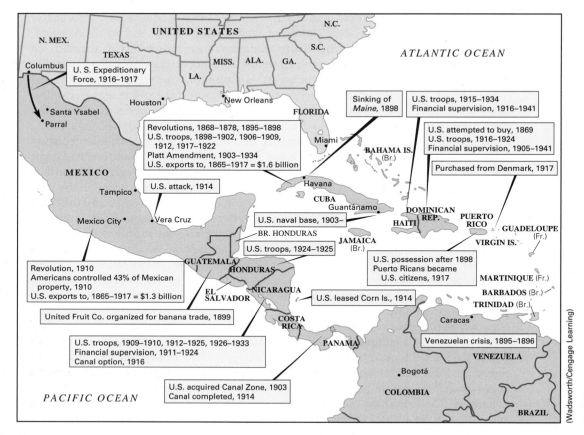

MAP 22.1 U.S. Hegemony in the Caribbean and Latin America, 1900–1941

Through many interventions, territorial acquisitions, and robust economic expansion, the United States became the predominant power in Latin America in the early twentieth century. Acting on Theodore Roosevelt's assertion of a U.S. right to combat "wrongdoing" in Latin America and the Caribbean, the United States dispatched troops to the region, where they met nationalist opposition.

A second crisis flared in 1904 when several European nations threatened to invade the Dominican Republic, a Caribbean island nation that had also defaulted on its debts. Roosevelt reacted swiftly. If any nation intervened, he believed, it should be the United States. While denying territorial ambitions in the region, Roosevelt in December 1904 declared that "chronic wrongdoing" by any Latin American nation would justify U.S. intervention.

This pronouncement has been called "the Roosevelt Corollary" to the 1823 Monroe Doctrine, which had warned European powers against meddling in Latin America. Now Roosevelt asserted that "wrongdoing" (a word he left undefined) gave the United States the right to step in. Suiting actions to words, the Roosevelt administration took over the Dominican Republic's customs service for two years and managed its foreign debt. Roosevelt once summed up his foreign-policy approach by quoting what he said was an African proverb, "Speak softly and carry a big stick."

The foreign policy of the Taft administration (1909–1913) focused on advancing American commercial interests, a policy some called "dollar diplomacy." A U.S.-backed revolution in Nicaragua in 1911 brought to power Adolfo Díaz, an officer of an American-owned mine. Washington, fearing growing British influence in Nicaragua, also worried that a foreign power might build a canal across Nicaragua to rival the Panama Canal. American bankers lent Díaz's government $1.5 million, in exchange for control of Nicaragua's national bank, customs service, and railroad. When a revolt against Díaz broke out in 1912, Taft sent marines to protect the bankers' investment. Except for one brief interval, they remained until 1933.

In Asia, too, Roosevelt and Taft sought to project U.S. power and advance American business interests. In 1900, exploiting the turmoil caused by the Boxer uprising, Russian troops occupied Manchuria, and Russia promoted its commercial interests by building railroads. This alarmed the Japanese, who also had designs on Manchuria and nearby Korea. Japan and Russia went to war in 1904 after a surprise Japanese attack destroyed Russian ships anchored in a Manchurian port. As Japan completely dominated Russia, an Asian power for the first time checked European imperialist expansion.

Roosevelt, while pleased to see Russian expansionism challenged, believed that a Japanese victory would disrupt the Asian balance of power and threaten America's position in the Philippines. Accordingly, he invited Japan and Russia to a peace conference at Portsmouth, New Hampshire. In September 1905, the two rivals signed a peace treaty. Russia recognized Japan's rule in Korea and made other territorial concessions. After this outcome, curbing Japanese expansionism—peacefully, if possible—became America's major objective in Asia. For his role in ending the war, Roosevelt received the Nobel Peace Prize.

In 1906, U.S.-Japanese relations soured when the San Francisco school board, reflecting prejudice against Asian immigrants, assigned all Asian children to segregated schools. When Japan angrily protested, Roosevelt summoned the school board to Washington and persuaded them to reverse this discriminatory policy. In return, in 1908 the administration negotiated a "gentlemen's agreement" with Japan by which Tokyo voluntarily halted Japanese emigration to America. Racist attitudes and discriminatory laws against Japanese in California continued to poison U.S.-Japanese relations, however.

While Californians warned of the "yellow peril," Japanese journalists, eyeing America's military strength and involvement in Asia, spoke of a "white peril." In 1907, Roosevelt ordered sixteen gleaming U.S. battleships on a "training operation" to Japan. Although officially friendly in intent, this "Great White Fleet" underscored America's naval might.

President Taft's policies in Asia extended the focus on dollar diplomacy, which in this case meant promoting U.S. commercial interests in China—the goal Secretary of State Hay had sought with his Open Door notes. A plan for a U.S.-financed railroad in Manchuria failed, however. Not only did U.S. bankers find the project too risky, but Russia and Japan signed a treaty carving up Manchuria for commercial purposes, freezing out the Americans.

Wilson and Latin America   Taking office in 1913, Woodrow Wilson criticized his Republican predecessors' expansionist policies. The United States, he pledged, would "never again seek one additional foot of territory by conquest." But he, too, soon intervened in Latin America. In 1915, after upheavals in Haiti and the Dominican Republic (two small nations sharing the Caribbean island of Santo Domingo), Wilson sent in U.S. marines, who brutally suppressed Haitians who resisted. A Haitian constitution favorable to U.S. commercial interests was overwhelmingly ratified in a 1918 vote supervised by the marines. The marines occupied the Dominican Republic until 1924 and Haiti until 1934 (see Map 22.1).

Events in Mexico triggered Wilson's most serious crisis in Latin America. Mexico had won independence from Spain in 1820, but the nation remained divided between a landowning elite and an impoverished peasantry. In 1911, rebels led by the democratic reformer Francisco Madero had ended the thirty-year rule of President Porfirio Díaz, a defender of the wealthy elite. Early in 1913, just as Wilson took office, Mexican troops loyal to General Victoriano Huerta, a full-blooded Indian, overthrew and murdered Madero.

Amid the chaos, Wilson tried to control events, protect U.S. investments, and safeguard U.S. citizens in Mexico and border towns. Forty thousand Americans had settled in Mexico under Díaz's regime, and U.S. investors had poured some $2 billion into Mexican oil wells and other ventures. Reversing long-standing U.S. practice of

Woodrow Wilson, Schoolteacher *This 1914 political cartoon captures the patronizing tone of Wilson's approach to Latin America, which planted the seeds of long-term resentments.*

(Granger Collection)

recognizing all governments, Wilson refused to recognize Huerta's "government of butchers." Authorizing arms sales to General Venustiano Carranza, Huerta's rival, Wilson ordered the port of Veracruz blockaded to prevent a shipment of German arms from reaching Huerta (see Map 22.1). Announced Wilson: "I am going to teach the South American republics to elect good men." In April 1914 seven thousand U.S. troops occupied Veracruz and battled Huerta's forces. Sixty-five Americans and approximately five hundred Mexicans were killed or wounded. Bowing to U.S. might, Huerta abdicated; Carranza took power; and the troops withdrew.

But turmoil continued. In January 1916, a bandit chieftain in northern Mexico, Pancho Villa, murdered sixteen U.S. mining engineers. Soon after, Villa's gang burned the town of Columbus, New Mexico, and killed nineteen inhabitants. Enraged Americans demanded action. Wilson dispatched a punitive expedition under General **John J. Pershing**. When Villa eluded Pershing and brazenly staged another cross-border raid into Texas, Wilson ordered 150,000 National Guardsmen to the border—a massive response that stirred anti-American feelings among Mexico's poor, for whom Villa was a folk hero. Villa ended his raids in 1920 when the Mexican government gave him a large land grant, but he was soon assassinated.

These involvements in Asia and Latin America illuminate the basic U.S. foreign-policy goal: to achieve a global order that would embrace American political values and welcome American business. President Wilson summed up this view in a 1916 speech to a business group in Detroit: "[C]arry liberty and justice and the principles of humanity wherever you go ... Sell goods that will make the world more comfortable and more happy, and convert them to the principles of America."

These early-twentieth-century engagements reflected the underlying worldview of the old-stock, upper-class men who directed U.S. foreign policy. Convinced of their ethnic, gender, and social superiority, they confidently promoted America's global economic and political interests while viewing with patronizing condescension the "backward" societies they sought to manipulate.

Meanwhile, a crisis unfolding in Europe challenged Wilson's dream of an American-based world order.

WAR IN EUROPE, 1914–1917

When war engulfed Europe in 1914, most Americans wished only to remain aloof, and President Wilson proclaimed U.S. neutrality. But by April 1917, economic considerations, cultural ties to England and France, visions of a world remade in America's image, and German violations of Wilson's definition of neutral rights all combined to suck America into the maelstrom.

The Coming of War   Although Western Europe was at peace through much of the nineteenth century, a series of ominous developments raised warning flags. In a short, sharp war in 1870–1871, an alliance of German states handed France a humiliating defeat. In the aftermath, Germany emerged as a powerful united nation ruled by Kaiser Wilhelm II. With many Germans convinced that Germany had lagged in the race for empire, Berlin's goal became modernization, expansion, and military power. Germany, Austria-Hungary, and

Italy signed a military-defense treaty in 1882. France, Great Britain, and Russia signed similar treaties in 1904 and 1907.

Meanwhile, the once-powerful Ottoman Empire, centered in Turkey, was weakening, leaving in its wake such newly independent nations as Romania, Bulgaria, and Serbia. Serbian patriots dreamed of expanding their boundaries to include Serbs living in neighboring Bosnia-Herzegovina. Serbia's ally Russia supported these ambitions. The Austro-Hungarian empire, based in Vienna, also dreamed of expansion as Ottoman power faded. In 1908, Austria-Hungary annexed (took over) Bosnia-Herzegovina, alarming Russia and Serbia.

In this volatile atmosphere, Archduke Franz Ferdinand of Austria visited Bosnia in June 1914. As Ferdinand and his wife rode in an open car through Bosnia's capital, Sarajevo, a young Bosnian Serb gunned them down. This act pushed a continent already poised for war over the precipice. Austria declared war on Serbia. Russia, aligned with Serbia by a secret treaty, mobilized for war. Austria's ally Germany declared war on Russia and France. Great Britain, linked by treaty to the latter two powers, declared war on Germany.

Thus began what contemporaries called the Great War, now known as World War I. On one side were Great Britain, Russia, and France, called the Allies. On the other were the Central Powers: Germany and Austria-Hungary. (Italy, despite its alliance with the Central Powers, joined the Allies in 1915.)

The Perils of Neutrality   President Wilson urged Americans to remain neutral "in thought as well as in action." Most citizens fervently agreed. A popular song summed up the mood: "I Didn't Raise My Boy to Be a Soldier." Carrie Chapman Catt and other feminists joined Jane Addams in forming the Woman's Peace Party. In New York City, fifteen hundred women marched to protest the war.

Neutrality proved difficult, however. Economic interests bound the United States and Britain. Many Americans had ancestral ties to England. Schoolbooks stressed the English origins of American institutions. The English language itself—the language of Shakespeare, Dickens, and the King James Bible—deepened the bond. British propaganda subtly stressed such links.

Many German-Americans, by contrast, sympathized with Germany, as did some Scandinavian immigrants. Irish-Americans speculated that a German victory might free Ireland from British rule. But these cultural and ethnic cross-currents did not at first override Wilson's commitment to neutrality. Most Americans saw staying out of the conflict as the chief goal.

Yet in 1917, America went to war. What caused this turnabout? Fundamentally, Wilson's vision of a peaceful, democratic, and capitalist world order conflicted with his neutrality. Such an international system would be impossible, he believed, if Germany won the war. Even an Allied victory would not ensure a transformed world order, Wilson became convinced, without a U.S. role in the postwar settlement. To shape the peace, America must fight the war.

These underlying ideas influenced Wilson's handling of the war's most troubling immediate challenge: neutral nations' rights. When the war began, Britain intercepted U.S. merchant ships bound for Germany, insisting that their cargo might aid

Germany's war effort. Wilson protested, especially when Britain, exploiting its naval advantage, declared the North Sea a war zone; planted it with explosive mines; and blockaded all German ports, choking off Germany's imports, including food.

But Germany, not England, ultimately pushed the United States into war. If Britannia ruled the waves, Germany controlled the ocean depths with its torpedo-equipped submarines, or U-boats. In February 1915, Berlin proclaimed the waters around Great Britain a war zone and warned off all ships. Wilson quickly responded: Germany would be held to "strict accountability" for any loss of U.S. vessels or lives.

On May 1, 1915, in a small ad in U.S. newspapers, the German embassy cautioned Americans against travel on British or French vessels. Six days later, a U-boat sank the British liner *Lusitania* off Ireland, killing 1,198 people, including 128 Americans. (The *Lusitania*, historians later discovered, was secretly carrying munitions destined for England.)

In three stern notes to Germany, Wilson demanded that Berlin stop unrestricted submarine warfare and pay reparations for the U.S. deaths in the *Lusitania* sinking. Publicly, he insisted that the United States could persuade the belligerents to recognize the principle of neutral rights without going to war. "There is such a thing as a man being too proud to fight," he said.

The *Lusitania* disaster exposed deep divisions in U.S. public opinion. Many Americans, now ready for war, ridiculed Wilson's "too proud to fight" speech. Theodore Roosevelt denounced the president's "abject cowardice." The National Security League, a lobby of bankers and industrialists, promoted stepped-up U.S. arms production and organized "preparedness" parades in major cities. By late 1915, Wilson himself called for a military buildup.

Lurid British propaganda (much of it false or exaggerated) screamed of atrocities committed by "the Huns" (a derogatory term for Germans). Intercepted German messages relating to espionage in U.S. factories further discredited the German cause.

Others, however, deplored the drift toward war. Some progressives warned that war fever was eroding support for reforms. The war, Jane Addams lamented, had destroyed the international movements to reduce infant mortality and improve care for the aged. Late in 1915, automaker Henry Ford chartered a vessel to take a group of pacifists to Scandinavia to persuade the belligerents to end the war by Christmas.

Divisions surfaced even within the Wilson administration. Secretary of State William Jennings Bryan, believing Wilson's *Lusitania* notes too hostile, resigned in June 1915. Under Bryan's weak successor, Robert Lansing, Wilson himself shaped U.S. policy.

Early in 1916, some Congressmen, seeking to avoid more *Lusitania*-type crises, introduced a bill to ban Americans from sailing on belligerents' ships. President Wilson successfully opposed it, however, insisting that the principle of neutral rights must be upheld.

For a time, Wilson's conciliatory approach seemed to work. Germany ordered its U-boats to spare passenger ships, and offered compensation for the Americans lost in the *Lusitania* sinking. In March 1916, however, a U-boat sank a French passenger ship in the English Channel, injuring several Americans. When Wilson threatened to break diplomatic relations—a step toward war—Berlin pledged not to attack merchant vessels without warning, provided that Great Britain, too, observed "the rules of international law." Ignoring this qualification, Wilson announced Germany's acceptance of American demands, and the crisis eased.

Meanwhile, U.S. banks' support for the Allies eroded the principle of neutrality. Early in the war, Secretary of State Bryan had rejected banker J. P. Morgan's request to extend loans to France. Such loans, said Bryan, would violate "the true spirit of neutrality." But economic considerations undermined this policy. In August 1915, Treasury Secretary William G. McAdoo warned Wilson that Allied purchases of American munitions and farm products were essential "[t]o maintain our prosperity." Only substantial loans to England, agreed Secretary of State Lansing, could prevent serious domestic economic problems, including "unrest ... among the laboring classes." The neutrality principle must not "stand in the way of our national interests," warned Lansing.

Swayed by such arguments and personally sympathetic to the Allies, Wilson permitted Morgan's bank to lend $500 million to the British and French governments. By April 1917, U.S. banks had lent the Allies $2.3 billion, in contrast to $27 million to Germany.

The land war, meanwhile, had settled into a grim stalemate. A September 1914 German drive into France bogged down along the Marne River. The two sides then dug in, constructing trenches across France from the English Channel to the Swiss border. For more than three years, this line scarcely changed. A German offensive in February 1916 began with the capture of two forts near the town of Verdun and ended that June when the French recaptured the same two forts, now nothing but rubble, at a horrendous cost in human life. Trench warfare became a nightmare of mud, rats, artillery bursts, and random death.

The war dominated the 1916 presidential election, which pitted Wilson against Republican Charles Evans Hughes, a former New York governor. Somewhat confusingly, Hughes criticized Wilson's lack of aggressiveness while rebuking him for policies that risked war. Theodore Roosevelt campaigned more for war than for the Republican ticket. The only difference between Wilson and the bearded Hughes, Roosevelt jeered, was a shave. While Hughes did well among Irish-Americans and German-Americans, Wilson eked out a narrow victory, aided by women voters in western states that had adopted woman suffrage. The Democrats' winning campaign slogan, "He kept us out of war," revealed the strength of popular peace sentiment as late as November 1916.

The United States Enters the War   In January 1917, Germany resumed unrestricted submarine warfare. Even if the United States declared war as a result, German strategists believed, the U-boat campaign could bring victory before American troops reached the front.

Events now rushed forward. Wilson broke diplomatic relations on February 3. During February and March, U-boats sank five American ships. A coded telegram from German foreign secretary Arthur Zimmermann to Germany's ambassador to Mexico, intercepted by the British, promised that if Mexico declared war on the United States, Germany would help restore Mexico's "lost territories" of Texas, Arizona, and New Mexico. The "Zimmermann telegram" further inflamed the war spirit in America.

Events in Russia also helped create favorable conditions for America's entry into the war. In March 1917, Russian peasants, industrial workers, intellectuals inspired by

Western liberal values, and communist revolutionaries joined in an uprising that overthrew the country's repressive czarist government. A provisional government under the liberal Alexander Kerensky briefly seemed to promise a democratic Russia, making it easier for President Wilson to portray the war as a battle for democracy.

On April 2, before a joint session of Congress, Wilson called for a declaration of war. Applause rang out as Wilson described his vision of America's role in creating a postwar international order to make the world "safe for democracy." As the speech ended, Republican senator Henry Cabot Lodge of Massachusetts, a staunch political foe, rushed forward to shake the president's hand.

After a short debate, the Senate voted 82 to 6 for war. The House agreed, 373 to 50. German violation of U.S. neutrality, reinforced by American ideological commitments, cultural affinities, and economic considerations had propelled the nation into the war. British propaganda and the "preparedness" campaign mounted by U.S. financial and corporate interests had played a role as well.

Mobilizing at Home, Fighting in France, 1917–1918

Compared to its effects on Europe, the war only grazed America. Russia suffered heavily. France, Great Britain, and Germany fought for more than four years; the United States, for nineteen months. Their armies suffered casualties of 70 percent or more; the U.S. casualty rate was 8 percent. The fighting left parts of France and Belgium brutally scarred; North America was physically untouched. Nevertheless, the war profoundly affected America. It changed not only those who participated in it directly, but also the home front and the nation's government and economy.

Raising, Training, and Testing an Army
April 1917 found America's military woefully unprepared. The regular army consisted of 120,000 men, few with combat experience, and an aging officer corps, plus eighty thousand National Guard members. Ammunition reserves were paltry. The War Department was a jungle of jealous bureaucrats, one of whom hoarded thousands of typewriters as the war approached.

While army chief-of-staff Peyton C. March brought order to the bureaucracy, Wilson's secretary of war, Newton D. Baker, a former mayor of Cleveland, concentrated on raising an army. Baker lacked administrative talent but was a public-relations genius. The **Selective Service Act** of May 1917 required all men between twenty-one and thirty (later expanded to eighteen through forty-five) to register with local draft boards. Mindful of the Civil War draft riots, Baker planned the draft-registration day, June 5, 1917, as a "festive and patriotic occasion."

By the war's end, more than 24 million men had registered, of whom nearly 3 million were drafted. Volunteers and National Guardsmen swelled the total to 4.3 million. Training camps gave combat instruction and introduced recruits to military discipline. Volunteer organizations built morale through shows, games, and recreational activities. The American Library Association contributed books. YMCA volunteers offered classes in literacy, French slang, and Bible study. In Plattsburgh, New York, local women opened a "Hostess House" to give homesick recruits a touch of domesticity. The idea soon spread to other communities near military camps.

The War Department closely monitored recruits' off-duty behavior. The **Commission on Training Camp Activities** presented films, lectures, and posters on the dangers of alcohol and prostitution. Any soldier disabled by venereal (sexually transmitted) disease, one poster warned, "is a Traitor!" Officers confined trainees to camp until nearby towns closed brothels and saloons.

Beginning in December 1917, recruits also underwent intelligence testing. Psychologists eager to demonstrate the usefulness of their new field claimed that measuring recruits' "intelligence quotient" (IQ) could help win the war by identifying potential officers and those best suited to handle more specialized assignments.

When many recruits received very low scores, editorial writers reacted with alarm. In fact, the results mostly revealed recruits' lack of formal education and the tests' cultural biases. One question asked whether *mauve* was a drink, a color, a fabric, or a food. Another asked in which city a particular automobile was built. The testing also reinforced racial and ethnic stereotypes: native-born recruits of northern European origins scored highest; African-Americans and recent immigrants lowest.

In short, the training camps not only turned civilians into soldiers, but also reinforced the Progressive Era's moral-control campaigns (see Chapter 21) and signaled changes ahead, including a vogue for standardized testing.

Some twelve thousand Native Americans served in the **American Expeditionary Force** (AEF). While some reformers eager to preserve Indian culture argued for all-Indian units, military officials integrated Native Americans into the general army. Some observers predicted that the wartime experience would hasten Indians' assimilation into mainstream American life, considered a desirable goal at the time.

Some blacks resisted the draft, especially in the South (as discussed later in this chapter), but most followed W. E. B. Du Bois's advice urging African-Americans to "close ranks" and support the war. More than 260,000 blacks volunteered or were drafted, and some 50,000 went to France. Racism pervaded the military, as it did American society. The navy assigned blacks only to menial positions, and the marines excluded them altogether.

Black troops in some camps endured abuse. One racist senator from Mississippi warned that the sight of "arrogant, strutting" black soldiers would trigger race riots. Tensions exploded in Houston in August 1917 when black soldiers stationed at nearby Camp Logan, goaded by abuse from local whites, including police officers, seized weapons, marched into town, and fatally shot sixteen whites, including four policemen. After court-martial trials, nineteen black soldiers were hanged and sixty-one sentenced to life imprisonment.

Organizing the Economy for War   World War I helped shape modern America. The war furthered such key later developments as an expanded government role in the economy; the growth of new professional and managerial elites; and the spread of mass production, corporate consolidation, and product standardization.

The war led to unprecedented government economic oversight and corporate regulation, long advocated by Populists and progressives. In 1916, Congress created an advisory body, the Council of National Defense, to oversee the government's military preparedness program. After war was declared, this council set up the **War Industries Board** (WIB) to coordinate military purchasing and ensure production efficiency. President Wilson reorganized the WIB in March 1918 and put the Wall Street financier Bernard Baruch in charge. Under Baruch, the WIB allocated raw materials, established production priorities, and induced competing companies to standardize and coordinate their products and processes to save scarce commodities.

With congressional authorization, Wilson set up two more new agencies, the Fuel Administration and the Food Administration. The Fuel Administration controlled coal output, regulated fuel prices and consumption, and introduced daylight-saving time—an idea first proposed by Benjamin Franklin. The Food Administration, headed by Herbert Hoover, oversaw the production and allocation of wheat, meat, and sugar to ensure supplies for the army as well as for the desperately food-short Allies. Born in poverty in Iowa, Hoover had prospered as a mining engineer in Asia. He was organizing food relief in Belgium when Wilson brought him back to Washington.

These agencies relied on voluntary cooperation, reinforced by government propaganda. Food Administration posters and ads urged Americans to conserve food. Housewives signed pledges to observe "Meatless Monday" and "Wheatless Wednesday." Slogans such as "Serve Beans by All Means" promoted substitutes for scarce commodities.

Harriot Stanton Blatch, daughter of woman's-rights pioneer Elizabeth Cady Stanton, headed the Food Administration's Speakers' Bureau, which spread the administration's conservation message. Blatch also organized the Woman's Land Army, which recruited women to replace male farm workers.

In all, nearly five thousand government boards supervised home-front activities. These included the National War Labor Board, which resolved labor-management disputes that jeopardized production, and the Railroad Administration, headed by Treasury Secretary William McAdoo. When a railroad tie-up during the winter of 1917–1918 threatened the flow of supplies to Europe, the Railroad Administration stepped in and soon transformed the thousands of miles of track operated by competing companies into an efficient national system.

American business, much criticized by progressive reformers, utilized the war emergency to improve its image. Corporate executives ran regulatory agencies. Factory owners distributed prowar propaganda to workers. Trade associations coordinated war production.

The war hastened the process of corporate consolidation and economic integration. In place of trustbusting, the government now encouraged cooperation and mergers among businesses. "Instead of punishing companies for acting in concert," one magazine observed, "the government is now in some cases forcing them to unite."

Overall, the war was good for business. Despite wartime tax increases, profits soared. After-tax profits in the copper industry, for example, jumped from 12 percent in 1913 to 24 percent in 1917.

The old laissez-faire suspicion of government, already weakened, eroded further in 1917–1918. The wartime regulatory agencies disappeared quickly after the war, but their influence lingered. In the 1930s, when the nation faced a different crisis, the government activism of World War I would be remembered (as discussed in Chapter 24).

As the U.S. military mobilized for combat, Allied prospects looked bleak. German U-boats were battering Allied shipping. French troops mutinied in the spring of 1917 after suffering ghastly casualties. Later that year, the Italian army suffered a disastrous defeat at Caporetto near the Austrian border and a British offensive along the French-Belgian border gained only four miles at a cost of many thousands killed and wounded. A breakthrough in military technology came in November 1917 when the British mobilized three hundred tanks along a six-mile section of the front near Cambrai, France, shattering the German defenses. Still the stalemate continued.

Russia, ill-prepared for war, had suffered devastating setbacks as well, contributing to the revolutionary upheaval. The communist faction of the revolution, the Bolsheviks (Russian for "majority"), gained strength when its top leaders, including Vladimir Lenin and Leon Trotsky, returned from exile abroad. On November 6, 1917 (October 24 by the Russian calendar), a Bolshevik coup overthrew Alexander Kerensky's provisional government and effectively removed Russia from the war. Early in 1918, the Bolsheviks signed an armistice with Germany, the Treaty of Brest-Litovsk, freeing thousands of German troops on the Russian front for fighting in France.

In these desperate circumstances, U.S. aid to the Allies initially consisted of munitions and convoys to protect Allied ships. The first U.S. troops, designated as the Allied Expeditionary Force (AEF), reached France in October 1917. Eventually about 2 million American soldiers served in France under General John J. Pershing. A West Point graduate and commander of the 1916 expedition against Pancho Villa, Pershing was an iron-willed officer with a ramrod bearing, steely eyes, and trim mustache. The death of his wife and three of their children in a fire in 1915 had further hardened him. (Ironically, Pershing was of German origin; his family name had been Pfoersching.)

Most men of the AEF at first found the war a great adventure. Plucked from towns and farms, they sailed for Europe on crowded freighters or, for a lucky few, captured German passenger liners. Once in France, railroad freight cars marked "HOMMES 40, CHEVAUX 8" (forty men, eight horses) took them to the front. Then began the routine of marching, training—and waiting.

The African-Americans with the AEF worked mainly as mess-boys (mealtime aides), laborers, and stevedores (ship-cargo handlers). Although discriminatory, the latter assignments vitally aided the war effort. Sometimes working twenty-four hours nonstop, black stevedores efficiently unloaded supply ships. Some whites of the AEF pressed the French to treat African-Americans as inferiors, but most ignored this advice and related to blacks without prejudice. This eye-opening experience would remain with black veterans after the war.

While most African-American troops served behind the front lines, regiments of the all-black 92nd and 93rd infantry divisions saw action under French command in the Second Battle of the Marne and the Meuse-Argonne campaign near the war's end. France awarded the Croix de Guerre, a military honor, to the entire 369th infantry regiment, nicknamed the "Harlem Hellfighters," and gave several hundred black U.S. soldiers individual decorations for bravery. German propaganda leaflets described U.S. racism and urged African-American soldiers to defect, but none did.

Only in death was the AEF integrated, however: graves in military cemeteries were not racially segregated.

In the air, a scant fifteen years after the Wright brothers' first flight, German and Allied planes dropped bombs, reported on troop movements, and engaged in deadly aerial dogfights (see Going to the Source). Germany's legendary "Red Baron," Manfred von Richthofen, downed eighty Allied planes before his luck ran out in April 1918. As early as 1916, American volunteers joined a French air unit known as the Lafayette Escadrille (squadron). The U.S. Army's air corps was established early in 1918. America's output of planes lagged, however, despite pressure from Secretary of War Baker—a rare war-production failure.

Continuing the military's policy of close moral oversight, AEF officials warned troops of the danger of venereal disease. "A German bullet is cleaner than a whore" declared one poster. When the French government offered to provide prostitutes for the AEF (as was the French practice), Newton Baker exclaimed, "For God's sake, don't show this to the President, or he'll stop the war."

The YMCA, Red Cross, and Salvation Army, including many female volunteers, provided a touch of home. Some 16,500 U.S. women served directly in the AEF as nurses, telephone operators, canteen workers, and secretaries.

In March 1918, when Germany launched a major offensive, the Allies created a unified command under French general Ferdinand Foch. Some Americans participated in the fighting around Amiens and Armentières that slowed the German advance.

The French and British wanted to continue this pattern of absorbing the Americans into existing units. But for both military and political reasons (including assuring a strong U.S. voice at the peace table), Pershing and his superiors in Washington insisted that the AEF fight in "distinct and separate" units. Pershing, favoring aggressive combat, abhorred the defensive mentality ingrained by three years of trench warfare.

The Germans' spring offensive resumed in May along the Aisne River, where they broke through to the Marne and faced a nearly open route to Paris, fifty miles away. On June 4, as the French government prepared to evacuate, American forces arrived in strength. Parts of three U.S. divisions and a marine brigade helped stop the Germans at the town of Château-Thierry and nearby Belleau Wood. (An AEF division at full strength consisted of twenty-seven thousand men and one thousand officers, plus twelve thousand support troops.)

The German offensive had punched several deep holes (called salients) in the Allied line. With the help of some eighty-five thousand American troops, the Allies at enormous cost halted a German attack on the cathedral city of Rheims between two of these salients (see Map 22.2). This battle proved to be the war's turning point.

American soldiers now endured the filth, vermin, and dysentery familiar to veterans of the trenches. Many would never forget the terror of combat. As shells streaked overhead, one recalled, "We simply lay and trembled from sheer nervous tension." Some collapsed emotionally and were hospitalized for "shell shock."

Deadly poison gas (first used by the Germans in 1915) often hung in the air, and rats scurried in the mud. "We are not men anymore, just savage beasts," wrote a young American. Death came in many forms, and without ceremony.

GOING TO THE SOURCE

World War I in the Air

Though World War I was mainly a ground and sea conflict, it also saw the beginnings of air combat by small planes that engaged in reconnaissance and some bombing missions. This memoir by Lieutenant E. C. Leonard describes a September 1918 bombing raid on German positions during the Meuse-Argonne offensive, in which he was the gunner and bombardier on a two-person aircraft in an eight-plane squadron.

Our wheels left the ground at nine o'clock and we rose into the fog, straining our eyes for the sight of another plane ... The ground faded out of sight and we were swallowed up in the mist. It was like another world. It lasted but for a minute, thank goodness. The sun began to grow brighter and suddenly we burst into daylight and blue sky....

We were nearing the objective now and ... getting ready to drop the bombs.... I leaned over the side with my hand on the release, watching for the bombs to drop from the plane ahead. In a few moments I saw them fall from the next plane and pulled the lever and marked up 448 pounds more of TNT for the Germans. At the release of weight, our plane gave a jump forward as if glad of the chance to hit the Hun....

[As the planes turn homeward, two waves of yellow-and-black German Fokker aircraft attack them.] They slid around our heavier machines like yellow jackets, swerving up for an instant to let a stream of bullets go at us and then taking a new position.... [Like a] nest of angry hornets, they came diving right through the middle of our formation, shooting a steady stream of fire.... [Leonard shoots down two Fokkers, but is knocked out of action when a bullet hits him in the neck.]

Suddenly our plane dropped into a nose spin. My first thought was that "Coop" [the pilot] had been shot and that in a very few seconds we would hit the ground and be through with everything. I slipped down on the seat unconscious, but only for an instant. When I

Bodies, packs, rifles, photos of loved ones, and letters from home sank indiscriminately into the all-consuming mud. Worsening the horror, thousands of men on both sides died of influenza, in a pandemic that began in the war zone and quickly spread (as discussed later in this chapter).

Religious and ethical principles faded as men struggled to survive. "Love of thy neighbor is forgotten," recalled one, with "all the falsities of a sheltered civilization." The war's brutality would shape the literature of the 1920s as writers such as Ernest Hemingway stripped away the illusions obscuring the reality of mass slaughter.

Turning the Tide

The Allied counteroffensive began in July 1918. About 270,000 U.S. soldiers joined the drive to push the Germans back from the Marne. Rain pelted down as the AEF moved into position. One wrote in his diary, "Trucks, artillery, infantry columns, cavalry, wagons, caissons, mud, MUD, utter confusion." Another 100,000 AEF troops joined a parallel British counterattack in the Somme region.

regained my senses, we were still falling in a spin but "Coop" had unfastened his safety belt and was standing up with one foot over the sides in the act of jumping overboard. And no wonder, for his cockpit was a mass of flames from the motor which was on fire. It was a question of dying an easy death by jumping overboard, or of burning to death…. He did not know whether I was dead or alive, but when he saw me open my eyes, he did not hesitate. Rather than desert a wounded and helpless comrade, he stepped back into what seemed, at the time, the certainty of burning to death.

We came out of the spin upside down and went into a side slip in a fruitless endeavor to extinguish the flames. By this time his hands were so badly burned that the stick slipped from his fingers and he had to use knees and elbows to work the controls. Finally by diving straight down with the motor turned on as much as it would go, the almost impossible was accomplished, and the flames put out….

We landed in a large field, barely missing some telephone wires…. "Coop" landed the machine with the control stick between his knees and elbows. Although

we hit the ground with force enough to send the plane up on its nose and break the wings, neither of us was thrown out. The machine was pretty well shot up. The motor was a wreck. There were bullet holes all over the plane … and long gashes in the fabric. Surely a Divine providence must have guided the bullets from the vital parts.

Questions

1. What led Coop to change his mind about jumping from the burning plane?

2. On the basis of this account, how did World War I aerial combat compare to trench warfare, as described elsewhere in this chapter?

Go to www.cengagebrain.com for additional primary sources on this period.

Source: Martin M. Evans, editor, *American Voices of World War I: Primary Source Documents, 1917–1920* (Chicago: Fitzroy Dearborn Publishers, 2001), 129–131.

In early September, as fighting continued on all fronts, Foch authorized an AEF campaign to close a German salient around the town of St. Mihiel on the Meuse River, 150 miles east of Paris (see Map 22.2). Pershing assembled nearly five hundred thousand American and one hundred thousand French soldiers. Shelling of German positions began at 1:00 A.M. on September 11. Recorded an American in his diary, "[I]n one instant the entire front … was a sheet of flame, while the heavy artillery made the earth quake." Within four days, the salient was closed. Although some German units had already withdrawn, St. Mihiel still cost seven thousand U.S. casualties.

In late September, 1.2 million Americans joined the struggle to drive the Germans from the Meuse River and the Argonne Forest north of Verdun. The AEF was assigned to cut the Sedan-Mezières Railroad, a vital German supply route protected by three long, heavily fortified trenches, called Stellungen. The fighting was long and fierce but the AEF at last overran the dreaded Stellungen. In early November the Sedan-Mezières Railroad was cut. The AEF had fulfilled its assignment, at a cost of 26,277 dead.

The successful Meuse-Argonne offensive ended the war. On November 11, 1918, Germany surrendered.

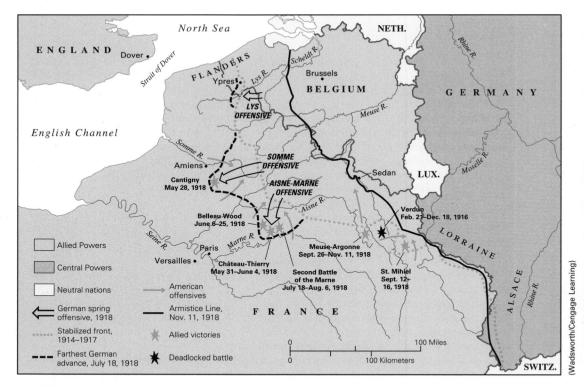

MAP 22.2 The United States on the Western Front, 1918

American troops first saw action in the campaign to throw back Germany's spring 1918 offensive in the Somme and Aisne-Marne sectors. The next heavy American engagement came that autumn as part of the Allies' Meuse-Argonne offensive, which ended the war.

PROMOTING THE WAR AND SUPPRESSING DISSENT

In their own way, the war's domestic effects matched the battlefield in importance. Spurred by government propaganda, patriotic fervor gripped America. The war fever, in turn, encouraged ideological conformity and smothered dissent. Fueling the repressive spirit, government authorities and private vigilante groups hounded socialists, pacifists, and other dissidents, trampling citizens' constitutional rights.

Advertising the War

President Wilson viewed home front support as crucial to military success. "It is not an army we must shape and train for war, it is a nation," he declared. The administration drew on the new professions of advertising and public relations to pursue this goal.

(National Archives)

The Fog of War. U.S. Troops on the Western Front, June 26, 1918 *The reality of combat differed from the idealized images offered in home front propaganda. As the war's final stage began, these American soldiers attacked entrenched German positions in Alsace, a disputed region along the French-German border near Switzerland (see Map 22.2). They are firing a 37mm. machine gun, a weapon of deadly accuracy with a maximum range of a mile and a half.*

Treasury Secretary William McAdoo orchestrated government bond drives, called Liberty Loans, that financed about two-thirds of the war's $35.5 billion cost.

Posters exhorted citizens to "Fight or Buy Bonds." Liberty Loan parades featured flags, banners, and marching bands. Charlie Chaplin and other movie stars promoted the cause. Schoolchildren purchased "thrift stamps" convertible into war bonds.

Patriotic war songs reached millions through phonograph recordings. Beneath the ballyhoo ran a note of coercion. Only "a friend of Germany," McAdoo warned, would refuse to buy bonds.

The balance of the government's war costs came from taxes. Under authority granted by the recently ratified Sixteenth Amendment, Congress imposed wartime income taxes that reached 70 percent at the top level. War-profits taxes, excise taxes on liquor and luxuries, and increased estate taxes also helped finance the war.

Journalist George Creel headed the government's wartime propaganda agency, the **Committee on Public Information** (CPI). While claiming merely to report facts, Creel's committee in reality publicized the government's version of events and discredited all who questioned that version. One CPI division distributed posters drawn by leading illustrators. Another wrote propaganda releases that appeared in the press as "news" with no indication of their source. Popular magazines published CPI ads warning of spies, saboteurs, and anyone who "spreads pessimistic stories" or "cries for peace." Theaters screened CPI films bearing such titles as *The Kaiser: The Beast of Berlin*.

The CPI poured foreign-language pamphlets into immigrant neighborhoods and supplied prowar editorials to the foreign-language press. At a CPI event at Mount Vernon on July 4, 1918, an Irish-born tenor sang "The Battle Hymn of the Republic" while immigrants from thirty-three nations filed reverently past George Washington's tomb. CPI posters in factories attacked the socialists' charge that this was a capitalists' war. Samuel Gompers of the American Federation of Labor headed a prowar "Alliance for Labor and Democracy" with CPI funding. CPI volunteers called "Four-Minute Men" gave prowar pep talks to movie audiences.

Teachers, writers, editors, and religious leaders overwhelmingly supported the war. These custodians of culture saw the conflict as a struggle to defend threatened values. Historians wrote essays contrasting German brutality with the Allies' ideals. In *The Marne* (1918), expatriate American writer Edith Wharton expressed her love for France. The popular war poems of Alan Seeger, who volunteered to fight for France and died in action in 1916, portrayed the conflict as a noble crusade. An artillery barrage was for him "the magnificent orchestra of war."

Progressive reformers who had applauded Wilson's domestic program now cheered his war. Herbert Croly, Walter Lippmann, and others associated with the *New Republic* magazine zealously backed the war. In gratitude, administration officials regularly briefed them on the government's war policies.

The educator John Dewey endorsed the war in a series of *New Republic* essays. Progressive intellectuals must accept reality and shape it toward positive social goals, he wrote, not withdraw in self-righteous isolation. The war, he went on, presented exciting "social possibilities." The government's wartime activism could be channeled to reform purposes when peace returned. Internationally, America's participation in the war would transform an imperialistic struggle into a global democratic crusade.

Wartime Intolerance and Dissent   Responding to the propaganda, some Americans lashed out at all things German. Reports of sabotage by German agents, including mysterious fires at munitions plants in New Jersey and Pennsylvania, fanned the flames of fear. Libraries banished German books; towns with German names changed them. An Iowa politician charged that "90 percent of all the men and women who teach the German language are traitors." Some restaurant menus replaced hamburgers with "liberty sandwiches." The Boston Symphony Orchestra dismissed its German-born conductor. The Philadelphia Orchestra banned all German music since Brahms. A popular evangelist, Billy Sunday, proclaimed, "If you turn hell upside down you will find 'Made in Germany' stamped on the bottom."

The zealots also targeted American citizens suspected of pro-German or antiwar sentiments. Some were forced to kiss the flag or recite the Pledge of Allegiance. An Ohio woman accused of disloyalty was wrapped in a flag, marched to a bank, and compelled to buy a war bond. A Cincinnati mob horsewhipped a pacifist minister. Theodore Roosevelt branded antiwar Senator Robert La Follette "an unhung traitor." Columbia University fired two antiwar professors.

In Bisbee, Arizona, in July 1917, two thousand armed vigilantes calling themselves the Citizens Protective League forced twelve hundred striking copper miners, some of whom belonged to the antiwar Industrial Workers of the World (IWW), onto a freight train that dumped them in the New Mexico desert without food, water, or shelter. Without doubt, declared Theodore Roosevelt, "the men deported from Bisbee were bent on destruction and murder."

In Collinsville, Illinois, in April 1918, a mob lynched a German-American coal miner, Robert Prager. When a jury freed the ringleaders, a jury member shouted, "Nobody can say we aren't loyal now." The *Washington Post* condemned the lynching but saw it as evidence of a "wholesome awakening" in the American heartland. President Wilson criticized Prager's murder when the German press publicized it, but the administration's strident attacks on radicals and war critics created the climate that led to such actions. In a June 1917 speech urging home-front vigilance, Wilson declared ominously: "Woe be to the man or group of men that seeks to stand in our way." A New York newspaper, advising direct action against war opponents, added: "You do not require any official authority.... [T]he only badge you need is your patriotic fervor."

Despite the persecution, many Americans persisted in opposing the war. Some had sentimental or ancestral ties to Germany. Others were religious pacifists, including Quakers, Mennonites, and Jehovah's Witnesses. Montana Congresswoman Jeannette Rankin, a pacifist and the first woman elected to Congress, opposed the declaration of war. "I want to stand by my country," she declared, "but I cannot vote for war."

Of some sixty-five thousand men who registered as conscientious objectors (COs), twenty-one thousand were drafted. Assigned to noncombat duty on military bases, these COs often experienced harsh treatment. Those who rejected this alternative went to prison. Woodrow Wilson scorned the pacifists. "[M]y heart is with them, but my mind has contempt for them," he declared; "I want peace, but I know how to get it, and they do not."

Socialist leaders such as Eugene Debs and Victor Berger denounced the war as a capitalist struggle for markets, with the soldiers as cannon fodder. The government's decision for war, they insisted, reflected Wall Street's desire to protect its loans to England and France. Other socialists supported the war, however, dividing the party.

The war split the women's movement as well. Some leaders joined Jane Addams in opposition, others endorsed the war while keeping their own goals in view. Carrie Chapman Catt, president of the National American Woman Suffrage Association (NAWSA), had helped start the Woman's Peace Party in 1915. But she supported U.S. entry into the war in 1917, sharing to some extent Wilson's vision of a more liberal postwar world order. Catt continued to fight for woman suffrage, however, as NAWSA's "number one war job." For this, some superpatriots accused her of disloyalty.

Draft resistance extended beyond the ranks of conscientious objectors. An estimated 2.4 to 3.6 million young men failed to register. Others who did register either did not appear when drafted or deserted from training camp. The rural South saw high levels of draft resistance. The urban elites who ran the draft boards were more inclined to excuse young men of their own class from service than poor farmers, white or black, fueling class resentment. In June 1918, a truck carrying soldiers pursuing draft evaders in rural Georgia crashed when a bridge collapsed, killing three. Investigators found that the bridge had been deliberately sabotaged.

African-Americans had added reasons to oppose the draft. Of southern blacks who registered, one-third were drafted, in contrast to only one-quarter of whites. White draft boards justified this by arguing that black families could more easily spare a male breadwinner. As an Alabama board observed: "[I]t requires more for a white man and his wife to live than it does a negro man and his wife, due to their respective stations in life." But racial bias worked in complex ways: some southern whites, fearful of arming black men even for military service, favored drafting only whites.

One war critic, Randolph Bourne, a young journalist, rejected John Dewey's argument that reformers could direct the war to their own purposes. "If the war is too strong for you to prevent," he asked, "how is it going to be weak enough for you to ... mould to your liberal purposes?" Many prowar intellectuals eventually agreed. By 1919, Dewey conceded that the war, far from promoting reform, had encouraged reaction and intolerance. Bourne did not live to see his vindication, however. He died of influenza in 1918, aged thirty-two.

Suppressing Dissent by Law   Wartime intolerance surfaced in federal laws and official actions. The **Espionage Act** of June 1917 set fines and prison sentences for a variety of loosely defined antiwar activities. The **Sedition Amendment** (May 1918) imposed stiff penalties on anyone convicted of using "disloyal, profane ... or abusive language" about the government, the Constitution, the flag, or the military.

Wilson's attorney general, Thomas W. Gregory, used these laws to suppress dissent. Opponents of the war, proclaimed Gregory, should expect no mercy "from an outraged people and an avenging government." Under the federal legislation and similar state laws, authorities arrested some fifteen hundred pacifists, socialists, IWW leaders, and other war critics. One socialist, Rose Pastor Stokes, received a ten-year prison sentence (later commuted) for telling an audience, "I am for the people, and the government is for the profiteers." Eugene Debs spent three years in prison for a speech discussing the economic causes of the war.

Under the Espionage Act, Postmaster General Albert S. Burleson banned socialist periodicals, including *The Masses*. In January 1919 Congressman-elect Victor Berger was convicted for publishing antiwar articles in his socialist newspaper, the *Milwaukee Leader*. (The Supreme Court reversed Berger's conviction in 1921.) Socialist Norman Thomas complained that Burleson "didn't know socialism from rheumatism," and Upton Sinclair protested to President Wilson that no one of Burleson's "childish ignorance" should wield such power. Still, Wilson did little to restrain the Postmaster General's excesses.

A patriotic organization called the American Protective League and local "Councils of Defense" claiming vague governmental authority further enforced ideological conformity. A group called "Boy Spies of America" recruited young patriots. The 1917 takeover in Russia by Bolsheviks who believed in a one-party state and preached the overthrow of capitalism deepened suspicion of domestic radicals. Could the United States itself fall to communism, some fearful Americans wondered.

In three 1919 decisions, the U.S. Supreme Court upheld the Espionage Act convictions of war critics despite the First Amendment guarantee of free speech. In *Schenck v. United States*, Justice Oliver Wendell Holmes, Jr., writing for a unanimous court, justified such repression in cases where a person's speech posed a "clear and present danger" to the nation. When the war ended, Wilson vetoed a bill repealing the Espionage Act, increasing the likelihood that the miasma of conformity and suspicion would linger into the postwar era.

ECONOMIC AND SOCIAL TRENDS IN WARTIME AMERICA

In many diverse ways, the war affected the lives of millions of Americans, including industrial workers, farmers, women, and blacks. Another of the war's byproducts, a deadly influenza pandemic, took a grievous toll. Some Progressive Era reforms advanced, but overall the war weakened the reform movement.

Boom Times in Industry and Agriculture   World War I benefited the U.S. economy. From 1914 to 1918, factory output grew by more than one-third. Even with many men in uniform, the civilian work force expanded by 1.3 million between 1916 and 1918, thanks to new jobs in shipbuilding, munitions, steel, and other war-related industries. Prices rose, but so did wages. Even unskilled workers enjoyed wartime wage increases averaging nearly 20 percent. Samuel Gompers urged a moratorium on strikes. Some IWW members and maverick AFL locals ignored this advice, but with the economy booming, most workers observed the no-strike request.

The war's social impact took many forms. Job seekers pouring into industrial centers strained housing, schools, and municipal services. Consumption of cigarettes, which soldiers and workers could carry in their shirt pockets more easily than pipes or cigars, more than tripled. Reflecting wartime prosperity, automobile production jumped from 460,000 in 1914 to 1.8 million in 1917, then dipped briefly in 1918 as steel went for military production.

Farmers profited, too. With European farm production disrupted, U.S. agricultural prices, including cotton, corn, and other commodities, more than doubled between 1913 and 1918, and farmers' real income rose significantly. This agricultural boom proved a mixed blessing, however. Farmers who borrowed heavily to expand production faced a credit squeeze when farm prices fell after the war. In the 1920s and 1930s, hard-pressed farmers would look back to the war years as a golden age of prosperity.

Blacks Migrate Northward   An estimated half-million African-Americans moved north during the war, and most settled in cities. Each day, fresh arrivals poured into Philadelphia, New York, Detroit, and Pittsburgh. Chicago's black population grew from forty-four thousand in 1910 to 110,000 in 1920, Cleveland's from eight thousand to thirty-four thousand.

With European immigration choked off by the war, booming industries hired more black workers. Some companies sent agents south to recruit black workers. African-American newspapers like the *Chicago Defender* spread the word, as did letters and word-of-mouth reports. One southern black, newly settled near Chicago, wrote home, "Nothing here but money, and it is not hard to get." A Pittsburgh newcomer presented a more balanced picture: "They give you big money for what you do, but they charge you big things for what you get." As economic opportunity beckoned, impoverished southern blacks welcomed the prospect of securing jobs in a region where racism seemed less oppressive. By 1920, 1.5 million African-Americans were working in northern factories and other urban-based jobs.

This vast population movement had profound social ramifications. Churches and storefront missions sprang up to serve deeply religious migrants from the South. As organizers for the National Association for the Advancement of Colored People built a national network of local branches, membership surged from 9,000 before the war to nearly 100,000 by the early 1920s. NAACP leaders pointed to African-American support for the war to buttress their demand for equality. The struggle against racism faltered in the 1920s, but the population movements and heightened race consciousness of the war years laid the groundwork for the civil-rights movement that lay ahead. The concentration of blacks in New York City set the stage for the Harlem Renaissance, a cultural flowering of the 1920s (covered in Chapter 23).

Still, African-American newcomers in northern cities faced severe challenges. White workers resented the labor competition, and white home-owners lashed out as blacks moved into "their" neighborhoods. Tensions exploded on July 2, 1917, in East St. Louis, Illinois, home to thousands of recently arrived southern blacks. In a coordinated attack, a white mob torched black homes and shot the fleeing residents. At least thirty-nine blacks died, including a two-year-old who was shot and thrown into a burning house.

A few weeks later, an NAACP silent march down New York's Fifth Avenue protested racist violence. One banner echoed Wilson's phrase justifying U.S. involvement in the war: "Mr. President, Why Not Make AMERICA Safe for Democracy?"

Women in Wartime

From one perspective, World War I seems a uniquely male experience. Male politicians led their nations into war. Male officers ordered other men into battle. Yet war touches all of society, not just half of it. The war affected women differently, but still profoundly.

Feminist leaders like Carrie Chapman Catt hoped that the war would lead to full equality and greater opportunity for women. For a time, these goals seemed attainable. In addition to the women holding AEF clerical positions and in wartime volunteer agencies, about 1 million women worked in industry. Thousands more held other jobs, from streetcar conductors to bricklayers. "Out of ... repression into opportunity is the meaning of the war to thousands of women," wrote Florence Thorne of the American Federation of Labor in 1917.

A key victory for the woman-suffrage movement came in November 1917 when New York voters amended the state constitution to permit women to vote. In Washington, members of Alice Paul's National Woman's Party (see Chapter 21) picketed the White House and posted banners criticizing President Wilson for opposing woman suffrage at home while championing democracy abroad. Several protesters were jailed and force-fed when they went on a hunger strike. Pressured by all wings of the suffrage movement, Wilson declared that women's war service had earned them the right to vote. In 1919, barraged by pro-suffrage petitions, the House and Senate overwhelmingly passed the **Nineteenth Amendment** granting women the vote. Ratification soon followed.

Beyond this victory, however, the war did little to better women's status permanently. Relatively few women entered the work force for the first time in 1917–1918; most simply moved to better-paying jobs. But even in these jobs, most earned less than the men they replaced. As for the women in the AEF, the War Department refused their requests for military rank and benefits.

At the war's end, many women lost their jobs to returning veterans. The New York labor federation advised, "The same patriotism which induced women to enter industry during the war should induce them to vacate their positions after the war." Male streetcar workers in Cleveland went on strike to force women conductors off the job. In 1920, the percentage of U.S. women in the paid labor force was actually slightly lower than it had been in 1910.

Public-Health Crisis: The 1918 Influenza Pandemic   Along with the war's other effects, the nation in 1918 reeled under an outbreak of influenza (or "flu"), a highly contagious viral infection. The **influenza pandemic**, spread by a particularly deadly strain of the virus, killed an estimated

(American Red Cross)

Battling Influenza, 1918 *Red Cross workers like these in Philadelphia and other public-health professionals mobilized to combat a deadly epidemic that claimed over half a million American lives.*

50-100 million people worldwide. Despite public-health advances, medical science had few weapons against influenza in 1918.

Originating in Africa, the virus spread from battlefields in France to U.S. military camps, striking Fort Riley, Kansas, in March 1918 and quickly advancing to other bases and the urban population. In September, a health official visiting Camp Devens in Massachusetts wrote, "I saw hundreds of young stalwart men in uniform coming into ... the hospital.... The faces wore a bluish cast, a cough brought up blood-stained sputum. In the morning, the dead bodies are stacked about the morgue like cord-wood."

The flu hit the cities hard. After a September Liberty Loan rally in Philadelphia, doctors reported 635 new influenza cases. Many cities forbade public gatherings. In the worst month, October, influenza killed 195,000 Americans. The total U.S. death toll reached about 550,000, over six times the number of AEF battle deaths in France.

The development of a flu vaccine in the 1940s and of antibiotics to control influenza's secondary infections reduced the severity of later outbreaks, but flu pandemics remain a threat. In 2004, using tissue preserved from two U.S. soldiers who had died of influenza in 1918 and from the frozen corpse of another victim buried in the Alaska tundra, scientists successfully synthesized the 1918 virus for research purposes.

The War and Progressivism   The war had mixed effects on Progressive Era reform movements. It strengthened progressivism's coercive, moral-control aspect, including the drive to prohibit alcohol consumption. Pointing out the German origins of large breweries such as Pabst, Schlitz, and Anheuser-Busch, prohibitionists hinted that beer was a German plot to undermine American fitness. With food conservation a high priority, they stressed the wastefulness of using grain to make liquor. The **Eighteenth Amendment** establishing national prohibition, which passed Congress in December 1917, was widely seen as a war measure. Ratified in 1919, it went into effect on January 1, 1920.

As we have seen, the war also strengthened the Progressive Era antiprostitution campaign. Congress appropriated $4 million to combat venereal disease among soldiers and war workers. The War Department closed red-light districts near military bases, including New Orleans's famed Storyville. (As Storyville's jazz musicians moved northward, jazz reached a national audience.) In San Antonio, a major military hub, an antiprostitution leader reflected the war mood when he declared, "We propose to fight vice ... with the cold steel of the law, and to drive in the steel from the point to the hilt until the law's supremacy is acknowledged."

In the wartime climate of "vigilance," the antiprostitution drive expanded to a broader policing of morals. Female lecturers for the Commission on Training Camp Activities urged unmarried young women to practice chastity. "Do Your Bit to Keep Him Fit" one pamphlet advised. Wartime "protective bureaus" in major cities monitored women's behavior. In Boston, female social workers hid in the Common after dark to apprehend young women dating soldiers from nearby bases.

All this moral-reform activity convinced some that traditional codes of sexual behavior, weakening before the war, had been restored. One antiprostitution crusader exulted, "Young men of today … are nearer perfection in conduct, morals, and ideals than any similar generation…. Their minds have been raised to ideals that would never have been attained save by the heroism of … the World War."

Labor reforms advanced as well. The Railroad Administration and the **War Labor Board** (WLB), spurred by progressives, encouraged workers to join unions and guaranteed unions' right to bargain with management. The WLB also pressured factory owners to introduce the eight-hour workday, end child labor, and open their plants to safety and sanitation inspectors. Under these favorable conditions, union membership rose from 2.7 million in 1916 to more than 5 million by 1920. Several state legislatures, eager to advance the war effort, passed wage-and-hour laws and other measures benefiting factory workers.

The **Bureau of War Risk Insurance** (BWRI), created in 1917 to aid soldiers' families, established a precedent of government help for families at risk. As Julia Lathrop, head of the Federal Children's Bureau, observed, "The least a democratic nation can do, which sends men into war, is to … [care for] the families." By the war's end, over two million families were receiving regular BWRI checks.

Overall, however, at least in the short run, the war weakened the Progressive Era's powerful social-justice impulse. While the war brought stricter regulation of the economy—a key progressive goal—business interests often dominated the regulatory agencies, and these agencies were quickly dismantled after the war. The government's repression of radicals and antiwar dissenters fractured the fragile coalition of left-leaning progressives, women's groups, trade unionists, socialists, and politicians that had supported the prewar reforms, and ushered in a decade of reaction. The 1918 midterm election signaled the shift, as the Democrats lost both houses of Congress to a deeply conservative Republican Party.

Nevertheless, taking a longer view, reform energies, after diminishing in the 1920s, would reemerge in the depression decade of the 1930s (covered in Chapter 24). As Franklin D. Roosevelt's New Deal took shape, the memory of such World War I agencies as the War Industries Board, the War Labor Board, and the Bureau of War Risk Insurance provided ideas and inspiration.

JOYOUS ARMISTICE, BITTER AFTERMATH, 1918–1920

The euphoria that greeted the November 1918 armistice proved short lived. Having defined America's war aims in lofty terms, Woodrow Wilson dominated the 1919 peace conference but failed in his most cherished objective—American membership in the League of Nations. Amid a sour climate of racism and intolerance, the voters in 1920 repudiated Wilsonian idealism and internationalism and elected a conservative Republican as president.

Wilson's Fourteen Points; The Armistice　President Wilson took America to war determined to put his personal stamp on the peace. He and his reform-minded supporters believed that U.S. participation could transform a sordid squabble for power and empire into a crusade for a transformed world order. Wilson recruited a group of advisers to translate his vision into specific war aims. The need for such a statement grew urgent after the Bolsheviks, having seized power in Russia, published the self-serving secret treaties negotiated by European powers before the war.

Addressing Congress in January 1918, Wilson summed up U.S. war aims in four-teen points. Eight of these promised the subject peoples of the Austro-Hungarian and Ottoman empires the right of self-determination—that is, the freedom to choose their own political futures. A ninth point insisted that imperial disputes should consider the interests of the colonized peoples. The remaining five points offered Wilson's larger postwar vision: a world of free navigation, free trade, reduced armaments, openly negotiated treaties, and "a general association of nations" to resolve conflicts peacefully. The **Fourteen Points** solidified American support for the war, especially among liberals. They seemed proof that America was fighting for noble motives, not selfish aims.

In early October 1918, facing defeat, Germany proposed an armistice based on Wilson's Fourteen Points. The British and French hesitated, but when Wilson threatened to negotiate a separate peace, they agreed. Meanwhile, in Berlin, Kaiser Wilhelm II had abdicated and a German republic had been proclaimed.

In the early morning of November 11, 1918, the Allied commander Marshal Foch and his German counterparts signed an armistice ending hostilities at 11:00 A.M. Rockets burst over the front that night, not in anger but in relief and celebration. In America, cheering throngs (some wearing masks against the influenza epidemic) filled the streets. "Everything for which America has fought has been accomplished," Wilson proclaimed.

As troop ships ferried the soldiers home, Captain Harry Truman of Missouri described his feelings in a letter to his fiancée:

> I've never seen anything that looks so good as the Liberty Lady in New York Harbor … [T]he men … have been in so many hard places that it takes something real to give them a thrill, but when the band … played "Home Sweet Home" there were not many dry eyes. The hardest of hard-boiled cookies even had to blow his nose a time or two.

The Versailles Peace Conference, 1919

Unwisely, Wilson decided to lead the U.S. delegation to the peace conference himself. The strain of long bargaining sessions would take its toll on his frail nerves. Wilson compounded his mistake by naming only one Republican to the delegation, an elderly diplomat with little influence in the party. Selecting more prominent Republicans might have spared Wilson future grief. The Democrats' loss of Congress in 1918 offered a further ill omen.

Nevertheless, crowds cheered and ships' whistles blared on December 4, 1918, as the *George Washington*, a converted German liner, left New York, bearing Wilson to Europe—the first sitting U. S. president to go abroad. The giddy mood continued when Wilson reached Europe. Shouts of "Voodrow Veelson" rang out as he rode up the Champs-Élysées, Paris's ceremonial boulevard. In England, children spread flowers in his path. In Italy, a local official compared him to Jesus Christ.

The euphoria faded once the peace conference began at the palace of Versailles near Paris, where, 136 years before, diplomats had signed the treaty ending the Revolutionary War. Joining Wilson were the other Allied heads of state: Italy's

Vittorio Orlando; France's aged and cynical Georges Clemenceau; and England's David Lloyd George, whom Wilson called "slippery as an eel." Japan participated as well.

The French and British came to the **Versailles Peace Conference** determined to punish Germany for their nations' wartime losses. Their vindictive agenda bore little relation to Wilson's liberal vision. As Clemenceau remarked, "God gave us the Ten Commandments and we broke them. Mr. Wilson has given us the Fourteen Points. We shall see."

Differences quickly surfaced. Italy demanded a port on the eastern Adriatic Sea. Japan insisted on the trading rights it had seized from Germany in the Chinese province of Shandong (Shantung). Clemenceau and Lloyd George were obsessed with revenge. At one point, an appalled Wilson threatened to leave the conference.

Reflecting this toxic climate, the peace treaty the sullen German delegation signed was harshly punitive. Germany was disarmed, stripped of its colonies, forced to admit sole blame for the war, and saddled with staggering reparation payments. France regained border provinces lost to Germany in 1871 and took control for fifteen years of Germany's coal-rich Saar Basin. The treaty demilitarized Germany's western border and transferred a slice of eastern Germany to Poland. These provisions cost Germany one-tenth of its population and one-eighth of its territory. The treaty granted Japan's Shandong claims and gave Italy a slice of Austria that contained two hundred thousand German-speaking inhabitants. These harsh terms, bitterly resented in Germany, planted the seeds of World War II.

Some provisions did reflect Wilson's themes of democracy and self-determination. Germany's former colonies went to the various Allies under a "mandate" or trusteeship system that in theory promised eventual independence. The treaty also recognized the independence of Poland and the Baltic states of Estonia, Latvia, and Lithuania (seized by Germany in its 1918 peace treaty with Bolshevik Russia). Separate treaties provided for the independence of Czechoslovakia and Yugoslavia, new nations carved from the Austro-Hungarian and Ottoman empires.

Palestine, a part of the Ottoman Empire, went to Great Britain under a mandate arrangement. In 1917, after gaining military control of Palestine, the British had issued the Balfour Declaration supporting a Jewish "national home" in the region while also acknowledging the rights of the non-Jewish Palestinians.

But the statesmen of Versailles ignored the aspirations of colonized peoples in Asia and Africa—people like Ho Chi Minh. A young Vietnamese nationalist who would later lead his nation, Ho tried unsuccessfully to secure Vietnamese independence from France.

Nor did the peacemakers come to terms with revolutionary Russia. Indeed, in August 1918 a fourteen-nation Allied army, including some seven thousand U.S. troops, had landed at Russian ports, ostensibly to protect Allied war equipment. In fact, the aim was to overthrow the new Bolshevik regime, whose communist ideology terrified European and American leaders. President Wilson, having welcomed the liberal Russian revolution of March 1917, viewed the Bolshevik coup and Russia's withdrawal from the war as a betrayal of his hopes for a democratic Russia. The Versailles treaty reflected this hostility. Its territorial provisions for Eastern Europe were designed to weaken communist Russia. Not until 1933 would the United States recognize the Soviet Union.

The Fight over the League of Nations

Dismayed by the treaty's vindictive features, Wilson focused on his one shining achievement at Versailles—a treaty provision, or covenant, creating a new international organization, the **League of Nations**. The League covenant embodied Wilson's vision of a new world order of peace and justice.

But Wilson's League faced major hurdles. A warning shot came in February 1919 when thirty-nine Republican senators and senators-elect, including powerful Henry Cabot Lodge, signed a letter rejecting the League in its present form. To reject the League covenant, Wilson retorted defiantly, would destroy the Versailles treaty's "whole vital structure."

When Wilson sent the treaty to the Senate for ratification in July 1919, Lodge bottled it up in the Foreign Relations Committee. To rally popular opinion, Wilson left Washington in September for a national speaking tour. Covering more than nine thousand miles by train, Wilson defended the League before large and friendly audiences. People wept as he described his visits to American war cemeteries in France and sketched his vision of a new world order.

But the trip exhausted Wilson, and on September 25 he collapsed in Colorado. His train sped back to Washington, where on October 2, he suffered a severe stroke. Wilson spent the rest of his term mostly in bed or in a wheelchair, a reclusive invalid, his fragile emotions betraying him into tearful outbursts and irrational, self-defeating actions. He broke with close advisers, refused to see the British ambassador, and dismissed Secretary of State Lansing, accusing him of disloyalty. In January 1920, he rejected his physician's advice to resign.

Wilson's first wife had died in 1914. His strong-willed second wife, Edith Galt, played a crucial behind-the-scenes role during this crisis. She concealed Wilson's condition from the public, controlled his access to information, and decided who could see him, barring cabinet members, diplomats, and congressional leaders. When one leader seeking a meeting urged Mrs. Wilson to consider "the welfare of the country," she snapped, "I am not thinking of the country now, I am thinking of my husband." (The Twenty-fifth Amendment, addressing issues of presidential disability, was not adopted until 1967.)

Against this grim backdrop, the League drama unfolded. On September 10, 1919, the Foreign Relations Committee at last sent the treaty to the Senate, but with a series of amendments. The Senate split into three groups. First were Democrats who supported the treaty without changes, including U.S. membership in the League of Nations. Second were Republican "Irreconcilables," led by Hiram Johnson of California, Wisconsin's Robert La Follette, and Idaho's William Borah, who opposed the League absolutely. Intensely nationalistic, they feared that League membership would restrict U.S. freedom of action and entangle America with corrupt foreign powers. Finally, a group of Republican "Reservationists," led by Lodge, demanded amendments as a condition of their support. The Reservationists especially objected to Article 10 of the League covenant, which pledged each member nation to defend the independence and territorial integrity of all other members. This provision, they believed, limited America's sovereignty and infringed on Congress's constitutional power to declare war.

Had Wilson compromised, the Senate would probably have ratified the Versailles treaty, including the League covenant, with amendments. But Wilson, ill and unyielding, instructed Senate Democrats to reject the Foreign Relations Committee's version of the treaty, which now included Lodge's reservations. Although international-law specialists argued that these reservations would not prevent U.S. participation in the League, Wilson stood firm.

Despite Wilson's speaking tour, the public did not rally behind the League, thanks in part to the reactionary mood his own administration had helped create. As the *Nation* magazine observed, "If [Wilson] loses his great fight for humanity, it will be because he was deliberately silent when freedom of speech and the right of conscience were struck down in America."

On November 19, 1919, pro-League Democrats, obeying Wilson's instructions, and anti-League Irreconcilables joined forces to defeat the proposed measure that included Lodge's reservations. A second vote in March 1920 produced the same result. The United States would not join the forty-four nations who in January 1920 launched the League of Nations, the forerunner of the United Nations. What might have been Wilson's crowning achievement had turned to ashes.

Racism and Red Scare, 1919– 1920   The war's strident patriotism left a bitter aftertaste. The years 1919–1920 brought new racial violence and anti-radical hysteria. Seventy-six blacks were lynched in 1919, the worst toll in fifteen years. The victims included ten veterans, several still in uniform. In Omaha, a mob inflamed by sensational newspaper stories seized a black prisoner from the courthouse, hanged him from a lamppost, dragged his bodythrough the streets, and burned it. Henry Fonda, a future film actor, witnessed the lynching as a fourteen-year-old. "It was the most horrendous sight I'd ever seen," he later recalled.

The worst violence exploded in Chicago, where simmering racial tension erupted on a hot afternoon in July 1919. When a black youth swimming at a Lake Michigan beach drowned after whites had pelted him with stones, black neighborhoods erupted in fury. A thirteen-day reign of terror followed as white and black marauders engaged in random attacks and arson. Black gangs stabbed an Italian peddler; white gangs pulled blacks from streetcars and shot or whipped them. The outbreak left fifteen whites and twenty-three blacks dead, over five hundred injured, and more than a thousand families, mostly black, homeless.

Wartime antiradicalism crested in a postwar Red Scare. (Communists were called "reds" because of the red flag favored by revolutionary organizations.) A rash of strikes in 1919 deepened overwrought fears of a communist takeover in America. When the IWW and other unions called a general strike in Seattle, the panicky mayor accused the strikers of seeking to "duplicate the anarchy of Russia" and called for federal troops to maintain order. Anxiety crackled again in April, when various public officials received packages containing bombs. One severely injured a senator's maid; another damaged the home of Attorney General A. Mitchell Palmer. When 350,000 steelworkers went on strike in September, mill owners ran newspaper ads denouncing the leaders as "Red agitators."

Antiradical paranoia also infected politics. In 1919, the House of Representatives refused to seat Milwaukee socialist Victor Berger, recently indicted under the Espionage Act. Milwaukee voters promptly reelected him, but the House stood firm. The New York legislature expelled several socialist members. The Justice Department set up an antiradical division under young J. Edgar Hoover, future head of the Federal Bureau of Investigation, who ordered the arrest of hundreds of suspected communists and radicals. In December 1919, the government deported 249 Russian-born aliens, including Emma Goldman, a prominent lecturer and birth-control advocate.

On January 2, 1920, in a Justice Department dragnet coordinated by Wilson's politically ambitious Attorney General, A. Mitchell Palmer, federal marshals and local police raided the homes of suspected radicals and the headquarters of radical organizations in thirty-two cities. Without search warrants or arrest warrants, they arrested more than four thousand persons (some 550 were eventually deported) and seized a horde of papers. Boston police paraded arrested persons through the streets in handcuffs and chains and jammed them into unsanitary cells without formal charges or the opportunity to post bail.

Gripped by anticommunist hysteria, Palmer luridly described the menace he believed his raids had averted: "The blaze of revolution was sweeping over every American institution of law and order ... eating its way into the homes of the American workman, its sharp tongues of revolutionary heat ... licking at the altars of the churches, leaping into the belfry of the school bell, crawling into the sacred corners of American homes ... burning up the foundations of society."

The hysteria soon subsided. When a bomb exploded in New York City's financial district in September 1920, killing thirty-eight people, most Americans saw the deed as the work of an isolated fanatic, not evidence of approaching revolution.

The Election of 1920

As the 1920 election approached, the invalid Wilson, lost in fantasy, considered seeking a third term, but was dissuaded. Few heeded his call to make the election a "solemn referendum" on the League. "The bitterness toward Wilson is everywhere ...," wrote a Democratic campaign worker; "he hasn't a friend."

The Democratic convention in San Francisco nominated James M. Cox, the mildly progressive governor of Ohio. As Cox's running mate they chose the young assistant secretary of the navy, Franklin D. Roosevelt, who possessed a potent political name.

The confident Republicans, meeting in Chicago, nominated Senator **Warren G. Harding** of Ohio, an amiable politician of little distinction. As one GOP leader observed, "There ain't any first raters this year.... We got a lot of second raters, and Harding is the best of the second raters." For vice president, they chose Massachusetts governor Calvin Coolidge, who had won attention in 1919 with his denunciation of a Boston policemen's strike.

Harding's vacuous campaign speeches reminded one critic of "an army of pompous phrases moving over the landscape in search of an idea." But many voters welcomed his reassuring promise of a return to "normalcy," and he won in a landslide. Nearly a million citizens defiantly voted for socialist Eugene Debs, still imprisoned for his earlier antiwar speeches.

The election dashed all hope for American entry into the League of Nations. Senator Lodge expressed grim satisfaction that the voters had ripped "Wilsonism" up by the roots. The sense of high purpose Wilson had evoked in April 1917 seemed remote indeed as Americans turned to a new president and a new era.

CHRONOLOGY
1899–1920

1899 First U.S. Open Door note seeking access to China market.
Boxer Rebellion erupts in China.

1900 Second U.S. Open Door note.

1904 President Theodore Roosevelt proclaims
"Roosevelt Corollary" to Monroe Doctrine.

1905 Roosevelt mediates the end of the Russo-Japanese War.

1906 At the request of Roosevelt, San Francisco ends segregation of Asian schoolchildren.
Panama Canal construction begins.

1911 U.S.-backed revolution in Nicaragua.

1912 U.S. Marines occupy Nicaragua.

1914 U.S. troops occupy Veracruz, Mexico.
Panama Canal opens.
World War I begins.
President Wilson proclaims American neutrality.

1915 U.S. Marines occupy Haiti and the Dominican Republic.
Woman's Peace Party organized.
British liner *Lusitania* sunk by German U-boat.
Wilson permits U.S. bank loans to Allies.

1916 U.S. punitive expedition invades Mexico, seeking Pancho Villa.
Germany pledges not to attack merchant ships without warning.
Wilson reelected.

1917 U.S. troops withdraw from Mexico.
Germany resumes unrestricted U-boat warfare;
United States declares war. Selective Service Act sets up national draft.
War Industries Board, Committee on Public Information, and Food Administration created.
Espionage Act passed.
War Risk Insurance Act authorizes payments to servicemen's dependents.
NAACP march in New York City protests upsurge in lynchings.
Bolsheviks seize power in Russia; Russia leaves the war.
New York State passes woman-suffrage referendum.
U.S. government operates the nation's railroads.
Striking miners forcibly expelled from Bisbee, Arizona.

1918 Wilson outlines Fourteen Points.
Sedition Amendment passed.
Global influenza pandemic takes heavy toll in United States.
National War Labor Board created.
American forces see action at Château-Thierry, Belleau Wood, St. Mihiel, and Meuse-Argonne campaign.
Republicans win control of both houses of Congress (November 5).
Armistice signed (November 11).

1919 Eighteenth Amendment added to the Constitution (prohibition).
Peace treaty, including League of Nations covenant, signed at Versailles.
Supreme Court upholds silencing of war critics in *Schenck v. United States*.

Upsurge of lynchings; racial violence in Chicago.
Wilson suffers paralyzing stroke.
Versailles treaty, with League covenant, rejected by Senate.

1920   "Red raids" organized by Justice Department.
Nineteenth Amendment added to the Constitution (woman suffrage).
Warren G. Harding elected president.

CONCLUSION

The early twentieth century saw intensifying U.S. involvement abroad. Focused initially on Latin America and Asia, this new globalism arose from a desire to export American values, promote U.S. business interests internationally, and extend the power of a newly confident, industrialized nation.

After initial neutrality, the nation's 1917 decision to enter the European war on the Allied side reflected a combination of cultural ties, economic interests, concern for neutral rights, and President Wilson's dream of a transformed world order emerging from the carnage.

By conservative estimates, World War I cost 10 million dead. Included in this toll were 112,000 American soldiers—forty-nine thousand in battle and sixty-three thousand from disease, mostly influenza. The toll of dead and injured reflected new technologies of warfare, from U-boat torpedoes and primitive aerial bombs to tanks, poison gas, and deadlier machine guns. The Allies won, but Wilson's visionary hopes, including American membership in the new League of Nations, went unrealized.

The war had far-reaching social, political, and economic effects. It advanced some reforms, notably woman suffrage and the campaigns against prostitution and alcohol. As war measures, the government expanded its regulatory power over corporations and took steps to ensure workers' well-being and right to organize. These initiatives offered models that would prove influential in the future.

But in a larger sense, the war undermined progressivism's openness to new ideas, its larger commitment to social justice, and its humanitarian concern for society's most vulnerable members. As government propaganda encouraged ideological conformity and fear of radicalism, the reform impulse withered. The reactionary climate intensified in the early postwar era.

The war at least temporarily improved the economic prospects of many workers, farmers, blacks, and women, and enhanced the standing of the corporate executives, psychologists, public-relations specialists, and other professionals who contributed their expertise to the cause. Internationally, despite the wrangles that kept America out of the League of Nations, the conflict underscored America's new status as a world power, and left the nation's businesses and financial institutions poised for global expansion.

Some of these changes endured; others proved fleeting. Cumulatively, however, their effect was profound. The nation that celebrated the armistice in November 1918 was very different from the one that Woodrow Wilson had solemnly taken into battle only nineteen months earlier.

23

COPING WITH CHANGE, 1920–1929

CHAPTER OUTLINE

• A New Economic Order • Standpat Politics in a Decade of Change
• Mass Society, Mass Culture • Cultural Ferment and Creativity • A Society
in Conflict • Hoover at the Helm

A NEW ECONOMIC ORDER

Fueled by new products and new ways of producing and selling goods, the economy surged in the 1920s. Not everyone benefited, and farmers suffered severe economic woes. Still, the overall picture appeared rosy. These economic changes influenced the decade's political, social, and cultural climate, as Americans confronted a changing society.

Booming Business, Ailing Agriculture

Recession struck in 1920 as Washington canceled wartime defense contracts and veterans reentered the job market. Recovery came by 1922, however, and for the next few years the nonfarm economy hummed. Unemployment fell to 3 percent, prices held steady, and the gross national product (GNP) grew by 43 percent from 1922 to 1929.

New consumer goods, including electrical products, fed the prosperity. By the mid-1920s, with more than 60 percent of the nation's homes electrified, new appliances, from refrigerators and vacuum cleaners to fans and razors, filled the stores. The manufacture and marketing of such appliances, as well as the construction of hydroelectric generating plants and equipment, provided a massive economic stimulus.

The automobile helped fuel the boom. Introduced before the war (see Chapter 21), automobiles spread like wildfire in the 1920s. By 1930, some 60 percent of U.S. families owned cars. Ford Motor Company led the market until mid-decade, when General Motors (GM) spurted ahead by touting comfort and color (Ford's Model T came only in black). GM's lowest-priced car, named for French automotive designer Louis Chevrolet, proved especially popular. In 1927 **Henry Ford** introduced the stylish Model A in various colors. By the decade's end, the automobile industry accounted for about 9 percent of all manufacturing wages and had stimulated such industries as rubber, gasoline and motor oil, advertising, and highway construction.

The stock market reflected the prevailing prosperity, and then far outran it. As the decade ended, a speculative frenzy gripped Wall Street (covered in Chapter 24).

The business boom reverberated globally. To supply overseas markets, Ford, GM, and other corporations built production facilities abroad. U.S. firms acquired foreign factories or sources of raw materials. U.S. meatpackers built plants in Argentina; Anaconda Copper bought Chile's biggest copper mine; the mammoth United Fruit Company established plants across Latin America. But true economic globalization lay far ahead. Economic nationalism prevailed in the 1920s, as the industrialized nations, including the United States, erected high tariff barriers. The Fordney-McCumber Tariff (1922) and the Smoot-Hawley Tariff (1930) pushed U.S. tariffs to all-time highs, helping domestic manufacturers but stifling foreign trade.

While prosperity lifted overall wage rates, workers benefited unequally, reflecting regional variations and discriminatory employment practices. The variation between North and South loomed largest. In 1928, unskilled laborers in New England earned an average of forty-seven cents an hour, in contrast to twenty-eight cents in the South. Textile corporations moved south seeking lower wage rates, devastating New England mill towns. African-Americans, women workers, Mexican-Americans, and recent immigrants clustered at the bottom of the wage scale. For farmers, wartime prosperity gave way to hard times. Grain prices plummeted when government purchases for the army dwindled, European agriculture revived, and America's high tariffs depressed agricultural exports. As tractors and other new machinery boosted farm production, the resulting surpluses further weakened prices. Farmers who had bought land and equipment on credit during the war felt the squeeze as payments came due.

New Modes of Producing, Managing, and Selling

Productivity increased dramatically in the 1920s. New assembly-line techniques boosted industrial workers' per capita output by some 40 percent. At Ford plants near Detroit, workers stood in place and performed repetitive tasks as chains conveyed the vehicles past them.

Assembly-line work influenced employees' behavior. Managers discouraged individual initiative. Even conversation or laughter could distract workers from their task. Ford employees learned to speak without moving their lips and adopted an expressionless mask that some called "Fordization of the face." Job satisfaction diminished. Assembly-line labor did not foster the pride that came from farming or mastering a craft. Nor did it offer much prospect of advancement. In Muncie, Indiana, factories employing over four thousand workers announced only ten openings for foremen in 1924–1925.

U.S. mass-production methods had a global impact. *Fordism* became a synonym worldwide for assembly-line manufacturing. In Russia, which purchased twenty-five thousand Ford tractors in the 1920s, people "ascribed a magical quality to the name of Ford," a visitor reported.

Business consolidation, spurred by the war, continued. By the late 1920s, over a thousand companies a year vanished through merger. Corporate giants dominated the major industries: Ford, GM, and Chrysler in automobiles; General Electric and Westinghouse in electricity; and so forth. Samuel Insull, president of Chicago's Commonwealth Edison Company, controlled a sprawling empire of local power companies. By 1930, one hundred corporations controlled nearly half the nation's business. Without actually merging, companies that made similar products formed trade associations to coordinate prices, market share, and product specifications.

As U.S. capitalism matured, management structures evolved. Corporations set up separate divisions for product development, market research, economic forecasting, employee relations, and so on, each under a professional manager.

The shift to a consumer economy affected wage policies. Rather than paying the lowest wages possible, business leaders now realized that higher wages increased consumers' buying power. Henry Ford had led the way in 1914 by paying his workers five dollars a day, well above the average for factory workers. Other companies soon followed suit.

(Archive/Getty Images)

"Honey, Where Did You Park the Car?" *Hundreds of identical Fords jam Nantasket Beach near Boston on a Fourth of July in the early 1920s.*

New systems for distributing goods emerged. Automobiles reached consumers through dealer networks. By 1926, nearly ten thousand Ford dealerships dotted the nation. Chain stores accounted for about 25 percent of retail sales by 1930. The A&P grocery chain boasted 17,500 stores. Department stores grew more inviting, with remodeled interiors and attractive displays. Air conditioning, a recent invention, made department stores (as well as movie theaters and restaurants) welcome havens on summer days.

Advertising and credit sales further stimulated the consumer economy. In 1929, corporations spent nearly $2 billion on radio, billboard, newspaper, and magazine ads, and advertising companies employed some six hundred thousand people. Chicago advertising baron Albert Lasker owned the Chicago Cubs and his own golf course. Advertisers used celebrity endorsements, promises of social success, and threats of social embarrassment. Beneath a picture of a sad young woman, a Listerine mouthwash ad proclaimed: "She was a beautiful girl and talented too.... Yet in the one pursuit ... foremost in the mind of every girl and woman—marriage—she was a failure." Her problem was "halitosis," or bad breath. The remedy, of course, was Listerine, and lots of it.

Portraying a fantasy world of elegance, pleasure, and limitless abundance, ads aroused desires that the advertisers promised to fulfill. One critic in 1925 described the advertisers' "dream world":

> [S]miling faces, shining teeth, schoolgirl complexions, cornless feet, perfect fitting [underwear], distinguished collars, wrinkleless pants, odorless breath, regularized bowels, ... charging motors, punctureless tires, perfect busts, shimmering shanks, self-washing dishes, backs behind which the moon was meant to rise.

The advertisers even defined America's essential meaning in terms of its abundance of material goods and consumers' "freedom of choice" in the marketplace. Buying more and more products, they claimed, fulfilled the "pursuit of happiness" promised in the Declaration of Independence, and was thus the duty of all good citizens.

A few critics challenged the advertisers' cultural dominance. In *Your Money's Worth* (1927), Stuart Chase and F. J. Schlink punctured advertisers' exaggerated claims. One observer called the book "the *Uncle Tom's Cabin* of the consumer movement." The *Consumers' Research Bulletin*, launched by Chase and Schlink in 1929, tested products and reported the results to consumers.

Easy credit further lubricated the economy. Earlier, credit had typically involved pawnbrokers, bank loans, or informal arrangements between buyers and sellers. Now retailers routinely offered credit plans for big-ticket items such as automobiles, furniture, and refrigerators.

Business values saturated 1920s' culture. "America stands for one idea: Business," proclaimed the *Independent* magazine in 1921; "Thru business, ... the human race is finally to be redeemed." Presidents Harding and Coolidge praised corporate America and hobnobbed with business leaders. Magazines profiled business tycoons. A 1923 opinion poll ranked Henry Ford as a leading presidential prospect. In *The Man Nobody Knows* (1925), ad man Bruce Barton described Jesus Christ as a managerial genius who "picked up twelve men from the bottom ranks of business and forged them into an organization that conquered the world."

Although more women worked outside the home in the 1920s, their proportion of the total female population held steady at about 24 percent. Male workers dominated the auto plants and other assembly-line factories.

Women who did enter the workplace faced wage discrimination. In 1929, for example, a male trimmer in the meatpacking industry received fifty-two cents an hour; a female trimmer, thirty-seven cents. The weakening of the union movement hit women workers hard. By 1929, the proportion of women workers belonging to unions fell to a minuscule 3 percent.

Most women workers, especially recent immigrants and members of minority groups, held low-paying, unskilled positions. By 1930, however, some 2 million women were employed in corporate offices as secretaries, typists, or filing clerks, although rarely at higher ranks. Indeed, office-space arrangements often segregated male managers and female clerks.

Nearly fifty thousand women received college degrees in 1930, almost triple the 1920 figure. Of these female graduates who joined the workforce, many entered such traditional "women's professions" as nursing, librarianship, and school teaching. With medical schools limiting the number of women students to 5 percent of their total enrollment, the number of women physicians actually declined from 1910 to 1930. A handful of women, however, following the lead of Progressive Era trailblazers, pursued postgraduate education to become faculty members in colleges and universities.

Marginalized in the workplace, women were courted as consumers. In the decade's advertising, glamorous women smiled behind the steering wheel, swooned over new appliances, and smoked cigarettes in romantic settings. (One ad man promoted cigarettes for women as "torches of freedom.") In the advertisers' dream world, housework became an exciting challenge. As one ad put it, "Men are judged ... according to their power to delegate work. Similarly the wise woman delegates to electricity all that electricity can do."

Struggling Labor Unions in a Business Age   Organized labor struggled in the 1920s. Union membership fell from 5 million to 3.4 million in the decade. Several factors underlay this decline. For one thing, despite inequities and regional variations, overall wage rates rose, reducing the incentive to join a union. Further, the union movement's strength lay in traditional crafts and older industries like printing, railroading, mining, and construction. These unions were ill-suited to the new mass-production factories.

Management hostility further weakened organized labor. Henry Ford hired thugs to intimidate union organizers. In 1929, anti-union violence flared in North Carolina, where textile workers faced low wages, long hours, and appalling work conditions. In Marion, deputy sheriffs shot and killed six striking workers. In Gastonia, the communist-led National Textile Workers Union organized the strike. The mill's absentee owners refused to negotiate and evicted strikers from their company-owned homes. When armed thugs in league with the owners raided an encampment of strikers, the police chief was shot, possibly by one of his own deputies. In the end, these strikes failed, and the textile industry remained nonunion.

As wartime antiradical sentiments persisted, opponents of labor unions often smeared them with the "communist" label, whether accurate or not. The antiunion campaign took subtler forms as well. Manufacturers' associations renamed the non-union shop the "open shop" and dubbed it the "American Plan" of labor relations. Some corporations provided cafeterias and recreational facilities for employees or sold them company stock at reduced prices. Corporate publicists praised "welfare capitalism" (the term for this anti-union strategy) as evidence of employers' benevolent concern for their workers.

Black membership in labor unions stood at only about eighty-two thousand by 1929, mostly miners, dockworkers, and railroad porters. The American Federation of Labor officially prohibited racial discrimination, but most AFL unions in fact barred African-Americans. Corporations often hired jobless blacks as strike-breakers, increasing organized labor's hostility toward them.

Standpat Politics in a Decade of Change

With Republicans in control of Congress and the White House, politics reflected the decade's business orientation. Unsettled by rapid social change, voters turned to conservative candidates who seemed to represent stability and traditional values. In this climate, would-be reformers and exploited groups had few political options.

The Evolving Presidency: Scandals and Public-Relations Manipulation
While white southerners and urban immigrants remained heavily Democratic, the Republican Party continued to attract northern farmers, businesspeople, many white-collar workers and professionals, and some skilled blue-collar workers. The GOP also benefited from the antiradical mood that fueled the early postwar Red Scare (see Chapter 22) and the anti-union campaign. Exploiting such fears, the Republican-led New York legislature set up a committee to investigate "seditious activities" and required loyalty oaths of public-school teachers.

With Republican progressives having bolted to Theodore Roosevelt in 1912, GOP conservatives controlled the 1920 convention and nominated Ohio Senator **Warren G. Harding** for president. As a young newspaper editor, Harding had married the local banker's daughter, who helped manage his 1914 Senate campaign. A genial backslapper, he enjoyed good liquor, a good poker game, and at least one long-term extramarital affair. In the election, Harding swamped his Democratic opponent James M. Cox. After the stresses of war and Wilson's moralizing, voters welcomed Harding's bland oratory.

Harding made some notable cabinet selections: Henry C. Wallace, the editor of an Iowa farm periodical, as secretary of agriculture; **Charles Evans Hughes,** former New York governor and 1916 presidential candidate, secretary of state; and **Andrew Mellon,** a Pittsburgh financier, treasury secretary. **Herbert Hoover,** the wartime food czar, became secretary of commerce.

Harding also made some disastrous appointments: his political manager, Harry Daugherty, as attorney general; a Senate pal, Albert Fall of New Mexico, as secretary of the interior; a wartime draft dodger, Charles Forbes, as Veterans' Bureau head. Such men set the low ethical tone of Harding's presidency. By 1922, Washington rumor hinted at corruption in high places. "I have no trouble with my enemies," Harding told an associate; "[b]ut ... my goddamn friends ... keep me walking the floor nights." In summer 1923, vacationing in the West, Harding suffered a heart attack and died in a San Francisco hotel.

A 1924 Senate investigation exposed the scandals. Charles Forbes, convicted of stealing Veterans' Bureau funds, evaded prison by fleeing abroad. The bureau's top lawyer committed suicide, as did an aide to Attorney General Daugherty accused of influence peddling. Daugherty himself narrowly escaped conviction in two criminal trials. Interior Secretary Fall went to jail for leasing government oil reserves, one in Teapot Dome, Wyoming, to oilmen in return for a $400,000 bribe. Like "Watergate" in the 1970s, **"Teapot Dome"** became a shorthand label for a tangle of scandals.

With Harding's death, Vice President **Calvin Coolidge,** on vacation in Vermont, took the presidential oath by lantern light from his father, a local magistrate. After entering local politics in Massachusetts, Coolidge had been elected Massachusetts governor in 1918 and secured the Republican vice-presidential nomination in 1920.

Coolidge's image as "Silent Cal," a Yankee embodiment of old-fashioned virtues, was carefully crafted. The advertising executive Bruce Barton, an early master of political image-making, guided Coolidge's bid for national office in 1919–1920. Having persuaded a Boston publisher to issue a book of Coolidge's speeches, Barton sent autographed copies to key GOP convention delegates. Barton planted pro-Coolidge articles in magazines and in other ways marketed his candidate just as advertisers were marketing soap, socks, and cereal. The very name *Calvin Coolidge*, he wrote in a *Collier's* magazine article building brand recognition, "seems cut from granite; one could almost strike sparks with such a name, like a flint." Targeting newly enfranchised women, Barton composed a "Message to Women" published under Coolidge's name in *Woman's Home Companion*.

Long before Franklin D. Roosevelt's "fireside chats" of the 1930s (covered in Chapter 24), Bruce Barton understood the political potential of radio. He advised Coolidge to speak conversationally in his radio addresses, avoiding earlier politicians' spread-eagle oratory. Wrote an admirer of Barton: "No man is his equal in [analyzing] the middle-class mind and directing an appeal to it."

Republican Policy Making in a Probusiness Era   While Coolidge raised the ethical tone of the White House, the probusiness policies, symbolized by high tariffs, continued. Prodded by Treasury Secretary Mellon, Congress lowered income-tax rates for the wealthy from their high wartime levels. Lower tax rates for the well-to-do, Mellon argued, would actually increase revenues by reducing the incentive to seek tax shelters. He also contended that tax cuts for high income earners encouraged business investment and thus benefited everyone. In the same probusiness spirit, the Supreme Court under Chief Justice William Howard Taft (appointed by Harding in 1921) overturned a federal ban on child labor passed in 1919.

While promoting corporate interests, Coolidge opposed government assistance for other Americans. This position faced a test in 1927 when torrential spring rains caused severe flooding on the Mississippi River. Soil erosion resulting from poor farming practices worsened the flood conditions, as did ill-considered engineering projects aimed at draining the river's natural floodplain for development purposes. One official described the river as "writh[ing] like an imprisoned snake" within its artificial confines. From Cairo, Illinois, to the Gulf of Mexico, water poured over towns and farms, flooding twenty-seven thousand square miles. Hundreds died, and the toll of the homeless, including many African-Americans, reached several hundred thousand. Disease spread in makeshift refugee camps. Floodwaters swept over New Orleans's low-lying black neighborhoods.

President Coolidge rejected calls to aid the victims. The government had no duty to protect citizens "against the hazards of the elements," he declared. Coolidge did, however, sign the Flood Control Act of 1928 funding levee construction along the Mississippi.

Another test of Coolidge's anti-government ideology came when hard-pressed farmers rallied behind the **McNary-Haugen Bill,** a price-support plan under which the government would purchase the surplus of six basic farm commodities—cotton, corn, rice, hogs, tobacco, and wheat—at their average price in 1909–1914 (when farm prices were high). The government would then sell these surpluses abroad at market prices and recover the difference, if any, through a tax on domestic sales of these commodities. Coolidge twice vetoed the McNary-Haugen bill, warning of "the tyranny of bureaucratic regulation and control." The government must not favor a single interest group, he argued—even though corporations had long benefited from high tariffs and other measures. These vetoes led many angry farmers to vote Democratic in 1928. In the 1930s, New Deal planners would draw upon the McNary-Haugen approach in shaping farm policy (as discussed in Chapter 24).

Independent Internationalism   The Harding and Coolidge administrations continued to oppose U.S. membership in the League of Nations. Coolidge did support U.S. membership in the new International Court of Justice (the World Court), but the Republican-controlled Congress imposed unacceptable reservations, and the U.S. did not join.

Backing away from Woodrow Wilson's idealistic view of America's global destiny, the Republican administrations of the 1920s pursued foreign policies that served America's economic interests—an approach historians have called independent internationalism. Despite postwar Europe's battered economies, Washington demanded repayment of $22 billion in Allied war debts and German reparation payments. A study commission in 1924 reduced these claims, but high U.S. tariffs and Europe's economic problems, including runaway inflation in Germany, made repayment of even the lower claims unrealistic. When Adolf Hitler took power in Germany in 1933 (covered in Chapter 25), he repudiated all reparations payments.

The Republican administrations worked to protect U.S. corporate interests in Latin America. In Mexico, the U.S. State Department vigorously opposed the efforts of a new revolutionary government to regain control of oilfields earlier granted to U.S. companies and to restrict landholding by foreign interests. In Nicaragua, President Coolidge in 1926 sent U.S. Marines to put down an insurrection against the country's president, Adolfo Diàz, who had close ties to a U.S.-owned gold-mining company.

One notable diplomatic achievement was the **Washington Naval Arms Conference.** After the war ended, the United States, Great Britain, and Japan edged toward a dangerous (and costly) naval-arms race. In 1921, Secretary of State Hughes called a Washington conference to address the problem. He startled the delegates by outlining a specific ratio of warships among the world's naval powers. Great Britain, Japan, Italy, and France accepted Hughes's plan, and agreed to halt battleship construction for ten years. The United States and Japan also pledged to respect each other's territorial holdings in the Pacific. Although this treaty ultimately failed to prevent World War II, it did represent an early arms-control effort.

Another U.S. peace initiative was mainly symbolic. In 1928, the United States and France, eventually joined by sixty other nations, signed the Kellogg-Briand Pact renouncing aggression and outlawing war. Lacking enforcement mechanisms, this high-sounding document accomplished little.

Progressive Stirrings, Democratic Party Divisions

The reform spirit survived in Congress. The **Sheppard-Towner Act** (1921) funded rural prenatal and baby-care centers staffed by public-health nurses. The Federal Radio Commission, created by Congress in 1927, extended the regulatory principle to this new industry. A reform-minded Nebraska senator, George Norris, prevented the Coolidge administration from selling a wartime federal hydroelectric plant to Henry Ford at bargain prices. In the 1930s, this Alabama plant would become part of the Tennessee Valley Authority, a key New Deal agency.

In the 1922 midterm election, labor and farm groups joined forces to defeat some conservative Republicans. In 1924, this alliance revived the Progressive Party and nominated Senator Robert La Follette for president. The Socialist Party and the American Federation of Labor endorsed La Follette.

The 1924 Democratic convention in New York City split between urban and rural wings. By one vote, the delegates defeated a resolution condemning the **Ku Klux Klan** (discussed later in this chapter). While the party's Protestant southern wing favored former Treasury Secretary William G. McAdoo, the big-city delegates championed New York's Catholic governor **Alfred E. Smith,** of Irish, German, and Italian immigrant origins. This split mirrored deep divisions in the nation. After 102 ballots, the exhausted delegates nominated an obscure New York corporation lawyer, John W. Davis.

Calvin Coolidge, aided by media adviser Barton, easily won the Republican nomination. The GOP platform praised the high protective tariff and urged tax cuts and reduced government spending. Amid general prosperity, Coolidge polled about twice Davis's total. La Follette's 4.8 million votes cut into the Democratic total, contributing to Coolidge's landslide victory.

Women and Politics in the 1920s: Achievements and Setbacks

Reformers' hope that woman suffrage would transform politics survived briefly after the war. Polling places shifted from saloons to schools and churches. The 1920 major-party platforms endorsed several measures proposed by the League of Women Voters. The Women's Joint Congressional Committee (WJCC), a coalition of activist groups, lobbied for child-labor laws, protection of women workers, maternal health care, and federal support for education. The WJCC played a key role in passage of the Sheppard-Towner Act and in congressional enactment of a constitutional amendment banning child labor in 1924.

As former suffragists scattered across the political spectrum, however, the movement lost focus. The League of Women Voters, drawing middle-class and professional women, played a role in the formation of the WJCC, but otherwise abandoned feminist activism, focusing instead on nonpartisan studies of civic issues. Alice Paul's National Woman's Party proposed a constitutional amendment guaranteeing women equal rights, but other reformers argued that it could jeopardize laws protecting women workers. Politically active African-American women battled racial discrimination rather than addressing feminist issues; Hispanic women in the Southwest focused on labor-union organizing.

The reactionary political climate intensified this retreat from feminist activism. Patriotic groups accused Jane Addams and other woman's-rights leaders of communist sympathies. Younger women, bombarded by ads defining liberation in terms of consumption, rejected the prewar feminists' civic engagement. One in 1927 criticized earlier suffragists' lack of "feminine charm" and their "constant clamor about equal rights."

The reforms backed by women's groups proved short-lived. The Supreme Court struck down child-labor and women's-protective laws. Few states ratified the constitutional amendment banning child labor, as critics accused its supporters, including the WJCC, of undermining the free-enterprise system. The Sheppard-Towner Act, denounced by the American Medical Association for weakening physicians' monopoly of health care, expired in 1929.

MASS SOCIETY, MASS CULTURE

Amid this conservative political climate, major transformations were reshaping society. Assembly lines, advertising, new consumer products, and innovations in mass entertainment and corporate organization all fueled the ferment. While some welcomed these changes; others recoiled in fear.

Cities, Cars, Consumer Goods

In the 1920 census, the urban population (defined as persons living in communities of twenty-five hundred or more) surpassed the rural (see Figure 23.1). The United States had become an urban nation.

Urbanization affected different groups in different ways. African-Americans migrated cityward in massive numbers, especially after the 1927 Mississippi River floods. By 1930, more than 40 percent of the nation's 12 million blacks lived in cities, 2 million of them in urban centers of the North and West (see Figure 23.2). The first black congressman since Reconstruction, Oscar De Priest of Chicago, won election in 1928.

For many women, city life meant eased housework thanks to laborsaving appliances. Store-bought clothes replaced hand-sewn apparel. Home baking and canning declined as bakeries and supermarkets proliferated.

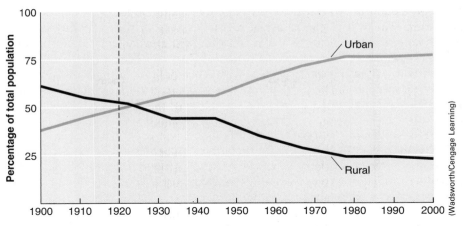

FIGURE 23.1 The Urban and Rural Population of the United States, 1900–2000

The urbanization of America in the twentieth century had profound political, economic, and social consequences.

Source: Census Bureau, Historical Statistics of the United States, *updated by relevant* Statistical Abstracts of the United States, *and U.S. Dept. of Transportation, Federal Highway Administration.*

For social impact, nothing matched the automobile. In *Middletown* (1929), a study of Muncie, Indiana, Robert and Helen Lynd reported one resident's comment: "Why … do you need to study what's changing this country? I can tell you … in just four letters: A-U-T-O."

The A-U-T-O's social impact proved decidedly mixed, including traffic jams, parking problems, and highway fatalities (more than twenty-six thousand in 1924). In some ways, the automobile brought families together. As family vacations became more common, tourist cabins and roadside restaurants sprang up. But the automobile also eroded family cohesion and parental authority. Young people could borrow the car to catch a movie, attend a distant dance, or park in a secluded lovers' lane.

Middle- and upper-class women welcomed the automobile. They could now drive to work, attend meetings, visit friends, and gain a sense of independence. Stereotypes of feminine delicacy faded as women mastered this new technology. As an automotive magazine editorialized in 1927, "[E]very time a woman learns to drive, … it is a threat to yesterday's order of things."

Automobiles offered farm families easier access to neighbors and to the city, lessening rural isolation. The automobile's country cousin, the tractor, increased productivity and reduced the physical demands of farming. Yet increased productivity did not always mean increased profits. And as farmers bought automobiles, tractors, and other mechanized equipment on credit, the rural debt crisis worsened.

Ads celebrated the freedom automobiles offered, in contrast to the fixed routes and schedules of trains and streetcars. Yet the automobile and other forms of motor transport also further standardized American life. Buses carried children to consolidated schools. Neighborhood grocery stores declined as people drove to supermarkets served by trucks bringing commercial foods from distant facilities. With the

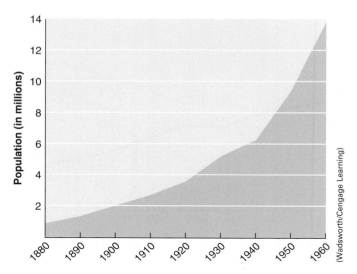

FIGURE 23.2 The African-American Urban Population, 1880–1960 (in Millions)

The increase in America's urban black population from under 1 million in 1880 to nearly 14 million by 1960 represents one of the great rural-urban migrations of modern history.

Source: Historical Statistics of the United States, Colonial Times to 1970 (Washington, D.C.: Bureau of the Census, 1975), vol. I, p. 12.

automobile came the first suburban shopping center (in Kansas City) and the first fast-food chain (A & W Root Beer).

Even at $300 or $400, and despite a thriving used-car market, automobiles remained too expensive for many. The "automobile suburbs" that sprang up beyond the streetcar lines attracted mainly the well-to-do, widening class divisions in American society.

Soaring Energy Consumption and Environmental Threats Electrification and the spread of motorized vehicles impacted America's natural resources and the environment. Electrical generating plants consumed growing quantities of coal. In 1929, U.S. refineries used over a billion barrels of petroleum to meet the gasoline and oil demands of the nation's 20 million cars.

Rising gasoline consumption underlay Washington's efforts to ensure U.S. access to Mexican oil and triggered feverish competition in the oilfields of Texas and Oklahoma. The natural gas found with petroleum seemed so abundant that it was simply burned off. In short, heavy fossil-fuel consumption, though small by later standards, already characterized America in the 1920s.

The wilderness that had inspired nineteenth-century artists and writers became more accessible as cars and improved roads gave easier access to national parks and once-pristine regions. While this development broadened the constituency for wilderness preservation, it also subjected the nation's parks and wilderness areas to heavy pressures as vacationers came to expect service stations, restaurants, hotels,

(Arizona Historical Society/Tucson AHS#62669)

Three Young Hispanic Women of Tucson, Arizona *In this posed photograph featuring an open touring car, these confident and fashionably dressed young women make their social aspirations clear.*

and other amenities. Worried by such contradictions, Secretary of Commerce Herbert Hoover in 1924 called a National Conference on Outdoor Recreation to consider ways to balance wilderness preservation and the decade's vacation-minded leisure culture (see Going to the Source).

The Sierra Club and other groups battled to protect wilderness and wildlife. In 1923, the Izaak Walton League, serving fishing enthusiasts, persuaded Congress to halt a development scheme to drain wetlands on the upper Mississippi. Instead, Congress declared this beautiful waterway a wildlife preserve. For too long, wrote preservationist Aldo Leopold in 1925, "a stump was our symbol of progress." However, few Americans in the expansive 1920s worried about the environmental issues that would occupy future generations.

Mass-Produced Entertainment   Prosperity and workplace drudgery stimulated leisure activities in the 1920s. In their free hours, Americans sought the fulfillment their jobs often failed to provide.

Mass-circulation magazines proliferated. By 1922, ten U.S. magazines boasted circulation of more than 2.5 million. The *Saturday Evening Post,* with its Norman Rockwell covers and fiction featuring small-town life, specialized in nostalgia. *Reader's Digest,* founded in 1921 by DeWitt and Lila Wallace, offered condensed versions of articles first published elsewhere. A journalistic equivalent of the Model T, the *Digest* offered standardized fare for mass consumption.

President Coolidge on the Importance of Outdoor Recreation

In 1924, Secretary of Commerce Herbert Hoover convened a National Conference on Outdoor Recreation in Washington, D. C. Here are extracts from President Coolidge's opening address to the conference.

[Most Americans once led] an active outdoor life in the open country.... Those days long ago passed away for most ... people. There is still ... a tremendous amount of manual labor, but to a large extent this has become specialized and too often would be designated correctly as drudgery.... [M]ore and more [workers] are engaged in purely clerical activities. All of this makes it more necessary than ever that we should stimulate every possible interest in out of door health-giving recreation....

Nearly every city is ... laying out spacious parks and playgrounds ... [and] providing recreation fields for ... outdoor games.... Golf courses and tennis courts abound.... [Cities must] get the children out of the alleys and off the streets into spacious open places where there is good sunlight and plenty of fresh air. Such an opportunity ... restores the natural balance of life and nourishes the moral fiber of youth....

A certain type of outdoor activity has been much developed in recent years and calls great throngs together, which may properly be designated as exhibition games.... [F]irst in importance [is] baseball, which is often known as the national game. Football and polo come in the same class.... [F]or creating an interest which extends to every age and every class, for giving ... a change of scene, a new trend of thought, and the arousing of new enthusiasm for the great multitude of our people, these have no superior....

The famous beauty and symmetry of the Greek race in its prime was due in no small part to their general participation in athletic games.... We can see in the gladiatorial shows of Rome, which degenerated into the butchery alike of beasts and men, the sure sign of moral decay.... It is altogether necessary that we keep our own

Book publishers expanded their market by selling through department stores or directly to the public via the Book-of-the-Month Club (founded 1926). While some criticized such mass-market ventures for debasing literary taste, they did help sustain a common national culture in an increasingly diverse society.

Radio and the movies similarly offered standardized cultural fare. The radio era began on November 2, 1920, when Pittsburgh station KDKA reported Warren Harding's election. In 1922, New York's WEAF began a regular news program, and a Newark station broadcast the World Series (the New York Giants beat the Yankees). Hundreds of new stations soon began operations, as radio fever gripped America.

In 1926, three corporations—General Electric, Westinghouse, and the Radio Corporation of America—formed the first radio network, the National Broadcasting Company (NBC). The Columbia Broadcasting System (CBS) soon followed. Testing popular taste through market research, the networks soon ruled broadcasting. Americans everywhere laughed at the same jokes, heard the same news, and absorbed the same commercials.

amusements and recreations within that field which will be prophetic, not of destruction, but of development.... [Most Americans prefer] clean and manly sports ... [and have] little appetite for that which is unwholesome or brutal....

[Industrial workers] need an opportunity for outdoor life and recreation no less than they need opportunity of employment. Side by side with the industrial plant should be the gymnasium and the athletic field. Along with the learning of a trade ... should go the learning of how to participate in the activities of recreation, by which life is made ... more rounded out and complete....

There is no better common denominator of a people [than] development of national interest in recreation and sports. In the case of a people which represents many nations, cultures and races, as does our own, a unification of interests and ideals in recreations is bound to wield a telling influence for solidarity of the entire population. No more truly democratic force can be set off against the tendency to class and caste than the democracy of ... sport....

I want to see all Americans have a reasonable amount of leisure. Then I want to see them educated to use such leisure for ... strengthening ... the quality of their citizenship. We can go a long way in that direction by getting them out of doors and really interested in nature ... [and] engaging them in games and sports.... We must make [America] a land of vision, a land of work, of sincere striving for the good, but we must [also] ... make it a land of wholesome enjoyment and perennial gladness.

Questions

1. In Coolidge's view, what conditions of modern life make outdoor recreation necessary, and what social benefits will result from such activities?

2. How do Coolidge's views compare with John Muir's? (See Chapter 21, Going to the Source.)

Go to www.cengagedbrain.com for additional primary sources on this period.

Source: John T. Woolley and Gerhard Peters, The American Presidency Project. www.presidency.ucsb.edu/ws/?pid=24169.

Some public-policy commentators advocated preserving radio as an educational and cultural medium, free of advertising, but commercial sponsorship soon won out. The first network comedy show, *Amos 'n Andy* (1928), enriched its sponsor, Pepsodent toothpaste. White actors played the black characters on the program, which softened the realities of a racist society with stereotyped caricatures of African-American life.

The movies migrated from the nickelodeons of the immigrant wards to elegant uptown pleasure palaces and reached all social classes. In 1922, facing protests about sexually suggestive movies, industry moguls named Postmaster General Will Hays, a former head of the Republican National Committee, to police movie morals. While enforcing a code of standards, Hays also promoted Hollywood films.

Despite charges of immorality, movies often reinforced conservative values. *The Ten Commandments* (1923), directed by Cecil B. De Mille (the son of an Episcopal clergyman), cautioned against breaking moral taboos. "America's sweetheart," Mary Pickford, with her look of frail vulnerability, played innocent girls in need of protection, reinforcing traditional gender stereotypes that many young women were challenging.

(Pickford herself sometimes played plucky young women facing danger courageously, and in real life she shrewdly managed her career and financial interests.)

Technical innovations kept moviegoers coming. Al Jolson's *The Jazz Singer* (1927) introduced sound. Walt Disney's cartoon *Steamboat Willy* (1928) not only introduced Mickey Mouse but also showed the potential of animation. By 1930, with weekly attendance approaching 80 million, the corporate giants Metro-Goldwyn-Mayer, Warner Brothers, and Columbia, relying on formulaic plots and typecast stars, produced most films. As U.S. business expanded abroad, Hollywood, too, sought overseas markets.

Like advertising, the movies created a dream world only loosely tethered to reality. One ad promised "all the adventure, ... romance, ... [and] excitement you lack in your daily life." These mass-produced fantasies shaped behavior and values, especially of the young. Hollywood, observed novelist John Dos Passos, offered a "great bargain sale of five-and-ten-cent lusts and dreams." Along with department stores, mass magazines, and advertising, the movies, too, stimulated consumption with alluring images of the good life, opening new vistas of consumer abundance.

The 1920s mass culture was a byproduct of urbanization. Even when advertisers, radio programmers, filmmakers, and magazine editors nostalgically evoked rural or small-town life, they did so from big-city offices and studios.

For all its influence, the new mass culture penetrated society unevenly. It had less impact in rural America, and met resistance among evangelical Christians suspicious of worldly amusements. Mexican-Americans preserved traditional festivals and leisure activities despite the "Americanization" efforts of non-Hispanic priests and well-intentioned outsiders. Working-class African-Americans flocked to concerts by performers outside the mass-culture mainstream like blues singers Bessie Smith and Gertrude "Ma" Rainey. Black-oriented "race records" catered to this specialized market.

Along with network shows, radio stations also broadcast farm reports, local news, church services, community announcements, and ethnic or regional music. Similarly, neighborhood movie theaters provided opportunities for socializing and for exuberant responses to the film. The *Chicago Defender*, voice of the city's black middle class, deplored the raucousness of movie theaters in black neighborhoods, where "during a death scene ... you are likely to hear the orchestra jazzing away." Despite the new mass culture, cultural diversity survived in the 1920s.

Celebrity Culture   Professional sports and media-promoted spectacles provided diversion as well. In 1921, Atlantic City promoters launched a bathing-beauty contest they grandly called the Miss America Pageant. Celebrities dominated professional sports: Babe Ruth of the New York Yankees, who hit sixty home runs in 1927; Ty Cobb, the Detroit Tigers' manager, whose earlier record of 4,191 hits still inspired awe; prizefighters Jack Dempsey and Gene Tunney, whose two heavyweight fights drew massive radio audiences. Ruth was a coarse, heavy-drinking womanizer; Cobb, a foul-tempered racist. Yet the alchemy of publicity transformed them into heroes with contrived nicknames: "the Sultan of Swat" (Ruth) and "the Georgia Peach" (Cobb).

This celebrity culture illuminates the stresses facing ordinary Americans in these years of social change. For young women uncertain about society's shifting expectations, beauty pageants offered one ideal to which they could aspire. For men confronting unsettling developments from feminism to Fordism, the exploits of sports heroes like Dempsey or Ruth could restore damaged self-esteem.

Celebrity worship crested in the response to **Charles Lindbergh,** a daredevil stunt pilot who flew solo across the Atlantic in his small single-engine plane, *The Spirit of St. Louis,* on May 20–21, 1927. A Minnesotan of Swedish ancestry, Lindbergh had entered a $25,000 prize competition offered by a New York hotel for the first nonstop New York-to-Paris flight. His success gripped the public's imagination. In New York, thousands cheered a ticker-tape parade. Radio, newspapers, magazines, and movie newsreels offered saturation coverage.

An instant celebrity, Lindbergh became a blank screen onto which people projected their hopes, fears, and ideologies. President Coolidge praised the flight as a triumph of U.S. business and corporate technology. Many editorial writers, by contrast, saw Lindbergh as proof that despite standardization and mechanization, the individual still counted. Others praised this native-born midwesterner of Scandinavian roots as more authentically American than the recent immigrants crowding the cities.

Overall, the new mass media had mixed social effects. Certainly, they promoted cultural standardization and uniformity of thought. But mass magazines, radio, and movies also helped forge a national culture and introduced new viewpoints and ways of behaving. Implicitly they conveyed a potent message: a person's immediate surroundings need not limit his or her horizons. If the larger world they opened for Americans was often superficial or tawdry, it could also be exciting and liberating.

CULTURAL FERMENT AND CREATIVITY

American life in the 1920s involved more than politics, assembly lines, and celebrity worship. Young people savored the postwar moment as engrained pieties and traditional ways faced challenges. As writers, artists, and musicians embraced the modernist spirit of cultural innovation, African-Americans created a cultural flowering known as the Harlem Renaissance.

The Jazz Age and the Postwar Crisis of Values   The war's disillusioned aftermath sharpened the cultural restlessness already bubbling in prewar America. The year 1918, wrote Randolph Bourne, marked "a sudden ... stop at the end of an intellectual era." Poet Ezra Pound hammered the same point in 1920. America had marched to war, he wrote, to save "a botched civilization; ... an old bitch gone in the teeth."

The postwar cultural ferment, summed up in the phrase "the Jazz Age," took many forms. Some young people—especially affluent college students—boisterously assailed middle-class standards of behavior. Grabbing the freedom offered by the automobile, they threw parties, drank bootleg liquor, and flocked to jazz clubs. Asked her favorite activity, a California college student replied, "I adore dancing; who doesn't?" Urged by advertisers, many young women defied prevailing taboos and took up cigarettes. For some, smoking became a feminist issue. As one female college student reasonably asked, "Why [should] men ... be permitted to smoke while girls are expelled for doing it?"

Young people also discussed sex more freely. Sigmund Freud, the Viennese physician who explored the sexual aspects of human psychology, enjoyed a popular vogue in the 1920s. Despite much talk about sex and charges of rampant immorality, however, the 1920s' "sexual revolution" is hard to pin down. Premarital intercourse remained exceptional and widely disapproved, especially for women.

What *can* be documented are changing courtship patterns. "Courting" had once been a formal prelude to marriage. The 1920s brought the more casual practice of "dating," whereby young people gained social confidence and a degree of sexual experience without necessarily contemplating marriage. Wrote novelist F. Scott Fitzgerald, "None of the Victorian mothers had any idea how casually their daughters were accustomed to be kissed." A Methodist bishop denounced new dances that brought "the bodies of men and women in unusual relation to each other." The 1920s saw greater erotic freedom, but within bounds, as most young people drew a clear line between permissible and taboo behavior.

For women, these changes in some ways proved liberating. Female sexuality was more openly acknowledged. Skirt lengths crept up; makeup became more acceptable; and the elaborate armor of petticoats and corsets fell away. The awesome matronly bosom mysteriously deflated as a more boyish figure became the fashion ideal.

An enduring twenties stereotype is "the flapper," the sophisticated, pleasure-mad young woman. (The term originated with a magazine illustration of a fashionable young lady whose rubber rain boots were open and flapping.) In the nineteenth century, the idealized woman on her moral pedestal had symbolized an elaborate complex of cultural ideals. The flapper, with her bobbed hair, defiant cigarette, lipstick, and short skirt, although a journalistic creation, similarly epitomized youthful rejection of entrenched stereotypes.

In some ways, however, 1920s' mass culture thwarted full gender equality nearly as effectively as had earlier Victorian stereotypes. Many young women, while rejecting older taboos, now molded their appearance according to standards dictated by fashion magazines. Advertisers and movies encouraged women to pursue a "glamorous" lifestyle by purchasing new fashions, cosmetics, silk stockings, and other consumer accessories. Further, the traditional double standard, which held women to a stricter behavior code, remained in force. Young men could boast of sexual exploits, but young women who "went all the way" or were reputed to be "fast" risked damaged reputations.

Around 1922, according to F. Scott Fitzgerald, adults embraced the rebelliousness of the young. As middle-aged Americans "discovered that young liquor will take the place of young blood," he wrote, "the orgy began." But such sweeping cultural generalizations can mislead. During the years of Fitzgerald's alleged national orgy, the divorce rate remained constant, and many conservative, religious Americans clung to traditional standards, rejecting alcohol and wild parties. Many farmers, industrial workers, blacks, Hispanics, and recent immigrants found economic concerns more pressing than the latest fads.

The "Jazz Age" was partially a media and literary creation. Fitzgerald's romanticized novel about affluent postwar youth, *This Side of Paradise* (1920), spawned many imitators. With his movie-idol good looks, Fitzgerald not only wrote about the Jazz Age but lived it. Yet if the Jazz Age stereotype obscured the complexity of

(Stock Montage)

F. Scott Fitzgerald and His Wife Zelda *While Fitzgerald chronicled the 1920s in his fiction, he and Zelda lived the high life in New York, Paris, and the French Riviera.*

the 1920s, it did capture a part of the postwar scene, especially the raucous new mass culture and the hedonism and materialism of the well-to-do as they basked in the era's prosperity.

Alienated Writers   Like Fitzgerald, many young writers found the decade's cultural turbulence energizing. Rejecting the old order's moralistic pieties, they also disliked the business pieties of the new order. In *Main Street* (1920), novelist Sinclair Lewis satirized the smugness and cultural barrenness of Gopher Prairie, a fictional mid-western town based on his native Sauk Centre, Minnesota. In *Babbitt* (1922), Lewis skewered a mythic larger city, Zenith, and the protagonist George F. Babbitt, a real-estate agent trapped in middle-class conformity.

H. L. Mencken, a journalist and critic, in 1924 launched the iconoclastic *American Mercury* magazine, an instant success with alienated intellectuals and college youth. Mencken championed writers like Lewis and Theodore Dreiser while ridiculing politicians, small-town America, Protestant fundamentalism, and the middle-class "Booboisie." His essays on Harding, Coolidge, and Bryan remain classics of political satire. Asked why he stayed in America, Mencken replied, "Why do people visit zoos?"

For the novelist Ernest Hemingway, seriously wounded in 1918 while a Red Cross volunteer on the Italian front, World War I was a watershed experience. In 1926, now an expatriate in Paris, Hemingway published *The Sun Also Rises,* portraying a group of American and English young people, variously damaged by the war, as they drift around Spain. His *A Farewell to Arms* (1929), loosely based on his own experiences, depicts the war's futility and politicians' empty rhetoric. In one passage, the narrator says,

> *I was always embarrassed by the words sacred, glorious, and sacrifice and the expression in vain. We ... had read them, on proclamations that were slapped up ... over other proclamations, now for a long time, and I had seen nothing sacred, and the things that were glorious had no glory and the sacrifices were like the stockyards at Chicago if nothing was done with the meat except to bury it.*

Although writers like Hemingway and Lewis blasted wartime hypocrisy and postwar vulgarity, they remained American at heart, striving to create a more authentic national culture. Even Fitzgerald, himself caught up in Jazz Age excesses, was fundamentally a moralist. His masterpiece, *The Great Gatsby* (1925), portrayed not only the party-filled lives of the decade's moneyed class, but also their superficiality, selfishness, and heedless disregard for the less fortunate.

Architects, Painters, and Musicians Confront Modern America

A burst of architectural creativity transformed the urban skyline in the 1920s. By 1930, New York City boasted four buildings more than fifty stories tall. Work on the 102-story Empire State Building, long the world's tallest building, began that year. The skyscraper, proclaimed one writer, "epitomizes ... American civilization." Cultural critic Lewis Mumford, by contrast, in *Sticks and Stones* (1924) and other works, deplored urban America's skyscrapers and automobile-clogged streets. Mumford preferred smaller communities and regional cultures to the congested cities and mass culture of 1920s' America.

The decade's leading painters took America—real or imagined—as their subject. While Thomas Hart Benton evoked a past of cowboys, pioneers, and riverboat gamblers, Edward Hopper portrayed faded towns and lonely cities of the present. Hopper's painting *Sunday* (1926), picturing a man slumped on the curb of an empty street of abandoned stores, conveyed both the bleakness and potential beauty of urban America.

The painter and photographer Charles Sheeler found inspiration in factories, including Henry Ford's plant near Detroit. The Italian immigrant Joseph Stella captured New York's vitality in such paintings as *The Bridge* (1926), an abstract representation of the Brooklyn Bridge. Wisconsin's Georgia O'Keeffe, who moved to New York City in 1918, evoked the allure of the metropolis in her paintings of the later 1920s.

The decade's creative ferment inspired composers as well. Ruth Crawford Seeger arranged American folksongs for the poet Carl Sandburg's *American Song-bag* (1927). Carl Ruggles set a Walt Whitman poem to music in 1923. And Frederick Converse's ambitious 1927 tone poem about the automobile, "Flivver Ten Million," featured such episodes as "May Night by the Roadside" and "The Collision."

Of all the musical innovations, jazz best captured the modernist spirit. The Original Dixieland Jass Band—white musicians imitating New Orleans' black jazz bands —had debuted in New York City in 1917, launching a vogue that spread by live performances, radio, and recordings. The white bandleader Paul Whiteman offered watered-down "jazz" versions of standard tunes, and white composers embraced jazz as well. George Gershwin's *Rhapsody in Blue* (1924) and *An American in Paris* (1928) revealed strong jazz influences.

Meanwhile, black musicians preserved authentic jazz and explored its potential. The 1920s recordings of trumpeter Louis Armstrong and his band decisively influenced the future of jazz. While the composer and bandleader Duke Ellington mesmerized audiences at Harlem's Cotton Club, Fletcher Henderson's band, featuring singer Ethel Waters and saxophonist Coleman Hawkins, held forth at New York's Roseland Ballroom. Pianists Fats Waller, Ferdinand "Jelly Roll" Morton, and Earl Hines demonstrated that instrument's jazz potential. Although much of 1920s' popular culture faded quickly, jazz endured.

The Harlem Renaissance

Jazz was only one of many black contributions to 1920s' American culture. The social upheavals of these years energized African-American cultural life, especially in New York City's Harlem. Once an elite white suburb, Harlem attracted many African-Americans during and after World War I, and by 1930 most of New York's 327,000 blacks lived within its boundaries. This concentration, plus the proximity of Broadway theaters, record companies, book publishers, and the NAACP's national headquarters, all contributed to the Harlem Renaissance.

This cultural flowering took varied forms. The Mississippi-born black composer William Grant Still, moving to Harlem in 1922, produced many works, including *Afro American Symphony* (1931). Painter Aaron Douglas and sculptor Augusta Savage explored the visual arts. Savage, moving from Florida to Harlem in 1921, opened a studio and later an art school.

The 1921 Broadway hit *Shuffle Along* launched a series of popular all-black musicals. Film-maker Oscar Micheaux featured black actors and black story lines. The multi-talented Paul Robeson gave vocal concerts; made films; and appeared on Broadway in Eugene O'Neill's *The Emperor Jones* and other plays.

Poet Langston Hughes incorporated African themes and southern black traditions in *The Weary Blues* (1926), and the Jamaican-born poet and novelist Claude McKay evoked Harlem's vibrant, sometimes sinister, nightlife in *Home to Harlem* (1928). In *Cane* (1923), Jean Toomer used poetry, drama, and fictional vignettes to convey the world of the rural black South. Novelist Nella Larsen, from the Danish West Indies, told of a mulatto woman's struggles in *Quicksand* (1928). In *The New Negro* (1925), Alain Locke, a philosophy professor at Howard University, assembled essays, poems, short stories, and artworks to document Harlem's cultural riches.

The white cultural establishment took notice. Book publishers and magazine editors courted black writers. Broadway producers mounted black shows. Whites jammed Harlem's jazz clubs. The 1929 Hollywood film *Hallelujah,* featuring an all-black cast, romanticized plantation life and dramatized the city's dangers. DuBose Heyward's 1925 novel *Porgy* (adapted for the stage by Heyward and his wife Dorothy) drew inspiration from Charleston's African-American community. George Gershwin's musical version, *Porgy and Bess,* premiered in 1935.

The Harlem Renaissance resonated internationally. Jazz won fans in Europe. Langston Hughes and Claude McKay found readers in Africa, Latin America, and Europe. The dancer and singer Josephine Baker, after debuting in Harlem, moved to Paris in 1925, where her highly erotic performances created a sensation.

With white support came misunderstanding and attempts at control. Rebellious young whites romanticized Harlem nightlife, ignoring the community's social problems. Some whites idealized black culture for its spiritual or "primitive" qualities. When Langston Hughes's poems addressed the gritty realities of black life in America, his wealthy white patron angrily withdrew her support. Wrote Hughes: "[S]he felt that [Negroes] were America's great link with the primitive.... But unfortunately I did not feel the rhythms of the primitive surging through me ... I was not Africa. I was Chicago and Kansas City and Broadway and Harlem."

The exuberance of the Harlem Renaissance faded as hard times hit in the 1930s. Nevertheless, it stands as a memorable cultural achievement. Future black writers, artists, musicians, and performers would owe a great debt to their predecessors of the 1920s.

A Society in Conflict

The social changes and tensions of the 1920s produced a fierce backlash. While Congress restricted immigration, highly publicized trials in Massachusetts and Tennessee cast a harsh spotlight on the nation's divisions. Millions of whites embraced the bigotry of a revived Ku Klux Klan, and many newly urbanized African-Americans rallied to Marcus Garvey, a magnetic black leader with a riveting message of racial pride. Prohibition stirred further controversy in this conflict-ridden decade.

Immigration Restriction   Fed by wartime super-patriotism and xenophobia, the impulse to remake America into a nation of like-minded, culturally homogeneous people revived in the 1920s.

The **National Origins Act** (1924) restricted annual immigration from any foreign country to 2 percent of the number of persons of that "national origin" in the United States in 1890. Since the great influx of southern and eastern Europeans had come later, this provision clearly aimed to reduce immigration from these regions. As Calvin Coolidge observed on signing the law, "America must be kept American."

In 1929, Congress changed the base year for determining "national origins" to 1920, but even under this formula, Poland's annual quota stood at a mere 6,524; Italy's at 5,802; and Hungary's, 869. This quota system, which survived to 1965, represented a counterattack by native-born Protestant America against the immigrant cities. Total immigration fell from 1.2 million in 1914 to 280,000 in 1929. The law excluded Asians and South Asians entirely.

Court rulings underscored the nativist message. In *Ozawa v. United States* (1922), the U.S. Supreme Court denied citizenship to a Japanese-born university student. In 1923, the Supreme Court upheld a California law limiting Japanese immigrants' right to own or lease farmland.

Needed Workers/ Unwelcome Aliens: Hispanic Newcomers

Extremely restrictive otherwise, the 1924 law did not limit immigration from the Western Hemisphere. Accordingly, immigration from Latin America (as well as from French Canada) soared. Poverty and political turmoil propelled thousands of Mexicans northward. By 1930, at least 2 million Mexican-born immigrants lived in the United States, mostly in the Southwest. California's Mexican-American population surged from 90,000 to nearly 360,000 in the 1920s.

Many of these immigrants worked in low-paid migratory agricultural jobs. Mexican labor sustained California's citrus industry. Cooperatives such as the Southern California Fruit Growers Exchange (which used the brand name "Sunkist") hired itinerant workers on a seasonal basis, provided substandard housing in isolated settlements, and fought the migrants' attempts to form labor unions.

Other Mexican immigrants settled in cities. Migrants to the Midwest worked not only in agriculture but also in the automobile, steel, and railroad industries. Retaining deep ties to "México Lindo" (Beautiful Mexico), they formed local support networks and cultural institutions. The Mexican-American community was divided, however, between recent arrivals and earlier immigrants who had become U.S. citizens. The strongest Mexican-American organization in the 1920s, the League of United Latin-American Citizens, ignored the migrant laborers of the Southwest.

Though deeply religious, Mexican-Americans found little support from the U.S. Catholic Church. Earlier, European Catholic immigrants had attended ethnic parishes and worshiped in their own languages, but church policy had changed by the 1920s. In parishes with non-Hispanic priests, Spanish-speaking Mexican newcomers encountered pressure to abandon their language and traditions.

In the larger society, Mexican immigrants faced ambivalent attitudes. Their labor was needed, but their presence angered nativists eager to preserve a "white" and Protestant nation. Would-be immigrants confronted strict literacy and financial tests, and in 1929 Congress made it a criminal offense to cross the border without following required immigration procedures. The flow continued, however, as an estimated one hundred thousand Mexicans arrived annually, legally and clandestinely, to fill the U.S. labor market's pressing demands.

Nativism, Anti-radicalism, and the Sacco-Vanzetti Case

The anti-immigration movement reflected deep ethnic, racial, and religious prejudice in 1920s' America. Anti-Semitic propaganda filled Henry Ford's weekly newspaper, the *Dearborn Independent*, distributed through Ford dealerships and mailed free to schools and libraries. The anti-Semitic articles were reprinted in pamphlets called *The International Jew.* Sued for defamation by a Jewish attorney, Ford in 1927 issued an evasive apology blaming subordinates.

Ethnic and antiradical prejudices pervaded the **Sacco-Vanzetti Case,** a Massachusetts murder case that began in April 1920, when robbers shot and killed a paymaster and guard at a South Braintree, Massachusetts, shoe factory. In 1921, a jury convicted two Italian immigrants, Nicola Sacco and Bartolomeo Vanzetti, of the crime. After many appeals and a review by a blue-ribbon panel of notables, they were electrocuted on August 23, 1927.

These bare facts hardly convey the passions the case aroused. Sacco and Vanzetti were anarchists, and the prosecution harped on their radicalism. The judge barely concealed his hostility to the pair, whom he privately called "those anarchist bastards." While conservatives supported the verdict, liberals and socialists protested. On the night of the electrocution, novelist John Dos Passos wrote a bitter poem that ended: *All right you have won you will kill the brave men our friends tonight ... all right we are two nations.*

Later research on Boston's anarchist community and ballistics tests on Sacco's gun pointed to their guilt. But the prejudices that tainted the trial remain indisputable, as does the case's symbolic importance in exposing the deep fault lines in 1920s' American society.

Fundamentalism and the Scopes Trial	An equally famous case in Tennessee highlighted another front in the decade's cultural wars: the growing prestige of science. While "individually powerless," wrote the Harvard philosopher Alfred North Whitehead in *Science and the*

Modern World (1925), scientists were "ultimately the rulers of the world." Many Americans welcomed the advance of science, but some religious believers found it threatening. Their fears had deepened as scholars had subjected the Bible to critical scrutiny, psychologists and sociologists had studied supernatural belief systems as expressions of human emotional needs, and biologists had embraced the naturalistic explanation for the variety of life forms on earth advanced in Charles Darwin's *Origin of Species* (1859).

While liberal Protestants had generally accepted these findings, evangelical believers had resisted. This gave rise to a movement called **fundamentalism,** after *The Fundamentals,* a series of tracts published in 1909–1914. Fundamentalists insisted on the Bible's inerrancy and literal truth, including the Genesis account of Creation.

In the early 1920s, fundamentalists targeted Darwin's theory of evolution. Many state legislatures considered barring public schools from teaching evolution, and several southern states enacted such laws. Texas governor Miriam "Ma" Ferguson personally censored textbooks that discussed evolution. "I am a Christian mother," she declared, "and I am not going to let that kind of rot go into Texas textbooks." Former Democratic presidential candidate William Jennings Bryan endorsed the antievolution cause.

In 1925, when Tennessee's legislature outlawed the teaching of evolution in the state's public schools, the American Civil Liberties Union (ACLU) offered to defend any teacher willing to challenge this law. A high-school teacher in Dayton, Tennessee,

John T. Scopes, encouraged by local businessmen and civic boosters, accepted the offer. After summarizing Darwin's theory to a science class, Scopes was arrested. Famed criminal lawyer Clarence Darrow headed the defense, while Bryan assisted the prosecution. Journalists poured into Dayton; a Chicago radio station broadcast the proceedings; and the **Scopes Trial** became a media sensation.

Cross-examined by Darrow, Bryan embraced the biblical version of creation and dismissed evolutionary theory. Although the jury found Scopes guilty (in a decision later reversed on a technicality), the trial exposed Fundamentalism to ridicule. When Bryan died of a heart attack soon after, H. L. Mencken wrote a scathing column contemptuously dismissing him and his fundamentalist admirers.

The Scopes Trial exposed the anxieties felt by many Americans. Bryan shrewdly appealed to citizens fearful of cultural forces beyond their control. Let parents and local communities decide what children are taught, he pled, evoking memories of his 1896 populist campaign defending common folk against the rich and powerful (see Chapter 20). Despite the setback in Dayton, Fundamentalism survived. Mainstream Protestant denominations grew more liberal, but many local congregations, radio preachers, Bible schools, new denominations, and flamboyant evangelists like Billy Sunday upheld the traditional faith. Southern and western states continued to pass antievolution laws, and textbook publishers modified their treatment of evolution to appease local school boards.

In Los Angeles, the charismatic Aimee Semple McPherson filled her cavernous Angelus Temple and reached thousands more by radio. Her followers, mainly transplanted midwesterners, embraced her fundamentalist theology while enjoying her theatrical sermons. (She once used a gigantic electric scoreboard to illustrate the triumph of good over evil.) At her death in 1944, her International Church of the Foursquare Gospel had more than six hundred branches in the United States and abroad.

The Ku Klux Klan   The tensions gripping American society of the 1920s also bubbled up in the form of a resurrected Ku Klux Klan (KKK). The original Klan of the Reconstruction South had eventually faded (see Chapter 16), but in 1915 hooded men gathered at Stone Mountain, Georgia, revived it. D. W. Griffith's glorification of the original Klan in his 1915 movie *The Birth of a Nation* provided further fuel.

In 1920, two Atlanta entrepreneurs plotted a national campaign to profit from the appeal of the Klan's ritual and its nativist, white-supremacist ideology. Their wildly successful scheme involved a ten-dollar membership fee divided among the salesman (called the Kleagle), the local sales manager (King Kleagle), the district sales manager (Grand Goblin), the state leader (Grand Dragon), and national leader (Imperial Wizard)—with a rake-off to themselves. The sale of Klan robes, masks, horse blankets, and bottled Chattahoochee River water (used in initiation rites) added to the take.

Preaching "100 percent Americanism," the Klan demonized blacks, Catholics, Jews, aliens, and, in some cases, women suspected of violating sexual taboos. Membership estimates for the KKK and its women's auxiliary in the early 1920s range as high as 5 million. From its southern base, the Klan spread through the

Midwest and across the country from Long Island to the West Coast. The white working class and lower middle class in cities with native-born Protestant majorities proved especially receptive. In 1922, Imperial Wizard Hiram Wesley Evans admitted the Klan's image as a haven of "hicks" and "rubes" and urged college graduates to support the great cause.

Although the Klan was basically a money-making scam riddled with corrupt and cynical leaders, observers commented on the ordinariness of the typical members. (Evans, a Texas dentist, called himself "the most average man in America.") The Klan's litany of enemies and its promise to restore the nation's lost purity—racial, ethnic, religious, and moral—appealed to economically marginal Protestants disoriented by a new social order of giant corporations, mass media, rebellious youth, and immigrant-filled cities. The rituals, parades, and night-time cross burnings added a jolt of drama and excitement to life's everyday routines.

But if individual Klan members seemed more needy than sinister, the Klan as a mass movement was menacing. Some KKK groups employed threats, beatings, and lynching in their quest to purify America. In several states, the Klan won political power. Oklahoma's Klan-controlled legislature impeached and removed an anti-Klan governor. The Oregon Klan elected a governor and enacted legislation requiring all children to attend public school, an attempt to destroy the state's Catholic schools.

The Klan collapsed with shocking suddenness. In March 1925, Indiana's Grand Dragon, David Stephenson, brutally raped his young secretary, who swallowed poison and died several weeks later. In prison, Stephenson revealed sordid details of political corruption. Its moral pretensions in shreds, the KKK faded. When civil-rights activism surged in the 1950s, however, the Klan would again rear its head.

The Garvey Movement   Among African-Americans who had fled southern rural poverty and racism only to experience discrimination and racism in the urban North, the 1920s produced a different kind of mass movement, led by **Marcus Garvey** and his Universal Negro Improvement Association (UNIA). Born in Jamaica in 1887, the son of a stonemason, Garvey founded UNIA in 1914 and soon after moved to Harlem. In a white-dominated society, Garvey glorified all things black. Urging black economic solidarity and capitalist enterprise as the lever of racial advance, he founded UNIA grocery stores and other businesses. Summoning blacks to return to "Motherland Africa," he established the Black Star Steamship Line to help them get there.

An estimated eighty thousand blacks joined UNIA, and thousands more felt the lure of Garvey's oratory, the excitement of UNIA parades and uniforms, and the appeal of economic self-sufficiency and a glorious future in Africa. Although centered in New York and other northern cities, the movement had chapters across the South as well. Garvey's popularity unsettled established black church leaders and roused opposition from the NAACP, which saw the African-American future in America, not Africa, and advocated racial integration rather than separation. W. E. B. Du Bois was among Garvey's sharpest critics.

The movement also highlighted social tensions in Harlem, where two streams of the African diaspora, one from the Caribbean, the other from the American

A UNIA parade in New York's Harlem, 1924 *Marcus Garvey's Universal Negro Improvement Association attracted many African-Americans in the 1920s. The banner reads: "THE NEW NEGRO HAS NO FEAR."*

South, converged. The resulting economic and political rivalry sharpened resistance to the UNIA, with its Jamaican founder and Caribbean leadership.

In 1923, a federal court convicted Garvey of fraud in the management of his Black Star Steamship Line. He was deported in 1927, and the UNIA collapsed. But this first mass movement in black America had revealed the social aspirations and activist potential of African-Americans in the urban North. "In a world where black is despised," commented an African-American newspaper after Garvey's fall, "he taught his followers that black is beautiful." Garvey is honored in his native island as a heroic forerunner of Jamaican independence from British Colonial rule.

The NAACP, meanwhile, remained active even in a decade of rampant racism. In some 300 branches nationwide, members kept the civil-rights cause alive and patiently laid the groundwork for legal challenges to segregation.

Prohibition: Cultures in Conflict

A bitter controversy over alcohol deepened the fissures in American society. As noted in Chapter 21, the Progressive Era **prohibition** campaign was both a legitimate effort to address social problems associated with alcohol abuse and a symbolic crusade by native-born Protestants to control the immigrant cities. These tensions persisted in the 1920s. When the Eighteenth Amendment took effect in 1920, prohibitionists rejoiced. Saloons closed, liquor advertising vanished, and arrests for drunkenness declined. Yet prohibition gradually lost support, and in 1933 it ended.

What went wrong? Essentially, prohibition's failure illustrates the difficulty in a democracy of enforcing a widely opposed law. The Volstead Act, the 1919 prohibition law, was underfunded and weakly enforced, especially in antiprohibition areas. New York, for example, repealed its prohibition-enforcement law as early as 1923. Would-be drinkers grew bolder as enforcement faltered. For many young people, alcohol's illegality increased its appeal. Challenging prohibition, declared one college student, represented "the natural reaction of youth to rules and regulations."

Rum-runners smuggled liquor from Canada and the West Indies, and every city harbored speakeasies selling alcoholic drinks. People concocted home brew, shady entrepreneurs sold flavored industrial-grade alcohol, and sacramental wine sales soared. By 1929, alcohol consumption reached about 70 percent of prewar levels.

Organized crime helped circumvent the law. Chicago, where gangsters battled to control the liquor business, witnessed 550 gangland killings in the 1920s. Speakeasies controlled by Chicago gangster Al Capone generated annual profits of $60 million. Although not typical, Chicago's crime wave underscored prohibition's failure. A reform designed to improve public morality was turning citizens into lawbreakers and mobsters into celebrities.

Prohibition, too, became a battleground in the decade's cultural wars. The "drys"—usually native-born Protestants—praised it. The "wets"—liberals, Jazz Age rebels, big-city immigrants—condemned it as moralistic meddling. At one college, the student newspaper suggested a campus distillery as the senior class gift.

Prohibition influenced the 1928 presidential campaign. While Democratic candidate Al Smith advocated repeal of the Eighteenth Amendment, Republican Herbert Hoover praised it as "a great social and economic experiment, noble in motive and far-reaching in purpose." Once elected, Hoover appointed a commission to study the issue. Its confusing 1931 report admitted prohibition's failure, but urged its retention. A journalist parodied the findings:

> *Prohibition is an awful flop.*
> *We like it.*
> *It can't stop what it's meant to stop.*
> *We like it.*
> *It's left a trail of graft and slime,*
> *It's filled our land with vice and crime,*
> *It don't prohibit worth a dime,*
> *Nevertheless we're for it.*

The Eighteenth Amendment was finally repealed in 1933, a relic of another age.

HOOVER AT THE HELM

Herbert Hoover, elected president in 1928, appeared well fitted to sustain the nation's prosperity. No standpat conservative like Harding and Coolidge, he brought to the White House a social and political philosophy that reflected his engineering background. He seemed the ideal president for the new technological age.

The Election of 1928   A Hollywood casting agent could not have chosen two individuals who better personified America's divisions than the 1928 presidential candidates, Al Smith and Herbert Hoover.

The Democratic party's urban-immigrant wing had gained strength since the deadlocked 1924 convention, and New York governor Al Smith easily won the nomination. A Catholic and a wet, Smith exuded the flavor of immigrant New York. Originally a machine politician and basically conservative, he had impressed reformers by backing social-welfare measures. His key advisors included several reform-minded women, notably Frances Perkins, head of the state industrial board.

Herbert Hoover won the Republican nomination after Coolidge chose not to run. Some conservative party leaders mistrusted the brilliant but aloof Hoover, who had never held elective office and had spent much of his adult life abroad. Born in Iowa and orphaned in boyhood, Hoover had put himself through Stanford University and made a fortune as a mining engineer in China and Australia. After his tour as wartime food administrator, he had served as secretary of commerce since 1921.

Disdaining conventional campaigning, Hoover instead issued "tons of reports on dull subjects" (as H. L. Mencken complained) and read radio speeches in a droning monotone that obscured the originality of his ideas. (Some Hoover strategists did make use of sound film to promote his cause.) Smith, by contrast,

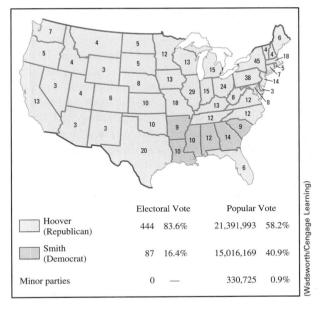

	Electoral Vote		Popular Vote	
Hoover (Republican)	444	83.6%	21,391,993	58.2%
Smith (Democrat)	87	16.4%	15,016,169	40.9%
Minor parties	0	—	330,725	0.9%

(Wadsworth/Cengage Learning)

MAP 23.1 The Election of 1928

Although Hoover won every state but Massachusetts and six Deep South states, Smith's 1928 vote in the Midwestern farm belt and the nation's largest cities showed significant gains over 1924.

campaigned spiritedly across the nation. This may have hurt him, however, because his big-city wisecracking and New York accent put off many voters.

The effect of Smith's Catholicism remains debatable. Hoover urged tolerance, and Smith himself denied any conflict between his religion and the duties of the presidency. His candidacy energized Catholic voters, but anti-Catholic prejudice also played a role. Rumors circulated that Smith would follow the Vatican's orders if he won. (A post-election joke had Smith sending the pope a one-word telegram, "Unpack."). The decisive issue was probably not popery but prosperity. Republican orators pointed to the booming economy and warned of "soup kitchens instead of busy factories" if Smith won. In his nomination-acceptance speech, Hoover grandly predicted "the final triumph over poverty."

Hoover won in a landslide, grabbing 58 percent of the vote and even making deep inroads in the Democratic South (see Map 23.1). However, the outcome also hinted at an emerging political realignment. Smith did well among hard-pressed Midwestern farmers angered by Coolidge's insensitivity to their plight. In northern cities, Catholic and Jewish wards voted heavily Democratic. Smith carried the nation's twelve largest cities, all of which had gone Republican in 1924. Should prosperity falter, the Republican Party faced trouble.

Herbert Hoover's Social Thought   Admirers dubbed Hoover "the Great Engineer." Although a self-made man, he did not uncritically praise the capitalist system. His Quaker background, humanitarian activities, engineering experience, and Republican loyalties combined to produce a unique social outlook, summed up in his 1922 book *American Individualism.*

Like Theodore Roosevelt (whom he had supported in 1912), Hoover opposed untrammeled free-market competition. Rational economic development, he insisted, demanded corporate cooperation in resource allocation, product standardization, and other areas. The economy, in short, should operate like an efficient machine. Believing in ethical business behavior, Hoover welcomed the growth of welfare capitalism. But above all, he advocated *voluntarism.* The efficient, socially responsible economic order he envisioned must arise from the voluntary action of capitalist leaders, not government coercion or labor-management power struggles.

Putting his philosophy into practice, Hoover as secretary of commerce had convened more than 250 conferences where business leaders discussed issues of common concern. He urged higher wages to increase consumer purchasing power, and in 1923 he persuaded the steel industry to adopt an eight-hour workday as an efficiency measure. During the 1927 Mississippi River floods, as President Coolidge did nothing, Hoover had visited the stricken area to mobilize private relief efforts.

A conservationist, Hoover as secretary of commerce had pushed for planned use of water resources and programs to combat the pollution of rivers and lakes. In 1922, he negotiated a compact among Western states to share Colorado River water. This agreement opened the way for a dam on the Colorado to provide hydroelectric power, control flooding, and supply water for irrigation. Construction of Hoover Dam began in 1930. (In an act of petty politics, Democrats changed the name to Boulder Dam in 1933, but Congress later restored the original name.)

TABLE 23.1 | PRESIDENTIAL VOTING BY SELECTED GROUPS IN CHICAGO, 1924, 1928, AND 1932

| | Percent Democratic | | |
	1924	1928	1932
Blacks	10	23	21
Czechoslovaks	40	73	83
Germans	14	58	69
Italians	31	63	64
Jews	19	60	77
Lithuanians	48	77	84
Poles	35	71	80
Swedes	15	34	51
Yugoslavs	20	54	67

Source: John M. Allswang, *A House for All Peoples: Ethnic Politics in Chicago*, 1890–1936 (Lexington: University Press of Kentucky, 1971).

Hoover's ideology had limitations. He showed more enthusiasm for cooperation among capitalists than among consumers or workers. His belief that capitalists would voluntarily embrace ethical behavior and pursue the general good reflected an exaggerated faith in the power of altruism in business decision making. His opposition to government economic intervention would prove disastrous when such intervention became urgently necessary.

Still, Hoover's presidency began promisingly. He created various commissions to gather data on recent social trends. At his urging, Congress created a Federal Farm Board to promote cooperative marketing. This, he hoped, would raise farm prices while preserving the voluntarist principle. Meanwhile, however, an economic crisis was approaching that would overwhelm and ultimately destroy his presidency.

CHRONOLOGY
1920–1929

1920–1921	Postwar recession.
1920	Warren G. Harding elected president. Radio station KDKA, Pittsburgh, broadcasts election returns. Sinclair Lewis, *Main Street*.
1921	Economic boom begins; agriculture remains depressed. Sheppard-Towner Act. *Shuffle Along*, all-black musical review.
1921–1922	Washington Naval Arms Conference.
1922	Supreme Court declares child-labor law unconstitutional. Fordney-McCumber Tariff restores high rates. Herbert Hoover, *American Individualism*.

1923	Harding dies; Calvin Coolidge becomes president.
	Teapot Dome scandals investigated.
	National Origins Act (immigration restriction).
1924	Calvin Coolidge elected president.
1925	Scopes Trial.
	Ku Klux Klan scandal in Indiana.
	Alain Locke, *The New Negro.*
	DuBose Heyward, *Porgy.*
	F. Scott Fitzgerald, *The Great Gatsby.*
1926	Book-of-the-Month Club founded.
	National Broadcasting Company founded.
	Langston Hughes, *The Weary Blues.*
	U.S. Marines intervene in Nicaragua.
1927	*The Jazz Singer*, first sound movie.
	Coolidge vetoes the McNary-Haugen farm bill.
	Henry Ford introduces the Model A.
	Ford apologizes for anti-Semitic publications.
	Execution of Sacco and Vanzetti.
	Charles A. Lindbergh's transatlantic flight.
	Marcus Garvey deported.
	Mississippi River flood.
1928	Herbert Hoover elected president.
1929	Federal Farm Board created.
	Sheppard-Towner program terminated.
	Textile strike in Gastonia, North Carolina.
	Ernest Hemingway, *A Farewell to Arms.*
	Claude McKay, *Home to Harlem.*

CONCLUSION

Repudiating the Wilsonian vision of America's postwar world role, the Republican administrations of the 1920s pursued a nationalistic foreign policy aimed at collecting war debts and protecting U.S. corporate interests in Latin America. The 1921 Washington Naval Arms Conference, though ultimately unsuccessful, represents the one diplomatic initiative of note in these years.

At home, the Twenties brought new entertainment media, consumer products, marketing strategies, and mass-production techniques. While enjoying widespread (if uneven) prosperity, Americans grappled with massive technological and social changes. Like jet-lagged travelers, they struggled to adapt to the new order. Skyscrapers, radio, automobiles, movies, and electrical appliances—all familiar today—were exciting novelties for this generation.

While the Harding and Coolidge administrations celebrated the corporate order and pursued probusiness policies, society seethed in ferment. Ironically, the same stresses that sparked social conflict also stimulated cultural creativity. Jazz Age youth; Mexican immigrants seeking a better life; native-born advocates of immigration restriction, prohibition, and Fundamentalism; white Protestant KKK members; blacks who rallied to Marcus Garvey; the artists and writers of the Harlem Renaissance; and the musicians, painters, and novelists who revitalized American culture were all, in their different ways, responding to the promise and uncertainties of modernity.

24

THE GREAT DEPRESSION AND THE NEW DEAL, 1929–1939

CHAPTER OUTLINE

• Crash and Depression, 1929–1932 • The New Deal Takes Shape, 1933–1935 • The New Deal Changes Course, 1935–1936 • The New Deal's End Stage, 1937–1939 • Social Change and Social Action in the 1930s • The American Cultural Scene in the 1930s

---

CRASH AND DEPRESSION, 1929–1932

The prosperity of the 1920s ended in October 1929 with the stock market collapse. The Wall Street crash, and the economic problems that underlay it, launched a depression that hit every household. President Hoover struggled to respond, but his commitment to private initiative and his horror of direct federal intervention limited his effectiveness. In November 1932, voters turned to the Democratic Party and its leader, Franklin Roosevelt. This set the stage for a vast federal response to the economic and social crisis.

Black Thursday and the Onset of the Depression
Stock prices had risen through much of the 1920s, but 1928–1929 brought a frenzied upsurge as speculators plunged into the market. In 1925, the market value of all stocks had stood at about $27 billion; by October 1929, it hit $87 billion. With stockbrokers lending buyers up to 75 percent of a stock's cost, credit or "margin" buying spread. The income-tax cuts promoted by Treasury Secretary Andrew Mellon had increased the flow of money into the market. Upbeat statements also fed the boom. In March 1929, former president Calvin Coolidge declared stocks "cheap at current prices." "Investment trusts," akin to today's mutual funds, lured novices into the market. The construction

industry faltered in 1928–1929, signaling a decline in the housing market and in business expansion.

In 1928, and again in September 1929, the Federal Reserve Board tried to dampen speculation by raising the interest rate on Federal Reserve notes. Early in 1929, the Fed warned member banks to restrain their lending. But with speculators paying up to 20 percent interest to buy more stock, lending institutions continued to loan money freely—equivalent to dumping gasoline on a raging fire.

The collapse came on October 24, 1929—"Black Thursday." As prices fell, some stocks found no buyers at all: they had become worthless. In the ensuing weeks, feeble upswings alternated with further plunges.

President Hoover, in the first of many optimistic statements, pronounced the economy "sound and prosperous." After a weak upswing early in 1930, the economy went into a long tailspin, producing a full-scale depression.

Economists probing the depression's underlying causes focus on structural problems that made 1920s' prosperity highly unstable. Agriculture remained depressed throughout the decade. In the industrial sector, wage increases lagged behind factory output, reducing consumer purchasing power. At the same time, assembly-line methods encouraged overproduction. By summer 1929, not only housing, but also the automobile, textile, tire, and other major industries were seriously overextended. Further, key industries such as railroads, steel, textiles, and mining lagged technologically in the 1930s and could not attract the investment needed to stimulate recovery.

Some economists, called monetarists, also blame the Federal Reserve System's tight-money policies in the early 1930s. This policy, they argue, strangled any hope of recovery by reducing the capital available to businesses for investment and growth.

All analysts link the U.S. depression to a global economic crisis. European economies, struggling with war-debt payments and a severe trade imbalance with the United States, collapsed in 1931, crippling the U.S. export market.

The worsening depression devastated the U.S. economy. From 1929 to 1932, the gross national product dropped from $104 billion to $59 billion. Farm prices, already low, fell by nearly 60 percent. By early 1933 more than fifty-five hundred banks had closed, and unemployment stood at 25 percent, or nearly 13 million workers (see Figure 24.1). In some cities, the jobless rate surged far higher. Many who still had jobs faced cuts in pay and hours.

Hoover's Response Historically, Americans had viewed depressions as similar to natural disasters: little could be done other than ride out the storm. President Hoover disagreed. Drawing upon his experience as U.S. food administrator in World War I and as secretary of commerce, Hoover initially responded boldly. But his belief in private initiative limited his options.

Hoover urged business leaders to maintain wages and employment. Viewing unemployment as a local issue, he advised city and state officials to create public-works projects. In October 1930, he set up an Emergency Committee for Employment to coordinate voluntary relief efforts. In 1931, he persuaded the nation's

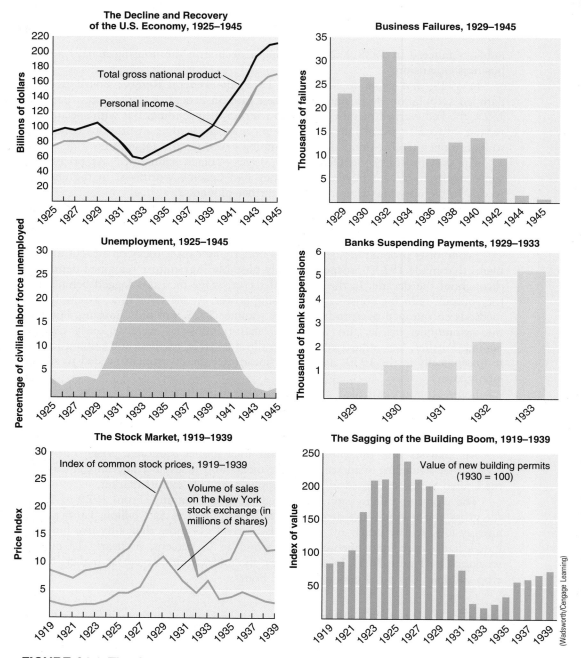

FIGURE 24.1 The Statistics of Hard Times

Figures on the gross national product, personal income, unemployment, the stock market, and business failures all show the Depression's shattering impact, with gradual and uneven improvement as the 1930s wore on.

Sources: Thomas C. Cochran, *The Great Depression and World War II: 1929–1945* (Glenview, Ill.: Scott, Foresman, 1968); *Historical Statistics of the United States, Colonial Times to 1970* (Washington, D.C.: U.S. Government Printing Office, 1975).

largest banks to create a private lending agency to help smaller banks make business loans.

Despite these initiatives, public opinion turned against Hoover. In the 1930 midterm election, the Republicans lost the House of Representatives and gave up eight Senate seats. In 1931, dreading a budget deficit, Hoover called for a tax increase, further angering hard-pressed Americans. That same year, despite their pledges, U.S. Steel and other big corporations slashed wages. The crisis swamped private charities and local welfare agencies. Philadelphia, with more than three hundred thousand jobless by 1932, cut weekly relief payments to $4.23 per family and then stopped them entirely.

In 1932, a presidential election year, Hoover swallowed his principles and took a bold step. In January, at Hoover's recommendation, Congress set up a new agency, the **Reconstruction Finance Corporation** (RFC), to make loans to banks and other lending institutions. By July, the RFC had pumped $1.2 billion into the economy. The RFC also granted $2 billion to state and local governments for job-creating public-works programs, and allocated $750 million for loans to struggling businesses.

Hoover supported these measures reluctantly, warning that they could lead to "socialism and collectivism." Blaming global forces for the depression, he argued that only international measures would help. His call for a moratorium on war-debt and reparations payments by European nations made sense, but seemed irrelevant to the plight of ordinary Americans. As Hoover urged self-help and local initiative and predicted recovery "just around the corner," his unpopularity deepened.

Mounting Discontent and Protest   An ominous mood spread as the jobless waited in breadlines, trudged the streets, and rode freight trains seeking work. Americans reared on the ethic of hard work and self-reliance found chronic unemployment deeply demoralizing.

The *New York Times* described "Hoover Valley"—a section of Central Park where jobless men lived in boxes and packing crates, keeping warm with layers of newspapers they bitterly called Hoover blankets. The suicide rate soared. In Youngstown, Ohio, a jobless father of ten whose family faced eviction jumped to his death from a bridge. Violence threatened in some cities when landlords evicted families unable to pay their rent.

Many farmers lost their lands because of tax delinquency, with Iowa and the Dakotas especially hard hit. At some forced farm auctions, neighbors bought the foreclosed farm for a trivial sum, and returned it to the evicted family.

In 1931, midwestern farmers organized a movement called the Farmers' Holiday Association to force prices up by withholding grain and livestock from the market. Dairy farmers angered by low prices dumped milk in Iowa and Wisconsin.

The most alarming protest came from World War I veterans. In 1924, Congress had voted veterans a bonus stretched over a twenty-year period. In June 1932, some ten thousand veterans, many jobless, descended on Washington to lobby for immediate payment of these bonuses. When Congress refused, most of the "bonus marchers" went home, but about two thousand stayed on, building makeshift shelters on the outskirts of Washington. President Hoover called in the army.

On July 28, troops commanded by General Douglas MacArthur and armed with tear gas, tanks, and machine guns drove the veterans from their camp and burned their shelters. A journalist described the scene:

> [The veterans and their families] wandered from street to street or sat in ragged groups, the men exhausted, the women with wet handkerchiefs laid over their smarting eyes, the children waking from sleep to cough and whimper from the tear gas in their lungs.... Their shanties and tents had been burned, their personal property destroyed, except for the few belongings they could carry on their backs.

To many Americans, this action symbolized the administration's heartlessness. American writers shared the despairing mood. In *The 42nd Parallel* (1930), John Dos Passos drew a dark panorama of the United States as money-mad, exploitive, and lacking spiritual meaning. Says one character: "Everything you've wanted crumbles in your fingers as you grasp it." In *Young Lonigan* (1932), James T. Farrell portrayed the empty existence of a working-class Irish-immigrant youth in Chicago. Jobless and betrayed by the American dream, he aimlessly wanders the streets.

Some radical novelists openly attacked the capitalist system. The Communist Party encouraged such fiction through writers' clubs and contests for working-class writers. Jack Conroy's *The Disinherited* (1933) dealt with life in the Missouri coal fields, where his own father and brother had died in a mine disaster.

The Election of 1932   Gloom pervaded the 1932 Republican convention that renominated Hoover. The Democrats gathered in Chicago, by contrast, scented victory. Their platform, crafted to erase the party divisions of the 1920s, appealed to urban voters with a call for repeal of prohibition, to farmers with support for aid programs, and to fiscal conservatives with demands for a balanced budget and spending cuts. Rejecting Al Smith, the party's 1928 candidate, the delegates nominated New York governor Franklin D. Roosevelt for president.

Breaking precedent, FDR flew to Chicago to accept the nomination in person. Despite a rousing speech pledging "a new deal for the American people," Roosevelt's campaign offered few specifics. He called for "bold persistent experimentation" and compassion for "the forgotten man at the bottom of the economic pyramid," yet he also attacked Hoover's "reckless" spending and insisted that "only as a last resort" should Washington play a larger depression-fighting role.

But Roosevelt exuded confidence, and above all he was not Hoover. On November 8, FDR and his running mate, Texas congressman John Nance Garner, received nearly 23 million votes, while Hoover received fewer than 16 million. Roosevelt carried every state but Pennsylvania and four in New England. Both houses of Congress went heavily Democratic.

How would Roosevelt use this impressive mandate? The nation waited.

THE NEW DEAL TAKES SHAPE, 1933–1935

The Roosevelt years began in a whirl of activity. An array of emergency measures reflected three basic goals: industrial recovery through business-government cooperation and pump-priming federal spending; agricultural recovery through crop reduction; and short-term emergency relief distributed through state and local agencies when possible, but directly by the federal government if necessary. These programs conveyed the sense of an activist government addressing urgent national problems. Hovering over the bustle loomed a confident Franklin Roosevelt, cigarette holder jauntily tilted upward, a symbol of hope. By 1935, however, the New Deal faced problems, and opposition was building.

Roosevelt and His Circle   FDR's inaugural address exuded confidence and hope. "The only thing we have to fear," he intoned, "is fear itself." In an outpouring of support, half a million letters deluged the White House.

Roosevelt seemed an unlikely popular hero. Like his distant cousin Theodore, FDR was of the social elite, with merchants and landowners among his Dutch-immigrant ancestors. He attended Harvard College and Columbia Law School. But as a state senator and governor, he had backed the Democratic Party's urban-immigrant wing. When the depression hit, he had introduced innovative measures in New York, including unemployment insurance and a public-works program. Intent on promoting recovery while preserving capitalism and democracy, Roosevelt encouraged competing proposals, compromised (or papered over) differences, and then backed the measures he sensed that Congress and the public would support.

Roosevelt brought to Washington a circle of advisers nicknamed the brain trust. It included Columbia University professor Rexford G. Tugwell and lawyer Adolph A. Berle. Shaped by the progressive reform tradition, Tugwell and Berle advocated federal economic planning and corporate regulation. But no single ideology or inner circle controlled the New Deal, for FDR sought a broad range of opinions.

Eleanor Roosevelt played a key role. A niece of Theodore Roosevelt, she had been active in settlement-house work and in Florence Kelley's National Consumers' League. Through her, FDR met reformers, social workers, and advocates of minority rights. Recalled Rexford Tugwell: "No one who ever saw Eleanor Roosevelt sit down facing her husband, and holding his eyes firmly, say to him 'Franklin, I think you should …,' or 'Franklin, surely you will not …' will ever forget the experience." Traveling ceaselessly, she was an astute observer for her wheelchair-bound husband. (A Washington newspaper once headlined "MRS. ROOSEVELT SPENDS NIGHT AT WHITE HOUSE.") In 1935, she began a newspaper column, "My Day."

Roosevelt's cabinet reflected the New Deal's diversity. Postmaster General James Farley, FDR's top political adviser, distributed patronage jobs, managed his campaigns, and dealt with state and local Democratic leaders. Secretary of Labor **Frances Perkins**, the first woman cabinet member, had served as industrial commissioner of New York. Interior Secretary **Harold Ickes** had organized liberal Republicans for Roosevelt in 1932. Secretary of Agriculture Henry A. Wallace held the same post his father had occupied in the 1920s. Treasury Secretary Henry Morgenthau, Jr., FDR's neighbor and political ally, though a fiscal conservative, tolerated the spending necessary to finance New Deal anti-depression programs.

Newcomers poured into Washington in 1933—former progressives, liberal-minded professors, bright young lawyers. They drafted bills, staffed government agencies, and debated recovery strategies. From this pressure-cooker environment emerged the laws, programs, and agencies gathered under a catch-all label: the New Deal.

(FDR Library)

Eleanor Roosevelt Visits a Nursery School in Des Moines Operated by the Works Progress Administration, June 1936 *Intensely shy as a young woman, Mrs. Roosevelt played an active, influential, and highly visible role during her years as First Lady.*

The Hundred Days   Between March and June 1933, a period labeled the "Hundred Days," Congress enacted more than a dozen key measures. Drawing upon precedents from the Progressive Era, World War I, and the Hoover presidency, these measures expanded Washington's involvement in America's economic life.

FDR first addressed the banking crisis. As borrowers defaulted, depositors withdrew savings, and homeowners missed mortgage payments, thousands of banks had failed, undermining confidence in the system. On March 5, Roosevelt ordered all banks to close for four days. At the end of this so-called bank holiday, he proposed an Emergency Banking Act. This law and a later one permitted healthy banks to reopen, set up procedures for managing failed banks, increased government oversight of banking, and required banks to separate savings deposits from investment funds. Congress also created the Federal Deposit Insurance Corporation (FDIC) to insure bank deposits up to five thousand dollars. Launching a series of radio talks, the president assured Americans that they could again trust their banks.

Other measures addressed the urgent problem of relief for Americans struggling to survive. Two new agencies assisted those who were losing their homes. The Home Owners Loan Corporation (HOLC) helped city-dwellers refinance their mortgages. The Farm Credit Administration provided loans to rural Americans.

Another early relief program, the **Civilian Conservation Corps** (CCC), employed jobless youths in environmentally friendly government projects such as reforestation, park maintenance, and erosion control. By 1935, half a million young men were earning thirty-five dollars a month in CCC camps—a godsend to desperate families.

The principal relief measure of the Hundred Days, the **Federal Emergency Relief Act**, appropriated $500 million for state and local relief agencies that had exhausted their funds. To head this program, FDR chose **Harry Hopkins**, the relief administrator in New York State, who soon emerged as a powerful New Deal figure.

While supplying immediate relief, the early New Deal also faced the larger challenge of promoting agricultural and industrial recovery. On the problem of low farm prices, the government advocated reduced production to push up farm income.

As a first step to cutting production, the government paid southern cotton planters to plow under much of their crop and midwestern farmers to slaughter some 6 million piglets and pregnant sows. Destroying crops and killing pigs amid widespread hunger proved a public-relations nightmare. Pursuing the same goal more systematically, Congress in May 1933 passed the Agricultural Adjustment Act. This law gave payments, called subsidies, to producers of the major farm commodities—including hogs, wheat, corn, cotton, and dairy products—in return for cutting production. A tax on grain mills and other food processors (a tax ultimately passed on to consumers) financed these subsidies. A new agency, the **Agricultural Adjustment Administration** (AAA), supervised the program.

The other key recovery measure of the Hundred Days, the National Industrial Recovery Act, appropriated $3.3 billion for large scale public-works projects to provide jobs and stimulate the economy. The **Public Works Administration** (PWA), headed by Interior Secretary Harold Ickes, ran this program.

This law also created the **National Recovery Administration** (NRA). The NRA brought together business leaders to draft codes of "fair competition" for their industries. These codes set production limits, prescribed wages and working conditions, and forbade price cutting and unfair competitive practices. The aim was to promote recovery by breaking the cycle of wage cuts, falling prices, and layoffs. This approach revived the trade associations promoted by Washington during World War I (see Chapter 22). Indeed, the NRA's head, Hugh Johnson, had served with the War Industries Board of 1917–1918. The NRA also echoed the theme of business-government cooperation that Herbert Hoover had encouraged as secretary of commerce in the 1920s.

Dependent on voluntary support by business and the public, NRA officials used parades, billboards, magazine ads, and celebrity events to persuade people to patronize companies that subscribed to an NRA code. Such companies displayed the NRA symbol, a blue eagle, and its slogan, "We Do Our Part."

While the NRA sought economic recovery, some New Dealers also saw its reform potential. Pressured by Labor Secretary Frances Perkins, the NRA's textile-industry code banned child labor. And thanks to New York senator Robert Wagner, Section 7a of the National Industrial Recovery Act affirmed workers' right to organize unions.

The Reconstruction Finance Corporation, dating from the Hoover years, remained active, lending large sums to banks, insurance companies, and even new business ventures. The early New Deal thus had a strong probusiness tone. In his speeches of 1933–1935, FDR always included business in the "all-American team" working for recovery.

A few early measures, however, took a tougher approach to business. A post–1929 antibusiness mood deepened when a Senate investigation revealed that none of the twenty partners of the powerful Morgan Bank had paid any income tax in 1931 or 1932. People jeered when the head of the New York Stock Exchange told a Senate committee considering regulatory measures, "You gentlemen are making a big mistake. The Exchange is a perfect institution."

Reflecting public support for tougher regulation, the Federal Securities Act of 1933 required corporations to inform the government fully on all stock offerings. This law also made executives personally liable for any misrepresentation of securities their companies issued. In 1934 Congress created the Securities and Exchange Commission (SEC) to enforce the new regulations.

The most innovative program of the Hundred Days was the **Tennessee Valley Authority** (TVA). This program had its origins in a government-built hydroelectric plant on the Tennessee River in Alabama that had powered a World War I munitions factory. In the 1920s, Senator George Norris of Nebraska had urged the use of this facility to supply electricity to nearby farmers.

Expanding Norris's idea, TVA advanced the economic and social development of the poverty-stricken Tennessee River valley. While creating construction jobs, TVA dams brought electricity to the region, provided recreational facilities, and reduced flooding and soil erosion. Under director David Lilienthal, TVA proved one of the New Deal's most popular and enduring achievements.

The outpouring of laws and new agencies during the Hundred Days suggests both the dynamism and the confusion of the New Deal. How all these new programs would work in practice remained to be seen.

Problems and Controversies Plague the Early New Deal

As the depression persisted, several early New Deal programs, including the NRA and the AAA, faltered. The NRA's problems related partly to the personality of the hard-driving, hard-drinking Hugh Johnson, who left in 1934. But the trouble went deeper. As the unity spirit of the Hundred Days faded, corporate America resisted NRA regulation. Code violations increased. Small businesses complained that the codes favored big corporations. The agency itself, meanwhile, became bogged down in drafting trivial codes. The shoulder-pad industry, for example, had its own code. Corporate trade associations used the codes to stifle competition and fix prices.

In May 1935, the Supreme Court unanimously ruled the NRA unconstitutional. The Court cited two reasons: first, the law gave the president regulatory powers that constitutionally belonged to Congress; second, the NRA regulated commerce inside states, violating the constitutional provision limiting federal regulation to *interstate* commerce. Few mourned. As a recovery measure, the NRA had failed.

The AAA, too, proved controversial. Farm prices did rise as production fell, and from 1933 to 1937 overall farm income increased by 50 percent. But the AAA did not help farm laborers or migrant workers; indeed, its crop-reduction payments actually hurt southern tenants and sharecroppers, who faced eviction as cotton planters removed acreage from production.

Some victims of this process resisted. In 1934, the interracial Southern Tenant Farmers' Union, led by the Socialist Party, emerged in Arkansas. Declared one black sharecropper at the organizing meeting: "The same chain that holds my people holds your people too.... [We should] get together and stay together." The landowners struck back, harassing union organizers.

While some New Dealers focused on raising total agricultural income, others took a more class-based approach and urged attention to the poorest farmers. Their cause was strengthened as a parching drought centered in the Oklahoma panhandle turned much of the Great Plains into a dust bowl (see Map 24.1). The rains failed in 1930, devastating wheat and livestock. In 1934, dust clouds spread eastward, darkening the skies over coastal cities. As a dense dust cloud passed over Washington, D.C., one legislator commented: "There goes Oklahoma." Through 1939, each summer brought a new scourge of dust (see Going to the Source).

Even night brought no relief. Recalled a Kansas woman, "A trip for water to rinse the grit from our lips, and then back to bed with washcloths over our noses. We try to lie still, because every turn stirs the dust on the blankets." Folk singer Woody Guthrie recalled his 1930s' boyhood in Oklahoma and Texas in a song called "The Great Dust Storm."

Battered by debt and drought, many families gave up. Nearly 3.5 million people left the Great Plains in the 1930s. Some migrated to nearby cities, further swamping relief rolls. Others packed their belongings into old cars and headed west. Though from various states, they all bore a derisive nickname, Okies. The plight of dust-bowl migrants further complicated New Deal agricultural planning.

Policy differences also plagued New Deal relief. As unemployment continued, Harry Hopkins argued for direct federal relief programs, rather than channeling funds through state and local agencies. Late in 1933, FDR named Hopkins to head a temporary agency, the Civil Works Administration (CWA). Through the winter the CWA funded short-term work projects for the jobless, but when spring came, FDR abolished it. Like his conservative critics, FDR feared creating a permanent underclass living on welfare. As local relief agencies ran out of money, however, further federal programs became inevitable.

MAP 24.1 The Dust Bowl

From the Dakotas southward to the Mexican border, farmers in the Great Plains suffered from a lack of rainfall and severe soil erosion in the 1930s, worsening the hardships of the Great Depression.

Hopkins and Harold Ickes, head of the Public Works Administration, competed to control federal relief policy. Large-scale PWA projects did promote recovery, but the cautious Ickes examined every proposal in minute detail, leaving relief funds stalled in the pipeline. Hopkins, by contrast, wanted to put people to work, even at make-work projects like raking leaves and collecting litter, and get money circulating. Given the urgent crisis, Hopkins's approach proved more influential.

Despite problems and rivalries, the public works programs of the PWA and WPA not only created jobs but reshaped the nation's infrastructure and promoted economic development. With projects throughout the nation, these agencies built dams, public buildings, airports, highways, bridges, viaducts, dams, water utilities, and sewage-treatment plants. The military factories and war-workers' housing construction of World War II and the public housing and interstate highway system of the postwar era would all reflect the legacy of these New Deal agencies.

1934–1935: Challenges from Right and Left   Despite the New Deal's initiatives, the depression persisted. In 1934 national income rose about 25 percent above 1933 levels but remained far below that of 1929. Millions had been jobless for three or four years. The rising frustration found expression in 1934 in nearly two thousand strikes, some communist-led.

With the NRA under attack, conflict flaring over farm policy, and relief spending growing, criticism mounted. Conservatives attacked the New Deal as socialistic. In 1934, several business leaders, joined by an embittered Al Smith, formed the anti-New Deal American Liberty League. Anti-Roosevelt jokes circulated among the rich, many of whom denounced him as a traitor to his class.

But the New Deal remained popular, reflecting both its promise and FDR's commanding political skills, enhanced by speechwriters and publicists. Pursuing his "national unity" theme, he exhorted Americans to join the battle for economic recovery just as they had united for war in 1917. Although Republican newspaper publishers remained hostile, FDR enjoyed good relations with the working press, and journalists responded with favorable stories.

Unlike Hoover, Roosevelt loved public appearances and took naturally to radio. Frances Perkins described his radio talks, nicknamed "fireside chats": "His head would nod and his hands would move in simple, natural, comfortable gestures. His face would smile and light up as though he were actually sitting ... with [his listeners]." Roosevelt's mastery of radio would provide a model for politicians of the television era.

The 1934 midterm election ratified the New Deal's popularity. Reversing the usual pattern, the Democrats increased their congressional majorities. As for FDR, Kansas journalist William Allen White observed, "He's been all but crowned by the people."

Despite this outcome, the political scene remained unstable. While conservatives criticized the New Deal for going too far, critics on the left attacked it for not going far enough and ridiculed Roosevelt's efforts to include big business in his "all-American team."

Demagogues peddled various nostrums. The Detroit Catholic priest and radio spellbinder Charles Coughlin viciously attacked FDR, made anti-Semitic allusions, and called for nationalization of the banks. For a time, Coughlin's National Union of Social Justice, attracted considerable support, mainly from the lower middle class.

Meanwhile, California doctor Francis Townsend proposed that the government pay all retired citizens two hundred dollars a month, requiring them to spend it within thirty days. This plan, Townsend insisted, would help the elderly, stimulate the economy, and create jobs by encouraging retirement. The scheme would have bankrupted the nation, but many older citizens rallied to Townsend's banner.

FDR's wiliest rival was Huey Long of Louisiana. A country lawyer elected governor in 1928, Long built highways, schools, and public housing while tolerating graft and political corruption. He roared into Washington as a senator in 1933, preaching his "Share Our Wealth" program: a 100 percent tax on all income over $1 million and appropriation of all fortunes over $5 million. Once this money was redistributed, Long promised, every family could enjoy a comfortable income. By 1935, he boasted 7.5 million supporters. His 1935 book, *My First Days in the White House,* made clear his ultimate goal. Long was assassinated that September, but his organization survived.

Battling back, Roosevelt regained the political high ground in 1935 with a fresh surge of legislation that rivaled that of the Hundred Days.

Dust Bowl Diary: Life on the Great Plains in the 1930s

The dust storms of the 1930s on the Great Plains, one of the twentieth century's major ecological disasters, resulted from a severe drought plus decades of farming practices that had destroyed the prairie grasses holding the soil in place. These excerpts from the diary of Ann Marie Low, a young school teacher, convey the reality of the Dust Bowl as she experienced it on her parents' farm near Kensal, North Dakota.

April 25, 1934. Last weekend was the worst dust storm we ever had.... [T]he air is just full of dirt coming, literally, for hundreds of miles. It sifts into everything. After we wash the dishes and put them away, so much dust sifts into the cupboard we must wash them again before the next meal. Clothes in the closets are covered with dust.... Newspapers say the deaths of many babies and old people are attributed to breathing in so much dirt.

May 21, 1934.... Saturday Dad, Bud [her brother], and I planted an acre of potatoes. There was so much dirt in the air I couldn't see Bud only a few feet in front of me.... The newspapers report that on May 10 ... [an] estimated 12,000,000 tons of Plains soil was dumped on [Chicago].

May 30, 1934 [returning home after a week away]. The mess was incredible! Dirt had blown into the house all week and lay inches deep on everything. Every towel and curtain was just black. There wasn't a clean dish or cooking utensil.... The cupboards had to be washed out to have a clean place to put them.... [E]very towel, curtain, piece of bedding, and garment had to be taken outdoors to have as much dust as possible shaken out before washing. The cistern is dry, so I had to carry all the water we needed from the well.... That evening Cap [her boyfriend] came to take me to the movie, as usual. Ixnay [No]. I'm sorry I snapped at Cap. It isn't his fault, or anyone's fault, but I was tired and cross. Life in

THE NEW DEAL CHANGES COURSE, 1935–1936

As the 1936 election neared, Roosevelt shelved the unity theme and championed the poor and the working class. His 1935 State of the Union address outlined six initiatives: expanded public-works programs, assistance to the rural poor, support for organized labor, benefits for retired workers and other at-risk groups, tougher business regulation, and heavier taxes on the well-to-do. These priorities translated into a bundle of reform measures some called "the Second New Deal". FDR's landslide victory in 1936 solidified a new Democratic coalition. The New Deal also addressed environmental issues and launched public-works and power projects that stimulated economic development in the American West.

Expanding Federal Relief   With unemployment still high, Congress passed the $5 billion Emergency Relief Appropriation Act in April 1935. Roosevelt swiftly set up the **Works Progress Administration** (WPA) under Harry Hopkins to funnel assistance directly to the jobless. Roosevelt insisted what the newspapers call "the Dust Bowl" is becoming a gritty nightmare.

July 9, 1934 [After a movie, Ann and Cap talk of marriage, but the discussion soon turns to their bleak economic prospects.] [Cap] is really a handsome man, ... [but] suddenly I seemed to see what his face will be someday—a tombstone on which is written an epitaph of dead dreams. I shivered. [Cap said] "Oh sweetheart, you are cold ..... I'll take you home." I didn't tell him I wasn't shivering from cold.

August 1, 1934. As far as one can see are brown pastures and fields which, in the wind, just rise up and fill the air with dirt. It tortures animals and humans, makes housekeeping an everlasting drudgery, and ruins machinery. The crops are long since ruined.... [A]ll subsoil moisture is gone. Fifteen feet down the ground is dry as dust. Trees are dying by the thousands. Cattle and horses are dying, some from starvation and some from dirt they eat on the grass.

July 11, 1936. Yesterday was 110° with a hot wind blowing. Today is the same. I'm writing this lying on the living room floor, dripping sweat and watching the dirt drift in the windows and across the floor. I've dusted this whole house twice today and won't do it again.

August 1, 1936. This is the worst summer yet. The fields are nothing but grasshoppers and dried-up Russian thistle.... There is one dust storm after another. It is the most disheartening situation I have seen yet. Livestock and humans are really suffering. I don't know how we keep going....

Questions

1. *Along with their economic toll, what does this diary reveal about the dust storms' emotional and psychological impact?*

2. *What was Ann's basic source of information for events outside her immediate community?*

Go to www.cengagebrain.com for additional primary sources on this period.

Source: From Dust Bowl Diary *by Ann Marie Low by permission of the University of Nebraska Press. Copyright 1984 by the University of Nebraska Press.*

that the WPA provide work, not handouts. Over its eight-year life, the WPA employed more than 8 million Americans and constructed or improved vast numbers of bridges, roads, post offices, and other public facilities.

The WPA also assisted writers, performers, and artists. The Federal Writers' Project (FWP) employed jobless writers nationwide to produce state and city guides and histories of ethnic and immigrant groups. In the South, research teams recorded the reminiscences of former slaves. Sterling Brown, the FWP's "Negro Affairs editor," worked to include African-American history and voices in FWP publications.

Under the WPA's Federal Music Project, unemployed musicians gave free concerts, often featuring American composers. Artists working for the Federal Arts Project designed posters, offered courses, and painted murals on public buildings.

The Federal Theatre Project (FTP) employed actors. One FTP project, the Living Newspaper, which dramatized current social issues, was criticized as New Deal propaganda. Nervous WPA officials canceled one FTP production, Marc Blitzstein's radical musical *The Cradle Will Rock* (1937), before the opening-night performance. The cast and audience defiantly walked to another theater, and the show went on.

Another 1935 agency, the National Youth Administration (NYA), provided job training for unemployed youth and part-time work for needy college students. Eleanor Roosevelt, viewing young people as the hope of the future, took particular pride in the NYA.

Harold Ickes's Public Works Administration, after a slow start, eventually completed some thirty-four thousand major construction projects, from New York City's Lincoln Tunnel to the awesome Grand Coulee Dam on the Columbia River. The PWA employed thousands of jobless workers.

All this relief spending generated large federal budget deficits, cresting at $4.4 billion in 1936. According to British economist John Maynard Keynes, governments should deliberately use deficit spending during depressions to fund public-works programs, thereby increasing purchasing power and stimulating recovery. The New Deal approach, however, was not Keynesian. Because every dollar spent on relief programs was counterbalanced by taxation or government borrowing, the stimulus effect was nil. FDR saw deficits as an unwelcome necessity, not a positive good.

The New Deal's second phase more frankly targeted workers, the poor, and the disadvantaged. Social-justice advocates like Frances Perkins and Eleanor Roosevelt encouraged this class-based emphasis, but so did political calculations. Looking to 1936, FDR's political advisers feared that the followers of Coughlin, Townsend, and Long could siphon off enough votes to cost him the election. This worry underlay FDR's 1935 political agenda.

The Second New Deal's agricultural policy addressed the plight of sharecroppers (a plight the AAA had helped create) and other poor farmers. The Resettlement Administration (1935) made loans to help tenant farmers buy their own farms and to enable displaced sharecroppers, tenants, and dust-bowl migrants to move to more productive areas.

The Resettlement Administration also funded two documentary films directed by Pare Lorenz. *The Plow That Broke the Plains* (1936) explained the farming practices that led to the dust bowl. *The River* (1938) dealt with the devastating effects of Mississippi River flooding, and the promise of New Deal flood-control projects. Lorenz's films rank among the outstanding cultural productions of the 1930s.

The Rural Electrification Administration, also started in 1935, made low-interest loans to utility companies and farmers' cooperatives to extend electricity to the 90 percent of rural America that still lacked it. By 1941, 40 percent of U.S. farms enjoyed electric power.

The agricultural-recovery program suffered a setback in January 1936 when the Supreme Court declared the Agricultural Adjustment Act unconstitutional. The processing tax that funded the AAA's subsidies, the Court held, was an illegal use of the government's tax power. To replace the AAA, Congress passed a soil-conservation act that paid farmers to plant grasses and legumes instead of soil-depleting crops such as wheat and cotton (which also happened to be the major surplus commodities).

Organized labor won a key victory in 1935, thanks to Senator Robert Wagner. During the New Deal's national-unity phase, FDR had criticized Wagner's campaign for a prolabor law as "special interest" legislation. But in 1935, when the

Supreme Court outlawed the NIRA, including Section 7a protecting union members' rights, as unconstitutional, FDR called for a labor law that would survive court scrutiny. The **National Labor Relations Act** of July 1935 (the Wagner Act) guaranteed collective-bargaining rights, permitted closed shops (in which all employees must join a union), and outlawed such management tactics as blacklisting union organizers. The law created the National Labor Relations Board (NLRB) to enforce the law and supervise shop elections. A wave of unionization soon followed (discussed later in this chapter).

The Second New Deal's more class-conscious thrust shaped other 1935 measures as well. The Banking Act strengthened the Federal Reserve Board's control over the nation's financial system. The Public Utilities Holding Company Act, targeting the sprawling public-utility empires of the 1920s, restricted gas and electric companies to one geographic region.

In 1935, too, Roosevelt called for steeper taxes on the rich to combat the "unjust concentration of wealth and economic power." Congress responded with a revenue act, also called the Wealth Tax Act, raising taxes on corporations and on the well-to-do. With its many loopholes, this law was not quite the "soak the rich" measure some believed, but it did express the Second New Deal's more radical spirit.

The Social Security Act of 1935; End of the Second New Deal The **Social Security Act** of 1935 stands out for its long-range significance. Drafted by a committee chaired by Frances Perkins, this measure drew upon Progressive Era ideas and European social-welfare programs. It established a mixed federal-state system of workers' pensions; unemployment insurance; survivors' benefits for victims of industrial accidents; and aid for disabled persons and dependent mothers with children.

Taxes paid partly by employers and partly by workers (in the form of sums withheld from their paychecks) helped fund the program. This cut in take-home pay contributed to a recession in 1937. But it made sense politically because workers would resist any threat to a pension plan they had contributed to. As FDR put it, "With those taxes in there, no damned politician can ever scrap my social security program."

The initial Social Security Act paid low benefits and bypassed farmers, domestic workers, and the self-employed. But it established the principle of federal responsibility for social welfare and laid the foundation for vastly expanded future welfare programs.

As 1935 ended, the Second New Deal was complete. Without embracing the panaceas of demagogues, FDR had addressed the grievances they had exploited. Although conservatives called the Second New Deal "anti-business," FDR insisted that he had saved capitalism through prudent reform. In earlier eras, the business class had dominated government, marginalizing other groups. Business interests remained influential in the 1930s, but the evolving New Deal also responded to other organized interest groups, including labor. And in 1935, with an election looming, New Deal strategists reached farther still, crafting legislation to aid sharecroppers, migrant workers, the disabled, the elderly, and others largely ignored by politicians of the past.

In the process, the New Deal enlarged the government's role in American life, as well as the power of the presidency. Building on precedents set by Theodore Roosevelt, FDR so dominated 1930s' politics that Americans now expected presidents to offer programs, address national issues, and shape the public debate. This decisively altered the power balance between the White House and Congress. Along with specific programs, the New Deal's importance thus also lay in how it enlarged the scope of the presidency and the social role of the state.

The 1936 Roosevelt Landslide and the New Democratic Coalition

FDR confidently faced the 1936 campaign. "There's one issue," he told an aide; "it's myself, and people must be either for me or against me."

The Republican candidate, Kansas governor Alfred Landon, a moderate fiscal conservative, proved an inept campaigner. ("Wherever I have gone in this country, I have found Americans," he revealed in one speech.) FDR, by contrast, responded zestfully when Republicans lambasted his alleged dictatorial ambitions or charged that the social security law would require all workers to wear metal dog tags. The forces of "selfishness and greed ... are united in their hatred for me," he declared at a tumultuous election-eve rally in New York City, "and I welcome their hatred."

In the greatest landslide since 1820, FDR carried every state but Maine and Vermont. Landon even lost Kansas. Pennsylvania went Democratic for the first time since 1856. The Democrats increased their majorities in Congress. Socialist Norman Thomas received under 200,000 votes, the Communist Party's presidential candidate only about 80,000. The Union Party, a coalition of Coughlinites, Townsendites, and Huey Long supporters, seemingly so formidable in 1935, polled under 900,000 votes.

The 1936 election signaled the emergence of a new Democratic coalition. Since Reconstruction, the Democrats had enjoyed three bases of support: the white South, parts of the West, and urban white ethnic voters. FDR retained these centers of strength. He rarely challenged state or local party leaders who produced the votes, whether or not they supported the New Deal.

Building on Al Smith's urban gains in 1928, FDR carried the nation's twelve largest cities in 1936. Aided by New Deal relief programs, many city-dwellers idolized Roosevelt. Cheering throngs greeted his visits to New York, Boston, or other cities. In filling New Deal positions, FDR often turned to the newer urban-immigrant groups, including Catholics and Jews.

Expanding the Democratic base, FDR also courted farmers and union members. Republican Midwestern farmers, won over by the New Deal's agricultural program, voted accordingly. FDR decisively carried Iowa, a GOP bastion, in 1936. Union members, too, joined the Roosevelt bandwagon that year, and unions pumped money into Roosevelt's campaign chest (though far less than business gave the Republicans). Despite his early criticism of the Wagner bill, FDR's reputation as a "friend of labor" proved unassailable.

African Americans came aboard as well. Although most southern blacks remained disfranchised, northern blacks could vote, and as late as 1932, two-thirds of them voted Republican, the party of Lincoln. The New Deal caused a historic shift. In 1936, 76 percent of black voters supported FDR.

***Marian Anderson at the Lincoln Memorial,* Painting by Betsy Graves Reyneau** *In the 1950s, Reyneau did a series of paintings of notable black Americans for a touring exhibit. This painting portrays Marian Anderson at the Lincoln Memorial on Easter Sunday, 1939, where her concert drew an audience of 75,000 and was broadcast nationally. Eleanor Roosevelt and Harold Ickes arranged the event after the Daughters of the American Revolution denied the use of Constitution Hall.*

(National Portrait Gallery, Smithsonian Museum, Washington, D.C./Art Resource, NY)

Economically, this shift made sense. New Deal relief programs greatly aided blacks. On racial-justice issues, however, the New Deal's record was mixed at best. Some NRA codes included racially discriminatory clauses, causing black activists to deride the agency as "Negroes Ruined Again." TVA and other New Deal agencies tolerated racial bias. Lynchings increased in the 1930s as some whites translated economic worries into racial violence, but Roosevelt kept aloof from an NAACP campaign to make lynching a federal crime. When southern Democratic senators killed such a bill in 1935, FDR, concerned about other legislative initiatives, did little. "[T]he Roosevelt administration [has] nothing for [blacks]," the NAACP concluded bitterly.

In limited ways, FDR did address racial issues. He cautiously tried to rid New Deal agencies of blatant racism. He appointed more than a hundred blacks to policy-level and judicial positions, including Eleanor Roosevelt's friend Mary McLeod Bethune as director of minority affairs in the National Youth

Administration. Bethune, a Florida educator, led the so-called black cabinet that linked the administration and black organizations. Roosevelt's Supreme Court appointees opposed racial discrimination in cases involving housing, voting rights, and other issues.

The New Deal also supported racial justice in symbolic ways. In 1938, when the participants in a conference in Birmingham, Alabama, were segregated in compliance with local statutes, Mrs. Roosevelt placed her chair halfway between the white and black delegates. In 1939, when the Daughters of the American Revolution barred black contralto Marian Anderson from performing in Washington's Constitution Hall, Mrs. Roosevelt and Harold Ickes arranged an Easter concert by Anderson at the Lincoln Memorial. Even symbolic gestures outraged many southern whites. When a black minister delivered the invocation at the 1936 Democratic convention, a South Carolina senator noisily stalked out.

Led by Molly Dewson, head of the Democratic Party's women's division, the New Deal also courted women voters. In the 1936 campaign, fifteen thousand women volunteers distributed flyers describing New Deal programs. "[W]e did not make the old-fashioned plea that our nominee was charming," she recalled; "We appealed to [women's] intelligence."

Dewson did not promote a specifically feminist agenda. The New Deal's economic programs, she argued, benefited both sexes. FDR did, however, appoint the first woman cabinet member, the first woman ambassador, and a number of female federal judges. Through Dewson's efforts, the 1936 Democratic platform committee reflected a fifty-fifty gender balance.

Despite the New Deal's symbolic gestures and appointment of a few blacks and women, racial and gender discrimination pervaded U.S. society in the 1930s, and Roosevelt, grappling with the depression, did relatively little to change things. That challenge would await a later time.

The Environment and the West   Environmental issues loomed large in the New Deal. While still in the New York Senate, FDR had sought logging regulation to protect wildlife. As president, he strongly supported the Civilian Conservation Corps' program of planting trees, thinning forests, and building hiking trails.

Soil conservation had high priority. The 1930s' dust storms resulted not only from drought, but from overgrazing and poor farming practices. For decades, Great Plains' wheat farmers had used tractors, combines, and heavy-duty plows called "sodbusters" to uproot the native prairie grasses that anchored the soil. When the rains failed, as they do in this drought-prone region, little remained to hold the soil in place, and parching winds whipped up devastating dust storms. By the 1930s, 9 million acres of farmland had been lost to erosion in the Great Plains, the South, and elsewhere.

In response, the Department of Agriculture's Soil Conservation Service promoted contour plowing, crop rotation, and soil-strengthening grasses. The Taylor Grazing Act of 1934 restricted the grazing on public lands that had exacerbated the problem. TVA dams helped control the floods that worsened erosion in the Tennessee valley.

New Deal planners also promoted national-park development, including Olympic National Park in Washington, Virginia's Shenandoah National Park, and Kings Canyon National Park in California. The administration also created some 160 new national wildlife refuges. FDR even closed a Utah artillery range near a nesting site of the endangered trumpeter swan!

The wilderness-preservation movement gained momentum in the 1930s, supported by such groups as the Wilderness Society (1935), started by environmentalist Aldo Leopold and others, and the National Wildlife Federation (1936), funded by firearms makers eager to preserve hunting areas. Pressured by such groups, Congress began to set aside protected wilderness areas. Building on these beginnings, the United States by 2008 had 704 officially designated national wilderness areas, comprising 107 million acres.

By later standards, the New Deal's environmental record was spotty. The decade's massive hydroelectric projects, while providing rural families with electricity, had serious ecological consequences. The Grand Coulee Dam, for example, destroyed salmon spawning on much of the Columbia River's tributary system. Other dams disrupted fragile ecosystems and the livelihoods of local residents, particularly Native American communities, who depended on them.

Viewed in context, however, the New Deal's environmental record remains impressive. While coping with the depression, the Roosevelt administration also focused a level of attention on environmental issues that had not been seen since the Progressive Era, and would not be seen again for a generation.

The New Deal impact on the West was profound, especially because the federal government owned a third or more of the land in eleven western states, and much more in some states. New Deal agencies and laws such as the Soil Conservation Service, the Taylor Grazing Act, and the Farm Security Administration (discussed shortly) set new rules for western agriculture, from prairie wheat fields and cattle ranges to California citrus groves and truck farms dependent on migrant labor.

The PWA and WPA built many large projects in the West, including thousands of public buildings, from courthouses and post offices to tourist facilities such as beautiful Timberline Lodge on Oregon's Mount Hood. Federal assistance also upgraded the highways linking the West to the rest of America, such as Route 66 from Chicago to Los Angeles.

Above all, the PWA in the West built dams—not only Grand Coulee, but also Shasta on the Sacramento River, Bonneville on the Columbia, Glen Canyon on the Colorado, and others. The PWA completed Hoover Dam on the Colorado, authorized by Congress in 1928 (see Chapter 23), well ahead of schedule. Despite their ecological downside, these great undertakings—among the largest engineering projects in history—supplied electricity to vast regions while contributing to flood control, irrigation, and soil conservation. (Las Vegas owed its post–World War II emergence as a gambling and entertainment mecca to power from nearby Hoover Dam.)

A New Deal initiative especially important for the West was Harold Ickes's National Planning Board, later renamed the National Resources Planning Board. This agency, which extended Herbert Hoover's promotion of multi-state water-resource planning in the West, facilitated state and regional management of water, soil, timber, and minerals.

THE NEW DEAL'S END STAGE, 1937–1939

Buoyed by his 1936 victory, Roosevelt proposed a controversial restructuring of the Supreme Court. After losing this fight, FDR confronted a stubborn recession and resurgent conservative opposition. With a few measures in 1937–1938, the New Deal ended.

FDR and the Supreme Court
In 1937, four of the Supreme Court's nine elderly justices were archconservatives who abhorred the New Deal. Joined by more moderate colleagues, these conservatives had struck down the NRA, the AAA, and progressive state laws. Roosevelt feared that the Social Security Act, the Wagner Act, and other key measures would meet a similar fate. Indeed, some corporate lawyers, convinced that the Social Security Act would be ruled unconstitutional, advised their clients to ignore it.

In February 1937, FDR proposed a bill that would have allowed him to appoint an additional Supreme Court member for each justice over age seventy, up to a total of six. Roosevelt blandly insisted that this would ease aging justices' heavy workload, but his political motivation was obvious.

Despite FDR's popularity, the press and public reacted with hostility. The Supreme Court's size, although unspecified in the Constitution, had held steady at nine since 1869, and thus seemed almost sacrosanct. Conservatives blasted FDR's "court-packing" scheme as a dangerous power grab. Even many Democrats disapproved. When the Senate voted down the scheme in July, FDR quietly dropped it.

But was this a defeat? Roosevelt's challenge to the Court, plus his 1936 electoral victory, sent powerful political signals that the justices heeded. In spring 1937, the Court upheld several New Deal measures, including the Wagner Act and a state minimum-wage law. Four conservative justices soon retired, enabling FDR to nominate successors of his choice and to create a judicial legacy that would long endure.

Overall, the New Deal era saw a fundamental shift in the Supreme Court's constitutional views. For decades, the court had interpreted very narrowly the Constitution's Commerce Clause (Article I, Sec. 8), which empowers the government to regulate business. After the 1930s, the court interpreted the Commerce Clause more broadly and proved much more receptive to business regulation and to the protection of individual rights as well as property rights.

The Roosevelt Recession
After a partial recovery, the economy dipped ominously in August 1937. Industrial production slumped. Unemployment again dominated the headlines. Federal policies that reduced consumer income contributed to this "Roosevelt recession." Social-security payroll taxes withdrew some $2 billion from circulation. The Federal Reserve Board had raised interest rates to forestall inflation, further contracting the money supply. FDR, meanwhile, concerned about mounting deficits, had cut back the New Deal relief programs.

Echoing Hoover, FDR assured his cabinet, "Everything will work out ... if we just sit tight." Meanwhile, however, some advisors had embraced John Maynard

Keynes's advocacy of deficit spending as the key to recovery. Aware that political rather than economic arguments carried more weight with FDR, they warned of a political backlash if conditions worsened. Convinced, FDR in April 1938 authorized new relief spending. By late 1938, unemployment had declined and industrial output increased. As late as 1939, however, more than 17 percent of the labor force remained jobless.

Final Measures;   Preoccupied by the Supreme Court fight, the recession, and
Growing   events abroad (covered in Chapter 25), FDR offered few
Opposition   domestic initiatives after 1936. Congress, however, enacted
                        several significant measures.

In 1937, Congress created the **Farm Security Administration** (FSA), replacing the under-funded Resettlement Administration. The FSA made low-interest loans to help tenant farmers and sharecroppers become farm owners. However, the FSA often rejected the poorest farmers' loan applications as too risky, weakening the program's impact.

The FSA operated camps offering shelter and medical services to impoverished migrant farm workers. FSA nurses and home economists provided practical advice on hygiene and housekeeping to poor farm families. The FSA also commissioned photographers to record the lives of migrant workers, tenant farmers, and dust-bowl refugees. These FSA photographs, published in various periodicals, helped shape a gritty documentary style that pervaded 1930s' popular culture, including movies and Henry Luce's photo magazine *Life,* launched in 1936. Today they comprise a haunting album of depression-era images.

Other measures set precedents for the future. The 1937 Housing Act appropriated $500 million for slum-clearance and public-housing projects that would vastly expand in the 1950s. The **Fair Labor Standards Act** of 1938 banned child labor and set a national minimum wage (initially forty cents an hour) and a maximum workweek of forty hours. This measure reflected not only humanitarianism but also some northern legislators' desire to undermine the competitive edge of the low-wage South. Despite many loopholes, the law helped exploited workers and underscored the government's role in regulating abusive workplace conditions.

In a final stab at raising farm income, the 1938 Agricultural Adjustment Act created a mechanism by which the government, in years of big harvests and low prices, would make loans to farmers and warehouse their surplus crops. When prices rose, farmers could sell these commodities and repay their loans. This complicated system set the framework of federal farm price support for decades.

Overall, New Deal farm policy produced mixed results. Large-scale growers benefited from government payments, but the cumbersome price-support mechanisms created many problems. The FSA assisted some tenants, sharecroppers, and small farmers (though often not the neediest), but did little to slow the long-term decline of family farms and the rise of agribusinesses. In reality, many small farmers dreamed of becoming large-scale commercial operators. Most did not succeed, however, and gradually left the land.

The New Deal's slower pace after 1935 also reflected the rise of an anti-New Deal congressional coalition of Republicans and conservative southern Democrats.

(Library of Congress)

A Camera's-Eye View of Depression-Era America *This 1937 image by Dorothea Lange, a photographer with the Farm Security Administration, pictures migrants from the Texas dust bowl gathered at a roadside camp near Calipatria in southern California.*

In 1937, this coalition rejected FDR's proposal to reorganize the executive branch. The plan made administrative sense, but critics again warned darkly of FDR's dictatorial ambitions.

In 1938–1939, conservative legislators slashed relief appropriations, cut corporate taxes, and killed the WPA's Federal Theatre Project for its alleged radicalism. Meanwhile, the House Un-American Activities Committee (created in 1937) investigated New Deal agencies for communist infiltration. The 1939 Hatch Act, barring federal employees from electoral campaigning, reflected conservatives' suspicions that WPA staff members were doubling as campaign workers. Indeed, Harry Hopkins and other public-works officials well understood these programs' electoral value, and political calculations influenced the allocation of PWA and WPA funds.

Although FDR campaigned in the 1938 midterm elections, the Republicans gained in the House and Senate and won a net of thirteen governorships. In the Democratic primaries Roosevelt opposed several anti-New Deal Democratic senators, but most defeated their primary challengers and went on to win in November. Highlighting foreign affairs in his January 1939 State of the Union message, FDR proposed no new domestic measures and merely noted the need to "preserve our reforms." The New Deal was over.

SOCIAL CHANGE AND SOCIAL ACTION IN THE 1930S

American life in the 1930s involved more than politics. The depression affected everyone, including the jobless and their families; working women; and all age groups. For industrial workers, African-Americans, Hispanics, and Native Americans, the crisis brought hard times but also encouraged organized resistance to exploitation and brought new legislative initiatives.

The Depression's Psychological and Social Impact The depression marked all who lived through it. Despite the New Deal, unemployment never fell below about 14 percent in the 1930s and was often considerably higher. A quarter of all farm families sought public or private assistance during the 1930s. Even the employed often had to take jobs below their level of training: college alumni pumped gas; business-school graduates sold furniture; a retired navy captain became a movie theater usher.

Psychologists described "unemployment shock": jobless persons who walked the streets seeking work and then lay awake at night worrying. When shoe soles wore out, cardboard or folded newspapers had to serve. Advertisements for mouthwashes, deodorants, and correspondence courses exploited feelings of shame and failure. Women's magazines described low-cost meals and other budget-trimming strategies. Habits of scrimping and saving acquired in the 1930s often survived into more affluent times. As Caroline Bird wrote in *The Invisible Scar* (1966), a social history of the 1930s, the depression for many boiled down to "a dull misery in the bones."

New York senator Robert Wagner called the working woman in the depression "the first orphan in the storm." Indeed, for the 25 percent of U.S. women employed in 1930, the depression brought difficult times. The female jobless rate exceeded 20 percent for much of the decade. Working women often took lower-paying jobs. Laid-off factory workers became waitresses. Jobless men competed with women even for such traditional "women's work" as library posts and school teaching.

Married women workers endured harsh criticism. Although most worked because of economic necessity, critics accused them of stealing men's jobs. Even Labor Secretary Frances Perkins urged married women to leave the labor market so more men could work. School boards fired married women teachers.

Women workers faced wage discrimination. In 1939, women teachers earned nearly 20 percent less than male teachers with comparable experience. Some NRA codes authorized lower pay for women. The minimum-wage provision of the Fair Labor Standards Act did not include the more than 2 million women who worked for wages in private households.

The late 1930s' unionization drive had mixed effects on women workers. Women employed in mass-production industries benefited, but the heavily female sectors of the labor force—textiles, sales, clerical and service work—resisted unionization. Male managers and even male union leaders opposed a campaign to unionize female clerical workers.

Despite the criticism, the percentage of married women in the workforce increased in the 1930s from under 12 percent to nearly 16 percent. The depression may actually have hastened the long-term movement of women into the workplace as married women took jobs out of necessity. When her husband stopped looking for work in 1932, one working wife explained, "[At] twenty-eight, with two little girls, ... I took a job as a salesclerk ..., and worked through the Depression."

As this story suggests, the depression affected family life. The birthrate fell in the early thirties as married couples postponed a family, and as birth-control devices became more readily available. The U.S. population in the 1930s grew by only 7 percent, in contrast to an average of 20 percent per decade from 1900 to 1930.

Family survival posed major challenges. Parents patched clothes, stretched food resources, and sought public assistance when necessary. In homes with a tradition of strong male authority, the husband's loss of a job could prove devastating. "I would rather turn on the gas and put an end to the whole family than let my wife support me," one man told a social investigator. Desertions increased, and the divorce rate spiked, hitting a then all-time high by 1940.

The depression spared neither old nor young. Bank failures wiped out the savings of older Americans. By 1935, a million citizens over sixty-five were on relief. One observer compared young people to runners waiting for a starting gun that never sounded. High-school enrollment increased as many youths, lacking job prospects, stayed in school. The marriage rate declined as anxious young people postponed this step. Commented Eleanor Roosevelt in 1934, "I have moments of real terror when I think we might be losing this generation."

Children found vacation plans canceled, birthdays with few presents, and mealtimes tense with anxious discussions. Depression-era children wrote sad letters to Eleanor Roosevelt. A Michigan high-school senior described her shame at lacking a graduation dress. "I give all I earn for food for the family," she explained. A thirteen-year-old Arkansas girl wrote, "I have to stay out of school because I have no books or clothes to ware."

Rediscovering traditional skills, depression-era families canned fruit and vegetables, painted their houses, and repaired their own cars. Many would later recall the 1930s as a time of simple, inexpensive pleasures and neighborly sharing of scant resources.

For the neediest—among them blacks, Hispanics, and southern sharecroppers—the depression imposed added misery on poverty-blighted lives. In *Native Son* (1940), novelist Richard Wright portrayed the desperate conditions in Chicago's black slums. Yet hope survived. Emotional resilience, habits of mutual aid, and survival skills honed over the years helped poor families cope. In New York's Harlem, a charismatic black religious leader calling himself Father Divine institutionalized this cooperative spirit by organizing kitchens that distributed free meals to the needy.

Industrial Workers Unionize   Of America's 7.7 million factory workers in 1930, most remained unorganized. Major industries such as steel, automobiles, and textiles had resisted workers' attempts to unionize. The conservative mood of the 1920s had further weakened the labor movement.

But with hard times and a favorable government climate, labor militancy surged in the 1930s. The Wagner Act's guarantee of workers' right to organize jolted the U.S. labor movement. The nation's major labor organization, the American Federation of Labor (AFL), had historically organized unions of skilled craftsmen rather than of all workers in a given industry (see Chapter 18). In the 1930s, that pattern changed. In November 1935, John L. Lewis of the United Mine Workers and Sidney Hillman of the Amalgamated Clothing Workers, frustrated by the AFL's slowness in organizing factory workers, started the Committee for Industrial Organization (CIO) within the AFL. CIO activists preached unionization in Pittsburgh steel mills, Detroit auto plants, Akron rubber factories, and southern textile mills. Unlike the narrowly restrictive AFL unions, CIO unions welcomed all workers in a particular industry, regardless of race, gender, or skill level.

In 1936 a CIO-sponsored organizing committee announced a strike to unionize the steel industry. (In fact, John L. Lewis had already secretly negotiated a settlement with the head of U.S. Steel.) In March 1937, U.S. Steel recognized the union, raised wages, and introduced a forty-hour workweek. Other big steel companies followed suit, and soon four hundred thousand steelworkers were union members (see Figure 24.2).

Other CIO organizers targeted General Motors, an anti-union stronghold. Their leader was a redheaded young autoworker and labor activist, Walter Reuther. Reuther's German-American father was a committed socialist, and when the depression hit, young Reuther rediscovered his radical roots. On December 30, 1936, employees at GM's plants in Flint, Michigan, stopped work and peacefully occupied the factories. This "sit-down" strategy (adopted so GM could not hire strikebreakers to keep the plants operating) paralyzed GM's production.

Although women workers did not participate in the plant occupation (to avoid gossip that might discredit the strike), they picketed outside. A Women's Auxiliary led by strikers' families provided meals, set up a speakers' bureau, and organized marches.

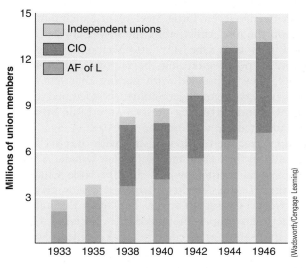

FIGURE 24.2 The Growth of Labor Union Membership, 1933–1946

The CIO's industrial unions grew rapidly with passage of the pro-union National Labor Relations Act in 1935. Union membership increased still more as war plants hired workers in the early 1940s.

Source: Historical Statistics of the United States, Colonial Times to 1970 (1975), 176–177.

GM sent spies to union meetings, called in police to harass the strikers, and threatened to fire them. A showdown with the police led to the formation of the Women's Emergency Brigade, whose members remained on twenty-four-hour alert for picket duty or to surround the plants in case of police raids.

GM asked President Roosevelt and Michigan's governor to send troops to expel the strikers, as Herbert Hoover had done with the bonus marchers. Both declined, however. Although the sit-down tactic troubled FDR, he refused to intervene.

On February 11, 1937, GM signed a contract recognizing the United Automobile Workers (UAW). Bearded workers who had vowed not to shave until victory was won streamed out of the plants. As Chrysler fell into line also, the UAW boasted more than four hundred thousand members. Unionization of the electrical and rubber industries advanced as well.

In 1938 the Committee for Industrial Organization broke with the AFL to become the **Congress of Industrial Organizations,** a 2-million-member association of industrial unions. In response, the AFL, too, began to adapt to the changed nature of the labor force. Overall, U.S. union membership shot from under 3 million in 1933 to over 8 million in 1941.

Some big corporations resisted. Henry Ford hated unions, and his tough lieutenant Harry Bennett organized a squad of union-busting thugs to fight the UAW. In 1937 Bennett's men viciously beat Walter Reuther and other UAW officials outside Ford's plant near Detroit. Not until 1941 did Ford finally yield to the union's pressure.

The Republic Steel Company, headed by a union hater named Tom Girdler, dug in as well. Even after the major steelmakers signed with the CIO, Republic and other smaller companies known collectively as "Little Steel" resisted. In May 1937, workers in twenty-seven Little Steel plants, including Republic's factory in Chicago, walked off the job. Anticipating the strike, Girdler had assembled an arsenal of guns and tear gas. On May 30, Memorial Day, a group of strikers approached over 250 police guarding the factory. When someone threw a large stick at the police, they responded with gunfire that left four strikers dead and scores wounded. An investigative committee condemned the killings as "clearly avoidable." In 1941, under growing pressure, the Little Steel companies, including Republic, finally accepted the CIO union.

Another holdout was the textile industry, with over six hundred thousand low-paid workers, mostly in the South and 40 percent female. A unionizing effort in the 1920s had failed owing to mill owners' hostility (see Chapter 23). In 1934, the AFL-affiliated United Textile Workers launched a new drive. Some four hundred thousand textile workers went on strike, but again the mill owners fought back. Anti-union Southern governors mobilized the National Guard. Several strikers were killed and thousands arrested. The strike failed, and the textile industry remained mostly non-union as the decade ended.

Indeed, despite the unionization surge, more than three-quarters of the nonfarm labor force remained unorganized in 1940, including low-paid manual laborers; domestic workers; and employees in department stores, offices, restaurants, and laundries—categories that included many women, blacks, and recent immigrants. Nevertheless, the unionization of many industrial workers ranks among the decade's memorable developments.

Why did powerful corporations yield to unionization after years of resistance? Workers' militancy and union organizers' tactical skill were crucial. But so was a changed government climate. Historically, the government had helped corporations break strikes. Although this still happened in the 1930s, as in the textile-industry strike, the Roosevelt administration and state officials generally refused to play the role of strikebreaker. New Deal labor laws made clear that Washington would no longer automatically back management in labor disputes. Once corporate managers realized this, unionization often followed.

Organized labor's successes in the later 1930s concealed some complex tensions. A core of activists, including communists and socialists, led the unionizing drive. Most rank-and-file workers were not political radicals, but once the CIO's militant minority showed the effectiveness of picket lines and sit-down strikes, workers signed up by the thousands. As they did, the radical organizers lost influence, and the unions became more conservative.

Black and Hispanic Americans Resist Racism and Exploitation   The depression stirred activism within the African-American and Hispanic communities. Although black migration northward slowed in the 1930s, four hundred thousand southern blacks moved to northern cities in the decade. By 1940, nearly one-quarter of America's 12 million blacks lived in the urban North.

Rural or urban, life was hard. Black tenant farmers and sharecroppers often faced eviction. Although some black industrial workers benefited from the CIO's nondiscriminatory policy, workplace racism remained a fact of life.

Over one hundred blacks died by lynching in the 1930s, and other miscarriages of justice continued, especially in the South. In 1931, an all-white jury in Scottsboro, Alabama, sentenced eight black youths to death on highly suspect rape charges. In 1935, after heavy publicity and an aggressive defense, the Supreme Court ordered a new trial for the "Scottsboro Boys" because they had been denied legal counsel and blacks had been excluded from the jury. Five of the group were again convicted, however, and served long prison terms.

But rising activism signaled changes ahead. The NAACP battled in courts and legislatures for voting rights and against lynching and segregation. Under the banner "Don't Shop Where You Can't Work," black protesters picketed businesses that refused to hire blacks, particularly in black neighborhoods. In March 1935, hostility toward discriminatory white-owned businesses in Harlem, intensified by anger over racism and joblessness, ignited a riot that caused heavy property damage and left three dead.

The Communist Party publicized lynchings and racial discrimination, and supplied lawyers for the "Scottsboro Boys," as part of a depression-era recruitment effort in the black community. But despite a few notable recruits (including the novelist Richard Wright), few blacks joined the party.

Other groups also faced discrimination. California continued to restrict landownership by Japanese-Americans. In 1934, Congress limited annual immigration from the Philippines to fifty, and offered free travel "home" for Filipinos long settled in the United States.

The more than 2 million Hispanic Americans confronted difficulties as well. Some were citizens with ancestral roots in the Southwest, but most were recent arrivals from Mexico or Caribbean islands such as Cuba and Puerto Rico (a U.S. holding whose residents are American citizens). While the Caribbean immigrants settled in East Coast cities, most Mexican newcomers worked as migratory agricultural laborers in the Southwest and elsewhere, or in midwestern steel or meatpacking plants.

As the depression deepened, Mexican-born residents endured rising hostility. "Okies" fleeing the dust bowl competed for jobs with Hispanic farm workers. By 1937 over half of Arizona's cotton workers were out-of-staters who had supplanted Mexican-born laborers. With their migratory work patterns disrupted, Mexican-Americans poured into the barrios (Hispanic neighborhoods) of southwestern cities. Lacking work, half a million returned to Mexico in the 1930s. Many did so voluntarily, but immigration officials and local authorities repatriated others. Los Angeles welfare officials announced free one-way transportation to Mexico. The savings in relief payments, they calculated, would more than offset the cost of sending *repatriados* to Mexico. Though the plan was "voluntary," those who remained were denied relief payments or jobs with New Deal work programs. Under federal and local pressure, an estimated seventy thousand Mexicans left Los Angeles in 1931 alone.

Mexican-American farm workers who remained endured appalling conditions and near-starvation wages. A wave of strikes (some led by Communist organizers) swept California. A labor organization called the Confederación de Uniones de Campesinos y Obreros Mexicanos (Confederation of Unions of Mexican Workers and Farm Laborers) emerged from a 1933 grape workers' strike. More strikes erupted in 1935–1936 from the celery fields and citrus groves around Los Angeles to the lettuce fields of the Salinas Valley.

Organizations like the citrus-growers' marketing cooperative Sunkist fought the unions, sometimes with violence. In October 1933, bullets ripped into a cotton pickers' union hall in Pixley, California, killing two men and wounding others. Resisting intimidation, the strikers won a 20 percent pay increase. Striking cotton pickers and other Mexican-American farm workers gained hard-fought victories as well. These strikes awakened at least some Americans to the plight of one of the nation's most exploited groups.

A New Deal for Native Americans   The 1930s also focused attention on the nation's 330,000 Native Americans, most of whom endured poverty, scant education, and poor health care. The 1887 Dawes Act (see Chapter 17) had dissolved the tribes as legal entities, allocated some tribal lands to individual Indians, and offered the rest for sale. By the 1930s, non-Indians held about two-thirds of the land that Indians had possessed in 1887. Indians had gained voting rights in 1924, but this did little to improve their lot.

In 1923, the reformer John Collier, who had lived among New Mexico's Pueblo Indians, founded the American Indian Defense Association to reverse the Dawes Act approach and to revitalize traditional Indian life. The National Council of American Indians, headed by Gertrude Bonnin, a Yankton Dakota Sioux, also pressed for reform.

Appointed commissioner of Indian affairs in 1933, Collier gathered funds from various New Deal agencies to construct schools, hospitals, and irrigation systems on reservations, and to preserve sites of cultural importance. The Civilian Conservation Corps employed twelve thousand Indian youths on projects on Indian lands.

Pursuing his vision, Collier drafted a bill to halt tribal land sales and restore the remaining unallocated lands to tribal control. Collier's bill also gave broad powers to tribal councils and required Indian schools to teach Native American history and handicrafts. Some Indian leaders criticized it as a plan to transform reservations into living museums and to isolate Native Americans from modern life. Some Indian property owners and entrepreneurs rejected the bill's tribalist assumptions. The bill did, indeed, reflect the idealism of well-meaning outsiders rather than the views of the nation's diverse Native American groups.

The **Indian Reorganization Act** of 1934, a compromise measure, halted tribal land sales and enabled tribes to regain title to unallocated lands. But Congress scaled back Collier's proposals for tribal self-government and dropped his proposals for renewing traditional tribal culture.

Of 258 tribes that voted on the law (a requirement for it to go into effect), 181 favored it, while 77 did not. America's largest tribal group, the 40,000-strong Navajo, voted no, largely because the law, to promote soil conservation, restricted grazing rights.

Indian policy remained contentious. But the law did recognize Indian interests and the value of cultural diversity. The restoration of tribes as legal entities laid the groundwork for later tribal business ventures as well as legal efforts to enforce long-ignored treaty rights (to be discussed in Chapter 30).

THE AMERICAN CULTURAL SCENE IN THE 1930s

Radio and the movies offered escapist fare amid the hard times of the 1930s, though some films addressed depression-era realities. Novelists, artists, playwrights, and photographers tended toward a highly critical view of capitalist America when the depression first struck, as we have seen. As the decade went on, however, a more positive view of America emerged, reflecting both optimism about the New Deal and apprehension about events abroad.

Avenues of Escape: Radio and the Movies   The standardization of mass culture continued in the 1930s. Each evening, Americans turned to their radios for network news, musical programs, and comedy shows. Radio humor flourished as Americans battled hard times. Comedians like Jack Benny and the husband-and-wife team George Burns and Gracie Allen attracted millions.

So, too, did the fifteen-minute afternoon domestic dramas known as soap operas (for the soap companies that sponsored them). Despite their assembly-line quality, these programs won a devoted audience, consisting mostly of housewives. Identifying with the radio heroines's troubles, female listeners gained temporary escape from their own difficulties. As one put it, "I can get through the day better when I hear they have sorrows, too."

The movies, with their low-priced tickets, remained extremely popular. In 1939, 65 percent of Americans went to the movies at least once a week.

Films of the early 1930s like *I Am a Fugitive from a Chain Gang* (1932) captured the grimness of the early depression. The popular Marx Brothers movies reflected the uncertainty of the Hoover years, when the economy and the social order itself seemed on the verge of collapse. In comedies like *Animal Crackers* (1930) and *Duck Soup* (1933), these vaudeville troupers of German-Jewish immigrant origins ridiculed authority and satirized the established order.

After Roosevelt took office, Warner Brothers studio (with close ties to the administration) made several topical films that presented the New Deal in a favorable light. These included *Wild Boys of the Road* (1933), about unemployed youth; *Massacre* (1934), on the mistreatment of Indians; and *Black Fury* (1935), dealing with striking coal miners.

Early thirties' gangster movies, inspired by real-life criminals like Al Capone, presented a different style of film realism. Films like *Little Caesar* (1930) and *The Public Enemy* (1931) offered gritty images of depression America: menacing streets; forbidding industrial sites; gunfights between rival gangs. (When civic groups protested the glorification of crime, Hollywood made the police and "G-men"—FBI agents—the heroes, while retaining the violence.) The movie gangsters played by Edward G. Robinson and James Cagney, variants of the Horatio Alger hero battling adversity, appealed to depression-era moviegoers.

Above all, Hollywood offered escape from depression-era realities. The publicist who claimed that the movies "literally laughed the big bad wolf of the depression out of the public mind" exaggerated, but cinema's escapist function in the 1930s is clear. Musicals such as *Gold Diggers of 1933* (with its theme song, "We're in the Money") offered dancing, music, and cheerful plots involving the triumph of pluck over adversity. In Frank Capra's *Mr. Deeds Goes to Town* (1936) and *Mr. Smith Goes to Washington* (1939), virtuous heroes representing "the people" vanquish entrenched interests. When color movies arrived in the late 1930s, they seemed an omen of better times ahead.

African-Americans appeared in 1930s' movies, if at all, mostly as stereotypes: the scatterbrained maid in *Gone with the Wind* (1939); the indulgent house servant played by tap dancer Bill Robinson and patronized by child star Shirley Temple in *The Little Colonel* (1935); the slow-witted "Stepin Fetchit" played in many movies by black actor Lincoln Perry.

In representing women, Hollywood offered mixed messages. While some 1930s' movie heroines found fulfillment in marriage and domesticity, other films challenged the stereotype. Joan Bennett played a strong-willed professional in *The Wedding Present* (1936). Katharine Hepburn portrayed independent-minded women in such films as *Spitfire* (1934) and *A Woman Rebels* (1936). Mae West, brassy and openly sexual, mocked conventional stereotypes in *I'm No Angel* (1933) and other 1930s hits.

The Later 1930s: Opposing Fascism; Reaffirming Traditional Values

The 1930s ended on a cautiously upbeat note. America had survived the depression. The social fabric remained whole; revolution had not come. As other societies collapsed into dictatorships, U.S. democracy endured. Writers, composers, and other cultural creators reflected the changed mood.

International developments and a domestic political movement known as the **Popular Front** influenced this shift. In the early 1930s, the U.S. Communist Party attacked Roosevelt and the New Deal. But in 1935, Russian dictator Joseph Stalin, fearing attack by Nazi Germany, called for a worldwide alliance, or Popular Front, against Adolf Hitler and his Italian fascist ally, Benito Mussolini. (Fascism is a form of government involving one-party rule, extreme nationalism, hostility to minority groups, and the suppression of dissent.) Parroting the new Soviet line, U.S. communists now praised FDR and summoned writers and intellectuals to the antifascist cause. Many noncommunists, alarmed by developments in Europe, responded.

The Spanish Civil War was the Popular Front's high-water mark. In July 1936, Spanish fascist general Francisco Franco began a military revolt against Spain's legally elected government, a coalition of left-wing parties. With aid from Hitler and Mussolini, Franco won backing from Spanish monarchists, landowners, industrialists, and the Catholic Church.

The Spanish Loyalists (that is, those loyal to Spain's elected government) won support from U.S. writers, artists, and intellectuals who backed the Popular Front, including the writer Ernest Hemingway, who visited Spain in 1936–1937. In contrast to his antiwar novels of the 1920s (see Chapter 23), Hemingway's *For Whom the Bell Tolls* (1940) told of a young American volunteer who dies while fighting with the Loyalists. For Hemingway, the Spanish Civil War offered a cause "in which you felt an absolute brotherhood with the others who were engaged in it."

The Popular Front collapsed in August 1939 when Stalin and Hitler signed a non-aggression pact. Overnight, enthusiasm for joining with communists under the "antifascism" banner faded. But while it lasted, the Popular Front influenced U.S. culture and alerted Americans to threatening events abroad.

The New Deal's programs for writers, artists, and musicians, as well as its turn leftward in 1935–1936, also contributed to the late 1930s' cultural shift. More positive views now replaced the cynical tone of the 1920s and early 1930s. In John Steinbeck's best-selling novel *The Grapes of Wrath* (1939), an uprooted dust-bowl family, the Joads, make their difficult way from Oklahoma to California along Route 66. Steinbeck stressed ordinary Americans' endurance, cooperation, and mutual support. As Ma Joad tells her son Tom, "They ain't gonna wipe us out. Why, we're the people—we go on." Made into a movie starring Henry Fonda, *The Grapes of Wrath* stands as a memorable cultural document of the later 1930s.

In 1936, journalist James Agee and photographer Walker Evans lived with Alabama sharecropper families while researching a magazine article. From this experience came Agee's masterpiece, *Let Us Now Praise Famous Men* (1941). Enhanced by Evans's photographs, Agee's work evoked the strength and decency of depression-era Americans.

On the stage, Thornton Wilder's *Our Town* (1938) lovingly portrayed early-twentieth-century life a New England town. William Saroyan's *The Time of Your Life* (1939) celebrated the foibles and virtues of a colorful group of patrons gathered in a San Francisco waterfront bar.

Composers, too, caught the spirit of cultural nationalism. In such works as *Billy the Kid* (1938), Aaron Copland drew upon American legends and folk melodies. George Gershwin's 1935 musical *Porgy and Bess,* based on DuBose and

Dorothy Heyward's 1920s' novel and play (see Chapter 23), brought this portrayal of black life in Charleston, South Carolina, to a larger audience.

Jazz gained popularity thanks to swing, a danceable style originated by pianist Fletcher Henderson and popularized by the bands of Count Basie, Benny Goodman, Duke Ellington, and others. The Basie band started at Kansas City's Reno Club, where, as Basie later recalled, "We played from nine o'clock in the evening to five or six the next morning.... [T]he boys in the band got eighteen dollars a week and I got twenty one." Moving to New York in 1936, Basie helped launch the swing era.

Benny Goodman, of a Chicago immigrant family, had played the clarinet as a boy at Jane Addams's Hull House. Challenging racial prejudices, Goodman included black musicians in his orchestra. The Goodman band's 1938 performance at New York's Carnegie Hall, a citadel of high culture, underscored jazz's growing cultural influence.

The later 1930s also saw a heightened interest in regional literature, painting, and folk art. Zora Neale Hurston's novel *Their Eyes Were Watching God* (1937) portrayed a black woman's search for fulfillment in rural Florida. William Faulkner's *Absalom, Absalom!* (1936) continued the saga of his mythic Yoknapatawpha County in Mississippi. Painters Thomas Hart Benton of Missouri (descended from a nineteenth-century senator of the same name), John Steuart Curry of Kansas, and Iowa's Grant Wood explored traditional and regional themes in their work.

Galleries displayed folk paintings, Amish quilts, and New England weather vanes. A 1938 show at New York's Museum of Modern Art introduced Horace Pippin, a black Philadelphia laborer partially disabled in World War I. In such paintings as *John Brown Going to His Hanging,* Pippin revealed a genuine, if untutored, talent. In 1939 the same museum featured seventy-nine-year-old Anna "Grandma" Moses of Hoosick Falls, New York, whose memory paintings of her farm girlhood enjoyed great popularity.

The surge of cultural nationalism heightened interest in American history. Visitors flocked to historical re-creations such as Henry Ford's Greenfield Village near Detroit and Colonial Williamsburg in Virginia, restored by John D. Rockefeller, Jr. Texans restored the Alamo in San Antonio, the "Cradle of Texas Liberty." Historical novels like Margaret Mitchell's Civil War epic *Gone with the Wind* (1936) became best sellers. These restorations and fictions often distorted history. Colonial Williamsburg and Mitchell's novel downplayed or romanticized slavery. "Texas Liberty" resonated differently for the state's Hispanic, African-American, and Indian peoples than it did for the white patriotic organizations that venerated the Alamo.

Streamlining and a World's Fair: Corporate America's Utopian Vision

A design style called streamlining also shaped the visual culture of the late 1930s. This style originated in the 1920s when industrial designers, inspired by the airplane, introduced flowing curves into the design of commercial products. Consumers loved streamlining—a vital business consideration during the depression. When Sears Roebuck streamlined its Coldspot refrigerators, sales surged. As products ranging from house trailers to pencil sharpeners and cigarette lighters emerged in sleek new forms, streamlining helped corporate America rebuild its image and present itself as the shaper of a better future.

Under the theme "The World of Tomorrow," the 1939 New York World's Fair represented the high point of the streamlining vogue and of corporate America's public-relations blitz. The Trylon and Perisphere, a soaring tapered tower and a globe that seemed to float on water symbolized the fair's futuristic theme. Inside the Perisphere, visitors found "Democracity," a revolving diorama portraying an idealized city of the future.

At Futurama, the General Motors exhibit, visitors entered a darkened auditorium where, amid piped-in music and a resonant recorded narration, a vision of America in the distant year 1960 slowly unfolded. A multilane highway network complete with cloverleaf exits and stacked interchanges dominated the imagined landscape. A brilliant public-relations investment, Futurama built support for the interstate highway system that would soon become a reality. Forget the depression and the bitter auto-workers' strike, GM's exhibit seemed to whisper; behold the exciting future we are preparing for you.

Also featuring such wonders as television and automatic dishwashers, the World's Fair portrayed "The World of Tomorrow" as a technological utopia created by America's corporations. A visit to the fair, a business magazine editorialized, "should convince [any doubters] that American business has been the vehicle which carried the discoveries of science and the benefits of machine production to … American consumers." The fair epitomized corporate America's version of the patriotism and hopefulness stirring in America as the 1930s ended.

But the hopefulness was tinged with fear, as danger loomed beyond the seas. The anxiety triggered by the menacing world situation surfaced on October 31, 1938, when CBS radio aired an adaptation of H. G. Wells's science-fiction story *War of the Worlds* directed by Orson Welles. In realistic detail, the broadcast reported the landing of a spaceship in New Jersey and aliens with ray guns advancing toward New York City. The show sparked a panic. Some terrified listeners jumped in their cars and sped off into the night. Others prayed. A few attempted suicide. Beneath the terror lay a more well-founded fear: of approaching war. For a decade, as America had battled the depression, the international situation had steadily worsened. By October 1938, another European war loomed on the horizon.

The panic triggered by Orson Welles's Halloween prank quickly faded, but the anxieties aroused by the all-too-real dangers abroad only escalated. By the time the New York World's Fair offered its hopeful vision of the future, the actual world of 1939 looked bleak indeed.

CHRONOLOGY

1929–1940

1929	Stock market crash; onset of depression.
1932	Reconstruction Finance Corporation.
	Veterans' bonus march.
	Franklin D. Roosevelt elected president.

1933	Repeal of Eighteenth Amendment.
	Civilian Conservation Corps (CCC).
	Federal Emergency Relief Act (FERA).
	Tennessee Valley Authority (TVA).
	Agricultural Adjustment Administration (AAA).
	National Recovery Administration (NRA).
	Public Works Administration (PWA).
1934	Securities and Exchange Commission (SEC).
	Taylor Grazing Act.
	Indian Reorganization Act.
1934–1936	Strikes by Mexican-American agricultural workers in the West.
1935	Supreme Court declares NIRA unconstitutional.
	Works Progress Administration (WPA).
	Resettlement Administration.
	National Labor Relations Act (Wagner Act).
	Social Security Act.
	NAACP campaign for federal antilynching law.
	Huey Long assassinated.
	Revenue Act raises taxes on corporations and the wealthy.
	Supreme Court reverses conviction of the "Scottsboro Boys."
	Harlem protests and riot.
1935–1939	Era of the Popular Front.
1936	Supreme Court declares AAA unconstitutional.
	Roosevelt wins landslide reelection victory.
	Autoworkers' sit-down strike against General Motors begins (December).
1937	Roosevelt's "court-packing" plan defeated.
	Farm Security Administration.
	GM, U.S. Steel, and Chrysler sign union contracts.
1937–1938	The "Roosevelt recession."
1938	Fair Labor Standards Act.
	Republicans gain heavily in midterm elections.
	Congress of Industrial Organizations (CIO) formed.
	Carnegie Hall concert by Benny Goodman Orchestra.
	Orson Welles' "War of the Worlds" radio broadcast.
1939	Hatch Act.
	Marian Anderson concert at Lincoln Memorial.
	John Steinbeck, *The Grapes of Wrath*.
1940	Ernest Hemingway, *For Whom the Bell Tolls*.

CONCLUSION

The stock-market crash and the Great Depression exposed major weaknesses in the U.S. and world economies. These ranged from chronically low farm prices and uneven income distribution to trade barriers, a glut of consumer goods, and a constricted money supply. As the crisis deepened, President Hoover struggled to respond. In 1932, with Hoover discredited, Franklin D. Roosevelt and his promised "New Deal" brought a surge of hope.

Initially focusing on immediate economic relief and recovery, Roosevelt welcomed big business in his depression-fighting coalition. By 1935, however, the New Deal adopted a more class-based approach. FDR now addressed the plight of the poor, including sharecroppers and migrants; pursued business regulation and higher taxes for the wealthy; and championed such fundamental reforms as Social Security, centerpiece of the welfare state, and the Wagner Act, guaranteeing workers' right to unionize. His smashing reelection victory in 1936 solidified FDR's Democratic coalition, including the white South, farmers, urban ethnics, union members, and African-Americans. By 1938, facing conservative opposition and menaces abroad, the New Deal's reformist energies faded.

The depression and the New Deal affected different groups in different ways. For citizens across the West and in the region served by TVA, public-works projects brought hydroelectric power and economic growth, while the New Deal also renewed attention to conservation and environmental issues. Women were told to stay home so jobless men could find work. Many resisted, however, and the female labor force expanded. For industrial workers, the decade's spirit of militance and favorable legislation brought a wave of strikes and unionization campaigns.

While African-Americans benefited from New Deal relief programs, the Roosevelt administration failed to address lynching and racial discrimination. Mexican-born farm laborers, facing deportation threats, organized strikes demanding better wages and working conditions. For Native Americans, New Deal legislation restored tribes' legal status, laying the groundwork for future enterprises and treaty claims.

American culture in the 1930s reflected the decade's economic and social realities. While movies and radio offered diversion, writers, painters, and other cultural creators initially expressed disillusionment over capitalism's failure. But as New Deal programs inspired hope, and as foreign threats loomed, the later 1930s brought a more upbeat and affirmative cultural climate.

The New Deal has its downside. Some programs failed, and recovery proved elusive. Only in 1943, as war plants boomed, did full employment return. On racial issues, symbolic gestures substituted for genuine engagement. But the New Deal's achievements remain impressive, reflecting an unprecedented level of governmental engagement with social and economic issues. FDR and his administration reshaped the role of the presidency, the Supreme Court, the nation's political agenda, and citizens' expectations of government's role in meeting urgent public needs.

Looming over the decade is the larger-than-life image of Franklin D. Roosevelt. Neither saint nor superman, FDR could be devious, superficial, and cavalier about details. But for most Americans of the 1930s—and most historians since—his strengths outweighed his liabilities. His experimental approach served a suffering nation well. He once compared himself to a football quarterback, deciding which play to call after seeing how the last one worked out.

Above all, Roosevelt's optimism inspired a demoralized people. "We Americans of today …" he told an audience of young people in 1939, "are characters in the living book of democracy. But we are also its author. It falls upon us now to say whether the chapters … to come will tell a story of retreat or a story of continued advance."

25

▼

AMERICANS AND A WORLD IN CRISIS, 1933–1945

CHAPTER OUTLINE

- The United States in a Menacing World, 1933–1939 • Into the Storm, 1939–1941 • America Mobilizes for War • The Battlefront, 1942–1944 • Liberating Europe • War and American Society • Triumph and Tragedy, 1945

THE UNITED STATES IN A MENACING WORLD, 1933–1939

Apart from improving relations with Latin America, the early administration of President Franklin D. Roosevelt (FDR) remained largely aloof from the crises in the world. Americans reacted ambivalently as Italy, Germany, and Japan grew more aggressive. Millions of Americans, determined not to stumble into war again, supported neutrality. Only a minority wanted the United States to help embattled democracies abroad. All the while, the world slid toward the precipice.

Nationalism and the Good Neighbor President Roosevelt at first put American economic interests above all else and showed little interest in international cooperation. He did, however, extend the internationalist approach of his predecessor in Latin America, where bitterness over "Yankee imperialism" ran high. FDR declared a **"Good Neighbor" policy,** renouncing any nation's right to intervene in the affairs of another. To that end, Roosevelt withdrew the last U.S. troops from Haiti and the Dominican Republic, and terminated the Platt Amendment, which had given the United States its right to intervene in Cuba since 1901.

An economic crisis in Cuba in 1933 brought to power a leftist regime that the United States opposed. Instead of sending in the marines, as earlier administrations might have done, the United States provided indirect aid to a conservative revolt led by Fulgencio Batista in 1934 that overthrew the radical government. American economic assistance would then allow Batista to retain power until his overthrow by Fidel Castro in 1959. In Mexico, a reform government came to power in 1936 and promptly nationalized several oil companies owned by U.S. and British corporations. While insisting on fair compensation, the United States refrained from military intervention and conceded Mexico's right to nationalize the companies. Subsequently, Mexico and the oil companies reached a compromise compensation agreement. Although the U.S. did little to improve social and economic conditions in Latin America, the better relations fostered by FDR did help the United States achieve hemispheric solidarity in World War II, and later in the Cold War.

The Rise of Aggressive States in Europe and Asia   Meanwhile, powerful forces raged across much of the world. As early as 1922, economic and social unrest in Italy enabled **Benito Mussolini** to seize power. Dictator until 1943, Mussolini suppressed dissent, imposed one-party rule, adopted anti-Semitic laws, and, hoping to recreate a Roman empire, invaded Ethiopia in 1935.

Borrowing the straight-armed Roman salute from Mussolini, **Adolf Hitler** in Germany proved yet more menacing. Hitler's National Socialist (Nazi) party had gained broad support as a result of the economic depression, fear of communism, and German resentment of the harsh Versailles treaty. In 1933 Hitler became Germany's chancellor. Crushing opponents and rivals, Hitler imposed a brutal dictatorship on Germany and began the pursuit of world domination he had proclaimed in his book *Mein Kampf (My Struggle)* (1923). He also instituted a program to purify the fatherland of Jews—whom he considered an "inferior race" responsible for Germany's defeat in World War I.

Violating the Versailles treaty, Hitler began rearming Germany in 1935. A year later, German troops reoccupied the Rhineland, a region between the Rhine River and France specifically demilitarized by the Versailles treaty. In 1938, as German tanks rolled into Vienna, Hitler proclaimed an *anschluss* (union) between Austria and Germany. London, Paris, and Washington murmured disapproval but took no action. An emboldened Hitler then claimed Germany's right to the Sudetenland, a part of neighboring Czechoslovakia containing 3 million ethnic Germans. British prime minister Neville Chamberlain and his French counterpart, insisting that their countries could not endure another war like that of 1914–1918, yielded to Hitler's demands in return for his assurance that Germany had no further territorial ambitions—a policy dubbed **appeasement**—at a conference in Munich in September 1938.

In Japan, meanwhile, militarists gained control of the government and launched a fateful course of expansion, sending troops into the northern Chinese province of Manchuria in 1931. Japan then initiated a full-scale war against China in 1937 and soon controlled key parts of that nation. Weak protests by Washington did little to deter Japan's plans for further aggression.

The American Mood: No More War

The feeble American response reflected the people's belief that the decision to go to war in 1917 had been a mistake. This conviction was rooted in the nation's isolationist tradition—its wish to avoid military and political entanglements in Old World quarrels—as well as in its desire to have the government focus on the problems of the depression, not foreign affairs. Popular books stressing American disillusionment with World War I's failure to make the world safe for democracy strengthened isolationist sentiment. So did a 1934–1936 Senate investigation headed by Republican Gerald P. Nye of North Dakota, which concluded that war profiteers, whom it called "merchants of death," had tricked the United States into World War I for financial gain. A January 1937 poll showed that 70 percent of the people believed that the United States should have stayed out of the war.

By the mid-1930s, an overwhelming majority of Americans thought that the "mistake" of intervention should not be repeated. In 1935–1937, a series of **Neutrality Acts** echoed the longing for peace. To prevent a repetition of 1917, these measures outlawed arms sales and loans to nations at war and forbade Americans to travel on the ships of belligerent powers. The high point of anti-war sentiment came in 1938 when Indiana congressman Louis Ludlow proposed a constitutional amendment requiring a national referendum on any U.S. declaration of war except in cases of direct attack. Only a direct appeal from FDR steeled Congress to reject the measure by the narrowest of margins.

With the public firmly isolationist and some American companies, like IBM, with large financial investments in German industry, confrontation with fascism came solely in sports. At the 1936 Olympics in Berlin, African-American track star Jesse Owens made a mockery of Nazi theories of racial superiority by winning four gold medals and breaking or tying three world records. In 1938, in a boxing match laden with symbolism, the black American Joe Louis knocked out German fighter Max Schmeling in the first round of their world heavyweight championship fight. Although Americans cheered Lewis, they still opposed any policies that might involve them in war.

The Gathering Storm: 1938–1939

On March 15, 1939, Nazi troops overran the rest of Czechoslovakia, violating the Munich accords. Five months after that, Hitler reached an agreement with Soviet Premier **Joseph Stalin** in the German-Soviet Nonaggression Pact that their nations would not fight one another and that they would divide Poland after Germany invaded it. No longer worried about waging war on two fronts, Hitler's troops attacked Poland. As expected, Britain and France declared war on Germany. World War II had begun.

Although isolationist sentiment remained strong in the United States, opinion began to shift. After the fall of Czechoslovakia, Roosevelt called for actions "short of war" to check fascism, and asked Hitler and Mussolini to pledge no further aggression. A jeering Hitler ridiculed FDR's message, while in Rome Mussolini mocked Roosevelt's physical disability, joking that the president's paralysis must have reached his brain. Roosevelt, however, did more than send messages. In

October 1938, he asked Congress for a $300 million military appropriation; in November, he instructed the Army Air Corps to plan for an annual production of 20,000 planes; in January 1939, he submitted a $1.3 billion defense budget. Hitler and Mussolini, he said, were "two madmen" who "respect force and force alone."

America and the Jewish Refugees   Hitler and the Nazis had translated their hatred of Jews into official policy. The Nuremberg Laws of 1935 stripped Jews of the rights of German citizenship and increased restrictions on Jews in all spheres of German educational, social, and economic life. This campaign of hatred reached a violent crescendo on November 9–10, 1938, when the Nazis unleashed *Kristallnacht* (Night of the Broken Glass), a frenzy of arson, destruction, and looting against Jews throughout Germany.

No longer could anyone mistake Hitler's malignant intent. Jews, who had been leaving Germany since 1933, streamed out by the hundreds of thousands, seeking haven. Between 1933 and 1938, sixty thousand fled to the United States. Most Americans condemned the Jews' persecution, but only a minority favored admitting more refugees. Congress rejected all efforts to liberalize the immigration law, with its discriminatory quotas, and FDR did little to translate his sympathy for the Jews into effective policies.

The consequences of such attitudes became clear in June 1939, when the *St. Louis*, a German liner jammed with 950 Jewish refugees, asked permission to put its passengers ashore at Fort Lauderdale, Florida. Immigration officials refused this request and, according to the *New York Times*, a Coast Guard cutter stood by "to prevent possible attempts by refugees to jump off and swim ashore." The *St. Louis* turned slowly away from the lights of America and sailed back to Europe, where most of its passengers would die from Nazi brutality.

INTO THE STORM, 1939–1941

Following the lightning German victories in western Europe in spring 1940, President Roosevelt's policy of neutrality to keep America out of war gave way to a policy of economic intervention. He knew that extending increasing amounts of aid to those resisting aggression by the so-called Rome-Berlin-Tokyo Axis, as well as his toughening conduct toward Germany and Japan, could, as he said, "push" the United States into the crisis of worldwide war. Japan's attack on the U.S. fleet at Pearl Harbor would provide the push.

The European War   The war in Europe began on September 1, 1939, as Nazi armies poured into Poland and the *Luftwaffe* (German air force) devastated Polish cities. Two days later, Britain and France, honoring commitments to Poland, declared war on Germany. Although FDR invoked the Neutrality Acts, he would not ask Americans to be impartial in thought and deed.

(Thomas McAvoy/TimeLife Pictures/Getty Images)

Isolationism Versus Interventionism *In front of the White House in 1941, an American soldier grabs a sign from an isolationist picketing against the United States entering the war in Europe. A diverse group, isolationists ran the gamut from pacifists who opposed all wars, to progressives who feared the growth of business and centralized power that a war would bring, to ultra-rightists who sympathized with fascism and/or shared Hitler's anti-Semitism.*

Tailoring his actions to the public mood, which favored both preventing a Nazi victory and staying out of war, FDR persuaded Congress in November to amend the Neutrality Acts to allow the belligerents to purchase weapons from the United States if they paid cash and carried the arms away in their own ships. But "cash-and-carry" did not stop the Nazis. In spring 1940, Hitler unleashed a *blitzkrieg* (lightning war) against Denmark, Norway, the Netherlands, Belgium, and Luxembourg. The Nazi *wehrmacht* (war machine) swept all the way to the English Channel in a scant two months. In early June, the British evacuated most of their army at Dunkirk, and on June 22, France surrendered.

Hitler then took aim against Great Britain, terror-bombing British cities in hopes of forcing a surrender or, failing that, preparing the ground for a cross-channel invasion. With thousands of civilians killed or wounded and much of London in smoking ruins, British Prime Minister **Winston Churchill** pleaded for American aid. Most Americans, shocked at the use of German air power against British civilians, favored such aid. But a large and vocal minority opposed it as wasteful of materials needed for U.S. defenses or as a ruse to lure Americans into a war not vital to their interests.

From Isolation to Intervention   In the United States in 1940, news of the "Battle of Britain" competed with speculation about whether FDR would break with tradition and run for an unprecedented third term. Not until the eve of the Democrats' July convention did he reveal that, given the world crisis, he would consent to a "draft" from his party. The Axis threat clinched his renomination and similarly led the Republicans to nominate Wendell Willkie of Indiana, an all-out internationalist who championed greater aid to Britain.

Adroitly playing the role of a national leader too busy with defense and diplomacy to engage in partisan politics, FDR forged a coalition cabinet. For secretary of war, he selected Henry Stimson, a conservative who had held major posts under previous Republican presidents, and he chose Frank Knox, who had been Landon's running mate on the GOP ticket in 1936, as secretary of the navy. Both men had abhorred the New Deal, but that mattered less to Roosevelt than their willingness to oppose isolationism and to support aiding the Allies against Hitler. The president also signed the Selective Service and Training Act, the first peacetime draft in U.S. history, and approved a dramatic increase in defense funding. In September, with Willkie's support, Roosevelt engineered a "destroyers-for-bases" swap with England, sending fifty vintage American ships to Britain in exchange for leases on British air and naval bases in the Western Hemisphere.

These moves infuriated isolationists, particularly the America First Committee. Largely financed by Henry Ford, and featuring Charles Lindbergh as its most popular speaker, the AFC insisted "Fortress America" could stand alone. But a majority of Americans reassured by the president's promise never to "send an American boy to fight in a foreign war," chose Roosevelt for a third term.

Roosevelt now called on the United States to become "the arsenal of democracy." He proposed a **"lend-lease"** program to allow the U.S. to lend or lease war materiel to any nation vital to America's security. While Roosevelt likened the plan to loaning a garden hose to a neighbor whose house was on fire, isolationist Senator Robert Taft compared it to chewing gum: after a neighbor uses it, "you don't want it back." Congress, however, approved lend-lease in March 1941, and supplies began to flow across the Atlantic. When Hitler's armies invaded the Soviet Union in June 1941, FDR dispatched supplies to the Soviets, despite American hostility toward communism. To defeat Hitler, FDR said, "I would hold hands with the Devil."

To counter the menace of German submarines that threatened to choke the transatlantic supply line, Roosevelt in mid-1941 authorized the U.S. Navy to convoy British ships, with orders to destroy enemy ships if necessary. In August he met with Churchill aboard a warship off Newfoundland. They issued a statement, known as the **Atlantic Charter,** that condemned aggression, affirmed national self-determination, and endorsed the principles of collective security, free trade, and disarmament. After a German submarine fired at an American destroyer in September, Roosevelt authorized naval patrols to shoot on sight all Axis vessels operating in the western Atlantic. Now on a collision course with Germany, Roosevelt persuaded Congress in November to permit the arming of merchant ships and to allow the transport of lend-lease supplies to belligerent ports in war zones. Unprepared for a major war, America was nevertheless fighting a limited one, and full-scale hostilities seemed imminent.

Pearl Harbor and the Coming of War

Hitler's triumphs in western Europe encouraged Japan to expand farther into Asia. Seeing Germany as America's primary threat, Roosevelt tried to apply enough pressure to deter Japanese aggression without provoking Tokyo to war before the United States had built the "two-ocean navy" authorized by Congress in 1940. "I simply have not got enough navy to go around," he told Harold Ickes in mid-1941, "and every episode in the Pacific means fewer ships in the Atlantic."

The Japanese, too, hoped to avoid war but would not compromise their desire to create the Greater East Asia Co-Prosperity Sphere (an empire embracing much of China, Southeast Asia, and the western Pacific). Japan saw the United States as blocking its legitimate rise to power, while Americans viewed Japan's talk of national aspirations as a smokescreen to cloak aggression. Decades of "yellow-peril" propaganda had hardened U.S. attitudes toward Japan, and even those who were isolationist toward Europe tended to be interventionist toward Asia.

The two nations became locked in a deadly dance. In 1940, believing that economic coercion would force the Japanese out of China, the United States ended a long-standing trade treaty with Japan and banned the sale of aviation fuel and scrap metal to the Japanese. Tokyo responded by occupying northern Indochina, a French colony, and signing the Tripartite Pact with Germany and Italy in September, creating a military alliance, the Berlin-Rome-Tokyo Axis, that required each government to help the others in the event of a U.S. attack.

When the Japanese then overran the rest of Indochina in July 1941, Roosevelt froze all Japanese assets in the United States and clamped a total embargo on trade with Japan. Tokyo had two choices: submit to the United States to gain a resumption of trade for vital resources or conquer new lands to obtain them. In October, expansionist war minister General Hideki Tojo became Japan's prime minister. Tojo set the first week in December as the deadline for a preemptive strike if the United States did not yield. By late November, U.S. intelligence—deciphering Japan's top diplomatic code—alerted the Roosevelt administration that war was imminent. Eleventh-hour negotiations under way in Washington made no headway, and warnings went out to all commanders in the Pacific advising that a Japanese attack was imminent. U.S. officials believed the Japanese would strike British or Dutch possessions or even the Philippines—but the Japanese gambled on a knockout punch, hoping to destroy the U.S. Pacific Fleet at Pearl Harbor and compel Roosevelt, preoccupied with Germany, to seek accommodation with Japan.

Waves of Japanese dive-bombers and torpedo planes thundered across Hawaii's island of Oahu Sunday morning, December 7, 1941, bombing ships at anchor in Pearl Harbor and strafing planes parked wingtip to wingtip at nearby air bases. In less than three hours, eight battleships, three light cruisers, and two destroyers had been sunk or crippled, and 360 aircraft destroyed or damaged. The attack killed more than twenty-four hundred Americans and opened the way for Japan's advance toward Australia. Americans had underestimated the resourcefulness, skill, and daring of the Japanese. At the same time, Japanese leaders erred in counting on a paralyzing blow at Pearl Harbor. That miscalculation assured an aroused and united nation determined to avenge the attack.

Roosevelt called December 7 a "date which will live in infamy." On December 8, Congress declared war on Japan. (The sole dissenter was Montana's Jeannette Rankin, who had also cast a nay vote against U.S. entry into WWI). Three days later, Hitler declared war on the "half Judaized and the other half Negrified" Americans, and Mussolini followed suit. Congress immediately reciprocated without a dissenting vote. America faced a global war that it was not ready to fight.

After Pearl Harbor, U-boats wreaked havoc in the North Atlantic and prowled the Caribbean and the East Coast of the United States. Every twenty-four hours, five more Allied vessels went to the bottom. By the end of 1942, U-boat "wolf packs" had destroyed more than a thousand Allied ships, offsetting the pace of American ship production. The United States was losing the battle of the Atlantic.

Additionally, the war news from Europe and Africa was, as Roosevelt admitted, "all bad." Hitler's rule covered an enormous swath of territory, from the outskirts of Moscow and Leningrad—a thousand miles deep into Russia—to the Pyrenees on the French-Spanish border, and from northern Norway to the Libyan desert. In North Africa the German Afrika Korps swept toward the Suez Canal, the British oil lifeline. It seemed as if the Mediterranean would become an Axis sea and that Hitler would soon be in India to greet Tojo marching across Asia before the United States was ready to fight.

The Japanese inflicted defeat after defeat on Allied Pacific forces. Tojo followed Pearl Harbor with a rampage across the Pacific that put Guam, Wake Island, Hong Kong, Singapore, Burma, and the Netherlands East Indies under Japan's control by the end of April 1942. American forces in the Philippines, besieged for months on the island of Bataan, surrendered in May. Japan's rising sun flag blazed over hundreds of islands in the central and western Pacific, and over the entire eastern perimeter of the Asian mainland from the border of Siberia to the border of India.

AMERICA MOBILIZES FOR WAR

In December 1941, American armed forces numbered just 1.6 million, and war production accounted for only 15 percent of U.S. industrial output. Pearl Harbor changed everything. Congress passed a War Powers Act, granting the president unprecedented authority over all aspects of the war. Volunteers and draftees swelled the armed forces; by war's end, more than 15 million men and nearly 350,000 women would serve. More would work in defense industries. Mobilization required unprecedented coordination of the American government, economy, and military. In 1942, those responsible for managing America's growing war machine moved into the world's largest building, the newly constructed Pentagon. Like the Pentagon, which was intended to house civilian agencies after the war, American attitudes, behavior, and institutions would also be significantly altered by far-reaching wartime domestic changes.

**Organizing for
Victory**
To direct the military engine, Roosevelt formed the Joint Chiefs of Staff, made up of representatives of the army, navy, and army air force. (Only a minor "corps" within the army as late as June 1941, the air force would grow more dramatically than any other branch of the service, achieve virtual autonomy, and play a vital role in combat strategy.) The changing nature of modern warfare also led to the creation of the Office of Strategic Services (OSS), forerunner of the Central Intelligence Agency, to conduct the espionage required for strategic planning.

Roosevelt established the **War Production Board (WPB)** to allocate materials, limit the production of civilian goods, and distribute contracts. The newly created War Manpower Commission (WMC) supervised the mobilization of men and women for the military, war industry, and agriculture; the National War Labor Board (NWLB) mediated disputes between management and labor; and the **Office of Price Administration (OPA)** imposed strict price controls to check inflation.

Although a Nazi commander had jeered, "The Americans can't build planes, only electric iceboxes and razor blades," the United States achieved a miracle of war production in 1942. Car makers retooled to produce planes and tanks; a pinball-machine maker converted to armor-piercing shells. By late 1942, 33 percent of the economy was committed to war production. Whole new industries appeared virtually overnight. With almost all of the nation's crude-rubber supply now in Japanese-controlled territory, the government built some fifty new synthetic-rubber plants. By the end of the war, the United States, once the world's largest importer of crude rubber, had become the world's largest exporter of synthetic rubber.

America also became the world's greatest weapons manufacturer, producing more war materiel by 1944 than its Axis enemies combined: 300,000 military aircraft, eighty-six thousand tanks, 2.6 million machine guns, and 6 million tons of bombs "To American production," Stalin would toast FDR and Churchill, "without which the war would have been lost." The United States also built more than five thousand cargo ships and eighty-six thousand warships. Henry J. Kaiser, who had supervised the construction of the Boulder Dam, introduced prefabrication to cut the time needed to build ships. In 1941, the construction of a Liberty-class merchant ship took six months; in 1943, less than two weeks. By 1945, Kaiser, dubbed "Sir Launchalot," was completing a cargo ship every day.

Such breakneck production had costs. The size and powers of the government expanded as defense spending zoomed from 9 percent of gross national product (GNP) in 1940 to 46 percent in 1945; the federal budget soared from $9 billion to $98 billion. Federal civilian employees mushroomed from 1.1 million to 3.8 million. The executive branch, directing the war effort, grew the most; and an alliance formed between the defense industry and the military. (A generation later, Americans would call these concentrations of power the "imperial presidency" and the "military-industrial complex.")

"Dr. New Deal," in FDR's words, gave way to "Dr. Win the War." To encourage business to convert to war production and expand its capacity, the government guaranteed profits, provided generous tax write-offs and subsidies, and suspended antitrust prosecutions. "If you are going to try to go to war in a capitalist country," said Secretary of War Stimson, "you have to let business make money out of the process or business won't work." America's ten biggest corporations got a third of the war contracts, and two-thirds of all war-production spending went to the hundred largest firms, greatly accelerating trends toward economic concentration.

The War Economy   The United States spent more than $360 billion ($250 million a day) to defeat the Axis, ten times the cost of World War I. Wartime spending and the draft not only vanquished unemployment, but also stimulated an industrial boom that made most Americans prosper. It doubled U.S. industrial output and the per capita GNP, created 17 million new jobs, increased corporate after-tax profits by 70 percent, and raised the real wages or purchasing power of industrial workers by 50 percent (see Figure 25.1).

The federal government poured $40 billion into the West, making it an economic powerhouse, the center of massive aircraft and shipbuilding industries. California alone secured more than 10 percent of all federal funds; by 1945, nearly half the personal income in the state came from the federal government.

A dynamic Sun Belt, stretching from the coastal Southeast to the coastal Southwest, was the recipient of billions spent on military bases and the needs of the armed forces. The South's industrial capacity increased by 40 percent and per capita income tripled. Boom times enabled hundreds of thousands of sharecroppers and farm tenants to leave the land for better-paying industrial jobs. While the South's farm population decreased by 20 percent in the 1940s, its urban population grew 36 percent.

Full employment, a longer workweek, larger paychecks, and the increased hiring of minorities, women, and the elderly brought a middle-class standard of living to millions of families. In California the demand for workers in the shipyards and aircraft factories opened opportunities for thousands of Chinese-Americans previously confined to menial jobs within their own communities. In San Diego, 40 percent of retirees returned to work. Deafening factories hired the hearing-impaired, and aircraft plants employed dwarfs as inspectors because of their ability to crawl inside small spaces.

The war years produced the only significant shift toward greater equality in the distribution of income in the twentieth century. The earnings of the bottom fifth of all workers rose 68 percent, and those of the middle class doubled. The richest 5 percent, conversely, saw their share of total disposable income drop from 23 to 17 percent.

Large-scale commercial farmers prospered, benefiting from higher consumer prices and increased productivity thanks to improved fertilizers and more mechanization. As sharecroppers, tenants, and small farmers left the land for better-paying industrial jobs, the overall agricultural population fell by 17 percent. Farming became "agribusiness," and organized agriculture wielded power alongside organized labor, big government, and big business.

Organized labor grew mightier as union membership rose from 9 million to 14.8 million workers, in part because of the expansion of the labor force. Although the National War Labor Board attempted to limit wage increases to restrain inflation, unions negotiated unprecedented fringe benefits for workers, including paid vacation time and health and pension plans. As most workers honored the "no-strike" pledge that they had given immediately after Pearl Harbor, less than one-tenth of 1 percent of wartime working hours was lost to wildcat strikes. Those strikes,

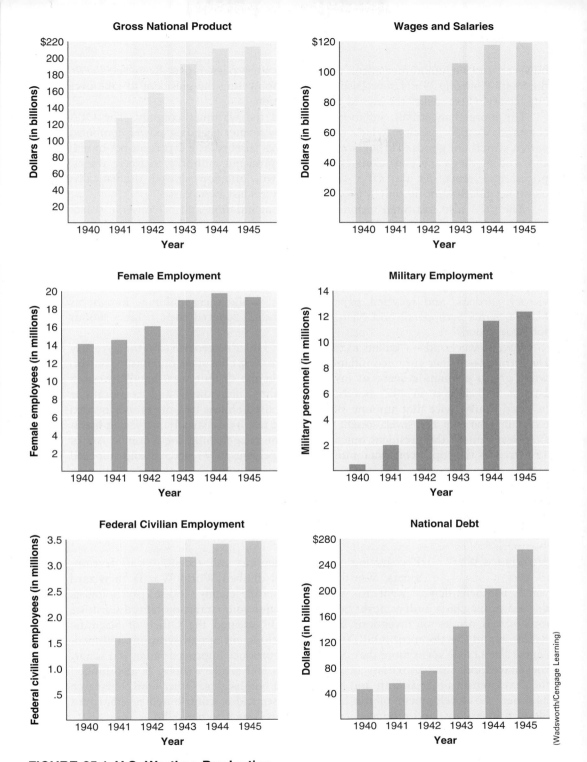

FIGURE 25.1 U.S. Wartime Production

Between 1941 and 1945, the economy grew at a remarkable pace.

(Wadsworth/Cengage Learning)

however, cost the union movement: in 1943, Congress passed, over Roosevelt's veto, the Smith-Connally War Labor Disputes act, empowering the president to take over any facility where strikes threatened war production.

Far more than strikes, inflation threatened the wartime economy. The OPA constantly battled inflation, which was fueled by greater spending power combined with a scarcity of goods. Throughout 1942, prices climbed at a 2-percent-per-month clip, and at the year's end, Congress gave the president authority to freeze wages, prices, and rents. As the OPA clamped down, inflation slowed dramatically: consumer prices went up only 8 percent in the war's last two years.

The OPA also instituted rationing to combat inflation and to conserve scarce materials. Under the slogan "Use it up, wear it out, make it do, or do without," the OPA rationed gasoline, coffee, sugar, butter, cheese, and meat. Americans endured "meatless Tuesdays" and cuffless trousers, ate sherbet instead of ice cream, and put up with imitation chocolate that tasted like soap and imitation soap that did not lather. Most Americans cheerfully formed carpools, planted victory gardens, and recycled paper and fats, while their children, known as "Uncle Sam's Scrappers" and "Tin-Can Colonels," scoured their neighborhoods for scrap metal.

Buying war bonds—"bullets in the bellies of Hitler's hordes!" said the Treasury Department—further curtailed inflation by decreasing consumer purchasing power, while giving civilians a sense of involvement in the distant war. Small investors bought $40 billion in "E" bonds, and wealthy individuals and corporations invested nearly twice that amount. Bond sales raised almost half the money needed to finance the war. Roosevelt sought to raise the rest by drastically increasing taxes. Congress refused the president much of what he sought. Still, the Revenue Act of 1942 raised the top income-tax rate from 60 percent to 94 percent and imposed income taxes on middle- and lower-income Americans for the first time. Beginning in 1943, the payroll-deduction system automatically withheld income taxes from wages and salaries. In 1945, the federal government collected nearly twenty times the tax revenue it had in 1940.

"A Wizard War"   Recognizing wartime scientific and technological developments, Winston Churchill dubbed World War II "a wizard war." Mathematicians went to work deciphering enemy codes, psychologists devised propaganda and, as never before, the major combatants mobilized scientists into virtual armies of invention. In 1941, FDR created the Office of Scientific Research and Development (OSRD) for the development of new weapons and medicines. The OSRD spent more than $1 billion to produce improved radar and sonar, rocket weapons, and proximity fuses for mines and artillery shells. It also funded the development of jet aircraft and high-altitude bombsights. Other OSRD research hastened the development of the laser and insecticides, contributed to improved blood transfusions, and produced "miracle drugs," such as penicillin.

The demand for greater accuracy in artillery required the kind of rapid, detailed calculations that only computing machines could supply. By 1944, navy personnel in the basement of Harvard's physics laboratory were operating IBM's Mark I, a cumbersome device fifty-one feet long and eight feet high that weighed five tons, and contained 760,000 parts. A second-generation computer, ENIAC (electronic numerical integrator and computer), soon reduced the time to multiply two tenth-place numbers from Mark I's three seconds to less than three-thousandths of a second.

Nothing saved the lives of more wounded servicemen than improvements in battlefield medical care. Military needs led to advances in heart and lung surgery, and to the use of synthetic antimalarial drugs to substitute for scarce quinine. So-called miracle drugs, antibiotics to combat infections, a rarity on the eve of war, would be copiously produced. The use of DDT cleared many islands of malaria-carrying mosquitoes. Along with innovations like the Mobile Auxiliary Surgical Hospital (MASH), science helped save tens of thousands of soldiers' lives and improved the health of the nation as well. Life expectancy rose by three years during the war.

The atomic bomb project began in August 1939 when Albert Einstein, a Jewish refugee and Nobel Prize–winning physicist, warned Roosevelt that Nazi scientists were seeking to use atomic physics to construct an extraordinarily destructive weapon. In 1941, FDR launched a massive Anglo-American secret program—the Soviets were excluded—to construct an atomic bomb. The next year, the participating physicists, both Americans and Europeans, achieved a controlled chain reaction under the University of Chicago football stadium and acquired the basic knowledge necessary to develop the bomb. By July 1945 this program, code-named the **Manhattan Project,** had employed more than 120,000 people and spent nearly $2 billion.

Just before dawn on July 16, 1945, a blinding fireball with "the brightness of several suns at midday" rose over the desert at Alamogordo, New Mexico, followed by a billowing mushroom cloud. Equivalent to twenty thousand tons of TNT, the blast from this first atomic explosion was felt a hundred miles away. "A few people laughed, a few people cried," recalled J. Robert Oppenheimer, the Manhattan Project's scientific director. "Most people were silent. I remembered the line from the Hindu scripture, the Bhagavad-Gita: 'Now I am become Death, the destroyer of worlds.'" The atomic age had dawned.

Propaganda and Politics   People as well as science and machinery had to be mobilized. To sustain a spirit of unity, the Roosevelt administration carefully managed public opinion. The Office of Censorship, established in December 1941, examined all letters going overseas and worked with publishers and broadcasters to suppress information that might damage the war effort, such as details of troop movements. Fearful of demoralizing the public, the government banned, until late 1943, the publication of any pictures of American war dead; then, worried about an overconfident public, it prodded the media to show American servicemen killed by the enemy.

To shape public opinion, FDR created the Office of War Information (OWI) in June 1942. The OWI employed more than four thousand writers, artists, and advertising specialists to explain the war and to counter enemy propaganda. The OWI depicted the war as a moral struggle between good and evil—the enemy had to be destroyed, not merely defeated. Hollywood films highlighted the heroism and unity of the American forces, while inciting hatred of the enemy. Films about the war portrayed the Japanese, in particular, as treacherous and cruel, as beasts in the jungle, as "slant-eyed rats." Jukeboxes blared songs like "We're Gonna Have to Slap the Dirty Little Jap." U.S. propaganda also presented the war as a struggle to preserve the "American way of life," usually depicted in images of small-town, middle-class, white Americans enjoying a bountiful consumer society.

While the Roosevelt administration concentrated on the war, Republican critics seized the initiative in domestic politics. Full employment and high wages undermined the Democrats' class appeal, and many of the urban and working-class voters essential to the Roosevelt coalition were serving in the armed forces and did not vote in the 1942 elections. Republicans gained nine seats in the Senate and forty-six in the House. A coalition of conservative Republicans and southern Democrats held power and, resentful of the wartime expansion of executive authority and determined to curb labor unions and welfare spending, it abolished the CCC and the WPA, and rebuffed attempts to extend the New Deal.

Despite the strength of the conservative coalition, the war expanded governmental and executive power enormously. As never before, Washington managed the economy, molded public opinion, funded scientific research, and influenced people's daily lives.

THE BATTLEFRONT, 1942–1944

America's industrial might and Soviet manpower turned the tide of war, and diplomacy followed in its wake. Allied unity diminished as the Axis weakened; increasingly, the United States, Britain, and the Soviet Union each sought wartime strategies and postwar arrangements best suited to its own interests.

LIBERATING EUROPE

After Pearl Harbor, British and American officials agreed to concentrate on defeating Germany first and then Japan. But they differed on where to mount an attack. Stalin demanded a second front, an invasion of western Europe to force Hitler to transfer troops west and thus relieve pressure on the Russians, who faced the full fury of the Nazi armies. Churchill insisted on clearing the Mediterranean before invading France, and he wanted American aid in North Africa to protect the Suez Canal. Roosevelt gave in to Churchill and American troops under General Dwight D. Eisenhower landed in Morocco and Algeria. Pushing eastward, they trapped the German and Italian armies being driven westward by the British, and in May 1943 some 260,000 German-Italian troops surrendered, despite Hitler's orders to fight to the death. All of Africa now lay in Allied hands (see Map 25.1).

Left alone to face two-thirds of the Nazi force, the Soviet Union hung on and, in the turning point of the European war, halted the German advance in the

MAP 25.1 World War II In Europe and Africa

The momentous German defeats at Stalingrad and in Tunisia in early 1943 marked the turning point in the war against the Axis. By 1945, Allied conquest of Hitler's "thousand-year" Reich was imminent.

protracted Battle of Stalingrad (August 1942–January 1943). As the Russian snow turned red with blood (costing each side more battle deaths in half a year than the United States suffered in the entire war), and its hills became "white fields," strewn with human bones, Soviet forces saved Stalingrad, defended Moscow, and relieved besieged Leningrad. The Red Army then went on the offensive along a thousand-mile front (see Map 25.1).

Although Stalin renewed his plea for a second front, Churchill again objected, and Roosevelt again agreed to a British plan: the invasion of Sicily. In summer

1943, Anglo-American forces overran Sicily in less than a month, leading the Italian military to depose, and then execute, Mussolini, and to surrender to the Allies on September 8. As Allied forces moved up the Italian peninsula, German troops poured into Italy. Facing elite Nazi divisions in strong defensive positions, the Allies spent eight months inching their way 150 miles to Rome and were still battling through northern Italy when the war in Europe ended in May 1945.

In 1943 and 1944, the United States and Britain turned the tide in the Atlantic and sent thousands of bombers over Germany. British and American air forces began round-the-clock bombardment, raining thousands of tons of bombs on German cities. In raids on Hamburg in July 1943, Allied planes dropping incendiary bombs created terrible firestorms, killing at least thirty-five thousand people and leveling the city, much as they had done earlier at Cologne and would do in February 1945 to Dresden, where an estimated sixty thousand people died.

Meanwhile, in July 1943, the Red Army, eating U.S. rations, marching in American-made boots, and driving Dodge and Ford trucks, engaged the Germans at Kursk. With a million men actively engaged on each side in the largest pitched battle of the war, Soviet soldiers won decisively and forced a German retreat. Advancing swiftly, they drove the Germans out of Soviet territory by mid-1944 and plunged into Poland, where the Soviets set up a puppet government. Late summer and early fall saw Soviet troops seize Romania and Bulgaria and aid communist guerillas under Josip Broz Tito in liberating Yugoslavia.

As the Soviets swept across eastern Europe, Allied forces opened the long-promised second front. On June 6, 1944—D-Day—nearly 200,000 Allied troops in the largest armada ever assembled landed in Normandy in northwestern France. Within six weeks, another million Allied troops had crossed the channel and waded ashore. Under General Eisenhower, the Allies liberated Paris in August and reached the German border by the end of summer.

In mid-December, as the Allies prepared for a full-scale assault on the German heartland, Hitler desperately threw his last reserves against American positions. The **Battle of the Bulge**—named for the "bulge" eighty miles long and fifty miles wide that Hitler's troops drove into the Allies' line—raged for nearly a month, and when it ended American troops stood on the banks of the Rhine. It had cost the United States 55,000 soldiers dead or wounded and 18,000 taken prisoner. But the way to Germany lay open, and the end of the European war was in sight.

War in the Pacific

The day after the Philippines fell to Japan in mid-May 1942, U.S. and Japanese fleets confronted each other in the Coral Sea off northeastern Australia, the first naval battle in history fought entirely from aircraft carriers. Both sides took heavy losses, but the Battle of the Coral Sea stopped the Japanese advance on Australia. Less than a month later, a Japanese armada turned toward Midway Island, the crucial American outpost between Hawaii and Japan. Because the U.S. Signal Corps had broken the Japanese naval code, Japan's plans and the locations of her ships were known. American carriers and their planes consequently won a decisive victory, sinking four Japanese carriers and destroying several hundred enemy planes.

Suddenly on the defensive, the stunned Japanese could now only try to hold what they had already won.

On the offensive, U.S. marines waded ashore at Guadalcanal in the Solomon Islands in August 1942. Facing fierce resistance as well as tropical diseases like malaria, the Americans needed six months to take the island, a bitter preview of the battles to come. As the British moved from India to retake Burma, the United States began a two-pronged advance toward Japan in 1943. The army, under General Douglas MacArthur, advanced north on the islands between Australia and the Philippines, and the navy and marines, under Admiral Chester Nimitz, "island-hopped" across the central Pacific to seize strategic bases and put Tokyo in range of American bombers. In fall 1944 the navy annihilated what remained of the Japanese fleet at the battles of the Philippine Sea and Leyte Gulf, giving the United States control of Japan's air and shipping lanes and leaving the Japanese home islands open to invasion (see Map 25.2).

| The Grand Alliance | President Roosevelt had two main goals for the war: the total defeat of the Axis at the least possible cost in American lives, and the establishment of a world order strong enough to |

ensure peace, open trade, and national self-determination in the postwar era. Aware that only a common enemy fused the Grand Alliance together, Roosevelt tried to promote harmony by concentrating on military victory and postponing divisive postwar matters.

Churchill and Stalin had other goals. Britain wanted neither the United States nor the Soviet Union to reshape and dominate the postwar world; it especially sought to retain its imperial possessions. As Churchill said, he had "not become the King's First Minister to preside over the liquidation of the British Empire." The Soviet Union wanted a permanently weakened Germany and a sphere of influence (a region whose governments can be counted on to do a great power's bidding) in eastern Europe. To hold together this fragile alliance, FDR relied on personal diplomacy to mediate conflicts.

The first president to travel by plane while in office, Roosevelt in January 1943 arrived in Casablanca, Morocco's main port, where he and Churchill resolved to attack Italy before invading France and proclaimed that the war would continue until the "unconditional surrender" of the Axis. By so doing, they sought to reduce Soviet mistrust of the West, which had deepened with the postponement of the second front. Ten months later, in Cairo, Roosevelt met with Churchill and Jiang Jieshi (Chiang Kai-shek), the anticommunist head of the Chinese government. To keep China in the war, FDR promised the return of Manchuria and Taiwan to China and a "free and independent Korea." From Cairo, FDR and Churchill continued on to Tehran, Iran's capital, to meet with Stalin. Here they set the invasion of France for June 1944, and agreed to divide Germany into zones of occupation and to impose reparations on the Reich. Most importantly to Roosevelt, Stalin pledged to enter the war against Japan after Hitler's defeat.

Roosevelt then turned his attention to domestic politics. Increasing conservative sentiment in the nation led him to drop the liberal Henry A. Wallace from the ticket

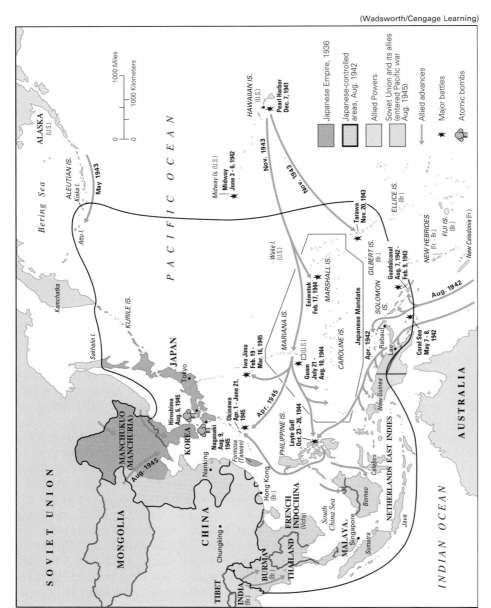

(Wadsworth/Cengage Learning)

MAP 25.2 World War II in the Pacific

American ships and planes stemmed the Japanese offensive at the Battles of the Coral Sea and Midway Island. Thereafter, the Japanese were on the defensive against American amphibious assaults and air strikes.

and accept Harry S. Truman as his vice-presidential candidate. A moderate senator from Missouri, now dubbed "the new Missouri Compromise," Truman restored a semblance of unity to the Democrats for the 1944 campaign. To compete, the Republicans nominated moderate and noncontroversial New York governor Thomas E. Dewey. The campaign focused more on personalities than on issues, and the still-popular FDR defeated his dull GOP opponent, but with the narrowest margin since 1916—winning 53 percent of the popular vote. A weary Roosevelt, secretly suffering from hypertension and heart disease, now directed his waning energies toward defeating the Axis and constructing an international peacekeeping system.

WAR AND AMERICAN SOCIETY

The crisis of war altered the most basic patterns of American life. Few families went untouched: more than 15 million Americans served in the armed forces, an equal number moved to find jobs, and millions of women went to work outside the home. As well, the war opened some doors of opportunity for African-Americans and other minorities, although many remained closed. It heightened minority aspirations and widened cracks in the wall of white racist attitudes and policy, while maintaining much of America's racial caste system, thereby tilling the ground for future crises.

The GIs' War   Most servicemen griped about regimentation and were more interested in dry socks than in ideology. They knew little of the big strategies, and cared less. They fought because they were told to and wanted to stay alive. Reluctant recruits rather than professional warriors, most had few aims beyond returning to a safe, familiar United States.

But the GIs' war dragged on for almost four years, transforming them in the process. Millions who had never been far from home traveled to unfamiliar cities and remote lands, shedding their parochialism. Sharing tents and foxholes with men of different religions, ethnicities, and classes, they experienced a "melting pot" effect that freed them from some prewar prejudices.

Besides serving with people they had never previously encountered, over a million GIs married overseas, broadening personal horizons and sowing the seeds of a more tolerant and diverse national culture. At the same time many GIs became evermore distrustful of foreigners and outsiders, and returned home obsessed with the flag as a symbol of patriotism.

Physical misery, chronic exhaustion, and, especially, intense combat took a heavy toll, leaving lasting psychological as well as physical wounds. Both American and Japanese troops saw the other in racist images, as animals to be exterminated, and brutality became as much the rule as the exception in "a war without mercy." Both sides machine-gunned hostile flyers in parachutes; both tortured and killed prisoners in cold blood; both mutilated enemy dead for souvenirs. In the fight against Germany, cruelties and atrocities also occurred, although on a lesser scale. A battalion of the second armored division calling itself "Roosevelt's Butchers" boasted that it shot all the German soldiers it captured. Some who served became cynical about human life; others, haunted by nightmares about the war, would long languish in veterans' hospitals.

The Home Front   Nothing transformed the social topography more than the vast internal migration of an already mobile people. About 15 million men moved because of military service, often accompanied by family members. Many other Americans moved to secure new economic opportunities, especially in the Pacific Coast states. Nearly a quarter of a million found jobs in the shipyards of the Bay area and at least as many in the aircraft industry that arose in the orange groves of southern California. More than one hundred thousand worked in the Puget Sound shipyards of Washington State and half as many in the nearby Boeing airplane plants. Others flocked to the world's largest magnesium plant in Henderson, Nevada, and to the Rocky Mountain Arsenal and Remington Rand arms plant outside Denver.

At least 6 million people left farms to work in urban areas, including several million southern blacks and whites. They doubled Albuquerque's population and increased San Diego's some 90 percent. This mass uprooting of people from familiar settings made Americans both more cosmopolitan and lonelier. Some who moved far from their hometowns left behind their traditional values. Housing shortages left millions living in converted garages and trailer camps, even in cars. Some workers in Seattle lived in chicken coops. The swarms of migrants to Mobile, Alabama, attracted by a new aluminum plant, two massive shipyards, an air base, and an army supply depot, transformed a sleepy fishing village into a symbol of urban disorder.

Overcrowding and wartime separations strained family and community life. High rates of divorce, mental illness, family violence, and juvenile delinquency reflected the disruptions caused in part by the lack of privacy, the sense of impermanence, the absence of familiar settings, and the competition for scarce facilities. Few boom communities had the resources to supply their swollen populations with transportation, recreation, and social services. Urban blight and conflicts between newcomers and old-timers accelerated.

While military culture fostered a sexist mentality, emphasizing the differences between "femininity" and "masculinity," millions of American women donned pants, put their hair in bandannas, and went to work in defense plants. Reversing a decade of efforts to exclude women from the labor force, the federal government urged women into war production in 1942. Songs like "We're the Janes Who Make the Planes" encouraged women to take up war work. Propaganda called upon them to take jobs and "release able-bodied men for fighting." More than 6 million women entered the labor force during the war, increasing the number of employed women to 19 million. Less than a quarter of the labor force in 1940, women constituted well over a third of all workers in 1945.

Before the war, most female wage earners had been young and single. By contrast, 75 percent of the new women workers were married, 60 percent were over thirty-five, and more than 33 percent had children under the age of fourteen. They tended blast furnaces, operated cranes, greased locomotives, drove taxis, welded

hulls, loaded shells, and worked in coke plants and rolling mills. On the Pacific Coast, more than one-third of all workers in aircraft and shipbuilding were women. **"Rosie the Riveter,"** holding a pneumatic gun in arms bulging with muscles, became the symbol of the woman war worker; she was, in the words of a popular song, "making history working for victory" (see Going to the Source).

Yet traditional attitudes and gender discrimination existed throughout the war. Women earned only about 65 percent of what men earned for the same work and labor unions often required women to give up their jobs to men returning from military service. One popular advertisement pictured a woman in overalls about to leave for work. Her daughter asks, "Mother, when will you stay home again?" The woman responds: "Some jubilant day, mother will stay home again doing the job she likes—making a home for you and daddy when he gets back."

The stigma attached to working mothers also shaped government resistance to establishing child-care centers for women employed in defense. "A mother's primary duty is to her home and children," the Labor Department's Children's Bureau stated. "This duty is one she cannot lay aside, no matter what the emergency." Funds for federal child-care centers covered fewer than 10 percent of defense workers' children, and the young suffered. Terms like "eight-hour orphans" and "latchkey children" described unsupervised children forced to take care of themselves. Fueling fears that the employment of women outside the home would cause the family to disintegrate, juvenile delinquency increased fivefold and the divorce rate zoomed from 16 per 100 marriages in 1940 to 27 per 100 in 1944.

The impact of war on women and the family proved multifaceted and even contradictory. As the divorce rate soared, so did marriage rates and birthrates. Although some women remained content to roll bandages for the Red Cross, more than three hundred thousand joined the armed forces and, for the first time in American history, were given regular military status and served in positions other than that of nurse. As members of the Women's Army Corps (WACs) and the Navy's Women Appointed for Volunteer Emergency Service (WAVES) they replaced men in such noncombat jobs as mechanics and radio operators, and served as mapmakers and ferry pilots. About a thousand women became civilian pilots with the WASPs (Women's Airforce Service Pilots).

Overall, women gained a new sense of their potential. The war proved their capabilities and widened their world. Recalled one war wife whose returning husband did not like her independence, "He had left a shrinking violet and come home to a very strong oak tree." Some of these women were among the 350,000 teachers who took better-paying war work or joined the armed services, leaving schools badly understaffed. Students, too, abandoned school in record numbers. High school enrollments sank as the full-time employment of teenagers rose from 900,000 in 1940 to 3 million in 1944.

The loss of students to war production and the armed services forced colleges to admit large numbers of women and to contract themselves out to the armed forces. Nearly a million servicemen took college classes in science, engineering, and foreign languages. Harvard University awarded four military-training certificates for every academic degree it conferred. The chancellor of one branch of the University of California announced that his school was "no longer an academic tent with military sideshows. It is a military tent with academic sideshows." Higher

GOING TO THE SOURCE

Women War Workers of Color

African American Fanny Christina Hill moved from Texas to Los Angeles in 1940, and found work as a live-in domestic, cleaning and cooking for a white family. In 1943, while her husband served in the military, she took a job with North American Aviation for sixty cents an hour.

Sometimes even if you're good, you just don't get the breaks if the color's not right. I could see where they made a difference in placing you in certain jobs. They had fifteen or twenty departments, but all the Negroes went to Department 17 because there was nothing but shooting and bucking rivets. You stood on one side of the panel and your partners stood on this side, and he would shoot the rivets with a gun and you'd buck them with the bar. That was about the size of it. I just didn't like it. I didn't think I could stay there with all this shooting and a'bucking and a'jumping and a'bumping. I stayed in

it about two or three weeks and then I just decided I did *not* like that. I went and told my foreman and he didn't do anything about it, so I decided to leave.... I went over to the union and they told me what to do. I went back inside and they sent me to another department where you did bench work and I liked that much better....

I must have stayed there nearly a year, and then they put me over in another department, "Plastics." ... I worked over there until the end of the war. Well, not quite the end, because I got pregnant, and while I was off having the baby the war was over....

When North American called me back, was I a happy soul! ... So, from sixty cents an hour, when I first hired in there, up to one dollar. That wasn't traveling fast, but it was better than anything else because you had hours to work by and you had benefits and you come home at night with your family. So it was a good deal.

education became more dependent on the federal government, and most universities sought increased federal contracts and subsidies. The universities in the West received some $100 billion from the Office of Scientific Research and Development, more money than had been spent on scientific research by all the western universities since their founding.

The war profoundly affected American culture. Spending on books and theater entertainment doubled. More than sixty million people (in a population of 135 million) attended movies weekly, and the film industry reached its zenith in 1945–1946. But as the war dragged on, people grew tired of war films, and Hollywood reemphasized romance and nostalgia with such stars as Katharine Hepburn and Judy Garland.

Similarly, popular music went from "Goodbye, Mama, I'm Off to Yokohama," the first hit of 1942, to songs of lost love and loneliness, like "They're Either Too Young or Too Old." By 1945, bitterness pervaded lyrics, and songs like "Saturday Night Is the Loneliest Night of the Week" revealed impatience for the war's end.

It made me live better. I really did. We always say that Lincoln took the bale off of the Negroes.... Well, my sister always said—that's why you can't interview her because she's so radical—"Hitler was the one that got us out of the white folks' kitchen."

Born in Mexico, Beatrice Morales Clift on was a married mother of four children when, over her husband's strenuous objections, she accepted a job offer from Lockheed in Los Angeles. Like Hill, she encountered resistance from male co-workers yet worked her way up to increasingly more skilled positions.

I felt proud of myself and felt good being that I had never done anything like that. I felt good that I could do something, and being that it was war, I felt that I was doing my part. I went from 65 cents to $1.05. That was top pay. It felt good and, besides, it was my own money. I could do whatever I wanted with it because my husband, whatever he was giving to the house, he kept on paying it. I used to buy clothes for the kids; buy little things that they needed. I had a bank account and I had a little saving at home where I could get ahold of the money right away if I needed it. Julio never asked about it. He knew how much I made; I showed him. If there was something that had to be paid and I had the money and he didn't, well, I used some of my money.

Questions

1. What effects did wartime employment have on these women's sense of themselves?

2. How might their wartime experiences have helped generate the civil rights and women's movements of the postwar era?

Go to www.cengagebrain.com for additional primary sources on this period.

Source: Sherna Berger Gluck, Rose the Riveter Revisited: Women, the War and Social Change, *Boston: Twayne, 1987. Reprinted with permission of the author.*

In bookstores, nonfiction ruled the roost and every newsmagazine increased its circulation. The Government Printing Office published Armed Services Editions, paperback reprints of classics and new releases; and the nearly 350 million copies distributed free to soldiers sped up the American acceptance of quality paperbacks, which were introduced in 1939 by the Pocket Book Company. Wendell Willkie's *One World* (1943) became the fastest-selling title in publishing history to that time, with 1 million copies snapped up in two months. A vision of a world without military alliances and spheres of influence, this brief volume expressed hope that an international organization would extend peace and democracy through the postwar world. Most startlingly, Willkie attacked "our imperialisms at home." Unless the United States ended its own racism, he concluded, nonwhites around the globe would rebuff its claim to world leadership.

An avid interest in wartime news also spurred the major radio networks to increase their news programs from 4 percent to nearly 30 percent of broadcasting time, and enticed Americans to listen to the radio an average of $4\frac{1}{2}$ hours a day. Daytime radio serials, like those featuring Dick Tracy tracking down Axis spies,

Rosie the Riveter

Memorialized in song and story, "Rosie the Riveter" symbolized the women war workers who assumed jobs in heavy industry to take up the slack for the absent 15 million men in the armed services. Here a very real Rosie the Riveter is doing her job in April 1943 at the Baltimore manufacturing plant for Martin PMB Mariners. Although sometimes scorned by male workers, the dedication and efficiency of most female workers won them the praise of male plant supervisors.

(National Archives)

reached the height of their popularity, as did juvenile comic books in which a platoon of new superheroes, including Captain America and Captain Marvel, saw action on the battlefield. Even Bugs Bunny donned a uniform to combat America's foes.

Racism and New Opportunities
Recognizing that the government needed the loyalty and labor of a united people, black leaders entered World War II determined to secure equal rights. In 1942, civil rights spokesmen insisted that African-American support of the war hinged on America's commitment to racial justice. They demanded a *"Double V"* campaign to gain victory over racial discrimination at home as well as over the Axis abroad. Membership in the NAACP multiplied nearly ten times, reaching half a million in 1945. The association pressed for legislation outlawing the poll tax and lynching, decried discrimination in defense industries and the armed services, and sought to end black disfranchisement. Its campaign for voting rights gained momentum when the Supreme Court, in *Smith v. Allwright* (1944), ruled the Texas all-white primary unconstitutional. The decision eliminated a bar that had existed

in eight southern states, although these states promptly resorted to other devices to minimize voting by blacks.

A new civil-rights organization, the Congress of Racial Equality (CORE), was founded in 1942. Employing the same forms of nonviolent direct action that Mohandas Gandhi used in his campaign for India's independence, CORE sought to desegregate public facilities in northern cities.

Also proposing nonviolent direct action, **A. Philip Randolph,** president of the Brotherhood of Sleeping Car Porters, in 1941 called for a "thundering march" of one hundred thousand blacks on Washington if the president did not end discrimination in the armed services and the defense industry. FDR agreed to compromise.

In June 1941, Roosevelt issued Executive Order 8802, the first presidential directive on race since Reconstruction. It prohibited discriminatory employment practices by federal agencies and by all unions and companies engaged in war-related work, and established the Fair Employment Practices Commission (FEPC) to monitor compliance. Although the FEPC lacked effective enforcement powers, booming war production and a labor supply depleted by military service resulted in the employment of some 2 million African-Americans in industry and two hundred thousand in the federal civil service. Between 1942 and 1945, the proportion of blacks in war production work rose from 3 to 9 percent. Black membership in labor unions doubled to 1.25 million, and the number of skilled and semiskilled black workers tripled. Formerly mired in low-paying domestic and farm jobs, some three hundred thousand black women found work in factories and the civil service. Overall, the average wage for African-Americans increased from $457 to $1,976 a year, compared with a gain from $1,064 to $2,600 for whites.

About 1 million African-Americans served in the armed forces. Wartime needs forced the military to end policies of excluding blacks from the marines and coast guard, restricting them to jobs as mess boys in the navy, and confining them to non-combatant units in the army. From just five in 1940—three of them chaplains—the number of black officers grew to over seven thousand in 1945. In 1944, both the army and navy began token integration in some training facilities, ships, and battle-field platoons.

The great majority of blacks, however, served throughout the war in segregated service units commanded by white officers. This indignity, made worse by the failure of military authorities to protect black servicemen off the post and by the use of white military police to keep blacks "in their place," sparked rioting on army bases. At least fifty black soldiers died in racial conflicts during the war. "I used to sing gospel songs until I joined the Army," recalled blues-guitar great B. B. King, "then I sang the blues."

Violence within the military mirrored growing racial tensions on the home front. As blacks protested against discrimination, many whites resisted blacks' efforts to improve their economic and social status. Race riots erupted in 1943 in Harlem, Mobile, and Beaumont, Texas. The bloodiest melee exploded in Detroit that year when white mobs assaulted blacks caught riding on trolleys or sitting in movie theaters and blacks smashed and looted white-owned stores and shops. After thirty hours of racial beatings, shootings, and burning, twenty-five African Americans and nine whites lay dead, more than seven hundred had been injured, and over $2 million of property had been destroyed. The fear of continued violence led to a greater emphasis on racial tolerance by liberal whites and to a reduction in the militancy of African-American leaders.

Yet the war brought significant changes that would eventually result in a successful drive for black civil rights. The migration of over seven hundred thousand blacks from the South turned a southern problem into a national concern. It created a new attitude of independence in African-Americans freed from the constraints of caste. As the growing numbers of blacks in northern cities began to vote, moreover, African-Americans could hold a balance of power in close elections. This prompted politicians in both major parties to extend greater recognition to blacks and to pay more attention to civil-rights issues.

African-American expectations of greater government concern for their rights also resulted from the new prominence of the United States as a major power in a predominantly nonwhite world. As Japanese propaganda appeals to the peoples of Asia and Latin America emphasized lynchings and race riots in the United States, Americans had to confront the peril that white racism posed to their national security. In addition, the horrors of Nazi racism discredited America's own white-supremacist attitudes and practices. A pluralist vision of American society now became part of official rhetoric, and of the liberal-left agenda. The contradiction between American ideals of freedom and equality and the actual state of African Americans became manifest. Swedish economist Gunnar Myrdal, in his massive study of race problems, *An American Dilemma* (1944), concluded that "not since Reconstruction had there been more reason to anticipate fundamental changes in American race relations . . . there is bound to be a redefinition of the Negro's status as a result of this War." Returning black veterans, and African-Americans who had served the nation on the home front, soon expected to gain all the rights enjoyed by whites.

War and Diversity   Wartime winds of change also brought new opportunities and difficulties to other minorities. More than twenty-five thousand Native Americans served in the armed forces, including 400 Navajo "code talkers" who confounded the Japanese by using their complex native language to relay messages between U.S. command centers. "Were it not for the Navajos, the Marines would never have taken Iwo Jima," one Signal Corps officer declared.

Another fifty thousand Indians left the reservation to work in defense industries, mainly on the West Coast. The Rosebud Reservation in South Dakota lost more than a quarter of its population to migration during the war. It was the first time most had lived in a non-Indian world, and the average income of Native American households tripled during the war. Such economic improvement encouraged many Indians to remain outside the reservation and to try to assimilate into mainstream life. But anti-Indian discrimination, particularly in smaller towns near reservations, such as Gallup, New Mexico, and Billings, Montana, forced many Native Americans back to their reservations, which had suffered severely from budget cuts during the war. Prodded by those who coveted Indian lands, lawmakers demanded that Indians be taken off the backs of the taxpayers and "freed from the reservations" to fend for themselves." To mobilize against the campaign to end all reservations and trust protections, Native Americans organized the National Congress of American Indians in 1944.

To relieve labor shortages in agriculture, caused by conscription and the movement of rural workers to city factories, the U.S. government negotiated an agreement with Mexico in July 1942 to import *braceros*, or temporary workers. Classified as foreign laborers rather than as immigrants, an estimated two hundred thousand *braceros*, half of them in California, received short-term contracts promising adequate wages, medical care, and decent living conditions. But farm owners frequently violated the terms of these contracts and also encouraged an influx of illegal migrants from Mexico desperate for employment. Unable to complain about their working conditions without risking arrest and deportation, hundreds of thousands of Mexicans were exploited by agribusinesses in Arizona, California, and Texas. At the same time, tens of thousands of Chicanos left agricultural work for jobs in factories, shipbuilding yards, and steel mills. By 1943, about half a million Chicanos were living in Los Angeles County, 10 percent of the total population. In New Mexico nearly 20 percent of Mexican-American farm laborers escaped from rural poverty to urban jobs. Even as their occupational status and material conditions improved, most Mexican-Americans remained in communities (*colonias*), segregated from the larger society and frequently harassed by the police.

Much of the hostility toward Mexican-Americans focused on young gang members who wore "zoot suits"—a fashion that originated in Harlem and emphasized long, broad-shouldered jackets and pleated trousers tightly pegged at the ankles. Known as *pachucos*, zoot-suited Mexican-Americans aroused the ire of servicemen stationed or on leave in Los Angeles who saw them as delinquents and draft dodgers. After a luridly publicized trial arising from a Mexican-American gang fight at a swimming hole called Sleepy Lagoon, and newspaper headlines of a Chicano "crime wave," bands of sailors and soldiers rampaged through Los Angeles in early June 1943, stripping *pachucos*, cutting their long hair, and beating them. Military authorities looked the other way. City police intervened only to arrest Mexican-Americans, and the city council made the wearing of a zoot suit a misdemeanor. Nothing was done about the substandard housing, disease, and racism Hispanics had to endure.

Unlike African-Americans, however, more than 350,000 Mexican-Americans served in the armed forces without segregation, and in all combat units. They volunteered in higher numbers than warranted by their percentage of the population and earned a disproportionate number of citations for distinguished service as well as seventeen Medals of Honor. Returning Mexican-American GIs joined established antidiscrimination groups, like the League of United Latin American Citizens (LULAC) and organized their own associations, like the American GI Forum, to press for equal rights.

Thousands of gay men and lesbians who served in the armed forces also found new wartime opportunities. The military officially barred those they defined as "sexual perverts," but owing to the urgency of building a massive armed forces, just four to five thousand men out of eighteen million examined for induction were excluded because of homosexuality. For the vast majority of gays not excluded, being emancipated from traditional expectations and the close scrutiny of family and neighbors, and living in overwhelmingly all-male or all-female environments, brought freedom to meet like-minded gay men and women. Like other minorities, many gays saw the war as a chance to prove their worth under fire. Yet some suspected of being gay were dishonorably discharged, sent to psychiatric hospitals, or imprisoned in so-called queer stockades. In 1945, gay veterans established the Veteran's Benevolent Association, the first organization in the United States to combat discrimination against homosexuals.

The Internment of Japanese-Americans   Far more than any other minority in the United States, Japanese-Americans suffered grievously during the war. About thirty-seven thousand first-generation Japanese immigrants (Issei) and nearly seventy-five thousand native-born Japanese-American citizens (Nisei) were interned in "relocation centers" guarded by military police—a tragic reminder of the fragility of civil liberties in wartime.

The **internment of Japanese-Americans** reflected forty years of anti-Japanese sentiment on the West Coast, rooted in racial prejudice and economic rivalry. Nativist politicians and farmers who wanted Japanese-American land had long decried the "yellow peril." Following the attack on Pearl Harbor they whipped up the rage of white Californians, aided by a government report falsely blaming Japanese-Americans in Hawaii for aiding the Japanese naval force. Patriotic associations and many newspapers clamored for evacuating the Japanese-Americans, as did the army general in charge of the Western Defense Command, who proclaimed, "It makes no difference whether he is an American citizen or not. . . . I don't want any of them."

In February 1942, President Roosevelt gave in to the pressure and issued Executive Order 9066, authorizing the removal from military areas of anyone deemed a threat. Although not a single Japanese-American was apprehended for espionage or sedition and neither the FBI nor military intelligence uncovered any evidence of disloyal behavior by Japanese-Americans, the military ordered the eviction of all Nisei and Issei from the West Coast. Only Hawaii was excepted. Despite the far larger number of Hawaiians of Japanese ancestry, as well as of Japanese living in Hawaii, no internment policy was implemented there, and no sabotage occurred.

Forced to sell all they owned at whatever prices they could obtain, Japanese-Americans lost an estimated $2 billion in property and possessions. Tagged with numbers rather than names, they were herded into barbed-wire-encircled detention camps in the most desolate parts of the West and Great Plains—places, wrote one historian, "where nobody had lived before and no one has lived since." Few protested the incarceration. Stating that it would not question government claims of military necessity during time of war, the Supreme Court upheld the constitutionality of the evacuation in the *Korematsu* case (1944). By then the hysteria had subsided, and the government had begun a program of gradual release, allowing some Nisei to attend college or take factory jobs (but not on the West Coast); about eighteen thousand served in the military. The 442nd regimental combat team, entirely Japanese-American, became the most decorated unit in the military.

In 1982, a special government commission concluded in its report, *Personal Justice Denied*, that internment "was not justified by military necessity." It blamed the Roosevelt administration's action on "race prejudice, war hysteria, and a failure of political leadership" and apologized to Japanese-Americans for "a grave injustice." In 1988, Congress voted to pay twenty thousand dollars in compensation to each of the nearly sixty-two thousand surviving internees; and in 1998 President Bill Clinton further apologized for the injustice by giving the nation's highest civilian honor, the Presidential Medal of Freedom, to Fred Korematsu, who had protested the evacuation decree all the way to the Supreme Court.

TRIUMPH AND TRAGEDY, 1945

Spring and summer 1945 brought stunning changes and new crises. In Europe, a new balance of power emerged after the collapse of the Third Reich. In Asia, continued Japanese reluctance to surrender led to the use of atomic bombs. And in the United States, a new president, Harry S. Truman, presided over both the end of World War II and the beginning of the Cold War and the nuclear age.

The Yalta Conference   By the time Roosevelt, Churchill, and Stalin met in the Soviet city of Yalta in February 1945, the military situation favored the Soviet Union. The Red Army had overrun Poland, Romania, and Bulgaria; driven the Nazis out of Yugoslavia; penetrated Austria, Hungary, and Czechoslovakia; and was massed just fifty miles from Berlin. American forces, in contrast, were still recovering from the Battle of the Bulge and facing stiff resistance on the route to Japan. The Joint Chiefs of Staff, contemplating the awesome cost in American casualties of invading Japan, insisted that Stalin's help was worth almost any price. And Stalin was in a position to make demands. The Soviet Union had suffered most in the war against Germany, it already dominated eastern Europe, and, knowing that the United States did not want to fight a prolonged war against Japan, Stalin had the luxury of deciding whether and when to enter the Pacific war.

The **Yalta accords** reflected these realities. Stalin again vowed to declare war on Japan "two or three months" after Germany's surrender, and in return Churchill and Roosevelt reneged on their arrangement with Jiang Jieshi and promised the Soviet Union concessions in Manchuria and the territories it had lost in the Russo-Japanese War (1904) (see Chapter 22). The Big Three delegated a final settlement of the German reparations issue to a postwar commission, and left vague the matter of partitioning Germany and its eventual reunification. The conference also vaguely called for interim governments in eastern Europe "broadly representative of all democratic elements" and for eventual freely elected permanent governments. On the matter dearest to FDR's heart, the negotiators accepted a plan for a new international organization and agreed to a founding conference of the new United Nations in San Francisco in April 1945.

Stalin proved adamant about the nature of the postwar Polish government. Twice in the twentieth century German troops had used Poland as a springboard for invading Russia. Stalin would not expose his land again, and after the Red Army had captured Warsaw in January 1945 he installed a procommunist regime and brutally subdued the anticommunist Poles. Conservative critics would later charge that FDR "gave away" eastern Europe. Actually, the Soviet Union gained little it did not already control, and short of going to war against the Soviets while still battling Germany and Japan, FDR could only hope that Stalin would keep his word.

(National Archives)

Young Niesi Evacuees at the Turlock Assembly Center *Awaiting their turn for baggage inspection on May 2, 1942, these children would be interned in remote "relocation centers" along with 37,000 first-generation Japanese immigrants (Issei) and some 75,000 native-born Japanese-American (Niesi) citizens of the United States. Hastily uprooted from their homes, farms, and stores, most lost all their property and personal possessions, and spent the war under armed guard.*

Victory in Europe　　As the Soviets prepared for their assault on Berlin, American troops crossed the Rhine at Remagen in March 1945 and encircled the Ruhr Valley, Germany's industrial heartland. Churchill now proposed a rapid thrust to Berlin. But Eisenhower and Roosevelt saw no point in risking high casualties to rush to an area of Germany already designated as the Soviet occupation zone. So Eisenhower advanced methodically along a broad front until the Americans met the Russians at the Elbe River on April 25. By then, the Red Army had taken Vienna and reached the suburbs of Berlin. On April 30, as Soviet troops approached his headquarters, Hitler committed suicide. Berlin fell to the Soviets on May 2, and on May 8 a new German government surrendered unconditionally.

Jubilant Americans celebrated Victory in Europe (V-E) Day less than a month after they had mourned the death of their president. On April 12, an exhausted President Roosevelt had abruptly clutched his head, moaned that he had a "terrific headache," and fell unconscious. A cerebral hemorrhage ended his life. As the nation grieved, Roosevelt's unprepared successor assumed the burden of ending the war and dealing with the Soviet Union.

"I don't know whether you fellows ever had a load of hay or a bull fall on you," Harry Truman told reporters on his first full day in office, "but last night the moon, the stars, and all the planets fell on me." An unpretentious politician awed by his new responsibilities, Truman struggled to continue FDR's policies. But Roosevelt had made no effort to familiarize his vice president with world affairs. Perhaps sensing his own inadequacies, Truman adopted a tough pose toward adversaries. In office less than two weeks, he lashed out at Soviet ambassador V. M. Molotov that the United States was tired of waiting for the Russians to allow free elections in Poland, and he threatened to cut off lend-lease aid if the Soviet Union did not cooperate. The Truman administration then reduced U.S. economic assistance to the Soviets and stalled on their request for a $1 billion reconstruction loan. Simultaneously, Stalin strengthened his grip on eastern Europe, ignoring the promises he had made at Yalta.

The United States neither conceded the Soviet sphere of influence in eastern Europe nor tried to end it. Although Truman still sought Stalin's cooperation in establishing the United Nations and in defeating Japan, Soviet-American relations deteriorated. By June 1945, when the Allied countries succeeded in framing the United Nations Charter, hopes for a new international order had dimmed, and the United Nations emerged as a diplomatic battleground. Truman, Churchill, and Stalin met at Potsdam, Germany, from July 16 to August 2 to complete the postwar arrangements begun at Yalta. But the Allied leaders could barely agree to demilitarize Germany and to punish Nazi war criminals. Given the diplomatic impasse, only military power remained to determine the contours of the postwar world.

The Holocaust

When news of the **Holocaust**—the term later given to the Nazis' extermination of European Jewry—first leaked out in early 1942, many Americans discounted the reports. Not until November did the State Department admit knowledge of the massacres. A month later, the American broadcaster Edward R. Murrow, listened to nationwide, reported on the systematic killing of millions of Jews, "It is a picture of mass murder and moral depravity unequalled in the history of the world. It is a horror beyond what imagination can grasp. . . . There are no longer 'concentration camps'—we must speak now only of 'extermination camps.'"

Most Americans considered the annihilation of Europe's 6 million Jews beyond belief. There were no photographs to prove it, and, some argued, the atrocities attributed to the Germans in World War I had turned out to be false. So few took issue with the military's view that the way to liberate those enslaved by Hitler was by speedily winning the war. Pleas by American Jews for the Allies to bomb the death camps and the railroad tracks leading to them fell on deaf ears. In fall 1944, U.S. planes flying over Auschwitz in southern Poland bombed nearby factories but left the gas chambers and crematoria intact, in order, American officials explained, not to divert air power from more vital raids elsewhere. "How could it be," historian David Wyman has asked, "that Government officials knew that a place existed where 2,000 helpless human beings could be killed in less than an hour, knew that this occurred over and over again, and yet did not feel driven to search for some way to wipe such a scourge from the earth?"

How much could have been done remains uncertain. Still, the U.S. government never seriously considered rescue schemes or searched for a way to curtail the Nazis' "final solution" to the "Jewish question." Its feeble response was due to its overwhelming focus on winning the war as quickly as possible, congressional and public fears of an influx of destitute Jews into the United States, Britain's wish to placate the Arabs by keeping Jewish settlers out of Palestine, and the fear of some Jewish-American leaders that pressing the issue would increase anti-Semitism at home. The War Refugee Board managed to save the lives of just two hundred thousand Jews and twenty thousand non-Jews. Six million other Jews, about 75 percent of the European Jewish population, were gassed, shot, and incinerated, as were several million gypsies, communists, homosexuals, Polish Catholics, and others deemed unfit to live in the Third Reich.

"The things I saw beggar description," wrote General Eisenhower after visiting the first death camp liberated by the U.S. army. He sent immediately for a delegation of congressional leaders and newspaper editors to make sure Americans would never forget the gas chambers and human ovens. Only after viewing the photographs and newsreels of corpses stacked like cordwood, boxcars heaped with the bones of dead prisoners, bulldozers shoving emaciated bodies into hastily dug ditches, and liberated, barely-alive living skeletons lying in their own filth, their vacant, sunken eyes staring through barbed wire, did most Americans see that the Holocaust was no myth.

The Atomic Bombs

Meanwhile, the war with Japan ground on. Early in 1945, an assault force of marines invaded Iwo Jima, 700 miles from Japan. In places termed the "Meat Grinder" and "Bloody Gorge," the marines savagely battled thousands of Japanese soldiers hidden in tunnels and behind concrete bunkers and pillboxes. Securing the five-square-mile island would cost the marines nearly twenty-seven thousand casualties, and one-third of all the marines killed in the Pacific. In June, American troops waded ashore on Okinawa, 350 miles from Japan and a key staging area for the planned U.S. invasion of the Japanese home islands. Death and destruction engulfed Okinawa as waves of Americans attacked nearly impregnable Japanese defenses head-on, repeating the bloody strategy of World War I. After eighty-three days of fighting on land and sea, twelve thousand Americans lay dead and three times as many wounded, a 35 percent casualty rate, higher than at Normandy.

The appalling rate of loss on Iwo Jima and Okinawa weighed on the minds of American strategists as they thought about an invasion of the Japanese home islands. The Japanese Cabinet showed no willingness to give up the war despite Japan's being blockaded and bombed daily (on March 9–10 a fleet of B-29s dropped napalm-and-magnesium bombs on Tokyo, burning sixteen square miles of the city to the ground and killing some eighty-four thousand). Japanese military leaders insisted on fighting to the bitter end; surrender was unthinkable. Japan possessed an army of over two million, plus up to four million reservists and five thousand kamikaze aircraft, and the U.S. Joint Chiefs estimated that American casualties in invasions of Kyushu and Honshu (the main island of Japan) might exceed 1 million.

The successful detonation of history's first nuclear explosion at Alamagordo in mid-July gave Truman an alternative. On July 25, while meeting with Stalin and Churchill in Potsdam, Truman ordered the use of an atomic bomb if Japan did not surrender before August 3. The next day, in the **Potsdam Declaration,** he warned Japan to surrender unconditionally or face "prompt and utter destruction." Japan refused, and on August 6, a B-29 bomber named *Enola Gay* took off from the Marianas island of Tinian and dropped a uranium bomb on Hiroshima. It plunged the city into what Japanese novelist Masuji Ibuse termed "a hell of unspeakable torments." The 300,000-degree centigrade fireball incinerated houses and vaporized people. More than sixty thousand died immediately from the blast, and another seventy-five thousand died from burns and radiation poisoning by late 1945. On August 8, Stalin declared war on Japan, and U.S. planes dropped leaflets on Japan warning that another bomb would be dropped if it did not surrender. Japan refused. Its military leaders preferred death to surrender. The next day, at high noon, the *Bock's Car* flattened Nagasaki with a plutonium bomb, killing over thirty-five thousand, and injuring more than sixty thousand. On August 14, Japan accepted the American terms of surrender, which implicitly permitted the emperor to retain his throne but subordinated him to the U.S. commander of the occupation forces. General MacArthur received Japan's surrender on the battleship *Missouri* on September 2, 1945. The war was over.

While Americans at the time overwhelmingly backed the atomic bombings of Japan as the necessary way to end the war quickly and with the least cost in lives, many critics later contended that Japan would have soon surrendered without the horrendous bombing. Some believed that racist American attitudes toward the Japanese motivated the decision to drop the bombs. As war correspondent Ernie Pyle wrote, "The Japanese are looked upon as something inhuman and squirmy—like some people feel about cockroaches or mice." While racial hatred undoubtedly stirred exterminationist sentiment, those involved in the Manhattan Project had regarded Germany as the target; and considering the ferocity of the Allied bombings of Hamburg and Dresden, there is little reason to assume that the Allies would not have dropped atomic bombs on Germany had they been available. By 1945, the Allies as well as the Axis had abandoned restraints on attacking civilians.

Other critics maintain that demonstrating the bomb's terrible destructiveness on an uninhabited island would have moved Japan to surrender. We will never know for sure. American scientists rejected a demonstration bombing because the United States had an atomic arsenal of only two bombs and they did not know whether the mechanism for detonating them in the air would work. A large number of those critical of Truman's decision believe that the president, aware of worsening relations between the United States and the USSR, ordered the atomic attack primarily to end the Pacific war before Stalin could enter it and share in the postwar occupation of Japan. At the same time, its use might also intimidate Stalin into making concessions in eastern Europe. Referring to the Soviets, President Truman noted just before the atomic test at Alamogordo, "If it explodes, as I think it will, I'll certainly have a hammer on those boys." Truman's new secretary of state, James

(AP Photos)

Atomic Bombs Bring Relief and Joy to Some *These U.S. servicemen, like many others, hearing the news of the atomic bombs and the Japanese surrender, expressed their relief and joy that they would soon be safely coming home rather than having to participate in an invasion of Japan.*

Byrnes, thought that the bomb would "make Russia more manageable" and would "put us in a position to dictate our own terms at the end of the war."

Although the president and his advisers believed that the atomic bombs would strengthen their hand against the Soviets, the foremost reason for Truman's decision was to shorten the war and save American lives. As throughout the war, American leaders in August 1945 relied on production and technology to win the war with the minimum loss of American life. Every new weapon was put to use; the concept of "total war" easily accommodated the bombing of civilians; and the atomic bomb was one more item in an arsenal that had already wreaked enormous destruction on the Axis. In "Operation Thunderclap," the Allies had obliterated miles of German and Japanese cities, making no pretense of distinguishing military and civilian targets. The rules of war that had once stayed the use of weapons of mass destruction against enemy civilians no longer prevailed. Before Hiroshima, the United States had already crossed the threshold into mass murder from the air.

No responsible official counseled that the United States should sacrifice American servicemen to lessen death and destruction in Japan, or not use a weapon developed with 2 billion taxpayer dollars. To the vast majority of Americans, the atomic bomb was, in Churchill's words, "a miracle of deliverance" that saved Allied lives. So E. B. Sledge and his comrades in the First Marine Division, slated to take part in the first wave of the invasion of Japan's home islands, breathed "an indescribable sense of relief." Hearing the news of the atomic bombs and Japan's surrender, Sledge wrote, they sat in stunned silence:

> We remembered our dead. So many dead. So many maimed. So many bright futures consigned to the ashes of the past. So many dreams lost in the madness that engulfed us. Except for a few widely scattered shouts of joy, the survivors of the abyss sat hollow-eyed and silent, trying to comprehend a world without war.

The atomic bombs ended the deadliest war in history. A truly global conflict, involving over half the world's peoples, with armies ranging over continents and navies fighting on every ocean, the war affected women, men, and children as victims of civilian bombing campaigns, as war workers, as slave laborers and comfort women. Neither side gave much quarter in seeking to destroy the other's will and resources. Some fifty million died—more than half of them noncombatants. The Soviet Union lost roughly twenty million people, China fifteen million, Poland six million, Germany four million, and Japan two million. Much of Asia and Europe was rubble. Some four hundred thousand American servicemen had also perished, and, although physically unscathed, the United States had changed profoundly—for better and worse.

CHRONOLOGY
1931–1945

1931–1932	Japan invades Manchuria and creates a puppet government.
1933	Adolf Hitler becomes chancellor of Germany and assumes dictatorial powers.
1934–1936	Nye Committee investigations.
1935–1937	Neutrality Acts.
1937	Japan invades China.
1938	Germany annexes Austria; Munich Pact gives Sudetenland to Germany. *Kristallnacht*, night of Nazi terror against German and Austrian Jews.
1939	Nazi-Soviet Pact. Germany invades Poland; World War II begins.
1940	Germany conquers the Netherlands, Belgium, France, Denmark, Norway, and Luxembourg. Germany, Italy, and Japan sign the Tripartite Pact. Selective Service Act. Franklin Roosevelt elected to an unprecedented third term.
1941	Lend-Lease Act. Roosevelt establishes the Fair Employment Practices Commission (FEPC). Germany invades the Soviet Union.

Japan attacks Pearl Harbor; the United States enters World War II.
War Powers Act.

1942   Battles of Coral Sea and Midway halt Japanese offensive.
Internment of Japanese-Americans.
Revenue Act expands graduated income-tax system.
Allies invade North Africa (Operation TORCH).
First successful atomic chain reaction.
CORE founded.

1943   Soviet victory in Battle of Stalingrad.
Coal miners strike; Smith-Connally War Labor Disputes Act.
Detroit and Los Angeles race riots.
Allied invasion of Italy.
Roosevelt, Churchill, and Stalin meet in Tehran.

1944   Allied invasion of France (Operation Overlord).
U.S. forces invade the Philippines.
Roosevelt wins fourth term.
Battle of the Bulge.

1945   Yalta Conference.
Battles of Iwo Jima and Okinawa.
Roosevelt dies; Harry S. Truman becomes president.
Germany surrenders.
Truman, Churchill, and Stalin meet in Potsdam.
United States drops atomic bombs on Hiroshima and Nagasaki; Japan surrenders.

CONCLUSION

Most Americans, and their government, initially responded to the war clouds over Asia and Europe by reaffirming their isolationism. As one senator proclaimed, prior to the vote that defeated Roosevelt's effort to have the United States join the World Court, "To hell with Europe and the rest of those nations!" Not till the Japanese attack on the American fleet at Pearl Harbor, more than two years after the war in Europe had begun, did the United States enter the fray, and even then it waited until Hitler and Mussolini declared war on it before joining the armed struggle engulfing the world. Once engaged, the Americans rapidly went on a war footing. Mobilization transformed the scope and authority of the federal government, vastly expanding presidential powers. It ended the unemployment of the depression and made American industry more productive than it had ever been, and most Americans more prosperous than they had ever been. It tilted the national economic balance toward the South Atlantic, Gulf, and Pacific coasts. It accelerated trends toward bigness in business, agriculture, and labor. It involved the military in the economy and education as never before.

To achieve an unconditional victory, with the least possible cost in American lives, Roosevelt concentrated on defeating Germany first yet delaying a second front in Europe until Soviet forces had routed the German army in eastern Europe. Meanwhile, half a world way, a two-pronged American offensive, across the central Pacific and north from Australia, brought Japan to the brink of defeat. On the home front, the war catalyzed vital changes in racial and social relations, sometimes intensifying prejudices against minorities and women, but also broadening educational and employment opportunities that widened their public spheres and heightened their expectations. Fighting and winning the greatest war in history, moreover, restored American faith in capitalism and democratic institutions. It was a vital coming-of-age experience for an entire generation that did much to give postwar American society a confident, "can-do" spirit, optimistic for the "American Century" that they knew lay ahead.

The awesome development and use of an atomic bomb bolstered that spirit and enabled the United States to defeat Japan promptly, to try to force the Soviets to be more manageable, and to avoid an invasion of the Japanese home islands that might cost untold thousands of American casualties. The mass destruction of the war and total defeat of the Axis, however, brought new crises to cloud the bright dawn of peace. The world's two superpowers—the United States and the U.S.S.R—soon squared off in a Cold War that would see the United States play a role in global affairs inconceivable to most Americans just five years before.

26

THE COLD WAR ABROAD AND
AT HOME, 1945–1960

ANTICOMMUNISM AND CONTAINMENT, 1946–1953

The smoldering antagonisms between Moscow and Washington at war's end continued to flare. The "shotgun wedding" that joined the United States and the USSR in an alliance to defeat Hitler dissolved into a struggle to fill the power vacuums left by the defeat of the Axis, the exhaustion and bankruptcy of Western Europe, and the crumbling of colonial empires in Asia and Africa. Misperception and misunderstanding mounted as the two powers sought greater security, each feeding the other's fears, causing a cycle of distrust and animosity. The Cold War resulted.

Polarization and Cold War The destiny of Eastern Europe, especially Poland, stood at the heart of the strife between the United States and the USSR. Wanting to end the Soviet Union's vulnerability to invasions from the West, Stalin insisted on a demilitarized Germany and a buffer zone of nations friendly to Russia along its western flank. He considered a Soviet sphere of influence in Eastern Europe essential to Russian security, a just reward for bearing the brunt of the war against Germany, and no different than the American spheres of influence in Western Europe, Japan, and Latin America. Stalin also believed that Roosevelt and Churchill had implicitly accepted a Soviet zone in Eastern Europe at the Yalta Conference.

With the Red Army occupying half of Europe at war's end, Stalin installed pro-Soviet puppet governments in Bulgaria, Hungary, and Romania, and supported the establishment of communist regimes in nominally independent Albania and Yugoslavia. Ignoring the Yalta Declaration of Liberated Europe, Stalin barred free elections in Poland and brutally suppressed Polish democratic parties. Poland, he said, was "not only a question of honor for Russia, but one of life and death."

Stalin's insistence on dominance in Eastern Europe collided with Truman's unwillingness to concede Soviet supremacy beyond Russia's borders. What Stalin saw as critical to Russian security Truman viewed as a violation of national self-determination, a betrayal of democracy, and a cover for communist aggression. Only a new world order based on the self-determination of all nations working in good faith within the United Nations, Truman maintained, could guarantee peace. He believed that accepting the "enforced sovietization" of Eastern Europe would betray American war aims and condemn nations rescued from Hitler's tyranny to another totalitarian dictatorship. In addition, Truman feared that the Democratic Party would invite political disaster if he reneged on the Yalta agreements. The Democrats counted on winning most of the votes of the 6 million Polish-Americans and millions of other Americans of Eastern European origin, who remained keenly interested in the fates of their homelands. He resolved not to appear "soft on communism."

Combativeness fit the temperament of the feisty Truman. Eager to demonstrate his command, the president matched Stalin's intransigence on controlling Poland with his own demands for Polish free elections. Encouraged by America's monopoly of atomic weapons and its position as the world's economic superpower, the new president hoped the United States could control the terms of the postwar settlement. His foreign policy sought, in the words of a November 1945 State Department document, to "establish the kind of world we want to live in."

The Iron Curtain Descends   As Truman's assertiveness deepened Stalin's mistrust of the West, the Soviet Union tightened its grip on Eastern Europe, stepped up its confiscation of materials and factories from occupied territories, and forced its satellite nations (countries under Soviet control) to close their doors to American trade and influence. In a February 1946 speech that the White House considered a "declaration of World War III," Stalin asserted that there could be no lasting peace with capitalism.

Two weeks later, **George F. Kennan,** an American diplomat in Moscow, wired a long telegram to the State Department. A leading student of Russian affairs, Kennan described Soviet expansionism as "like a toy automobile, wound up and headed in a given direction, stopping only when it meets some unanswerable force." Therefore, U.S. policy must be the "long-term, patient but firm and vigilant containment of Russian expansive tendencies." Truman, who had already insisted the time had come "to stop babying the Soviets" and "to get tough with Russia," accepted Kennan's advice. **Containment**—a policy uniting military, economic, and diplomatic strategies to curb, or "contain," any further Soviet communist expansion—became Washington gospel.

In early March 1946, Truman accompanied Winston Churchill to Westminster College in Missouri, where the former British prime minister warned of a new threat to democracy. Stalin, he said, had drawn an "iron curtain" across the eastern half of Europe. To meet the threat of further Soviet aggression, Churchill called for an alliance of the English-speaking peoples and the maintenance of an Anglo-American monopoly of atomic weapons: "There is nothing the Communists admire so much as strength and nothing for which they have less respect than for military weakness."

As mutual hostility escalated, the Soviets and Americans rushed to develop doomsday weapons. In 1946, Congress established the Atomic Energy Commission (AEC) to spur both nuclear energy and nuclear weaponry. The AEC, however, devoted more than 90 percent of its effort to atomic bombs. By 1950, one AEC adviser reckoned, the United States "had a stockpile capable of somewhat more than reproducing World War II in a single day."

Thus, less than a year after American and Soviet soldiers had jubilantly met at the Elbe River to celebrate Hitler's defeat, a Cold War emerged. It would be waged by economic pressure, nuclear intimidation, propaganda, subversion, and proxy wars (fought by governments and peoples allied to the principals rather than directly by the principals themselves). It would affect American life as decisively as any military engagement the nation had fought.

Containing Communism   On February 21, 1947, Britain informed the United States that it could no longer afford to assist Greece and Turkey in their struggles against communist insurgents in the eastern Mediterranean. The harsh European winter, the most severe in memory, heightened the sense of urgency in Washington. The economies of Western Europe had come to a near halt. Famine and tuberculosis plagued the continent. European colonies in Africa and Asia had risen in revolt. Cigarettes and candy bars circulated as currency in Germany, and the communist parties in France and Italy appeared ready to topple democratic coalition governments. Truman resolved to meet the challenge. But congressional leaders balked, agreeing to support the president only if he could "scare hell out of the country" to gain popular backing for meeting the Soviet threat.

Truman could and did. On March 12, 1947, addressing a joint session of Congress, he asked for $400 million in military assistance to Greece and Turkey while announcing the **Truman Doctrine**. Instead of mentioning that the aid would go to a right-wing, military-dominated Greek regime and an autocratic Turkey, the Truman Doctrine pictured the matter as a global struggle, pitting "freedom" and "liberty" against "oppression" and "terror," in which the policy of the United States would be to support free peoples everywhere "resisting attempted subjugation by armed minorities or by outside pressures." The Truman Doctrine and the funds appropriated by Congress helped the Greek monarchy to defeat the rebel movement and Turkey to stay out of the Soviet orbit. Moreover, it endured long after the crisis in the Mediterranean. It proclaimed the nation's intention to be a global policeman—everywhere on guard against advances by the Soviet Union and its allies—and it laid the foundation for American foreign policy for much of the next four decades.

To back up the new international initiative, Congress passed the **National Security Act of 1947,** unifying the armed forces under a single Department of Defense, creating the National Security Council (NSC) to advise the president on strategic matters, and establishing the Central Intelligence Agency (CIA) to gather information abroad and engage in covert activities in support of the nation's security. Congress also approved the administration's proposal for massive U.S. assistance for European recovery in 1947. Advocated by Secretary of State George C. Marshall, and thus called the **Marshall Plan,** the European Recovery Plan (ERP) aimed to combat the "hunger, poverty, desperation" that spawned communism. Truman correctly guessed that the Soviet Union and its satellites would refuse to take part in the plan, because of the controls linked to it, and accurately foresaw that Western European economic recovery would expand sales of American goods abroad and promote prosperity in the United States.

Although denounced by the Left as a "Martial Plan" and by isolationist voices on the Right as a "Share-the-American-Wealth Plan," the Marshall Plan more than fulfilled its sponsors' hopes. By 1952, industrial production had risen 200 percent in Western Europe, and the economic and social chaos that communists had exploited had been overcome in the sixteen nations that shared the $17 billion in aid provided by the ERP. Its slogan, "Prosperity Makes You Free," had been vindicated, and, not incidentally, Western Europe had become a major center of American trade and investment.

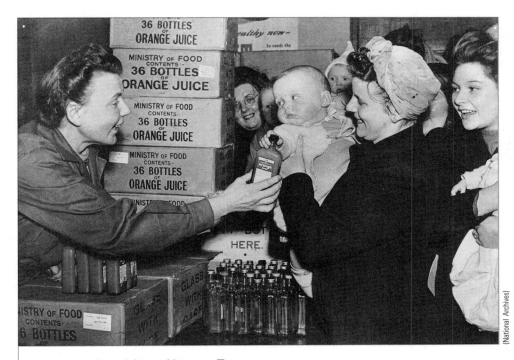

(National Archives)

American Food for a Hungry Europe *Grateful English mothers line up for orange juice sent by the United States to assist Europeans devastated by the Second World War.*

Confrontation in Germany

The Soviet Union reacted to the Truman Doctrine and the Marshall Plan by tightening its grip on Eastern Europe. Communist takeovers added Hungary and Czechoslovakia to the Soviet bloc in 1947 and 1948, and Stalin set his sights on Germany. The 1945 Potsdam Agreement had divided Germany into four separate zones (administered by France, Great Britain, the Soviet Union, and the United States) and created a joint four-power administration for Germany's capital, Berlin, lying 110 miles within the Soviet-occupied eastern zone. As the Cold War intensified, the Western powers moved toward uniting their zones into an anti-Soviet West German state. Stalin responded in June 1948 by blocking all surface traffic into Berlin.

Truman resolved neither to abandon Berlin nor to shoot his way into the city and possibly trigger World War III. Instead, he ordered a massive airlift of supplies to the city (the **Berlin airlift**). American cargo planes landed in West Berlin every three minutes around the clock, bringing the mountain of food and fuel necessary

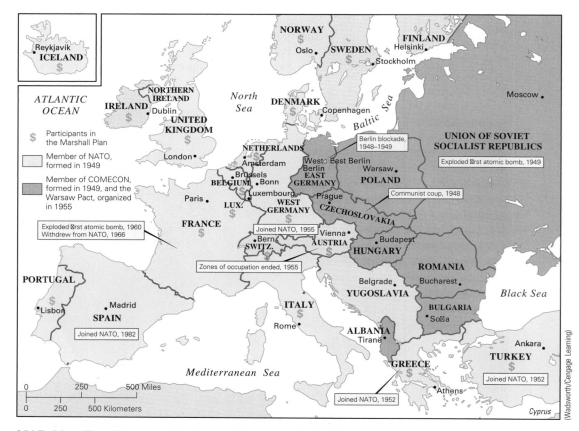

MAP 26.1 The Postwar Division of Europe, 1945–1989

The wartime dispute between the Soviet Union and the Western Allies over Poland's future hardened after World War II into a Cold War that split Europe into competing American and Russian spheres of influence. Across an "iron curtain," NATO countries faced the Warsaw Pact nations.

The Berlin Airlift, 1948 *German children watching an American plane in "Operation Vittles" bring food and supplies to their beleaguered city. The airlift kept a city of 2 million people alive for nearly a year and made West Berlin a symbol of the West's resolve to contain the spread of Soviet communism.*

to provide the blockaded city with a precarious lifeline. In May 1949, the Soviets ended the blockade. Stalin's gambit had failed. The airlift highlighted American determination and technological prowess, revealed Stalin's readiness to use innocent people as pawns, and dramatically heightened anti-Soviet feeling in the West. Continuing fears of a Soviet attack on Western Europe and public support for "firmness and increased 'toughness' in relations with Russia" then led Truman to push for a rearmed West German state and an Atlantic collective security alliance.

In May 1949, the United States, Britain, and France ended their occupation of Germany and approved the creation of the Federal Republic of Germany (West Germany). A month earlier, ten Western Europe nations had signed the North Atlantic Treaty, establishing a military alliance with the United States and Canada in which "an armed attack against one or more of them . . . shall be considered an attack against them all." After overwhelming Senate approval, the United States officially joined the **North Atlantic Treaty Organization (NATO)**, marking the formal end of America's long tradition of avoiding entangling alliances abroad.

Truman ranked the Marshall Plan and NATO as his proudest achievements, convinced that if the latter had been in existence in 1914 and 1939, the world would have been spared two disastrous wars. Accordingly, he spurred Congress to authorize the deployment of U.S. troops in Europe and $1.3 billion for military assistance to NATO nations. The Soviet Union responded by creating the German Democratic Republic (East Germany) in 1949, exploding its own atomic bomb that same year, and forming in 1955 an Eastern bloc military alliance—the Warsaw Pact (see Map 26.1). The United States and Soviet Union had divided Europe into two armed camps.

The Cold War in Asia   Moscow-Washington hostility also carved Asia into contending camps. The Russians created a sphere of influence in Manchuria, the Americans denied Moscow a role in postwar Japan, and both partitioned a helpless Korea.

As head of the U.S. occupation forces in Japan, General Douglas MacArthur oversaw that nation's transformation from an empire in ruins into a prosperous democracy. In 1952, the occupation ended, but a military security treaty allowed the U.S. to retain its Japanese bases and brought Japan under the American "nuclear umbrella." In further pursuit of containment, the United States helped crush a pro-communist insurgency in the Philippines and aided French efforts to reestablish colonial rule in Indochina (Vietnam, Laos, and Cambodia), despite American declarations in favor of national self-determination and against imperialism.

In China, however, U.S. efforts to block communism failed. The Truman administration first tried to mediate the civil war between the nationalist government of Jiang Jieshi and the communist forces of **Mao Zedong,** hoping to arrange a coalition government that would end the bloody conflict raging since the 1930s. It also sent nearly $3 billion in aid to the nationalists between 1945 and 1949. But American dollars could not prevent the surrender of Jiang's armies to Mao's forces or the collapse of the nationalists' corrupt regime, whose remnants fled to the island of Taiwan.

Mao's establishment of the communist People's Republic of China (PRC) shocked Americans. The most populous nation in the world, seen as a counterforce to communism and a market for American goods, had become "Red China." Although Truman blamed Jiang's defeat on his failure to reform China, most Americans were unconvinced. China's "fall" especially embittered conservatives who believed that America's interests lay in Asia, not Europe. Their pressure influenced the administration's refusal to recognize the PRC, block its admission to the United Nations, and proclaim Jiang's nationalist regime in Taiwan the legitimate government of China.

In September 1949, as the "Who lost China" debate raged, the president announced that the Soviet Union had exploded an atomic bomb. The loss of their nuclear monopoly shattered Americans' illusions of invincibility and increased their fear of communism.

Ordinary Americans sought safety in civil defense. Public schools held air-raid drills, teaching students to "duck and cover"—dive under their desks and shield their eyes against atomic blasts. "We took the drills seriously," recalled novelist Annie Dillard; "surely Pittsburgh, which had the nation's steel, coke, and aluminum, would be the enemy's first target." Four million Americans volunteered to be Sky Watchers, looking for Soviet planes. More than a million purchased or constructed their own family bomb shelters. Those who could not afford a bomb shelter were advised by the Federal Civil Defense Administration to "jump in any handy ditch or gutter . . . bury your face in your arms . . . never lose your head."

In January 1950, stung by charges that he was "soft on communism," Truman ordered the development of a fusion-based hydrogen bomb (H-bomb), a thousand times more destructive than an atomic bomb. In November 1952, the United States exploded its first H-bomb, completely vaporizing one of the Marshall Islands in the

Pacific, carving a mile-long, 175-foot-deep crater in the ocean floor, and spilling radioactive dust over thousands of square miles. "You would swear the whole world was on fire," a sailor wrote home. Nine months later, the Soviets detonated their own H-bomb. The balance of terror escalated.

So, too, did nuclear-generated environmental and health problems. Nuclear tests left minimally protected U.S. soldiers and South Pacific islanders exposed to radiation, and radioactive debris from atomic tests contaminated vast areas of Colorado, Utah, Nevada, and Washington. Although the AEC insisted the fallout was harmless, many people exposed to radiation, as well as unborn children, would pay the cost of an out of control arms race poisoning the atmosphere.

In April 1950, a committee appointed by the president issued a sweeping analysis of U.S. defense policy. **National Security Paper 68 (NSC-68)** emphasized the Soviet Union's aggressive intentions, territorial greed, and military strength. To counter the Soviets' "design for world domination," NSC-68 urged massive increases in America's nuclear arsenal, vigorous covert action by the CIA, and open-ended increases in the defense budget to resist Communist expansion anywhere and everywhere. Secretary of State Acheson characterized NSC-68 as "the fundamental paper" defining American foreign policy into the foreseeable future. The United States now approached the Cold War as a military confrontation. By the end of 1950, Congress had tripled the defense budget of the self-proclaimed "world policeman."

The Korean War, 1950–1953   After World War II, the United States and Soviet Union temporarily divided Korea, which had been controlled by Japan since the Russo-Japanese War of 1904, at the thirty-eighth parallel. This line then solidified into a de facto border between the Soviet-backed Democratic People's Republic of Korea in the north and the American-supported Republic of Korea, or South Korea, each claiming the sole right to rule all of Korea.

On June 25, 1950, North Korean troops swept across the thirty-eighth parallel to attack South Korea (see Map 26.2). Truman decided to fight back, viewing the assault as Stalin's test of U.S. will and containment policy. "Korea is the Greece of the Far East," Truman maintained. "If we are tough enough now, if we stand up to them like we did in Greece . . . they won't take any next steps." Mindful of the failure of appeasement at Munich in 1938, he believed the communists were doing in Korea exactly what Hitler and the Japanese had done in the 1930s: "Nobody had stood up to them. And that is what led to the Second World War." Having been accused of "selling out" Eastern Europe and "losing" China, Truman needed to prove he could stand up to "the Reds."

Without consulting Congress, Truman ordered air and naval forces to Korea from their bases in Japan on June 27. That same day, he asked the United Nations to authorize action to repel the invasion. Because the Soviets were boycotting the Security Council to protest the UN's unwillingness to seat Mao's China, and could not use their veto power, Truman gained approval for a UN "police action" to restore South Korea's border. He appointed General Douglas MacArthur to command the UN effort and ordered American ground troops into what now became the **Korean War**. The Cold War had turned hot.

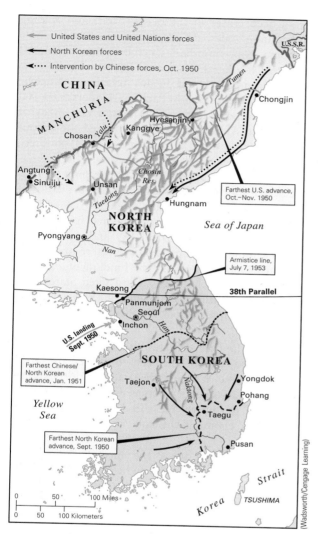

MAP 26.2 The Korean War, 1950–1953

The experience of fighting an undeclared war for the limited objective of containing communism confused the generation of Americans who had just fought an all-out war for the total defeat of the Axis. General MacArthur spoke for the many who were frustrated by the Korean conflict's mounting costs in blood and dollars: "There is no substitute for victory."

North Korean forces initially routed the outnumbered American and South Korean troops. Then, in mid-September, with UN forces cornered on the southeastern tip of the Korean peninsula, struggling to avoid being pushed into the sea, MacArthur executed a brilliant amphibious maneuver, landing his troops at Inchon, 150 miles behind North Korean lines. Within two weeks, UN forces drove the North Koreans back across the thirty-eighth parallel. Basking in victory,

MacArthur persuaded Truman to let him go beyond the UN mandate to repel aggression and to cross the border to liberate all of Korea from communism.

As UN troops approached the Yalu River—the boundary between Korea and China—the Chinese warned that they would not "sit back with folded hands and let the Americans come to the border." Dismissing the threat as "hot air," MacArthur deployed his forces in a thin line below the river. On November 25, thirty-three Chinese divisions (about 300,000 men) counterattacked, driving MacArthur's forces back below the thirty-eighth parallel in what *Time* magazine called "the worst military setback the United States has ever suffered." By March 1951, the fighting had deadlocked at roughly the original dividing line between the two Koreas. "We were eyeball to eyeball," recalled Bev Scott, one of the first black lieutenants to head a racially integrated infantry squad.

> *Just 20 meters of no man's land between us. We couldn't move at all in the daytime without getting shot at. . . . It was like World War I. We lived in a maze of bunkers and deep trenches. . . . There were bodies strewn all over the place. Hundreds of bodies frozen in the snow. We could see the arms and legs sticking up. Nobody could get their dead out of there.*

Stalemated, Truman reversed course and sought a negotiated peace based on the original objective of restoring the integrity of South Korea. MacArthur rocked the boat, however, urging that he be allowed to seek total victory even at the risk of an all-out war with China. Truman refused: "We are trying to prevent a world war—not to start one." He sought a limited war for a limited objective: to hold the line in Korea. But MacArthur would not accept a stalemate. When he bluntly and repeatedly criticized Truman's limited war—the "appeasement of Communism"—the president fired the general to protect civilian control of the military. Public opinion, however, backed the general. To Americans accustomed to unconditional victory, the very idea of limited war was baffling. Mounting casualties for no apparent purpose at places named Heartbreak Ridge or Pork Chop Hill added anger to the mix. Despite warnings from the chairman of the Joint Chiefs of Staff that MacArthur's proposals would result in "the wrong war at the wrong place in the wrong time and with the wrong enemy," a growing number of Americans agreed with MacArthur that "There is no substitute for victory," and listened sympathetically to Republican charges that communist agents controlled American policy.

Truman, meanwhile, found himself bogged down in Korea, unable to win a victory or craft a peace. After two more years of fighting, the two sides reached an armistice in July 1953 that left Korea divided. The "limited" conflict cost the United States 54,246 lives (about 33,700 of them battlefield deaths), another 103,284 wounded, and some $54 billion. The Chinese lost 900,000 men, and the two Korean armies lost 800,000. As in World War II, massive U.S. "carpet bombing" killed at least a million civilians and left North Korea looking like a moonscape.

The Korean War had major consequences. It accelerated implementation of NSC-68 and the expansion of the containment doctrine into a global commitment. From 1950 to 1953, defense spending zoomed from $13 billion to $60 billion—from one-third to two-thirds of the entire federal budget—the U.S. army grew from half a million men to 3.6 million, and the American atomic stockpile mushroomed from 150 to 750 nuclear warheads. The United States acquired new bases

(© Bettmann/Corbis)

A Racially Integrated Unit in the Korean War *The Korean War was the first war in U.S. history in which most soldiers fought in racially integrated units. President Truman ordered the integration of the armed forces in 1948, despite the opposition of many military officers, and the successful performance of African-Americans in Korea accelerated acceptance of military integration.*

around the world, committed itself to rearm West Germany, and joined a mutual-defense pact with Australia and New Zealand. Increased military aid flowed to Jiang Jieshi on Taiwan and to France's fight against communist insurgents in Indochina.

Truman's intervention in Korea preserved a precarious balance of power in Asia and stepped up the administration's commitment to the anticommunist struggle. Containment, originally advanced to justify U.S. aid to Greece and Turkey, had become the ideological foundation for a major war in Korea and, ominously, for a deepening U.S. involvement in Vietnam. Truman's actions enhanced the powers of an already powerful presidency and set a precedent for future undeclared wars. They also augmented an economic boom, intensified the second Red Scare, and fostered Cold War attitudes that lasted long after the war ended.

THE TRUMAN ADMINISTRATION AT HOME, 1945–1952

The Cold War profoundly changed the United States for better and for worse. It weakened the nation's commitment to civil liberties while propelling research in medicine and science that, for the most part, made lives longer and better. It spurred more than a quarter of a century of economic growth and prosperity, the longest such period in American history. That, along with a vast expansion of higher education, enabled many Americans to become middle class, diminishing support for federal regulation of business and the expansion of the welfare state.

The Cold War context, vastly different than the context in which FDR operated, largely determined the domestic record of Truman as well as of Presidents Dwight Eisenhower and John Kennedy.

TRUMAN'S DOMESTIC PROGRAM

Americans' hunger for the fruits of affluence left them with little appetite for extending the New Deal. Truman agreed. "I don't want any experiments," he confided. "The American people have been through a lot of experiments and they want a rest." His only major domestic accomplishment in the Seventy-ninth Congress was the **Employment Act of 1946.** It committed the federal government to ensuring economic growth and established the Council of Economic Advisers to confer with the president and formulate policies for maintaining employment, production, and purchasing power. Congress, however, gutted both the goal of full employment and the enhanced executive powers to achieve that objective.

Congressional eagerness to dismantle wartime controls worsened the nation's chief economic problem: inflation. Consumer demand outran the supply of goods, intensifying the pressure on prices. The Office of Price Administration (OPA) sought to hold the line by enforcing price controls, but food producers, manufacturers, and retailers opposed continuing wartime controls. While some consumers favored the OPA, others deplored it as an irksome relic of wartime regulations. In June 1946, Truman vetoed a bill that would have extended the OPA's life, but deprived it of power, effectively ending all price controls. Consequently, food costs rose 16 percent within a week and the price of beef doubled. "PRICES SOAR, BUYERS SORE, STEERS JUMP OVER THE MOON," headlined the *New York Daily News*.

Congress then passed, and Truman signed, a second bill extending price controls in weakened form. Protesting any price controls, however, farmers and meat producers threatened to withhold food from the market. Knowing that "meatless voters are opposition voters," Truman lifted controls on food prices just before the 1946 midterm elections. When Democrats fared poorly anyway, Truman ended all price controls. By then, the consumer price index had jumped nearly 25 percent since the end of the war.

Sharp price rises and shrinking paychecks shorn of overtime goaded organized labor to demand higher wages. More than 4.5 million workers went on strike in 1946. When a United Mine Workers walkout paralyzed the economy for forty days, Truman ordered the army to seize the mines. A week later, after Truman had pressured owners to grant most of the union's demands, the miners returned to work, only to walk out again six months later. Meanwhile, on the heels of the first mine workers settlement, railway engineers and trainmen announced they would shut down the nation's railroad system for the first time in history. "If you think I'm going to sit here and let you tie up this whole country," Truman shouted at the heads of the two unions, "you're crazy as hell." In May, he asked Congress for authority to draft workers who struck vital industries. Before he could finish his speech, the unions gave in. Still, Truman's threat alienated labor leaders.

By the fall of 1946, Truman had angered most major interest groups. Less than a third of Americans polled approved of his performance. "To err is Truman," some gibed. Summing up the public discontent, Republicans asked, "Had enough?" In the 1946 elections, they captured twenty-five governorships and, for the first time since 1928, won control of both houses of Congress.

The public mood reflected more than just economic discontent. Under the surface, laughter at stores advertising atomic sales or bartenders mixing atomic cocktails ran a new, deep current of fear, symbolized by the rash of "flying saucer" sightings that had begun after the war. An NBC radio program depicted a nuclear attack on Chicago in which most people died instantly. "Those few who escaped the blast, but not the gamma rays, died slowly after they had left the ruined city," intoned the narrator. "No attempt at identification of the bodies or burial ever took place. Chicago was simply closed." There was much talk of urban dispersal—resettling people in small communities in the country's vast open spaces—and of how to protect oneself in a nuclear attack. The end of World War II had brought an uneasy peace.

The Eightieth Congress, 1947–1948   Many Republicans in the Eightieth Congress interpreted the 1946 elections as a mandate to reverse the New Deal. As "Mr. Republican," Senator Robert A. Taft of Ohio, declared, "We have got to break with the corrupting idea that we can legislate prosperity, legislate equality, legislate opportunity." Congress defeated Democratic bills to raise the minimum wage and to provide federal funds for education and housing and, capitalizing on the national consensus for curbing labor union power generated by the waves of postwar strikes, passed the **Taft-Hartley Act** in 1947. Officially the Labor-Management Relations Act, it barred the closed shop—a workplace where all employees had to join the union; outlawed secondary boycotts—strikes against suppliers of a targeted business; required union officials to sign anticommunist loyalty oaths; and permitted the president to call a cooling-off period to delay strikes that might endanger national safety or health. The act weakened organizing drives in the nonunion South and West, hastening the relocation of labor-intensive industries, such as textiles, from the Northeast and Midwest to the Sunbelt, and it drove leftist leaders out of the CIO, weakening organized labor as a force for social justice.

Truman vetoed the bill, and Congress easily overrode the veto. Yet Truman had taken a major step in regaining organized labor's political support and reforging FDR's New Deal coalition. Now an unabashed liberal, Truman urged Congress to repeal Taft-Hartley and to provide federal aid to education and housing, national health insurance, and high farm-price supports. To woo ethnic voters of Eastern European descent, Truman railed against Soviet communism; and to court Jewish-American voters, as well as express his deep sympathy toward Holocaust survivors, he overrode the objections of the State Department, which feared alienating the oil-rich Arab world, and extended diplomatic recognition to the new state of Israel within hours of its establishment in May 1948.

Still, Truman's chances for victory dimmed as southern segregationists, alarmed by the president's support for civil rights, bolted the Democrats and nominated Governor Strom Thurmond of South Carolina as the candidate of the States' Rights ("Dixiecrat") party, a significant step toward the eventual breakup of the

Democratic political coalition of southern conservatives and northern liberals. Further diminishing Truman's chances, leftwing Democrats joined with communists to launch a new Progressive Party headed by former vice president Henry A. Wallace. To capitalize on Democratic divisions, Republicans played it safe, nominating the moderate governor of New York, Thomas E. Dewey, for president, and of California, Earl Warren for vice president. Confident of victory, Dewey ran a complacent campaign designed to offend the fewest people. Truman, in contrast, campaigned aggressively, blasting the "no-good, do-nothing" Republicans as "gluttons of privilege." Pollsters applauded Truman's spunk but predicted a Dewey victory.

Instead, the president won the biggest electoral upset in U.S. history. The Progressives and Dixiecrats, ironically, helped Truman. Their radicalism kept most moderates safely in the Democratic fold. Most importantly, Truman succeeded as the defender of the New Deal against the party of Herbert Hoover and the depression. Accordingly, the Roosevelt coalition—organized labor, farmers, urban ethnics, blacks, and most white southerners—held together one more time.

The Fair Deal   Despite his slim victory, Truman proposed a vast liberal agenda—the **Fair Deal**—that included civil rights, national health-care legislation, and federal aid to education. Unlike New Deal liberalism, the Fair Deal counted on continual economic growth. An expanding economic pie would mean a bigger piece for most Americans (so they would not resent helping those left behind) and more tax revenue for the government (so it would have the funds to pay for more social-welfare programs).

Despite prosperity, the bipartisan conservative coalition of northern Republicans and southern Democrats, which had largely controlled Congress since 1938, rejected the Fair Deal. While extending some existing programs, such as the minimum wage and Social Security, and authorizing the construction of 800,000 units of low-income housing, Congress would go no further. Special interest groups, such as the American Medical Association and the National Association of Manufacturers, lobbied extensively against what they called "creeping socialism," and prosperity sapped public enthusiasm for liberal initiatives. By 1950, Truman was once again subordinating domestic issues to foreign policy.

THE POLITICS OF ANTICOMMUNISM

As the Cold War worsened, some Americans concluded that the roots of the nation's difficulties abroad lay in domestic treason and subversion. How else could the communists have taken China and built an atomic bomb? Millions of fearful Americans enlisted in a crusade that equated dissent with disloyalty and blamed scapegoats for the nation's problems.

Similar intolerance had prevailed in the Red Scare of 1919–1920 (see Chapter 22), but the Second Red Scare lasted longer, affected more people, and had greater consequences. It took root in the creation of the House Committee on Un-American Activities—later called the House Un-American Activities Committee (HUAC)—in 1938 to ferret out Fascists, but it quickly became a platform for right-wing denunciations of the New Deal as a communist plot. After World War II, mounting numbers of conservative Democrats and Republicans found it popular to climb aboard the anti-Red bandwagon.

The **Second Red Scare** influenced both governmental and personal actions. Millions of Americans were subjected to security investigations and loyalty oaths. Anticommunist extremism destroyed the Left, undermined labor militancy, and discredited liberalism. It spawned a "silent generation" of college students and ensured anticommunist foreign-policy rigidity.

Loyalty and Security   The U.S. Communist Party had claimed eighty thousand members during the Second World War, and no one knew how many of its members or sympathizers occupied sensitive government positions. In mid-1945, a raid on the offices of a procommunist magazine revealed that classified documents had been stolen from government offices. Ten months later, the Canadian government exposed a major spy network that had passed American atomic secrets to the Soviets during the war. Republicans accused the Democratic administration of being "soft on communism."

A week after his Truman Doctrine speech of March 1947, the president issued Executive Order 9835 establishing the Federal Employee Loyalty Program to root out subversives in the government. It authorized the Attorney General to prepare a list of "subversive" organizations and made association with such groups grounds for dismissal. The drive for security overran civil liberties, as those suspected could neither face their accusers nor require investigators to reveal sources.

Mere criticism of American foreign policy could result in an accusation of disloyalty. People lost jobs because they liked foreign films, associated with radical friends, or favored the unionization of federal workers. "Of course the fact that a person believes in racial equality doesn't prove he's a communist," mused an Interior Department Loyalty Board chairman, "but it certainly makes you look twice, doesn't it?" Of the 4.7 million jobholders and applicants who underwent loyalty checks by 1952, 560 were fired or denied jobs, and several thousand resigned or withdrew their applications. Although Loyalty Board probes uncovered no evidence of espionage or subversion, it spread fear among government employees. "If communists like apple pie and I do," claimed one federal worker, "I see no reason why I should stop eating it. But I would."

The Anticommunist Crusade   The very existence of a federal loyalty probe fed fears of domestic subversion. It promoted hysteria about communist infiltrators and legitimated a witch-hunt for subversives. College administrators cooperated with the FBI in spying on students and faculty, universities banned controversial speakers, and popular magazines featured articles like "Reds Are After Your Child." By the end of Truman's term, thirty-nine states had created loyalty programs. Few had any procedural safeguards. Schoolteachers, college professors, and state and city employees throughout the nation had to sign loyalty oaths or lose their jobs. No one knows for sure how many were dismissed, denied tenure, or drifted away, leaving behind colleagues too frightened to speak out.

In 1947, blurring distinctions between dissent and disloyalty, between radicalism and subversion, the **House Un-American Activities Committee** (HUAC) held widely publicized hearings to expose communist infiltration of Hollywood. When some prominent film directors and screenwriters, dubbed the Hollywood Ten, refused to testify about past political associations, claiming the free-speech protections of the First Amendment, HUAC had them cited for contempt of Congress and sent to federal prison. Despite HUAC's failure to prove that Hollywood had produced "flagrant communist propaganda films," blacklists in the motion picture industry and in radio broadcasting quickly followed. They barred the employment of those with a questionable past or those who had associated, however remotely, with others deemed "subversive" or "un-American" (see Going to the Source). They silenced many talented people, and prompted the entertainment media either to shun controversial issues or to tilt politically to the right.

HUAC also frightened the labor movement into expelling communists and avoiding progressive causes. Fearful of appearing "red," or even "pink," most unions shunned politics to focus on securing better pay and benefits for their members.

The 1948 presidential election campaign also fed national anxieties. Truman lambasted Wallace as a Stalinist dupe and the GOP dubbed the Democrats "the party of treason." To blunt such accusations, Truman's Justice Department prosecuted eleven top leaders of the American Communist Party under the Smith Act of 1940, which outlawed any conspiracy advocating the overthrow of the government. The Supreme Court upheld the Smith Act's constitutionality (*Dennis v. United States*, 1951), declaring that Congress could curtail freedom of speech if national security required such restriction. Ironically, the Communist Party was fading into obscurity at the very time politicians magnified its threat. By 1950, its membership had shrunk to fewer than thirty thousand.

McCarthyism

Nothing set off more alarms of a diabolic Red conspiracy than the matter of **Alger Hiss and Whittaker Chambers,** discussed at the beginning of this chapter. That an eminent official such as Hiss had been disloyal intensified the widespread fears of a communist underground in the government. Then, a month after Hiss's perjury conviction, another spy case shocked Americans. In February 1950, the British arrested Klaus Fuchs, a German-born scientist involved in the Manhattan Project, for passing atomic secrets to the Soviets in 1944–1945. His confession led to the arrest of an American who then named his brother-in-law and sister, **Julius and Ethel Rosenberg,** as co-conspirators in the wartime spy network. The Rosenbergs insisted they were victims of anti-Semitism being prosecuted for their leftist beliefs. But in March 1951, a jury found them guilty of conspiring to commit espionage, and in June 1953 they each died in the electric chair—the first American civilians to lose their lives for espionage.

The release of classified documents in the 1990s, from the archives of the former Soviet Union, confirm that Hiss did pass secret information to the Soviets and that Julius Rosenberg, who described himself as a "soldier of Stalin," was part of a spy ring that gave the USSR data on America's atomic bomb project. Ethel Rosenberg, however, appears to have been merely, "a lever" to pressure Julius into naming other spies.

By 1950, when few Americans could separate fact from fantasy regarding the communist threat, the spy cases tarnished liberalism and fueled other loyalty

GOING TO THE SOURCE

Remembering the Hollywood Blacklist

In 1947, attorney Bartley Crum helped represent the Hollywood Ten before HUAC. In 1997, Crum's daughter, Patricia Bosworth, wrote to the *New York Times* about her memories of the subsequent blacklist and its effects on the people involved. Bosworth emphasizes the chilling hardships that HUAC's assault on civil liberties brought down on individuals.

I first learned about the Hollywood blacklist on Nov. 24, 1947. I remember the exact moment. I was standing with my father, Bartley Crum, by a phone booth near Union Square in San Francisco, feeding him nickels and dimes while he made a series of intense phone calls to Dore Schary, who was the head of MGM.

If you're wondering why he had to make calls from a pay phone, it's because our house was bugged by the F.B.I. At that point I was too young to quite grasp the bugged calls, but I did know that my father had been one of six lawyers who had just defended the "Hollywood 10" in front of the House Un-American Activities Committee (HUAC) in Washington.

These were the writers, directors, and producers who had been subpoenaed to testify about their political beliefs. But they stood on their First Amendment rights and refused to reveal whether they were Communists. After the hearings, in October, the Hollywood 10 were indicted for contempt, sent to jail, and "blacklisted" from working in Hollywood.

On that foggy afternoon in San Francisco so long ago, my father stopped making phone calls and turned to me to try to explain why the Hollywood 10 would have to be sacrificed to appease HUAC. It was the start of the Red Scare and America's paranoia about Russia and Communism.

Today, almost nobody I know has anything but the vaguest memories of the Hollywood blacklist. Nobody remembers that HUAC continued its investigations into the film community well into 1956 and that hundreds of witnesses were called to testify and to inform on colleagues to prove their loyalty and their patriotism.

Back in the 50s, there wasn't any talk of selling out when blacklisted writers, just out of jail, huddled in our living room.

investigations. Only a conspiracy, it seemed, could explain U.S. setbacks. Frustrated by unexpected failure in the 1948 election, Republicans eagerly exploited the fearful mood and accused the "Commiecrats" of selling out America.

In February 1950, Republican senator **Joseph R. McCarthy** of Wisconsin, desperate for an issue on which to run for reelection in 1952, and parroting a speech given by Richard Nixon, boldly told a West Virginia audience that "the bright young men who were born with silver spoons in their mouths" had betrayed America. McCarthy was referring to the State Department. "I have in my hand 205 cases of individuals," he asserted as he waved a laundry list, "who would appear to be either card carrying members or certainly loyal to the Communist Party, but who nevertheless are still helping to shape our foreign policy." McCarthy subsequently lowered his number to 57, then to 10, and then to one "policy risk." McCarthy never released any names or proof. A Senate committee found McCarthy's accusations "a fraud and a hoax," but he persisted, making so many accusations that the facts could never catch

Instead, my father's conversations with them focused on the meaning of loyalty and questions about censorship and how one could survive in the writers' black market. All the best writers had been blacklisted, and everyone was writing under pseudonyms and being paid in cash; it was hard to open a bank account, impossible to get life insurance. Nobody had enough money. Everyone was being hounded by the F.B.I.

My father was being hounded too. Because he had defended the Hollywood 10 and taken on numerous loyalty cases as well, he was labeled subversive. He was followed relentlessly by the F.B.I., and our phones remained tapped. My father was even put on the F.B.I. security index, which meant that in the event of an "emergency" he would be put in a concentration camp. He lost most of his clients. Close to bankruptcy and in despair, my father informed on two colleagues already known to be Communists. In 1959, he committed suicide.

The cold war lasted until 1991. During much of the time between the 1950's and then HUAC was still active in various forms. Many movie executives were afraid to stand up for anything, least of all blacklisted writers. And nobody wanted to seem soft on Communism.

Today there are still threats to our freedom of expression, many of them the work of self-appointed guardians of decency. We can put them in historical context by remembering the blacklist of the 1950's.

Questions

1. *What were some of the consequences of defying the House Un-American Activities Committee?*

2. *In what ways does the postwar assault on domestic radicalism shed light on developments in American life today? How is it similar? How does it differ?*

Go to www.cengagebrain.com for additional primary sources on this period.

Source: Patricia Bosworth's books include biographies of Marlon Brando and the photographer Diane Arbus as well as the memoir "Anything Your Little Heart Desires—An American Family Story." It's the story of her father Bartley Crum, but it's also a cultural history of the 40s and 50s about the fall of liberalism and the dawn of the Cold War and the political turmoil that ensued, which created an environment of anti-communist hysteria that ruined many lives full of promise. This letter first appeared in the *New York Times*, April 20, 1997. Copyright © 1997 by Patricia Bosworth. Reprinted with permission.

up. "McCarthyism" became a synonym for personal attacks on individuals by means of indiscriminate allegations and unsubstantiated charges.

As the Korean War dragged on, McCarthy's efforts to "root out the skunks" escalated. He ridiculed Secretary of State Dean Acheson as the "Red Dean" and charged George Marshall with having "aided and abetted a communist conspiracy so immense as to dwarf any previous such venture in the history of man." McCarthyism especially appealed to midwestern Republicans opposed to Democratic internationalism and restrictions on business. For many in the American Legion and the Chambers of Commerce, anticommunism was a weapon of revenge against liberals—a means to regain the dominance that conservatism formerly held in American life. McCarthy also won a devoted following among blue-collar workers who felt that all true Americans detested "communists and queers" and among Catholic ethnics, who sought acceptance as "100 percent Americans" through a show of anticommunist zeal. Countless

Americans also shared McCarthy's scorn for State Department liberals as the "bright young men who are born with silver spoons in their mouths." And McCarthy's conspiracy theory offered a simple answer to the perplexing questions of the Cold War: the fault is in Washington.

McCarthy's political power rested on both the Republican establishment and Democratic fears of antagonizing him. In the 1950 elections, when he helped Republicans defeat Democrats who had denounced him, McCarthy appeared invincible. Few dared incur his wrath.

Over Truman's veto, Congress in 1950 adopted the **McCarran Internal Security Act,** which required organizations deemed communist by the attorney general to register with the Department of Justice. It also authorized the arrest and detention during a national emergency of "any person as to whom there is reason to believe might engage in acts of espionage or sabotage." In addition, the McCarran-Walter Immigration and Nationality Act of 1952, also adopted over Truman's veto, maintained the quota system that severely restricted immigration from southern and eastern Europe and from Asia, but did end the ban on Japanese immigration and made Issei eligible for naturalized citizenship. In the name of national security, moreover, the law increased the attorney general's authority to exclude or deport "undesirable" aliens, particularly those suspected of homosexuality or supporting communism.

The Election of 1952

In 1952, public apprehension about the loyalty of government employees combined with frustration over the Korean stalemate to sink Democratic hopes to their lowest level since the 1920s. Truman's approval rating plummeted to 23 percent, the lowest ever recorded by a president. Popular resentment of Truman's handling of the Korean War and revelations of bribery by his political associates gave the GOP ammunition for charging the Democrats with "plunder at home, and blunder abroad" and for campaigning on the "K1 C2" slogan—"Korea, Communism, and Corruption."

With Truman too unpopular to run for reelection, dispirited Democrats drafted Governor Adlai Stevenson of Illinois and, to appease southern white voters, nominated segregationist Senator John A. Sparkman of Alabama for vice president But Stevenson could not dissociate himself from Truman, and his lofty speeches appealed primarily to intellectuals, not the average voter. Above all, Stevenson could not overcome the sentiment that twenty years of Democratic rule was enough.

Compounding Democratic woes, the GOP nominated the hugely popular war hero **Dwight D. Eisenhower.** Essentially apolitical, he answered the call of the moderate wing of the Republican Party in 1952 and accepted the nomination. As a concession to the hard-line anticommunists in the party, "Ike" chose as his running mate Richard Nixon, who had won a seat in the Senate in 1950 by red-baiting his opponent, Helen Gahagan Douglas, as "pink right down to her underwear."

Eisenhower and Nixon proved unbeatable. With a captivating grin and an unimpeachable record of public service, Eisenhower projected both personal warmth and the vigorous authority associated with military command. At the same time, Nixon kept public apprehensions at the boiling point. Accusing the

Democrats of treason, he charged that the election of "Adlai the appeaser . . . who got a Ph.D. from Dean Acheson's College of Cowardly Communist Containment" would bring "more Alger Hisses, more atomic spies."

Less than two weeks before the election, Eisenhower dramatically pledged to "go to Korea" to end the stalemated war. It worked: 62.7 percent of those eligible to vote (compared to just 51.5 percent in 1948) turned out in 1952 and gave the Republican ticket 55 percent of the ballots. Ike cracked the Solid South, carrying thirty-nine states (and 442 electoral votes). Enough Republicans rode his coattails to give the GOP narrow control of both houses of Congress.

The Downfall of Joseph McCarthy   Although he despised Joseph McCarthy, Eisenhower thought it beneath his dignity to "get into the gutter with that guy." He also understood the usefulness of anticommunism as a GOP campaign issue. In 1953, 185 of the 221 House Republicans sought a seat on HUAC. So Ike allowed McCarthy to grab plenty of rope in hopes that the demagogue would hang himself. He did.

In 1954, McCarthy accused Army officials of harboring communist spies and trying to blackmail his investigating committee. The resulting Army-McCarthy hearings—the first Senate hearings broadcast nationally on the new medium of television—brought McCarthy down. For more than a month, millions witnessed McCarthy's boorish behavior on television. His contemptuous combativeness repelled viewers. He behaved like the bad guy in a TV western, observed novelist John Steinbeck: "He had a stubble of a beard, he leered, he sneered, he had a nasty laugh. He bullied and shouted. He looked evil." When the hearings ended in June, the spell of the inquisitor had been broken. That December, the Senate voted 67 to 22 to censure McCarthy for contemptuous behavior. This powerful rebuke demolished McCarthy as a political force. In 1957, he died from an alcohol-related illness, ignored by the media that had made him powerful. He had uncovered no communists, but had ruined careers and made the United States look pitifully fearful to the rest of the world. Still, the paranoia he exploited lingered. Congress annually funded HUAC into the 1960s, and state and local governments continued to require loyalty oaths from teachers. Accusations of communism remained a useful charge to hurl at one's opponents. To protect themselves, individuals and organizations continued to avoid any hint of radicalism. Just to be safe, the Cincinnati Reds renamed their baseball team the "Redlegs."

McCarthyism also remained a rallying call of conservatives disenchanted with the postwar consensus. Young conservatives like William F. Buckley, Jr., and groups like the Christian Anti-Communist Crusade, continued to claim that domestic communism was a major subversive threat. The John Birch Society denounced Eisenhower as a conscious agent of communism and equated liberalism with treason. Although few saw the conspiratorial dangers that the John Birch Society did, Barry Goldwater, George Wallace, and Ronald Reagan, among others, would later use its anticommunist, antigovernment rhetoric to advantage. Stressing victory over communism, rather than its containment, the self-proclaimed "new conservatives" (or radical Right, as their opponents called them) criticized the "creeping socialism" of Eisenhower, advocated a return to traditional moral standards, and condemned the liberal rulings of the Supreme Court.

Joseph McCarthy, The Terror of Washington *Although McCarthy never produced any credible evidence to support his charges, his reckless anticommunist demagoguery pinned the Democrats with being responsible for "twenty years of treason," and made suspect any politician, group, or cause that could be described as "leftist."*

"Modern Republicanism" Most Americans in the 1950s did not venture that far right. They voted for a president who would steer a moderate course and got what they wanted. Rarely in history has a president better fit the national mood than "Ike." Exhausted by a quarter-century of upheaval, Americans craved stability and peace. And Eisenhower, projecting the image of a plain but good man, delivered. He gave a people weary of partisanship a sense of unity; he set a quieter, less angry national mood, a moderate tone between conservatism and liberalism; he inspired confidence and comforted people in an anxious, demanding age.

Born on October 14, 1890, in Denison, Texas, Eisenhower grew up in Abilene, Kansas, in a poor, religious family. More athletic than studious, he graduated from the U.S. Military Academy at West Point in 1915. In directing the Allied invasion of North Africa in 1942 and of western Europe in 1944, he revealed himself to be a brilliant war planner and an efficient, diplomatic executive. His approach to the presidency reflected his wartime leadership style. He concentrated on major matters, delegated authority, and worked to reconcile contending factions. His restrained view of presidential authority and his low-key style, combined with frequent fishing and golfing vacations, led Democrats to scoff at Eisenhower as a leader who "reigned but did not rule."

The image of passivity, however, masked a "hidden-hand" presidency that enabled him to work successfully behind the scenes. More pragmatic than ideological, the president wished to reduce taxes, contain inflation, and when necessary, check downturns by stimulating the economy. After the Democrats retook Congress in 1954, Eisenhower supported extending social-security benefits, raising the minimum wage, adding 4 million workers to those eligible for unemployment benefits, and providing federally financed public housing for low-income families. He also approved construction of the St. Lawrence Seaway, linking the Great Lakes and the Atlantic Ocean, and creation of the Department of Health, Education, and Welfare. In 1956, Eisenhower backed the largest and most expensive public-works program in American history: the Interstate Highway Act, authorizing construction of a 41,000-mile system of expressways that would soon snake across America, accelerating suburban growth, heightening dependence on imported oil, and contributing to urban decay and air pollution.

Republicans renominated Ike by acclamation in 1956, and voters gave him a landslide victory over Democrat Adlai Stevenson. With the GOP crowing, "Everything's booming but the guns," the president won by the greatest popular majority since FDR's victory in 1936.

The Cold War Continues

Eisenhower essentially maintained Truman's containment policy. Stalin's death in 1953 and Eisenhower's veiled threat to use nuclear weapons broke the Korean stalemate. The armistice signed in July 1953 set the boundary between North and South Korea once again at the thirty-eighth parallel. Some Americans claimed that communist aggression had been thwarted and containment vindicated; others condemned the truce as peace without honor.

Ike and Dulles   Eager to ease Cold War hostilities, Eisenhower first had to quiet the GOP right wing's clamor to roll back the Red tide. To do so, he chose as his secretary of state **John Foster Dulles,** a rigid, humorless Presbyterian who advocated a holy war against "atheistic communism," including "instant, massive retaliation" with nuclear weapons. Dulles called for "liberation" of the captive peoples of Eastern Europe and for unleashing Jiang Jieshi against communist China. Believing that the Soviet Union understood only force, Dulles insisted on the necessity of "brinksmanship," the art of never backing down in a crisis—even at the risk of war.

Such saber rattling pleased the Right, but Eisenhower preferred conciliation, partly to keep the cost of containment at a manageable level and partly because the Soviet Union had tested its own hydrogen bomb in 1953. Eisenhower refused to translate Dulles's rhetoric into action. The United States did nothing to check the Soviet interventions that crushed uprisings in East Germany (1953) and Hungary (1956). There would be no rolling back Red power in Eastern Europe.

As multimegaton thermonuclear weapons replaced atomic bombs in U.S. and Soviet arsenals, and both nations developed intercontinental ballistic missiles (ICBMs) to deliver such bombs, Eisenhower worked to reduce the probability of mutual annihilation. He proposed "atoms for peace," whereby both superpowers would contribute fissionable materials to a new UN agency for use in industrial projects. In the absence of a positive Soviet response, the government constructed an electronic air defense system to provide early warning of a missile attack.

Work also began on commercial nuclear plants in the mid-1950s, promising electricity "too cheap to meter." However, most money continued to go for nuclear research that was military. Radioactive fallout from atomic tests, especially the 1954 U.S. tests that spread strontium 90 over a wide area, heightened world concern about the nuclear-arms race. In 1955, Eisenhower and Soviet leaders met in Geneva for the first East-West conference since World War II. Discussions produced no concrete plan for arms control, but mutual talk of "peaceful coexistence" led reporters to hail the "spirit of Geneva." In March 1958, Moscow suspended atmospheric tests of nuclear weapons, and the United States followed suit.

But the Cold War continued. Dulles negotiated mutual-defense pacts with forty-three nations, and created SEATO in 1954, extending collective security agreements between the United States and Australia, New Zealand, Pakistan, the Philippines, and Thailand. Rather than trying to match the communists "man for man, gun for gun," Eisenhower's "New Look" defense program reduced conventional forces and emphasized nuclear weapons. Promising "more bang for the buck," it succeeded in reducing the defense budget yet spurred the Soviets to seek "more rubble for the ruble" by enlarging their nuclear stockpile.

Meanwhile, the focus of the Cold War shifted from Europe to the Third World, the largely nonwhite developing nations. There, the two superpowers waged war by proxy, using local guerrillas and military juntas to do their fighting for them. There, too, the CIA fought covert wars against those thought to imperil American interests.

CIA Covert Actions   Established in 1947 to conduct foreign intelligence gathering, the CIA soon began to carry out undercover operations to topple regimes friendly to communism. By 1957, half its personnel and 80 percent of its budget were devoted to "covert action." To woo influential foreign thinkers away from communism, the CIA also sponsored intellectual conferences and jazz concerts. It bankrolled anticommunist cultural events, subsidized magazines to publish articles supporting the United States, and recruited college students and businessmen traveling abroad as "fronts" in clandestine CIA activities.

In 1953, the CIA orchestrated a coup to overthrow the government of Iran. Fearing that the prime minister, who had nationalized the oil fields, might open oil-rich Iran to the Soviets, the CIA replaced him with the pro-American Shah Reza Pahlavi. The United States gained a loyal ally on the Soviet border, and Western oil companies prospered when the Shah made low-priced oil available to them. But Iranian hatred of America took root—a hostility that would haunt the United States into the twenty-first century.

The CIA also intervened in Philippine elections in 1953 to ensure a pro-American government. The following year, a CIA-supported band of mercenaries in Guatemala overthrew the elected communist-influenced regime, which had seized land from the American-owned United Fruit Company. The new pro-American government restored United Fruit's properties and trampled political opposition. "Our traditional ideas of international sportsmanship," Eisenhower noted privately in 1955, "are scarcely applicable in the morass in which the world now flounders."

Troubles in the Third World   Eisenhower first followed Truman's course of aiding France in its battle with Indochinese insurgents. When that failed, he pinned his hopes on the CIA-installed President Ngo Dinh Diem to keep South Vietnam an independent anticommunist nation tied to the United States. That policy, too, appeared to be faltering as he left office (to be further discussed in Chapter 28). He faced his greatest crisis, however, in the Middle East. In 1954, Gamal Abdel Nasser came to power in Egypt, determined to modernize his nation. To woo him, the United States offered financing for a dam at Aswan to harness the Nile River. But when Nasser purchased arms from Czechoslovakia, John Foster Dulles canceled the loan, and Nasser nationalized the British-controlled Suez Canal.

Viewing the canal as the lifeline of its empire, Britain, in alliance with France, which feared Arab nationalism in their Algerian colony, and with Israel, which feared the Egyptian arms buildup, attacked Egypt to retake the canal in October. Angered that America's three closest allies had not consulted him, and fearful that such military action would drive the Arab world and its precious oil to the Russians, Eisenhower forced his allies to withdraw their troops. Given gas-hungry Americans' need to avoid alienating the Arab world, the United States did nothing as Egypt retook the Suez Canal and built the Aswan Dam with Soviet support.

The **Suez crisis** had major consequences. It swelled Third World antiwestern sentiment, and the United States replaced Britain and France as the protector of western interests in the Middle East. Determined to guarantee the flow of oil to the West from Iran, Iraq, Kuwait, and Saudi Arabia, which had some 60 percent of the world's known reserves, the president announced the **Eisenhower Doctrine** in 1957—a proclamation that the United States would send military aid and, if necessary, troops to any Middle Eastern nation threatened by "Communist aggression."

Such interventions intensified anti-American feelings in Third World nations. Angry crowds in Peru and Venezuela spat at Vice President Nixon and stoned his car in 1958. In 1959, Fidel Castro overturned a dictatorial regime in Cuba and confiscated American properties without compensation. He then established close economic and military ties with the Soviet Union. If the United States dared intervene, Soviet premier Nikita Khrushchev warned, he would defend Cuba with nuclear weapons. "The Monroe Doctrine has outlived its time," Khrushchev said.

A tougher blow came on May 1, 1960, two weeks before a scheduled summit conference between Eisenhower and Khrushchev, when Soviet air defenses shot down a U.S. spy plane far inside their border. Khrushchev displayed the captured CIA pilot and the photos taken of Soviet missile sites. Eisenhower refused to apologize, and the summit collapsed.

The Eisenhower Legacy   Just before leaving office, Eisenhower offered Americans a farewell and a warning. The demands of national security, he stated, had produced the "conjunction of an immense military establishment and a large arms industry." Swollen defense budgets had yoked American economic health to military expenditures, and military contracts had become the staff of life for research scholars, politicians, and America's largest corporations. This combination of interests, Eisenhower believed, exerted enormous leverage and threatened the traditional subordination of the military in American life. "We must guard against the acquisition of unwarranted influence . . . by the **military-industrial complex.** The potential for the disastrous rise of misplaced power exists and will persist."

The president concluded that he had avoided war but that lasting peace was not in sight. Most scholars agreed. Eisenhower ended the Korean War, avoided direct intervention in Vietnam, initiated relaxing tensions with the Soviet Union, and suspended atmospheric nuclear testing. At the same time, he presided over an accelerating nuclear-arms race and a Cold War that encircled the globe. So, too, would his successor.

CHRONOLOGY
1945–1960

1946	George Kennan's "long telegram."
	Winston Churchill's "iron curtain" speech.
	Republicans win control of Congress.
1947	Truman Doctrine.
	Federal Employee Loyalty Program.
	Taft-Hartley Act.
	National Security Act.
	HUAC holds hearings on Hollywood.
1948	State of Israel founded.
	Berlin airlift.
	Congress approves Marshall Plan to aid Europe.
	Communist leaders put on trial under the Smith Act.
	Truman elected president.

1949	North Atlantic Treaty Organization (NATO) established.
	East and West Germany founded as separate nations.
	Communist victory in China; People's Republic of China established.
	Soviet Union detonates an atomic bomb.
1950	Soviet spy ring at Los Alamos uncovered.
	Joseph McCarthy launches anticommunist crusade.
	Korean War begins.
	McCarran Internal Security Act.
	Truman accepts NSC-68.
1951	Julius and Ethel Rosenberg convicted of espionage.
1952	First hydrogen bomb exploded.
	Dwight D. Eisenhower elected president.
1953	Korean War truce signed.
1954	Army-McCarthy hearings.
1956	Suez Crisis.
	Eisenhower re-elected.
1957	Eisenhower Doctrine announced.
1959	Fidel Castro comes to power in Cuba.
1960	U-2 incident.

CONCLUSION

After nearly two decades of depression and war, the end of World War II meant the beginning of a new era of hope for most Americans. At the same time, an assertive United States, eager to protect and expand its influence and power in the world, sought to contain a Soviet Union obsessed with its own security and self-interest. Stalin's aggressive posture toward Eastern Europe and the Persian Gulf was met by an American policy of containment, in whose name the United States aided Greece and Turkey, established the Marshall Plan, airlifted supplies into Berlin for a year, approved the creation of the Federal Republic of Germany (West Germany), established NATO, implemented NSC-68, financed France's war in Vietnam, and went to war in Korea. The resulting stalemate would last for four decades, define American politics and society, transform the U.S. economy, and condition the thinking of a generation.

The Cold War obsession with communism, as well as postwar prosperity, weakened the appeal of liberal reform. In a political climate far more conservative than that of the 1930s, New Deal measures remained in place, but Truman's Fair Deal to assist the disadvantaged with new initiatives in education, health insurance, and civil rights failed. Anticommunist hysteria squashed the Left and narrowed the range of politically acceptable ideas. Most importantly, Truman's actions at home and abroad fed America's fear of communism, which grew with the president's responses to the Soviet detonation of an atomic bomb, the fall of China to the communists, the invasion of South Korea, and Truman's own loyalty probe to root out subversive government workers. Witch-hunts for communism in American life and the discovery of a Soviet atomic spy ring added to the paranoia. In this atmosphere, Truman's actions encouraged others to seek scapegoats for American failures abroad and legitimated conservative accusations that equated dissent with disloyalty.

As the Cold War continued throughout the 1950s, continuity would also mark the domestic and foreign policies of Truman's successor. Dwight Eisenhower, in the main, pursued a centrist course in domestic affairs. While tilting to the right in favoring private corporations, the Eisenhower administration left New Deal reforms in place, expanded existing social-welfare benefits, and employed Keynesian deficit spending to curtail economic recessions. The president made no effort to hamper labor unionization and proposed construction of a vast interstate highway system.

Eisenhower also followed Truman in his determination to contain communism abroad, while putting new emphasis on the need to avoid nuclear war and to fight communism in the Third World. Gaining short-term victories in local conflicts, often by clandestine means, Ike and Secretary of State Dulles largely ignored the nationalist yearnings and socioeconomic deprivations of local peoples and increasingly allied the United States with reactionary, repressive regimes.

27

AMERICA AT
MIDCENTURY, 1945–1961

POSTWAR JITTERS

The immediate concerns of most Americans following V-J Day centered on "bringing the boys home" and avoiding a return to the Great Depression. The steep decline in defense spending and factory jobs caused many to fear demobilization and the reconversion to a peacetime economy. Strife between labor and management, as well as inflation and shortages, intensified the anxiety. But by 1947, consumer spending and the Cold War had begun to spur a quarter-century of economic growth and prosperity, the longest such period in American history.

Demobilization and Reconversion   When the war ended, GIs and civilians alike wanted those who had served overseas "home alive in '45." Troops demanding transport ships barraged Congress with threats of "no boats, no votes." In December 1945, postcards deluged the White House with the message "Bring the Boys Home by Christmas." Truman bowed to popular demand, and by 1948, American military strength had dropped from 12 million to just 1.5 million.

Returning veterans faced readjustment problems intensified by a soaring divorce rate and a drastic housing shortage. Many feared the return of mass unemployment and economic depression as war plants closed. Defense spending dropped from $76 billion in 1945 to under $20 billion in 1946, and more than a million defense jobs vanished. By the end of the decade more women were working outside the home than during World War II. Most took jobs in traditional

(© Bettmann/Corbis)

Veterans at Pennsylvania State College *The Serviceman's Readjustment Act of 1944 (the so-called GI Bill), included among its various programs financial assistance for every veteran of the Second World War who sought further education. Some 8 million veterans would eventually study at technical institutes, trade schools, and universities.*

women's fields, especially office work and sales, to pay for family needs. Although the postwar economy created new openings for women in the labor market, many public figures urged women to seek fulfillment at home. Popular culture romanticized married bliss and demonized career women as a threat to social stability.

The GI Bill of Rights

The Servicemen's Readjustment Act of 1944, commonly called the GI Bill of Rights or **GI Bill,** was designed to forestall the expected recession by easing veterans back into the work force, and to reward the "soldier boys" for their wartime service. The GI Bill gave veterans priority for many jobs, occupational guidance, and if need be, fifty-two weeks of unemployment benefits. It also provided low-interest government loans to some 4 million returning GIs who were starting businesses or buying homes, helping to fuel a baby boom, suburbanization, and a record demand for new goods and services.

The government also promised to pay up to four years of further education or job training for veterans. By 1946, flush with stipends of sixty-five dollars a month —ninety dollars for those with dependents—and up to five hundred dollars a year for tuition and books, 1.5 million veterans were attending college, spurring a huge increase in higher education and the creation of many new colleges. By 1947, veterans made up over half of all college students.

To make room for the millions of GIs pursuing higher education after the war, many colleges limited the percentage of women admitted or barred students from out of state. The percentage of female college graduates dropped from 40 percent in 1949 to 25 percent in 1950. By then, most women who might have been students were the working wives of the 8 million veterans who took advantage of the GI Bill to go college.

The GI Bill democratized higher education. By 1956, nearly 10 million veterans had used the GI Bill to enroll in vocational training programs and colleges (most the first in their families to do so). No longer a citadel of privilege, universities awarded twice as many degrees in 1950 as in 1940, propelling millions of veterans into the middle class. Two decades later, these more affluent and educated veterans expected their children to follow suit. Higher education became an accepted part of the American Dream.

| The Economic Boom Begins | In addition to the assistance given returning servicemen, a 1945 tax cut of $6 billion spurred corporate investment in new factories and equipment and helped produce an eco- |

nomic boom (see Figure 27.1). Further kindling postwar prosperity, Americans spent much of the $135 billion they had saved from wartime work and service pay to satisfy their desire to consume, and sales of homes, cars, and appliances skyrocketed. Scores of new products—televisions, high-fidelity phonographs, filter cigarettes, automatic transmissions, freezers, and air conditioners—became hallmarks of the middle-class lifestyle.

The Bretton Woods Agreement (1944) among the Allies had set the stage for the United States to become economic leader of the noncommunist world. It created the International Monetary Fund (IMF) to stabilize exchange rates by valuing ("pegging") other currencies in relation to the U.S. dollar; established the International Bank for Reconstruction and Development (World Bank) to help rebuild war-battered Asia and Europe; and laid the groundwork for the 1947 General Agreement on Tariffs and Trade (GATT) to break up closed trading blocs and expand international trade. Since the United States largely controlled and funded these powerful economic institutions, they gave the United States an especially favorable position in international trade and finance.

With many nations in ruins, American firms could import raw materials cheaply; with little competition from other industrial countries, they could increase exports to record levels. U.S. economic dominance also resulted from wartime advances in science and technology, which significantly increased the productivity of American workers, and led to revolutionary developments in such industries as electronics and plastics.

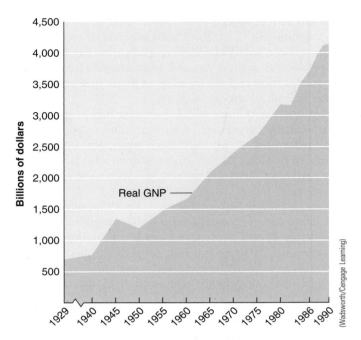

FIGURE 27.1 Gross National Product, 1929–1990

Following World War II, the United States achieved the highest living standard in world history. Between 1950 and 1970, the real GNP, which factors out inflation and reveals the actual amount of goods and services produced, steadily increased. However, in 1972, 1974–1975, 1980, and 1982, the real GNP declined.

Source: Economic Report of the President, 1991.
Note: Data shown in 1982 dollars.

THE AFFLUENT SOCIETY

In 1958, the economist John Kenneth Galbraith published *The Affluent Society*, a study of postwar America whose title reflected the broad-based prosperity that made the 1950s seem the fulfillment of the American Dream. By the end of the decade, about 60 percent of American families owned homes; 75 percent, cars; and 87 percent, at least one TV. Government spending, a huge upsurge in productivity, and steadily increasing consumer demand pushed the gross national product (GNP) up 50 percent. The United States achieved the world's highest living standard ever. By 1960, the average worker's income, adjusted for inflation, was 35 percent higher than in 1945. With just 6 percent of the world's population, the United States produced and consumed nearly half of everything made and sold on Earth.

The New Industrial Society

Federal spending constituted a major source of economic growth, nearly doubling in the 1950s to $180 billion. Just 1 percent of the GNP in 1929, federal expenditures reached 17 percent by the mid-1950s. These funds built roads and

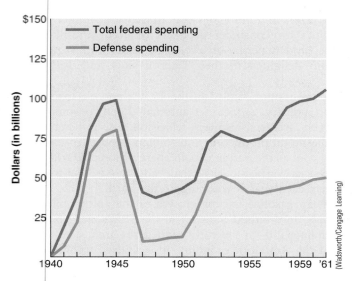

FIGURE 27.2 National Defense Spending, 1941–1960

In 1950, the defense budget was $13 billion, less than a third of the total federal outlay. In 1961, defense spending reached $47 billion, fully half of the federal budget and almost 10 percent of the gross national product.

Source: From America's History Volume II 4e by James A. Henretta et al. Copyright © 2000 by Bedford/St. Martin's. Reproduced by permission of Bedford/St. Martin's.

airports, financed home mortgages, supported farm prices, and provided stipends for education. More than half the federal budget—10 percent of the GNP—went to defense spending (see Figure 27.2). These expenditures made the federal government the nation's main financier of scientific and technological research and development (R&D).

For the West, especially, it was as if World War II never ended, as the new Air Force Academy in Colorado Springs signified. Politicians from both parties in California sought contracts for Lockheed, those from Texas labored for General Dynamics, and those from Washington State kept defense funds flowing to Boeing. By the late 1950s, California alone received half the space budget and a quarter of all major military contracts. By then, Denver had the largest number of federal employees outside Washington, D.C.; Albuquerque boasted more Ph.D. degrees per capita than any other U.S. city; and over a third of workers in Los Angeles depended on defense industries. Utah, once the Mormon dream of an agricultural utopia, received the nation's highest per capita expenditures on space and defense research. Government spending transformed the mythic West of individualistic cowboys, miners, and farmers into a West of bureaucrats, manufacturers, and scientists dependent on federal funds.

Science became a ward of the state, with government funding and control transforming both the U.S. military and industry. Financed by the Atomic Energy Commission (AEC) and utilizing navy scientists, the nation's first nuclear-power plant came on line in 1957. The chemical industry continued its wartime growth.

As chemical fertilizers and pesticides contaminated ground water supplies, and as the use of plastics for consumer products reduced landfill space, Americans—unaware of the hidden perils—marveled at fruits and vegetables covered with Saran Wrap and delighted in their Dacron suits and Teflon-coated pots and pans.

Electricity consumption tripled in the 1950s, and electronics became the fifth-largest American industry, as factories automated and consumers purchased electric washers and dryers, freezers, blenders, television sets, and stereos. Cheap oil fueled expansion. Domestic oil production and foreign imports rose steeply, and by 1960 oil had replaced coal as the nation's main energy source. Hardly anyone paid attention when a physicist warned in 1953 that "adding 6 billion tons of carbon dioxide to the atmosphere each year is warming up the Earth."

Plentiful, cheap gasoline fed the growth of the automobile and aircraft industries. The nation's third-largest industry in the 1950s, aerospace depended heavily on defense spending and on federally funded research. The automobile industry, still the titan of the American economy, also utilized technological R&D. Where machines had earlier replaced some human workers, automation now controlled the machines. Between 1945 and 1960, the industry halved the number of hours and workers required to produce a car.

The Age of Computers

The computer was a major key to the technological revolution. To decipher secret Axis codes, International Business Machines (IBM) in 1944 produced the Mark I calculator, a cumbersome device with five hundred miles of wiring. In late 1945, to improve artillery accuracy, the military devised ENIAC, the first electronic computer. Still unwieldy, with eighteen thousand vacuum tubes, ENIAC could perform five thousand calculations per second. Next came the development of operating instructions, or programs, that could be stored inside the computer's memory; the substitution of printed circuits for wires; and in 1948, at Bell Labs, the invention of tiny solid-state transistors that ended reliance on radio tubes.

Sales of electronic computers to industry rose from twenty in 1954 to more than a thousand in 1957 and more than two thousand in 1960. Major manufacturers used them to monitor production lines, track inventory, and ensure quality control. In government, computers were as indispensable to Pentagon strategists playing war games as they were to the Census Bureau and the Internal Revenue Service. By the mid-1960s, more than thirty thousand mainframe computers would be used by banks, hospitals, and universities. Further developments led to the first integrated circuits and to what would ultimately become the Internet, fundamentally changing the nature of work as well as its landscape.

The development of the high-technology complex known as Silicon Valley began in 1951 as Stanford University utilized its science and engineering faculties to design and produce products for the Fairchild Semiconductor and Hewlett-Packard companies. This relationship became a model followed by other high-tech firms. Soon apricot and cherry orchards throughout the Santa Clara valley gave way to industrial parks filled with computer firms and pharmaceutical laboratories.

ENIAC, the Electronic Numerical Integrator and Computer *The co-conceiver and designer of ENIAC, Dr. John W. Mauchly of the University of Pennsylvania's School of Electrical Engineering publicly unveiled the first general-purpose electronic computer in February 1946.*

Initially a far cry from dirty eastern factories, these campus-like facilities would eventually choke the valley with traffic congestion, housing developments, and smog. Similar developments would follow the military-fueled research complexes along Boston's Route 128, near Austin, Texas, and in North Carolina's Research Triangle.

The Costs of Bigness   Rapid technological advances accelerated the growth and power of big business. In 1950, twenty-two U.S. firms had assets of more than $1 billion; ten years later more than fifty did. By then, one-half of 1 percent of all companies earned more than half the total corporate income in the United States. The wealthiest became oligopolies, swallowing up weak competitors. Three television networks monopolized the nation's airwaves; three automobile and three aluminum companies produced more than 90 percent of America's cars and aluminum; and a handful of firms controlled the lion's share of assets and sales in steel, petroleum, chemicals, and electrical machinery. Corporations acquired overseas facilities to become "multinational" enterprises, and formed "conglomerates" by merging companies in unrelated industries: International Telephone and Telegraph (ITT) branched out from communications into car rental, home building, motel chains, insurance, and more. Growth and consolidation meant greater bureaucratization. "Executives" replaced "capitalists." Success required conformity not creativity, teamwork not individuality. According to sociologist David Riesman's *The Lonely Crowd* (1950), the new "company people" were "other-directed," eager to follow the cues from their peers and not think innovatively or act independently. In the old nursery rhyme "This Little Pig Went to Market," Riesman noted, each pig went his own way. "Today, however, all little pigs go to market; none stay home; all have roast beef, if any do; and all say 'we-we.'"

Changes in American agriculture paralleled those in industry. Farming grew increasingly scientific and mechanized. Technology halved the work hours necessary to grow crops between 1945 and 1960, causing many farm families to migrate to cities. In 1956 alone, one-eleventh of the farm population left the land. Meanwhile, heavily capitalized farm businesses, running "factories in the field," prospered by using more machines and chemicals.

Until the publication of Rachel Carson's *Silent Spring* in 1962, few Americans understood the extent to which fertilizers, herbicides, and pesticides poisoned the environment. Carson, a former researcher for the Fish and Wildlife Service, dramatized the problems caused by use of the insecticide DDT and its spread through the food chain. Her depiction of a "silent spring" caused by the death of songbirds from DDT toxicity led many states to ban its use. The federal government followed suit. But the incentives for cultivating more land, and more marginal land, led to further ravages. The Army Corps of Engineers and the Bureau of Reclamation dammed the waters of the West, turning the Columbia and Missouri Rivers into rows of slack-water reservoirs, killing fish and wildlife as well as immersing hundreds of square miles of Indian tribal lands.

Blue-Collar Blues

Consolidation also transformed the labor movement. In 1955, the merger of the AFL and CIO brought 85 percent of union members into a single federation. Although labor leadership promised aggressive unionism, organized labor fell victim to its success at the bargaining table. Higher wages, shorter workweeks, paid vacations, health-care coverage, and automatic wage hikes tied to the cost of living led most workers to view themselves as middle class rather than the proletariat.

A decrease in the number of blue-collar workers further sapped labor militancy. Most of the new jobs in the 1950s were in the service sector and in public employment, which banned collective bargaining by labor unions, and automation cut membership in the coal, auto, and steelworkers' unions by more than half. In 1956, for the first time in U.S. history, white-collar workers outnumbered blue-collar workers. Although most service jobs were as routinized as any factory job, few unions sought to woo white-collar workers. The percentage of the unionized labor force dropped from a high of 36 percent in 1953 to 31 percent in 1960, and kept falling.

Prosperity and the Suburbs

As real income (adjusted for inflation) rose, Americans spent less of their income on necessities and more on powered lawnmowers and air conditioners. They heaped their shopping carts with frozen, dehydrated, and fortified foods. When they lacked cash, they borrowed. In 1950, Diner's Club issued the first credit card; American Express followed in 1958. Installment buying, home mortgages, and auto loans tripled Americans' total private indebtedness in the 1950s. In its effort to convince people to buy what they did not need, business spent more on advertising than the nation did on public schools Thrift and savings were no longer depicted as virtues.

Suburban America   Urged to "Buy Now, Pay Later," Americans purchased 58 million new cars during the 1950s. Manufacturers enticed people to trade in and up by offering flashier models, two-tone color, tail fins, and extra-powerful engines—like Pontiac's 1955 "Sensational Strato-Streak V-8," which could go more than twice as fast as any speed limit. Seat belts remained an unadvertised extra-cost option. The consequences were increases in highway deaths, air pollution, oil consumption, and "autosclerosis"—clogged urban arteries.

In addition to "auto mania," government policy spurred white Americans' exodus to the suburbs (see Figure 27.3). Federal spending on highways skyrocketed from $79 million in 1946 to $2.6 billion in 1960, putting once-remote areas within "commuting distance" for city workers (see Technology and Culture). The income tax code stimulated home sales by allowing deductions for home-mortgage interest payments and for property taxes. Both the Federal Housing Administration (FHA) and Veterans Administration (VA) offered low-interest loans; and both continued to deny loans to blacks who sought to buy homes in white neighborhoods. In 1960, suburbia was 98 percent white.

In 1947, some thirty miles from midtown Manhattan on Long Island, Alfred and William Levitt used the mass-production construction techniques they perfected during the war to construct standardized 720-square-foot houses as quickly as possible. All 17,000 looked alike. Deeds to the property required door chimes, not buzzers, prohibited picket fences, mandated regular lawn mowing, and even specified when the wash could be hung to dry in the backyard. All the town streets curved at the same angle. A tree was planted every twenty-eight feet. The Levitts then built a second, larger Levittown in Bucks County, Pennsylvania, and a third in Willingboro, New Jersey.

Other contractors followed suit, and 85 percent of the 13 million new homes built in the 1950s were in the suburbs. In the greatest internal migration in the nation's history, some 20 million Americans moved to the suburbs in the decade—making the suburban population equal to that of the central cities. Although social

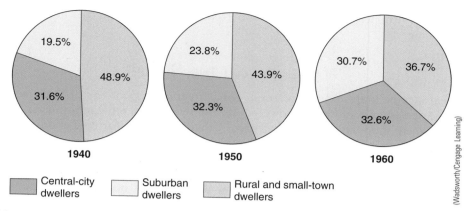

FIGURE 27.3 **Urban, Suburban, and Rural Americans, 1940–1960**

In the fifteen years following World War II, more than 40 million Americans migrated to the suburbs, where, as one father put it, "a kid could grow up with grass stains on his pants." Over the same period, fourteen of the fifteen largest U.S. cities lost population.

Source: Adapted from U.S. Bureau of the Census, *Current Censuses,* 1930–1970 (Washington, D.C.: U.S. Government Printing Office).

critics lampooned the "ticky-tacky" houses in "disturbia," suburban life embodied the American dream for many families who longed for their own home, good schools, safe streets, and neighbors like themselves.

Americans also moved South and West, into the Sunbelt, lured by job opportunities, the climate, and the pace of life. California, where the population went from 9 to 19 million between 1945 and 1964, supplanted New York as the most populous state. Los Angeles boasted the highest per capita ownership of private homes and cars of any city. Initially designed to lure shoppers downtown, the highway system instead had become the road to a home in the suburbs (see Map 27.1).

Industry, too, headed south and west, drawn by low taxes, low energy costs, and anti-union right-to-work laws. Senior citizens similarly headed to the easier climate. Both brought a conservative outlook. By 1980, the population of the **Sunbelt,** which stretched from the old Confederacy across Texas to southern California, exceeded that of the North and East. The political power of the Republican Party rose accordingly.

Consensus and Conservatism Not everyone embraced the conformity of 1950s consumer culture. Intellectuals found an audience for their attack on "organization men," incapable of independent thought bent on getting ahead by going along, and on "status seekers" pursuing external rewards to compensate for inner insecurities. Others, like Riesman, took aim at "other-directed" conformists and "an America of mass housing, mass markets, massive corporations, massive government, mass media, and massive boredom." Riesman described modern Americans as conformists, shaped by the opinions of their peers rather than by their own consciences, and lacking the inner resources

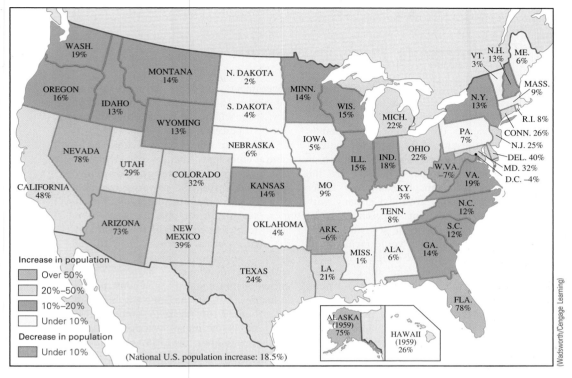

MAP 27.1 Rise of the Sunbelt, 1950–1960

The years after the Second World War saw a continuation of the migration of Americans to the Sunbelt states of the Southwest and the West Coast.

to dare be different. Some took aim at the consumerist middle class: "all items in a national supermarket—categorized, processed, labeled, priced, and readied for merchandising."

This social criticism oversimplified reality. It ignored ethnic and class diversity, the acquisitiveness and conformity of earlier generations, and the currents of dissent swirling beneath the surface. But it rightly spotlighted the elevation of comfort over challenge, and of private pleasures over public affairs. The decade was, in the main, a time of political passivity and preoccupation with personal gain.

Togetherness, the Baby Boom, and Domesticity   After years of separation and loss, Americans yearned for emotional security as well as material success, and more than ever, they looked to family as a bastion of stability in an insecure world. In 1954, *McCall's* magazine coined the term *togetherness* to celebrate the "ideal" couple: the man and woman who centered their lives on home and children. Confident in continued economic prosperity and influenced by popular culture, Americans in mid-century wed at an earlier age than had their parents (one woman in three married by age nineteen), and had

TECHNOLOGY & CULTURE

The Interstate Highway System

As a young captain after World War I, Dwight Eisenhower had been given the task of accompanying a convoy of army trucks across the country. The woefully inadequate state of the roads for military transport dismayed him then as much as he would later be impressed by the German autobahns that allowed Hitler to deploy troops around Germany with incredible speed. Not surprisingly, when he became president, he sought a transportation system that would facilitate the rapid movement of the military, as well as increase road safety and aid commerce. The arms race with the Soviet Union, moreover, necessitated a network of highways for evacuating cities in case of a nuclear attack—a change, according to the *Bulletin of the Atomic Scientists*, from "Duck and Cover" to "Run Like Hell."

In 1954, Eisenhower set up a high-powered commission to recommend a highway program that would cost as much as a war. He appointed an army general to head it to emphasize the connection between highways, national defense, and the concerns Americans had about their security. The next year, with the entire federal budget at $71 billion, Eisenhower asked Congress for a $40 billion, forty-one-thousand-mile construction project, to be financed by government bonds. Conservative Republicans, fearful of increasing the federal debt, balked. So Ike switched to a financing plan based on new gasoline, tire, bus, and trucking taxes. The federal government would use the taxes to pay 90 percent of the construction costs in any state willing to come up with the other 10 percent.

Millions of suburbanites commuting to central cities loved the idea of new multi-lane highways. So did motorists dreaming of summer travel; the powerful coalition of automobile manufacturers, oil companies, asphalt firms, and truckers, who stood to benefit financially the most; and the many special interests in virtually every congressional district, including real-estate developers, shopping mall entrepreneurs, engineers, and construction industries. Indeed, the interstate highway bill promised something to almost everybody except the inner-city poor. It sailed through Congress in 1956, winning by voice vote in the House and by an 89 to 1 margin in the Senate.

The largest and most expensive public-works scheme in American history, the interstate highway system was designed and built as a single project for the entire country, unlike the haphazard development of the canal and railroad networks. It required taking more land by eminent domain than had been taken in the entire history of road building in the United States. Expected increases in highway use, speed of travel, and weight of loads necessitated drastic changes in road engineering and materials. Utilizing the technological advances that had produced high-quality concrete and asphalt, diesel-powered roadbed graders, reinforced steel, and safely controlled explosives,

more babies sooner. The fertility rate (the number of births per thousand women), eighty in 1940, peaked at 123 in 1957, when an American baby was born every seven seconds. That year, America's rapidly increasing population matched India's; the number of children per family had risen to 3.2, from 2.4 in 1945, and one-third of the population was under the age of 15.

construction crews built superhighways with standardized twelve foot-wide lanes, ten-foot shoulders, and median strips of at least thirty-six feet in rural areas. Terrain in which a dirt trail was difficult to blaze was laced with cloverleaf intersections and some sixteen thousand exits and entrances. More than fifty thousand bridges, tunnels, and overpasses traversed swamps, rivers, and mountains. Road curves were banked for speeds of seventy miles per hour, with grades no greater than 3 percent and minimum sight distances of six hundred feet. The massive amounts of concrete poured, Ike later boasted, could have made "six sidewalks to the moon" or sixty Panama Canals.

The network of four-to-eight-lane roads linking cities and suburbs made it possible to drive from New York to San Francisco without encountering a stoplight. It more than fulfilled the initial hopes of most of its backers, enormously speeding the movement of goods and people across the country, invigorating the tourist industry, providing steady work for construction firms, enriching those who lived near the interstates and sold their lands to developers, and hastening suburban development.

The freeways that helped unify Americans by increasing the accessibility of once-distant regions also helped homogenize the nation with interchangeable shopping malls, motels, and fast-food chains. In 1955, Ray Kroc, who supplied the Multi-mixers for milk shakes to the original McDonald's drive-in in San Bernardino, California, began to franchise similar family restaurants beside highways, each serving the same standardized foods under the instantly recognizable logo of the golden arches. By century's end, McDonald's would be the world's largest private real-estate enterprise, as well as the largest food provider, serving more than 40 million meals daily in a hundred countries.

Moreover, the expressways boosted the interstate trucking business and hastened the decline of the nation's railroad lines and urban mass-transportation systems. The highways built to speed commuters into the central cities—"white men's roads through black men's bedrooms," said the National Urban League—often bulldozed minority neighborhoods out of existence or served as barriers between black and white neighborhoods. The beltways that lured increasingly more residents and businesses to suburbia eroded city tax bases which, in turn, accelerated urban decay, triggering the urban crisis that then furthered suburban sprawl. The interstates had locked the United States into an ever-increasing reliance on cars and trucks, drastically increasing air pollution and American dependence on a constant supply of cheap and plentiful gasoline.

Questions for Analysis

1. *Why did Congress authorize the construction of an interstate highway system?*
2. *Describe some of the unintended consequences of the new highway system.*

New antibiotics subdued once deadly childhood diseases like diphtheria and whooping cough, streptomycin drastically reduced tuberculosis, and the Salk and Sabin vaccines ended the dread of polio. The decline in childhood mortality helped raise American life expectancy from 65.9 years in 1945 to 70.9 years in 1970. Coupled with the "baby boom," it led to a 19 percent population spurt during the

1950s—a larger jump than in any previous decade. The sheer size of the **baby-boom generation** (the 76 million Americans born between 1946 and 1964) ensured its impact and historical importance. Its needs and expectations at each stage of life would be as contorting as the digestion of a pig by a boa constrictor. First came the bulge in baby carriages; in the 1950s, school construction boomed; and in the 1960s, college enrollments soared. Then in the 1970s—as the baby boomers had their own families—home construction peaked. The 1980s and 1990s brought a surge in retirement investments, and the twenty-first century a preoccupation with health matters. In the 1950s, the baby boom also made child rearing a foremost concern, reinforcing the idea that women's place was in the home. No one did more to emphasize the necessity for women to be full-time mothers than **Dr. Benjamin Spock**. Only the Bible outsold his *Common Sense Book of Baby and Child Care* (1946) in the 1950s. Spock urged mothers not to work outside the home, in order to create an atmosphere of warmth and intimacy for their children. Crying babies were to be comforted; breast-feeding came back into vogue. Spock's advice also led to a more "democratic" family and to a "permissive" approach to child-rearing in which kids ruled the roost.

The postwar emphasis on family togetherness renewed the ideal of domesticity in defining—and constraining—the role of women. As we saw in Chapter 25, an advertisement during the war pictured a woman in overalls about to leave for work proclaiming, "Some jubilant day, mother will stay home again doing the job she likes—making a home for you and daddy when he gets back." With Daddy back, popular culture glorified marriage and parenthood as never before, emphasizing a woman's role as a helpmate to her husband and a full-time mother to her children. Television mostly pictured women as at-home mothers. *Life* magazine lauded Marjorie Sutton for marrying at sixteen, cooking and sewing for the family, raising four children, being a pillar of the PTA and Campfire Girls, and working out on a trampoline "to keep her size 12 figure."

Education reinforced these notions. Girls were encouraged to study typing and cooking and cautioned not to "miss the boat" of marriage by pursuing higher education. "Men are not interested in college degrees but in the warmth and humanness of the girls they marry," stressed a textbook on the family. More men than women went to college in the 1950s, and only one-third of college women completed a degree.

Women both embraced and repudiated the domestic ideal as profound changes accelerated. By 1952, 2 million more women worked outside the home than had during the war; and by 1960, twice as many did as in 1940. In 1960, one-third of the labor force was female, and one out of three married women worked outside the home. Of all women workers that year, 60 percent were married, while 40 percent had school-age children. Most held so-called "pink collar" jobs in the service industry—secretary or clerk, waitress or hairdresser. Their median wage was less than half that for men.

Most women worked to augment family income, not to challenge stereotypes. White women mostly filled clerical positions, while African-Americans held service jobs in private households and restaurants. Some women, as during World War II, developed a heightened sense of expectations and empowerment as a result of employment. Transmitted to their daughters, their experience would fuel a feminist resurgence in the late 1960s.

Religion and Education   "Today in the U.S.," *Time* claimed in 1954, "the Christian faith is back in the center of things." Evangelist **Billy Graham,** Roman Catholic Bishop Fulton J. Sheen, and Protestant minister Norman Vincent Peale all had syndicated newspaper columns, bestselling books, and radio and television programs. Each promoted a potent mixture of religious salvation and aggressive anticommunism. Hollywood religious extravaganzas, such as *Ben Hur* and *The Ten Commandments*, were the biggest box-office hits of the 1950s, while television promoted the slogan that "the family that prays together stays together." Congress added "under God" to the Pledge of Allegiance and required "IN GOD WE TRUST" to be put on all U.S. currency. While church membership doubled to 114 million between 1945 and 1960, the *intensity* of faith diminished for many people, as mainstream churches downplayed sin and evil, and preached Americanism and fellowship.

Similarly, education swelled in the 1950s yet seemed less rigorous than in earlier decades. Primary school enrollment rose by 10 million in the 1950s (compared with 1 million in the 1940s). California opened a new school every week throughout the decade and still faced a classroom shortage. The proportion of college-age Americans in higher education climbed from 15 percent in 1940 to more than 40 percent by the early 1960s. "Progressive" educators promoted sociability and self-expression over science and history. The "well-rounded" student became more prized than the highly skilled or intelligent student. Surveys of college students found them conservative, conformist, and careerist, a "silent generation" seeking security and comfort.

Few university faculty challenged the reigning thought of the day or addressed the problems of those in need. Historians downplayed class conflicts and highlighted the pragmatism of most Americans. Consensus—the widely shared agreement on most matters of importance, especially respect for private property, individualism, and equal opportunity—was frequently depicted as central to America's history and greatness.

Postwar Culture   American culture reflected both the spirit of prosperity and the Cold War. Enjoying more leisure time and fatter paychecks, Americans spent one-seventh of the GNP on entertainment. Spectator sports boomed, new symphony halls opened, and book sales doubled.

With the opening of a major exhibit of abstract expressionists by the Museum of Modern Art in 1951, New York replaced Paris as the capital of the art world. Like the abstract canvases of Jackson Pollock and the cool jazz of trumpeter Miles Davis, introspection and improvisation characterized the major novels of the era. The personal yearnings of characters in John Updike's *Rabbit Run* (1960), typically, had little to do with the political engagement and social realism of literature in the 1930s. Southern, African-American, and Jewish-American writers turned out the decade's most vital fiction. William Faulkner continued his dense saga of Yoknapatawpha County, Mississippi, while Eudora Welty evoked southern small-town life in *The Ponder Heart* (1954). The black experience found memorable expression in James Baldwin's *Go Tell It on the Mountain* (1953) and Ralph Ellison's *Invisible Man* (1951). Bernard Malamud's *The Assistant* (1957) explored the Jewish immigrant world, and Philip Roth's *Goodbye Columbus* (1959) dissected the very different world of upwardly mobile Jews.

Hollywood reflected the diminished interest in political issues, churning out westerns, musicals, and costume spectacles. Most films about contemporary life portrayed Americans as one happy white, middle-class family. Minorities and the poor remained invisible, and women appeared largely as "dumb blondes" or cute helpmates. Still, as TV viewing soared, movie attendance dropped 50 percent, and a fifth of the nation's theaters became bowling alleys and supermarkets by 1960.

The Television Culture   No cultural medium ever grew so huge so quickly as television. In 1946, just one in 18,000 households had a TV set; by 1960, nine of ten households had at least one TV, and more Americans had televisions than had bathrooms (see Figure 27.4).

Business capitalized on the phenomenon. The three main radio networks—ABC, CBS, and NBC—gobbled up virtually every TV station in the country and, just as in radio, they profited by selling time to advertisers who wanted to reach the largest possible audiences. *TV Guide,* introduced in 1952, soon outsold all other periodicals. First marketed in 1954, the TV dinner altered the nation's eating habits. When Walt Disney produced a show on Davy Crockett in 1955, stores could not keep up with the massive demand for "King of the Wild Frontier" coonskin caps. It seemed that TV could sell anything.

Initially, TV showcased talent and creativity. Opera performances appeared in prime time, as did political dramas and documentaries like Edward R. Murrow's

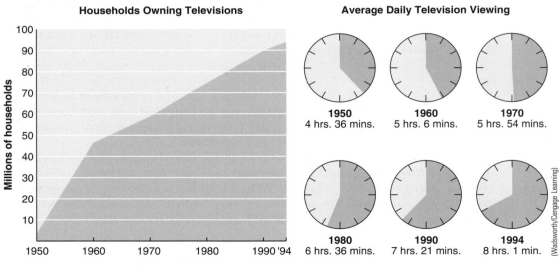

FIGURE 27.4 The Television Revolution, 1950–1994

As televisions became commonplace in the 1950s, TV viewing altered the nature of American culture and politics.

Source: Statistical Abstracts of the United States.

See It Now. Early situation comedies such as *The Life of Riley* and *The Goldbergs* featured ethnic working-class families. But as the price of TV sets came down and the chill of McCarthyism spread, the networks' caution and appetite for a mass audience transformed TV into a celebration of conformity and consumerism. Controversy went off the air. Most situation comedies, like *Father Knows Best* and *The Adventures of Ozzie and Harriet*, portrayed perfectly coiffed moms who loved to vacuum in high heels, frisky yet obedient kids, and all-knowing dads. Even Lucille Ball and Desi Arnaz in *I Love Lucy*—which no network initially wanted because its all-American redhead was married to a Cuban—had a baby and left New York for suburbia.

Decrying TV's mediocrity in 1961, the head of the Federal Communications Commission called it "a vast wasteland." A steady parade of soaps, unsophisticated comedies, and violent westerns led others to call TV the "idiot box."

Measuring television's impact is difficult. Different people read the "texts" of TV (or of movies or books) in their own way and so receive their own messages from the medium. While TV bound some to the status quo, it raised expectations of others. It functioned both as a conservator and as a spur to change. In the main, television reflected existing values and institutions. It stimulated the desire to be included in American society, not to transform it. It spawned mass fads for Barbie dolls and hula hoops, and spread the message of consumerism. It reinforced gender and racial stereotypes, rarely showing African-Americans and Latinos—except in servile roles or prison scenes. It extolled male violence in fighting evil; and it portrayed women as either zany madcaps or self-effacing moms. While promoting professional baseball and football into truly national phenomena, TV decreased the audience of motion picture theaters and of general interest magazines like *Life*.

Television also changed political life. Politicians could effectively appeal to the voters over the heads of party leaders, and appearance mattered more than content. The millions watching Senator Estes Kefauver grill mobsters about their ties to city governments made him a serious contender for the presidency. At least 20 million watched Senator Joseph McCarthy bully and demean witnesses. Richard Nixon reached 58 million and saved his political career with his appeal in the "Checkers" speech, answering charges that he had received gifts and money from California businessmen. Eisenhower's pioneering use of brief "spot advertisements" clinched his smashing presidential victories. And in 1960, John F. Kennedy's "telegenic" image played a major role in his winning the presidency.

Overall, television helped produce a more national, homogenized culture, diminishing provincialism and regional differences. It vastly increased the cost of political campaigning while decreasing the content level of political discussion. It also shortened attention spans. And its overwhelming portrayal of a contented citizenry reinforced complacency and hid the reality of "the other America."

SEEDS OF DISQUIET

Late in the 1950s, apprehension ruffled the calm surface of American life. Questions about the nation's values and goals, periodic recessions, rising unemployment, and the growing national debt made Khrushchev's boast that "your grandchildren will live under communism" ring in American ears. The growing alienation of

American youth and a technological breakthrough by the Soviet Union further diminished national pride.

Sputnik   On October 4, 1957, the Soviet Union launched the first artificial satellite, *Sputnik* ("Little Traveler"). Weighing 184 pounds and only twenty-two inches in diameter, *Sputnik* dashed the American myth of unquestioned technological superiority. When *Sputnik II*, carrying a dog, went into a more distant orbit on November 3, Democrats charged that Eisenhower had allowed a "technological Pearl Harbor."

The Eisenhower administration disparaged the Soviet achievement, but behind the scenes pushed to have the American Vanguard missile launch a satellite. On December 6, with millions watching on TV, Vanguard rose six feet in the air and exploded. Newspapers ridiculed America's "Flopnik."

Eisenhower did not laugh. He more than doubled the funds for missile development and established the Science Advisory Committee, whose recommendations led to the creation of the National Aeronautics and Space Administration (NASA) in July 1958. By decade's end, the United States had launched several space probes and successfully tested the Atlas intercontinental ballistic missile (ICBM).

Spurred by *Sputnik*, Americans embarked on a crash program to improve American education. The National Defense Education Act (1958) for the first time provided direct federal funding to higher education, especially to improve the teaching of the sciences, mathematics, and foreign languages. Far more funds went to university research to ensure national security. By 1960, the U.S. government was funneling $1.5 billion to universities, a hundred-fold increase over 1940, and nearly a third of scientists and engineers on university faculties worked full-time on government research, primarily defense projects. Some observers dubbed it the "military-industrial-educational complex."

A Different Beat   Few adults considered the implications of affluence for the young, or the consequences of having a teenage generation stay in school instead of working. Few pondered how the young would respond to growing up in an age when traditional values like thrift and self-denial had declining relevance, or to maturing when young people had the leisure and money to shape their own subculture. Little attention was paid to the decline in the age of menarche (first menstruation), or the ways that the relatively new institution of junior high school affected the behavior of youth. Despite talk of family togetherness, busy fathers paid little attention to their children, and mothers sometimes spent more time chauffeuring their young than listening to them. Much of what adults knew about teenagers (a noun that first appeared in the 1940s but was not commonly used until the 1950s) they learned from the mass media, which focused on the sensational and the superficial.

Accounts of juvenile delinquency abounded, portraying high schools as war zones, city streets as jungles, and teenagers as zip-gun-armed hoodlums. In truth, teenage crime had barely increased. But male teenagers sporting black-leather motorcycle jackets, their hair slicked into "ducktails," aroused adult alarm.

As dismaying to parents, young Americans embraced rock-and-roll. In 1952, Cleveland radio host Alan Freed, having observed white teenagers dancing to rhythm-and-blues records by such black performers as Chuck Berry and Bo Diddley, started a new radio program, "Moondog's Rock and Roll Party," to play "race music." In 1954, Freed took the program to New York, creating a national craze for "rock-and-roll," the very term that had been used in blues songs for sexual intercourse.

Just as white musicians in the 1920s and 1930s had adapted black jazz for white audiences, white performers in the 1950s transformed the heavy beat and suggestive lyrics of rhythm-and-blues into "Top Ten" rock-and-roll. In 1954, Bill Haley and the Comets dropped the sexual allusions from Joe Turner's "Shake, Rattle, and Roll," added country-and-western guitar riffs, and had the first major white rock-and-roll hit. When Haley performed "Rock Around the Clock" in *The Blackboard Jungle*, a 1955 film about juvenile delinquency, many parents linked rock-and-roll with crime. Red hunters saw it as a communist plot to corrupt youth. Segregationists claimed it was a ploy "to mix the races." Psychiatrists feared it was "a communicable disease." Churches condemned it as the "devil's music."

"If I could find a white man who had the Negro sound and the Negro feel," said Sam Phillips, the owner of Sun Records in Memphis, "I could make a million dollars." He made it by finding **Elvis Presley**. Born in Tupelo, Mississippi, Elvis melded the Pentecostal music of his boyhood with the powerful beat and sexual energy of rhythm-and-blues. In songs like "Hound Dog" and "All Shook Up" he transformed the bland pop music that youth found wanting into a proclamation of teenage "separateness." Presley's gyrating pelvis and bucking hips—exuding sexuality—shocked middle-class adults, but the more adults condemned rock-and-roll, the more teenagers relished its assault on mainstream values. Record sales tripled between 1954 and 1960, and Dick Clark's *American Bandstand* became the decade's biggest TV hit. The songs for black artists written by the Jewish songwriters Jerry Leiber and Mike Stoller, the rocking versions of Mexican folk music by East Los Angeles' Richie Valens (Valenzuela), and Little Richard dancing on his piano nourished the roots of the coming youth revolt.

Portents of Change

Teens cherished rock-and-roll for defying adult propriety. They elevated characters like James Dean in *Rebel Without a Cause* (1955) to cult status for rejecting society's mores. They delighted in *Mad* magazine's ridiculing of the phony and pretentious in middle-class America. They customized their cars to reject Detroit's standards. All were signs of their distinctiveness from the adult world.

Nonconformist writers known as the **Beats** expressed a more fundamental revolt against middle-class society. In Allen Ginsberg's *Howl* (1956) and Jack Kerouac's *On the Road* (1957), the Beats scorned the conformity, religion, family values, and materialism of "square" America. They romanticized society's outcasts —the mad ones, wrote Kerouac, "the ones who never yawn or say a commonplace thing, but burn, burn, burn like fabulous yellow roman candles exploding like spiders across the stars." They glorified uninhibited sexuality and spontaneity in the search for "It," the ultimate authentic experience.

The mass media scorned the Beats, as they did all dissenters. But some college youth admired their rejection of conformity. They read poetry and listened to jazz, and some students even protested capital punishment and demonstrated against the continuing investigations of the House Un-American Activities Committee. Others decried the nuclear-arms race. In 1958 and 1959, thousands participated in Youth Marches for Integrated Schools in Washington. Together with the Beats and rock music, this vocal minority of the "silent generation" heralded a youth movement that would explode in the 1960s.

THE OTHER AMERICA

"I am an invisible man," declared the African-American narrator of Ralph Ellison's *Invisible Man*; "I am invisible, understand, simply because people refuse to see me." Indeed, few middle-class white Americans perceived the extent of social injustice in the United States. "White flight" from cities to suburbs physically separated races and classes. New expressways walled off ghettos and rural poverty from middle-class motorists speeding by. Popular culture focused on affluent Americans enjoying the "good life." But poverty and racial discrimination were rife and dire, and the struggles for social justice intensified.

Poverty and Urban Blight   Although the percentage of poor families (defined as a family of four with a yearly income of less than three thousand dollars) declined from 34 percent in 1947 to 22 percent in 1960, 35 million Americans remained below the "poverty line." Eight million senior citizens existed on annual incomes below one thousand dollars. A third of the poor lived in depressed rural areas, where 2 million migrant farm workers experienced the most abject poverty. Observing a Texas migratory-labor camp in 1955, a journalist reported that 96 percent of the children had consumed no milk in the previous six months; eight out of ten adults had eaten no meat; and most slept "on the ground, in a cave, under a tree, or in a chicken house."

The bulk of the poor huddled in decaying inner-city slums. Displaced southern blacks and Appalachian whites, Native Americans forced off reservations, and newly arrived Hispanics strained cities' inadequate facilities. Nearly two hundred thousand Mexican-Americans were herded into San Antonio's Westside barrio. A local newspaper described them as living like cattle in a stockyard. As described by Michael Harrington in *The Other America: Poverty in the United States* (1962), the poor lived trapped in a vicious cycle of want and a culture of deprivation. Unable to afford good housing, a nutritious diet, and doctors, the poor got sick more often and for longer than more affluent Americans. Losing wages and finding it hard to hold steady jobs, they could not pay for the decent housing, good food, or doctors that would keep them from getting and staying sick. Children of the poor started school disadvantaged, quickly fell behind, and, lacking encouragement or expectation of success, dropped out. Living with neither hopes nor skills, the poor bequeathed a similar legacy to their children.

The pressing need for low-cost housing went unanswered. "Slum clearance" generally meant "Negro clearance," and "urban renewal" meant "poor removal,"

(National Archives)

In a Kentucky Mining Town *Life was not the "nifty fifties" for many Americans. Nearly one in four lived below the poverty line, which was calculated by the federal government to be $2,973 for a family of four in 1959. The bottom 20 percent of Americans then owned only 0.05 percent of the nation's wealth.*

as developers razed low-income neighborhoods to put up parking garages and expensive housing. Bulldozers razed the Los Angeles barrio of Chavez Ravine to make way for Dodger Stadium. Landlords, realtors, and bankers deliberately excluded nonwhites from decent housing. Half of the housing in New York's Harlem predated 1900. A dozen people might share a tiny apartment with broken windows, faulty plumbing, and gaping holes in the walls. Harlem's rates of illegitimate births, infant deaths, narcotics use, and crime soared above the averages for the city and the nation. "Where flies and maggots breed, where the plumbing is stopped up and not repaired, where rats bite helpless infants," black social psychologist Kenneth Clark observed, "the conditions of life are brutal and inhuman."

Latinos and Latinas   High unemployment on the Caribbean island and the advent of direct air service to New York in 1945 brought a steady stream of Puerto Ricans to the city, where they could earn four times the average wage on the island. From seventy thousand in 1940 to a quarter of a million in 1950 and then nearly a million in 1960, El Barrio in

New York City's East Harlem had a larger Puerto Rican population and more bodegas than San Juan.

In New York, Puerto Ricans suffered from inadequate housing, employment, and schools, and from police harassment. Like countless earlier immigrants, they gained greater personal freedom in the United States while losing the security of a strong cultural tradition. Family frictions flared in the transition to unaccustomed ways. Parents felt upstaged by children who learned English and obtained jobs that were closed to older Puerto Ricans. The relationship between husbands and wives changed as women found readier access to jobs than did men. Yet, however much they tried to embrace American ways, many could not enjoy the promise of the American Dream because of their skin color and language. Increasingly, they turned to organizations like Antonia Pantoja's Puerto Rican Association for Community Affairs (PRACA), which sought to end discrimination against Puerto Ricans and *Nuyoricans*—their children born in New York City.

Mexican-Americans suffered the same indignities. Most were underpaid and segregated from mainstream American life. The presence of countless "undocumented aliens" compounded their woes.

After World War II, new irrigation systems added 7.5 million acres to the agricultural lands of the Southwest, stimulating demand for cheap Mexican labor. In 1951, to stem the resulting tide of illegal Mexican immigrants, Congress reintroduced the wartime "temporary worker" program that brought in seasonal farm laborers (*braceros*). Many stayed without authorization, joining a growing number of Latinos who entered the country illegally.

During the 1953–1955 recession, the U.S. government deported some 3 million allegedly undocumented entrants during the Eisenhower administration's "Operation Wetback" (*wetback* being a term of derision for illegal Mexican immigrants who supposedly swam across the Rio Grande to enter the United States). Periodic round-ups, however, did not stop the millions of Mexicans who continued to cross the poorly guarded border. The **bracero program** itself peaked in 1959, admitting 450,000 workers. Neither the *Asociación Nacional México-Americana* (founded in 1950) nor the older League of United Latin American Citizens (LULAC) could stop the exploitation or widespread violations of the rights of Mexican-American citizens.

The Mexican-American population of Los Angeles County doubled to more than six hundred thousand, and the *colonias* of Denver, El Paso, Phoenix, and San Antonio grew proportionately as large. The most rural of all major ethnic groups in 1940, 85 percent of Mexican-Americans lived in urban areas by 1970. As service in World War II gave Hispanics an increased sense of their own American identity and of their claim on the rights of American citizens, urbanization provided better educational and employment opportunities. Unions like the United Cannery, Agricultural, Packing and Allied Workers of America brought higher wages and better working conditions for their Mexican-American members. Middle-class organizations included LULAC, the Unity League, and the GI Forum (established in 1949 after a funeral parlor in Texas refused to bury a deceased Chicano veteran). These groups campaigned to end discrimination and segregation and won important court decisions that declared school segregation of Mexican-Americans unconstitutional (*Mendez*, 1947, and *Delgado*, 1948) and ended their exclusion from Texas jury lists (*Hernandez*, 1954).

The mobilization of Hispanic voters led to the election of the first Mexican-American mayor, in El Paso in 1958. Latinos also took pride in baseball star Roberto Clemente and their growing numbers in the major leagues, in Nobel Prize winners like biologist Severo Ochoa, and in Anthony Quinn and other Hollywood stars. But the existence of millions of undocumented aliens and the continuation of the *bracero* program stigmatized all Hispanics. Their median income was less than two-thirds that of Anglos. At least a third lived in poverty.

Native Americans   Native Americans remained the poorest minority, with a death rate three times the national average. Unemployment rates on reservations during the 1950s reached a staggering 70 to 86 percent for some tribes. Congress again changed course, moving away from New Deal efforts to reassert Indian sovereignty and cultural autonomy and back toward the goal of assimilation. Between 1954 and 1962, Congress terminated treaties and withdrew financial support from sixty-one reservations. Proponents claimed such measures would increase "Indian self-sufficiency," but this termination policy, which reduced federal services, sold off tribal lands, and pushed Indians off the reservations, was disastrous. First applied to the Menominees of Wisconsin and the Klamaths of Oregon, who owned valuable timberlands, it further impoverished the tribes and transferred more than 500,000 acres of Native American lands to non-Indians.

To lure Indians off the reservations and into urban areas, and to speed the sale of Indian lands to developers, the government established the Voluntary Relocation Program. It provided Native Americans with moving costs, assistance in finding housing and jobs, and living expenses until they obtained work. "We're like wheat," said one Hopi woman who went to the city. "The wind blows, we bend over. . . . You can't stand up when there's wind."

By 1960, about sixty thousand Indians had been relocated to cities. Some became middle class, generally losing their Indian identity in the process; some ended up on state welfare rolls, living in rundown shantytowns and addicted to alcohol; and nearly a third returned to their reservations. The National Congress of American Indians vigorously opposed termination, and most tribal politicians advocated Indian sovereignty, treaty rights, federal trusteeship, and the special status of Indians.

THE CIVIL RIGHTS MOVEMENT

The integration of baseball in 1947, spearheaded by the brilliant Jackie Robinson, symbolized a new robustness in the fight against racial discrimination and segregation in the postwar era. The war had heightened African-American expectations for racial equality, and demands included a permanent Fair Employment Practices Commission (FEPC), the outlawing of lynching, and the right to vote.

The Politics of Race   Fearful of black assertiveness in seeking the vote and in mobilizing grassroots forces, white racists accelerated their repression and violence. In 1946, whites killed several black veterans in Georgia for daring to vote and blinded a black soldier for failing to sit in the rear of a bus in South Carolina. In Columbia, Tennessee, also in 1946, a white riot against blacks who were insisting on their rights led to the arrest of seventy African-Americans and the jailhouse lynching of two of the prisoners.

These events horrified President Truman. Aware of the importance to the Democratic party of the growing African-American vote, Truman also realized how much white racism damaged U.S. relations with much of the world. Genuinely believing that every American should enjoy the full rights of citizenship, Truman in late 1946 established the **President's Committee on Civil Rights** to investigate race relations. The committee's report, *To Secure These Rights,* published in 1947, called for the eradication of racial discrimination and segregation and proposed antilynching and antipoll tax legislation and enactment of a permanent FEPC. Boldly, Truman in February 1948 sent a special message to Congress urging lawmakers to enact most of the committee's proposals. Although Truman's subsequent actions would fall short of his rhetoric, the president insisted on closing the gap between the nation's ideals and its racist practices and issued executive orders barring discrimination in federal employment and creating a committee to ensure "equality of treatment and opportunity" for all persons in the armed services.

Jim Crow in Court   During the Truman presidency, moreover, the Supreme Court declared segregation in interstate bus transportation unconstitutional (*Morgan* v. *Virginia,* 1946) and outlawed restrictive housing covenants that forbade the sale or rental of property to minorities (*Shelley* v. *Kraemer,* 1948). Soon thereafter, reflecting the growing determination of black Americans to demand their rights, the NAACP's chief attorney, Thurgood Marshall, abandoned the call for greater equality within "separate but equal" under which, for example, a county in South Carolina with segregated schools could, and did, provide $179 in public funds per white student but only $43 per black student. Instead, Marshall undertook a direct attack on segregation itself. He pursued a strategy built on an earlier federal court ruling that had prohibited the segregation of Mexican-American children in California schools as well as on decisions in 1950 in which the Supreme Court significantly narrowed the possibility of separate law school and graduate education being constitutional.

In May 1954, the new Chief Justice appointed by Eisenhower, **Earl Warren** (1953), speaking for a unanimous Court, reversed the "separate but equal" doctrine of *Plessy v. Ferguson* (see Chapter 20) in the landmark case of ***Brown v. Board of Education of Topeka.*** Overturning more than sixty years of legal segregation, the Supreme Court ruled that separate educational facilities for blacks and whites were "inherently unequal," denying black children the "equal protection of the laws" guaranteed by the Fourteenth Amendment, and thereby unconstitutional. A year later, however, the Court decreed that school desegregation should proceed "with all deliberate speed"—an oxymoron that implied gradualism.

In the border states, some African-American and white students sat side by side for the first time in history. But in the South, where segregation was deeply entrenched in law and custom, politicians vowed resistance, and Eisenhower refused to press them to comply: "I don't believe you can change the hearts of men with laws or decisions." Although not personally racist, Ike never publicly endorsed the *Brown* decision and privately called his appointment of Earl Warren "the biggest damn fool mistake I ever made."

Encouraged by the president's indecisiveness, White Citizens' Councils organized to defend segregation and the Ku Klux Klan revived. Declaring *Brown* "null, void, and of no effect," southern legislatures adopted a strategy of "massive resistance" to thwart compliance with the law. They closed down or denied state aid to school systems that desegregated and enacted pupil-placement laws that permitted school boards to assign black and white children to different schools. In 1956, more than a hundred members of Congress signed the **Southern Manifesto,** denouncing *Brown*, and that year not a single African-American attended school with whites in the Deep South, and few did so in the Upper South.

The Laws of the Land

Southern resistance reached a climax in September 1957. Although the Little Rock school board had accepted a federal court order to desegregate Central High School, Arkansas governor Orval E. Faubus mobilized the state's National Guard to block enforcement and bar nine African-American students from entering the school. After another court order forced Faubus to withdraw the guardsmen, an angry mob of whites blocked the black students' entry.

Eisenhower, believing he had to uphold federal authority, nationalized the Arkansas National Guard, augmented by a thousand federal troops, to protect the African-American students for the rest of the academic year. He thus became, albeit reluctantly, the first president since Reconstruction to use federal troops to enforce the rights of blacks. Local authorities, however, shut down Little Rock's public schools the next year, and by decade's end, fewer than 1 percent of African-American students in the Deep South attended desegregated schools.

Clearly, court victories alone would not end Jim Crow. Nor would weak legislation. The Civil Rights Act of 1957, the first since Reconstruction, established a permanent commission on civil rights with broad investigatory powers, but did little to guarantee the ballot to blacks; and the Civil Rights Act of 1960 only slightly strengthened the first measure's enforcement provisions. At best, these bills implied a changing view of race relations by the federal government, which further encouraged blacks to fight for their rights.

Mass Protest in Montgomery

To sweep away the separate but rarely equal Jim Crow facilities in the South, African-Americans turned to new tactics, organizations, and leaders. They utilized nonviolent direct-action protest to engage large numbers of blacks in their own freedom struggle and to arouse white America's conscience.

In the 1950s, racism still touched even the smallest details of daily life. In Montgomery, Alabama, black bus riders had to surrender their seats so that no white rider would stand. Although they were more than three-quarters of all passengers, African-Americans had to pay their fares at the front of the bus, leave, and reenter through the back door, sit only in the rear, and then give up their seats to any standing white passengers.

(AP Images/Arkansas Democrat/Will Counts)

Little Rock, 1957 *Elizabeth Eckford, age fifteen, one of the nine black students to desegregate Central High School, endures abuse on her way to school, September 4, 1957. Such scenes of angry whites jeering, screaming, and threatening African-American students were televised to the nation, showing the human suffering caused by racist hatred in the South. By so doing, television made Americans aware of the stark consequences of racism. Forty years later, the young white woman shouting insults in this picture asked for forgiveness.*

On December 1, 1955, **Rosa Parks**, for many years an officer of the Montgomery NAACP and a veteran of civil rights protests in the 1930s and 1940s, refused to get up so that a white man could sit. "I was not tired physically," she later wrote. "No, the only tired I was, was tired of giving in." Her arrest sparked Jo Ann Robinson of the Women's Political Council, and other blacks who had been engaged in the freedom struggle in Montgomery, to propose a boycott of the buses—the beginning of the mass phase of the civil-rights movement. They founded the Montgomery Improvement Association (MIA) to organize the protest, and elected **Martin Luther King, Jr.**, a twenty-seven-year-old African-American minister, to lead the boycott. "There comes a time when people get tired," declared King, articulating the anger of Montgomery blacks, "tired of being segregated and humiliated; tired of being kicked about by the brutal feet of oppression." The time had come, he continued, to cease being patient "with anything less than freedom and justice." "My soul has been tired for a long time," an old woman told a minister who had stopped his car to offer her a ride; "now my feet are tired, and my soul is resting." Montgomery African-Americans trudged the streets, organized car pools, and raised thousands of dollars to carry on the fight, and when city leaders would not budge, blacks persisted for more than a year until the Supreme Court ordered the buses desegregated.

The Montgomery bus boycott demonstrated African-American strength and determination. It shattered the myth that African-Americans approved of segregation and that only outside agitators opposed Jim Crow. It affirmed the possibility of social change and inspired protests elsewhere in the South. It vaulted Dr. King, whose oratory simultaneously inspired black activism and touched white consciences, into the national spotlight. As no one before, King presented the case for black rights in a vocabulary that echoed both the Bible and the freedom values of the Founding Fathers.

King's philosophy of civil disobedience fused the spirit of Christianity with the strategy of achieving racial justice by nonviolent resistance. Casting aside the legalistic strategies of the NAACP, direct action gave every African-American an opportunity to demonstrate the moral evil of racial discrimination. King's insistence on nonviolence also diminished the likelihood of bloodshed. Preaching that blacks must lay their bodies on the line to provoke crises that would force whites to confront their racism, King urged his followers to love their enemies. By so doing, he believed, blacks would convert their oppressors and bring "redemption and reconciliation." In 1957, King and a group of black ministers formed the Southern Christian Leadership Conference (SCLC) "to carry on nonviolent crusades against the evils of second-class citizenship." Yet more than on leaders, the movement's triumphs in the decade ahead would depend on the thousands of ordinary people who marched, rallied, and demonstrated extraordinarily in grassroots protest movements.

New Tactics for a New Decade   Foreshadowing the massive grass-roots activism to come, four black college students in Greensboro, North Carolina, entered the local Woolworth's on February 1, 1960, and sat down at the whites-only lunch counter, defying segregation. "We don't serve colored here," the waitress replied when the freshmen ordered coffee and doughnuts. The blacks remained seated. They would not be moved.

Impatient yet hopeful, the students would not accept the inequality their parents had endured. Inspired by the earlier black struggles for justice, as well as by successful African independence movements, they vowed to sit-in until they were served. Six months later, after prolonged sit-ins, boycotts, and demonstrations by hundreds of students, and violent white resistance, Greensboro's civic leaders grudgingly allowed blacks to sit down at hitherto segregated restaurants and be served.

Meanwhile, the courageous example of the Greensboro "coffee party" catalyzed similar sit-ins throughout the border states and Upper South. Black students confronted humiliations and violence: they endured beatings, cigarette-burnings, tear-gassing, and jailing in their sit-ins to desegregate eating facilities, as well as in their "kneel ins" in churches, "sleep ins" in motel lobbies, "wade ins" on restricted beaches, "read ins" at public libraries, "play ins" at city parks, and "watch ins" at segregated movie theaters. Yet they stayed true to nonviolent principles and refused to retaliate.

The determination of the students transformed the struggle for racial equality. Their activism and commitment emboldened black adults and other youths to act. Their assertiveness desegregated facilities and generated a sense of self-esteem and strength. "I myself desegregated a lunch counter, not somebody else, not some big man, some powerful man, but little me," claimed a student. By year's end, nearly fifty thousand people had participated in demonstrations, desegregating lunch counters and other public facilities in 126 southern cities. Each victory convinced others that "nothing can stop us now."

Newly encouraged and emboldened, the Congress of Racial Equality (CORE), which had been founded in WWII, organized a "freedom ride" through the Deep South in spring 1961 to dramatize the flouting of federal court decisions banning segregation in interstate transportation facilities. It aroused white wrath. Mobs beat the Freedom Riders in Anniston, Alabama, burning their bus, and mauled the protestors in Birmingham, making the **Freedom Rides** front-page news. A week later, scores of racist southerners in Montgomery beat Freedom Riders with bats and iron chains, generating international publicity and indignation, which ultimately forced the Interstate Commerce Commission to require the desegregation of all interstate carriers and terminals.

Many of the Freedom Riders were members of the **Student Nonviolent Coordinating Committee (SNCC)**. Formed in April 1960 by participants in the sit-ins, SNCC (known as "Snick") stressed both the nonviolent civil disobedience strategy of Martin Luther King, Jr., and the need to stimulate local activism and leadership. Within months, SNCC volunteers spread out into Mississippi, organizing voting-rights campaigns and sit-ins, and in fall 1961 it chose Albany, Georgia, as the site of a campaign to desegregate public facilities and secure the vote. Despite King's involvement, wily local authorities avoided the overt violence that had won the freedom riders national sympathy. The Albany movement collapsed; but the lesson of Albany, and of the Freedom Rides, had been learned: only the provocation of vicious white racist violence generated national publicity and forced the federal government to intervene to protect the rights of African-Americans. The young activists who learned that lesson and how to use the media skillfully would chart the course of the 1960s.

CHRONOLOGY
1952–1961

1944	Servicemen's Readjustment Act (GI Bill).
1946	ENIAC, the first electronic computer, begins operation.
1947	Levittown, New York, development started.
	Jackie Robinson breaks major league baseball's color line.
	President's Committee on Civil Rights issues *To Secure These Rights*.

1948	Bell Labs develops the transistor.
1950	*Asosiación Nacional México-Americana* established.
1953	Earl Warren appointed chief justice.
	Operation Wetback begins.
1954	*Brown v. Board of Education of Topeka.*
	Father Knows Best begins on TV.
1955	Salk polio vaccine developed.
	AFL-CIO merger.
	Elvis Presley ignites rock-n-roll.
	James Dean stars in *Rebel Without a Cause.*
	Montgomery bus boycott begins.
1956	Interstate Highway Act.
1957	Little Rock school-desegregation crisis.
	Soviet Union launches *Sputnik.*
	Peak of baby boom (4.3 million births).
	Southern Christian Leadership Conference founded.
1958	National Defense Education Act.
	National Aeronautics and Space Administration (NASA) founded.
1960	Sit-ins begin.
	Suburban population almost equals that of central city.
1961	Freedom Rides begin.

Conclusion

A far more complex era than that implied in the stereotype of the "nifty fifties," the decade encompassed contradictions. Although mightier than any nation had ever been and basking in a level of material comfort previously unknown in world history, many Americans felt uneasiness as the Cold War continued and prosperity brought unsettling changes.

The postwar era was one of unparalleled affluence for most Americans. Building on the accumulated savings and pent-up demand for consumer goods after the Second World War, high levels of government spending, the GI Bill, and new technologies that increased productivity spurred an economic boom. Prosperity further enriched the rich, transformed the working class into the middle class, and left the poor isolated on a remote island of deprivation and powerlessness in "the other America."

Overall, the postwar United States, with its burgeoning suburbia and cornucopia of consumerism, seemed the very model of contentment and complacency—what Americans considered the good life. Despite the criticism by the Beats and intellectuals of conservatism and conformity, despite the alienation and rebelliousness of young people questioning their parents' embrace of the status quo, most middle-class whites ignored the seeds of disquiet along with the inequities in

American society. Enjoying their private pleasures, they rejected radicalism, condoned the income disparity and persistent prejudice minorities encountered, extolled a benign and optimistic religion, lauded mass culture, and idealized traditional gender roles, domesticity, and togetherness. Busy working and consuming, they left for a future decade the festering problems of hidden poverty, urban decay, and racial injustice.

Still, the cracks in the picture of a placid people widened. Unrest competed with consensus. Although racism remained omnipresent, the seeds of struggle, planted in the 1930s and the Second World War, flowered in new campaigns to end racial discrimination and segregation. In the courts, the NAACP ceased requesting that separate facilities be equal and instead insisted that true equality required desegregation. And in the streets, Martin Luther King, Jr., SNCC, and CORE employed the techniques of nonviolent civil disobedience to attack Jim Crow, bringing some gains and stimulating an insurgency that spurred further challenges to make the nation live up to its ideals.

28

LIBERALISM, CIVIL RIGHTS,
AND WAR IN VIETNAM,
1960–1975

CHAPTER OUTLINE

• The Kennedy Presidency, 1961–1963 • The Continuing Struggle for
Black Equality, 1961–1968 • The Expanding Movement for Equality
• Liberalism Ascendant, 1963–1968 • The Vietnam Crusade, 1961–1967

THE KENNEDY PRESIDENCY, 1961–1963

Projecting an image of youthful vigor, **John F. Kennedy** personified the self-confident liberal who believed that an activist state could improve life at home and confront the communist challenge abroad. His wealthy father, Joseph P. Kennedy, seethed with ambition and instilled in his sons a passion to excel and to rule. Despite a severe back injury, John Kennedy served in the navy in World War II and came home a war hero. He then used his charm and his father's connections to win election in 1946 to the House of Representatives from a Boston district where he had never lived. Although Kennedy earned no distinction in Congress, Massachusetts voters sent him to the Senate in 1952 and overwhelmingly reelected him in 1958.

By then, Kennedy had a beautiful wife, Jacqueline, and a Pulitzer Prize for *Profiles in Courage* (1956), written largely by a staff member. Despite the political liability of his Roman Catholic faith, he won a first-ballot victory at the 1960 Democratic convention. Just forty-three years old, he sounded the theme of a "New Frontier," exhorting Americans to "get this country moving again."

A New Beginning	"All at once you had something exciting," recalled a University of Nebraska student. "You had a guy who had little kids and who liked to play football on his front lawn. Kennedy

was talking about pumping new life into the nation and steering it in new directions." But most voters, middle aged and middle class, wanted the stability and security of Eisenhower's "middle way" promised by the Republican candidate, Vice President Richard M. Nixon. Although scorned by liberals for his McCarthyism, Nixon was better known and more experienced than Kennedy, identified with the still-popular Ike, and a Protestant.

Nixon fumbled his opportunity, agreeing to meet his challenger in televised debates. More than 70 million tuned in to the first televised debate between presidential candidates, a broadcast that secured the dominance of television in American politics. Nixon, sweating visibly, appeared haggard and insecure; in striking contrast, the tanned, telegenic Kennedy radiated confidence. Radio listeners judged the debate a draw, but the far more numerous television viewers declared Kennedy the victor. He shot up in the polls, and Nixon never recovered.

Kennedy also benefited from an economic recession in 1960, and from his choice of a southern Protestant, Senate Majority Leader Lyndon B. Johnson, as his running mate. Still, the election was the closest since 1884. Only 120,000 votes separated the two candidates. Kennedy's religion cost him millions of popular votes, but his capture of 80 percent of the Catholic vote in the closely contested midwestern and northeastern states delivered crucial Electoral College votes, enabling him to squeak to victory.

Kennedy's inauguration set the tone of a new era. Taking office in the pale sun and icy wind, he trumpeted that: "the torch has been passed to a new generation of Americans." In sharp contrast to Eisenhower's reliance on businessmen (see Chapter 27), Kennedy surrounded himself with liberal intellectuals. He seemed more a celebrity than a politician. Aided by his wife, he adorned his presidency with the trappings of culture and excellence, inviting distinguished artists to perform at the White House and studding his speeches with quotations from Emerson. Awed by his grace and taste, as well as by his wit and wealth, the media extolled him as a vibrant leader and adoring husband. The public knew nothing of his fragile health, frequent use of mood-altering drugs to alleviate pain, and extramarital affairs.

Kennedy's Domestic Record

Media images obscured Kennedy's lackluster domestic record. The conservative coalition of Republicans and southern Democrats that had stifled Truman's Fair Deal similarly doomed the New Frontier. Lacking the votes, JFK rarely pressed Congress for social legislation.

JFK made stimulating economic growth his domestic priority; he combined higher defense expenditures with investment incentives for private enterprise. In 1961, he persuaded Congress to boost the defense budget by 20 percent. He vastly increased America's nuclear stockpile, strengthened the military's conventional forces, and established the Special Forces ("Green Berets") to engage in guerrilla warfare. By 1963, the defense budget reached its highest level as a percentage of total federal expenditures in the entire Cold War era. Kennedy also persuaded Congress to finance a "race to the moon," which Americans would win in 1969 at a cost of more than $25 billion. Most importantly, Kennedy took his liberal advisers' Keynesian advice to call for a huge cut in corporate taxes, which would greatly increase the deficit but would presumably provide capital for business to invest, stimulating the economy and thus increasing tax revenues.

When the Kennedy presidency ended tragically in November 1963, the proposed tax cut was bottled up in Congress. But Kennedy's spending on technology and the military had already doubled the 1960 rate of economic growth and decreased unemployment, triggering the United States' longest uninterrupted economic expansion.

The boom would both cause further ecological damage and provide the affluence that enabled Americans to care about the environment. Environmental protection would build on an older conservation movement, emphasizing the efficient use of resources, a preservation movement (focusing on preserving "wilderness"), and the fallout scare of the 1950s, which raised questions about the biological well-being of the planet. The publication in 1962 of Rachel Carson's *Silent Spring* (see Chapter 27), documenting the hazards of pesticides, intensified concern. Additionally, postwar prosperity made many Americans less concerned with increased production and more concerned with the quality of life. In 1963, Congress passed a Clean Air Act, regulating automotive and industrial emissions. After decades of heedless pollution, Washington hesitantly began to address environmental problems.

Cold War Activism

Proclaiming in his inaugural address that "we shall pay any price, bear any burden, meet any hardship," to assure the "success of liberty," Kennedy launched a major military buildup and surrounded himself with Cold Warriors who shared his belief that American security depended on superior force and the willingness to use it. He also increased economic assistance to Third World countries to counter the appeal of communism. The Peace Corps, created in 1961, exemplified the New Frontier's liberal anticommunism. By 1963, five thousand Peace Corps volunteers were serving two-year stints as teachers, sanitation engineers, crop specialists, and health workers in more than forty Third World nations.

In early 1961, a crisis flared in Laos, a tiny nation in Southeast Asia where a civil war between American-supported forces and Pathet Lao rebels seemed headed toward a communist triumph. In July 1962, Kennedy agreed to a face-saving compromise that restored a neutralist government but left communist forces dominant in the countryside. The accord stiffened Kennedy's resolve not to allow further communist gains in Asia, especially in South Vietnam.

Spring 1961 brought Kennedy's first major foreign-policy crisis. Despite his military advisers thinking it had little chance of success, he approved a CIA plan, drawn up in the Eisenhower administration, to invade Cuba. In April, fifteen hundred anti-Castro exiles, "La Brigada," stormed Cuba's Bay of Pigs, expecting their arrival to trigger a general uprising to overthrow Fidel Castro and eliminate a communist outpost on America's doorstep. It was a fiasco. Deprived of air cover by Kennedy's desire to conceal U.S. involvement, the invaders had no chance against Castro's superior forces.

In July 1961, on the heels of the Bay of Pigs failure, Kennedy met with Soviet premier Nikita Khrushchev, who threatened war unless the West retreated from Berlin (see Chapter 26). A shaken Kennedy returned to the United States and declared the defense of West Berlin essential to the Free World. He doubled draft calls, mobilized reservists, and called for vastly increased defense spending. The threat of nuclear war escalated until mid-August, when the Soviets constructed a wall to seal off East Berlin and end the exodus of brains and talent to the West. The Berlin Wall became a concrete symbol of communism's denial of personal freedom until it fell in 1989.

To the Brink of Nuclear War   In mid-October 1962, aerial photographs revealed that the Soviet Union had built bases for intermediate-range ballistic missiles (IRBMs) in Cuba, capable of striking U.S. soil. Smarting from the Bay of Pigs disaster, fearing unchecked Soviet interference in the Western Hemisphere, and believing his credibility at stake, Kennedy responded forcefully. In a somber televised address, he announced that the United States would "quarantine" Cuba—impose a naval blockade—to prevent delivery of more missiles and would dismantle by force the missiles already in Cuba if the Soviets did not do so.

The world held its breath. The two superpowers appeared on a collision course toward nuclear war. Two thousand government officials eligible to go to the secret nuclear war relocation site, buried deep in a Virginia mountainside, were issued special badges of admission. (When Chief Justice Warren asked where was the pass for Mrs. Warren, and was told there was no provision for family, he returned his pass.)

Meanwhile, Soviet technicians worked feverishly to complete the missile launch pads, and Soviet missile-carrying ships steamed toward the blockade. B-52s armed with nuclear bombs took to the air, and nearly a quarter-million troops assembled in Florida to invade Cuba. Secretary of State Dean Rusk gulped, "We're eyeball to eyeball."

"I think the other fellow just blinked," a relieved Rusk remarked on October 25. Kennedy received a message from Khrushchev promising to remove the missiles if the United States pledged never to invade Cuba. As Kennedy prepared to respond positively, a second, more belligerent message arrived from Khrushchev insisting that American missiles be withdrawn from Turkey as part of the deal. Hours later, an American U-2 reconnaissance plane was shot down over Cuba. Some of the president's advisers urged an immediate invasion, but the president, heeding Robert Kennedy's advice, decided to accept the first message and ignore the second one. The next morning, Khrushchev pledged to remove the missiles in return for Kennedy's noninvasion promise. Less publicly, Kennedy subsequently removed U.S. missiles from Turkey.

Only after the end of the Cold War did the Russians disclose that Soviet forces in Cuba had possessed thirty-six nuclear warheads as well as nine tactical nuclear weapons for battlefield use, and that Soviet field commanders had independent authority to use these weapons. Moreover, the Soviets had already had the capability to launch a nuclear strike from Cuba. Speaking in 1992, former secretary of defense Robert McNamara recalled the pressure for an invasion: "No one should believe that U.S. troops could have been attacked by tactical nuclear warheads without the U.S.'s responding with nuclear warheads. ... And where would it have ended? In utter disaster."

Chastened by coming to the brink of nuclear war, Kennedy and Khrushchev installed a telephone "hot line" so that the two sides could communicate instantly in future crises and then agreed to a treaty outlawing atmospheric and undersea nuclear testing. These efforts signaled a new phase of the Cold War, later called détente, in which the superpowers moved from confrontation to negotiation. Concurrently, the **Cuban missile crisis** escalated the arms race by convincing both sides of the need for nuclear superiority.

The Thousand-Day Presidency   On November 22, 1963, during a trip to Texas to shore up the president's reelection chances, John and Jackie Kennedy rode in an open car along Dallas streets lined with cheering crowds. Shots rang out. The president slumped, dying, his skull and throat shattered. Soon after, aboard Air Force One, Lyndon B. Johnson was sworn in as president.

Grief and disbelief numbed the nation, as most Americans spent the next four days in front of TV sets staring at replays of the murder of accused assassin Lee Harvey Oswald; at the somber state funeral, with the small boy saluting his father's casket; at the grieving family lighting an eternal flame at Arlington National Cemetery. Few who watched would forget. Kennedy had helped make television central to American politics; now, in death, it made him the fallen hero-king of Camelot.

(JACK BEERS/The Dallas Morning News)

Jack Ruby Shooting Lee Harvey Oswald *Two days after Oswald's arrest for the assassination of President John Kennedy, as television cameras filmed his transfer to a different jail, Dallas nightclub owner Jack Ruby stepped from a crowd of onlookers and fatally shot Oswald.*

More admired in death than in life, JFK ranked as one of the very few "great" presidents, in the view of a public that associated him with a spirit of energy and innovation. While Kennedy loyalists continue to stress his intelligence and his ability to change and grow, his detractors point to his lack of achievements, the discrepancy between his public image and his private philandering, his aggressive Cold War tactics, and his vast expansion of presidential powers.

Kennedy's rhetoric expressed the new liberalism, but he frequently compromised with conservatives and segregationists in Congress; economic expansion came from spending on missiles and the space race, not on social welfare and human needs. Partly because his own personal behavior made him beholden to FBI director J. Edgar Hoover, JFK allowed the agency to infringe on civil liberties, even as the CIA plotted with the Mafia to assassinate Fidel Castro. (Scholars are still trying to untangle the plots and policies that enmeshed the Kennedy brothers, Hoover, organized crime, and the national security agencies.)

Internationally, Kennedy left a mixed record. He signed the world's first nuclear-test-ban treaty, yet initiated a massive arms buildup. He compromised on Laos but deepened U.S. involvement in Vietnam. He came to question the need for confronting the Soviet Union yet insisted on U.S. global superiority and aggressively prosecuted the Cold War. Yet, JFK inspired Americans to expect greatness, aroused the poor and the powerless, and stimulated the young to activism. Dying during the calm before the storm, he left his successor soaring expectations at home and a deteriorating entanglement in Vietnam.

THE CONTINUING STRUGGLE FOR BLACK EQUALITY, 1961–1968

Following the lunch-counter sit-ins and Freedom Rides, civil-rights activists eager to climb the next steps of racial justice pressed Kennedy to act; and the president continued to stall. Viewing civil rights as a thorny thicket to avoid, not as a moral issue, Kennedy feared it would split the Democratic Party, immobilize Congress in filibusters, and jeopardize his reelection. Yet the Movement persisted until it had achieved de jure, or legal, equality; made protest respectable; and become an inspiration and model of activism for aggrieved others.

The African-American Revolution

As television coverage of the struggle for racial equality brought mounting numbers of African-Americans into the movement, civil-rights leaders beseeched Kennedy to intervene. They realized it would take decades of blood and bravery to dismantle segregation piecemeal; only comprehensive national legislation, backed by the power of the federal government, could guarantee full citizenship for African-Americans. To achieve this goal, they needed a crisis that would outrage the conscience of the white majority and force the president's hand.

Determined to expose the violent extremism of southern racism and provoke a crisis, Martin Luther King launched nonviolent marches, sit-ins, and pray-ins in Birmingham, Alabama. In the most rigidly segregated big city in America, nicknamed "Bombingham" for the many past acts of violence against civil-rights protestors, few doubted Police Commissioner Eugene "Bull" Connor's pledge that "blood would run in the streets of Birmingham before it would be integrated."

When jailed for instigating a march that a local court had prohibited, King penned the "Letter from Birmingham Jail." It detailed the humiliations of racial discrimination and segregation; vindicated the nonviolent struggle against Jim Crow; and justified civil disobedience to protest unjust laws.

In May, thousands of schoolchildren, some only six years old, joined King's crusade. Connor lost his temper. He unleashed his men—armed with electric cattle prods, high-pressure water hoses, and snarling attack dogs—on the nonviolent youthful demonstrators. The ferocity of Connor's attacks, caught on camera and television, horrified the world.

"The civil-rights movement should thank God for Bull Connor," JFK remarked. "He's helped it as much as Abraham Lincoln." Connor's vicious tactics seared the nation's conscience and pushed Kennedy to help negotiate a settlement that ended the demonstrations in return for desegregating stores and hiring black workers. By mid-1963, the rallying cry "Freedom Now!" reverberated across the nation as the protests grew. Increasingly concerned about America's image abroad as well as the "fires of frustration and discord" raging at home, Kennedy feared that if the government did not act, blacks would turn to violence. When Governor George Wallace refused to allow two black students to enter the University of Alabama in June 1963, Kennedy forced Wallace—who had pledged "Segregation now! Segregation tomorrow! Segregation forever!"—to capitulate to a court desegregation order.

On June 11, the president went on television to define civil rights as "a moral issue" and to declare that "race has no place in American life or law." A week later, Kennedy proposed a bill outlawing segregation in public facilities and authorizing the federal government to withhold funds from programs that discriminated. As the bill bogged down in Congress, civil-rights adherents planned to march on Washington to muster support for the legislation.

The March on Washington, 1963   The idea for a March on Washington had originally been proposed by A. Philip Randolph in 1941 to protest discrimination against blacks in the defense mobilization (see Chapter 25). Twenty-two years later, a quarter of a million people, including fifty thousand whites, converged on Washington, D.C. After a long, sweltering day of speeches and songs, Martin Luther King took the podium to remind Americans that the hopes generated by the Emancipation Proclamation had still not been fulfilled, and to reiterate his dream of true brotherhood, in which blacks would be an integral, equal part of American society, not embittered opponents of it.

With one of the greatest American speeches ever, portrayed at the beginning of this chapter, King turned a political rally into a historic event. But not even that quelled the rage of white racists. In September, the Ku Klux Klan bombing of a black church in Birmingham killed four girls attending Sunday school. (Not until 2002 was the last of the four main suspects brought to justice.) And southern obstructionism still kept the civil-rights bill stymied in Congress.

Civil Rights at
High Tide Kennedy's assassination, however, brought to the White House a southerner, Lyndon Johnson, who knew he had to prove himself on the race issue or the liberals "would get me.... I had to produce a civil rights bill that was even stronger than the one they'd have gotten if Kennedy had lived."

It would take all of LBJ's legislative skills, brave bipartisanship by Republicans like Representative William McCulloch of Ohio and Senator Everett Dirksen of Illinois, and the massed efforts of civil rights workers, churches, and unions to win passage of the **Civil Rights Act of 1964**—the most significant civil-rights law in U.S. history. The law banned racial discrimination and segregation in public accommodations; outlawed bias in federally funded programs; granted the federal government new powers to fight school segregation; and created the Equal Employment Opportunity Commission (EEOC) to enforce the ban on job discrimination.

The Civil Rights Act did not address the right to vote. So CORE and SNCC activists, believing the ballot held the key to power for southern blacks, mounted a major campaign to register black voters. They organized the Mississippi Freedom Summer Project of 1964 to focus on the state most hostile to black rights. Although 42 percent of Mississippi's population, blacks comprised only 5 percent of the registered voters. A thousand college-student volunteers assisted blacks in registering to vote and in organizing "Freedom Schools" that taught black history and emphasized African-American self-worth. Harassed by Mississippi law-enforcement officials and Ku Klux Klansmen, the volunteers endured the firebombing of black churches and of movement headquarters, as well as arrests and even murders.

The civil-rights workers enrolled nearly sixty thousand disfranchised blacks in the Mississippi Freedom Democratic Party (MFDP). In August 1964, they took their case to the national Democratic convention, seeking to be seated as the proper delegation. "I was beaten till I was exhausted," Fannie Lou Hamer, the twentieth child of poor sharecroppers, told the convention. "All of this on account we wanted to register, to become first class citizens. If the Freedom Democratic party is not seated now, I question America." The MFDP was not seated. To stop a threatened walkout by southern white delegates, Johnson forged a compromise that the MFDP rejected. Within SNCC, the failure of the Democrats to support seating the MFDP delegates proved to be a turning point in their disillusionment with liberalism.

Most blacks still shared the optimism of Martin Luther King, and more than 90 percent of African-American voters cast their ballots for the Democrats in 1964, leaving Johnson and the liberals in firm control. Determined to win a strong voting-rights law, King and the SCLC organized mass protests in Selma, Alabama, in March 1965. Blacks were half the population of Dallas County, where Selma was located, but only 1 percent were registered to vote.

King knew he again had to create a crisis to pressure Congress to act. He masterfully provoked Selma's county sheriff, Jim Clark to brutally beat and arrest thousands of black protestors.

When civil-rights activists sought to march from Selma to Montgomery, to petition Governor George Wallace, Alabama state police stormed into the defenseless marchers, who were clubbed, shocked with cattle prods, and tear-gassed. Showcased on TV, the spectacle provoked national outrage and support for a voting rights bill.

Signed by the president in August 1965, the **Voting Rights Act** invalidated the use of any test or device to deny the vote and authorized federal examiners to register voters in states that had disfranchised blacks. The law dramatically expanded black suffrage, boosting the number of registered black voters in the South from 1 million in 1964 to 3.1 million in 1968, and transformed southern politics (see Map 28.1).

The number of blacks holding office in the South swelled from fewer than two dozen in 1964 to nearly twelve hundred in 1972, including half the seats on Selma's city council and the first two African-Americans elected to Congress from the former Confederacy since the nineteenth century. Electoral success brought jobs for African-Americans, contracts for black businesses, and improvements in facilities and services in black neighborhoods. Most importantly, as Fannie Lou Hamer recalled, when African-Americans could not vote, "white folks would drive past your house in a pickup truck with guns hanging up on the back and give you hate stares.... Those same people now call me Mrs. Hamer."

Fire in the Streets   The civil-rights movement changed, but did not revolutionize race relations. It ended de jure racial discrimination and segregation, broke the white monopoly on political power in the South, and galvanized a new black sense of self-esteem. It raised hopes for the possibility of greater change and legitimated protest. But its inability to move beyond opportunity to achievement, to gain equality as a result, not just a right, underscored the limitations of liberal change, especially in the urban ghetto. The movement did little to change the deplorable economic conditions of many African-Americans, and the anger bubbling below the surface boiled over.

On August 11, 1965, five days after the signing of the Voting Rights Act, a scuffle between white police and blacks in Watts, the largest African-American district in Los Angeles, ignited the most destructive race riot in decades. For six days, blacks looted shops, firebombed white-owned businesses, and sniped at police officers and firefighters, leaving in their wake thirty-four dead, nine hundred injured, and four thousand arrested.

Watts proved to be just a prelude to a succession of "long hot summers." In 1966, rioting erupted in more than a score of northern ghettos, forcing whites to heed the squalor of the slums and the brutal behavior of police in the ghetto—problems the civil-rights movement had ignored. Frustrated by the allure of America's wealth portrayed on TV and by what seemed the empty promise of civil-rights laws, black mobs stoned passing motorists, ransacked stores, torched white-owned buildings, and hurled bricks at the troops sent to quell the disorder.

The following summer, black rage at oppressive conditions and impatience with liberal change erupted in 150 racial skirmishes and forty riots—the most intense and destructive period of racial violence in U.S. history. In Newark, New Jersey, twenty-seven people died and more than eleven hundred were injured. The following week, Detroit went up in smoke in the decade's worst riot. By the time the Michigan National Guard and U.S. army paratroopers quelled the riot, forty-three people had died, two thousand were injured, and seven thousand had been arrested. Then in 1968, following the assassination of Martin Luther King

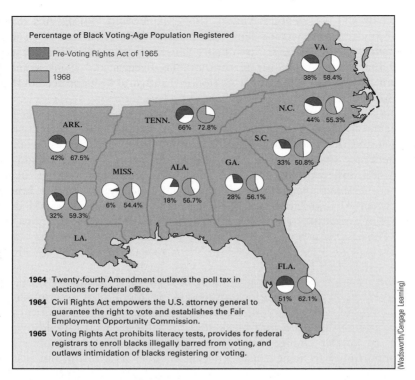

Percentage of Black Voting-Age Population Registered

■ Pre-Voting Rights Act of 1965

□ 1968

VA. 38% 58.4%

N.C. 44% 55.3%

TENN. 66% 72.8%

ARK. 42% 67.5%

S.C. 33% 50.8%

MISS. 6% 54.4%

ALA. 18% 56.7%

GA. 28% 56.1%

LA. 32% 59.3%

FLA. 51% 62.1%

1964 Twenty-fourth Amendment outlaws the poll tax in elections for federal office.

1964 Civil Rights Act empowers the U.S. attorney general to guarantee the right to vote and establishes the Fair Employment Opportunity Commission.

1965 Voting Rights Act prohibits literacy tests, provides for federal registrars to enroll blacks illegally barred from voting, and outlaws intimidation of blacks registering or voting.

(Wadsworth/Cengage Learning)

MAP 28.1 Voter Registration of African-Americans in the South, 1960–1968

As blacks overwhelmingly registered to vote as Democrats, some former segregationist politicians, among them George Wallace, started to court the black vote, and many southern whites began to cast their ballots for Republicans, inaugurating an era of real two-party competition in the South.

(discussed in Chapter 29), black uprisings flared in the ghettos of a hundred cities. The 1964–1968 riot toll included two hundred dead, seven thousand injured, forty thousand arrested, and at least $500 million in property destroyed—mostly white-owned stores and tenements that exemplified exploitation in the ghetto.

A frightened, bewildered nation asked why rioting occurred just when blacks achieved many of their goals. Militant blacks saw the uprisings as revolutionary violence to overthrow a racist, reactionary society. The Far Right thought them evidence of a communist plot. Conservatives described them as senseless outbursts by troublemakers. The administration's National Advisory Commission on Civil Disorders (known as the Kerner Commission) indicted white racism for fostering an "explosive mixture" of poverty, slum housing, poor education, and police brutality. The commission recommended increased federal spending to create new jobs for urban blacks, construct additional public housing, and end de facto (existing in practice, but not in law) school segregation in the North. Johnson and Congress, however, aware of the swelling white backlash, ignored the advice, and most whites approved their inaction.

"Black Power"   For many young African-Americans, liberalism's response to racial inequality proved "too little, too late." The demand for **Black Power** sounded in 1966 paralleled the fury of the urban riots; it expressed the eagerness of young activists for militant self-defense and rapid social change. The slogan encapsulated both their bitterness toward a white society that blocked their aspirations and their rejection of King's commitment to nonviolence, racial integration, and alliances with white liberals.

Derived from a long tradition of black nationalism, autonomy, and race pride, Black Power owed much to the rhetoric and vision of Malcolm X. A former drug addict and street hustler, Malcolm X had converted to the Nation of Islam, or the Black Muslim faith, while in prison. Founded in Detroit in 1931 by Elijah Poole (who took the Islamic name Elijah Muhammad), the Black Muslims insisted that blacks practice self-discipline and self-respect, and they rejected integration. Malcolm X accordingly urged African-Americans to separate themselves from the "white devil" and to relish their African roots and their blackness. Blacks, he asserted, had to rely on armed self-defense and had to seize their freedom "by any means necessary." "If ballots won't work, bullets will," he said. Malcolm X's assassination by members of the Nation of Islam in February 1965, after he had broken with Elijah Muhammad, did not still his voice. *The Autobiography of Malcolm X* (1965) became the main text for the rising Black Power movement.

Bobby Seale and Huey Newton

Founded by Bobby Seale and Huey Newton in Oakland, California, in response to police brutality against African-Americans, the Black Panther Party was organized along semi-military lines and advocated fighting for black justice, in Newton's words, "through the barrel of a gun."

(AP Images)

Two days after winning the world heavyweight championship in 1964, boxer Cassius Clay shocked the sports world by announcing his conversion to the Nation of Islam and his new name, Muhammad Ali. Refusing induction into the armed services on religious grounds, Ali was found guilty of draft evasion, stripped of his title, and exiled from boxing for three and a half years during his athletic prime. Inspired by the examples of Ali and Malcolm X—and bitter at the failure of the established civil-rights organizations to achieve a fundamental distribution of wealth and power—young, urban African-Americans abandoned nonviolence and reform. In 1966, CORE and SNCC changed from interracial organizations committed to achieving integration nonviolently to all-black groups advocating racial separatism and Black Power "by any means necessary."

The Black Panther Party for Self-Defense, founded in Oakland, California, in 1966 by Huey P. Newton and Bobby Seale, urged blacks to become "panthers— striking by night and sparing no one." Despite sponsoring community centers and school breakfast programs, the Panthers attained national notoriety from their paramilitary style and shootouts with the police. A violent and often illegal campaign of repression by federal, state, and local authorities left some Black Panthers dead and more in prison, further splintering the black–white civil-rights alliance and contributing to the rightward turn in politics.

The Black Power movement failed to alleviate the poverty and racism afflicting African-Americans, and the concept remained amorphous—ranging from notions of black capitalism to local control of schools to revolutionary schemes to overthrow the American system. But Black Power celebrated black pride and stressed the importance of black self-determination as no mass movement had done before. Scores of new community self-help groups and self-reliant black institutions exemplified it, as did the establishment of black studies programs at colleges, the mobilization of black voters to elect black candidates, and the encouragement of racial self-esteem—"black is beautiful." As never before, African-Americans rejected skin bleaches and hair straighteners, gave their children Islamic names, and gloried in soul music. "I may have lost hope," SCLC leader Jesse Jackson had students repeating with him, "but I am ... somebody ... I am ... black ... beautiful ... proud ... I must be respected." This message, and Black Power's critique of American society, resonated with other marginalized groups, and helped shape their protests.

The Struggle Goes On   As a result of civil-rights activism, millions of blacks experienced significant upward mobility. In 1965, black students accounted for less than 5 percent of total college enrollment; by 1990, the figure had risen to 12 percent, close to their proportion in the general population. By 1990, some 46 percent of black workers held white-collar jobs. TV's *Cosby Show*, a late-1980s comedy in which Bill Cosby played a doctor married to a lawyer, portrayed this upwardly mobile world.

Outside this world lay the inner-city slums, inhabited by perhaps a third of the black population. Here, up to half the young people never finished high school, and the jobless rate soared as high as 60 percent, owing to suburbanization and deindustrialization. In 1980, the poverty rate among African-Americans stood at 32 percent, three times the rate for non-Hispanic whites.

Cocaine and other drugs pervaded the inner cities. Some black children recruited as lookouts for drug dealers eventually became dealers themselves. With drugs came violence. In the 1980s, a young black male was six times as likely to be murdered as a young white male. Drug abuse affected all social levels, including yuppies and show-business celebrities; but drug use and trafficking particularly devastated the inner cities. Serious social problems among those left behind in the inner cities, as well as upward mobility and educational advances by African-Americans, would continue into the twenty-first century (as discussed in Chapter 31).

To compensate for past racial discrimination in employment and education, some cities set aside a percentage of building contracts for minority businesses, industries adopted hiring goals and recruitment training program, and many educational institutions reserved slots for minority applicants. These so-called **affirmative action** programs faced court challenges, however. In *University of California Regents v. Bakke* (1978), the Supreme Court declared racial quotas unconstitutional, yet also held that universities might consider race as a factor in admission "to remedy disadvantages cast on minorities by past racial prejudice."

THE EXPANDING MOVEMENT FOR EQUALITY

Native Americans, Hispanic Americans, and Asian-Americans were similarly affected by liberalism. They, too, were inspired by Kennedy's rhetoric, by Johnson's actions, and by the assertive outlook of Black Power. Each followed the black lead in challenging the status quo, demanding full and equal citizenship rights, and emphasizing group identity and pride. And like blacks, each group saw its younger members push for ever more radical action.

Native-American Activism

In 1961, representatives of sixty-seven tribes drew up a Declaration of Purposes criticizing the termination policy of the 1950s (see Chapter 27), and in 1964 hundreds of Indians lobbied in Washington for their inclusion in the War on Poverty (covered later in this chapter). Indians suffered the worst poverty, the highest disease and death rates, and the poorest education and housing of any American group. President Johnson responded by establishing the National Council on Indian Opportunity in 1965, which funneled more federal funds onto reservations than any previous program. Promising to erase "old attitudes of paternalism," Johnson advocated Indian self-determination, "the right of the First Americans to remain Indians while exercising their rights as Americans."

Militant Native Americans, meanwhile, began to organize. By 1968, younger Indian activists, calling themselves "Native Americans," demanded "Red Power." They protested the lack of protection for Indian land and water rights and the desecration of Indian sacred sites. They mocked Columbus Day and staged sit-ins against museums that housed Indian bones. They established reservation cultural programs to reawaken spiritual beliefs and teach native languages. The Navajo and Hopi protested strip-mining in the Southwest; the Taos Pueblo organized to reclaim the Blue Lake sacred site in northern New Mexico; and the Puyallup held "fish-ins" to assert old treaty rights to fish in the Columbia River and Puget Sound.

The most militant group, the **American Indian Movement (AIM),** was founded in 1968 by Chippewas, Sioux, and Ojibwa living in Minnesota. Among its goals was preventing police harassment of Indians in urban "red ghettos." In November 1969, AIM occupied Alcatraz Island in San Francisco Bay, and held it for nineteen months. The occupation helped foster a new sense of identity among American Indians. As one participant glowed, "we got back our worth, our pride, our dignity, our humanity."

Building on their occupation of Alcatraz, AIM briefly occupied the Bureau of Indian Affairs in Washington in 1972, and in 1973 took over a trading post at Wounded Knee, South Dakota, site of an 1890 Indian massacre by the U.S. army (see Chapter 17). In response to spreading protests, the **Indian Self-Determination Act of 1974** granted tribes control of federal aid programs on the reservations and oversight of their own schools.

AIM's militancy aroused other Native-Americans to be proud of their heritage. Their members "had a new look about them, not that hangdog reservation look I was used to," Mary Crow Dog remembered, and they "loosened a sort of earthquake inside me." Many of the eight hundred thousand who identified themselves as Indians in the 1970 census did so for the first time, and by 1990 their number had soared to 1.7 million. This upsurge reflected ethnic pride, as well as the economic advantages associated with tribal membership. Under a 1961 law permitting them to buy or develop land for commercial projects, tribes launched ventures ranging from gambling resorts to mining and logging operations. Many also reasserted long-ignored treaty rights, resulting in a gain of 40 million acres and nearly $1 billion for Alaskan Indians in 1971 and a 1980 award of $107 million to the Sioux for South Dakota lands taken from them illegally.

Although high rates of joblessness, alcoholism, and disease persisted among Indians, renewed pride and progress in asserting treaty rights offered hope. In the popular culture, movies such as *Little Big Man* (1970) and *Dances with Wolves* (1990), while idealizing Indians, represented an improvement over the negative stereotypes of earlier films.

Hispanic-Americans Organize

As earlier in American history, immigration swelled the ranks of minority groups in the second half of the twentieth century. Of enormous significance, President Johnson proposed and Congress enacted the **Immigration Act of 1965,** abolishing the national-origins quotas of the 1920s. Annual legal immigration began an increase from 250,000 to well over a million, and the vast majority of new immigrants came from Asia and Latin America. The Latino, or Hispanic-American, population increased from 4.5 percent in 1970 to nearly 12 percent in 2000. Less than 1 percent of the U.S. population in 1960, Asian-Americans (discussed in the next section) comprised more than 4 percent in 2000. During the 1960s, these groups contributed to the general spirit of activism.

Like Native-Americans, Latinos—the fastest-growing minority—became impatient with their establishment organizations, which had been unable to better their dismal conditions: a median annual wage half the poverty level; a functional illiteracy rate of 40 percent among Mexican-American adults; and de facto segregation common throughout the Southwest. As they turned to the more militant tactics of the civil-rights movement, Latinos found a charismatic leader in **César Estrada Chávez.**

Born on an Arizona farm first cultivated in the 1880s by his grandfather, Chávez grew up a migrant farm worker, joined the U.S. navy in World War II, and then devoted himself to gaining union recognition and improved working conditions for the mostly Mexican-American farm laborers in California. A magnetic leader who, like Martin Luther King, blended religion with nonviolent resistance to fight for social change, Chávez led his followers in the Delano vineyards of the San Joaquin valley to strike in 1965. He and United Farm Workers (UFW) cofounder Dolores Huerta organized consumer boycotts of table grapes to dramatize the farm workers' struggle, often referred to as *La Causa.*

Chavez and Huerta made *La Causa* part of the struggle of the entire Mexican-American community and of the larger national civil-rights movement. For the first time, farm workers gained the right to unionize to secure better wages; by mid-1970, two-thirds of California grapes were grown under UFW contracts. Just as the UFW flag featured an Aztec eagle and the Virgin of Guadalupe, Chávez combined religion, labor militancy, and Mexican heritage to stimulate ethnic pride and politicization.

Also in the mid-1960s, young Hispanic activists began using the formerly pejorative terms **Chicano and Chicana** to express a militant collective identity. "Our main goal is to orient the Chicano to *think* Chicano so as to achieve equal status with other groups, not to emulate the Anglo." Rejecting assimilation, Chicano student organizations came together in 1967 in *El Movimiento Estudiantil Chicano de Aztlan (MEChA).* MEChA demanded bilingual education and more Latino teachers in high schools as well as Chicano studies programs and organizations at colleges.

Similar zeal led poet Rodolfo "Corky" Gonzales to found the Crusade for Justice in Colorado in 1965 to fight police brutality and foster Chicano culture. It led Reies Lopez Tijerina to form the *Alianza Federal de Mercedes* in New Mexico to reclaim land usurped by whites in the 1848 Treaty of Guadalupe Hidalgo. It also led Jose Angel Gutierrez and others in Texas to create an alternative political party in 1967, *La Raza Unida,* to elect Latinos and instill cultural pride. Across the West, Hispanic-American activists created the "brown is beautiful" vogue and the paramilitary Brown Berets, with conceptual roots in the Black Panthers.

Similarly inspired, Puerto Ricans in New York City founded the Young Lords. Modeled on the Black Panthers, the Young Lords published a newspaper, started drug treatment programs, and even hijacked ambulances and occupied a hospital to demand better medical services in the South Bronx.

Meanwhile, a steady influx of immigrants, both legal and illegal, continued to arrive in the United States. Where most had once come from Europe, some 45 percent now came from the Western Hemisphere and 30 percent from Asia. As in the past, economic need drew these newcomers. Mexico's chronic poverty forced many to seek jobs in the north. But life in the United States was often harsh. In 1980, some 26 percent of persons of Hispanic origin in the United States lived in poverty, twice the national rate. Despite adversity, Hispanic newcomers preserved their language and traditions, influencing U.S. culture in the process.

Millions of Hispanic immigrants lacked official documentation. Many sweated in the garment trades, cleaned houses, held low-paying service-sector jobs, and labored in agricultural fields. The **Immigration Reform and Control Act of 1986,** an update of the 1965 Immigration Act, outlawed the hiring of undocumented immigrants but offered legal status to aliens who had lived in the United States for five years.

Asian-American Activism   Among the rapidly climbing number of immigrants from Asia, some, like the Hmong (pronounced "mong"), the indigenous people of Indochina who had supported the United States in the Vietnam War, came mainly for political reasons; others, like those from South Korea and the Philippines, came primarily for economic betterment. Valuing education, many Asian immigrants advanced academically and economically. The younger generation, torn between new and old, sought to balance family and group loyalties with the appeal of the larger society beyond.

Like their counterparts, young activists with roots in East Asia rejected the term *Oriental* in favor of *Asian-American,* to signify their ethnic consciousness. Formed at the University of California in 1968, the **Asian American Political Alliance** encouraged Asian-Americans to claim their own cultural identity and, in racial solidarity with their "Asian brothers and sisters," to protest against the U.S. war in Vietnam.

As did other ethnic groups, Asian-American students marched, sat in, and went on strike to gain courses on Asian-American studies or to protest repressive dictatorships in their homeland. Others focused on improving the lives of Asian-Americans in need or on agitating to force the United States to make restitution for the internment of Japanese Americans during World War II.

None of these movements for ethnic pride and power, in later decades, would sustain the fervent activism and media attention they attracted in the late sixties. But by elevating the consciousness and nurturing the confidence of the younger generation, each contributed to the empowerment of its respective group and to the politics of identity that would continue to grow in importance.

LIBERALISM ASCENDANT, 1963–1968

Although a New Dealer in the 1930s, **Lyndon Baines Johnson** came to be distrusted by liberals as "a Machiavelli in a Stetson" and regarded as a usurper by Kennedy loyalists. He had become the 36th President of the United States through the assassination of a popular president in his home state. Though just nine years older than JFK, he seemed a relic of the past, a back-room wheeler-dealer, as crude as Kennedy was smooth.

Yet Johnson had substantial political assets. He had served in Washington almost continuously since 1932, accruing enormous experience and a close association with the Capitol Hill power brokers. He excelled at wooing allies, neutralizing opponents, forging coalitions, and achieving results.

Demonstrating his determination to prove himself to liberals, Johnson deftly handled the transition of power, won a landslide victory in 1964, and guided through Congress the greatest array of liberal legislation in U.S. history, surpassing the New Deal. Needing to outdo JFK, even FDR, LBJ had both great talents and glaring flaws. His swollen yet fragile ego could not abide the sniping of Kennedy loyalists—and the press. Wondering aloud, "Why don't people like me?" Johnson labored to make the American Dream a reality for everyone and to vanquish all

The LBJ Treatment

Not content unless he could wholly dominate friend as well as foe, Lyndon Johnson used his body as well as his voice to bend others to his will and gain his objectives.

(Lyndon B. Johnson Presidential Library)

foes at home and abroad. Ironically, in seeking consensus and adoration, Johnson divided the nation and left office repudiated.

Johnson Takes Over   Calling for quick passage of the tax-cut and civil-rights bills as a memorial to JFK, Johnson used his skills to win passage of the Civil Rights Act of 1964 and a $10 billion tax-reduction bill, which produced a surge in capital investment and personal consumption that further spurred economic growth and shrank the budget deficit. More boldly, Johnson declared "unconditional **war on poverty** in America."

Largely invisible in an affluent America, according to Michael Harrington's *The Other America* (1962), some 40 million people lived in a "culture of poverty," lacking the education, medical care, and employment opportunities that most Americans took for granted. To be poor, Harrington asserted, "is to be an internal alien, to grow up in a culture that is radically different from the one that dominates the society."

LBJ championed a campaign to bring these "internal exiles" into the mainstream. Designed to offer a "hand up, not a handout," the Economic Opportunity Act established the Office of Economic Opportunity to fund and coordinate such programs as a job corps to train young people in marketable skills; VISTA (Volunteers in Service to America), a domestic peace corps; Project Head Start, to provide compensatory education for preschoolers from disadvantaged families; an assortment of public-works and training programs; and a Community Action Program to encourage the "maximum feasible participation" of the poor in decisions that affected them.

Summing up his goals in 1964, Johnson offered his vision of the **Great Society**. First must come "an end to poverty and racial injustice." In addition, it would be a place where all children could enrich their minds, where people would be in contact with nature, and where all would be "more concerned with the quality of their goals than the quantity of their goods."

The 1964 Election

Johnson's Great Society horrified the "new conservatives," such as William F. Buckley and the college students of Young Americans for Freedom (YAF). The most persuasive criticism came from Arizona senator **Barry Goldwater**. A western outsider fighting the power of Washington and a fervent anticommunist, Goldwater advocated as little federal governmental intervention in the economy as possible and opposed government efforts to expand and protect civil rights and liberties.

Johnson's jibe that civil rights leaders would have to wear sneakers to keep up with him evoked no laughter from southern segregationists or from blue-collar workers in northern cities who dreaded the integration of their neighborhoods, schools, and workplaces. Their support of Alabama's segregationist governor George Wallace in the spring 1964 Democratic presidential primaries heralded a "white backlash" against the civil-rights movement.

Buoyed by this backlash, conservatives gained control of the GOP in 1964. They nominated Barry Goldwater for the presidency and adopted a platform totally opposed to liberalism. Determined to offer the nation "a choice not an echo," Goldwater lauded his opposition to civil-rights legislation, denounced the War on Poverty, and accused the Democrats of a "no-win" strategy in the Cold War, hinting that he might use nuclear weapons against Cuba and North Vietnam. His stance appealed most to those angered by the Cold War stalemate, by the erosion of traditional moral values, and by the increasing militancy of African-Americans. But his charge that the Democrats had not pursued total victory in Vietnam allowed Johnson to appear the apostle of restraint: "We are not going to send American boys nine or ten thousand miles from home to do what Asian boys ought to be doing for themselves."

LBJ won a landslide victory, 43 million votes to Goldwater's 27 million. The GOP lost thirty-eight congressional and two Senate seats. Many proclaimed the death of conservatism. But Goldwater's coalition of economic, social, and religious conservatives, and anti-integrationist whites, presaged the Right's future triumph. It transformed the Republicans from a moderate, eastern-dominated party to one decidedly conservative, southern, and western. It built a national base of financial support for conservative candidates; catalyzed the creation of new conservative publications and think-tanks; energized volunteers like Phyllis Schlafly to campaign for Goldwater and stay involved in politics; and mobilized future leaders of the party, like Ronald Reagan. But in the short run, the liberals controlled all three branches of government.

The Great Society   "Hurry, boys, hurry," LBJ urged his aides. "Get that legislation up to the hill and out. Eighteen months from now ol' Landslide Lyndon will be Lame-Duck Lyndon." Johnson flooded Congress with liberal proposals, and got most of what he requested.

The Eighty-ninth Congress expanded the War on Poverty and passed the Voting Rights Act. It enacted **Medicare** to provide health insurance for the aged under social security and a **Medicaid** health plan for the poor. By 1975, the two programs would be serving 47 million people and account for a quarter of the nation's health-care expenditures. The legislators also appropriated funds for public education and housing and for aid to Appalachia and inner-city neighborhoods. They created new cabinet departments of transportation and of housing and urban development as well as the National Endowments for the Arts and the Humanities. The first president to send a special message on the environment to Congress, Johnson won the enactment of measures to control air and water pollution, protect endangered species, set aside millions of acres of wilderness, and preserve the natural beauty of the American landscape. As noted, Congress enacted the Immigration Act of 1965, abandoning the quota system enacted in the 1920s that had discriminated against Asians and southern and eastern Europeans, and transforming America's racial and ethnic kaleidoscope.

The Great Society improved the lives of millions. The proportion of the poor in the population dropped from 22 percent in 1960 to 13 percent in 1969, infant mortality declined, and African-American family income rose from 54 percent to 61 percent of white family income. The percentage of blacks living below the poverty line plummeted from 40 percent to 20 percent. Great Society programs gave those on the bottom reason to hope and a sense of entitlement to a fair share of the American Dream. But because Johnson oversold the Great Society and Congress underfunded it, rising expectations outdistanced results.

For many in need, the Great Society remained more a dream than a reality. The war against poverty, Martin Luther King, Jr., asserted, was "shot down on the battlefields of Vietnam." The Asian war diverted LBJ's attention from liberal reforms and devoured tax dollars that might have gone to the Great Society. Yet the perceived liberality of federal spending and the "ungratefulness" of rioting blacks, as well as the intrusive rulings of the Supreme Court, alienated many middle- and working-class whites. The Democrats' loss of forty-seven House seats in 1966 ended the sway of congressional liberalism.

The Liberalism of the Warren Court   The Supreme Court, led by Chief Justice Earl Warren, far more liberal than public opinion or Congress, supported an activist government to protect the disadvantaged and accused criminals and expanded individual rights to a greater extent than ever before in American history.

In landmark cases, the Court prohibited Bible reading and prayer in public schools, limited local power to censor books and films, and overturned state bans on contraceptives. It ordered states to apportion legislatures on the principle of "one person, one vote," increasing the representation of urban minorities.

The Court's upholding of the rights of the accused in criminal cases, at a time of soaring crime rates, particularly incensed many Americans. Criticism of the Supreme Court reached a climax in 1966 when it ruled in *Miranda v. Arizona* that police must advise suspects of their right to remain silent and to have counsel during questioning. In 1968, presidential candidates Richard Nixon and George Wallace would win favor by promising to appoint judges who emphasized "law and order" over individual liberties.

THE VIETNAM CRUSADE, 1961–1967

The activist liberals who boldly tried to uplift the downtrodden also went to war to contain communism in Vietnam. The nation's longest war, and most controversial, would shatter the liberal consensus and divide the United States as nothing had since the Civil War.

Origins and Causes   American involvement in Vietnam grew out of the containment policy to stop the spread of communism. First as a means of strengthening our anti-Soviet ally France, President Truman authorized U.S. aid for French efforts to reestablish its colonial rule in Indochina. After the outbreak of war in Korea, with all of Asia now viewed as a Cold War battleground, Truman ordered vastly increased assistance for the French army fighting the Vietminh, a broad-based Vietnamese nationalist coalition led by the communist Ho Chi Minh. By 1954, the United States was paying three-quarters of the French war costs in Vietnam.

But the French were losing. In early 1954, the Vietminh besieged twelve thousand French troops in the valley of Dienbienphu. France appealed for U.S. intervention, and some American officials toyed with the idea of a nuclear strike, which President Eisenhower flatly rejected. In May, the French surrendered at Dienbienphu. An international conference in Geneva arranged a cease-fire and divided Vietnam at the seventeenth parallel, pending elections in 1956 to choose the government of a unified nation.

Although unwilling to go to war, Eisenhower would not accept a communist takeover of Vietnam. In what became known as the **domino theory**, Eisenhower warned that, if Vietnam fell to the communists, then Thailand, Burma, Indonesia, and ultimately all of Asia would follow. The United States refused to sign the Geneva Peace Accords and in late 1954 created the Southeast Asia Treaty Organization (SEATO), a military alliance patterned on NATO (see Chapter 26).

In June 1954, the CIA installed Ngo Dinh Diem, a fiercely anticommunist Catholic, as premier and then president of an independent South Vietnam. CIA agents helped him eliminate political opposition and block the election to reunify Vietnam specified by the Geneva agreements. As Eisenhower later admitted, "possibly 80 percent of the population would have voted for the communist Ho Chi

Minh as their leader." Washington pinned its hopes on Diem to maintain a non-communist South Vietnam with American dollars rather than American lives.

But the autocratic Diem's Catholicism alienated the predominantly Buddhist population, and his refusal to institute land reform and end corruption spurred opposition. In December 1960, opponents of Diem coalesced in the communist-led **National Liberation Front (NLF)**. Backed by North Vietnam, the insurgency soon controlled half of South Vietnam.

Kennedy and Vietnam   Following the 1962 compromise settlement in Laos, President Kennedy resolved, as had President Eisenhower, not to give further ground in Southeast Asia. Fearing the likely success of the NLF, which sought to overthrow the American puppet government in Saigon and unify the country under communist rule, JFK ordered massive shipments of weaponry to South Vietnam. He stepped up clandestine operations against the North and increased the number of American forces stationed in Vietnam from less than seven hundred in 1960 to more than sixteen thousand by late 1963. Like Eisenhower, he believed that letting "aggression" go unchecked would lead to wider wars (the Munich analogy), and that the communist takeover of one nation would lead to others going communist (the domino theory). Kennedy resolved to prove that wars of national liberation were doomed to fail and to show the world that the United States was not the "paper tiger" that Mao Zedong (Mao Tse-tung) mocked.

To counter Vietcong, or NLF gains in the countryside, the United States used both chemical defoliants to destroy vegetation and deprive the Vietcong of natural cover, and napalm bombs—whose petroleum jelly burned at 1,000 degrees and clung to whatever it touched, including human flesh. It also forcibly uprooted Vietnamese peasants and moved them into fortified villages, or "strategic hamlets," to prevent infiltration by the Vietcong. But South Vietnamese president Diem rejected American pressure to gain popular support through reform measures, instead crushing demonstrations by students and Buddhists. By mid-1963, Buddhist monks were setting themselves on fire to protest Diem's repression, and Diem's own generals were plotting a coup.

Frustrated American policy makers concluded that only a new government could prevent a Vietcong victory and secretly encouraged the coup to overthrow Diem. On November 1, South Vietnamese military leaders captured and murdered Diem and his brother, the head of the secret police. Although the United States promptly recognized the new government (the first of nine South Vietnamese regimes in the next five years), it too made little headway against the Vietcong. JFK now faced two unpalatable alternatives: increase the combat involvement of American forces or withdraw and seek a negotiated settlement.

What Kennedy would have done remains unknown. Less than a month after Diem's death, John Kennedy himself fell to an assassin's bullet. His admirers contend that by late 1963 he favored the withdrawal of American forces after the 1964 election. "It is their war … it is their people and their government who have to win or lose the struggle," he proclaimed. Yet the president then restated the domino theory and promised that America would not withdraw from the conflict. Indeed, the speech he was to give the day he was killed warned, specifically, about Vietnam, "We dare not weary of the task." Virtually all his closest advisers held that an American victory in Vietnam was essential to check communism in Asia. National Security Adviser McGeorge Bundy, Secretary of Defense Robert McNamara, and Secretary of State Dean Rusk would counsel Kennedy's successor accordingly.

Lyndon Johnson's Endless War   Now Johnson had to choose between intervening decisively or withdrawing from a conflict that three previous presidents had insisted the communists must not win. Privately describing Vietnam as "a raggedy-ass fourth-rate country" undeserving of American blood and dollars, LBJ feared that an all-out American military effort might lead to World War III and foresaw that full-scale engagement in "that bitch of a war" would destroy "the woman I really loved—the Great Society." Yet Johnson also accepted the domino theory and Munich analogy and saw both the nation's and his own credibility as on the line. He worried that a pullout would make him appear cowardly, threaten his liberal agenda, and leave him vulnerable to conservative accusations that he was "soft" on communism.

Trapped between unacceptable alternatives, feeling like "a catfish who had just grabbed a big juicy worm with a right sharp hook in the middle of it," Johnson escalated a Vietnamese civil war into America's war, hoping that U.S. firepower would force Ho Chi Minh to the bargaining table. But the North Vietnamese and NLF calculated that they could gain more by outlasting the United States than by negotiating. In 1964, Johnson took steps to impress North Vietnam with American resolve and to block his opponent, Barry Goldwater, from capitalizing on Vietnam in the presidential campaign. He ordered the Pentagon to prepare for air strikes against North Vietnam; appointed General Maxwell Taylor, an advocate of escalation, as ambassador to Saigon; and had his advisers draft a congressional resolution authorizing an escalation of American military action. In early August, North Vietnamese patrol boats allegedly clashed with two U.S. destroyers in the Gulf of Tonkin (see Map 28.2). Privately surmising that the "navy might have been shooting at whales out there," Johnson publicly announced that Americans had been victims of Hanoi's "open aggression on the high sea." Never admitting that the U.S. ships took part in covert raids against North Vietnam, Johnson ordered retaliatory air strikes on North Vietnamese naval bases and asked Congress to pass the prepared resolution giving him the authority to "take all necessary measures to repel any armed attack" on American forces "and to prevent further aggression." Assured that this meant no "extension of the present conflict," the Senate passed the Gulf of Tonkin Resolution 88 to 2, and the House 416 to 0.

Privately, LBJ called the resolution "grandma's nightshirt—it covered everything." Although it was initially designed to deflect Goldwater's charge that he was weak on communism, Johnson also considered the resolution a blank check to commit U.S. forces if that became necessary. Yet he assured the public during the 1964 campaign that he would neither deploy American troops to fight in Vietnam nor extend the war by bombing North Vietnam.

Both assurances were short-lived. Early in 1965, Johnson ordered "Operation Rolling Thunder," the sustained bombing of North Vietnam. It would lead to the dropping of eight hundred tons of bombs a day on North Vietnam between 1965 and 1968, three times the tonnage dropped by all the combatants in World War II. Yet it neither forced Hanoi to negotiate nor stopped the flow of soldiers and supplies coming from North Vietnam via the so-called Ho Chi Minh Trail (see Map 28.2).

Unable to turn the tide by bombing, Johnson committed U.S. combat troops. Adopting a "meat-grinder" or attrition strategy, Johnson sought to inflict unacceptable casualties on the communists to force them to the peace table. Johnson

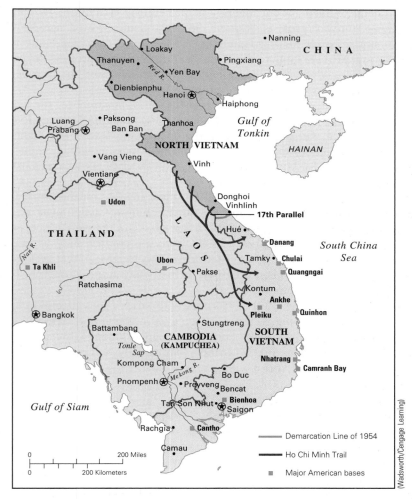

MAP 28.2 The Vietnam War, to 1968

Wishing to guarantee an independent, noncommunist government in South Vietnam, Lyndon Johnson remarked in 1965, "We fight because we must fight if we are to live in a world where every country can shape its own destiny. To withdraw from one battlefield means only to prepare for the next."

sent 485,000 troops (a greater military force than the U.S. had deployed in Korea) to Vietnam by the end of 1967. But superiority in numbers and weaponry did not defeat an enemy that could choose when and where to attack and then melt back into the jungle. Determined to battle until the United States lost the will to fight, Hanoi matched each American troop increase with its own. No end was in sight.

First among pacifists and socialists, then on college campuses, and lastly in the wider society, a growing number of Americans opposed the war. In March 1965, students and faculty at the University of Michigan staged the first teach-in to raise questions about U.S. intervention. Later that spring, twenty-five thousand people, mainly students, rallied in Washington to protest the escalation. In 1966, large-scale campus antiwar protests erupted. Students demonstrated against the draft and university research for the Pentagon. They proved only a prelude to 1967's massive Spring Mobilization to End the War in Vietnam protests in New York and San Francisco, which drew half a million participants, and the October demonstrations at the Pentagon by another hundred thousand.

Intellectuals and clergy joined the chorus of opposition to the war. Some decried the massive bombing of an underdeveloped nation; some doubted the United States could win at any reasonable cost; some feared the demise of the Great Society and liberalism. In 1967, prominent critics, including Senator Robert Kennedy and Martin Luther King, spurred hundreds of thousands to participate in antiwar protests.

Critics also noted that the war's toll fell most heavily on the poor. Owing to college deferments, the use of influence, and a military-assignment system that shunted the better-educated to desk jobs, lower-class youths were twice as likely to be drafted and, when drafted, twice as likely to see combat duty as middle-class youths. About 80 percent of the enlisted men who fought in Vietnam came from poor and working-class families; only two of the twelve hundred men in Harvard's class of 1970 served in Vietnam.

TV coverage of the war further eroded support. Scenes of children maimed by U.S. bombs and of dying Americans, replayed nightly, laid bare the horror of war and undercut the optimistic reports of government officials. Americans shuddered as they watched U.S. troops, supposedly winning the hearts and minds of the Vietnamese, burn villages and leave thousands of civilians mutilated or dead.

Yet for every protestor shouting "Hell No, We Won't Go!" many more war supporters affixed bumper stickers reading "America, Love It or Leave It!" Until 1968, most Americans either supported the war or remained undecided. "I want to get out, but I don't want to give up" expressed a widespread view. They were not prepared to accept a communist victory over the United States.

Equally disturbing was how polarized the nation had grown. **"Hawks"** would accept little short of total victory, whereas **"doves"** insisted on negotiating, not fighting. Civility vanished. As Johnson termed his critics "nervous Nellies" and refused to de-escalate, demonstrators paraded past the White House chanting, "Hey, hey, LBJ, how many kids did you kill today?" By 1968, the president had become a virtual prisoner in the White House, unable to speak in public without being shouted down. So ended an era of hope and liberalism.

The Tet Offensive and a Shaken President

In January 1968, liberal Democratic senator **Eugene McCarthy** of Minnesota, a Vietnam War critic, announced he would challenge LBJ for the presidential nomination. Pundits scoffed that McCarthy had no chance of unseating Johnson, who had won the presidency in 1964 by the largest margin in U.S. history. The last time such an insurgency had been attempted, in 1912, even the wildly popular Teddy Roosevelt had failed. Yet McCarthy persisted, determined that at least one Democrat should enter the primaries on an antiwar platform.

Suddenly, on January 31—the first day of Tet, the Vietnamese New Year—America's hopes for victory in Vietnam sank, and with them LBJ's political fortunes. NLF and North Vietnamese forces mounted a huge offensive, attacking more than a hundred South Vietnamese cities and towns, and even the U.S. embassy in Saigon. U.S. and South Vietnamese troops repulsed the offensive, inflicting a major military defeat on the communists, who failed to unleash a general uprising against the government in Saigon or to hold any South Vietnamese city. With the Viet Cong largely decimated, the brunt of the fighting now had to be borne by North Vietnamese troops.

Victory, however, came at an enormous psychological cost. The dramatic initial reports of the media, highlighting communist success and the immense scope of the Tet offensive, undercut Administration claims of imminent victory, of "light at the end of the tunnel." They deepened the growing mood of gloom about the war and intensified doubts that the United States could win at an acceptable cost. Public approval of the president's conduct of the war fell to just 26 percent in the immediate aftermath of Tet.

After Tet, moreover, McCarthy's criticism of the war won many new sympathizers. *Time, Newsweek,* and influential newspapers published editorials urging a negotiated settlement. The nation's premier newscaster, Walter Cronkite of CBS, observed that, at best, the war would end in a stalemate. "If I've lost Walter," LBJ sighed, "then it's over. I've lost Mr. Average Citizen." The number of Americans who described themselves as prowar "hawks" slipped from 62 percent in January to 41 percent in March, while the antiwar "doves" jumped from 22 percent to 42 percent.

Beleaguered, Johnson pondered a change in American policy. When the Joint Chiefs of Staff sought 206,000 additional troops, he turned to old friends for advice. Former secretary of state and venerable Cold Warrior Dean Acheson told him, "the Joint Chiefs of Staff don't know what they're talking about." Clark Clifford, once a hawk and now secretary of defense, concluded "that the military course we were pursuing was not only endless but hopeless."

Meanwhile, nearly five thousand college students had swarmed to New Hampshire to stuff envelopes and ring doorbells for Eugene McCarthy in the nation's first primary contest. "Clean for Gene," they cut their long hair and dressed conservatively so as not to alienate potential supporters. McCarthy astonished the experts by winning nearly half the popular vote in a state usually regarded as conservative.

After this upset, twice as many students converged on Wisconsin to canvass its more liberal voters. Expecting Johnson to lose, Senator **Robert Kennedy**, also promising to end the war, entered the Democratic contest. Projecting the family's glamour and magnetism, Kennedy was the one candidate who Johnson feared could deny him renomination. Indeed, millions viewed Kennedy as the rightful heir to the White House. Appealing to minorities, the poor, and working-class ethnic whites, Kennedy became, according to a columnist, "our first politician for the pariahs, our great national outsider."

On March 31, Johnson surprised a television audience by announcing a halt to the bombing in North Vietnam. Adding that he wanted to devote all his efforts to the search for peace, LBJ then announced startlingly, "I shall not seek, and I will not accept, the nomination of my party for another term as your president." Embittered by the personal abuse he had endured and reluctant to polarize the nation further, LBJ inaugurated peace negotiations and called it quits. Both physically and emotionally spent, LBJ lamented, "The only difference between the [John F.] Kennedy assassination and mine is that I am alive and it has been more torturous." Two days later, pounding the final nail into Johnson's political coffin, McCarthy trounced the president in the Wisconsin primary.

Ignored and often forgotten in retirement, Johnson died of a heart attack in January 1973—on the same day the Paris Peace Accords ended America's combat role in Vietnam. In many ways a tragic figure, he had carried out Vietnam policies shaped by his predecessors and received little acclaim for his enduring domestic achievements, especially in civil rights and reducing poverty. Although he often displayed high idealism and generosity of spirit, the enduring image of LBJ remained that of a crude, overbearing politician with an outsized ego that masked deep insecurities.

Nixon's War   Following his election in 1968, President Richard Nixon plotted a strategy of détente—reduced tensions—with the USSR and China that hinged on ending the Vietnam War. He understood that the war had sapped American military strength, hurt the economy, hindered U.S. relations abroad, and devastated Lyndon Johnson. "I'm not going to end up like LBJ, holed up in the White House afraid to show my face on the street. I'm going to stop the war. Fast."

Announcing the Nixon Doctrine in August 1969, the president redefined America's role in the Third World as that of a helpful partner rather than a military protector. It reflected the president's recognition of war weariness by both the electorate and troops in Vietnam. Johnson's decision to negotiate rather than escalate had left American troops with the sense that little mattered except survival. Morale plummeted. Discipline collapsed. Racial conflict became commonplace. And the army reported hundreds of cases of "fragging"—enlisted men killing officers and noncommissioned officers. By war's end, 20 percent of the Americans who served in Vietnam, nearly 500,000, had received less-than-honorable discharges—a measure of the desertion rate, soaring drug usage, antiwar sentiment in the military, and immaturity of the troops (the average U.S. soldier in Vietnam was just 19, seven years younger than the average GI in World War II).

The toll of atrocities against the Vietnamese also mounted. Instances of Americans dismembering enemy bodies, torturing captives, and murdering civilians came to light. In March 1968, an army unit led by an inexperienced lieutenant, William Calley, massacred several hundred South Vietnamese in the hamlet of My Lai.

Soldiers gang-raped girls, lined up women and children in ditches and shot them, and burned the village. Revelations of such incidents, and the increasing number of returned soldiers who joined Vietnam Veterans Against the War, undercut the already-diminished support for the war. At the same time, news coverage fed the strong and growing opposition to the war abroad (see Going to the Source).

Despite pressure to end the war, Nixon proved no more willing than his predecessors to accept defeat. Seeking "peace with honor," he acted on three fronts. First: "Vietnamization," replacing American troops with South Vietnamese. It was hardly a new idea; the French had tried *jaunissement* or "yellowing" in 1951, and it had not worked. By 1972, U.S. forces had been cut from half a million to thirty thousand. Second: bypassing South Vietnamese leaders, Nixon sent Kissinger to negotiate directly, and secretly, with North Vietnam's foreign minister, Le Duc Tho. Third: to force the communists to compromise despite the U.S. troop withdrawal, Nixon escalated the bombing of North Vietnam and secretly ordered air strikes on Cambodia and Laos. He told an aide,

> I want the North Vietnamese to believe I've reached the point where I might do anything to stop the war. We'll just slip the word to them that "for God's sake, you know Nixon is obsessed about communism. We can't restrain him when he's angry—and he has his hand on the nuclear button"—and Ho Chi Minh himself will be in Paris in two days begging for peace.

The secret B-52 raids neither made Hanoi beg for peace nor disrupted communist supply bases. They did, however, undermine the stability of Cambodia, and increase North Vietnam infiltration of troops into that tiny republic. "To show our enemy that we were still serious about our commitment in Vietnam," Nixon ordered a joint U.S.-South Vietnamese incursion into Cambodia at the end of April 1970. The invaders seized large caches of arms and bought time for Vietnamization. But the costs were high. It ended Cambodia's neutrality, widened the war throughout Indochina, and provoked massive American protests, culminating in student deaths at Kent State University and Jackson State (discussed in Chapter 29).

In February 1971, Nixon had South Vietnamese troops invade Laos to destroy communist bases there. The South Vietnamese were routed. Emboldened, North Vietnam mounted a major campaign in April 1972—the Easter Offensive—the largest since 1968. Nixon retaliated by mining North Vietnam's harbors and unleashing B-52s on its major cities: "The bastards have never been bombed like they are going to be bombed this time."

America's Longest War Ends   The 1972 bombing helped break the impasse in the Paris peace talks, stalemated since 1968. In late October, just days before the 1972 presidential election, Kissinger announced that "peace is at hand." The cease-fire agreement he had secretly negotiated with Le Duc Tho required the withdrawal of all U.S. troops, provided for the return of American prisoners of war, and allowed North Vietnamese troops to remain in South Vietnam.

Kissinger's negotiation sealed Nixon's reelection, but South Vietnam's President Thieu refused to sign a cease-fire permitting North Vietnamese troops to remain in the South. An angry Le Duc Tho then pressed Kissinger for additional concessions,

GOING TO THE SOURCE

Images of Vietnam

(AP Images)

It is often said that a picture is worth a thousand words. These photographs show a crying, naked Vietnamese girl running down a road, her body burned by napalm, and a South Vietnamese police chief summarily executing a prisoner he believed to be a Vietcong. These images appeared on the front pages of newspapers and on television broadcasts around the world within a day after they were

and Nixon retaliated with massive B-52 raids. The 1972 Christmas bombing of Hanoi and Haiphong, the most destructive of the war, roused fierce opposition but broke the deadlock. Nixon's secret reassurance to Thieu that the United States would "respond with full force should the settlement be violated by North Vietnam" ended Saigon's recalcitrance.

The Paris Accords, signed in late January 1973, essentially restated the terms of the October truce. The agreement ended hostilities between the United States and North Vietnam, but left unresolved the differences between North and South Vietnam, guaranteeing that Vietnam's future would still be settled on the battlefield.

(AP Images)

taken. Subsequently they were reproduced and refashioned in an array of media. Note how they could be used as a means of persuasion, of judgment on the war, of critical reflection.

Questions

1. *What makes these images so powerful and such successful examples of visual culture?*

2. *What do they expose—and what goes unstated?*

3. *How might they have affected public opinion regarding the war?*

Go to www.cengage.com for additional primary sources on this period.

After the "decent interval" that Kissinger and Nixon had insisted upon, North Vietnamese troops in the spring of 1975 overran South Vietnam, took control of Saigon, and forced American helicopters to airlift the last remaining officials out of the besieged U.S. embassy.

America's longest war had ended in defeat. It had left fifty-eight thousand American dead and three hundred thousand wounded. The expenditure of at least $150 billion (more than $700 billion in 2009 dollars) had damaged the economy, diverted resources from reform, and triggered huge budget deficits and inflation. It shattered the liberal consensus and inflamed dissent and conflict, indelibly scarring a generation. The war also distanced the U.S. from its allies and alienated many in the world. "No more Vietnams" decided many in the military: the U.S. should not fight abroad unless its national security was clearly at stake, there was demonstrable public support, and it had the necessary means to accomplish the goal.

Virtually all who survived, wrote one marine veteran, returned "as immigrants to a new world. For the culture we had known dissolved while we were in Vietnam, and the culture of combat we lived in so intensely … made us aliens when we returned." Beyond media attention on the psychological difficulties of readjusting to civilian life, which principally fostered an image of them as disturbed and dangerous, the nation paid little heed to its Vietnam veterans—reminders of a war that Americans wished to forget.

Eager "to put Vietnam behind us," few gave much thought to the 2 million Vietnamese casualties, or to the suffering in Laos, or the price paid by Cambodia. In 1975, the fanatical Khmer Rouge (Cambodian communists), led by Pol Pot, took power and turned Cambodia into a genocidal "killing field," murdering some 2 million, an estimated third of the population.

"We've adjusted too well," complained Tim O'Brien, a veteran and novelist of the war. "Too many of us have lost touch with the horror of war…. It would seem that the memories of soldiers should serve, at least in a modest way, as a restraint on national bellicosity. But time and distance erode memory. We adjust, we lose the intensity. I fear that we are back where we started. I wish we were more troubled."

CHRONOLOGY
1960–1975

1960	John F. Kennedy elected president.
1961	Peace Corps and Alliance for Progress created. Bay of Pigs invasion. Berlin Wall erected.
1962	Cuban missile crisis.
1963	Civil-rights demonstrations in Birmingham. March on Washington. Test-Ban Treaty between the Soviet Union and the United States. Kennedy assassinated; Lyndon B. Johnson becomes president.
1964	Freedom Summer in Mississippi. Civil Rights Act. Gulf of Tonkin incident and resolution. Economic Opportunity Act initiates War on Poverty. Johnson elected president. Bombing of North Vietnam and Americanization of the war begin.
1965	Assassination of Malcolm X. Civil-rights march from Selma to Montgomery. César Chávez's United Farm Workers strike in California. Teach-ins to question U.S. involvement in war in Vietnam begin. Voting Rights Act. Watts riot in Los Angeles.

1966 SNCC and CORE call for Black Power.
Black Panthers formed.
Massive antiwar demonstrations.

1967 Race riots in Newark, Detroit, and other cities.

1968 Vietnam peace talks open in Paris.
Richard Nixon elected president.

1970 United States invades Cambodia.

1971 United States and South Vietnam invade Laos.

1973 Vietnamese cease-fire agreement signed.

1974 Indian Self-Determination Act.

1975 South Vietnam surrenders following North Vietnam's capture of Saigon.

CONCLUSION

Kennedy's liberal rhetoric captivated the media and obscured a so-so domestic record. Stymied by the conservative coalition in Congress, Kennedy did more to stimulate hope than to achieve change. Others would force changes from the bottom up, and the next president, Lyndon Johnson, would persuade Congress to make a reality of the liberal ideal of an activist government promoting a fairer life for all Americans.

Fed up with the more legalistic, cautious strategy of the civil-rights movement in the past, young African-Americans in the 1960s initiated a new direct action phase in black America's struggle for equal rights. Their activism, bubbling up from the local level, and Martin Luther King's stirring oratory and leadership, led to the landmark Civil Rights and Voting Rights Acts, which ended the legality of racial discrimination and black disfranchisement, provided greater equality of opportunity for African-Americans, and nurtured the self-esteem of blacks. However, the laws left untouched the maladies of the urban black ghetto. There, unfulfilled expectations and frustrated hopes exploded into rioting, which helped trigger a white backlash that undermined support for the liberal agenda.

For Kennedy's successor, Lyndon Johnson, that agenda meant Great Society legislation promoting health, education, voting rights, urban renewal, immigration reform, federal support for the arts and humanities, protection of the environment, and a war against poverty—the most sweeping liberal measures since the New Deal, and a significant enlargement in the role of the federal government in the lives of most Americans. Although the aggressiveness and violence of some blacks, and the Great Society's vast expansion of governmental powers and expenditures, helped shatter the liberal consensus, many liberal programs endured. Most Americans still supported Social Security and Medicare, favored a safety net of benefits for those truly in need, and did not want an unmanaged economy or a polluted environment.

Still, in the riot-torn streets of the "long hot summers," and, above all, the rice paddies of Vietnam, the liberal consensus exploded. To prevent South Vietnam from being taken over by the communists, Kennedy significantly increased the number and fighting role of American advisers in Vietnam and gave the green light for a coup to overthrow Diem, the unpopular head of the government in Saigon. Inheriting a deteriorating limited war from Kennedy, LBJ also chose to escalate America's involvement, hoping to force North Vietnam to negotiate a compromise. Three years later, a half-million American troops were stationed in Vietnam, and the United States was dropping more bombs on Vietnam than had been dropped in World War II. Still, the United States was no closer to achieving its objective, and Richard Nixon would fare no better. Although the nation had not been so deeply divided since the Civil War, Nixon's determination to prevent the United States from appearing a "pitiful helpless giant," kept the war dragging on for four more years, with increasing American casualties and destruction in Indochina, until he accepted the limitations of U.S. power and bowed to the resolution of the North Vietnamese. Yet, the bitterness engendered by the war, and its unprecedented— and, for many, humiliating—defeat, would linger, and the liberal idealism articulated by King would remain a dream.

29

A TIME OF UPHEAVAL, 1961–1980

CHAPTER OUTLINE

• Coming Apart • The Countercultural Rebellion • Feminism and a Values Revolution • A Divided Nation • Successes Abroad, Crises at Home • A Troubled Nation and Presidency

---

COMING APART

By the 1960s, the number of American students pursuing higher education had risen from 1 million in 1940 to 8 million. More than half the U.S. population was then under age thirty. Breaking with its forty-year tradition, *Time* magazine in 1967 selected the entire baby-boom generation as its "Man of the Year." Their sheer numbers gave the young a collective identity and guaranteed that their actions would have impact. And not just in the United States. Major student demonstrations shook the governments of Japan, Korea, Turkey, and Venezuela in 1960, and many, many more would follow.

Most baby boomers followed conventional paths. They sought a secure place in the system, not its overthrow. They preferred beer to drugs, and football to political demonstrations. They joined fraternities and sororities and majored in subjects that would equip them for the job market. Whether or not they went to college—and fewer than half did—the vast majority had their eyes fixed on a good salary, and a new car with a bumper sticker proclaiming "My Country— Right or Wrong."

Many politically engaged young people mobilized on the right, joining organizations like Young Americans for Freedom (YAF), which by 1970 boasted fifty thousand members—far more than any other student group. Rather than John Kennedy, these youths idolized Barry Goldwater, who embodied the traditional values and muscular anticommunism they cherished. YAF would be the seedbed of a new generation of conservatives who later gained control of the GOP, yet it was overshadowed in the 1960s by young activists in the New Left.

Toward a New Left   Although a tiny minority of youth, an insurgent band of leftist students got the lion's share of attention. Initially hopeful, they welcomed the idealism of the civil-rights movement, supported the campaign against nuclear testing, answered the rousing call of President Kennedy for service to the nation, and admired the mavericks and outsiders of the fifties.

In June 1962, some sixty students adopted the Port Huron Statement, a broad critique of American society and a call for more genuine human relationships. Proclaiming themselves "a new left," they organized the **Students for a Democratic Society (SDS),** which envisioned a nonviolent youth movement transforming the United States into a "participatory democracy" in which individuals would control the decisions that affected their lives. SDS assumed this could lead to the end of consumerism, militarism, and racism.

The generation of activists who found their agenda in the Port Huron Statement had their eyes opened by the police dogs in Birmingham, the assassination of President Kennedy, and the escalating war in Vietnam. Most never joined SDS but associated with what they vaguely called "the Movement" or "the New Left." Unlike the Leftists of the 1930s, they rejected Marxist ideology and emulated SNCC's style. Many became radicalized by the rigidity of campus administrators and mainstream liberalism's inability to achieve swift, fundamental change. Only a radical rejection of the liberal consensus, they presumed, could restructure society and create a genuinely democratic nation.

From Protest to Resistance   Returning from the Mississippi Freedom Summer to the Berkeley campus of the University of California in fall 1964, Mario Savio and other student activists tried to solicit funds and recruit volunteers near the campus gate, a spot traditionally open to political activities. Prodded by local conservatives, university administrators suddenly banned such practices; but when police arrested one of the activists, students surrounded the police car and kept it from moving. Savio then founded the **Berkeley Free Speech Movement (FSM),** a coalition of student groups insisting on the right to campus political activity. Likening the university to an impersonal machine, and its students to interchangeable machine parts, Savio insisted that "when the operation of the machine becomes so odious, makes you so sick to heart, you've got to put your bodies upon the gears and upon the wheels ... and you've got to make the machine stop until we're free." More than a thousand students then sat-in on the administrative "gears." Their arrests led to more demonstrations and a strike by nearly 70 percent of the student body.

The conservative former movie star Ronald Reagan, running for governor in 1966, vowed to "clean up the mess at Berkeley," with its "Beatniks, radicals and filthy speech advocates" and its "sexual orgies so vile I cannot describe them." But the demands and tactics of the FSM reverberated on campuses nationwide. Students disenchanted with filing into impersonal buildings to endure lectures from remote professors initiated a wave of protests seeking greater involvement in university affairs. Their objectives changed the character of American higher education: curricular reform, the end of rules regulating dormitory life, and the admission of more minority students.

Flower Power at the March on the Pentagon *The year 1967 brought the start of truly significant nationwide protest against the Vietnam War. In October, an estimated 100,000 people attended an antiwar rally in Washington, and many sought to "invade" the Pentagon, the nerve center of the American war effort.*

The escalation of the war in Vietnam, and the abolition of automatic student deferments from the draft in January 1966, transformed the protests into a *mass* social movement. Popularizing the slogan "Make Love—Not War," SDS organized some 200 new chapters and harassed campus recruiters for the Dow Chemical Company, the chief producer of flesh-burning napalm and the defoliant Agent Orange, used on Vietnam forests. In 1967, urging a shift "From Protest to Resistance," SDS supported draft resistance and civil disobedience in selective service centers. By 1968, it claimed one hundred thousand members on three hundred campuses and attracted a half-million antiwar protesters to its spring Mobilization to End the War in Vietnam, remembered for the chants of "Burn cards, not people" (meaning draft cards) and "Hell no, we won't go!"

That spring, at least forty thousand students on a hundred campuses demonstrated against war and racism. In April, the SDS chapter at Columbia University demanded the university end all its military research projects, and the Students' Afro-American Society insisted it stop the construction of a new gymnasium, claiming that it encroached on the Harlem community. Shouting "Gym Crow must go," a thousand students barricaded themselves inside five campus buildings, declaring them "revolutionary communes" and holding them for six days. "Up against the wall, motherfucker," SDS's leader told the Columbia president. "This is a stickup."

Outraged by the brutality of the police who retook the buildings by storm, the moderate majority of Columbia students joined a sympathy boycott of classes that shut down the university. Elsewhere, students in Czechoslovakia, France, Germany, Ireland, Italy, Japan, Mexico, and South Korea expressed their own revolutionary bombast. Their protests far exceeded in size and ferocity anything that occurred in the United States. In part, the turbulence of the young reflected the sheer numbers of the postwar baby boom in many nations, which produced a heightened sense of the power of youth, higher levels of expectations and impatience, and a huge number of university students attracted to nonconformity and even rebellion. Satellite technology and new portable video cameras now made it easy to instantly transmit student uprisings in one nation to students around the globe.

The year 1969 saw the high point of the Movement with the New Mobilization, a series of huge antiwar demonstrations culminating in mid-November with a March Against Death. Three hundred thousand protestors descended on Washington to march in a candle-lit parade, carrying signs with the names of soldiers killed or villages destroyed in Vietnam. By 1972, antiwar sentiment would be nationwide. In contrast to the apolitical students of the 1950s, youth in the 1960s proved themselves able to challenge the authorities and inequities of American society.

Kent State and Jackson State   Although revulsion against the war continued to grow after Richard Nixon assumed office in 1969, his periodic announcements of troop withdrawals from Vietnam brought a lull in campus demonstrations. On April 30, 1970, however, the U.S. invasion of Cambodia jolted a war-weary nation and reawakened student protest.

At Kent State University in Ohio, as elsewhere, antiwar students broke windows and torched the ROTC building. Nixon branded them "bums," his vice president compared them to Nazi storm troopers, and the Ohio governor slapped martial law on the university. Three thousand National Guardsmen in full battle gear rolled onto the campus in armored personnel carriers. The next day, as six hundred Kent State students demonstrated, Guardsmen in Troop G, poorly trained in crowd control, fired on students retreating from tear gas, leaving four dead and eleven wounded. None was a campus radical.

Ten days later, Mississippi state patrolmen, responding to a campus protest, fired into a women's dormitory at a black college, **Jackson State,** killing two students and wounding a dozen. Nationwide, students exploded in anger against the violence, the war, and the president. More than four hundred colleges and universities, many of which had seen no previous unrest, shut down as students boycotted classes. The war had come home.

The nation was polarized. Most students blamed Nixon for widening the war, yet more Americans blamed the victims for the campus violence and criticized students for undermining U.S. foreign policy. Patriotism, class resentment against privileged college students, and a fear of social chaos underlay the condemnation of protesters. Many Kent townspeople shared the view of a local merchant that the guard had "made only one mistake—they should have fired sooner and longer." A local ditty promised, "The score is four, and next time more."

Legacy of Student Frenzy The campus disorders after the invasion of Cambodia were the final spasm of a tumultuous, now fragmenting, movement. When a bomb planted by antiwar radicals destroyed a science building at the University of Wisconsin in summer 1970, killing a graduate student, most deplored the tactic. With the resumption of classes in the fall, the fad of "streaking"—racing across campus in the nude—more reminiscent of the 1920s than the 1960s, heralded a change in the student mood. By then, Nixon had significantly reduced the draft calls and the entire conscription system was soon to be ended, decreasing student opposition to the war. Some antiwar activists turned to other causes, or to communes, careers, and parenthood. A handful of radicals went underground, committing terrorist acts that justified the government's repression of the remnants of the antiwar movement. The New Left fell victim to government harassment, to its own internal contradictions, and to Nixon's winding down the Vietnam War.

The consequences of campus upheavals outlived the New Left. Student radicalism spurred the resentment of millions of Americans, helping shatter the liberal consensus. It gave religious evangelicals, southern segregationists, and blue-collar workers yet another reason to vote conservative, and propelled Republicans like Ronald Reagan to prominence. "If it takes a bloodbath, let's get it over with," he declared of militants in 1966. "No more appeasement!"

At the same time, the New Left helped mobilize campuses into a force that the government could not ignore, and it made continued U.S. involvement in Vietnam difficult. The Movement also liberalized many facets of campus life and made university governance less authoritarian: virtually ending dress codes and curfews; making ROTC an elective rather than a requirement; and forcing the increased recruitment of minority students and the proliferation of Black Studies programs. Such changes, however, fell short of the New Left vision of remaking society and politics. While masses of students could be mobilized in the short run for a particular cause, only a few made long-term commitments to Movement activism. The generation that the New Left had hoped would be the vanguard of radical change preferred pot to politics, and rock to revolution.

THE COUNTERCULTURAL REBELLION

The alienation and hunger for change that drew some youths into radical politics led others to cultural rebellion, to personal rather than political change, to discarding middle-class conformity, careerism, and sexual repression. A San Francisco journalist termed these young people **"hippies."** Hippies disdained consumerism. Preferring to make what they needed and share it with others, they tried not to want what they did not have. They donned simple garments and let their hair grow long. Love, cooperation, and immediate gratification became their mantra.

Many hippies joined communes and tribes that glorified liberation, helped bring ecology and alternative medicine into the mainstream, and disdained decorum. In urban areas such as San Francisco's Haight Ashbury or Chicago's Old Town—"places where you could take a trip without a ticket"—communards experimented with drugs, mysticism, and uninhibited sexuality. Historian Theodore Roszack called them "a **'counter culture'** … a culture so radically disaffiliated from the mainstream assumptions of our society that it scarcely looks to many as a culture at all, but takes on the alarming appearance of a barbarian intrusion."

Hippies and Drugs   Illustrative of the gap between the two cultures, one saw marijuana as a "killer weed," a menace to health and life, and the other thought it a harmless social relaxant. At least half the college students in the late sixties tried marijuana, and a minority used mind-altering drugs, particularly LSD. The high priest of LSD, Timothy Leary, preached "Tune in, turn on, drop out." On the West Coast, novelist Ken Kesey and his followers, the Merry Pranksters, conducted "acid tests" (distributing free tablets of LSD in orange juice), and created the "psychedelic" craze of Day-Glo-painted bodies gyrating to electrified rock music under flashing strobe lights.

Many youths distanced themselves from middle-class respectability, flaunting outrageous personal styles ("do your own thing") and shaggy beards; expressing contempt for consumerism by wearing surplus military clothing or torn jeans; and expanding the language to include *bummer, far-out,* and *groovy.* Typical of the generation that had been schooled in the deprivation and duty of the 1930s and 1940s, newly elected Governor Ronald Reagan of California responded by defining a hippie as one "who looked like Tarzan, walked like Jane, and smelled like Cheetah."

Musical Revolution   "This the dawning of the age of Aquarius," sang the cast of 1968's *Hair,* and the nation pulsed with music that both echoed and developed a separate generational identity, a distinct youth culture. In the early 1960s, the revived popularity of folk music mirrored youth's search for an "authentic" alternative to what they considered an artificial consumer culture. Expressing their idealism in protesting war and racism, Bob Dylan sang hopefully of changes "blowin' in the wind" and indignantly of changes that would "shake your windows and rattle your walls."

"Beatlemania" swept the country in 1964. The Beatles would soon be joined by Motown rhythm-and-blues black performers and eardrum-shattering acid rockers—extolling "sex, drugs, and rock-and-roll" for a generation at war.

In August 1969, 400,000 young people gathered for the **Woodstock festival** in New York's Catskill Mountains to celebrate their vision of freedom and harmony. For one long weekend, they reveled in rock music and openly shared drugs and sexual partners. One magazine claimed it "the model of how good we will all feel after the revolution." Many heralded Woodstock as the dawning of an era of love and peace—the Age of Aquarius.

Its luster had already dimmed. "Freedom's just another word for nothing left to lose," sang Janis Joplin, one of a number of rock stars who would soon die of drug addiction. The pilgrimage of "flower children" to the Haight and to New York's East Village in the mid-sixties had brought in their wake a train of rapists and organized-crime dope peddlers. In late 1969, hippie Charles Manson and his "family" of runaways ritually murdered a pregnant movie actress and four of her friends, and the Rolling Stones hired the Hell's Angels motorcycle gang to guard them at their rock concert at the Altamont Raceway near San Francisco. While the

Stones snarled "Street Fighting Man," the Hell's Angels terrorized spectators and stabbed and stomped a young black man to death. In 1970, the Beatles disbanded. John Lennon sang, "The dream is over."

Advertisers awoke to the economic potential of the youth culture, using "revolution" to sell cars and jeans. Rock groups, commanding huge fees, became big business. Yogurt and granola appeared in supermarkets. Although cynics concluded that counterculture values were not deeply held, the culture's attitudes and beliefs continued to influence American society long after the 1960s. Self-fulfillment remained a popular goal, the questioning of conventional values and authority became commonplace, and the repressive sexual standards of the 1950s did not return.

The Sexual Revolution   The counterculture's "if it feels good, do it" approach fit the hedonistic and permissive ethic of the 1960s, leading to a revolution in sexual norms. Although the AIDS epidemic and the graying of the baby boomers in the late 1980s chilled the ardor of promiscuity, liberalized sexual mores were more publicly accepted than ever before, making full gender equality and gay liberation realizable goals.

Many commentators linked the increase in sexual permissiveness to "the Pill"—an oral contraceptive that freed women from the threat of pregnancy. It became available in 1960, and by 1970, ten million women were taking it. Still other women used the intrauterine device (IUD, later banned as unsafe) or the diaphragm. Many universities ended their rules on dormitory visits and living off campus, allowing more women to explore and enjoy their sexuality, but also increasing pressures from men for women to have sex lest they be labeled "frigid" and unliberated. Some states legalized abortion. In New York, one fetus was legally aborted for every two babies born in 1970. The Supreme Court's *Roe v. Wade* (1973) decision struck down all remaining state laws infringing on a woman's constitutional right to abortion during the first trimester (three months) of pregnancy.

The Supreme Court also threw out most laws restricting any "sexually explicit" art with "redeeming social importance." Mass culture exploited the new permissiveness. *Playboy* featured ever-more-explicit erotica, and women's periodicals encouraged readers to enjoy recreational sex. *The Joy of Sex* (1972)—a "Gourmet Guide to Love Making"—became a fixture in middle-class bedrooms. Hollywood filled movie screens with scenes of couples having sex; Broadway presented plays featuring full-frontal nudity and mock orgies; and even television presented dramas about, and frank discussions of, once-forbidden topics. Attitudinal changes brought behavioral changes, and vice versa. Cohabitation—living together without marriage—became thinkable to average middle-class Americans. Some marital counselors even touted "open marriage" (in which spouses are free to have sex with other partners) and "swinging" (sexual sharing with other couples) as cures for stale relationships. Some Americans' tolerance for unconventional, unrestrained sexuality had changed dramatically by the mid-1970s.

Overall, the baby boomers transformed sexual relations as much as racial relations. The institutions of marriage and family would be fundamentally altered. Freer social norms and language spread throughout much of American society. But what some hailed as liberation others bemoaned as moral decay. Offended by open sexuality and its preferences, and by "topless" bars and X-rated theaters, many Americans applauded politicians who promised a war on immorality. The public association of the counterculture and the sexual revolution with student radicalism and ghetto riots swelled the tide of conservatism in the 1970s.

FEMINISM AND A VALUES REVOLUTION

The rising tempo of social activism also stirred a new spirit of self-awareness and dissatisfaction among educated women. Although one of the last of the major social movements to emerge in the 1960s, the Second wave of Feminism outlasted the others and profoundly altered the economic and legal status of women, as well as attitudes about gender roles and sexual relationships.

A Second Feminist Wave   Several events fanned the embers of women's discontent into flames. Unprecedented numbers of women were going to college and employed outside the home. In 1963, the report of John Kennedy's Presidential Commission on the Status of Women documented occupational inequities similar to those endured by minorities. Women received less pay than men for comparable work; and they made up only 7 percent of the nation's doctors and less than 4 percent of its lawyers. The women who served on the presidential commission successfully urged that the Civil Rights Act of 1964 prohibit gender-based as well as racial discrimination in employment.

Dismayed by the Equal Employment Opportunity Commission's reluctance to enforce the ban on sex discrimination in employment, these women formed the **National Organization for Women (NOW)** in 1966. A civil-rights group for women, NOW labored "to bring women into full participation in the mainstream of American society." It lobbied for equal opportunity, filed lawsuits against gender discrimination, and mobilized public opinion against sexism.

NOW's prominence owed much to the publication of journalist Betty Friedan's critique of domesticity, *The Feminine Mystique* (1963), which posed what Friedan called "the problem that has no name"—the frustration of educated, middle-class wives and mothers who had subordinated their own aspirations to the needs of men. Friedan urged women to pursue careers that would establish their own independent identity and would "fulfill their potentialities as human beings."

Still another catalyst for feminism came from the involvement of younger women in the civil-rights and anti-Vietnam War movements. These activists had gained confidence in their own potential, an ideology to understand oppression, and experience in the strategy and tactics of organized protest. They also became conscious of their own second-class status, as they were sexually exploited and relegated to menial jobs by male activists. In the words of the civil rights movement's Casey Hayden: the "assumptions of male superiority are as widespread and deep-rooted and every much as crippling to the woman as the assumptions of white supremacy are to the Negro."

Although small in number, young women who shared such thoughts would soon create a women's liberation movement more critical of sexual inequality than NOW.

**Women's
Liberation**   In 1968, militant feminists adopted "consciousness-raising" as a recruitment device and a means of transforming women's perceptions of themselves and society. Tens of thousands of women assembled in small groups to share experiences and air grievances. They learned that others felt dissatisfaction similar to their own: "When I saw that what I always felt were my own personal hangups was as true for every other woman in that room as it was for me! Well, that's when my consciousness was raised." Women came to understand that their personal, individual problems were in fact shared problems with social causes and political solutions—"the personal is political." This new consciousness opened eyes and minds and begot a sense that "sisterhood is powerful."

Women's liberation groups employed a variety of publicity-generating, confrontational tactics. In 1968, radical feminists crowned a sheep Miss America to dramatize their belief that beauty pageants enslaved women "in high-heeled, low-status roles" and set up "freedom trash cans" in which women could discard girdles, make-up, and other "women-garbage." They demanded inclusion in the Boston Marathon, no longer accepting the excuse that "it is unhealthy for women to run long distances." Overcoming male condescension, they established health collectives and shelters for abused women, created day-care centers and rape crisis centers, founded abortion-counseling services and women's studies programs. Publishing nearly five hundred new feminist publications, they fought negative portrayals of women in the media and advertising. Terms like *male chauvinist pig* entered the vocabulary and those like *chicks* exited.

In August 1970, feminists joined in the largest women's rights demonstration ever. Commemorating the fiftieth anniversary of woman suffrage, the Women's Strike for Equality brought out tens of thousands of women to parade for the right to equal employment and safe, legal abortions. By then, the women's movement had already ended newspapers' practice of listing employment opportunities under separate "Male" and "Female" headings, and pressured banks to issue credit to women in their own name.

In the 1970s, feminists focused especially on three issues: equal treatment in education and employment, access to abortion, and passage of the **Equal Rights Amendment (ERA)** barring discrimination on the basis of sex. In 1972, Title IX of the Education Amendments Act prohibited educational institutions that received federal funds from discriminating on the basis of sex. Women gained entry to the U.S. military academies in 1976; and at the state and local levels they won laws expanding what constituted rape as well as greater protection for victims of domestic violence and more effective prosecution of abusers. Many single-sex colleges became coeducational. The percentage of female students in medical schools rose from 8 to 24 percent and in law schools from 5 percent to 40 percent in the 1970s. By century's end, women would constitute about 20 percent of all state and federal legislators.

The right to control their own sexuality and to make the decisions regarding having children became feminist rallying cries. In addition to using "the Pill," some women challenged demeaning obstetrical practices. Others explored alternatives to hospital births and popularized alternatives to radical mastectomy for breast cancer. And many, aware of the dangers of illegal abortions, pushed for their legalization, achieved in *Roe v. Wade*. Perhaps the most controversial ruling

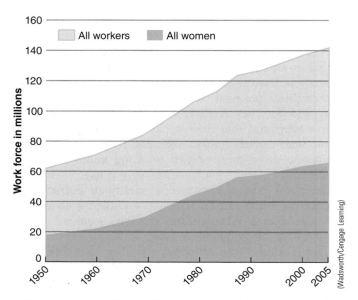

FIGURE 29.1 Women in the Work Force, 1950–2005

After 1960, the numbers of American women who were wage earners surged upward. Both the women's movement and economic pressures encouraged this trend.

Source: U.S. Department of Labor, Bureau of Labor Statistics *(www.bls.gov).*

of the century, *Roe v. Wade* and the subsequent doubling of abortions, to 1.5 million by 1980, triggered an enormous backlash from social conservatives and from Catholics and Protestants, many of whom felt abortion the moral equivalent of murder. Abortion opponents would seek a "right to life" amendment to the Constitution and simultaneously energize Phyllis Schlafly's "STOP ERA" campaign.

In 1972, both houses of Congress passed the ERA with little opposition and, within a year, twenty-eight of the necessary thirty-eight states approved the proposed amendment. Its ultimate adoption seemed self-evident. Then Schlafly, a Republican organizer and working-woman herself, took up the fight. Her monthly newsletter, *The Phyllis Schlafly Report*, added antifeminism to its traditional attacks on communism and on federal social programs. Her accusation that feminism was just self-centeredness, and her affirmation of traditional gender roles, struck a responsive chord with many men as well as with working-class women who felt estranged from the largely upper-middle-class feminist movement. Schlafly charged that the ERA would force women into combat roles in the military, necessitate "unisex toilets," promote lesbianism, and "deprive women of a right, benefit, or exemption that they now enjoy." Her relentless assault eroded support and helped kill the amendment. Selling millions of records, country artist Tammy Wynette sang "Don't Liberate Me, Love Me."

While the number of women working outside the home leaped from under 20 million in 1960 to nearly 60 million by 1990 (see Figure 29.1), women's wages still lagged behind those of men, the workplace remained gender-segregated, and the "glass ceiling" that limited their ability to rise beyond a certain corporate level remained in place. As divorce and out-of-wedlock births became more common, the number of women heading families increased; by 1980, only 15 percent of American families with children had a father who worked and a mother who stayed at home. Children now constituted the bulk of the poor, and sociologists wrote about the "feminization of poverty."

Evidenced by the rising divorce rate in the 1970s, from one-third to one-half of the marriages occurring annually, complex issues of role-sharing befuddled middle-class families too. Women who worked still bore primary responsibility for their homes and family. Yet day-care centers for working women became commonplace; grown women were no longer "girls"; gender-neutral terms (for example firefighter in place of firemen), came into vogue; and the ideal male changed from swashbuckler to one more "in touch with his feelings." Few pined for the era when child care, housework, and volunteerism had defined "women's sphere." American women had learned, according to historian Gerda Lerner:

> that they belong to a subordinate group; that they have suffered wrongs as a group; that their condition of subordination is not natural, but societally determined; that they must join with other women to remedy these wrongs; and finally, that they must and can provide an alternative vision of societal organization in which women as well as men will enjoy autonomy and self-determination.

Gay Liberation   Like feminists, gay men and women were emboldened by the new sexual openness to assert their values, and stimulated by the other protest movements in the sixties, **gay liberation** emerged publicly in 1969. During a routine raid by New York City police, the homosexual patrons of the Stonewall Inn, a gay bar in Greenwich Village, unexpectedly fought back fiercely. The furor triggered a surge of "gay pride," a new sense of identity and self-acceptance, and widespread activism. "We reject society's attempt to impose sexual roles and definitions of our nature," asserted the Gay Liberation Front. "We are going to be who we are."

By 1973, approximately eight hundred openly gay groups campaigned for equal rights, for incorporating lesbianism into the women's movement, and for removing the stigma of immorality and depravity attached to being gay. That year, the American Psychiatric Association officially ended its classification of homosexuality as a mental disorder. More and more gay men and women "came out of the closet," proudly acknowledging their sexual orientation.

In 1977, "Gay Pride" parades drew seventy-five thousand marchers in New York City and three hundred thousand in San Francisco. More taboos fell as Elaine Noble, an avowed lesbian, won a seat in the Massachusetts legislature in 1974, and Harvey Milk, an openly gay candidate, was elected to the San Francisco board of supervisors in 1977. In 1987, Massachusetts congressman Barney Frank publicly acknowledged his homosexuality.

As gay activism spread from big cities on the coasts to small communities in Middle America, organizations like the National Gay Task Force, founded in 1973 (and later renamed the National Gay and Lesbian Task Force), demanded the repeal of anti-gay laws and passage of legislation protecting homosexuals' civil rights. Responding to the pressure, many states and cities repealed laws against same-sex relations between consenting adults and, like the U.S. Civil Service Commission in 1975, barred job discrimination on the basis of sexual orientation.

Like feminism, the gay liberation movement came under attack from conservatives, who feared that protecting gay rights encouraged immoral behavior. In 1977, singer Anita Bryant led a successful campaign to repeal a Miami law banning discrimination against homosexuals, prompting similar antigay campaigns in other cities.

Environmental Activism   Building on the concerns raised in the early sixties, environmentalists also carried the tide of reform into the 1970s. Following the first Earth Day in April 1970, which attracted some 20 million participants, large numbers of Americans began to focus on ecology and the interaction of humans with their environment. For the first time, the media began to highlight acid rain, global warming, nuclear waste disposal, and other human-caused environmental hazards. Well-publicized disasters greatly furthered concern. Cleveland's Cuyahoga River burst into flames, and Lake Erie "died," both contaminated by decades of toxic chemical dumping. A huge oil spill fouled the coast of Santa Barbara, and many Americans choked on the air they breathed while dead fish floated in local rivers and beaches closed owing to sewage contamination.

Environmental advocacy groups gained many fresh recruits. Older organizations such as the Sierra Club and the Audubon Society continued their efforts to preserve natural areas for habitat protection and the recreational and aesthetic pleasures of future generations. Newer groups such as Greenpeace and Friends of the Earth worked against threats to ecological balance. Founded in 1971 when Canadian activists protested a planned U.S. nuclear test on an island in the Bering Sea, Greenpeace established its U.S. branch a year later, working to preserve old-growth forests and protect the world's oceans. By 2000, it had 250,000 U.S. members. The Save the Whales campaign, launched by the Animal Welfare Institute in 1971, opposed the slaughter of the world's largest mammals by fleets of floating processing factories that made dog-and-cat food.

President Nixon responded to popular pressures by signing bills for cleaner air and water, for reducing toxic wastes, and for the further protection of endangered species and wilderness. He also signed bills creating the Occupational Safety and Health Administration (OSHA), to enforce health and safety standards in the workplace, and the Environmental Protection Agency (EPA), which required federal agencies to prepare an environmental-impact analysis for all proposed projects.

Environmentalists also targeted the nuclear-power industry, adopting techniques from the civil-rights and antiwar campaigns to protest at planned nuclear facilities. The movement crested in 1979 when a partial meltdown crippled the **Three Mile Island** nuclear-power plant in Pennsylvania. A Jane Fonda movie released at the same time, *China Syndrome*, portrayed a fictitious but plausible nuclear-power disaster caused by a California earthquake. Deepening public concerns about nuclear power encouraged citizen groups like the Clamshell Alliance in New England to stop new atomic power plants from going online.

However, at a time of concern over an energy crisis, and of rising unemployment, Americans divided over environmental issues like construction of the Trans-Alaska Pipeline in 1973 and whether or not to abandon atomic power, offshore oil drilling, and restrictions on logging. A popular bumper stick read: "If You're Hungry and Out of Work, Eat An Environmentalist." Yet other Americans sought a healthy lifestyle that promoted less consumption. Cigarette smoking declined. Organic food consumption increased. A jogging craze swept the middle-class.

The "Me Decade" Whatever political views Americans held, personal pursuits and self-fulfillment largely shaped 1970s American society. Journalist Tom Wolfe dubbed this turn from the public sphere the "Me Decade," and many citizens—reacting to defeat in Vietnam, an economic downturn, and the corruption of public officials—retreated inward, following the advice of Robert Ringer's best-seller *Looking Out for Number One*.

Highly individualistic pet causes flourished, as did new faiths. Some young people practiced Transcendental Meditation or joined the Reverend Sun Myung Moon's Unification Church. Others embraced the International Society for Krishna Consciousness, whose shaved-head, saffron-robed followers added an exotic note in airports and on college campuses. Several thousand rural communes arose as some counterculture veterans sought to escape the urban-corporate world, practice organic farming, revive old technologies, and live in harmony with nature. Most communes proved short-lived.

Journalists discovered the "Yuppie" (young urban professional), preoccupied—often obsessed—with physical fitness and consumer goods. Yuppies jogged and bicycled, ate pesticide-free natural foods, and in a process known as gentrification, purchased and restored rundown inner-city apartments, often displacing poor and elderly residents in the process. Self-indulgence appeared to be their hallmark, and many identified with conservatism's priority on, above all, individual rights.

As baby boomers continued to sing "We want the world, and we want it now!" the 1970s saw the rise of punk rock, an aggressively anti-establishment genre promoted by groups like the Sex Pistols. Tejano music spread from Texas to win national popularity thanks to performers such as Selena Quintanilla. Rap or hip-hop, whose free-form improvised recitations had roots in Jamaican reggae music and West African storytelling traditions, emerged from poor black New York City neighborhoods. And disco music spotlighted the desire to dance on one's own and to pursue individual rather than societal goals.

In the cultural arena, much but not all reflected the era's malaise. Along with films featuring the madness of the war in Vietnam and corruption in high places, blockbuster movies like *Jaws* (1975), *Rocky* (1976), and *Star Wars* (1977) offered escapist fare. *Happy Days*, the top TV show of 1976–1977, evoked nostalgia for the 1950s. The TV series *Dallas*, chronicling the steamy affairs of a Texas oil family, captivated millions, as did numerous other hit programs featuring characters that defied traditional morality. And beginning in 1971 and gaining popularity throughout the decade, *All in the Family* featured a blue-collar working stiff, Archie Bunker, raging against "girls with skirts up to here" and "men with hair down to there," as well as just about everything else associated with the 1960s. Whether those who laughed were rejecting Archie's bigoted politics or endorsing his tirades against big government and social disorder may never be known. But the character his creator meant to be a cultural and political dinosaur actually forecast a shift to the right, a backlash against "the sixties."

A DIVIDED NATION

By 1968, the combined stresses and strains in American society had produced the most tumultuous era in the United States since the Civil War. The tensions that year resulted in riots, fiery demonstrations, two stunning assassinations, Lyndon Johnson's retreat in Vietnam and from politics, and an election that marked the demise of liberalism.

Assassinations and Turmoil   Three days after the Wisconsin primary, a bullet from a sniper's high-powered rifle killed Martin Luther King, Jr., as he stood on a motel balcony in Memphis, Tennessee. Because of his increasing concern about poverty in America and his plans for an upcoming Poor People's Campaign, King had gone there to support striking black sanitation workers. The presumed assassin, James Earl Ray, an escaped convict and white racist, would confess, be found guilty, and then recant, leaving aspects of the killing unclear. As in the assassination of John F. Kennedy, it seemed unworthy that one misfit was alone responsible. What was clear in 1968: the civil rights movement had lost its preeminent leader, and its way. As the news spread, black ghettos in more than a hundred cities burst into violence. Twenty blocks of Chicago's West Side went up in flames, and Mayor Richard Daley ordered police to shoot to kill arsonists. In Washington, D.C., under night skies illuminated by seven hundred fires, army units in combat gear set up machine-gun nests outside the Capitol and White House. It would take seventy-five thousand troops to quell the riots, which left 46 dead, three thousand injured, and nearly twenty-seven thousand in jail.

Entering the race as the favorite of the party bosses and labor chieftains, LBJ's vice president, **Hubert Humphrey,** turned the contest for the nomination into a three-cornered scramble. **Eugene McCarthy** remained the candidate of the "new politics"—a moral crusade against war and injustice directed to affluent, educated liberals. **Robert Kennedy** campaigned as the tribune of the less privileged, the sole candidate who appealed to both the white ethnic working class and the minority poor. In early June, after his victory in the California primary, the brother of the murdered president was himself assassinated by a troubled Palestinian, Sirhan Sirhan.

The deaths of King and Kennedy frustrated untold Americans. The murders denied them a fundamental democratic right, the right to choose their own leaders. "I won't vote," a youth said. "Every good man we get, they kill." "People just dropped out," the civil rights movement's John Lewis observed, "I think some people were afraid to hope again, afraid to get involved." "Where have you gone, Joe DiMaggio?" sang a wistful Paul Simon. Although Kennedy's death cleared the way for Humphrey's nomination, increasing numbers of Democrats turned to third-party candidate George Wallace's thinly veiled appeal for white supremacy or to

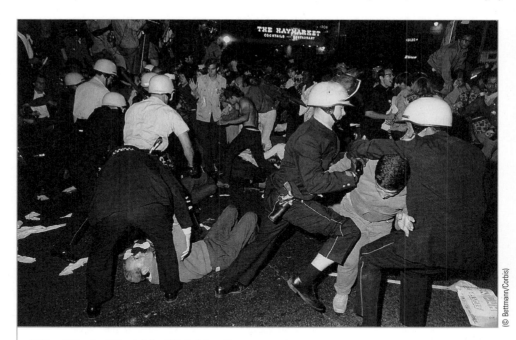

(© Bettmann/Corbis)

"The Whole World Is Watching" *Photographs and televised pictures of Chicago police beating and gassing antiwar protesters and innocent bystanders at the Democratic convention in 1968 linked Democrats in the public mind with violence and mayhem. The scenes made Republican Richard Nixon a reassuring presence to those he would term "the silent majority."*

the GOP nominee Richard M. Nixon. The Republican appealed to those disgusted with inner-city riots and antiwar demonstrations. He claimed to have a "secret plan" to end the war, lambasted the liberal decisions of the Warren Court, and derided hippies and protestors. Nixon also said he would heed "the voice of the great majority of Americans, the forgotten Americans, the non-shouters, the non-demonstrators, those who do not break the law, people who pay their taxes and go to work, who send their children to school, who go to their churches, ... who love this country." Tapping the same wellsprings of anger and frustration, Wallace pitched a fiery message to southern segregationists and working-class northerners, denouncing welfare mothers, antiwar demonstrators, and black militants. If elected, Wallace vowed to throw "over-educated, ivory-tower" federal bureaucrats "into the Potomac," and to crack down on "long-hair, pot-smoking, draft-card-burning youth."

In August 1968, violence outside the Democratic National Convention in Chicago reinforced the appeal of both Wallace and Nixon. Determined to avoid the rioting that wracked Chicago after King's assassination, Mayor Richard Daley had denied demonstrators permits to march or engage in meaningful protest and given police a green light to attack "the hippies, the **yippies,** and the flippies." On August 28, as a huge national television audience looked on and protesters chanted

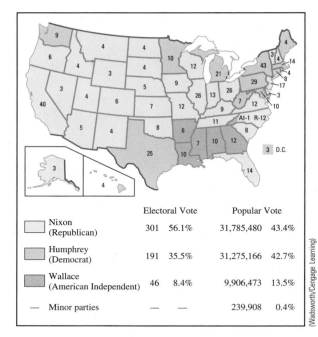

	Electoral Vote		Popular Vote	
Nixon (Republican)	301	56.1%	31,785,480	43.4%
Humphrey (Democrat)	191	35.5%	31,275,166	42.7%
Wallace (American Independent)	46	8.4%	9,906,473	13.5%
— Minor parties	—	—	239,908	0.4%

(Wadsworth/Cengage Learning)

MAP 29.1 The Election of 1968

"The whole world is watching," Daley's bluecoats took off their badges and clubbed demonstrators, tossed tear gas at bystanders, and bloodied reporters and photographers. The police's brutal response to the protestors' taunting obscenities and rage tore the Democrats apart and created an image of them as the party of dissent and disorder. Although a federal commission later described the melee as a "police riot," 70 percent of Americans supported the police violence against the protestors. Hubert Humphrey, who for years had dreamed of becoming president, had received a nomination that appeared worthless.

Conservative Resurgence   Nixon capitalized on the televised turmoil to attract the support of voters desperate for "law and order." Portraying himself as the candidate of the Silent Majority, he criticized the Supreme Court for safeguarding criminals and radicals, vowed to get people off welfare rolls and on payrolls, promised to crack down on "pot, pornography, protest, and permissiveness," and asserted that "our schools are for education—not integration."

Reaching out even more bluntly to working-class whites, George Wallace stoked their fury against "bearded anarchists, smart-aleck editorial writers, and pointy-headed professors looking down their noses at us." Promising to keep peace in the streets, he vowed that "if any demonstrator ever lays down in front of my car, it'll be the last car he'll ever lie down in front of." Although many shared his views, few believed he had any chance of winning, and either did not vote or switched to his opponents. Still, 14 percent of the electorate—primarily young, lower-middle-class, small-town workers—cast their votes for Wallace.

In a narrow outcome with large consequences, Nixon and Humphrey split the rest of the vote almost evenly (see Map 29.1). But with Humphrey receiving just 38 percent of the white vote and not even close to half the labor vote, the long-dominant New Deal coalition was shattered. The buoyant sense of liberalism that all was possible had evaporated. The electorate clearly sought stability, not further social change.

The 57 percent of the electorate who chose Nixon or Wallace would dominate American politics for the rest of the century. While the Democratic Party fractured into a welter of contending groups, the Republicans attracted a new majority, many of whom lived in the Sunbelt—the metropolitan South, the sun country of Florida, the desert Southwest and Texas, and populous southern California. Kevin Phillips, whose advice to Nixon to focus on Sunbelt voters was published in 1969 as *The Emerging Republican Majority,* described its residents as "the pleasure-seekers, the bored, the ambitious, the space-age technicians and the retired—a super-slice of the rootless, socially mobile group known as the American middle class." Phillips also recognized the attraction of Sunbelt attitudes—on government spending, defense, race, and taxes—to residents in the suburbs and ethnic working-class neighborhoods of the North. So did the authors of *The Real Majority,* who deeply impressed Nixon with their assertion that the new key to a winning coalition was the "47 year old Catholic housewife in Dayton, Ohio whose husband is a machinist." Although she and her blue-collar husband had always voted Democratic, they would defect to the Republicans because of the couple's conservative views on black rioters, antiwar protesters, pornography, and drugs. Wooing these voters—who he named the Silent Majority in a 1969 speech—became the centerpiece of Nixon's political strategy.

A Matter of Character   A Californian of Quaker roots, Richard Milhous Nixon was elected to Congress as a navy veteran in 1946. He won prominence for his role in the HUAC investigation of Alger Hiss (see Chapter 26) and advanced to the Senate in 1950 by accusing his Democratic opponent of disloyalty. He served two terms as Eisenhower's vice president, but lost the presidential race to Kennedy in 1960 and a run for the California governorship in 1962. Ignoring what seemed a political death sentence, Nixon campaigned vigorously for GOP candidates in 1966 and won his party's nomination and the presidency in 1968.

Nixon yearned to be remembered as an international statesman, but domestic affairs kept intruding. He tried to reform the welfare system and solve complex economic problems. But the underside of Nixon's personality appealed to the darker recesses of the nation and intensified the fears and divisions among Americans.

Although highly intelligent, he displayed the rigid self-control of a man monitoring his own every move. When the private Nixon emerged, he was suspicious, insecure, seeking vengeance. His conviction that enemies lurked everywhere, waiting to destroy him, verged on paranoia. He sought to annihilate his Democratic opponents, to "get them on the ground ... stick our heels in, step on them hard ... crush them, show them no mercy."

The classic outsider, reared in pinched surroundings, physically awkward, unable to relate easily to others, Nixon remained fearful, even at the height of his power, that he would never be accepted. At the beginning of his administration, however, his strengths stood out. He spoke of national reconciliation, took bold initiatives internationally, and dealt with domestic problems responsibly.

Symbolic of his positive start, the nation celebrated the first successful manned mission to the moon. On July 21, 1969, the Apollo 11 lunar module, named *Eagle,* descended to the Sea of Tranquility. As millions watched on television, astronaut **Neil Armstrong** walked on the moon's surface and proclaimed, "That's one small step for man, one giant leap for mankind." Five more lunar expeditions followed, and in 1975 the space race essentially ended with the United States and the Soviet Union engaging in cooperative efforts to explore the rest of the universe.

The first newly elected president since 1849 whose party controlled neither house of Congress, Nixon cooperated with the Democrats to increase social-security benefits, build subsidized housing, expand the Job Corps, and grant the vote to eighteen-year-olds. As noted earlier, the president also approved new laws to protect the environment and worker safety.

Conservatives grumbled as government grew larger and more intrusive and as race-conscious employment policies, including affirmative-action quotas, were mandated for all federal contractors. Conservatives grew still angrier when Nixon unveiled the Family Assistance Plan (FAP) in 1969. A bold effort to overhaul the welfare system, FAP proposed a guaranteed minimum annual income for all Americans. Caught between liberals who thought the income inadequate and conservatives who disliked it on principle, FAP died in the Senate.

A Troubled Economy

Nixon inherited the fiscal consequences of President Johnson's effort to wage the Vietnam War and finance the Great Society by deficit financing—to have both "guns and butter." Facing a "whopping" budget deficit of $25 billion in 1969 and an inflation rate of 5 percent (see Figure 29.2), Nixon cut government spending and encouraged the Federal Reserve Board to raise interest rates. The result was a combination of inflation and recession that economists called "stagflation" and Democrats termed "Nixonomics."

Accelerating inflation lowered the standard of living of many families and sparked a wave of strikes as workers sought wage hikes to keep up with the cost of living. It encouraged the wealthy to invest in art and real estate rather than technology and factories. Hence, more plants shut down, industrial jobs dwindled, and many displaced workers lost their savings, their health and pension benefits, and their homes.

Throughout 1971, Nixon lurched from policy to policy. Declaring "I am now a Keynesian," he increased deficit spending to stimulate the private sector, which resulted in the largest budget deficit since World War II. Then, Nixon devalued the dollar to correct the balance-of-payment deficit. Finally, he imposed a freeze on wages, prices, and rents, a short-term fix that gave the economy a shot in the arm until after the 1972 election. Then Nixon again reversed course, replacing controls with voluntary—and ineffective—guidelines. Inflation zoomed as the **Organization**

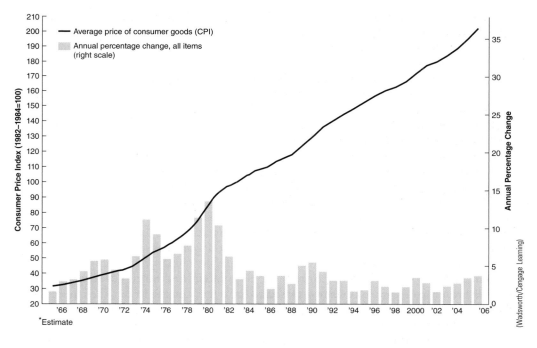

FIGURE 29.2 Inflation, 1965–2006

Inflation, which had been moderate during the two decades following the Second World War, began to soar with the escalation of the war in Vietnam in the mid-1960s. In 1979 and 1980, the nation experienced double-digit inflation in two consecutive years for the first time since World War I.

of Petroleum Exporting Countries (OPEC), a group of Third World nations that had joined together to set production levels and prices, launched an embargo that raised the price of crude oil, and sluggish growth dogged the economy throughout the decade.

Law and Order   Despite his public appeals for unity, Nixon hoped to divide the American people in ways that would bring about a realignment in politics and create a new Republican majority coalition. His "southern strategy" sought to attract Dixie's white Democrats into the GOP fold, while his stands on crime, drugs, antiwar protestors, and black militants wooed blue-collar laborers and suburbanites—voters whom political strategist Kevin Phillips described as "in motion between a Democratic past and a Republican future." To outflank George Wallace, Nixon opposed court-ordered busing and took a tough stand against campus unrest and black radicalism.

To combat the militants he despised, Nixon had the IRS audit their tax returns, the Small Business Administration deny them loans, and the National Security Agency illegally wiretap them. The FBI worked with local law officials to disrupt and immobilize the Black Panthers, the CIA illegally investigated and compiled dossiers on thousands of American citizens, and the Justice Department prosecuted antiwar activists and black radicals in highly publicized trials. Nixon himself drew up an "enemies list" of adversaries to be harassed by the government.

In 1970, Nixon widened his offensive against the antiwar movement by approving the Huston Plan, which would use the CIA and FBI in various illegal activities, such as wiretapping and break-ins to gather or plant evidence. But FBI chief J. Edgar Hoover opposed the plan as a threat to the bureau's independence. Blocked, Nixon secretly created his own White House unit to discredit his opposition and ensure executive secrecy. Nicknamed **"the plumbers"** because of their assignment to plug government leaks, and to undermine opposition to the president, the team was headed by former FBI agent G. Gordon Liddy and former CIA operative E. Howard Hunt.

The plumbers first targeted Daniel Ellsberg, a former Defense Department analyst who had given the press the **Pentagon Papers,** a secret chronicle of U.S. involvement in Vietnam. On June 13, the *New York Times* began publishing the Pentagon Papers, revealing a long history of White House lies to Congress, foreign leaders, and the American people. Although the papers contained nothing about his administration, Nixon, fearing that they would undermine trust in government and establish a precedent for publishing classified material, sought to bar their publication. The Supreme Court, however, ruled that publication of the Pentagon Papers was protected by the First Amendment. Livid, Nixon directed the Justice Department to indict Ellsberg for theft and ordered the plumbers to break into the office of Ellsberg's psychiatrist in search of information to discredit the man who had become a hero to the antiwar movement.

The Southern Strategy   Nixon especially courted whites upset by the drive for racial equality. The administration opposed extension of the Voting Rights Act of 1965, sought to cripple enforcement of the Fair Housing Act of 1968, pleaded for the postponement of desegregation in Mississippi's schools, and filed suits to prohibit the busing of children as a means of desegregating public schools. In 1971, when the Supreme Court upheld "forced" busing as a constitutional and necessary tactic in *Swann v. Charlotte-Mecklenburg Board of Education* Nixon, the new champion of the white South, asked Congress to enact a moratorium on busing. By so doing, Nixon also appealed to northern whites, in such cities as Boston and Denver, who opposed court-ordered busing plans.

The strategy of wooing angry and fearful whites also dictated Nixon's Supreme Court nominations. To reverse the Warren court's liberalism, he sought strict constructionists, judges who would not "meddle" in social issues or be "soft" on criminals. In 1969 he appointed Warren Burger as chief justice. Although the Senate then twice rejected southern conservatives nominated by Nixon, the president succeeded in appointing Harry Blackmun of Minnesota, Lewis Powell of Virginia, and William Rehnquist of Arizona. Along with Burger, they steered the Court in a centrist direction, ruling liberally in most cases involving abortion, desegregation, and the death penalty, while shifting to the right on civil liberties, community censorship, and police power.

As the 1970 congressional elections neared, Nixon encouraged his vice president, Spiro T. Agnew, to step up attacks on "hooligans, hippies, and radical liberals." Agnew assailed the Democrats as "sniveling hand-wringers" and the news media as "nattering nabobs of negativism." Liberals deplored Agnew's alarming alliterative allegations, but many others found them on target. The 1970 elections were a draw, with the GOP losing nine House seats and winning two Senate seats.

Successes Abroad, Crises at Home

Above all else, Nixon focused on foreign affairs. Considering himself a master of *realpolitik*—a pragmatic approach stressing national interest rather than ethical goals—he sought to check Soviet expansionism and to limit the nuclear-arms race and reduce superpower conflict. To achieve a new era of **détente**—reduced tensions—with the communist world, Nixon chose **Henry Kissinger,** a refugee from Hitler's Germany and professor of international relations, who shared Nixon's penchant for secrecy and for the concentration of decision-making power in the White House.

In his second inaugural, Nixon pledged "to make the next four years the best four years in America's history." Ironically, they would rank among its sorriest. His vice president would resign in disgrace; his closest aides would go to jail; and he would serve barely a year and a half of his second term before resigning to avoid impeachment.

Détente   Having entered into negotiations to end the war in Vietnam (see Chapter 28), Nixon pursued détente with the Soviet Union and a turnabout in Chinese-American affairs. These developments, the most significant shift in U.S. foreign policy since the start of the Cold War, created a new relationship among the United States, the Soviet Union, and China.

Presidents from Truman to Johnson had refused to recognize the People's Republic of China, to allow its admission to the United Nations, and to permit American allies to trade with it. But by 1969, a widening Sino-Soviet split made the prospect of improved relations with both nations attractive to Nixon, who hoped to have "closer relations with each side than they did with each other." In June 1971, Kissinger began secret negotiations with Beijing, laying the groundwork for Nixon's historic February 1972 trip to China "to seek the normalization of relations." The first visit ever by a sitting American president to the largest nation in the world, it ended more than twenty years of Chinese-American hostility. Full diplomatic recognition followed in 1979.

Equally significant, Nixon went to Moscow in May 1972 to sign agreements with the Soviets on trade, technological cooperation, and the limitation of nuclear weapons. Fear of a Sino-American alliance and a desire to slow the incredibly expensive arms race made the Soviet Union eager for better relations with the U.S. The **Strategic Arms Limitation Treaty (SALT I)** froze each side's offensive nuclear missiles for five years, and committed both countries to strategic equality rather than nuclear superiority; and the Anti-Ballistic Missile (ABM) Treaty restricted the deployment by both sides of nationwide missile-defense systems. Although they did not end the arms race, the treaties symbolized a first step toward that goal, reduced Soviet-American tensions and, in an election year, enhanced Nixon's stature.

Shuttle Diplomacy   Not even better relations with China and the Soviet Union ensured global stability. In the Middle East, Israel, fearing an imminent Arab attack, launched a preemptive strike on its neighbors in 1967, routing them in six days, and seizing Sinai and the Gaza Strip from Egypt, the West Bank and East Jerusalem from Jordan, and Syria's Golan Heights. Israel promised to give up the occupied lands in exchange for a negotiated peace, but the Arab states refused to negotiate with Israel or to recognize its right to exist. Palestinians, many of them refugees since the creation of Israel in 1948, turned to the Palestine Liberation Organization (PLO), which demanded Israel's destruction.

War exploded again in 1973 when Egypt and Syria attacked Israel on the Jewish high holy day of Yom Kippur. Only massive shipments of military supplies from the United States enabled a reeling Israel to stop the assault. In retaliation, the Arab states embargoed shipments of crude oil to the United States and its allies. As the five-month embargo and following spike in oil prices sharply intensified inflation, it dramatized U.S. dependence on foreign energy sources.

The dual shocks of the energy crisis at home and rising Soviet influence in the Arab world spurred Kissinger to engage in "shuttle diplomacy." Flying from one Middle East capital to another for two years, he negotiated a cease-fire, pressed Israel to cede some captured territory, and persuaded the Arabs to end the oil embargo. Although Kissinger's diplomacy left the Palestinian issue festering, it successfully excluded the Soviets from a major role in Middle Eastern affairs.

Nixon-Kissinger *realpolitik* based American aid on a nation's willingness to oppose communism, not on the nature of its government. Thus, the Nixon administration liberally supplied arms and assistance to the shah of Iran, the white supremacist regime of South Africa, and President Ferdinand Marcos in the Philippines. It also furnished aid to antidemocratic regimes in Argentina, Brazil, and South Korea, as well as to Portuguese colonial authorities in Angola.

When Chileans elected a Marxist, Salvador Allende, president in 1970, the CIA secretly funded opponents of the leftist regime. The United States also cut off economic aid to Chile. In 1973, a military junta overthrew the Chilean government and killed Allende. Nixon quickly recognized the new dictatorship, and economic aid and investment again flowed to Chile.

The Election of 1972   Nixon's reelection appeared certain. He faced a deeply divided Democratic Party and counted on his diplomatic successes and the winding down of the Vietnam War to win over moderate voters. He expected his southern strategy and law-and-order posture to attract Wallace voters. Nixon's only possible worry, another third-party candidacy by Wallace, vanished on May 15, 1972, when Wallace was shot during a campaign stop. Paralyzed from the waist down, Wallace withdrew from the race, leaving Nixon a monopoly on the white backlash.

The Senate's most outspoken dove, **George McGovern** of South Dakota, capitalizing on antiwar sentiment, blitzed the Democratic primaries. He gained additional support from new party rules requiring state delegations to include minority, female, and youthful delegates in approximate proportion to their numbers. Actress Shirley MacLaine approvingly described California's delegation as "looking like a couple of high schools, a grape boycott, a Black Panther rally, and four or five politicians who walked in the wrong door." A disapproving labor leader complained about "too much hair and not enough cigars at this convention," but McGovern won the nomination on the first ballot.

Perceptions of McGovern as inept and radical drove away all but the most committed supporters. McGovern had to drop his vice-presidential running mate, Thomas Eagleton, when it became known that Eagleton had received electric-shock therapy for depression. Subsequently, McGovern suffered the embarrassment of having several prominent Democrats publicly decline to run with him. McGovern's endorsement of decriminalization of marijuana, immediate withdrawal from Vietnam, and pardons for those who had fled the United States to avoid the draft exposed him to GOP ridicule as the candidate of the radical fringe.

Remembering his narrow loss to Kennedy in 1960 and too-slim victory in 1968, Nixon left no stone unturned. To do whatever was necessary to win, he appointed his attorney general, John Mitchell, to head the Committee to Re-Elect the President (CREEP). Millions of dollars in campaign contributions financed "dirty tricks" to create dissension in Democratic ranks and paid for an espionage unit, led by Liddy and Hunt, to spy on the opposition. In 1972, it received Mitchell's approval to wire-tap telephones at the Democratic National Committee headquarters in Washington's Watergate apartment and office complex. However, a security guard foiled the break-in to install bugs in June 1972. Arrested were James McCord, the security coordinator of CREEP, and several other Liddy and Hunt associates.

Dirty tricks went from a scandal to a constitutional crisis when Nixon abused the power of his office to cover up wrongdoing and hinder criminal investigations. Asserting that "no one in the White House staff, no one in this administration, presently employed, was involved in this bizarre incident," Nixon coached associates on what they should tell investigators, authorized the payment of hush money and hints of a presidential pardon to buy the silence of those arrested, and directed the CIA to halt the FBI's investigation on the pretext that it would damage national security.

With the McGovern campaign a shambles and Watergate seemingly contained, Nixon amassed nearly 61 percent of the popular vote and an overwhelming 520 electoral votes. Supported primarily by minorities and low-income voters, McGovern carried only Massachusetts and the District of Columbia. The election solidified the 1968 realignment. Nevertheless, the GOP gained only twelve seats in the House and lost two in the Senate, demonstrating the growing difficulty of unseating incumbents, the rise in ticket-splitting, and the decline of both party loyalty and voter turnout. Only 55.7 percent of eligible voters went to the polls (down from 63.8 percent in 1960).

The Watergate Upheaval   The scheme to conceal links between the White House and the accused Watergate burglars had succeeded during the 1972 campaign. But after the election, federal judge "Maximum John" Sirica, known for his tough treatment of criminals, used the threat of heavy sentences to pressure one burglar into confessing that the White House knew in advance of the break-in and that the defendants had committed perjury during the trial. Two *Washington Post* reporters, Carl Bernstein and Bob Woodward, were investigating, following clues furnished by a secret informant named **"Deep Throat"**—identified in 2005 as FBI Deputy Director Mark Felt. Woodward and Bernstein wrote a succession of front-page stories tying the break-in to illegal contributions and "dirty tricks" by CREEP.

In February 1973, the Senate established the Special Committee on Presidential Campaign Activities to investigate, and one stunning revelation after another poured forth. The hearings revealed the existence of a White House "enemies list," the president's use of government agencies to harass opponents, and administration favoritism in return for illegal campaign donations. Both the president's special counsel and the acting head of the FBI testified to the involvement of the White House in the Watergate break-in, forcing Nixon to announce the resignation of his principal aides and the appointment of a special Watergate prosecutor with broad powers of investigation and subpoena. Then the most dramatic bombshell, the disclosure that Nixon taped every conversation in the Oval Office, meant there was an incontrovertible record of "what the president knew and when he knew it."

When the special prosecutor insisted on access to the tapes, Nixon ordered the Attorney General to fire him. The Attorney General and the number two man in the Justice Department refused and were dismissed in what became known as the "Saturday night massacre." More than 150,000 telegrams poured into the White House, and eighty-four members of Congress sponsored sixteen different bills of impeachment. The House Judiciary Committee began impeachment proceedings, and Congress went to the Supreme Court to demand access to the original tapes.

Adding to Nixon's woes, Vice President Agnew pleaded no contest—"the full equivalent to a plea of guilty," according to the trial judge—to charges of income tax evasion and solicitation of bribes, both as governor of Maryland and as vice president. Agnew left office in October 1973 with a fine and suspended sentence, and was replaced, under provisions of the Twenty-fifth Amendment, by House Minority Leader Gerald R. Ford of Michigan.

A President Disgraced   In late July 1974, the Supreme Court ruled unanimously in *United States v. Nixon* that the unedited tapes must be turned over to Congress, and the House Judiciary Committee adopted three articles of impeachment. They charged Nixon with obstruction of justice for impeding the Watergate investigation; abusing the powers of the presidency by using federal agencies to harass citizens and deprive them of their rights; and contempt of Congress for refusing to obey a congressional subpoena for the tapes. Checkmated, Nixon surrendered the subpoenaed tapes.

The tapes produced the "smoking gun" proving that Nixon had ordered the cover-up, obstructed justice by hindering the criminal investigation of the break-in, and lied about his role for more than two years. The revelations confirmed many Americans' distrust of government and cynicism about politics, hastening their disengagement from public affairs.

In trying to explain Watergate, some historians point to the increasing expansion of presidential power, "the imperial presidency," stretching back several decades. Others argue that Nixon simply got caught and that his liberal foes forced him to pay a higher price for his misdeeds than had other presidents. Most focus on Nixon himself and his obsession to destroy his hated adversaries. Whatever the cause of America's most dramatic political scandal, Richard Nixon, certain the Senate would vote to convict him once impeached, became the first president to resign—and Gerald Ford took office as the nation's first chief executive who had not been elected either president or vice president.

A Troubled Nation and Presidency

In the aftermath of the Vietnam debacle and Richard Nixon's disgrace, Presidents **Gerald Ford** and **Jimmy Carter** grappled with inflation, recession, and industrial stagnation as well as humiliations abroad and, for Carter, a maddening hostage crisis. The confident 1950s and early 1960s, when prosperous America had savored its role as the Free World's leader, ready to "pay any price, bear any burden, meet any hardship," now seemed remote, even foolhardy. A nation convinced that it was immune to the historical forces that constrained other societies now confronted sobering new realities—particularly significant foreign competition and an energy crisis—beyond its control.

Panic at the Pump
In 1973–1974, Americans sat in their cars and waited in long lines to buy gasoline at skyrocketing prices. Angry and frustrated, motorists fought each other and battled with police. At one service station with no gas to sell, a driver threatened the attendant, "You are going to give me gas or I will kill you." The nation had long taken cheap, abundant energy for granted, yet remained heavily dependent on the third of its oil it imported. This vulnerability became apparent when Arab nations, angered by Nixon's support of Israel during the 1973 war, cut off the supply of oil to the West. Then the seven Arab members of OPEC, quadrupled the cost of a barrel of oil from $3 to $12 in 1976. OPEC would almost triple it again, to $34 in 1979, pushing the price of a gallon of gas over $1 for the first time, a price barrier many had thought unreachable. Overall, consumer prices would more than double in the 1970s, with inflation soaring to 14 percent. It battered American families and turned hard-pressed taxpayers against the welfare programs adopted during past Democratic administrations.

Disturbing economic developments forced millions of Americans in the 1970s to, according to a magazine, "Learn to Live with Less," less energy and jobs, less possibilities and power. Unemployment ranged between 6 and 10 percent, nearly twice the usual postwar level, and the federal deficit soared from $8.7 billion in 1970 to $72.7 billion in 1980. Federal borrowing to cover the deficit increased the costs of all businesses that had to borrow, which worsened the rising price spiral and the galloping inflation rate that had resulted from President Johnson's attempt to fund both the Vietnam War and the Great Society without raising taxes. Moreover, in 1971 the dollar, long the strongest currency in the world, fell to its lowest

The Energy Crisis *The Arab embargo on oil shipments to the United States, begun in 1973, revealed America's dependence on Middle Eastern oil reserves and the end of its unchallenged economic dominance in the world. In the wake of energy shortages and dramatic increases in heating oil and gas prices, both unemployment and inflation increased dramatically, underlining the extent to which Americans no longer could shape their economic future alone.*

(AP Images)

level since 1949, and the U.S. posted its first trade deficit—importing more than it exported—in almost a century.

Most acutely, higher costs and greater foreign competition ravaged the manufacturing regions of the Midwest and Northeast, soon to be called the "Rust Belt." The automobile industry was especially hard hit by soaring gasoline prices that boosted sales of more fuel-efficient foreign imports, mainly from Japan. U.S. purchases of foreign cars grew from 2 million in 1970 to 4 million in 1989. Chrysler, the third largest automaker, was saved from bankruptcy only by a $1.2 billion federal loan guarantee. Facing severe production cutbacks, the Big Three carmakers eliminated the jobs of one in three autoworkers between 1978 and 1982.

Several factors contributed to industrial decline in the United States: aging machinery, inefficient production methods, complacent management, and fierce competition from foreign companies paying lower wages, especially in the countries of the Pacific Rim. American-based manufacturers moved their high-wage jobs overseas. In one five-year period, 1979–1983, 11.5 million U.S. workers lost jobs because of plant closings and cutbacks. Although new employment opportunities opened in the so-called "knowledge-based" industries (and would lead to an uneven economic revival later in the century), many industrial workers lacked the skills to fill these jobs. They joined a growing pool of the unemployed and underemployed in communities dependent on manufacturing.

With the loss of industrial jobs, the union movement weakened. In 1960, 31 percent of U.S. workers belonged to unions; thirty years later, that figure had been virtually halved to 16 percent, with further declines ahead. Some workers did join unions in these years, mainly teachers, public employees, and service workers, many of whom were female. Service-sector unionization, however, only slowed, but did not reverse, the overall decline of union membership. A union official lamented "a nation of hamburger stands ... a country stripped of industrial capacity and meaningful work ... a service economy."

Gerald Ford, Caretaker

Former Michigan congressman Gerald Ford became vice president after Agnew resigned in disgrace, and then president after Nixon resigned to avoid impeachment. Conveying a likable decency and acknowledging he was "a Ford not a Lincoln," he urged Americans to move beyond the "long national nightmare" of Watergate rather than look backward in recrimination. But the honeymoon quickly ended as many Americans reacted with outrage when Ford pardoned Nixon for "any and all crimes" committed while in office, meaning that Nixon would neither have to assume responsibility nor face prosecution for his actions.

Economic problems, particularly inflation, dogged Ford's presidency. To curtail the worsening inflationary spiral, in October 1974, Ford unveiled a program of voluntary price restraint dubbed "Whip Inflation Now" (WIN), but prices continued upward. When the Federal Reserve Board tried to cool the economy by raising interest rates, a severe recession resulted. Unemployment approached 11 percent by 1975, more than twice the postwar average. Then Ford tried tax cuts to stimulate business activity. They made inflation worse and did little to promote employment. As oil and gas prices soared, Americans for the first time since World War II struggled to curb energy consumption. Congress set fuel-efficiency standards for automobiles in 1975 and imposed a national speed limit of fifty-five miles per hour.

National morale sank further in late April 1975 when the South Vietnamese government fell, and television chronicled desperate helicopter evacuations from the U.S. embassy in Saigon (soon renamed Ho Chi Minh City). A few weeks later, Cambodia seized a U.S. merchant ship, the *Mayagüez*. Ford ordered a military rescue, which freed the thirty-nine *Mayagüez* crew members but cost the lives of forty-one U.S. servicemen. As the nation entered the election year 1976—also the bicentennial of the Declaration of Independence—Americans found little reason for optimism.

Jimmy Carter, Outsider

Gerald Ford won the 1976 Republican nomination, turning back a strong challenge from former California governor Ronald Reagan, who opposed détente. Jimmy Carter, a Georgia peanut grower and former governor, effectively used the media to bypass party machines and sweep the Democratic primaries by stressing his honesty, his status as a Washington outsider, and his evangelical Christian faith.

With his running mate, Minnesota senator Walter Mondale, Carter won a narrow victory, 50 to 48 percent in the popular vote and 297 to 240 in the Electoral College. He garnered the votes of the less well-off, African-Americans, southerners, and those disgusted by Watergate. Underscoring his rejection of Nixon's "imperial presidency," Carter walked with his wife Rosalyn in the inaugural parade from the Capitol to the White House; enrolled his daughter, Amy, in a largely black, Washington, D.C. public school; and held a two-hour "call-in," answering questions phoned in by people from every part of the country. In an echo of Roosevelt's fireside radio chats, he delivered some TV speeches wearing a sweater and seated by a fireplace.

Despite the populist symbolism and gestures of inclusiveness, Carter never shaped a clearly liberal agenda. Reflecting his training as an engineer, he proved better at analyzing details than at defining broad goals. Lacking both the Washington experience and the inclination to deal with the capitol's key political players, he distanced himself from reformist Democrats and could not break legislative gridlock. At heart a fiscal conservative, he favored cutting federal spending. "Government cannot solve our problems," he asserted in his second State of the Union address. "It cannot eliminate poverty, or provide a bountiful economy, or reduce inflation, or save our cities, or cure illiteracy, or provide energy." Accordingly, Carter left unresolved the major economic and social problems of the 1970s, especially, **"stagflation"**—the anomaly of economic stagnation combined with price inflation—which topped 20 percent in 1979.

Carter further disappointed liberals by beginning deregulation—the removal of government controls on the airline, railroad, and trucking industries, as well as on oil and natural gas prices—and by failing to adopt an effective energy policy. Angered by rising gasoline prices and increasing dependence on foreign oil—over 40 percent by 1980—Americans demanded energy self-sufficiency (see Going to the Source). Carter proposed a program that barely reduced oil consumption, grandiosely calling it the "moral equivalent of war"; most Americans sneered at it as MEOW. His failures contributed immensely to the destruction of what remained of the liberal coalition and enormously boosted the fortunes of political conservatism.

In Niagara Falls, New York, where for years the Hooker Chemical and Plastics Corporation had dumped tons of waste in a district known as Love Canal, Carter confronted a major environmental crisis. In 1953, Hooker had covered the landfill with earth and sold it to the city. Homes and schools sprang up, but residents complained of odors and strange substances oozing from the soil. In the late 1970s, tests confirmed that toxic chemicals, including deadly dioxin, were seeping into buildings, polluting the air, and discharging into the Niagara River. Medical researchers found elevated levels of cancer, miscarriages, and birth defects among Love Canal residents.

In 1978, President Carter authorized federal funds to relocate Love Canal families, and in 1980 he declared the situation a national emergency, freeing more federal money for relocation and clean-up. As his presidency ended, Carter signed legislation creating a federal "Superfund" to clean up the nation's most polluted sites. In addition, the **Alaska Lands Act** set aside more than 100 million acres of public land for parks, wildlife refuges, and national forests and added twenty-six rivers to the nation's Wild and Scenic River System. These two bills proved to be Carter's rare successes. As a consequence of his own ineptness and the sharp conservative turn in the political climate, Carter, groused one legislator, "couldn't get the Pledge of Allegiance through Congress."

Carter's foreign-policy record proved only somewhat better. As a candidate, he had urged more emphasis on protecting human rights worldwide, in contrast to Henry Kissinger's dominant focus on U.S. national interests. His secretary of state, Cyrus Vance, worked to combat human rights abuses by some, but not all, American allies who committed them, and Carter did raise public awareness of human rights issues.

The president particularly sought resolution of the lingering dispute over control of the Panama Canal. Since 1964, when anti-American riots had rocked Panama, U.S. diplomats had been working on a new canal treaty that would address Panama's grievances. The Carter administration completed negotiations on treaties transferring full control over the canal to Panama by 2000. The Senate ratified the treaties over the objections of conservatives; Ronald Reagan had earlier said of the canal, "we bought it, we paid for it, it's ours and we're going to keep it."

Toward the Soviet Union, Carter first showed conciliation, but toughness ultimately won out. In 1979, Carter and the Soviet leader Leonid Brezhnev signed a new Strategic Arms Limitation Treaty (SALT II), limiting each side's nuclear arsenals. Senate ratification stalled, however, when Cold Warriors who had never accepted détente attacked the treaty for allegedly favoring the Soviets. Support dissolved entirely in late December 1979 when the Soviets invaded Afghanistan. Many Americans saw the invasion as proof of Moscow's expansionist designs. Carter revived registration for the military draft, boycotted the 1980 Summer Olympics in Moscow, and embargoed grain shipments to Russia.

The Middle East and Iran   Carter's best and worst moments came in the Middle East. Following Egyptian leader Anwar el-Sadat's unexpected trip to Israel in 1977 to negotiate with Israeli prime minister Menachem Begin, Carter hosted both leaders for two weeks at Camp David, the presidential retreat in Maryland. The resulting **Camp David Accords,** and the formal peace treaty that followed, led to Israel's withdrawal from the Sinai Peninsula, captured in the 1967 war; for its part, Egypt recognized Israel as a nation, the first Arab country to do so.

Carter's efforts for a broader Middle Eastern peace failed, however. The other Arab states rejected the Camp David Accords, Israel continued to build Jewish settlements in territories it occupied, and Islamic fundamentalists assassinated Sadat in 1981. Peace remained as elusive as ever.

Still less successful was Carter's policy toward Iran. For years, Iran had been ruled by Shah Mohammed Reza Pahlavi, who had come to power in 1953 with CIA help (see Chapter 26). Washington viewed the shah's repressive, pro-U.S. regime as a bulwark against Soviet expansion and a source of abundant oil reserves. Iran's Shiite Muslims, however, inspired by their exiled spiritual head,

Carter and Stockman on Energy

In his first presidential speech on energy, Jimmy Carter sought to win the support of the American people for conservation and for governmental solutions. In response, Congressman David Stockman (R-Mich.) argued against federal intervention and for allowing unfettered global markets to provide abundant energy.

Carter on energy: Our national energy plan is based on 10 fundamental principles. The first principle is that we can have an effective and comprehensive energy policy only if the Government takes responsibility for it and if the people understand the seriousness of the challenge and are willing to make sacrifices....

The third principle is that we must reduce our vulnerability to potentially devastating embargoes. We can protect ourselves from uncertain supplies by reducing our demand for oil, by making the most of our abundant resources such as coal, and by developing a strategic petroleum reserve....

The fifth principle is that we must be fair. Our solutions must ask equal sacrifices from every region, every class of people, and every interest group. Industry will

have to do its part to conserve just as consumers will. The energy producers deserve fair treatment, but we will not let the oil companies profiteer.

The sixth principle, and the cornerstone of our policy, is to reduce demand through conservation.... Conservation is the quickest, cheapest, most practical source of energy. Conservation is the only way we can buy a barrel of oil for about $2. It costs about $13 to waste it.

The seventh principle is that prices should generally reflect the true replacement cost of energy. We are only cheating ourselves if we make energy artificially cheap and use more than we can really afford.... .

The ninth principle is that we must conserve the fuels that are scarcest and make the most of those that are plentiful. We can't continue to use oil and gas for 75 percent of our consumption, as we do now, when they only make up 7 percent of our domestic reserves. We need to shift to plentiful coal, while taking care to protect the environment, and to apply stricter safety standards to nuclear energy.

The tenth and last principle is that we must start now to develop the new,

Ayatollah Ruhollah Khomeini, overthrew the shah's government early in 1979. The shah fled Iran and Khomeini returned in triumph, imposing strict Islamic rule.

On November 4, 1979, after Carter admitted the shah to the United States for cancer treatment, Khomeini supporters stormed the U.S. embassy in Tehran and seized 66 American hostages, demanding the return of the shah in exchange for the captured Americans. Thus began a 444-day ordeal that virtually paralyzed the Carter administration. Night after night, TV images of blindfolded hostages, anti-American mobs, and U.S. flags being burned rubbed American nerves raw. A botched rescue attempt in April 1980, in which several U.S. helicopters malfunctioned and eight GIs died, added to the nation's humiliation, and to the public's view of Carter as an ineffective bumbler. Not until January 20, 1981, the day Ronald Reagan took office as the new president, did the Iranian authorities release the hostages.

unconventional sources of energy that we will rely on in the next century.

Stockman's response: At bottom, the notion that "home grown energy is better" implies a radical rejection of the global trading system and the law of comparative advantage [that some nations can more efficiently produce certain commodities, such as oil] on which it is premised.... The result would be substantial, unnecessary loss in national output, and an artificially high domestic-energy-cost structure which would reduce the competitiveness of our exports and increase the cost-advantage of imports....

Overall, the planet's accessible natural hydrocarbon reserves readily exceed 20 trillion barrels. This is the equivalent of five centuries of consumption at current rates.... The case for fossil-fuel exhaustion simply cannot rest on physical scarcity or the stinginess of the planet.

... It is time to discard our medieval energy maps. There is no region filled with lurking dragons and other perils on the far side of the ocean. So rather than institute a politically imposed and bureaucratically managed and enforced regime of domestic-energy autarky [a policy based on authoritarian power], we need do little more than decontrol domestic energy prices, dismantle the energy bureaucracy, and allow the U.S. economy to equilibrate at the world level. Energy supply and demand will take care of itself... and by thus encouraging full integration of the U.S. economy into the world marketplace's search for the least-cost-development sequence of our planet's prodigious remaining energy resources, we will produce the highest possible level of domestic economic growth and welfare.

Questions

1. How do the two men differ on the causes and solution of the energy crisis?

2. Explain how the goals of Carter's energy proposals might conflict with his economic and environmental goals?

Go to www.cengagebrain.com for additional primary sources on this period.

Source: *Jimmy Carter, "The Energy Problem," April 18, 1977, Public Papers of the Presidents of the United States: Jimmy Carter, 1977–1981; and David Stockman, "The Wrong War? The Case Against a National Energy Policy,"* Public Interest, 53 (Fall 1978).

As with Herbert Hoover in the early 1930s, Americans turned against the remote figure in the White House. When Carter's approval rating sagged to 26 percent in mid-1979 (lower than Nixon's when he resigned as a result of Watergate), he retreated to Camp David and emerged to deliver a TV address that blamed the American people's "crisis of confidence" for leading them to doubt the meaning of their own lives, the future, and the nation's purpose and abilities. He also castigated them for worshipping "self-indulgence and consumption," so that a person "is no longer defined by what one does, but by what one owns." But when a cabinet reshuffle was all that followed, most Americans thought the helpless Carter was the problem. The 1980 Democratic convention glumly renominated Carter, but defeat in November loomed. A successful post-presidential career of public service would do much to restore Carter's reputation and bring him the Nobel Peace Prize in 2002. But in 1980, most Americans hungered for a new president and changed policies.

CHRONOLOGY
1964–1974

1964   Berkeley Free Speech Movement (FSM).
The Beatles arrive in the United States.

1965   Ken Kesey and Merry Pranksters stage first "acid test."

1966   Abolition of automatic student deferments from the draft.

1967   March on the Pentagon.
Israeli-Arab Six-Day War.

1968   Tet offensive.
Martin Luther King, Jr., assassinated; race riots sweep nation.
Students take over buildings at Columbia University.
Robert F. Kennedy assassinated.
Violence mars Democratic convention in Chicago.
Vietnam peace talks open in Paris. Richard Nixon elected president.

1969   Apollo 11 lands first Americans on the moon.
Nixon begins withdrawal of U.S. troops from Vietnam.
Woodstock festival.

1970   United States invades Cambodia.
Students killed at Kent State and Jackson State Universities.
Beatles disband.
Earth Day first celebrated.

1971   *Swann v. Charlotte-Mecklenburg Board of Education.*
New York Times publishes Pentagon Papers.
Nixon institutes wage-and-price freeze.
South Vietnam invades Laos with the help of U.S. air support.

1972   Nixon visits China and the Soviet Union.
SALT I agreement approved.
Break-in at Democratic National Committee headquarters in
Watergate complex.
Nixon reelected president.

1973   Vietnam cease-fire agreement signed.
Senate establishes special committee to investigate Watergate.
President Salvador Allende ousted and murdered in Chile.
Vice President Spiro Agnew resigns; Gerald Ford appointed
vice president.
Roe v. Wade.
Yom Kippur War; OPEC begins embargo of oil to the West.
Saturday Night Massacre.

1974   House Judiciary Committee votes to impeach Nixon.
Nixon resigns; Ford becomes president.

CONCLUSION

Baby boomers took material comfort and their own importance for granted. Longing for meaning in their lives, as well as personal liberty, they sought a more humane democracy, a less racist and consumerist society, and an end to the war in Vietnam. Failing to get what they wanted quickly, the New Left became increasingly radical and violent. Most of the young, however, were more interested in "sex, drugs, and rock-and-roll." Ultimately, the student movement and counterculture helped prod the United States into becoming a more tolerant, diverse, and permissive society. They helped pave the way for the environmental movement and spurred an end to America's longest war—which had cost the nation dearly in lives and dollars, in turning Americans against one another and in diverting society from pressing needs.

The youth rebellion, racial rioting, and the Tet offensive in Vietnam brought politics to a boil in 1968. The year of assassinations and turmoil cost Democrats the White House and triggered a conservative resurgence and major political realignment. Pursuing the national interest by *realpolitik*, President Richard Nixon and Henry Kissinger undertook secret negotiations with North Vietnam to end hostilities. At the same time, they opened the way for reduced tensions with China and the Soviet Union, enhancing the world outlook for peace, while also giving economic and military assistance to anticommunist dictatorships.

Equally vital to his political success, Nixon wooed whites upset by civil strife and by hippies and radicals. He emphasized law and order to attract the silent majority concerned with the upsurge of criminality and breakdown of traditional values, and he played upon middle-class resentment of rising taxes to pay for the federal largess going to minorities and the poor. Following a "southern strategy," he nominated conservatives for the Supreme Court, opposed extension of the Voting Rights Act and school busing for racial integration, and cracked down on militant blacks and young radicals.

In 1972, the secret schemes Nixon had put in place to spy upon and destroy those who opposed his Vietnam policies began to unravel. His obsession for secrecy and his paranoia about opponents brought his downfall. The arrest of the Watergate burglars and the subsequent attempted cover-up of White House involvement led to revelations of a host of "dirty tricks" and criminal acts, the indictment of nearly fifty Nixon administration officials and the jailing of a score of his associates, and a House Judiciary Committee vote to impeach the president. To avoid certain conviction, a disgraced Nixon resigned on August 9, 1974. Neither his successor, Gerald Ford, nor Jimmy Carter restored confidence in the White House. The national government seemed helpless as the plague of inflation, energy crisis, recession, and deindustrialization swept the land. The deepening public disenchantment with politicians and disillusionment with government, which had led Dorothy Burlage and millions of others to turn inward, would last throughout the 1970s and into the next century.

30

A CONSERVATIVE REVIVAL AND THE
END OF THE COLD WAR, 1980–2000

> **CHAPTER OUTLINE**
>
> • A Conservative Shift in American Culture and Politics • Domestic Drift and
> a New World Order • Domestic and Global Issues at Century's End
> • Moderation, White House Scandal, and a Disputed Election, 1996–2000
> • Economic and Cultural Trends at Century's End

A CONSERVATIVE SHIFT IN AMERICAN CULTURE AND POLITICS

Ronald Reagan won the presidency in 1980 riding the conservative tide that had been building for years. Domestically, Reagan and his congressional allies enacted tax cuts and deregulatory measures reflecting their free-market, small-government ideology. The Reagan era began with a recession and ended with a stock-market crash. In between, though, inflation eased and the overall economy improved. Reagan's economic policies produced mounting federal deficits, however, while economic inequities, inner-city problems, and stubborn unemployment persisted.

An avid Cold Warrior, Reagan boosted military spending and adopted a tough stance toward Russia. Like presidents before and since, he also faced crises in the Middle East. The administration's secretive efforts to overthrow a leftist regime in Latin America triggered a constitutional crisis in Reagan's second term. But a dramatic easing of Cold War tensions, symbolized by Reagan's meeting in Moscow with Soviet leader Mikhail Gorbachev, ended his presidency on a high note.

Conservative Cultural Trends in the 1970s The 1960s was a polarizing decade. While the counterculture and antiwar protests drew media attention, many Americans deplored what they viewed as the decade's radical excesses. As we saw in Chapter 29, Richard Nixon exploited this disaffection to win the White House in 1968.

938

Even earlier, William F. Buckley had launched the conservative *National Review* magazine (1955); founded Young Americans for Freedom (1960); and started a conservative TV talk show, *Firing Line,* in 1966. Barry Goldwater's 1964 presidential campaign, though unsuccessful, gave evidence of conservatism's latent strength.

In local communities, especially in the fast-growing South and West (see Chapter 27, Map 27.1), conservatives came together and mobilized politically. Think tanks like the Heritage Foundation, founded by the Colorado beer baron Joseph Coors in 1973, helped conservatives solidify their ideology.

Southern California's Orange County, recently transformed from ranches and citrus groves to suburban developments, vividly illustrates this process. Orange County conservatives—mostly upwardly mobile white evangelical Protestants—were intensely anticommunist, dismayed by 1960s' radicals, and suspicious of the "liberal elites" dominating the media and national politics. Recognizing their common agenda, these conservatives organized locally into a potent political force. Foreshadowing changes ahead nationally, Orange County helped elect Ronald Reagan governor of California in 1966 and in 1978 rallied behind Proposition 13, a state referendum mandating deep cuts in property taxes.

Conservatives mobilized around specific issues, especially abortion. As noted in Chapter 29, in the wake of *Roe v. Wade,* "right to life" activists pressed for a constitutional amendment outlawing abortion. Led by Roman Catholic and conservative Protestant activists, "pro-life" advocates rallied, signed petitions, and picketed abortion clinics and pregnancy-counseling centers.

Responding to the pressure, Congress in 1976 ended Medicaid funding for most abortions, effectively denying this procedure to the poor. Handing conservatives another victory, President Nixon in 1972 had vetoed a bill setting up a national network of day-care centers, criticizing its "communal approach to child-rearing." The Equal Rights Amendment, denounced by Phyllis Schlafly and other conservatives, died in 1982—three states short of ratification.

To conservatives, gay and lesbian activism foretold society's moral collapse. "God ... destroyed the cities of Sodom and Gomorrah because of this terrible sin," thundered TV evangelist Jerry Falwell. In 1977, singer Anita Bryant led a successful campaign against a Miami ordinance protecting homosexuals' civil rights. "God created Adam and Eve, not Adam and Bruce," she pointed out. Soon after, *Good Housekeeping* magazine readers voted Bryant "the most admired woman in America." Other cities, too, reversed earlier measures protecting gay rights.

In 1978, as the backlash intensified, a member of the San Francisco board of supervisors fatally shot gay activist and board-member Harvey Milk and Milk's political ally, Mayor George Moscone. When the killer received a light sentence, riots erupted in the city. (Thirty years later, actor Sean Penn won an Academy Award for his starring role in a film celebrating Milk's career as a gay activist.)

The conservative movement also gained strength from the rapid growth of evangelical Protestantism, with its emphasis on strict morality, biblical authority, and a "born again" conversion experience. Evangelical denominations such as the Assemblies of God and the Southern Baptist Convention grew explosively in the 1970s and 1980s, as did independent suburban megachurches. Meanwhile, liberal denominations whose ministers had rallied behind the civil-rights and antiwar movements lost members.

Evangelicals had supported antislavery and other social reform before the Civil War. Their modern-day successors also preached reform, but of a conservative variety. Jerry Farwell's Moral Majority, founded in 1979 as a "pro-life, pro-family, pro-moral, and pro-America" crusade, supported conservative candidates. So did Pat Robertson, founder of the Christian Broadcasting Network. Tim LaHaye of San Diego, another leading evangelical preacher, was also active in mobilizing grass-roots support for conservative causes. In 1981, LaHaye founded the Council for National Policy, a secretive political lobby.

While battling abortion, homosexuality, and pornography, often in alliance with conservative Catholics, evangelicals also attacked the Supreme Court's 1962 *Engel v. Vitale* decision banning organized prayer in public schools as a violation of the First Amendment. Evangelicals also advocated home schooling and private Christian schools to shield children from what they saw as the public schools' permissiveness and secularist (nonreligious) values.

Christian bookstores, radio stations, and TV evangelists fueled the revival. Falwell's *Old Time Gospel Hour*, Robertson's *700 Club*, Jim and Tammy Bakker's *PTL* (Praise the Lord) program, and Jimmy Swaggart's telecasts from Louisiana attracted a loyal following. The so-called electronic church suffered after 1987 amid sexual and financial scandals, but the evangelical resurgence continued. In a world of change, evangelicals found certitude and a sense of community in their shared faith. In the process, they profoundly influenced late-twentieth-century American life.

Not all evangelicals were political conservatives. Most African-American evangelicals retained their Democratic Party loyalties. In general, however, resurgent evangelicalism strengthened the larger conservative movement of the 1970s. Ronald Reagan rode this powerful conservative tide to the White House.

Conservatism Triumphant: The 1980 Election

Reagan grew up in Dixon, Illinois, the son of an alcoholic father and a devout mother. In 1937, after a stint as a radio sports announcer, he went to Hollywood for a screen test. His fifty-four films proved forgettable, but he gained political experience as president of the Screen Actors' Guild. A New Dealer in the 1930s, Reagan moved rightward in the 1950s, and in 1954 became the General Electric Company's corporate spokesperson. In a 1964 TV speech for Barry Goldwater, he lauded American individualism and the free-enterprise system. As governor of California (1967–1975), he espoused conservative ideas and denounced campus demonstrators, but also proved open to compromise.

In the 1980 Republican primaries, Reagan bested his principal opponent, George H. W. Bush (father of the later President George W. Bush), whom he then chose as his running mate. Belying his sixty-nine years, he campaigned vigorously against President Jimmy Carter, seeking a second term. In the election, Reagan garnered 51 percent of the vote to 41 percent for the Carter-Mondale ticket (An independent candidate, liberal Republican John Anderson, collected most of the balance.)

Republicans gained eleven Senate seats, winning a majority for the first time since 1955, and trimmed thirty-five seats from the Democrats' majority in the House of Representatives. The Republican successes revealed the power of conservative political action committees (PACs) whose computerized mass mailings focused on emotional issues like abortion and gun control.

Benefiting from the erosion of Democratic strength in the South fostered by George Wallace and Richard Nixon, Reagan carried every southern state except Carter's own Georgia. He also swept every state west of the Mississippi except Minnesota and Hawaii. Over half of white blue-collar workers, once solidly Democratic, voted Republican. Of FDR's New Deal coalition, only black voters remained solidly Democratic.

Jerry Falwell's pro-Reagan Moral Majority registered an estimated 2 million new voters in 1980 and 1984. The organization disbanded after 1984, but Pat Robertson's Christian Coalition took its place, mobilizing evangelicals to elect candidates to town councils and school boards as a stepping stone to expanded national influence.

Reagan embraced the conservative movement's cultural agenda, evoking a somewhat mythic era when American life had seemed simpler and traditional values had prevailed. But other factors also underlay Reagan's appeal. Voters frightened by stagflation welcomed his promise that tax cuts would stimulate the economy. Reagan's anti-government rhetoric and dismissal of social-welfare programs like Lyndon Johnson's War on Poverty resonated with white middle-class and blue-collar Americans. Like his one-time political hero Franklin Roosevelt, Reagan promised a new deal. But unlike FDR's, Reagan's new deal meant individualism, smaller government, lower taxes, and untrammeled free enterprise.

Reagan, a seasoned actor and public speaker, wrapped these themes into an appealing message of moral affirmation and support for "traditional values." At a time of national malaise, he seemed confident and assured. His unabashed patriotism, calls for military strength, and praise of America's greatness soothed the battered psyche of a nation traumatized by Vietnam, Watergate, and the frustrations of the Ford and Carter years. Some found Reagan's core ideology negative and mean-spirited. But in 1980, a majority of voters embraced his hopeful message.

Population changes contributed to Reagan's success. While New York City, Chicago, Detroit, and other Democratic strongholds in the Northeast and Midwest lost population in the 1970s, Texas, California, Florida, and other more conservative Sunbelt states grew.

Enacting the Conservative Domestic Agenda Reagan's economic plan, dubbed "Reaganomics" by the media, boiled down to the belief that the free-enterprise system, if freed from heavy taxes and regulations, would achieve wonders of productivity. Reagan proposed a 30 percent cut in federal income taxes over three years. Trimming this proposal slightly, Congress voted a 25 percent cut: 5 percent in 1981, 10 percent in 1982 and 1983.

To partially counterbalance the lost revenues, Congress slashed more than $40 billion from domestic spending. Not since FDR's Hundred Days of 1933 had government shifted gears so dramatically. Economists warned that the tax cut would produce huge federal deficits, but Reagan insisted that lower tax rates would stimulate business growth, pushing up tax revenues. In the Republican primaries, George

Bush had ridiculed Reagan's rosy predictions as "voodoo economics," but as vice president he tactfully remained silent.

Business deregulation had begun under Carter, but Reagan extended it into new areas such as banking, the savings-and-loan industry, and communications. The secretary of transportation cut regulations aimed at improving air quality and fuel economy.

Interior Secretary James Watt of Wyoming opened federal wilderness areas, forest lands, and coastal waters to oil, gas, and timber companies and cut back on environmental and endangered species protections. Watt earlier spearheaded the so-called Sagebrush Rebellion, a campaign by ranchers, farmers, and mineowners to shift federal lands in the West to state and county control. The Sierra Club and other environmental organizations protested Watt's policies and circulated petitions demanding his ouster. After various public-relations gaffes, Watt resigned in 1983.

Reagan had little sympathy for organized labor. In 1981, when the Professional Air Traffic Controllers Organization (PATCO) went on strike, Reagan invoked the 1948 Taft-Hartley law against strikes by federal employees and ordered them back to work. When more than eleven thousand PATCO members defied the order, Reagan fired them and barred them permanently from federal employment. Reagan acted within the law, but other federal workers had struck in the past without such dire retribution.

To combat continuing inflation (see Chapter 29), the Federal Reserve Board pushed up interest rates. This harsh medicine, coupled with falling oil prices, pushed the inflation rate down from double digits to around 4 percent by 1983. But high interest rates also brought on a recession. By late 1982, unemployment stood at 10 percent. Reagan's cuts in social programs worsened the plight of the poor, including inner-city blacks and Hispanics. The Fed's policy also hurt U.S. exports. As foreign investors bought Treasury bonds to earn high U.S. interest rates, the dollar rose in value, making U.S. export goods more expensive. With exports declining and U.S. consumers buying cars, TVs, and stereo systems made in Japan and elsewhere, the trade deficit soared to $111 billion in 1984.

Facing a recession and rising federal budget deficits, Reagan in 1982–1983 slowed military spending, approved emergency job programs, restored some spending on social programs, and authorized tax increases disguised as "revenue-enhancement measures." Nevertheless, the recession hurt Reagan's popularity, and in the 1982 midterm elections, the Democrats regained twenty-six House seats.

By 1983, an economic rebound was underway. Encouraged by tax cuts and lower inflation, consumer spending increased and the stock market surged. Money managers like Ivan Boesky, an apparent genius at stock transactions, became celebrities. E. F. Hutton and other brokerage firms lured new investors. Corporate mergers proliferated. Savings-and-loan (S&L) companies, newly deregulated and flush with deposits from eager investors, ladled out billions to developers planning shopping malls, condominiums, and retirement villages.

The Wall Street frenzy had an unsavory underside. In 1985, E. F. Hutton officials pled guilty to illegal fund manipulation. Ivan Boesky went to prison after a 1986 conviction for insider trading (profiting through advance knowledge of corporate actions). The high-flying S&L industry would collapse in 1988 (as detailed later in this chapter). The 1987 film *Wall Street* captured the spirit of the decade.

As protagonist Gordon Gekko, a hard-driving speculator played by Michael Douglas, puts it: "Greed, for lack of a better word, is good. Greed is right, greed works. Greed ... captures the essence of the evolutionary spirit."

On October 19, 1987, the stock market crashed, reducing the paper value of the nation's stocks by 20 percent overnight. The market soon recovered, but the collapse had a sobering effect on giddy investors.

Even during the boom, systemic economic problems persisted. Federal budget deficits—the predictable consequence of Reagan's tax cuts and military spending—surpassed $200 billion in 1985 and 1986. Budget deficits, the trade deficit, and a savings-and-loan crisis related to deregulation must rank among Reagan's economic legacies. Further, many Americans missed out on the boom times.

Reagan also shaped the Supreme Court. His 1981 selection of Sandra Day O'Connor as the first woman Supreme Court justice won praise. He nudged the high court in a conservative direction in 1986 by elevating William Rehnquist, a Nixon appointee, to the chief justiceship upon the retirement of Warren Burger, and nominating Antonin Scalia to replace him. Scalia would prove one of the Court's most outspokenly conservative members and a champion of the view that the "original intent" of the Constitution's eighteenth-century framers ruled out any later judicial interpretations responding to changing social realities.

When another vacancy opened in 1987, Reagan nominated Robert Bork, a judge and legal scholar whose abrasive personality and inflexible views led the Senate to reject him. Reagan's next nominee withdrew after he admitted smoking marijuana as an adult. Reagan's third choice, Anthony Kennedy, a conservative California jurist, won quick confirmation.

The Cold War Heats Up   The late 1970s' deterioration in U.S.-Soviet relations worsened during Reagan's first term. Addressing a convention of evangelicals, the president demonized the Soviet Union as an "evil empire." Anti-Soviet fury exploded in September 1983 when the Russians shot down a Korean passenger plane that strayed into their airspace, killing all 269 aboard.

Insisting that post–Vietnam America had grown dangerously weak, Reagan launched a major military expansion. The Pentagon's budget nearly doubled, reaching more than $300 billion by 1985. The buildup included nuclear weapons. Secretary of State Alexander Haig spoke of using "nuclear warning shots" in a conventional war; other officials mused about the "winnability" of nuclear war. Despite protests across Europe, the administration deployed 572 nuclear missiles in Western Europe in 1983, fulfilling a NATO decision to match Soviet missiles in Eastern Europe. The Federal Emergency Management Agency issued a nuclear-war defense plan whereby city-dwellers would flee to nearby small towns. A Defense Department official proposed backyard shelters as adequate protection in a nuclear war. "With enough shovels," he asserted, "everybody's going to make it."

Such talk, coupled with the military buildup and Reagan's anti-Soviet rhetoric, sparked a grass-roots campaign for a multinational freeze on the manufacture and deployment of nuclear weapons. Antinuclear protesters packed New York's Central

Park in June 1982. That November, voters in nine states, including California and Wisconsin, approved nuclear-freeze referenda.

To counter the freeze campaign, Reagan in March 1983 proposed the **Strategic Defense Initiative** (SDI), a computerized antimissile system involving space based lasers and other high-tech components. Critics quickly dubbed the scheme "Star Wars." Experts warned of monumental technical hurdles and the danger of further escalating the nuclear-arms race. Nevertheless, Reagan prevailed, and Congress authorized a costly SDI research program.

Fearing communist gains in Latin America, the administration backed El Salvador's ruling military junta in its brutal suppression of a leftist insurgency supported by Fidel Castro's Cuba (see Map 30.1). In Nicaragua, Reagan vigorously opposed the Sandinista insurgents who overthrew dictator Anastasio Somoza in 1979. The Sandinistas, Reagan claimed, were turning Nicaragua into a communist state like Cuba. In 1982, the CIA organized and financed an anti-Sandinista guerrilla army, called the contras, based in neighboring Honduras and Costa Rica. The contras, with links to the hated Somoza regime, conducted raids, planted mines, and carried out sabotage inside Nicaragua that killed many civilians.

Fearing another Vietnam, Congress late in 1982 voted a yearlong halt in U.S. military aid to the contras, and in 1984 imposed a two-year ban. Ignoring these prohibitions, the White House secretly continued to funnel money contributed by

(© Bill Gentile/Corbis)

Anti-Sandinista Contras on Patrol in Nicaragua, 1987 *Under Reagan, the CIA recruited, financed, and equipped an army to overthrow Nicaragua's leftist Sandinista regime. This support continued clandestinely despite congressional prohibitions, leading to the so-called Iran-contra scandal.*

(Wadsworth/Cengage Learning)

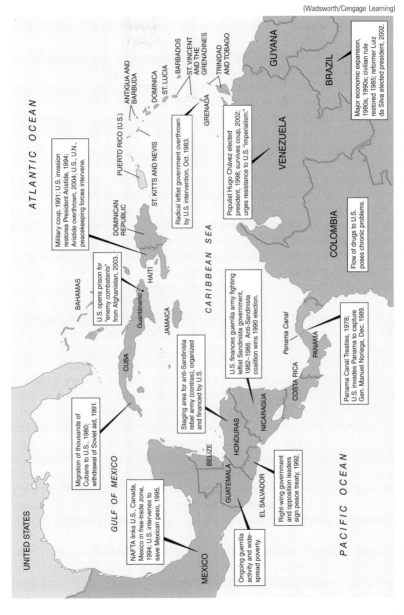

MAP 30.1 The United States in Central America and the Caribbean, 1978–2006

Plagued by poverty, population pressures, repressive regimes, and drug trafficking, this region has experienced turmoil and conflict—but also some hopeful developments—in recent decades.

Map labels:

UNITED STATES

ATLANTIC OCEAN

GULF OF MEXICO

NAFTA links U.S., Canada, Mexico in free-trade zone, 1994; U.S. intervenes to save Mexican peso, 1995.

MEXICO

Ongoing guerrilla activity and widespread poverty.

Migration of thousands of Cubans to U.S. 1980; withdrawal of Soviet aid, 1991.

BAHAMAS

CUBA

U.S. opens prison for "enemy combatants" from Afghanistan, 2003.

Guantánamo

HAITI

Military coup, 1991; U.S. invasion restores President Aristide, 1994; Aristide overthrown, 2004; U.S., U.N. peacekeeping forces intervene.

DOMINICAN REPUBLIC

PUERTO RICO (U.S.)

ST. KITTS AND NEVIS

ANTIGUA AND BARBUDA

DOMINICA

ST. LUCIA

BARBADOS

ST. VINCENT AND THE GRENADINES

GRENADA

Radical leftist government overthrown by U.S. intervention, Oct. 1983.

TRINIDAD AND TOBAGO

JAMAICA

CARIBBEAN SEA

BELIZE

GUATEMALA

HONDURAS

Staging area for anti-Sandinista rebel army (contras), organized and financed by U.S.

U.S. finances guerrilla army fighting leftist Sandinista government, 1982–1988. Anti-Sandinista coalition wins 1990 election.

EL SALVADOR

Right-wing government and opposition leaders sign peace treaty, 1992.

NICARAGUA

COSTA RICA

Panama Canal

PANAMA

Panama Canal Treaties, 1978; U.S. invades Panama to capture Gen. Manuel Noriega, Dec. 1989.

PACIFIC OCEAN

COLOMBIA

Flow of drugs to U.S. poses chronic problems.

VENEZUELA

Populist Hugo Chávez elected president, 1998; survives coup, 2002; urges resistance to U.S. "imperialism."

GUYANA

BRAZIL

Major economic expansion, 1980s, 1990s; civilian rule restored 1985; reformer Luiz da Silva elected president, 2002.

right-wing groups and foreign governments to the contras. When this subterfuge became known, a major scandal resulted.

Reagan's one unqualified success in Latin America involved the tiny island of Grenada, where a 1983 coup had installed a pro-Castro government. In October 1983, two thousand U.S. troops invaded Grenada and substituted a pro-U.S. government.

Pursuing its anticommunist campaign on the other side of the globe in Afghanistan, the Reagan administration (extending a policy started by President Carter) secretly funneled funds and equipment to Islamic fighters, called mujahadeen, battling to expel Russian troops that had invaded Afghanistan in 1979 in an effort to prop up an unpopular pro-Russian government. Ironically, young **Osama bin Laden,** a wealthy Saudi Arabian who would later become a deadly foe of America, was also helping to finance the mujahadeen, putting him and the United States briefly on the same side.

Reagan's anticommunist fervor and determination to make America "stand tall" again in the world had broad appeal. So did his tax cuts and celebration of the nation's free-enterprise system. Americans also liked Reagan's upbeat style, typified by his jaunty response in March 1981 when a ricocheting bullet fired by a deranged young man struck him in the chest. Rushed to the hospital, Reagan insisted on walking in. "Please tell me you're all Republicans," he quipped to physicians. (The attack disabled Reagan's press secretary, James Brady, who with his wife Sarah later joined the campaign for stricter gun control.)

With Reagan's approval ratings rising as the recession faded, he and Vice President Bush were enthusiastically renominated at the 1984 Republican convention. Staged for TV, the convention accented themes of patriotism, prosperity, and Reagan's personal charm.

The Democratic hopefuls included civil-rights leader Jesse Jackson. In the Democratic primaries, Jackson garnered 3.5 million votes and won five southern states. But former vice president Walter Mondale captured the nomination with backing from party leaders, labor unions, and other traditional Democratic constituencies. His vice-presidential choice, New York congresswoman Geraldine Ferraro, became the first woman to run on a major-party presidential ticket.

Reagan's ideological and personal appeal, combined with prosperity and the continued support of "Reagan Democrats," proved decisive. Reagan and Bush won 59 percent of the popular vote and carried every state but Mondale's Minnesota plus the District of Columbia. The Republicans' post–1968 dominance of the White House—interrupted only by Jimmy Carter's single term—continued.

In 1985, frustrated by the Democrats' image as a "big government" and "tax-and-spend" party, Arkansas governor Bill Clinton, Tennessee senator Al Gore, and others formed the more centrist **Democratic Leadership Council** (DLC). Clinton would later use the DLC as a springboard for a presidential bid.

Reagan's second-term achievements included the 1986 Immigration Reform and Control Act (see Chapter 29) and a tax-reform law making the system less complicated. These were overshadowed, however, by a White House scandal involving the abuse of executive power and by a dramatic easing of Cold War hostilities.

The Iran-Contra Scandal and a Thaw in U.S.-Soviet Relations

The worst crisis of Reagan's presidency, the so-called **Iran-contra scandal,** began obscurely in 1986 when a Beirut newspaper reported that in 1985 the United States had shipped, via Israel, 508 antitank missiles to Iran, America's avowed enemy. Admitting the sale, Reagan claimed the goal had been to encourage "moderate elements" in Tehran and to gain the release of U.S. hostages held in Lebanon by pro-Iranian groups. In February 1987, a presidentially appointed investigative panel blamed Reagan's chief of staff, Donald Regan, who resigned.

Next came the revelation that Oliver North, a National Security Council aide in the White House, had secretly diverted profits from the Iran arms sales to the Nicaraguan contras despite Congress's ban on such aid. To hide this crime, North and his secretary had altered and destroyed incriminating documents.

In May 1987, a congressional investigative committee opened hearings on the scandal. North, resplendent in his marine uniform, boasted of his patriotism, and National Security Adviser John Poindexter testified that he had deliberately concealed the scheme from President Reagan. The committee found no proof that Reagan knew of illegalities, but criticized the lax management and contempt for the law that pervaded the White House. In 1989, North was convicted of obstructing a congressional inquiry and destroying and falsifying official documents. (The conviction was later reversed on a technicality.) Although less damaging than Watergate, the Iran-contra scandal dogged the administration's final years.

Other scandals plagued Reagan's second term. Attorney General Edwin Meese resigned in 1988 amid charges of using his influence to promote ventures from which he hoped to profit. In 1989 came revelations that former interior secretary James Watt and other prominent Republicans had collected hundreds of thousands of dollars for using their influence to help housing developers seeking federal subsidies. Reagan's popularity seemed unaffected; some dubbed him the Teflon president—nothing stuck to him.

Reagan's second term also brought a dramatic warming in Soviet-American relations. At meetings in Europe in 1985 and 1986, Reagan and Soviet premier Mikhail Gorbachev revived the stalled arms-control process. Beset by economic problems at home and by spreading unrest in Eastern Europe, Gorbachev worked to reduce superpower tensions while pursuing his ambitious goals: restructuring the economy, loosening Moscow's grip in Eastern Europe, and bringing more openness to Russia's government.

In December 1987, in Washington, Reagan and Gorbachev signed the **Intermediate-range Nuclear Forces (INF) Treaty,** eliminating twenty-five hundred U.S. and Soviet missiles from Europe. This, in turn, led to Reagan's historic visit to Moscow in May 1988, where the two leaders strolled in Red Square.

Some Reaganites protested as their hero embraced the world's top communist. But Reagan cheerfully pointed to Gorbachev's reforms and argued that the "evil empire" was becoming more benign. Most Americans welcomed improved relations with Moscow.

The INF treaty and Reagan's trip to Moscow marked a significant thaw in the Cold War. Historians still debate the relative importance of Reagan's military buildup versus the Soviet Union's internal weaknesses in producing this outcome.

Whatever the final judgment on that point, that one of America's most dedicated Cold Warriors presided over the early stages of the Cold War's demise remains a striking irony of recent U.S. history.

Conflict and Terrorism in the Middle East and Beyond

For U.S. diplomats, the Middle East remained a major challenge. Though far away, events in this region directly affected U.S. security, economic interests, and international relations. In 1980, Iraq under strongman Saddam Hussein invaded its neighbor Iran. The incoming Reagan administration, hoping to slow the spread of Islamic fundamentalism as represented by Iran's anti-American Ayatollah Khomeini, backed Iraq in what would prove to be an eight-year war. (Two decades later, the United States would invade Iraq to overthrow Saddam Hussein, covered in Chapter 31.)

As the administration confronted the ongoing conflict among Israel, the Palestinians, and Israel's Arab foes, it faced conflicting interests. The United States gave its ally Israel large annual grants in military aid and other assistance, while also providing aid to Egypt and the Palestinians and importing oil from Saudi Arabia and other Arab states.

In June 1982, when extremists linked to the Palestinian Liberation Organization (PLO) shot and critically wounded Israel's ambassador to Great Britain, Israeli troops under Defense Minister Ariel Sharon attacked PLO bases in southern Lebanon and forced its leaders, including chairman Yasir Arafat, to evacuate the country.

As part of this operation, a Lebanese Christian militia, with Sharon's approval, invaded two Palestinian refugee camps thought to harbor PLO terrorists. Here they massacred hundreds of residents, including women and children. Years later, in the 2008 animated documentary *Walzing with Bashir,* Israeli filmmaker Ari Folman recalled this invasion, and the refugee-camp massacre, as remembered by Israeli soldiers.

In September 1982, Reagan ordered two thousand marines to Lebanon as part of a multinational force to keep peace among the country's religious and political factions. On October 23, 1983, a Shiite Muslim crashed an explosives-filled truck into a U.S. barracks, killing 239 marines. Reagan had never made clear how the deployment served U.S. interests, and early in 1984 he withdrew the surviving marines.

In 1987, Palestinians launched an *intifada,* or uprising, against Israeli occupation of Gaza and the West Bank, Palestinian territories occupied by Israel since the 1967 war. In response, Secretary of State George Shultz (who had replaced Alexander Haig in 1982) proposed negotiations leading to an independent Palestinian state. Israel refused to negotiate until the *intifada* ended, however, and the Palestinians rejected Shultz's proposals for not assuring Palestinian interests. Over U.S. objections, Jewish settlement continued in the occupied territories.

A deadly byproduct of the Middle East conflict was a series of bombings, assassinations, hijackings, and hostage-takings by anti-Israel and anti-American terrorists. At the 1972 Summer Olympics in Munich, Palestinian gunmen killed eleven Israeli athletes. In 1985, terrorists set off bombs in the Vienna and Rome airports and hijacked a TWA flight en route from Athens to Rome, holding the crew and 145 passengers hostage for seventeen days and killing one passenger, a U.S. sailor. That same year, armed men demanding the release of Palestinians held by Israel hijacked an Italian cruise ship, dumping a wheelchair-bound Jewish-American passenger into the sea.

A 1986 bombing of a Berlin club popular with Americans killed two GIs and injured others. Accusing Libyan strongman Muammar al-Qaddafi of masterminding this and other attacks, Reagan ordered the bombing of Libyan military sites. But the attacks continued. In December 1988, a bomb detonated aboard Pan Am flight 103, en route from London to New York. It crashed near Lockerbie, Scotland, killing all 259 aboard, including many Americans. In 1991, the United States and Great Britain indicted two Libyan officials in the attack. In 1999, Qaddafi released the two for trial. A Scottish court sitting in the Netherlands acquitted one, but convicted the other and imposed a life sentence.

This terrorism reflected bitter religious and political divisions. Hatred of Israel, and even denial of its right to exist, gripped parts of the Muslim world. Radical Islamic clerics called for *jihad* (holy war in defense of Islam) against a secular West that seemed increasingly dominant militarily, economically, and culturally. The stationing of U.S. troops in Saudi Arabia, as well as expanding Jewish settlements in the Palestinian territories, also fed the anger that fueled terrorist attacks.

Despite terrorist attacks and festering problems in the Middle East, many Americans felt confident about the nation and its stature in the world as Reagan's term ended. After Nixon's disgrace, Ford's caretaker presidency, and Carter's rocky tenure, Reagan's two terms restored a sense of stability to U.S. politics. Domestically, Reagan compiled a mixed record. Inflation eased, and the economy improved after 1982. But the federal deficit soared, and the reduction of the government's regulatory role planted the seeds of future problems. Despite Reagan's antigovernment rhetoric, on his watch the federal budget and bureaucracy continued to grow.

Building on Richard Nixon's strategy, Reagan exploited the anxieties of middle-class white voters. He dismissed the social activism of the 1960s, criticized affirmative-action programs, and ridiculed the welfare system by recounting urban legends about Cadillac-driving "welfare queens."

To Reagan's critics, at best his presidency seemed an interlude of nostalgia and drift. Reagan's celebration of individual freedom, they charged, could readily morph into self-centered materialism. Apart from individualism, anticommunism, and flag-waving patriotism, they contended, Reagan offered few common goals around which all Americans could rally.

In 1988, former chief of staff Donald Regan, still smarting over his forced resignation, published a memoir that portrayed Reagan as little more than an automaton: "Every moment of every public appearance was scheduled, every word was scripted, every place where Reagan was expected to stand was chalked with toe marks."

Reagan's admirers praised him for reasserting the values of self-reliance and free enterprise, criticizing governmental excesses, and restoring national pride. The mood at the 1984 Summer Olympics in Los Angeles, they suggested, when exuberant American fans had waved flags and chanted "USA, USA" captured the nation's newly discovered confidence. Reagan's militant anticommunism and military build-up, they contended, hastened the Soviet collapse and America's Cold War victory. Alzheimer's disease darkened Reagan's post-presidential years, but "the Reagan revolution" still influences American politics.

DOMESTIC DRIFT AND A NEW WORLD ORDER

George H. W. Bush, elected president in 1988, was a patrician in politics. Son of a Connecticut senator, a Yale graduate, and World War II bomber pilot, he entered the Texas oil business, served in Congress, lost a Senate race, and was a U.N. ambassador and CIA director before becoming Reagan's running mate in 1980. As president, Bush reacted decisively when Iraq invaded Kuwait, but he proved less impressive on domestic issues.

1988: The Conservative Momentum Continues Easily winning the 1988 Republican presidential nomination, Bush in his acceptance speech called for a "kinder, gentler America" and pledged, "Read my lips: no new taxes." As his running mate, he selected Indiana senator Dan Quayle, son of a newspaper publisher.

On the Democratic side, Jesse Jackson again did well in the primaries, but Massachusetts governor Michael Dukakis, winning in New York and California, captured the nomination. As his running mate, Dukakis chose Texas senator Lloyd Bentsen.

In the campaign, Bush emphasized prosperity and improved Soviet relations, while distancing himself from the Iran-contra scandal. A TV commercial aired by Bush supporters, playing on racist stereotypes, featured a black convict who committed rape and murder after his release under a Massachusetts prisoner-furlough program.

Dukakis emphasized his managerial skills, pointed to holes in the "Swiss-cheese" Reagan economy, and urged "Reagan Democrats" to return to the fold. But Dukakis seemed wooden, and his focus on competence rather than ideology made it difficult for him to define his political vision. Both candidates relied on sound bites and TV-oriented "photo opportunities." Bush visited flag factories and military plants. Dukakis proved his toughness on defense by posing in a tank. Editorial writers deplored the "junk-food" campaign.

Bush won, carrying forty states and garnering 54 percent of the vote. Dukakis prevailed in only ten states plus the District of Columbia. The Democrats, however, retained control of Congress.

The Cold War Ends; Global Challenges Persist As Bush took office, the Soviet Union's collapse, heralded by the opening of the Berlin Wall, proceeded with breathtaking rapidity. East Germany's communist regime imploded. The Baltic republics annexed by Moscow in 1940—Estonia, Latvia, and Lithuania—declared independence. The other Soviet republics moved toward autonomy as well.

In July 1991, President Bush and Mikhail Gorbachev signed a treaty reducing their nuclear arsenals by 25 percent. Secretary of Defense Dick Cheney proposed a 25 percent reduction in U.S. military forces over five years. NATO announced major troop reductions.

In August 1991, die-hard communists tried to overthrow Gorbachev. But thousands of Muscovites, rallied by Boris Yeltsin, president of the Russian Republic, protectively surrounded Moscow's parliament building, and the coup failed. Exuberant crowds toppled statues of Lenin and Stalin. Gorbachev, overwhelmed by forces he himself had unleashed, soon resigned, and Boris Yeltsin filled the power vacuum.

The Cold War was over. Speaking at Pearl Harbor on December 7, 1991, fifty years after the Japanese attack that propelled the United States into World War II, President Bush proclaimed: "[N]ow we stand triumphant—for a third time this century—this time in the wake of the Cold War. As in 1919 and 1945, we face no enemy menacing our security."

But even as Americans savored the moment, a host of new problems arose. As the Soviet Union fragmented into a loose federation of independent nations, Secretary of State James Baker, a longtime Bush family friend, worked to ensure the security of nuclear missiles based in Russia and in newly independent Ukraine, Belarus, and Kazakhstan, and to prevent rogue states or terrorists from acquiring nuclear materials or know-how from these countries.

For decades, the superpowers had backed client states and rebel insurgencies around the world. As the Cold War faded, prospects brightened for resolving some local disputes. In Nicaragua, Bush abandoned the U.S.-funded contra war against the leftist Sandinista government. In the Philippines, a former U.S. colony and longtime military ally, the United States closed two U.S. naval bases under pressure from the Philippines legislature.

Meanwhile, South Africa's policy of racial segregation—apartheid—provoked worldwide protests, vocally supported by U.S. black leaders and campus activists. In 1986, over Reagan's veto, Congress had joined other nations in imposing economic sanctions against white-ruled South Africa, including a ban on U.S. corporate investment. Yielding to these pressures and to an anti-apartheid campaign in South Africa itself, the South African government in 1990 released black leader Nelson Mandela after years in prison. When South Africa scrapped its apartheid policy in 1991, President Bush lifted the sanctions. In 1994, Mandela was elected president and his party, the African National Congress, assumed power.

In 1989, Chinese troops brutally crushed a pro-democracy demonstration in Beijing's Tiananmen Square, killing several hundred students and workers. The Bush administration curtailed diplomatic contacts, but Bush, committed to expanding U.S. trade, did not break diplomatic relations or cancel trade agreements with Beijing.

The Persian
Gulf War, 1991

On August 2, 1990, Iraq invaded neighboring Kuwait. Iraq's dictator, Saddam Hussein, viewed Kuwait's ruling sheiks as Western puppets and asserted Iraq's historic claims to Kuwait's vast oil fields.

During the Iran-Iraq War, the United States had backed Iraq. But now, confronted by Iraq's invasion of Kuwait, an important oil-producing nation, Bush responded decisively. Assembling a force of more than five hundred thousand U.S. troops, Bush also built a multi-nation coalition, including five in the Persian Gulf, which contributed additional troops.

When Saddam ignored UN economic sanctions and a resolution demanding Iraq's withdrawal by January 15, 1991, both houses of Congress endorsed military action. Most Democrats voted against war, however, favoring continued economic sanctions. Memories of Vietnam stirred as Americans debated another war.

Beginning on January 16, U.S. bombers pounded Iraqi troops, supply depots, and command centers in Iraq's capital, Baghdad. In retaliation, Saddam fired Soviet-made Scud missiles against Tel Aviv and other Israeli cities, as well as against Riyadh, the capital of Saudi Arabia, which supported the U.S.-led war. As TV viewers watched distant explosions filmed through greenish aircraft bombsights, and shots of interceptor missiles streaking off to attack incoming Scuds, the war seemed hardly real, almost resembling a video game.

On February 23, two hundred thousand U.S. troops moved across the desert toward Kuwait (see Map 30.2). Thousands of Iraqi soldiers fled or surrendered. U.S. forces destroyed thirty-seven hundred Iraqi tanks while losing only three. With Iraqi resistance crushed, President Bush declared a cease-fire, and Kuwait's ruling family returned to power. U.S. casualties numbered 148 dead—including thirty-five killed inadvertently by U.S. firepower—and 467 wounded. Iraqi military casualties were estimated at twenty-five thousand to sixty-five thousand. The Iraqi government claimed that U.S. bombs also killed twenty-three hundred civilians.

For President Bush, the **Persian Gulf War** proved that Americans were prepared to use force to pursue national interests. "By God, we've kicked the Vietnam syndrome once and for all," he declared.

Bush and his national-security advisors rejected the urging of some who favored invading Iraq itself and overthrowing Saddam Hussein. Such an invasion, they feared, could lead to an extended and costly occupation. The UN did impose "no-fly zones" on Iraqi aircraft, and a somewhat chastened Saddam granted UN inspectors access to his weapons-production facilities. Nevertheless, Saddam's army brutally suppressed antigovernment uprisings by Iraq's Shiite Muslims and ethnic Kurds.

Troubles at Home: Economic Woes, Racial Tensions, Environmental Threats

As for Bush's domestic record, a rare accomplishment was the **Americans with Disabilities Act** of 1990. Supported by Bush, this law barred discrimination against disabled persons in hiring or education. As in the earlier civil-rights movement, Congress acted following demonstrations and lobbying by the disabled and their advocates. Thanks to this law, job opportunities for handicapped persons increased and public schools enrolled more physically or developmentally impaired children. Otherwise, the Bush years saw more problems than achievements on the home front.

By the early 1990s, the impact of Reagan-era tax cuts and deregulation began to hit home. First came the collapse of the savings-and-loan (S&L) industry, provider of home loans and a modest but secure return to depositors. In the late 1970s, as inflation had pushed up interest rates, the S&Ls had offered higher interest

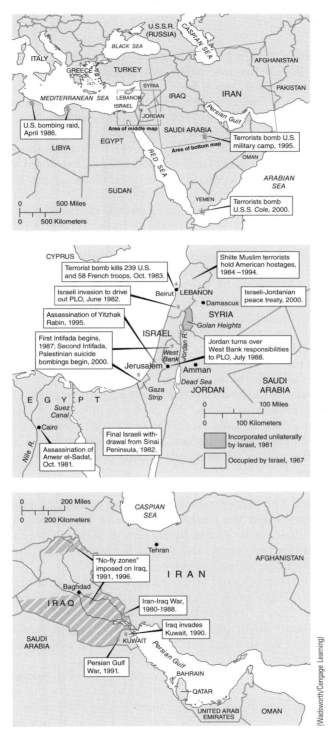

MAP 30.2 The Mideast Crisis, 1980–2000

With terrorist attacks, the Iran-Iraq War, the Persian Gulf War, and the ongoing struggle between Israel and the Palestinians, the Middle East was the site of almost unending violence and conflict in these years.

to retain investors, even though the S&L's assets were mostly in fixed-rate mortgages. Following the Reagan tax cuts, money flowed into S&Ls with their attractive rates. Meanwhile, in the deregulatory fervor, Congress eased the rules governing S&Ls, enabling them to make loans on risky real-estate ventures. As recession hit, many of these investments went bad. In 1988–1990, nearly six hundred S&Ls failed, especially in the Southwest, wiping out depositors' savings.

Because the government insures S&L deposits, the Bush administration in 1989 set up a program to repay depositors and sell hundreds of foreclosed office towers and apartment buildings in a depressed market. Estimates of the bailout's cost topped $400 billion.

Meanwhile, the federal deficit continued to mount, thanks in part to Reagan's tax cuts and military spending. In 1990, Congress and the administration agreed on a deficit-reduction plan involving spending cuts and tax increases. Bush's retreat from his "no new taxes" pledge angered voters. Despite this plan, the 1992 deficit neared $300 billion, thanks to the Persian Gulf War, S&L bailout, and soaring welfare and Medicare payments.

Making matters worse, another recession struck in 1990. Retail sales slumped; housing starts fell. General Motors, battered by Japanese imports, laid off more than seventy thousand workers—a foretaste of worse to come. By 1992, the jobless rate exceeded 7 percent and the ranks of Americans living in poverty had risen alarmingly. If 1984 was "morning in America," wrote a columnist, quoting a Reagan campaign slogan, this was "the morning after."

The recession worsened inner-city poverty and despair. In April 1992, an outbreak of arson and looting in Watts, the predominantly black district of Los Angeles and scene of rioting in 1965 (see Chapter 28), left forty persons dead and millions in property damage. The immediate cause was outrage over a jury's acquittal of four white police officers whose brutal beating of a black motorist had been captured on videotape.

Underlying the outbreak, too, was tension between local residents and Korean-American shopkeepers. The black filmmaker Spike Lee anticipated just such a scenario in his 1989 movie *Do the Right Thing,* set in the predominantly black Bedford-Stuyvesant district of Brooklyn. In the film, a dispute between the Italian-American owner of a pizza restaurant and a local black youth escalates into a full-scale riot that the police combat with heavy-handed brutality.

America's environmental worries increased during Bush's presidency. In March 1989, a giant oil tanker, the *Exxon Valdez,* ran aground in Alaska's Prince William Sound, spilling more than 10 million gallons of oil. The accident fouled coastal habitats, killed thousands of sea otters and shore birds, and jeopardized Alaska's fisheries. Bush deplored the spill, but insisted that America's energy-hungry economy required ever more quantities of oil, coal, and natural gas.

That summer, air pollution in many U.S. cities exceeded federal standards. A 1991 Environmental Protection Agency study found that pollutants were eroding the atmosphere's ozone layer, which reduces cancer-causing solar radiation. Growing numbers of scientists also warned of global warming related to increasing levels of carbon dioxide in the atmosphere and the role of human activity in causing it (see Chapter 31, Beyond America).

Aftermath of the Exxon Valdez disaster *An oil-soaked cormorant after the 1989 oil spill in Alaska's Prince William Sound.*

(CHRIS WILKINS/AFP/Getty Images)

Squeezed between growing environmental concern and his party's free-market ideology and links to the energy industries, Bush signed a stricter Clean Air Act passed by the Democratic Congress in 1990, but otherwise backed oil exploration in Alaskan wilderness preserves, proposed to open protected wetlands to developers, and largely ignored a 1992 UN conference in Rio de Janeiro addressing global environmental issues.

Of President Bush's two Supreme Court nominations, David Souter, a New Hampshire judge of moderate views, won easy confirmation. With Clarence Thomas, however, Bush continued Reagan's effort to push the court to the right. Bush nominated Thomas in 1991 to replace Thurgood Marshall, a black who as an NAACP lawyer had played a role in the historic *Brown* school desegregation case (see Chapter 27). Thomas, also African-American, supported right-wing causes and, as head of the Equal Employment Opportunity Commission (EEOC) under Reagan, had opposed affirmative-action programs. Noting his weak judicial qualifications, critics charged Bush with playing racial politics.

In the Senate confirmation hearings, a former staff member at EEOC, Anita Hill, accused Thomas of sexual harassment. Thomas narrowly won confirmation, but Republican efforts to discredit Hill's testimony alienated many women, and their resentment appeared to play a role when women candidates did well in the 1992 elections.

On the Court, Thomas allied with Antonin Scalia, Chief Justice Rehnquist, and other Republican-appointed justices who supported expanded executive power and a strict interpretation of the Constitution. Sometimes joined by moderates Sandra Day O'Connor or Anthony Kennedy, the conservative bloc narrowed the rights of arrested persons; curbed death-penalty appeals; cut back affirmative-action programs; and, in *Planned Parenthood v. Casey* (1992), upheld a Pennsylvania law imposing restrictions on abortion providers.

1992: America's Voters Choose a New Course   Given President Bush's popularity after the Persian Gulf War, many top Democrats opted out of the 1992 presidential race. But Arkansas Governor **William (Bill) Jefferson Clinton** took the plunge. Fending off reports of marital infidelity, Clinton won the nomination. As his running mate, he chose Tennessee senator **Albert (Al) Gore, Jr.**

President Bush quashed a primary challenge by conservative columnist Pat Buchanan, but at the Republican convention, underscoring the party's rightward turn, Buchanan and evangelist Pat Robertson gave divisive, hard-line speeches on contested cultural issues. A third-party candidate, H. Ross Perot, founder of a Texas data-processing firm, insisted he could easily solve the nation's economic problems. He proposed electronic "town meetings" at which the public would govern directly. At his peak of popularity, nearly 40 percent of the voters backed Perot, but his eccentricities and thin-skinned response to criticism cost him support.

Bush attacked Clinton for evading the Vietnam-era draft and promised more attention to domestic issues in a second term. Clinton hammered on the recession and the problems of the middle class. He pledged to work for a national health-care system, welfare reform, environmental protection, and economic growth.

Clinton won 43 percent of the vote to Bush's 38 percent. Perot's 19 percent was the best for a third-party candidate since Teddy Roosevelt in 1912. Clinton did well in the South, carried Ohio and other swing states, and lured back many blue-collar and suburban "Reagan Democrats." The recession, Bush's lackluster domestic record, and the divisive Perot campaign all helped Clinton. With Democrats now in control of Congress and the White House, an end to the much-deplored "Washington gridlock" seemed possible.

Thirty-eight African-Americans and seventeen Hispanics won congressional seats. The new Senate included six women and the House forty-seven. California became the first state with two women senators, Barbara Boxer and Dianne Feinstein. Illinois elected the first African-American woman senator, Carol Moseley Braun.

Apart from the Persian Gulf War, President Bush's single term proved unmemorable. A *New York Times* editorial, judging him "shrewd and energetic in foreign policy..., clumsy and irresolute at home," went on: "The domestic Bush flops like a fish, leaving the impression that he doesn't know what he thinks or doesn't much care, apart from the political gains to be extracted from an issue."

DOMESTIC AND GLOBAL ISSUES AT CENTURY'S END

Clinton's presidency soon encountered setbacks, notably the failure of an ambitious national health-care plan, and the 1994 midterm election produced a Republican

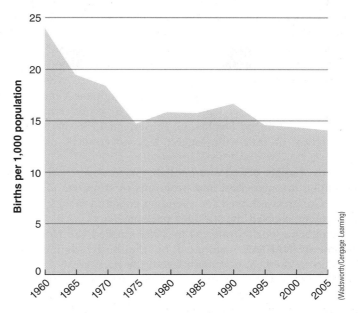

(Wadsworth/Cengage Learning)

FIGURE 30.1 The American Birthrate, 1960–2005

Families of five or six children or more were once common in the United States, and the birthrate remained high in the baby-boom years of the later 1940s and the 1950s. (The nearly 80 million children of the baby boomers, born between 1982 and 1995, were dubbed "echo boomers.") The U.S. birthrate fell dramatically from 1960 to the mid-1970s, rose slightly, and then resumed its downward trend after 1990.

Source: National Center for Health Statistics, U.S. Dept. of Health and Human Services.

landslide. The newly energized congressional Republicans pursued their conservative agenda, including—with Clinton's cooperation—sweeping welfare reform.

Clinton preferred domestic issues, but world events dictated attention to foreign policy. Abroad, four key challenges loomed: promoting stability in the former Soviet Union; improving relations between Israel and the Palestinians; addressing security threats posed by nuclear proliferation and Islamic terrorism; and protecting U.S. trade and investment interests (covered in this chapter's last section).

Trade, Gay Rights, Health Care: Clinton's Mixed Record

Born in Arkansas in 1946, Bill Clinton was part of the baby-boom generation that admired Elvis and came of age in the era of JFK, Vietnam, and the Beatles. After college and a fellowship at Oxford University, he attended Yale Law School where he met his future wife, Hillary Rodham. Returning to Arkansas, he was elected governor at age thirty-two. Now, at forty-six, he was president.

As a founder of the New Democratic Coalition—moderates eager to shed the party's "ultraliberal," "tax and spend" reputation—Clinton in his campaign stressed middle-class concerns and muted the party's traditional attention to the poor and social-justice issues. Seeking middle ground on abortion, he said it should be "safe, legal, and rare." He strongly endorsed environmental protection; indeed, his running mate, Al Gore, in 1992 published an environmental manifesto, *Earth in the Balance* (see Going to the Source).

Committed to the woman's movement, Clinton named women to head several cabinet departments and advisory panels. To fill a Supreme Court vacancy in 1993, he nominated Judge Ruth Bader Ginsberg. (When a second vacancy arose in 1994, Clinton chose moderate liberal Stephen G. Breyer.) In 1996, he named Madeleine K. Albright as secretary of state—the highest U.S. government office ever held by a woman.

To reduce the budget deficit and combat the recession, Clinton proposed military spending cuts, tax increases, and programs to stimulate job creation and economic growth. Congress adopted the spending cuts and tax increases, but with the economy improving, shelved the stimulus package.

With Clinton's support, Congress in 1993 ratified the **North American Free Trade Agreement (NAFTA),** negotiated by the Bush administration. This pact admitted Mexico to the U.S.-Canadian free-trade zone created earlier. While Ross Perot and others warned that U.S. jobs would flee to Mexico, NAFTA backers, including most economists, predicted a net job gain as Mexican markets opened to U.S. products.

Other early Clinton initiatives failed, however. Fulfilling a campaign pledge to gay-rights organizations, Clinton proposed to end the ban on gays in the military. When religious conservatives and some military leaders protested, he backed off. A study commission crafted a compromise, summed up in the phrase "Don't ask, don't tell." It continued the ban, but also barred officers from querying service members about their sexual orientation.

Health-care reform proved an even greater minefield. With Medicare costs exploding, and millions of citizens lacking health insurance, this issue stood high on Clinton's "to do" list, and he appointed his wife **Hillary Rodham Clinton** to head a healthcare task force. Working in secret, this group devised a sweeping plan for universal health insurance. Cost-containment provisions included health-care purchasing cooperatives, caps on insurance premiums, and limits on Medicare/Medicaid payments to physicians. Higher tobacco taxes would cover start-up expenses.

Lobbyists for physicians, insurance and tobacco companies, and other special interests rallied the opposition. By fall 1994, the ambitious plan was dead. Clinton had misread public complaints about the existing system as support for radical change. But soaring costs and dissatisfaction with the status quo guaranteed that this issue would remain on the political agenda.

Jolted by these setbacks, Clinton in 1994 turned to issues with broad voter appeal: crime and welfare reform. His anticrime bill included a ban on assault weapons and funds for more prisons and police officers. After partisan maneuvering, Congress enacted a bill similar to Clinton's proposal.

Clinton's welfare-reform bill put a two-year limit on payments from the federal welfare program, Aid to Families with Dependent Children (AFDC). After that, able-bodied recipients would have to find work, in a public-service job if necessary. The bill included job training and child-care provisions, measures to force absent fathers ("deadbeat dads") to support their offspring; and procedures to bar unmarried welfare mothers who had more babies from automatically receiving increased payments. In 1995, having regained control of Congress, Republicans shaped their own, even tougher bill (discussed shortly).

The approaching midterm election found the administration mired in problems. Republican critics publicized the Clintons' earlier involvement in a murky Arkansas real-estate speculation, the Whitewater Development Company. The 1993 suicide of assistant White House counsel Vincent Foster, the Clintons' close friend, attracted conspiracy theorists. In 1994, Paula Jones, an Arkansas state employee, sued Clinton for alleged sexual harassment during his governorship.

Favorable economic news helped Clinton somewhat. By 1994, the unemployment rate had fallen, inflation remained low, and the federal deficit was dropping. In October 1994, however, an ominous 58 percent of Americans told pollsters that they felt no better off despite the economic upturn.

Radio commentator Rush Limbaugh won fans for his jeering attacks on the Clintons and liberals in general. The religious Right remained a potent political force. Pat Robertson's **Christian Coalition,** with hundreds of chapters nationwide, controlled several state Republican parties.

Conservative Resurgence and Welfare Reform: 1994–1996   Bill Clinton had run as a "new Democrat," but by 1994 Republicans tarred him as an old Democrat of the big-government, "tax-and-spend" variety, beholden to gays, feminists, and other "special interests." The failed health-care plan, they charged, simply perpetuated the New Deal/Great Society style of top-down reform.

A network of conservative organizations, from the Christian Coalition to the National Rifle Association, helped re-energize the rightward swing in U.S. politics. Direct-mail campaigns and conservative radio commentators tirelessly hammered such hot-button issues as abortion, gun control, gay rights, school prayer, "radical feminism," sex education, and an alleged erosion of "family values."

Republican congressman **Newt Gingrich** of Georgia mobilized the discontent. In September 1994, about three hundred Republican congressional candidates signed Gingrich's "Contract with America" pledging to support tax cuts, tougher crime laws, antipornography measures, a balanced-budget amendment, and other reforms. The Contract nationalized the midterm election, normally fought on local issues.

In November, voters gave the GOP control of both houses of Congress for the first time since 1954 and increased the number of Republican governors. In Texas, George W. Bush, son and namesake of the former president, defeated a popular Democratic governor. Evangelicals, mobilized by politicized preachers like Falwell and Robertson, turned out in large numbers, mostly to vote Republican.

In the Senate, North Carolina's reactionary Jesse Helms became chairman of the Foreign Relations Committee, and ninety-two-year-old Strom Thurmond of South Carolina, presidential candidate of the segregationist States' Rights Party in 1948, headed the Armed Services Committee. In the House of Representatives, a jubilant horde of 230 Republicans, seventy-three of them newly elected, chose Newt Gingrich as Speaker, made Rush Limbaugh an "honorary member," and set

GOING TO THE SOURCE

Al Gore Reflects on Our Relation to Nature

In 1992, the year he was elected vice president, Al Gore published *Earth in the Balance: Ecology and the Human Spirit.* While this best-selling work mostly discussed specific environmental hazards and proposed remedies, Gore here reflects more broadly on modern society's relationship to the natural world.

Civilization has become astonishingly complex, but as it grows ever more elaborate, we feel increasingly distant from our roots in the earth. In one sense, civilization itself has been on a journey from its foundations in the world of nature to an ever more contrived, controlled, and manufactured world.... [T]he price has been high. At some point during this journey we lost our feeling of connectedness to the rest of nature. We now dare to wonder: Are we so unique and powerful as to be essentially separate from the earth?

Many of us act—and think—as if the answer is yes. It is now all too easy to regard the earth as a collection of "resources" having an intrinsic value no larger than their usefulness at the moment. Thanks in part to the scientific revolution, we organize our knowledge of the natural world into smaller and smaller segments and assume that the connection between these separate compartments aren't really important. In our fascination with the parts of nature, we forget to see the whole.

The ecological perspective begins with a view of the whole, an understanding of how the various parts of nature interact in patterns that tend toward balance and persist over time. But ... we are part of the whole too, and looking at it ultimately means looking at ourselves. And if we do not see that the human part of nature has an increasingly powerful influence over the whole of nature—that we are, in effect, a natural force just like the winds and the tides—then we will not be able to see how dangerously we are threatening to push the earth out of balance....

about enacting the Contract with America. A constitutional amendment requiring a balanced federal budget passed the House but narrowly failed in the Senate. House Republicans also targeted the Public Broadcasting System and the National Endowment for the Arts, suspected of a liberal bias. Fulfilling the antipornography pledge, Congress passed a Communications Decency Act strengthening the government's censorship powers. (In 1997, the Supreme Court ruled it unconstitutional.)

The torrent of bills, hearings, and press releases recalled the heady days of the early New Deal and Lyndon Johnson's Great Society. Now, however, the activist energy came from the conservative side of the political spectrum.

The architect of this revolution, Newt Gingrich, stumbled in 1995 when he accepted, then returned, a $4.5 million advance from a publishing house owned by Rupert Murdoch, a media tycoon with interests in federal legislation. Gingrich's network of political action groups, dubbed "Newt, Inc.," funded by corporations and conservative foundations, also drew critical scrutiny.

Turning to welfare reform, congressional Republicans criticized the existing system on both economic and public-policy grounds. AFDC, with 14.2 million women and children on its rolls cost about $125 billion in 1994, including direct

Even though it is sometimes hard to see their meaning, we have by now all witnessed surprising experiences that signal the damage from our assault on the environment.... But our response to these signals is puzzling. Why haven't we launched a massive effort to save our environment? ... Why do some images startle us into immediate action ... [while] other images, though sometimes equally dramatic, produce instead a kind of paralysis?...

Now that our relationship to the earth has changed so utterly, we have to see that change and understand its implications.... [T]he startling images of environmental destruction now occurring all over the world ... are symptoms of an underlying problem broader in scope and more serious than any we have ever faced. Global warming, ozone depletion, the loss of living species, deforestation—they all have a common cause: the new relationship between human civilization and the earth's natural balance....

[T]he faith that is so essential to restore the balance now missing in our relationship to the earth is the faith that we do have a future. We can believe in that future and work to achieve it and preserve it, or we can whirl blindly on, behaving as if one day there will be no children to inherit our legacy. The choice is ours; the earth is in the balance.

Questions

1. *In Gore's view, how have science and technology altered the way we view nature?*

2. *Considering economic, political, and cultural factors, how would you answer Gore's rhetorical question: "Why haven't we launched a massive effort to save our environment?"*

Go to www.cengagebrain.com for additional primary sources on this period.

payments, food stamps, and Medicaid benefits, a sharp jump since 1989. Though dwarfed by the benefits enjoyed by the middle class through social security, Medicare, farm subsidies, and various tax loopholes, this still represented a budgetary drain. On public-policy grounds, the critics contended that the welfare system encouraged irresponsible social behavior and trapped recipients in a multigenerational cycle of dependence. Many linked the soaring rate of out-of-wedlock births to AFDC policies that paid mothers higher benefits for each child.

As a consensus emerged on the existing system's flaws, debate focused on how to change it. While Clinton favored federally funded child care and job-training programs to ease the transition from welfare to work, Republicans argued that businesses, the states, and private agencies could best provide these services. Clinton vetoed two welfare bills that lacked the safeguards he thought essential.

At last, amidst another presidential campaign, Clinton signed the **Welfare Reform Act of 1996.** Reversing sixty years of welfare policy, the law replaced AFDC with block grants to states to develop their own programs within funding limits and guidelines restricting recipients to two years of continuous coverage, with a five-year lifetime total.

Advocates for the poor warned of the effects on inner-city children whose mothers lacked education or job skills, but many observers rated welfare reform at least a qualified success. From 1996 to 2005, the number of families on welfare fell by 57 percent and the birthrate among unmarried women leveled off. The percentage of unmarried mothers in the work force rose from around 48 percent in 1996 to around 65 percent in 2000, although many held low-paying, unskilled jobs, and changed jobs frequently.

A Pandora's Box of Dangers in a Post–Cold War World   As we have seen, global crises and challenges persisted despite the Cold War's end. In Yugoslavia, an unstable nation comprised of Serbia, Bosnia, Croatia, and other enclaves, the ruling communist party collapsed in 1990. As Yugoslavia broke apart, Serbian forces incited by Serbia's president Slobodan Milosevic launched a campaign of "ethnic cleansing" in neighboring Bosnia. Supported by Bosnia's ethnic Serbs, they killed or drove out Muslims and Croats. In August 1995, after UN peacekeepers failed to stop the killing, a joint U.S. and NATO operation launched air strikes against Bosnian Serb targets.

Later in 1995, the Clinton administration flew the leaders of Bosnia's warring factions to Dayton, Ohio, for talks. The resulting Dayton Accords imposed a cease-fire and created a governing framework for Bosnia. Clinton committed twenty thousand U.S. troops to a NATO operation to enforce the cease-fire.

In 1998, when Serbian forces attacked Muslims in Serbia's southern province, Kosovo, Clinton approved U.S. bombing of Serbian facilities in Kosovo and in Serbia itself, including Belgrade, the capital, as part of a NATO response. As Serb forces withdrew from Kosovo, U.S. troops joined a NATO occupying force, and refugees slowly returned. In 2001, a new Serbian government, eager for Western aid, delivered Slobodan Milosevic to a war-crimes tribunal at the Hague. The trial ended inconclusively with Milosevic's death in 2006.

Russia, meanwhile, invaded the breakaway Islamic republic of Chechnya in 1995. This war proved unpopular in Russia, and the Clinton administration watched anxiously as President Boris Yeltsin's position weakened. Hard times and corruption linked to Russia's hasty conversion to a free-market economy further undermined Yeltsin.

Despite Yeltsin's erratic behavior, compounded by alcoholism, the Clinton administration continued to support him, and used diplomacy, economic aid, and technical assistance to assure the safe disposal of deactivated nuclear weapons throughout the former Soviet Union. In 1999, the administration backed Russia's admission to the Group of Seven (G-7), the world's leading industrialized nations. In the same year, however, over Russia's protests, the United States supported NATO's decision to admit three new members from the former Soviet bloc— Hungary, Poland, and the Czech Republic. With Yeltsin's resignation in December 1999, Prime Minister Vladimir Putin, a former agent of the KGB, the Soviet secret police, succeeded him as president, opening a new chapter in the tortured history of U.S.-Russian relations.

In the Israeli-Palestinian conflict, of vital concern to America, prospects brightened in 1993 when Israeli and Palestinian negotiators meeting in Norway agreed on a timetable for peace. The so-called Oslo Accords provided for a Palestinian state, the return of Israeli-held land in the West Bank and Gaza, and further talks on Palestinian refugees' claims and the final status of Jerusalem (see Map 30.2). In 1994, President Clinton presided as Israeli Prime Minister Yitzhak Rabin and Yasir Arafat of the PLO signed the agreement at the White House.

After hopeful beginnings, however, this initiative failed. In 1995, a young Israeli opposed to the Oslo Accords assassinated Rabin. Israel's next election brought to power Benjamin Netanyahu of the hard-line Likud Party. Suicide bombings in Israel by Palestinian extremists in 1996–1997 triggered retaliatory attacks. Under U.S. pressure, Netanyahu agreed to withdraw Israeli forces from some West Bank areas in return for security guarantees. But as attacks continued, Netanyahu halted the withdrawal. By 2000, the West Bank and Gaza had an estimated two hundred thousand Jewish settlers, with accompanying checkpoints, security forces, and limited-access highways making existence difficult for Palestinians.

In July 2000, Clinton invited Arafat and Israel's new prime minister, Ehud Barak, of the more moderate Labour Party, for talks at Camp David. Barak made major concessions, reportedly including acceptance of a Palestinian state; Israeli withdrawal from most of the West Bank and all of Gaza; and the transfer of Jerusalem's Temple Mount, sacred to both Muslims and Jews, to a vaguely defined "religious authority." In return, the PLO would end hostilities and give up further claims on Israel.

Arafat rejected Barak's offer, however, and the summit failed. In September, hundreds of Israeli soldiers and police briefly occupied Temple Mount, symbolically asserting Israel's control of the site. The Palestinians launched a new *intifada*, and in 2001 Israelis elected the hard-liner Ariel Sharon prime minister. As Clinton left office, the conflict raged on.

Iraq also claimed Clinton's attention. In 1997, when Saddam Hussein barred UN inspectors from facilities suspected of research on chemical and nuclear weapons, Clinton dispatched ships, bombers, and troops to the Persian Gulf and sought support for a multinational military strike. But France, Russia, and various Arab states resisted, and the stand-off continued.

Other nations, too, posed threats of nuclear proliferation. Neither India nor Pakistan, at odds over the disputed region of Kashmir, had signed the 1968 Nuclear Nonproliferation Treaty. In 1988, India tested a "nuclear device" and Pakistan soon followed. Both the Bush and Clinton administrations imposed sanctions on the two countries, but the threat of nuclear confrontation in this volatile region remained urgent.

North Korea, despite having signed the Nonproliferation Treaty, also pursued nuclear-weapons development and missile testing. In 1994, facing UN economic sanctions and the loss of $9 billion in international assistance, North Korea pledged to halt its nuclear-weapons program. In 1999, confronting famine and economic crisis, North Korea suspended missile testing in return for an easing of U.S. trade and travel restrictions. The country's nuclear intentions remained worrisome, however.

Terrorism: "The War of the Future"   Attacks by anti-American Islamic extremists continued. A February 1993 bomb blast in a parking garage beneath one of the towers of New York's World Trade Center killed six persons, injured hundreds, and forced fifty thousand workers to evacuate. Five Islamic militants were arrested, and three, including the alleged mastermind, a blind Egyptian Muslim extremist known for his hatred of America, were convicted of murder and given life sentences.

The terrorist threat extended to Africa. In 1992, President Bush committed twenty-six thousand U.S. troops to a UN humanitarian mission in Somalia, a predominantly Muslim East African nation beset by civil war and famine. As the warring factions battled, forty-four Americans were killed, including eighteen in Mogadishu, Somalia's capital. President Clinton withdrew the U.S. force in 1994, and the UN mission ended a year later. Later evidence implicated Islamic extremists directed by Osama bin Laden in the killings. Son of a wealthy Saudi contractor, bin Laden had been expelled from Saudi Arabia in 1991 and settled in Sudan, where he financed construction and agricultural projects but also plotted anti-Western terrorist activities.

On August 7, 1998, simultaneous bomb blasts at the U.S. embassies in Nairobi, Kenya, and Dares-Salaam, Tanzania, killed 220—including twelve Americans. U.S. intelligence again pinpointed bin Laden, by now organizing terrorist training camps in Afghanistan. Clinton ordered cruise missile strikes on one of these Afghan camps as well as on a suspected chemical-weapons factory in Sudan allegedly financed by bin Laden. A U.S. grand jury charged bin Laden with complicity in the embassy attacks and the earlier killing of GIs in Somalia.

Declared Secretary of State Albright: "We are involved here in a long-term struggle..., This is, unfortunately, the war of the future." Underscoring Albright's grim assessment, on October 12, 2000, a bomb aboard a small boat in the harbor of Aden, Yemen, ripped a gaping hole in the U.S. destroyer *Cole,* killing seventeen sailors (see Map 30.2).

Defining America's Role amid Global Changes   As Americans confronted these myriad international dangers, the peaceful post–Cold War era that many had anticipated seemed a cruel mirage. The Soviet adversary had collapsed, but crises still flared around the world. Like firefighters battling many small blazes rather than a single conflagration, policy makers now wrestled with a baffling tangle of issues.

Amid the complexities, some larger trends could be discerned. Economic and even cultural **globalization** played an ever greater role. International trade and finance increasingly shaped America's foreign-policy interests. American movies, popular music, and television programs (including the sermons of U.S. televangelists) reached a worldwide audience in an age of instant telecommunications.

Along with globalization, however, came a widening chasm that divided the prosperous, comparatively stable industrialized world from societies marked by poverty, disease, illiteracy, and explosive population growth. This vast gulf helped spawn resentment, hatred, and terrorism.

Ancient ethnic hatreds burst into violence as the bipolar Cold War world fragmented. The lethal conflict in the former Yugoslavia was far from unique. Similar clashes erupted in many regions. In the African nation of Rwanda, as many as a million people perished in genocidal violence in 1994, as militias of the ruling Hutu ethnic group massacred members of the once-dominant Tutsi group. Thousands more fled in panic, creating a refugee crisis. (The 2004 film, *Hotel Rwanda,* about a courageous Rwandan hotel manager who sheltered over a thousand Tutsi refugees, conveyed the horror of the genocide.) Traumatized by the Somalia fiasco, President Clinton did not intervene.

Resurgent religious fundamentalism intensified the global unrest. As Muslim fundamentalists denounced Western liberalism and secularism, a small but lethal minority embraced violence as a religious duty. In India, violence erupted in 1992 when Hindu fundamentalists destroyed an ancient Muslim mosque they claimed had been built on an even more ancient Hindu shrine. Meanwhile, some ultrareligious Israeli Jews (supported by U.S. Christian fundamentalists) claimed a divine right to the West Bank and Jerusalem's Temple Mount, with its sacred Muslim shrines, on the basis of biblical texts.

Confronting such complexities, some U.S. citizens simply gave up. In a 1997 poll, only 20 percent of Americans said they followed foreign news, down sharply from the 1980s, with the biggest drop among young people. TV coverage of events abroad fell by more than 50 percent from 1989 to 1995.

Newt Gingrich's 1994 Contract with America largely ignored foreign policy, and key Republican legislators pushed isolationist views. Jesse Helms, as chair of the Senate Foreign Relations Committee, denounced the United Nations, criticized environmental treaties, and belittled UN peacekeeping efforts and America's foreign-aid program. Congressional Republicans refused to pay $1 billion in past UN dues. Bending to such pressures (and to Pentagon objections), Clinton in 1998 declined to sign a multinational treaty banning land mines, even though these mines remain deadly for years, often killing or maiming children.

Despite isolationist currents, however, opinion polls indicated that most Americans supported internationalist approaches to global problems and acknowledged America's continued role in a troubled world. The U.S. part in negotiating the Dayton Accords that brought a fragile peace to Bosnia offered a noteworthy instance of this role. Another came in 1995 when President Clinton appointed former Democratic senator George Mitchell as a special envoy to Northern Ireland to promote negotiations between Catholics favoring independence and Protestants advocating continued ties to Great Britain. Mitchell's efforts were rewarded in 1998 when the two sides signed a peace agreement.

With the Cold War's end, the United Nations, long hostage to the superpowers' conflict, seemed better positioned to fulfill the role its supporters had envisioned in 1945. Indeed, by 2000, more than forty thousand UN peacekeepers and civilian personnel were deployed in fifteen world trouble spots. A complex network of UN agencies addressed global environmental, nutritional, public-health, and human-rights issues. The UN-sponsored International Court of Justice at the Hague adjudicated disputes between nations and tried perpetrators of mass violence in Bosnia, Rwanda, Liberia, and elsewhere.

MODERATION, WHITE HOUSE SCANDAL, AND A DISPUTED ELECTION, 1996–2000

Straddling the political center, Bill Clinton won reelection in 1996. Along with sending U.S. forces to Kosovo and the final stab at resolving the Israeli-Palestinian dispute, his second term saw a battle over tobacco-industry regulation and a sex scandal that led to his impeachment. A disputed presidential election in 2000 deepened the nation's divisions.

**Clinton Battles
Big Tobacco and
Woos Political
Moderates** Bill Clinton won the nickname "the Comeback Kid" following a long-shot victory in the 1992 New Hampshire primary, and after the 1994 Republican landslide he again hit the comeback trail. In a 1995 budget battle, Clinton outmaneuvered House Speaker Newt Gingrich, who annoyed voters by twice allowing a partial government shutdown.

As the 1996 electoral campaign began, Kansas senator Bob Dole, a partially disabled World War II veteran, won the Republican nomination after General Colin Powell, the popular former chairman of the Joint Chiefs of Staff, declined to run. Fundraising scandals marred Clinton's reelection campaign. After an event at a Los Angeles Buddhist temple attended by Vice President Al Gore, priests and nuns sworn to poverty contributed over a hundred thousand dollars to the Democratic cause, apparently from Asian businessmen seeking favor with the administration. But the seventy-three-year-old Dole ran a lackluster campaign, and Clinton won with 49 percent of the vote to Dole's 41 percent. (Ross Perot garnered 8 percent.) The Republicans retained control of Congress, but proved more subdued than after their 1994 triumph.

Tobacco regulation, a major public-health issue, loomed large as Clinton's second term began. In 1997, facing lawsuits by former smokers and by states saddled with medical costs linked to smoking-related diseases, the tobacco industry agreed to pay some $368 billion in settlement. The agreement limited tobacco advertising, especially when directed at young people.

Since the agreement required government approval, the debate shifted to Washington. Legislators from tobacco states defended the industry, but the Clinton administration backed a bill imposing tougher penalties, higher cigarette taxes, and stronger antismoking measures. The bill's supporters documented the industry's manipulation of nicotine levels and targeting of children. The industry struck back with a $40 million lobbying campaign and heavy contributions to key politicians, killing the bill. The Republican Party, commented Arizona Republican senator John McCain, appeared to be "in the pocket of the tobacco companies." In 1998, the tobacco industry and most states reached a new settlement, scaled back to $206 billion.

Pursuing his middle-of-the-road strategy, Clinton in his January 1998 State of the Union address offered some initiatives to help the poor, such as enrolling the nation's 3 million uninsured children in Medicaid, but mostly highlighted proposals attractive to the middle class (college-tuition tax credits; extending Medicare to early retirees) and fiscal conservatives (reducing the national debt; shoring up social security). Some liberals dismissed the speech as "Progressivism Lite," but it had broad appeal.

Further, Clinton's economic policies contributed to the decade's prosperity and in 1998 produced the first federal budget surplus in nearly thirty years. Under normal circumstances, Clinton's record would have assured that his presidency, despite early missteps, would end in a glow of success.

**A Media Field
Day as Scandal
Grips the White
House** But conditions were not normal. Even as Clinton spoke, scandal swirled around his presidency. Adultery charges had long clung to Clinton, and now he faced Paula Jones's sexual-harassment suit, dating from his days as Arkansas governor.

Seeking to document a pattern of sexual harassment, Jones's lawyers quizzed Clinton about rumors linking him to a young White House intern, Monica Lewinsky. Under oath, Clinton and Lewinsky denied everything. As the rumors became public, Clinton denounced them as false. Hillary Clinton blamed "a vast right-wing conspiracy." Clinton settled Paula Jones's suit by paying her $850,000, but problems remained. In telephone conversations illegally taped by her "friend" Linda Tripp, Lewinsky had described a White House affair with Clinton. Tripp passed the tapes to Kenneth Starr, an independent counsel investigating the Clintons' Arkansas real-estate dealings. Fitting Tripp with a recording device, the FBI secured further Lewinsky evidence.

Starr's inquiry now shifted to whether Clinton had committed perjury in his Paula Jones testimony and persuaded Lewinsky to lie. In August, after a promise of immunity, Lewinsky admitted the affair to a grand jury. As the scandal unfolded in tabloid headlines, late-night television jokes, and Internet humor, Clinton in a brief TV address conceded "inappropriate" behavior but attacked Starr as politically motivated.

In a September 1998 report to the House Judiciary Committee, Starr recommended Clinton's impeachment for perjury, influencing others to commit perjury, and obstructing justice by coaching his secretary on his version of events. The Judiciary Committee, on a party-line vote, forwarded four articles of impeachment to the House of Representatives. In a similarly partisan vote, the House approved and sent to the Senate two articles of impeachment: perjury and obstruction of justice.

The public, however, sent the Republicans an ominous message: Clinton's approval ratings rose, and the Democrats gained five House seats in the 1988 midterm elections. Few believed the president's actions met the Constitution's "high crimes and misdemeanors" standard for removal from office. With the economy booming and Clinton's political program generally popular, voters appeared willing to tolerate his personal flaws. Further, many saw him as the target of Republican zealots.

The trial began in January 1999. With Chief Justice William Rehnquist presiding, House Republicans presented their case. White House lawyers dismissed the charges as a "witches' brew of speculation." On February 12, the Senate rejected both charges, and the trial ended. In November, Newt Gingrich, a leader of the impeachment effort but now embroiled in his own ethical controversies, resigned as Speaker and left Congress.

While the impeachment failed, the scandal tarnished Clinton's reputation. Still facing legal liability as he left office in January 2001, the president admitted to perjury, paid a $25,000 fine, and lost his law license for five years.

2000: Divided Nation, Disputed Election   As the 2000 campaign approached, the Democrats nominated Vice President Al Gore for the top job. Distancing himself from the Lewinsky scandal, Gore chose as his running mate Connecticut senator Joseph Lieberman, who had denounced Clinton's behavior.

In the Republican contest, Arizona's somewhat maverick senator John McCain, a Vietnam-era prisoner of war, made a strong bid. But Texas governor **George**

W. Bush, with powerful backers, a familiar name, and a folksy manner, won the nomination. His running mate, Dick Cheney, had been defense secretary in the first Bush administration. The environmentally-minded Green Party nominated consumer advocate Ralph Nader.

Both Gore and Bush courted the center while trying to hold their bases. For Bush, this base included corporate interests, energy companies, religious conservatives, and so-called Reagan Democrats in the middle class and blue-collar ranks. Gore's base included liberals, academics and professionals, union members, environmentalists, feminists, and African-Americans. The Hispanic vote remained divided.

Gore boasted of the nation's prosperity and pledged to extend health-care coverage and protect social security. In TV debates, Gore was more articulate and knowledgeable, but some found him rather pompous. Demonstrating his independence, Gore kept Clinton at arm's length, despite the president's popularity.

Bush, with little experience outside Texas, was widely seen as a lightweight, dependent on family influence. As Texas's former Democratic governor Ann Richards quipped, "George was born on third base and thought he had hit a home run." Calling himself a "compassionate conservative," Bush subtly reminded voters of Clinton's misdeeds by promising to restore dignity to the White House. Polls showed that most voters agreed with Gore on the issues, but preferred Bush as a person.

On election day, Gore won the popular vote by more than 500,000. But the all-important Electoral College outcome came down to Florida, where a handful of votes separated the two candidates.

Flaws in Florida's voting process quickly emerged. In Palm Beach County, a poorly designed ballot led several thousand Gore supporters to vote for Pat Buchanan, running on Ross Perot's Reform Party ticket. In counties with many black voters, antiquated voting machines rejected thousands of ballots in which the paper tabs, called "chads," were not fully punched out. When election officials began a hand count of rejected ballots, Bush's lawyers sued to prevent it.

On November 21, the Florida Supreme Court, with a preponderance of Democrats, unanimously ruled that the ongoing recount should constitute the official result. Bush's legal team appealed to the U.S. Supreme Court. Despite a long-established precedent that state courts should decide electoral disputes, the justices accepted the case. On November 26, ignoring the unresolved legal dispute, Florida's secretary of state, Katherine Harris, certified the original, contested Florida vote, awarding Bush the state. (Harris was co-chair of Bush's Florida campaign and a political ally of Florida governor Jeb Bush, the candidate's brother.)

After further legal maneuvering, the Supreme Court on December 12, by a 5-to-4 vote, halted the re-count and let Harris's ruling stand. Gore conceded the next day. Five Supreme Court justices (all Republican appointees) had made George W. Bush president. Third-party candidate Ralph Nader also helped Bush win. Had the nearly 100,000 Floridians who voted for Nader not had that option, Gore would almost certainly have won the state and the presidency.

The election produced an evenly divided Senate, giving Vice President Cheney the deciding vote. Hillary Rodham Clinton, the first presidential spouse to pursue an independent political career, won election as senator from New York. The Republicans narrowly held the House of Representatives.

The Florida Election Dispute *A Fort Lauderdale judge scrutinizes a partially punched-out ballot in late November 2000.*

(© Bettmann/Corbis)

ECONOMIC AND CULTURAL TRENDS AT CENTURY'S END

The 1990s saw sustained economic growth, increased productivity, falling unemployment, low inflation, and the first federal budget surplus in years. Economic globalization fueled U.S. economic growth, but when foreign economies faltered, the American economy stumbled as well.

As corporate profits surged and the stock market soared, America exuded a glow of abundance amid leisure-time diversions and get-rich-quick enthusiasm. But real wages lagged, many workers lacked the skills valued by the emerging knowledge-based economy, and the gap between the super wealthy and most Americans widened. A continuing AIDS epidemic, outbursts of violence, and bitter cultural disagreements also characterized American society as the twentieth century ended.

An Uneven Prosperity   From 1992 to 2000, the unemployment rate fell from 7.5 percent to 4 percent. The gross domestic product, a key economic indicator, rose nearly 40 percent in the decade (see Figure 30.2). The boom had varied sources, but the revolution in information technology was crucial.

Wall Street stock prices far outran many companies' actual earnings prospects. From under 3,000 in 1991, the Dow Jones Industrial Average approached 12,000 by early 2001. By 1998, nearly half of U.S. families owned stock directly or through their pension plans. Leisure pursuits and consumer spending burgeoned.

In 2000, Americans spent $105 billion on new cars; $107 billion on video, audio, and computer equipment; and $81 billion on foreign travel. A few economists raised cautionary flags. In 1996, Federal Reserve Board chairman Alan Greenspan warned of "irrational exuberance" in the stock market, but with little effect.

Surging information technology (IT) stocks fed the boom. The NASDAQ composite index, loaded with technology stocks, shot up from under 500 in 1991 to over 5,000 by early 2000. Some stock offerings by unknown IT start-up companies hit fantastic levels, turning young entrepreneurs into paper millionaires.

As the stock market roared on, companies sought to improve their profitability through mergers and acquisitions. In 2000, communications giant Viacom swallowed CBS for $41 billion. In one super merger, Internet company America Online (AOL) acquired Time-Warner (the product of earlier mergers) for $182 billion.

The prosperity was spotty, however. From 1979 to 1996, the share of the total national income going to the wealthiest 20 percent of Americans increased by 13 percent, while the share going to the poorest 20 percent *dropped* by 22 percent. Commented economist Richard Freeman in 1998: "The U.S. has the most unequal distribution of income among advanced countries—and the degree of inequality has increased more here than in any comparable country."

Adjusted for inflation, the buying power of the average worker's paycheck fell or remained flat from 1986 to 2000. As corporations maintained profits by downsizing, cost cutting, and exporting jobs overseas, workers faced uncertain times. The growing service sector included not only white-collar positions, but also low-paying jobs in fast-food outlets, custodial work, car washes, telemarketing, and so forth. Only 13.5 percent of the labor force was unionized in 2000, eroding this means by which workers had historically bettered their wages and job conditions. As unions grew weaker, protests by labor leaders failed to prevent Congress's ratification of the 1993 NAFTA treaty.

Job market success increasingly required special training, posing problems for displaced industrial workers, welfare recipients entering the labor force, and those lacking advanced education. Overall employment statistics also obscured racial and ethnic variables. In 2000, the jobless rate for blacks and Hispanics remained significantly higher than the rate for whites. As shifting immigration patterns created an increasingly diverse American population (as further discussed in Chapter 31), some newcomers with training in special skills found well-paying positions, but many took low-paying, unskilled jobs with few benefits or long-term prospects. In short, while many Americans prospered during these boom years, millions more experienced minimal gains or none at all.

As the economy boomed and banks passed out credit cards like candy, consumer debt soared alarmingly. Unscrupulous finance companies offered would-be homeowners mortgages they could ill afford, often at low "teaser" rates that rose sharply after a year or two. The deregulation of business and banking that began in the late 1970s and continued through the Clinton years (and beyond) encouraged these dangerous trends. Credit buying and the deregulation mania gave the economy a glow of prosperity, but also laid the groundwork for a harsh recession (see Chapter 31).

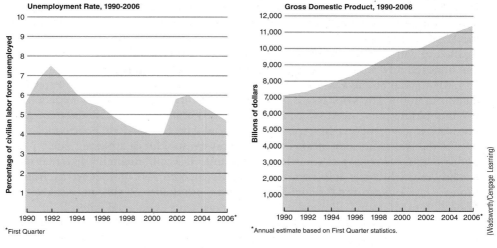

FIGURE 30.2 The U.S. Economy, 1990–2006

The unemployment rate fell, and the gross domestic product rose during the boom years of the 1990s. As recession hit in 2001, however, the jobless rate increased and the GDP flattened.

Source: Unemployment Rate chart: Bureau of Labor Statistics, U.S. Department of Labor; GDP: U.S. Department of Commerce. http://www.bea.gov/bea/dn/gdplev.xls. *The GDP figures are in constant dollars, adjusted for inflation.*

America and the World Economy   As the NAFTA agreement showed, trade issues ranked high on Clinton's agenda. When the U.S. trade deficit hit $133 billion in 1993, including a $59 billion trade gap with Japan, Clinton, like his predecessor, pressured the Japanese to buy more U.S. goods.

Multinational economic considerations increasingly shaped U.S. foreign policy. Despite China's human rights abuses and one-party rule, Clinton welcomed Chinese president Jiang Zemin in 1997 and visited China in 1998. This reflected economic realities. In 2000, U.S. imports from China surpassed $100 billion, making it America's fourth largest trading partner, after Canada, Mexico, and Japan.

In 1997–1998, a banking and credit crisis threatened the booming export economies of Thailand, South Korea, Indonesia, and other Asian nations, and indirectly jeopardized the U.S. economy. The International Monetary Fund, a Washington-based agency to which the United States is the largest contributor, put together a $40 billion bailout package to stabilize the situation. As the crisis spread to Japan, the Clinton administration pressed that country to undertake economic reforms. When Brazil and Argentina also sank into recession, U.S. prosperity looked increasingly vulnerable. All this underscored how deeply the United States had become enmeshed in a complex global economy.

Affluence and a Search for Heroes   The economic boom produced vast wealth for some and an orgy of consumption that set the decade's tone. Wall Street and Silicon Valley spawned thousands of youthful millionaires.

Surveying the lifestyles of the newly rich in 1997, *Vanity Fair* magazine described New York as "the champagne city, making the brash consumption of the 1980s look like the depression." Elegant restaurants offered absurdly expensive cigars and wines; exclusive shops sold $13,000 handbags. In 1999, the nation's top one hundred advertisers spent $43 billion promoting their goods.

Attendance at the Disney theme parks in Florida and California neared 30 - million in 2000. The sales of gas guzzling sport-utility vehicles (SUVs) soared. When a White House press secretary was asked in 2001 if people should reduce consumption to conserve energy, he replied, "[I]t should be the goal of policy makers to protect the American way of life—the American way of life is a blessed one."

The boom encouraged a hard-edged "winner take all" mentality like that of the Gilded Age, when the rich turned their backs on the rest of society. In *Bowling Alone: The Collapse and Revival of American Community* (2000), political scientist Robert Putnam found diminished civic engagement; weakened interest in public affairs; and a more self-absorbed, individualistic society. *The Prayer of Jabez* (2000), a best-selling motivational book, cited a shepherd's prayer recorded in the Bible ("Bless me indeed, and enlarge my territory") as a key to success. "If Jabez had worked on Wall Street," wrote the author, "he might have prayed 'Lord, increase the value of my investment portfolio.'"

(Cal Warlick)

The Mcmansion: Domestic Architecture As Conspicuous Consumption *As some Americans grew rich in the boom years of the 1980s and 1990s, ostentatious and pretentious houses, nicknamed McMansions, sprang up across the country.*

The mass culture offered escapist fare. The 1997 film *Titanic* grossed $600 million. The top-rated TV show of 1999–2000, *Who Wants to Be a Millionaire?*, celebrated raw greed. So-called reality shows like *Survivor* offered viewers a risk-free taste of challenges that contemporary American life itself conspicuously lacked, at least for the privileged insulated from life's harsher realities.

Millions followed TV coverage of the 1995 trial of O. J. Simpson, a former football star accused of killing his former wife and her friend. The 1996 murder of a six-year-old Colorado girl whose parents had pushed her into child beauty pageants similarly mesmerized the public. The Clinton sex scandals often seemed little more than another media diversion in a sensation-hungry decade.

But the popular culture also offered evidence of more complex social crosscurrents. Some critics interpreted *Titanic,* which sided with its working-class hero in steerage against the rich snobs in first class, as a comment on America's widening class differences. One even called the movie "an exercise in class hatred." Dissatisfaction with a materialistic culture and money-driven politics, some suggested, found expression in bestselling books about past heroes and more heroic times, such as Stephen Ambrose's *Eisenhower* (1991); David McCullough's *Truman* (1993); and Tom Brokaw's *The Greatest Generation* (1998), about the GIs who fought in World War II.

The 2001 film *Pearl Harbor,* argued critic Frank Rich, reflected a longing "for what is missing in our national life: some cause larger than ourselves." Concluded Rich: "Even those Americans who are...foggy about World War II...know intuitively that it was fought over something more blessed than the right to guzzle gas."

The AIDS Epidemic Rages On; Outbursts of Violence Stir Concern	Beneath the glow of prosperity, darker currents stirred. The AIDS crisis continued its deadly course. By 2000, U.S. deaths surpassed 458,000, with more new cases of AIDS and HIV, an infection that often precedes full-blown AIDS, diagnosed each year. As knowledge about preventive measures spread and medications were developed to treat HIV, the crisis

abated somewhat by the early twenty-first century—but it was far from over. Tony Kushner's two-part play *Angels in America* (1991–1992), and the long-running rock musical *Rent* (1996), an update of the opera *La Bohème,* explored the human and cultural impact of AIDS. As the disease spread worldwide, Africa was particularly hard hit.

A popular 1999 film, *American Beauty,* and TV's *The Sopranos,* an HBO series about a mobster and his family, explored dark impulses and a violent substratum in American life. The violence was not limited to pop-culture fantasy. True, overall crime rates fell nearly 20 percent between 1992 and 2000—a decline that experts attributed to prosperity, a drop in the young male population, the waning crack cocaine epidemic, and tougher sentencing rules. (The prison population approached 2 million by 2000.) But violent outbursts punctuated the decade. Gun deaths exceeded twenty-eight thousand in 2000. In April 1999, two students at Columbine High School near Denver fatally shot twelve students and a teacher before committing suicide. After this massacre, President Clinton called for stricter gun-control laws, but the National Rifle Association fought such efforts.

The violence sometimes arose from the culture wars. In 1998, two youths tortured and murdered a gay student at the University of Wyoming, Matthew Shepard, because of his sexual orientation. As the abortion controversy raged, some "pro-life" advocates turned violent. In the 1990s, at least five physicians who performed abortions or staff members at clinics providing this service were murdered, and other clinics were bombed.

On April 19, 1995, in the decade's worst incident of mass violence, explosives concealed in a rental truck demolished a federal office building in Oklahoma City, killing 168, including nineteen children in a day-care center. Police soon arrested Timothy McVeigh, a Gulf War veteran obsessed with conspiracy theories. McVeigh, convicted of murder, was executed in 2001. A co-conspirator, Terry Nichols, received a life sentence.

The **Oklahoma City bombing** came precisely two years after an April 1993 government raid on the Waco, Texas, compound of the Branch Davidians, an apocalyptic religious sect led by David Koresh, charged with firearms violations. An earlier confrontation at Waco had left four government agents and six Davidians dead. The April raid ended tragically when fires inside the compound, probably set by Koresh and others, killed some eighty Davidians as federal tanks moved in. Timothy McVeigh boasted that his Oklahoma City attack represented retaliation for Waco.

Culture Wars: A Broader View   While the 1990s' culture wars typically did not descend into violence, they did involve fierce contests that some viewed as a struggle for the nation's soul. During the Cold War, the ideological menace had centered in Moscow. Now, many Americans projected the same black-and-white worldview onto the homefront culture, and searched for the enemy within.

The struggle unfolded on many fronts, from televangelists' programs, bookstore shelves, and radio talk shows to school-board protests and demonstrations at family-planning clinics. Some endorsed a constitutional amendment permitting prayer in public school classrooms; others criticized history textbooks as insufficiently patriotic or excessively multicultural. In 1995, the Smithsonian Institution radically scaled back a planned exhibit marking the fiftieth anniversary of the atomic bombing of Hiroshima and Nagasaki when politicians and veterans' organizations criticized it for graphically documenting the bombs' human toll and for presenting differing contemporary views of the bombings.

As gays and lesbians grew more vocal politically (and more visible in the media), conservatives resisted their demands for equality. The Southern Baptist Convention, America's largest Protestant denomination, urged a boycott of Disney World for unofficially sponsoring "Gay Pride" days.

The fast-growing evangelical movement denounced the nation's alleged moral decline. In 1997, thousands of men representing a conservative Protestant movement called Promise Keepers rallied in Washington, D.C., for a day of prayer, hymn singing, and pledges to reclaim leadership of their families. Bill Clinton's misdeeds underscored for conservatives the moral rot they saw eating away at America. Activists even complained about Republican politicians who courted their votes but ignored their agenda once in power.

Pat Robertson's *The New World Order* (1991) interpreted world history as a vast conspiracy that will soon end in the rule of the Antichrist. The best-selling *Left Behind* series of novels (1995–2004), coauthored by the conservative activist

Tim LaHaye, described an approaching end time when satanic forces will take over America and the world, until Jesus Christ returns to destroy all evildoers and establish a righteous kingdom.

But for whom did the culture warriors speak? In *One Nation After All* (1998), sociologist Alan Wolfe found most contemporary Americans surprisingly tolerant of diverse views and lifestyles. "[T]here is little truth to the charge that middle-class Americans, divided by a culture war, have split into two hostile camps," Wolfe concluded. "Middle-class Americans, in their heart of hearts, are desperate that we once again become one nation."

CHRONOLOGY
1980–2000

1980	Ronald Reagan elected president.
1981	Major cuts in taxes and domestic spending. Large increases in military budget.
1982	Equal Rights Amendment dies. CIA funds contra war against Nicaragua's Sandinistas. Central Park rally for nuclear weapons freeze.
1983	239 U.S. marines die in Beirut terrorist attack. U.S. deploys Pershing II and cruise missiles in Europe. Reagan proposes Strategic Defense Initiative (Star Wars). U.S. invasion of Grenada.
1984	Reagan defeats Walter Mondale to win second presidential term.
1984–1986	Congress bars military aid to contras.
1985	Rash of airline hijackings and other terrorist acts.
1986	Congress passes South African sanctions. Immigration Reform and Control Act.
1987	Congressional hearings on Iran-contra scandal. Stock-market crash.
1988	Reagan trip to Moscow. George H. W. Bush elected president.
1989	Massive Alaskan oil spill by *Exxon Valdez*. Supreme Court, in several 5-to-4 decisions, restricts civil-rights laws. China's rulers crush prodemocracy movement. Berlin Wall is torn down.
1990	Federal Clean Air Act strengthened. Americans with Disabilities Act passed. Iraq invades Kuwait. Recession (1990–1993). Germany reunified; Soviet troops start withdrawal from Eastern Europe.
1991	Persian Gulf War (Operation Desert Storm). Hearings on Clarence Thomas's Supreme Court nomination. Collapse of Soviet Union.

1992	Supreme Court in *Planned Parenthood v. Casey* approves abortion restrictions but upholds *Roe v. Wade*.
	President Bush commits U.S. troops in Somalia.
	Bill Clinton elected president.
1993	Congress approves NAFTA treaty.
	Economy expands, stock market surges (1993–2000).
	Clinton health-care reform plan fails (1993–1994).
	Eighty Branch Davidians die in fire as federal agents raid compound in Waco, Texas.
	World Trade Center bombing kills six.
1994	Christian Coalition gains control of Republican Party in several states.
	Yasir Arafat and Yitzhak Rabin sign Oslo Accords at White House.
	Clinton withdraws U.S. forces from Somalia.
	United States joins the World Trade Organization (WTO).
	Republicans proclaim "Contract with America" and win control of House and Senate; Newt Gingrich becomes Speaker.
1995	Oklahoma City federal building bombed.
	Dayton Accords achieve cease-fire in Bosnia; Clinton commits U.S. troops to enforce agreement.
1996	Welfare Reform Act.
	Clinton defeats Robert Dole to win second presidential term.
1997	Congressional battle over tobacco industry regulation.
1998	Clinton impeached by House of Representatives in sex scandal.
1999	Senate dismisses impeachment charges.
	Columbine High School shootings.
	U.S. and NATO forces intervene in Kosovo.
2000	George W. Bush wins presidency when Supreme Court ends Florida election dispute.

CONCLUSION

Conservative mobilization dating to the 1950s and accelerating in the 1970s prepared the way for Ronald Reagan's election as president in 1980. Many Americans welcomed Reagan's optimism, patriotism, conservative cultural values, and political ideology stressing free enterprise and smaller government coupled with military might and aggressive anticommunism. Tax cuts, less business regulation, military spending increases, and rhetorical attacks on the Soviet Union marked Reagan's first term.

The Iran-contra scandal, involving the administration's secret military aid to Iran and illegal funding of a campaign to overthrow Nicaragua's leftist regime, preoccupied the nation in 1987 but left Reagan largely unscathed. U.S.-Soviet relations improved dramatically during Reagan's second term as Soviet leader Mikhail Gorbachev, facing economic and political problems at home and unrest in the Soviet sphere, took conciliatory steps that signaled the Cold War's end. However, conflict in the Middle East and an upsurge of terrorism foretold fresh hazards ahead.

The 1980s, though bracketed by a recession and a stock-market crash, saw a boom that brought prosperity to many. However, a persistent trade gap, massive federal deficits linked to Reagan's tax cuts, and a continuing erosion of factory jobs raised warning flags.

Reagan's successor, George H. W. Bush, mobilized an international coalition to drive Iraqi forces from Kuwait. Domestically, however, Bush proved ineffectual, and in 1992 he lost to Arkansas governor Bill Clinton, a Democratic moderate.

The failure of Clinton's sweeping health-care reform plan, coupled with other missteps, laid the groundwork for a Republican landslide in the 1994 midterm elections. Adapting to the more conservative political climate, Clinton signed a welfare-reform bill sponsored by Republicans. A rebounding economy and stock-market boom helped Clinton's political standing. While the good times benefited some, inner-city residents and displaced industrial workers did not share in the general prosperity.

Internationally, the Clinton administration worked to combat nuclear proliferation and joined in multinational efforts to halt ethnic violence in the Balkans. Clinton stood aside as genocidal slaughter overwhelmed Rwanda, however, and despite his peacemaking efforts, the Israeli-Palestinian conflict raged on.

Caught in lies intended to conceal an embarrassing sex scandal, Clinton was impeached by a partisan House of Representatives. Though he escaped removal from office, his reputation suffered. In the disputed 2000 presidential election, finally resolved by the Supreme Court, George W. Bush, son of the former President Bush, defeated Vice President Al Gore.

In a nation awash with new wealth, conspicuous consumption set the cultural tone of the 1990s. However, the continuing scourge of AIDS and outbursts of violence, from school shootings to a catastrophic bombing in Oklahoma City, coupled with angry cultural dissension and a sometimes poisonous political climate, left many citizens feeling apprehensive as the nation entered a new century. Despite the culture wars, however, signs of reconciliation could also be seen.

31

GLOBAL DANGERS, GLOBAL
CHALLENGES, 2001 TO THE PRESENT

CHAPTER OUTLINE

• America Under Attack: September 11, 2001, and Its Aftermath • Politics
and the Economy as a New Century Begins • Debating Iraq and Confronting
Other Global Challenges • Social and Economic Trends in Contemporary
America • A Floundering Administration Yields to a Renewed Vision

---

AMERICA UNDER ATTACK: SEPTEMBER 11, 2001, AND ITS AFTERMATH

On September 11, 2001, a devastating attack horrified the nation. President George
W. Bush mobilized a multinational coalition to invade Afghanistan, stronghold of
al Qaeda, the organization responsible. Bush also secured new laws and reorga-
nized federal agencies to tighten homeland security. Accusing Iraq's dictator
Saddam Hussein of complicity in the 9/11 attacks, Bush launched an invasion of
Iraq as well.

**A New
Administration,
a Day of Horror**
Assuming the presidency in January 2001, George W. Bush
named **Colin Powell,** former head of the Joint Chiefs of
Staff, as secretary of state, making him the highest-ranking
African-American to serve in a presidential administration.
Condoleezza Rice, a Russian specialist at Stanford University, also African-
American, became national security adviser. Other appointees were, like Vice Presi-
dent **Richard (Dick) Cheney,** veterans of earlier Republican administrations with
corporate ties. Secretary of Defense **Donald Rumsfeld** held the same post under
President Ford and later headed a pharmaceutical company. Ultraconservative
John Ashcroft became attorney general.

Launching his administration, Bush proposed education reforms, tax cuts favoring the wealthy, an energy bill shaped by the energy industries, and initiatives welcomed by his conservative Christian base (as discussed later in this chapter). Apart from this, Bush seemed unfocused and attentive mainly to his core supporters. As the year wore on, his approval ratings fell. This changed dramatically on **September 11, 2001,** a day of horror that energized the administration and dominated Bush's remaining years in office.

On that morning, three commercial airliners hijacked by terrorists slammed into the Pentagon and the twin towers of New York's World Trade Center. As the blazing towers collapsed, 2,752 men and women met their deaths, including nearly 350 firefighters and twenty-three police officers. The Pentagon attack left 245 dead on the ground. A fourth plane crashed in Pennsylvania when heroic passengers overpowered the hijackers. Nearly 250 passengers and crew in the four planes perished. When investigators identified the nineteen hijackers as Muslims from the Middle East, President Bush urged Americans to distinguish between a few terrorists and the world's 1.2 billion Muslims, including some 6 million in the United States. Islamic leaders worldwide repudiated the attacks, although demonstrators in some Arab cities and Palestinian refugee camps celebrated.

As the nation mourned, political divisions faded. The World War II anthem "God Bless America" enjoyed renewed popularity. "United We Stand" proclaimed billboards and bumper stickers. The damaged New York Stock Exchange reopened after six days, but consumer confidence remained fragile. The airline and hospitality industries reeled as jittery travelers canceled trips. Anxiety increased in October, when letters containing deadly anthrax spores appeared in the offices of NBC News, two senators, and a tabloid newspaper. Five persons, including two postal workers, died from anthrax-tainted mail. In 2008, Dr. Bruce Ivins—a researcher at a U.S. Army biological defense research laboratory at Fort Detrick in Frederick, Maryland—committed suicide after the FBI identified him as the likely perpetrator.

Confronting al Qaeda in Afghanistan

President Bush declared the attacks an "act of war," and on September 14 the Senate unanimously authorized Bush to use "all necessary and appropriate force" to retaliate and to prevent future terrorist attacks. The President's approval ratings neared 90 percent. On September 20, before a joint session of Congress, Bush blamed **al Qaeda** ("the base"), an organization headed by Osama bin Laden in Afghanistan. Bin Laden, already under indictment for the 1998 attack on U.S. embassies in Africa, had long denounced America for supporting Israel and for stationing "infidel" troops on Saudi soil.

Bush also targeted the Taliban, a Pakistan-based Muslim fundamentalist movement that controlled Afghanistan since 1996. This U.S. effort enjoyed NATO backing and broad international support, led by British prime minister Tony Blair. Pakistan's military government endorsed Bush's decision to invade despite Taliban enclaves in Pakistan's border regions. On October 7, a U.S.-led coalition of forces launched the attack.

The Taliban soon surrendered Kabul, the Afghan capital (see Map 31.1), and by mid-December, the U.S.-led coalition claimed victory. Hundreds of captured prisoners were sent to the U.S. base in **Guantánamo Bay,** Cuba. In June 2002, with U.S. support, Afghan tribal leaders named an interim prime minister, Hamid Karzai. However, Osama bin Laden, Taliban leader Mullah Omar, and many al Qaeda loyalists retreated to Afghanistan's mountainous border with Pakistan—prepared to fight on.

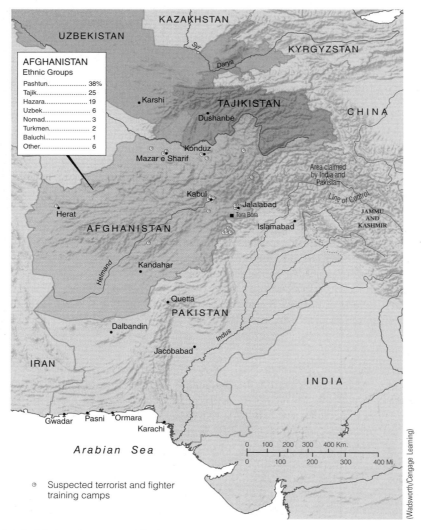

MAP 31.1 Afghanistan and Pakistan

After the attacks of September 11, 2001, U.S. and NATO forces attacked the terrorist organization al Qaeda, based in Afghanistan. The country's radical Islamist Taliban regime was overthrown, but many fighters retreated to the mountains along the Afghanistan-Pakistan border. Afghanistan remained violent and unsettled, and al Qaeda leader Osama bin Laden was still at large.

A Grieving Nation *Rescuers remove a flag-draped body from the ruins of the World Trade Center.*

Tightening Home-Front Security   Congress late in 2001 created the Transportation Security Administration to oversee an expanded force of twenty-eight thousand airport security personnel. Over the protests of civil liberties advocates and some local officials, the Justice Department rounded up hundreds of Middle Easterners in the United States, some for minor visa violations, and held them without filing charges or even revealing their names.

The **USA-Patriot Act,** the administration's sweeping antiterrorist bill passed by Congress in October 2001, granted the government authority to monitor telephone and e-mail communications. Civil libertarians and others protested this expansion of federal power. (Congress renewed the Patriot Act in 2005, with some added civil liberties safeguards.)

Further questions arose as the media reported missed clues before the 9/11 attack. Through the summer of 2001, President Bush's daily security briefings included warnings of an al Qaeda plot to hijack a U.S. airliner. In August 2001, the FBI bungled a Minnesota flight school's warning that a suspicious person named Zacarias Moussaoui wanted to enroll. (Later linked to the 9/11 plot, Moussaoui was arrested, tried, and sentenced to life imprisonment.)

In November 2002, Congress created a new cabinet level **Department of Homeland Security,** which absorbed the Federal Emergency Management Agency (FEMA), the Immigration and Naturalization Service, and other agencies. The FBI and the CIA remained independent, however. Skeptics questioned whether such a bureaucratic reshuffling actually increased security.

In 2003, Bush named a bipartisan commission to examine pre-9/11 intelligence failures. Its report pinpointed communication lapses between the FBI and the CIA and urged a restructuring of U.S. intelligence operations. In 2005, Bush appointed a Director of National Intelligence to coordinate the government's fifteen different intelligence agencies. Nevertheless, when the commission's cochair was asked about homeland security in 2006, he replied: "A lot of the things we need to do... to prevent another 9/11 just simply aren't being done." Critics noted, for example, that most incoming shipping containers went unchecked.

War in Iraq, 2003–2004 Although Afghanistan remained unstable and Osama bin Laden uncaptured, the administration's attention shifted elsewhere. In his January 2002 State of the Union address, President Bush called Iran, Iraq, and North Korea an "axis of evil." He especially targeted Iraq's ruler, Saddam Hussein, weakened but still in power following the 1991 Persian Gulf War. In a barrage of coordinated speeches and interviews, Cheney, Rumsfeld, Rice, and other officials accused Saddam of complicity in the 9/11 attacks and of developing nuclear, chemical, and biological weapons. The Bush administration clearly believed an invasion of Iraq was necessary and justified.

This focus on Iraq was orchestrated by a close-knit group of Republican **neoconservatives,** including Cheney, Rumsfeld, and their key aides. (The term, meaning "new conservatives," originally applied to Democrats who switched to the Republican Party when the Democratic Party moved leftward in the 1960s.)

Throughout the Cold War, some hardliners rejected George Kennan's Containment doctrine, advocating instead a policy of overwhelming U.S. military superiority and aggressive challenges to Soviet power. With the Soviet Union's collapse, neoconservatives shifted focus but continued to advocate the aggressive projection of U.S. power worldwide. Any actual or potential threat to America's global interests, they insisted, must be resisted by all available means, including preemptive military action. While NATO and other alliances had their uses, and the UN might sometimes serve U.S. purposes, America must primarily act alone in defense of its interests.

These neoconservatives had little patience with the "soft diplomacy" of winning hearts and minds, courting world opinion, or spreading U.S. values of democracy and freedom by example rather than by force. For them, the traditional foreign policy goal of resolving conflict by compromise conveyed weakness. The point was not to negotiate with adversaries, but to defeat them.

Neoconservatives attacked presidents Carter and Clinton as overly preoccupied with world opinion and too reluctant to use U.S. military power. But they also criticized Republicans: Nixon and Kissinger for their amoral "realism" in dealing with China and the Soviet Union; Reagan-era diplomats for diluting Reagan's "evil empire" rhetoric with an over-reliance on diplomacy; and the first President Bush for failing to overthrow Saddam Hussein in the Persian Gulf War.

In the Middle East, neoconservatives focused on defending Israel, assuring the flow of oil to meet U.S. energy needs, and promoting democracy, in the belief that democracies are less likely than repressive regimes to engage in military aggression.

Ending Saddam Hussein's dictatorship, they believed, was crucial to advancing U.S. interests in the region.

George W. Bush's election gave neoconservatives the opportunity to put their ideology into practice. Although Cheney, Rumsfeld, and their top aides were its real architects, the administration's foreign policy approach, particularly in Bush's first term, came to be called the "Bush Doctrine" because Bush was its public spokesperson, clothing it with an aura of religious certitude. America must "rid the world of evil" he proclaimed after 9/11. "The liberty we prize," he added in his 2003 State of the Union address, "is not America's gift to the world, it is God's gift to humanity." Defense Secretary Rumsfeld adorned Iraq combat reports he prepared for Bush with biblical passages proclaiming the triumph of righteousness.

Although a majority of Americans initially supported military intervention in Iraq, the action proved controversial from the outset. Critics challenged the administration to prove its claims. A preemptive war would violate U.S. principles, they charged, and could drag on for years, outrage the Muslim world, and divert attention from Afghanistan. Great Britain's Tony Blair backed the administration, but other NATO allies, along with most Arab leaders, objected.

Nevertheless, in October 2002, Congress authorized President Bush to "defend the national security... against the continuing threat posed by Iraq." While Republicans supported the resolution, Democrats were divided, with some fearful of opposing a resolution Bush called vital to American security. As Lyndon Johnson had cited the Gulf of Tonkin Resolution to justify his Vietnam War escalation, so President Bush used this resolution to justify invading Iraq.

Bolstered by the 2002 midterm elections, in which Republicans regained control of the Senate and increased their House majority, the administration pushed its Iraq invasion plans. The Americans would be welcomed as liberators, predicted Vice President Cheney. Victory would be a "slam dunk," the CIA director assured Bush. In a February 2003 UN speech, Secretary of State Colin Powell, relying on CIA evidence, insisted that Saddam Hussein was developing weapons of mass destruction (WMDs).

On March 19, 2003, U.S. cruise missiles hit Baghdad. Two days later, U.S. and British troops invaded southern Iraq, populated by Shi'ite Muslims, brutally oppressed by Saddam. Securing the region's oil fields, the invaders moved north (see Map 31.2). Despite unexpected guerrilla resistance, the U.S. commander, General Tommy Franks, foresaw quick victory. In early April, U.S. troops occupied Baghdad and toppled a large statue of Saddam. As the regime fell and Saddam fled, basic municipal services collapsed and widespread looting erupted.

On May 1, aboard the aircraft carrier *Abraham Lincoln* off San Diego, President Bush declared: "[M]ajor combat operations in Iraq have ended." A banner behind him proclaimed "Mission Accomplished." Bush named Paul Bremer, a Foreign Service officer, to administer affairs in Iraq. In December, Saddam was captured. In two trials before a special tribunal of Iraqi judges, Saddam was convicted of human-rights abuses in genocidal attacks on Iraq's Kurdish and Shi'ite populations. He was hanged in December 2006. Human-rights organizations criticized procedural aspects of the trials, and Saddam's hardcore supporters protested, but the outcome otherwise met general approval.

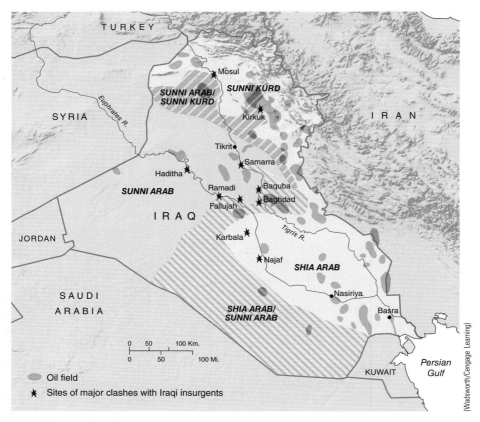

(Wadsworth/Cengage Learning)

MAP 31.2 Iraq

With Saddam Hussein's overthrow by U.S.-led forces in 2003, violence erupted among Iraq's ethnic and religious groups, including the majority Shia Muslims concentrated in the southeast and the minority Sunni Muslims, who ruled the country under Saddam.

Iraq's Sunni Muslims, though a minority, long dominated Iraqi politics. Resenting their loss of power, they mobilized to expel the invaders. Radical Muslim fighters from outside Iraq added to the unrest. So did a young anti-American Shi'ite cleric, Moqtada al-Sadr, popular among Baghdad's poor.

Conditions worsened through 2004, with frequent kidnappings, suicide bombings, and deadly highway blasts caused by improvised explosive devices (IEDs). In June, Bremer transferred power to a provisional Iraqi government, but little changed. By September, the toll of U.S. dead in Iraq passed one thousand. The campaign the Bush team had launched so confidently seemed bogged down. Secretary of State Powell, who privately opposed the war, resigned in November. Bush named Condoleezza Rice to replace him.

Politics and the Economy as a New Century Begins

While pursuing the post–9/11 "war on terror," the early Bush administration also proposed tax cuts and other domestic legislation reflecting its conservative ideology. Debate over these measures unfolded amid a recession and a cascade of bankruptcies and corporate scandals.

Economic Reverses and Corporate Scandals   George W. Bush's presidency began with a short but sharp recession. The high flying Silicon Valley IT companies led the downturn. An estimated 250 such businesses collapsed in a few months. As the market value of the surviving companies plummeted, instant millionaires watched their portfolios shrivel.

The recession soon spread. The stock market fell by 24 percent. Industrial production dropped; unemployment rose. By mid-2003, 2.6 million workers had lost their jobs. The Bush administration, having inherited a budget surplus, now projected years of deficits. To stimulate recovery, the Federal Reserve Board cut interest rates eleven times in 2001, to a forty-year low. A wave of corporate bankruptcies and scandals in the energy and telecommunications fields further eroded investor confidence. Houston's Enron Corporation, with close ties to the administration, was an early casualty. A marketer of electric power that had moved into utilities and telecommunications, Enron in 2000 claimed revenues of $101 billion and ranked seventh among America's corporations. The end came with brutal swiftness in 2001 when Enron filed for bankruptcy and admitted to falsifying profit reports. More than five thousand jobless Enron workers also lost their retirement funds, consisting mostly of Enron stock. Shortly before the collapse, the company's top officials sold their Enron stock, profiting handsomely. In 2006, a Houston jury convicted Enron founder Kenneth Lay and the company's CEO Jeffrey Skilling on multiple counts of fraud and conspiracy. The company's logo—a crooked "E"—seemed appropriate.

In 2002, America's second-largest telecommunications company, WorldCom, admitted to falsifying its annual reports, filed for bankruptcy, and fired seventeen thousand employees. WorldCom's CEO, convicted of securities fraud, received a twenty-five-year prison sentence.

In September 2002, Dennis Kozlowski, the CEO of Tyco, an industrial-products company, was indicted for looting the company of $600 million, including $2 million for his wife's birthday party on a Mediterranean island. Along with a prison sentence, Kozlowski was fined $70 million and ordered to repay Tyco $134 million.

Declared a Wall Street investment banker: "I cannot think of a time when business… has been held in less repute." The University of Maryland business school organized field trips to penitentiaries where imprisoned executives lectured students on honesty. Responding to public anger, Congress in July 2002 imposed stricter financial reporting rules on corporations and toughened criminal penalties for business fraud.

Recovery began in 2003, stimulated by heavy consumer spending (much of it on credit), and a booming housing market. But prosperity was spotty. While the average real income of the nation's richest 1 percent increased by more than 12 percent in 2004, that of the remaining 99 percent grew by only 1.5 percent. Real wages remained flat and job creation weak. Observed economist Paul Krugman: "It's a great economy if you're a high-level corporate executive or someone who owns a lot of stock. For most other Americans, economic growth is a spectator sport." By mid-2006, even this uneven recovery faltered, and the jittery stock market again sank. The worst recession since the 1930s lay ahead.

The Republican Domestic Agenda   In February 2001, President Bush proposed $1.6 trillion in income-tax cuts over a ten-year period. Though the measure reduced all rates, wealthy taxpayers received the highest percentage reduction. The cuts would stimulate investment, Bush argued. Democrats attacked the bill for favoring the rich, and warned that such deep cuts would produce even larger federal deficits.

In May, Congress passed a $1.35 trillion tax cut somewhat less slanted toward the rich. Mounting budget deficits predictably followed, erasing the surplus Clinton had achieved. Nevertheless, the Republican-led Congress cut taxes further in 2003 and 2005.

The administration's 2001 energy bill emerged from secret meetings of oil and gas executives with Vice President Cheney (a former head of energy company Halliburton). Enron's Kenneth Lay, a major GOP contributor, played a key role. The bill eased environmental regulations on energy companies and provided tax incentives to expand coal, oil, nuclear power, and natural gas production, including drilling in Alaska's **Arctic National Wildlife Refuge** (ANWR).

The bill Congress eventually passed in 2005 granted generous tax breaks to energy companies, exempted them from some environmental laws, and eased the permit process for drilling or mining on public lands. Congress rejected drilling in ANWR and offered tax credits for purchasing hybrid vehicles and energy-efficient appliances. Incentives for research on renewable and cleaner energy sources, including ethanol made from corn, pleased corn-belt politicians. Despite lobbying by environmental groups, Congress did not tighten vehicle fuel-efficiency requirements. Overall, the law pleased the energy companies that helped draft it.

Bush's education program, labeled **"No Child Left Behind,"** passed by Congress in 2001 with bipartisan support, required states to administer standardized reading and math tests in grades four and eight. Schools that failed to raise test scores were required to introduce remedial programs. If test scores still failed to improve, schools faced the loss of federal funds and other penalties. Critics worried that teachers would focus too exclusively on the tested subjects. Others warned of federal intrusion in public education, traditionally a local matter. As test data accumulated, results proved mixed.

Reflecting Republicans' preference for private-sector solutions to social problems, the administration also supported school vouchers, by which children in poorly performing public schools could receive grants to enroll in private schools, mostly church-sponsored. Milwaukee introduced vouchers in 1990, but such programs met court challenges, on grounds that they violated the First Amendment separation of church and state. While many supported the voucher idea as a creative response to public-school problems, others, including the teachers' unions, criticized vouchers for draining tax dollars from the public schools and allowing private schools to "cherry pick" the most promising applicants. Congressional Democrats rejected Bush's call for a federally-funded voucher program.

Many education reformers also supported charter schools, which gain exemption from many regulations governing traditional public schools in exchange for agreeing to contracts, typically for a 3–5 year period, mandating specific student achievement goals. By 2009, charter schools across the nation enrolled more than a million students. This attention to school reform suggested that the nation's public education system did, indeed, need strengthening—particularly in a globalizing economy and an information-based job market.

Rewarding his conservative religious supporters, Bush created an Office of Faith-Based and Community Initiatives to funnel tax dollars to church-run social programs. Grants went to antiabortion groups, organizations promoting teenage sexual abstinence, and evangelical prison ministries. A charity operated by televangelist Pat Robertson received $22 million.

President Bush pleased abortion opponents by restricting stem-cell research. Stem cells are produced during an early stage of human embryo development, and fertility clinics often have "surplus" fertilized embryos. Since stem cells can develop into more specialized human cells, they are valuable for medical research. Some anti-abortion groups oppose research using fertilized embryos, however. In 2001, Bush barred federal funding for research involving stem cells harvested from human embryos in the future.

(John Domines/Time Life Pictures/Getty Images)

Musk Oxen in Alaska's Arctic National Wildlife Refuge *Proposals by the George W. Bush administration to permit oil drilling in the refuge stirred controversy.*

Committed to a free-market ideology, Bush's appointees throughout the federal bureaucracy reduced regulatory oversight of business and finance and weakened environmental and consumer protection laws.

Campaign Finance Reform and the 2004 Election

Reform-minded legislators who deplored the role of money in politics targeted so-called soft money contributions to political parties that then flowed on to specific candidates. In the 2000 election, soft money contributions reached $400 million. Big contributors ranged from (mostly Republican) business lobbies, anti-abortion groups, and the National Rifle Association to (mostly Democratic) labor unions, trial lawyers, and teachers' unions.

In 2002, President Bush signed a campaign finance reform bill cosponsored by Arizona Republican senator John McCain and Wisconsin Democrat Russell Feingold. Among other provisions, it banned soft money contributions and restricted TV "issue ads" designed to influence elections. As big contributors sought ways around the law, its impact remained uncertain. In 2007, the Supreme Court, on First Amendment free speech grounds, restricted the law's ban on pre-election "issue ads."

As the 2004 election approached, Howard Dean, a former Vermont governor, emerged as the early frontrunner for the Democratic presidential nomination. Criticizing the Iraq War and appealing directly to voters as Jimmy Carter had done in 1976, Dean built a following via the Internet, especially on college campuses. His campaign faded, however, when he trailed in the Iowa primary behind senators **John Kerry** of Massachusetts and John Edwards of North Carolina. Nevertheless, Dean tapped into growing opposition to the Iraq War and demonstrated the Internet's political potential.

Kerry won the nomination, and chose Edwards, a former trial lawyer, as his running mate. Democratic strategists hoped Kerry's distinguished Vietnam War record would neutralize charges of Democratic weakness on defense while underscoring Bush's avoidance of service in Vietnam. Kerry, a Catholic, wooed pro-Bush evangelicals. "I don't wear my religion on my sleeve," he said, "but faith has given me values and hope to live by." Bush and Cheney, raising some $150 million from corporations and wealthy individual donors, again headed the Republican ticket.

Although Kerry had voted for the Patriot Act and initially supported the Iraq War, he now accused Bush of misleading the nation and criticized parts of the Patriot Act as threats to civil liberties. He also called for stricter environmental laws, tougher fuel-efficiency standards, and support for renewable energy.

President Bush defended both the Iraq War and the Patriot Act. Citing Kerry's changing positions, Republicans accused him of "flip-flopping" and indecisiveness. Anti-Kerry TV commercials, funded by a shadowy group called Swift Boat Veterans for Truth supposedly independent of the Republican campaign, questioned his Vietnam record.

The candidates' differences on abortion, the death penalty, gun control, and other issues reflected national divisions. The issue of same-sex marriage loomed large. In 2004, San Francisco's mayor challenged California law by marrying same-sex couples, and the Massachusetts Supreme Court ruled that banning same-sex marriage violated the state constitution's equal rights clause. The issue energized religious conservatives, who applauded Bush's call for a constitutional amendment banning gay marriage. Antigay marriage referenda, on the ballot in eleven states, passed in all eleven. Bush carried nine of the eleven, including Ohio, a key swing state that determined the election's outcome.

Bush won a second term, garnering 50.7 percent of the popular vote. Republicans gained a net of four Senate seats and four House seats. A tax-cutting president seen as a leader in the "war on terror" and a defender of embattled conservative cultural values had eked out a razor-thin victory.

Democrats took heart from the fact that Kerry won 55 percent of voters under thirty, a growing cohort. In Illinois, a charismatic young African-American Democratic state legislator, Barack Obama, won election to the U.S. Senate.

The election highlighted the Internet's political role. During the campaign and after, MoveOn.org, a website initially launched to oppose President Clinton's impeachment and later devoted to rallying opposition to the Iraq War, raised funds and mobilized e-mails and telephone calls on behalf of liberal candidates and causes. While conservative organizations had long built support through magazines, direct mail, and talk radio, liberals appeared to have the edge in Internet-based activism, especially among young people.

Conservative political groups and those on the religious right, some dating to the 1970s, remained active. But so did progressive organizations such as People for the American Way, Planned Parenthood, the Sierra Club, and Emily's List (which supported women candidates who endorsed liberal and feminist goals). Even among evangelical Christians, support for Bush was not unanimous. Jim Wallis of the evangelical Sojourners movement espoused social justice and the search for peace in his books and *Sojourners* magazine.

DEBATING IRAQ AND CONFRONTING OTHER GLOBAL CHALLENGES

As the Iraq conflict dragged on, home-front support eroded. Revelations of prisoner abuse, illegal spying on U.S. citizens, and serious distortions in the administration's case for invading Iraq sapped Bush's standing at home and abroad. The Israeli-Palestinian struggle, nuclear proliferation threats, and concern about global warming posed further challenges.

The Continuing Struggle in Iraq In his second inaugural address in January 2005, Bush described the Iraq War as part of a noble campaign to "[end] tyranny in our world." In Iraq, however, conditions worsened. Sunni insurgents in Baghdad and in Sunni strongholds north of the capital battled to prevent a Shiite-dominated government. A November 2004 anti-insurgent operation in Fallujah involved approximately ten thousand U.S. and Iraqi forces. Typically, however, the insurgents returned after the troops withdrew. Followers of the radical Shi'ite cleric Moqtada al-Sadr attacked Sunnis, GIs, journalists, and foreign contractors alike. Muslim militants from elsewhere, attracted by the U.S. presence and calling themselves al Qaeda in Mesopotamia (the region's ancient name), added to the unrest.

Despite billions in U.S. funds, reconstruction lagged, and basic municipal services remained unpredictable. A subsidiary of the Halliburton Company, once headed by Vice President Cheney, with $3.6 billion in no-bid reconstruction contracts, faced accusations of fraud. Oil exports, vital to Iraq's economy, remained below prewar levels.

Political progress proved equally difficult. Sunnis boycotted a January 2005 election, resulting in a Shi'ite-dominated National Assembly. The prime minister came from a religious party with links to Moqtada al-Sadr. Sunnis accused Shi'ite militias and Interior Ministry "death squads" of kidnapping and killing Sunni leaders and detonating car bombs in Sunni neighborhoods. In February 2006, suicide bombers destroyed the revered Golden Dome Shi'ite mosque in Samarrah, dating to 944 C.E., triggering anti-Sunni reprisal attacks. (The Kurds in northern Iraq, hoping for an independent Kurdish state, remained aloof from the Sunni-Shi'ite sectarian violence.)

As thousands of refugees fled Iraq or sheltered in makeshift camps, an Iraqi leader lamented: "If this is not civil war, then God knows what civil war is." In April 2006, a new Shi'ite prime minister, Nouri al-Maliki, urged "national reconciliation," but the chaos continued. As other coalition forces withdrew, the United States bore the brunt of anti-insurgency fighting.

Sagging Support at Home   Under these circumstances, American public opinion turned decisively against the war. In November 2005, Pennsylvania Democratic congressman Jack Murtha urged immediate withdrawal from Iraq. A decorated Vietnam War veteran, Murtha initially supported the war but now labeled it "a flawed policy, wrapped in an illusion." Similar calls came from across the political spectrum. Even conservative writer William Buckley bluntly declared: "[T]he American objective in Iraq has failed."

The popular culture mirrored the nation's divisions. Michael Moore's anti-Bush satirical documentary *Fahrenheit 9/11* packed movie theaters in 2004. Singers including Bruce Springsteen, Neil Young, John Mellencamp, Ani DiFranco, and the Dixie Chicks country trio expressed opposition to the administration's policies. Bush supporters posted Internet lists urging boycotts of scores of Hollywood stars, including George Clooney, Susan Sarandon, Robert Redford, and Sean Penn, who vocally opposed Bush and the Iraq War.

On the other hand, conservative media voices such as radio personality Rush Limbaugh, as well as Bill O'Reilly and other commentators on Rupert Murdoch's Fox TV channel, supported the president along with many evangelical religious leaders. In an already polarized cultural and political climate, Bush's foreign and domestic policies further divided America.

Under critical scrutiny, the administration's arguments for invading Iraq—Saddam Hussein's alleged WMD program and his connections to the 9/11 attacks—crumbled. After the invasion, investigators found no WMDs. President Bush's claim in his 2003 State of the Union address that Iraq had imported uranium from Africa proved false, and Saddam's alleged role in the 9/11 attacks remained unproven. A Senate inquiry found that Vice President Cheney and other administration officials pressured the CIA to link Saddam to al Qaeda and focused on intelligence supporting their case while ignoring contradictory data.

Defense Secretary Rumsfeld's prewar assurances that a small U.S. force equipped with high-tech weaponry would achieve quick victory proved tragically wrong. When Army chief of staff General Eric Shineski told Congress in March 2003 that success in Iraq would require several hundred thousand troops, Rumsfeld derided this estimate. In a 2006 book, retired general Bernard Trainor blamed Iraq's postinvasion descent into chaos on poor advance planning. Nevertheless, Bush initially rejected calls for Rumsfeld's dismissal. "I am the decider, and I decide what is best," declared Bush in April 2006, "and what's best is for Don Rumsfeld to remain as secretary of defense."

Shocking evidence of prisoner mistreatment deepened home-front uneasiness. In 2004, photographs surfaced showing the abuse and sexual humiliation of Iraqis held by U.S. forces at Baghdad's Abu Ghraib prison. Further evidence soon revealed a broader pattern of prisoner abuse, approved at the highest level, including at Guantánamo, where more than five hundred prisoners from Afghanistan were held without trial. In a secret 2002 memo, Justice Department lawyer John Yoo argued that the Geneva Conventions protecting prisoners of war did not apply to persons the president designated as "enemy combatants." The only interrogations constituting torture, Yoo wrote, were those causing "death, organ failure, or serious impairment of bodily functions." All else was permissible.

Yoo's "torture memo," approved by White House counsel (and future attorney general) Alberto Gonzales, became public in 2004, unleashing more controversy. The International Red Cross and prisoner rights organization Amnesty International denounced as torture interrogation techniques at Guantánamo, including "water boarding," in which the victim is nearly drowned. UN agencies, along with Great Britain and other allies, urged Bush to close the Guantánamo prison. The army, however, called its interrogation techniques "safe, secure, and humane," and the administration claimed the right to hold these prisoners without trial as long as the open-ended "war on terrorism" continued. Evidence also surfaced that the CIA had secretly flown some detainees to an uncertain fate in Egyptian and Eastern European prisons.

In 2005, Congress passed legislation proposed by Senator John McCain forbidding "cruel, inhuman, and degrading" treatment of prisoners. McCain himself had been tortured as a POW in Vietnam. Bush signed the bill, but issued a "signing statement" asserting, in effect, that he was not bound to obey it.

This was one of many such pronouncements by which the president "interpreted" bills he was signing, even though the Constitution gives presidents no authority to interpret laws as they choose. The *New York Times,* criticizing Bush's "out-of-control sense of his powers in combating terrorism," editorialized in May 2006: "This president seems determined not to play by any rules other than the ones of his own making."

Americans also learned in 2005 that President Bush in 2002 had secretly authorized the National Security Agency (NSA), a government body created in 1952, to tap U.S. citizens' overseas phone calls and e-mails without securing a warrant as required by law. John Yoo, the author of the so-called "torture memo," also crafted a Justice Department memo justifying this action. In defense of this warrantless surveillance, Bush and Attorney General Gonzales argued that the 2001 congressional resolution authorizing the president to use "all necessary and appropriate force" to prevent future attacks covered almost anything the administration chose to do. Evidence also surfaced that the NSA had tapped domestic as well as foreign phone calls and e-mails and that the FBI had targeted peace groups and journalists for surveillance. These invasions of privacy disturbed not only the American Civil Liberties Union, but many ordinary citizens as well. The American Library Association protested legislation permitting investigators to access library patrons' record of book borrowing and Internet use.

In *Hamdi v. Rumsfeld* (2004), the Supreme Court addressed the Bush administration's claim that "enemy combatants" could be held indefinitely. This case involved a U.S. citizen captured in Iraq in 2001 and held thereafter without trial or legal counsel. Eight of the justices agreed (though on various grounds) that the government had violated Hamdi's Fifth Amendment right to due process. Four justices went further, declaring that all alleged enemy combatants, whether U.S. citizens or not, had the right to trial.

In response to criticism, the Bush administration set up special military tribunals, not bound by the customary rules of courtroom procedure, to try the Guantánamo prisoners. In 2006, the Supreme Court rejected this approach, however, ruling that such tribunals violated both the Constitution and the Geneva Conventions.

In March 2006, *Time* magazine reported that in November 2005, U.S. marines killed twenty-four unarmed Iraqi men, women, and children after a roadside IED killed one of their unit. As this and other atrocities came to light, memories of the Vietnam era massacre at My Lai stirred uneasily. Amid a cascade of disturbing news, the reputation not only of the Bush administration but of America itself suffered.

The Bush Administration and the Israeli-Palestinian Conflict   Central to U.S.-Muslim relations was America's support for Israel and Washington's response to Jewish settlements in the West Bank and Gaza. This issue also complicated America's relations with its European allies, many of which supported the Palestinian cause and criticized Israel's occupation of territories outside its borders. On this issue, the Bush administration accomplished little. As the Palestinian *intifada* (uprising) continued, Israeli Prime Minister Ariel Sharon demanded an end to the violence before resuming talks, while Palestinian leader Yasir Arafat insisted that protests would continue so long as Israel fostered Jewish settlements in Palestinian territory. In 2002, Israel began a security barrier, partially extending into the West Bank, to control access and prevent suicide attacks.

The Bush administration proposed a so-called "road map to peace" in 2003, but it did not push the initiative, and little changed. In 2005, Israel withdrew Jewish settlements from Gaza, but in January 2006 Palestinian elections gave victory to the radical Hamas organization, which condoned attacks on Israel and even denied Israel's right to exist. Taking control of Gaza, Hamas rejected a call by the United

States, the EU, Russia, and the UN, collectively called the Quartet, to renounce violence and recognize Israel.

Meanwhile, Hezbollah, a militant Lebanon-based Shi'ite organization supported by Iran and Syria, killed or kidnapped several Israeli soldiers and lobbed rockets into northern Israel. In retaliation, Israel invaded Lebanon in July 2006 and bombed not only Hezbollah bases but also bridges, highways, and Beirut's airport, causing heavy casualties and property damage. The Israelis soon withdrew, however, leaving Hezbollah intact and claiming victory.

As Hamas militants in Gaza fired rockets into border towns, Israel in December 2008 launched a full-scale air and ground assault on Gaza, jammed with 1.5 million people. Over thirteen hundred Gazans died, many women and children among them, including forty at two UN schools. The Israelis withdrew after three weeks, leaving Hamas in power and the underlying conflict no nearer solution.

In eight years, the Bush administration did little to push the negotiations that offered the only prospect of resolving a contentious struggle that jeopardized Israel's security, damaged U.S. interests in the region and beyond, and left the Palestinians demoralized and impoverished.

America Confronts Growing Nuclear Threats   The danger of nuclear proliferation, a grave world threat, worsened in these years. Impoverished and isolated North Korea, ruled by an eccentric dictator, Kim Jong Il, withdrew from the Nuclear Non-Proliferation Treaty and in 2006 tested both a long-range missile and a nuclear weapon. Stop-and-start negotiations appeared to make some progress, but North Korea exploded an even more powerful bomb in May 2009 and fired more missiles, stirring alarmed protests from many nations, including the United States.

Iran, meanwhile, pursued a uranium-enrichment program, allegedly for nuclear power development. Under UN pressure, Iran suspended this program in 2004 but resumed it in 2006 after the election of Mahmoud Ahmadinejad as president. An Islamic fundamentalist, Ahmadinejad taunted America, called the Holocaust a myth, and denied Israel's right to exist. Secretary of State Rice worked with the UN and European allies to induce Iran to open its program to inspection or face economic sanctions, but the stand-off continued. An Iranian long-range missile test in May 2009 deepened uneasiness about its intentions and posed new dilemmas for the United States.

Citing these threats, the Bush administration spent billions on a ground-based version of President Reagan's missile-defense system (see Chapter 30). This program violated the 1972 Anti-Ballistic Missile (ABM) Treaty, but in 2002 the United States and Russia allowed the ABM treaty to lapse, while pledging further reductions in their nuclear arsenals. However, Russian president Vladimir Putin vigorously opposed the administration's plans to build radar facilities in Poland and the Czech Republic as part of its missile-defense program.

In 2006, President Bush agreed to provide fuel and parts for India's nuclear power reactors even though India refused to sign the Nuclear Non-Proliferation Treaty and barred UN inspectors from its nuclear weapons facilities. Critics warned that this would encourage other nations to pursue nuclear weapons programs.

Meanwhile, political instability in Pakistan, a nuclear power, intensified fears of deepening nuclear dangers stalking the world.

A Widening Trade Gap and China's Rising Economic Power   The 2007 U.S. trade deficit approached $800 billion. This massive imbalance mainly reflected imports of oil, automobiles (mostly Japanese), and consumer goods from China. The 2007 trade deficit with China alone surged to $256 billion.

U.S. manufacturers complained that China artificially manipulated its currency, the yuan, to make Chinese exports cheaper. However, big-box discounters welcomed low-priced Chinese imports. When U.S. textile manufacturers pressured President Bush to impose quotas on clothing imported from China, Wal-Mart and other discount chains fought the effort.

China's 2007 gross domestic product (GDP) of $7 trillion ranked second in the world, after the United States. Some economists predicted that China's GDP would surpass America's in twenty years. For China to sustain its growth and provide a higher living standard for its people, the U.S. market was crucial. On exchange visits in 2005 and 2006, President Bush and China's leaders acknowledged the two nations' economic interdependence, while recognizing strains in the relationship. Critics targeted China's repressive regime, poor quality-control on export goods, and massive greenhouse gas emissions. (As host of the 2008 Olympic Games, China did reduce Beijing's notorious air pollution, at least temporarily.)

Environmental Hazards Become a Global Concern   Three Mile Island, Love Canal, and the *Exxon Valdez* disaster (see Chapters 29 and 30) underscored modern technology's environmental risks. Acid rain carrying pollutants from U.S. factories and vehicle emissions damaged Appalachian forests and Canadian lakes. As fluorocarbons from aerosol cans, air conditioners, and other sources depleted the atmosphere's protective ozone layer, increased solar radiation posed skin cancer risks. A 1986 nuclear power plant explosion at Chernobyl in the Ukraine and a 1984 disaster in Bhopal, India, in which deadly gases from a U.S.-owned chemical plant killed seventeen hundred people, highlighted the global scope of these risks. Polluted water caused untold deaths in poor countries.

Environmental hazards included the problem of radioactive waste disposal. In 2002, President Bush designated Nevada's Yucca Mountain as the storage site for nuclear wastes that will remain deadly for thousands of years. But as Nevada politicians protested and scientists warned of seismic activity and water seepage in the area, the project stalled. Meanwhile, dangerous byproducts of dismantled weapons and aging nuclear power plants accumulated in temporary sites across the nation.

Above all, **global warming** loomed as a grave threat (see Beyond America). The United States, with less than 5 percent of the world's population, accounts for 25 percent of global energy consumption, primarily from fossil fuels widely viewed as contributing to global warming. A 2005 EPA study found significant increases in average U.S. motor vehicles emissions since 1980, mainly because federal emissions standards exempted light trucks and SUVs.

Despite mounting evidence, the Bush administration downplayed the environmental impact of fossil fuel consumption. Energy conservation might be a "sign of personal virtue," said Vice President Cheney, but had little place in shaping public policy. The administration rejected calls for stricter emissions standards, weakened enforcement of existing regulations, and marginalized government scientists who questioned its policies. In 2002, Bush dismissed an EPA study on the human role in global warming as "a report put out by the bureaucracy."

A 1997 UN conference on global warming held in Kyoto, Japan, set strict emission targets for industrialized nations. President Clinton signed the **Kyoto Accords** but did not submit the document for Senate ratification, fearing defeat. President Bush repudiated the agreement entirely, on the grounds that it would hurt the U.S. economy and did not include developing nations such as China and India.

At a follow-up conference, delegates crafted a new agreement to meet U.S. objections, but to no avail. The revised Kyoto Accords went into effect in 2005, with only the United States, Australia, India, and China remaining aloof.

Time and again, the Bush administration sought to undermine environmental protection laws. As late as November 2008, in its final months, the administration opened thousands of acres near fragile national park sites in Utah to oil and gas exploration. Bush's environmental record, charged the head of the EPA under President Nixon, "represents a radical rollback of environmental policy going back... many, many years."

Hollywood filmmakers both reflected and contributed to global warming fears. In Kevin Kostner's *Waterworld* (1995), rising sea levels inundate the whole world except for a few islands—former mountain peaks—where isolated communities struggle to survive. In *The Day After Tomorrow* (2004), a scientist (Dennis Quaid) witnesses a massive collapse of the Antarctic ice shelf while studying ice cores. He tries desperately to warn the world and to save his son as the Atlantic engulfs New York City. While such popular culture productions heightened public awareness of global warming, critics charged that they exploited the issue while wildly distorting the actual risks.

SOCIAL AND ECONOMIC TRENDS IN CONTEMPORARY AMERICA

As a new century began, long-term population shifts to the South and West and continued immigration from Asia and Latin America, with other developments, brought significant changes to U.S. society. Upward mobility continued, but so did poverty and inequality. Profound economic changes benefited some but disadvantaged others, including inner-city residents and displaced industrial workers, widening the economic gap between those at the top and the rest of society.

An Increasingly Diverse People   Americans have long been a people on the move, and this mobility continues. The West's population increased by 10.4 million in the 1990s. California grew by more than 4 million; Maricopa County, Arizona (which includes Phoenix), by nearly 1 million. The South expanded by nearly 15 million in the decade. Across the Midwest and Great Plains, by contrast, populations remained stable and even declined.

Global Warming as a Worldwide Challenge

As long ago as 1957, Roger Revelle, director of the Scripps Institution of Oceanography in San Diego, co-authored a scientific paper warning of rising carbon dioxide levels in the atmosphere and attributing the increase in part to combustion of fossil fuels (coal, oil, and natural gas). Global warming could result, the article cautioned.

In the decades since, the conclusions of this farsighted paper have been verified. The Earth's average temperature rose by one degree Fahrenheit in the twentieth century, and the rate of increase shot up after 1970. The century's ten hottest years came after 1985, and 2005 was the hottest year ever recorded.

Rising carbon dioxide levels have also been documented by many studies, including ice-core sampling. In the 1990s, U.S., Russian, and French scientists extracted a two-mile-long ice core in Antarctica and measured carbon dioxide levels in trapped air bubbles over a 440,000-year span. In 2005, European researchers reported on ice cores extending back 650,000 years. Both teams found current carbon dioxide levels at an all-time high. Throughout these incredibly long time spans, carbon dioxide levels remained within a range of 180 to 300 parts per million. However, beginning around 1950, the level crept up. In 2005, it reached 380 parts per million.

The connection between carbon dioxide levels and global warming is clear as well. Just as the glass roof of a greenhouse traps the sun's heat, so carbon dioxide and other "greenhouse gases" blanketing the Earth prevent solar heat from escaping.

Further, despite some skeptics, most scientists now agree that human pursuits involving increasing use of fossil fuels in factories, homes, and motor vehicles have contributed significantly to the rising levels of atmospheric carbon dioxide. In a 2005 report, the leading scientific bodies of the United States, Canada, France, Italy, Germany, Great Britain, Japan, China, India, Russia, and Brazil attributed "most of the warming in recent decades...to human activities."

The United States is the world's major producer of carbon dioxide emissions from fossil fuels, followed by China, Russia, Japan, and India. This is clearly a global issue. Throughout the world, growing numbers of factories belching smoke and motorized vehicles spewing exhaust worsen the problem. In 2005, annual carbon dioxide emissions in the United States and Japan were about 20 percent greater than in 1990. In the same fifteen-year period, however, India's annual emissions more than doubled, and China's soared by a startling 237 percent. The burning of vast tracks of the Amazonian rainforest to create more grazing land has placed Brazil high on the list of greenhouse gas producers as well.

In moderate levels, greenhouse gases pose no threat; indeed, they are essential. Without their warming effect, the Earth would be a frozen waste. But the recent surge, now widely linked to human activity, brings serious hazards—present and potential.

Photographs transmitted by two Russian satellites launched in 2002 reveal that Antarctica's icecap is melting at a rate of thirty-six cubic miles per year, with a similar melt-off in the Greenland and Arctic Ocean icecaps. As polar ice has melted, sea levels have risen. Storm surges are destroying homes in Shishmaref, an Inupiat village in northwestern Alaska, as a protective sea-ice barrier melts. In 2002, the residents voted to move farther inland to preserve their community.

As the permafrost weakens in Alaska and northern Canada, highways buckle and cracks develop in houses. The stability of Alaska's oil pipeline from Prudhoe Bay to Valdez is threatened. In northern Iceland, vast lagoons have appeared as glaciers recede. In the Swiss and Austrian Alps, deadly avalanches, shrinking glaciers, and melting permafrost threaten the economy of a region dependent on skiers, tourists, and mountain climbers.

Beyond such immediate effects, global warming is impacting the Earth's delicate ecological balance. Examples abound:

- The mountain pine beetle, advancing northward as Alaska and western Canada grow warmer, has devastated millions of acres of spruce forest.
- Antarctica's penguin population has dramatically declined since 1950, as melting ice reduces breeding areas.
- The U.S. Interior Department placed polar bears on the endangered species list in 2008, as warming threatened their Arctic habitat.
- In 2005, amphibian disease experts documented a massive decline in rare Latin American frog species because of a spreading fungus attributed to global warming.
- Australian researchers report dying coral reefs as ocean temperatures rise.

Projections of future trends offer further cause for concern. Even with preventive measures, carbon dioxide levels are predicted to increase for years. Climatologists using computer simulations foresee continued global temperature increases for at least a century. The resulting polar melting could increase sea levels up to five feet, endangering coastal cities from Boston and New York to Mumbai and Hong Kong. In low-lying Bangladesh, flooding could displace 6 million people.

Climatic changes could radically disrupt agricultural production and extend the range of disease-causing organisms. Rising ocean temperatures could affect fisheries and generate ferocious tropical storms.

Global warming has triggered a global response. The 1997 Kyoto Accords represent a major multinational commitment to reducing greenhouse gases. Brazil in 2008 announced a bold plan to protect the Amazonian rainforest. China, India, and other developing nations are addressing the issue as well, though environmental objectives often clash with economic goals.

Many international organizations and hundreds of Internet websites publicize the issue. Al Gore's *Earth in the Balance* reached a vast audience (see Chapter 30, Going to the Source), and his 2006 book and Academy-Award-winning film *An Inconvenient Truth* further documented the dangers of global warming. Germany's environmental minister ordered six thousand DVDs of the film for showing in German schools. Other nations took similar steps. In 2007, Gore and the UN's Intergovernmental Panel on Climate Change jointly received the Nobel Peace Prize for promoting awareness of global warming.

Research on alternative energy sources, including solar, wind, and thermal, is accelerating as is work on more fuel-efficient hybrid vehicles. The United States and many other nations have set emissions standards for factories and vehicles.

Whether this international response will match the magnitude of the challenge remains an urgent question as the global community confronts its future.

Questions for Analysis

1. *What are some possible long-term consequences of global warming?*

2. *What international responses have addressed the problem of greenhouse gas emissions?*

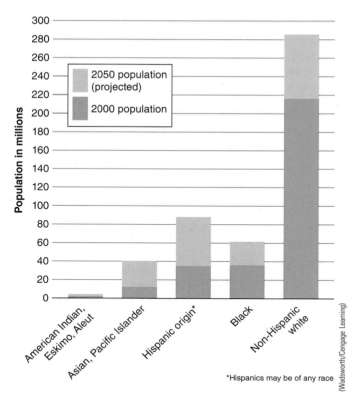

FIGURE 31.1 U.S. Population by Race and Hispanic Origin, 2000 and 2050 (Projected)

By 2050, the Census Bureau projects, non-Hispanic whites will constitute only about half the total U.S. population.

Source: U.S. Census Bureau, 2004.

Household patterns changed as well. The proportion of "traditional" families headed by a married heterosexual couple fell from 74 percent in 1960 to under 50 percent in 2007. Commented the *New York Times*: "[T]he nuclear family is not the only kind of family..... In modern America no type of family can really be recognized to the exclusion of all others."

Heavy immigration from Asia and Latin America reversed a long decline in the proportion of foreign-born persons in the population. From a low of about 5 percent in 1970, this figure neared 13 percent in 2008. The 2009 U.S. population of more than 305 million was about 13 percent Hispanic, 12 percent black, 4 percent Asian, and 1 percent American Indian (see Figure 31.1). The nation's Hispanics— nearly 60 percent of Mexican origin, with Puerto Ricans, Cubans, and Salvadorans comprising most of the balance—are predicted to make up 25 percent of the population by 2050. Some 6 million Muslims, mainly from the Middle East and North Africa, add to the ethno-religious mix.

These demographic changes offer more than an interesting snapshot of contemporary American society. They have far-reaching political, economic, and cultural implications and offer a preview of a dynamic future nation very different from that of yesterday or today.

Upward Mobility and Social Problems in a Multiethnic Society

African-American median household income in 2007 approached $35,000. Although below the national median of around $50,700, this represented a substantial gain, in constant dollars, since 1990. College-educated blacks enjoyed significantly higher earnings, and 57 percent of black high school graduates in 2005 went on to college. TV's long-running *Cosby Show* (1984–1992), starring Bill Cosby as an obstetrician and his wife (Phylicia Rashad) as an attorney, offered a fictional version of this upwardly mobile group of African-Americans.

But many inner-city blacks confront a different reality, including bleak job prospects, poor schools, and drug-related crime. The black unemployment rate of nearly 10 percent in 2008 (already well above the national rate) was far higher among high school dropouts and youths lacking a college education. Prison statistics for ill-educated young black males, often involving drug-related offenses, were similarly bleak.

Inner-city black women face risks of drug use, HIV/AIDS infection, and out-of-wedlock pregnancy. In 2006, more than 70 percent of black births were to unmarried women, almost twice the percentage in 1970. Many of these unmarried mothers were teenagers, reducing their prospects for education and employment. (Out-of-wedlock births to white women also rose, but at a far lower rate.)

Inner-city churches and community organizations addressed the multiple social problems of their neighborhoods. In 2006, a group of big-city mayors demanded action to curb the plague of illegal guns.

Among Native Americans, renewed tribal pride and activism continued, including federal lawsuits to enforce long-ignored Indian treaties. Tribal gambling casinos, approved by Congress in 1988, proliferated. By 2008, about four hundred casinos generated more than $18 billion in annual income. Some tribal leaders lamented the social problems casinos sometimes brought in their wake, but casino income did help fund tribal schools, museums, job training, and substance-abuse programs.

The Hispanic population resisted sweeping generalizations. While Mexican-Americans concentrated in the Southwest, many lived elsewhere. Cubans, Puerto Ricans, and Haitians (mostly of African origin), resided mainly in Florida, New York, New Jersey, and Illinois.

Hispanic households' median income neared $40,000 by 2008, and unemployment among Hispanics dropped from 9 percent in 1995 to 5.6 percent in 2007. However, in 2007, 21.5 percent lived in poverty, many in troubled inner-city neighborhoods. Religion and family loom large in Hispanic culture, but stressful social conditions took their toll. (See also the discussion, later in this chapter, of immigration reform during the Bush administration.)

In 2007, more than five thousand Hispanics held elective public office, including Los Angeles mayor Antonio Villaraigosa. Ten million Hispanics streamed to the polls in 2008, making them an increasingly important constituency. In 2009, filling a Supreme Court vacancy, President Barack Obama nominated Sonia Sotomayor, a U.S. district court judge of Puerto Rican descent. Born in New York City, Sotomayor was reared by her mother after her father's death and went on to compile a brilliant college and law school record. Despite some controversy she won Senate confirmation by a 68-31 vote.

Of the nation's 13 million Asian-Americans in 2007, 75 percent had arrived since 1980. Prizing education and supported by family networks, many followed a trajectory of academic achievement and upward mobility. Nearly 50 percent of adult Asian-Americans hold college degrees, and among high school graduates, the college enrollment rate nears 90 percent.

By 2050, demographers predict, given baby-boom mortality and comparative fertility rates, non-Hispanic whites will constitute only about half the U.S. population. Non-Hispanic whites, while still a plurality, will simply be another minority. Many Americans of mixed origins, like the golfer Tiger Woods, of Thai, Chinese, African-American, and American Indian ancestry, resist being pigeonholed. From 1970 to 2005, the number of black-white married couples in the United States rose from 65,000 to 422,000. The total number of biracial married couples among all racial groups exceeds 2 million. Recognizing these realities, the Census Bureau now permits citizens to check more than one racial category, or none at all.

With the graying of the baby-boom generation (those born between 1946 and 1964), America is also aging. In 2007, the highest-circulation U.S. magazine was *AARP,* read by 24 million members of the American Association of Retired Persons. The proportion of Americans over sixty-five, about 13 percent in 2009, is projected to reach 20 percent by 2050—a statistic with profound implications for health care, Social Security and Medicare funding, and other economic and social issues.

The "New Economy" and the Old Economy

In the early twentieth century, industrial production replaced agriculture as America's economic engine. The century's end saw an equally profound transformation: the rise of a professional and service-based economy. Farming and manufacturing continued, of course, but with far fewer workers.

In the U.S. work force of 146 million in 2007, about 60 percent held white-collar jobs, ranging from sales clerks, office workers, and teachers to physicians, lawyers, engineers, computer programmers, and business executives. Service-sector employees in health care, custodial work, restaurants, and so forth accounted for another 16 percent. Only 23 percent worked in manual-labor fields that as recently as 1960 had dominated the labor market: manufacturing, farming, construction, trucking, etc.

This transformation had mixed effects. Young people with education, skills, and contacts did well in the new electronics, programming, and telecommunications fields and in the burgeoning corporate and financial services sectors. For others, supermarkets, car washes, fast-food outlets, and discount superstores provided entry-level jobs, but few long-term prospects.

The computer-based information revolution has had economic ramifications as well. Newspaper circulation fell 16 percent between 1985 and 2006. Even major papers such as the *New York Times* and newsmagazines like *Newsweek* faced problems as Americans turned to TV or online news sources—which for some meant Jon Stewart's satirical *Daily Show* on TV's Comedy Central. The new technologies impacted the music industry as well. CD sales fell by 17.5 percent from 1998 to 2007, as fans downloaded songs electronically to their laptops or iPods.

The economic transformation summed up by the term "globalization" complicated all these changes. America's economy has long been enmeshed in transnational patterns of trade and investment, of course, but this involvement has vastly accelerated in recent decades. Today's large corporations and financial institutions are all global in scope. Thanks to regional trading blocs such as NAFTA and multinational agreements administered by the **World Trade Organization (WTO),** the production and marketing of goods now largely ignores national boundaries. The WTO, created in 1995 as successor to an earlier body set up in 1947, monitors and promotes trade among its 153 member nations. The flow of capital among financial institutions is similarly global in scope.

The economic well-being of all Americans, whether worker, consumer, or investor (or all three), increasingly depends on developments beyond the nation's borders. As imports replaced American-made products and U.S. manufacturers shifted operations overseas to cut labor costs, displaced workers faced unemployment or lower-wage service-sector jobs. Union membership by 2007 sank to only 12 percent of the labor force, leaving workers even more vulnerable. The recession that hit in 2008 worsened the impact of these longer-term trends.

The decline of the U.S. auto industry typifies the pattern. After losing sales because of rising gasoline prices in the 1970s (see Chapter 30), American carmakers had returned to profitability with gas-guzzling SUVs and light trucks. But as gas prices again spiked upward after 2000, car buyers turned to more fuel-efficient imports, particularly Japan's Toyota, Honda, and Nissan. By mid-2007, foreign carmakers had captured over half the U.S. market—a historic first.

Foreign automakers set up U.S. production plants, mostly in the South and West, and mostly nonunion. By 2008, Toyota employed thirty-six thousand workers in fourteen U.S. plants and supported thousands more through its dealerships, parts suppliers, and advertising agencies.

At GM, a century-old icon of America's industrial might, annual losses spurted to nearly $39 billion in 2008. GM's stock price tumbled, and the company shed tens of thousands of jobs. Said one GM engineer: "This once was the premier company... to work for. You were at the top of the heap, the major leagues....Today, you know this company is crumbling around you."

From 2005 through mid-2008, GM, Chrysler, and Ford eliminated nearly 150,000 jobs and closed thirty-five plants, causing pain across America. As recession hit, even the foreign automakers suffered. By 2008, facing plunging sales and a yawning deficit, Toyota contemplated jobs cuts in its U.S. plants. "In the past our flexibility was only upward," said a Toyota executive; "To manage downward flexibility is obviously more challenging."

Economists continued to defend globalization as beneficial for America overall, lowering consumer prices and opening world markets for U.S. exports, from agricultural commodities, heavy machinery, scrap metal, and airplanes to films and communications gadgets. But for displaced workers, this was cold comfort. In addition to the impact on U.S. industrial workers, human rights activists charged that

corporations in a "race to the bottom" open factories in poor countries where workers, often young women, live in prison-like barracks and work long hours for low
wages with no benefits. Such factories often are environmental polluters as well.

Amid economic worries and a "war on terror," post–9/11 popular culture
reflected crosscurrents of anxiety and escapism. Rupert Murdoch's Fox TV network, while rallying support for Bush, also offered the top-rated *American Idol*
program, in which amateur vocalists competed for audience votes. Such shows,
along with long-running syndicated game shows *Jeopardy* and *Wheel of Fortune*
and the contrived scenarios of so-called "reality" programs, provided distraction
from the stress of contemporary life. A longing to obliterate shadowy enemies perhaps contributed to the success of fantasy movies such as *Spider-Man 3* (2007) and
The Incredible Hulk (2008), in which comic-book superheroes battle menacing
foes. In *Halo 3*, the best-selling videogame of 2007, players combat an array of
intergalactic religious fanatics bent on destroying civilization.

A FLOUNDERING ADMINISTRATION YIELDS TO A RENEWED VISION

President Bush's second term brought multiple setbacks, including the administration's ineffectual response to a devastating hurricane. Two Supreme Court appointments extended Bush's conservative legacy, but lobbying scandals, soaring federal
deficits, and discontent with his domestic and foreign policies, capped by a severe
recession, all eroded Bush's standing. The watershed 2008 election suggested a
renewed national resolve to fulfill the enduring vision of what America might yet
become.

Mixed Record, Mounting Deficits, and Disaster in New Orleans   In 2003, Congress enacted Bush's proposal to pay part of seniors' prescription drug expenses under the federal Medi-care program. Though older citizens welcomed the help in paying for their medications, many grumbled as they battled the red tape. Democrats charged that the plan mainly benefited drug firms and insurance companies.

George W. Bush, leader of a party historically committed to fiscal prudence and
balanced budgets, presided over spending levels unprecedented in American history.
The prescription drug benefit helped push the government's share of Medicare costs
to $179 billion in 2007, more than five times the 1990 figure. Medicare and social
security costs, plus Bush's tax cuts, the Iraq and Afghan wars, and interest payments on the national debt, produced yawning federal deficits from 2002 on. Worsening the problem, Congress members of both parties continued the time-honored
practice of quietly inserting into spending bills pet projects known as "earmarks"
that benefited their districts.

Foreign investors funded the mushrooming federal debt by purchasing U.S.
government bonds. China, awash in dollars—thanks to its U.S. exports—held
nearly $700 billion in U.S. government bonds by 2008.

Launching his second term, Bush proposed a partial privatization of social
security, the New Deal pension program. The social security system faced severe
budgetary strains as the baby boom generation grew older. Under Bush's plan,

people could shift some of their social security funds to private investment accounts. After much debate of pros and cons, however, the proposal failed to win acceptance. Most citizens preferred a government program to the uncertainties of the market.

The administration stumbled again over immigration policy. Of the estimated 11 million illegal immigrants in the United States, most from Mexico or elsewhere in Latin America, many worked in a low-wage "shadow economy" as farm laborers, janitors, motel cleaners, nursing-home attendants, or employees in food-processing plants. In 2005, the administration proposed a bill by which these workers could eventually gain legal status. The debate that erupted revealed deep divisions in U.S. public opinion and within Bush's own party. Supporters invoked America's tradition of welcoming newcomers. Undocumented immigrants, they argued, did the unpleasant but essential work shunned by others. Businesses employing immigrants supported the bill. But opponents denounced the plan as "amnesty" for lawbreakers. Deport them, they argued, and the law of supply-and-demand would push up wages for the jobs they held, increasing opportunities for U.S.-born workers. Post 9/11 fears of terrorism contributed to the pressure for tougher immigration controls.

Late in 2005, the House of Representatives, with strong Republican support, defied the administration by passing a tough immigration bill criminalizing illegal aliens and requiring their deportation; strengthening the U.S.-Mexican border; and making it a felony for anyone, including ministers, priests, and health-care providers, to help undocumented immigrants.

The reaction was swift. Religious leaders denounced the bill. Protesters, supported by Spanish-language radio and TV, marched in Los Angeles and other cities. The bill's supporters mobilized as well. Radio personality Rush Limbaugh angrily denounced the marches. Others protested against "Nuestro Himno," a Spanish version of "The Star-Spangled Banner." In the Southwest, volunteers organized a vigilante-like "Minuteman Project" to patrol the border.

With the Hispanic vote in play (some called it "the sleeping giant of American politics"), politicians proceeded cautiously. In the Senate, a bipartisan bill funded tougher border controls, but also established procedures by which undocumented immigrants could secure citizenship. Defying the White House, a bloc of Senate Republicans defeated the compromise bill.

Shelving hopes for reform, the Bush administration cracked down on illegal immigration. In 2006, Bush signed a bill to build a 700-mile reinforced fence along the U.S.-Mexican border. Federal agents raided plants employing undocumented Hispanics. A raid in Iowa led to the arrest of nearly four hundred workers, many of whom were deported. In 2008, the Supreme Court struck down an administration effort to deny deportees legal representation. While some applauded the administration's harsh policies, humanitarian and civil rights groups protested, noting the impact on children and disrupted families. A 2008 film, *The Visitor,* portrayed the human consequences of rigidly enforced deportation policies.

The administration took another hit in August 2005, when **Hurricane Katrina** struck the Gulf Coast, taking as many as fourteen hundred lives, inflicting heavy property damage, disrupting shipping on the Mississippi River, and smashing oil refineries and offshore oil rigs. New Orleans suffered most. Much of the city lies

New Orleans in the Aftermath of Hurricane Katrina, September 1, 2005
Four days after the city's levees burst and flood waters devastated their homes, New Orleans residents await evacuation to the Superdome, which quickly became a scene of nightmarish conditions as thousands of desperate people crowded in.

below sea level, protected by levees. Over the years, developers drained surrounding marshland, destroying a buffer against storm surges.

As New Orleans' levees burst under Katrina's storm surge, rampaging water flooded the lower wards, populated mainly by poor blacks. Many residents drowned or died awaiting rescue. Others lost homes and possessions. The elderly, hospitalized, and nursing home residents suffered most. Thousands poured into New Orleans's Superdome, which soon became a squalid disaster zone.

Washington's response was appallingly inadequate. Despite a local FEMA official's urgent warnings of collapsing levees, neither Homeland Security director Michael Chertoff nor President Bush recognized the emergency. FEMA head Michael Brown, a political appointee with no disaster experience, proved hopelessly inept. Though praised by Bush ("Heck of a job, Brownie"), he soon resigned. The distribution of emergency relief funds involved massive fraud and ineptitude. FEMA spent $900 million on twenty-six thousand mobile homes, many of which sat unused. Despite the reorganization of the national security bureaucracy after 9/11, Hurricane Katrina revealed the same pattern of missed warnings, failed communication, and bumbling response. Many blamed Washington as New Orleans neighborhoods stood silent, their streets lined with empty, mud-caked houses, their residents scattered.

Extending Republican Influence: From the Supreme Court to K Street

In July 2005, Supreme Court justice Sandra Day O'Connor, a key swing vote in close decisions, announced her retirement. To replace her, Bush nominated federal judge John Roberts, who had held posts in the Reagan administration. When Chief Justice Rehnquist died in September, Bush nominated Roberts as chief justice. He won easy Senate confirmation while revealing little about his judicial philosophy.

To fill the second vacancy, Bush first chose White House counsel Harriet Miers, a longtime Texas friend. Widely criticized as unqualified, Miers soon withdrew. Bush next nominated Samuel Alito, Jr. As a Justice Department lawyer in the Reagan administration, and later as a federal judge, Alito had espoused the broad view of executive powers that the Bush administration used to justify its post–9/11 actions at home and abroad. Alito won confirmation, 58 to 42.

With Roberts and Alito joining Scalia and Thomas as a bloc of four reliably conservative justices, Justice Anthony Kennedy emerged as the swing vote in close decisions. Prochoice advocates feared (and abortion opponents hoped) that the high court's growing conservative strength would threaten *Roe v. Wade,* the 1973 ruling upholding abortion rights. Although it remained highly contentious, opinion polls showed broad support for *Roe v. Wade*, with about 55 percent endorsing legal abortions with certain restrictions, 24 percent favoring no legally imposed restrictions at all, and 20 percent believing that all abortions should be banned. In *Gonzales v. Carhart* (2007), the Supreme Court, on a 5 to 4 vote, upheld a 2003 Congressional ban on late-term abortions. In the decision, however, the majority cited *Roe v. Wade* as a guiding precedent, thus implicitly reaffirming that ruling.

As Supreme Court politics attracted notice, so did the influence of Washington lobbyists. (This term stems from the era when individuals representing special interests would crowd the lobbies of the Capitol and state legislatures.) Long a part of American politics, lobbyists' influence increased during the ascendancy of Texas Republican Congressman Tom "the Hammer" DeLay, who became House majority leader in 2003. From 2000 to 2005, the ranks of registered Washington lobbyists expanded from around fifteen thousand to nearly thirty-three thousand, with many more unregistered ones. Implementing a plan dubbed "the K Street project" (after the Washington street where many lobbyists had offices), DeLay extracted campaign contributions from lobbyists and pressured them to hire Republican staffers—often members of legislators' families. This reflected a broader GOP effort, originating with White House political strategist Karl Rove, to create a permanent Republican majority.

An eruption of scandals in 2005 focused attention on lobbyists and money's role in politics. In September, DeLay resigned as majority leader, and soon left Congress altogether, after a grand jury indicted him for violating Texas election laws by engineering a redistricting scheme that benefited Republicans. In November, a California Republican congressman admitted accepting more than $2 million in bribes and unreported campaign contributions from defense contractors. In December, a federal grand jury indicted Jack Abramoff, a Washington lobbyist with ties to DeLay. Abramoff had collected millions from corporations trying to influence legislation, including $82 million from Indian tribes seeking casino licenses or to prevent rival tribes from getting licenses. Laundered through dummy organizations, this money paid for dinners, expensive gifts, campaign donations, and golf junkets for Congress members—including some Democrats—while Abramoff siphoned off millions for himself.

Pleading guilty, Abramoff went to prison. Both he and DeLay had close White House connections, but President Bush denied any wrongdoing. As public disgust mounted, politicians scrambled to return tainted contributions and regulate lobbyists more strictly.

A Shifting Political Landscape: The 2006 Election and Beyond   In the 2006 midterm election, voters rendered a stinging judgment on the Bush administration and the Republican-led Congress. Even President Bush admitted that his party had taken a "thumping." Democrats gained thirty-two House seats, retaking control for the first time in twelve years. Democrats also narrowly won control of the Senate, 51 to 49. The number of women senators rose to sixteen, a record high. For the first time since 1994, Democrats won a majority of governorships. In Massachusetts, Democrat Deval Patrick became only the second African-American elected governor since Reconstruction.

The Democratic victories brought new congressional leadership, including Nancy Pelosi of San Francisco as Speaker of the House, the first woman to hold that post. "Today we have made history," Pelosi told fellow Democrats at a post-election party; "Now let us make progress."

The election results signaled discontent with the nation's direction, and especially over the Iraq War. Consequently, President Bush fired Defense Secretary Rumsfeld and named Robert Gates his successor. A former CIA director, Gates had served on a blue-ribbon Iraq Study Group whose 2006 report criticized both the decision to invade Iraq and the administration's conduct during the war. Vice President Cheney's influence had diminished as well, as Secretary of State Rice and other administration officials challenged the imprisonments without trial, harsh interrogation techniques, sweeping domestic surveillance, and other policies promoted by Cheney after 9/11.

By the end of 2007, more than four thousand GIs had been killed in Iraq and more than thirty thousand wounded, many severely. After five years, the war's costs had soared to around $600 billion, with billions more projected. The documented number of Iraqi civilians killed approached 100,000, with some estimates ranging far higher.

Advised by General David Petraeus, the new commander in Iraq, Bush in 2007 ordered more troops to Iraq. With additional GIs patrolling Baghdad and other trouble spots, violence declined. An uneasy cease-fire by Shi'ite militias, and cooperation by Sunni clan leaders in combating insurgents, helped as well. Assassinations, suicide bombings, and IED attacks continued, but U.S. military deaths in Iraq for 2008 fell to 314, down sharply from previous years. In November 2008, the Iraqi parliament ratified an agreement with Washington for the withdrawal of U.S. combat forces from urban centers by mid-2009 and their complete withdrawal by 2012. The conflict, already longer than World War II, was winding down at last.

In December 2008, Bush made a final visit to Baghdad. At a news conference with Prime Minister Maliki, an Iraqi journalist hurled his shoes at the president—a gesture of contempt in Arabic societies—while shouting, "This is for widows and orphans and all those killed in Iraq!" The president shrugged off the incident. "That's what happens in free societies," he commented, "where people try to draw attention to themselves."

Despite some encouraging developments, the situation, in General Petraeus's words, remained "fragile and reversible." Historically a patchwork of ethnic and religious groups ruled by successive Persian, Greek, and Arab invaders, and then by British colonial administrators after World War I, Iraq had achieved independence only in 1932. Whether it could function as a democracy, avoiding either fragmentation or renewed despotism, remained unknown.

Despite Bush's claim that Saddam Hussein's overthrow justified the war, most Americans continued to view it as a disastrous mistake. A Taliban resurgence in Afghanistan strengthened this view. The Iraq adventure, many concluded, had diverted essential resources from the more vital conflict in Afghanistan. Reports of poor care in veterans' hospitals, delays in processing wounded veterans' claims, and massive fraud in the Iraq reconstruction program deepened public anger over the war.

Other controversies plagued Bush's final years in office. In March 2007, Vice President Cheney's chief of staff went to prison after his conviction for perjury and obstruction of justice. The conviction related to an investigation of charges that Cheney's office had revealed to reporters the identity of a covert CIA agent, as part of a campaign to discredit her husband, a critic of the administration's pre-war claims about Iraq's nuclear weapons program.

In August 2007, Attorney General Alberto Gonzales resigned amid an uproar over the hiring and firing of U.S. attorneys and Justice Department lawyers for blatantly political reasons rather than competence and experience. Gonzales' approval of the Justice Department's "torture memo" and of illegal FBI spying during his tenure as White House counsel added to the firestorm of criticism.

As Bush's presidency wound down, his approval ratings sank to around 25 percent—close to the lowest ever recorded for any president and a steep decline from their stratospheric levels after 9/11. What caused this reversal? Beyond the unpopular Iraq War and related issues of torture, unlimited detention, and violations of citizens' rights, many saw an arrogant, go-it-alone approach that damaged America's standing worldwide. Critics also targeted the administration's dismissal of scientific evidence on global warming, the politicization of the Justice Department and other federal agencies, the secretive power exercised by Vice President Cheney and a small circle of like-minded advisors, and the dominance of narrow partisanship and rigid ideology in shaping administration policies. To his opponents, Bush's simplistic, black-and-white worldview, preference for snap decisions based on gut instincts, and reluctance to admit mistakes further limited his effectiveness.

The Economist, a respected London-based magazine that endorsed Bush in 2000, reached a harsh judgment as his term ended: "He leaves the White House as one of the least popular and most divisive presidents in American history,... [and] the most partisan... in living memory.... [C]ontent to be president of half the country..., he devoted his presidency to feeding the Republican coalition that elected him.... [G]ood policy repeatedly took a back seat to Mr. Bush's overweening political ambition. Both the country and, ultimately, the Republican Party are left the worse for it."

Millions of Americans continued to support Bush, of course. The Iraq invasion, tax cuts, educational reforms, promotion of international trade, and free-market suspicion of government regulation all had their admirers. Bush himself defended his record, insisting that even his most controversial post–9/11 actions aimed to protect the country from terrorists. Citing Harry Truman's post-presidential popularity, he suggested rather wistfully that he, too, would be vindicated by history.

The Republican party retained a large core of loyal supporters. In 2008, despite Bush's unpopularity and a charismatic Democratic candidate, 46 percent of the electorate voted Republican. For the moment, however, the party's fortunes stood at a low ebb.

Recession Strikes the U.S. and World Economies

Deepening the national malaise, a recession began in 2007 and quickly worsened. The downturn started in the real estate market. Beginning in the late 1990s, housing prices spiked upward, especially in California, Florida, the Southwest, and Northeast. The bubble burst in 2007. As real estate prices tumbled, homebuilding and commercial developments stalled.

The crisis soon spread, worsened by lax governmental regulation. In 1999, Congress repealed the Glass-Steagall Act, a 1933 law designed to regulate bank practices and protect depositors. Introduced by Republicans, the repeal won bipartisan support and was signed by President Clinton. Freed of regulatory constraints, investment banks could now acquire unregulated financial services companies and indulge in other forms of financial wheeling and dealing. Even banking activities that were still regulated received little scrutiny in the free-market mood of the era.

During the real estate boom, banks and lending companies extended mortgages to homebuyers who could barely afford them. With slogans like "No credit? No problem" and low initial interest rates that quickly jumped higher, predatory lenders lured first-time home buyers, many of them black and Hispanic. By 2008, nearly 30 percent of all mortgages were rated as "subprime." These risky mortgages were then sold to Wall Street investment banks or other financial institutions that bundled or "securitized" them into stock offerings purchased by educational institutions, pension funds, mutual funds, and foreign banks. Decades of deregulation, driven by free-market ideology, had fostered a climate that encouraged both predatory lending and the marketing of highly risky securities.

As the real estate market weakened, homeowners facing exorbitant mortgage payments could neither sell their homes nor refinance their mortgages. Many defaulted, leaving empty, neglected houses and a sea of foreclosure signs behind. As homeowners defaulted, the value of the securities based on these mortgages collapsed, bringing the entire credit structure to its knees. Wall Street banks and financial services companies found themselves holding securities, now re-labeled "toxic assets," they could not sell, and whose actual market value no one knew.

Wall Street's largest banks faced disastrous losses, with some nearing insolvency. Giant Lehman Brothers collapsed, while Citigroup faltered badly. Struggling to survive, the big banks stopped lending, fearing further losses. As credit froze, the broader economy suffered. Business activity slowed; jittery consumers cut spending.

The already weakened U.S. auto companies teetered toward bankruptcy. The Dow Jones stock market average, after soaring above 14,000 in October 2007, sank to under 8,000 by March 2009, wiping out billions in investors' assets.

The recession hit home as Americans saw their savings, property values, and retirement funds shrivel, and as companies announced layoffs. In 2008, 2.6 million workers lost their jobs, the highest rate of loss in sixty years. By September 2009, the unemployment rate stood at 9.8 percent. Even this figure did not include discouraged jobseekers who had stopped looking or involuntary part-time workers. In Michigan, home of the U.S. auto industry, the jobless rate passed 15 percent. The downturn affected even the high-flying IT sector, as mighty Microsoft and the giant chipmaker Intel announced layoffs.

Despite some hopeful signs, by autumn 2009 recovery from the worst recession since the Great Depression seemed likely to be slow and uneven. College students worried about their prospects. For displaced workers and unskilled youth, an already tough job market looked even grimmer.

The recession struck an economy whose benefits, as already noted, were very unevenly distributed. While some had profited handsomely from the Bush tax cuts, the soaring stock market, and the boom in financial services and innovative electronics technologies, most Americans' real income remained flat through the Bush years. The surge in consumer spending was largely financed with plastic. Total consumer debt in 2008, excluding mortgages, approached $2.6 trillion. After a decade when both Washington and American consumers had plunged deeply into debt, the chickens now came home to roost. In 2008, U.S. banks wrote off $41 billion in unpaid credit-card debt. Analysts predicted the total would approach $100 billion in 2009 as the recession bit deeper.

The administration in its waning months grappled with the crisis. In July 2008, despite his party's free-market beliefs, President Bush signed a bill that helped homeowners refinance their mortgages, tightened mortgage-lending regulations, and strengthened federal oversight of two privately owned but government-supported home-loan agencies—nicknamed Fannie Mae and Freddie Mac. With the heads of Treasury and the Federal Reserve calling for a Wall Street bailout, Congress late in 2008 appropriated $700 billion to provide more capital to the investment banks and thereby stimulate the economy. As the Treasury Department ladled out the first $350 billion, it imposed few rules on what the banks must do with the money, and most simply used it to stabilize their own balance sheets rather than making loans to stimulate recovery.

Revelations of the bloated earnings of the financiers who had caused the crisis deepened public anger. In 2004–2007, the CEO of Countrywide Finance, a giant subprime mortgage lender, made $270 million. As late as December 2008, after fourth-quarter losses of $15 billion, Merrill Lynch's CEO doled out millions in bonuses to company executives and spent $2.2 million redecorating his office. A familiar pattern of greed and excess in the upper reaches of American capitalism— as millions faced desperate times—was again unfolding.

In an era of globalization, a crisis that began in the United States quickly spread. Banks in Europe and Asia tightened credit as the U.S. securities in their portfolios lost value. China was doubly hard hit as its billions in U.S. securities plunged in value and its exports of consumer goods to the United States dried up.

Meanwhile, plunging oil prices battered the economies of oil-producing nations, from Venezuela to Russia and the Middle East.

The recession did help soften longstanding cultural conflicts over matters of personal behavior and belief. Differences over abortion, gay marriage, school prayer, and similar issues remained, but as economic worries deepened, their emotional intensity somewhat diminished. More tolerant views among the younger generation, documented in opinion polls, contributed to the waning of the culture wars as well.

A New Beginning and an Enduring Spirit
With the recession deepening voter discontent, Democratic prospects looked good as the 2008 election approached. Among the Democratic presidential contenders, New York senator and former first lady **Hillary Clinton** emerged as the frontrunner. In the field of challengers, **Barack Obama,** an African-American senator from Illinois, seemed an improbable long shot.

An array of Republican hopefuls reflected the party's varied constituencies, but Arizona senator **John McCain** outlasted the rest. A Vietnam War bomber pilot who spent six years in a Hanoi prison, McCain had built a reputation in the Senate as a party maverick on some issues. As running mate he chose Alaska governor Sarah Palin, an evangelical Christian with a populist touch who had bucked her state's Republican establishment to win the governorship after serving as a small-town mayor. After an initial buzz of excitement, Palin struck many as ill-informed and unqualified.

In the Democratic contest, Barack Obama won the Iowa primary and emerged as a formidable candidate. He built powerful grass-roots support, especially among young people attracted by his cool demeanor and inspiring speeches. Energized by Internet websites and by rallies that attracted thousands, Obama backers volunteered to phone and ring doorbells. They also contributed millions to his campaign, far outstripping McCain's fundraising efforts. Winning the nomination after a grueling series of primaries pitting him against a determined Hillary Clinton, Obama chose as his running mate Delaware senator Joseph Biden, a foreign-affairs specialist.

McCain, downplaying his differences with the Bush administration, stressed his patriotism and conservative credentials, called for victory in Iraq, and courted evangelical Christians despite his earlier criticism of some politicized preachers as "agents of intolerance." In TV debates, the seventy-two-year-old McCain sometimes seemed out of touch, especially on economic matters, while the youthful, articulate Obama exuded confidence. When divisive pronouncements by his black minister stirred controversy, Obama delivered a thoughtful address on race that won favorable comment. Obama hammered the Bush administration's failures and emphasized his themes of change, hope, and overcoming partisan divisions in a cooperative, pragmatic spirit.

Winning a resounding victory, Obama captured 53 percent of the popular vote and a solid Electoral College majority, carrying not only the crucial swing states of Florida, Ohio, Pennsylvania, Michigan, and Colorado, but also Virginia and North Carolina, long Republican strongholds. Along with overwhelming black support, he won 67 percent of the Hispanic vote, a 14 percent increase over John Kerry's 2004 total. As the Democrats widened their majorities in both houses of Congress, Karl Rove's "permanent Republican majority" slipped away. Bush's unpopularity, the recession, and Obama's strengths as a campaigner had proven decisive. Among 18- to 24-year-olds, only 32 percent voted for McCain—an ill omen for Republicans' future hopes.

Around the world, people savored the historic moment. More than 140 years after the Emancipation Proclamation, half a century beyond the civil rights struggles of the 1950s and 1960s, an African-American won the presidency. Obama himself marveled in his inaugural address that sixty years earlier, his father could have been denied service in Washington restaurants.

Barack Obama was born in Hawaii in 1961, the son of a Kenyan university student and his white wife, an anthropologist from Kansas. The couple soon separated, and Obama was reared by his mother and grandparents. After college and Harvard Law School, he worked as a community organizer in Chicago rather than joining a law firm, and in 1996 won election to the Illinois legislature. His wife Michelle, also a lawyer, traced her southern ancestry to slavery days.

In his inaugural address, delivered before a vast throng in Washington and a global radio and television audience, President Obama rejected what he called the "worn out dogmas" that blocked bold responses to urgent problems. Implicitly targeting the Bush administration's excesses in the war on terrorism, he said: "We reject as false the choice between our safety and our ideals.... Those ideals still light the world, and we will not give them up for expedience's sake.... [O]ur power alone cannot protect us, nor does it entitle us to do as we please."

"[S]turdy alliances and enduring convictions," he continued, were as important as military might in achieving security. America's "patchwork heritage" of differing ethnicities and national origins, of "Christians and Muslims, Jews and Hindus and nonbelievers," was no liability, he declared, but a great asset as the nation sought to restore its battered reputation in an equally diverse world.

Obama named Hillary Clinton secretary of state. She quickly appointed two seasoned diplomats as special envoys to address the volatile Afghanistan and Pakistan region and the Israeli-Palestinian conflict, the source of such tension in U.S.-Muslim relations. Within days of his inauguration, Obama ordered the Guantánamo prison closed and granted an interview to Al-Arabiya, a popular Arabic-language television network. Obama's choice as Attorney General, Eric Holder, forthrightly declared in his Senate confirmation hearing that water boarding, the interrogation technique used on some Guantánamo prisoners, constituted torture and would not be allowed.

In a speech in Prague in April 2009, Obama pledged to work toward the goal of a world free of nuclear weapons. North Korea's nuclear tests, Iran's secretive nuclear program, and the dangerous instability of nuclear-armed Pakistan underscored the urgency of this issue.

Obama lifted Bush's ban on stem-cell research and named Steven Chu, a Nobel laureate in physics and advocate of alternative energy sources, to lead the Department of Energy. To head the EPA, he chose Lisa Jackson, an authority on environmental protection issues. Reversing Bush-administration policy, Obama announced that by 2016 all new automobiles, light trucks, and SUVs would be required to meet the tougher fuel-efficiency standards already adopted by California and other states. Obama also urged redoubled work on alternative energy sources to reduce the nation's reliance on fossil fuels—a diminishing resource—and to cut the emissions that contribute to global warming.

The new Treasury Secretary Timothy Geithner, formerly president of the Federal Reserve Bank of New York, and economist Lawrence Summers, named head of the White House National Economic Council, led Obama's recession-fighting team. (Ironically, both had supported the deregulatory legislation that helped lay the groundwork for the crisis.)

In February, Obama signed a $787 billion economic-stimulus bill. It channeled $120 billion to states for highways, bridges, rapid transit, and other infrastructure projects; appropriated additional billions for school construction and energy-related projects; and cut taxes for middle- and lower-income Americans while restoring higher rates for upper-income earners. Ominously, despite Obama's pleas for bipartisanship, only three Senate Republicans voted for the bill.

Obama also insisted that future distributions from the Wall Street bailout package must include rules assuring that banks actually channeled the funds into the credit market, to promote recovery. He also called for limits on executive compensation in return for federal money. When the *New York Times* revealed that Wall Street executives had pocketed $18.4 billion in bonuses in 2008 while their banks received government bailout money, Obama denounced the news as "outrageous."

While the administration threw a lifeline to the ailing auto industry in the form of a multibillion emergency bailout, Obama created a White House task force to oversee the industry's long-term restructuring. Chrysler filed for bankruptcy, though a takeover by the Italian automaker Fiat brightened its long-term prospects. As once mighty General Motors filed for bankruptcy as well, Americans realized the depth of the crisis facing this core domestic industry. A 2009 "cash for clunkers" program, granting government-funded rebates to car owners who traded gas guzzling older vehicles for more fuel-efficient models, provided at least a temporary boost to auto sales.

Despite the economic crisis, Obama pursued his top domestic goal: health-care reform, to control runaway costs while extending coverage to the uninsured. Securing cost-cutting pledges from the drug industry, health insurers, hospital associations, and other key players, Obama called on Congress to enact comprehensive health-care legislation.

Reform momentum soon slowed, however. As Congress members returned to their districts, they confronted agitated voters fearful of change. Some critics resorted to scare tactics, conjuring visions of government "death panels" that would deny care to the elderly or terminally ill. As they had since President Truman's day, opponents warned of "socialized medicine" and "a government-run health care system," even though Medicare, the federal health-insurance program for the elderly, enjoyed broad popularity. The pharmaceutical and health-insurance industries, profiting handsomely under the present system, opposed any cost-control regulations beyond what they had already voluntarily pledged.

Reform proponents, by contrast, pointed to the millions of uninsured Americans, the loss of coverage that often came with unemployment, insurance companies' denial of coverage to high-risk applicants, and the spiraling overall costs of U.S.

President Obama Proposes Stricter Oversight of Financial Institutions *At the White House in June 2009, the president proposes tougher regulation of financial institutions, to safeguard against the practices that led to a major crisis in 2008. He is joined by Treasury Secretary Timothy Geithner (left) and Federal Reserve Board chairman Ben Bernanke.*

health care in contrast to other nations with comparable or superior medical outcomes.

Despite Obama's call for bipartisan cooperation, party divisions hardened. Indeed, even Democrats were divided. Congressional Democrats from conservative districts or states, often thinly populated rural areas, nicknamed "blue dog" Democrats, favored a cautious, incremental approach. Democratic liberals, by contrast, supported a "public option," a government health insurance program, supplementing the private system, that would serve the uninsured and provide a yardstick for efficient, lower cost coverage. Fiscal conservatives warned that such a program would worsen already soaring budget deficits. The August 2009 death of Massachusetts Democratic senator Edward Kennedy, a champion of healthcare reform, inspired advocates to redouble efforts. Despite opposition, a reform measure seemed likely to pass, though its precise provisions remained unclear.

Meanwhile, the eight-year war in Afghanistan ground on, with increasingly uncertain prospects. With some 68,000 G.I.s deployed in that country (plus about 38,000 NATO troops), U.S. fatalities by early October 2009 neared nine hundred, with more than 2,500 wounded. As the Islamic fundamentalists known as the Taliban regained control in southern Afghanistan, they weakened the U.S.-backed government of President Hamid Karzai and destabilized neighboring Pakistan as well. Rampant government corruption, accusations of fraud in an August 2009 election, and Afghanistan's leading role in the cultivation of opium poppies from which heroin is manufactured further complicated the picture.

President Obama declared the Afghan struggle a "war of necessity" even as casualties mounted, America's NATO allies reduced their commitment, and homefront support eroded. Ironically, antiwar sentiment was strongest in Obama's own party, while conservative Republicans provided a core of support. Obama's well wishers recalled nervously how the Vietnam War had undermined Lyndon Johnson's domestic program, and how the Iraq War had eroded George W. Bush's effectiveness. When President Obama was unexpectedly awarded the Nobel Peace prize in October 2009, after only nine months in office, it was widely viewed as a gesture of support for his good intentions and an expression of hope for the future—a hope widely shared in a war-weary nation and world.

The nation faced uncertain times, but with a history of overcoming challenges and discovering sources of renewal. As President Obama declared in his inaugural address: "The time has come to reaffirm our enduring spirit, to choose our better history, to carry forward that precious gift... passed on from generation to generation: the God-given promise that all are equal, all are free, and all deserve a chance to pursue their full measure of happiness."

CHRONOLOGY
2001–2009

2001	Bush administration repudiates Kyoto protocol on emission standards. Congress passes $1.35 trillion tax cut bill. Stock market falls; wave of corporate bankruptcies and scandals. Congress passes No Child Left Behind Act. U.S. withdraws from ABM (Anti-Ballistic Missile) Treaty and pursues missile-defense system. Terrorist attacks on World Trade Center, Pentagon (September 11). U.S. and allied forces overthrow Taliban regime in Afghanistan. Captured fighters and others imprisoned at Guantánamo Bay, Cuba. USA-Patriot Act passed.
2002	McCain-Feingold Campaign Reform Act passed. Department of Homeland Security created. Bush authorizes warrantless spying by National Security Administration. Republicans gain in midterm elections.
2003	U.S. and coalition forces invade Iraq (March 21). North Korea withdraws from Nuclear Non-Proliferation Treaty. Prescription-drug benefits added to Medicare.
2004	Revelation of abuses at Baghdad's Abu Ghraib prison. George W. Bush wins second term, defeating John Kerry.
2005	Congress passes Energy Act. Trade deficit and budget deficit hit record levels. Bush names John Roberts and Samuel Alito to Supreme Court. Hurricane Katrina devastates New Orleans. Lobbyist Jack Abramoff indicted on multiple criminal charges.

2006   Tom DeLay resigns House seat.
Widespread criticism of government response to Hurricane Katrina.
Radical Hamas organization wins Palestinian elections.
Iran resumes nuclear enrichment program.
U.S. sells India nuclear fuel and reactor parts.
Administration's immigration-reform bill fails; arrests and deportation of illegal immigrants increase.
Democrats gain control of both houses in midterm elections.
Resignation of Defense Secretary Donald Rumsfeld.

2007   Bush sends more troops to Iraq; violence declines.
Real estate market falls; recession begins.

2008   United States and Iraq set timetable for U.S. troop withdrawals.
Military situation in Afghanistan worsens.
Recession deepens; major banks fail; job losses increase.
Congress passes bank bailout legislation.
Barack Obama, America's first African-American president, is elected; Democrats make gains.
Gaza rockets hit Israel; Israel responds with major military attack causing heavy civilian casualties.

2009   President Obama orders closing of Guantánamo prison.
Obama reverses Bush administration on vehicle emissions, stem-cell research.
Congress enacts broad economic stimulus package as recession worsens.

CONCLUSION

Reeling from the attacks of September 11, 2001, Americans supported President Bush's call for attacking al Qaeda terrorists and their Taliban protectors in Afghanistan, and Congress approved the administration's antiterrorism legislation. The proposed invasion of Iraq, promoted as an antiterrorism measure, also won approval, but quickly proved divisive.

On the domestic front, Congress passed Bush's proposed tax cut favoring the wealthy; an energy bill mainly drafted by the nation's oil, coal, and gas companies; and an education bill requiring universal testing in core subjects.

Support for the open-ended "war on terrorism" eroded amid worsening violence in Iraq, skepticism about the administration's case for invading Iraq, abuses of military prisoners and denial of their legal rights, and domestic spying in the name of security. The long-running Israeli-Palestinian conflict and nuclear-proliferation threats further challenged the administration. Despite mounting evidence, the Bush administration rejected international efforts to address global warming.

The social changes and technological innovations characteristic of the United States continued in the new century, with sustained migration to the South and West, high levels of Hispanic and Asian immigration, the graying of the baby-boom generation, and popular new communications technologies. Declining industrial production and an emergent information-based and service economy opened new opportunities but also disrupted the lives of many workers. Tax cuts, a stock market boom, and growth in the electronic technology and financial services sectors benefited some, but far from all, in these years. As globalization brought a tide of imported goods, the U.S. economy experienced strains, especially the troubled auto industry, and credit-card purchases created mountainous levels of consumer debt.

As federal deficits soared, the administration experienced setbacks in Bush's second term, including failed efforts to privatize social security and to reform immigration policy. The government's response to Hurricane Katrina, influence-peddling scandals, and continued damaging revelations relating to the Iraq War and domestic spying intensified doubts about the administration's competence and even its willingness to abide by the rule of law. As the administration lost support, Democrats made substantial gains in the 2006 midterm elections. As President Bush's approval ratings sank, an economic recession deepened public uneasiness.

In 2008, Democratic presidential candidate Barack Obama won a resounding—and historic—victory, becoming the United States's first African-American president. In addition, Democrats made sweeping gains at all levels. Taking office as the economic crisis worsened and challenges loomed globally, Obama pledged to set a new course for America at home and abroad.

What, then, is the "enduring vision" of our title? There is, of course, no single vision, but many. That is part of America's meaning. Nor is this a vision of a foreordained national destiny unfolding effortlessly, but rather of successive generations' often frustrating struggle to better their common life as a people. At their best, these shared aspirations are rooted in hope, not fear. In 1980, Jesse de la Cruz, a Mexican-American activist for California's migrant workers, summed up her philosophy: "Is America progressing toward the better?... With us, there's a saying: *La esperanza muere al ultimo*. Hope dies last. You can't lose hope. If you lose hope, that's losing everything."

Appendix A

THE DECLARATION
OF INDEPENDENCE

THE UNANIMOUS DECLARATION OF THE THIRTEEN UNITED STATES OF AMERICA

When in the Course of human events it becomes necessary for one people to dissolve the political bands which have connected them with another, and to assume among the Powers of the earth, the separate and equal station to which the Laws of Nature and of Nature's God entitle them, a decent respect to the opinions of mankind requires that they should declare the causes which impel them to the separation.

We hold these truths to be self-evident, that all men are created equal, that they are endowed by their Creator with certain unalienable Rights, that among these are Life, Liberty and the pursuit of Happiness. That to secure these rights, Governments are instituted among Men, deriving their just Powers from the consent of the governed. That whenever any Form of Government becomes destructive of these ends, it is the Right of the People to alter or to abolish it, and to institute new Government, laying its foundation on such principles and organizing its Powers in such form, as to them shall seem most likely to effect their Safety and Happiness. Prudence, indeed, will dictate that Governments long established should not be changed for light and transient causes; and accordingly all experience hath shewn, that mankind are more disposed to suffer, while evils are sufferable, than to right themselves by abolishing the forms to which they are accustomed. But when a long train of abuses and usurpations, pursuing invariably the same Object evinces a design to reduce them under absolute Despotism, it is their right, it is their duty, to throw off such Government, and to provide new Guards for their future security. Such has been the patient sufferance of these Colonies; and such is now the necessity which constrains them to alter their former Systems of Government. The history of the present King of Great Britain is a history of repeated injuries and usurpations, all having in direct object the establishment of an absolute Tyranny over these States. To prove this, let Facts be submitted to a candid world.

Text is reprinted from the facsimile of the engrossed copy in the National Archives. The original spelling, capitalization, and punctuation have been retained. Paragraphing has been added.

He has refused his Assent to Laws, the most wholesome and necessary for the public good.

He has forbidden his Governors to pass Laws of immediate and pressing importance, unless suspended in their operation till his Assent should be obtained; and when so suspended, he has utterly neglected to attend to them.

He has refused to pass other Laws for the accommodation of large districts of people, unless those people would relinquish the right of Representation in the Legislature, a right inestimable to them and formidable to tyrants only.

He has called together legislative bodies at places unusual, uncomfortable, and distant from the depository of their Public Records, for the sole Purpose of fatiguing them into compliance with his measures.

He has dissolved Representative Houses repeatedly, for opposing with manly firmness his invasions on the rights of the People.

He has refused for a long time, after such dissolutions, to cause others to be elected; whereby the Legislative Powers, incapable of Annihilation, have returned to the People at large for their exercise; the State remaining in the mean time exposed to all the dangers of invasion from without, and convulsions within.

He has endeavoured to prevent the Population of these States; for that purpose obstructing the Laws for Naturalization of Foreigners; refusing to pass others to encourage their migrations hither, and raising the conditions of new Appropriations of Lands.

He has obstructed the Administration of Justice, by refusing his Assent to Laws for establishing Judiciary Powers.

He has made Judges dependent on his Will alone, for the tenure of their offices, and the amount and payment of their salaries.

He has erected a multitude of New Offices, and sent hither swarms of Officers to harass our People, and eat out their substance.

He has kept among us, in times of peace, Standing Armies without the Consent of our legislatures.

He has affected to render the Military independent of and superior to the Civil Power.

He has combined with others to subject us to a jurisdiction foreign to our constitution, and unacknowledged by our laws; giving his Assent to their Acts of pretended Legislation:

For Quartering large bodies of armed troops among us:

For protecting them, by a mock Trial, from Punishment for any Murders which they should commit on the Inhabitants of these States:

For cutting off our Trade with all parts of the world:

For imposing Taxes on us without our Consent:

For depriving us in many cases, of the benefits of Trial by Jury:

For transporting us beyond Seas to be tried for pretended offences:

For abolishing the free System of English Laws in a neighbouring Province, establishing therein an Arbitrary government, and enlarging its Boundaries so as to render it at once an example and fit instrument for introducing the same absolute rule into these Colonies:

For taking away our Charters, abolishing our most valuable Laws, and altering fundamentally the Forms of our Governments:

For suspending our own Legislatures, and declaring themselves invested with Power to legislate for us in all cases whatsoever.

He has abdicated Government here, by declaring us out of his Protection, and waging War against us.

He has plundered our seas, ravaged our Coasts, burnt our towns, and destroyed the lives of our people.

He is at this time transporting large Armies of foreign Mercenaries to compleat the works of death, desolation and tyranny, already begun with circumstances of Cruelty and perfidy scarcely paralleled in the most barbarous ages, and totally unworthy the Head of a civilized nation.

He has constrained our fellow Citizens taken Captive on the high Seas to bear Arms against their Country, to become the executioners of their friends and Brethren, or to fall themselves by their Hands.

He has excited domestic insurrections amongst us, and has endeavoured to bring on the inhabitants of our frontiers, the merciless Indian Savages, whose known rule of warfare, is an undistinguished destruction of all ages, sexes and conditions.

In every stage of these Oppressions We have Petitioned for Redress in the most humble terms: Our repeated Petitions have been answered only by repeated injury. A Prince, whose character is thus marked by every act which may define a Tyrant, is unfit to be the ruler of a free People.

Nor have We been wanting in attentions to our British brethren. We have warned them from time to time of attempts by their legislature to extend an unwarrantable jurisdiction over us. We have reminded them of the circumstances of our emigration and settlement here. We have appealed to their native justice and magnanimity, and we have conjured them by the ties of our common kindred to disavow the usurpations, which, would inevitably interrupt our connections and correspondence. They too have been deaf to the voice of justice and of consanguinity. We must, therefore, acquiesce in the necessity, which denounces our Separation, and hold them, as we hold the rest of mankind, Enemies in War, in Peace Friends.

We, therefore, the Representatives of the United States of America, in General Congress, Assembled, appealing to the Supreme Judge of the world for the rectitude of our intentions, do, in the Name, and by Authority of the good People of these Colonies, solemnly publish and declare, That these United Colonies are, and of Right ought to be Free and Independent States; that they are Absolved from all Allegiance to the British Crown, and that all political connection between them and the State of Great Britain, is and ought to be totally dissolved; and that, as Free and Independent States, they have full Power to levy War, conclude Peace, contract Alliances, establish Commerce, and to do all other Acts and Things which Independent States may of right do. And for the support of this Declaration, with a firm reliance on the protection of divine Providence, we mutually pledge to each other our Lives, our Fortunes and our sacred Honor.

Appendix B

THE CONSTITUTION OF THE UNITED STATES OF AMERICA

We the People of the United States, in Order to form a more perfect Union, establish Justice, insure domestic Tranquility, provide for the common defence, promote the general Welfare, and secure the Blessings of Liberty to ourselves and our Posterity, do ordain and establish this Constitution for the United States of America.

Article I

Section 1   All legislative Powers herein granted shall be vested in a Congress of the United States, which shall consist of a Senate and House of Representatives.

Section 2   The House of Representatives shall be composed of Members chosen every second Year by the People of the several States, and the Electors in each State shall have the Qualifications requisite for Electors of the most numerous Branch of the State Legislature.

No Person shall be a Representative who shall not have attained to the Age of twenty five Years, and been seven Years a Citizen of the United States, and who shall not, when elected, be an Inhabitant of that State in which he shall be chosen.

Representatives and direct Taxes[1] shall be apportioned among the several States which may be included within this Union, according to their respective Numbers, which shall be determined by adding to the whole Number of free Persons, including those bound to Service for a Term of Years, and excluding Indians not taxed, three fifths of all other Persons.[2] The actual Enumeration shall be made within three Years after the first Meeting of the Congress of the United States, and within every subsequent Term of ten Years, in such Manner as they shall by Law direct. The Number of Representatives shall not exceed one for every thirty Thousand, but each State shall have at Least one Representative; and until such enumeration shall be made, the State of New Hampshire shall be entitled to chuse three; Massachusetts eight; Rhode Island and Providence Plantations one; Connecticut five; New York six; New Jersey four; Pennsylvania eight; Delaware one; Maryland six; Virginia ten; North Carolina five; South Carolina five; and Georgia three.

When vacancies happen in the Representation from any State, the Executive Authority thereof shall issue Writs of Election to fill such Vacancies.

Text is from the engrossed copy in the National Archives. Original spelling, capitalization, and punctuation have been retained.

The House of Representatives shall chuse their Speaker and other Officers; and shall have the sole Power of Impeachment.

Section 3   The Senate of the United States shall be composed of two Senators from each State, chosen by the Legislature thereof, for six Years; and each Senator shall have one Vote.[3]

Immediately after they shall be assembled in Consequence of the first Election, they shall be divided as equally as may be into three Classes. The Seats of the Senators of the first Class shall be vacated at the Expiration of the second Year, of the second Class at the Expiration of the fourth Year, and of the third Class at the Expiration of the sixth Year, so that one third may be chosen every second Year; and if Vacancies happen by Resignation, or otherwise, during the Recess of the Legislature of any State, the Executive thereof may make temporary Appointments until the next Meeting of the Legislature, which shall then fill such Vacancies.[4]

No Person shall be a Senator who shall not have attained to the Age of thirty Years, and been nine Years a Citizen of the United States, and who shall not, when elected, be an Inhabitant of that State for which he shall be chosen.

The Vice President of the United States shall be President of the Senate, but shall have no Vote, unless they be equally divided.

The Senate shall chuse their other Officers, and also a President pro tempore, in the Absence of the Vice President, or when he shall exercise the Office of President of the United States.

The Senate shall have the sole Power to try all Impeachments. When sitting for that Purpose, they shall be on Oath or Affirmation. When the President of the United States is tried, the Chief Justice shall preside: And no Person shall be convicted without the Concurrence of two thirds of the Members present.

Judgment in Cases of Impeachment shall not extend further than to removal from Office, and disqualification to hold and enjoy any Office of honor, Trust or Profit under the United States: but the Party convicted shall nevertheless be liable and subject to Indictment, Trial, Judgment and Punishment, according to Law.

Section 4   The Times, Places and Manner of holding Elections for Senators and Representatives, shall be prescribed in each State by the Legislature thereof, but the Congress may at any time by Law make or alter such Regulation, except as to the Places of chusing Senators.

The Congress shall assemble at least once in every Year, and such Meeting shall be on the first Monday in December, unless they shall by Law appoint a different Day.[5]

Section 5   Each House shall be the Judge of the Elections, Returns and Qualifications of its own Members, and a Majority of each shall constitute a Quorum to do Business; but a smaller Number may adjourn from day to day, and may be authorized to compel the Attendance of absent Members, in such Manner, and under such Penalties as each House may provide.

Each House may determine the Rules of its Proceedings, punish its Members for disorderly Behaviour, and, with the Concurrence of two thirds, expel a Member.

Each House shall keep a Journal of its Proceedings, and from time to time publish the same, excepting such Parts as may in their Judgment require Secrecy; and the Yeas and Nays of the Members of either House on any question shall, at the Desire of one fifth of those Present, be entered on the Journal.

Neither House, during the Session of Congress, shall, without the Consent of the other, adjourn for more than three days, nor to any other Place than that in which the two Houses shall be sitting.

Section 6   The Senators and Representatives shall receive a Compensation for their Services, to be ascertained by Law, and paid out of the Treasury of the United States. They shall in all Cases, except Treason, Felony and Breach of the Peace, be privileged from Arrest during their Attendance at the Session of their respective Houses, and in going to and returning from the same; and for any Speech or Debate in either House, they shall not be questioned in any other Place.

No Senator or Representative shall, during the Time for which he was elected, be appointed to any civil Office under the Authority of the United States, which shall have been created, or the Emoluments whereof shall have been encreased during such time; and no Person holding any Office under the United States, shall be a Member of either House during his Continuance in Office.

Section 7   All Bills for raising Revenue shall originate in the House of Representatives; but the Senate may propose or concur with Amendments as on other Bills.

Every Bill which shall have passed the House of Representatives and the Senate shall, before it become a Law, be presented to the President of the United States; If he approve he shall sign it, but if not he shall return it, with his Objections to that House in which it shall have originated, who shall enter the Objections at large on their Journal, and proceed to reconsider it. If after such Reconsideration two thirds of that House shall agree to pass the Bill, it shall be sent, together with the Objections, to the other House, by which it shall likewise be reconsidered, and if approved by two thirds of that House, it shall become a Law. But in all such Cases the Votes of both Houses shall be determined by yeas and Nays, and the Names of the Persons voting for and against the Bill shall be entered on the Journal of each House respectively. If any Bill shall not be returned by the President within ten Days (Sundays excepted) after it shall have been presented to him, the Same shall be a Law, in like Manner as if he had signed it, unless the Congress by their Adjournment prevent its Return, in which Case it shall not be a Law.

Every Order, Resolution, or Vote to which the Concurrence of the Senate and House of Representatives may be necessary (except on a question of Adjournment) shall be presented to the President of the United States; and before the Same shall take Effect, shall be approved by him, or being disapproved by him shall be repassed by two thirds of the Senate and House of Representatives, according to the Rules and Limitations prescribed in the Case of a Bill.

Section 8   The Congress shall have power To lay and collect Taxes, Duties, Imposts and Excises, to pay the Debts and provide for the common Defence and general Welfare of the United States; but all Duties, Imposts and Excises shall be uniform throughout the United States;

To borrow Money on the credit of the United States;

To regulate Commerce with foreign Nations, and among the several States, and with the Indian Tribes;

To establish an uniform Rule of Naturalization, and uniform Laws on the subject of Bankruptcies throughout the United States;

To coin Money, regulate the Value thereof, and of foreign Coin, and fix the Standard of Weights and Measures;

To provide for the Punishment of counterfeiting the Securities and current Coin of the United States;

To establish Post Offices and post Roads;

To promote the Progress of Science and useful Arts, by securing for limited Times to Authors and Inventors the exclusive Right to their respective Writings and Discoveries;

To constitute Tribunals inferior to the supreme Court;

To define and punish Piracies and Felonies committed on the high Seas, and Offences against the Law of Nations;

To declare War, grant Letters of Marque and Reprisal, and make Rules concerning Captures on Land and Water;

To raise and support Armies, but no Appropriation of Money to that Use shall be for a longer Term than two Years;

To provide and maintain a Navy;

To make Rules for the Government and Regulation of the land and naval Forces;

To provide for calling forth the Militia to execute the Laws of the Union, suppress Insurrections and repel Invasions;

To provide for organizing, arming, and disciplining, the Militia, and for governing such Part of them as may be employed in the Service of the United States, reserving to the States respectively, the Appointment of the Officers, and the Authority of training the Militia according to the discipline prescribed by Congress;

To exercise exclusive Legislation in all Cases whatsoever, over such District (not exceeding ten Miles square) as may, by Cession of particular States, and the Acceptance of Congress, become the Seat of the Government of the United States, and to exercise like Authority over all Places purchased by the Consent of the Legislature of the State in which the Same shall be, for the Erection of Forts, Magazines, Arsenals, dock-Yards, and other needful Buildings;—And

To make all Laws which shall be necessary and proper for carrying into Execution the foregoing Powers, and all other Powers vested by this Constitution in the Government of the United States, or in any Department or Officer thereof.

Section 9 The Migration or Importation of such Persons as any of the States now existing shall think proper to admit, shall not be prohibited by the Congress prior to the Year one thousand eight hundred and eight, but a Tax or duty may be imposed on such Importation, not exceeding ten dollars for each Person.

The Privilege of the Writ of Habeas Corpus shall not be suspended, unless when in Cases of Rebellion or Invasion the public Safety may require it.

No Bill of Attainder or ex post facto Law shall be passed.

No Capitation, or other direct, Tax shall be laid, unless in Proportion to the Census or Enumeration herein before directed to be taken.

No Tax or Duty shall be laid on Articles exported from any State.

No Preference shall be given by any Regulation of Commerce or Revenue to the Ports of one State over those of another: nor shall Vessels bound to, or from, one State, be obliged to enter, clear, or pay Duties in another.

No Money shall be drawn from the Treasury, but in Consequence of Appropriations made by Law, and a regular Statement and Account of the Receipts and Expenditures of all public Money shall be published from time to time.

No Title of Nobility shall be granted by the United States: And no Person holding any Office of Profit or Trust under them, shall, without the Consent of the Congress, accept of any present, Emolument, Office, or Title, of any kind whatever, from any King, Prince, or foreign State.

Section 10   No State shall enter into any Treaty, Alliance, or Confederation; grant Letters of Marque and Reprisal; coin Money; emit Bills of Credit; make any Thing but gold and silver Coin a Tender in Payment of Debts; pass any Bill of Attainder, ex post facto Law, or Law impairing the Obligation of Contracts, or grant any Title of Nobility.

No State shall, without the Consent of the Congress, lay any Imposts or Duties on Imports or Exports, except what may be absolutely necessary for executing its inspection Laws: and the net Produce of all Duties and Imposts, laid by any State on Imports or Exports, shall be for the Use of the Treasury of the United States; and all such Laws shall be subject to the Revision and Controul of the Congress.

No State shall, without the Consent of Congress, lay any Duty of Tonnage, keep Troops, or Ships of War in time of Peace, enter into any Agreement or Compact with another State, or with a foreign Power, or engage in War, unless actually invaded, or in such imminent Danger as will not admit of delay.

Article II

Section 1   The executive Power shall be vested in a President of the United States of America. He shall hold his Office during the Term of four Years, and, together with the Vice President, chosen for the same Term, be elected, as follows:

Each State shall appoint, in such Manner as the Legislature thereof may direct, a Number of Electors, equal to the whole Number of Senators and Representatives to which the State may be entitled in the Congress: but no Senator or Representative, or Person holding an Office of Trust or Profit under the United States, shall be appointed an Elector.

The Electors shall meet in their respective States, and vote by Ballot for two Persons, of whom one at least shall not be an Inhabitant of the same State with themselves. And they shall make a List of all the Persons voted for, and of the Number of Votes for each; which List they shall sign and certify, and transmit sealed to the Seat of the Government of the United States, directed to the President of the Senate. The President of the Senate shall, in the Presence of the Senate and House of Representatives, open all the Certificates, and the Votes shall then be counted. The Person having the greatest Number of Votes shall be the President, if such Number be a Majority of the whole Number of Electors appointed; and if there be more than one who have such Majority, and have an equal Number of Votes, then the House of Representatives shall immediately chuse by Ballot one of them for President; and if no Person have a Majority, then from the five highest on the List the said House shall in like Manner chuse the President. But in chusing the President, the Votes shall be taken by States, the Representation from each State having one Vote; A quorum for this Purpose shall consist of a Member or Members from two thirds of the States, and a Majority of all the States shall be necessary to a Choice. In every Case, after the Choice of the President, the Person having the greatest Number of Votes of the Electors shall be the Vice President. But if there should remain two or more who have equal Votes, the Senate shall chuse from them by Ballot the Vice President.[6]

The Congress may determine the Time of chusing the Electors, and the Day on which they shall give their Votes; which Day shall be the same throughout the United States.

No Person except a natural born Citizen, or a Citizen of the United States, at the time of the Adoption of this Constitution, shall be eligible to the Office of President, neither shall any Person be eligible to that Office who shall not have attained to the Age of thirty five Years, and been fourteen Years a Resident within the United States.

In Case of the Removal of the President from Office, or of his Death, Resignation, or Inability to discharge the Powers and Duties of the said Office, the Same shall devolve on the Vice President, and the Congress may by Law provide for the Case of Removal, Death, Resignation or Inability, both of the President and Vice President, declaring what Officer shall then act as President, and such Officer shall act accordingly, until the Disability be removed, or a President shall be elected.[7]

The President shall, at stated Times, receive for his Services, a Compensation, which shall neither be encreased nor diminished during the Period for which he shall have been elected, and he shall not receive within that Period any other Emolument from the United States, or any of them.

Before he enter on the Execution of his Office, he shall take the following Oath or Affirmation:—"I do solemnly swear (or affirm) that I will faithfully execute the Office of President of the United States, and will to the best of my Ability, preserve, protect and defend the Constitution of the United States."

Section 2   The President shall be Commander in Chief of the Army and Navy of the United States, and of the Militia of the several States, when called into the actual Service of the United States; he may require the Opinion, in writing, of the principal Officer in each of the executive Departments, upon any Subject relating to the Duties of their respective Offices, and he shall have Power to grant Reprieves and Pardons for Offences against the United States, except in Cases of Impeachment.

He shall have Power, by and with the Advice and Consent of the Senate, to make Treaties, provided two thirds of the Senators present concur; and he shall nominate, and by and with the Advice and Consent of the Senate, shall appoint Ambassadors, other public Ministers and Consuls, Judges of the supreme Court, and all other Officers of the United States, whose Appointments are not herein otherwise provided for, and which shall be established by Law; but the Congress may by Law vest the Appointment of such inferior Officers, as they think proper, in the President alone, in the Courts of Law, or in the Heads of Departments.

The President shall have Power to fill up all Vacancies that may happen during the Recess of the Senate, by granting Commissions which shall expire at the End of their next Session.

Section 3   He shall from time to time give the Congress Information of the State of the Union, and recommend to their Consideration such Measures as he shall judge necessary and expedient; he may, on extraordinary Occasions, convene both Houses, or either of them, and in Case of Disagreement between them, with Respect to the Time of Adjournment, he may adjourn them to such Time as he shall think proper; he shall receive Ambassadors and other public Ministers; he shall take Care that the Laws be faithfully executed, and shall Commission all the Officers of the United States.

Section 4   The President, Vice President and all civil Officers of the United States, shall be removed from Office on Impeachment for, and Conviction of, Treason, Bribery, or other high Crimes and Misdemeanors.

Article III

Section 1   The judicial Power of the United States, shall be vested in one supreme Court, and in such inferior Courts as the Congress may from time to time ordain and establish. The Judges, both of the supreme and inferior Courts, shall hold their Offices during good Behaviour, and shall, at stated Times, receive for their Services, a Compensation, which shall not be diminished during their Continuance in Office.

Section 2   The judicial Power shall extend to all Cases, in Law and Equity, arising under this Constitution, the Laws of the United States, and Treaties made, or which shall be made, under their Authority;—to all Cases affecting Ambassadors, other public Ministers and Consuls;—to all Cases of admiralty and maritime Jurisdiction;—to Controversies to which the United States shall be a Party;—to Controversies between two or more States;—between a State and Citizens of another State;[8]—between Citizens of different States,—between Citizens of the same State claiming Lands under Grants of different States, and between a State, or the Citizens thereof, and foreign States, Citizens or Subjects.

In all Cases affecting Ambassadors, other public Ministers and Consuls, and those in which a State shall be Party, the supreme Court shall have original Jurisdiction. In all the other Cases before mentioned, the supreme Court shall have appellate Jurisdiction, both as to Law and Fact, with such Exceptions, and under such Regulations as the Congress shall make.

The Trial of all Crimes, except in Cases of Impeachment, shall be by Jury; and such Trial shall be held in the State where the said Crimes shall have been committed; but when not committed within any State, the Trial shall be at such Place or Places as the Congress may by Law have directed.

Section 3 Treason against the United States, shall consist only in levying War against them, or in adhering to their Enemies, giving them Aid and Comfort. No Person shall be convicted of Treason unless on the Testimony of two Witnesses to the same overt Act, or on Confession in open Court.

The Congress shall have Power to declare the Punishment of Treason, but no Attainder of Treason shall work Corruption of Blood, or Forfeiture except during the Life of the Person attainted.

Article IV

Section 1 Full Faith and Credit shall be given in each State to the public Acts, Records, and judicial Proceedings of every other State. And the Congress may by general Laws prescribe the Manner in which such Acts, Records and Proceedings shall be proved, and the Effect thereof.

Section 2 The Citizens of each State shall be entitled to all Privileges and Immunities of Citizens in the several States.

A Person charged in any State with Treason, Felony, or other Crime, who shall flee from Justice, and be found in another State, shall on Demand of the executive Authority of the State from which he fled, be delivered up, to be removed to the State having Jurisdiction of the Crime.

No Person held to Service or Labour in one State, under the Laws thereof, escaping into another, shall, in Consequence of any Law or Regulation therein, be discharged from such Service or Labour, but shall be delivered up on Claim of the Party to whom such Service or Labour may be due.

Section 3 New States may be admitted by the Congress into this Union; but no new State shall be formed or erected within the Jurisdiction of any other State, nor any State be formed by the Junction of two or more States, or Parts of States, without the Consent of the Legislatures of the States concerned as well as of the Congress.

The Congress shall have Power to dispose of and make all needful Rules and Regulations respecting the Territory or other Property belonging to the United States; and nothing in this Constitution shall be so construed as to Prejudice any Claims of the United States, or of any particular State.

Section 4 The United States shall guarantee to every State in this Union a Republican Form of Government, and shall protect each of them against Invasion; and on Application of the Legislature, or of the Executive (when the Legislature cannot be convened) against domestic Violence.

Article V

The Congress, whenever two thirds of both Houses shall deem it necessary, shall propose Amendments to this Constitution, or, on the Application of the Legislatures of two thirds of the several States, shall call a Convention for proposing Amendments, which, in either Case, shall be valid to all Intents and Purposes, as Part of this Constitution, when ratified by the Legislatures of three fourths of the several States, or by Conventions in three fourths thereof, as the one or the other Mode of Ratification may be proposed by the Congress; Provided that no Amendment which may be made prior to the Year One thousand eight hundred and eight shall in any Manner affect the first and fourth Clauses in the Ninth Section of the first Article; and that no State, without its Consent, shall be deprived of its equal Suffrage in the Senate.

Article VI

All Debts contracted and Engagements entered into, before the Adoption of this Constitution, shall be as valid against the United States under this Constitution, as under the Confederation.

This Constitution, and the Laws of the United States which shall be made in Pursuance thereof; and all Treaties made, or which shall be made, under the Authority of the United States, shall be the supreme Law of the Land; and the Judges in every State shall be bound thereby, any Thing in the Constitution or Laws of any State to the Contrary notwithstanding.

The Senators and Representatives before mentioned, and the Members of the several State Legislatures, and all executive and judicial Officers, both of the United States and of the several States, shall be bound by Oath or Affirmation, to support this Constitution; but no religious Test shall ever be required as a Qualification to any Office or public Trust under the United States.

Article VII

The Ratification of the Conventions of nine States, shall be sufficient for the Establishment of this Constitution between the States so ratifying the Same.

Done in Convention by the Unanimous Consent of the States present the Seventeenth Day of September in the Year of our Lord one thousand seven hundred and Eighty seven and of the Independence of the United States of America the Twelfth. In witness whereof We have hereunto subscribed our Names,

Articles in Addition to, and Amendment of, the Constitution of the United States of America, Proposed by Congress, and Ratified by the Legislatures of the Several States, Pursuant to the Fifth Article of the Original Constitution.

Amendment I[9]

Congress shall make no law respecting an establishment of religion, or prohibiting the free exercise there-of; or abridging the freedom of speech, or of the press; or the right of the people peaceably to assemble, and to petition the Government for a redress of grievances.

Amendment II

A well regulated Militia, being necessary to the security of a free State, the right of the people to keep and bear Arms shall not be infringed.

Amendment III

No Soldier shall, in time of peace, be quartered in any house, without the consent of the Owner, nor in time of war, but in a manner to be prescribed by law.

Amendment IV

The right of the people to be secure in their persons, houses, papers, and effects, against unreasonable searches and seizures, shall not be violated, and no Warrants shall issue, but upon probable cause, supported by Oath or affirmation, and particularly describing the place to be searched, and the persons or things to be seized.

Amendment V

No person shall be held to answer for a capital or otherwise infamous crime, unless on a presentment or indictment of a Grand Jury, except in cases arising in the land or naval forces, or in the Militia, when in actual service in time of War or public danger; nor shall any person be subject for the same offence to be twice put in jeopardy of life or limb; nor shall be compelled in any criminal case to be a witness against himself, nor be deprived of life, liberty, or property, without due process of law; nor shall private property be taken for public use, without just compensation.

Amendment VI

In all criminal prosecutions, the accused shall enjoy the right to a speedy and public trial, by an impartial jury of the State and district wherein the crime shall have been committed, which district shall have been previously ascertained by law, and to be informed of the nature and cause of the accusation; to be confronted with the witnesses against him; to have compulsory process for obtaining witnesses in his favor, and to have the Assistance of Counsel for his defence.

Amendment VII

In suits at common law, where the value in controversy shall exceed twenty dollars, the right of trial by jury shall be preserved, and no fact tried by a jury, shall be otherwise reexamined in any Court of the United States, than according to the rules of the common law.

Amendment VIII

Excessive bail shall not be required, nor excessive fines imposed, nor cruel and unusual punishments inflicted.

Amendment IX

The enumeration in the Constitution, of certain rights, shall not be construed to deny or disparage others retained by the people.

Amendment X

The powers not delegated to the United States by the Constitution; nor prohibited by it to the States, are reserved to the States respectively, or to the people.

Amendment XI[10]

The Judicial power of the United States shall not be construed to extend to any suit in law or equity, commenced or prosecuted against one of the United States by Citizens of another State, or by Citizens or Subjects of any Foreign State.

Amendment XII[11]

The Electors shall meet in their respective States and vote by ballot for President and Vice-President, one of whom, at least, shall not be an inhabitant of the same State with themselves; they shall name in their ballots the person voted for as President, and in distinct ballots the person voted for as Vice-President, and they shall make distinct lists of all persons voted for as President, and of all persons voted for as Vice-President, and of the number of votes for each, which lists they shall sign and certify, and transmit sealed to the seat of the government of the United States, directed to the President of the Senate;—The President of the Senate shall, in the presence of the Senate and House of Representatives, open all the certificates and the votes shall then be counted;—The person having the greatest number of votes for President, shall be the President, if such number be a majority of the whole number of Electors appointed; and if no person have such majority, then from the persons having the highest numbers not exceeding three on the list of those voted for as President, the House of Representatives shall choose immediately, by ballot, the President. But in choosing the President, the votes shall be taken by states, the representation from each state having one vote; a quorum for this purpose shall consist of a member or members from two-thirds of the states, and a majority of all the states shall be necessary to a choice. And if the House of Representatives shall not choose a President whenever the right of choice shall devolve upon them, before the fourth day of March next following, then the Vice-President shall act as President, as in the case of the death or other constitutional disability of the President.—The person having the greatest number of votes as Vice-President, shall be the Vice-President, if such number be a majority of the whole number of Electors appointed, and if no person have a majority, then from the two highest numbers on the list, the Senate shall choose the Vice-President; a quorum for the purpose shall consist of two-thirds of the whole number of Senators, and a majority of the whole number shall be necessary to a choice. But no person constitutionally ineligible to the office of President shall be eligible to that of Vice-President of the United States.

Amendment XIII[12]

Section 1   Neither slavery nor involuntary servitude, except as a punishment for crime whereof the party shall have been duly convicted, shall exist within the United States, or any place subject to their jurisdiction.

Section 2   Congress shall have power to enforce this article by appropriate legislation.

Amendment XIV[13]

Section 1   All persons born or naturalized in the United States, and subject to the jurisdiction thereof, are citizens of the United States and of the State wherein they reside. No State shall make or enforce any law which shall abridge the privileges or immunities of citizens of the United States; nor shall any State deprive any person of life, liberty, or property, without due process of law; nor deny to any person within its jurisdiction the equal protection of the laws.

Section 2   Representatives shall be apportioned among the several States according to their respective numbers, counting the whole number of persons in each State, excluding Indians not taxed. But when the right to vote at any election for the choice of electors for President and Vice-President of the United States, Representatives in Congress, the Executive and Judicial officers of a State, or the members of the Legislature thereof, is denied to any of the male inhabitants of such State, being twenty-one years of age, and citizens of the United States, or in any way abridged, except for participation in rebellion, or other crime, the basis of representation therein shall be reduced in the proportion which the number of such male citizens shall bear to the whole number of male citizens twenty-one years of age in such State.

Section 3   No person shall be a Senator or Representative in Congress, or elector of President and Vice-President, or hold any office, civil or military, under the United States, or under any State, who, having previously taken an oath, as a member of Congress, or as an officer of the United States, or as a member of any State legislature, or as an executive or judicial officer of any State, to support the Constitution of the United States, shall have engaged in insurrection or rebellion against the same, or given aid or comfort to the enemies thereof. But Congress may by a vote of two-thirds of each House, remove such disability.

Section 4   The validity of the public debt of the United States, authorized by law, including debts incurred for payment of pensions and bounties for services in suppressing insurrection or rebellion, shall not be questioned. But neither the United States nor any State shall assume or pay any debt or obligation incurred in aid of insurrection or rebellion against the United States, or any claim for the loss or emancipation of any slave; but all such debts, obligations, and claims shall be held illegal and void.

Section 5   The Congress shall have the power to enforce, by appropriate legislation, the provisions of this article.

Amendment XV[14]

Section 1   The right of citizens of the United States to vote shall not be denied or abridged by the United States or by any State on account of race, color, or previous conditions of servitude—

Section 2   The Congress shall have power to enforce this article by appropriate legislation.

Amendment XVI[15]

The Congress shall have power to lay and collect taxes on incomes, from whatever source derived, without apportionment among the several States, and without regard to any census or enumeration.

Amendment XVII[16]

The Senate of the United States shall be composed of two Senators from each State, elected by the people thereof, for six years; and each Senator shall have one vote. The electors in each State shall have the qualifications requisite for electors of the most numerous branch of the State legislatures.

When vacancies happen in the representation of any State in the Senate, the executive authority of such State shall issue writs of election to fill such vacancies: *Provided,* That the legislature of any State may empower the executive thereof to make temporary appointments until the people fill the vacancies by election as the legislature may direct.

This amendment shall not be so construed as to affect the election or term of any Senator chosen before it becomes valid as part of the Constitution.

Amendment XVIII[17]

Section 1   After one year from the ratification of this article the manufacture, sale, or transportation of intoxicating liquors within, the importation thereof into, or the exportation thereof from the United States and all territory subject to the jurisdiction thereof for beverage purposes is hereby prohibited.

Section 2   The Congress and the several States shall have concurrent power to enforce this article by appropriate legislation.

Section 3   This article shall be inoperative unless it shall have been ratified as an amendment to the Constitution by the legislatures of the several States, as provided in the Constitution, within seven years from the date of the submission hereof to the States by the Congress.

Amendment XIX[18]

Section 1   The right of citizens of the United States to vote shall not be denied or abridged by the United States or by any State on account of sex.

Congress shall have power to enforce this article by appropriate legislation.

Amendment XX[19]

Section 1   The terms of the President and Vice-President shall end at noon on the 20th day of January, and the terms of Senators and Representatives at noon on the 3rd day of January, of the years in which such terms would have ended if this article had not been ratified; and the terms of their successors shall then begin.

Section 2   The Congress shall assemble at least once in every year, and such meeting shall begin at noon on the 3rd day of January, unless they shall by law appoint a different day.

Section 3   If, at the time fixed for the beginning of the term of the President, the President elect shall have died, the Vice-President elect shall become President. If a President shall not have been chosen before the time fixed for the beginning of his term, or if the President elect shall have failed to qualify, then the Vice-President elect shall act as President until a President shall have qualified; and the Congress may by law provide for the case wherein neither a President elect nor a Vice-President elect shall have qualified, declaring who shall then act as President, or the manner in which one who is to act shall be selected, and such person shall act accordingly until a President or Vice-President shall have qualified.

Section 4   The Congress may by law provide for the case of the death of any of the persons from whom the House of Representatives may choose a President whenever the right of choice shall have devolved upon them, and for the case of the death of any of the persons from whom the Senate may choose a Vice-President whenever the right of choice shall have devolved upon them.

Section 5   Sections 1 and 2 shall take effect on the 15th day of October following the ratification of this article.

Section 6   This article shall be inoperative unless it shall have been ratified as an amendment to the Constitution by the legislatures of three-fourths of the several States within seven years from the date of its submission.

Amendment XXI[20]

Section 1   The eighteenth article of amendment to the Constitution of the United States is hereby repealed.

Section 2   The transportation or importation into any State, Territory, or possession of the United States for delivery or use therein of intoxicating liquors, in violation of the laws thereof, is hereby prohibited.

Section 3   This article shall be inoperative unless it shall have been ratified as an amendment to the Constitution by conventions in the several States, as provided in the Constitution, within seven years from the date of the submission hereof to the States by the Congress.

Amendment XXII[21]

No person shall be elected to the office of the President more than twice, and no person who has held the office of President, or acted as President, for more than two years of a term to which some other person was elected President shall be electesd to the office of the President more than once.

But this Article shall not apply to any person holding the office of President when this Article was proposed by the Congress, and shall not prevent any person who may be holding the office of President, or acting as President, during the term within which this Article becomes operative from holding the office of President or acting as President during the remainder of such term.

Amendment XXIII[22]

Section 1   The District constituting the seat of Government of the United States shall appoint in such manner as the Congress may direct:

A number of electors of President and Vice President equal to the whole number of Senators and Representatives in Congress to which the District would be entitled if it were a State, but in no event more than the least populous State; they shall be in addition to those appointed by the States, but they shall be considered, for the purposes of the election of President and Vice President, to be electors appointed by the State; and they shall meet in the District and perform such duties as provided by the twelfth article of amendment.

Section 2   The Congress shall have power to enforce this article by appropriate legislation.

Amendment XXIV[23]

Section 1   The right of citizens of the United States to vote in any primary or other election for President or Vice President, or for Senator or Representative in Congress, shall not be denied or abridged by the United States or any State by reason of failure to pay any poll tax or other tax.

Section 2   The Congress shall have power to enforce this article by appropriate legislation.

Amendment XXV[24]

Section 1   In case of the removal of the President from office or of his death or resignation, the Vice President shall become President.

Section 2   Whenever there is a vacancy in the office of the Vice President, the President shall nominate a Vice President who shall take office upon confirmation by a majority vote of both Houses of Congress.

Section 3   Whenever the President transmits to the President pro tempore of the Senate and the Speaker of the House of Representatives his written declaration that he is unable to discharge the powers and duties of his office, and until he transmits them a written declaration to the contrary, such powers and duties shall be discharged by the Vice President as Acting President.

Section 4   Whenever the Vice President and a majority of either the principal officers of the executive department or of such other body as Congress may by law provide, transmit to the President pro tempore of the Senate and the Speaker of the House of Representatives their written declaration that the President is unable to discharge the powers and duties of his office, the Vice President shall immediately assume the powers and duties of the office of Acting President.

Thereafter, when the President transmits to the President pro tempore of the Senate and the Speaker of the House of Representatives his written declaration that no inability exists, he shall resume the powers and duties of his office unless the Vice President and a majority of either the principal officers of the executive department or of such other body as Congress may by law provide, transmit within four days to the President pro tempore of the Senate and the Speaker of the House of Representatives their written declaration that the President is unable to discharge the powers and duties of his office. Thereupon Congress shall decide the issue, assembling within forty-eight hours for that purpose if not in session. If the Congress, within twenty-one days after receipt of the latter written declaration, or, if Congress is not in session, within twenty-one days after Congress is required to assemble, determines by two-thirds vote of both Houses that the President is unable to discharge the powers and duties of his office, the Vice-President shall continue to discharge the same as Acting President; otherwise, the President shall resume the powers and duties of his office.

Amendment XXVI[25]

Section 1   The right of citizens of the United States, who are eighteen years of age or older, to vote shall not be denied or abridged by the United States or by any State on account of age.

Section 2   The Congress shall have power to enforce this article by appropriate legislation.

Amendment XXVII[26]

No law, varying the compensation for the service of the Senators and Representatives, shall take effect, until an election of Representatives shall have intervened.

NOTES

1. Modified by the Sixteenth Amendment.
2. Replaced by the Fourteenth Amendment.
3. Superseded by the Seventeenth Amendment.
4. Modified by the Seventeenth Amendment.
5. Superseded by the Twentieth Amendment.
6. Superseded by the Twelfth Amendment.
7. Modified by the Twenty-fifth Amendment.
8. Modified by the Eleventh Amendment.
9. The first ten amendments were passed by Congress September 25, 1789. They were ratified by three-fourths of the states December 15, 1791.
10. Passed March 4, 1794. Ratified January 23, 1795.

11. Passed December 9, 1803. Ratified June 15, 1804.
12. Passed January 31, 1865. Ratified December 6, 1865.
13. Passed June 13, 1866. Ratified July 9, 1868.
14. Passed February 26, 1869. Ratified February 2, 1870.
15. Passed July 12, 1909. Ratified February 3, 1913.
16. Passed May 13, 1912. Ratified April 8, 1913.
17. Passed December 18, 1917. Ratified January 16, 1919.
18. Passed June 4, 1919. Ratified August 18, 1920.
19. Passed March 2, 1932. Ratified January 23, 1933.
20. Passed February 20, 1933. Ratified December 5, 1933.
21. Passed March 12, 1947. Ratified March 1, 1951.
22. Passed June 16, 1960. Ratified April 3, 1961.
23. Passed August 27, 1962. Ratified January 23, 1964.
24. Passed July 6, 1965. Ratified February 11, 1967.
25. Passed March 23, 1971. Ratified July 5, 1971.
26. Passed September 25, 1789. Ratified May 7, 1992.

Index

AAA, *see* **Agricultural Adjustment Administration**
ABM, *see* Anti-Ballistic Missile (ABM) Treaty
Abolition and abolitionists, 312–315; free soil, 420; soldiers in Civil War and, 455–456; Southern view of, 432; *Uncle Tom's Cabin*, 417; women's rights and, 316–317
Abortion: conservatives and, 939; nineteenth century, 282–283; sexual revolution and, 911
Abramoff, Jack, 1005–1006
Abu Ghraib, 991
Acoma Indians, 42
Acorns, 13
Adams, Abigail, 175, 221
Adams, John, 144, 151, 152, 154, 172, 174, 181; election of 1800 and, 215–216; Indian removal and, 261; President, 213; vice-presidency, 196, 197
Adams, John Quincy, 398, 402; presidency, 289–291; Secretary of State, **254–255**
Adams-Onis (Transcontinental) Treaty, 254–255, 260, 388
Adams, Samuel, 139, 145, 147, 151
Addams, Jane, 592–593, 636, 643, 682, 683, 718
Adena, 11
Administration of Justice Act, 150
Advertising, 551, 712; political, 715; WWI propaganda and, 692–694
AEF, *see* **American Expeditionary Force**
Affirmative action, 885
Afghanistan: Obama and, 1013–1014; Reagan and, 946; Soviet invasion, 933, 946; U.S. invasion, 979–980 (map), 1007
AFL, *see* **American Federation of Labor**

Africa: colonization by free blacks, 312–313; Rwanda, 964; slave trade and, 30–33 *See also* West Africa
African-Americans: advance in WWII, 802–804; after Reconstruction, 620–624; antagonism toward, in Reconstruction, 492–494; appeals for liberty, 149; "black codes", 483–484; blackface, 597; Black Power, 883–974; Carolinas, legal harassment of in, 104; Christianity and, 376–378; churches, 277, 496, 655; in Civil War, 461–462; Democratic coalition and, 758–760, 941; diversity of population and, 999; draft and, 696; emergence from slavery, 375–379; education and, 277; exodus from South, 508, 654; farmers' movements and, 619, 621; freedmen, under Reconstruction, 491; Garveyism, 734–735; ghettos, 581–582; Harlem Renaissance, 729–730; inequality and free, 277; Jim Crow, demise of, 866–867; in labor unions, 566, 714; legal status post-Revolution, 224; life under slavery, 366–375; Los Angeles riots, 954; loyalists among, 160; lynching, 620–621, 655, 705, 759, 769; migrations, 495, 623, 697–698; military service and, 176, 803; Missouri Compromise and free, 253; Montgomery bus boycott, 866–868; music, in antebellum south, 378–379; New Deal and, 759–760; organization of, 656; poverty among, post-WWII, 862–863; Progressive racism

and, 654–656; protest, in civil rights movement, 878–879; Protestantism and, 119; ragtime and, 597–598; resistance to racism, 769; Revolution and, 175–178; self-help among community, 225–226; Spanish-American war and, 635; sports, discrimination in, 595; suffrage, 481, 485, 486–487, 488–489, 508, 620, 880–881; urban life, opportunities in, 371–373; WWI and, 686, 688–689; WWII and women workers, 800–801. *See also* Segregation; Race and Racism; Slavery
African Methodist Church, 277
Africans: in Chesapeake society, 58–59; enslaved, 36. *See also* Slavery
Agee, James, 773
Agent Orange, 907
Agnew, Spiro, 928
Agricultural Adjustment Administration (AAA), 749; failures of, 751
Agriculture: origin and spread of, 6–7; *See also* Farms and farming.
Aguinaldo, Emilio, 637
AIDS, 973
AIM, *see* **American Indian Movement**
Airplanes, 651; in WWI, 689, 690–691
Alaska: gold rush in, 529–530; Native Americans in, 14; Seward's purchase of, 501
Alamo, 391
Alaska Lands Act, 933
Alcohol and alcoholism: Eighteenth Amendment, 671, 700; Native Americans and, 69; Progressive regulation and, 652; prohibition, 735–736; reformers and, 310–311; saloons, 594